THE CAMBRIDGE URBAN HISTORY OF BRITAIN

VOLUME I

600–1540

The first volume of *The Cambridge Urban History* surveys the history of British towns from their post-Roman origins in the seventh century down to the sixteenth century. It provides the first ever detailed overview of the course of medieval urban development, and draws on archaeological and architectural as well as documentary sources. The volume combines thematic analysis with regional and national surveys, with full coverage of developments in England, Scotland and Wales. The international team of contributors represent historical, geographical and archaeological expertise, and the whole marks a major step forward in the understanding of the medieval British town.

Part I examines historiographical tradition and the origins of British towns. Parts II and III focus on the early and later medieval periods respectively, and Part IV contains a sequence of systematic regional surveys. Extensively illustrated with maps, figures and pictorial evidence, this volume of *The Cambridge Urban History* is complete with ranking lists of towns and an extensive bibliography.

The editor D. M. PALLISER is Professor of Medieval History in the School of History at the University of Leeds. He has published more than forty books, articles and pamphlets on urban history between the tenth and the sixteenth century.

THE CAMBRIDGE URBAN HISTORY OF BRITAIN

GENERAL EDITOR

PROFESSOR PETER CLARK (*University of Leicester*)

The three volumes of *The Cambridge Urban History of Britain* represent the culmination of a tremendous upsurge of research in British urban history over the past thirty years. Mobilising the combined expertise of nearly ninety historians, archaeologists and geographers from Britain, continental Europe and North America, these volumes trace the complex and diverse evolution of British towns from the earliest Anglo-Saxon settlements to the mid-twentieth century. Taken together they form a comprehensive and uniquely authoritative account of the development of the first modern urban nation. *The Cambridge Urban History of Britain* has been developed with the active support of the Centre for Urban History at the University of Leicester.

VOLUME I 600–1540
EDITED BY D. M. PALLISER (*University of Leeds*)
ISBN 0 521 44461 6

VOLUME II 1540–1840
EDITED BY PETER CLARK (*University of Leicester*)
ISBN 0 521 43141 7

VOLUME III 1840–1950
EDITED BY MARTIN DAUNTON (*University of Cambridge*)
ISBN 0 521 41707 4

Advisory committee

THE CAMBRIDGE URBAN HISTORY OF BRITAIN

VOLUME I
600–1540

EDITED BY
D. M. PALLISER

PUBLISHED BY THE PRESS SYNDICATE OF THE UNIVERSITY OF CAMBRIDGE
The Pitt Building, Trumpington Street, Cambridge, United Kingdom

CAMBRIDGE UNIVERSITY PRESS
The Edinburgh Building, Cambridge CB2 2RU, UK
40 West 20th Street, New York, NY 10011–4211, USA
10 Stamford Road, Oakleigh, Melbourne 3166, Australia
Ruiz de Alarcón 13, 28014 Madrid, Spain
Dock House, The Waterfront, Cape Town 8001, South Africa

http://www.cambridge.org

First published 2000

Printed in the United Kingdom at the University Press, Cambridge

Typeset in Bembo 10/12½ *System* QuarkXPress™ [SE]

A catalogue record for this book is available from the British Library

ISBN 0 521 44461 6 hardback

Contents

Plates

Between pages 537 and 538

Maps

Figures

Tables

Contributors

Grenville Astill: Professor of Archaeology, University of Reading
Caroline M. Barron: Reader in the History of London, Royal Holloway College, University of London
Julia Barrow: Senior Lecturer in History, University of Nottingham
John Blair: Fellow of the Queen's College, Oxford
Richard Britnell: Professor of Medieval History, University of Durham
Bärbel Brodt: Forschungsstipendiatin der Deutschen Forschungsgemeinschaft, University of Münster
James Campbell: Professor and Lightbody Fellow and Tutor in Medieval History, Worcester College, Oxford
E. Patricia Dennison: Director of the Centre for Scottish Urban History, University of Edinburgh
David Ditchburn: Lecturer in History, University of Aberdeen
Barrie Dobson: Emeritus Professor of Medieval History, University of Cambridge
Alan Dyer: Senior Lecturer in History, University of Wales, Bangor
Christopher Dyer: Professor of Medieval Social History, University of Birmingham
Elizabeth Ewan: Associate Professor, Department of History, University of Guelph
Ralph A. Griffiths: Professor of Medieval History, University of Wales, Swansea
David A. Hinton: Professor of Archaeology, University of Southampton
Richard Holt: Førsteamanuensis i middelalderhistorie, University of Tromsø
Derek Keene: Director of the Centre for Metropolitan History, Institute of Historical Research, University of London
Jennifer Kermode: Senior Lecturer in History, University of Liverpool
Maryanne Kowaleski: Professor of History, Fordham University, New York City
D. M. Palliser: Professor of Medieval History, University of Leeds
S. H. Rigby: Reader in History, University of Manchester
Gervase Rosser: Fellow and Tutor of St Catherine's College, Oxford

John Schofield: Curator, Architecture, Museum of London
Grant G. Simpson: Formerly Reader in Scottish History, University of Aberdeen; now a heritage consultant
T. R. Slater: Reader in Historical Geography, University of Birmingham
Geoffrey Stell: Head of Architecture, Royal Commission on Ancient and Historical Monuments, Scotland

Preface by the General Editor

British cities and towns at the end of the twentieth century are at a turning-point: their role, developed over hundreds of years, is being challenged. The redevelopment of bigger city centres in the 1960s, and of many small county and market towns during subsequent decades, has eroded much of the ancient palimpsest, the mixture of public and private buildings, high streets and back lanes, which has given them for so long a sense of place, of physical coherence and individual communal identity.[1] The decline of traditional urban industries, increasingly at the mercy of global forces, has been partially redressed by the expansion of the service sector, but the recent arrival of American-style out-of-town shopping malls has contributed to the contraction of retailing in the old central areas of towns, even affecting the business of their medieval markets, while shopping parades in the suburbs are littered with empty premises.

Just as economic activity has begun to decamp from the city, so the cultural and leisure life of town centres is being threatened by the migration of cinemas and other entertainment to the urban periphery, and the decay of municipal provision. Fundamental to the weakening position of British cities in recent times has been the erosion of municipal power and autonomy, first through the transfer of key civic functions to the state during and after the second world war and, more recently, through a brutal assault by Conservative governments of the 1980s and 1990s on the financial position of town halls and their ability to sustain their civic responsibilities. It is little wonder that, in this problematic urban world, issues of social exclusion and environmental degradation seem increasingly stark, their effects impacting on the whole of national society.

Of course, the decline of the city is not a uniquely British phenomenon. Throughout much of Western Europe there has been a loss of momentum, a

[1] Such changes have also destroyed much of the archaeological record, the buried archives of towns, so essential for understanding their early history.

decay of confidence, manifested but hardly resolved by the endless spate of European conferences, research programmes and official reports on the subject, almost an industry in itself. However, the problems and pressures seem particularly acute in Britain, raising questions about how far their current difficulties reflect longer-term structural factors related to the processes by which Britain became the first modern urban nation. Is the peripheralisation of economic and cultural activity the logical conclusion of the spatial fragmentation of British cities, including suburbanisation, which has been occurring since 1800? Why have so many of Britain's great cities fared so badly in the twentieth century? Is this related to the nature of the rapid urbanisation and industrialisation from the late eighteenth century, based on low human capital formation and cheap fuel, which made it difficult to maintain growth once other countries began to exploit cheap fuel as well?

And yet if at least some of the problems of Britain's present-day cities and towns may be rooted in the past, the historic experience of our urban communities encourages us to believe that, given greater autonomy both of leadership and funding, they can generate an effective response to many of the current challenges. As we shall see in this series, past periods of urban decline, with all their attendant social, political and other difficulties, have often been reversed or moderated by changes of economic direction by towns, whether in the late middle ages through the expansion of service trades, in the seventeenth century through the development of specialist manufacturing and leisure sectors or in the early twentieth century through the rise of new, often consumer-oriented industries. At the present time, general images of urban decline and dereliction are countered, however selectively, by the rise of the Docklands area as the new international financial quarter of the capital, by the renewed vitality of Glasgow, Manchester and Newcastle as regional capitals, by the tourist success of towns like Bath and York marketing their civic heritage, by the social harmony and cultural vibrancy of a multi-ethnic city such as Leicester. Propelled by a strong sense of civic pride, Britain's urban system has shown, over time, a powerful capacity to create new opportunities from changing circumstances, a capacity that remains as crucial now as in the past. Certainly if many of the modern challenges to society have an urban origin then urban solutions are imperative.

Undoubtedly, Britain is an ancient urban country, remarkable for the longevity and, for much of the time, relative stability of its urban system. Though the early city barely outlasted the Romans' departure from these shores, after the seventh and eighth centuries a skeleton of urban centres developed in England, which was fully fleshed out by the start of the fourteenth century, headed by London, already a great European city, but with a corpus of established shire and market towns: the pattern established by 1300 was remarkably stable until the start of the nineteenth century. Scottish and Welsh towns were slower to become fully established and even in the early modern period new market burghs were founded in Scotland, but by the eighteenth century the island had a strong, generally affluent and increasingly integrated network of towns, which was to provide the essential springboard for the urban and industrial take-off of the nineteenth century. From the Georgian era cities and towns were centres of manufacturing and commercial expansion, public improvement and enlightenment; they were the centre stage for the enactment of a British identity. In Victoria's reign the city with its political rallies, crafts and factories, railways, gothic town halls, societies and civic amenities threatened to swallow up the country. Whether one should see the growing fascination with the countryside after 1918, that fashionable, if fanciful pursuit of Ambridge, as a new kind of anti-urbanism, or rather as the ultimate post-urban annexation of the countryside and its incorporation into the cultural hinterland of the city, remains in hot debate.[2] But the interwar period was, despite the problems of the biggest industrial cities, a time of considerable prosperity and community pride for many cities and towns up and down the country. Even in the aftermath of the second world war, many of the traditional functions and relationships of the British urban system survived – at least until the 1960s.

This is a good time for a systematic historical investigation of the rise of British cities and towns over the *longue durée*. Not just because understanding urban society is too important a task to be left to contemporary sociologists, geographers and planners, but because of the flourishing state of British urban history. Though earlier scholarly works existed, the last thirty years have seen a revolution in our understanding of the complexity of the social, political and other functions of towns in the past, of the social groups and classes that comprised the urban population, of the relationships within the urban system and between cities and the wider society, whether countryside, region or state. Initially most sonorous for the Victorian period and orchestrated by that brilliant academic conductor, H. J. (Jim) Dyos, in company with Asa Briggs and Sydney Checkland, the new concert of urban historians has increasingly embraced the early modern and medieval periods, a historiographical story explained in detail in the introductions to the separate volumes. The result is that for the first time we can follow the comparative evolution of English, Scottish and Welsh towns from the seventh to the twentieth century, traversing those conventional divisions of historical labour, particularly at the close of the middle ages and the end of the eighteenth century. Mobilising the expertise of historians, geographers, archaeologists, landscape historians and others, the modern study of urban history has always sought to pursue a wide-ranging agenda, aiming, so far as possible, to comprehend communities in the round, to see the interrelation of the different parts, even if such ambitions cannot always be fully achieved.

[2] P. Mandler, 'Against "Englishness": English culture and the limits to rural nostalgia', *TRHS*, 6th series, 7 (1997), 155–75.

Here urban history offers an important methodological alternative to the more fragmented study of specific urban themes, which, through micro-studies focusing on the most interesting sources and communities, runs the risk of seeing issues, social groups or particular towns in isolation, out of meaningful context. Thickets of knowledge of this type are the bane of sustained and innovative scholarly research, and have contributed much to the distancing of academic literature from the public domain. Strikingly, the last few years have seen a renewed or enhanced recognition of the overarching importance of the urban variable, both dependent and independent, in the many different areas of social, business, demographic and women's history.

In the fertile tradition of urban history, the three volumes of the *Cambridge Urban History of Britain* are the product of a collaborative project, with a good deal of friendship, fellowship, hard talking and modest drinking amongst those involved. The idea for such a series was discussed at Leicester as early as 1977, at a convivial lunch hosted by Jim Dyos, but it was not until 1990 that a proposal was made to launch the series. An advisory board was established, editors agreed and several meetings held to plot the structure of the volumes, the contributors and the publishing arrangements. Since then regular meetings have been held for particular volumes, and the discussions have not only produced important dividends for the coherence and quality of the volumes, but have contributed to the better understanding of the British city in general. The involvement of colleagues working on Scotland has been particularly fruitful.

This series of volumes has had no earmarked funding (though funding bodies have supported research for individual chapters), and the editors and contributors are grateful to the many British and several North American universities for funding, directly and indirectly, the research, travel and other costs of contributors to the enterprise. Through its commitment to the Centre for Urban History, which has coordinated the project, the University of Leicester has been a valued benefactor, while Cambridge University Press, in the friendly guise of Richard Fisher, has been enormously helpful and supportive over the long haul of preparation and publication. The fact that the series, involving nearly ninety different contributors, has been published broadly on schedule owes a great deal to the energy, high commitment and fathomless interpersonal skills of my fellow editors, David Palliser and Martin Daunton (to whom I have been heavily indebted for wise and fortifying counsel), to the collective solidarity of the contributors, as well as to the generous support and patience of partners and families.

Thirty years ago in his introduction to *The Study of Urban History* Dyos declared that 'the field is as yet a very ragged one, and those in it are a little confused as to what they are doing'.[3] Plausibly, the volumes in the present series show that current students of urban history are less confused and somewhat

[3] H. J. Dyos, ed., *The Study of Urban History* (London, 1968), p. 46.

better dressed intellectually, having access to an extensive wardrobe of evidence, arguments and ideas, with a broad comparative and temporal design. The picture of the British town becomes ever more complex, as our greater knowledge recognises variety where once only uniformity was evident. However, we are at last nearer the point of uncovering the spectrum of historical processes, which have shaped our many cities and towns, making the urban past more intelligible and accessible, not just to academics, but to those townspeople whose identification with their own contemporary communities at the turn of the millennium is being so constantly and fiercely questioned.

Acknowledgements

In a collaborative volume of this kind, the contributors and I would like to thank fellow contributors for their helpful comments and suggestions. I am particularly grateful to Christopher Dyer and Terry Slater who took over the Midlands chapter after the successive withdrawal of two other contributors. I am also much indebted to the General Editor, Peter Clark, for his constant support and advice; to Maria Di Stefano and Christine Cascarino for their help in getting the volume to press; and to Richard Fisher and his colleagues at Cambridge University Press for their unfailing helpfulness, and for their tolerance in coping with unavoidable delays to the submission of the final text. I would also like to thank Linda Randall for her superb copy-editing of the whole volume and Auriol Griffith-Jones for compiling the index. I owe it to those contributors who met the original deadlines to add that final texts were submitted between December 1996 and January 1999.

The editor, contributors and publisher gratefully acknowledge the assistance of the following persons and institutions in the provision of illustrative material, and their kind permission to reproduce same: Plate 1: Museum of Oxford; Plate 2: Somerset County Council Museums Service; Plates 3, 16 and 17: Guildhall Library and Art Gallery, London; Plate 4: reproduced by courtesy of Fife Council Museums West, Dunfermline Museum; Plate 5: Southampton Museums Services; Plate 6: Bristol Record Office; Plate 7: Crown copyright, National Monuments Record; Plates 8 and 13: Museum of London; Plate 9: Conway Library, Courtauld Institute of Art; Plate 10: Shakespeare Birthplace Trust, Stratford-upon-Avon; Plates 11 and 15: Ashmolean Museum, Oxford; Plate 12: reproduced by courtesy of the Guildry of Dunfermline; Plate 14: York City Art Gallery; Plate 18: Crown copyright, RCAHMS; Plate 19: Clothworkers' Company; Plate 20: reproduced by kind permission of the Corporation of London (Guildhall Library, Print Room); Plates 22 and 23: Crown copyright: Royal Commission on the Ancient and Historical Monuments of Wales; Plate 24: reproduced by permission of the Trustees of the National Library of Scotland; Plate 25: the Master and Fellows of Corpus Christi College, Cambridge.

Abbreviations

Ag.HEW	*The Agrarian History of England and Wales*
Annales ESC	*Annales: économies, sociétiés, civilisations*
Antiq. and Arch. Soc.	Antiquarian and Archaeological Society
AO	Archives Office
APS	*The Acts of the Parliaments of Scotland*, ed. T. Thomson and C. Innes (1814–75)
Arch. (and Hist.) J	Archaeological (and Historical) Journal
Arch. (and Hist.) Soc.	Archaeological (and Historical) Society
Arch. and NHSoc.	Archaeological and Natural History Society
BAHT	*British Atlas of Historic Towns*
BL	British Library
Bull. IHR	*Bulletin of the Institute of Historical Research* (now *Historical Research*)
C	Proceedings in the Court of Chancery, Public Record Office
CBA	Council for British Archaeology
CBA Res. Rep.	Council for British Archaeology, Research Reports
CCh.R	*Calendar of Charter Rolls*
CCR	*Calendar of Close Rolls*
CIPM	*Calendar of Inquisitions Post Mortem*
CPR	*Calendar of Patent Rolls*
DNB	*Dictionary of National Biography*
E	Exchequer Records, Public Record Office
Ec.HR	*Economic History Review*
EHR	*English Historical Review*
ER	*The Exchequer Rolls of Scotland*, ed. J. Stuart *et al.* (1878–1908)
GSt.	*Guildhall Studies in London History*
HJ	*Historical Journal*

HMC	Historical Manuscripts Commission
HMSO	Her Majesty's Stationery Office
HR	*Historical Research*
J	*Journal*
JEcc.Hist.	*Journal of Ecclesiastical History*
JMed.H	*Journal of Medieval History*
JUH	*Journal of Urban History*
LJ	*London Journal*
LMAS	London and Middlesex Archaeological Society
Med. Arch.	*Medieval Archaeology*
New DNB	*New Dictionary of National Biography*
NHist.	*Northern History*
PIMSST	Pontifical Institute of Mediaeval Studies, Studies and Texts
P&P	*Past and Present*
PRO	Public Record Office, London
Proc.	*Proceedings*
Proc. Soc. Antiq. Scot.	*Proceedings of the Society of Antiquaries of Scotland*
RCAHMS	Royal Commission on Ancient and Historical Monuments and Constructions of Scotland
RCHM	Royal Commission on Historical Monuments
RMS	*Registrum Magni Sigilli Regum Scotorum*, ed. J. M. Thomson *et al.* (1882–1914)
RO	Record Office
RRS	*Regesta Regum Scottorum*, ed. G. W. S. Barrow *et al.* (1960–)
RS	Rolls Series
SHist.	*Southern History*
SHR	*Scottish Historical Review*
SP	State Papers Domestic, Public Record Office
SR	*Statutes of the Realm*, ed. A. Luders *et al.*
SRO	Scottish Record Office, Edinburgh
TLMAS	*Transactions of the London and Middlesex Archaeological Society*
TRHS	*Transactions of the Royal Historical Society*
UH	*Urban History*
UHY	*Urban History Yearbook*, now *Urban History*
VCH	*Victoria County History*

· PART I ·

Introductory

· 1 ·

Introduction

D. M. PALLISER

THE HISTORY of British towns[1] is a very distinctive one in a European – even in a world – perspective. Until the eighteenth century most of them were small by international standards, yet in the nineteenth century Britain became the first country in the world to urbanise, that is, to have more than half of its population living in towns. The divide is neatly measured by the 1851 census, which showed (depending on urban definitions and boundaries) about 54 per cent of English and Welsh people, and 52 per cent of Scots, town dwellers. No one, therefore, questions the importance of British towns and urbanisation in the last two centuries, and it is indeed possible to write British history since 1850 from an urban point of view.[2] For the pre-industrial period the subject has understandably seemed less important, since though southern Britain at least has had towns for most of the last two millennia, for much of that long period they were relatively small: relative, that is, both to contemporary continental cities, and to modern towns. Visitors from Venice judged late medieval London to be the only important British city, while Patrick Collinson has described Tudor towns (other than London) as 'small-scale Toytowns and Trumptons' compared to the great imperial cities of Germany and the Netherlands.[3]

Yet if London stood alone in the first division of European pre-industrial cities, other British towns were not therefore unimportant. They housed a substantial

The section on Scottish historiography is by E. Patricia Dennison and Grant G. Simpson.

[1] 'Town' is used throughout these volumes to mean 'that sort of place which, however it was governed and however small its population, fulfilled the functions which are normally implied by the modern use of the word "town" in British English, "city" in American English, *ville* in French, *Stadt* in German, and *città* in Italian': S. Reynolds, *Kingdoms and Communities in Western Europe 900–1300*, 2nd edn (Oxford, 1997), p. 157.

[2] Notably by P. J. Waller, *Town, City and Nation: England 1850–1914* (Oxford, 1983).

[3] D. M. Palliser, 'Urban society', in R. Horrox, ed., *Fifteenth-Century Attitudes: Perceptions of Society in Late Medieval England* (Cambridge, 1994), p. 132; P. Collinson, *The Birthpangs of Protestant England* (Basingstoke, 1988), p. 32.

minority of the population (at least in England), larger than is generally believed. Though some writers have put the urban proportion of the population at only 5 or 10 per cent as late as 1500, the best recent estimates are considerably higher: up to 10 per cent in 1086, 15 or more per cent by 1300, 20 per cent in 1377, and after perhaps a fall in the fifteenth century, a return to about 20 per cent by 1524.[4] Furthermore, they were regular places of resort for the rural majority, whether for economic, social, administrative, judicial or ecclesiastical purposes, and 'it is easy to forget that . . . towns can often seem more important to those who visit them than those who live there'.[5] Nearly everyone, for instance, lived within easy reach of a market town by the thirteenth century, at least over the greater part of England. This volume is full of examples of the relationships between town and country in the middle ages, a natural feature of an island much of which was becoming commercialised as early as the tenth and eleventh centuries. Studying British and European urbanisation 'requires a lengthy look backward in time. The answers to many questions about the nature of contemporary European cities lie in the medieval period, not in the modern industrial era.'[6]

The work reviewed here, and in Volume II, should help to dispel any lingering 'suspicion that urbanization in the centuries before the period of classic industrial revolution is too petty for study'.[7] The importance of our theme – indeed of the theme of all three volumes of the *Urban History of Britain* – was justified long ago by James Tait: to trace urban growth 'from the advent of the town-hating Angles and Saxons down to these latter days, when five-sixths of the population of Great Britain are massed upon pavements' was, he said in 1922, 'a task worthy of the best powers of an historian of institutions'.[8] We might put this slightly differently now. One of the myths dispelled by modern scholarship is that the English peoples who invaded Britain in the fifth and sixth centuries were 'town-hating' folk, but none the less the collapse of Roman urban centres left them little opportunity to live in towns. Now we would perhaps emphasise towns as social and economic communities, and not think of them only as boroughs or institutions. Nevertheless, as a reminder of the huge growth of towns over nearly fourteen centuries, and the consequences it has entailed, Tait's programme can hardly be bettered.

(i) THE IDENTIFICATION AND IMPORTANCE OF TOWNS

An issue to be faced at the outset is that of definitions: what are meant by a town, and by the middle ages? Whatever may be true of later periods, there are great

[4] R. H. Britnell, *The Commercialisation of English Society, 1000–1500*, 2nd edn (Manchester, 1996), pp. 49, 115, 170; C. Dyer, 'How urbanized was medieval England?', in J.-M. Duvosquel and E. Thoen, eds., *Peasants and Townsmen in Medieval Europe* (Ghent, 1995), pp. 169–83.

[5] R. B. Dobson, 'The risings in York, Beverley and Scarborough, 1380–1381', in R. H. Hilton and T. H. Aston, eds., *The English Rising of 1381* (Cambridge, 1984), p. 142.

[6] P. M. Hohenberg and L. H. Lees, *The Making of Urban Europe 1000–1950* (Cambridge, Mass., 1985), p. 1. [7] Waller, *Town, City and Nation*, p. vii.

[8] J. Tait, *The Medieval English Borough* (Manchester, 1936), p. 358 (from a paper first given in 1922).

difficulties in agreeing on an urban definition valid for all the centuries usually labelled 'medieval'. Over the long time span concerned, functions of 'central places' changed, and definitions valid for one century might not help for another. The functions later concentrated in multi-purpose towns were often separated in the early middle ages, with a royal centre in one, a major church in another and perhaps a market, mint or port in a third. 'A settlement growing up around a royal and / or ecclesiastical site in the seventh or eighth century should not be judged as non-urban by the criteria applicable to a later Saxon burh, just as these latter places should not be judged by the standards of later medieval towns'.[9] The literature is also confused by the relationship between places with a legal, and those with a socio-economic, identity, between 'borough' and 'town'; and if we adopt a socio-economic definition, as we broadly shall, there is the problem of evidence: criteria in terms of population, or of economic and social structure, cannot be applied in the precise and quantitative way that they can for recent centuries.

A definition is, fortunately, no more than an aid to thought: it has no intrinsic value. As Karl Popper has warned, 'a definition cannot establish the meaning of a term any more than a logical derivation can establish the truth of a statement: both can only shift this problem back'.[10] Nevertheless, a working definition may be helpful, and the one we have adopted here – at least for the high and later middle ages – is that of Susan Reynolds. The first part is functional: 'a town is a permanent and concentrated human settlement in which a significant proportion of the population is engaged in non-agricultural occupations . . . A town therefore normally lives, at least in part, off food produced by people who live outside it.' The second part is social: 'the inhabitants of towns normally regard themselves, and are regarded by the inhabitants of predominantly rural settlements, as a different sort of people'. This is, as she recognises, a loose definition, not because it is defective, but because definitions are human constructs and have unclear boundaries.[11] We are persuaded that such a definition as hers is a better aid to analysis than taking refuge in a 'bundle of criteria' (*Kriterienbündel*) of the kind favoured in some archaeological surveys, 'one of the less useful concepts that has come to Britain from abroad'.[12]

Our definition of 'middle ages' is that almost universally employed in Western Europe, and in North America, to mean the millennium, or thereabouts, between the fall of the Western Roman Empire and the Renaissance. It may seem

[9] J. Haslam, *Early Medieval Towns in Britain* (Princes Risborough, 1985), p. 6.

[10] K. R. Popper, *The Open Society and its Enemies*, 4th edn (London, 1962), vol. II, pp. 19–21.

[11] S. Reynolds, 'The writing of medieval urban history in England', *Theoretische Geschiedenis*, 19 (1992), 49–50.

[12] Carolyn M. Heighway, ed., *The Erosion of History* (London, 1972), p. 9; M. Biddle, 'Towns', in D. M. Wilson, ed., *The Archaeology of Anglo-Saxon England* (London, 1976), p. 100; Reynolds, 'The writing of medieval urban history', 49.

superfluous to say that, but a surprising number of British scholars still define the middle ages as beginning in 1066, thus absurdly relegating the six centuries of the 'Anglo-Saxon' period to a kind of limbo. The middle ages are taken here to begin in Britain with the collapse of Roman imperial power around 409–11, though since that collapse seems to have entailed the almost complete disappearance of urban life, our story really begins with the revival of urban life in the seventh century. The other terminal date is the mid-sixteenth century, when the Protestant Reformation marks a decisive break in British urban life. The nine centuries we cover are, of course, only very imperfectly designated by the single term 'medieval': there were enormous changes over that time, and we have recognised this by dividing our chronological treatment into two, with the break at around 1300. It makes, of course, for very unequal time spans, but it can be justified not only by the imbalance in the surviving documentary sources, but also, and more importantly, by the major changes in British social and economic life at the turn of the thirteenth and fourteenth centuries. It certainly makes for a better division than the Norman Conquest of England, which is a meaningless divide for Scotland and Wales, and which even in many aspects of English urban life marked no break at all.[13]

We have attempted to balance the volume in terms of what is important – trying, certainly, to summarise established knowledge and recent research, but also to draw attention to problems and lacunae. We have also drawn extensively upon the evidence of archaeology and urban morphology as well as documentary sources, a procedure which is especially (though not only) important for the period before the twelfth century when documentary evidence for most towns is sparse. The point is worth stressing because a document-based approach dominated British medieval urban history until recently, to its considerable impoverishment.

We have also been concerned to envisage urban history in terms of people and places as well as institutions. It is unfortunate that Tait's brilliant *Medieval English Borough* (1936), like much other work published before the 1960s, is concerned so exclusively with constitutions and institutions: as H. M. Colvin has remarked, 'it is as much the failure to envisage towns as actual places as any defect of scholarship' that makes it 'so unsatisfactory an introduction to urban history'.[14] Carl Stephenson's *Borough and Town* (1933), to which Tait's book was partly a rejoinder, had at least the merit of a stimulating topographical chapter with plans, however much he was wrong – and Tait right – over the application of Henri Pirenne's insights to English towns. Helen Cam, in a perceptive and critical review of part of Stephenson's argument, commended him for

[13] See e.g. S. Reynolds, *An Introduction to the History of English Medieval Towns* (Oxford, 1977), pp. 42–3; S. Reynolds, 'English towns of the eleventh century in a European context', in P. Johanek, ed., *Die Stadt im 11. Jahrhundert* (Münster, 1995), pp. 7–10.

[14] H. M. Colvin, review in *Med. Arch.*, 6–7 (1962–3), 363.

asserting 'very rightly' that urban evolution 'must be approached from the side of topography'.[15] However, Tait's approach was reinforced by the work of F. M. Stenton, especially his massively influential *Anglo-Saxon England* (1943, 1947, 1971), with his 'literary approach which relied so little on illustrations, plans, or excavation reports'.[16] It has not been possible to illustrate this volume as extensively as we would wish, but we hope to have succeeded in reflecting some of the riches of archaeological and topographical work which have made us more aware of towns 'as actual places' over the past generation or so. Likewise, we must remember always that towns were communities of people, and we have drawn on as much evidence as possible to put townspeople into the centre of the story – not only the relatively well-recorded mayors and town councillors, but so far as possible the ordinary men, women and children they represented. However, we have also tried to avoid the excesses of some recent scholarship which is concerned so exclusively with people and places as to exclude the old, constitutional approach altogether. It is not possible to make sense of medieval towns without considering their government and institutions, their customs and by-laws. Boroughs, charters and guilds should not be excluded by the new urban history.

(ii) HISTORIOGRAPHY: ENGLAND AND WALES

It may help, as background to our present state of knowledge of medieval towns, to sketch the history of the subject. Some investigations of the urban past can be traced back to the later middle ages, including the civic chronicles of London, and the topographical descriptions of towns by William of Worcester in the 1470s, and by John Leland in the 1530s and 1540s.[17] Detailed descriptions of the urban fabric and its past came together first in Tudor London, with the conjunction of early drawings by Wyngaerde, a huge printed plan of the city, probably also by Wyngaerde (1553–9), and John Stow's *Survey of London*, begun about the same time though not published until 1598.[18] Many other histories of English towns followed in the seventeenth and eighteenth centuries, usually with a medieval and constitutional bias, with at least 150

[15] C. Stephenson, *Borough and Town* (Cambridge, Mass., 1933); H. Cam, *Liberties and Communities in Medieval England* (London, 1963), pp. 1, 3.

[16] D. Hill, 'The Saxon period', in J. Schofield and R. Leech, eds., *Urban Archaeology in Britain* (CBA Res. Rep., 61, 1987), p. 46.

[17] J. H. Harvey, ed., *William Worcestre: Itineraries 1478–1480* (Oxford, 1969); L. Toulmin Smith, ed., *The Itinerary of John Leland in or about the Years 1535–1543* (London, 1907–10).

[18] M. Holmes, 'An unrecorded map of London', *Archaeologia*, 100 (1966), 105–28; S. P. Marks, *The Map of Mid-Sixteenth Century London* (London Topographical Society 100, 1964); M. Holmes, 'A source-book for Stow?', in A. E. J. Hollaender and W. Kellaway, eds., *Studies in London History presented to Philip Edmund Jones* (London, 1969), pp. 275–85; P. D. A. Harvey, *Maps in Tudor England* (London, 1993), pp. 73–7.

being published between 1701 and 1800, and another 90 in the first two decades of the nineteenth century.[19]

Many early histories were antiquarian and uncritical, but the same period initiated real historical research on English towns, even if largely confined to legal and constitutional aspects. Thomas Madox's *Firma Burgi* (1726) is still of great value, while a century later the debate over municipal reform produced *The History of the Boroughs and Municipal Corporations of the United Kingdom* by Merewether and Stephens (1835), still useful despite its bias.[20] Victorian scholars discovered the social and economic dimensions of the subject, revived the serious study of townscape and topography which Stow had pioneered, and in some cases attempted what would now be called rescue archaeology. E. A. Freeman published good local studies (notably *Towns and Districts*, 1883), and launched a series of *Historic Towns* in 1887. His contemporary John Richard Green used town plans helpfully in his *Conquest of England* (1883), and we have his widow's testimony of a day spent with him in Ancona, where 'as was his habit, he made his way first to the Town-hall, and from the fragments of Greek and mediaeval carving built into its walls, from harbour and pier, from names of streets, and the cathedral crypt, he extracted century by century some record of the old municipal life'.[21] The quotation comes from Alice Green's own masterpiece, *Town Life in the Fifteenth Century* (1894), which has, astonishingly, 'not yet been superseded by a work of equivalent length and depth of treatment'.[22] By the turn of the century, major publishing enterprises were beginning to tackle the history and historical fabric of towns systematically, notably the Survey of London (started in 1896), the Victoria History of the Counties of England (founded in 1899) and the Royal Commission on Historical Monuments (1908).

The true founders of medieval English urban history, however, were F. W. Maitland (1850–1906) and Charles Gross (1857–1909), both inspired in part by German scholarship. Gross developed his Göttingen doctoral dissertation into *The Gild Merchant* (1890), besides compiling a *Bibliography of British Municipal History* (1897): both are still standard works a century later.[23] Maitland published much on the legal and constitutional history of boroughs, including *Township and*

[19] R. Sweet, *The Writing of Urban Histories in Eighteenth-Century England* (Oxford, 1997), p. 9. Welsh town histories are generally later in date: the first known was written (but not published) *c.* 1669, and the earliest published examples are Newcombe's on Denbigh (1829) and Ruthin (1836): R. A. Griffiths, ed., *Boroughs of Mediaeval Wales* (Cardiff, 1978), pp. 1, 2.

[20] C. Gross, *A Bibliography of British Municipal History* (New York, 1897), nos. 158, 79. Gross' *Bibliography*, reissued in 1966 (2nd edn., with preface by G. H. Martin, Leicester, 1966), is still the definitive guide to pre-1897 literature. G. H. Martin and S. McIntyre, *A Bibliography of British and Irish Municipal History*, was designed to supplement rather than supersede Gross; only vol. 1, *General Works* (Leicester, 1972) has yet appeared, and not the promised succeeding volumes listing post-1897 work on individual towns.

[21] A. S. Green, *Town Life in the Fifteenth Century* (London, 1894), vol. 1, p. xiii.

[22] R. Holt and G. Rosser, eds., *The Medieval Town* (London, 1990), p. 2.

[23] C. Gross, *The Gild Merchant* (Oxford, 1890); Gross, *Bibliography*.

Borough (1898); he also encouraged Mary Bateson, who edited two volumes of *Borough Customs* (1904–6), while Gross' pupil Morley Hemmeon published the definitive analysis of burgage tenure (1914).[24] Bateson had also published an exemplary edition of the earliest Leicester records in 1899, a year which may be taken as initiating really reliable editions of borough archives, for it also saw publication of the first volume of Reginald Sharpe's *Calendar of Letter Books of the City of London*.[25] Others inspired to enter the field were E. A. Lewis, who published the first synthesis of Welsh burghal history, and Adolphus Ballard, who initiated a series of digests of urban charters, continued after his death by James Tait.[26]

The 1920s and 1930s were dominated by the rival work of Stephenson and Tait, already briefly noticed. It is unfortunate that Stephenson had invested much of his work in arguing for a late (post-Conquest) development of urban life in England, an argument Tait was able to refute, because the result was that Tait was perceived to have 'defeated' Stephenson, whereas both books still have great merit, and moreover Stephenson's is much the more readable.[27] G. H. Martin has commented that 'the subject is a difficult one, and Tait made it sound difficult'.[28] That may be why publication of Tait's book signalled, if it did not cause, a thirty-year period when relatively little of the first rank was published, apart from constitutional analyses by Martin Weinbaum.[29]

Little recognised at the time, however, serious work was beginning in medieval urban archaeology. In Oxford between the 1930s and 1950s important discoveries were made by R. L. Bruce-Mitford, E. M. Jope and W. A. Pantin, and other 'rescue archaeology', as it would later be called, was undertaken after 1945 on sites cleared by bombing, providing important medieval evidence in London, Canterbury and elsewhere.[30] Pantin became one of the founders of the Society

[24] F. W. Maitland, *Domesday Book and Beyond* (Cambridge, 1897), pp. 172–219; F. Pollock and F. W. Maitland, *The History of English Law before the Time of Edward I*, 2nd edn (Cambridge, 1898), esp. vol. I, pp. 634–88; F. W. Maitland, *Township and Borough* (Cambridge, 1898); F. W. Maitland and M. Bateson, eds., *The Charters of the Borough of Cambridge* (Cambridge, 1901); M. Bateson, ed., *Borough Customs* (Selden Society, 18, 21, 1904–6); M. de W. Hemmeon, *Burgage Tenure in Mediaeval England* (Cambridge, Mass., 1914).

[25] M. Bateson, ed., *Records of the Borough of Leicester* ([London], 1899–1905); R. R. Sharpe, ed., *Calendar of Letter Books of the City of London* (London, 1899–1912).

[26] E. A. Lewis, *The Mediæval Boroughs of Snowdonia* (London, 1912); A. Ballard, ed., *British Borough Charters 1042–1216* (Cambridge, 1913); A. Ballard and J. Tait, eds., *British Borough Charters 1216–1307* (Cambridge, 1923).

[27] For a judicious appraisal of Tait and Stephenson, see Martin and McIntyre, *Bibliography*, pp. xxxvi–xxxvii.

[28] G. H. Martin, 'The English borough in the thirteenth century', in Holt and Rosser, eds., *The Medieval Town*, p. 32.

[29] M. Weinbaum, *The Incorporation of Boroughs* (Manchester, 1937); M. Weinbaum, ed., *British Borough Charters, 1307–1660* (Cambridge, 1943).

[30] W. A. Pantin, 'The recently demolished houses in Broad Street, Oxford', *Oxoniensia*, 2 (1937), pp. 171–200; W. Grimes, *The Archaeology of Roman and Medieval London* (London, 1968); P. Ottaway, *Archaeology in British Towns* (London, 1992), p. 10.

for Medieval Archaeology (1956), as well as the author of the first modern study of town house plans in an early volume of its journal,[31] and it was partly owing to the Society that the serious study of medieval towns revived in the 1960s, accompanied by much topographical and archaeological work alongside the traditional documentary fare. Early fruits included M. R. G. Conzen's pioneering analyses of the town plans of Alnwick, Newcastle, Ludlow and Conwy, and publication of the first British volume of the *Atlas of Historic Town Plans of Western Europe* (1969); the first major urban excavation programme in Britain under Martin Biddle at Winchester (1961–71); Maurice Beresford's detailed analyses of planted towns in England, Wales and Gascony; and his catalogue, in conjunction with H. P. R. Finberg, of all known English boroughs.[32]

Since 1970, research and publication in all of these areas has advanced apace. Colin Platt and Susan Reynolds provided the first scholarly surveys of English medieval towns for a generation, closely followed by Ralph Griffiths and others for Wales; [33] their work helped to inspire an increased output of monographs on individual towns, editions of urban records and more recently some excellent surveys incorporating much of the new archaeological data.[34] New research has been inspired by a series of lively debates about major issues: the extent of urban continuity in the post-Roman period; the nature of revived town life, including the role of *emporia, burhs* and minsters; the relationship of 'feudalism' and towns; the nature of urban communities; the role of women; the existence of urban oligarchy; and the extent of late medieval urban decline. The last controversy, though probably irresolvable, led to very fruitful investigations. Surviving medieval buildings have been thoroughly described in comprehensive inventories of Salisbury, Stamford and York,[35] though regrettably such inventories have now been discontinued; and an Urban Morphology Group at the University of Birmingham is building on Conzen's work. And the growing body of archaeological data is now

[31] W. A. Pantin, 'Medieval English town-house plans', *Med. Arch.*, 6–7 (1962–3), pp. 202–39.

[32] M. R. G. Conzen, *Alnwick, Northumberland* (Publications of the Institute of British Geographers, 27, 1960); M. R. G. Conzen, 'The plan analysis of an English city centre', *Proc. of the I. G. U. Symposium in Urban Geography, Lund 1960* (Lund, 1962); M. R. G. Conzen, 'The use of town plans in the study of urban history', in H. J. Dyos, ed., *The Study of Urban History* (London, 1968), pp. 113–30; *BAHT*, I: M. Biddle, 'The study of Winchester: archaeology and history in a British town, 1961–1983', *Proc. of the British Academy*, 69 (1983), 93–135; M. Beresford, *New Towns of the Middle Ages* (London, 1967); M. W. Beresford and H. P. R. Finberg, *English Medieval Boroughs* (Newton Abbot, 1973).

[33] C. Platt, *The English Medieval Town* (London, 1976); Reynolds, *English Medieval Towns*; Griffiths, ed., *Boroughs of Mediaeval Wales*; I. Soulsby, *The Towns of Medieval Wales* (Chichester, 1983).

[34] E.g. Ottaway, *Archaeology in British Towns*; J. Schofield and A. Vince, *Medieval Towns* (London, 1994).

[35] RCHM (England), *Ancient and Historical Monuments in the City of Salisbury: Volume One* (London,1980); RCHM (England), *Salisbury: The Houses of the Close* (London, 1993); RCHM (England), *An Inventory of Historical Monuments in the Town of Stamford* (London, 1977); RCHM (England), *An Inventory of the Historical Monuments in the City of York* (London, 1962–81).

increasingly being synthesised, not only in excavation site reports, but also in works setting the finds in surveys more accessible to the urban historian, including fine surveys of the buildings, furnishings and artefacts of London, Winchester and Norwich.[36] It is therefore a lively and developing subject at the time of writing, though by the same token it is not an easy time to take stock.

(iii) HISTORIOGRAPHY: SCOTLAND

The nineteenth century bequeathed to us a series of studies of individual towns. Many tended to be strongly antiquarian in approach, and at times rested on scholarship which was unduly influenced by local patriotism. More valuable in the long term has been the work of the Scottish Burgh Records Society, which between 1868 and 1911 produced twenty-six volumes of record material, much of it on Edinburgh and Glasgow and the Convention of Royal Burghs. The nineteenth-century tradition produced massive results in an elaborate study, on which he had been working since the 1880s, David Murray's *Early Burgh Organisation in Scotland*.[37] This had the merit of displaying considerable grasp of the archival, constitutional and topographical evidence, but his approach to his subject was diffuse, and his theory of origins, that burghs evolved from pre-existing agricultural communities, was based more on assumption and analogy than on evidence.

The sparseness of early evidence, and some failures of clarity on the part of earlier writers, left the field open in the mid-twentieth century for a strong concentration on constitutional aspects. A useful short survey appeared in W. Mackay Mackenzie's *The Scottish Burghs*. As the title implies, he saw 'burgh' rather than 'town' as the principal element of the subject, and dismissed the David Murray approach with the crisp opinion that 'the key-word to the burgh is creation, not growth'.[38] W. Croft Dickinson's magisterial introduction to the early records of Aberdeen analysed the Scottish burghs as a whole, but concentrated heavily on the royal burghs and touched only occasionally on the economic background.[39] Further constitutional attention was applied in the valuable and accurate handlist of Scottish burghs by George S. Pryde.[40] By this era the history of Scottish medieval towns had come to be viewed in a strongly institutional light.

[36] J. Schofield, *Medieval London Houses* (New Haven, 1995); M. Biddle *et al.*, *Object and Economy in Medieval Winchester* (Oxford, 1991); S. Margeson, *Norwich Households: The Medieval and Post-Medieval Finds from Norwich Survey Excavations 1971–1978* (East Anglian Archaeology 58, Norwich, 1993).

[37] D. Murray, *Early Burgh Organisation in Scotland, as Illustrated in the History of Glasgow and of Some Neighbouring Burghs* (Glasgow, 1924).

[38] W. M. Mackenzie, *The Scottish Burghs* (Edinburgh, 1949), p. 14.

[39] W. Croft Dickinson, ed., *Early Records of the Burgh of Aberdeen, 1317, 1398–1407* (Scottish History Society, 1957).

[40] G. S. Pryde, *The Burghs of Scotland* (London, 1965).

In the last quarter-century physical evidence has been given much greater attention, an approach stimulated by the work of urban geographers such as Ian Adams, and by George Gordon and Brian Dicks' *Scottish Urban History*.[41] Nicholas Brooks and G. Whittington were, moreover, pointing a way forward, with their article on St Andrews, for assessments of town growth by the use of documentary, cartographic and archaeological evidence.[42] Archaeological investigation, also, in early towns commenced in Scotland in the early 1970s, albeit at first on a fairly small scale. The steady stream of excavations which has followed, especially in Perth and Aberdeen, and the resulting published reports,[43] have contributed vastly to knowledge of the subject: buildings, possessions, pottery, diet, health and other topics have been illuminated on particular sites. It is, perhaps, inevitable, if regrettable, that syntheses are slow to appear in print, as archaeologists generally prefer to build up from minutiae rather than attempt 'the big picture'; a general overview of urban archaeology in Scotland would be welcome.

The Scottish Burgh Survey Series, funded by the then Scottish Development Department, produced some fifty reports on the archaeology and history of individual towns. The historical research of Anne Turner Simpson and the archaeological overview of Robert Gourlay and Sylvia Stevenson were not, however, closely intermeshed. Two perceptive short surveys, by A. A. M. Duncan and G. W. S. Barrow, emphasised the stimulus of trade and the need for a good location as fundamental to early urban activity, and viewed the crown's grant of privileges to a community as a comprehensible but formal part of the process.[44] Elizabeth Ewan then attempted to fit the urban archaeological material with the documentary evidence for towns as a whole.[45]

Michael Lynch's 'Whatever happened to the medieval burgh?' pointed to a new approach to urban history, and in 1988 the entire subject was given a notable stimulus in a set of essays on *The Scottish Medieval Town,* edited by Lynch, together with Michael Spearman and Geoffrey Stell,[46] a volume which both summarised current ideas and pointed the way ahead towards areas requiring investigation. Spearman's contribution on Perth, for example, was the first published topographical analysis

[41] I. H. Adams, *The Making of Urban Scotland* (London, 1978); G. Gordon and B. Dicks, eds., *Scottish Urban History* (Aberdeen, 1981).

[42] N. P. Brooks and G. Whittington, 'Planning and growth in the medieval Scottish burgh: the example of St Andrews', *Transactions, Institute of British Geographers*, new series, 2 (1977), 278–95.

[43] J. C. Murray, ed., *Excavations in the Medieval Burgh of Aberdeen, 1973–81* (Society of Antiquaries Monograph Series, 2 (1982); P. Holdsworth, ed., *Excavations in the Medieval Burgh of Perth, 1979–81* (Society of Antiquaries of Scotland Monograph Series, 5, 1987).

[44] A. A. M. Duncan, *Scotland* (Edinburgh, 1975), chs. 18, 19; G. W. S. Barrow, *Kingship and Unity* (London, 1981), ch. 5.

[45] E. Ewan, *Townlife in Fourteenth-Century Scotland* (Edinburgh, 1990).

[46] M. Lynch, 'Whatever happened to the medieval burgh?', *Scottish Economic and Social History*, 4 (1984), 5–20; M. Lynch, M. Spearman and G. Stell, eds., *The Scottish Medieval Town* (Edinburgh, 1988).

of an early Scottish town, following the lines of the seminal study of Alnwick by Conzen.[47] Individual studies of particular towns continued to be undertaken, with results appearing either in print or in thesis form: Glasgow, Dunfermline, Dundee, Selkirk, Leith and Montrose, for example, have all been the subjects of detailed studies on a variety of aspects.[48] Indeed, the individuality of towns, as against a sameness of appearance, has come to be given more emphasis.

An interdisciplinary approach to the study of individual towns has been adopted by the new series of Burgh Surveys. These are funded by Historic Scotland and produced in the Centre for Scottish Urban History, Department of Scottish History, Edinburgh University, with Pat Dennison as historian and Russel Coleman as archaeologist. Documentary, archaeological and cartographic evidence is allied to other visual remnants of the built environment in an attempt to recreate the historic town.[49] And by the year 2000 a two-volume history of the town of Aberdeen, funded by Aberdeen District Council, will add substantially to our knowledge of town life in Scotland.[50]

(iv) PLAN OF THE VOLUME

This volume, like its successors, is designed to provide an authoritative and up-to-date account of British towns within its period, looking at their nature and functions, their origins and development, and the relationships between towns, between towns and their hinterlands and between towns and the state. We have been especially keen to draw wherever appropriate on sources and disciplines other than document-based history, and the balance of our team of authors reflects that. Archaeology, architecture, urban morphology and other disciplines provide vital evidence where documents are lacking, and often greatly enrich our knowledge even after urban documentation becomes available.

[47] Conzen, *Alnwick*.

[48] A. Gibb, *Glasgow: The Making of a City* (London, 1983); J. McGrath, 'The administration of the burgh of Glasgow' (PhD thesis, University of Glasgow, 1986); S. Stevenson and E. P. D. Torrie, *Historic Glasgow, the Archaeological Implications of Development* (Scottish Burgh Survey, 1990); J. McGrath, 'The medieval and modern burgh', in T. M. Devine and G. Jackson, eds., *Glasgow* (Glasgow, 1995), vol. I, pp. 17–62; E. P. D. Torrie, 'The gild of Dunfermline in the fifteenth century' (PhD thesis, University of Edinburgh, 1984); E. P. D. Torrie, *Medieval Dundee* (Dundee, 1990); J. M. Gilbert, ed., *Flower of the Forest: Selkirk, a New History* (Galashiels, 1985); S. Mowat, *The Port of Leith: Its History and Its People* (Edinburgh, n.d. *c.* 1995); G. Jackson and S. G. E. Lythe, *The Port of Montrose: A History of its Harbour Trade and Shipping* (Tayport, 1993).

[49] Fifteen towns were assessed in 1994–7: Kirkcaldy, Stranraer, Cumnock, Hamilton, Musselburgh, Dunblane, Coupar-Angus, Stornoway, Melrose, Dalkeith, Forfar, Dumbarton, Linlithgow, Nairn and North Queensferry. Pat Dennison and Russel Coleman are the authors, and the surveys are published by Historic Scotland in association with Scottish Cultural Press. Aberdeen has also been the subject of a survey: E. P. Dennison and J. Stones, *Historic Aberdeen* (Scottish Burgh Survey, 1997).

[50] E. P. Dennison, D. Ditchburn and M. Lynch, eds., *A New History of Aberdeen* vol. I (East Linton, forthcoming); H. Fraser and C. Lee, eds., *ibid.*, vol. II (East Linton, forthcoming).

Temporal and spatial coverage provide even more problems than for the early modern and later modern periods which are the subjects of the following volumes. The 'middle ages', as defined above and as followed in this volume, represents a span of time about twice as long as the periods covered by Volumes II and III combined, and changes over that time were enormous. It is true that the bulk of surviving urban archives is much less than for post-medieval times, but the 'buried archives' of archaeology have added enormously to our knowledge over the past generation or so. It has not been easy in a single volume to do justice to it all, though we hope that the bibliographical references we provide will enable readers to explore much more of it.

The British coverage of the volume also creates problems, for historians have usually discussed English, Scottish and Welsh towns separately – for the very good reason that medieval Britain was a geographical expression and not a united state. The context of the earliest towns and central places was one of a multiplicity of small states which only gradually coalesced into the kingdoms of England and Scotland. Once they did so, these two kingdoms developed their own political and administrative systems, so that the framework for English boroughs and Scottish burghs was never quite the same: the recent work on Scottish medieval towns listed above has stressed not only many similarities with English towns but also striking differences arising from their political, social and ecclesiastical as well as geographical context – the greater uniformity of burgh law and custom in Scotland, for instance, or the more unified voice of the towns in Scottish national politics (at least by the fifteenth century).[51] The Welsh context was even more complex, since although medieval Wales was 'an identifiable geographical unit' by the time that towns developed, 'it had never known political unity other than the hegemony temporarily imposed by military might':[52] even when the last independent principality was conquered by the English king Edward I the country remained divided under different systems of administration. For these reasons a number of chapters have been written jointly by English and Scottish experts, while Part IV includes separate surveys of Welsh and Scottish towns.

The structure of the volume balances the main themes of urban history against these temporal and spatial dimensions. Parts II and III take a broadly chronological approach, dividing the nine centuries or so under discussion, very unequally, in the decades either side of 1300, for reasons already stated: where we have to distinguish the two broad periods, we use 'early middle ages' for the period before 1300, and 'later middle ages' for the fourteenth, fifteenth and early sixteenth centuries. Within each part the structure is approximately the same, to allow for comparisons between the two periods: an introductory survey is

[51] E.g. Lynch, Spearman and Stell, eds., *The Scottish Medieval Town*, pp. 11–13.

[52] R. R. Davies, *Conquest, Coexistence, and Change* (Oxford, 1987), pp. 4, 14.

followed successively by accounts of towns in a political, social and economic context (in the broad sense of those terms); by surveys of the interlocking themes of culture and the Church; by discussion of the physical fabric or townscape; and then by a series of three or four chapters considering the different levels and types of town from London – then as later the largest British town – to the smallest of market towns. In Part IV we shift our focus to the geographical context, looking at the different regions and states within which the towns were located – six English and Welsh regions, and a separate survey of Scotland – where the stress is on the patterns and distinctions between towns in different parts of Britain rather than over time. Finally, a conclusion sums up some of the main themes and findings identified in the volume, and an appendix of ranking tables of towns acts as a point of reference for the volume as a whole.

We hope that the evidence presented here, some of it for the first time, will demonstrate abundantly how much change and development took place over the long time span we cover, so easy to foreshorten when lumping together medieval and early modern towns as 'pre-industrial' in the manner of Gideon Sjoberg, whose model, as Peter Clark rightly remarks, 'is only of limited value for the analysis of the Western European . . . town'.[53] David Nicholas, whose richly detailed survey of the medieval European city was published as our volume was being completed,[54] stresses the same point: he divides the medieval centuries, like us, at around 1300 to stress the great changes of the later medieval period, and his conclusion emphasises how greatly urban life changed between the fourth and fifteenth centuries: 'the Roman city when it survived at all was only a central core of a settlement that was far more complex socially, economically and topographically than its ancient predecessor had been . . . The urban pattern of the modern period was clearly recognisable by 1450.'[55] That may be to stress progress and increasing complexity a little too strongly – he himself surveys evidence for retrogression in English towns in the fifteenth century – but he is surely right to stress the great distance in character as well as in time between Roman and late medieval. British towns by 1450, and even more by 1540, had come a long way, and much of what we would find if we could visit an early sixteenth-century town would be nearer to modern urban life than to the distant revival of town life in the early seventh century.

[53] G. Sjoberg, *The Preindustrial City* (New York, 1960); P. Clark, 'Introduction: the early modern town in the west', in P. Clark, ed., *The Early Modern Town: A Reader* (Harlow, 1976), p. 2.

[54] D. Nicholas, *The Growth of the Medieval City: From Late Antiquity to the Early Fourteenth Century* (Harlow, 1997); D. Nicholas, *The Later Medieval City 1300–1500* (Harlow, 1997).

[55] Nicholas, *The Later Medieval City*, p. 344.

· 2 ·

The origins of British towns

D. M. PALLISER

THE *Cambridge Urban History* begins with the seventh century because that was when permanent town life, on our definition, began in southern Britain. However, it would be wrong to plunge into the story of medieval British towns without at least some discussion of previous urban life in this island. The long Roman occupation of *Britannia* had entailed the introduction and development of towns on the Mediterranean model, and some scholars have argued that the occupation of some of those towns was never interrupted. The current consensus is for discontinuity at least of urban life if not of occupation; but no one doubts the importance of the infrastructure left by the Romans: the town sites, the road network linking them and in many cases the very shape of streets and town centres. This Roman prologue, as it were, is therefore of importance to later developments. Before it is faced, however, a little should be said of the possibility of recognisably urban settlements even before the Roman occupation.

Neolithic farming communities first appeared in Britain around 3500 bc,[1] and by 3000 bc they were established in many areas. This development of settled agriculture led to the need for 'central places' and meeting places in the Neolithic and Bronze Ages, though to nothing yet recognisably urban as it did in the Middle East at the same time. The Iron Age, however (*c.* 500 BC–AD 50 in southern Britain), witnessed the development of tribal states with, probably, some form of central authority, accompanied by forms of settlement which may be interpreted as genuinely proto-urban. Hill-forts, which originated in the Bronze Age if not the Neolithic, became common in many parts of Britain. They were traditionally interpreted as temporary refuges (German *Fluchtburgen*), but it is now clear that some were occupied in peacetime, and some large ones,

[1] English-speaking pre-historians and archaeologists now distinguish between dates BC (calendar years) and bc (radiocarbon years).

including Danebury (Hants.), 'were intensively settled, even to the extent of a simple form of street system'. These are often seen as places which the Romans forced the Britons to abandon in favour of new towns nearby, though 'in some areas this had already occurred before the Roman occupation, while in others it did not occur till considerably later, if at all'.[2] In at least one case, *Sorbiodunum* (Old Sarum), the hill-fort was successively occupied – as Roman town, West Saxon *burh* and Norman cathedral city – until the thirteenth century. Even closer to proto-towns may have been the large defended settlements of the major tribal states in the lowlands, notably Wheathampstead (Herts.), probably the stronghold captured by Caesar in 54 BC, and Colchester and *Verulamium*, at both of which coins were struck by King Cunobelin (*c.* AD 10–40). 'What went on in these vast areas remains obscure', remarked A. L. F. Rivet, but 'although they cannot properly be called cities, some of the Britons were already accustomed to central settlements on a truly regal scale.'[3] Finally, pre-Roman Britain seems also to have had landing-places which may be characterised as ports, through which there was regular trade with the continent.

Some writers have gone so far as to argue that 'by the end of the Iron Age there was in southern and eastern Britain a complex urban society', whereas one of the latest writers to survey Romano-British towns states flatly that 'in the year 43 there were no settlements in Britain which could properly be described as towns'.[4] The second statement is nearer the general opinion, and the first seems overstated however one defines 'urban'. Certainly the Romans, who invaded South-East Britain in AD 43, regarded themselves as bringing in more advanced forms of society and settlement based upon the city-state (*civitas*), with the countryside as an adjunct of the town. *Britannia*, like other Roman provinces, was divided into *civitates*, of which at least sixteen are well attested.[5] The structure was based as far as possible on existing areas, with nearly every *civitas* having a capital on or close to the site of its tribal predecessor. Thus Leicester and Silchester appear to have been laid out on the sites of pre-Roman centres, while in other cases the old focus was deliberately replaced (e.g. Dorchester in place of Maiden Castle). Above the *civitas* capitals in status were the privileged towns of Roman citizens called *coloniae* and *municipia*, though it is not clear from the accidents of surviving inscriptions how many towns acquired those privileges. The only *coloniae* under the early Empire, when the term was confined to foundations for retired army veterans, were Colchester, Lincoln and Gloucester, but later other towns could be promoted to this rank – York certainly acquired it by

[2] P. Salway, *Roman Britain* (Oxford, 1981), p. 13.

[3] A. L. F. Rivet, 'Summing-up: some historical aspects of the Civitates of Roman Britain', in J. S. Wacher, ed., *The Civitas Capitals of Roman Britain* (Leicester, 1966), pp. 102–3.

[4] J. V. S. Megaw and D. D. A. Simpson, *Introduction to British Prehistory* (Leicester, 1979), p. 421; G. de la Bédoyère, *English Heritage Book of Roman Towns in Britain* (London, 1992), p. 15.

[5] A. L. F. Rivet, *Town and Country in Roman Britain*, 2nd edn (London, 1964), pp. 135, 176.

AD 237, and London must surely have done so earlier. The only certain *municipium* was *Verulamium*, but evidence points to others acquiring the same status, such as Leicester.[6] The difference between them and other urban communities ceased to matter in the third century, when the distinction between citizens and non-citizens was virtually abolished.

There is, however, only limited usefulness in identifying Roman towns, like their medieval successors, in terms of contemporary categories. No fewer than six different Latin terms were used for British urban sites, not all of them with precise legal meanings.[7] It is, perhaps, better to think of the towns of the province in terms of their size, complexity and infrastructure. John Wacher discusses twenty-one settlements which had sufficient specialised functions (administrative, social, economic, etc.) to be considered urban, as well as having planned layouts; while he and Barry Burnham have also analysed another fifty-four settlements from the wide range of sites often grouped together as 'small towns' (Map 2.1).[8] What is remarkable about these seventy-five places is how many were also towns in the medieval period, and indeed have remained urban ever since. As Rivet put it well:

> Colchester, Gloucester, Lincoln and York, Canterbury, Winchester, Chichester, Dorchester and Leicester, Cambridge and Worcester, all revived after the Dark Ages and are still county towns today. The implication of this must surely be that these places, both as administrative centres and as markets, were as well sited as they could be in relation to the agricultural exploitation of Britain not only in Roman conditions but in the conditions that prevailed in the Middle Ages and later . . . The pattern is strikingly modern.[9]

However, a geographical limitation must be stressed in here introducing a work covering Britain as a whole. None of Wacher's and Burnham's Roman towns lay north of Hadrian's Wall, and only two in Wales. In the rest of Britain the Iron Age pattern of settlement continued to evolve without the injection of Mediterranean city life.

Even within the urbanised part of *Britannia*, a caveat must be entered against identifying Roman towns too closely with their medieval and modern successors. Their sites may often have been the same; they may often have been centred round a group of public buildings in the same way, and laid out in the same way, as many medieval towns; but their chief functions may have been rather different. Medieval towns are in this volume characterised in primarily socio-economic

[6] Salway, *Roman Britain*, p. 575; J. S. Wacher, *The Towns of Roman Britain*, 2nd edn (London, 1995), pp. 18, 19. [7] Wacher, *Towns of Roman Britain*, pp. 15, 16.

[8] *Ibid.*, pp. 82–407; B. C. Burnham and J. Wacher, *The 'Small Towns' of Roman Britain* (London, 1990), *passim*.

[9] Rivet, *Town and Country*, p. 76. His statement is substantially true: two of his examples, Canterbury and Colchester, while not 'county towns today', were certainly the administrative centres of their counties throughout the middle ages.

Map 2.1 The towns of Roman Britain
Source: J. S. Wacher, *The Towns of Roman Britain*, 2nd edn (London, 1995), p. 22.

terms, following Reynolds' definition, and that is valid for at least some British towns since the seventh century: the *wic* or *emporia* of London, York, Ipswich and *Hamwic* were all, at least in part, economically specialised communities. Greco-Roman cities have, however, been generally viewed since Werner Sombart as functionally very different, 'political and military capitals, more consumers than producers of goods and services, that exploited the rural environs to which they were linked juridically and socially'.[10] That is confirmed by the curious fact that villas were more numerous around secondary towns than around *civitas* capitals: it seems likely that the land around the capitals (as around

[10] D. Nicholas, *The Growth of the Medieval City* (Harlow, 1997), p. 3, citing Sombart and Hopkins.

the *coloniae*) was farmed from the towns, whereas in medieval times it was the smaller towns which were more likely to have a significant agricultural sector.[11] Sombart's model of Greco-Roman urbanism is broadly that accepted by Chris Wickham and Guy Bois in their different accounts of the transition from the ancient world to 'feudalism': the details of their arguments are beyond the scope of this discussion, but they both point the way to an ancient system in which towns and the economy played a very different role from that in both medieval and modern times.[12] The differences should, however, not be overstressed: despite the greater predominance of governmental functions and public services, 'much of what went on in Roman towns was what went on in later towns: commerce and manufacture'.[13]

What happened to the towns of Roman Britain is difficult to establish, despite over a century of archaeological investigation (part of the town of *Viroconium*, Wroxeter, was excavated as early as 1860). Some towns seem to display signs of decline, or at least of shrinkage, well before the end of Roman occupation, and there has long been a temptation to argue that, because the towns more or less disappeared in the fifth century, they must have been in decline in the fourth, or even in the third, century; but it may be that the pattern was in fact one of 'stabilisation and transition' rather than 'stagnation and depression'.[14] There were certainly major barbarian attacks in 367, and Ammianus Marcellinus notes that Theodosius, having repelled the attacks, restored cities as well as forts, though many town defences have now been shown to have been improved and strengthened over a long period, too lengthy to be all connected with his alleged restorations.[15] Nor did towns all become mere defensive strongpoints. Environmental archaeology has recently shown that at Lincoln commercial food processing, and perhaps heated buildings, survived into the late fourth century.[16]

However, Simon Esmonde Cleary has assembled much archaeological evidence to argue for 'a marked recession in activity in Roman Britain', including the abandonment of urban buildings, well before the end of imperial rule in *c.* 409–11. The structure of the province depended on the maintenance of the army through taxation, and the raising of that taxation from the rural economy via towns. All of this, functioning with difficulty between *c.* 380 and 410, collapsed suddenly 'in the generation or so after 411. In that time the towns, the villas, the industries and the other material evidence diagnostic of Roman

[11] Rivet, 'Summing-up', p. 105; Salway, *Roman Britain*, pp. 587, 596. Two recent regional surveys of the South-East have confirmed that the majority of villas did not cluster round major towns: *British Archaeology*, 31 (1998), 5.

[12] C. Wickham, 'The other transition', *P&P*, 103 (1984), 3–36; G. Bois, *The Transformation of the Year One Thousand* (Manchester, 1992), pp. 70–93. Cf. also Philip Jones, *The Italian City-State: From Commune to Signoria* (Oxford, 1997), pp. 17–46, for a vigorous differentiation of ancient and medieval towns.

[13] J. Campbell, ed., *The Anglo-Saxons* (Oxford, 1982), p. 10.

[14] De la Bédoyère, *Roman Towns in Britain*, p. 76.

[15] Wacher, *Towns of Roman Britain*, p. 78.

[16] *British Archaeology*, 5 (June 1995), p. 4.

Britain disappeared.'[17] It is true that Constantius' *Life of St Germanus* has been taken to imply that municipalities may still have been functioning in 429, and probably still in the 430s, but a careful analysis of his text shows that it does *not* imply the continuing existence of urban life.[18] As to *why* town life should have disappeared in the fifth century, views are still sharply divided, with some historians seeing the traditional agents of invasion, genocide, famine and epidemics as the causes, while others prefer to stress continuity of population but with a 'systems collapse' in which demoralised Britons allowed themselves to be 'acculturated' to the society and economy of a minority of successful but primitive invaders. Yet other writers deny any sudden collapse of urban life, whether through breakdown, conquest or economic crisis.[19]

Differing interpretations of the ending of Roman town life depend chiefly on archaeology, since documentary records are both scanty and problematic. Unfortunately, the more abundant archaeological evidence is also problematic because of the lack of reliable dating materials: the official importation of coinage in large quantities seems to have ended in or by 402, while factory-made pottery also disappeared in the early fifth century, both of them clear evidence of a 'commercial collapse'.[20] There is therefore no easy way of dating fifth-century deposits. Furthermore, overlying early and mid-Roman layers in many towns are deposits of what is usually termed 'dark earth', deposits of dark-coloured loam often mixed with building material. This is frequently interpreted as evidence of a sharply reduced urban occupation in late Roman towns, but it seems increasingly likely that the earth, whenever and however it was formed, has destroyed and absorbed late Roman buildings and made impossible an analysis of stratification and dating for the fourth and early fifth centuries.[21] The chronologies proposed by archaeologists, not surprisingly in these circumstances, differ widely. Esmonde Cleary would see urban occupation ending by *c.* 430 at latest, whereas others have stressed casual but significant finds suggesting a much later end in at least some towns: for instance, 'a brand-new water-main' was 'constructed in normal Roman fashion' in *Verulamium*, dated by Sheppard Frere and Peter Salway to perhaps about 450 or even later, with the implication that 'urban life continued in *Verulamium* in some form into the second half of the century',

[17] S. Esmonde Cleary, *The Ending of Roman Britain* (London, 1989), pp. 131, 161; his dating bracket of *c.* 409–11 is better than the standard date of 410 in many British textbooks: see e.g. Salway, *Roman Britain*, pp. 433–45.

[18] E. A. Thompson, *Saint Germanus of Auxerre and the End of Roman Britain* (Woodbridge, 1984), pp. 8–10. Thompson's conclusions, and his revised date for Germanus' second visit, are unfortunately not taken into account by Wacher in his revised edition: *Towns of Roman Britain*, p. 409.

[19] E.g. R. Reece, 'Town and country: the end of Roman Britain', *World Archaeology*, 12 (1980), 77–92; R. Reece, 'The end of the City in Roman Britain', in J. Rich, ed., *The City in Late Antiquity* (London, 1992), pp. 136–44; P. Dixon, '"The cities are not populated as once they were"', in Rich, ed., *The City in Late Antiquity*, pp. 145–60.

[20] Salway, *Roman Britain*, p. 456.

[21] B. Yule, 'The "dark earth" and late Roman London', *Antiquity*, 64 (1990), 620–8.

though one sceptical critic notes that it is 'rather a lot to read into a single pipe'.[22] At Wroxeter, even later dates have been suggested for a final period of settlement when timber-framed buildings were erected in and around the baths complex, but the dating is still controversial.[23]

Frere, indeed, went so far as to suggest that the majority of important towns 'never ceased to be occupied', but this is hard to substantiate on present evidence.[24] There are certainly possibilities for survival, or early revival, of important central functions in some towns – a royal palace or a church adapting or succeeding a Roman structure – but *urban* occupation properly understood is another matter. The evidence is best at Canterbury, significantly the site of the first English cathedral in 597. There 'sunken-featured buildings', presumed to be those of English immigrants, have been found from as early as the mid- to late fifth century.[25] Nevertheless, even there the cumulative evidence of recent excavations suggests at best that the town remained without a break a centre from which authority was exercised: 'there was no continuity of *occupation* from the Roman to Anglo-Saxon periods'.[26] Dodie Brooks, in a survey of the evidence nationally, concludes that 'the principal towns of Roman Britain were deserted by the mid fifth century, and remained so for at least a hundred years', though in a specific study of Canterbury she concludes that the gap between Roman and English settlement may there have been much shorter, perhaps as little as twenty years.[27]

In short, though the nature of the English conquest of southern Britain in the fifth and sixth centuries is still debated, there is much support for the traditional view that urban life on our definition was extinguished. Nevertheless, many former Roman towns seem to have remained important as centres of authority, especially in the West where Britons long continued to rule from Roman towns. The well-known *Chronicle* entry of 577, for example, seems to identify three British kings overthrown in that year as ruling from Gloucester, Cirencester and Bath. Admittedly, one of those cities has often been cited as a classic case of a

22 Salway, *Roman Britain*, p. 459; Wacher, *Towns of Roman Britain*, p. 238; de la Bédoyère, *Roman Towns in Britain*, p. 125.

23 See e.g. R. White, 'Wroxeter, rich in a wealthy land', *British Archaeology*, 17 (1996), 7. Wacher, *Towns of Roman Britain*, p. 377, is more cautious, dating the final phases only to 'beyond 388'.

24 S. S. Frere, 'The end of towns in Roman Britain', in Wacher, ed., *Civitas Capitals*, pp. 87–100 (quotation from p. 87). The best summaries are now D. A. Brooks, 'A review of the evidence for continuity in British towns in the 5th and 6th centuries', *Oxford J of Archaeology*, 5 (1986), 77–102; D. A. Brooks, 'The case for continuity in fifth-century Canterbury re-examined', *Oxford J of Archaeology*, 7 (1988), 99–114; Wacher, *Towns of Roman Britain*, pp. 408–21; and P. Ottaway, *Archaeology in British Towns* (London, 1992), pp. 109–19.

25 K. Blockley *et al.*, *Excavations in the Marlowe Car Park and Surrounding Areas* (Canterbury Archaeological Trust: Archaeology of Canterbury, 5, 1995), pp. 280–350. I am grateful to D. A. Hinton for information on the Canterbury evidence.

26 Ottaway, *Archaeology in British Towns*, p. 112 (my italics).

27 Brooks, 'Review of the evidence', 99; Brooks, 'Case for continuity', 113.

Roman town quickly becoming a cluster of crumbling buildings linked by streets overgrown with vegetation. That is because of the later Old English poem, *The Ruin*, which is usually thought to have been inspired by the appearance of Bath (*Aquae Sulis*):

> The fortified places have fallen asunder; the works of giants crumble.
> Roofs have fallen, towers have tumbled;
> The barred gate[?] is plundered; frost is on the mortar;
> Gaping shelters against storms are split open and fallen . . .[28]

The point of the poem, however, is that it was probably written by a monk steeped in the Roman literary tradition and familiar with ruined Roman buildings as part of his everyday life, not as something alien.[29]

Certainly the Roman period cannot be viewed as an irrelevance, a false start only, in the history of British urbanism. The continuous history of town life, from the seventh century onwards, is saturated with its Roman inheritance, and it is impossible to treat the new urban pattern as if it had been developed on a *tabula rasa*. It is no coincidence that many major English towns arose on, or adjacent to, the sites of Roman predecessors, or that many cathedrals were planted in Roman towns. Not only were those towns often in good natural positions, but they also had defences which could be patched up, buildings which could be re-used and a good network of roads linking them. There is no geographical determinism about this: there had been no major settlement in the lower Thames valley in the Iron Age, and so the very creation of London, and consequently of a web of main roads radiating from it, are entirely a legacy of Rome, and a legacy of enduring importance. The same is true of York, where there had been no significant centre before the Romans, but which endured for many centuries as the leading northern centre once the Romans had made it so. Both London and York, along with many other Roman towns, seem to have survived the end of Roman rule as centres of authority, and as pre-urban nuclei from which true town life could revive and spread.[30] Had southern Britain never experienced its lengthy Roman occupation, the medieval – and modern – pattern of towns and communications might have been completely different.[31]

[28] J. F. Benton, *Town Origins* (Boston, Mass., 1968), p. 47.

[29] I owe this point to Christopher Dyer. Cf. also below, p. 150.

[30] See e.g. Campbell, ed., *The Anglo-Saxons*, p. 39; P. S. Barnwell, '*Hlafaeta, ceorl, hid* and *scir*: Celtic, Roman or Germanic?', *Anglo-Saxon Studies in Archaeology and History*, 9 (1996), 56–8.

[31] For a recent survey stressing 'the enduring and constantly renewed influence of the Roman world' in post-Roman Britain, see M. Archibald *et al.*, 'Heirs of Rome: the shaping of Britain AD 400–900', in L. Webster and M. Brown, eds., *The Transformation of the Roman World AD 400–900* (London, 1997), pp. 208–48.

· PART II ·

The early middle ages 600–1300

· 3 ·

General survey 600–1300

GRENVILLE ASTILL

FOR MOST of the period under review the data allow a qualitative, rather than a quantitative, approach to towns and, therefore, important issues such as the relative size of towns can be addressed only in an oblique fashion. From the late tenth century an indication of the relative intensity of urban development can be gained from, first, the coin evidence and, then, Domesday Book, followed by the taxation records. While the documentary record increases from the twelfth century, it is largely 'external' to the town itself and reflects the growth and interests of central government; historical evidence is, therefore, mainly concerned with the process of creating and administering towns. A major exception are the urban surveys which survive for a small number of towns and start in the later thirteenth century.[1]

Much new information has come from archaeological fieldwork, but this, like the documentary material, has a bias towards the larger towns. The proportion of any town that has been excavated is very small, and consequently it is difficult to assess the validity of the sample.[2] Excavated evidence can show the diversity of a town through information about the urban fabric, including communal structures such as defences and churches, as well as domestic and industrial buildings, and about the inhabitants themselves and the kind of environment they lived in. Where it is possible to draw upon the results of a number of archaeological excavations in the same town, aspects of the urban economy can be discussed, such as the range and organisation of industries and

[1] G. H. Martin, 'The English borough in the thirteenth century', *TRHS*, 5th series, 13 (1963), 123–44; D. M. Palliser, 'Sources for urban topography: documents, buildings and archaeology', in M. W. Barley, ed., *Plans and Topography of Medieval Towns in England and Wales* (CBA Res. Rep., 14, 1976), pp. 1–7.

[2] For example the 1961–71 excavation campaign at Winchester sampled 'just under 2%' of the intramural city, M. Biddle, 'The study of Winchester: archaeology and history in a British town, 1961–1983', *Proc. of the British Academy*, 69 (1983), 96.

trading patterns.[3] Considerable progress has also been made through the spatial analysis of towns such that it is possible to show that many towns, including newly planned foundations, often had a long and complex development; it often remains, however, to put a chronology to these spatial changes.[4]

The main problem for at least half of the period concerned is that an adequate outline for the development of towns has yet to be produced. Between the seventh and tenth centuries it is difficult to identify any urban settlement, if that is defined as a place in which were concentrated a variety of attributes that distinguished it from surrounding settlements, for example in terms of its administrative, economic or military function. Instead, there appear to be a variety of locations which performed sufficient of one or more of these functions for each to be regarded as a distinctive, a central, place. An evolutionary model of urban development thus seems inappropriate. In any one area central-place functions may well have been distributed among several settlements, some of which went on to acquire a more recognisably urban character, while others returned to being 'normal' rural settlements. A possibility is that the function of some central places lapsed in the face of changed economic or political circumstances, only to resume later and develop into fully fledged towns. This last consideration is particularly important because a considerable number of places which were to become towns have long periods for which there is no evidence to indicate their character. How do we deal with places, for example, which were central places between say 650 and 850, and reappear in our sources as towns in the twelfth or thirteenth centuries? The question is relevant for several of our major types of central places. What was the function of those Roman cities before they became bishops' sees, and why were some selected as religious centres and not others? Similarly, not all minsters or *villae regales* became later medieval towns, but when and how did the successful towns become differentiated from the rest? The temptation is to treat these lapses in the historical record as if they were periods when the settlements became more complex incrementally – the continuity argument – but there are often no grounds for these assumptions.

In such an apparently fluid situation, it is necessary to try to isolate the factors which contributed to, and ultimately resolved, the medieval urban process. The attempt runs the risk of denying that the real character of the urban process depended as much on a complex intermeshing of these factors as the factors themselves, but it is nevertheless a necessary starting point which also serves to highlight differences of approach. There are essentially three major strands, crudely summarised as political, religious and economic, which have been used to elucidate the urban sequence: first, the development of kingship and the English state, secondly, the Church and, thirdly, the 'quickening' of the economy.

[3] Recent surveys include J. Schofield and R. Leech, eds., *Urban Archaeology in Britain* (CBA Res. Rep., 61, 1987); J. Schofield and A. Vince, *Medieval Towns* (Leicester, 1994).

[4] See below, pp. 158–66.

The relative emphasis can deny or accentuate the similarities between the British and continental experiences.

First, it is clear that from the seventh century royal power was consolidated in larger territorial units, allied to an increased interest in the productivity of land at a time when other sources of wealth, often derived from warfare or exchange, were becoming less reliable. Nevertheless, the small scale and personal nature of the kingdoms' social structures, underpinned by 'networks of negotiation' which involved the recycling of surpluses, militated against the kings' ability to create a resource base.[5] In the course of the eighth century, attempts were made to increase royal surplus in order to achieve a greater degree of authority and independence, as in Mercia. Such power was exercised from particular places which became instruments or agents of this power.[6] The complexity of these agencies increased as the mechanisms of central government developed, and this complexity is best documented from *c.* 900 in terms of political and economic regulation. What were initially centres for tribute collection and periodic consumption could, for example, develop more thoroughgoing regulatory activities which would include the administration of justice, tax raising and the institution of a mint, as well as the supervision and protection of trading activities, including specially appointed officials, as reflected in the laws of Edward the Elder, Athelstan, Edgar and Cnut.[7] Centres could also acquire a military function by becoming a garrison for troops and a refuge for the surrounding area, as detailed in the Burghal Hidage.[8] Although all these activities had an economic dimension, they were primarily indicators of political development, so that such centres were seen as part of the political restructuring, and indeed their physical character may have been intended to make an ideological statement.[9]

Secondly, many of these 'political' attributes were delegated or granted to the Church, so that from at least the eighth century the locations of cathedrals and minsters had acquired a character that differentiated them from other settlements. Indeed, the permanent residence of a religious community, rather than a periodic royal presence, would have increased the administrative and

[5] B. A. E. Yorke, *Kings and Kingdoms in Early Anglo-Saxon England* (London, 1990), pp. 9–19, 157–78; C. Wickham, 'Problems of comparing rural societies in early medieval western Europe', *TRHS*, 6th series, 2 (1992), 241–4.

[6] Wickham, 'Problems of comparing rural societies', 244–6; N. P. Brooks, 'The development of military obligations in eighth- and ninth-century England', in P. Clemoes and K. Hughes, eds., *England before the Conquest* (Cambridge, 1971), pp. 69–84; J. Haslam, 'Market and fortress in England in the reign of Offa', *World Archaeology*, 19 (1987), 76–93; R. Hodges, *The Anglo-Saxon Achievement* (London, 1989), pp. 115–49.

[7] H. R. Loyn, 'Towns in late Anglo-Saxon England: the evidence and possible lines of enquiry', in Clemoes and Hughes, eds., *England before the Conquest*, pp. 122–3; see below, pp. 51–60.

[8] The most recent discussion is D. Hill and A. Rumble, eds., *The Defence of Wessex* (Manchester, 1996).

[9] As for example in M. O. H. Carver, *Arguments in Stone* (Oxford, 1993), pp. 17–18, 63–77.

consumption roles. In some cases the distinction is not necessary, as both royal and religious centres were located close together, and were thus mutually supportive.[10] The problem then becomes how to separate royal and religious influence, and which came first; often this is impossible, as reflected in the disputed (secular or religious?) aristocratic status of the excavated complex at Northampton.[11] After the Norman Conquest the royal initiative in town formation and regulation was increasingly shared with, or delegated to, lay and ecclesiastical lords with the result that urban development became inextricably linked with the increasing seigneurialisation of the country, leading to a multiplication of town creations.[12]

The third explanation for urbanisation is based on a general economic expansion. An increase in long-distance trade from the late seventh century was underpinned by an intensification of agricultural production, allied to population growth. Centres were needed from which to articulate and supervise the resulting trading network. It is still not clear if such a demand for urban centres had arisen organically as a result of expansion in the countryside, or if indeed towns were created as part of a royal policy to orchestrate and control rural production.[13] The evidence presented below, however, shows that the pace of economic development had pronounced temporal and geographic variations which indicate that the economy exercised a far from positive or continuous influence on town growth.

(i) 600–800

These three themes, individually or collectively, produced a variety of distinctive settlements which have been termed 'central places', 'centres of authority' or 'proto-urban settlements', and it is necessary to ask how they related to the existing settlement pattern. The most obvious places to start are the Roman towns. 'England was exceptional in having been Roman and yet in not preserving Roman Christianity, a Romance language or other discoverable Roman institutions.'[14] What relevance, then, did Roman towns have for the English in the sixth or seventh centuries? As economic activity was negligible, it is customary, following the work in northern France and Germany, to argue that some towns retained a political and administrative importance as 'centres of authority'. Canterbury and London may have had royal residences in the late

[10] J. Blair, 'Minster churches in the landscape', in D. Hooke, ed., *Anglo-Saxon Settlements* (Oxford, 1988), pp. 35–50.

[11] See comments in D. A. Hinton, *Archaeology, Economy and Society* (London, 1990), p. 45; J. Blair, 'Palaces or minsters? Northampton and Cheddar reconsidered', *Anglo-Saxon England*, 25 (1996), 98–108.

[12] M. Beresford, *New Towns of the Middle Ages* (London, 1967), pp. 327–38.

[13] Summarised in Hodges, *Anglo-Saxon Achievement*, pp. 186–202.

[14] S. Reynolds, *An Introduction to the History of English Medieval Towns* (Oxford, 1977), p. 22.

sixth to late seventh centuries, and these have also been postulated at Winchester and York. No explicit archaeological evidence has been forthcoming, and there is always the possibility, based on later material, that such a royal complex was extramural. However, it is important to emphasise that even if such royal sites were established inside some Roman towns, they were in the minority and that, in order to facilitate the exercise of power, most 'palaces' were located in the countryside in order to be an effective element in the contemporary settlement pattern.[15]

Both archaeological and historical evidence indicates that religion reclaimed Roman towns: they were incorporated into the seventh-century framework of Christianity. Whereas previously the location of bishops' sees in Roman towns was interpreted as a recognition of the existing secular power structure, it is possible (as is true of other religious foundations) that there was a conscious and symbolic use of the Roman past. The uncertainty is perhaps indicated by rival, secular or ecclesiastical, interpretations of the medieval origin of Winchester. A primarily religious function for both York and Worcester between the seventh and ninth centuries has been proposed.[16]

Yet Roman towns were not invariably selected to be religious centres. They may well have been chosen for ideological reasons, but this was not sufficiently consistent to be regarded as a deliberate policy – the prevailing power or settlement structure did not allow that. But, by assuming roles as centres for the collection of tribute, and of consumption, some Roman towns once again became differentiated.

For the same reasons some royal estate centres are seen as potential central places, but there is not a great deal of evidence. Some royal sites of the eighth and ninth centuries were production centres, such as the salt workings at Droitwich; and others were clearly processing large agricultural surpluses, to judge from the cornmills at Tamworth and Old Windsor.[17] But, just as with the Roman towns, there is a growing tendency to emphasise the importance of religious institutions such as minsters for the development of incipient towns, although it must be said that most of the evidence is considerably later and topographic in nature. The excavations at the eighth- and ninth-century monasteries such as Hartlepool, Wearmouth, Jarrow and Whitby demonstrate the

[15] M. Biddle, 'Towns', in D. M. Wilson, ed., *The Archaeology of Anglo-Saxon England* (London, 1976), pp. 105–10; M. Welch, *Anglo-Saxon England* (London, 1992), p. 104.

[16] Biddle, 'Towns', pp. 118–19, 114; B. A. E. Yorke, 'The foundation of the Old Minster and the status of Winchester in the seventh and eighth centuries', *Proc. of the Hampshire Field Club and Arch. Soc.*, 38 (1982), 75–83; Carver, *Arguments in Stone*, pp. 59–60; N. J. Baker, *et al.*, 'From Roman to medieval Worcester: development and planning in the Anglo-Saxon city', *Antiquity*, 66 (1992), 65–74, and see below, pp. 128, 247–8.

[17] J. Bond and A. Hunt, 'The town: *c.* 400–1900', in S. Woodiwiss, ed., *Iron Age and Roman Salt Production and the Medieval Town of Droitwich* (CBA Res. Rep., 81, 1992), pp. 186–7; P. Rahtz and R. Meeson, *An Anglo-Saxon Watermill at Tamworth* (CBA Res. Rep., 83, 1992), pp. 9–12, 156.

diverse economic activities that were pursued at such places.[18] And such activities needed expertise and commodities from other regions of England and the continent. This was nothing new – many imported materials came into this country, mainly through Kent, by the sixth century via, presumably, small ports of entry which were probably no more than periodic beach markets. Few have been recognised archaeologically, but a candidate is Sarre, with its rich weapon burials and (later) toll exemption, which Fordwich also had from 675. The excavated coastal monasteries at Whitby, Jarrow and Hartlepool suggest that such houses directly managed their own trading, while the mid-eighth-century exemption from tolls shows that some Kentish churches traded (for at least some of the time) via London.[19]

The introduction of silver coinage in the late seventh century, and the rapid expansion of its use, especially with the secondary series of *sceattas* from *c.* 710–15, are indications of the extent to which the country was engaged in exchange, particularly the South and East. *Sceattas* are generally regarded as unsuitable and unnecessary for everyday transactions within rural society. Their distribution suggests they were primarily used in the raising and conversion of tribute, and in regional and continental exchange. *Sceattas* occur in the locality of known royal and aristocratic sites, and churches and minsters, thus confirming the special character of such centres of authority. They have also been found close to river and road crossings and at hill-forts, all potential sites of fairs. Some particular types of *sceatta* were in use over a wide area, and demonstrate that England was integrated into a North Sea commercial zone: examples of the 'porcupine' series have not only been found in England, but also in the Low Countries, the Rhineland and Denmark.[20]

From about 700 until the mid-ninth century this trade had been augmented by large coastal and riverine settlements, for example London, *Hamwic*, York and Ipswich, which were some of the largest and most densely occupied sites in England. They matched similar *wics* on the southern Channel, North Sea and

[18] Blair, 'Minster churches in the landscape', pp. 40–50; R. Shoesmith, *Hereford City Excavations*, vol. II (CBA Res. Rep., 46, 1982), pp. 29–31; R. Daniels, 'The Anglo-Saxon monastery at Church Close, Hartlepool', *Archaeological J*, 145 (1988), 158–210; R. Cramp, 'Monastic sites', in Wilson, ed., *Archaeology of Anglo-Saxon England*, pp. 223–41. Other possible examples include Brandon and Flixborough, but the foundations failed to survive beyond the ninth century: R. Carr, A. Tester and P. Murphy, 'The middle Saxon settlement at Staunch Meadow, Brandon', *Antiquity*, 62 (1988), 371–7; C. Lovelock, 'A high-status Anglo-Saxon settlement at Flixborough, Lincolnshire', *Antiquity*, 72 (1988), 158–60.

[19] J. Hines, 'North Sea trade and the proto-urban sequence', *Archaeologia Polona*, 32 (1994), 15–17; Hinton, *Archaeology*, p. 57; S. Kelly, 'Trading privileges from eighth-century England', *Early Medieval Europe*, 1 (1992), 3–28.

[20] See below, pp. 221–2 and 245; D. M. Metcalf, 'Monetary circulation in southern England in the first half of the eighth century', in D. Hill and D. M. Metcalf, eds., *Sceattas in England and the Continent* (Oxford, 1984), pp. 27–47; D. M. Metcalf, *Thrymsas and Sceattas in the Ashmolean Museum, Oxford*, vol. III (London, 1994), p. 308.

Baltic Sea coasts: those which had most contact with England are likely to have been Dorestad and Quentovic, supplemented by smaller ports on the beaches to the north of the Rhine mouth. Together, they indicate a recrudescence of trade between these areas in the eighth and most of the ninth centuries at a time when contacts with the Mediterranean world were minimal.

Wic settlements have been interpreted as the means by which a flow of prestige goods came into the hands of kings in order to maintain the stability of the social and political structure which was dependent on the recycling of surplus or gift giving. This view was supported largely by evidence for settlement planning and by the quantities of imported pottery that had been recovered. There is, however, little difference in the material culture from other contemporary inland sites, and the units of production, as far as craftworking is concerned, appear to be the same.[21] As a result, some see the king's role in *wics* as being essentially indirect. The ports were under his control and he supervised, regulated and taxed the exchanges which took place there. The *wics* started to operate at a time when kings were trying to increase their control over their kingdoms' resources, and they recognised, albeit belatedly, how extensive was the long-distance trade and decided to exploit it. It was, perhaps, the change in the nature of kingship rather than the state of international contacts that was the context for the rise of the *emporia*; otherwise it is difficult to see why *wics* had not been developed earlier because the trade had clearly existed before. It is also unlikely that the *emporia* functioned entirely to provide the kings with prestige goods at a time when royal authority was increasingly exercised through land grants and not gifts. The *wic* may represent a relatively short-lived experiment in the exercise of royal power, similar perhaps to the granting of exemption from tolls at about the same time.[22] That royal attempts to control and concentrate long-distance trade were not totally effective is indicated by the independent activities of the monasteries already referred to, but also because around the south and east coasts collections of *sceattas* have been found which probably indicate that small-scale trading continued to take place at beach markets, as for example at North Ferriby, and perhaps Selsey.[23]

Eighth- and ninth-century England, then, appears to have had two types of place which were differentiated from rural settlements in terms of economic and administrative function: the *wic* and the central place. Both are to be seen developing within the context of the changing nature of kingship and the development of the Church. Centres of authority existed and were also for collection and consumption and, to judge from the distribution of *sceattas*, for exchange.

[21] See below, pp. 218–22, for details.

[22] Hines, 'North Sea trade', 15–23; Kelly, 'Trading privileges', 3–28.

[23] E. Pirie, 'Some Northumbrian finds of *sceattas*', in Hill and Metcalf, eds., *Sceattas in England*, pp. 209–11; J. Munby, 'Saxon Chichester and its predecessors', in J. Haslam, ed., *Anglo-Saxon Towns in Southern England* (Chichester, 1984), pp. 317–22.

They included places which were later to become differentiated from one another: former Roman towns, new diocesan centres, *villae regales* and minsters. The *wics* were formalised and regulated trading places whose occupants and merchants were probably supplied from royal lands via the centres of authority. This two-part proto-urban hierarchy probably existed alongside earlier, small-scale, trading arrangements which continued and were perhaps developed by some monasteries.

The provisioning of *wics*, and the documentary evidence for renders, may be interpreted as a more aggressive, royal, approach to resource management, but it is more commonly regarded as evidence for the increase in agricultural production. To a certain extent this is confirmed by evidence for agricultural intensification during the eighth and ninth centuries. New areas were brought into use for the first time – in the Fens and in high valleys such as Teesdale – and the exploitation of river and marine resources increased. It is also possible that this intensification was associated with some changes in the pattern of rural settlement as shown by the abandonment of early Saxon settlements on outlying areas.[24]

(ii) THE NINTH AND TENTH CENTURIES

Evidence for economic expansion during the late eighth and ninth centuries is, however, fugitive. Growth in *Hamwic*, for example, had apparently dissipated by the ninth century. The Offan silver penny and the subsequent issues did not have such a widespread distribution as the secondary *sceattas*, suggesting that there was a decline in the volume of exchange at this time: this is also indicated by the absence of later coins in the assemblages coming from the 'prolific' *sceatta* coastal sites. Such evidence may point to a contraction in economic activity in England, and between the English kingdoms and the continent. The change may well have started before, but was almost certainly hastened by, the Viking raids from the 790s.[25] Most of the *wic* sites appear to have been abandoned by the mid-ninth century, and it is thought that the population was relocated – in the case of London and York within the refurbished Roman walls. It is, however, not just a case of displacement of population, because in the case of London the resettled intramural area was considerably smaller and less occupationally diverse than *Lundenwic*, which would again suggest a significantly different economic situation.[26]

[24] Summarised in G. Astill, 'An archaeological approach to the development of agricultural technologies in medieval England', in G. Astill and J. Langdon, eds., *Medieval Farming and Technology: The Impact of Agricultural Change in Northwest Europe* (Leiden, 1997), pp. 196–204.

[25] D. A. Hinton, 'Coins and commercial centres in Anglo-Saxon England', in M. A. S. Blackburn, ed., *Anglo-Saxon Monetary History* (Leicester, 1986), p. 18.

[26] A. Vince, 'The economic basis of Anglo-Saxon London', in R. Hodges and B. Hobley, eds., *The Rebirth of Towns in the West AD 700–1050* (CBA Res. Rep., 68, 1988), p. 72.

Difficulties from within and without seem to have coincided with, or perhaps stimulated, a more aggressive kingship, which is seen most obviously in Mercia with the inclusion of borough work in charters from the mid-eighth century, and at least one physical embodiment of centralised coercion, Offa's Dyke. Further indications are the fortification of some centres of authority, perhaps in the early ninth century. The bishop's seat at Hereford was enclosed by a defensive circuit and an integrated street system; at Tamworth the site of a royal palace was extended and protected by new defences. Some centres of authority, then, acquired a military function, were apparently garrisoned by troops and offered refuge for the surrounding population; this is as far as the archaeological evidence will take us.[27]

Debate continues about the extent to which a military reorganisation of some proto-urban centres was accompanied by an increase in economic activity. Some, for example, have taken the documentary and archaeological evidence for an increase in royal authority with the, mostly undated, topographic evidence for planned street systems to argue for a royal town-planning exercise which was rewarded by immediate economic growth. Others have separated the act of defence (and perhaps the laying out of streets) from the, later, development as an economic centre. The problem is to reconcile the evidence for a sluggish economy with an interpretation of these central places as thriving towns.[28]

The defended centre of authority was, however, a characteristic response in the ninth century to the combined effect of a developing kingship and the external threat of the Vikings. While the earliest examples come from Mercia, the later Wessex evidence is more complete because of the Burghal Hidage, which details the organisation of the ninth-century defensive arrangements; it indicates a burgeoning royal authority which was developing its powers of taxation at the same time as having to assume responsibility for the protection of the populace in the face of attack.[29] A distinction is commonly made between burghal forts and towns, and the evidence for a planned street system in the latter has often been regarded as the critical indication that *burhs* were intended to be towns as well as garrisons. The distinction may have been overdrawn: it is undeniable that the forts were larger and sited in unsuitable positions to become economic centres. It does not, however, follow that the 'towns' achieved this status immediately. The renovation of the old Roman centres such

[27] Brooks, 'The development of military obligations', pp. 69–84; D. Hill, *An Atlas of Anglo-Saxon England* (Oxford, 1981), p. 75; Shoesmith, *Hereford City Excavations*, II, pp. 70–80; Rahtz and Meeson, *An Anglo-Saxon Watermill*, pp. 4–5.

[28] Biddle, 'Towns', pp. 120–34; Hodges, *Anglo-Saxon Achievement*, pp. 194–200; G. G. Astill, 'Towns and town hierarchies in Saxon England', *Oxford J of Archaeology*, 10 (1991), 95–117.

[29] N. P. Brooks, 'England in the ninth century: the crucible of defeat', *TRHS*, 5th series, 29 (1979), 17–20; N. P. Brooks, 'The administrative background to the *Burghal Hidage*', in Hill and Rumble, eds., *The Defence of Wessex*, pp. 128–50.

as Winchester, Bath or Exeter, and the laying out of defences and streets at 'new' sites such as Wallingford or Cricklade indicate an intention, but was it realised? Some sites for the burghal towns were carefully chosen: they were already distinctive places, usually centres of authority, which thus had a potential for economic development. In some cases the royal intention was clear – Alfred created new mints at Winchester, Exeter, Oxford and Gloucester, king's officials were appointed – but these actions may constitute more of a political statement because they were not always accompanied by 'urban' development. The essentially agricultural occupation, of timber buildings and byres, within the walls at Gloucester, for example, remained unchanged for most of the later ninth and tenth centuries. A considerable proportion of Cricklade's intramural area lay vacant, a situation which might indicate a provision for the periodic billeting of a garrison rather than a permanent, urban, occupation. Although it is difficult to date late Saxon deposits within *burhs*, it does seem unlikely that evidence for urbanisation occurred before the later tenth century. The archaeological evidence for most of the ninth-century *burhs* then indicates a clear military purpose, with pretensions to urban status which may not have been met for nearly another century. But we should also be aware that the documentary evidence for dense and diverse occupation commensurate with urban conditions is not always reflected in the archaeological record, and this is the case with Canterbury. Winchester, by the ninth century, is unusual because it seems so precocious in its urban development, as reflected in its refurbished Roman defences, its new street system and its intramural and suburban occupation. The original aristocratic character of the seventh- and eighth-century settlement may have become more socially diverse in the ninth, but large tenements were still granted to lay and ecclesiastical lords, who may have used them as 'urban manors'.[30]

Most *burhs* appear to have been no more economically differentiated than the centres of authority – indeed some *burhs* previously had this status. One suspects that the impetus for specialised settlements lay entirely with the king's and the aristocracy's needs. The state of the economy could not support a complex urban structure, and indeed the bulk of the rural population had no need of anything more sophisticated than centres of authority. It is significant that the most economically diverse sites in ninth-century England were to be located at aristocratic sites and central places; in other words, the present evidence suggests that proto-urban centres satisfied aristocratic needs and had little relevance for the majority of the population, a pattern that some also see in Domesday. The connection between the aristocracy and the *burh* was not only economic, however, for this

[30] Excavations in individual *burhs* are summarised in Astill, 'Towns and town hierarchies', 104–8; M. Biddle and D. Keene, 'Winchester in the early middle ages', in M. Biddle, ed., *Winchester in the Early Middle Ages* (Oxford, 1976), pp. 341, 452–4.

would underestimate the importance and size of the garrisons, and that the king's thegns may have resided within the *burhs*.[31]

The coinage, however, shows few signs of economic growth in the ninth and early tenth centuries. In the face of declining silver stocks, the reform of the coinage in the early tenth century appears to have had little effect and pennies continued to have a limited circulation and can hardly have been used in everyday transactions. Coin finds remain low, and coin loss was similar in *burhs* to excavated palace and aristocratic sites – another indication that the level of trading at both types of site remained approximately the same. The excavated sites of Cheddar, Faccombe Netherton and Goltho also revealed a variety of specialised industrial and agricultural activities, demonstrating that these centres retained an important position in the economic life of tenth-century England. Yet levels of exchange may have remained low because some religious centres failed to survive, or took a long time to recover from, the ravages of the ninth century. The sample is small, but few of the excavated monastic sites continued into the tenth century. Reduced or stagnant internal trade may well have been matched by a decline in overseas exchange, for tenth-century assemblages from *burhs*, even those on the coast, are remarkable for their lack of imported pottery.[32]

If it was the intention of the Wessex kings to promote the essentially military installations into towns, their lack of success was not reversed by the expansion and growing unification of the kingdom. The Æthelflædan *burhs* have not received a great deal of archaeological attention, but the excavator of Stafford concluded that it was 'little more than a fort, whose immediate and strategic needs were served by a cantonment of tradesmen retained at its gates'.[33] Even after Edward the Elder's reconquest (and refortification) of the Danelaw, the output of the southern mints, including London and Winchester, remained stable whereas those in the Danelaw, and Chester in particular, were extremely active. Trading may have shifted away from the traditional southern English links with the Low Countries and the Rhineland to the northern English contacts with the Scandinavian kingdoms across the North and Irish Seas.[34]

The new trade axis appears to coincide with a change to a more urban form of settlement in some northern central places. Foremost were the creation of enduring properties, a densely packed occupation and evidence of a considerable range of industrial activity. Such attributes were present in York and Lincoln from the late ninth/early tenth century, with a clear intensification in the later tenth century; it was also the time when there is remarkable evidence for industry from

[31] R. Fleming, 'Rural elites and urban communities in late Saxon England', *P&P*, 141 (1993), 3–26; Brooks, 'England in the ninth century', 18–19.

[32] Hinton, 'Coins and commercial centres', pp. 18–22; Vince, 'The economic basis', pp. 90–2.

[33] M. O. H. Carver, *Underneath English Towns* (London, 1987), p. 56.

[34] D. M. Metcalf, 'The monetary history of England in the tenth century viewed in the perspective of the eleventh century', in Blackburn, ed., *Anglo-Saxon Monetary History*, pp. 134–5.

Stamford and Thetford and, in the case of the latter, dense occupation. Consistent, but more fragmentary, evidence comes from Chester and Norwich.[35]

Urbanisation was, it seems, more apparent in the North-East and the East Midlands than the South. The reduced minting and trading activity in the South was contrasted in the North by a sustained period of trading with the Scandinavian areas which probably underpinned the prolific minting of coin in the region. The extensive evidence for overseas contact in places like York and Chester goes a long way to justify this interpretation, but this urban growth could not just have been sustained by long-distance trade. Places such as Lincoln and Thetford have congested and diverse occupation areas, but do not have extensive evidence of continental trade; their industries – ceramic and metal-working – would have catered for demand in the surrounding areas, not abroad.

(iii) THE LATER TENTH AND ELEVENTH CENTURIES

The southern mints, dominated by London, re-established their productivity and, as a consequence, Chester's control of Irish trade was increasingly challenged by Bristol and Exeter. Active trading with the Low Countries and the Rhineland was resumed, and both increased minting and trade are probably to be associated with the exploitation of new sources of silver in the Harz mountains. The change virtually coincides with Edgar's reform of the coinage in 973, after which mint signatures are consistently included on coins. This new information allows for the first time a geographical expression of coin production; this has been obtained either on the basis of the number of moneyers working at each mint (as a percentage of the whole working in any one reign) or as the output of each mint as a percentage of total national output for each issue of coinage. The problem is that the geography of minting is not the same as the geography of regional consumption or indeed marketing. The activity of mints was invariably related to the processing of, usually imported, silver (coin) which leads to the primacy of ports in any distribution. So the ranking of towns says less about the productivity of the surrounding region than the country's external relationships. An independent source for the latter is imported pottery, which again became prolific in the late tenth and early eleventh centuries.[36]

The coinage can, then, be used to rank the towns of late Saxon England, but its utility is perhaps more limited than the rankings based on later taxation records. It does, however, give an interesting distribution. York, for example, was the most northerly mint and it existed in virtual isolation. There were nine other regional minting centres: largest by far was London, followed by Lincoln, Winchester, Stamford, Chester, Thetford, Exeter, Canterbury and Norwich. The second rung

[35] See below, pp. 225–30, for details of individual towns.

[36] See Astill, 'Towns and town hierarchies', 112–13, for details.

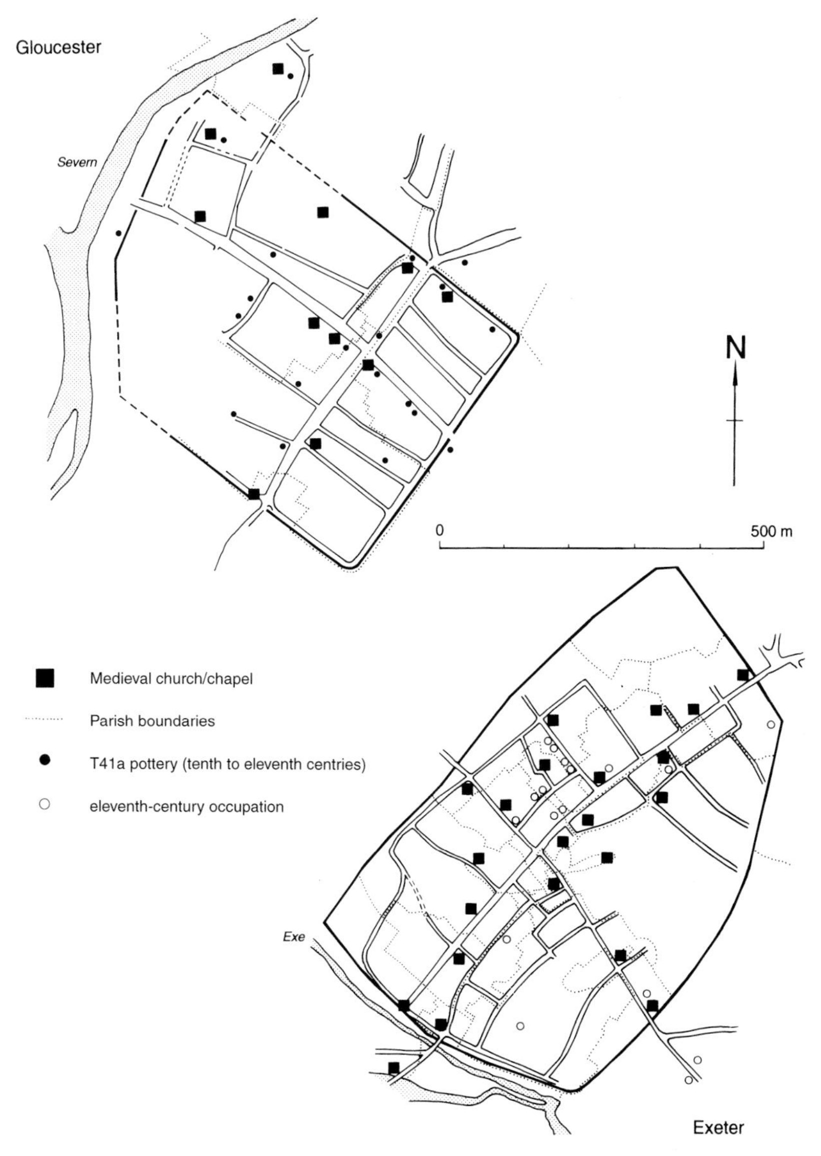

Figure 3.1 Later Saxon Gloucester and Exeter
Source: after G. G. Astill, 'Towns and town hierarchies in Saxon England', *Oxford J of Archaeology*, 10 (1991), 106.

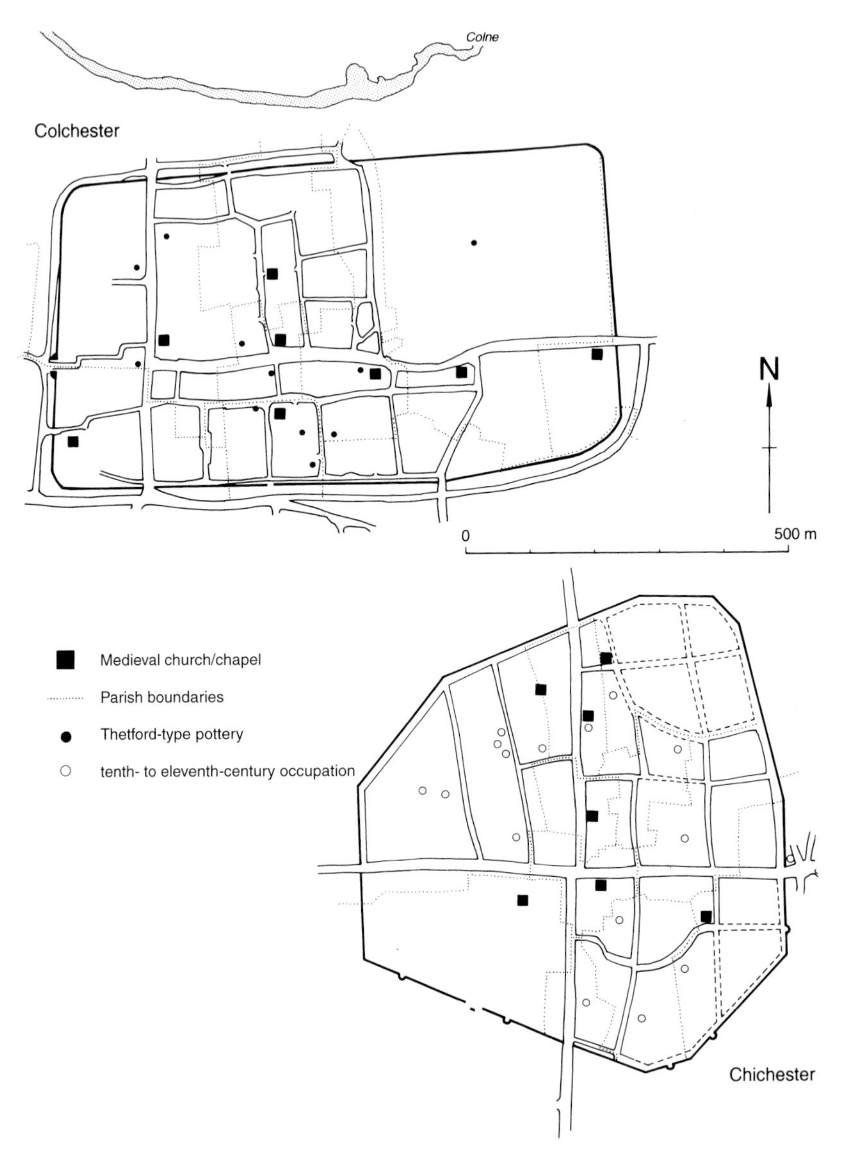

Figure 3.2 Later Saxon Colchester and Chichester
Source: after G. G. Astill, 'Towns and town hierarchies in Saxon England', *Oxford J of Archaeology*, 10 (1991), 107.

was essentially the county towns, usually *burhs*, followed by smaller mints which were located on royal estates, a particular concentration being in Somerset, and on the southern coast. The large number of mints, larger than was really necessary given the strong royal control over coinage, gives some indication of the extent to which coins were being used increasingly in transactions.[37]

The apparent revival of the southern economy led to a rapid development of the southern *burhs*. By the early eleventh century, most of the *burhs* exhibited all the characteristics of urbanised settlements: built-up street frontages, dense nature of the occupation, a large number of churches, variety of industries, especially ceramics, the prominence of imports in pottery assemblages and a growth of suburbs. As with the North fifty years or so earlier, this revival was not just a result of the revival of continental trade; it also reflects a further intensification in the countryside, but the evidence is largely indirect. Foremost amongst these indications must be the start of the 'great rebuilding' of churches in stone which has considerable implications for the mobilisation of resources. But there are also signs in the colonisation and allotment of reclaimed land in Somerset and Essex, probably in the later tenth century, and readjustments in the settlement pattern which may be associated in some parts of the country with the development of nucleated settlements.[38]

There are also strong indications of a readjustment in the urban network which has not yet been fully researched – in some ways the late tenth and early eleventh centuries are the least studied, although the ranking of towns between 973 and 1066 on the basis of numismatic evidence tends to emphasise continuity rather than change. The most obvious changes occur in the reign of Ethelred II in response to the Danish invasion. The creation of what have been termed 'emergency *burhs*', usually by the recommissioning of Iron Age hill-forts, has been regarded as an act of military expediency; while this was no doubt the case, it also gives an insight into the nature of contemporary urbanism. First, it emphasises the continued military importance of *burhs*, for the creation of hill-top defences should also probably be associated with the improvement of the fortifications in established *burhs* such as Wareham, Cricklade, Wallingford and Christchurch. Secondly, some emergency *burhs* were probably intended for more permanent occupation. The transfer of moneyers from Ilchester to South Cadbury or from Wilton to Old Sarum could be regarded as a prudent, temporary, measure, but the construction of stone

[37] Summarised in *ibid.*, 98–100, and see below, Appendix 1b, for a list based on D. M. Metcalf, *An Atlas of Anglo-Saxon and Norman Coin Finds c. 973–1086* (London, 1998), pp. 293–301.

[38] Vince, 'The economic basis', pp. 90–2; R. Morris, *Churches in the Landscape* (London, 1989), pp. 162–7; R. Gem, 'The English parish church in the eleventh and early twelfth centuries: a great rebuilding?', in J. Blair, ed., *Minsters and Parish Churches* (Oxford, 1988), pp. 21–30; S. Rippon, 'Medieval wetland reclamation', in M. Aston and C. Lewis, eds., *The Medieval Landscape of Wessex* (Oxford, 1994), pp. 242–7; S. Rippon, 'Essex *c.* 700–1066', in O. Bedwin, ed., *The Archaeology of Essex* (Chelmsford, 1996), p. 125.

defences and churches indicates an intention to create a more permanent settlement, as indeed Old Sarum became. The urban network of *c.* 1000 was still in a process of formation and adjustment. The intention, stated in Athelstan's laws, to concentrate the marketing, minting and defensive functions in one place was, no doubt, close to being fulfilled. But there were still parts of the country, for example north Somerset or central Wiltshire, where these three activities took place in separate locations, reflecting perhaps the low level of economic differentiation which had taken place between towns, *burhs* and centres of authority in these regions. That the relocation of some of the *sedes* into the larger towns occurred only in the eleventh century perhaps indicates how extended was this centralising, urban, movement which was still incomplete at the Norman Conquest.[39]

An increased differentiation can also be seen in the centres of authority, especially those where religious foundations had been reformed and revived. Æthelwold's refoundation of Abingdon in the 950s with an enlarged endowment meant that it exercised a powerful economic influence reflected in the ten merchants recorded in Domesday, and on a larger scale there were the ambitious urban projects at the gates of Bury St Edmunds and perhaps St Albans and Ely. Secular centres may have had less impact because their role as collecting centres may have lapsed with the disappearance of food rents, and their administrative responsibilities had either been weakened through alienation or assumed by the *burhs*.[40]

(iv) THE LATER ELEVENTH TO TWELFTH CENTURIES

The century after the Norman Conquest sees the development of many trends of the preceding period, in particular continued urban growth and the increasing concentration of central-place functions within single urban settlements, which gave a greater stability to the hierarchy of towns. The similarity in the ranking of towns based on the coin evidence between 973 and 1066 and that recorded in Domesday (Map 3.1) makes this point, and also confirms a three-part hierarchy of regional, county and minor centres.[41]

[39] M. Aston, 'The towns of Somerset', in Haslam, ed., *Anglo-Saxon Towns in Southern England*, pp. 188, 173–4; J. Haslam, 'The towns of Wiltshire', in Haslam, ed., *Anglo-Saxon Towns in Southern England*, pp. 94–102, 122–8, 140; J. Campbell, 'The Church in Anglo-Saxon towns', in D. Baker, ed., *The Church in Town and Countryside* (Oxford, 1979), pp. 132–3.

[40] G. Astill, 'The towns of Berkshire', in Haslam, ed., *Anglo-Saxon Towns in Southern England*, p. 65; M. Atkin, 'The Anglo-Saxon urban landscape in East Anglia', *Landscape History*, 7 (1985), 31–2; Beresford, *New Towns*, p. 326; P. H. Sawyer, 'The royal *tūn* in pre-Conquest England', in P. Wormald, D. Bullough and R. Collins, eds., *Ideal and Reality in Frankish and Anglo-Saxon Society* (Oxford, 1983), p. 281.

[41] D. M. Metcalf, 'The ranking of boroughs: numismatic evidence from the reign of Ethelred II', in D. Hill, ed., *Ethelred the Unready* (Oxford, 1978), pp. 159–212; Hill, *Anglo-Saxon Atlas*, p. 130; G. H. Martin, 'Domesday Book and the boroughs', in P. H. Sawyer, ed., *Domesday Book* (London, 1985), pp. 155–9.

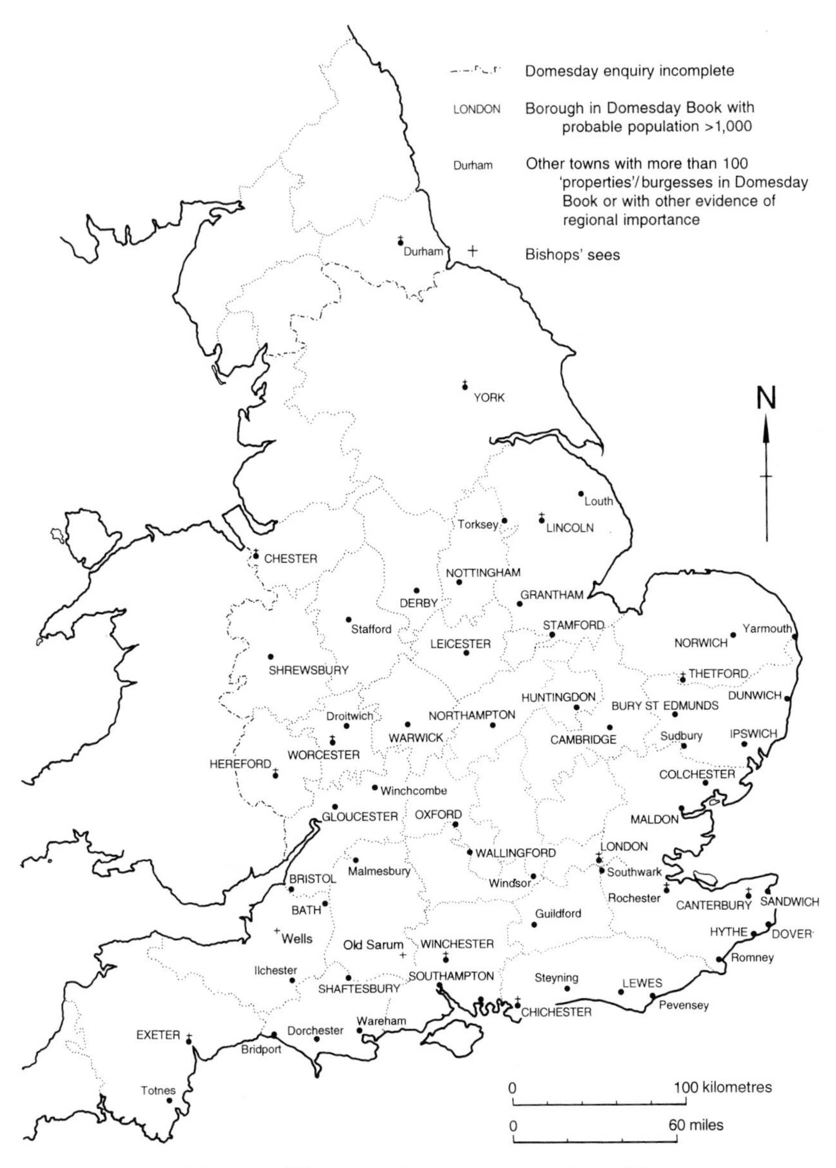

Map 3.1 The more important towns in 1086
Source: after S. Reynolds, *An Introduction to the History of English Medieval Towns* (Oxford, 1977), p. 35.

The Conquest did, however, demonstrate in a stark way how the town's function as an agency of central government could be increased. The major and strategically important towns quickly became instruments of royal control through the construction of castles in the core of the urban areas; it is perhaps no accident that the most systematically recorded towns in Domesday were those in which castles were built. Damage to the urban fabric, both residential and religious, could be extensive and cause a dramatic rearrangement of the urban topography; this was particularly the case where Norman designs included the promotion of a town to a diocesan centre, as at Lincoln and Norwich, where the new cathedral precinct swept away much of the late Saxon town. Such rearrangements stimulated extensive suburban development along the major access routes, as in Norwich, York and Canterbury, rather than a more intensive use of backlands.[42]

The later eleventh century is also the time when the first definite signs of urbanisation occur in Wales and Scotland. In the case of Wales, urban development was principally part of the Anglo-Norman invasion and colonisation. Towns were sited primarily for military purposes, although they were often in locations which served as a focus for the local population, such as *trefi* or ecclesiastical sites. The urban community invariably comprised a colony of imported burgesses – usually English or Flemish – which existed in the shadow of a castle; over 78 per cent of medieval Welsh towns had a castle at their core. Most of the early foundations (colonised from Chester, Shrewsbury and Hereford) were in the southern Marches and along the South and West coasts, such as Chepstow, Monmouth, Brecon, Cardiff and Tenby, and during most of the twelfth century the majority of the new foundations were in these regions' lordships – Glamorgan, Gwent and Pembroke.[43]

The documentary evidence tends to concentrate the period of Scottish town creation and growth in the twelfth century, and in particular during the reign of David I (1124–53). However, it is probable that this phase of town foundation was preceded by a period of urbanisation which was taking place at least by the eleventh century. It is noticeable, for example, that many of the twelfth-century burghs were grafted on to settlements which were already economically differentiated from rural settlements as royaltouns and strongholds (Edinburgh, Stirling, Dunbarton, Dunbar) or as kirktouns (St Andrews, Brechin). In addition, there are signs that some places which received charters in the twelfth century had already been trading settlements a hundred years before, for example Dunfermline and Aberdeen. David I's creation of royal burghs was, therefore, a process whereby some of these trading settlements were 'promoted' through the

[42] See below, pp. 60; C. Drage, 'Urban castles', in Schofield and Leech, eds., *Urban Archaeology in Britain*, pp. 119–25; B. Ayers, *Norwich* (London, 1994), pp. 30–5; T. Tatton-Brown, 'The towns of Kent', in Haslam, ed., *Anglo-Saxon Towns in Southern England*, p. 9.

[43] See below, pp. 695–7; I. Soulsby, *The Towns of Medieval Wales* (Chichester, 1983), pp. 3–11, 34.

acquisition of burghal status. The burghs appear to have been an integral part of a royal policy to increase political and economic control in the core areas of the kingdom – most of the burghs were concentrated in the east and south-west of Scotland. During the twelfth century the practice of town creation was adopted by both secular and ecclesiastical lords under royal authorisation (Glasgow, Arbroath, Dundee), but the country does not seem to have shared in the great urban expansion of the thirteenth century. Scottish towns shared some of the urban characteristics common in other parts of Europe – the association of castle and town, and the importation of foreign burgesses. But they had the distinctive economic advantage of having a marketing monopoly over their rural hinterlands.[44]

It is difficult to assess the economic condition of English towns during the later eleventh century: destruction, and the reduction in size, of urban areas would no doubt have caused immediate problems, but in some cases this may have been offset by the introduction of mercantile colonies. In the short term, the initiation of such huge building campaigns would have created a demand for ancillary services, and over a longer time scale the concentration in one place of communities associated with cathedral, castle and palace would have created a large centre of consumption: the extent of the intramural area occupied by such institutions in Winchester, for example, emphasises the importance of royal and aristocratic consumption in the life of such cities.[45]

Charting the effect of royal and aristocratic consumption on the character of towns is problematic. There are, however, strong indications that the fabric of English towns continued to change from the later eleventh to the thirteenth century and beyond. The industrial basis of some towns, for example, continued to alter. Domesday and archaeological data show that the main locus for pottery manufacture was shifting from the towns, especially those in the East, to the countryside. The increasing complexity, size and congestion of some towns may have made them increasingly unsuitable for such industries. The perception of unsuitability may have been shared both by those townspeople who wished to exercise communal regulation over activities within towns, and by potters who sensed a change in demand for their wares and one which could be better catered for by moving. Similarly, the craft and processing functions which were characteristic of pre-Conquest aristocratic sites no longer appear in the archaeological record of their eleventh- and twelfth-century counterparts. In such

[44] See below, pp. 719–24; R. M. Spearman, 'Early Scottish towns: their origins and economy', in S. Driscoll and M. Nieke, eds., *Power and Politics in Early Medieval Britain and Ireland* (Edinburgh, 1988), pp. 104–8; I. H. Adams, *The Making of Urban Scotland* (London, 1978), pp. 14–16, 22–4; R. Fox, 'Urban development, 1100–1700', in G. Whittington and I. Whyte, eds., *An Historical Geography of Scotland* (London, 1983), pp. 74–6.

[45] Summarised in M. Biddle, 'Early Norman Winchester', in J. Holt, ed., *Domesday Studies* (Woodbridge, 1987), pp. 315–21.

circumstances towns would be an appropriate location for such activities, but it is surprising to find that there is less evidence for craft activities, particularly metalworking, in towns after than before the Norman Conquest. The progressive reduction in the number of towns which could mint coin during the twelfth century may have resulted in a concentration of metalworkers in those which continued as mints to the detriment of other towns which found their industrial base depleted.[46] A silver shortage in the late eleventh to twelfth century may also have hindered town growth: coin loss in towns remains low in the twelfth century. There is, thus, an apparent discrepancy between the extensive evidence for investment in the political and religious infrastructures of the larger towns, and the sparse indications of a diverse occupational structure and economic growth.

The essentially institutional character of towns of this period is also apparent lower down the urban hierarchy. In many places the intention was to associate the foundation of a castle or monastery with the creation of a small town, as had already occurred with the defence of the Marches and the colonisation in Wales. But castle towns were not confined to sensitive or disputed areas but were present in most parts of the country indeed; there was a clear tradition of founding a castle, monastery and town on one site. The extent to which these settlements merely represented urban aspirations rather than urban activity can only be determined by future work, but, as with the larger towns, the consistent association of institutions and urbanism suggests that the primary stimulus for economic growth was the consumption of aristocratic households. The exceptions to this trend were those towns which were extensively engaged in overseas trade, for example Southampton and Bristol.[47]

(v) THE LATER TWELFTH AND THIRTEENTH CENTURIES

For the late twelfth (from about 1180) to the mid-thirteenth century there is a remarkable concurrence of evidence to demonstrate a period of rapid urban growth. New classes of documentary material allow a much better appreciation of urban development. The larger towns show clear signs of a growing independence in terms of self-government, the development of laws and craft regulation. Taxation records allow for the first time a view of the post-Conquest urban hierarchy, headed by a London of European city size, followed a long way behind by regional centres – York, Norwich, Lincoln, Bristol, Northampton, Canterbury, Dunwich, Exeter and Winchester, and then the county and smaller towns. It is the latter which seem to be a particularly distinctive feature of this period – some

[46] Summaries in: M. R. McCarthy and C. M. Brooks, *Medieval Pottery in Britain AD 900–1600* (Leicester, 1988), pp. 63–70; Hinton, *Archaeology*, pp. 104–9, 141.

[47] M. W. Thompson, 'Associated monasteries and castles in the middle ages', *Archaeological J*, 143 (1986), 305–21; G. G. Astill, 'Archaeology and the smaller medieval town', *UHY* (1985), 48.

2,500 markets and 500 boroughs were probably created in England alone. The same was true in Wales where the new towns concentrated in the south and east and continued to be attached to castles, while the existing towns were extended and had their defences rebuilt in stone, often occasioned by Welsh attacks.[48] This evidence for urban development and growth was not just an accident of central government documentation. Other extensive evidence exists to demonstrate a huge growth in marketing, associated with a period of rising inflation and direct demesne farming. Almost for the first time there was a need for the rapidly growing rural population to have access to markets, not only to buy, but also to sell commodities in order to gain currency with which to pay dues and taxes. We can also see that the nature of trading was often socially determined. Local markets were used by the majority of the population for most of their needs, but magnates, for example, used all levels of the urban hierarchy as they were prepared to pay the increased costs of transportation in order to obtain luxuries. Such behaviour reflects growing specialisation, and the association of particular towns with particular commodities, but it also demonstrates that some of the most intense trading was periodic and took place at fairs, some of which, like St Ives, were divorced from the large towns.[49]

This period of increased marketing coincides with the introduction of the Short Cross penny, reinforced by new silver stocks; as the loss rate of these coins is higher than previous issues, it is likely to be another indication of increased exchange. Important changes in material culture also occur at this time; the increased production and sophistication of pottery, for example, was a response to an increased and more discerning demand, while the renewed production of small metal objects is a reflection of the increased demand among the artisan and rural populations. An important change in jointing techniques, first recorded in the larger towns at the end of the twelfth century, heralded a more sophisticated timber framing which allowed an increase in the height of buildings, another response to the increased pressure on space in the burgeoning towns.[50]

This period of growth had a dramatic effect on the urban fabric of large towns. The growing identity and self-regulation of the larger towns resulted in a physical display of this independence. The construction of defences, or perhaps more frequently barriers in the form of bars or gates, was an important way of defining the urban area as well as achieving a greater control over commercial

[48] Martin, 'The English borough', 123–44; see below, pp. 264–70. The ranking is based on the aids of Henry II, R. A. Donkin, 'Changes in the early middle ages', in H. C. Darby, ed., *A New Historical Geography of England* (Cambridge, 1973), pp. 132–5, and cf. Appendix 3 below; see below, pp. 696–8; Soulsby, *Towns of Medieval Wales*, pp. 12–13.

[49] See below, pp. 108–12; R. H. Britnell, *The Commercialisation of English Society, 1000–1500*, 2nd edn (Manchester, 1996), pp. 79–90; C. Dyer, 'The consumer and the market in the later middle ages', *Ec.HR*, 42 (1989), 305–20.

[50] See Astill, 'An archaeological approach', pp. 212–13, for summary discussion.

transactions. In the past, it was customary to date these attempts at urban definition to the same time as the levying of murage grants from the thirteenth century, but recent archaeological work would suggest that the process was under way in the twelfth century.[51] Suburban growth, too, is another characteristic of this period, with sprawling occupation along the major approach roads – the emphasis was clearly on the need to secure new frontage space rather than develop the tenement backs which were relegated to the disposal of rubbish. Periods of suburban growth were often punctuated by the construction of hospitals, which were another indication of the growing self-confidence of urban communities. The pressure on space is also reflected at river and coastal ports by the increasing use of, and growing sophistication of construction, of waterfronts. Both an attempt to increase space and to facilitate shipping, quay construction is an important index to the economic activity of towns, and it is noticeable that in major ports such as London or Newcastle the greatest phase of waterfront construction occurs between the twelfth and mid-thirteenth centuries. The importance of overseas trade particularly with regions bounded by the North Sea is demonstrated by the increase in east coast ports (and their greater tax burden), especially from the early twelfth century with places like Lynn, and then Newcastle and Yarmouth. The relative importance of towns within Britain is also indicated by the locations chosen for the foundations of the mendicant orders.[52]

The reorientation of the economy is most obvious in some county towns by a change in topography. Tenth- and eleventh-century towns usually betray their origins by the way the built-up area is centred on the cathedral or castle, reflecting the stimulus for urban growth. But later developments within these towns demonstrate that the balance of consumption has swung from the aristocracy to the artisan and rural population. Market areas were no longer constructed or enlarged at the gates of the castles, but were located on the periphery of the built-up area, often where the major approach roads met, in a position which would be most advantageous for whole communities to trade, as for example seems to have occurred at Hereford, Northampton and Oxford.[53]

The redefinition of urban space in this period of growth is also apparent in the location and arrangement of small towns. No longer were they sited at the

[51] See below, pp. 236–8; J. Bond, 'Anglo-Saxon and medieval defences', in Schofield and Leech, eds., *Urban Archaeology in Britain*, pp. 92–116.

[52] D. Keene, 'Suburban growth', in Barley, ed., *Plans and Topography of Medieval Towns*, pp. 71–82; G. Milne reviews the material in 'Waterfront archaeology in British towns', in Schofield and Leech, eds., *Urban Archaeology in Britain*, pp. 192–200; L. Butler, 'The houses of the mendicant orders in Britain', in P. V. Addyman and V. E. Black, eds., *Archaeological Papers from York Presented to M. W. Barley* (York, 1984), pp. 123–36; and see below, pp. 144–5.

[53] Shoesmith, *Hereford City Excavations*, II, pp. 94–5; T. G. Hassall, 'Archaeology of Oxford city', in G. Briggs, J. Cook and T. Rowley, eds., *The Archaeology of the Oxford Region* (Oxford, 1986), p. 124.

gates of abbeys or castles, but more usually at nodes in the communication system, often at the boundaries of different blocks of landscape or *pays*, in order to maximise the possibility of trading among the local population. Often existing settlements were extended in order to trade effectively, but others were new creations. The siting of such towns paid little attention to parochial structure. Both promoted and new towns were arranged in such a way as to increase their chances of survival – large open market areas were created, with maximal use of the main street frontage. To a certain extent this was also true of Wales. From the later thirteenth century there is clear evidence for the creation of towns in Welsh lordships such as Gwynedd which developed without castles or defences, as at Nefyn. But this was also the time of the great surge in castle and town foundations, especially in North Wales where it was primarily associated with Edward I's conquest, but was also emulated by Marcher lords and in the south-west. The continued dependence of towns on castles and garrisons for their urban status is emphasised by the failure of some towns once military support was withdrawn, as at Diserth, Cefnllys and Newport (Dyfed).[54]

So profound and rapid was the expansion in this period that there were bound to be failures, either as a result of faulty siting or of overcrowding. As in previous periods, some failed as a result of changed circumstances, and this was not limited to the small towns. Winchester was relegated to the role of a county town when it ceased to be a favoured royal residence; it did not have a sufficiently broadly based economy to retain its pre-eminence without the institutional support of the monarchy.[55]

By the end of the thirteenth century the urban network was at its maximum extent; its genesis and development had taken place with neither an even pace nor geographical consistency. For at least half of the period discussed in this chapter, progress towards a mature medieval urban form had barely started, reflecting the uneven development of the economy and the major institutions. By the late tenth century internal and overseas developments converged to create the conditions for a profound period of urban growth, but this was in turn overshadowed by the massive and rapid expansion in the late twelfth and early thirteenth centuries which ensured that the town was fully embedded in medieval society.

[54] See below, pp. 264–70, 695–8; Soulsby, *Towns of Medieval Wales*, pp. 24, 106, 130; K. Murphy, 'Excavations in three burgage plots in the medieval town of Newport, Dyfed, 1991', *Med. Arch.*, 38 (1994), 55–82.

[55] Beresford, *New Towns*, pp. 290–315; D. Keene, *Survey of Medieval Winchester* (Winchester Studies, 2, Oxford, 1985), vol. 1, pp. 88–105.

· 4 ·

Power and authority 600–1300

JAMES CAMPBELL

THE EXERCISE of power and authority in, through and over towns is fundamental to the evolution of the English state. State and towns were linked so intimately that the process or progress of each depended on the other.

(i) POWER AND AUTHORITY IN PRE-CONQUEST TOWNS

Our earliest sources are suggestive, if meagre. A law of Hlothere and Eadric, kings of Kent (673 x 686), specifies: 'If a man of Kent buys property in London he shall have two or three trustworthy men or the king's *wicgerefa* (*wic* reeve) as witness.'[1] The *wic* element relates to London as a major trading place; royal authority was already linked to the regulation of trade. Narrative sources put royal officials in the context of an urban site. Bede, writing *c.* 731 on Edwin of Northumbria (616–33), mentions a royal *prefectus*, obviously an important man, at Lincoln.[2] A *Life* of Cuthbert (written 699 x 705) mentions *civitatis praepositus* at Carlisle in 685.[3] Maybe such men exercised authority simply *in* a former Roman place, somewhat more probably in but chiefly *from* one. Such Roman centres could survive as centres of authority, if more doubtfully with other functions. Bede is explicit that Canterbury was the *metropolis* of the whole *imperium* of Æthelbert of Kent.[4] London and York apparently enjoyed comparable

I gratefully acknowledge the help of Professors G. H. Martin and Derek Keene in writing this chapter. All errors are my own.

[1] F. L. Attenborough, ed., *The Laws of the Earliest English Kings* (Cambridge, 1922), pp. 22–3.

[2] B. Colgrave and R. A. B. Mynors, eds., *Bede's Ecclesiastical History of the English Nation*, rev. edn (Oxford, 1991), pp. 192–3.

[3] B. Colgrave, ed., *Two Lives of St Cuthbert* (Cambridge, 1940), pp. 122–3.

[4] Colgrave and Mynors, eds., *Ecclesiastical History*, pp. 74–5; cf. D. G. Russo, *Town Origins and Development in Early England c. 400–950 A.D.* (Westport, Conn., 1998), p. 104 and n.

status.[5] The governmental status of some lesser places is attested by the names of early West Saxon shires. Hampshire (*Hamtunscir*, first mentioned *s. a.* 755 in the *Chronicle*, composed *c.* 891) takes its name from *Hamtun*, the royal centre at or near modern Southampton. Compare the relation of the names of Wiltshire and Somersetshire to Wilton and Somerton. Such places must have been among the more important of the *villae* or *vici regalis*, royal *tuns*, centres of royal authority often with an urban future. The distribution and location of English towns has been determined not by geography alone, but also by the needs and schemes of rulers, sometimes very early rulers. The possibility that some early rulers consciously founded towns cannot be excluded. For example the major (and apparently planned) *emporium* at *Hamwic* could have been founded by the king of Wessex.[6]

What was the nature of the internal governance of places of significance? Scanty evidence has to be eked out by inference. Some major trading places, *emporia*, of the seventh and eighth centuries were far too big to have been run simply by a *wicgerefa*. Fairly complex organisation must have been needed, for example, for Mercian kings to levy tolls in eighth-century London.[7] More, if little, is known about the internal arrangements of early Canterbury than about those of any other English place. Thus in an eighth-century charter its inhabitants appear as a collectivity, the *burhware*, owning a wood.[8] The place-name Burwash, occurring in a mid-ninth-century charter as *Burwaramers* ('*burh* men's marsh'), tells a similar tale.[9] In another ninth-century charter the *burhware* are divided into inner (*innan*) and outer (*utan*) groups.[10] Maybe the latter comprised men whose principal interests lay outside Canterbury. If so their being *burhware* could have reflected a status and function for Canterbury indicated in its name: 'the fortification of the people of Kent'. A yet more interesting mid-ninth-century charter refers to a *cnihtengild* at Canterbury.[11] It is unclear what a *cniht* was; possibly we have here an association of young men or of junior nobles.[12] What such early Kentish charters suggest is some complexity in the society, and it may be in the government, of Canterbury. For most significant places no more

[5] Russo, *Town Origins and Development*, pp. 142–3; P. Godman, ed., *Alcuin: The Bishops, Kings and Saints of York* (Oxford, 1982), line 204. [6] Russo, *Town Origins and Development*, pp. 140–1.

[7] S. Kelly, 'Trading privileges from eighth-century England', *Early Medieval Europe*, 1 (1992), 1–26.

[8] W. de Gray Birch, ed., *Cartularium Saxonicum* (London 1885–93), vol. 1, p. 344, no. 248. P. H. Sawyer, *Anglo-Saxon Charters*, rev. edn by S. E. Kelly (n.p., 1994), no. 125, refers to comments including one questioning the authenticity of the charter; Cf. also J. Tait, *The Medieval English Borough* (Manchester, 1936), pp. 8–10, cf. p. 14.

[9] E. Ekwall, ed., *The Concise Oxford Dictionary of English Place-Names*, 4th edn (Oxford, 1960), s.v., p. 76. [10] Tait, *Medieval English Borough*, p. 9 and n.

[11] *Ibid.*, p. 12, cf. pp. 81, pp. 119–22. S. Reynolds, *An Introduction to the History of English Medieval Towns* (Oxford, 1977), p. 13, points out that the association could be one of non-townsmen.

[12] J. Bosworth and T. N. Toller, *An Anglo-Saxon Dictionary* (Oxford, 1898); and T. N. Toller, *Supplement* (Oxford, 1921), s.v. *cniht*.

can be said than that a royal reeve had authority there, perhaps shared with some communal authority.

Our knowledge of towns, their origin and functioning in relation to power and authority improves from about 900. The key document is the Burghal Hidage belonging either to Edward the Elder's time (899–924) or to the later years of his predecessor Alfred.[13] It lists thirty-three places nearly all in Wessex and attributes a hidage to each. An appendix to one version relates the hidage to the number of men needed to maintain the fortification concerned. Many but not all of the places concerned were or became towns.[14] The Burghal Hidage provides the fullest early evidence for the systematic organisation of a relationship between military needs and towns or proto-towns. Other sets of fortresses were constructed by Edward the Elder in connection with his conquest of the Danelaw and by his sister and her husband for the defence of Mercia.[15] Some of these fortifications became towns, though many did not. The annals of the period refer to the men of various towns as comprising significant military forces.[16] This raises a question which remains important, and not fully answerable, for centuries to come. How far do such references relate to townsmen, in an approximately modern sense, who were armed, how far to aristocrats or gentlemen living in or associated with towns? It could be that (as Professor Platt has suggested) in the tenth century towns were often the preserve of men who were also significant rural landowners and that the urban power of such 'gradually diminished' in the eleventh and twelfth centuries.[17]

Our best starting point for investigation of the relationship between towns and government in the tenth and eleventh centuries is Domesday Book (Map 3.1). Although omitting London and Winchester, Domesday provides for some hundred places more or less information such as historians regard as providing indications of 'urban status'.[18] The extent to which towns of certain kinds were integral to government is plain above all from the administrative map of the Midlands. By 1066 there were sixteen shires between Thames and Humber, and west of East Anglia and Essex, which took their names from their shire towns. In seven of these shires the shire town was the only Domesday place with any urban status. The layout of the Midland shires is such that a river forms the spine of each and the shire town lies at a nodal point on the river

[13] D. Hill and A. Rumble, eds., *The Defence of Wessex* (Manchester, 1996). The crucial evidence for the 'one man from every hide' formula of one version of the Burghal Hidage relating to maintenance rather than to garrisoning is an obvious parallel in P. Morgan, ed., *Domesday Book Cheshire* (Chichester, 1978), f. 262v. [14] Tait, *Medieval English Borough*, p. 18. [15] *Ibid.*, p. 24.

[16] C. Plummer, ed., *Two of the Saxon Chronicles Parallel* (Oxford, 1892–9), vol. I, pp. 84, 86, 87, 88, 98–9, 101; A. P. Smyth, *Alfred the Great* (Oxford, 1995), pp. 136–7.

[17] C. Platt, *The English Medieval Town* (London, 1976), p. 22.

[18] H. C. Darby, *Domesday England* (Cambridge, 1977), pp. 363–8. For Domesday boroughs in general, most recently, G. H. Martin, 'The Domesday boroughs', in A. Williams and R. W. H. Erskine, eds., *Domesday Book Studies* (London, 1987), pp. 56–60, and above, pp. 42–4.

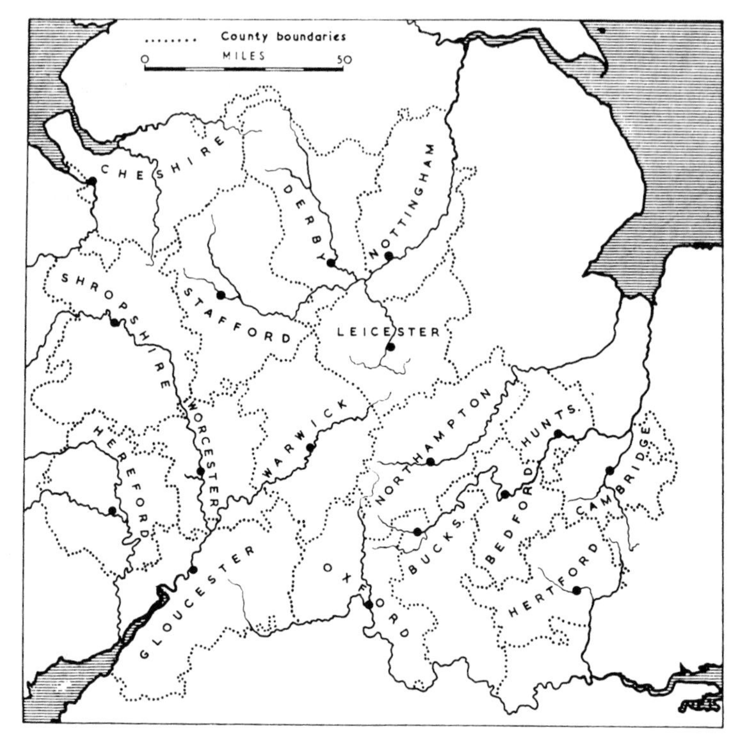

Map 4.1 The Midland counties and county towns in relation to rivers
Source: C. B. Fawcett, *Provinces of England*, revised edn, W. G. East and S. W. Wooldridge (London, 1960), p. 59.

system (Map 4.1).[19] This closely organised relationship between towns and provincial government was largely created by the tenth-century kings. In Wessex itself there had been a comparable system but the importance of some of its former shire-centres had faded. Elsewhere in the East and South-East some shires had no organised centre. The most peculiar case is that of Essex. When Essex was a kingdom, London was its head. Beheaded after the seventh century, it had no defined focus (Colchester was in too awkward a corner), and this could account for the curious rise in the thirteenth century of the seigneurial borough of Chelmsford to some of the functions of a shire town.[20]

The relationship between towns and the shires appears in various ways. In a number of shires there is a relationship between land holdings in the body of the shire and the tenure of certain properties in the shire town. The significance of this relationship is debated, but relates, *inter alia*, to the maintenance of urban

[19] C. B. Fawcett, *Provinces of England*, rev. edn by W. G. East and S. W. Wooldridge (London, 1960), p. 59. [20] H. Grieve, *The Sleepers and the Shadows* (Chelmsford, 1988–94), vol. 1, pp. 11–15.

defences.[21] Towns appear to be associated with a system or systems of economic control and monopoly within shires. We have no more than fragmentary indications of these; they may possibly have been confined to the Midlands. Our clearest hint of the existence of such systems comes from a writ of Henry I of 1130 or 1131, specifying the privileges of Cambridge.[22] These privileges differ greatly from those found in the numerous urban charters issued later in the century. The writ states that no vessel shall ply at any quay in Cambridgeshire except at Cambridge. Carts are to be laden nowhere but there, and toll shall be taken nowhere but there. Comparable if generally less explicit indications of a relationship between urban privilege and shire organisation are to be found elsewhere;[23] and there was undoubtedly in some shires an intimate connection between urban status and the collection of toll not only in the town itself but also at places at a considerable distance. Although none of the directly relevant evidence is pre-Conquest it is, nevertheless, likely that it relates to a pre-Conquest system which fell largely into desuetude during the twelfth century. The efforts of tenth-century kings to confine commercial transactions at more than a low level to towns speak for a concern to integrate political authority and economic control.[24] The apparent system of shire-related urban monopolies could indicate an even more thoroughgoing effort. The twelfth- and thirteenth-century Scottish practice whereby certain towns were granted important elements of trade monopoly within a wide related area seems to echo the system found in England; perhaps its ultimate origins were English.[25] Powerful evidence for the urban dimension of economic control is of course the elaborate coinage system sternly ordered by kings (particularly after the reform near the end of Edgar's reign) and crystallised round a close framework of mints, the most important of which were in towns.[26] Significantly, the names of the two great towns of Norwich and Bristol first appear in the historical record on coins. Royal control of the currency powerfully reinforces Domesday, in demonstrating the complex and, one has to say,

[21] F. W. Maitland, *Domesday Book and Beyond* (Cambridge, 1897), pp. 186–91, is a classic account; Tait, *Medieval English Borough*, pp. 21–6, a classic rejoinder; cf. Darby, *Domesday England*, pp. 309–13. Maps illustrating these connections may be found in the relevant volumes of the *Domesday Geography* series by H. C. Darby and others.

[22] F. W. Maitland and M. Bateson, eds., *The Charters of the Borough of Cambridge* (Cambridge, 1901), pp. 2–3; C. Johnson and H. A. Cronne, eds., *Regesta Regum Anglo-Normannorum, 1066–1154* (Oxford 1913–69), vol. II, *Regesta Henrici Primi* (1956), no. 1728, p. 256.

[23] E.g., when Henry I confirmed to Beverley a grant by the archbishop of York 'according to the free laws and customs of the burgesses of York' he added freedom of toll throughout Yorkshire, Johnson and Cronne, eds., *Regesta*, II, no. 1137.

[24] Tait, *Medieval English Borough*, p. 28; cf. E. O. Blake, ed., *Liber Eliensis* (Camden Society, 3rd series, 92, 1962), p. 100.

[25] A. Ballard, ed., *British Borough Charters 1042–1216* (Cambridge, 1913), pp. 169–70 (Perth), 170 (Aberdeen), 170 (Inverness); P. G. B. McNeill and H. L. MacQueen, eds., *Atlas of Scottish History to 1707* (Edinburgh, 1996), pp. 234–5.

[26] H. R. Loyn, 'Boroughs and mints A.D. 900–1066', in R. H. M. Dolley, ed., *Anglo-Saxon Coins* (London, 1961), pp. 122–35.

sophisticated command of the late Anglo-Saxon state. That control was largely mediated through towns.

What was the internal government of a late Anglo-Saxon town? Plainly, there were great distinctions between, at extremes, London at the top and, at the bottom, small places with vestigial Domesday traces of 'urban status'. Some major towns were anomalous in their government as in other matters. An example is that of the one important town whose lord was neither the king nor a great monastery, Dunwich. Dunwich was mainly the property of a major nobleman, Eadric of Laxfield, but important authority was exercised from the royal centre at Blythburgh, nearby.[27] Dunwich cannot have fitted a pattern, nor can such a major ecclesiastical town as Bury St Edmunds. If there was a pattern, it will chiefly be found in early shire towns and above all those of the lands between the Thames and the Humber, the old English boroughs which strike the keynote in our municipal history, such that each was a military centre and a political centre, the market and the centre of government of a shire.[28] Often towns of this kind were regarded as hundreds in themselves. It may well indeed be that, particularly in the Midlands, the establishment of the town-centred shires and of a neat plan of hundreds or wapentakes was part of the same tenth-century operation.[29] The major old English towns may have largely conformed to a pattern such that the authority of their courts corresponded to that of a rural hundred. The intermediate authority between the borough and the king would then be, by the eleventh century, the sheriff. There are, indeed, good Domesday indications for sheriffs being responsible for collecting the revenues from towns, though this was not always so and in at least one case (there could easily have been others) he farmed this responsibility out to the inhabitants, or to some of them.[30]

It is characteristic of early English urban history that scattered evidence shows a bewildering relationship between uniformity and diversity and suggests more than it proves. One example of the problem of the relationship between hundredal jurisdiction and urban jurisdiction comes from Norwich. Norwich records include a series of thirteenth- and fourteenth-century rolls, recording proceedings of courts leet, the earliest dating from 1288.[31] The city was divided into four leets, each with a court, which dealt with minor offences, some involving economic regulation. In this Norwich presented a close parallel to East Anglian hundreds of whose internal organisation we know. It was common for a hundred to be divided into four leets, each with its own court. One could hardly have a better

[27] A. Rumble, ed., *Domesday Book: Suffolk* (Chichester, 1986), vol. I, ff. 311^{b}–312^{a} (6/84, 6/89).

[28] F. W. Maitland, *Township and Borough* (Cambridge, 1898), pp. 36–42; Maitland, *Domesday Book and Beyond*, pp. 186–90.

[29] Maitland, *Township and Borough*, p. 41 n. 2.

[30] Tait, *Medieval English Borough*, pp. 123–4.

[31] W. Hudson, ed., *Leet Jurisdiction in the City of Norwich in the Thirteenth and Fourteenth Centuries* (Selden Society, 5, 1892).

illustration of how even a very big town could have a 'hundredal' organisation. Two observations must be made here. One, were it not for the survival of these rolls from what must once have been an older and longer series, it would be impossible to trace the internal organisation of thirteenth-century Norwich. Two, one of the four leets is that of the French borough which was not established until after the Conquest; if Norwich as a hundred may well antedate the Conquest, then its internal organisation was modified extensively after 1066.

Consideration of the internal organisation and jurisdiction of significant English towns in the late Anglo-Saxon period is important because it casts a long shadow forward. The likely relationship between urban and hundredal jurisdiction has relevance for commercial jurisdiction. When King Edgar specifies the number of witnesses, both for large towns and for small, he also specifies the number of witnesses needed in a hundred.[32] This is a reminder that hundred courts, to the extent that they had witnessing functions, probably had a commercial role; there may have been complicated relationships between the hundredal system and local markets.[33] Yet the conception of integration between town and country jurisdiction has to reckon with an earlier eleventh-century reference to a distinction between *burhriht* and *landriht* (town law and country law).[34] Such a distinction would be compatible with the mysterious reference in a law of Edgar (repeated by Cnut) to a *burh* court meeting three times a year.[35] It is made transparent that this court is not, as one might otherwise have thought, a shire court meeting in the *burh*. It is not easy to avoid acceptance of Mary Bateson's thesis that the allusion is to special borough courts corresponding to the special courts which much later borough custumals record as being held two or three times annually and distinguishable from a 'borough as hundred' court.[36] The constitutions and organisation of towns as they emerge into the fitful light of medieval documentation were often variously indebted developments from the late Anglo-Saxon period.

That such developments did not always last is to be seen in the case of the Five Boroughs. The collectivity of the Five Boroughs – Derby, Leicester, Lincoln,

[32] A. J. Robertson, ed., *The Laws of the Kings of England from Edmund to Henry I* (Cambridge, 1925), pp. 32–3 (IV Edgar 3–6).

[33] R. H. Britnell, 'English markets and royal administration before 1200', *Ec.HR*, 2nd series, 31 (1978), 183–96. (Professor Britnell doubts a systematic connection between hundreds and markets; but his evidence does not exclude the distinct possibility of such a relationship, albeit incomplete.)

[34] Tait, *Medieval English Borough*, p. 40; cf. T. Wright, *Anglo-Saxon and Old English Vocabularies*, 2nd edn, ed. R. P. Wülker (London, 1884), vol. II, p. 49, for *anre burge riht* as a translation for *ius civile*. The early twelfth-century private compilation *Leges Henrici Primi* says that a penalty could be affected by the offence's having been committed in a town (*civitas*): ed. L. J. Downer (Oxford, 1972), pp. 214–15 (68/2). Reynolds, *Introduction*, pp. 92–3, is important here.

[35] Robertson, ed., *Laws of the Kings of England*, pp. 26–7, 182–3 (III Edgar 5.1, II Cnut 18).

[36] Tait, *Medieval English Borough*, pp. 31–2.

Nottingham, and Stamford – occupies a curious place in the history of local government. It is mentioned four times. The *Anglo-Saxon Chronicle* states that King Edmund in 954 regained the land of the Five Boroughs, and mentions them again under 1013 and 1015.[37] It has been generally assumed that these references provide a clue to the organisation of part of the Danelaw before it passed under English rule. In any case the fourth reference, in a law of Æthelred II, reveals the five boroughs court as part of an ordered hierarchy.[38] This law refers to a scale of penalties for breach of the peace, descending from the court of the Five Boroughs through the court of one borough down through the wapentake into, at the bottom, the *ealahuse* (literally 'alehouse'; but 'village hall' might well be better). This particular hierarchy disappeared; no later trace of a court of the Five Boroughs remains to us. But urban-centred administrative experiments probably of tenth-century date left a long mark. Thus, the three Ridings of Yorkshire converged, by obvious design, on the city of York.

In these and in other regards the towns of Domesday show diversity and uniformity, antiquity and modernity, related in imperfectly documented and baffling ways. There is much to surprise us. Take the peculiar case of the relations between the city of Exeter and William the Conqueror in 1068. Ordericus Vitalis, *c.* 1120, says that in 1067 the *cives* of Exeter resisted William, appealed to other cities and said they would not swear fealty to him nor admit him to their city.[39] All they would do was pay him tribute 'according to ancient custom'. This is a very vague statement. But Domesday shows it related to something real, and remarkable; for the survey states that at the time of Edward the Confessor Exeter paid geld only when London, Winchester and York did so.[40] Other passages indicate special arrangements and privileges for other towns. Thus Bedford, unlike other comparable shire towns, may have been exempt from geld.[41] Thanks to Domesday, we know that ports among the Cinque Ports already owed ship service such as they owed much later; and that this was already rewarded by important fiscal privileges.[42] The Domesday records of specialised renders from towns tell of particular royal arrangements with particular towns, for example Norwich's render of a bear and dogs.[43] A chartered town was a post-Conquest phenomenon. A privileged town was earlier. Some of the urban privileges of which Domesday tells us, for example those given in regard to taxation, disap-

[37] Plummer and Earle, eds., *Two of the Saxon Chronicles*, I, pp. 110, 143, 146.

[38] Robertson, ed., *Laws of the Kings of England*, pp. 64–5 (III Æthelred I, 1); cf. C. Hart, *The Danelaw* (London and Rio Grande, 1992), pp. 19–20; D. Roffe, ed., *Stamford in the Thirteenth Century* (Stamford, 1994), pp. 7–8.

[39] M. Chibnall, ed., *The Ecclesiastical History of Orderic Vitalis* (Oxford, 1968–80), vol. II, pp. 210–15.

[40] C. Thorn and F. Thorn, eds., *Domesday Book: Devon* (Chichester, 1985), vol. I, f. 100a (C/4).

[41] *Nunquam fuit hidata*, J. Morris, ed., *Domesday Book: Bedfordshire* (Chichester, 1977), f. 209ᵃ (B).

[42] K. M. E. Murray, *The Constitutional History of the Cinque Ports* (Manchester, 1935), pp. 21–22; Tait, *Medieval English Borough*, pp. 125–6.

[43] P. Brown, ed., *Domesday Book: Norfolk* (Chichester, 1984), vol. I, f. 117ᵃ (1/61).

peared before the epoch of continuous fiscal record. Others retained a long, shadowy history. A possible case in point is the privileged functions performed by London, Winchester, Canterbury, the Cinque Ports and Oxford in connection with coronations and, in particular, the coronation feast. These ceremonial functions, though not evidenced until the twelfth century, well may antedate the Conquest and, if so, suggest a high status for towns within the Anglo-Saxon polity.[44]

Town communities play an active part in the story of the Norman Conquest as related in the *Carmen* attributed to Guy of Amiens. The men of Winchester advise Queen Edith to yield; the men of Dover and of Canterbury offer the keys of their strongholds; and 'others did the same, fearing for their rights'.[45] Even if the *Carmen* is as late as *c.* 1150, it gives a view of towns earlier than the era of the urban charter. Its author saw towns as communities with powers of independent action. His account of the surrender of London in the aftermath of the Conquest is arresting.[46] He describes an important man, crippled by wounds, negotiating with William on behalf of London. He probably implies that this man was called Ansgardus, and certainly states that a man of this name should have a prominent role in a possible settlement. The author had serious information about London in 1066; his reference to Ansgardus, heavily overdramatised though it may be, proves this. 'Ansgar' must be Esgar the Staller who is known to have had an important position in London in Edward the Confessor's reign, possibly as portreeve. Most of his lands were acquired by Geoffrey de Mandeville, and the later claims of the de Mandeville family to high position in London must derive ultimately from Esgar.[47]

That a nobleman was very important in London does not mean that the city's elite were not also of great weight. The London negotiations with the Conqueror belong to a context in which there was a London claim, both before and after the Conquest, to participate in the choice of a king.[48] This is first heard of in the *Chronicle* which says that in 1016 the *burhware* and those of the *witan* who were in London elected Edmund as king. According to 'Florence' the nobles who sought to make Edgar king in 1066 acted *cum civibus Londiniensibus et butsecarlis*. The Londoners' claim is made explicit in William of Malmesbury's account of the reign of Stephen. He says that the *maiores natu* of London said that it was their right and special privilege that when a king died they should provide

[44] J. H. Round, *The King's Serjeants and Officers of State* (London, 1911), pp. 168–72, 328–9; Murray, *Cinque Ports*, p. 20; H. E. Salter, *Medieval Oxford* (Oxford Historical Society, 100, 1936), pp. 18–19.

[45] C. Morton and H. Muntz, eds., *The Carmen de Hastingae Proelio of Guy, Bishop of Amiens* (Oxford, 1972), pp. 38–41; cf. Guillaume de Poitiers, *Histoire de Guillaume le conquérant*, ed. R. Foreville (Paris, 1952), p. 224.

[46] Morton and Muntz, eds., *The Carmen de Hastingae Proelio*, pp. 42–7.

[47] C. N. L. Brooke and G. Keir, *London 800–1216* (London, 1975), pp. 37–9, 191–7, 213–18.

[48] M. McKisack, 'London and the succession to the crown during the middle ages', in R. W. Hunt, W. A. Pantin and R. W. Southern, eds., *Studies in Medieval History Presented to F. M. Powicke* (Oxford, 1948), pp. 76–89.

another. Doubtless they overstated their case. But their claims relate to circumstances such that London (and other) towns of Edward the Confessor's England were more than aggregations of population ruled by royal agents.

The importance of towns to the Conqueror is demonstrated by the distribution of William's castles. London was dominated by the Tower, a mighty castle-palace unparalleled north of the Alps. Two lesser castles, probably baronial, accompanied it in the west of the city. Two castles were built at York. Of William's thirty-one other royal castles, twenty-two were in shire towns.[49] There could be no more powerful demonstration of the importance of the shire town to William than that in eastern England the distribution of royal castles related not to the defence of the coast (notwithstanding the Danish threat) but to the control of the shire towns.

It is an interesting question as to how far there were written pre-Conquest records relating to the royal towns. There was at least one such; the survey of the royal property in Winchester of Henry I's reign derives, demonstrably, from one made in the time of Edward the Confessor.[50] Such a Domesday account as that of Colchester has the air of deriving from written records which could easily have had pre-Conquest antecedents,[51] as have the surviving post-Conquest urban surveys, only somewhat later than, and independent of, Domesday: those for Gloucester (*c.* 1096–1101) and Winchcombe.[52]

(ii) FROM DOMESDAY BOOK TO THE LATE TWELFTH CENTURY

The relationship between the organisation of power in towns and that of power over towns in the century after Domesday is no less important than ill-documented. Salient features come into sight only fleetingly. Internally generated records from English towns are absent until the late twelfth century. One of our main sources after 1100 is, of course, the charters granted to towns by the king and other lords. The earliest urban charters contrast with those of a later date. In the early period, the privileges and advantages of a town, particularly a royal town, did not usually derive from charters. Nearly all the relevant so-called borough charters of Henry I relating to towns are writs alluding to or confirming municipal rights but not claiming to create them. A case in point is the writ relating to

[49] R. A. Brown, H. M. Colvin and A. J. Taylor, *The History of the King's Works* (London, 1963), pp. 119–32, esp. p. 22.

[50] F. Barlow, 'The Winton Domesday', in M. Biddle, ed., *Winchester in the Early Middle Ages* (Oxford, 1976), pp. 9–10.

[51] A. Rumble, ed., *Domesday Book: Essex* (Chichester, 1983) ff. 104^{a}–107^{b} (B).

[52] H. Ellis, *A General Introduction to Domesday Book* (London, 1833), vol. II, pp. 445–7. For such records, or possible records, in general, S. P. J. Harvey, 'Domesday Book and Anglo-Norman governance', *TRHS*, 5th series, 25 (1975), pp. 180–1.

the privileges in regard to Cambridgeshire trade enjoyed by Cambridge. William I's writ to London, claimed as the first English urban charter, is essentially confirmatory.[53] The charters which most closely resemble later grants of urban privilege of the kind which create rather than (or as well as) confirm are those issued by great lords to places under their control. If the first charter to Burford, that of Robert fitz Hamon, is as early as 1087, it is the earliest charter of this kind to survive in England.[54] The extent to which urban status and privilege existed independently of charter is indicated not only by what we learn from Domesday and by some of the circumstances of the Conquest, but also by indications in early twelfth-century documents. Thus a charter from Henry I to Bury St Edmunds refers to the burgesses as if they were coordinate in authority with the abbot.[55] Another writ suggests that the burgesses of Huntingdon were regarded as a group with known rights.[56] It appears that the burgesses of Exeter were, as a collectivity, granting property in the earlier twelfth century.[57] A remarkable list of the laws and customs of Newcastle-upon-Tyne, drawn up in Henry II's reign, claims, plausibly, to relate to Henry I's. It includes privileges, some of which were to become common, or perhaps already were common, in many towns. They include an early statement that a *rusticus* who lives in the borough for a year and a day without being claimed by his lord was free to remain.[58] This document is an approach to a borough custumal, the only post-Domesday example of such earlier than the thirteenth (or very late twelfth) century. The study of borough customs has not prospered since the seminal publications of Mary Bateson and Morley Hemmeon.[59] But we know enough to apprehend the extent of the variation of urban custom on such matters as devise and of the idiosyncracy of urban custom on such matters as punishment. A likely implication of such divergences is that town customs could derive from an epoch long before that of the town charter.

Knowledge of internal town government up to and during the eleventh century is thin. In some or many towns the urban court may be descended from a hundred court. In some towns there may have been courts meeting less often, with greater powers. Such a reference as one to the *witan* in the smaller boroughs

[53] Robertson, ed., *Laws of the Kings of England*, pp. 230–1; D. A. E. Pelteret, ed., *Catalogue of English Post-Conquest Vernacular Documents* (Woodbridge, 1990), pp. 47–51.

[54] C. Gross, *The Gild Merchant* (Oxford, 1890), vol. II, p. 29; R. M. Gretton, *The Burford Records* (Oxford, 1920), pp. 10, 301.

[55] Johnson and Cronne, eds., *Regesta*, II, no. 644, cf. M. D. Lobel, *The Borough of Bury St Edmunds* (Oxford, 1935), pp. 9–10.

[56] Johnson and Cronne, eds., *Regesta*, II, no. 1359.

[57] B. Wilkinson, *The Mediæval Council of Exeter* (Manchester, 1931), p. xviii.

[58] W. Stubbs, ed., *Select Charters and Other Illustrations of English Constitutional History*, 9th edn, corrected, ed. H. W. C. Davis (Oxford, 1951), pp. 132–3; cf. D. C. Douglas and G. W. Greenaway, eds., *English Historical Documents 1042–1189* (London, 1953), no. 298; cf. Reynolds, *Introduction*, p. 100.

[59] M. Bateson, ed., *Borough Customs* (Selden Society, 18, 21, 1904–6), M. de W. Hemmeon, *Burgage Tenure in Mediaeval England* (Cambridge, Mass., 1914).

of Devonshire presumably refers to courts or/and to councils (at this date the distinction may well be one without a difference) formal or informal.[60] In four Danelaw towns (Stamford, Lincoln, Cambridge and York) and one probably under Scandinavian influence, Chester, in Domesday and/or in later sources there appear 'lawmen' or 'judices'.[61] What their functions were and how far these had been at some stage the same from town to town is unknown. In three towns this office appears in the thirteenth century as hereditary and attached to the tenure of particular properties.[62] If the diversity of urban customs suggests their antiquity, the rights to which they refer, especially in relation to civil litigation, suggest the early importance of urban jurisdictions. By the time of the custumals towns' criminal jurisdiction was generally very limited; though this may not always have been the case earlier, and towns could enjoy independence in criminal cases in so far as their citizens could enjoy privileges relating to the location and/or procedures of trials in royal courts.[63] Urban courts were administrative as well as judicial bodies. Here relationships to the king's reeves mattered. From at latest Edward the Confessor's reign until the late twelfth century most English towns were under the ultimate authority (under the king) of the shire-reeve, the sheriff. This was specially important in fiscal matters. We have, however, references *c.* 900 to reeves particularly associated with a town and in contexts suggesting that they were men of importance: 896 the *wicgerefa* of Winchester; 906 the *gerefa* at Bath.[64] Little is, however, known of the urban reeve from the late Anglo-Saxon period and through the twelfth century. If, during this period, he was a local man, then a town could have had more self-government *de facto* than it did *de jure*. Thus it is important that, at least from the twelfth century, the administration of London was largely in the hands of Londoners, often of English extraction.[65]

A most powerful element in the relationship between king and towns was money. The annual farm, paid either via the sheriff or directly, represented in principle regular revenues from tolls, quit-rents, etc. At the time of Domesday most towns paid danegeld (alias heregeld). By the time of the first Pipe Roll (1129–30) this levy had been replaced by a different one. Some thirty towns paid round sums termed *auxilia* or *dona*.[66] The levy appears to have been annual in

[60] Tait, *Medieval English Borough*, pp. 31–2.

[61] *Ibid.*, pp. 43–4; A. Ballard, *The Domesday Boroughs* (Oxford, 1904), pp. 51–4. At least some of the lawmen in Lincoln inherited their positions and some were, or were well connected with, major landowners in the shire, cf. Hart, *Danelaw*, pp. 267–72.

[62] Tait, *English Medieval Borough*, p. 124 n.

[63] If the charter of Henry I to London is genuine (cf. p. 67 n. 98 below), then the grant of the right to appoint local justiciars would have had important implications in regard to criminal justice, A. H. Thomas, ed., *Calendar of Early Mayors' Court Rolls of the City of London* (Cambridge, 1924), p. x.

[64] Plummer, ed., *Two of the Saxon Chronicles Parallel*, I, pp. 90, 94.

[65] S. Reynolds, 'The rulers of London in the twelfth century', *History*, 57 (1972), 337–57.

[66] J. A. Green, *The Government of Henry I* (Cambridge, 1986), p. 76; C. Stephenson, *Borough and Town* (Cambridge, Mass., 1933), pp. 159–66.

that period, although there were elements of variation as to both the number of towns taxed and the sums levied. This system reappears (though not on an annual basis) when we once again have Pipe Rolls, from 1155 on. From 1168 the tax was transformed from being one on a limited number of towns, nearly all ancient shire towns, to a levy on all the royal demesne, rural and urban, and including some sixty towns. This tax, which from the late twelfth century was called 'tallage', was levied at frequent, but irregular, intervals by all Henry's successors until Edward I.[67] Under Edward it was replaced by taxes on movables. The 'Dialogue of the Exchequer' (*c.* 1178) gives an account of the method by which this tax was levied which is important for the understanding of twelfth-century urban organisation.[68] Royal justices (i.e. senior administrators) go to each borough or city. If the citizens offer a sum 'worthy of a prince' then they are responsible for raising it. If the citizens do not make an adequate offer then the justices will raise what sum they think fit, allocated as they think fit. These arrangements suggest that it was normal for townsmen to have considerable powers of independent deliberation and administrative action.

An important feature of the taxation system from 1168 on was its association of towns with royal demesne, or 'ancient demesne'.[69] Both towns and other royal demesne, or former demesne, were specially burdened and also especially privileged. This is an important reminder that the distinction between a *burgus*, with its *burgenses* and other places, although recognised by contemporaries, has to be placed in the context of variations and complications of legal status. At the top of the scale of settlements there were places which were unquestionably *burgi*, at the bottom there were places which were definitely not. In between there were areas of ambiguity. The phenomenon of the so-called 'manorial borough' is an old one: such a seigneurial establishment as early thirteenth-century Chelmsford, much more than a mere village but governed as a manor, is in the line of succession in which by the early nineteenth century great cities could lack royal charters but have constitutions which were ultimately manorial. For contemporary administrators (as for us) there was no plain or easy distinction to be drawn between 'town' and 'non-town'. There was a continuum across which different defining lines (often wavering lines) could be drawn in different circumstances.[70] Here it is important to notice how many English towns have grown from centres of estate administration, commonly, but not always, royal, and with origins not infrequently going back to systems of control and administration in the early

[67] S. K. Mitchell, *Taxation in Medieval England* (New Haven, 1951), pp. 236–399.

[68] C. Johnson, ed., *Dialogus de Scaccario* (Oxford, 1950), pp. 108–9.

[69] Mitchell, *Taxation in Medieval England*, pp. 238–9; R. S. Hoyt, *The Royal Demesne in English Constitutional History* (Ithaca, 1950), pp. 107–25.

[70] S. Webb and B. Webb, *The Manor and the Borough*, introduction by B. Keith-Lucas (London, 1963), esp. vol. II, pp. 127–211; cf. Tait, *Medieval English Borough*, p. 263. For Chelmsford, Grieve, *The Sleepers and the Shadows*.

Anglo-Saxon centuries; monastic sites may have been notably important in this regard.[71]

An institution common to many towns was the guild merchant, an association of townsmen for commercial and social purposes, with a defined membership, and with certain exclusive rights or, anyway, claims.[72] In some towns, above all those which were early under the authority of a lord other than the king, the guild merchant was the institution from which later civic organisation largely derived. Some towns are not known ever to have had a guild merchant; Norwich for example. But an early guild merchant could easily exist without getting into any surviving record. For example, the earliest Burford charters refer to a guild merchant at Oxford well before any other record does so.[73] That there was a guild merchant at Huntingdon *c.* 1120 is only known from the *Life* of Christina of Markyate.[74] For her biographer the essence of the association was festive: the biographer calls the merchant guild (*gilda mercantium*) a feast (*festum*). The dinner-table, the ale-butt and the wine barrel were essential to civic life.

Not only merchants had guilds. *Cnihtengilds* are mentioned in or before the twelfth century in a number of towns.[75] The relationship between '*cniht*' and '*knight*' is a complicated one. But yet again the related questions are raised of how far noblemen and gentlemen lived in towns and how far towns were reservoirs of military force. By 1086 the lawmen of Cambridge were assumed to be furnished with a horse and the arms of a knight.[76] No doubt in the eleventh and twelfth centuries there were links of considerable intimacy between men of landed consequence and at least some English towns. Thus a burgess named Dunning was conspicuous at Cambridge early in the twelfth century. He was the grandfather of Hervey fitz Eustace who was *c.* 1200 the first known mayor of Cambridge. Hervey's seal bore a mounted knight with a drawn sword and he had lands in the rural part of the shire.[77] Could the men of Cambridge have provided a military force with which to reckon? Near contemporaries higher and lower on the urban scale certainly could. When William fitz Stephen said that London disposed of 20,000 horse and 60,000 foot, civic pride had doubtless addled his statistics.[78] But when Henry of Huntingdon said that in 1145 Stephen marched on Faringdon 'with a formidable and numerous body of Londoners' we might consider believing him.[79] Jordan

[71] A. Everitt, 'The primary towns of England', in his *Landscape and Community in England* (London, 1985), pp. 93–108; cf. Tait, *Medieval English Borough*, pp. 14, 29 and pp. 31–2 above.

[72] Gross, *Gild Merchant*; Reynolds, *Introduction*, pp. 82–93.

[73] Gross, *Gild Merchant*, II, pp. 27–8; Salter, *Medieval Oxford*, pp. 34–5.

[74] C. H. Talbot, ed., *The Life of Christina of Markyate*, with additional material (Oxford, 1987), pp. 48–9.

[75] Tait, *Medieval English Borough*, pp. 12, 81, 119–22.

[76] A. Rumble, ed., *Domesday Book: Cambridgeshire* (Chichester, 1981), f. 189a (B/32).

[77] Maitland, *Township and Borough*, pp. 164–6.

[78] J. C. Robertson and J. B. Sheppard, eds., *Materials for the History of Thomas Becket* (RS, 1875–85), vol. III, p. 4.

[79] D. Greenway, ed., *Henry, Archdeacon of Huntingdon, Historia Anglorum* (Oxford, 1996), pp. 746–7.

Fantosme describes the importance to Henry II of the loyalty of the citizens of London and stresses how formidable and well armed they were.[80] A striking example of the military importance of the men of a tiny town comes from the North. Richard de Lucy's charter for Egremont, *c.* 1200, treats his burgesses almost as knights. They are to find twelve armed men for the defence of the castle for forty days. They are to give him an aid for knighting one of his sons, another for marrying one of his daughters, another for ransoming him and another when the knights of his lands contribute.[81]

The warlike experience of English townsmen in the twelfth century was largely to be found on the sea and overseas. Such experience may have helped determine urban aspiration. Consider an account of the siege of Lisbon in 1147.[82] It speaks of the assembly of a crusading fleet at Dartmouth, one of whose four divisions was largely English. This was under the command of Hervey de Glanvill. But also involved in command was a kind of representative council such that each thousand seamen chose two representatives.[83] This is the first certain reference to an elected representative assembly in English history. The fleet sailed off to Lisbon which was still in Moorish hands and under siege by the king of Portugal. The siege was successful and the English played a large part in its success, the men of Ipswich being well to the fore.[84] It is of interest that the representatives of the English fleet treated the king of Portugal with what a modern commentator calls 'democratic effrontery'.[85]

A different link between towns and military activity is provided by the castle guard. At least in the first generations after 1066 the king's castles were garrisoned by knights, provided by tenants-in-chief.[86] Thus the abbeys of Ely and of Bury had to provide castle guard at Norwich; one owed forty, the other fifty knights.[87] So, in such a garrison centre as Norwich a considerable number of knights (? with their families) from wide areas would always be present. Maybe the grandeur of the central hall of Norwich Castle relates partly to the life of such men.[88] Similarly, the reference in Domesday for Nottingham to twenty-five houses attributed to *equites* as opposed to *mercatores* may refer to the knights of the garrison; if not, it indicates the presence of other resident knights.[89] For many boroughs the involvement with the landed interest may be explained in

[80] R. C. Johnston, ed., *Jordan Fantosme's Chronicle* (Oxford, 1981), pp. 68–9, 120–1.

[81] J. Nicholson and R. Burn, *The History and Antiquities of the Counties of Westmorland and Cumberland* (London, 1777), vol. II, pp. 526–8.

[82] C. W. David, ed., *De expugnatione Lyxbonensi* (New York, 1936). [83] *Ibid.*, pp. 56–7.

[84] *Ibid.*, p. 160. [85] *Ibid.*, p. 13.

[86] F. M. Stenton, *The First Century of English Feudalism*, 2nd edn (Oxford, 1961), ch. 6.

[87] H. M. Chew, *The Ecclesiastical Tenants-in-Chief* (Oxford, 1932), pp. 101–2; E. Miller, *The Abbey and Bishopric of Ely* (Cambridge, 1951), p. 155.

[88] Brown, Colvin and Taylor, *King's Works*, I, pp. 39, 47–8, II, pp. 73–5; T. A. Heslop, *Norwich Castle Keep: Romanesque Architecture and Social Context* (Norwich, 1994).

[89] J. Morris, ed., *Domesday Book: Nottingham* (Chichester, 1977), f. 280.

terms of Maitland's general observation that 'The shire maintains the burh, the burh defends the shire.'[90] In such a case as that of Oxford where 'six bishops, besides abbots and counts and mighty men of war have houses in it and men in it', the landed presence may relate to the town's having been not only a local capital but also a centre for national meetings.[91]

The urban charters of Henry II's reign suggest a royal policy. They relate to some thirty towns.[92] In eighteen cases the earliest surviving grant (commonly the only grant) dates from between 1154 and 1158. The principal purport of all these is to confirm privileges as they were under Henry I. These generally included exemptions from toll, the right to a guild merchant and *consuetudines*. Most of these charters are very brief. Three, however, say something of Henry's motives. That for Wallingford says it is made 'in consideration of the service and great labour which they sustained for me in the securing of my hereditary right in England'.[93] That for Exeter says not only that the city's good customs from the time of Henry I are confirmed, but that bad customs introduced since his time are abolished.[94] The Norwich charter says that anyone who during Stephen's reign removed himself from their customs and payments (*consuetudinibus eorum et scottis*) is to return to his society and customs.[95] The Wallingford charter suggests something of the political weight which a town could have. Those for Exeter and Norwich indicate that developments later seen as undesirable happened in Stephen's reign. There is other evidence for this. The extreme example is the grant by Matilda to Geoffrey de Mandeville in 1141 making him sheriff and hereditary justice in London, Essex and Hertfordshire and stating that she would make no peace or agreement with the burgesses of London without his agreement 'for they are his mortal enemies'.[96] Comparable is the grant made to Stephen's son William in accordance with the agreement between Henry and Stephen of 1153, whereby Henry confirms to William the castle and *villae* (i.e. the Norman as well as the English borough) of Norwich.[97] These extreme cases seem to relate to something uncommonly like division of the kingdom. The long series of charters to major towns granted by Henry II in his earliest years stands for a policy of reinforcing some-

[90] Maitland, *Township and Borough*, p. 37.

[91] *Ibid.*, p. 45. The evidence for national meetings at Oxford is strongest for the late Anglo-Saxon period, Salter, *Medieval Oxford*, pp. 16–17.

[92] Ballard, ed., *British Borough Charters 1042–1216*, pp. xxv–xl and *passim*.

[93] Gross, *Gild Merchant*, II, pp. 244–5.

[94] Ballard, ed., *British Borough Charters 1042–1216*, p. 6.

[95] W. Hudson and J. C. Tingey, eds., *The Records of the City of Norwich* (Norwich, 1906–10), vol. I, p. 1.

[96] H. A. Cronne and R. H. C. Davis, eds., *Regesta Regum Anglo-Normannorum*, vol. III, *Regesta 1135–54* (Oxford, 1968), no. 175, p. 100; cf. Brooke and Keir, *London 800–1216*, pp. 37–9, 191–2.

[97] Cronne and Davis, eds., *Regesta*, III, no. 272, pp. 97–9; cf. Hudson and Tingey, eds., *Records of Norwich*, I, p. xv. This mediatisation of a major town to a magnate was paralleled under William II, Tait, *Medieval English Borough*, pp. 154–5.

thing threatened, the immediate royal connection with towns as major elements in the English polity.

The most important of Henry II's urban transactions had to be with London. The story is complicated by the disputed nature of a charter alleged to have been granted by Henry I and surviving only in a private collection of about 1200.[98] The powers granted were formidable indeed. For example the citizens were allowed to farm the shrievalty of London and Middlesex and to choose their own justices. Henry I's reign lies in the relatively short period during which there were local justiciars in England; the charter's giving London the right to appoint such an official may speak for its authenticity; and if it is authentic it follows that London was then granted more extensive jurisdictional independence than ever it later enjoyed. The evidence of the Pipe Roll of 1130 certainly indicates that London was, at that time, in an unusually privileged position, farming its own revenues and, apparently, responsible for choosing the sheriff of Middlesex.[99] There is good evidence for London's having a commune of some kind in Stephen's reign.[100] Although Henry II's one known charter to London (1155) confirms the rights the city had enjoyed under Henry I, there is no sign of his ever allowing it anything like the powers indicated by the charter attributed to Henry I.

There are two particular features of Henry II's relationship with towns and townsmen which had lasting (and to an extent linked) roles in the relationship between kings and towns. One is the importance of men of urban origin in the administration. Becket was a leading example. The phenomenon was not a new one. For example, it has been shown how a particular London family, that of Deorman, provided minters (and probably other royal functionaries) from well before the Conquest until well into the twelfth century.[101] Second, in his early, difficult, years, Henry was borrowing considerable sums from merchants, above all William Cade of St-Omer and William Trentegeruns of Rouen.[102] The relationship between royal success and urban loans could have been still older. For all we know William the Conqueror's amazing capacity to keep his forces together for months on end, as Harold could not, may have been sustained by credit. Certainly by the 1150s the operations of power and the availability of credit are becoming intimately connected. Jews became the dominant lenders to the king. This gave special importance to the Jews in towns. First appearing in

[98] Esp. C. N. L. Brooke, G. Keir and S. Reynolds, 'Henry I's charter for the city of London', *J of the Society of Archivists*, 4 (1973), 558–78; C. W. Hollister, 'London's first charter of liberties: is it genuine?', *J of Medieval History*, 6 (1980), 289–306.

[99] Tait, *Medieval English Borough*, pp. 156–7.

[100] Brooke and Keir, *London 800–1216*, pp. 35–6.

[101] P. Nightingale, 'Some London moneyers and reflections on the organisation of English mints in the eleventh and twelfth centuries', *Numismatic Chronicle*, 142 (1982), pp. 34–50.

[102] H. G. Richardson, *The English Jewry under the Angevin Kings* (London, 1960), pp. 150–60. It is interesting that the security for such loans included the right to farm the revenues of important towns, *ibid.*, p. 54.

the late eleventh century, they became, within a hundred years, a major economic force and of great importance for royal finance; by far the most economically important inhabitants of such a town as Norwich in the later part of Henry II's reign were Jewish.[103]

Henry II's dominions stretched far beyond England. When he thought about towns he must have thought about France as well as England. When Richard of Devizes wrote that Henry would under no circumstances concede a commune, he may reflect this wider knowledge. An informed king of England could well regard a communal movement as a terrible danger. A good demonstration of this comes in Ordericus Vitalis' account of the urban rebellion at Rouen (probably in 1090). The leader of the rebel townsmen, Conan, was rich, had a strong military household and seemed to be doing very well. But he failed, and was captured. According to Orderic, the future Henry I took him to the top of a tall tower and pushed him over the edge to his death.[104] Any well-informed ruler would know about whatever it was that lay behind this story, or about the Flemish crisis of 1124, or about many another incident, and could see the urban scene as rich both in problems and in possibilities. Henry II, not uncharacteristically, avoided urban troubles. The Pipe Rolls record fines on two towns, Gloucester and York, for setting up communes.[105] The term commune and the implications of setting one up doubtless varied in their implications. In an urban context three things were of the essence. One, an urban organisation which was distinct from and might seek to alter existing structures (Plate 1); two, an oath taken by the participants; and three, in consequence, the whiff of sedition. A key problem for Henry II's government could well have been that of averting urban sedition while not only exploiting the towns, but also harnessing the interests and energies of their ruling groups in ways which would sustain a modernised version of the outstandingly successful Anglo-Saxon state. Elements of these royal attempts, in general successful, may be seen in the Assize of Clarendon, and in the Assize of Arms.[106] The Assize of Clarendon (1166) emphasised urban responsibilities towards the judicial system: no one in a town with a house, or land or a soke should receive anyone there without accepting responsibility for producing him for justice if required or for having him in frankpledge. A different emphasis emerges from the Assize of Arms (1181). There the burgesses appear in conjunction with 'the whole community of freemen' and each is to have a strengthened jacket, a helmet and a lance.

Not the least important, but the least appreciated, of the Henrician legislation enforced in and by towns were the assizes of bread and ale.[107] The assize of bread

[103] *Ibid.*, V. D. Lipman, *The Jews of Medieval Norwich* (London, 1967), ch. 6.

[104] Chibnall, ed., *Ecclesiastical History*, IV, pp. 220–7.

[105] Tait, *Medieval English Borough*, pp. 176–7.

[106] Stubbs, ed., *Select Charters*, pp. 170–3, 183–4.

[107] A. S. C. Ross, 'The assize of bread and ale', *Ec.HR*, 2nd series, 9 (1956–7), 332–42; P. Studer, ed., *The Oak Book of Southampton* (Southampton Record Society, 10–12, 1923), pp. xxi–xxix; Ballard, ed., *British Borough Charters 1042–1216*, pp. 157–9.

was a system of regulating bread prices by relation to the price of grains. Thus the weight of a half-penny loaf or a penny loaf would be determined by the going grain prices locally. This system of price control for a major commodity was of importance in England for many centuries. Some kind of municipal regulation of bread and ale would seem to go back to the reign of Henry I, if not further. The 'assize' as national legislation is not evidenced until the 1170s and the first references to municipal responsibility for its enforcement come from *c.* 1200. Its long importance thereafter is attested both by municipal records and by municipal riots. In all pre-modern polities the control of the prices of basic foodstuffs were of ultimate importance. The introduction of such a system in England must have mattered a lot. Its incidence and organisation were above all urban.

(iii) FROM THE LATE TWELFTH CENTURY TO THE EARLY FOURTEENTH

The reigns of Richard I and of John see urban movements no less important than cloudy and complicated. Within one generation some fifty English towns were given charters, many, it seems, for the first time.[108] The leading characteristic of nearly all these charters was the grant of a privilege hitherto very rare. This was the fee-farm, the right to pay the town's dues to the king in the form of an annual sum, fixed in perpetuity. Henry I may have granted such a privilege to London and to Lincoln. If so, neither concession had proved permanent. Henry II had allowed a number of towns to farm their revenues, but always on a revocable basis. Now numerous towns gained charters granting the privilege long withheld.[109] These charters could include other privileges, for example that of electing the town reeve. Even when they do not do so explicitly, they could be taken to entail more than was formally specified. The leading instance here is that of Ipswich. It was granted a charter with the privilege of the fee-farm on 25 May 1200. The charter says nothing about a council, but a month later the citizens established a council and shortly afterwards regulated its election; and made other arrangements indicating a new sense of independence.[110] This Ipswich instance is specially important because it demonstrates that it was by no means necessarily the case that a charter of the type granted to Ipswich represented little more than a compulsorily expensive confirmation of what already existed *de facto*.

Why was there such a wave of such grants to towns at this time? Partly to raise money. Four tallages were levied in Richard's reign, seven in that of John.[111]

[108] Ballard, ed., *British Borough Charters 1042–1216*, pp. xx–xl and *passim*.

[109] Tait, *Medieval English Borough*, pp. 139–93. T. Madox, *Firma Burgi* (London, 1726), remains fundamental.

[110] Tait, *Medieval English Borough*, pp. 270–1.

[111] Mitchell, *Taxation in Medieval England*, pp. 285–320, 330. (Not all towns were taxed on every occasion.)

There was an element of consultation (probably *de facto* of consent) in such grants and new charters must have helped to sweeten townsmen. Furthermore, they paid for such charters, up to £100 or more. But it is likely that we should see a wider significance in the charter grants, and judge them as part of a royal attempt to secure the alliance and good will of elements in society which had wealth and armed force at their disposal and sometimes knowledge of, and temptations towards, foreign and seditious possibilities. A context for such a 'political' explanation is provided by the ordinance on defence in the crisis year of 1205.[112] It specifies that there should be *communa* throughout the realm, communes of shires, hundreds, cities, boroughs and groups of minor vills. Every male aged more than twelve was to take an oath for the honour of God and fidelity to the king and for the security of the realm. This effort for a national rally shows how in concessions to towns there may have been a royal concern to win hearts and swords as much as pounds and marks. That urban liberties could be seen in a general national context is made plain by Magna Carta, clause 13, guaranteeing the liberties and free customs not only of London but also of all other cities, towns, *villae* and ports.[113] There was an aspiring, even revolutionary, mood. Men in London were studying old laws and old claims and doubtless associating them with new demands.[114] There was certainly an innovatory climate elsewhere; witness the case of Ipswich. Discussion on how revolutionary this climate was relates to a neglected debate between, on the one hand, Maitland, on the other, Round and Tait.[115] Maitland saw the development of urban constitutions in this period as in large measure evolutionary. Round and Tait were more inclined to see the changes brought about in so many towns between 1190 and 1216 as introducing new elements with foreign origins. Thus where a mayor appears, as he often does, they see him as a new kind of officer responsible to the burgesses and without that element of responsibility to the crown characterising the reeves or, in the thirteenth century, the bailiffs. H. E. Salter, the great historian of Oxford, in a rare flight of wit, said that *c.* 1200 'there seems to have been a general impression that a mayor would bring the millennium'.[116]

The study of the organisation of power in towns of the thirteenth century is helped by the appearance of new or newly surviving kinds of record; and complicated by the certainty that far more such records have been lost than

[112] W. Stubbs, ed., *The Historical Works of Gervase of Canterbury* (RS 1879–80), vol. II, pp. 96–7; cf. Reynolds, *Introduction*, p. 103.

[113] W. S. McKechnie, *Magna Carta: A Commentary on the Great Charter of King John*, 2nd edn., revised (Glasgow, 1914), pp. 240–8.

[114] M. Bateson, 'A London municipal collection of the reign of John', *EHR*, 17 (1902), 480–511, 707–30.

[115] F. Pollock and F. W. Maitland, *The History of English Law before the Time of Edward I*, 2nd edn., (Cambridge, 1898), vol. I, pp. 656–60; Tait, *Medieval English Borough*, pp. 286–93, 348; J. H. Round, *The Commune of London* (London, 1899), pp. 241–51.

[116] Salter, *Medieval Oxford*, pp. 48–9.

have survived. The earliest internally produced records from an English town to survive are lists of free members of the guild at Leicester dating from the 1190s. Similar records appear at Wallingford and Shrewsbury not much later. Shrewsbury has accounts, cast on a weekly basis, from the 1240s, and Shrewsbury would have been an unlikely pioneer in this. Evidence, usually the indirect evidence of somewhat later custumals, shows that some towns were keeping records of their by-laws as they passed them. In London the oldest surviving rolls recording property transfers, the Husting rolls, date from 1252 and were probably not the first such; and there is evidence for earlier financial and apprenticeship records there. Similar enrolments in other towns appear later in the century. The presence of these straightforward systems of land registration must have had economic importance.[117]

A negative implication of such records is that royal charters to towns are an imperfect guide as to their government. Sometimes we learn of constitutional developments more from incidental references than from royal charters. An interesting case is that of Canterbury. It was unusual among considerable towns in not gaining a grant of the fee-farm until 1234. Yet, as William Urry suggested, a change of the kind commonly associated with the grant of the fee-farm quite possibly came in about 1200.[118] Previously the bailiffs held office for long periods; afterwards they change almost annually; with the likely implication that now they were being elected. In such matters it is important to emphasise diversity. One example: such was the popularity of the office of mayor that some twelve towns, other than London, are mentioned as having one before 1220, and by 1300 a mayor was the leading officer in most leading towns.[119] Nevertheless, there were major exceptions, the most striking of which was that the great city of Norwich did not have a mayor until 1404.

Reservations are essential, but generalisations are possible. In the thirteenth century as mayors became common it is not unusual to find that a town has a sworn council (often of twelve or twenty-four) to advise the mayor. It is questionable whether such councils had continuous rather than somewhat intermittent and fluctuating lives and how far, *de facto*, they were really new. It is a further question how far there were other assemblies with more or less authority. The frequent use in thirteenth-century documents of terms indicating 'the whole

[117] For urban records the bibliographies by Gross and by Martin and McIntyre are indispensable. G. H. Martin, 'The English borough in the thirteenth century', *TRHS*, 5th series, 13 (1963), 123–44, is a valuable survey; cf. G. R. Elton, *England 1200–1640* (London, 1962), pp. 119–28. *House of Commons Letters and Papers 1931–2*, vol. x, pp. 663–94, provides a summary list. See also G. H. Martin, 'The registration of deeds of title in the medieval borough' in D. A. Bullough and R. L. Storey, eds. (Oxford, 1971), pp. 151–73. For London also W. Cunningham, *The Growth of English Industry and Commerce during the Early and Middle Ages*, 5th edn. (Cambridge, 1910), pp. 617–18; A. H. Thomas, ed., *Calendar of Plea and Memoranda Rolls 1364–81* (Cambridge, 1929), p. xxx.

[118] W. Urry, *Canterbury under the Angevin Kings* (London, 1967), pp. 84–5.

[119] Tait, *Medieval English Borough*, p. 291 n. 4.

community' or the like often conceals more than it reveals. Certainly in some towns there were in the late thirteenth century assemblies for some purposes which were rather widely attended.[120]

The most important authorities in thirteenth-century provincial towns were their courts. In the twelfth century courts and councils are thought to have been essentially the same thing in the sense that all effective local functions not discharged by royal officers were performed by the undifferentiated borough court. If so there was a thirteenth-century movement towards bifurcation of function between court and council. The essence of an English borough was jurisdictional. Normally in a significant provincial town the borough court had jurisdiction over disputes relating to property in the town, the regulation of municipal life in general, the wills of the burgesses, various elements of commercial law and low grade police jurisdiction. A most important thing about municipal courts was the frequency with which they sat. Twelfth- and early thirteenth-century charters for London and a number of other important towns state that the principal court is to be held weekly.[121] An advantage of municipal justice was that it was available often (and probably cheaply).

What municipal courts could not do was important. With very few exceptions English towns did not enjoy major criminal jurisdiction. Thus, even such a city as Norwich had no criminal franchise higher than that which enabled it to execute a thief caught in the act. When, in 1285, the city authorities made the mistake of attempting to execute a thief not caught in the act, they lost their liberties for several months.[122] Edward I's government kept municipal aspiration well reined in. If the criminal jurisdiction enjoyed by towns was minor, nevertheless it mattered for convenience of ordinary life. The Norwich leet rolls show how the minor courts of the subdivisions of a town could have a flourishing and important existence in relation to police and economic control.[123] Subdivisions of towns could have distinct institutional life. Four towns have subdivisions recorded in Domesday Book, other towns appear with such divisions afterwards, though these may have been significantly older.[124] Thus Canterbury was divided into six *berthae* by the end of the twelfth century at the latest. These resembled the wards of London as each had its alderman and a court which seems to have corresponded to that of a hundred in its responsibility for the maintenance of frankpledge and was also used for the recording of sales and conveyances.[125] Such an organisation could be created at a rather late date. Thus, a system of wards and aldermen was introduced into Exeter in 1281 'by order of the Justices in

[120] *Ibid.*, ch. 10, for this paragraph.

[121] Ballard, ed., *British Borough Charters 1042–1216*, pp. 142–3; Thomas, ed., *Calendar of Early Mayors' Court Rolls*, p. ix.

[122] Hudson and Tingey, eds., *Records of Norwich*, I, nos. LIX, LXXXVI, pp. 214, 220–2.

[123] Hudson, ed., *Leet Jurisdiction, passim.* [124] Darby, *Domesday England*, p. 294.

[125] Urry, *Canterbury*, pp. 91–100; Brooke and Keir, *London 800–1216*, pp. 170–1.

Eyre and by consent of the whole city'.[126] Other towns were subdivided in various ways. Durham included a set of what were essentially independent boroughs, at least two of which had separate charters.[127] Hereford was composed of four separate fees.[128] Not only in London but also in provincial towns individual lords, churches or burgesses could have limited jurisdiction ('soke') over particular areas.[129] Any cathedral city would contain a large area exempt from municipal jurisdiction. A town such as Oxford with the misfortune to contain a university could find its jurisdiction trammelled.

Their limited criminal jurisdiction is but one reminder of how unindependent English towns, one and all, were. They remained in the most important ways completely under the authority of the crown. Things went very ill with the bailiffs of a town which failed to pay its farm, for they faced a large element of individual liability.[130] A main function of their officers was to carry out royal commands. Towns might have their individual governmental arrangements, but these were much subject to royal control. Thus, in 1219 one of the 'twenty-four' at Lincoln found himself in mercy for going against the other twenty-three.[131] Towns were required to bestir themselves to provide goods and services required by the crown. One example among many: in 1218 the mayor of Lincoln was ordered to provide 200 pickaxes and 1,000 ropes to be used immediately in siege engines.[132] Most shipbuilding for royal war-fleets was undertaken by towns. The role of towns in organising purveyance of food for the royal household was hardly less. If an English town was one which enjoyed exemptions from some of the ordinary routines of royal jurisdiction it was also one on which the requirements of royal administration were concentrated. Urban fortification was an important instance of the relationship between urban needs and demands and those of king and country. The construction of new town walls was fairly common in the thirteenth century, in areas threatened by the Welsh; later, as French invasion threatened, in the South and East normally the municipality undertook the work and the crown helped towards the cost by allowing special tolls, 'murage', to be levied.[133]

Such circumstances help to determine the relationships between English provincial towns and the crown in the thirteenth century. Other factors were as follows. The crown continued to grant, or sell, charters of privilege. There were a few further grants of the fee-farm; fifty towns had gained this privilege by 1300.

[126] Wilkinson, *Mediaeval Council of Exeter*, p. xxxii.

[127] M. Bonney, *Lordship and the Urban Community* (Cambridge, 1990), pp. 41–9.

[128] M. D. Lobel, 'Hereford', p. 7, in *BAHT*, I.

[129] Brooke and Keir, *London 800–1216*, pp. 150, 155–7; for provincial examples, Tait, *Medieval English Borough*, pp. 43, 97; Platt, *The English Medieval Town*, p. 22; Roffe, ed., *Stamford in the Thirteenth Century*, pp. 20–4.

[130] C. R. Young, *The English Borough and Royal Administration, 1130–1307* (Durham, N.C., 1961), pp. 18–19. [131] *Ibid.*, p. 77. [132] *Ibid.*, p. 98.

[133] H. L. Turner, *Town Defences in England and Wales* (London, 1970), esp. pp. 28–46.

It was common for thirteenth-century towns to receive the privilege of 'return of writs'.[134] This meant that judicial writs relating to inhabitants of the town were not dealt with by the sheriff but their serving and return were delegated to the municipal authorities. It could be that in this towns were paying to obtain written confirmation of privileges already enjoyed. Urban consciousness may have been affected by the establishment of houses of friars in most towns during the last three generations of the century. The presence of religious institutions invariably with urban connections and with an urban commitment not shared by other orders maybe had a political effect. If friars were friends to towns, monks could be enemies. There were serious disturbances in such monastic towns as Bury, St Albans and Dunstable, during the Barons' Wars (as later in the reigns of Edward II and Richard II).[135] Recurrent tension between the crown and the towns is demonstrated in the frequency with which major towns were seized into the king's hand. The frequency and the long periods of such royal domination particularly in Edward I's reign could make one suppose that Edward had a general policy of suppressing urban liberties, a suspicion reinforced by the marked limitations on the privileges he gave to his new town of Hull.[136] If so, there is a suggestive parallel with the concern of Louis IX to control and regulate French towns.[137]

It was not enough for Edward I to control towns. He needed to use and conciliate them too. This is indicated by two related movements: a change in the system of taxing towns and the summons of urban representatives to national assemblies. Henry III had levied tallage fourteen times; his son did so only once, replacing it by more widely based taxes on movables.[138] Kings had summoned urban representatives to assemblies on occasions, perhaps fairly numerous occasions, in the twelfth and earlier thirteenth centuries.[139] But emphasis on Simon de Montfort as an originator of urban parliamentary representation is justified. In summoning urban representatives to his assembly in 1265 he recognised the political weight of towns. This could have owed something to his experience of urban activity in Gascony.[140] The point was not lost on his more legitimate successors in authority. In 1268 Henry III summoned to treat before the council the mayor, the bailiffs and six important burgesses from each of twenty-seven towns.[141] In Edward

[134] A. Ballard and J. Tait, eds., *British Borough Charters 1216–1307* (Cambridge, 1923), pp. 171–2.

[135] N. M. Trenholme, *The English Monastic Boroughs* (University of Missouri Studies, 2, no. 3, 1927).

[136] *VCH*, Yorkshire: East Riding, 1, pp. 11–20.

[137] C. Petit-Dutaillis, *The Feudal Monarchy in France and England* (London, 1936), pp. 314–18.

[138] Mitchell, *Taxation in Medieval England*, pp. 330–1, 358.

[139] A. B. White, 'Some early instances of concentration of representatives in England', *American Historical Review*, 9 (1913–14), 735–50.

[140] J. R. Maddicott, *Simon de Montfort* (Cambridge, 1994), pp. 106–23, 284–9, 314–18, 366, 388; C. Bémont, *Simon de Montfort, Earl of Leicester 1208–1265*, new edn, trans. E. F. Jacob (Oxford, 1930), pp. 73–128.

[141] M. McKisack, *The Parliamentary Representation of English Boroughs during the Middle Ages* (Oxford, 1932), pp. 2–3.

I's reign town representatives were summoned to at least fourteen assemblies.[142] By the end of the reign parliament had developed in such a way as to suggest, of burgesses (and knights), 'that their presence was coming to be regarded as so desirable as often to be almost indispensable'.[143] Normally only London representatives were summoned directly; everywhere else it was left to the sheriff to summon the towns in his shire to provide two representatives each. Definition was left to him; and minor places, hardly more than villages, became involved. The total number of places summoned for one assembly or another was less than 166, the average number represented in the relevant Edwardian parliaments 86 or more.[144] Something to weigh is that the representatives of the town were associated with those of the shires. I believe that in no other European assembly of estates were town representatives put together with what in most of western Europe would have been regarded as the lower nobility. Here there may be an association of forces and classes with a long history, going back to epochs in which the relationship of towns to the shires and the gentry raises so many possibilities and problems.

Edward had another interest in towns: their use as instruments for the control of conquered lands. He summoned a special assembly of townsmen to advise him on the organisation of Berwick, probably the richest element in his Scottish conquest.[145] In Wales the organisation of new towns went hand in hand with the construction of his castles. In particular, at Conwy and Caernarfon a domineering new castle was integrated with a new walled town.[146]

London was dominant among English towns. The thirteenth century was its 'age of iron'.[147] Its political weight was made plain in the 1190s. In Richard I's absence on crusade his brother John bought the city's support by granting it a commune. It was probably in association with this that the city was first headed by a mayor. John made further concessions to London in 1199: amongst them the reduction of the city's farm to an old, and in inflationary times absurdly low, rate of £300. The king's concern to identify the municipal aspiration to the support of royal authority is visible in the 'oath of commune', 1193: those taking it were to be loyal to King Richard against all men, and to keep his peace; but they were *also* to 'hold the commune' and to be obedient to the mayor and his *skivini*, though this was to be *in fide regis*.[148] Londoners' loyalty was supposed to straddle two horses, not guaranteed to gallop in the same direction. In the long run this was accomplished, but not in the short. London played an active part in

[142] E. B. Fryde, D. E. Greenway, S. Porter and R. I. Roy, *Handbook of British Chronology*, 3rd edn (London, 1986), pp. 545–52. [143] McKisack, *Parliamentary Representation*, p. 23.

[144] *Ibid.*, p. 11. [145] *Ibid.*, p. 8 and n.6.

[146] R. R. Davies, *Conquest, Coexistence and Change* (Oxford, 1987), pp. 371–3.

[147] The phrase is that of G. A. Williams, *Medieval London* (London, 1963), p. 9. His account of thirteenth-century London politics, though somewhat over-dogmatic, has been substantially followed below.

[148] J. H. Round, *The Commune of London and Other Studies* (London, 1899), pp. 235–6.

the opposition to John, while the mayor was one of the twenty-five great men appointed to oversee the execution of the charter. The Londoners supported Louis VIII's invasion of England. The most conspicuous of the king's opponents, Robert fitz Walter, was, as lord of Baynard's Castle, hereditary leader of London's troops.[149]

Throughout the thirteenth century there was frequent discord between king and city. London was repeatedly taken into the king's hand; the longest period of suspension of normal city government was between 1285 and 1298. The causes of tension were various. Hostility towards the privileges of Henry III's favoured abbey of Westminster played a part, as in 1239. London politics could be exceedingly complicated: for example in 1258 the king's agent, Mansel, tried to use the semi-popular folkmoot against the leading men of the city. Such complication made itself felt during the hectic years of the Barons' Wars. Not for the last time the city authorities sought to perch on the fence. Not for the last time there were radical currents and tides which swept caution away. By 1263 London was committed to de Montfort. The London troops fought for him, and suffered badly at Lewes in 1264. Next year the Londoners found they had backed the wrong horse. The city was fined heavily; it did not regain its elective mayor and sheriffs until 1270. But if London was hardly a biddable city for the king, it was, with its detested neighbour, Westminster, more and more the capital of his kingdom.[150]

London, by its very size, was altogether exceptional in England. At the beginning of the fourteenth century it was probably rising towards 100,000 inhabitants. Because London was big it needed a great deal of administration and justice. By the end of the thirteenth century the London courts had an elaboration and overlapping complexity which, *inter alia*, indicates the antiquity of some of the arrangements. Numerously attended assemblies related to the ancient folkmoot still played a significant part, especially in times of crisis. The centuries-old court of Husting met weekly with extremely important functions, including that of the registration of property transfers, which must have done much to solidify the economic life of the city. The courts of the mayor and of the sheriffs had extensive overlapping jurisdictions; particularly important was their capacity to give quick justice in commercial cases, not least to foreign merchants.[151] The city was served by a substantial bureaucracy.[152]

However firmly under royal control, London had important characteristics of an active and innovative city-state. This is particularly apparent in its legislative activity: not least in the extent to which it anticipated similar legislation not only

[149] Brooke and Keir, *London 800–1216*, p. 52, for John's razing of the castle.

[150] T. F. Tout, 'The beginnings of a modern capital. London and Westminster in the fourteenth century' in his *Collected Papers* (Manchester, 1934), vol. III, pp. 249–75; Williams, *Medieval London*, pp. 307–14.

[151] Williams, *Medieval London*, pp. 36–7, 80–4, 95–6, 256–7; Thomas, ed., *Calendar of Early Mayors' Court Rolls*.

[152] Williams, *Medieval London*, pp. 95–105.

in other towns, but also nationally. One of the earliest pieces of post-Conquest economic legislation to survive is the London assize of building, some of which must go back at least to the reign of John and some of which may be older.[153] *Inter alia* it is one of the first known English attempts to regulate wages. The London ordinances of 1285 involved extensive economic regulation; similarly with those of York in 1301.[154] (Both sets were issued when the city concerned was in the hand of the king.) The background to the statutory regulation of forestalling via JPs from 1364 is one of urban efforts to the same end from the fourteenth century.[155] Indeed the office of JP may itself have a partly London origin. The legislative innovations of Edward III, the effort at wide economic regulation, the reorganisation of the local judicial system can be seen as the general extension to the countryside of systems of organisation and control which had originated in towns, and especially in London.

Such urban developments may well have been influenced by close involvement, above all London involvement, with foreign parts. Relations with Normandy, naturally, became particularly close after the Conquest. We are told that 'many natives of the chief towns of Normandy, Rouen and Caen, moved to London, and chose a dwelling there; because it was a better place for their trade and better stored with the goods in which they were accustomed to deal';[156] and Thomas Becket's father was one of these. There seem to have been important connections between the constitutional development of London and that of Rouen.[157] German influence became hardly less important: one of the most important of all London's leaders in the thirteenth century, Arnold fitz Thedmar, had German grandparents who had settled in London in about 1180.[158] By the time of Edward I the most important foreign influence was Italian. Its importance is expressed by the inclusion in the London *Liber Custumarum* (*c.* 1300) of the Florentine Brunetto Latini's *Trésor*, revised to make it applicable to the mayor.[159] An apparent provincial instance of Italian influence appears in the York ordinances of 1301, which includes provision for the regulation of doctors which have no known English, but at least one contemporary Italian, counterpart.[160] The history of sumptuary legislation in England is an instructive one. Such laws appear in Spain, Italy and France in the thirteenth century. The first known English examples are from London from near the end of the century; in a national form sumptuary legislation appears in 1336 and 1337 and, much more extensively, in 1363.[161]

153 H. M. Chew and W. Kellaway, eds., *London Assize of Nuisance 1301–1431, a Calendar* (London Record Society, 10, for 1974, 1973), pp. ix–xi.

154 Williams, *Medieval London*, pp. 255–6.

155 Thomas, ed., *Calendar of Early Mayors' Court Rolls*, *passim*.

156 Robertson and Sheppard, eds., *Materials for the History of . . . Becket*, IV, p. 81.

157 Round, *The Commune of London*, pp. 243–51.

158 Williams, *Medieval London*, p. 44.

159 *Ibid.*, pp. 312–13.

160 M. Prestwich, *York Civic Ordinances 1301* (Borthwick Paper, 49, York, 1976), esp. pp. 1–5, 28.

161 *Lexikon des Mittelalters* (Munich and Zurich, 1980–98) s.v. *Kleiderordnungen*; Williams, *Medieval London*, p. 197.

The high point of London's medieval career as a revolutionary city came with its support for the coup by which Queen Isabella and Mortimer deposed Edward II in 1326–7. After terrible riot and bloodshed, the Londoners, led by their mayor, Hamo de Chigwell, won unprecedented success. In January 1327 very many of the great men of the kingdom were forced to come to the Guildhall to swear loyalty to the new king and observance of the liberties of the city. Those liberties were much increased by a new charter in 1327.[162] Not the least of what they gained was the right to be taxed at the rural rather than the urban rate. Thus London's tax assessment in 1334, and for long afterwards, was £733 6s 8d., a derisory sum for so great a metropolis.[163]

Until very nearly the end of the long reign of Edward III there was no conflict with or within London approaching in ferocity those in the time of his father, grandfather and great-grandfather. Under Edward I it was common for major provincial towns to be taken into the king's hand. In his grandson's reign this was no longer so. Gwyn Williams said that after the trauma of 1326–7 London was newly 'integrated into the . . . national community'.[164] The substantial element of truth in the sweeping phrase applies beyond London. Another way of putting it would be to say that under Edward III the style and climate of government changed, largely, it may well be, because the king's success in gaining a permanent and mighty increase in the customs tax on wool as the Hundred Years War began softened the need to harass individual men and communities, urban communities not least.

It is tempting to use biological metaphor when one generalises about the organisation of power and authority in and over early English towns. The English urban scene in 1300 was the product of long evolution. The towns can be categorised by genus and by species. The older types of animal had had long lives and so manifested distinct individualities. Particularly, but not only, in London such individuality may have been not so very different (not in power, but in distinctness and historically affected complexity) from that of a state. It is a question, no less interesting than unsolved, as to how far the individualities of town constitutions as they were until the Municipal Corporations Act of 1835 took the mark of distant pasts. For example, how remote were the ultimate origins of the large number (and strong privileges) of the freemen of Norwich? Something we can be certain of is that the determining milieu in which all these creatures had grown up was that of a powerful state to whose life they were integral.

[162] Williams, *Medieval London*, pp. 298–300.

[163] R. E. Glasscock, ed., *The Lay Subsidy of 1334* (London, 1975), pp. 187–8.

[164] Williams, *Medieval London*, p. 299.

· 5 ·

Society and population 600–1300

RICHARD HOLT

(i) PROTO-URBAN POPULATIONS

IN THE early middle ages only a few rudimentary urban societies were to be found in Britain. Bede could describe eighth-century London as a market well frequented by its many visitors arriving by land and by sea – the reference is presumably to *Lundenwic*, to the west of the Roman city – and it is also known that there were extensive trading settlements or *wics* at other sites.[1] By 800 *Hamwic*, Southampton's predecessor which was perhaps half the size of contemporary London, had streets laid out in a regular grid over a considerable area of some 100 acres (40 ha); it was fairly densely settled by a population living by trade and commodity manufacturing that could have been reckoned in thousands.[2] Whether this was a settled community of permanent residents capable of evolving a distinct social structure, however, remains uncertain, and the casual manner in which the dead were disposed of may point to a society in which many inhabitants were transients and social bonds remained undeveloped.[3] Other proto-urban centres existed in places with a range of central-place functions. Many of the former *civitas* capitals and *coloniae* of the Roman period became the setting for major public buildings such as royal palaces or important early churches, and in some cases an appreciable population composed of thegns, priests and their many retainers and servants would have gathered. Although at

[1] Bede, *Ecclesiastical History*, ed. B. Colgrave and R. A. B. Mynors (Oxford, 1969), p. 142 (ii. 3).

[2] P. V. Addyman, 'Saxon Southampton: a town and international port of the 8th to the 10th century', in H. Jankuhn, W. Schlesinger and H. Steuer, eds., *Vor- und Frühformen der Europäischen Stadt im Mittelalter* (Göttingen, 1973), vol. 1, p. 223; P. E. Holdsworth, ed., *Excavations at Melbourne Street, Southampton, 1971–76* (CBA Res. Rep., 33, 1980), p. 1; John H. Williams, 'A review of late Saxon urban origins and development', in M. L. Faull, ed., *Studies in Late Anglo-Saxon Settlement* (Oxford, 1984), pp. 25–34.

[3] A. Morton, 'Burial in middle Saxon Southampton', in S. Bassett, ed., *Death in Towns* (Leicester, 1992), pp. 68–77.

this distance impossible to measure, such city populations presumably totalled some hundreds of individuals; at a small number of central places the resident population could have considerably exceeded that size.

For Canterbury, fragments of evidence for such a substantial proto-urban population provide insights into the social structure that was manifestly well established by the mid-ninth century. From the earliest English period, it has been suggested, the site of this former Roman city had been the focus of the estates of Kent's noble families, a practice similar to that observed in the Rhineland during the early middle ages. The situation within Canterbury becomes clearer during the ninth century, by which time charters conveying city land began to be issued. The indications of a flourishing land market in small plots implies a thriving population, as does the local custom or by-law – dating from before 868 – requiring that a space of at least two feet (0.6 m) be left between each house to allow for the eaves-drip. Development was thus already sufficiently dense to require regulation, with at least some plot-owners having apparently built along the whole of their frontages. Properties were being subdivided, and sold in parcels; and, most importantly, it is implied that the *burhwara*, the borough inhabitants or burgesses, had their own court to establish and enforce *folcriht*, the body of local law. Already the people had formed themselves into some sort of corporate organisation: they held common water-meadows along the banks of the Stour, as well as arable lands; their rights to take wood in their own woods were defined. Regulation of their communal rights and responsibilities could presumably have been accomplished only through regular meetings in a borough court. The implication of the names and status of witnesses to a damaged charter of about 860, amplified by evidence from a century later, is that the population saw itself in terms of particular groupings or fraternities: the *innan burhware*, or burgesses resident within Canterbury; the *utan burhware*, or those living outside (a group it has been suggested were nobles and others normally resident outside the city but who nevertheless had interests in Canterbury). The *micle gemettan* were probably the many retainers of greater men; the *cniahta gegildan* or guild of *cnihtas* has been identified with the *ceapmannegild* or merchant guild of burgesses of the eleventh century, although there is no evidence that at this earlier date it fulfilled the same role.[4] Such evidence can convey neither the size of this city population, nor even how this formal social classification translated into practice; unquestionably, however, even at this early date Canterbury was inhabited by a distinct community with its own institutions and a capacity for communal action. However, there is nothing to suggest that by 900 this city was living primarily by commerce; this was not yet unequivocally an urban society, but a population inhabiting what had once been, and soon would be again, an urban setting.

[4] N. P. Brooks, *The Early History of the Church of Canterbury* (Leicester, 1984), pp. 27–30.

(ii) THE INHABITANTS OF THE BOROUGHS

The provision of streets within *burhs* or boroughs, postulated at Winchester, Gloucester, Worcester and elsewhere, was designed in part at least to accommodate a commercial population.[5] The agreement concerning the fortification of Worcester, made in the 890s between the city's bishop and Æthelred of Mercia, talks of the Church's rights in the market and in the streets; specified fines for dishonest trading imply the existence or perhaps just the expectation of a settled population engaged in commerce.[6] The legal terminology of the tenth century, which equated the port or trading place with the borough, strengthens the impression that a truly urban population was emerging, as does archaeological evidence of growing activity both in the English boroughs and those of the Danelaw.[7]

Historical evidence for the identity of the townspeople is sparse, but none the less illuminating. At Worcester, for instance, successive bishops – still effectively lords of the city – pursued a policy of granting house-plots in the borough to their retainers. Several leases of rural lands issued by Bishop Oswald between 963 and his death in 992 were accompanied by messuages in the city; whilst providing maintenance for both clerical and lay members of his household, the bishop was also making provision for their continued residence in the city where they served him. Their town house was no less essential than the agricultural lands from which they drew their income. No other contemporary lord can be observed rewarding so many of his retainers in this way, but it is only the accident of survival that makes Oswald's many surviving leases a unique series.

Oswald's policy continued that of his predecessors, as later evidence points to earlier bishops having associated land in Worcester with grants of rural estates, and the bishops of the eleventh century continued the practice. Other great lords too, including the king, continued to attach Worcester properties to rural estates until the time of the Conquest, although in fact many of these appurtenant town properties escaped mention in Domesday Book. The recorded total of only eleven manors with appurtenant houses in Worcester, in addition to the ninety

5 M. Biddle and D. Hill, 'Late Saxon planned towns', *Antiquaries J*, 51 (1971), 70–85; C. Heighway, 'Anglo-Saxon Gloucester', in *VCH, Gloucestershire*, IV, pp. 5–12; N. J. Baker and R. A. Holt, 'The city of Worcester in the tenth century', in N. P. Brooks and C. Cubitt, eds., *St Oswald of Worcester* (London, 1996), pp. 129–46; N. J. Baker *et al.*, 'From Roman to medieval Worcester: development and planning in the Anglo-Saxon city', *Antiquity*, 66 (1992), 65–74.

6 F. E. Harmer, *Select English Historical Documents of the Ninth and Tenth Centuries* (Cambridge, 1914), no. 13; translated in D. Whitelock, ed., *English Historical Documents*, vol. I, 2nd edn (London, 1979), pp. 540–1.

7 F. W. Maitland, *Domesday Book and Beyond* (Cambridge, 1897), p. 196 n.1; F. Liebermann, *Die Gesetze der Angelsachsen* (Halle, 1903–16), vol. I, pp. 146–9, 196–7; A. Vince, 'The urban economy in Mercia in the 9th and 10th centuries', in *Archaeology and the Urban Economy: Festschrift to Asbjørn E. Herteig* (Arkeoligiske Skrifter fra Historisk Museum, Universitetet i Bergen, 5, Bergen, 1989), pp. 136–59.

houses in the city held from the bishop's manor of Northwick, might have been no more than a fraction of the true total.[8]

A predominant feature of the population of tenth-century Worcester, therefore, like that of Canterbury a century before, was the considerable number of households belonging to the episcopal and royal retainers settled in the city. Owing their military, ecclesiastical or administrative service within Worcester, presumably these men had much of the surplus from their estates delivered to them in the city for consumption or for sale. Doubtless the upper layer of urban society which these people and their households constituted in the greater shire towns was more prominent than the community of craftsmen and others living primarily by trade whose activities have been detected by archaeology.[9] The several urban guilds whose regulations survive from this period are more likely to have been associations, certainly in origin, of aristocratic townsmen and their dependants: the tenth-century regulations of the thegns' guild of Cambridge, for instance, were designed for a membership apparently preoccupied with the service they owed to their lords, and with the consequences of bloodshed.[10]

Domesday Book confirms that before 1066 the thegnly class had routinely owned urban land, and involved itself in urban affairs; there were at least superficial parallels, therefore, with the more urbanised parts of Europe such as Italy or Flanders where the ruling class was at home in both town and country.[11] The aristocracy's urban houses and estates at the time of the Conquest brought profits of justice from tenants: perhaps fines from offences they committed, and doubtless forfeitures too. Many lords had sake and soke within their own urban houses and those of their tenants, and some had the rights to take tolls. Their town estates could thus produce a useful income, as well as providing a base for their frequent visits to the borough for meetings of courts, and for business and trading transactions.[12] It was this latter function that was diminishing in importance, according to Domesday Book; by 1086 most aristocratic urban land had been let for housing, producing the curious situation recorded in all the shire towns of numerous burgesses holding their tenements from the lords of rural manors.

(iii) URBAN POPULATION IN 1086

The extent of this first phase of medieval urbanisation can be seen in the number and size of the towns recorded in 1086 (Map 3.1). Domesday Book's treatment

[8] Baker and Holt, '*Worcester in the tenth century*', pp. 129–46; Great Domesday ff. 180d, 176a, 177b, 177c, 177d, 178a, 180c, 180d, 182b.

[9] There are other known grants of urban land to thegns in Winchester, Oxford, Warwick and Chichester: J. M. Kemble, *Codex Diplomaticus Aevi Saxonici* (London, 1839–48), nos. 673, 1144, 1235, 746, 705, 724, 663.

[10] Whitelock, ed., *English Historical Documents*, pp. 603–5.

[11] C. J. Wickham, *Early Medieval Italy* (London, 1981), pp. 85–8; R. H. Hilton, *English and French Towns in Feudal Society* (Cambridge, 1992), pp. 88–91.

[12] R. Fleming, 'Rural elites and urban communities in late-saxon England', *P&P*, 141 (1993), 3–37.

of towns is inconsistent and tantalising; nevertheless with some 112 places identified as having urban characteristics it is plain that England had already acquired a substantial urban population. Estimates of the size of individual towns based on the recorded number of houses or of tenants (as presented in Appendix 2) must of necessity be cautious, producing minimal figures; even by that reckoning, however, some thirty-six towns had a population greater than 1,000. Domesday Book's national coverage means that these estimates must remain our points of reference for the numbers of urban inhabitants in 1086; yet alternative – and in each case considerably higher – estimates can be proposed for those few towns where there is alternative evidence. A population figure of 6,000 has been suggested for Canterbury, well in excess of the figure that might be calculated from the Domesday Book total of 451 burgesses.[13] Elsewhere, and for whatever reason, Domesday Book failed to record many urban tenements. Surveys of Gloucester and Winchcombe, made within ten or fifteen years of Domesday Book, demonstrate that the 1086 burgess totals had been serious underestimates.[14] It is not possible to tell how often underrecording had occurred elsewhere; just as seriously, the translation of numbers of burgesses into population estimates can provide only the crudest approximations. The well-studied city of Winchester provides an example: although not recorded in Domesday Book, it was surveyed in the years just prior to the Conquest when it had an estimated 1,130 tenements. The growing city had about 1,300 tenements by the early twelfth century, and translating these figures into a population following the established method of using a multiplier of perhaps 4.5 to represent an average household size, plus an allowance of 10 per cent for families in excess of tenements, provides a figure of 5,500 for late Anglo-Saxon Winchester, and about 6,500 for *c.* 1110. However, on the evidence of the more certain size of Winchester's population during later centuries, it has been proposed that twelfth-century Winchester actually had more like 12,000 people.[15] Better evidence from other towns might indicate that such reassessment would be more generally appropriate, with many more of these estimates from Domesday Book requiring substantial revision upwards.

More useful, perhaps, than the individual numerical estimates is the deduced ranking of towns from Domesday Book. Below London, the greater English towns were York, Lincoln and Norwich; Winchester too, although not in Domesday Book, and Thetford – soon to go into a spectacular decline. Bristol, it has been suggested, may already have been a major town, although certain evidence for its prominence comes only from the following century.[16] The

[13] Brooks, *Early History of the Church of Canterbury*, p. 32.

[14] J. S. Moore, ed., *Domesday Book: Gloucestershire* (Chichester, 1982), Appendix, Evesham K.

[15] M. Biddle, 'Early Norman Winchester', in J. C. Holt, ed., *Domesday Studies* (Woodbridge, 1987), pp. 311–31.

[16] C. C. Dyer, 'St Oswald and 10,000 West Midland peasants', in Brooks and Cubitt, eds., *St Oswald of Worcester*, p. 182n.

distribution of the larger towns and indeed of much of the urban population, is very marked: northern and western towns were less numerous, with East Anglia and the South-East of England – followed by the Midlands – being the most urbanised regions. That was the pattern for Britain as a whole: the earliest evidence for urban development in Scotland dates from the twelfth century, while in Wales towns first appeared as an aspect of Anglo-Norman colonisation. Over England as a whole, Domesday Book records about 7 per cent of households as urban, although after due allowance is made for its obvious shortcomings in recording towns of all sizes – even its total of 112 being probably far from complete – perhaps 10 per cent of England's population in 1086 lived in towns. That suggested figure includes the already substantial suburban population which has been identified as living outside a number of towns and which Domesday Book identifies as communities of cottagers or smallholders.[17]

(iv) BOROUGH SOCIETY AFTER THE CONQUEST

Although conveying little of the complexity of the urban society that had developed by 1086, Domesday Book acknowledges that the inhabitants of the greater towns at least had established a common identity and were capable of representing their collective interests to king or lord. Moreover, it is plain that this had been a development of the pre-Conquest period, and owed little or nothing to the new political regime.[18] An objective measure of social stratification is apparent in most of the larger towns, with inhabitants of lesser status specified separately: at Ipswich, for instance, there were 110 burgesses, 100 poor burgesses, 32 bordars and 8 villeins; at Norwich there were 665 burgesses and 480 bordars. There was also a new borough there, inhabited mainly by 124 Frenchmen and their households; planted communities of the conquerors were not common, and were generally small, such as the 24 Frenchmen of Dunwich who held tenancies in the town along with 316 burgesses, 80 men and 178 poor men – all presumably English.[19] The ethnic impact of the Conquest on urban society generally was not great; even in the leading royal city of Winchester the Conquest did not entail any drastic replacement of population. Leading citizens there – the reeves and the moneyers – continued to have English names until they ceased to be fashionable in the twelfth century, and most property continued to be held by English tenants. In the greatest commercial centre, London, the community retained its English identity, just

[17] H. C. Darby, *Domesday England* (Cambridge, 1977), pp. 87–91, 337, 364–8; C. Dyer, 'How urbanised was medieval England?', in J.-M. Duvosquel and E. Thoen, eds., *Peasants and Townsmen in Medieval Europe* (Ghent, 1995), p. 172; C. Dyer, *Everyday Life in Medieval England* (London, 1994), pp. 241–55.

[18] S. Reynolds, 'Towns in Domesday Book' in Holt, ed., *Domesday Studies*, pp. 306–8.

[19] A. Farley, ed., *Domesday Book*, (London, 1783), vol. II, pp. 116, 290, 311–12.

as in York and Lincoln where Englishmen continued to fill the important public offices.[20]

With the rapid growth in the size of settled urban communities living by trade and manufacturing, distinctive urban institutions became more prominent. There was general recognition that townspeople should hold urban land freely, and personal freedom had become by the twelfth century – if not much earlier – the hallmark of the borough.[21] The superior urban property of 1086 and before, whether described as a *mansura*, a *haga* or haw, or just as a *domus* or house, was clearly in most cases held freely for a cash rent; the term 'burgage' came to predominate after the Conquest, just as the townsman enjoying the range of urban liberties was a 'burgess' (though usually a 'citizen' in the cathedral cities). The many variations in local law and custom – particularly those recorded in Domesday Book and during the twelfth century – demonstrate the diverse origins of both burgage tenure and the status of the medieval burgess. But behind differences of detail lay a considerable and apparently growing uniformity, so that by the end of the twelfth century the charters granted to new and existing towns shared broad assumptions as to the nature and extent of urban liberties.[22] Even in those towns whose liberties were not to be formally recognised by charter during the middle ages free tenure of land prevailed, accepted by most lords as a privilege essential to a population engaged in commerce.[23]

The burgage could be bought and sold, or subdivided; any serious restrictions were to protect not the lord's interests but those of the heirs, whose rights generally applied only to inherited land – not to land a burgess had purchased. Whilst in the greater towns burgages might be held from a variety of lords with interests in the town, as Domesday Book shows, the rights of lords over their tenants withered away; the burgage rent or landgable became no more than a symbol of a lordship[24] that was losing its meaning in the face of the growing identity of the community of burgesses, with its own courts and institutions. Crucially, by the twelfth century and doubtless before, burgess status was perceived to confer commercial and legal privileges that were denied to outsiders or to lesser residents of the town; equally, it implied the sharing of burdens common to the whole burgess community, and a voice in the deliberations of

[20] Biddle, 'Early Norman Winchester', pp. 325–8; S. Reynolds, 'The rulers of London in the twelfth century', *History*, 57 (1972), 337–57; F. Hill, *Medieval Lincoln* (Cambridge, 1948), pp. 52–3; A. Williams, *The English and the Norman Conquest* (Woodbridge, 1995), pp. 205–6.

[21] J. Tait, *The Medieval English Borough* (Manchester, 1936), p. 85.

[22] A. Ballard, ed., *British Borough Charters 1042–1216* (Cambridge, 1913), *passim*.

[23] As for instance in the case of Birmingham: R. A. Holt, *The Early History of the Town of Birmingham* (Dugdale Society Occasional Papers, 30, 1985), pp. 5–9; R. H. Britnell, *The Commercialisation of English Society, 1000–1500*, 2nd edn (Manchester, 1996), p. 147.

[24] Tait, *Medieval English Borough*, pp. 96,100–2. M. de W. Hemmeon, *Burgage Tenure in Mediaeval England* (Cambridge, Mass., 1914), pp. 64–77 and *passim*.

the community that was denied to others.[25] The distinction made in Domesday Book between burgesses and non-burgess inhabitants of the towns points to a tenurial difference that already in 1086 had widely recognised social implications.

Tenancy of a messuage in burgage conferred burgess status, but was clearly not the sole qualification nor, in time, the only route to the liberty of the borough. Formal acceptance by the burgess community was also required, as in twelfth-century Tewkesbury for instance.[26] In every town this must have entailed a public commitment to uphold the common interest of the community. Among the privileges and duties of the burgess, some charters assumed that the individual would be in scot and lot with his fellows, others that he would be in their guild; whether in practice there was any difference is to be doubted.[27] Town air did make free, but only up to a point; the few borough charters that recognised the personal freedom of any rural immigrant who remained unchallenged or unclaimed by his lord for a year and a day, as at Pembroke, were greatly outnumbered by those specifying that the clause applied only to those accepted as burgesses by the rest of the community.[28] The formula which came to be established in common law was that the serf had to have been received into the burgesses' community or guild to be considered freed from villeinage – explicitly to be more than just resident within the borough.[29] The privilege was obviously of more value to the established burgess wishing to travel the countryside unharassed than to the servile immigrant too poor to buy property or to be accepted into the merchant community. Throughout the middle ages lords continued to claim, when they could, chevage payments from those of their servile tenants who emigrated to towns, although in practice most migrants from the countryside must have taken advantage of their anonymity in the town to shake off their servile past.[30]

Recent work by historians on the life experience of medieval townspeople is strictly applicable only to the later medieval centuries. Evidence from before 1300 is generally lacking, with small-town society paradoxically better recorded than the larger towns with their more ambitious record keeping. Knowledge of the urban population is restricted in the main to those matters that required regulation by law, although certain basic premises may be assumed. Unquestionably the family-based household was – as in medieval society generally – both social

[25] Tait, *Mediaeval English Borough*, pp. 86–96; see for instance the mid-twelfth-century customs of Newcastle-upon-Tyne and Bury St Edmunds: D. C. Douglas and G. W. Greenaway, eds., *English Historical Documents*, vol. II, 2nd edn (London, 1981), pp. 1034–6, 1040–1.

[26] A. E. Bland, P. A. Brown and R. H. Tawney, eds., *English Economic History: Select Documents* (London, 1914), pp. 116–19.

[27] Douglas and Greenaway, eds., *English Historical Documents*, pp. 1030–2, 1038–9, 1042–3.

[28] Ballard, ed., *British Borough Charters 1042–1216*, pp. 103–5.

[29] Tait, *Medieval English Borough*, pp. 223–4; G. D. G. Hall, ed., *Glanvill, Tractatibus de Legibus et Consuetudinibus Regni Anglie qui Glanvilla Vocatur* (London, 1965), p. 58.

[30] Such payments could still be claimed from serfs emigrating to towns as late as the fifteenth century, as for instance at Churchdown in Glos.: Gloucestershire County RO, D621.M1.

and economic unit. Commodities were manufactured in family workshops, and behind the publicly recorded society of households headed by men or widows there stood a working population of younger men, women and children. Wage earners and live-in servants supplemented the family labour force, and women worked alongside men at probably most tasks. The formal apprenticeship agreements recorded from the fourteenth century onwards, and which stipulated length and conditions of service, are unlikely to have marked any material difference in the work or status of young people within the household.[31]

The choice of marriage partner, accordingly, had far more than domestic implications, and women were doubtless valued for their industrial skills and experience. Urban laws of inheritance, differing in detail from town to town, not only acknowledged the interests of the heirs but also often acted to maintain the household after the death of its head. The principal restraint upon the freedom of devise theoretically bestowed by tenure in burgage was the widow's right of free-bench, or rather the variety of dower rights that went under that title. In some towns – for instance London or Ipswich – the widow retained control of her home, and thus of the family business, for the term of her life or until her remarriage; elsewhere, as at Nottingham, she might be entitled to a half share.[32] It was clearly envisaged that the widow would share the house with the heir, and the main Scottish burgh law realistically stipulated the parts of the house each party was to have.[33] The heir was not always the burgess's eldest surviving son; in some towns the traditional custom was ultimogeniture or inheritance by the youngest son. Whatever its origins, this was again a provision that favoured the continuity of the stable household, as the heir would so often have been a minor still in his mother's care. In such cases the family would have avoided the sudden upheaval in relationships following on the inheritance and subsequent marriage of the eldest son, and the intrusion of a new mistress into the household. The antiquity of the custom is demonstrated by its application at Nottingham to property subject to English law, but not to tenements in the French borough established after the Conquest where inheritance was in the first place to the eldest brother; at Leicester in 1255 it was replaced by primogeniture, with the full approval of the burgesses and apparently at their request.[34]

Twelfth-century records show the expanding urban communities acting independently of their lords, and seeking to develop the institutions of self-government. Often the binding institution of the community was the merchant

[31] E. Lipson, *The Economic History of England*: vol. I: *The Middle Ages*, 8th edn (London, 1945), pp. 324–8.

[32] M. Bateson, ed., *Borough Customs* (Selden Society, 18, 21, 1904–6), vol. II, pp. 123, 126; W. H. Stevenson, ed., *Records of the Borough of Nottingham 1155–1625* (Nottingham, 1882–9), vol. I, pp. 121–2, 170.

[33] Bateson, ed., *Borough Customs*, II, p. 125.

[34] Stevenson, ed., *Records of the Borough of Nottingham*, I, pp. 175, 189, III, p. 406; M. Bateson, ed., *Records of the Borough of Leicester* ([London], 1899–1905), vol. I, p. 49.

guild, the organised body of merchants and others which regulated the economic life of the town and perhaps much else besides. There are eleventh- and early twelfth-century references to such guilds in York, Oxford, Lincoln, Leicester, Beverley and several smaller towns; in Scotland, too, the recognition of a merchant guild was a feature of early charters – several from the twelfth century – to Edinburgh, Perth, Aberdeen, Roxburgh, Dundee, Inverness and elsewhere.[35] A guild could act as a legitimate representative of the townspeople, acting on their behalf: in 1147, for instance, the 'citizens of Oxford of the commune of the city and of the guild of merchants' could convey land belonging to the community.[36] Presumably the institution had evolved as the commercial population of the town grew in numbers and influence, and the widespread occurrence of merchant guilds by 1200 points to their having been a natural expression of urban solidarity. The precise extent to which the growing commercial communities of the eleventh and twelfth centuries turned to the merchant guild as the principal means of pursuing their common interests is, however, unclear.[37] Just as unclear is the nature of the evolving relationship between guild and borough community. Many twelfth-century guilds may not have been entirely urban in character; charters to Lincoln (1157) and Pembroke (1154–89) for instance, as well as to most of the Scottish burghs, provide for merchant guilds that could confer the privileges of membership upon merchants resident within the town's hinterland – a recognition that the mercantile community might not yet have been wholly urban.[38] Nor do we know how socially inclusive or exclusive most of these twelfth-century guilds were – although even if they ostensibly embraced all of a town's settled population effective control must have lain with the wealthier townsmen.

The willingness of the crown, by the end of the twelfth century, to concede the right of election of urban officials and the perpetual farm of the borough had the effect of giving formal recognition to the urban social hierarchy. Generally, royal charters of liberties were addressed simply to the burgesses, although John's charter of 1200 to Gloucester recognised the existing focus of the community and was directed to 'my burgesses of the merchant guild', a formula echoing royal grants of earlier decades made to the citizens of the merchant guild of Winchester.[39] Such a grant of municipal autonomy legitimated the authority of the leading townsmen, as can be observed happening at Ipswich. A unique description of the arrangements made to implement the provisions of

[35] Ballard, ed., *British Borough Charters 1042–1216*, *passim*.

[36] Tait, *Medieval English Borough*, p. 226.

[37] C. Gross, *The Gild Merchant* (Oxford, 1890), *passim*; Tait, *Medieval English Borough*, pp. 222–34.

[38] Ballard, ed., *British Borough Charters 1042–1216*, pp. 204–5.

[39] W. H. Stevenson, ed., *Calendar of the Records of the Corporation of Gloucester* (Gloucester, 1893), p. 6; Douglas and Greenaway, eds., *English Historical Documents*, pp. 1043–4; Tait, *Medieval English Borough*, p. 229.

the royal charter of 1200 details how a dozen men assumed all the offices of the borough. The limited role allowed to the rest of the community in making these arrangements was to express their unanimous approval when requested to do so at mass meetings.[40]

(V) INDUSTRIAL RELATIONS AND DISSENT

There can have been no essential differences between this formal induction of a burgess oligarchy, empowered to govern their town and to regulate the economic activities of the rest of the community, and what happened elsewhere. The virtually identical institutions of self-government granted to other towns likewise had the appearance of representing the whole burgess body, but in reality served to extend the authority of those who already dominated a highly stratified urban society. It would be mistaken, therefore, to exaggerate the extent to which the merchant guilds of the twelfth century and the successor borough administrations effectively united the urban population. It has been asserted that the ordinary townspeople accepted rule by their social superiors, regarding them as a natural aristocracy,[41] and certainly there will be truth in that assessment; even so, dissatisfaction with the conduct of the ruling group could be expressed in forthright terms, and where the relationship between rulers and those they ruled had commercial implications there is evidence of sustained conflicts of interest.

Most prominent was the struggle for control of the cloth industry between craft producers and merchants. The latter were successful in gaining control of the processes of production and marketing of cloth in the major cloth-producing towns, but the records convey very little of the likely intensity of the conflict.[42] During the twelfth century the crown had been prepared to grant commercial privileges apparently to any craft guild willing to pay the substantial sum demanded in return. The weavers of York, for instance, received confirmation some time before 1173 of their ancient liberties, and particularly of their monopoly within Yorkshire of making coloured cloth – saving the privileges of the weavers of other named boroughs – in return for the considerable annual payment of £10. In London, the weavers had their guild confirmed between 1155 and 1158, with all the liberties it had possessed during the reign of Henry I including the right of the guild to control the craft within and around London – a privilege they evidently thought worth an annual payment of two marks of gold or £12. The cordwainers of Oxford likewise around 1175 received confirmation of their guild's ancient right to a monopoly of their craft within

[40] Gross, *Gild Merchant*, II, pp. 116ff; translated into English in J. F. Benton, *Town Origins* (Boston, Mass., 1968), pp. 65–6.

[41] S. Reynolds, *An Introduction to the History of English Medieval Towns* (Oxford, 1977), p. 138.

[42] E. M. Carus-Wilson, 'The English cloth industry in the late twelfth and early thirteenth centuries', in E. M. Carus-Wilson, *Medieval Merchant Venturers* (London, 1954), pp. 211–38.

their town.[43] Because other, similar, guilds are known only from their annual payments recorded in the Pipe Rolls, there is no certain information of the privileges that most enjoyed. But such substantial payments – £12 from the weavers of Winchester, £6 each from the fullers of Winchester, the weavers of Oxford and the weavers of Lincoln, and £2 from the weavers of Huntingdon, for example – can have been made only to purchase effective control of their craft within their town: the power to determine all matters relating to their product, its marketing and the recruitment and working conditions of the labour force.[44] Doubtless there were more craft guilds in the twelfth century than these. Unauthorised guilds may have gone undetected, and there were guilds approved by the crown that were not recorded in the Pipe Rolls because they did not pay their annual fines to the sheriff – for instance, £1 from the guild of Gloucester weavers had been assigned to St Augustine's Abbey, Bristol, by Stephen. During the thirteenth century the Gloucester weavers continued to pay a further £1 annually to the town administration, suggesting that before 1200 this payment had been collected by the crown-appointed town reeves.[45] That was a situation that might have applied elsewhere, with many more craft guilds paying annual fines to local royal or seigneurial officials.

Town governments of the thirteenth century, dominated as they were by the mercantile interest, were openly hostile to the guilds of clothworkers. In 1202 the privileges of the London weavers came under attack from the city administration, which attempted to buy out their privileges from the crown; harsh civic regulations governing the weavers and fullers of Winchester, Oxford, Marlborough and Beverley, and said to be derived from those of London, were collected together at about this time.[46] In both Winchester and Beverley, laws forbade weavers and fullers from dyeing or selling cloth outside the town; in Winchester – where the authorities in 1205 took over the liability to pay the annual farms of the weavers and fullers to the crown – it was stipulated that the clothworkers could sell only to the city's merchants. In Marlborough it was laid down that weavers and fullers could work only for the *prudes humes* or 'good men' of the town; in Oxford the *prudes humes* were to control the craft. Forbidden in all four of the towns to become burgesses unless they forswore their

[43] Douglas and Greenaway, eds., *English Historical Documents*, pp. 1014–15, 1043; Ballard, ed., *British Borough Charters 1042–1216*, pp. 254, 207, 208.

[44] J. Hunter, ed., *Pipe Roll of 31 Henry I* (Record Commission, 1833), pp. 2, 48, 109. Pipe Rolls from 1158 onwards have been published by the Pipe Roll Society, 1884– . The references to guilds in the Pipe Roll of 1179–80 are conveniently brought together in Bland, Brown and Tawney, eds., *English Economic History*, pp. 114–16.

[45] *CChR 1300–26*, p. 378; W. H. Stevenson, ed., 'The records of the corporation of Gloucester', in *Historical Manuscripts Commission, Report 12, Appendix 9* (London, 1891), p. 420.

[46] Ballard, ed., *British Borough Charters 1042–1216*, p. 208; R. R. Sharpe, ed., *Calendar of Letter-Books of the City of London* (London, 1889–1912), C, p. 55; G. Unwin, *The Gilds and Companies of London*, 4th edn (London, 1963), pp. 45–6.

craft, weavers and fullers were furthermore debarred even from giving evidence against burgesses – thus preventing them from taking legal proceedings against the merchants on whom they were forced to be dependent.[47] The thirteenth-century records of the merchant guild of Leicester show such regulations in operation, whilst the guild – with all the authority of the borough – also rigorously stipulated the fees the master weavers and fullers could take from the merchant clothiers for the cloth they were commissioned to make.[48] And as if to demonstrate the essentially parallel development of Scottish and English urban society during this period, the charter confirming Perth's merchant guild – dated to the years before 1214 – specifically excluded the fullers and weavers from the liberty, as did Aberdeen's a few years later, and Stirling's in 1226. By the same charters, the right to make dyed cloth or to cause it to be made was restricted to burgesses of the burgh, thus forcing the workers in all but the cheapest cloth to surrender their independence to the merchant clothiers.[49]

The phrasing of these Scottish burgh charters was more specific than that of their English counterparts, but the authority given the English borough administrations was used to achieve the same effect. How far was the imposition of mercantile control on the clothworkers generally symptomatic of industrial and class relationships in the larger towns? There is no evidence to suggest that any other group of workers was legally constrained in quite the same way, but borough governments were nevertheless suspicious of attempts in some of the larger provincial towns to establish craft guilds. At Norwich, guilds were forbidden under the terms of royal charters of 1256 and 1285; and although the city authorities were forced to relent and allow them in 1286, they were able to insist that the guilds accept officials imposed by the city authorities. By 1300 there were guilds of tanners, shoemakers, fullers, saddlers and chandlers.[50] The scarcity of references to craft guilds in most similar towns until the fourteenth century reflects this antagonism towards organised labour; when guilds did in time become more common, it was to be – at least in part – as organs placing the master craftsmen within the hierarchy of borough government, and enforcing the standardisation of wage levels and working conditions.[51]

There is some evidence of overt expressions of class antagonism, and dissatisfaction with the activities of town rulers; behind such cases as we know of may

[47] A. F. Leach, ed., *Beverley Town Documents* (Selden Society, 14, 1900), pp. 134–5; D. Keene, *Survey of Medieval Winchester*, 2 vols. (Winchester Studies, 2, Oxford, 1985), vol. 1, p. 296.

[48] Bateson, ed., *Records of the Borough of Leicester*, 1, pp. 106, 168 and passim; E. Miller and J. Hatcher, *Medieval England: Towns, Commerce and Crafts, 1086–1348* (London, 1995), p. 365; Carus-Wilson, 'The English cloth industry', *passim*.

[49] Ballard, ed., *British Borough Charters 1042–1216*, pp. 205, 210–11; A. Ballard and J. Tait, eds., *British Borough Charters 1216–1307* (Cambridge, 1923), pp. 278, 285.

[50] Ballard and Tait, eds., *British Borough Charters 1216–1307*, p. 283.

[51] R. Holt and G. Rosser, eds., *The Medieval Town* (London, 1990), Introduction, pp. 9–10; R. H. Hilton, 'Towns in English medieval society', in *ibid.*, pp. 19–28.

have lain much greater discontent, given the difficulty both the poorer burgesses and those excluded from the borough community must have had in making themselves heard and having their grievances recorded. From Oxford a list of complaints came in 1257 from the 'lesser commune', detailing abuses of power on the part of thirty-two named 'great burgesses' who were evidently in effective control of the town. One of the grievances was that men could work as weavers only on the oligarchy's terms, so that the protest was at least in part against the merchants' control of cloth production; other grievances were the oligarchy's policies of forcing even poor workmen to pay to join the merchant guild, and of levying tallages unfairly. The complainants were anonymous, but the prevailing tenor of their grievances shows them to have been people who were themselves employers of labour or traders in the market, rather than wage labourers or the very poor.[52] Similar though less specific complaints from the ordinary burgesses about the wealthy men who ruled them came from other towns, including Grimsby in 1258, Northampton in 1276 and Cambridge in 1291, the main grievance being unjust taxation.[53] Typical was the protest to the parliament of 1290 from a group calling itself the 'community of Gloucester', complaining that the *potentes ville* were abusing their power by imposing unreasonable levels of tallage.[54] Again, these protests at the behaviour of the town oligarchies were coming not from those at the bottom of urban society but from the middle rank of burgesses, who clearly resented their exclusion from power.

(vi) THE JEWISH COMMUNITY

Jewish people entered England in the years following the Norman Conquest, and retaining their distinct religious and cultural identity they came in time to form communities in most of the major English towns. There is no evidence for Jewish settlement anywhere in Britain during the pre-Conquest period, and no reason to question the received version of events: that Jewish families – many of them from the established Jewish community at Rouen – moved to England following the influx of the new French ruling class. Their special role was the supply of credit to both the lay and the ecclesiastical aristocracy, whilst their profitability to the crown ensured a sufficient level of protection until the middle years of the thirteenth century.[55]

Their relations with other townspeople were probably never easy; it is instances of disharmony of which we hear most, the occasions when prejudice and mistrust turned to accusation or violence. That could have been only one aspect of a more complex relationship, however, and the reluctance of the Jewish

[52] *Calendar of Inquisitions Miscellaneous*, vol 1, 1219–1307, pp. 79–83.

[53] Miller and Hatcher, *Medieval England: Towns, Commerce and Crafts*, p. 359.

[54] *Rotuli Parliamentorum* (Record Commission, 1783), vol. 1, p. 47b.

[55] H. G. Richardson, *The English Jewry under Angevin Kings* (London, 1960), pp. 1–22.

communities to withdraw into defensible ghettoes – even after the serious attacks made on them in many towns in 1189–90–suggests that fear of their Christian neighbours was not uppermost in their minds. Nevertheless, the fact of such attacks and of numerous actions against individuals or groups of Jews leaves little doubt that in every town Jewish families led separate lives from their social peers in the Christian community. Jews and Christians might often be business partners, and there are glimpses of situations where there was mutual respect and perhaps friendship, but the impossibility of non-Christians ever being assimilated into Christian society remained.[56] Indeed, anti-Jewish sentiment apparently increased over the years, and was doubtless shared by most Christians. It was at the request of the local townspeople that Jews were excluded from Newcastle in 1234, from Derby in 1261 and from Bridgnorth in 1274.[57]

In 1130 the Jewish community was still firmly based in London, where probably all English Jews then lived. The decade or so following, however, saw Jewish populations established in other towns, so that by 1159 there were eleven separate communities to be taxed.[58] After London the wealthiest was at Norwich, where Jewish residents had been accused of the ritual murder of a Christian boy in 1144. Similar accusations were made in Gloucester in 1168, Bury St Edmunds in 1181 and Bristol in 1183.[59] Widespread anti-Jewish riots in 1189 and 1190 were provoked by people with a range of motives, but clearly many townspeople were more than ready to participate in massacring Jews at York, London, Norwich and elsewhere.[60] Although several apparently new Jewish communities were established during the thirteenth century, the riots marked the real end of the period of expansion into the major towns; after 1200, there were seventeen recognised communities where Jews could live and transact business, at Bristol, Cambridge, Canterbury, Colchester, Exeter, Gloucester, Hereford, Lincoln, London, Northampton, Norwich, Nottingham, Oxford, Stamford, Winchester, Worcester and York. Later communities established at Bedford, Dorchester, Marlborough, Warwick and Wilton were clearly less important, and both here and at the smaller Jewish communities briefly recorded during the twelfth century such as Thetford and Bungay the permanent Jewish population may have been very small indeed.[61]

Even the largest provincial communities were never substantial. By the time of their expulsion in 1290, the number of English Jews had fallen, it has been

[56] Richardson, *The English Jewry*, pp. 23–49.

[57] R. B. Dobson, 'The Jews of medieval Cambridge', *Jewish Historical Studies*, 32 (1990–2), 17; C. Roth, *A History of the Jews in England*, 3rd edn (Oxford, 1964), pp. 58, 82.

[58] K. T. Streit, 'The expansion of the English Jewish community in the reign of King Stephen', *Albion*, 25 (1993), 177–92.

[59] J. Edwards, 'The church and the Jews in English medieval towns', in T. R. Slater and G. Rosser, eds., *The Church in the Medieval Town* (Aldershot, 1998), pp. 43–54.

[60] R. B. Dobson, *The Jews of Medieval York and the Massacre of March 1190* (Borthwick Paper, 45, York, 1974).

[61] Richardson, *The English Jewry*, pp. 13–20.

estimated, to between 2,000 and 3,000; their population had been greater before the preceding period of increasing state harassment, but whether it had ever reached the 4,000–5,000 that has been suggested seems unlikely.[62] The Jewish cemetery at York, in use from soon after 1177 until 1290, contained an estimated total of no more than a thousand burials of which more than a third were of infants; by implication, the adult population during most of that century had not been extensive.[63] At its greatest extent in the early thirteenth century, the Norwich community contained perhaps 150 to 200 people.[64] But despite its small size, Jewish society was no less stratified by wealth than was Christian urban society. Taxation records listing the payments made by individual Jews reveal the great wealth of a few prominent families, the moderate wealth of others and the poverty of many more Jews who were too poor to be taxed in any but a poll tax such as those levied for the support of converts in the 1280s.[65] Beside the great money-lenders there must have been many pawnbrokers; there were Jewish physicians, goldsmiths and other craftsmen, as well as retailers, whilst many of the poorer Jews presumably found employment as servants to the wealthy households in their own community.[66]

(vii) SMALL-TOWN SOCIETY

It has been suggested that by 1300 at least half of the urban population lived in the many small towns that had sprung up.[67] Some of these smaller urban communities may already have been long-established; in all likelihood, a number of emerging urban societies were either unidentified or at best imperfectly described in Domesday Book. The grant of liberties to Burford in Oxfordshire by its lord at some time during the twenty years following 1086 – burgage tenure, and the trading privileges of the guild merchant of Oxford – may have marked the absolute beginning of the town's history; it is equally likely that there was already a nucleus of people living by trade and manufacturing. The value of the manor in 1086 – £13 – was a high one, and within the large tenant population recorded as twenty-two *villani* and eighteen *bordarii* there may have been a nascent burgess element.[68] But could such a society be construed as urban? An urban presence within the great royal manor of Tewkesbury was recognised in

[62] V. D. Lipman, *The Jews of Medieval Norwich* (London, 1967), pp. 36–8.

[63] J. M. Lilley *et al.*, *The Jewish Burial Ground at Jewbury* (The Archaeology of York, 12/3, 1994), pp. 526–33.

[64] Lipman, *The Jews of Medieval Norwich*, pp. 38–48.

[65] M. Adler, *Jews of Medieval England* (London, 1939), p. 302.

[66] Richardson, *The English Jewry*, pp. 26–7; J. Hillaby, 'The Worcester Jewry, 1158–1290: portrait of a lost community', *Transactions of the Worcestershire Arch. Soc.*, 12 (1990), 73–122.

[67] R. H. Hilton, 'The small town and urbanisation: Evesham in the middle ages', *Midland History*, 7 (1982), 1–8, and repr. in R. H. Hilton, *Class Conflict and the Crisis of Feudalism* (London, 1985), p. 187.

[68] Douglas and Greenaway, eds., *English Historical Documents*, p. 1034; Farley, *Domesday Book*, I, f. 156b.

1086, where a market had been founded before the Conquest (during the time of Queen Edith, after 1045) and thirteen burgesses together rendered £1 a year. Given such a small number, and the lack of any indication that the total of urban households was greater than that, it is hard to imagine Tewkesbury in 1086 as a place with any but the most rudimentary urban functions. Successive earls of Gloucester, apparently from the late eleventh century onwards, acknowledged the commercial privileges of the Tewkesbury burgesses, as well as their tenurial and legal liberties, and their right to regulate their own affairs through their own court.[69] These were privileges designed to meet the needs of an evolving community, not least by providing the legal means for them to regulate their relationships with each other. Crucially, through their court they appointed their own town officials, and could determine which strangers might, or might not, be allowed to join their community. A charter conferring basic urban liberties might not make a new town, but was clearly of great importance in nurturing the development of a distinctive urban society.

Twelfth-century evidence from Evesham points to how such an urban society might be growing. A town in many ways comparable with Tewkesbury, it too had its origins in the decades before the Conquest. Its commercial character was recognised with the grant of the privileges of a port and the right to a market in 1055; as may also have been the case with the rent of the burgesses of Tewkesbury, the £1 its inhabitants rendered to Evesham Abbey in 1086 has every appearance of being an agreed amount, collected and paid over by an organised body of burgesses. A rental of the town from only a century after Domesday Book lists 231 tenants of the abbey, settled in four distinct quarters of the town. Twenty-nine lived in the 'new borough', apparently a sign of recent expansion. The town must have had a population of at least 1,000 in the late twelfth century, and doubtless many more as not all the town's householders would have held their tenements directly from the abbey. Moreover, Evesham had acquired a transpontine suburb. Beyond the Avon, the abbey's manor of Bengeworth contained twenty-eight *bordarii*, all but two paying a rent of 12d. and including at least two smiths and a weaver. In that quarter of the borough named simply as 'Evesham' – evidently the old core of the town from before the Conquest – there were ninety-six tenants, an indication perhaps of the original extent of the town, and demonstrating the degree to which it had grown in little more than a century.[70]

By 1200, there is abundant evidence of the expansion of the urban sector throughout England and those parts of Wales coming under English rule.[71] The

[69] Farley, *Domesday Book*, I, f.163c; Bland, Brown and Tawney, eds., *English Economic History*, pp. 116–19.

[70] W. D. Macray, ed., *Chronicon Abbatiae de Evesham* (RS, 1863), p. 75; Farley, *Domesday Book*, I, f.175c; BL, Cotton MS Vesp. BXXIV, ff.42–5v, 34.

[71] M. W. Beresford and H. P. R. Finberg, *English Medieval Boroughs* (Newton Abbot, 1973), pp. 38–40.

significant population growth of established towns is implied by their continued physical expansion, both intensively and extensively. The evidence for greater density of population within towns is matched by the abundant evidence for suburban growth during the twelfth and thirteenth centuries.[72]

More impressive evidence of the growth in the urban population is the large number of towns recorded now for the first time. By the end of this long phase of expansion, in the early fourteenth century, some 500 settlements showing urban characteristics had emerged in England alone.[73] Yet with only limited evidence for a truly urban life within so many of these little communities – recognition of their status resting in many cases on the survival of a charter of liberties, or the recorded existence of borough courts and borough law, or even just on references to burgage tenure – it might be questioned how far these were really towns. The fact of their burghality does not necessarily imply a truly urban community, just as there were flourishing towns at this time which clearly had no need of a charter of liberties from their lord, and whose burghality, in consequence, might be legally doubtful.

The few studies of small-town society that have been possible cannot by themselves dispel such doubts, although they demonstrate how readily a distinctively urban society could establish itself in even the smallest and least well-favoured new town. Evidence for the origins and early development of Stratford-on-Avon, the archetypal English small town, establishes how the bishop of Worcester's foundation of the borough in 1196 was indeed the beginning of the urban settlement. He planned and built it upon a new site, distinct from the older village site around the parish church; within a couple of generations, there was a diverse population of immigrants and the children of immigrants. With at least 234 households, the new town had an estimated population in excess of 1,000 living by a wide range of craft skills, and which had already demonstrated a sense of community with its foundation of the Holy Cross guild. Through the guild the burgesses built their own place of worship at the centre of the town, and from this basis went on to create the social institutions that would give form and solidarity to their community.

Analysis of the surnames of the burgesses of 1251 has shown Stratford to have been a town mainly of artisans. Both the diversity of occupations and the absence of producers or suppliers of luxury goods stresses that the economic role of these craftsmen was to supply the simple needs of the people of the surrounding countryside. The lack of scope for specialisation in any particular product would have prevented the growth of any large, local industries dominated by mercantile interests. Whilst it had its wealthier burgesses, therefore, Stratford seems to have

[72] D. Keene, 'Suburban growth', in M. W. Barley, ed., *The Plans and Topography of Medieval Towns in England and Wales* (CBA Res. Rep., 14, 1976), and reprinted in Holt and Rosser, ed., *The Medieval Town*, pp. 97–119.

[73] Beresford and Finberg, *English Medieval Boroughs*, pp. 38–40.

lacked the powerful merchant class which so dominated the society and economy of the larger towns.[74]

Yet as a market town serving a prosperous locality, Stratford was not at the lowest level of urbanisation. At less than half its size, and lacking its powerful guild, the Worcestershire borough of Halesowen might better fit that description. Even here, though, we can observe a society recognisably urban in its interests and its structure, as the unique evidence for Halesowen's people demonstrates. Halesowen had a market and fair in the 1220s and by 1270 had been granted a charter of liberties by its lord, the Premonstratensian abbey of Halesowen. The fortuitous survival of the greater number of its court records from 1272 onwards makes Halesowen a remarkable exception to the general pattern of poorly documented small towns, and has provided a rich source of information relating to the everyday life and activities of this otherwise undistinguished community.[75] In their commercial activities, the people of Halesowen did nothing unusual or unexpected; theirs was as typical a small town as could be found, and all the more important for that fact. Particularly valuable in the court rolls is the mass of detail concerning social relationships. Within a very few years of the town's formal beginnings a stable burgess community had become established, consisting of up to a hundred settled families. Many held tenements by burgage tenure, with the commercial liberties that implied; alternatively, individuals acquired rights to trade legally either by taking out the liberty of the borough on an annual or lifetime basis, or by paying an annual rent for the right to set up a stall. Family interrelationships over two or more generations can be established in about eighty cases, and reveal a pattern that was more varied than we might expect.

The town's population in the decades around 1300 has been estimated at 600, although the total must have fluctuated with the ebb and flow of migrants for whom residence in Halesowen was often brief. The evident stability of the community is surprising, given the continued influx of immigrants which the court rolls record. Many were poor and regarded as undesirable entrants to the borough, although usually little was done to enforce the removal of illegal residents. The majority were women: in the 1270s they amounted to some 65 per cent of illegal immigrants, and as many as 75 per cent thereafter. Presumably driven by lack of opportunity in the countryside, they saw even in this small urban economy the possibility of living by trade, and in Halesowen most found employment as petty retailers or in making and supplying food and drink. So while this remained a male-dominated society, many women here (and doubtless also in similar small

[74] E. M. Carus-Wilson, 'The first half-century of the borough of Stratford-upon-Avon', *Ec.HR*, 2nd series, 18 (1965), 46–63, and rep. in Holt and Rosser, eds., *The Medieval Town*, pp. 49–70.

[75] R. H. Hilton, 'Small town society in England before the Black Death', *P&P*, 105 (1984), 53–78, and repr. in Holt and Rosser, eds., *The Medieval Town*, pp. 71–96, from which all the following evidence for Halesowen is drawn.

towns) were engaged in activities on their own behalf rather than as associates of husbands or fathers. Women must have appreciably outnumbered men in the adult population, and were able to lead independent lives: of the many women active in a variety of trades, some headed households in which men seem to have played no more than a transient role.

The relationship between townspeople and their lord was close and often uneasy. Abbots of Halesowen were clearly reluctant to concede all of the privileges of the borough of Hereford which they had promised to their burgesses of Halesowen by their charter, and until 1300 demanded labour services as a punishment for petty offences. They even claimed dues from the burgesses which elsewhere would have implied their lack of personal freedom: both marriage fines and *leyrwite* – the fine for fornication – were imposed, whilst burgesses were sometimes regarded as serfs whose property was liable to appropriation – at least in theory – by the lord. According to the court rolls, the burgesses of the thirteenth century offered only verbal resistance to this high-handed behaviour, which came to an end during the fourteenth century as abbots and town established a more distant relationship.

At the apex of Halesowen society was a small group of men, filling the public offices of the town and conducting the day-to-day administration. This was the group deemed worthy to serve as jurors in the borough court, who presented offenders, adjudicated on issues and questions of custom, and who doubtless initiated ordinances issued in the name of the court or the community. From the jurors came the candidates for the offices of bailiff, ale-taster and catchpoll, who collected any monies due to the court. By contrast with the situation in the greater towns, this was no small, exclusive elite based solely on wealth and family; the jurors were drawn from the established families of the town, with most of them providing at least one juror over time. Through the court the community could take concerted action in the interests of all: frequent ordinances were issued to control nuisances, and pollution of the water supply; the quality, and not just the weight, of bread was an issue, and the attempts to control and exclude undesirable and disreputable immigrants doubtless met with the approval of the established members of the community.

Disputes between individuals were common, and frequently led to violence. Women, although in a majority and generally economically active, rarely initiated attacks on others; they were responsible for no more than 15 per cent of assaults in the decades before 1300, though they were frequently the victims of male violence. When it came to vituperation and defamation, however, women were as active as men, using terms of abuse nearly always of a sexual nature: *meretrix* or 'whore' was most commonly used by women, along with 'thief' or – less commonly – 'witch'. On occasion women impugned the sexual morals of the canons of Halesowen, or mocked men for effeminacy. Abuse was taken seriously by the court, and there is no doubt of the peculiar hurtfulness of such insults in a society where great value was set on married respectability but where more casual liaisons were common – particularly among the shifting population of poor migrants. Undue sensitivity to suggestions of irregular sexual relations points to a fear of losing a fragile reputation within a small community.

(viii) THE EMERGENCE OF URBAN SOCIETY IN WALES

The Halesowen model of small-town society may not apply to the minor towns of Scotland about which we know so little, and is certainly not directly applicable to the towns of Wales. There, the circumstances and political implications of urbanisation ensured that still in 1300 many urban populations would retain an ethnic identity distinct from that of their hinterland. Military as well as commercial considerations had dictated the siting of most new towns, founded by kings and Marcher lords in the course of asserting their control over their newly acquired lands. At the core of Welsh urban societies were communities of immigrant burgesses with English names, for whom strong walls and the lord's castle offered security from the hostility of a dispossessed native people. At a number of towns – perhaps in practice at every English town in Wales – the English burgess was expected to play a military role, guarding the town or serving the lord in local campaigns. At Denbigh, for instance, it was specified that military service in person or through a proxy was a condition of holding a burgage, and at Swansea the burgesses had a guaranteed right to half the booty when they went on campaign.[76] In England, such service was only very rarely specified in post-Conquest charters, as for instance at Egremont in the northern border county of Cumberland.[77]

Thus the divide between urban and rural society was marked more intensely in Wales than elsewhere, and frequently found expression in outright hostility during the period before 1300; there are recorded instances of both castles and towns being attacked and destroyed. Urban growth was clearly retarded, and the suggestion that Wales in 1300 had an urban population approaching 50,000 or as much as a sixth of its total population may be an exaggeration. On close examination, of the 105 or more towns of medieval Wales apparently no more than 60 show any indication of a truly urban population before 1300. Borough status, a market charter and some rudimentary planning were not enough to make a town, and rentals recording often little more than twenty burgages plainly show that many of these boroughs still, at the end of the thirteenth century, had not succeeded in nurturing an autonomous urban economy or society. Towns of any size were very few in number and were still in the main a feature of those parts of the Marches where English rule was most firmly established. Thirteenth-century Welsh urban

[76] R. R. Davies, *Conquest, Coexistence and Change* (Oxford, 1987), pp. 165–6, 421; Ballard and Tait, eds., *British Borough Charters 1216–1307*, pp. 114–15; Ballard, ed., *British Borough Charters 1042–1216*, p. 89.

[77] Ballard, ed., *British Borough Charters 1042–1216*, p. 90.

populations defy precise measurement; even so, very few places escape classification as small towns in English terms – that is, taking a population of 2,000 as the dividing line. With 420 burgesses in the 1290s Cardiff cleared that hurdle, although whether evidently thriving towns such as Carmarthen, Cowbridge, Holt, Haverfordwest, Tenby, Chepstow, Usk, Newport or Monmouth did so yet is debatable. Urbanisation came later than in England, and many towns in Wales were still growing rapidly in the decades either side of 1300; life in towns evidently became more attractive with the political stability that accompanied undisputed English control of the principality.[78]

The promotion of new towns for strategic rather than economic advantage came to an end, effectively, with the establishment in the 1280s of the Edwardian fortified boroughs of North Wales following the defeat of Gwynedd. Elsewhere in Wales, the closing years of the thirteenth century saw urban communities becoming less obviously alien and unwelcome intrusions, and more clearly identified with their localities. Ethnically Welsh towns were appearing, such as Welshpool; given a foundation charter by its Welsh lord before 1245, it had become a town of 106 taxpayers in the 1290s.[79] This and other Welsh towns were wholly commercial in character, and the greater part of their populations had presumably arrived through immigration from the immediate locality on the same pattern as the smaller English towns. But like the smallest of the 'English' boroughs in Wales, few such places could have evolved a social structure of any complexity before 1300; from their size and rudimentary topography the impression is that many were little more than rural marketing centres, nucleated settlements often associated with an ancient church.[80]

(ix) URBAN LIVING STANDARDS AND MORTALITY

For many of those moving into the expanding towns of the twelfth and thirteenth centuries, lack of appropriate skills or financial resources meant there was little prospect of economic security through regular employment. Driven by rural poverty rather than attractive prospects of urban wealth, they faced the prospect of living by casual labour or street trading. Doubtless their living conditions and their diet were appreciably worse than those of better-situated men and women; so, whilst there is abundant archaeological evidence that townspeople generally ate better food than did their rural counterparts, that certainly did not imply an adequate diet at every social level.[81] The impressive quantities of

[78] I. Soulsby, *The Towns of Medieval Wales* (Chichester, 1983), pp. 19–23, 62–3.

[79] Soulsby, *Towns of Medieval Wales*, p. 268. However, by the 1290s many of the inhabitants of Welshpool bore English names: Davies, *Conquest, Coexistence and Change*, p. 165.

[80] Soulsby, *Towns of Medieval Wales*, *passim*.

[81] C. Dyer, *Standards of Living in the Later Middle Ages* (Cambridge, 1989), pp. 196–202; J. Schofield and A. Vince, *Medieval Towns* (London, 1994), pp. 189–96.

butchered animal bones found in urban excavations, and the common occurrence of a profuse variety of fruit pips among other vegetable remains in urban cesspools, together with the remains of a wide range of marine and freshwater fish, testify to an urban diet that could be rich and varied. By contrast, the evident need for close regulation of the price and quality of urban foodstuffs indicates a situation where even a small increase in the price of the staple, bread, could leave many hungry, and where even the most unwholesome of victuals found buyers among those unable to afford something better.[82]

But if it was the poorest townspeople who felt the worst effects of an inadequate diet, other aspects of the urban environment affected everyone. The effects of the concentration of population have always made towns especially vulnerable to the spread of disease; and the frequency with which the remains of intestinal parasites are found in excavated cesspools suggests that the whole urban population must have been so afflicted; however superior an individual's diet might have been, it was impossible to avoid its contamination.[83] In the same way, the superior housing of the wealthier townspeople did not necessarily provide healthier living conditions. Even the wealthiest merchants chose to live and trade at the same premises, a practice they shared with the master craftsmen engaged in manufacturing production. With only rudimentary environmental controls, it was inevitable that much of the urban population suffered overcrowding, poor sanitary arrangements and drainage, and inadequate water supplies.[84]

Evidence for the lethal effects of overcrowding on the pre-1300 urban population comes entirely from archaeology, and most eloquently from the small number of urban cemeteries of this period that have been investigated using modern techniques of excavation and analysis. The cemetery of St Nicholas Shambles in London, for instance, produced 234 skeletons dating from the eleventh and twelfth centuries. Of those individuals for whom a date at death could be calculated with sufficient confidence, 94 per cent died before they were forty-five – a sombre statement of the high level of urban mortality, even allowing for a considerable margin of accuracy. The cemetery of St Helen on the Walls, York, produced a much larger sample, of 1,041 individuals, from a period of some six centuries, from the tenth to the sixteenth. Any conclusions from this cemetery are less specific to any particular period of the middle ages; nevertheless, the estimate that 91 per cent of the individuals had died before they were sixty again points to a persistent pattern of high mortality, as does the evidence that over a quarter had died before reaching adult years. Men lived longer than women: by the age of thirty-five, as many as 56 per cent of the women had died compared with only 36

[82] Schofield and Vince, *Medieval Towns*, pp. 193–6; Hilton, *English and French Towns in Feudal Society*, pp. 78–81.
[83] Schofield and Vince, *Medieval Towns*, p. 200.
[84] P. V. Addyman, 'The archaeology of public health at York, England,' *World Archaeology*, 21 (1989), 244–63; E. L. Sabine, 'Latrines and cesspools of medieval London', *Speculum*, 9 (1934), 303–21.

per cent of the men.[85] As a contrast, the cemetery of York's medieval Jewish community provided evidence from a closely defined period, and for an identified social group. The permission granted in 1177 to Jews outside London to establish their own cemeteries, provided they were in extramural locations, marks the official beginning of the Jewbury cemetery; interments ended there with the expulsion of 1290 and the sale of the land. In all, 476 individuals were identified, from an estimated total of around 1,000 burials. A quarter of the excavated burials were of children aged ten or less, yet even so it was deduced that many infant graves had escaped detection. Three out of five adult women died between the ages of twenty and forty; the equivalent figure for men was 53 per cent, a smaller difference than that observed at St Helen on the Walls. But just as in the wider urban population, Jewish old people were a rarity: women and men over fifty were respectively only 3 per cent and 5 per cent of the Jewish community.[86]

(x) IMMIGRATION INTO TOWNS

There is insufficient evidence from this period to allow comparison between the urban birth rate and the death rate, just as it is impossible to make any accurate assessment of the volume of immigration. Unquestionably the urban population was growing, but how far this was achieved by natural increase and how far by immigration is unclear. The latter was an important factor in urban expansion; the appearance of so many new towns during the twelfth and thirteenth centuries demonstrates considerable population movement from countryside to town, and between towns. Urban surnames often referred to a place of family origin, and a sufficiently large sample of such names will indicate the area from which a town drew its population. Many of the burgess families of Stratford in 1251 had surnames showing that they had come from a host of Warwickshire villages, nearly all within a sixteen mile radius of the new town. The population of Halesowen, similarly, was essentially local, and it would seem that very few small towns drew their immigrants from beyond their market area.[87] Not surprisingly, larger towns showed greater pulling power, although the importance of the local market area remained: York, according to its freemen's rolls for the latter part of the thirteenth century, drew 60 per cent of its immigrants from within a distance of twenty miles; around 1300, almost 70 per cent of immigrants into Norwich and Leicester came from the same distance. Immigrants to Gloucester showed the same pattern, with two-thirds travelling no more than twenty miles, and half

[85] Schofield and Vince, *Medieval Towns*, pp. 197–8; W. White, *Skeletal Remains from the Cemetery of St Nicholas Shambles* (London and Middlesex Arch. Soc., Special Paper, 9, 1988); J. D. Dawes and J. R. Magilton, *The Cemetery of St Helen-on-the-Walls, Aldwark* (The Archaeology of York, 12/1, 1980), p. 63. [86] Lilley, *et al.*, *The Jewish Burial Ground at Jewbury*, pp. 305–11, 427–35.

[87] Carus-Wilson, 'The first half-century of Stratford-upon-Avon', pp. 58–60; Hilton, 'Small town society in England', p. 77.

travelling fourteen miles or less.[88] A few immigrants came from places a hundred miles or more away. But every town's immigration pattern must have been affected by that of its neighbours: Gloucester was only thirty-two miles from Bristol, where a rather different pattern prevailed, with 50 per cent of immigrants travelling distances of up to thirty miles, and a quarter of the total coming from places more than sixty miles away.[89]

An inherent bias of such figures is that they are inevitably compiled from lists of the more substantial householders: freemen's registers, or those who paid tallage or subsidies. These are the immigrants who had found at least moderate prosperity and social position, and who must for the most part have come to the town already possessing useful skills or placed by their families as apprentices in the better crafts. By contrast, many of those who entered towns to escape rural poverty – even starvation, in the most extreme cases – perhaps followed a different migration pattern. The evidence for Halesowen included the poor as well as the comfortably-off, and both originated in the town's immediate hinterland; but during the early modern period the destitute might tramp long distances from town to town in search of employment, and probably the opportunities offered by the larger medieval towns encouraged a similar pattern of behaviour.[90] Whether as domestic servants or as casual labourers the poor and unskilled were a major component of the urban labour force, although without property or long-term employment their period of residence in any particular town may have been limited. Some, doubtless, were seasonal migrants, travelling between town and countryside as employment opportunities presented themselves.

(xi) CONCLUSION

Population estimates derived from the taxation figures presented in Appendix 4 indicate the extent to which England had become urbanised by 1300. Uncertainty as to the proportion of people liable to property taxation means that such estimates can never be precise, but a recent suggestion that 20 per cent of the population were by now living in towns is likely to be correct. On the evidence of a range of local sources, London by now had more than 80,000 people, in all probability, while Norwich may have reached 20,000.[91] But these large

[88] P. McClure, 'Patterns of migration in the late middle ages: the evidence of English place-name surnames', *Ec.HR*, 2nd series, 32 (1979), 178, 180–1; R. A. Holt, 'Gloucester: an English provincial town during the later middle ages' (PhD thesis, University of Birmingham, 1987), pp. 163–5.

[89] S. Penn, 'The origins of Bristol migrants in the early fourteenth century: the surname evidence', *Transactions of the Bristol and Gloucestershire Arch. Soc.*, 101 (1983), 128–9.

[90] McClure, 'Patterns of migration in the late middle ages', 167–82; Penn, 'The origins of Bristol migrants in the early fourteenth century', 123–30.

[91] D. Keene, 'A new study of London before the Great Fire', *UHY* (1984), 11–21; E. Rutledge, 'Immigration and population growth in early fourteenth-century Norwich: evidence from the tithing roll', *UHY* (1988), 15–30.

cities were exceptional, and perhaps half of the urban population was to be found in small towns of fewer – often far fewer – than 2,000 inhabitants. Elsewhere in Britain, virtually all of the urban population lived in towns of this size. Population estimates for the Welsh towns suggest that by the fourteenth century the level of urbanisation in Wales might have approached England's;[92] the situation in Scotland is far less clear. Edinburgh, Perth, Aberdeen and Dundee were regarded abroad as the outstanding Scottish towns, but their prominence as wool-exporting centres may not have been matched by any great increase in their population.[93] The total contrast between the urbanisation of Lowland Scotland and the eastern coast, and the failure of towns to develop throughout the whole of the Highland region, was more marked than in any other neighbouring parts of Britain.[94]

Whilst much of this growth was relatively recent, especially in Wales, it was the earlier centuries of the period that had seen the emergence of a distinct urban society in England. The initial phases of urbanisation had been swift, and social patterns and organisation that become visible to the historian mainly during the thirteenth century and later clearly owe much to the preceding centuries of development. The remarkable degree of uniformity shown by urban institutions is indicative of the shared experiences and interests of townspeople, but also reflects the antiquity of urban society. Greater knowledge of the pre-Conquest boroughs would allow a clearer appreciation of the extent to which the urban social pattern was forming its distinct identity during the earliest phase of town foundations and growth. By 1300 the populations of English towns stood at their highest medieval level, and English urban society had grown to maturity.

[92] Dyer, 'How urbanised was medieval England?', pp. 173–4, 179; Soulsby, *Towns of Medieval Wales*, p. 23.

[93] M. Lynch, M. Spearman and G. Stell, eds., *The Scottish Medieval Town* (Edinburgh, 1988), pp. 5–6.

[94] E. Ewan, *Townlife in Fourteenth-Century Scotland* (Edinburgh, 1990), map 1, following p. 116.

· 6 ·

The economy of British towns 600–1300

RICHARD BRITNELL

(i) DEMAND FOR URBAN GOODS AND SERVICES

NO DEFINITION of the word town is very convenient for the analysis of medieval economies. It is tempting to take the contemporary term *burh* or *burgus* as a proxy, but this needs resisting because there was so little consistency or stability in the way the word was used.[1] Population levels might serve as a guide if they were reliably known for each town, but they are not. Differences of taxable wealth are on record, and for 1334 can be charted for most of England, but they depend upon the size of the assessed area and the social distribution of wealth to such an extent that there is considerable overlap between places with 'urban' features (craftsmen, traders, marketing institutions) and places dependent solely on rural pursuits. It will be assumed here, first, that a necessary condition for being considered a town is that a settlement should have some institutional apparatus for regular local or long-distance trade; from the eleventh century onwards this would normally mean at least a weekly market. Secondly, a settlement with this institutional provision is classifiable as a town if its income depends to a perceptible degree upon the sale of manufactures and services to buyers external to the body of townsmen.[2] Buyers external to the urban community, in this context, may mean large households or bodies of administrative personnel adjacent to the town; describing such purchasers as external is justifiable because large households of all kinds normally drew most of their income from outside the town in which they were placed. Alternatively, external buyers were people from nearby rural settlements, wanting basic manufactures

[1] E. Miller and J. Hatcher, *Medieval England: Towns, Commerce and Crafts, 1086–1348* (London, 1995), pp. 18–30, 279–85; S. Reynolds, *An Introduction to the History of English Medieval Towns* (Oxford, 1977), pp. 24, 31–6, 91–2. In the following text *burh* and *burgus* will be rendered as 'borough' for England and 'burgh' for Scotland.

[2] This definition is similar to, but somewhat narrower than, that in Reynolds, *Introduction*, pp. ix–x.

and services that their own communities could not supply. Or, thirdly, external buyers were people from far away, dependent upon merchants to act as intermediaries for the supply of some distinctive speciality of the exporting town. Even a small town might illustrate all these aspects of demand; the citizens of Wells in the thirteenth century supplied the bishops and chapter of Wells, they operated weekly markets and annual fairs where they traded with people from the surrounding countryside, and merchants there dealt in wool and cloth over longer distances.[3] Examination of each of these three components of demand in greater detail can help to explain some varying patterns of urban growth between 600 and 1300.

Landlords stood to benefit more than other social classes from commercial development and the rising demand for land that accompanied it during the period 600–1300. The vast inequalities of income in medieval society need to be remembered in any analysis of urban development, whether as a general phenomenon or in some particular case. Until the tenth century English towns were predominantly centres of power, and their trade was mostly to satisfy the needs of lords and their servants.[4] But even after that, though other sources of demand increased in importance, the presence of large households remained an important feature in urban development. The least ambiguous examples of this are monastic towns, since monastic communities were continuously resident in a single set of buildings, which meant that they were both permanent centres of consumption and administrative centres. Because most large secular households were itinerant, the significance of their administrative headquarters often outweighed that of their lord's domestic consumption, as in the case of the Scottish royal burghs of the twelfth century. Nevertheless, the headquarters of lordships may be analysed in much the same way as monastic centres, since they created similar on-going opportunities for employment even if the lord's family was not always present. In many cases it would be difficult, and artificial, to assess the relative importance of the 'domestic' and 'administrative' components of demand.

Canterbury and York had recognisably urban features by the late eighth century and both were major ecclesiastical centres.[5] The continuing importance of monasteries for urban development is suggested by the very names of Westminster, St Albans, Bury St Edmunds and Peterborough, and there are numerous other examples of pre-Conquest settlements of craftsmen and tradesmen with a religious house at their core – as at Shaftesbury, Malmesbury and Durham.[6] In Wales there may have been some urban development by the monastic foundation of Caerwent

[3] D. G. Shaw, *The Creation of a Community* (Oxford, 1993), p. 33.

[4] G. G. Astill, 'Towns and town hierarchies in Saxon England', *Oxford J of Archaeology*, 10 (1991), 95–117.

[5] D. Hill, 'Towns as structures and functioning communities through time: the development of central places from 600 to 1066', in D. Hooke, ed., *Anglo-Saxon Settlements* (Oxford, 1988), p. 200.

[6] M. Bonney, *Lordship and the Urban Community* (Cambridge, 1990), pp. 12–17.

in the tenth century.[7] In Scotland, too, some of the earliest urban or proto-urban centres were attached to important churches, as at St Andrews and Brechin.[8] Lay dignitaries, too, contributed to the development of town life. In the days when there were many kings in Britain there were many royal seats; London, Canterbury, Winchester and York were all prominent central places of government in the seventh and eighth centuries, and Winchester was substantially redeveloped as a royal town in the late ninth century.[9] In the North, Bamburgh was the centre of Northumbrian royal power up to 954 and became a seat of the earls of Northumbria thereafter. Late Saxon and Norman boroughs often benefited from the presence of earls. Exeter had a street known in the twelfth century as 'Irlesbyri' ('earl's dwelling'), and there was an equivalent 'Earlesburgh' in York. The larger towns were the homes of lesser landowners as well, at least for part of the year.[10]

After the Norman invasion of 1066, the colonisation of Britain by Norman landlords was a major stimulus to the spread of boroughs. New monasteries sometimes deliberately created settlements of tradesmen and craftsmen at their gates, as at Battle.[11] Many new towns were attached to royal and baronial castles. Some of these remained very small developments, like the little castle boroughs of New Buckenham (Norfolk) or Pleshey (Essex). Yet in areas with little previous experience of town life, Norman colonisation could be decisive in promoting urban development on a feudal pattern, and in this context castles constituted a prominent part of the scene. Amongst the most successful examples of this was the royal borough of Newcastle-upon-Tyne, which began to grow in the late eleventh century, but there were many lesser northern examples, like Alnwick, Barnard Castle, Kendal, Morpeth and Richmond.[12]

This association between new towns and castles becomes stronger the farther away from southern England one looks. It is prominent in the South-West.[13] It is also a striking feature of the early urban development of Wales, where out of twenty-nine new towns of the period 1086–1200 listed by Professor Beresford, twenty-four were castle boroughs.[14] A good example of such development is

[7] W. Davies, *An Early Welsh Microcosm: Studies in the Llandaff Charters* (London, 1978), pp. 61–2.

[8] B. Dicks, 'The Scottish medieval town: a search for origins', in G. Gordon and B. Dicks, eds., *Scottish Urban History* (Aberdeen, 1983), pp. 42–3.

[9] M. Biddle, ed., *Winchester in the Early Middle Ages* (Oxford, 1976), p. 450; M. Biddle, 'Towns', in D. M. Wilson, ed., *The Archaeology of Anglo-Saxon England* (London, 1976), pp. 110, 114, 116–17, 120.

[10] R. Fleming, 'Rural elites and urban communities in late Saxon England', *P&P*, 141 (1993), 23–5.

[11] E. Searle, *Lordship and Community* (Toronto, 1974), pp. 69–88.

[12] M. Beresford, *New Towns of the Middle Ages* (London, 1967), pp. 432, 472–4, 518; R. H. Britnell, 'Boroughs, markets and trade in northern England, 1000–1216', in R. H. Britnell and J. Hatcher, eds., *Progress and Problems in Medieval England* (Cambridge, 1996), pp. 50–1.

[13] A. Preston-Jones and P. Rose, 'Week St Mary: town and castle', *Cornish Archaeology*, 31 (1992), 143–53.

[14] Beresford, *New Towns*, pp. 534–74.

Cardigan, where a castle was first built by Gilbert fitz Richard of Clare soon after 1110, and by 1136 there was a small town there and a bridge. The Clare family bolstered their presence at Cardigan by founding a priory there before 1165. In origin, therefore, Cardigan was a colonial venture, but in 1165 it was captured by Rhys ap Gruffydd, who developed the castle and made the town the capital of a vigorous Welsh lordship. The town remained small – in 1268 it had about 110 burgesses – but it pioneered urban life and formal trading institutions in Ceredigion. Even Edward I's later borough of Aberystwyth, though on the coast and clearly intended from the start to develop some commercial role, depended heavily for its prosperity on the castle and its garrison.[15] Because the early Welsh boroughs were so dependent upon colonial considerations, their subsequent history was exceptionally liable to be affected by political change.[16]

The Scottish experience was analogous to that of Wales, but differed because of the active role of kings in the creation of the earliest towns. As in Wales, there is little recognisable town life before the twelfth century, and when towns first occur they are closely associated with patterns of lordship, mostly royal. The word and the idea of the burgh were here imported – like the feudal institutions that were introduced into Scotland at the same time. Many of the earliest royal burghs were attached to royal castles, and most of them were administrative centres of some significance. Berwick, Crail, Dunfermline, Edinburgh, Linlithgow, Perth, Roxburgh and Stirling, all occur both as burghs and at the head of 'shires' under David I (1124–53) or his successor Malcolm IV (1153–65), and there was a sheriffdom of Haddington, another early burgh, in 1184.[17] A few other early Scottish burghs were founded by bishops in their cathedral cities, like St Andrews (*c.* 1145–50) and Glasgow (*c.* 1170–90).[18]

These examples show the close relation between patterns of lordship and the formation of towns, but do not sufficiently explain the link. Large households derived many of their basic supplies from their estates rather than from markets through much of the period. Luxury goods, too, could not be expected in a small town, and had to be acquired from afar. In the Anglo-Saxon period, and later, landlords commonly traded directly through their own agents, often with their own ships.[19] Later, between the eleventh and the thirteenth centuries,

[15] R. A. Griffiths, *Conquerors and Conquered in Medieval Wales* (New York and Stroud, 1994), pp. 277–88, 309, 313.

[16] R. R. Davies, *Lordship and Society in the March of Wales, 1282–1400* (Oxford, 1978), pp. 321–37.

[17] *Regesta Regum Scottorum*, ed. G. W. S. Barrow *et al.*, (Edinburgh, 1960–), vol. I, pp. 37, 40, 45–9; I. H. Adams, *The Making of Urban Scotland* (London, 1978), p. 22. For the Scottish shire, or soke, see G. W. S. Barrow, *The Kingdom of the Scots* (London, 1973), pp. 7–68.

[18] G. W. S. Barrow, *Kingship and Unity* (London, 1981), pp. 88, 92.

[19] S. Kelly, 'Trading privileges from eighth-century England', *Early Medieval Europe*, I (1992), 3–28; R. H. Britnell, 'Sedentary long-distance trade and the English merchant class in the thirteenth century', in P. R. Coss and S. D. Lloyd, eds., *Thirteenth Century England, V* (Woodbridge, 1995), p. 138.

access to imported goods became heavily dependent on seasonal fairs. The main fairs, as they had developed by the thirteenth century, were close by long-established towns – Stamford (Lent), St Ives (Easter), Boston (July), Lynn (late July), Winchester (September), Westminster (October), Northampton (November) and Bury St Edmunds (December).[20] By their very nature, however, they involved extensive travelling by most buyers and sellers, or their agents. At the end of the thirteenth century Durham Priory was buying furs and haberdashery at Darlington fair and wine and spices at Boston.[21] By this time the commercial role of these great fairs was dwindling, as merchants in each part of the country realised their ability to find customers for their wares all year round rather than through the limited period when local fairs were being held. In the later thirteenth century, for example, the royal household switched into purchasing fabrics and spices through London rather than through provincial fairs, to the benefit of those merchants who imported into the city and kept stocks there.[22] Even after the decline of the fairs, however, the availability of internationally traded products was restricted to the larger towns, and magnates were unlikely to do a great deal of business elsewhere.[23]

Though great households did not buy a large part of their requirements directly through local markets, their presence was nevertheless important for the formation of towns. There were several possible reasons for this. First, such households generated a considerable demand for household services of many kinds, both menial and professional, and the resulting coming together of dependants could be sufficiently large to constitute the core of a landless or nearly landless community. For example, at Abingdon Abbey in 1185 there were at least eighty servants, most of whom received much of their food from the monks.[24] Secondly, though large households might depend upon materials and provisions drawn from afar, they often required local craftsmen to work them. This was the case not only with construction and repairs to buildings, but also with carpentry, tailoring and repairs to all sorts of equipment and utensils.[25] Thirdly, they often employed local people in the business of procuring supplies. Some landlords went over earlier than others to receiving cash rather than produce from their estates, and in these circumstances the provisioning of their households required contracts with local dealers.[26] Even households that lived mostly from their own estates, like Durham Priory, required textiles, wine and other

[20] E. W. Moore, *The Fairs of Medieval England* (Toronto, 1985), p. 10.

[21] Bonney, *Lordship*, p. 171.

[22] G. A. Williams, *Medieval London*, 2nd edn (London, 1970), pp. 107–8.

[23] C. Dyer, *Everyday Life in Medieval England* (London, 1994), pp. 263–5.

[24] B. Harvey, *Living and Dying in England, 1100–1540* (Oxford, 1993), p. 151; D. Keene, *Survey of Medieval Winchester* (Winchester Studies, 2, Oxford, 1985), vol. I, p. 323.

[25] Bonney, *Lordship*, pp. 90–1, 156–7; G. Rosser, *Medieval Westminster 1200–1540* (Oxford, 1989), pp. 150–5.

[26] Keene, *Survey*, I, p. 103.

imported goods to be commercially supplied.[27] Fourthly, large households commonly attracted a stream of visitors who needed temporary accommodation or other services. From the late Saxon period some towns became centres of pilgrimage because of the relic collections they housed, and for towns like Winchester, Westminster, Canterbury, York and Durham this business long remained an important source of trade.[28] Glasgow, too, originated as an ecclesiastical centre and benefited from the pilgrim traffic to St Kentigern's tomb.[29] Other visitors were drawn to towns in the course of litigation or the performance of public services like the payment of taxes.

The demand of large households and administrative authorities was undoubtedly a stimulus to urban growth, especially in the earliest phases of development. Yet almost all towns, however small, had a broader commercial basis than that. In order to be more than an enclave of craftsmen and tradesmen depending on a single buyer, a town had to be able to supply goods and services to its neighbours. This was the single most general source of urban growth between about 880 and 1300, because of the expansion of the rural economy during that period. The expenditure of rural landlords increased as their cash incomes rose, and it seems that there was also some increase in the standards of living of the wealthier peasantry. Such demand was chiefly for cheap woollen cloth, leather goods and other basic merchant goods such as salt, tar, iron and fish.[30]

The relationship between Anglo-Saxon boroughs and patterns of local trade is a topic of considerable uncertainty, because many were created in wartime as centres of defence and administration rather than of trade. To identify them as a network of price-setting markets requires a hazardous leap of faith over the silences of the written texts. Nevertheless, some centres, whether called boroughs or not, did come to attract traders from neighbouring settlements, and were provided with an appropriate institutional apparatus.[31] Urban growth in the period *c.* 880–930 at York, Lincoln and perhaps some other towns of the Danelaw would be difficult to explain without reference to some increase in local interdependence between town and country.[32] The best evidence for

[27] Bonney, *Lordship*, pp. 157–8.

[28] Biddle, ed., *Winchester*, pp. 308, 461; Fleming, 'Rural elites and urban communities', 29–31; Bonney, *Lordship*, pp. 10, 16, 24; B. Dobson, 'The later middle ages, 1215–1500', in G. E. Aylmer and R. Cant, eds., *A History of York Minster* (Oxford, 1977), pp. 85–6; Rosser, *Medieval Westminster*, pp. 35–6, 150, 216.

[29] N. F. Shead, 'Glasgow: an ecclesiastical borough', in M. Lynch, M. Spearman and G. Stell, eds., *The Scottish Medieval Town* (Edinburgh, 1988), pp. 116–17.

[30] R. H. Britnell, 'Commercialisation and economic development in England', in R. H. Britnell and B. M. S. Campbell, eds., *A Commercialising Economy* (Manchester, 1995), pp. 20–1.

[31] R. H. Britnell, 'English markets and royal administration before 1200', *Ec.HR*, 2nd series, 31 (1978), 183–96.

[32] Biddle, 'Towns', p. 137; M. Biddle and D. Hill, 'Late Saxon planned towns', *Antiquaries J*, 51 (1971), 78–85.

exchanges of this type is that of pottery, some of which travelled many miles from its urban point of manufacture.[33] Many boroughs and markets of the Domesday survey must have exemplified the interdependence of town and country, in the absence of any other explanation of their urban characteristics. The renewed prominence of town building in the period *c.* 1080–1220 through most of Britain is more likely to have depended on the growth of the rural economy than increasing landlord expenditure or the expansion of overseas trade.[34]

The satisfactory organisation of trade between towns and their rural neighbours required the establishment of regular markets and market rules. From the late eleventh century, at least, towns also commonly had annual fairs to attract more specialised traders over longer distances. Little is known about how these operated before the thirteenth century, and there is no reason to suppose that there was any universal set of customs. From 1066, if not earlier, kings of England asserted the right to license all new markets, and they were followed in this respect by kings of Scots from David I onwards.[35] From that time we know increasingly more about where there were markets and fairs, and when they were held. The bigger the resident community a market place served the more trade it would attract and the more money it would make for its licensee. The residents were normally free to trade without paying tolls, but rents were charged for stalls in the market and for the use of distinctive market facilities like weighing apparatus. Outsiders were charged tolls on their trade according to some regular tariff; an early list of toll charges from the new town of Cardiff dates from the mid-twelfth century. In addition, fines were charged for offences against market rules.[36] This possibility of making money from the development of a town and its trade was undoubtedly a consideration that encouraged kings and other landlords to engage in urban development. Some new towns – like Stratford-on-Avon, founded in 1196 – were quite unrelated to the requirements of a large household or administrative centre, and increasingly in the course of the twelfth and thirteenth centuries landlords founded such new towns as an aspect of estate improvement. Markets and fairs were sometimes created to serve existing settlements, and sometimes in order to develop new ones. In Essex, the modern Witham (originally the new town of 'Wulvesford'), Harwich (originally a market in Dovercourt), Manningtree (originally a market at 'Sheningho'),

[33] J. Campbell, 'Was it infancy in England? Some questions of comparison', in M. Jones and M. Vale, eds., *England and her Neighbours, 1066–1453: Essays in Honour of Pierre Chaplais* (London, 1989), pp. 10–11; Fleming, 'Rural elites and urban communities', 19–20.

[34] Britnell, 'Boroughs, markets and trade', pp. 62–4; S. Reynolds, 'Towns in Domesday Book', in J. C. Holt, ed., *Domesday Studies* (Woodbridge, 1987), pp. 308–9.

[35] *Regesta Regum Scottorum*, ed. Barrow *et al.*, I, no. 90, p. 170.

[36] Griffiths, *Conquerors and Conquered*, p. 339; Miller and Hatcher, *Medieval England: Towns Commerce and Crafts*, pp. 155–80, 259–60.

modern Epping (originally a new foundation on Epping Heath, away from old Epping) and Billericay (originally a market in Great Burghstead) are all first known from royal grants of markets and fairs at dates between 1212 and 1253.[37]

The expansion of demand over even longer distances, beyond nearby villages, is also well attested for the period 600–1300 though its magnitude is unknown. Towns differed very greatly in the extent to which they benefited from such mercantile activity. Especially in Anglo-Saxon and Norman England, a commercial impetus to urban growth was closely associated with large households, with their conspicuous consumption of imported goods.[38] But inevitably the clearest archaeological traces of such trade are at ports. The coast of Kent showed signs of commercial development at least as early as the eighth century, and a trading settlement at Southampton that grew up beside the River Itchen was one of England's largest towns at that time. There is documentary evidence of maritime trade from a hithe in London in the second quarter of the eighth century.[39] The beginnings of the development of Ipswich as a port is also probably from this early period.[40] Setbacks to overseas trade in the period of Viking attacks, *c.* 830–80 were soon followed by vigorous revival. When King Alfred refounded London in 886, Queenhithe was developed on the banks of the Thames. Alfred also developed Exeter as a borough and a port, probably recognising its potential for the export of tin.[41] Trade increased around the southern shores of England through the following hundred years, and the number of trade-dependent coastal towns increased. All the towns of eleventh-century Kent except Canterbury were by the sea or near river mouths, and Fordwich, Sandwich, Dover, Hythe and New Romney were significant ports.[42] In the North overseas contacts contributed powerfully to the development of York, where excavations in the late Saxon deposits of Coppergate have produced the remains of artefacts from as far away as Byzantium and the Middle East.[43] The continuing development of trade on the coast and river estuaries through the twelfth and thirteenth centuries encouraged both the expansion of earlier ports and the creation of new ones, chiefly on the North Sea coast and the southern shores of England opposite France. Some

[37] R. H. Britnell, 'Essex markets before 1350', *Essex Archaeology and History*, 13 (1981), 15–21.

[38] P. Nightingale, *A Medieval Mercantile Community* (New Haven and London, 1995), p. 53.

[39] T. Dyson and J. Schofield, 'Saxon London', in J. Haslam, ed., *Anglo-Saxon Towns in Southern England* (Chichester, 1984), pp. 292–3; P. Holdsworth, 'Saxon Southampton', in Haslam, ed., *Anglo-Saxon Towns in Southern England*, p. 335; T. Tatton-Brown, 'The Anglo-Saxon towns of Kent', in Hooke, ed., *Anglo-Saxon Settlements*, pp. 213–21.

[40] Biddle, 'Towns', pp. 144–5n; J. G. Hurst, 'The pottery', in Wilson, ed., *Archaeology of Anglo-Saxon England*, p. 303.

[41] T. Dyson, 'King Alfred and the restoration of London', *LJ*, 15 (1990), 99–110; J. R. Maddicott, 'Trade, industry and the wealth of King Alfred', *P&P*, 123 (1989), 19–35.

[42] Tatton Brown, 'Anglo-Saxon towns of Kent', pp. 221–32. On New Romney, see M. Gardiner, 'Old Romney: an examination of the evidence for a lost Saxo-Norman port', *Archaeologia*, 114 (1994), 329–45.

[43] R. Hall, 'The making of Domesday York', in Hooke, ed., *Anglo-Saxon Settlements*, p. 241.

of these latest developments rapidly assumed dominant regional positions. Newcastle-upon-Tyne, Hull, Boston, Lynn, Portsmouth and Poole all came into existence between the Norman Conquest and the end of the twelfth century.[44]

In Wales, Cardiff was first developed as a borough by Robert fitz Hamo simultaneously, so far as we know, with the founding of a castle there between 1090 and 1107, but the fact that it rapidly became the most successful of all Welsh boroughs owes much to its development as a port. By 1185 the borough was worth about £48 a year to its lord, and twice that sum by 1262. Carmarthen, founded by an Anglo-Norman castle by 1116, also benefited from its location on the River Tywi to develop as a port, and it was another of the most flourishing of the Welsh boroughs.[45] Outside the region of Anglo-Norman colonisation, the court of the princes of Gwynedd fostered urban and commercial development at Llanfaes on Anglesey, and Nefyn, on the Lleyn peninsula, from the late twelfth century until Edward I's conquest of Wales.[46]

The coastal trade of Scotland was not great enough to encourage urban development much before the twelfth century, but Perth provides an early example of its relevance thereafter. Here there was already a commercial nucleus in the early twelfth century, before the building of a castle on the northern side of the town. By about 1124 a settlement existed at Watergate, and King David I was collecting tribute (*cain*) from shipping there.[47] Aberdeen, Dundee and Berwick were also able to benefit from sea-borne trade and fishing, and there were yet smaller ports at places like St Andrews, Crail and Inverkeithing. Some towns set back from the coast nevertheless had associated ports that enabled them to develop as mercantile centres from the twelfth century. Edinburgh was trading through Leith from this time, and Linlithgow had similar access to the sea at Bo'ness.[48] In the thirteenth century Aberdeen, Perth and Berwick each constituted the focus of an economic region, though Berwick's maritime trade was appreciably greater than that of the other two.[49]

Most of the new ports of the medieval period were established by 1200. However, overseas trade continued to expand to the end of the period under discussion – it has been estimated that the value of England's overseas trade increased at least threefold between 1204 and 1309[50] – and the implication that

[44] Beresford, *New Towns*, pp. 428–9, 447–9, 463–5, 467–8, 473–4, 511–12, 515–16.

[45] *Ibid.*, p. 553; Griffiths, *Conquerors and Conquered*, pp. 175, 177, 338–40.

[46] See below, pp. 696–8; E. M. Besly, 'Short cross and other medieval coins from Llanfaes, Anglesey', *British Numismatic J*, 65 (1995), 47.

[47] R. M. Spearman, 'The medieval townscape of Perth', in Lynch, Spearman and Stell, eds., *The Scottish Medieval Town*, pp. 47–8.

[48] A. A. M. Duncan, *Scotland* (Edinburgh, 1975), p. 506; A. Stevenson, 'Trade with the south', in Lynch, Spearman and Stell, eds., *The Scottish Medieval Town*, pp. 182, 191.

[49] M. Lynch and A. Stevenson, 'Overseas trade: the middle ages to the sixteenth century', in P. McNeil and H. L. MacQueen, eds., *Atlas of Scottish History to 1707* (Edinburgh, 1996), p. 238.

[50] Miller and Hatcher, *Medieval England: Towns, Commerce and Crafts*, p. 214.

up to 1300 long-distance trade remained a source of urban growth is supported by both the expansion of older port towns and the creation of a few significant new ones. By 1300 Newcastle-upon-Tyne, Boston and Lynn were amongst England's ten wealthiest towns, and mercantile trade had also contributed powerfully to the growth of London. The port town of Hull, originally founded by Meaux Abbey in the twelfth century, was significantly expanded by Edward I in 1293. Amongst the new port towns of the thirteenth century were Weymouth, Harwich and Liverpool in England, and Aberystwyth in Wales, though none of these could compare in 1300 with the foundations of the Anglo-Norman period.[51]

Throughout the period 600–1300 the principal commodities exported from British ports were agricultural products (especially wool and hides) and mineral products (especially tin) derived from rural areas. Scottish exports were principally hides, wool and woolfells, though they also included fish.[52] At all times the proportion of British urban manufactures that was exported was minute. The main contribution of overseas demand to urban incomes in the thirteenth century, and probably throughout the period, was accordingly in supporting mercantile occupations that linked markets abroad to supplies from the hinterland. Many inland towns had a wool merchant or two by the later thirteenth century.[53] In the course of the period merchants developed practices that permitted the reduction of transaction costs, and increased the security of their livelihood, and they emerged as a recognisable interest group in the government of towns and of the realm.[54] Their prominence was enhanced by the growing importance of customs duties in the king's finances after 1275. Except in the major port towns, however, overseas trade was an interest subordinate to local trade, and the smaller towns often had no one who could be confidently described as a merchant. In the late twelfth and early thirteenth centuries there was an ephemeral surge in the export of woollen textiles, and this increased employment in a number of inland English towns – notably York and Beverley in Yorkshire, Lincoln, Louth and Stamford in Lincolnshire, Leicester and Northampton in the East Midlands.[55] However, the international reputation of English cloth was not maintained through the thirteenth century, so that the manufacture of superior cloths became a depressed sector of urban economies by 1300.[56]

[51] See below, p. 755; Beresford, *New Towns*, pp. 429–30, 435, 461, 511–12, 515–16, 537.

[52] Stevenson, 'Trade with the south', pp. 185–6.

[53] T. H. Lloyd, *The English Wool Trade in the Middle Ages* (Cambridge, 1977), pp. 51–2.

[54] Britnell, 'Sedentary long-distance trade', pp. 135–7.

[55] E. M. Carus-Wilson, *Medieval Merchant Venturers*, 2nd edn (London, 1967), pp. 211–38.

[56] E. Miller, 'The fortunes of the English textile industry in the thirteenth century', *Ec.HR*, 2nd series, 18 (1965), 68–70.

(ii) THE SUPPLY OF LABOUR, FOOD AND MATERIALS

Urban growth between 600 and 1300 depended upon the willingness of men and women to move into a position where they relied upon market relationships for their livelihood, selling manufactures and services in exchange for food and raw materials, either directly or through the medium of monetised exchange. In other words, the towns that grew did not depend for their growth on an exceptionally high rate of natural increase, but upon an exceptionally high capacity to attract migrants.[57] In general the more mercantile boroughs were those that exercised the strongest pull, but special efforts were made in areas of colonisation to draw new burgesses from a distance, and some of the Welsh and Scottish towns depended heavily upon their chartered liberties to attract migration over long distances. Urban development in Wales was strongly associated with the immigration of English settlers, so much so that Gerald of Wales reported in the 1190s that 'the Welsh do not live in towns, villages or castles'. Even in 1300 Cardiff was a predominantly English town; all the jurors who provided information for a survey of the town in 1295 were of English origin.[58] A new wave of English urban settlers in the last quarter of the thirteenth century followed Edward's I's invasions of 1277 and 1282–3, which led to another wave of numerous important borough foundations, most notably at Caernarfon and Conwy.[59] Some of Scotland's early burghs were similarly centres of English habitation, according to William of Newburgh, and his view gains support from the evidence of the personal names of early settlers. The political significance of the Scottish towns was quite different from that of the Welsh, however, because they were not imposed by conquest, and the proportion of burgesses who were native was significantly large from the start. As far as one can tell, both in Scotland and Wales there were also Flemish craftsmen amongst the early townsmen.[60]

The proportion of households dependent upon supplying manufactures and services increased very significantly between 600 and 1300, and a large proportion of them were located in towns of various sizes because of the reduced costs and reduced risks of trade that urban life provided. Even in Wales it is estimated that by the 1290s the urban proportion may have been almost as high as in England.[61] The circumstances governing townward migration over this period of 700 years doubtless varied considerably, and our knowledge of fluctuations in the urban labour market, and the changing conditions that governed them, is woefully poor. Some towns in some periods attracted labour from the countryside because of the superior condition of employment to be obtained there; that

[57] Miller and Hatcher, *Medieval England: Towns, Commerce and Crafts*, pp. 330–6.

[58] R. R. Davies, *Conquest, Coexistence and Change* (Oxford, 1987), pp. 97, 162; Griffiths, *Conquerors and Conquered*, p. 344.

[59] M. C. Prestwich, *Edward I* (London, 1988), p. 216.

[60] Barrow, *Kingship and Unity*, pp. 92–3; Duncan, *Scotland*, pp. 476–8.

[61] See below, p. 681.

is quite likely to have been the case in the vicinity of growing towns during the period 880–930 and again in the late twelfth and early thirteenth centuries, which were seemingly periods of dynamic urban development and expanding overseas trade. At other times, as in the later thirteenth century, rural unemployment drove men into the towns in pursuit of casual work or alms, driving down wage levels there. In such circumstances large numbers of town dwellers contributed little or nothing to urban incomes, depending on begging and almsgiving for much of their subsistence; the poor scrambled for the alms handed out at funerals and anniversaries and the weakest went to the wall.[62]

Whatever the truth about changes in urban wealth may be, urban populations were higher around 1300 than at any time in the medieval period. Although a large proportion of these people lived on very low incomes they were fed except in occasional years of famine, so the period around 1300 was also one of exceptionally high urban demand for food and raw materials. This relates well to what is known of the agrarian economy of this period, which saw the commercial exploitation of land carried to a high degree. At a rough guess, in a normal year around 1300 about a third of all the grain harvested in southern England (by value) was made available for sale, though not all of this was for urban consumption. This estimate is based on the assumption that some 6–8 per cent of the kingdom's total harvest was sold by parish rectors out of parochial tithes, that 12 per cent was sold by demesne officials from demesne lands and that 12–20 per cent was sold by peasant households from their family holdings.[63]

Medieval towns never depended wholly upon trade with external suppliers for their requirements of food, animal feed and raw materials. Many had fields and pastures in which their inhabitants had an interest; indeed, pasture rights were often one of the most important features of free status as a burgess. 'Cambridge had fields as Lower Heyford had fields.'[64] In Colchester in 1301, 39 per cent of taxpayers were assessed on grain and livestock only, implying that they may have depended upon sales of agrarian produce for income.[65] To the extent that townsmen produced their own foodstuffs their dependence upon trade with external suppliers was reduced, and so was their degree of urbanity by the criteria we have adopted. The rustic features of Colchester in this period are strikingly illustrated in the agrarian conflicts waged by

[62] Harvey, *Living and Dying*, p. 23.

[63] R. H. Britnell, 'La commercializzazione dei ceriali in Inghilterra dal 1250 al 1350', *Quaderni storici*, 96 (1997), p. 639.

[64] Miller and Hatcher, *Medieval England: Towns, Commerce and Crafts*, pp. 26–7, 257–8; F. W. Maitland, *Township and Borough* (Cambridge, 1898), p. 4.

[65] *Rotuli Parliamentorum* (Record Commission, 1783), vol. 1, pp. 228–38, 243–65. This calculation includes taxpayers from Mile End but excludes those from Greenstead, West Donyland and Lexden.

burgesses of the town with the manorial lords within the bounds of their jurisdiction.[66]

Even a town of this kind, however, was not self-sufficient in foodstuffs. Though grain figures prominently in Colchester's tax assessment of 1301, the total volume of vendible stocks recorded there amounts to no more than 133 quarters of rye and 26 quarters of wheat – perhaps enough to keep the town in bread for a fortnight – and this record cannot therefore be used to argue that the town was self-sufficient. To set against it, there is the accusation against eleven burgesses in 1334 that within the previous four months they had evaded paying toll on 530 quarters of grain intended for resale. Local manorial accounts supply direct evidence that even in years of low prices Colchester's grain supply depended upon substantial purchases from rural suppliers. Meat and dairy produce, too, was brought in from the countryside around. Fish supplies depended both upon Colchester fishermen and upon supplies from other fishing ports.[67] If the provisioning of Colchester relied upon regular trade, this is likely to be true of many other English towns of the period; Colchester ranked only fifty-third amongst English towns in 1334 in terms of its taxable wealth.[68] Evidence from elsewhere in medieval Europe shows that the larger the population of a town the smaller the share of the population dependent upon agricultural income. At the top end, London is estimated to have required around 175,000 quarters of grain a year, which it drew from many parts of the surrounding counties.[69]

Fuel was another commodity whose supply affected the potential of towns to grow. By 1300 it is estimated that London required annually 141,000 tons of firewood.[70] Analysis of this market is complicated by the range of different fuels used in different parts of England, Wales and Scotland, and the paucity of evidence of prices. Firewood, peat, charcoal and sea coal were all used in different parts of the country. In southern England the sale of faggots as fuel became a commercial part of the operations of some manors with woodlands, though it was rarely a major operation. Peat was the commonest fuel in the towns of Scotland. In London and some other towns local supplies were augmented to some extent by the shipment of coal from north-eastern England, though coal burning gave rise to complaints of pollution. Archaeological evidence shows that in addition to these more predictable fuels townsmen used waste matter, such as

[66] R. H. Britnell, *Growth and Decline in Colchester, 1300–1525* (Cambridge, 1986), pp. 30–1; R. H. Britnell, 'The fields and pastures of Colchester, 1280–1350', *Essex Archaeology and History*, 19 (1988), 163–4.

[67] Britnell, *Growth and Decline*, pp. 15, 39–45; R. H. Britnell, 'Production for the market on a small fourteenth-century estate', *Ec.HR*, 2nd series, 19 (1966), 382–3.

[68] See below, p. 756.

[69] B. M. S. Campbell, J. A. Galloway, D. Keene and M. Murphy, *A Medieval Capital and its Grain Supply* (Historical Geography Research Series, 30, London, 1993).

[70] J. A. Galloway, D. Keene and M. Murphy, 'Fuelling the city: production and distribution of firewood and fuel in London's region, 1290–1400', *Ec.HR*, 49 (1996), 455.

old straw and spoiled fodder.[71] Any town of any size depended on trade for fuel supplies, and urban markets sometimes designated a special area for its sale.[72] Fuel supplies do not crop up as a major concern in the literature concerning medieval towns, however, and it could not be claimed on present evidence that contemporaries perceived much of a problem.

Urban growth in the thirteenth century was more inhibited by problems of food supply. Prices of grain rose between the late twelfth century and the early fourteenth, and probably rose more than incomes towards the end of the period.[73] Urban authorities, and ultimately the king, came to treat the supply of foodstuffs as a problem requiring regulatory intervention, so that measures were introduced to prevent scarcity and high prices.[74] The agrarian evidence suggests that from the mid-thirteenth century it was becoming more difficult in most parts of England to increase the food supply simply by increasing the area under crops, which meant that urban growth was becoming more dependent upon improved methods in agriculture or imports from abroad.[75] When harvests failed because of bad weather, as notoriously between 1315 and 1318, a larger number of people were at risk of starvation than when towns were smaller.[76]

(iii) MONEY AND CREDIT

The development of town life between 600 and 1300 was facilitated by developments in the monetary system that constitute the most unambiguous evidence for the growth of commercial activity in the medieval economy. These developments may be divided between two distinct aspects, first the expansion of the volume of coinage, which was the primary monetary medium, and secondly the improvement of institutional arrangements for the creation and sanctioning of credit relationships.

At the beginning of the period there was no regulated currency system anywhere in Britain; the only coins in use were surviving Roman issues and imitations of them, together perhaps with a few gold pieces brought in from the

[71] E. Ewan, *Townlife in Fourteenth-Century Scotland* (Edinburgh, 1990), p. 22; J. Hatcher, *The History of the British Coal Industry*, vol. I: *Before 1700* (Oxford, 1993), pp. 24–5; J. Schofield and A. Vince, *Medieval Towns* (London, 1994), p. 114.

[72] D. L. Farmer, 'Woodland and pasture sales on the Winchester manors in the thirteenth century: disposing of a surplus or producing for the market?', in Britnell and Campbell, eds., *Commercialising Economy*, pp. 123–4; Keene, *Survey*, I, p. 265; O. Ogle, 'The Oxford market', in M. Burrows, ed., *Collectanea II* (Oxford Historical Society, 16, 1890), pp. 13–14, 119.

[73] D. L. Farmer, 'Prices and wages', in H. E. Hallam, ed., *Ag.HEW*, vol. II (Cambridge, 1988), pp. 772–9.

[74] Britnell, *Commercialisation*, pp. 90–7; R. H. Britnell, '*Forstall*, forestalling and the Statute of Forestallers', *EHR*, 102 (1987), 89–102.

[75] E. Miller and J. Hatcher, *Medieval England: Rural Society and Economic Change, 1086–1348* (London, 1978), p. 54.

[76] I. Kershaw, 'The great famine and agrarian crisis in England, 1315–1322', in R. H. Hilton, ed., *Peasants, Knights and Heretics: Studies in English Social History* (Cambridge, 1976), pp. 90, 92–3.

Table 6.1 *Estimates of money stock in circulation in England c. 1000–1311*

Year	Currency in circulation £
973–1059	25,000
1086	37,500
1205	250,000
1218	300,000
1247	400,000
1278	674,000
1298	600,000
1311	1,100,000

Sources: N. J. Mayhew, 'Modelling medieval monetisation', in Britnell and Campbell, eds., *Commercialising Economy*, pp. 62, 72; N. J. Mayhew, 'Money and prices in England from Henry II to Edward III', *Agricultural History Review*, 35 (1987), 125.

continent. Following a period when additions to the money stock were restricted to small numbers of uninscribed *sceattas*, royal minting began in at least two English kingdoms soon after 750, but in 800 there were still only three mints with anything resembling a continuous tradition – at Canterbury, London and somewhere in East Anglia.[77] The currency stock increased from very low levels through the ninth and tenth centuries, and the eleventh-century economy was outstanding at the time for the volume and quality of the coinage in circulation, but there was dramatic expansion still to come. This may be seen from Table 6.1, which demonstrates that at the end of the thirteenth century the volume was about thirty-six times higher than it generally was in the eleventh century. Although Wales had no currency of its own, its economy became increasingly monetised, and in Scotland, too, there was a considerable expansion of the coinage in circulation. There was no Scottish coinage as such till the reign of David I, who began minting Scottish pennies to a distinctive design from 1136. From only a few thousand pounds in the early 1190s, the Scots coinage in circulation increased to about £50,000–£60,000 or more in the mid-thirteenth century and £130,000–£180,000 around 1280.[78] The princes of

[77] P. Grierson and M. Blackburn, *Medieval European Coinage*, vol. 1: *The Early Middle Ages (5th–10th Centuries)* (Cambridge, 1986), pp. 284–93.

[78] I. Stewart, 'The volume of early Scottish coinage', in D. M. Metcalf, ed., *Coinage in Medieval Scotland (1100–1600)* (British Archaeological Reports, 45, British Series, 1977), pp. 65–72; E. Gemmill and N. Mayhew, *Changing Values in Medieval Scotland* (Cambridge, 1995), p. 140.

Gwynedd initiated a coinage at Rhuddlan in the late twelfth century, imitating the English issues of the time, but this was not continued after the first few decades of the thirteenth century; most of the increasing number of coins circulating in thirteenth-century Wales were from English mints.[79]

The close relationship between the emergent monetary system and the needs of urban economies is evident from the organisation of minting activity, which rested on the assumption that mints needed to be located in boroughs all across the country. There were usually at least sixty mints operating in late Anglo-Saxon England, between them spanning the range from some very minor centres of local trade, such as Horndon-on-the-Hill (Essex), Cadbury (Somerset) and Cissbury (Sussex), to the major towns of the period. Until 1279 moneyers put their names on the coins they struck, and the number of moneyers in operation simultaneously is one of the best indicators available of the relevant importance of different towns. Over twenty London moneyers are known for the years 1042–66, twice as many as for any other town.[80] Between the eleventh century and the end of the thirteenth improvements in the circulation of currency reduced the necessity for mints in small market towns and led to an increasing concentration of activity, notably in London. The number of mints was halved to only thirty at the time of Henry II's first coinage and further reduced to only eleven for Edward I's recoinage of 1279.[81]

The history of credit institutions is chiefly a subject for the period after 1100. It involved more than purely commercial requirements for ready money. Landowners of all sorts were amongst those who required to borrow on the security of their lands, and the kings of England, too, were consistently dependent upon credit for the management of their realms by the end of the period. Although Jewish money-lenders were established in many English towns between the mid-twelfth century and 1275, when they were forbidden to practise usury, most of their business was oriented towards the landed interest of the surrounding countryside.[82] Nevertheless, much of the development of credit relates to the needs of townsmen and merchants, particularly towards the very end of the period under study. Procedures for the recovery of debt through borough and national courts went through a series of refinements through the formal development of the plea of debt as a regular form of action. In 1275 merchants were protected against the arbitrary distraint of their goods – which had been one of the costs of the rising efficacy of local jurisdiction for debt. But the institutions through which debt was contracted and sanctioned were greatly

[79] Besly, 'Short cross and other medieval coins', 55.

[80] F. M. Stenton, *Anglo-Saxon England*, 2nd edn (Oxford, 1947), pp. 529–30.

[81] D. M. Stenton, *English Society in the Early Middle Ages*, 4th edn (Harmondsworth, 1965), pp. 166–70.

[82] R. C. Stacey, 'Jewish lending and the medieval English economy', in Britnell and Campbell, eds., *Commercialising Economy*, pp. 85–7, 95–7.

increased by statutory measures in 1283 and 1285 (the Statute of Acton Burnell and the Statute of Merchants) which facilitated the formal registration of debts in borough courts and simplified the procedures by which debts so registered could be recovered.[83]

(iv) URBAN EMPLOYMENT AND CHANGES IN RANK SIZE

The growth of towns between 600 and 1300 rested upon their capacity to produce a wide variety of goods and services to satisfy the various sorts of demand that have been considered. Apart from basic household supplies, wealthy households required luxury manufactures, often requiring considerable skill to make, exotic foodstuffs, often requiring commercial expertise to supply, and a wide range of personal services. If such demand was high enough it created the possibility of a wide range of highly specialised crafts and trades. The majority of rural consumers bought a narrower range of goods and services, though the aggregate demand for each good and each service permitted a high degree of occupational specialisation. Distant markets were likely to require some very specific commodity from particular towns, and so permitted regional as well as occupational specialisation. Urban development might be written, had we the detailed knowledge to do so, as the development and proliferation of occupational skills in response to these different commercial opportunities.

The differing sizes of town corresponded not only to differences in their degree of self-sufficiency but also in the range of their skills and specialities. This was greatest, predictably, where opportunities for serving large households, supplying the surrounding region and in servicing overseas trade coexisted. The occupational make-up of medieval towns is difficult to reconstruct even after the remarkable rise of urban record keeping from the thirteenth century onwards, and for earlier periods the demonstration of any proposition such as this one must be of an impressionistic nature. Nevertheless, having identified a tanner, a fuller, a bargee, a parchmentmaker, a cordwainer, a saddler, a lorimer, a currier, a waferer and a bell-founder in the early charters of St Paul's Cathedral, and having been impressed by the number of goldsmiths working in London in the early twelfth century, Stenton was surely right to conclude that the evidence of Norman London was distinguished 'both by the variety of occupations represented at an early date and by the number of persons following the same calling at the same time'.[84]

Table 6.2 shows the distribution of primary occupations amongst the citizens of York, Winchester and Norwich at the end of the period under observation as it appears on evidence derived from occupational descriptions alone. It suggests

[83] T. F. T. Plucknett, *Legislation of Edward I* (Oxford, 1949), pp. 136–43.

[84] F. M. Stenton, *Preparatory to Anglo-Saxon England*, ed. D. M. Stenton (Oxford, 1970), p. 43.

Table 6.2 *Occupations of some citizens in York, Norwich and Winchester around 1300*

	York 1307–19 % N=1,951	Norwich 1285–1311 % N=717	Winchester 1300–39 % N=421
Trade			
Food and drink	23	18	21
Other	17	29	28
Industry			
Textiles and clothing	12	16	20
Leather and leather goods	18	20	9
Metals	13	8	4
Other	6	2	1
Services			
Transport	4	1	3
Building	4	5	5
Other	3	1	9

Source: Miller and Hatcher, *Medieval England: Towns, Commerce and Crafts*, p. 326.

that the food trades and clothing industries (textiles and leather) accounted for at least half of the employment of these towns, and this underrepresents the importance of these activities since traders in textiles, textile requirements, hides and skins are included amongst 'other' traders. However, these broad groupings cover a wide range of different activities. Even the smaller towns of medieval Britain maintained a surprisingly wide range: Durham deeds of the thirteenth century have produced fifty-three different occupational descriptions. As many as sixty-seven occupations can be identified from Winchester sources of the thirteenth century, and they include such seemingly specialised crafts as hatmaking, bottle-making and soapmaking.[85] Occupational names are misleading in the degree of rigidity and continuity that they suggest. The growth of towns inevitably required repeated, complex adaptations to new possibilities of trade and specialisation. Entrepreneurial activity in this economy operated at the level of the individual, self-employed householders as they put together combinations of agrarian, commercial and industrial activity that would support them with an adequate income. The ingenuity of which people were capable is barely perceptible to the historian, who can rarely get beyond the description of an individual townsman as 'smith' or 'carpenter'. The innovations or special skills that might

[85] Bonney, *Lordship*, p. 269; Keene, *Survey*, I, pp. 252–65.

be concealed behind occupational descriptions are usually imperceptible, as is the range of different activities with which they might be combined. Archaeological and iconographic analysis implies that varying technical methods and styles of manufacture may be covered by the same occupational description, and documentary evidence shows both that many townsmen owned at least some land and that throughout the middle ages there were men and women who practised more than one craft.[86]

The middle ages, though a period of urban growth, was not one in which all towns had even prospects of prosperity, and across the long period from 600 to 1300 there were numerous shifts in the relative position of different towns and different regions. The creation of new towns affected the economies of older ones, as when Boston's growth limited the prospects for Lincoln.[87] The construction of bridges sometimes decisively altered the relative attractiveness of different river crossings, and caused one town to grow at the expense of another, as when a new bridge at Ware (Herts.) threatened the townsmen of Hertford.[88] Other adjustments resulted from changes in the coastline, which reduced the attractiveness of particular havens relative to others. The town of Dunwich, one of the most important in Britain in the late twelfth century when it paid tallage on a level with Winchester and Lincoln, decayed as a result of marine incursions and the deterioration of its harbour.[89] The founding of new abbeys or castles could lead to alterations in the balance of advantages between different trading centres; the founding of Reading Abbey in 1121 is said to have favoured the development of Reading at the expense of Wallingford.[90] By contrast, the withdrawal of a source of demand for political or administrative reasons could damage a town's economy. Winchester's decline in importance as a royal centre retarded its prospects for development in the twelfth and thirteenth centuries.[91] No general formula can be given for rates of urban development, but two observations in particular are worth making. One is that at every stage in this period the fortunes of towns were shaped to a large degree by the decisions of landlords rather than entrepreneurial choices of townsmen. Investment in urban development and infrastructure, the location of large households, garrisons and armies, and the choice of schemes for provisioning them, were all predominantly matters for decision by the king, the magnates and the greater churches. Such decisions were obviously not arbitrary, but they introduce an element of chance into the history of urban development that was sometimes fundamental to their fortunes, as when the bishop of Salisbury removed his cathedral city from Old Sarum to the new town of Salisbury. Secondly, Table 6.3 suggests that nine out of the wealthiest

[86] Britnell, *Growth and Decline*, pp. 17, 38; Hurst, 'Pottery', pp. 283–348; Keene, *Survey*, I, p. 250; Schofield and Vince, *Medieval Towns*, pp. 111–12, 126.

[87] F. Hill, *Medieval Lincoln* (Cambridge, 1965), pp. 314–20.

[88] *VCH*, Hertfordshire, III, p. 499.

[89] *The Bailiffs' Minute Book of Dunwich, 1404–1430*, ed. M. Bailey (Suffolk Records Society, 34, 1992), pp. 1–2.

[90] Stenton, *English Society*, p. 189.

[91] Keene, *Survey*, I, p. 88.

Table 6.3 *The twenty wealthiest English towns in 1334, with changes in ranking since 1086*

Rank in 1334	Town	Rank in 1086	Rank in 1334	Town	Rank in 1086
1	London	1	11	Lynn	—
2	Bristol	*	12	Salisbury	—
3	York	2	13	Shrewsbury	—
4	Newcastle	—	14	Winchester	3= or 6
5	Boston	—	15	Canterbury	13
6	Norwich	4 or 5	16	Hereford	—
7	Yarmouth	—	17	Southampton	—
8	Oxford	10=	18	Gloucester	10=
9	Lincoln	3=	19	Ipswich	—
10	Coventry	—	20	Beverley	—

Notes: Rank in 1334 is based on the subsidy assessment of that year. Rank in 1086 is from the assessment of the probable rank ordering of the farms of the first fourteen towns in Biddle, ed., *Winchester in the Early Middle Ages*. The asterisk by Bristol signifies that the town may have been amongst the top twenty, but none of the other towns in the table was likely to be in this category. Among royal boroughs, larger farms than those from Yarmouth and Shrewsbury were paid in 1086 by Dover, Dunwich, Hereford, Huntingdon, Stamford and Wilton.
Sources: M. Biddle, ed., *Winchester in the Early Middle Ages* (Oxford, 1976), p. 500; J. Tait, *The Medieval English Borough* (Manchester, 1936), p. 184; below, Appendixes 2 and 4.

twenty English towns in 1334 were seaport or estuary towns, that only three of these (London, Bristol, Gloucester) are likely to have had any comparable status amongst English towns in 1086, that three (Newcastle, Boston, Lynn) were new towns of the post-Conquest period and that a further three (Yarmouth, Southampton, Ipswich) had risen into the top twenty only after 1086.

Though the area of Britain where there was significant urban development more than doubled between 1066 and 1300, at the end of this period the largest fifty British towns, probably all with populations of 3,000 or more, lay south and east of a line drawn from Newcastle in north-eastern England to Plymouth in the South-West. Cornwall, Wales, north-western England and Scotland were lands of small towns. Cardiff, the largest of the Welsh boroughs, had 405 burgage tenures in 1262, implying a population of perhaps fewer than 2,000, and Carmarthen was only half this size. The Edwardian boroughs of North Wales were still minute; Caernarfon had no more than about 300–400 people.[92]

[92] Beresford, *New Towns*, p. 553; Griffiths, *Conquerors and Conquered*, pp. 180, 340; K. Williams-Jones, 'Caernarvon', in R. A. Griffiths, ed., *Boroughs of Mediaeval Wales* (Cardiff, 1978), p. 83.

Berwick, the largest town in Scotland, had only 84 burgesses in 1291,[93] though its total population was probably several thousands. The growth and multiplication of towns had not altered the fact that the southern and eastern parts of Britain were both much more populous, wealthier and better located for mercantile enterprise than the North and West. Underlying all the economic development and changing fortunes of the period this contrast remained an inevitable consequence of the different economic potential of different parts of the island.

(v) THE REGULATION OF TRADE

The expansion of commercial and industrial activity has been accompanied throughout history by an increase in the body of regulation to prevent fraud, restrictive practices, pollution of the environment and other abuses of public confidence. In England, royal legislation touched on trading practices, quite apart from the numerous provisions incorporated in individual borough charters from the Anglo-Norman period onward. The prices of bread and ale were regulated in accordance with the price of grain from the 1190s, for example, and similar regulations were subsequently in force in Scottish towns.[94] In Scotland, the multiplication of new burghs under David I was accompanied by the compilation of assizes to regulate trade both within the burgh and without. During the following century the body of law relating to Scottish townsmen and trade increased, much of it as a result of royal initiative, and it was written down in individual burgh charters and in some more general formulations. The best known of these, the *Leges Burgorum*, is first known from a late thirteenth-century manuscript; it is of complex origins and includes material of both the twelfth and thirteenth centuries.[95]

Many medieval rules of trade have remained important over longer periods, and have modern analogies, because they represent collective attempts to reduce the normal costs and attendant risks of commercial activity. These, if successful, favour the growth of towns and trade, and can therefore be regarded as contributing to the historical processes by which commercialisation has occurred. Such are the attempts to control weights and measures and to guard against fraud that have been a recurrent feature of government policy from the tenth century onwards.[96]

It is difficult to evaluate much of the great body of medieval regulations very positively by absolute criteria of public interest, however. One of its prime objects was to protect the interests of particular social groups, as in the case of the many rules by which burgesses of the twelfth and thirteenth centuries were

[93] Barrow, *Kingship and Unity*, p. 94.

[94] Britnell, *Commercialisation*, pp. 94–5, Duncan, *Scotland*, pp. 499–500; Gemmill and Mayhew, *Changing Values*, pp. 30–53.

[95] H. L. MacQueen and W. J. Windram, 'Laws and courts in the burghs', in Lynch, Spearman and Stell, eds., *The Scottish Medieval Town*, pp. 208–12.

[96] Britnell, *Commercialisation*, pp. 25, 90–1.

privileged at the expense of non-burgesses. Amongst early urban liberties there are traces of chartered territorial monopolies, whereby trade within particular zones was restricted to borough markets. This system – whose early extent and operations is very unclear from the scanty documentation relating to it – was apparently in decay in England during the twelfth century, but in Scotland such urban monopolies have left very many more traces, and continued to function all through the middle ages. A burgh there characteristically had a virtual monopoly of trade and clothmaking within its hinterland.[97]

Even the abandonment of territorial monopolies in England did not equalise the terms on which burgesses traded with outsiders. In many towns, in both England and Scotland, the urban trading class was allowed to form a 'guild merchant', with chartered privileges to protect its interests.[98] Levels of toll payable on market transactions varied according to the origins and status of the transacting parties. At certain hours of the day trading in formal markets was restricted to burgesses, and rationing schemes were operated both to limit competition for supplies between burgesses and to favour them against others. Regulations to protect trade in the market place against forestallers – that is, traders who monopolised produce by buying it up on its way to market – became more formalised in the thirteenth century throughout Britain, but even they were used as a cover to protect the interests of burgesses against outsiders.[99] Urban regulations systematically favoured the interests of consumers against those of producers. One consequence of this was to ensure that for many rural traders urban market places were a second- or third-best option, and at all times a vast amount of trade was conducted away from the towns.[100] In other words, the cost-reducing advantages of regulated markets that towns offered were considerably reduced by the many market imperfections that were deliberately built into the regulatory system.

[97] Britnell, 'English markets', 194–5; Duncan, *Scotland*, pp. 474–5; Ewan, *Townlife*, p. 65.

[98] Duncan, *Scotland*, pp. 488–9, 491, 497; Miller and Hatcher, *Medieval England: Towns, Commerce and Crafts*, pp. 290–8.

[99] Britnell, '*Forstall*', 89–102; R. H. Britnell, 'Price-setting in English borough markets, 1349–1500', *Canadian J of History*, 31 (1996), 2–15; Duncan, *Scotland*, p. 499.

[100] Miller and Hatcher, *Medieval England: Towns, Commerce and Crafts*, pp. 155–9.

· 7 ·

Churches, education and literacy in towns 600–1300

JULIA BARROW

AS IN many other parts of Europe, churches are often the key to explaining the revival or emergence of towns in Britain in the earlier middle ages; nor did they cease to be influential once the towns were well established, but, on the contrary, continued to dominate many smaller towns, or to be powerful forces in larger ones, as landlords, consumers and patrons of the arts. Not least among the last was architecture: churches were usually the most important features in the landscape, being usually the tallest structures, often topographically the most extensive, and architecturally the most innovative. While defining the role of churches in towns is fairly straightforward in the earlier middle ages, exploring culture is much harder, chiefly because it is difficult to define a specifically urban culture before the end of the thirteenth century. The 'high culture' of courts and major churches did not necessarily require, though it often enjoyed, an urban setting, while popular culture is not only hard to divide into urban and rural forms but is also poorly documented for this period. None the less, it is possible to discern one cultural area where towns played an active role towards the end of this period: that is the growth of literacy and the development of education. Accordingly, this chapter will be broken up into four sections of unequal length: first, a short summary of the role of churches in the embryonic towns of the 600–900 period; secondly, an overview of churches in towns as they expanded or were created in the tenth and eleventh centuries; thirdly, an overview of the diversification of ecclesiastical institutions in towns in the twelfth and thirteenth centuries, and fourthly, a sketch of three separate aspects of urban culture: schools, the increasing use of the written word by townspeople and the development of the genre of urban panegyric.

(i) CHURCHES IN PROTO-TOWNS 600–900

Churches were of unquestionable importance for the survival or the emergence of urban or proto-urban sites in this period. The subject is dealt with in detail elsewhere in this volume[1] and so only a brief recapitulation is necessary here. First, churches played a large part in revivifying many of the Roman cities and towns: the end of the sixth century and the seventh century saw the establishment of episcopal churches or monastic communities in former Roman large towns such as Canterbury, Rochester, London, York, Gloucester and Leicester, and also in Bath, a Roman spa town, and Worcester, which had been a small Roman industrial town.[2] At Canterbury, Worcester and perhaps also Gloucester these new foundations apparently joined earlier churches, perhaps of the fifth or sixth centuries,[3] but these older establishments were quickly overshadowed by the new cathedrals and monasteries. Although reuse of Roman architectural features was quite common, especially to provide suitable accommodation for baptism,[4] uninterrupted use of sites is rare. Above all it has so far been impossible to prove that any Roman church site in any Roman town which was revived as a town in the middle ages was reused for a later church, even though Lincoln may be a partial exception to this, if the construction built in the forum in the fourth century was a church. Even this uncertain site, however, lacks continuity, since it lacked buildings in the fifth and sixth centuries and was only subsequently used as a church site again in the seventh or eighth.[5] What sixth- and seventh-century churchmen doubtless principally sought was the protection of city walls, often the most durable of Roman remains; they may also have thought that ideally bishops ought to have their see-churches based in cities, though the siting of several early sees away from Roman sites, even where these existed in the vicinity, for example Lichfield rather than *Letocetum*, and Hereford rather than *Magnis*,[6]

[1] See below, pp. 246–53.

[2] N. P. Brooks, *The Early History of the Church of Canterbury* (Leicester, 1984), esp. pp. 8–9; T. Tatton-Brown, 'The towns of Kent', in J. Haslam, ed., *Anglo-Saxon Towns in Southern England* (Chichester, 1984), pp. 1–36 at 12; M. Biddle, 'A city in transition, 400–800', in *BAHT*, III, pp. 20–9 at 23; A. G. Dickens, 'York before the Norman Conquest', in *VCH*, City of York, pp. 2–24 at 4; C. Heighway, 'Anglo-Saxon Gloucester, *c.* 680 to 1066', in *VCH*, Gloucestershire IV, pp. 5–12 at 7; B. Cunliffe, 'Saxon Bath', in Haslam, ed., *Anglo-Saxon Towns in Southern England*, pp. 345–58 at 345–8; N. J. Baker, *et al.*, 'From Roman to medieval Worcester: development and planning in the Anglo-Saxon city', *Antiquity*, 66 (1992), 65–74 at 69.

[3] Brooks, *The Early History of the Church of Canterbury*, p. 17; S. Bassett, 'Churches in Worcester before and after the conversion of the Anglo-Saxons', *Antiquaries J*, 69 (1991), 225–56; S. Bassett, 'Church and diocese in the West Midlands: the transition from British to Anglo-Saxon control', in J. Blair and R. Sharpe, eds., *Pastoral Care before the Parish* (Leicester, 1992), pp. 13–40 at 22–6; R. M. Bryant, 'St Mary de Lode, Gloucester', *Bulletin of the Council for British Archaeology Churches Commission*, 13 (1980), 15–18; Heighway, 'Anglo-Saxon Gloucester', p. 6.

[4] S. Foot, '"By water in the spirit": the administration of baptism in early Anglo-Saxon England', in Blair and Sharpe, eds., *Pastoral Care before the Parish*, pp. 171–92 esp. 181–2; J. Blair, 'Anglo-Saxon minsters: a topographical review', in *ibid.*, pp. 226–66.

[5] M. J. Jones, 'The latter days of Roman Lincoln', in A. G. Vince, ed. *Pre-Viking Lindsey* (Lincoln, 1993), pp. 14–28.

[6] M. Gelling, *Signposts to the Past*, 2nd edn (Chichester, 1988), pp. 57–9, 100; M. Gelling, *The West Midlands in the Early Middle Ages* (Leicester, 1992), p. 162.

shows that the stipulations of canon law could where necessary be overlooked. Within Roman fortifications the major churches often stood alone in the seventh and eighth centuries, though they may sometimes have been joined by royal residences and the *hagae* of great noblemen, as has been argued in the case of London and suggested for Canterbury.[7] At York, in addition to the minster, which almost certainly stood in the walled area, at least one church, St Mary Bishophill Junior, for which sculptural and epigraphic evidence survives, was built in the old Roman *colonia* across the Ouse in the middle Saxon period;[8] indeed the eighth-century foundation of *Alma Sophia*, mentioned in Alcuin's York poem, may also have been built in the *colonia*, later becoming the priory of Holy Trinity.[9]

Secondly, major churches seem to have played a larger role than lay manorial centres or royal palaces in creating 'central places', what Alan Everitt defined as 'Banburys', the nuclei from which many subsequent towns, big and small, emerged.[10] Ecclesiastical communities, unlike itinerant kings, were constantly present, and in addition to their economic impact on the surrounding region as consumers and landlords they also acquired pastoral authority.[11] Several churches were also significant shrines.[12] In the seventh century kings and magnates began deliberately to choose to be buried in churches,[13] thus increasing the latter's influence, not least because people lower down the social scale adopted the custom.

There is one type of urban settlement in this period, however, in which the significance of churches is hard to discern: this is the *emporium*.[14] However, *emporia* do not necessarily seem to have lacked churches – *Hamwic* may have had

[7] Biddle, 'A city in transition, 400–800', pp. 22–3; Brooks, *Early History of the Church of Canterbury*, p. 23.

[8] R. K. Morris, 'Churches in York and its hinterland: building pattern and stone sources in the eleventh and twelfth centuries', in J. Blair, ed. *Minsters and Parish Churches* (Oxford, 1988), pp. 191–9, at 192.

[9] R. K. Morris, 'Alcuin, York and the Alma Sophia', in L. A. S. Butler and R. K. Morris, eds., *The Anglo-Saxon Church* (CBA Res. Rep., 60, 1986), pp. 80–9; Alcuin, *The Bishops, Kings and Saints of York*, ed. P. Godman (Oxford, 1982), pp. 118–21, lines 1507–20.

[10] J. Blair, 'Minster churches in the landscape', in D. Hooke, ed., *Anglo-Saxon Settlements* (Oxford, 1988), pp. 35–58; A. Everitt, 'The Banburys of England', *UHY* (1974), pp. 28–38.

[11] See debate on this topic by E. Cambridge and D. Rollason, 'The pastoral organization of the Anglo-Saxon Church: a review of the "Minster Hypothesis"', *Early Medieval Europe*, 4 (1995), 87–104, and J. Blair, 'Ecclesiastical organization and pastoral care in Anglo-Saxon England', *Early Medieval Europe*, 4 (1995), 193–212.

[12] S. Bassett, 'A probable Mercian royal mausoleum at Winchcombe, Gloucestershire', *Antiquaries J*, 65 (1985), 82–100, esp. 85; J. Blair, 'St Frideswide reconsidered', *Oxoniensia*, 52 (1987), 71–127; J. Blair, 'St Frideswide's monastery: problems and possibilities', in J. Blair, ed., *St Frideswide's Monastery at Oxford*, *Oxoniensia*, 53 (1988), 221–58 at 226.

[13] D. A. Bullough, 'Burial, community and belief in the early medieval West', in P. Wormald, ed., *Ideal and Reality in Frankish and Anglo-Saxon Society* (Oxford, 1983), pp. 177–201 at 192, 196–7.

[14] R. Morris, *Churches in the Landscape* (London, 1989), p. 189.

two or even three at the turn of the eighth and ninth centuries.[15] Doubtless it was the ephemeral nature of many of the *wic* settlements which deprived their churches of lasting influence, though at *Hamwic* one of the churches may have had continuing importance: in the high middle ages and later the church of St Mary on the abandoned *emporium* site exercised its right to bury all the citizens of Southampton, a sign of superior parochial status suggestive of long existence, even though archaeological evidence that St Mary's existed in the middle Saxon period is so far lacking.

(ii) CHURCHES IN TOWNS 900–1100

During the ninth century military necessity forced the Mercian kings to defend some of their settlements with fortifications, or borough-works; one of these was the strategic site of Hereford, where a ditch and gravel bank, later replaced with turf and timber walls, were constructed to surround a square space divided into quarters by two streets.[16] The cathedral, which had existed in Hereford since at least *c.* 800, and probably since the creation of the diocese in the late seventh century, was allotted one of these quarters.[17] Fortified urban sites were established in large numbers in Wessex and elsewhere from the late ninth century onwards.[18]

The role of ecclesiastical establishments in all these new or newly fortified urban sites varied according to two factors: the previous history of each site and the region within which it lay. Alfred and Edward the Elder, probably largely responsible for choosing sites of *burhs* in Wessex, disapproved of powerful churches in them, except nunneries. In Winchester, it was of course impossible to uproot the cathedral (Old Minster) and senseless not to make use of the Roman walls; instead, Edward (who was carrying out the wishes of his parents) planted two other major churches, New Minster and Nunnaminster, near the cathedral, as a sign of royal power.[19] Otherwise, it is striking how many cathedrals and newly reformed male monastic houses in tenth-century Wessex fail to coincide with *burhs*. Sees for Somerset, Wiltshire and Devon were established in the early tenth century on sites outside the burghal network, at Wells, Ramsbury and Crediton. Sherborne, the seat of a bishop since 705, was not fortified. By

[15] A. Morton, 'Burial in middle-Saxon Southampton', in S. Bassett, ed., *Death in Towns* (Leicester, 1992), pp. 68–77.

[16] R. Shoesmith, ed., *Hereford City Excavations, Volume 2: Excavations on and Close to the Defences* (London, 1982), pp. 76–9.

[17] P. Sims-Williams, *Religion and Literature in Western England, 600–800* (Cambridge, 1990), pp. 90–1.

[18] See above, p. 53, and below, pp. 225–30.

[19] M. Biddle, '*Felix urbs Winthonia*', in D. Parsons, ed., *Tenth-Century Studies* (London and Chichester, 1975), pp. 123–40; see also B. A. E. Yorke, 'The bishops of Winchester, the kings of Wessex and the development of Winchester in the ninth and early tenth centuries', *Proc. of the Hampshire Field Club and Arch. Soc.*, 40 (1984), 61–70.

1066 Malmesbury was a small borough but it does not occur in the Burghal Hidage.[20] By contrast, perhaps because nuns were felt to require protection, and also because abbesses were often royal princesses and kings may therefore have regarded them as manipulable, Alfred's foundations for women at Wilton (890) and Shaftesbury (*c.* 888) were both placed in boroughs from the outset; furthermore, Wareham is recorded as having an abbess in 982.[21] Evidently Alfred, Edward the Elder and their successors wished to prevent bishops and abbots from developing seats of economic and political influence in towns. It is worth stressing this point because elsewhere in Europe, and, indeed, in other parts of England, for example at Worcester,[22] bishops played an active role in urbanisation in this period.

In western Mercia Æthelred and Æthelflæd often encouraged a plurality of major churches inside fortified urban sites: at Shrewsbury, which first emerges into the light of day in this period though it must already have enjoyed a long existence, they were probably responsible for founding St Alkmund's to add to St Chad's and St Mary's which probably predate their time; at Chester, they appear to have refounded one church and perhaps rededicated it to St Werburgh. At Gloucester, doubtless to rival the abbey of St Peter's, they founded a new church, destined to be their own mausoleum, to which Æthelflæd had relics of St Oswald brought from Bardney. The movement of relics from eastern to western England, and the building of new churches in which to place them, were an important feature of Æthelflæd's policy of urbanisation: relics were clearly being used to create a sense of identity for each town.[23]

In the Danelaw, contrary to the usual perceptions of Viking paganism and savagery, many churches in central places seem to have survived unscathed, though often losing endowments.[24] The eastern Mercian and East Anglian sees, however, were disrupted, Leicester and Lindsey being merged and transferred to Dorchester-on-Thames, while Elmham and Dunwich were also merged and temporarily put under the control of the bishop of London in the first half of the tenth century. These dramatic diocesan disruptions, usually attributed to Viking hostility to the church, are more probably to be explained as a deliberate policy of the kings of Wessex, who would have been anxious to curb the

[20] Great Domesday, ff. 64c, 67d.

[21] In general on late Saxon nuns, see B. Yorke, 'Sisters under the skin', *Reading Medieval Studies*, 15 (1989), 95–117.

[22] Baker *et al.*, 'From Roman to medieval Worcester'.

[23] S. Bassett, 'Anglo-Saxon Shrewsbury and its churches', *Midland History*, 16 (1991), pp. 1–23, at 9; A. Thacker, 'Chester and Gloucester: early ecclesiastical organisation in two Mercian burhs', *N Hist.*, 18 (1982), 199–211, here 203–4; D. Rollason, *Saints and Relics in Anglo-Saxon England* (Oxford, 1989), pp. 153–4.

[24] Cf. R. A. Hall, 'The Five Boroughs of the Danelaw: a review of present knowledge', *Anglo-Saxon England*, 18 (1989), 149–206'; D. Hadley, 'Conquest, colonization and the Church: ecclesiastical organization in the Danelaw', *HR*, 69 (1996), 109–28, esp. 113.

influence of the Danish armies over the Church.[25] Furthermore, Danish settlers and their descendants certainly encouraged the foundation of numerous small local churches in the tenth and eleventh centuries, many of them urban. Scandinavian influence is visible in a wealth of Anglo-Scandinavian funerary sculpture and, later, in the name-forms preserved in inscriptions celebrating church foundation or rebuilding surviving from York and Lincoln.[26]

To discuss the impact of churches on the social and political life of towns in this period it is sensible to divide them into two groups: first, the major churches, that is the cathedrals, the monastic houses which had been reformed or newly founded in the tenth and eleventh centuries, and sizeable establishments of secular clerics such as those of St Werburgh's or St John's in Chester,[27] and, secondly, all the smaller churches.

Larger churches made an impact on the urban scene by virtue of their existence – they took up space – as well as through the influence their communities could exercise politically, jurisdictionally and economically. All major churches required large areas of land for their church buildings and graveyards and to house members of their communities and servants. This accommodation might, as in the cases of churches served by secular clerks in Shrewsbury and Chester, consist of separate houses, or alternatively of claustral buildings.[28] Although the use of the term immunity did not take root in England before the Conquest,[29] the idea that churches and their graveyards should be sanctuaries was recognised in Anglo-Saxon legislation, and fines for breach of sanctuary or *ciricgriþ* were graded according to the importance of the church concerned.[30] Evidence for how the spaces around churches were protected survives for Winchester.[31]

[25] J. Barrow, 'English cathedral communities and reform in the late tenth and the eleventh centuries', in D. Rollason, M. Harvey and M. Prestwich, eds., *Anglo-Norman Durham 1093–1193* (Woodbridge, 1994), pp. 25–39, here 26–9.

[26] Morris, *Churches in the Landscape*, pp. 169–73; J. Lang, *Corpus of Anglo-Saxon Stone Sculpture*, vol. III, *York and Eastern Yorkshire* (Oxford, 1991), pp. 53–120; E. Okasha, *Handlist of Anglo-Saxon Non-Runic Inscriptions* (Cambridge, 1971), pp. 92–3, 131.

[27] Great Domesday, ff. 263a–b; Thacker, 'Chester and Gloucester', pp. 201, 204; on secular minsters in general see J. Blair, 'Secular minster churches in Domesday Book', in P. H. Sawyer, ed., *Domesday Book* (London, 1985), pp. 104–42.

[28] Great Domesday, I ff. 252b, 253a, 263a–b; *Symeonis Monachi Opera Omnia*, ed. T. Arnold, (R S, 1882–5), vol. I, p. 113; D. Rollason, 'Symeon of Durham and the community of Durham in the eleventh century', in C. Hicks, ed., *England in the Eleventh Century* (Stamford, 1992), pp. 183–96 at 192–3.

[29] P. Wormald, 'Lordship and justice in the early English kingdom: Oswaldslow revisited', in W. Davies and P. Fouracre, eds., *Property and Power in the Early Middle Ages* (Cambridge, 1995), pp. 114–36; N. Hurnard, 'The Anglo-Norman franchises', *EHR*, 64 (1949), 289–323, 433–60.

[30] VIII Æthelred, c. 5.1, and Northumbrian Priests' Law, *c.* 19 (D. Whitelock, M. Brett and C. N. L. Brooke, eds., *Councils and Synods with Other Documents relating to the English Church 1* (Oxford, 1981), vol. I, pp. 390, 456; *Be griþe 7 be munde* (F. Liebermann, ed., *Die Gesetze der Angelsachsen* (Halle, 1903–16), vol. I, p. 471); see also literature cited at n. 54 below.

[31] F. Barlow, M. Biddle, O. von Feilitzen and D. J. Keene, *Winchester in the Early Middle Ages* (Winchester Studies, 1, Oxford, 1976), p. 308.

However, the size and shape of precincts were liable to alteration: Norwich Cathedral carved a large precinct for itself out of a previously inhabited part of the town from 1096; Christ Church Canterbury expanded its precinct by steady accretions in this period; Exeter's one, by contrast, seems to have shrunk; Worcester Cathedral redefined its precinct, probably under Bishop Oswald (961–92), to exclude lay settlement, and at Winchester large precincts were formed 963 x 970 under Bishop Æthelwold to accommodate the three principal churches.[32] Although these areas were walled or fenced this was not intended to exclude lay people completely; their presence, at any rate at important feasts, was welcomed. Many cathedrals and abbeys exercised pastoral care over some urban inhabitants: at Worcester, for example, it was normal in the eleventh century for the monks to preach to the townspeople.[33]

One of the most lucrative pastoral uses of precincts was burial; major churches often claimed a burial monopoly within the walls of a borough, and cathedrals would encourage richer people in the rest of the diocese to seek burial in their graveyards.[34] Sometimes, as we see from various documents of the eleventh century, lay people grouped together into guilds in association with a great church to provide burial and memorial services for each other; this was by no means an exclusively urban phenomenon, as some guilds (Abbotsbury and Bedwyn) were rural, but one guild, though rural, was associated with the minster in Exeter, one was based at Exeter and another at Cambridge (though in the latter case the church which received offerings for prayers was St Etheldreda's in Ely).[35]

Furthermore, major churches were very often powerful landlords within towns. To take some examples from Domesday, the bishop of Worcester had ninety houses, Bath Abbey had twenty-four burgesses, and the bishop of Hereford had ninety-eight houses in the time of King Edward. Bishops or abbeys might also control jurisdiction in parts of towns, and a few were allowed

[32] J. Campbell, 'Norwich', 8, in *BAHT*, II; Brooks, *Early History of the Church of Canterbury*, p. 15; W. Urry, *Canterbury under the Angevin Kings* (London, 1967), pp. 204–7; J. Allan, C. Henderson and R. Higham, 'Saxon Exeter', in Haslam, ed., *Anglo-Saxon Towns in Southern England*, p. 395; N. Baker and R. Holt, 'The city of Worcester in the tenth century', in N. P. Brooks and C. Cubitt, eds., *St Oswald of Worcester* (London, 1996), pp. 129–46 at 142–3; J. Barrow, 'The community of Worcester 961–*c*. 1100', in Brooks and Cubitt, eds., *St Oswald of Worcester* pp. 84–99; Barlow, Biddle, von Feilitzen and Keene, *Winchester in the Early Middle Ages*, p. 322 and fig. 9.

[33] William of Malmesbury, *Vita Wulfstani*, ed. R. R. Darlington (Camden Society, 3rd series, 40, 1928), pp. 13–14; E. Mason, *St Wulfstan of Worcester c. 1008–1095* (Oxford, 1990), pp. 67–8; G. Rosser, 'The cure of souls in English towns before 1000', in Blair and Sharpe, eds., *Pastoral Care before the Parish*, pp. 267–84; M. Franklin, 'The cathedral as parish church: the case of southern England', in D. Abulafia, M. Franklin and M. Rubin, eds., *Church and City 1000–1500: Essays in Honour of Christopher Brooke* (Cambridge, 1992), pp. 173–98.

[34] J. Barrow, 'Urban cemetery location in the high middle ages', in Bassett, ed., *Death in Towns*, pp. 78–100; B. Kjølbye-Biddle, 'Dispersal or concentration: the disposal of the Winchester dead over 2000 years', in *ibid*., pp. 210–47, esp. 224–33.

[35] G. Rosser, 'The Anglo-Saxon gilds', in Blair, ed., *Minsters and Parish Churches*, pp. 31–4.

to employ their own moneyer.[36] York was one of the few large towns where churchmen had extensive powers: here, according to Domesday and another late eleventh-century text, *The Rights and Customs of the Archbishops of York*, the archbishop controlled one of the shires (equivalent to wards) into which the town was divided in the late eleventh century. He also had a share of tolls.[37] Canon law texts connected with the diocese of York in the eleventh century further illustrate the extent to which bishops might regulate the activities of townsmen: the *Northumbrian Priests' Law* (chapters 55–6) proscribed travel and trade on Sundays but specified that travelling on the eves of feasts was permissible within a certain radius of York in times of hostility. The treatise known as *Episcopus* (chapter 6) tells bishops to take responsibility for checking measures and weigh-beams in boroughs, and even though its prescriptions are drawn from much older continental canon law collections, its language suggests that it had contemporary and local validity.[38] Elsewhere in England the powers of ecclesiastics were more limited either because royal power was more extensive or because urban settlements associated with bishops were too small to be significant.

Smaller churches, though in a different way, made their presence felt in towns. In comparison with most of the rest of Europe, medieval English towns were unusually rich in parish churches, and this has sometimes been seen as a specifically English phenomenon,[39] but a similar state of affairs prevailed in Denmark and towns of Scandinavian origin in Ireland, especially Dublin. Plurality of parishes was not true of all English towns, but only of those which became decisively urbanised before the mid-eleventh century.[40] Although documentary evidence for most of these churches is very sparse before Domesday (and often for some time thereafter), archaeological evidence, where available, shows that most were founded over the period *c.* 950–*c.* 1100. St Mark's, Lincoln, was built originally in the tenth century as a one-celled wooden structure; St Helen's on the Walls, York, was also of tenth-century origin.[41] The mushrooming of churches can be related in part to the relative size of towns in the eleventh century: by 1200 London (about 110) had between two and three times as many as Winchester (57), York (over 40), Norwich (57) and Lincoln (48), each of which had about two or three times as many as the towns with the next largest

[36] Cf. Great Domesday ff. 173c, 89d, 181c.

[37] D. M. Palliser, *Domesday York* (Borthwick Paper, 78, York, 1990), p. 28.

[38] Whitelock, Brett and Brooke, eds., *Councils and Synods* I, pp. 463–4, 419.

[39] C. N. L. Brooke, 'The missionary at home: the Church in the towns 1000–1250', *Studies in Church History*, 6 (1970), 59–83.

[40] Morris, *Churches in the Landscape*, p. 169; cf. also J. Campbell, 'The Church in Anglo-Saxon towns', in J. Campbell, *Essays in Anglo-Saxon History* (London, 1986), pp. 139–54.

[41] B. J. J. Gilmour and D. A. Stocker, *St Mark's Church and Cemetery* (The Archaeology of Lincoln, 13/1, 1986); J. R. Magilton, *The Church of St Helen-on-the-Walls, Aldwark* (The Archaeology of York, 10/1, 1980), p. 18.

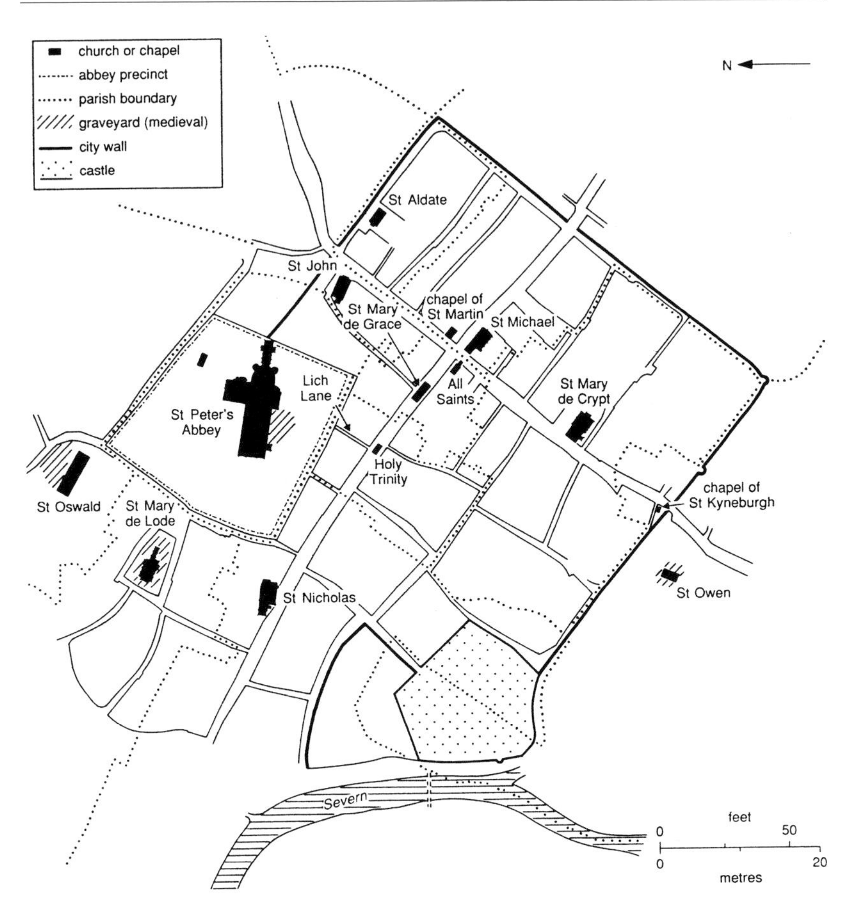

Figure 7.1 The churches and graveyards of twelfth-century Gloucester
Sources: Julia Barrow, 'Urban cemetery location in the high middle ages', in S. Bassett, ed., *Death in Towns* (Leicester, 1992), p. 85.

numbers of parish churches, Exeter (22), Oxford (20), Bristol (18) and Huntingdon (16). There were rather fewer parish churches in Gloucester (11), Worcester (10), Chester (9 parishes; a tenth, first recorded 1224, is probably earlier), Northampton (9) and Hereford (6 parishes, one of them based in the cathedral) (Figures 7.1, 7.2 and 7.3).[42] However, demographic factors, though important, were not the only ones which counted: the extent to which pre-existing churches could retain control over new foundations was significant too. Older churches were more successful in doing this in western Mercia, Wessex and Kent than their counterparts in eastern England. One sign of this is the fact

[42] Cf. Morris, *Churches in the Landscape*, pp. 178, 188, 191; some of the figures have been altered.

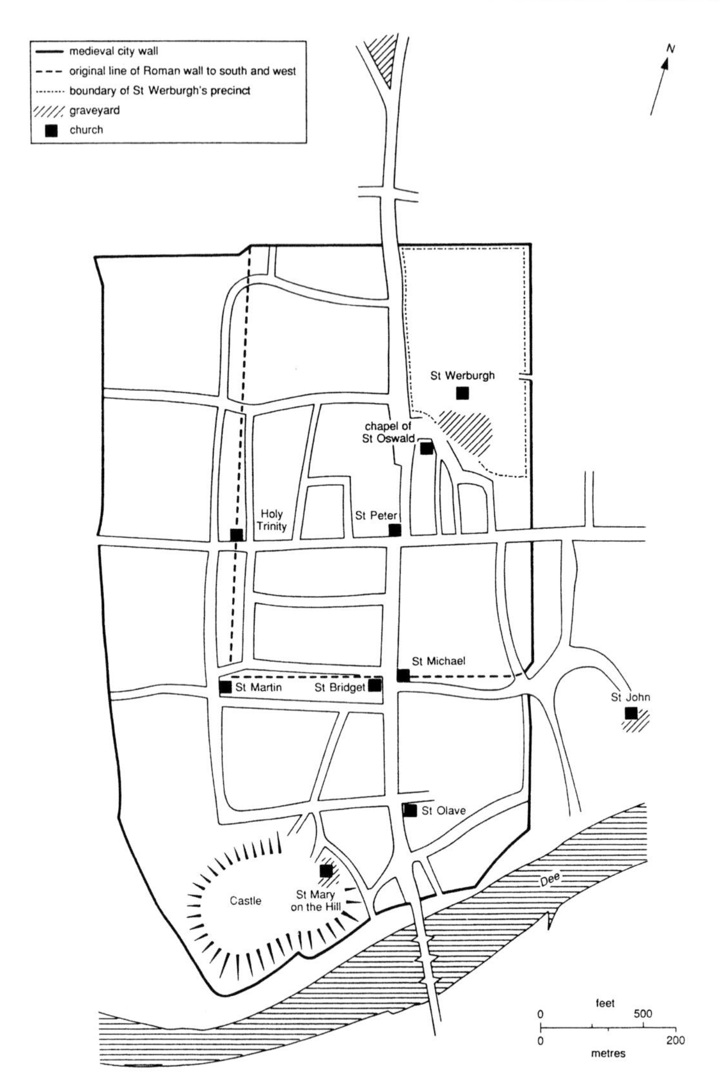

Figure 7.2 The churches and graveyards of medieval Chester
Sources: Julia Barrow, 'Urban cemetery location in the high middle ages', in S. Bassett, ed., *Death in Towns* (Leicester, 1992), p. 83.

that many small churches founded in eastern towns in the tenth and eleventh centuries were laid out from the start in extensive graveyards, which meant that they were independent of the parochial authority of any other church in the town. Small intramural churches in Wessex and western Mercia, by contrast, often lacked burial rights until late in the middle ages, being subordinate in parochial terms to the (usually) oldest church in the town; they were often sited on

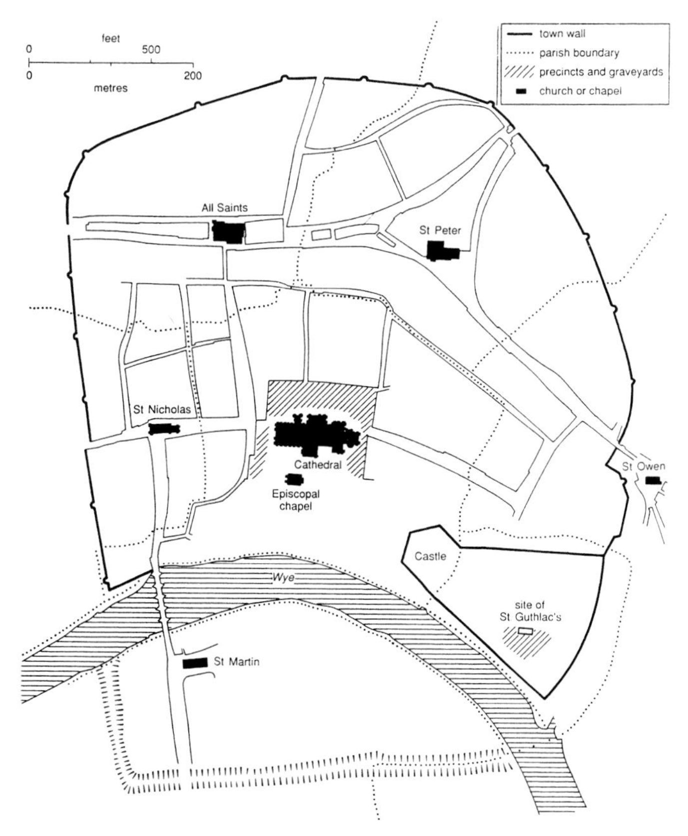

Figure 7.3 The churches, parishes and graveyards of medieval Hereford
Sources: Julia Barrow, 'Urban cemetery location in the high middle ages', in S. Bassett, ed., *Death in Towns* (Leicester, 1992), p. 82.

street corners or at or even on top of gateways, sites which afforded them prominence without the expense of a graveyard.

Gate churches still exist in Bristol, and in the eleventh and twelfth centuries churches near or on gates were to be found in Chester, Oxford, Canterbury and Gloucester.[43] London perhaps had churches near gates before the Conquest. They might, according to Jeremy Haslam, represent an early stage of parish creation since their parishes were often both extramural and intramural; they may

[43] N. Alldridge, 'Aspects of the topography of early medieval Chester', *J of the Chester Arch. Soc.*, 64 (1981), pp. 5–31 at 17, 28; B. Durham, C. Halpin and N. Palmer, 'Oxford's northern defences', *Oxoniensia*, 48 (1983), 13–40 at 14–18, 33; P. Blockley, 'Excavations at Riding Gate, Canterbury', *Archaeologia Cantiana*, 107 (1989), 117–54 at 136–7; 'Interim report on work carried out in 1988 by the Canterbury Archaeological Trust', *Archaeologia Cantiana*, 106 (1988), 129–97 at 161–8; Heighway, 'Anglo-Saxon Gloucester', p. 11.

perhaps have been founded as the religious counterpart of the wards into which burgesses were divided for urban defence.[44] However, in most towns they are not earlier than the eleventh century, and in any case they were swiftly joined by other churches, making the eventual pattern of parish boundaries in each town untidy. Several urban churches, like St Martin's, Oxford, may have originated as private chapels in the *hagae* of noblemen;[45] others, according to archaeological evidence, were founded on the sites of what had been small houses or workshops, like All Saints, Oxford, and St Nicholas Shambles and St Nicholas Acon in London.[46] Evidence for founders and owners of such churches is rare in western areas of England before the twelfth century, but richer in eastern areas, where we have inscriptions for a few churches in York and Lincoln and some information in Domesday Book. Domesday entries for Huntingdon and Ipswich show several churches changing hands frequently in the eleventh and early twelfth centuries, being bought and sold by priests and by landholders and burgesses of both sexes.[47] The *Northumbrian Priests' Law* proscribed such sales.[48] Clearly small churches were well integrated into the economic and social fabric of boroughs long before the late eleventh century.

Churches also played a major role in the tenth and eleventh centuries in the development of small towns which were able to achieve the status of boroughs in the late eleventh and the twelfth centuries. Perhaps the commonest starting point for the growth of these towns was the existence of a rural cathedral such as Wells or of a major monastic house such as St Albans.[49] It is possible that in Scotland and Wales those churches which were focal points for pilgrimage and for royal burial encouraged small settlements in this period.[50] An important advantage enjoyed by churches in encouraging urban growth was their right to claim that the area within a certain radius of the church was sanctuary: this is well documented for Wales where the concept of *nawdd* (protection) was 'territorialised' as *noddfa* (sanctuary) in Welsh laws, and for the North of England, where areas of sanctuary (*griþ*) around major churches such as Hexham,

[44] J. Haslam, 'Parishes, churches, wards and gates in eastern London', in Blair, ed., *Minsters and Parish Churches*, pp. 35–43.

[45] E.g. St Martin's, Oxford: *VCH*, Oxfordshire, IV, p. 384.

[46] T. G. Hassall *et al.*, 'Excavations at Oxford 1973–4: sixth and final interim report', *Oxoniensia*, 39 (1974), 54–7; A. Vince, *Saxon London* (London, 1990), pp. 72–3; R. Fleming, 'Rural elites and urban communities in late Saxon England', *P&P*, 141 (1993), 3–37 at 31–2.

[47] Great Domesday, ff. 208a, and Little Domesday, f. 290a–b; cf. Campbell, 'The Church in Anglo-Saxon towns', pp. 149–50.

[48] Whitelock, Brett and Brooke, eds., *Councils and Synods*, I, p. 452, drawing on Theodulf's *Capitula*, c. XVI.

[49] W. J. Rodwell, 'Wells, the cathedral and city', *Current Archaeology*, 73 (1980), 42–3; Great Domesday, I, f. 135c.

[50] A. Macquarrie, 'Early Christian religious houses in Scotland: foundation and function', in Blair and Sharpe, eds., *Pastoral Care before the Parish*, pp. 110–33 at 121, 132; and H. Pryce, 'Pastoral care in early medieval Wales', in *ibid.*, pp. 41–62 at 60, 45.

Durham, Ripon and Beverley were confirmed in twelfth-century and later charters.[51] The area under protection might be divided into zones of increasing penalty for committing crimes within the sanctuary as one moved towards the church, the outermost zone being marked with crosses. Evidence for Scottish examples of sanctuary is very scanty, but St Andrews, Brechin and Dunkeld (to take a few examples) might have resembled Irish monastic towns in this respect as they did in others. The concept of *ciricgriþ* or sanctuary survived the Norman Conquest in monastic towns not only in northern England but also in the South, though here the terminology current in France, *leuca* or *leuga* ('league') was adopted. Domesday Book shows that Bury St Edmunds had between 1066 and 1086 used much of its *leuca* to house its own knights, merchants and craftsmen.[52] Battle Abbey, newly founded by William I to give thanks for his victory, was granted its own *leuga*, within which it settled inhabitants in 'house-sites with fixed dimensions' (*certis dimensionibus mansiones*) before the early years of the reign of Henry I, when a rental was compiled.[53] Areas protected by sanctuary were favoured sites for markets;[54] not surprisingly, therefore, several abbeys and minsters set up market places in this period, sometimes with streets and house-plots.[55]

(iii) CHURCHES IN TOWNS 1100–1300

In this period the network of churches reached its widest extent before the nineteenth century, both because of new foundations in existing towns and because many new towns were set up, usually with their own churches; in addition to this process of consolidation, churches developed new forms of outreach into the urban community.

Up to about the middle of the twelfth century, the creation of new parish churches continued vigorously. Many existing towns were extended, often with large new market places, and churches might be set up nearby, as in Bristol or Nottingham, or actually in the market place, as in Norwich (St Peter Mancroft)

[51] W. Davies, 'Adding insult to injury', in W. Davies and P. Fouracre, eds., *Property and Power* (Cambridge, 1995), p. 144; D. Hall, 'The sanctuary of St Cuthbert', in G. Bonner, C. Stancliffe and D. Rollason, eds., *St Cuthbert, his Cult and his Community to A.D. 1200* (Woodbridge, 1989), pp. 425–36; see also G. Rosser, 'Sanctuary and social negotiation in medieval England', in J. Blair and B. Golding, eds., *The Cloister and the World* (Oxford, 1996), pp. 57–79.

[52] Little Domesday, II, f. 372a; see also M. D. Lobel, 'The ecclesiastical banleuca in England', in *Oxford Essays in Medieval History Presented to H. E. Salter* (Oxford, 1934), pp. 122–40.

[53] *The Chronicle of Battle Abbey*, ed. E. Searle (Oxford, 1980) pp. 50–1 and also 52–8.

[54] Cf. literature cited by Barrow, 'Urban cemetery location', pp. 91–3.

[55] G. Astill, 'The towns of Berkshire', in Haslam, ed., *Anglo-Saxon Towns in Southern England*, pp. 53–86 at 73–4; W. J. Rodwell, 'Wells, the cathedral and city', *Current Archaeology*, 73 (1980), 42–3; J. N. Croom, 'The topographical analysis of medieval town plans: the examples of Much Wenlock and Bridgnorth', *Midland History*, 17 (1992), 16–38 at 27, on Much Wenlock.

and Hereford (St Peter's and All Saints).[56] Church dedications, where they can be combined with archaeological and architectural evidence, are helpful in pinpointing the dates of new foundations: the very end of the eleventh and the twelfth centuries saw an inrush of Nicholases, Lawrences, Leonards, Giles, Mary Magdalens, Margarets and Catherines.[57] Of course, dedications were quite often altered, but none the less new ones frequently occur in churches which have no fabric earlier than the twelfth century. One dedication hitherto unknown in England was combined with an architectural form, also hitherto unknown in England, in the round churches dedicated to Holy Sepulchre in Northampton and Cambridge, which reflect the impact of the Crusades.[58] After *c.* 1150 the formation of new parishes more or less ceased: by now the process was strictly under the control of the local diocesan, who was usually unwilling to disturb the rights of existing parishes unless there were pressing reasons for doing so.[59] Some non-parochial chapels were built, but on the whole the energies of lay benefactors were channelled into rebuilding existing churches: many urban parish churches were rebuilt in the twelfth century and further enlarged, often with aisles and side chapels, in the thirteenth.

For great churches in towns too, it was a time of consolidation and ever bigger and better building. The last quarter of the eleventh century and the opening of the twelfth saw the replacement of most major Anglo-Saxon churches with Romanesque models, characterised by length and uninterrupted vistas. To obtain the space necessary for the new churches with their much larger floorplans, neighbouring buildings had to be sacrificed, and the older fashion of having groups or pairs of churches together, as for example St Peter's and St Mary's at Worcester and New Minster and Old Minster at Winchester, was abandoned. The monks of New Minster moved to a new site just outside Winchester at Hyde, and at Worcester Bishop Wulfstan pulled down Oswald's church of St Mary and replaced it; the old cathedral of St Peter's at Worcester also disappeared, though its precise fate is uncertain.[60] The Normans, shocked to find many cathedrals in settlements little better than villages, moved sees to urban centres,[61] sometimes without creating adequate space for them. In the late twelfth century Lincoln Cathedral outgrew its quarters within the old Roman walled area and spread

[56] Cf. literature cited by Barrow, 'Urban cemetery location', p. 92 n. 80, to which add M. Barley and I. F. Straw, 'Nottingham', p. 3, in *BAHT*, I.

[57] F. Arnold Forster, *Studies in Church Dedications or England's Patron Saints*, 3 vols. (London, 1899); discussion in A. Binns, *Dedications of Monastic Houses in England and Wales 1066–1216* (Woodbridge, 1989), esp. pp. 22–31.

[58] RCHM (England), *An Inventory of the Historical Monuments in the City of Cambridge* (London, 1959), vol. II, pp. 255–6; and RCHM (England), *An Inventory of Archaeological Sites and Churches in Northampton* (London, 1985), pp. 59–61.

[59] Brooke, 'The missionary at home', pp. 72–3.

[60] Barlow, Biddle, von Feilitzen and Keene, *Winchester in the Early Middle Ages*, pp. 308–12, 317; Philip Barker, *A Short Architectural History of Worcester Cathedral* (Worcester, 1994), pp. 11–35.

[61] Frank Barlow, *The English Church, 1066–1154* (London, 1979), pp. 47–8.

along the ridge of the hill;[62] Salisbury Cathedral had no room to expand on its hilltop in Old Sarum and its canons plotted an escape to the flat water-meadows below, where they could build on a scale rivalling Wells and Winchester: they won permission to do this in March 1219, and rushed to build their new cathedral, together with a carefully laid out new town.[63]

The period 1100–1300 was an active one for urban formation in Britain, above all in Scotland and Wales which had not hitherto seen urbanisation on any serious scale. Royal burghal foundations in Scotland, for which the peak period was the twelfth century, tended to acquire a parish church at the outset, as in the cases of Perth, Edinburgh (St Giles), and Stirling (Holy Rude); at Perth, it is possible that an existing church was taken over by the burgh, perhaps with a change of site, while at Edinburgh and Stirling the new settlements were quickly detached from the older parishes (St Cuthbert's under the Castle and St Ninian's) within which their sites had lain.[64] Episcopal burghs were more variable: at St Andrews there was a parish church by 1144, but until the late middle ages it lay in the cathedral precinct rather than in the town, while in Glasgow, which only started to become truly urbanised in the final quarter of the twelfth century, part of the cathedral served as the parish church.[65] The much smaller burghs of barony were often unable to create parishes for themselves or to persuade existing parish churches to move into the built-up area. In Wales new boroughs usually grew up next to castles, but they themselves might be built near old *clas* churches, such as Carmarthen. Quite commonly, *clas* churches lying in or near new towns would be converted into Benedictine or Augustinian priories (for example, Carmarthen, turned first into a cell of Battle Abbey and then into an Augustinian priory), or new priories might be founded, as at Brecon and Cardigan. Parish churches for the inhabitants were usually established separately, though at Cardigan the priory church served a double purpose.[66] A characteristic of towns newly founded in the twelfth century, or newly attaining urban status then, is that they had no more than two or three and sometimes only one parish church in the middle ages. Where there was only one this might, however, be large, with numerous side chapels which would to some extent compensate for the lack of other churches. New towns would be more likely to have more

[62] P. Kidson, 'Architectural history', in D. Owen, ed., *A History of Lincoln Minster* (Cambridge, 1994), pp. 14–46 at 26–7.

[63] T. Cocke and P. Kidson, *Salisbury Cathedral: Perspectives on the Architectural History* (London, 1993); RCHM (England), *Ancient and Historical Monuments in the City of Salisbury*, vol. I (London, 1980), pp. xxxii–xl at xxxii.

[64] I. B. Cowan, 'The emergence of the urban parish', in M. Lynch, M. Spearman and G. Stell, eds., *The Scottish Medieval Town* (Edinburgh, 1988), pp. 82–98, here 90, 92.

[65] *Ibid.*, p. 87; N. F. Shead, 'Glasgow: an ecclesiastical burgh', in Lynch, Spearman and Stell, eds., *The Scottish Medieval Town*, pp. 116–32 at 122.

[66] R. A. Griffiths, *Conquerors and Conquered in Medieval Wales* (Stroud, 1994), pp. 173–4, 176, 178, 280–2; F. G. Cowley, *The Monastic Order in South Wales 1066–1349* (Cardiff, 1977), pp. 13–14.

than one parish if there were a pre-existing church or if there were a castle with its own liberty for which a separate church might be created.[67]

The roles played by religious houses in towns became more varied during the twelfth and thirteenth centuries. Long-established abbeys and cathedrals continued to be, as they had always been, landlords and consumers. Their activities as urban landlords began now to be better documented as more and more land transactions in towns came to be recorded in charters. In several of the larger towns, major churches claimed jurisdiction over particular areas or particular inhabitants, as for example Hereford Cathedral.[68] In those small towns which owed their existence to the stimulus of a monastic house or a cathedral (for example, Abingdon, Reading, Sherborne, Cirencester, Glastonbury, Bury St Edmunds, Peterborough, St Albans and Salisbury), there was no possibility open to the burgesses of appeal to a rival lord, and although many of these towns received charters from their ecclesiastical lords the liberties granted were usually restricted: for example the abbot or bishop might demand the right to veto officials chosen by the burgesses, or insist on having his own official preside over the borough court. Relations between the two sides would break down periodically, sometimes leading to violence, though usually only on a small scale.[69] Major churches might often be minor landlords in towns other than those in which they were sited: David I granted to several Scottish abbeys one or two messuages each in different towns, usually including Berwick and Roxburgh. Dunfermline Abbey acquired messuages from David in Berwick, Edinburgh, Stirling, Dunfermline and Perth, and tofts from William the Lion in Kinghorn and Montrose.[70]

The diversity of religious provision in towns (as also in the countryside) increased markedly from the end of the eleventh century onwards. Hospitals, not exclusively, but none the less overwhelmingly, an urban phenomenon, were founded in ever-increasing numbers from the late eleventh century onwards, with hundreds existing by 1300.[71] At first essentially the work of great men such

[67] Cf. Salisbury: RHCM, *City of Salisbury*, p. xxxviii; Berwick: Cowan, 'The emergence of the urban parish', p. 91; Bridgnorth: Croom, 'The topographical analysis', 21.

[68] G. Rosser, 'Conflict and community in the medieval town: disputes between clergy and laity in Hereford', in T. R. Slater and G. Rosser, eds., *The Church in the Medieval Town* (Aldershot, 1998), 20–42, esp. 23–5.

[69] N. M. Trenholme, *The English Monastic Boroughs* (University of Missouri Studies, 2, no. 3, 1927); *VCH*, Wiltshire, VI, pp. 94–5; cf. also D. G. Shaw, *The Creation of a Community: The City of Wells in the Middle Ages* (Oxford, 1993).

[70] *Registrum de Dunfermelyn: Liber Cartarum Abbatie Benedictine Sacrosancte Trinitatis et Beate Margarete Regine de Dunfermelyn* (Bannatyne Club, Edinburgh, 1842), pp. 3–4, 32–3, 37; Wendy Stevenson, 'The monastic presence: Berwick in the twelfth and thirteenth centuries', in Lynch, Spearman and Stell, eds., *The Scottish Medieval Town*, pp. 99–115 at 99–100.

[71] See R. M. Clay, *The Medieval Hospitals of England* (London, 1909); R. Gilchrist, 'Christian bodies and souls: the archaeology of life and death in later medieval hospitals', in Bassett, ed., *Death in Towns*, pp. 101–18.

as Henry of Blois (St Cross, Winchester, 1136) or Rahere (St Bartholomew's, London, 1123), by the middle of the twelfth century they were also being founded by burgesses such as Aslac of Killinghow, whose Hospital of St Mary the Virgin, Westgate, Newcastle-upon-Tyne, was founded before 1155. At the end of the twelfth century the money-lender Gervase of Southampton founded God's House, Southampton. St Ethelbert's Hospital, Hereford, was founded in the 1220s by a well-to-do cleric, Elias of Bristol, a canon of Hereford.[72] About a quarter of all hospitals were leper houses and most of the rest catered for the aged and infirm; the leper houses tended to be built at a distance of two or three miles outside towns, the rest often on the periphery of urban settlement.[73] Hospitals usually stood in precincts, within which accommodation would be provided separately for the brothers or sisters serving the house and for the inmates, who would sleep in long dormitories, a feature which influenced hospital plans down to the twentieth century. Dormitories were usually intended to serve simultaneously as chapels, and thus normally had an altar at one end, although in the infirmary building of St Leonard's Hospital, York, as rebuilt in the mid-thirteenth century, the chapels protruded laterally.[74]

Some new religious orders were introduced into England, Scotland and Wales particularly with towns in mind. The earliest of these was the order of Augustinian canons; although by the late twelfth century its houses in England were predominantly rural, many of its earliest foundations in England, during the reign of Henry I, were urban, particularly in those shire towns lacking Benedictine foundations or cathedrals. Very often they would take over pre-existing minsters of secular clerks (for example, the minster in Cirencester, St Frideswide's in Oxford and St Oswald's in Gloucester). The original purpose behind such foundations may perhaps have been to encourage the canons to assist with pastoral care in towns, though if so it was unsuccessful, for the care of souls was usually quickly delegated to vicars and chaplains. By the middle of the twelfth century some of these urban Augustinian houses were moving into the countryside to take advantage of better sites; these however often lay very near towns, allowing the canons to take a strong interest in urban life, which they were the more inclined to do since a large part of their revenues was made up of urban rents.[75] In Scotland and Wales Augustinian foundations sometimes served as the nuclei of new towns: for example, Edinburgh's Holyrood established the burgh of Canongate, 1128, and

[72] *Early Deeds Relating to Newcastle upon Tyne*, ed. A. M. Oliver (Surtees Society, 137, 1924), pp. 9–11; *The Cartulary of God's House, Southampton*, ed. J. M. Kaye (Southampton Records Series, 19, 20, 1976), vol. 1, pp. xxv–xxxi; for St Ethelbert's, Hereford, see *Charters and Records of Hereford Cathedral*, ed. W. W. Capes (Hereford, 1908), pp. 56–61.

[73] Gilchrist, 'Christian bodies and souls', pp. 100, 115–16.

[74] P. H. Cullum, 'St Leonard's Hospital, York: the spatial and social analysis of an Augustinian Hospital', in R. Gilchrist and H. Mytum, eds., *Advances in Monastic Archaeology* (British Archaeological Reports, British Series, 227, 1993), pp. 11–18, here 16.

[75] D. Postles, 'The Austin canons in English towns, *c.* 1100–1350', *Historical Research*, 66 (1993), 1–20.

St Andrews Cathedral community became Augustinian, and established its burgh *c.* 1150.

Orders of friars were almost exclusively urban, not only in original intention but also in continued practice (Map 7.1). The Dominicans and Franciscans began to found houses in England from the 1220s and in other parts of Britain soon after;[76] they and two other orders of mendicants, the Carmelites and the Augustinians, which came into being somewhat later, achieved considerable popularity in England, where, by 1300, nine towns, Cambridge, Lincoln, London, Lynn, Newcastle-upon-Tyne, Norwich, Oxford, Winchester and York, had houses of each of these four orders, while twenty-seven towns had houses of both Dominicans and Franciscans. This was also true of Cardiff, and in Scotland the chief burghs had two or three friaries each.[77] These houses were almost exclusively male: convents of mendicant nuns were rare in Britain, were not necessarily urban and, with the exception of the short-lived Franciscan house at Northampton (1252–72), began to be founded only at the very end of the thirteenth century; none was established in Scotland before the late fifteenth century.

Kings and magnates were prominent among the benefactors of mendicant houses: all the London friaries received generous grants from Henry III and Edward I, while the Perth Blackfriars was founded by Alexander II and was closely associated with the Scottish royal dynasty. Convents of friars would be sited either immediately outside the walls or on remaining empty spaces just inside them, as at Chester, for example;[78] indeed the siting of friaries is a fairly good guide to the extent of closely built-up settlement in the thirteenth century. Their precincts would provide space for large graveyards, for friars frequently were prepared to bury the poor cheaply or even for nothing, while the rich might choose to be buried in mendicant cemeteries for pious motives.[79] By the end of the thirteenth century the mendicants were beginning to introduce a distinctive new form of church into Britain, which gave more space for congregations listening to sermons.[80] By this time they had become sufficiently

[76] D. Knowles and R. N. Hadcock, *Medieval Religious Houses*, 2nd edn (London, 1971); W. A. Hinnebusch, *The Early English Friars Preachers* (Rome, 1951); L. Butler, 'The houses of the mendicant orders in Britain: recent archaeological work', in P. V. Addyman and V. E. Black, eds., *Archaeological Papers from York Presented to M. W. Barley* (York, 1984), pp. 123–36; Barrie Dobson, 'Mendicant ideal and practice in late medieval York', in *ibid.*, pp. 109–22.

[77] Knowles and Hadcock, *Medieval Religious Houses*; Butler, 'The houses', p. 124; and cf. Dobson, 'Mendicant ideal and practice', p. 111, who lists the thirteen English towns which had four or more friaries by the Dissolution.

[78] S. W. Ward, 'The monastic topography of Chester', in Gilchrist and Mytum, eds., *Advances in Monastic Archaeology*, pp. 113–26; cf also R. B. Harbottle, 'Excavations at the Carmelite Friary, Newcastle upon Tyne, 1965 and 1967', *Archaeologia Aeliana*, 4th series, 46 (1968), 163–223.

[79] S. Bassett, C. Dyer and R. Holt, 'Introduction', in Bassett, ed., *Death in Towns*, pp. 6–7; Dobson, 'Mendicant ideal and practice', p. 116.

[80] Butler, 'The houses', pp. 129–31, with literature cited; Ward, 'The monastic topography of Chester', pp. 120–1.

well established to undertake large-scale building enterprises, mostly for themselves but sometimes with a wider impact on the community at large, for example conduits.[81]

(iv) SCHOOLS

Before the end of the eleventh century there does not seem to have been a strong link between schools and towns. Religious communities would run schools for their own inmates, male or female, who would, whether as child-oblates in reformed Benedictine monasteries, or as the sons of married clergy in secular minsters, be educated within the precinct.[82] The two most prominent schools in late Anglo-Saxon England, those of Old Minster in Winchester and Christ Church in Canterbury, happened to be urban, but this was coincidental. More personal, less institutional forms of education existed also: some Anglo-Saxon legislation suggests that a priest could take on the training of a young clerk as a personal responsibility, and a similar system seems to have survived well into the twelfth century in remote parts of Wales, to judge from a charter of Bishop David of St Davids (1148–76).[83]

From about 1100, however, schools in an urban context begin to be referred to in large numbers in England, and in much smaller numbers from the middle of the twelfth century in Scotland. During the course of the twelfth century it is likely that nearly every shire town or town of equivalent size and many smaller ones in England acquired schools, while in Scotland there was a parallel development at Perth, Stirling, Roxburgh, Linlithgow and St Andrews.[84] The schools in question were all associated with major churches, whether cathedrals, monasteries or minsters, but by the early twelfth century pupils no longer formed an integral part of male communities and in most cases were not intending to join them (nunneries, by contrast, continued to provide education within the cloister). Schools were therefore often held outside the precinct. Schools attached to male monastic houses were not run by a member of the community, but by a schoolmaster appointed by the monks. A similar process occurred in secular cathedrals between the middle of the twelfth century and *c.* 1200, as the title of the dignitary in charge of the schools switched from *magister scholarum* to

[81] C. J. Bond, 'Water management in the urban monastery', in Gilchrist and Mytum, eds., *Advances in Monastic Archaeology*, pp. 43–78 at 57–63.

[82] Cf. *The Waltham Chronicle*, ed. L. Watkiss and M. Chibnall (Oxford, 1994), p. 20.

[83] Whitelock, Brett and Brooke, eds., *Councils and Synods*, I, pp. 318 and cf. 424, 426; *St Davids Episcopal Acta, 1085–1280*, ed. J. Barrow (South Wales Record Society, 13, 1998), pp. 53–4.

[84] N. Orme, *English Schools in the Middle Ages* (London, 1973), p. 170; on Perth and Stirling, *Registrum de Dunfermelyn*, pp. 56–7, nos. 93, 94; on Roxburgh, Scottish RO, Papal Bulls, no. 3 (Lucius III, 25 March) and, on Linlithgow and St Andrews, *Liber Cartarum Prioratus Sancti Andree in Scotia* (Bannatyne Club, Edinburgh, 1841), pp. 63, 316–18.

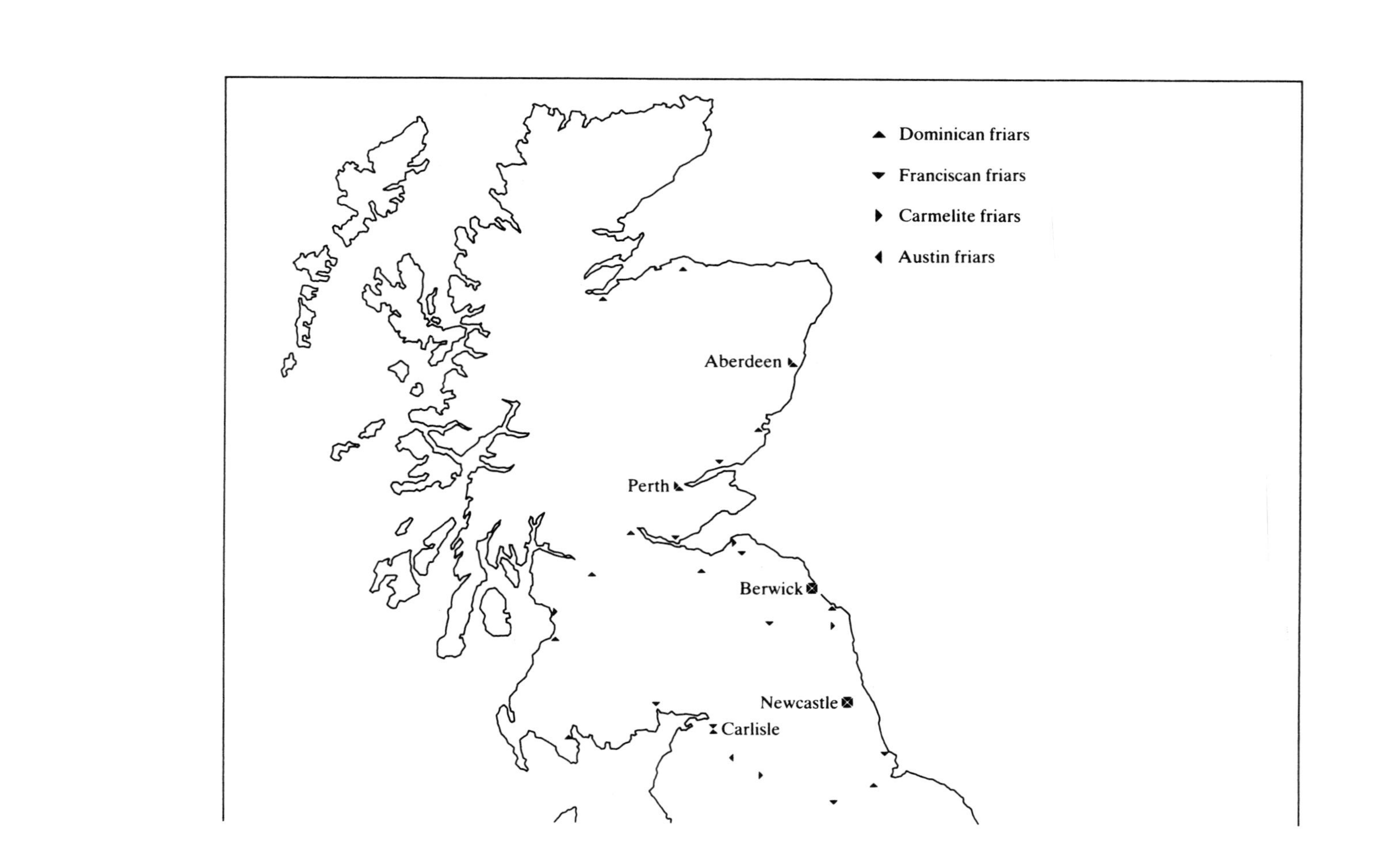
Dominican friars
Franciscan friars
Carmelite friars
Austin friars
Aberdeen
Perth
Berwick
Newcastle
Carlisle

Map 7.1 The four main orders of friars in British towns
Source: Janet Burton, *Monastic and Religious Orders in Britain, 1000–1300* (Cambridge 1994), pp. 116–17.

chancellor, reflecting, very often, a shift in duties away from teaching to appointing the schoolmaster.[85] Since much of the surviving evidence for the existence of schools in the twelfth century consists of charters sought by monasteries from bishops to confirm their monopoly over schools in particular towns, it is clear that providing education brought profits. Pupils would have been drawn not only from towns but also from the countryside, for they often had to board. The main motive for establishing schools in towns may well have been the availability of lodgings, either rented from townspeople, or hostels provided charitably for poor scholars, for example by Abbot Samson of Bury.[86]

Most of these schools would have concentrated on Latin grammar, but several, above all the cathedral schools, taught all the liberal arts with theology and occasionally medicine and law, for example, Lincoln, Salisbury and Hereford.[87] During the second half of the twelfth century, the schools of Northampton (from the 1170s) and of Oxford (from the late 1180s, but essentially only after about 1190) developed into higher schools.[88] Since, for most of this period, higher schools rented rooms from churches and other landlords and possessed few movables, they could easily pack up and move to other surroundings in times of trouble. The early school of Oxford, which seems to have grown out of the gatherings of clerics at ecclesiastical legal disputes, rather than out of a school dependent on a single monastery, had few ties. In 1209 its scholars fled to Cambridge as a protest against the summary hanging of two students, and likewise in 1238 and again in the 1260s scholars left Oxford for Northampton.[89] However, the especial suitability of Oxford as a place to study canon law (because ecclesiastical disputes were commonly heard there) ensured its reinstatement in 1214, while equally the fact that the archdeacons of Ely, and probably also the bishops, held their courts in Cambridge preserved the Cambridge schools after 1214.[90] During the thirteenth century, although many Oxford scholars found lodgings independently (they were called 'chamberdeacons'), the practice of lodging in a hall run by a master of arts became common. During the second

[85] D. Greenway, 'The false *Institutio* of St Osmund', in D. Greenway, C. Holdsworth and J. Sayers, eds., *Tradition and Change: Essays in Honour of Marjorie Chibnall* (Cambridge, 1985), pp. 77–101 at 85.

[86] *The Chronicle of Jocelin of Brakelond*, ed. H. E. Butler (London and Edinburgh, 1949), p. 45; Orme, *English Schools in the Middle Ages*, p. 178.

[87] R. W. Hunt, 'English learning in the late twelfth century', *TRHS*, 4th series, 19 (1936), 19–42; T. Webber, *Scribes and Scholars at Salisbury Cathedral* (Oxford, 1992).

[88] H. G. Richardson, 'The schools of Northampton in the twelfth century', *EHR*, 56 (1941), 595–605; R. W. Southern, 'From schools to university', in J. I. Catto, ed., *The History of the University of Oxford*, vol. I: *The Early Oxford Schools* (Oxford, 1984), pp. 1–36, esp. 12–17.

[89] Richardson, 'The schools of Northampton', 597; D. R. Leader, *A History of the University of Cambridge*, vol. I: *The University to 1546* (Cambridge, 1988), pp. 16–19.

[90] J. A. Brundage, 'The Cambridge faculty of canon law and the ecclesiastical courts of Ely', in P. Zutshi, ed., *Medieval Cambridge: Essays on the Pre-Reformation University* (Woodbridge, 1993), pp. 21–45.

half of the thirteenth century the earliest colleges were endowed, but as yet these had little impact on the student population.[91]

(v) LITERACY IN TOWNS

While the extent of literacy in towns was doubtless still rather limited in this period (indeed the schools which have just been discussed may well have catered more for the sons of rural landowners than for those of prosperous townspeople), the interest shown in the written word by townsmen and townswomen from the twelfth century onwards was considerable, and tangible evidence for it survives in the charters which they issued from the middle of the twelfth century onwards to record their property transactions. Although charters issued personally by urban inhabitants of non-knightly rank are relatively few up to the 1170s or 1180s, during the 1190s and early 1200s the numbers increased about twenty or thirtyfold.[92] In the last quarter of the twelfth century a growing confidence in their legal powers can be seen in the introduction of clauses of corroboration and warranty. Parallel to the growth in the output of charters went, naturally enough, an increase in the ownership of seals, so that, by *c.* 1200, these must have been normal possessions for all men and women who owned property, even if they were of fairly modest social status. The seals tended to be small and simple, and the popularity of certain devices (above all birds and fleur-de-lis) suggests some standardisation in their manufacture.[93] There seems to have been no attempt by secular or ecclesiastical authorities to limit the expansion in the production of private charters or the use of private seals, and indeed churches probably welcomed the development, since it facilitated sales and benefactions to them. Towns with cathedrals or great monasteries were in any case especially well provided with freelance scribes, who already by *c.* 1100 were commonly being hired to perform the tasks formerly done by monastic scriptoria.[94] The production of books and charters probably began to be especially associated with towns from the later twelfth century onwards, though the countryside was not

[91] J. I. Catto, 'Citizens, scholars and masters', and J. R. L. Highfield, 'The early colleges', both in Catto, ed., *The History of the University of Oxford*, I, at pp. 151–92 and pp. 225–63 respectively.

[92] Cf., among a wide range of sources, *Westminster Abbey Charters, 1066–c. 1214*, ed. E. Mason (London Record Society, 25, 1988); *Early Charters of the Cathedral Church of St Paul, London*, ed. M. Gibbs (Camden Society, 3rd series, 58, 1939); *The Registrum Antiquissimum of the Cathedral Church of Lincoln*, vol. VIII, ed. K. Major (Lincoln Record Society, 51, 1958); in general on the ownership of seals by people of modest means, see P. D. A. Harvey, 'Personal seals in thirteenth-century England', in I. Wood and G. A. Loud, eds., *Church and Chronicle in the Middle Ages* (London and Rio Grande, 1991), pp. 117–27.

[93] See seal descriptions in works listed in n. 92 above; cf. also M. T. Clanchy, *From Memory to Written Record: England 1066–1307*, 2nd edn (Oxford, 1993), pp. 315–17.

[94] Clanchy, *Memory to Written Record*, p. 117; R. M. Thomson, *Manuscripts from St Albans Abbey, 1066–1235* (Woodbridge, 1982), vol. I, p. 13; J. J. G. Alexander, *Medieval Illuminators and their Methods of Work* (New Haven and London, 1992), pp. 12–25.

deprived of access to scribes, not least because many rural settlements were within easy distance of towns.

(vi) URBAN PANEGYRIC

Writing descriptions of towns was rare in England until the twelfth century, and unknown in Scotland or Wales until much later. Bede's interest in topographical description was slow to find imitators in England, though the relative shortage of narrative sources between the eighth and the eleventh centuries partly explains this. York, however, was briefly described by Alcuin in his poem *The Bishops, Kings and Saints of York* of the late eighth century and by Byrhtferth, who incorporated a short sketch of York into his *Vita Sancti Oswaldi*, written *c.* 1000.[95] After Alcuin's *York* poem, the next free-standing work thought to describe an identifiable English town is the fragmentary Old English poem *The Ruin*, composed at some point before the late tenth century; its references to hot baths suggest that the poet was visualising Bath. However, its portrayal of ruined fortifications and the transience of earthly pleasures is generalised and echoes Augustine's views on the transience of earthly cities. By contrast, the *Durham* poem of *c.* 1100, also in Old English, is certainly a eulogy of Durham; however, it says nothing about the living population or the buildings but instead remarks on the natural surroundings and gives a list of the saints whose relics are preserved there. In both works the past is significant but is dehistoricised: the *Ruin* attributes the building of the fortifications to 'giants', not to the Romans, while *Durham* treats the saints as living forces and does not set them in a historical context.[96]

English writers were not slow in European terms to develop an interest in the history of towns, but were less well able to supply historical details about them. This can be largely explained by the almost complete absence, in England, of the genre of *gesta episcoporum* ('deeds of bishops', in other words histories of individual dioceses), popular in parts of France and the Empire, and sometimes consciously leading to the evolution of urban history, as at Trier with its *Gesta Treverorum* of the early twelfth century. Alcuin's *York* poem, as has been recently pointed out by Simon Coates,[97] was a fairly early example of this genre, but it found no successors in England until the early twelfth century, when William of Malmesbury attempted, with his *Gesta Pontificum*, to fill this gap for all English dioceses. For most of them he found it impossible to say much about their origins;

95 Alcuin, *Bishops, Kings and Saints of York*, pp. 4–7, lines 19–45.

96 *The Exeter Book*, ed. G. P. Krapp and E. van K. Dobbie (London, 1936), pp. 227–9; D. R. Howlett, 'The shape and meaning of the Old English poem "Durham"', in Rollason, Harvey and Prestwich, eds., *Anglo-Norman Durham*, pp. 485–95.

97 S. Coates, 'The bishop as benefactor and civic patron: Alcuin, York and episcopal authority in Anglo-Saxon England', *Speculum*, 71 (1996), 529–58, at 548.

none the less he defines each see-town clearly, Bedan-fashion, according to its settlement type (for example, Wells is a *villa*, York an *urbs*, Winchester a *civitas*). He refers to Roman remains, with an inscription, at Carlisle (discussed as part of the archdiocese of York), and mentions the story that Gloucester (described as part of the diocese of Worcester) was named after the Emperor Claudius.[98]

More influential in the development of interest in the urban past was Geoffrey of Monmouth's *Historia Regum Britanniae* (1136), a spoof history parodying William's antiquarian pretensions, which provided origin stories for several towns. In the case of Gloucester, Geoffrey retained William's explanation, though dressing it up in more romantic terms. For several other towns, however, he projected their origins much further back into the past, notably London, which he said had been founded as *Trinovantum* or 'New Troy' by Brut the Trojan, and later renamed Kaerlud after King Lud, after whom Ludgate was also named (Geoffrey was parodying his contemporaries' zeal for etymology).[99] The work had an unusually large circulation and was translated into French soon after its composition; thus it was not long before its urban origin stories were finding eager local audiences. Both William and Geoffrey, in very different ways, created an appetite for descriptions, historical and otherwise, of towns, and already in the second half of the twelfth century we see some of the results of this. Geoffrey's origin myths are specifically referred to by at least two of the authors writing about English towns in the late twelfth century, William fitz Stephen and Lucian of Chester. William inserted a description of London, with its cathedral, thirteen conventual houses, 126 parish churches (this number must include several lying outside the city) and three schools, into his *Life of Thomas Becket*, London being the saint's birthplace; William made his debt to Geoffrey of Monmouth clear by referring to the Brut legend.[100] Lucian, a monk of Chester Abbey, portrayed Chester as being spiritually defended by the patron saints of its churches, and refers in passing to Geoffrey's explanations of the names Leicester and Gloucester.[101] Less consciously an urban eulogy, but none the less in a similar mould, is a poem by a contemporary of Lucian, Simon de Freine, a canon of Hereford Cathedral, addressed to Gerald of Wales, which praises Hereford as a home of various branches of learning.[102] During this period literary descriptions

[98] William of Malmesbury, *Gesta Pontificum*, ed. N. E. S. A. Hamilton R S, (1870), pp. 193, 208, 158, 208–9 and 291.

[99] *The Historia Regum Britannie of Geoffrey of Monmouth, I, Bern, Burgerbibliothek, MS. 568*, ed. N. Wright (Cambridge, 1984), esp. pp. 14–5 (London) and 44 (Gloucester); V. I. J. Flint, 'The *Historia Regum Britannie* of Geoffrey of Monmouth: parody and its purpose. A suggestion', *Speculum*, 54 (1979), 447–68.

[100] *Materials for the History of Thomas Becket*, ed. J. C. Robertson, (RS, 1875–85), vol. III, pp. 2–13.

[101] *Liber Luciani de Laude Cestrie*, ed. M. V. Taylor (Record Society for the Publication of Original Documents Relating to Lancashire and Cheshire, 64, 1912), esp. p. 64.

[102] The poem is printed in two separate parts in *Giraldus Cambrensis Opera*, ed. J. S. Brewer, J. F. Dimock and G. F. Warner (RS, 1861–91), vol. I, pp. 382–3; and Hunt, 'English learning', 36–7.

of towns tended to concentrate on their setting (the *locus amoenus* topos occurs in practically all these works) and on churches, religious allegory and saints' cults rather than attempting comprehensive coverage: detailed topographical accounts (if we except fiscal surveys) were a thing of the future. None the less by far the most significant development for the future seems to have been the creation of urban myths, principally by Geoffrey of Monmouth. Even though Geoffrey was writing for a courtly audience, the stories in his work swiftly reached a much wider public, and by the later middle ages were helping to forge a sense of identity in many towns.[103]

(vii) CONCLUSION

By the late twelfth century towns had clearly established themselves as the centres of education and literacy, and were providing an audience capable of appreciating origin myths and religious symbolism. Major churches in towns seem to have been the main factor in this development – mostly not deliberately, but coincidentally, through the employment they gave to freelance scribes and through their establishment of schools, intended in the first instance to produce revenue for themselves. The ecclesiastical presence was a strong one in towns throughout this period, sustaining proto-urban existence at the very beginning and fostering a wide range of spiritual and charitable activities by the end.

[103] Cf. also G. Rosser, 'Myth, image and social process in the English medieval town', *UH*, 23 (1996), 5–25.

· 8 ·

The topography of towns 600–1300

D. M. PALLISER, T. R. SLATER AND E. PATRICIA DENNISON

SURVEYING THE topography of towns before 1300 inevitably draws heavily on the disciplines of archaeology and plan analysis, rather than on documents and standing buildings, which are predominantly late medieval. Fortunately, the proliferation of urban excavations since the 1970s has produced a huge volume of topographical material, telling us much more about the siting, phases and layout of many towns than could be learnt from documents alone. This does not mean that we should neglect the value of early documents, however brief and laconic: the expert excavator of medieval Paris, Michel Fleury, demonstrates from personal experience 'la nécessité d'allier constamment les données des sources écrites à celles que fournissent les fouilles archéologiques'.[1] Nevertheless, there is much detail that we could never have gleaned of early medieval topography without excavation, and for the very earliest periods for the most crucial facts – whether a town site remained inhabited, or whether it was relocated – such evidence is all we have. It is therefore important that major discoveries of the past few years be built into general syntheses as soon as possible, and that is one of the purposes of this volume.

Most Roman town sites were also urban in the middle ages, and in most cases the Roman core lies beneath the modern town centre. However, to move from those premises to the conclusion of 'continuity of site if not of urbanism' is to go beyond the evidence. It is now clear that, of the four most important towns of the earliest post-Roman period, Ipswich was without a Roman past, while London and York developed on open sites outside the Roman walls before shifting back into the fortified area in the ninth and tenth centuries. *Hamwic* was different again: it developed on an open site south-west of its Roman predecessor, but when trouble threatened in the ninth century, the population moved, not back to the Roman site but further south-west to create a new

[1] M. Fleury, *Point d'archéologie sans histoire: The Zaharoff Lecture for 1986–7* (Oxford, 1988), p. 2.

fortified settlement of Southampton. Other towns with Roman predecessors had varied experiences: St Albans, for instance, was built over a hill-top extra-mural cemetery containing the tomb of England's proto-martyr, overlooking the site of *Verulamium*, while Cambridge developed partly within the deserted Roman town but, very early on, also across the Cam into what became the medieval town centre. A non-Roman site could shift its centre of gravity in the same way: the latest interpretation of Norwich is of a fortified 'North *wic*' on the north bank of the Wensum, established before 917, but supplanted in importance before 1066 by a new, planned centre on the opposite bank.[2]

Maurice Beresford, discussing the rarity of urban relocations from the eleventh century, says reasonably enough that 'Streets, houses and public buildings do not transplant easily': yet that does not explain why such shifts occurred in the early middle ages. Helen Clarke and Björn Ambrosiani, discussing the same phenomenon in Scandinavia, note that until *c.* 1000 'towns were built entirely of timber and their movement would not have entailed much capital loss to their founders or overlords'. However, they concede that the explanation may not necessarily hold for English towns: 'Hamwic had a stone church (St Mary) during its period of occupation, and York and London were probably in the same situation.' At any rate, the migration of urban settlements is unusual in England after the tenth century: Salisbury and New Winchelsea stand out in the thirteenth century as rare exceptions. However, the centre of gravity of a large town could well shift given sufficient pull: thus new market places at Northampton and Norwich, laid out after the Conquest, provided the impetus for such a move; the centre of Reading shifted eastwards after the abbey was founded in 1125; while Beresford's study provides numerous examples of smaller post-Conquest towns which 'migrated' towards a road or bridge as traffic shifted direction.[3]

In Scotland, too, there are numerous examples of movement away from the original urban nucleus, for geographical or economic reasons. The early settlement at Dundee clustered around the castle and Seagait to the east well into the fourteenth century. By about 1400, the town had reoriented westwards, towards a better harbour site and St Mary's church, founded in 'a field' outside the settlement (Figure 8.1).[4] Similarly, the original nucleus of lay settlement at St Andrews was probably close to Kinrimund, the site of the leading Pictish royal monastery from the mid-eighth century and the seat of the chief bishopric from

[2] B. S. Ayers, 'The cathedral site before 1096', in I. Atherton, E. Fernie, C. Harper-Bill and H. Smith, eds., *Norwich Cathedral* (London, 1996), pp. 63–71. For the *wic* sites at *Hamwic*, Ipswich, London and York see below, pp. 188–9, 218–22.

[3] M. Beresford, *New Towns of the Middle Ages* (London, 1967), pp. 104–41; H. Clarke and B. Ambrosiani, *Towns in the Viking Age* (Leicester, 1991), pp. 88, 138; the same points are made in the 2nd edn (Leicester, 1996), except that the reference to York and London (p. 138) is deleted.

[4] Dundee District Archive and Record Centre MS CC1, no. 15; J. Dowden, ed., *The Chartulary of the Abbey of Lindores, 1159–1479* (Scottish History Society, 1903), p. 3; E. P. D. Torrie, *Medieval Dundee* (Dundee, 1990), pp. 51, 53.

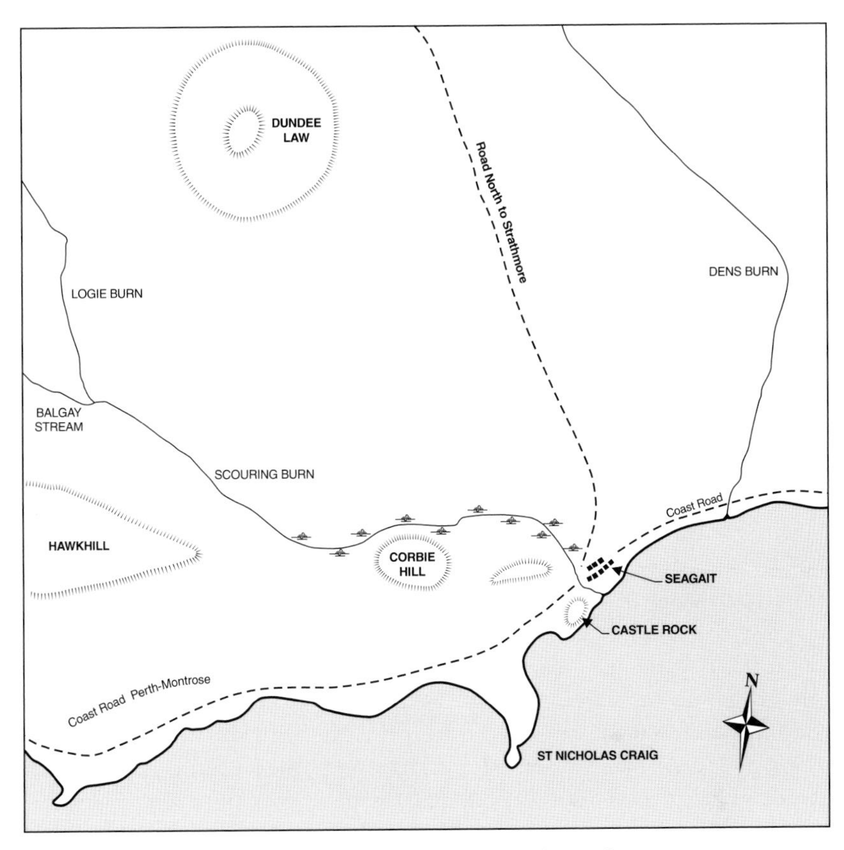

Figure 8.1 The development of Dundee
Eleventh century

the early tenth century. This settlement was to form the core of the burgh established by Bishop Robert sometime between 1144 and 1153; and it was here that the first market cross stood. As the burgh expanded, however, another market was permitted further west; and sometime between 1189 and 1198 the market cross, and focal point of the burgh, was transferred to the new site.[5] Aberdeen also follows this pattern: Castlegate, the fifteenth-century market centre of the medieval town, being in all probability a later development, after economic expansion necessitated an enlarged market area and a consequent shift of focus from the early urban site.[6]

[5] N. P. Brooks and G. Whittington, 'Planning and growth in the medieval Scottish burgh: the example of St Andrews', *Transactions, Institute of British Geographers*, new series, 2 (1977), 278–95; SRO, MS Black Book of St Andrews', f. 35.

[6] E. P. D. Torrie, 'The early urban site of New Aberdeen: a reappraisal of the evidence', *Northern Scotland*, 12 (1992), 1–18.

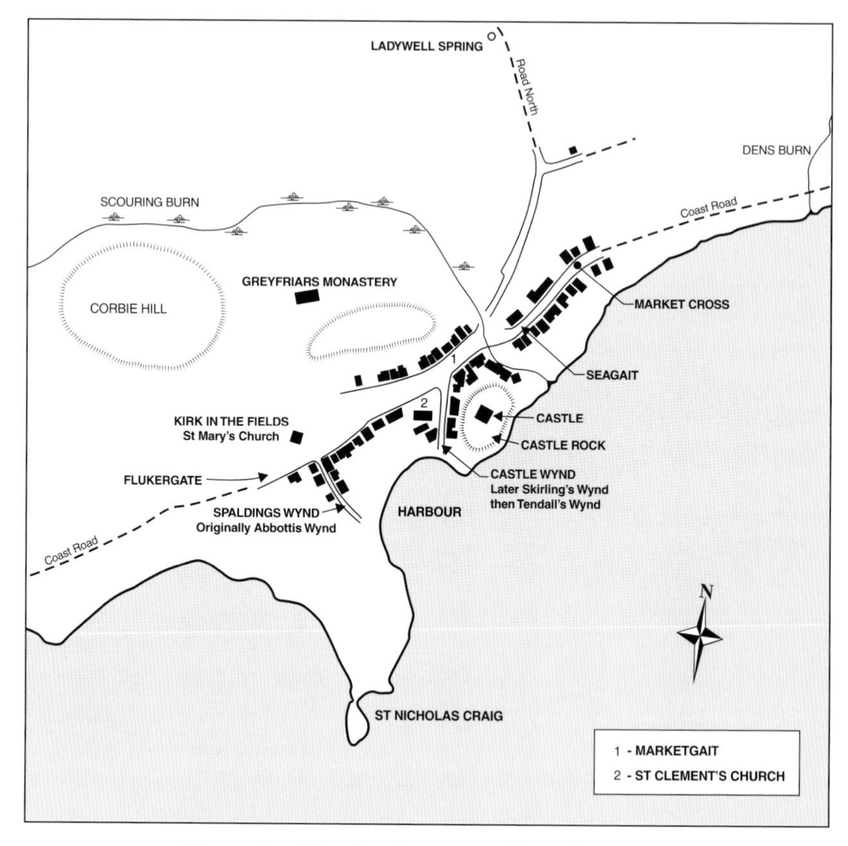

Figure 8.1 The development of Dundee (*cont.*)
Thirteenth century

A general feature of the siting of towns was their relationship to communications – to roads and, even more, to water: nearly all large towns before the rise of Coventry were situated on an estuary or navigable river. Many, indeed, followed their Roman predecessors in being sited some way inland at a fording or bridging point on a major river (London, Lincoln, York), and non-Roman towns did so also (Norwich, Glasgow). Though there were always coastal ports too, many of these – at least on the east coast – came later. 'Ports actually on the coast, such as Orwell, Dunwich, Great Yarmouth, Lynn, Boston and Hull, often begin their development at around the time of the Conquest or later.'[7] Certainly the new towns founded after the Conquest included many seaports: on Beresford's figures 27 per cent of all English foundations were sea or estuarine ports, and 23 per cent of Welsh foundations.[8] Of Scottish burghs founded before

[7] J. Campbell, ed., *The Anglo-Saxons* (Oxford, 1982), p. 175.

[8] Beresford, *New Towns*, p. 121.

Figure 8.1 The development of Dundee (*cont.*)
Fifteenth century

1314, somewhere in the region of 43 per cent were ports, albeit many were very small. A number of ports were established on sand spits. Yarmouth was the most successful, but Harwich and Ravenser are other east coast examples, the last destroyed by coastal erosion in the 1340s.[9] Coastal erosion also caused the rapid decline of Dunwich, whilst new shingle banks were responsible for the decline of both Old and New Winchelsea.

Spectacular defensible sites are rather less common than in some parts of Europe: the volcanic plugs of Edinburgh and Dumbarton Castles are perhaps the best known, together with the incised meander site of Durham's cathedral and castle. Gentler meander sites are common elsewhere, however, including Shrewsbury and Warkworth. River cliffs were often used for castle sites and towns sometimes followed: Chepstow is a notable case. The confluence of rivers

[9] *Ibid.*, pp. 513–14.

provides a similar defensible promontory, though often at risk of flooding as at York, Monmouth, Bristol and Reading. Where the subsidiary stream was only small its defensive properties could be enhanced by damming it: the promontory site of Pembroke is an example, while Stafford and Newcastle-under-Lyme were partly bounded by artificial lakes in this way.

(i) CHRONOLOGY

Whatever the truth about post-Roman continuity of urban life, there can be no doubt of the enduring importance of Roman sites and layouts. Most larger Roman towns were planned on a grid and within defences, and elements of their layout have clearly continued to influence the topography of their medieval successors. Parts of many towns, including London, York, Chester, Lincoln and Winchester, still reflect the lines of Roman walls and streets. However, the nature and extent of the Roman heritage have been very variable. At Wroxeter, sub-Roman timbered buildings were laid out exactly on Roman alignments while, later, St Andrew's church was built within a corner of the walled site and exactly on the Roman street alignment: 'that ought to mean that it was founded, not in a long-deserted urban wasteland, but in a living settlement of some importance'.[10] However, Wroxeter later ceased to be urban; and at Winchester, where there was apparently a break in urban occupation, the regular medieval street pattern does not correspond to the Roman grid, except where the survival of walls and gates dictated an identical through-route.[11] York and Chester may stand for intermediate cases: in both, there is no clear evidence of urban continuity, but in both, later occupants made use of several central streets exactly (or almost exactly) on Roman alignments. In some cases the adherence to Roman routes may have been dictated by the survival of Roman buildings, in use or as ruins, until the eleventh and twelfth centuries. William of Malmesbury tells of a Roman hall in Carlisle not demolished until the twelfth century, 'the only description from this period of Roman buildings still standing in England'.[12]

No overall pattern of development is yet clear among the earliest post-Roman towns. Too little is yet known of the layout of the *wic* settlements of London and York; Ipswich seems to have developed in a sprawling way, but with a deliberate grid plan of streets superimposed on it around 800,[13] while *Hamwic* appears to have been regularly planned on a grid from the start. Even less is known of the smaller *wics,* such as Fordwich or Sandwich, which served the kingdom of Kent, though the latter has the characteristic plot pattern of port towns noted above whilst Greenwich and Woolwich, further up the Kentish bank of the

[10] S. Bassett, 'Medieval ecclesiastical organisation in the vicinity of Wroxeter and its British antecedents', *J of the British Archaeological Association*, 145 (1992), 1–28.

[11] M. Biddle and D. Hill, 'Late Saxon planned towns', *Antiquaries J*, 51 (1971), 70–85.

[12] J. Campbell, *Essays in Anglo-Saxon History* (London, 1986), p. 215.

[13] *Ex inf.* K. Wade.

Thames, and Dover, are noted only in the place-name literature as probable trading places of this kind.[14] The principal topographical characteristic of *wics* is their elongated beach location with landing stages extending out into the water. Of other types of town emerging before the Viking invasions, there seems again to be no common pattern. Early episcopal towns include both Canterbury, where the Roman intramural street system vanished and a small, irregular town developed round the cathedral precinct in the north-east quadrant of the defences, and Hereford, with a regular plan from *c.* 700. The many smaller towns or proto-towns based on royal vills or minsters, at least in the English Midlands, reveal no common pattern, though some, such as Bampton, reflect the sub-circular plans which have been found in the monastic towns of Ireland.[15] However, there may also have been a series of *burhs* developed by Offa of Mercia in the eighth century. Haslam makes a case for these as new foundations with defences and street systems 'on a more or less rectilinear plan', though excavations at Kingsbury (St Albans) have shown little development of this kind. Some towns may have originated as minster-towns and later been reorganised as *burhs*: at Oxford, Wareham and Hereford the minster came before *burh* defences.[16]

The later pre-Conquest period (*c.* 850–1066) is a little clearer, and the evidence more abundant (Figures 3.1 and 3.2). The best-known group of towns are the *burhs* of Wessex and English Mercia: nearly all the larger ones were regularly planned, some at least in modules of the standard perch.[17] While regular planning goes back to Hereford and *Hamwic*, it is with ninth- and tenth-century Wessex that it becomes a major element in towns for the first time since the Roman occupation. The crucial period was probably the reigns of Alfred and Edward the Elder; documentary evidence from London implies part of an orthogonal street grid by the 890s (Plate 3), while a coin of Edward the Elder was found lying on the surface of one of Winchester's planned streets.[18] Beresford's survey of town plantations is here seriously misleading, for it is a survey of post-Conquest plantations and planning: he allows only three before 1066 out of 172 English plantations, though he does briefly discuss the *burhs*.[19]

[14] W. F. H. Nicolaisen, M. Gelling and M. Richards, *The Names of Towns and Cities in Britain* (London, 1970), pp. 197, 207.

[15] J. Blair, 'Minster churches in the landscape', in D. Hooke, ed. *Anglo-Saxon Settlements* (Oxford, 1988), pp. 35–58; H. B. Clarke and A. Simms, eds., *The Comparative History of Urban Origins in Non-Roman Europe* (British Archaeological Reports, International Series, 255, 1985).

[16] J. Haslam, *Early Medieval Towns in Britain* (Princes Risborough, 1985), p. 19; J. Haslam, 'Market and fortress in England in the reign of Offa', *World Archaeology*, 19 (1987), 76–93; J. Blair, 'St Frideswide's monastery: problems and possibilities', *Oxoniensia*, 53 (1988), 224.

[17] P. Crummy, 'The system of measurement used in town planning from the ninth to the thirteenth centuries', in S. C. Hawkes, D. Brown and J. Campbell, eds., *Anglo-Saxon Studies in Archaeology and History* (British Archaeological Reports, British Series, 72, 1979), pp. 149–63.

[18] M. Biddle, ed., *Winchester in the Early Middle Ages* (Oxford, 1976); see below, pp. 225–6.

[19] Beresford, *New Towns*, pp. 324–8.

There were also new or enlarged towns, often fortified, in the Danelaw at the same period as the West Saxon *burhs*, but they were apparently planned, if at all, in more piecemeal fashion. Thus York seems to have expanded, on both banks of the Ouse, in loosely planned segments, and there is only limited evidence for standard burgage layout.[20] James Campbell, contrasting Winchester's 'neat grid' with 'the sprawling tangle of Norwich' which 'says more about evolution than about planning', suggests that the differences 'are part of a pattern of distinction between east and west, which owes much to the policies and attitudes of the kings of the house of Wessex'.[21] In addition to the fortified towns of both Wessex and the Danelaw, the tenth and eleventh centuries saw the development of many lesser towns. Jeremy Haslam sees a whole group of new towns founded at the gates of monasteries, which 'generally consisted of triangular market places lined with burgage plots outside the main abbey gate'.[22]

The Norman Conquest may have had less impact on English towns than was once thought. Nevertheless, the planting of castles in almost every shire town, and in many others, caused much destruction of houses and realignment of town centres, including the laying out of new market places in Norwich, Northampton and Warwick; while Archbishop Lanfranc's insistence on moving cathedrals from lesser towns to greater was decisive for the fortunes of some towns. The other major changes of the post-Conquest period – the rapid growth of existing towns and the founding of many new ones – would have happened with or without a Conquest, and were part of a Europe-wide economic expansion. Some towns acquired new suburbs, like Lincoln's Newport; others had large extensions to their centres, like the 'French borough' at Nottingham. And between the Conquest and 1300 many 'new towns' were created, sometimes on green-field sites, though more often by the promotion or expansion of existing settlements, or by adding a planned urban unit to an existing village as at Olney and Stratford. Altogether, over 150 English towns planted between 1066 and 1300 are listed by Beresford, and other examples such as Lichfield have been identified since he wrote. In Wales, the picture is still more striking: there were no towns before the Normans invaded, but between 1071 and 1310, seventy-seven towns were planted.[23] The most dramatic examples came at the end of the period, with Edward I's conquest of Gwynedd and his imposition of a ring of planned and fortified towns round Snowdonia.

[20] D. M. Palliser, 'York's west bank', in P. V. Addyman and V. E. Black, eds., *Archaeological Papers from York Presented to M. W. Barley* (York, 1984), pp. 101–8; R. A. Hall, *English Heritage Book of Viking Age York* (London, 1994), pp. 55–81; P. Ottaway (forthcoming) for York's burgage layout.

[21] Campbell, ed., *The Anglo-Saxons*, pp. 174–5.

[22] Haslam, *Early Medieval Towns in Britain*, p. 50.

[23] Beresford, *New Towns*, pp. 328, 330, 341–2; C. C. Taylor, 'The origins of Lichfield', *Trans. of the South Staffordshire Arch. and Hist. Soc.*, 10 (1969), 43–52.

The earliest definite evidence for Scottish towns comes as late as the twelfth century, but there is much to suggest that towns, or at least proto-urban settlements, were established in the eleventh century.[24] One of the primary benefits bestowed on burghs was exemption from tolls and some customs due to the crown; and, in consequence, the right to trade freely. Although non-burghal markets were not unknown, the near-monopoly of trading rights by burghs meant that any town that was to flourish was essentially burghal. The only two settlements designated as burghs prior to 1124 were Berwick and Roxburgh. They were soon followed by Edinburgh, Dunfermline and Perth, all in existence by 1130. By 1153, thirteen burghs had been founded by the crown, two by other lords (both ecclesiastical) and a further two, Haddington and Renfrew, passed between the king and a private lord. A further twenty-two were added by 1214 – thirteen royal foundations, seven of other lords and two passing from the crown to another lord. The following century saw a further six royal burghs and nine dependent on other lords, making fifty-four burghs in total.[25]

(ii) THE SHAPE OF TOWNS

The physical elements that make up a town's plan are threefold: the system of through-roads, access streets, back lanes and footways; the plot pattern of tenements and other units of ownership and occupation; and the buildings occupying those plots. The research by M. R. G. Conzen, with his experience of central European scholarship, long ago showed that models of town development based only on street plans were inadequate. He demonstrated that almost all towns in the medieval period, including classic medieval 'planned' towns such as Salisbury, Ludlow, Bury St Edmunds and Stratford, have composite plans which reflect the periods of growth, standstill and decline of the urban economy and the decisions of individuals and corporate bodies in developing, adapting or replacing urban topographical elements.[26] Most shire towns have particularly complex developmental histories. Recent work on Worcester, for example, has shown how the bishop was responsible for large-scale earth-moving operations in the late ninth century to infill the Roman ditch and expand the city northwards; that the king then developed a planned *burh* beyond this; and that the cathedral

[24] See below, pp. 718–20.

[25] P. McNeill and R. Nicholson, eds., *An Historical Atlas of Scotland, c. 400–c. 1600* (St Andrews, 1975), pp. 132–4.

[26] M. R. G. Conzen, *Alnwick, Northumberland* (Publications of the Institute of British Geographers, 27, 1960); M. R. G. Conzen, 'The plan-analysis of an English city centre', in K. Norborg, ed., *Proceedings of the I.G.U. Symposium in Urban Geography, Lund 1960* (Lund, 1962), pp. 383–414; M. R. G. Conzen, 'The use of town plans in the study of urban history', in H. J. Dyos, ed., *The Study of Urban History* (London, 1968), pp. 113–30; M. R. G. Conzen, 'Morphogenesis, morphological regions and secular human agency in the historic townscape, as exemplified by Ludlow', in D. Denecke and G. Shaw, eds., *Urban Historical Geography* (Cambridge, 1988), pp. 253–72.

priory laid out a planned one-street suburb northwards along the ridge in the twelfth century.[27] Other, smaller-scale, developments were occurring in between these significant episodes of town planning, leading to the complex later medieval plan which survived with comparatively little change into the industrial era. Similarly, the plan of Maidstone, one of Alan Everitt's 'primary' towns, has been shown recently to consist of at least eight developmental phases, four of which were clearly planned.[28]

It is inadequate to talk of a town growing 'organically'. The physical growth of a town depends on the decisions of individuals or corporate bodies to develop or redevelop land with buildings which are subsequently put to urban economic purposes. To this extent all towns were 'planned'. The differences between medieval towns are to be found in the scale at which these individual or corporate decisions were taken. A smallholder dividing his property on the suburban edge of a market town into plots for building three or four small cottages had a different effect upon the topography of the town from the bishop of Salisbury decreeing that the town of Old Sarum should be relocated and redesigned to a regular planned layout with market place, rectangular street grid and regular plot series.

The simplest of town plans in Britain is the small, new-planned, medieval borough of the twelfth or thirteenth centuries consisting of a single street, widening in its centre to provide space for a market place, with a plot series of tenements on either side of the street, the plots being at least three times as long as they are wide (Figure 8.2). To the rear of the plots there is frequently a narrow back access lane or footpath which is often, too, the physical expression of the invisible administrative boundary of the legal entity of the borough; more definitive markers in terms of crosses or bars were sometimes to be found at either end of the main street. Often, a later chapel and a market cross or house provided the dominant corporate buildings. These 'planted towns' fill the pages of Beresford's *New Towns* and are easily the most common type of English town plan. However, Beresford also demonstrated that even these simple planned towns are often more complex than they seem at first since most had existing attributes which encouraged their lords to think of urban foundation in the first place. Thus a crossroads location, as at Moreton-in-Marsh or Wellington, or a river crossing site such as Totnes, inevitably led to a more complex plan with tenements laid out along two axes rather than one. A pre-existing minster or castle would tend to provide a focus for marketing activity, and often led to the

[27] N. J. Baker *et al.*, 'From Roman to medieval Worcester: development and planning in the Anglo-Saxon city', *Antiquity*, 66 (1992), 65–74; N. J. Baker and T. R. Slater, 'Morphological regions in English medieval towns', in J. W. R. Whitehand and P. J. Larkham, eds., *Urban Landscapes: International Perspectives* (London, 1992), pp. 43–68.

[28] A. Everitt, 'The Banburys of England', *UHY* (1974), 28–38; P. Clark and L. Murfin, *The History of Maidstone: The Making of a Modern County Town* (Stroud, 1995), p. 23.

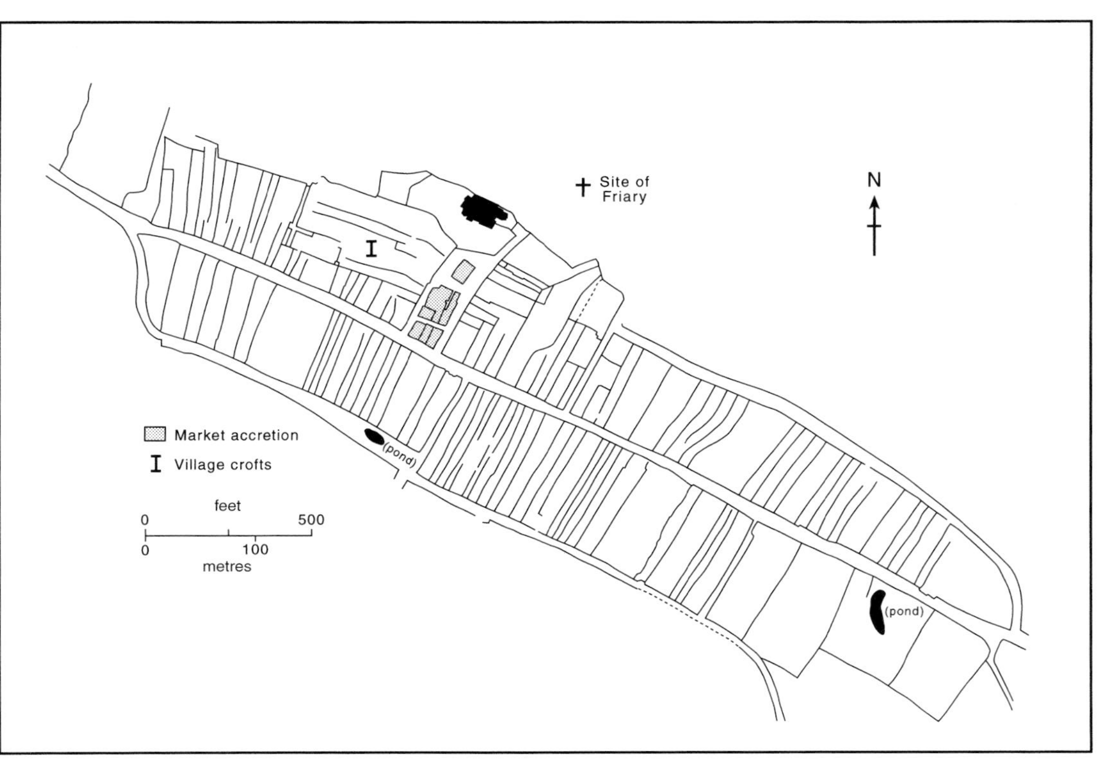

Figure 8.2 Atherstone (War.): a good example of the single-street planned towns of the twelfth and thirteenth centuries.

development of more formalised market places with rectangular or triangular shapes at their gates.

None the less, the single street with tenements on each side is a useful model with which to begin. Some important towns were developed with almost no other plan attributes. Durham, for example, despite, or perhaps because of, the spectacular site of the town spreading over the meander core of the River Wear, and its equally spectacular cathedral and castle dominating that site, comprises some six separate single-street plan units laid out on either side of the approach roads to the central market square, the only unusual attribute being that each was legally a separate borough. Similarly, Burton-on-Trent, another town dominated by a Benedictine monastery, with a seemingly complex partial grid street plan, in fact consists of five separate twelfth- and thirteenth-century developments by successive abbots, each of which consisted of a single street with tenements on either side.[29] In central Europe, the parallel street plan, with two streets and their tenements, normally of equal status and laid out side by side, is a further variant of this plan type, but such a plan is far less common in Britain. It has been recognised in the final phase of development of Bridgnorth (Figure 8.3), in Hedon and in the Redcliff suburb of Bristol.[30]

The grid plan might be seen as a further development of those towns with tenements laid out along two axial streets at right angles. Despite the frequency with which grid-planned towns are referred to in the literature, especially that related to the history of town planning, they are far from common in Britain. They are associated with periods when royal control was predominant (the Wessex *burhs*, or Edward I's North Welsh boroughs, for example) or with especially powerful lords (Abbot Baldwin at Bury St Edmunds in the 1070s, or Bishop Richard at Salisbury in the 1220s, for example). Even more uncommon than a grid-planned town is one in which the street grid is orthogonal. New Winchelsea is exceptional in England in the rectangularity of its street grid and plot pattern, and derives from the experience of Edward I's surveyors in laying out the castle boroughs of North Wales such as Flint and Caernarfon.[31] Most grid-planned towns laid out before the thirteenth century paid as much attention to the underlying topography and pre-existing morphological frame of lanes, field boundaries and existing properties as they did to the orthogonality of the grid. Thus the three by three street grid of the

[29] M. Bonney, *Lordship and the Urban Community* (Cambridge, 1990); T. R. Slater, 'Medieval town-founding on the estates of the Benedictine Order in England', in F.-E. Eliassen and G. A. Ersland, eds., *Power, Profit and Urban Land* (Aldershot, 1996), pp. 70–92.

[30] T. R. Slater, 'English medieval new towns with composite plans: evidence from the Midlands', in T. R. Slater, ed., *The Built Form of Western Cities* (Leicester and London, 1990), pp. 60–82; T. R. Slater, 'Medieval new town and port: a plan-analysis of Hedon, East Yorkshire', *Yorkshire Archaeological J*, 57 (1985), pp. 23–41; M. D. Lobel, *BAHT*, II, *Bristol*, pp. 6–7.

[31] Beresford, *New Towns*, pp. 3–28.

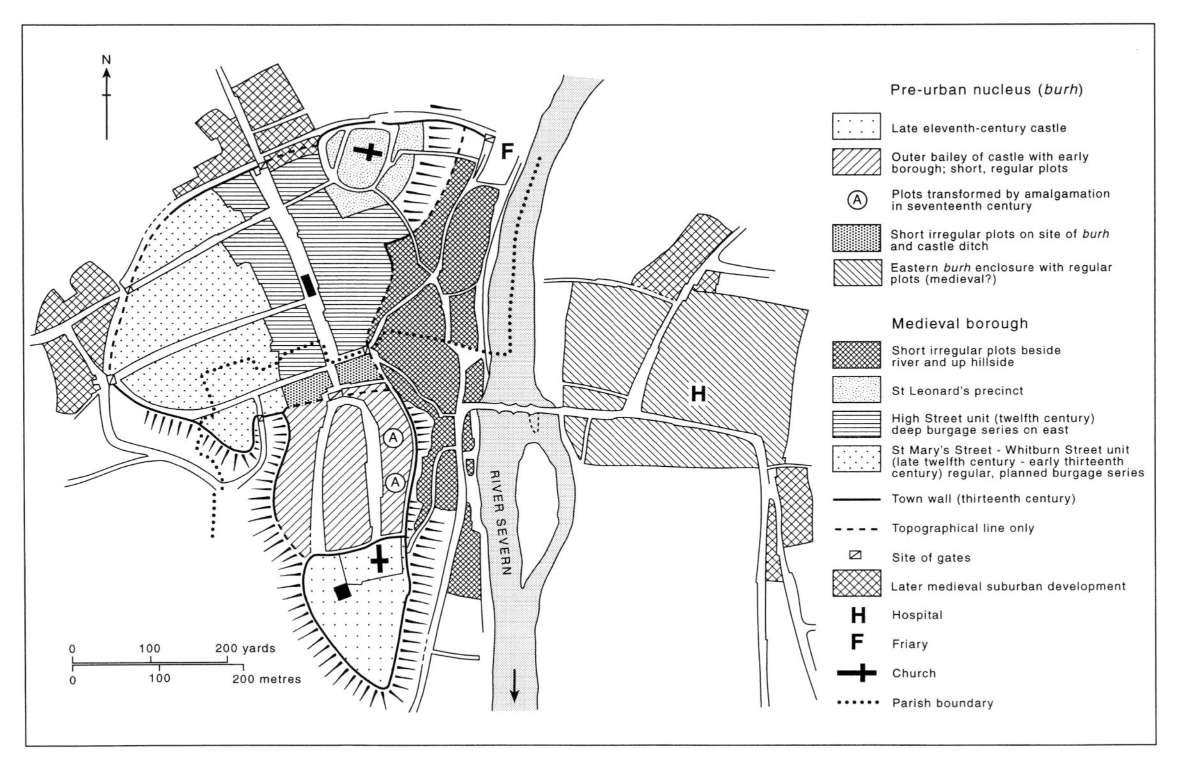

Figure 8.3 Bridgnorth (Salop.): careful analysis reveals a composite plan with six major plan units, two of them with distinctive subdivisions.

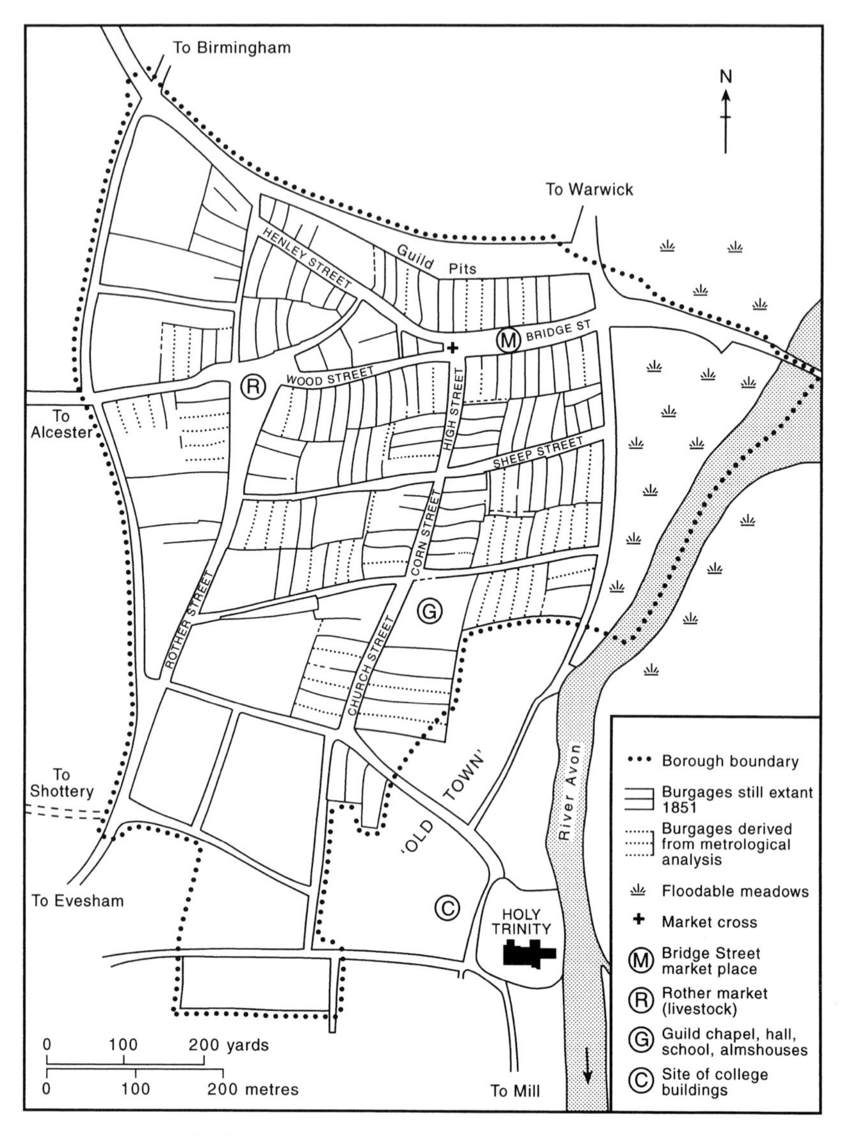

Figure 8.4 Stratford-on-Avon (War.): reconstruction of its plan as laid out by the bishop of Worcester in 1196

new borough of 1196 at Stratford was distorted into parallelogram form to fit the terrace gravels which raised the site above the flood plain, whilst the rectangularity of the plots was further distorted by the sinuous curves of the underlying open-field ridge and furrow (Figure 8.4). Similarly, the street grid of Bury St Edmunds was disrupted by the pre-existing sinuosity of Angel Lane, and the tenements in the centre of Burton-on-Trent were adapted to fit into an ancient cattle driftway.[32] A further variant on the grid plan is provided by the much-discussed plan of Ludlow where the streets which make up the grid were of different width, reflecting different functions; the broad Mill Street and Broad Street, with their grand properties, were thus very different from Raven Lane and Bell Lane, which were back lanes in their function and building fabric, a difference which Hope failed to recognise in his very early analysis of this town plan.[33] In Scotland, more elaborate grid-like plans are found in Perth and Crail, although both are composite plans which probably originated as single streets.[34]

(iii) MARKET PLACES

The market place is, topographically speaking, simply a variant street type; however, given the size of many medieval market places they give distinctive form to many towns both large and small. At least one central market place is often thought to have been essential for a medieval town, but John S. Schofield and Alan V. Vince suggest that 'older towns, like London and Lincoln, had their markets in the streets because they developed their main frontages at a time when large open spaces were not required' or could be provided extramurally, whereas from the twelfth century 'virtually all new towns had a market-place as a centre of activity'.[35] The explanation may be rather that older larger towns had a multiplicity of markets in different streets, whereas the later tendency was to collect them all into one or two open spaces. The broad street (rectangular or lozenge-shaped) such as those at Newnham, Chipping Sodbury and Chipping Campden, is probably the most common type, even in large towns such as London's Cheapside and York's Pavement which both acted as wide market streets, though they were never the only markets. The other geometric variants were the orthogonal square or rectangle, the triangle and semi-circle. This last is associated with towns founded in or beside castle baileys, the most notable cases being Devizes and Richmond (Yorks.). Pleshey, which failed to develop as a town, might be regarded as an example of the earliest phase of such a plan. Square or rectangular market places are associated with grid plans. The great rectangular market places at Bury and Salisbury are especially notable, but not all grid plans have such a market place: Harwich, for example, does not, nor do the Welsh bastides of Edward I where marketing took place outside the walls. Triangular

[32] T. R. Slater, 'Domesday village to medieval town: the topography of medieval Stratford-upon-Avon', in R. Bearman, ed., *The History of an English Borough* (Stroud, 1997), pp. 30–42; Slater, 'Medieval town-founding', p. 77; T. Rowley, *The Norman Heritage, 1066–1200* (London, 1983), pp. 76–7, for plan of Bury.

[33] Conzen, 'Morphogenesis, morphological regions'; Slater, 'English medieval new towns'; W. H. StJ. Hope, 'The ancient topography of Ludlow', *Archaeologia*, 61 (1909), 383–9.

[34] M. Spearman, 'The medieval townscape of Perth', in M. Lynch, M. Spearman and G. Stell, eds., *The Scottish Medieval Town* (Edinburgh, 1988), pp. 42–59.

[35] J. Schofield and A. Vince, *Medieval Towns* (London, 1994), p. 51.

market places seem to be especially characteristic of monastic towns, perhaps because the abbey gateway could provide an effective architectural display of power with such a shape. The Conqueror's new town at Battle is particularly notable in this respect. The great market place of Coventry was similar and the prior later built a new street focusing on the cathedral priory gate on the opposite side of the market place. The large triangular market places at St Albans and Evesham, with broad street beyond, are other well-known Benedictine examples. Triangular markets are to be found also in towns founded by monastic lords, as at Northleach, and early minster sites, such as the vast market and green at Witney. However, minster-town market places are more usually smaller irregular triangles such as those at Bampton or Tetbury. The association with monastic towns is not exclusive, however. Triangular market places also derive from road junctions, as at Alnwick and the great suburban St Giles market and fairground at Oxford, and quite a large number of Welsh towns have triangular market places, including Tenby and Haverfordwest. The large triangular market place at Doncaster derives from an urban extension which included a new market place on the fringe of the built-up area, whilst the market at Hereford derives from both a road junction location and a decision to relocate the market in the years immediately after the Conquest.[36] In Scotland there is no evidence of early market specialisation, although it is known that market places might be in open spaces, as at Inverkeithing, Haddington and Musselburgh, for example, or in linear street markets, as in Dunfermline.

The buildings associated with market places are distinctive. First, since they were public spaces, market places were normally the locations of disciplinary functions such as pillories, stocks and, frequently, prisons. The town hall often fronted the market place in those towns that were self-governing communities, though not to the extent that is found in other European countries; more usual in Britain was a booth hall or court house which served a variety of functions, both legal and administrative. Many market places are dominated by churches and, in the high medieval period, the naves of these churches often provided the

[36] M. Aston and J. Bond, *The Landscape of Towns* (London, 1976), pp. 78–96; Blair, 'Minster churches'; Conzen, *Alnwick, Northumberland*; Essex County Council, *Historic Towns in Essex, an Archaeological Survey* (Chelmsford, 1983), p. 74; J. Hillaby, 'The boroughs of the bishops of Hereford in the late thirteenth century', *Transactions, Woolhope Naturalists Field Club*, 40 (1970), 1–9; R. Leech, *Small Medieval Towns in Avon* (Bristol, 1975), pp. 9–13; R. Leech, *Historic Towns in Gloucestershire* (Bristol, 1981), pp. 12–5, 62–4; K. D. Lilley, 'Coventry's topographical development: the impact of the priory', in G. Demidowicz, ed., *Coventry's First Cathedral* (Stamford, 1994), pp. 72–96; K. D. Lilley, *The Norman Town in Dyfed, a Preliminary Study of Urban Form* (Urban Morphology Research Monograph Series, 1, University of Birmingham, 1996), pp. 23–35, 71–9; *BAHT*, I; E. Searle, *Battle Abbey and its Banlieu* (Toronto, 1980); T. R. Slater, 'Ideal and reality in English episcopal medieval town planning', *Transactions, Institute of British Geographers*, new series, 12 (1987), 191–203; T. R. Searle, 'Doncaster's town plan: an analysis', in P. C. Buckland, J. R. Magilton and C. C. Hayfield, eds., *The Archaeology of Doncaster*, vol. II: *The Medieval Town* (British Archaeological Reports, British Series, 1989) pp. 43–61; I. Soulsby, *The Towns of Medieval Wales* (Chichester, 1983), pp. 29–42.

meeting space for secular functions. In new-founded towns of the twelfth and thirteenth centuries these churches were often chapels of earlier-founded rural parish churches and stood in the market place without churchyards, but many grew to be large and wealthy institutions. Holy Trinity, Hull, is perhaps the best-known example, but St Saviour's, Dartmouth, is another. Elsewhere, churches surrounded by a churchyard are prominent in the midst of the market place. This is normally a sign of early market functions developing in or around the church on Sundays; Birmingham, with St Martin's-in-the-Bullring filling the southern end of the market is an example. A central water supply in terms of a well or pump, sometimes provided by the lord or a friary, as in Lichfield, was another common feature though, again, not to the same extent as in continental Europe. The most common feature of medieval market places, however, is what is normally called market infill, or market accretion; narrow strips of shop buildings with no yards or garden ground, separated by equally narrow lanes with names such as 'The Shambles'. These were formerly thought to derive from a process whereby market stalls became successively more permanent structures. However, documentary evidence has shown that in almost every case they are deliberate creations by the ground landlord to increase the rent roll. Townspeople protested at such action by the abbot of Cirencester in the thirteenth century, for example, and the infilling of the market place at Coventry can also be documented. In Ludlow, one row of the four strips which fill the eastern end of the market consisted of warehouses rather than shops.[37]

(iv) PLOT PATTERNS

Towns in which the plots have a length to depth ratio of more than six to one give them a very different texture from those with shorter plots. The little research devoted to plot patterns suggests that there is a distinct chronology and geography of urban plot patterns. Very elongated plots are associated with eastern England and with early foundation, whereas shorter plots are associated with the new towns of the twelfth and thirteenth century; very broad plots are characteristic of the 'Newland' suburbs established by some lords in the thirteenth and fourteenth centuries, as at Witney and Pershore.[38] Archaeological

[37] *VCH*, Yorkshire: East Riding, I; Conzen, *Alnwick, Northumberland* (2nd edn, 1969), pp. 126–7; R. Holt, *The Early History of the Town of Birmingham 1166 to 1600* (Dugdale Society Occasional Papers, 30, 1985); Lilley, 'Coventry's topographical development'; D. Lloyd and M. Moran, *The Corner Shop: The History of Bodenhams from the Middle Ages* (Birmingham, 1978); T. R. Slater, 'The town and its regions in the Anglo-Saxon and medieval periods', in A. D. McWhirr, ed., *Studies in the Archaeology and History of Cirencester* (British Archaeological Reports, British Series, 30, 1976), pp. 81–108; H. Thorpe, 'Lichfield: a study of its growth and function', *Staffordshire Historical Collections for 1950–51* (1954), 139–211.

[38] C. J. Bond and A. M. Hunt, 'Recent archaeological work in Pershore', *Vale of Evesham Historical Society Research Papers*, 6 (1977), 23–6.

research, for example in Worcester, suggests that the early Anglo-Saxon *haga* plots in the *burhs* were also broad plots which were subdivided into the characteristic urban strip plots only later.[39] Excavations have shown that plot boundaries consisted of ditches, fences, earth banks, live hedges or brushwood, or walls. Evidence of physical boundaries in Scotland running the length of the plots has been found in the form of gulleys and wattle fencing. Most of the tofts were delimited at the rear with fencing, or 'heid dykes', often broken with small 'back yetts', giving access to the burgh's common land beyond.[40] Excavations have also shown that plot boundaries are extremely long-lived features in many towns and that, once established, they continued unchanged into the industrial era, even where the original plot was subdivided many times over. The processes of plot subdivision and amalgamation are extremely complex in any larger town. Where back lanes provide access, plots can be divided transversely as well as longitudinally, increasing that complexity. Such processes have been reconstructed in places such as Winchester and Cheapside (London), where documentary and archaeological sources have been combined enabling plot change to be related to changing patterns of ownership, occupation and use. In smaller towns, such processes of change can also sometimes be reconstructed, as in Ludlow or Wells, but more usually they need to be inferred from the plan evidence as at Stratford.[41]

The main reason why urban plots became shorter in the twelfth and thirteenth centuries may be related to the increasingly urban use to which they were put. In the tenth and eleventh centuries people living in towns used their land in rural style for growing produce and pasturing animals overnight, whilst rubbish disposal in pits was another major use. By 1100, however, such large areas of land were thought no longer necessary, and most new-founded towns had plots of between one quarter and half an acre in size (0.1–0.2 ha). The dimensions of the plots are often documented in foundation charters either in areal or linear measures.

A particularly distinctive type of plot series is associated with many port towns. Excavations in London and elsewhere have shown that this type of plot series is related to the successive reclamation of the harbour front over time by the tipping of rubbish and the construction of new wharves further out into the water. The resultant plots contained long narrow tenements divided by narrow lanes running from the earliest harbour-front street back to the current wharf.

[39] Baker and Slater, 'Morphological regions'.

[40] P. Holdsworth, ed., *Excavations in the Medieval Burgh of Perth, 1979–1981* (Society of Antiquaries of Scotland, Monograph Series, 5, 1987), pp. 78, 82, for example.

[41] D. Keene, *Survey of Medieval Winchester* (Winchester Studies, 2, Oxford, 1985); D. Keene, 'The character and development of the Cheapside area', *Transactions of the London and Middlesex Arch. Soc.*, 41 (1990), 178–93; D. Lloyd, *Broad Street, its Houses and Residents through Eight Centuries* (Birmingham, 1979); A. J. Scrase, 'Development and change in burgage plots: the example of Wells', *J of Historical Geography*, 15 (1989), 349–65; Slater, 'Ideal and reality'.

Such plans can be found on the Stour harbour frontage of Sandwich, beside the River Hull in Hull, alongside the Thames in London and beside the Tyne in Newcastle, for example. The distinctive plan of Yarmouth with its narrow 'Rows' is a variant of this plan, which can also be found elsewhere around the coasts of northern Europe.

There are few documentary references to the ways in which urban properties or whole towns were laid out, or to the individuals who were responsible; for the most part the technicalities of the planning process must be inferred from the plan itself, and from such archaeological evidence as there is. The Wessex *burhs* demonstrate a concern to focus merchant properties along the axial roads, and to provide rear access to properties, at least in the case of Winchester; all show the importance of rapid access to the defences via an intramural road; while the regularity of the street grids shows that these places were conceived as an integrated whole, even if subsequently there needed to be adaptations to fit existing features such as minsters. It also seems clear that defence was of greater significance than trade, at least in the earliest years.

The monastic towns of the tenth and eleventh centuries show a greater concern with trade. The St Albans *Chronicle* reports the tradition that Abbot Wulsin, about 950, diverted the road from *Verulamium* through his new town in front of the abbey, and marked the diversions with new churches. It also makes reference to the provision of timber for settlers to build their houses.[42] The creation of larger walled precincts with ceremonial gateways from the 1060s often led to a second phase of planning with streets being closed or diverted to allow for enlargement; the Longport suburb of Canterbury was rebuilt in this way: the new grid plan at Bury was associated with such a precinct enlargement and street diversion, and similarly at Peterborough.

As secular and ecclesiastical lords began to develop new towns in the twelfth and thirteenth centuries, more information becomes available. The bishop of Worcester granted burgage tenure at Stratford in 1196; the plots of land so granted were specified as being 3.5 x 12 perches (18 x 60m). These were quite small plots (less than ¼ acre (0.1 ha)) in one respect, but their width was sufficient to allow holders to divide them into halves or thirds and to sub-let at a profit. A Worcester rental half a century later shows that this process of division was well underway since many landholders are recorded as in possession of half or one third of a burgage. In key locations such as street corners, subdivision could take place crossways as well as lengthways and in the centre of Stratford there were properties equivalent to only one ninth of an original burgage by the fourteenth century. Access to most of the plots in Stratford was from the street frontage; there were no back lanes. However, despite these processes of division, and

[42] H. T. Riley, ed., *Gesta Abbatum Monasterii Sancti Albani I–III* (RS, 1867–69), vol. I, p. 22, vol. III, p. 366.

sometimes of amalgamation, many of the initial plot boundaries survived through to the present retaining those initial dimensions.[43] The process of laying out burgages on the ground has also been traced archaeologically and can be seen most clearly in those towns which were comparative failures since the first stage of development is the only stage. The little market settlement founded at Chipping Dassett in 1267 had plots four perches wide and half an acre in area which were divided by shallow ditches. The same was true in the extension to Hedon in the 1130s, where the excavation and documentary evidence are in agreement that the initial layout was of plots 20 x 8 perches (100.6 x 39.6m) or one statute acre. The excavations show that some of the plots there had been divided in half quite soon after the initial development but there was little further division afterwards.[44]

The success of a new town foundation was not necessarily assured by the act of foundation, and most lords seem to have devised incentives to encourage settlers in the early years. Some may have followed the example of the abbot of St Albans, though there are few records of the provision of building materials. More provided land rent free for a period of from three to seven years. There are indications that in some towns the central plots were granted to estate officials and were sometimes of above average size, but there are few variants on the burgage rent which, by the twelfth century, was fixed at 12d. per year in almost all new planned towns whatever the size of the plot. In many Scottish burghs, too, there was a quite deliberate planning of streets and burgages, often respecting natural features, such as rivers, marshes and hills. There is evidence of deliberate importation of planners from other towns. St Andrews was laid out by Mainard the Fleming, who had previously planned Berwick, and Glasgow by Ranulf from Haddington.[45]

(v) DEFENCES

The pre-existence of Roman urban defences may have been particularly important in Britain, where the proportion of towns walled in the Roman period was, it has been asserted, 'without parallel elsewhere in the Empire'.[46] Though some of the earliest English towns were on non-Roman sites, many were located either inside or just outside Roman defences, and this became an important factor when the pressure of Scandinavian raids and invasions made defences imperative.

[43] Slater, ' Ideal and reality'; Slater, 'Domesday village'.

[44] *Medieval Settlement Research Group Annual Report*, 2 (1987), 24–5; C. C. Hayfield and T. R. Slater, *The Medieval Town of Hedon, Excavations 1975–1976* (Hull, 1984), pp. 12–16.

[45] A. C. Lawrie, ed., *Early Scottish Charters Prior to 1153* (Glasgow, 1905), no. 169; J. D. Marwick, ed., *Charters and Other Documents relating to the City of Glasgow* (Glasgow, 1894–7), vol. I, pt II, p. 5.

[46] J. Bennett, *Towns in Roman Britain*, 2nd edn (Princes Risborough, 1984), p. 29.

Nicholas Brooks has traced the history of the three 'common burdens' imposed by pre-Conquest kings, one of which was 'borough work' or the upkeep of *burh* defences. They were normally specified as incumbent on estates granted by royal charter, certainly from the mid- to late eighth century in Mercia and Kent, and from the mid-ninth in Wessex.[47] These communal defences were usually of earth and timber except where Roman walls survived, though Hereford and Oxford both built new defences at least partly in stone. That is not surprising, for shire towns played a key role in the West Saxon system of burghal defence, and all estates were expected to help with borough work for their shire town. The picture is less clear for the Danelaw: York's defences seem to have been repaired and extended by the Danish conquerors, but elsewhere traces of possible defences have been located only at Stamford and Nottingham, and even there 'it is not absolutely certain that they date to the period of Scandinavian control'.[48] Systematic defences of *burh* type were probably extended into this area only under Æthelflæd and Edward the Elder, as the Anglo-Saxon *Chronicle* implies. Nevertheless, the total number of towns with defences before 1066 was considerable. C. J. Bond accepts over 100 for the period 500–1066, whether Roman circuits wholly or partly reused, or new post-Roman defences. The figure is perhaps too high – it includes some uncertain examples, and several cases of more than one circuit within the same urban area (e.g. two at Thetford, and two or three at Norwich), but it is still an impressive total.[49]

The Norman Conquest introduced the new element of castles alongside communal defences; initially, at least, they were intended to overawe the inhabitants and most are located in one corner of the existing defences, allowing the garrison immediate access to open country. Where the town had its own walls, the two were usually linked in a common defensive circuit. The strategic location was everything and in many towns large numbers of houses were demolished to make way for the castle; in Worcester it took over part of the cathedral close. Many smaller towns, however, especially seigneurial boroughs, began with a castle, the lord of which would then encourage a settlement of traders and craftsmen outside the gate. Sometimes they would build defences of their own linked to the castle, but many such towns had no walls. In Wales and the borders, these early boroughs were often located within the castle bailey on rather inhospitable sites and it was only later that townspeople moved outside; the earliest phase of Bridgnorth is of this kind. C. Drage, who has made the first specialised study of urban castles, suggests that the term should be used for those castles

[47] N. P. Brooks, 'The development of military obligations in eighth- and ninth-century England', in P. Clemoes and K. Hughes eds., *England before the Conquest* (Oxford, 1971), pp. 69–84.

[48] R. A. Hall, *Viking Age Archaeology in Britain and Ireland* (Princes Risborough, 1990), p. 23.

[49] M. J. Jones and C. J. Bond, 'Urban defences', in J. Schofield and R. Leech, eds., *Urban Archaeology in Britain* (CBA Res. Rep., 61, 1987), pp. 95–8.

established within existing towns, and that 'castle boroughs' should define those where castles preceded towns.[50]

The Normans also repaired or enlarged communal defences, or created new ones, in many English towns, as well as extending them to Wales. Most were of earth and timber, but some gates and sections of walls were of stone by the twelfth century, or even earlier (Bootham Bar, York, has an eleventh-century core). Other towns were defended only by a ditch at the rear of the tenements, but this could be a substantial earthwork. Lichfield and St Albans had defences of this kind. From the thirteenth century, however, many towns built new circuits in stone, often for prestige as much as for defence. This late dating may explain why, unlike many continental towns, English ones rarely enlarged their circuit once it was of stone: 'the pattern in England is simpler because in the Norman period castles protected towns, and because most stone walls were built between 1250 and 1350, at the time of maximum urban expansion'. Indeed, it has been suggested that 'only Bristol, Lincoln, Norwich and York developed extensions in several directions which resemble the concentric rings of defences seen in continental cities'.[51] It should be added that many towns never acquired walls. Bond has counted 211 English and 55 Welsh towns with 'some sort of communal defences' between 500 and 1600, but some of those were not kept up after 1066; and even this full total represents well under half of all English and Welsh towns, wherever one draws the urban threshold.[52]

In Scotland, there is little evidence of highly defensive enclosing walls. Most typical was a form of wooden palisading, perhaps reinforced with a ditch, as in Linlithgow, for example, which was not even sufficiently secure to be able to withstand a strong wind. Even Berwick, one of Scotland's most important burghs, was protected merely by a ditch and palisade, although the latter may have been relatively substantial for purposes of defence. The function of such defences was, however, primarily to afford a measure of security from thieves for the townsman and his stock. The one early exception to this was Perth, whose 'wallis war all of stane' by 1312, and possibly earlier.[53] The encircling palisading, as opposed to the stone walls of Perth, and the town ports, which were more of the nature of simple bars than truly gates, were of more psychological than physical importance. They served to define the town limits, to set the town apart from the surrounding countryside.

[50] Slater, 'English medieval new towns'; C. Drage, 'Urban castles', in Schofield and Leech, eds., *Urban Archaeology in Britain*, pp. 117–32.

[51] M. W. Barley, 'Town defences in England and Wales after 1066', in M. W. Barley, ed., *The Plans and Topography of Medieval Towns in England and Wales* (CBA Res. Rep., 14, 1976), p. 68; Schofield and Vince, *Medieval Towns*, p. 36.

[52] Jones and Bond, 'Urban defences', p. 92.

[53] J. Bain *et al.*, eds, *Calendar of Documents relating to Scotland* (Edinburgh, 1881–1986), vol. IV, p. 459; J. Barbour, *The Bruce*, ed. W. W. Skeat (Scottish Text Society, 1894), vol. IV, p. 221.

In short, in both England and Scotland only a minority of towns were walled, in sharp contrast not only to Ireland, but also to continental western Europe, where almost all large towns were defended by 1200. Isidore of Seville had defined a city (*urbs*) as 'made by its walls', and German and French medievalists still tend to assume a similar definition. Yet some major towns, such as Cambridge, Ipswich and Reading, were undefended, or were at best protected by earthworks. For England, though not for Scotland, the explanation seems to have been a combination of a strong crown, general internal peace and limited urban autonomy.[54]

(vi) PUBLIC SPACE

In towns, as in villages, space can be divided into public, communal and private. Public space, where everyone had rights, included, in towns, the streets, lanes, market place and rights of way.[55] Communal space, where in the countryside villagers had rights, 'although the ownership of the land is usually vested in the lord of the manor', also had its urban equivalents: most early founded towns had their commons, strays and other public spaces over which grazing and other rights were confined to the townspeople, or even to freemen or burgesses only. Private space, of course, accounted for the largest part of the urban area, and included most house-plots as well as most ecclesiastical and commercial buildings. In Scotland, the town's common lands included the crofts for growing produce, although many necessities were grown in the backlands of tofts; grazing lands; and common land where peat and turf might be collected for both thatching and heating.

The equivalent to the lord of the manor was the lord of the town (often but not always the king), and he retained rights over the land in towns even when he had granted them self-government, though they were not always clearly defined. Much of Maitland's brilliant *Township and Borough* is an attempt to answer the apparently simple question of what King John really did when he granted the town of Cambridge to its burgesses: did he, for instance, intend that they should become owners of all land in the town 'not held in severalty'? Certainly the University argued later (in 1601) that John's charter had 'never carried the soil', and gave the townsmen no right 'to build and pester every lane and corner of the towne with unholsome and base cottages'.[56]

[54] D. M. Palliser, 'Town defences in medieval England and Wales', in A. Ayton and J. L. Price, eds., *The Medieval Military Revolution* (London, 1995), pp. 105–20; C. Coulson, 'Battlements and the bourgeoisie: municipal status and the apparatus of urban defence in later medieval England', in S. Church and R. Harvey, eds., *Medieval Knighthood, V* (Woodbridge, 1995), pp. 119–95; cf. also B. Brodt, *Städte ohne Mauern* (Paderborn, 1997).

[55] B. K. Roberts, *The Making of the English Village* (Harlow, 1987), p. 20.

[56] F. W. Maitland, *Township and Borough* (Cambridge, 1898), pp. 3, 91.

Next to a street system and common lands, one of the earliest requirements of a developing town was at least one open space for public meetings and commercial transactions, whether a churchyard or a market place. This was the pattern in early medieval Italy, and it seems to have obtained in England. In London, the folkmoot was held in St Paul's churchyard; at Oxford, by 1172, the portmanmoot met in St Martin's churchyard, and at Ipswich in 1200, the first municipal elections were held at a gathering of *tota villata burgi* in St Mary's churchyard.[57] Churchyards were used for similar functions in Scotland – for striking bargains, handfasting and the like. Churchyards were not the only open spaces: there were also purely secular ones, some of them possibly very ancient. London's Roman amphitheatre, discovered under Guildhall Yard in 1988, may well have determined the site of an open-air assembly and then of the Guildhall. 'Guildhall Yard occupies the central part of the arena and has evidently been an open space and natural place of assembly throughout London's history.'[58] Similarly, the head courts of Scottish burghs, which all burgesses were obliged to attend, were often held in the open air.

Public buildings in the modern sense were few before 1300, and were largely confined to defences, bridges, churches and town halls. Bridges were linked to defences in that both were important for major towns, and the maintenance of both was covered by the 'king's three works'. Some Roman bridges may have continued in use for centuries, but before the Conquest new ones were being constructed in England. London Bridge is recorded by the tenth century, and Brooks has recently analysed the evidence for the maintenance and structure of Rochester bridge, built on the piers of its Roman predecessor. There was a bridge over the Tay, at Perth, by 1209; and Glasgow's first bridge over the Clyde was built sometime before 1286.[59] Lords of towns came early to need specialised buildings from which they could administer the town itself, the district dependent on it or, in the case of shire towns, the whole shire. When William I planted a castle in virtually every English county town, that normally became the administrative headquarters of the county, but the process was not always sudden or complete. At York, around 1150, the 'king's house' stood on the site of a possible pre-Conquest palace, and the county court seems still to have been held there about 1200, rather than in one of York's two royal

[57] C. N. L. Brooke and G. Keir, *London 800–1216* (London, 1975), p. 249; R. H. C. Davis, *From Alfred the Great to Stephen* (London, 1991), p. 267; C. Gross, *The Gild Merchant* (Oxford, 1890), vol. II p. 116.

[58] *BAHT*, III, p. 19; cf. N. Bateman, 'The London amphitheatre', *Current Archaeology*, 137 (1994), 164–71.

[59] N. P. Brooks, 'Rochester Bridge, AD 43–1381', in N. Yates and J. M. Gibson, eds., *Traffic Management and Politics: The Construction and Management of Rochester Bridge, AD 43–1993* (Woodbridge, 1994), pp. 1–40, 362–9; A. A. M. Duncan, *Scotland* (Edinburgh, 1975), p. 469; *Registrum Monasterii de Passelet* (Maitland Club, 1832), p. 400.

castles.[60] Such king's houses have nearly everywhere vanished without trace, but St Mary's Guildhall at Lincoln has been recently identified as probably a surviving range of the royal *hospicium* where Henry II held court in 1157.[61] Towns in seigneurial hands also needed administrative centres: for secular lords, as at Warwick or Leicester, these were doubtless housed in the castle, but bishops and abbots needed unfortified headquarters. By the 1160s, Beverley had a stone bishop's hall islanded in the larger market place, and in the thirteenth century a bishop's guildhall was similarly located in Salisbury.[62]

The word guildhall is a reminder, however, that townsmen enjoyed some autonomy through guilds, of which the guild merchant often became the precursor for self-governing town councils; and these bodies needed meeting places also. York had a guild merchant by 1128, apparently with a hall on Bishophill, and London had its guildhall by the second quarter of the twelfth century, on the same site as the later 'guildhall' or city hall, while numerous other English towns had town halls or guildhalls by the thirteenth century.[63] In Scotland, the *Statute Gilde*, the rulings of the guild of Berwick, the earlier part of which is attributed to 1249 and the later dated to 1281 x 1294, suggest an institution of some age. The Berwick guild appears, however, to be of a pre-thirteenth-century origin; Perth and Roxburgh are known to have had guilds before 1202, as they are referred to in a charter of Roger, bishop of St Andrews, when the guild of that burgh was established; a guild had probably been established by *c.* 1209 in Edinburgh; Dundee, Inverness and Inverkeithing had guilds by 1165? x 1214, to be followed soon after by Aberdeen, Ayr, Dumbarton and Stirling. When their guild houses were established is unclear, although it is known that Berwick had a guild house before 1249.[64] Other small municipal buildings or structures, which can in some cases be documented by 1300, included market crosses, tolbooths, prisons, stocks, pillories and gallows.

What would now be called public services accounted for very little before 1300. Water supplies, for example, came largely from rivers, streams and wells; and the bishop's pretext for moving from Old to New Sarum in 1219 included

[60] W. Farrer, ed., *Early Yorkshire Charters* (Edinburgh, 1914), vol. I, pp. 405–7; Palliser, 'York's west bank', pp. 103, 108.

[61] D. Stocker, *St Mary's Guildhall, Lincoln* (The Archaeology of Lincoln, 12/1, 1991), pp. 37–41.

[62] R. Horrox, 'Medieval Beverley', in *VCH*, Yorkshire: East Riding, VI, p. 14; RCHM (England), *Ancient and Historical Monuments in the City of Salisbury*, vol. I (London, 1980), p. xliv, and plate 8.

[63] Palliser, 'York's west bank', p. 107; D. M. Palliser, *Domesday York* (Borthwick Paper, 78, York, 1990), p. 25; C. M. Barron, *The Medieval Guildhall of London* (London, 1974), pp. 15–18; R. Tittler, *Architecture and Power* (Oxford, 1991), pp. 12, 29.

[64] MS B65/1/1, f. 35r, St Andrews University Library; E. P. Dennison, 'Gilds merchant pre 1500' in P. G. B. McNeill and H. L. MacQueen, eds., *Atlas of Scottish History to 1707* (Edinburgh, 1996), p. 125; 'Statute gilde', in C. Innes, ed., *Ancient Laws and Customs of the Burghs of Scotland* (Edinburgh, 1868), vol. I, p. 66.

the lack of well water in the former. Urban religious houses could arrange for piped water, but municipal pipes and conduits are scarcely recorded before the late middle ages. An exception is Bristol, where the piped supplies brought in for the monasteries and friaries also supplied the townspeople through public cisterns by the early thirteenth century.[65] The same is generally true of street cleansing, paving and refuse disposal, though that may reflect records rather than reality. The earliest (pre-Conquest) surface of at least one Oxford street was of stone paving, while in 1286 Lincoln arranged for 'the paving of the high road running through the said town'. London, at least, had early public latrines: 'the necessary house built at Queenhithe' by Queen Matilda for the citizens was enlarged in 1237, the reference implying a twelfth-century origin.[66]

(vii) ECCLESIASTICAL PRECINCTS AND BUILDINGS

Churches and other ecclesiastical buildings played a prominent part in towns, physically as well as institutionally:[67] in many towns they and their precincts occupied a large proportion of the urban area (Figure 8.5), and were often the only buildings more than two storeys high. Both in pre- and post-Conquest times the largest churches (cathedrals, minsters, monastic houses and collegiate churches) played a crucial role, taking up a dominant position within existing towns (like the huge hill-top cathedral which arose at Lincoln after the diocesan seat was moved there in 1072) and acting as pre-urban nuclei in other places, around which a town grew up or was laid out (e.g. Beverley, Bury St Edmunds, Glasgow and St Andrews). A cathedral, or a monastery which was lord of a town, could take up an enormous amount of ground with its ancillary buildings. At Canterbury, Christ Church's precinct grew to cover almost the whole quarter between Northgate and Burgate;[68] at York the cathedral precinct occupied nearly the whole of the Roman fortress area; and at Lincoln it shared the whole upper city with the royal castle. By the end of the period, many of the great precincts were enclosed, forming a city within a city with their own gates into the precinct; between 1285 and 1299 the bishops or chapters of Lincoln, York, Exeter, Wells and Lichfield were all licensed to crenellate their closes.

English cathedrals were almost by definition urban: Lanfranc's decision in 1072 to move several bishops' sees reflected that. Collegiate churches were also largely urban: forty of them were in towns, some of them in towns which owed their existence to the college, including the northern trio of Beverley, Ripon and Southwell. Benedictine monasteries and priories also tended to be urban or

[65] *BAHT*, II, *Bristol*, p. 9.

[66] C. Platt, *The English Medieval Town* (London, 1976), p. 48; *CPR 1234–37*, p. 564; *CPR 1281–92*, p. 260. [67] See above, pp. 127–45.

[68] See plan reproduced in D. M. Palliser, 'The medieval period', in Schofield and Leech, eds., *Urban Archaeology in Britain*, pp. 60, 61.

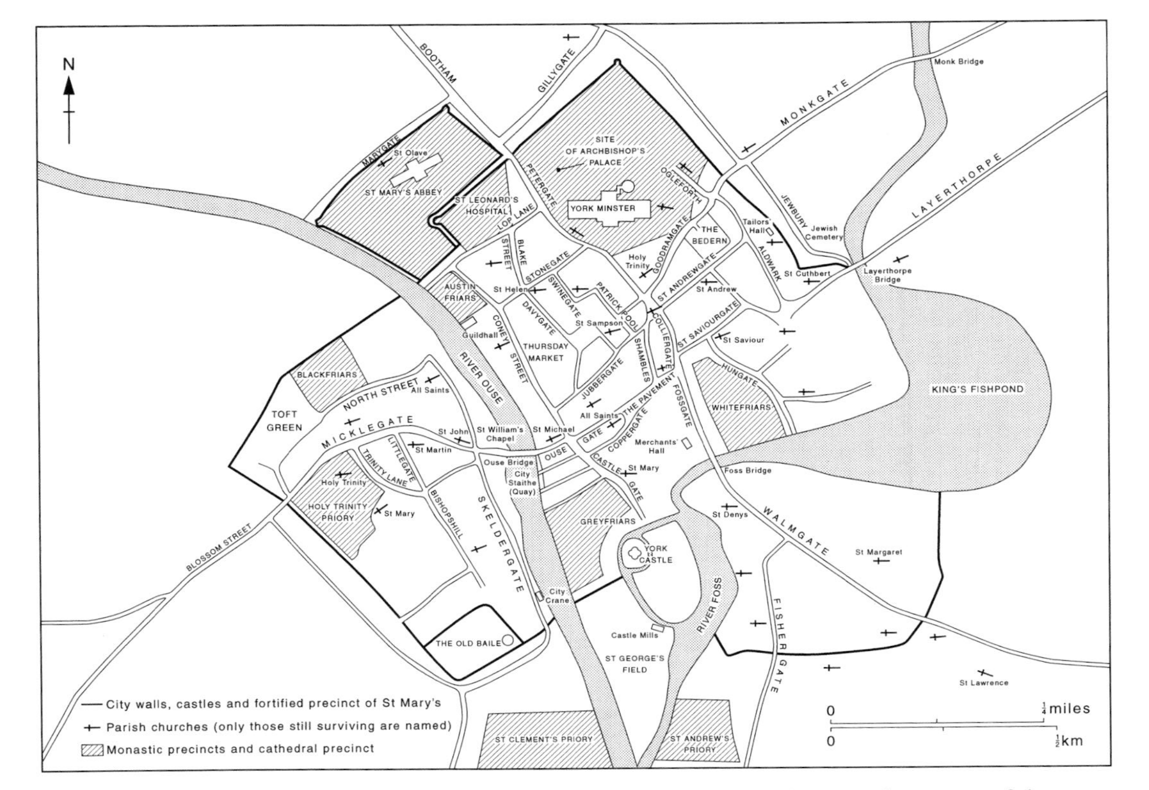

Figure 8.5 Collegiate and monastic precincts in medieval York, showing the extent of the ecclesiastical liberties exempt from civic jurisdiction

to give rise to towns, both before and after the Conquest: on Butler's figures, over 200 Benedictine houses out of 350 were urban, as were many Cluniac and Augustinian houses.[69]

Citeaux and its associated orders in the twelfth century, of course, deliberately chose remote rural locations, but in complete contrast the new mendicant orders of the thirteenth century were almost exclusively urban. The consequence was that large towns of early foundation acquired numerous monastic and mendicant houses: York had three Benedictine houses, one Gilbertine house and four friaries by 1300, all enclosed within their own precinct walls. In addition, there were, before the Black Death, an enormous number of urban hospitals – some 650 in England and Wales – and 'each town with a vigorous economic life could expect to maintain 3 or 4 foundations.'[70] Many were small and humble, but the major ones – including the four greater London hospitals, and St Leonard's at York – were large and well endowed, and with their own walled precincts. The majority of the later and smaller institutions were located at the urban fringe where large plots of land were more easily available whilst leper hospitals were normally beyond the built-up area. The same pattern may be seen in Scotland on a smaller scale. Unlike most of their counterparts in western Europe, however, religious houses in Scotland held much urban property. Grants to monasteries were made by all levels of society from the crown down; and by the thirteenth century religious houses were also purchasing holdings in burghs. By the end of the thirteenth century twenty-four houses held property in all of the fifty or so burghs. Some burghs might have had only one or two tenements possessed by a religious house; but others experienced a powerful monastic presence. Berwick, for example, was favoured by fifteen houses, some of which held more than one property in the town.[71]

Naturally, however, it was parish churches and chapels which were the main foci of most townspeople's loyalties. They were very numerous in the large, early-founded towns, their numbers being 'a rough measure of the relative importance of towns before 1100': they correspond roughly to the rank-size rule, with London followed by the provincial capitals of Winchester, Norwich, Lincoln and York.[72] The siting of churches varied considerably in these multi-parish towns. In West Midland cities where the main church had a monopoly of burials (Hereford, Chester, Gloucester, Worcester) popular sites were gates, street corners and even the middle of streets. In eastern England (e.g. Lincoln, York)

[69] L. A. S. Butler, 'Medieval urban religious houses', in Schofield and Leech, eds., *Urban Archaeology in Britain*, p. 167; A. H. Thompson, *The Cathedral Churches of England* (London, 1925), pp. 157–8; D. M. Palliser, 'The "minster hypothesis": a case study', *Early Medieval Europe*, 5 (1996), 207–14.

[70] Butler, 'Medieval urban religious houses', p. 169.

[71] W. B. Stevenson, 'The monastic presence: Berwick in the twelfth and thirteenth centuries', in Lynch, Spearman and Stell, eds., *The Scottish Medieval Town*, pp. 99–100.

[72] R. Morris, *Churches in the Landscape* (London, 1989), pp. 185, 188, 191.

'a more sprawling arrangement' allowed space for parish graveyards.[73] Smaller towns, and towns founded later like Coventry, had much smaller numbers: while towns founded after *c.* 1200 often had no parish church at all, but a chapel or chapels dependent on the surrounding rural parishes out of which they had been carved. Such was the case, for instance, with Hull, Market Harborough and many of the small Cornish boroughs. In Scotland, all towns were single parishes throughout the medieval period, although it might be argued that few truly urban parishes existed. There was often included within the parish a large proportion of parishioners from the surrounding rural hinterland, the division into parishes antedating the appearance of towns.[74] The earliest phases of urban churches, judging from recent excavations, were usually small single-cell buildings (in the case of St Mary, Tanner Street, Winchester, adapted from a domestic building), and some were certainly of timber (St Mary Bredin, Canterbury, is *ecclesia lignea* in a rental of *c.* 1180), though by the twelfth century stone was the norm. By the thirteenth century many had bell-towers, and the bells became useful markers for work as well as devotion. In 1301, York's fishmongers were forbidden to sell 'after Vespers is struck at the church of St Michael at Ouse Bridge until Prime is struck at the great church of St Peter on the next day.'[75]

(viii) DOMESTIC AND COMMERCIAL BUILDINGS

Though towns were often dominated physically and institutionally by royal, seigneurial and ecclesiastical buildings, the bulk of the urban fabric naturally comprised the buildings needed by townspeople for living and for earning a living – their houses, workshops, warehouses, inns, taverns and so on. For those before 1300, documentary and architectural evidence is scarce, and though archaeology is increasingly helping, very often the evidence is confined to foundations, and almost never is there surviving evidence for upper floors.

Many foundations of pre-Conquest buildings have now been excavated – over 600 in Ipswich, for instance, since 1974 – but few are yet published. They seem to have varied enormously, from sunken-floored buildings represented only by post-holes (like the earliest houses found at Canterbury and Ipswich) to substantial, reused Roman buildings, like the *petrosum aedificium* apparently still standing and inhabited in London in 889.[76] By the tenth century, substantial and

[73] J. Barrow, 'Urban cemetery location in the high middle ages', in S. Bassett, ed., *Death in Towns* (Leicester, 1992), p. 95.

[74] I. B. Cowan, 'The emergence of the urban parish', in Lynch, Spearman and Stell, eds., *The Scottish Medieval Town*, p. 82.

[75] M. Prestwich, *York Civic Ordinances*, 1301 (Borthwick Paper, 49, York, 1976), p. 13 (slightly adapted); T. Tatton Brown, 'Medieval parishes and parish churches in Canterbury', in T. R. Slater and G. Rosser, eds., *The Church in the Medieval Town* (Aldershot, 1998), pp. 236–71.

[76] D. Bullough, 'Social and economic structure and topography in the early medieval town', *Settimane di Studio del Centro Italiano di Studi sull' alto Medioevo*, 21 (1975 for 1974), 393.

well-constructed timbered houses can be demonstrated. From London come timbers reused in a later waterfront, exhibiting as yet unparalleled features of a timbered arcade, though evidence of London timbered buildings *in situ* has not been found before the eleventh century.[77] At Coppergate, York, four tenements, which were first built *c.* 910 of posts interlaced with wattles, were then rebuilt *c.* 973 with substantial uprights and supporting horizontal planks: the rebuilding has been interpreted as a means of enlargement through an upper storey, though only the semi-basement walls survive.[78]

Several excavated sites in London, Northampton, Lincoln and Durham suggest 'the emergence of the right-angled medieval house plan' and a degree of 'rectilinearity and organisation of properties' during the eleventh century.[79] Houses might be gable-end to the street, parallel, or in the case of grander properties, on courtyard lines, often with the main house towards the back of the plot and a row of shops in the front with a central gateway. Henry II in his charter to Scarborough (1155) demanded 6d. from each house 'whose sides are turned towards the street', but 4d. for those gable-end on. Classic examples of the former are the surviving Jew's House and Norman House at Lincoln, now dated respectively to the 1150s/1160s and 1180s.[80] They are also notable in two other ways: in being built of stone, a pattern increasingly common for wealthy townsmen in the twelfth and thirteenth centuries, and in combining domestic and commercial space: small shop units below, and domestic halls above. A variant on this pattern are the five stone halls terraced into the slope of Pride Hill, Shrewsbury, with commercial properties on the street front.[81] Stone houses were, however, always a small minority, and most substantial houses seem to have been timbered. The flimsy cottages of the urban poor have scarcely been studied or even identified from pre-1300 deposits, except in Winchester, though an early twelfth-century cob building at Wallingford has been excavated but not fully published.

In Scotland both archaeological and documentary evidence suggest that most urban buildings were of wood in this period. Fires were commonplace and houses rapidly reconstructed. Alexander II, in 1236, specifically permitted the townspeople of Ayr to take wood from the neighbourhood to build their houses.[82] This suggests little construction work in stone. Indeed, Froissart reported that the Scots were unconcerned about the devastation effected by the

[77] D. Goodburn, pers. comm.; J. Schofield, *Medieval London Houses* (New Haven, 1995), pp. 27–8.

[78] R. A. Hall, *English Heritage Book of Viking Age York* (London, 1994), p. 64.

[79] Schofield and Vince, *Medieval Towns*, p. 64.

[80] A. Ballard, ed., *British Borough Charters 1042–1216* (Cambridge, 1913), p. 47; R. Harris, 'The Jew's house and the Norman house', in M. Jones, ed., *Lincoln Archaeology 1992–3: 5th Annual Report of the City of Lincoln Archaeology Unit* (Lincoln, 1993), pp. 24–8.

[81] N. J. Baker, J. B. Lawson, R. Maxwell and J. T. Smith, 'Further work on Pride Hill, Shrewsbury', *Shropshire History and Archaeology*, 68 (1993), 3–64.

[82] W. S. Cooper, ed., *Charters of the Royal Burgh of Ayr* (Ayr, 1883), no. 6.

English, because to rebuild would take merely a matter of days, since all that was required was 'five or six poles and boughs to cover them'.[83] Archaeological excavations reinforce this view, although much of the research in this field, in Perth, St Andrews and Aberdeen, in particular, has been into backland sites, where the quality of housing would probably be poorer than on the frontages.[84] Twelfth- and thirteenth-century houses were little more than basic hut-type dwellings, made of stakes and interwoven wattles, with free-standing posts to support the walling. From the late thirteenth century, however, and as the town authorities revealed an increasing interest in plot layout and related planning matters, there is evidence of growing sophistication in house structures. Walls supported by free-standing posts were replaced by stake and wattle set in ground sills, first of wood and later of stone. This extra strength was reinforced by heavy clay, dung, mud or peat cladding on the walls. Increasing evidence of interior partition walls indicates different functional areas. Roofing continued, however, to be thatch of cut heather or turves of growing plants that offered water resistance. By the fourteenth century there is evidence of one stone house in Edinburgh, one in Aberdeen and three in Ayr, although others, undocumented, must have existed.[85] Early burgh laws laid down a standard of 20 feet (6 m) for a burgage frontage.[86] In practice, however, there was not always consistency. Excavations at Perth, for example, suggest 20 feet.[87] In Dunfermline, cartographic and sasine evidence indicate frontages of 22 feet, with a variant of between 20 and 25 feet (6–7.6 m).[88] Dundee's layout had much in common with the Dunfermline pattern,[89] whereas St Andrews had several variants, the most common being 36–8 feet (11–11.6 m) and 28–32 feet (8.5–9.8 m).[90]

Recent work is suggesting that, at least in London, there was a dramatic change in building technology around 1180–1220, when the technology of timber framing, lost since the Roman period, was redeveloped. This made multi-storey buildings possible, and allowed a considerable increase in population densities. It also meant that buildings became much more valuable since they lasted for more than a generation. In Paris in 1254, Henry III was much

[83] P. Hume Brown, ed., *Early Travellers in Scotland* (Edinburgh, 1891), p. 10.

[84] The work of the Scottish Urban Archaeological Trust in Perth and St Andrews, the Archaeological unit of the Aberdeen Museums and Art Gallery in Aberdeen and Scotia Archaeology in St Andrews should particularly be noted.

[85] J. Schofield, 'Excavations south of Edinburgh High Street', *Proc. of the Society of Antiquaries of Scotland*, 107 (1975–6), 180; W. C. Dickinson, ed., *Early Records of the Burgh of Aberdeen, 1317, 1398–1407* (Scottish History Society, 1957), p. 11; *Charters of the Friars Preacher of Ayr*, in *Archaeological and Historical Collections relating to Ayrshire and Gallaway* (n.p., 1881), nos. 10 and 12; E. Ewan, *Town Life in Fourteenth-Century Scotland* (Edinburgh, 1990), pp. 16–17.

[86] Fragmenta Collecta, *c.* 54, in Innes, ed., *Ancient Laws*.

[87] Spearman, 'Medieval townscape of Perth', pp. 55–6.

[88] R. J. D. Torrie, 'Central Dunfermline: an analysis of the 1988 road network and the geographical factors that determined its layout' (unpublished typescript, 1988).

[89] Torrie, *Medieval Dundee*, pp. 52–3.

[90] Brooks and Whittington, 'St Andrews', 288.

struck by elegant houses of four or more storeys, implying that he would not have seen these at home,[91] but by the late thirteenth century there were houses in Cheapside of three storeys plus a garret. Additional space could be obtained by jettying as well as by extra storeys: jettied buildings are recorded in London in 1246.[92]

The improvement in building technology may have been encouraged by a gradual if only partial conquest of the threat of fire. Fitz Stephen's opinion (1173–5) was that 'the only plagues of London are the immoderate drinking of fools and the frequency of fires.'[93] Certainly there are frequent records of major fires devastating whole towns down to the twelfth and thirteenth centuries, but it may be that the larger towns then took steps to minimise the risks – not by banning timbered houses, but by reducing the use of thatch and other flammable materials. In London, the first surviving building regulations, clearly intended in part to minimise fires, were drawn up in 1192 x 1212, with a further set issued by the mayor after a serious fire in 1212 and, although they were incompletely enforced (as late as 1302 the corporation were demanding that some thatched houses within the walls be reroofed with tiles), they may have made a substantial difference and, of course, imply that most buildings were by then substantial enough to take the weight of a tile roof.[94] Certainly London suffered no city-wide fire between 1212 and 1666: and other towns may have taken similar precautions, if not in the same explicit way: certainly there is no fire recorded as devastating an entire provincial town of the size of York, Norwich or Bristol in the thirteenth or fourteenth centuries.

Specialised shops for retail trade seem to have become common in London by the thirteenth century, and evidence from Lincoln has already been cited. This is not always easy to prove, since the word shop (*schopa*) meant 'workshop' as well as retail shop.[95] The documents also frequently use 'seld' (*selda*) for a retail outlet: thus Exeter's thirteenth-century customs provided for men living in the countryside but having selds in the city, and a Norwich man was fined for permitting outsiders to trade secretly 'within his seld.'[96] The word is often translated as 'booth' or 'stall', but that may be too loose in some cases: in London and

[91] H. R. Luard, ed., *Matthaei Parisiensis Monachi Sancti Albani, Chronica Majora* (RS, 1872–83), vol. V, p. 481.

[92] Schofield and Vince, *Medieval Towns*, p. 89.

[93] S. Reynolds *et al.*, eds., *Elenchus Fontium Historiae Urbanae*, vol. II, pt II (Leiden, 1988), p. 80.

[94] Schofield, *Medieval London Houses*, pp. 32–3 (correcting the traditional date of 1189 for the first regulations); R. R. Sharpe, ed., *Calendar of Letter Books . . . of the City of London: Letter Book C* (London, 1901), pp. 105–6.

[95] D. Keene, 'Shops and shopping in medieval London', in L. Grant, ed., *Medieval Art, Architecture and Archaeology in London* (British Archaeological Association Conference Transactions for 1984, 1990), pp. 29–46; Schofield and Vince, *Medieval Towns*, p. 135.

[96] M. Bateson, ed., *Borough Customs* (Selden Society, 18, 21, 1904–6), vol. I, pp. 112, 118; W. Hudson, ed., *The Leet Jurisdiction in the City of Norwich* (Selden Society, 5, 1892), p. 38.

Chester selds seem to have comprised large groups of privately owned stalls, bazaar-style.[97] A northern regional variant was 'dings', rows of small shops for letting, recorded in the Domesday account of York and in later references at Beverley and Hull.[98] Waterfront warehouses and quays also existed very early, although most of the surviving or excavated evidence is from the later middle ages as is the case in Scotland.

(ix) SUBURBS[99]

Strictly speaking, only defended towns had suburbs since the word implies an extramural location, especially at the European scale. However, in England it usefully defines those areas of towns beyond the administrative limits of the town as well as those areas outside defences. One of the more common types of suburb is the transpontine settlement, but these were often technically separate towns with their own borough privileges. Southwark, opposite London, is one of the earliest examples of this kind, but there are many others, because rivers frequently marked changes of landownership. Bridgetown Pomeroy, for example, stands across the Dart from Totnes and gained separate borough privileges in about 1250. It was sufficient of a success to be extended in 1268. The Redcliff and Temple suburb of Bristol is a more spectacular example which was not only outside the borough jurisdiction but, located on the south side of the Avon, was in Somerset rather than Gloucestershire. It grew rapidly in the twelfth century, acquired its own charter from Henry II in the 1160s and, by the early thirteenth century, was as prosperous as Bristol itself.[100]

Other suburbs were spread out along the principal approach roads to towns beyond the town gates and along the extramural roads that often ringed the defences. There are therefore characteristic plan forms with 'goose foot' patterns of roads coming together; narrow extramural roads lined with cottages which often encroached on the ditches, and broad single streets leading to the gate. Early markets or fairs were often located extramurally and led to later changes in the focus of the town as in Hereford and Northampton, or to the development of market places towards the fringe of the town simply because there was little space elsewhere as at Oxford and Stamford. Even if the provisions market was not in a suburban location, livestock markets often were for obvious reasons. Canterbury's *Hrythera ceap* shows this to have been so in pre-Conquest times, and similarly at Warwick. London's Smithfield was extramural, and at Stratford two market places were laid out from the start, the livestock market being on the edge

[97] Keene, 'Shops and shopping', pp. 38–9; Schofield, *Medieval London Houses*, p. 56.

[98] Palliser, *Domesday York*, p. 16.

[99] For many examples and plans of suburbs, see D. Keene, 'Suburban growth', in Barley, ed., *Plans and topography of Medieval Towns*, pp. 71–82, reprinted in R. Holt and G. Rosser, eds., *The Medieval Town* (London, 1990), pp. 97–118.

[100] Beresford, *New Towns*, p. 420; *BAHT*, II, *Bristol*, pp. 6–7.

of the borough. The breadth of approach roads was necessary for carts queuing to pay tolls at the gates or bars on market days; Biddle and Keene's detailed analysis of Winchester has demonstrated how blacksmiths and inns concentrated in these main approach roads in the twelfth century.[101] The sale of wood and hay seems to have been another common feature of these spaces. The majority of these suburbs had reached their greatest extent by the late twelfth century and many had already begun to shrink in size before the population decline of the fourteenth century. In most larger towns the suburbs were the location of hospitals, friaries and later monasteries, the former so that contagious diseases did not spread rapidly, the latter because of the difficulty of obtaining sufficiently extensive land. The vast majority of Scottish towns, however, did not develop suburbs in this period. Indeed, until into the seventeenth century, many towns retained their medieval limits.

This survey of urban topography before 1300 has, we trust, demonstrated how much has been learned over the past generation from interdisciplinary work. The British medieval town is often perceived in late medieval terms since, although the dominant public buildings – cathedrals and major churches, castles and town walls – are often survivals of the earlier period, almost all the surviving domestic buildings are of the fourteenth and fifteenth centuries at the earliest. It is very easy to picture a 'medieval city' in terms of, for instance, processions, pageants and plays performed against a backdrop of multi-storeyed timber-framed houses, and to forget that the physical environment, no less than the cultural context, is all of the very late middle ages. As the disciplines of archaeology and urban morphology continue to produce results on a large scale, they remind us ever more strongly how long was the history of the urban fabric in medieval Britain, and make us reflect that some early sixteenth-century townspeople lived in communities which had been urban for up to nine centuries, with all that that means in terms of the frequent renewal, destruction, repair and rebuilding of the urban fabric.

[101] W. Urry, *Canterbury under the Angevin Kings* (London, 1967), p. 108; N. P. Brooks, *The Early History of the Church of Canterbury* (Leicester, 1984), p. 32; Slater, 'Ideal and reality'; M. Biddle and D. J. Keene, 'Winchester in the eleventh and twelfth centuries', in Biddle, ed., *Winchester*, pp. 389–92, 433–4, 436.

· 9 ·

London from the post-Roman period to 1300

DEREK KEENE

(i) THE EARLY SETTLEMENT 400–900

IN THE late fourth century London, formerly one of the most substantial Roman cities north of the Alps, was the prime seat of authority in Britain and still a significant centre of urban life. Within a generation or two, following the withdrawal of imperial rule, the city had been virtually abandoned.[1] Yet later London owes much to its Roman predecessor. The carefully constructed site on the Thames, the bridge at the hub of an extensive road network and the ready access to a productive hinterland and to the river networks and markets of northern Europe endowed London with continuing potential as a place for business. The circuit of walls was to shape the city for centuries to come. Features within the walls, surviving as enclosures or as barriers to movement, influenced later settlement and may have marked seats of authority (Plate 3). During the fifth and sixth centuries this largely uninhabited site perhaps served as a focus for a zone of settlements within some twenty miles (32 km).[2] London persisted as a massive, but ruined, physical presence and as an idea in bureaucratic memory. Perhaps the most important element in the city's continuity is ideological: in the recognition of its power as the organising principle for a distinctive territory.

London comes more clearly into view in 601, when Pope Gregory envisaged that it would serve as the primatial see of England. Political reality no longer

[1] For recent work: B. Watson, ed., *Roman London: Recent Archaeological Work* (Journal of Roman Archaeology, Supplementary Series, 24, 1998); *LJ*, 20/2 (1995), republished in P. Garside, ed., *Capital Histories: A Bibliographical Study of London* (Aldershot, 1998). H. A. Harben, *A Dictionary of London* (London, 1918); C. N. L. Brooke and G. Keir, *London 800–1216* (London, 1975); *BAHT*, III; J. Schofield, 'The capital discovered: archaeology in the city of London', *UH*, 20 (1993), 211–24; and H. Creaton, ed., *Bibliography of Printed Works on London History to 1939* (London, 1994), are essential tools.

[2] *BAHT*, III, pp. 21–4; A. Vince, *Saxon London* (London, 1990), pp. 131–3.

matched Roman perceptions and London, in the province of the East Saxons, was under the overlordship of the king of Kent. Thus, in 604 the king himself established London's cathedral church of St Paul, although East Saxon apostasy was to break the episcopal succession for at least a generation. About 680 London was important for Kent: the archbishop did business there, the king had a hall and his officials supervised trade. The city could be characterised as the metropolis of the East Saxons. A landscape of authority was established within the city walls, comprising an enclosure around St Paul's, and an adjacent area to the north where the royal residence seems to have been.[3] By 700 London was again a major commercial centre, participating in a growing network of exchange, both inland and overseas. Sited at the margins of several kingdoms the city was attractive as a source of power. Kings of Mercia and Wessex extended their influence up to and beyond London, although it was primarily within the Mercian sphere, comprehending the dependent realm of Kent, that the settlement on the north bank of the Thames was to remain for 200 years.[4]

Throughout this time much of the city, as formally defined by the Roman wall, remained uninhabited. The entire area may have been an elite preserve, and its physical character, with substantial ruins blocking access from the river, made it difficult to adapt for renewed commercial use. For whatever reason, the commercial settlement was established outside the walls on an open site now associated with the Strand (Figure 9.1). It grew to occupy more than 150 acres (60 ha),[5] about a quarter of the area covered by the jurisdiction of the city from *c.* 1200 onwards, raising the possibility that at its peak *c.* 800 commercial London housed between 5,000 and 10,000 souls.

Much concerning the character of London in this period remains uncertain. The Strand settlement, densely built and carefully organised, was no mere appurtenance to a beach market. Enjoying an active trade with the region between Frisia and the Seine, it was probably the largest of the English *wic* trading settlements. Wine was probably a mainstay among its imports, which included pottery, glass and quern stones. Contacts with the district of Huy on the River Meuse suggest a trade in metals and possibly one in silks and spices. Exports included slaves and probably also agrarian produce and cloth. London artisans engaged in a range of manufactures.[6] Royal, aristocratic and ecclesiastical

[3] D. Whitelock, *Some Anglo-Saxon Bishops of London* (London, 1975); J. Campbell, 'The Church in Anglo-Saxon towns', *Studies in Church History*, 16 (1979), 119–35; W. Page, *London: Its Origin and Early Development* (London, 1929), pp. 127–9; *BAHT*, III, pp. 24–5; Vince, *Saxon London*, pp. 53–6; R. H. C. Davis, 'The college of St Martin-le-Grand and the anarchy, 1135–54', *London Topographical Record*, 23 (1972), 9–26.

[4] S. Keynes, 'The control of Kent in the ninth century', *Early Medieval Europe*, 2 (1993), 111–31.

[5] R. Cowie, 'A gazetteer of Middle Saxon sites in the Strand/Westminster area', *TLMAS*, 39 (1988), 37–46; R. Cowie, 'Archaeological evidence for the waterfront of Middle Saxon London', *Med. Arch.*, 36 (1992), 164–8.

[6] R. Cowie and R. L. Whytehead, with L. Blackmore, 'Two Middle Saxon occupation sites:

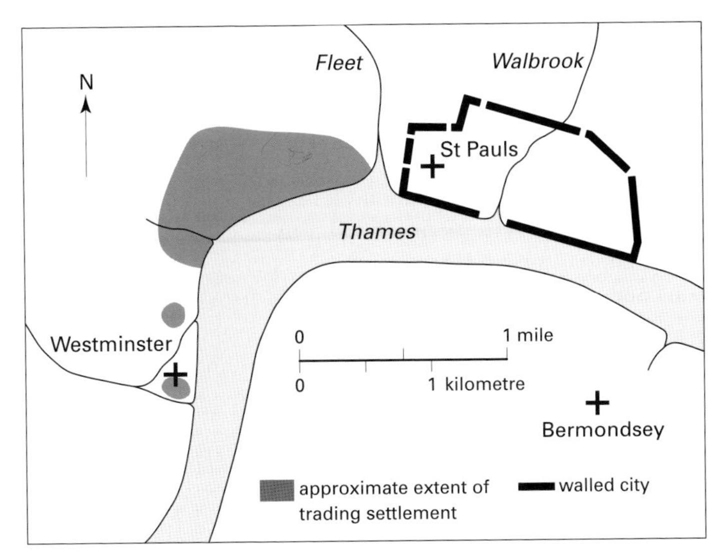

Figure 9.1 London in the seventh, eighth and ninth centuries
The extent of the settlement to the west of the walled city is based on information provided by the Museum of London Archaeology Service, 1998. The existence of churches at Bermondsey and Westminster is not certain.

demands undoubtedly stimulated London's commerce, but to see its economic life solely in terms of the acquisition of prestige goods for use as gifts and in display[7] is probably to exaggerate the role of a form of business which was to remain important in the city throughout the middle ages. A mixture of interests and commercial styles probably prevailed, including local trade in an open market, and merchants who traded both on their own account and as the dependants of powerful lords.

Nevertheless, the king's peace underwrote London's prosperity. Under Mercian rule the city occupied a pivotal point in a network which extended from Tamworth to the highly commercialised eastern parts of Kent, and thence to the continent. During the eighth century the bishops of London and Worcester and the monastery at Minster-in-Thanet obtained from the Mercian kings toll exemptions for their ships in London, and the Frankish abbey of St Denis may have had a base there.[8] In this light, the foundation by Earconwald, the seventh-century Kentish nobleman, later bishop of London, of the monastic houses at

excavations at Jubilee Hall and 21–22 Maiden Lane', *TLMAS*, 39 (1988), 47–163; R. L. Whytehead and R. Cowie, with L. Blackmore, 'Excavations at the Peabody site, Chandos Place, and the National Gallery', *TLMAS*, 40 (1993 for 1989), 35–176.

[7] Cf. R. Hodges, *Dark Age Economics* (London, 1982), and above, pp. 29–31.

[8] S. Kelly, 'Trading privileges from eighth-century England', *Early Medieval Europe*, 1 (1992), 3–28.

Barking and Chertsey[9] can be seen as an exercise in organising the resources of the immediate hinterland of the growing metropolis and in marking out London's territory at a time of political change. The continuing interest of the bishops of Worcester in London is also noteworthy, for they represented Mercian concerns. A mid-ninth-century bishop acquired a valuable property in the *wic* (*vicus*) of London, associated with the regulation of weights and measures and formerly held by the king's reeve.[10] In all likelihood it occupied a commanding position between the Strand and the river.

By 800 London's trading interest seems to have shifted northwards towards the Rhine. Coinage suggests a decline in its business from then on, and the most recent findings point to a shrinkage of settlement and the construction of a defensive ditch. Viking incursions, first touching London directly in 842, disrupted its trade and introduced a new element in the rivalry between Wessex and Mercia. Alfred's seizure of London from Viking control during the 880s was thus as much a triumph over Mercian interests. His purpose was presumably to establish a protected settlement, on the lines of the newly defensible towns of Wessex. This episode marks an important turning point in London's history: the Strand settlement was largely abandoned and from then on the walled city was to be the focus of London's commercial life.[11]

(ii) GROWTH OF THE RESTORED CITY 900–1300

At about this time groups of streets were laid out within the walls. The river frontage had a special place in the scheme, for the earliest identifiable streets led up into the city from landing-places which came to be focal points of trade. One, just below London Bridge, presumably served vessels from the estuary and overseas, while the other, above the bridge at the place now known as Queenhithe, was perhaps primarily intended for traffic with the Mercian hinterland. The earliest name for Queenhithe commemorates Alfred's son-in-law, the ruler of London and ealdorman of Mercia, who may also be remembered in the name Aldermanbury, a property which lay directly to the north near Wood Street and was perhaps associated with the royal residence. Continuity of interests is also indicated by the assignment of blocks of land near Queenhithe to the bishop of Worcester and the archbishop of Canterbury. New streets linked the waterfront to the street now known as Cheapside, probably laid out at the same time. This wide, straight street, running east from St Paul's along high, level ground, was

[9] Whitelock, *Some Anglo-Saxon Bishops*; Keynes, 'Control of Kent'; B. A. E. Yorke, *Kings and Kingdoms in Early Anglo-Saxon England* (London, 1990), pp. 45, 54–6. [10] *BAHT*, III, p. 29.

[11] T. Dyson, 'King Alfred and the restoration of London', *LJ*, 15 (1990), 99–110; Cowie and Whytehead, 'Jubilee Hall'; Whytehead and Cowie, 'Peabody site'; H. Pagan, 'Coinage in southern England, 796–874', in M. A. S. Blackburn, ed., *Anglo-Saxon Monetary History* (Leicester, 1986), pp. 45–65.

probably intended as the city's principal market place. Below the bridge, business was more exclusively focused on the river. Just above the bridge there is a group of streets laid out in an apparently regular fashion to either side of a spinal street or market, possibly in the years around 900. Thus, by the early tenth century the newly organised city of London seems to have contained several commercial nuclei. The western part of the city, protected by London Bridge, displays a coherent association between sites of power, the daily needs of the citizens, river trade and inland markets. The complex street plan was also influenced by the physical barrier of the Walbrook stream. London Bridge, on the site of its Roman predecessor, was another important element in the replanning of the city.[12] The bridgehead settlement of Southwark was a defended place in the early tenth century, and from then on developed as a dependency of London, but largely outside its jurisdiction.[13]

For much of the tenth century there is little evidence for London's overseas commerce. York, well integrated with the Scandinavian world, may have been the livelier place.[14] London's main traffic was inland along the Thames, and its contacts with the Oxford region were strong. By *c.* 1000, however, London was again an important site in a network of long-distance trade resembling that of the eighth century. This revival reflected the slow restoration of interrupted contacts, a steady growth in agrarian and industrial production (especially in northern France, the Low Countries and the eastern parts of England) and the stimulus to exchange provided by new supplies of silver. London was presumably one of the largest English recipients of German silver, shipped via Cologne with a wide range of other goods.[15] Towards the end of the tenth century London moved sharply ahead, as its relations with Winchester and its strategic role during the renewed Scandinavian invasions demonstrate.[16] London's reputed contribution to the Danegeld of 1018 amounted to a striking 13 per cent of the total for England, while throughout the period up to the Norman Conquest London was similarly prominent for its production of coin (Table 22.1). Whether that is a true measure of London's standing as a place of trade and population, whether that standing was set back or advanced under Cnut and

[12] Dyson, 'King Alfred'; K. Steedman, T. Dyson and J. Schofield, *Aspects of Saxo-Norman London*, vol. III: *The Bridgehead and Billingsgate to 1200* (LMAS Special Paper, 14, 1992), pp. 122–31 (and review in *LJ*, 20/2 (1995), 107–8); J. Schofield *et al.*, 'Medieval buildings and property development in the area of Cheapside', *TLMAS*, 41 (1993 for 1990), 39–238, esp. 178–83. The discussion in P. Nightingale, *A Medieval Mercantile Community* (New Haven and London, 1995), pp. 26–9, is fanciful.

[13] M. Carlin, *Medieval Southwark* (London, 1996), pp. 7–18.

[14] See below, pp. 226–8, 543–4.

[15] Vince, *Saxon London*, pp. 102–4; P. Spufford, *Money and its Use in Medieval Europe* (Cambridge, 1988), pp. 74–94.

[16] N. Banton, 'Monastic reform and the unification of tenth-century England', *Studies in Church History*, 18 (1982), 71–86; M. Biddle, ed., *Winchester in the Early Middle Ages* (Oxford, 1976), pp. 461, 556–7.

whether it was undermined after the Norman Conquest are matters for debate.[17] There is no doubt, however, that over the eleventh century as a whole London expanded rapidly, and that the process continued thereafter. Within the city there was a burst in the construction of houses and commercial buildings; many churches were erected which came to serve parish communities; on the waterfront the quays were restored, and what remained of the Roman riverside wall was removed. The main extension of the street network seems to belong to this period and records of 'new' streets indicate that the process was completed by the early thirteenth century.[18] The city also expanded beyond its original limit, which had followed a line some 220 yards (200 m) in front of the Roman wall: by 1200 its suburbs were defined by a boundary more or less identical to that of the modern city.[19] Extramural growth was extensive along the roads to the north, and greatest to the west, where by 1200 a network of side streets was developing beyond the city limit and building extended continuously as far as the abbey at Westminster, founded or refounded over 200 years before. Southwark became a substantial trading settlement in its own right.[20] London acquired a populous penumbra immediately beyond its jurisdiction: in 1334 Southwark, Westminster and adjacent hamlets were valued at 5 per cent of the city, more than the valuation of Southampton.[21]

The density of parish churches[22] provides clues as to the distribution of population and wealth in the city up to the mid-twelfth century. There were three areas of intense activity: in the neighbourhood of the Bridge; in a zone extending up from the river at Queenhithe into Wood Street; and in the central and eastern parts of Cheapside (Figure 9.2). By contrast, the northern, south-western and south-eastern parts of the city within the wall were less densely settled, as were the suburbs. One of the most distinctive expressions of the city's growth

[17] D. Metcalf, 'Continuity and change in English monetary history, *c.* 973–1086', *British Numismatic J*, 50 (1980), 20–49, and 51 (1981), 52–90; P. Nightingale, 'The origin of the court of Husting and the Danish influence on London's development into a capital city', *EHR*, 102 (1987), 559–78; Nightingale, *Medieval Mercantile Community*, p. 18 and n; P. Sawyer, 'Anglo-Scandinavian trade in the Viking age and after', in Blackburn, ed., *Anglo-Saxon Monetary History*, pp. 185–99; M. K. Lawson, *Cnut: The Danes in England in the early Eleventh Century* (London and New York, 1993), pp. 37, 82–3, 205–6. See below, p. 560.

[18] Steedman, Dyson and Schofield, *Aspects of Saxo-Norman London*; Schofield *et al.*, 'Medieval buildings', 178–83; J. Schofield, 'Saxon and medieval parish churches in the city of London', *TLMAS*, 45 (1994), 23–145.

[19] M. B. Honeybourne, 'The Fleet and its neighbourhood in early and medieval times', *London Topographical Record*, 19 (1947), 13–87, esp. 16–17; M. J. Gelling, 'The boundaries of the Westminster charters', *TLMAS* I (1953), 101–4; *BAHT*, III, pp. 77, 95 (s.n. Holborn Bars, Temple Bar).

[20] *BAHT*, III, pp. 40, 73 (s.n. Feweterlane); G. Rosser, *Medieval Westminster, 1200–1540* (Oxford, 1989), pp. 12–15; Carlin, *Southwark*, pp. 19–44.

[21] R. E. Glasscock, ed., *The Lay Subsidy of 1334* (London, 1975), pp. 187, 191, 298, 302.

[22] *BAHT*, III. See above, pp. 134–8.

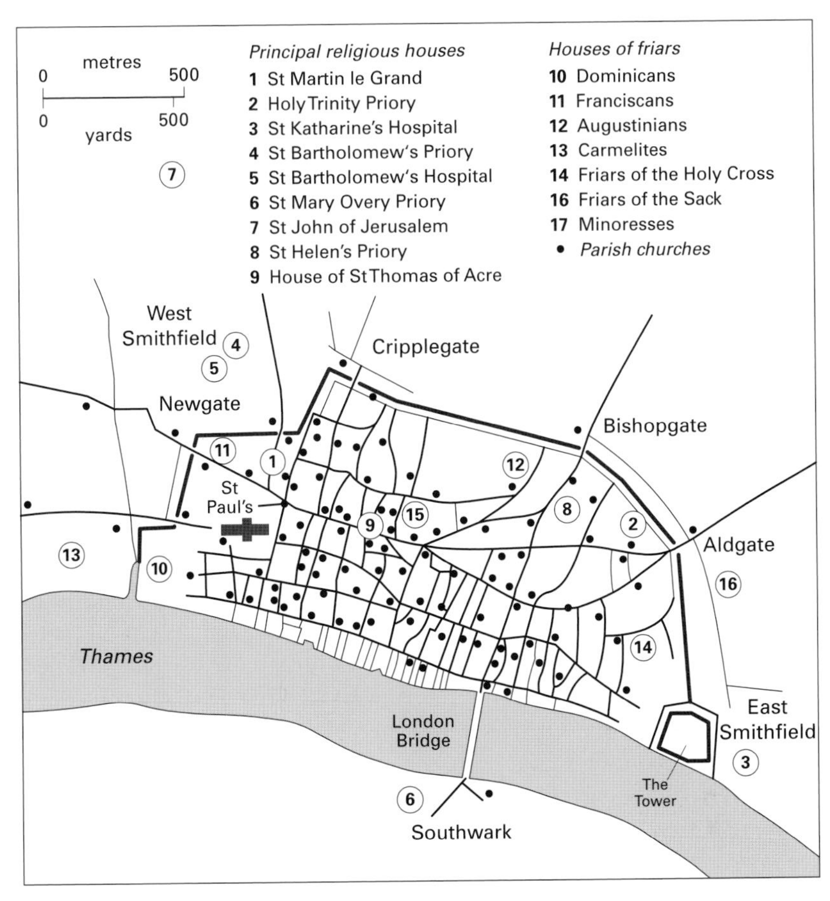

Figure 9.2 The City of London *c.* 1300
Source: BAHT, III. The streets are shown in simplified outline.

was on the waterfront, where, especially after 1100, the rebuilding of quays in more substantial form caused the land to be extended into the river, up to 100 yards or more in some places by 1300. This created a distinctive environment of narrow lanes leading down to the water, containing dwellings, warehouses, wine cellars and industrial installations. The busiest part of the waterfront lay between Queenhithe and the Bridge, and especially around Dowgate at the mouth of the Walbrook, which in and before the twelfth century was the focus for the trade in wine and other imported goods, and, possibly, moneying.[23]

[23] T. Dyson, *Documents and Archaeology: The Medieval London Waterfront* (London, 1989); *BAHT*, III, maps; D. Keene, 'New discoveries at the Hanseatic Steelyard in London', *Hansische Geschichtsblätter*, 107 (1989), 15–25; M. D. O'Hara, 'An iron reverse die of the reign of Cnut', in A. R. Rumble, ed., *The Reign of Cnut: King of England, Denmark and Norway* (London, 1994), pp. 231–82.

Developments in building during the twelfth and thirteenth centuries reveal London's wealth, the growth of infrastructure and responses to distinctive urban needs. Through the increasing employment of stone, London became more durable than it had been since Roman times. Stone cellars were built for the secure storage of goods. This, together with regulations concerning roofing materials and party walls, reduced the frequency of fires, which before 1200 had regularly devastated the city. Rules concerning the positioning of cess pits betray a concern for sanitary matters and a firm subsoil.[24] Above ground most houses were of timber, but changes in carpentry technique from around 1200 meant that it became possible to build high relatively cheaply, and so to accommodate a growing population without the lateral expansion which characterised earlier phases of growth.[25] In the Cheapside area and elsewhere the intensity of land use increased up to about 1315. Houses were subdivided, both horizontally and vertically; extra storeys were added; yards and gardens were built on; encroachment on to public spaces continued.[26] About 1300 it was thought that houses in the city commonly had two or three storeys over a cellar and were divided into several units of occupation. An English report of the much larger city of Paris about 1250 noted that the houses there were three or four storeys high.[27]

About 1300 medieval London reached a peak in size, and perhaps in aggregate wealth, from which, like the country as a whole, it subsequently declined. How large was London at that date? It is easier to demonstrate its exceptional scale in relation to other English towns than to estimate its absolute size. About 1100, to judge from the 110 or so parish churches within the city alone, fiscal indicators and mint outputs, London was about twice as populous and wealthy as the next English town. Its standing increased, for by the early fourteenth century it was five times wealthier than its nearest rival. London's primacy index (measuring its standing in relation to the next four cities) shows a similar trend, moving from around 0.8 in the eleventh century to 1.8 in 1334, when the city contained 1.9 per cent of English taxed wealth. The poll tax totals for 1377 indicate that London then contained 1.7 per cent of the assessed population of England: the proportion in 1300 may have been slightly lower, but that is far from

[24] J. Schofield, *Medieval London Houses* (New Haven, 1995), pp. 25–34; D. Keene, 'Fire in London: destruction and reconstruction, A.D. 982–1676', in M. Körner, ed., *Destruction and Reconstruction of Towns: Destruction by Earthquakes, Fire and Water* (Berne, 1999), pp. 187–211.

[25] G. Milne, *Timber Building Techniques in London, c. 900–c. 1400* (LMAS Special Paper, 15, 1992).

[26] D. Keene, 'A new study of London before the Great Fire', *UHY* (1984), 11–21; D. Keene, *Cheapside before the Great Fire* (London, 1985); D. Keene and V. Harding, *Historical Gazetteer of London before the Great Fire*, vol. I: *Cheapside* (Cambridge, 1987), *passim*; Schofield *et al.*, 'Medieval buildings', 178–93; H. M. Chew and M. Weinbaum, eds., *The London Eyre of 1244* (London Record Society, 6, 1970), pp. 136–53.

[27] H. T. Riley, ed., *Munimenta Gildhallae Londoniensis* (RS, 1859–62), vol. I, pp. 469–70; H. R. Luard, ed., *Matthaei Parisiensis Monachi Sancta Albani, Chronica Majora* (RS, 1872–83), vol. V, p. 481.

certain.[28] London's progress was almost certainly uneven. Some provincial ports and commercial centres probably had faster rates of growth, especially during the twelfth century, but there is no clear indication that at any stage London lost ground to the major provincial towns, for the fiscal indicators are too irregular and too subject to short-term political or military influences to provide more than a broad indication of trends.[29]

A dead-reckoning exercise based on property values and building densities in the heart of the city and in at least one suburb suggests that in 1300 conditions resembled those in 1550, when Londoners may have numbered about 80,000. Comparison with estimates for other English cities, and estimates of the population which could be sustained by the output of London's agrarian hinterland suggest that the population could have been that size or greater in 1300.[30] By the early sixteenth century a higher proportion of London's assessed wealth lay in extramural suburbs than had been the case in the early fourteenth, but that does not necessarily indicate a comparable shift in the distribution of population.[31] Estimating the population of medieval English cities and that of the country as a whole involves a wide margin of error. The poll tax figures provide the most reliable indicator of proportions. Thus, in 1300 if London had a population of 50,000 then the population of England was 2.9 million, while if London contained 80,000 inhabitants then England had 4.7 million, a national total which is low by comparison with many recent estimates.[32] Whatever the true figure, London was certainly a major city of the Latin West: much smaller than Paris or Milan, comparable to several of the greater Italian cities, and possibly larger than Ghent or Cologne. London's standing within Christian Europe had almost certainly been higher in 1100, when its merchants were more prominent. About 1200, when Paris was overtaking London and the Flemish cities were rivalling it

[28] D. Keene, 'Medieval London and its region', *LJ*, 14 (1989), 99–111; B. M. S. Campbell, J. A. Galloway, D. Keene and M. Murphy, *A Medieval Capital and its Grain Supply* (Historical Geography Research Series, 30, London, 1993), pp. 9–11.

[29] Biddle, ed., *Winchester*, pp. 500–1; J. F. Hadwin, 'The medieval lay subsidies and economic history', *Ec.HR*, 2nd series, 36 (1983), 200–17. A claim that London lost ground between 1213–14 and 1269 (P. Nightingale, 'The growth of London in the medieval economy', in R. Britnell and J. Hatcher, eds., *Progress and Problems in Medieval England* (Cambridge, 1996), pp. 89–106) is disingenuous since consideration of the assessments for 1255 would lead to the opposite conclusion. The exceptionally low level of London's assessment in 1269 is to be explained by its separate payments to the king and the Lord Edward in that year, by its recent payment of a large fine after the battle of Evesham, and by the departure of many Londoners with their goods so as to avoid taxation: T. Stapleton, ed., *De Antiquis Legibus Liber: Cronica Maiorum et Vicecomitum Londoniarum* (Camden Society, 1846), pp. 80, 107, 124.

[30] Campbell, Galloway, Keene and Murphy, *Medieval Capital*, pp. 43–5, 76–7.

[31] See below, pp. 558, 576. Arguments in Nightingale, *Medieval Mercantile Community*, and Nightingale, 'Growth of London', concerning spatial shifts in population and wealth within the city (not in themselves unlikely) misinterpret the evidence of property holding; the assertion there that the population in 1300 was 60,000 may be correct, but has no particular support from the evidence adduced.

[32] See above, p. 103.

in a way that they had not a century earlier, a contemporary who knew London's churches well said that they served 40,000 souls.[33] As a population estimate that is not unreasonable. It prompts speculation that in 1100 there had been at least 20,000 Londoners.

The most striking feature of London's position within the English urban hierarchy in 1300 was its extreme prominence and isolation. The nearest towns of any size were 60 miles (97 km) away.[34] England's second city, however defined, was more than 100 miles (161 km) from London, and even on the most generous estimate did not exceed 30,000 inhabitants. Immediately accross the sea, by contrast, there were four or five towns each with 30,000 or more inhabitants lying within 60 miles of Ghent.[35] Links between London and Flanders had long been close. London is thus to be visualised in two contexts. In England it was a primate city, distant from other major centres. Within that region unified by the Channel and the southern part of the North Sea, on the other hand, London was a large and relatively well-integrated participant in a highly urbanised network of intensive production and exchange. London's capacity for action in these two spheres was one of its unique characteristics as an English city.

(iii) COMMERCE AND MANUFACTURES

Trade was the foundation of London's power, and its share of English overseas trade was always large. Growth of wool and grain exports to Flanders favoured the east coast, and about 1200 London's share of the trade handled by eastern and south-eastern ports was probably not much greater than that of its nearest rival. By 1300, however, following a recent shift, it handled about 35 per cent of wool exports, and had perhaps doubled its share of overseas trade.[36] London's commerce was a microcosm of that of the kingdom as a whole, but it was distinguished by the scale of the demand that its inhabitants made upon the produce of the hinterland, by the wealth and status of the domestic consumers it supplied, by its distributive role and by its situation in relation to European trade routes on which Britain was the end of the line. It was the focus of a wide internal market for luxury goods. Around AD 1000, merchants were coming to London from Rouen (bringing whale products and wine), France (perhaps wine), Flanders (later, if not already, a source of woollen cloth), the Meuse valley (probably copper alloys, metal goods, silks and spices) and Ponthieu (later a source of agrarian produce, cloth and dyestuffs). The 'men of the Emperor', trading along the Rhine, enjoyed a privileged position and imported spices, grey

[33] Keene, 'Medieval London'. [34] See below, pp. 556–62.

[35] A. Derville, 'Le nombre d'habitants des villes de l'Artois et de la Flandre Wallonne (1300–1450)', *Revue du Nord*, 65 (1983), 277–99; W. Prevenier, 'La démographie des villes du comté de Flandre au XIIIe et XIVe siècles. Etat de la question. Essai d'interpretation', *Revue du Nord*, 65 (1983), 255–75. [36] Nightingale, 'Growth of London'.

and brown cloth (probably linen), gloves and presumably wine. Wool and other animal products were exported. Within a generation Scandinavia had probably been drawn into London's trade, and English merchants were active in northern Italy. By the early twelfth century London's spices and silks may have been supplied by English and Lorraine merchants who visited north-western Spain, as well as via Italy. London's wool exports to Flanders were by then substantial, but the export of English woollen cloth was also significant and was presumably handled by, among others, the Englishmen and Londoners who by the 1170s resided in Genoa and other Mediterranean ports. Lorraine merchants were prominent in London, and a contemporary noted the numerous Germans trading in the city. They brought wine, linens from Mainz and precious metals, stones and cloth (probably including silks) from Constantinople and Regensburg, a reference which suggests a supply route through Venice. They also brought 'mercery', comprising spices and wax, along with fustian.[37] London perhaps handled a traffic in tin, serving both its own metalworkers and the needs of Cologne and the Meuse valley.[38] Under Angevin rule the bulk of London's wine came to be supplied from Poitou and Gascony, links which in the thirteenth century promoted more direct contact between London and the Mediterranean. By the 1260s men from Cahors and Montpellier, Provençals and Italians had come to play the dominant role. Some of these merchants, with commercial interests extending from Italy to Norway, became major financiers in the city. Genoese established a sea route by which they traded directly to Flanders and London.[39]

Initially, merchants from outside the realm were confined to the waterfront zone, and their period of residence was strictly limited. Before 1200 this neighbourhood contained the 'seamen's church' and the famous cook shops which supplied their needs, while not long afterwards bathhouses and brothels were among services provided.[40] Such restrictions made it possible for the king's officers

[37] The key texts are a part of the law code known as IV Æthelred (A. J. Robertson, *The Laws of the Kings of England from Edmund to Henry I* (Cambridge, 1925), pp. 72–3) and what appear to be early twelfth-century regulations discussed in M. Bateson, 'A London municipal collection of the reign of John', *EHR*, 17 (1902), 480–511, 707–30, esp. 499–502. See also P. Nightingale, 'The London Pepperers' Guild and some twelfth-century trading links with Spain', *Bull.IHR*, 58 (1985), 123–32; Sawyer, 'Anglo-Scandinavian trade'; A. Sutton, 'Mercery through four centuries, 1130s–*c.* 1500', *Nottingham Medieval Studies*, 41 (1997), 100–25.

[38] A. Joris, *La ville de Huy au moyen âge: des origines à la fin du XIVe siècle* (Paris, 1959), pp. 242–4, 266; D. Keene, 'Metalworking in medieval London: an historical survey', *J of the Historical Metallurgy Society*, 30/2 (1996), 95–102.

[39] Brooke and Keir, *London 800–1216*, p. 266; T. H. Lloyd, *Alien Merchants in England in the High Middle Ages* (Brighton and New York, 1982); Nightingale, *Medieval Mercantile Community*, pp. 61–80, 104–5; D. Keene, 'William Servat', *New DNB* (forthcoming).

[40] D. Keene, 'Du seuil de la cité à la formation d'une économie morale: l'environment hanséatique à Londres, 1100–1600', in M. Aymard, J. Bottin and D. Calabi, eds., *Les étrangers dans la ville* (Paris, 1999), pp. 409–24.

effectively to exercise royal rights of pre-emption and to collect tolls. Moreover, they reserved the distributive trade within the city and beyond to Londoners and other Englishmen. By the 1120s London merchants appeared with luxury goods at the major provincial fairs, a role in which they remained prominent until the fairs' decline in the late thirteenth century. Some groups of aliens obtained privileges in the city. By the early twelfth century Danish and Norwegian traders had special rights of residence, and the Scandinavian cultural presence in London was strong, at least during the eleventh century.[41] Jews were present before 1100, and with the support of the early Norman kings had by the 1120s established a Jewish quarter close to Cheapside and the heart of the city's money market, in which they were to be important players up to *c.* 1250.[42] Rouen merchants had rights in London and other English markets by 1066, and Henry II at the opening of his reign granted similar privileges to the men of St-Omer. In the 1170s the king confirmed the men of Cologne in possession of their house on the river frontage, perhaps because of their role in the renewed flow of silver from Germany. From the mid-thirteenth century onwards Lübeck merchants active in the Baltic trade also used the property. The neighbourhood acquired a cluster of German, Flemish and Brabantine residents, while nearby there was an equally distinctive group of Gascons and southern Frenchmen primarily engaged in the wine trade. Some merchants from overseas acquired citizenship of London.[43] The principle of containing the visiting traders on the river frontage, or as lodgers in the houses of native citizens, broke down from the mid-thirteenth century onwards, especially as a small number of exceptionally wealthy Provençal and Italian merchants acquired houses close to the inland commercial heart of the city. Crown support for these outsiders, who provided vital services for the powerful, became one of the many bones of contention between king and citizens.[44] The cosmopolitan element in the population was a recognised characteristic of London and was cer-

[41] Bateson, 'Municipal collection', 500, 502; Brooke and Keir, *London 800–1216*, pp. 138–42; Nightingale, 'London Pepperers' Guild'; Nightingale, *Medieval Mercantile Community*, pp. 32–3, 106–7.

[42] J. Hillaby, 'The London Jewry: William I to John', *Jewish Historical Studies*, 33 (1992–4), 1–44; J. Hillaby, 'London: the 13th-century Jewry revisited', *Jewish Historical Studies*, 32 (1990–2), 89–158; R. Stacey, 'Jewish lending and the medieval English economy', in R. H. Britnell and B. M. S. Campbell, eds., *A Commercialising Economy* (Manchester, 1995), pp. 78–101; R. C. Stacey, *Politics, Policy, and Finance under Henry III, 1216–1245* (Oxford, 1987), pp. 154–9.

[43] Brooke and Keir, *London 800–1216*, pp. 265, 269–70; E. Perroy, 'Le commerce anglo-flamand au XIIIe siècle: la Hanse flamande de Londres', *Revue historique*, 252 (1974), 3–18; Spufford, *Money*, pp. 109–13; Keene, 'New discoveries'; Keene, 'Du seuil de la cité'; Keene, 'Servat'.

[44] Stapleton, ed., *De Antiquis Legibus*, p. 118; G. Williams, *Medieval London* (London, 1963), pp. 109–10, 117–18, 250–7 (all statements in this work should be treated with caution); Nightingale, *Medieval Mercantile Community*, pp. 91–6, 117–19; D. Keene, 'Wardrobes in the city: houses of consumption, finance and power', in M. Prestwich, R. Britnell and R. Frame, eds., *Thirteenth-Century England, VII* (Woodbridge, 1999), pp. 61–79.

tainly more prominent than in other towns.[45] Even so, those born overseas are likely to have represented less than a tenth of the city's population and most of them were probably humble immigrants from the Low Countries largely invisible in the records.[46]

London's merchants remained active abroad, although their share of the city's overseas trade is difficult to estimate. At the end of the century English merchants handled about 60 per cent of the city's wool exports, of which Londoners were perhaps responsible for half (i.e. 30 per cent of the total); Italians may have handled 20 per cent of the total; and the remainder was in the hands of German and Low Countries merchants. Before the dispute with Flanders in the 1270s Flemings had perhaps handled more than the Londoners. A tallage levied in 1304 points to the aliens' greater dominance of the city's economy overall: 60 per cent by value of the assessed chattels (perhaps predominantly money and stock in trade, both imported and for export) in the city was in the hands of a few merchants from the Mediterranean, and a further 7 per cent was in the possession of other aliens.[47] In the twelfth century and earlier the Londoners' share of the city's trade was probably much larger. London's exports were now more than ever dominated by wool destined mainly for Flanders.[48] Animal products, perhaps especially cheese and hides, were also significant exports, along with tin, pewter and sea coal. Corn, in which there was a substantial export trade from some English ports, was not a significant export from London, reflecting the large demand of its inhabitants.[49] To judge from the available information, which mostly concerns goods handled by aliens and purchases for the royal household, London's imports were dominated by cloth, mercery (principally fine textiles) and wine, while furs, copper, spices, iron, steel, weapons and armour represented the next largest categories by value. Since the twelfth century London had jealously protected its market in woad and other imported raw materials for cloth finishing, which sustained the city's industry and its distributive trade. Fish, including stockfish from Norway, was another large category but cannot readily be valued.[50] Between the eleventh and the late thirteenth century, as London was drawn into an expanding and progressively more integrated European market for raw materials and manufactured products, it seems that Londoners lost a share of their city's growing overseas trade, above all to Italians.

[45] Luard, ed., *Chronica Majora*, IV, p. 531, V, pp. 245–6.

[46] The pattern of immigration probably resembled that of the fifteenth century: J. L. Bolton, ed., *The Alien Communities of London in the Fifteenth Century* (Stamford, 1998), esp. pp. 8–10.

[47] T. H. Lloyd, *The English Wool Trade in the Middle Ages* (Cambridge, 1977), pp. 51, 56–8, 123; Lloyd, *Alien Merchants*, pp. 229–3.

[48] Nightingale, 'Growth of London', pp. 93–4; cf. Lloyd, *Wool Trade*, p. 123.

[49] PRO E122/68/18, 22, 23; E122/69/2; Campbell, Galloway, Keene and Murphy, *Medieval Capital*, pp. 27, 181.

[50] Bateson, 'Municipal collection', 725; Lloyd, *Alien Merchants*, pp. 53–4.

London was also by far the largest English centre for manufactures. Broadly, the distribution of its recorded crafts resembled that of other large towns.[51] Such a notion of occupational structure, however, does not provide the most useful insight into London's workshops: relatively few recorded Londoners had occupational names, which in any case are imperfect indicators of practice. Moreover, even around 1300, at least 80 per cent of the London workforce remains invisible, lacking the resources to be caught by tax listings (but not to be defined as impoverished on that account), not being within the franchise of the city, or excluded from view by virtue of their status as wives or servants. In addition, many lived on the fringes of the city and came in daily to trade or labour. Nevertheless, it is clear that London's size and wealth supported a greater variety of crafts, and more specialised activity within individual sectors, than elsewhere. Thus, around 1300, when it is possible roughly to compare London with cities such as Winchester, York, Norwich or Paris, the numbers of recorded occupations seems to have been in proportion to those cities' size. In the twelfth and thirteenth centuries London's character as a site for conspicuous consumption promoted crafts where there was a high input of skill using valuable raw materials. The national role of London goldsmiths and die-cutters demonstrates that this had been the case since the eleventh century.[52] In the thirteenth century this group of London craftsmen, along with other metalworkers, painters, embroiderers and sculptors, continued to meet the highest European standards.[53] London was also the site of simpler, but large-scale, manufacturing processes. In the thirteenth century the cheap cloth commissioned from the city's weavers by the burellers of Candlewick Street was widely distributed. A short distance away on the waterfront there was massive and sustained capital investment in the cloth-dyeing industry.[54] Tanners' yards occupied large areas outside the walls.[55]

[51] E. M. Veale, 'Craftsmen and the economy of London in the fourteenth century', in A. E. J. Hollaender and W. Kellaway, eds., *Studies in London History Presented to Philip Edmund Jones* (London, 1969), pp. 133–51; D. Keene, 'Continuity and development in urban trades: problems of concepts and the evidence', in P. J. Corfield and D. Keene, eds., *Work in Towns, 850–1850* (Leicester, 1990), pp. 1–16, esp. p. 7; E. Miller and J. Hatcher, *Medieval England: Towns, Commerce and Crafts, 1086–1348* (London, 1995), pp. 324–7.

[52] Brooke and Keir, *London 800–1216*, pp. 93–4, 283; P. Nightingale, 'Some London moneyers and reflections on the organization of English mints in the eleventh and twelfth centuries', *Numismatic Chronicle*, 142 (1982), 34–50; C. E. Challis, ed., *A New History of the Royal Mint* (Cambridge, 1992), pp. 78–9, 111–12.

[53] J. Alexander and P. Binski, eds., *Age of Chivalry: Art in Plantagenet England* (London, 1987), pp. 101–3, 115, 133, 152, 159–60, 167, 172, 273.

[54] E. M. Carus-Wilson, *Medieval Merchant Venturers* (London, 1954), pp. 213–14, 217–20; D. Keene, *Survey of Medieval Winchester* (Winchester Studies, 2, Oxford, 1985), vol. II, pp. 1097–8; Schofield, *London Houses*, pp. 218–19.

[55] D. Keene, 'Tanners' widows, 1300–1350', in C. M. Barron and A. F. Sutton, eds., *Medieval London Widows, 1300–1500* (London, 1994), pp. 1–27.

The occupational and social topography of the city[56] reflected the interaction between demands for space and successive stages in manufacture and distribution. London contained by far the largest and most sophisticated system of this kind in Britain. There were distinct neighbourhoods characterised by interdependent commodity markets and manufacturing crafts which formed extended 'communities of skill'. Key nodes for the exchange of information – especially in Cheapside, but also around Queenhithe, London Bridge, Billingsgate and Gracechurch – co-ordinated the requirements of householders, craftsmen, merchants, shoppers and aristocratic consumers, as well as markets in money and labour.[57] This system, embodying much social capital, was largely created over the three centuries up to 1300, and its influence was still apparent at the end of the twentieth century. London's retail trade was large. Shops are recorded in several English cities in the twelfth century, but only in London do we find the recognised profession of 'shopkeeper', one whose main business was the display and sale of goods. Many shops were devoted to both manufacture and distribution, but the extent of the space in Cheapside which in the thirteenth century was devoted to minute permanent trading sites in the street, in shops, and in the selds (bazaars) behind the shops, indicate that specialised retailing employed hundreds, if not thousands, of people, including many women. This and the archaeological evidence for the manufacture and use of cheap, serially-produced items of personal adornment indicates that the city contained a mass market for consumer products, perhaps from the eleventh century onwards, and certainly on a large scale by 1300.[58]

Supplying the basic needs of the population occupied a major share of the city's effort, as occupations and street-names show. London was notable for the multiplicity of its food markets: within the walls and without, near the river and inland, and to east and west of Walbrook.[59] Taverns, especially around Cheapside and near the waterfront, supplied large quantities of wine to consumers. Of high architectural quality, they were important meeting places for the elite. London had more taverns and brewers than any other English city. The exceptional scale of its trade in drink is also apparent in the substantial brewhouses, run by professional brewers, which by about 1300 had emerged in central commercial districts.[60]

[56] E. Ekwall, ed., *Two Early London Subsidy Rolls* (Lund, 1951), provides the best impression.

[57] A. Sutton, 'The silent years of London guild history before 1300: the case of the mercers', *HR*, 71 (1998), 121–41; Keene, 'Tanners' widows'; Keene, 'Metalworking'; Keene, 'Wardrobes'.

[58] D. Keene, 'Shops and shopping in medieval London', in L. Grant, ed., *Medieval Art, Architecture and Archaeology in London* (British Archaeological Association Conference Transactions for 1984, 1990), pp. 29–46; G. Egan and F. Pritchard, *Dress Accessories, c. 1150–c. 1450* (Medieval Finds from Excavations in London, 3, London, 1993), esp. pp. viii–ix.

[59] V. Harding, 'The London food markets', in I. Archer, C. Barron and V. Harding, eds., *Hugh Alley's Caveat: The Markets of London in 1598* (London Topographical Society, 137, 1988), pp. 1–15; Campbell, Galloway, Keene and Murphy, *Medieval Capital*, pp. 24–31, 81–107.

[60] Keene, *Survey*, 1, pp. 277; Keene, 'Wardrobes'. Keene and Harding, *Cheapside*, nos. 11/8, 10; 95/2–5, 18; 104/13, 20, 29–30, 32; 105/8, 11, 13–16, 19, 26; 145/1B, 36–7, 39.

The city authorities carefully regulated its internal market in grain, but there is little evidence that the mass of Londoners routinely suffered shortages. By contrast, the supply of wood fuel was more constrained and there are signs that London was on the verge of experiencing the type of fuel crisis which was to occur after 1550. There were, however, some years in which corn was in extremely short supply. In crisis years, such as 1258 and 1316–17, foodstuffs flowed into the city, where merchants stockpiled them so as to command the highest price. The poor flowed after them, seeking relief and, as in 1258, died in thousands in the streets.[61] London thus offered unique opportunities to gain reputation and grace through charity. The poor and disadvantaged were highly visible in distinctive locations: at Cripplegate (first recorded by name *c.* 1000), and later flowing through the streets towards distributions of doles, sometimes dying in the crush. Royal purchases of cheap cloth, shoes and food for the poor injected large sums into the city's workshops and markets. From about 1100 onwards the foundation of hospitals for the poor and the sick became a form of religious patronage in which magnates and the citizens developed complementary roles.[62]

London imparted a strong identity to its hinterland. That part of Mercia taken over by Wessex in 911 was described as 'the lands which belonged to' London and Oxford. Under Athelstan the city was the focus of a peace guild which served a territory extending well beyond the diocese. Those rural estates which in the eleventh century included property in London indicate that links between the city and the surrounding countryside were especially close within a radius of about 20 miles (32 km). Twelfth-century Londoners enjoyed hunting rights even further afield, although later they were limited to Middlesex.[63] By 1300 the city's demands had had strong influence on patterns in horticulture, woodland management and grain production within a region extending up to 50 miles (80 km) from the city where water transport was available and 25 miles when it was not, while the networks which supplied the city's livestock markets were more wide-ranging. Within this region small towns specialised in serving the London market, while rural and small-town industries also came to depend heavily on entrepreneurs and consumers in the city. The London market thus promoted

[61] H. R. Luard, ed., *Annales Monastici* (RS, 1864–9), vol. I, p. 166; Campbell, Galloway, Keene and Murphy, *Medieval Capital*, pp. 69, 89–90; J. A. Galloway, D. Keene and M. Murphy, 'Fuelling the city: production and distribution of firewood and fuel in London's region, 1290–1400', *Ec.HR*, 49 (1996), 447–72; W. C. Jordan, *The Great Famine: Northern Europe in the Early Fourteenth Century* (Princeton, 1996), pp. 156–62, 173–4.

[62] Ekwall, ed., *Subsidy Rolls*, p. 80; Brooke and Keir, *London 800–1216*, pp. 314–37.

[63] D. Whitelock, ed., *English Historical Documents*, vol. I: *500–1042*, 2nd edn (London, 1979), pp. 423–7; F. M. Stenton, 'Norman London', in D. M. Stenton, ed., *Preparatory to Anglo-Saxon England* (Oxford, 1970), pp. 23–47, esp. pp. 24–5; H. C. Darby and E. M. J. Campbell, eds., *The Domesday Geography of South-East England* (Cambridge, 1962), pp. 132–3; W. Illingworth and J. Caley, eds., *Rotuli Hundredorum* (London, 1812–18), vol. I, p. 419.

distinctive agrarian and industrial landscapes within a hinterland shaped largely by the lines of communication and by transport costs.[64]

Londoners regularly traded even further afield, at the great provincial fairs, at Yarmouth for herring, at Lynn and Hull for stockfish and Baltic goods, at Newcastle for the coal which by 1200 already made a significant contribution to the city's fuel supply, and in Norfolk for the light textiles which they sold in London and exported thence. London had a particularly close relationship with Canterbury and ports on the Strait of Dover.[65] The flow of people to London was shaped by these commercial links. Around 1300 London's migration field was by far the most extensive for any English city. Immigrants from the East Midlands and Norfolk were especially numerous, showing that local population densities could be as significant as trade for the composition of the metropolitan population.[66] The impact of the city is also apparent from the way in which Londoners turn up overseas. In the twelfth century they were prominent as crusaders and pilgrims, and resided in Genoa.[67] A London vintner, returning from Jerusalem in 1180, founded a college for clerks in Paris, a city where a century later people 'of London' were the largest group named by association with any town.[68] In thirteenth-century Dublin Londoners were a major force in the project to impose English civilisation on Ireland.[69]

(iv) POWER AND GOVERNMENT

London was likewise a source of order in home affairs. In the twelfth century the 'customs of London', or those 'of London and Winchester', set standards for other towns.[70] Those customs were well established *c.* 1000, when Londoners reported some of them to a royal inquiry. By that date London had taken precedence over

[64] See below, pp. 563–4.

[65] Stapleton, ed., *De Antiquis Legibus*, p. 79; H. E. Butler, ed., *The Chronicle of Jocelin of Brakelond* (London, 1949), pp. 75–7; Williams, *Medieval London*, pp. 161–5; Keene, 'Medieval London'; A. F. Sutton, 'The early linen and worsted industries of Norfolk and the evolution of the London mercers' company', *Norfolk Archaeology*, 40 (1987–9), 201–25; Nightingale, *Medieval Mercantile Community*, pp. 29–30; Galloway, Keene and Murphy, 'Fuelling the city'. See below, pp. 550, 580–1.

[66] E. Ekwall, *Studies in the Population of Medieval London* (Stockholm, 1956); P. H. Reaney, *The Origin of English Surnames* (London, 1967), pp. 345–51 and fig. IV; P. McClure, 'Patterns of migration in the late middle ages: the evidence of English place-name surnames', *Ec.HR*, 2nd series, 32 (1979), 167–82; Rosser, *Medieval Westminster*, pp. 183–6; Carlin, *Southwark*, pp. 144–8.

[67] W. Stubbs, ed., *Gesta Regis Henrici Secundi Benedicti Abbatis* (RS, 1867), vol. II, pp. 89–90, 115–18; C. W. David, ed., *De Expugnatione Lyxbonensi* (New York, 1936), pp. 55–7; Brooke and Keir, *London 800–1216*, pp. 270–1.

[68] H. Rashdall, *The Universities of Europe in the Middle Ages*, ed. F. M. Powicke and A. B. Emden, (Oxford, 1936), vol. I, pp. 501–2; Keene, 'Medieval London', 105.

[69] J.A. Watt, 'Dublin in the thirteenth century: the making of a colonial capital city', in P. R. Coss and S. D. Lloyd, eds., *Thirteenth Century England, I* (Woodbridge, 1986), pp. 150–7; P. Connolly and G. Martin, eds., *The Dublin Guild Merchant Roll, c. 1190–1265* (Dublin, 1992).

[70] See below, p. 565.

Winchester in setting the English system of measurement, and its court of Husting, later the focus of the city's jurisdiction in all matters concerning land and trade, set the national weight standard for silver. The ultimate authority for the customs of the city was the larger assembly, the folkmoot, which met three times a year in St Paul's churchyard.[71] That site, adjoining Cheapside, the early bullion market and the likely site of the royal palace, demonstrates the close association between the citizen assembly and the heart of power. By the twelfth century the Husting, an indoor assembly, met weekly, perhaps usually at the Guildhall which can first be identified at that time. Set back from the main areas of business, the Guildhall may have had a link with an earlier site of public authority.[72] The continuity in the character of London's customary regulations between the eleventh and the thirteenth century is testimony to their strength. Another important sign of the Londoners' cohesiveness is the guild of leading citizens, the *cnihtas*, whose rights and laws, said to extend back to the days of King Edgar, were confirmed by King Edward in 1042×44. Fifteen of their descendants in 1125 collectively assigned those rights, which included ward jurisdiction (covering defence, public order, sanitation and fiscal matters) in the suburb outside Aldgate, to the newly founded priory within. William the Conqueror's confirmation of the Londoners in their rights and customs is the earliest English civic charter.[73] Such rights and customs were not unique, but in London were exceptionally well secured. The care which monarchs took to acknowledge them demonstrates the degree to which they valued the city as a source of goods, money, armed men and popular acclaim. Indeed, the significance of London for its stock of armour and the power of its army recurs as a theme between the eleventh century and the later thirteenth.[74] Londoners were perceived, by themselves and others, as 'the chief men of the realm', and there was substance behind their claim in times of crisis to elect the king.[75] Throughout the twelfth and thirteenth centuries the monarch's relations with London set the tone for those with other English cities.

The strength of London also resided in those 'chief men' who regularly acted for the city in a variety of ways from the mid-eleventh century onwards. Powerful individuals and families can readily be identified, but it is far from clear

[71] Biddle, ed., *Winchester*, pp. 556–7; Brooke and Keir, *London 800–1216*, p. 249; Nightingale, 'Court of Husting'.

[72] W. D. Macray, ed., *Chronicon Abbatiae Rameseiensis* (RS, 1886), pp. 248–9; *BAHT*, III, pp. 23–4; C. M. Barron, *The Medieval Guildhall of London* (London, 1974), pp. 15–18; N. Bateman, 'The London amphitheatre', *Current Archaeology*, 12 (1994), 164–71.

[73] Stenton, 'Norman London', pp. 25, 32–3; F. E. Harmer, ed., *Anglo-Saxon Writs* (Manchester, 1952), pp. 231–4.

[74] Stenton, 'Norman London', pp. 28–9; Lawson, *Cnut*, p. 37; R. Johnston, ed., *Jordan Fantosme's Chronicle* (Oxford, 1981), p. 121; Stapleton, ed., *De Antiquis Legibus*, pp. 61–2.

[75] M. McKisack, 'London and the succession to the crown during the middle ages', in R. W. Hunt, W. A. Pantin and R. W. Southern, eds., *Studies in Medieval History Presented to Frederick Maurice Powicke* (Oxford, 1948), pp. 76–89.

how many they may have been in addition to the twenty-four aldermen of the wards, who first become visible as a coherent group during the twelfth century. Twelve 'better citizens' spoke with William Rufus at the beginning of his reign. In the twelfth century the terms 'barons', 'citizens', 'nobles' and *probi homines* of London appear at times to have been interchangeable and perhaps sometimes denoted that large number of inhabitants who assembled in the folkmoot. But the terms could also denote more restricted groups, and eventually the 'barons' came to be equated with the aldermen.[76] A London group equivalent to the committee of 'better burgesses' summoned at Winchester in *c.* 1110 would have contained some 300 individuals, 7 per cent of householders.[77] From the accounts of meetings in the thirteenth century, it seems that even greater numbers of Londoners (sometimes both men and women) met to do city business or to legitimate royal action. In 1258 an assembly of 864 men (possibly 7 per cent of householders) representing the wards was called to St Paul's for an inquiry into tallage assessments. That group appears to have been smaller than the *universa communitas* or the *populus* of London which at that time gathered in the folkmoot and elsewhere.[78] Throughout the thirteenth century, and especially during its last decades, *ad hoc* bodies of between 24 and about 100 individuals, representing the citizens as a whole and sometimes made up of the 'wealthier and wiser men' from each ward, met in conjunction with the aldermen, while the assemblies which 'received' the newly elected sheriffs could number around 300. Such loosely defined groups were perhaps equivalent to the *magnates* or *viri discreti* who earlier in the century had believed that they alone were capable of running the city's affairs and of maintaining its dignity. Eventually they took shape as the Common Council.[79]

In twelfth-century sources the landowning and official concerns of the leading citizens predominate, but some individual cases and what we know of the pattern of London's growth suggest that, as for their successors, the basis of their influence lay in commerce.[80] Prominent citizens were men, and occasionally widows, who invested heavily in large-scale trade and who had key roles in the money market. A major source of business was the supply of high-value imports and more basic goods and services to the magnates who maintained bases in London, although the significance of those clients is exaggerated by the survival of records. Nevertheless, such connections played an important part in mercantile and civic

[76] Stenton, 'Norman London', pp. 40–1; J. Tait, *The Medieval English Borough* (Manchester, 1936), pp. 256–9, 265–70; Brooke and Keir, *London 800–1216*, pp. 162–3.

[77] Biddle, ed., *Winchester*, p. 423; estimate based on the likely size of the two cities.

[78] Stapleton, ed., *De Antiquis Legibus*, pp. 16, 19, 31–2, 42.

[79] R. R. Sharpe, ed., *Calendar of the Letter-Books . . . of the City of London* (London, 1899–1912), *Letter-Book C*, pp. 1, 2, 4, 5, 23, 114; Tait, *Medieval English Borough*, pp. 302–16; Williams, *Medieval London*, pp. 37–42. See below, pp. 400–1.

[80] S. Reynolds, 'The rulers of London in the twelfth century', *History*, 57 (1972), 337–57; Nightingale, 'London moneyers'; Nightingale, *Medieval Mercantile Community*, pp. 23–42.

success, leading to commissions to act in household management, building projects and diplomacy, and to offices in the management of coinage or in local administration. Members of some London-based mercantile families in the twelfth and early thirteenth centuries had spectacular curial careers, rising to high positions in Church and state.[81] Among that minority of thirteenth-century aldermen for whom an occupation is recorded, the trades of draper, goldsmith and mercer clearly predominated. Towards the end of the century pepperers gained minor prominence in the group, but the trade in spices had long been important for leading Londoners and narrow specialism by commodity was not characteristic of leading merchants. Aldermen are also known to have sold wine and cloth and to have exported wool.[82]

Leading Londoners had large rent rolls in the city, and also land and country residences in the Home Counties or further afield. Landed and mercantile interests were closely intertwined, and it is likely that as in later centuries some leading merchant families had a landed origin. Several of those active in coinage and the exchange had property in Kent and Canterbury.[83] The London properties were commonly clustered near the principal residence. The city place-names Sabelinesbury and Bucklersbury commemorated such establishments of powerful twelfth-century families.[84] Parish churches, often proprietary churches associated with the residence, could be highly valued components of these estates, for which they might serve as administrative centres.[85] Some leading families were active in the city over many generations. One, engaged in moneying and luxury trade both within and outside the city, owning land in several counties, and including a canon of St Paul's among its members, can be traced in London from perhaps the beginning of the eleventh century to the mid-twelfth. The descent of the Cornhills runs from before 1100 well into the thirteenth century.[86] Other families with equally long careers as officeholders expressed their sense of identity through naming patterns and intermarriage. Yet the terms 'dynastic' and 'patrician' sometimes used to characterise the leading families in this period, in contrast to those of succeeding centuries, convey a misleading sense of the rigidity of London's social life, above all when invoked in explanations of civic politics.[87] It is clear, for example, that aldermanic office was not restricted to a closed group, and that the families of many leading men were prominent only for a

81 F. Barlow, *Thomas Becket* (London, 1986); *DNB*, s.n. Henry de Loundres.

82 A. B. Beaven, *The Aldermen of the City of London* (London, 1908–13), vol. I, pp. 371–9; M. Weinbaum, ed., *The London Eyre of 1276* (London Record Society, 12, 1976), pp. 82–3; Lloyd, *Wool Trade*, pp. 55–7.

83 W. Urry, *Canterbury under the Angevin Kings* (London, 1967), pp. 56–8; Williams, *Medieval London*, pp. 329–31.

84 E. Ekwall, *Street-Names of the City of London* (Oxford, 1954), pp. 194–7.

85 R. R. Sharpe, ed., *Calendar of Wills Proved and Enrolled in the Court of Husting, London, A.D. 1258–A.D. 1688* (London, 1889–90), vol. I, p. 18; Page, *London*, p. 141; Brooke and Keir, *London 800–1216*, p. 135.

86 Page, *London*, pp. 242–4; Nightingale, 'London moneyers'.

87 Notably in Williams, *Medieval London*.

short time. Moreover, the identification of individuals, their connections and even the significance of personal-names are more uncertain than often has been implied.

City property holding looms large in our knowledge of prominent Londoners. That reflects the survival of evidence, but in 1300 land, houses and rents probably contributed more to the wealth and longevity of leading London families than later. It made sense to retain control of sites in an expanding city. In the very different circumstances of the later middle ages, city property was perhaps less the generator of wealth which it may once have been. Lands and rents in London, however, were not the preserve of a secular elite, for a large share of the total rental of the city contributed to the incomes of religious institutions, while small rents were a vital financial resource for artisans and shopkeepers. Overall, London's property market was characterised by a fluidity and a sustained concentration of high value, which far exceeded those in any other English city.[88]

Londoners formed many group loyalties. Little is known of the secular functions of the city's 110 parish churches before 1300, but they probably played an important part in neighbourhood association, especially in the crowded heart of the city where some parishes contained fewer than fifty families. In John's reign the parishes within each ward were units of assembly for the city's army.[89] Twelfth-century Londoners formed fraternal organisations. Eighteen illicit guilds reported in 1179–80 covered a wide range in wealth and social standing: each had its alderman, at least four were associated with crafts, and the five bridge guilds had presumably been founded to support the rebuilding of London Bridge. Other guilds achieved public recognition. At least three twelfth-century artisan guilds enjoyed a more or less continuous existence into the fourteenth century. Guilds of weavers, bakers and, by the mid-thirteenth century, fishmongers exercised a regulatory authority, delegated by the crown, over those vital trades. Well before 1200 the saddlers' guild worshipped in the collegiate church of St Martin le Grand, close to the main focus of their trade. Tanners ceased to use their guildhall within Bishopsgate before 1190, but continued to maintain a society for the protection of their commercial interests until after 1350. The craft associations for which records proliferate from the 1260s onwards had deep roots in city life.[90]

City government derived its authority from the crown. Royal reeves had a recorded presence in the city from the seventh century onwards. They supervised the citizens' assemblies as well as the collection of the king's socage (elsewhere

[88] D. Keene, 'Landlords, the property market and urban development in medieval England', in F. E. Eliassen and G. A. Ersland, eds., *Power, Profit and Urban Land* (Aldershot, 1996), pp. 92–119.

[89] Bateson, 'Municipal collection', 728.

[90] Brooke and Keir, *London 800–1216*, pp. 278–82; Keene, 'Tanners' widows'; E. Veale, 'The "Great Twelve": mistery and fraternity in thirteenth-century London', *HR*, 64 (1991), 237–63.

usually described as landgable), profits of jurisdiction and the tolls due at the city gates, in the markets and at several points along the river, all revenues later contributing to the city's farm. From the eleventh century onwards they administered London and Middlesex together, and so came to be known as sheriffs rather than portreeves. By 1129 it was the practice for Londoners to participate in the choice of sheriffs. The farm for which the sheriffs were responsible amounted to well over £500 a year for much of the twelfth century and the bureaucratic element in the city's government was substantial.[91] Regalian interests were delegated to other bodies and officials. Significantly, in view of its earlier association with the ealdorman of Mercia, the large toll revenue from Queenhithe was kept separate from the farm.[92] The king's chamberlain of London, who supervised purchases for the king and exercised a jurisdiction over alien merchants, occupied an important independent position in the governance of the city and may at first have been closely associated with the palace.[93] Effectively to deal with London the king needed a powerful representative on the spot. Up to the twelfth century the bishop often served in that role. In the mid-eleventh century a staller, a nobleman in the royal household, was sometimes associated with the control of the city, where he stood after the bishop but above the reeves and leading citizens. After 1100 the justice of London, close to the king and at times also described as sheriff, occupied a similar position. Some justices also controlled several counties around the city. The small size of the pool of individuals and families from which sheriffs were chosen under Henry II suggests a similar intention to maintain a close link between the crown and a trustworthy group of city governors. The Norman castles also expressed the royal need to control the city. The lord of Baynard's Castle, as hereditary leader of the militia, had an influential role in city affairs. The Tower of London, erected in 1067, was thereafter enlarged and elaborated as both a symbol and an instrument of royal power. At several moments of crisis in the thirteenth century the king took the city into his hands and delivered it into the control of the constable of the Tower.[94]

When the king was in urgent need of cash or when his authority was challenged on the national stage, the Londoners' strength and cohesiveness enabled them to assert their power. Critical episodes were marked by their communal oaths sworn under Stephen and early in the reign of Richard I. The commune

[91] Brooke and Keir, *London 800–1216*, pp. 193–7, 212, 220; Reynolds, 'Rulers'; S. Reynolds, 'The farm and taxation of London, 1154–1216', *Guildhall Studies in London History*, 1/4 (1975), 211–28; C. W. Hollister, 'London's first charter of liberties: is it genuine?', *J Med. H.*, 6 (1980), 289–306; T. Madox, *The History and the Antiquities of the Exchequer* (London, 1711), p. 534; PRO SC6/917/1. [92] Harben, *Dictionary*, pp. 492–3.

[93] Page, *London*, pp. 122, 245, 260; W. Kellaway, 'The coroner in medieval London', in Hollaender and Kellaway, eds., *Studies*, pp. 75–91; Brooke and Keir, *London 800–1216*, p. 374.

[94] Stapleton, ed., *De Antiquis Legibus*, pp. 32, 106; Harmer, *Writs*, nos. 75, 105–6; Brooke and Keir, *London 800–1216*, pp. 193–222; Williams, *Medieval London*, pp. 235; D. Carpenter, 'King Henry III and the Tower of London', *LJ*, 19 (1994), 95–107.

of 1191 was quickly followed by the emergence of the mayor and the negotiation of a new relationship between the customary authority of the citizens and the royal governance of the city. The mayor embodied the interests of those powerful citizens who cast themselves as the leaders of London, but at the same time met the king's long-standing need for a stable institution through which he could address the many confusing interests within the city. London's mayoralty set a precedent soon followed in other English cities. Eventually, the office became the most important expression of the citizens' competence to run their own affairs under the king, and the office of sheriff came to be a duty rather than a source of power.[95]

Twelfth- and thirteenth-century London contained a honeycomb of separate jurisdictional interests in addition to those exercised on behalf of the crown. The most notable were the enclaves represented by the precincts of the religious houses. Less distinct were those blocks of land or rights enjoyed by powerful lords to whom the king had ceded rights represented by the term soke. The king's own soke included the public streets and those private properties where he retained a socage rent. Within the other sokes the jurisdiction of royal or civic officers was subject to restriction. The term soke, however, could also denote jurisdictions such as those exercised by the aldermen within the wards or by a craft over the practice of its trade, and sometimes simply denoted a unit of land and rent. The customs of London in land tenure and in other matters, as administered through the folkmoot and Husting, also applied within the sokes. Thus during the later twelfth and the thirteenth centuries, as the royal courts increased their strength and as the citizen body gained in coherence and capacity for action, the sokes lost the independence they had once enjoyed.[96]

From 1200 onwards the idea of unified civic administration in London came increasingly to supersede that of governance by a multiplicity of officials and institutions under the king. Civic government became increasingly elaborate. Courts under the mayor and under the sheriffs split off from Husting, providing more frequent and specialised sessions for the settlement of disputes, especially concerning trade. Record keeping became more prevalent. By 1200 an elaborate system for assessing the citizens' contributions to taxation according to the value and quality of their houses had come into being, and it was later the practice to archive the assessment rolls. Enrolment in the court of Husting of deeds and bequests concerning land in the city had begun by 1252, while twenty years earlier a public record of apprenticeships and admissions to the franchise had

[95] Brooke and Keir, *London 800–1216*, pp. 234–48; Williams, *Medieval London*, pp. 28–30.

[96] There is no satisfactory overall account of the London sokes, but see Stenton, 'Norman London', pp. 33–5; Page, *London*, pp. 127–58; A. H. Thomas, ed., *Calendar of Plea and Memoranda Rolls, A.D. 1364–1381* (Cambridge, 1929), pp. xv–xviii; H. M. Cam, ed., *The Eyre of London 14 Edward II, A.D. 1321* (Selden Society, 85–6, 1968–9), vol. 1, pp. lvi–lvii; P. Taylor, 'The bishop of London's city soke', *Bull.IHR*, 58 (1980), 174–82.

been established. New series of records proliferated during the strong mayoral and royal regimes of the last quarter of the century.[97]

As the mayoralty emerged, friction between more powerful and less powerful groups acquired a new focus. During the 1190s the levies which their leaders imposed on Londoners in order to meet royal financial demands prompted violent opposition under the spirited leadership of William fitz Osbert whose story, both as told by contemporaries and as reshaped in the mid-thirteenth century, throws much light on the realities and perceptions of city politics.[98] Thirteenth-century civic quarrels had similar roots, especially during the 1240s and 1250s when King Henry III, having exhausted other sources, began heavily to tax the city.[99] Many equated the mayoralty with an oppressive regime of aldermen and city magnates. The cross-cutting interests and alignments of families and individuals during these turmoils cannot readily be disentangled. Nevertheless, lineage, differences between established families and newcomers, the distribution of wealth, control of commerce and the workforce, and access to the patronage of the king and other powerful figures all played a part in promoting the violent struggles which broke out, above all at moments of national crisis. Sworn associations for the protection of group interests against the powerful were formed, said individually to contain hundreds, or thousands, of members. Strife often focused on the tendency of the powerful to off-load their share of the tax burden on to the poor. A related issue concerned the attempts by mercantile and entrepreneurial groups to organise craft production so as to meet their particular needs. These threatened both the profit of individual artisans and their collective regulatory powers. From the latter part of Henry III's reign onwards civic conflict thus tended to focus on issues concerning the crafts, while the crown's increasingly close relationship with alien merchants contributed to the tension. As in other English cities, the 1260s and early 1270s were especially critical, and groups were formed which tended to line up with the protagonists in national politics. Two mayors associated with 'popular' regimes granted regulatory privileges to large numbers of crafts, suppressed under subsequent mayors more closely aligned with aldermanic authority and the king.[100] The problems were not resolved, however,

[97] Stapleton, ed., *De Antiquis Legibus*, pp. 31–2; W. Cunningham, *The Growth of English Industry and Commerce during the Early and Middle Ages* (Cambridge, 1890), pp. 542–3; Bateson, 'Municipal collection', 508–10; A. H. Thomas, ed., *Calendar of Early Mayor's Court Rolls Preserved among the Archives of the City of London at the Guildhall* (Cambridge, 1924), pp. vii–xlv; Thomas, ed., *Plea and Memoranda Rolls*, p. xxx; Williams, *Medieval London*, pp. 77–84; G. Martin, 'The registration of deeds of title in the medieval borough', in D. A. Bullough and R. L. Storey, eds., *The Study of Medieval Records: Essays in Honour of Kathleen Major* (Oxford, 1971), pp. 151–93; D. Keene and V. Harding, *A Survey of Documentary Sources for Property Holding in London before the Great Fire* (London Record Society, 22, 1985), pp. 2–5.

[98] D. Keene, 'William FitzOsbert', *New DNB* (forthcoming).

[99] Cf. Luard, ed., *Chronica Majora*, v, p. 49.

[100] The lively account in Williams, *Medieval London*, contains many errors and forces the recorded events into a preconceived pattern. A useful approach is to compare the differing contemporary

and the position of craft guilds in relation to the franchise and government of the city remained at issue into the fourteenth century.[101]

(V) CULTURAL IDENTITY AND THE EMERGENCE OF THE CAPITAL

Struggles such as these sharpened the cultural and political profile of the city. In the eleventh century London's cultural identity seems relatively unformed, certainly by comparison with royal and ecclesiastical centres such as Winchester or Canterbury. Thus in 1100, despite its size and wealth, the city had only one major religious institution within its limits and only three more (two of them recently established) in the immediate vicinity. By 1200, however, London and its environs, with eighteen important religious houses, including seven hospitals, had conclusively emerged as the pre-eminent English concentration of innovative religious and charitable institutions. By 1300 the total had risen to thirty-three, including seven friaries and a further six hospitals. They conferred a new physical, spiritual and moral order on the sprawling metropolis. If London's friaries were a measure of its urban culture, there was no more urban place in Europe.[102] In the twelfth century the fame of the city's schools was a sign of its growing wealth and reputation and Londoners self-consciously interpreted their city with an awareness of both Roman and mythical pasts. Recycled classical rhetoric on metropolitan vice came readily to hand in condemning those sides of London life which undoubtedly attracted many to the city.[103] More sober records reveal staple elements of London life: people crowded together at home and in the streets, early and late; the dangers of oaths, drink and fires; riots against ethnic and religious minorities such as the Jews; and the vendetta and street-fight as expressions of political process.[104] Armed pilgrimage and naval expeditions had a special attraction for wealthy young Londoners. Violent games expressed Londoners' collective identity and became embroiled with larger issues. In 1222 a wrestling match between the citizens and the men of Westminster recalled the

viewpoints in Stapleton, ed., *De Antiquis Legibus* (note pp. 36, 55, 150–2); Luard, ed., *Chronica Majora*, IV and V; and Illingworth and Caley, eds., *Rotuli Hundredorum*, I, pp. 403–33.

[101] Veale, 'Great Twelve'; see below, pp. 405–6.

[102] Brooke and Keir, *London 800–1216*, pp. 293–337, provides a partial account. See below, pp. 565–8.

[103] Butler, ed., *Jocelin of Brakelond*, pp. 75–7; Stenton, 'Norman London', pp. 45–6; Brooke and Keir, *London 800–1216*, pp. 116–19, 181–2; J. Clark, 'Cadwallo, king of the Britons, the bronze horseman of London', in J. Bird, H. Chapman and J. Clark, eds., *Collectanea Londiniensia: Studies in London Archaeology and History Presented to Ralph Merrifield* (LMAS Special Paper, 8, 1978), pp. 194–9; J. Clark, 'A postscript', in *TLMAS*, 31 (1980), 96–7; J. Clark, 'Trinovantum – the evolution of a legend', *J Med. H.*, 7 (1981), 135–51.

[104] Stapleton, ed., *De Antiquis Legibus*, pp. 7, 50–1, 62, 99; Luard, ed., *Annales Monastici*, IV, pp. 141–2; Bateson, 'Municipal collection', 502, 720; R. B. Pugh, 'Laurence Ducket's murderers', *EHR*, 95 (1980), 331–8.

conflict of jurisdictions between the bishop of London and the abbot of Westminster and inflamed memories of London's recent support of Prince Louis against King John. Serious violence and destruction of property ensued. Royal officers forcibly took control of the city, and hanged one of the sheriffs.[105]

Saints contributed to the city's power. A contemporary could depict eleventh-century London, with slight inaccuracy, as that incomplete entity a city without saints. In the twelfth century a vision of St Bartholomew contributed to the mobilisation of resources for the priory and hospital founded in his honour, and the bishop's promotion of the cult of Earconwald may have been intended to furnish the city with a popular patron as well as to raise funds for rebuilding St Paul's after the fire of 1087.[106] Soon after 1170, however, the citizens found their own patron in the martyred Londoner, Thomas archbishop of Canterbury. The focus of the new cult was the site of the martyrdom, but London was a strong force in its development. William fitz Stephen's uniquely vivid portrayal of the city in the 1170s was written as an introduction to the life of a saint whose relationship with the king perhaps recalled that of the Londoners themselves. The cult quickly came to be identified with the civic enterprise of rebuilding London Bridge, and with the commune and mayoralty. About 1220, the year of Thomas' translation at Canterbury, he was portrayed on the splendid new seal of the barons of London as one of the city's two saintly protectors. At the same time the citizens acquired his birthplace in Cheapside so as to erect there a basilica, later an important setting for civic ceremonial. Thomas was claimed by the most powerful citizens, so perhaps those crowds of poor who in 1196 grovelled for the earth stained with the blood of William fitz Osbert were seeking a protector of their own.[107]

The arrival of Edward I as king in 1274 initiated a dramatic stage in the consolidation of London's civic culture. A detailed programme was put into effect, expressing ideals of social order and good government common to the city's leaders and the king. New notions of political science, as well as a sense that rule by the fit had been restored, lay behind the extensive codification of the city's customs and the deployment of texts such as Latini's *Tresor*. The programme, promoted both by mayors and when the city was under direct royal control between 1285 and 1298, restored the assize of bread, and provided for peace, public order, defence, the regulation of markets and crafts and the control of the strangers who in increasing numbers flocked to London. Masters, servants,

[105] Luard, ed., *Chronica Majora*, III, pp. 71–3; Luard, ed., *Annales Monastici*, III, pp. 78–9; D. Carpenter, *The Minority of Henry III* (Berkeley and Los Angeles, 1990), pp. 289–91; M. Weinbaum, ed., *The London Eyre of 1276* (London Record Society, 12, 1976), no. 116.

[106] Brooke and Keir, *London 800–1216*, pp. 325–8; E. G. Whatley, *The Saint of London: The Life and Miracles of St Erkenwald* (Medieval and Renaissance Texts and Studies, 58, Binghampton, 1989), pp. 57–66.

[107] Barlow, *Becket*, pp. 3–6, 12–15, 262; Keene and Harding, *Cheapside*, no. 105/18; D. Keene, 'Peter of Colechurch' and 'William FitzOsbert', *New DNB* (forthcoming).

apprentices and lodgers were to be registered as never before. A moral purpose is clear: the limits of the city were to be made secure, especially at night, and the unclean, such as whores and lepers, were to be expelled beyond them; standards were set for female dress. Under the royal regime the special rights of alien merchants were defined.[108] The anticipated arrival of King Edward prompted a comprehensive reordering of public space. Traders' stalls were cleared from Cheapside, thus enhancing its function as a processional way. New monuments marked out this space, such as the city's water conduit, constructed *c.* 1245, and the great cross commemorating Queen Eleanor erected in 1296. This encouraged new developments in civic ceremonial, building on the processions through the streets of the city and Westminster, accompanied by music, torches and dancing, which were a recorded feature of public celebrations by the 1230s, occasions for which streets were cleared of filth and obstructions.[109] Traders displaced from Cheapside were accommodated in a new wooden market house, which to judge from its name (*Hales*) was inspired by Parisian example. In this period too the city Guildhall was substantially rebuilt and provided with a new chapel, and the neglected finances of London Bridge put on a new footing.[110] Civic leaders involved in these developments expressed their solidarity in the musical and literary performances associated with the society known as the Puy, which followed a French model.[111] During the last years of the thirteenth century, there emerged a rich and varied civic culture with roots of its own and much in common with tastes at court.

Always a major gateway city, London nevertheless occupied, up to the eleventh century, a marginal site in the political geography of England. In the tenth century Winchester had a special role as a royal capital.[112] Under the Danish kings London perhaps established itself as a major focus of royal authority, as it certainly

[108] This important topic, touched on in Williams, *Medieval London*, esp. pp. 76–80, deserves a new assessment. Principal sources are: the 'assizes' and 'statutes' of Gregory of Rokesle, mayor, 1274–80 (Sharpe, ed., *Letter-Book A*, pp. 183–4, 204–5, 207–8, 215–19); the 'ordinances' of Henry le Waleys, mayor, 1282 (Sharpe, ed., *Letter-Book C*, pp. 84–5); the *Etablicementz* of the king, 1285 (Riley, ed., *Munimenta Gildhallae Londoniensis*, I, pp. 260–3, 275–6, 280–97, II, pp. 282–5, 502–3); and regulations of 1297 (H. T. Riley, ed., *Memorials of London and London Life in the XIIIth, XIVth, and XVth Centuries* (London, 1868), pp. 33–6).

[109] Illingworth and Caley, eds., *Rotuli Hundredorum*, I, pp. 408, 431; Stapleton, ed., *De Antiquis Legibus*, pp. 40, 87, 168; Luard, ed. *Chronica Majora*, III, pp. 334–6, 617, IV, pp. 261, 513, 736; Keene and Harding, *Cheapside*, no. 105/36.

[110] Illingworth and Caley, eds., *Rotuli Hundredorum*, I, pp. 403, 406, 415; W. Stubbs, ed., *Chronicles of the Reigns of Edward I. and Edward II.* (RS, 1882–3), vol. I, p. 90; Williams, *Medieval London*, pp. 86–7; Archer, Barron, and Harding, eds., *Hugh Alley's Caveat*, p. 4; Barron, *Guildhall*, pp. 20–1.

[111] A. F. Sutton, 'Merchants, music and social harmony: the London Puy and its French contexts *c.* 1300', *LJ*, 17 (1992), 1–17; A. F. Sutton, 'The Tumbling Bear and its patrons: a venue for the London Puy and mercery', in J. Boffey and P. King, eds., *London and Europe in the Later Middle Ages* (London, 1995), pp. 84–110.

[112] S. Keynes, ed., *The Liber Vitae of the New Minster and Hyde Abbey, Winchester* (Early English MSS in Facsimile, 26, Copenhagen, 1996), pp. 16–41.

did when Edward the Confessor rebuilt Westminster Abbey as his burial place and removed the royal palace from the city. The construction at Westminster of the largest royal hall in Europe, the misfortunes of Winchester and the twelfth-century characterisations of London as 'queen metropolis' and as *caput regni* all demonstrate that the city was of key significance for the kings who followed Edward. Given the peripatetic style of royal government, however, London could not command a central position in the Anglo-Norman and Angevin empires, despite its growing wealth. Under Henry II London succeeded Winchester as the chief English site for the royal treasure and Westminster became the principal seat of justice. London and Rouen were the two places where the king spent most time, but London remained in some senses peripheral and Westminster Abbey did not continue to attract substantial royal patronage. With the loss of Normandy in 1204, London's strategic position shifted, although up to the death of Henry III royal sentiment, and the antipathy between many Londoners and the crown, ensured that traditional patterns of royal residence persisted.[113]

Much as he may have detested citizen magnates, Henry III depended heavily on them for finance, and from the 1230s onwards perceived London as central to his standing as a Christian king. His was perhaps the most emotional and ambiguous relationship between any sovereign and the city, involving heavy exactions, confrontation and tearful pleas for loyalty. He saw London and Westminster with the Paris of Louis IX in mind, but the models of Rome and Jerusalem also contributed to the cultural and architectural programme which during his reign marked an important stage in the construction of the capital. At about the time of his marriage to Louis' sister-in-law he settled on the London Temple as the place for his burial, and in 1240 participated in ceremonies marking the completion of both the Temple church and St Paul's. Soon afterwards, however, he decided on the reconstruction of the more distant Westminster Abbey as a royal shrine. By that time the palace of Westminster was well on the way to being established as the fixed site of legal and financial administration, although the Temple and the Tower continued as repositories for treasure. King Henry's sense of the city and Westminster as places for the expression of monarchical ideals was apparent in 1244 when he supplied 20,000 meals for the poor at Westminster and 15,000 at St Paul's.[114]

Henry also promoted Westminster by establishing a new international fair, intended to generate revenue for the abbey by transferring trade from the city,

[113] Butler, ed., *Jocelin of Brakelond*, pp. 75–7; K. R. Potter, ed., *Gesta Stephani* (London, 1955), pp. 3, 7; Keene, 'Medieval London'; Nightingale, 'Court of Husting'; E. Mason, 'Westminster Abbey and the monarchy between the reigns of William I and John (1066–1216)', *JEcc.Hist.*, 4 (1990), 199–216; R. C. Stacey, *Receipt and Issue Roll for the Twenty-Sixth Year of the Reign of King Henry III, 1241–2* (Pipe Roll Society, new series, 49, 1992 for 1987–8), pp. v–xiv. See below, p. 561.

[114] Luard, ed., *Chronica Majora*, IV pp. 11, 49; H. M. Colvin, ed., *The History of the King's Works* (London, 1963), pp. 130–57; *VCH*, London, I, p. 468; T. F. Tout, *Chapters in the Administrative History of Medieval England* (Manchester, 1920–33), vol. I, pp. 196–7, 245–6; Stacey, *Politics*, p. 240.

and probably also to bring alien merchants to his doorstep. He had some success, although the commercial muscle of the Londoners subverted the enterprise and the service economy of Westminster stood in sharp contrast to the trade and manufactures of London.[115] The city of London emerged as the focal point in a ceremonial geography which expressed its position as a seat of commerce and kingship and emphasised the role of the Londoners as the prime assembly of the king's subjects. Foreign dignitaries, royal brides, the Blood and the Footprint of Christ and even an elephant were received at Dover or Canterbury, and progressed by land or water to London, where they were paraded through the city.[116] This elevation of London, and the periodic imposition of direct royal control, aggravated the tension between the monarch and the citizens and inclined many of them towards the baronial opposition. No wonder the Londoners pelted the queen from London Bridge as she fled in 1263, and that in his last years King Henry preferred to stay at his birthplace, Winchester.[117]

With Edward I royal attachment to Winchester abruptly ceased. He spent a much greater share of his time in or close to London than his predecessors had done, and his concern for the order of the kingdom included a vigorous policy for the city. He did not elaborate his father's cultural programme, but under the new regime London and Westminster enhanced their prestige as the seat of government. Moreover, the more frequent presence of the king, his council and their households contributed to a marked increase in the city's business and in its physical growth.[118] It was during Edward's reign that London came fully to be established as a capital city in the modern sense of the term: the focal point of English identity, language and law, the unchallenged seat of the state and the site where the severed heads of Welsh and Scots leaders were displayed.[119]

The interest of lay and ecclesiastical magnates in London paralleled that of the king. From before the Conquest they had maintained bases there so as to facilitate the sale of produce from their estates, the purchase of goods, the raising of cash and the exercise of political influence. All three motives are evident when, in the late eleventh century, the archbishop of Canterbury set up a business establishment in Cheapside and began occasionally to reside at Lambeth, where a permanent archiepiscopal residence was later set up, opposite Westminster.[120] Magnate houses proliferated in London after 1100, while those at Winchester faded away and lords based overseas shifted the business focus of their English

[115] Rosser, *Medieval Westminster*, pp. 97–115.

[116] Luard, ed., *Chronica Majora*, III, pp. 334–6, 617, IV, pp. 640–1, V, pp. 81–2; Stubbs, ed., *Chronicles*, I, p. 48; N. Vincent, 'Goffredo de Prefetti and the church of Bethlehem in England', *JEcc.Hist.*, 49 (1998), 213–35.

[117] H. R. Luard, ed., *Flores Historiarum* (RS, 1890), p. 482; Keene, *Survey*, I, pp. 88, 103.

[118] Keene, 'Medieval London'. [119] Stubbs, ed., *Chronicles*, I, pp. 90–1, 255.

[120] Brooke and Keir, *London 800–1216*, pp. 157–8; R. Fleming, 'Rural elites and urban communities in late Saxon England', *P&P*, 141 (1993), 3–37; Keene and Harding, *Cheapside*, no. 104/0.

estates to London. Many of these residences lay towards Westminster along the road from London, but the commercial attraction of the city is apparent from the way in which others clustered near the heart of trade. Even at the close of the thirteenth century magnates set up spacious dwellings at Holborn.[121] Such concerns, and the increasing flow of elite spending in London, are evident in the new type of aristocratic house known as the wardrobe which appeared in the heart of the city during this period. Imposing structures, wardrobes served as occasional residences and as sites for conducting financial business and for managing luxury consumption.[122] They exemplify the complexity of the late thirteenth-century capital, where interests of court, city and countryside interlocked, and show that the concentration of goods, money and information at the heart of the city was in key ways more powerful than royal patronage at Westminster. At the same time the cultures of London and Westminster operated within a common world of goods and ideas. Both drew inspiration from a multiplicity of sources, including monarchies and cities overseas. The city's mass market for products of all types, embodying the skills and requirements of its merchants, artisans and shopkeepers, was as important as elite patronage for the creation of a metropolitan culture. The increasing attraction of this dense cluster of interdependent functions was probably the main force behind London's rapid move forward as a centre of trade from the 1280s onwards.[123]

London's distinctiveness was rooted in its size and wealth, in the extent and diversity of its trade and manufactures, and in its close links with the continent. Its role as a capital city was secondary. Paris, by contrast, grew primarily because it was the seat of royal power. Over a long period London drew the monarchy to itself and by 1300 had made a fundamental contribution to shaping the state. As by far the most dominant city it drew in resources from a wide territory upon which it imposed coherent patterns. It set standards for social, commercial, municipal and cultural practice. Many of the most powerful individuals and institutions in the land found that they could most effectively prosecute their objectives through London. A central challenge in interpreting London is to assess its interaction with the provinces and their contribution to its life, within cultures and economies which varied regionally and were far from fully integrated. London had acquired a physical form, power, reputation and structures of government which were to endure for centuries, and which were distinct from its manifestation as a capital. That set up tensions between the liberty of London and the power of the nation, which had acquired many of the attributes of a city-state. Those tensions also have endured.

[121] Biddle, ed., *Winchester*, pp. 389–92; M. Chibnall, ed., *Charters and Custumals of the Abbey of Holy Trinity Caen* (British Academy, Records of Social and Economic History, new series, 5, London, 1982), pp. xxviii, 34, 90; Rosser, *Medieval Westminster*, pp. 16–32; Schofield, *London Houses*, pp. 34–5; Carlin, *Southwark*, pp. 19–44.

[122] Keene, 'Wardrobes'.

[123] Problems in North Sea trade also contributed: Nightingale, 'Growth of London'.

· 10 ·

The large towns 600–1300

DAVID A. HINTON

At the beginning of the seventh century, nowhere in Britain could have been described as a town, a place with permanent occupants whose life styles were distinct from those of rural contemporaries. Urbanism had become established at a few sites by *c.* 700, but even thereafter its progress was slow and intermittent.

Although vestiges of an urban past may have survived in fifth- and sixth-century Canterbury,[1] the new Church communities established inside and outside its walls after 597 did not stimulate rapid regeneration. An early seventh-century gold coin inscribed *Dorovernis Civitas* marks an aspiration to revive the city's status, and a valuable gold and garnet pendant and other objects have been found in extramural cemeteries and at intramural sites. Those who owned such things need not have lived within Canterbury, however, and occupation remained sporadic there, with one area that had already had post-Roman use even being abandoned. Sunken-featured buildings were still constructed in the style current since the early fifth century, but ground-level timber structures have also been found. Iron workers certainly continued to operate inside the walls,[2] and another craft, pottery making, was beginning to become more specialised, but the quality of the local clays probably caused it to be extramural.[3] Some demand for higher-quality products may have been developing, and the 675 charter reference to *Fordewicum* is usually taken to mean that a *wic* or landing-place was coming into use downstream from

[1] See above, p. 23.

[2] Excavation reports in the Canterbury Archaeological Trust's Archaeology of Canterbury series, and in *Archaeologia Cantiana*. See also L. Webster and J. Backhouse, eds., *The Making of England: Anglo-Saxon Art and Culture A.D. 600–900* (London, 1991), pp. 23–4, 26–7 and 36–7.

[3] A. Mainman and N. Macpherson-Grant, in K. Blockley *et al.*, *Excavations in the Marlowe Car Park and Surrounding Areas* (Archaeology of Canterbury, 5, 1995), pp. 816, 819–87, 895. For the Canterbury documentation, see above, pp. 52, 80.

Canterbury on the River Stour at Fordwich, where toll privileges were granted in the next century.[4]

(i) *EMPORIA*, *MERCIMONIA*, AND THE *WIC* SITES

Both the volume and the nature of archaeological discoveries suggest that by the early eighth century there were landing-places that were more than just fishing-villages whose inhabitants occasionally travelled further afield, or places where occasional beach-markets were held. Three, perhaps four, can certainly be called large towns by northern European standards (Figure 10.1). What Bede termed an *emporium* is presumably the area of some 150 acres (60 ha) upstream of the old Roman walls of London, known as *Lundenwic*.[5] Southampton (*Hamwic*, and a *mercimonium*) was perhaps smaller than *Lundenwic* at some 100 acres (42 ha); it was downstream of a Roman fort.[6] Ipswich (*Gipeswic* in 993, its earliest documentary mention) had no Roman site in the immediate area.[7] At York, another major bishopric and like London and Canterbury probably a minting-place for seventh-century gold coins, a scatter of mid-Saxon-period finds indicates some use of the Roman walled areas in the eighth century, but the main density has been found outside them, downriver at Fishergate, where excavation has revealed an intensively used complex of buildings and pits.[8] Whether this area covered as much ground as the other three *wic* sites has yet to be demonstrated. Although York was known as *Eoforwic* by the eleventh century, pre-Viking references to it are as a *civitas*, and the two texts that mention a Frisian merchant and Frisian ships in the same breath as York do not explicitly locate them there, so Fishergate may indeed have been quite a small *wic*, with perhaps another to serve the near-by 'minster' at Beverley yet to be discovered.

[4] On this, and on the *wic* sites' functions and trade generally, see above, pp. 32–3, 52. Also S. Kelly, 'Trading privileges from eighth-century England', *Early Medieval Europe*, 1 (1992), 3–28.

[5] See above, pp. 188–9, and R. Cowie, 'Archaeological evidence for the waterfront of middle Saxon London', *Med. Arch.*, 36 (1992), 164–8.

[6] A. D. Morton, ed., *Excavations at Hamwic*, vol. 1 (CBA Res. Rep. 84, 1992), and work by P. Andrews (Six Dials site), J. Bayley (metalworking), J. Bourdillon (animal bone), J. Coy (animal bone), M. Garner (Cook Street site), D. A. Hinton (metalwork), R. Hodges (pottery), J. R. Hunter and M. P. Heyworth (glass), D. M. Metcalf (coins), H. E. Pagan (coins) and J. Timby (pottery).

[7] K. Wade, 'The urbanisation of East Anglia: the Ipswich perspective', in J. Gardiner, ed., *Flatlands and Wetlands* (East Anglian Archaeology, 50, 1993), pp. 144–51; K. Wade, 'Ipswich', in R. Hodges and B. Hobley, eds., *The Rebirth of Towns in the West AD 700–1050* (CBA Res. Rep. 68, 1988), pp. 93–100. Unfortunately there are no full reports yet on any aspects of recent work in Ipswich, but I am grateful to my colleague Dale Serjeantson for showing me her unpublished typescript on the animal bone. See also below, pp. 641–2.

[8] R. L. Kemp, *Anglian Settlement at 46–54 Fishergate* (The Archaeology of York, 7/1, 1996), and monographs in the same series by A. J. Mainman (pottery), T. O'Connor (animal bone) and N. S. H. Rogers (artefacts). Also D. Phillips and B. Heywood, ed. M. O. H. Carver, *Excavations at York Minster*, vol. 1. *From Roman Fortress to Norman Cathedral* (London, 1995).

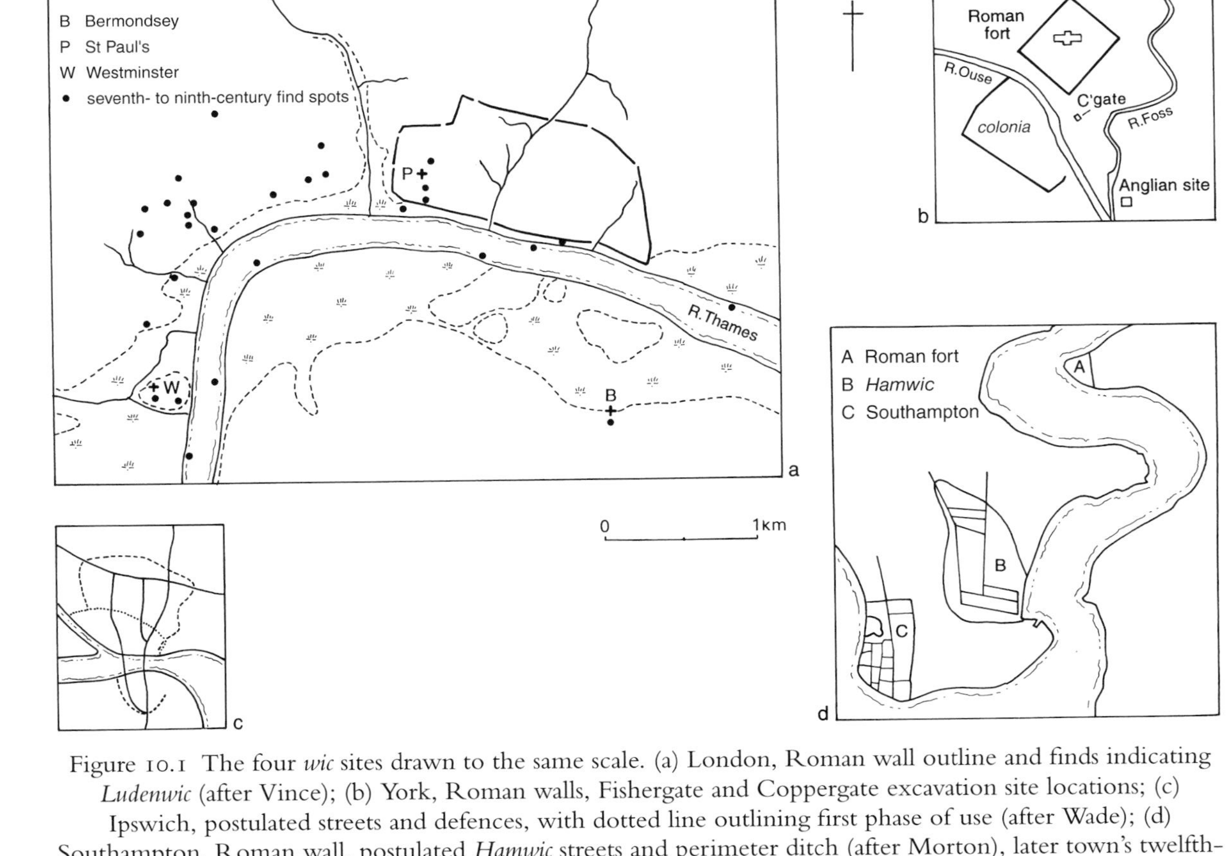

Figure 10.1 The four *wic* sites drawn to the same scale. (a) London, Roman wall outline and finds indicating *Ludenwic* (after Vince); (b) York, Roman walls, Fishergate and Coppergate excavation site locations; (c) Ipswich, postulated streets and defences, with dotted line outlining first phase of use (after Wade); (d) Southampton, Roman wall, postulated *Hamwic* streets and perimeter ditch (after Morton), later town's twelfth- to thirteenth-century streets and perimeter ditch. Drawn by K. Knowles.

All these sites probably offered low, shelving shorelines on which boats could be beached. In Ipswich, an effort was made to secure the river bank from erosion by a post-and-wattle revetment – very different from the sophisticated series of 'hards', quite soon developing into open-water jetties, at Dorestad.[9] They were provided with metalled streets, and *Hamwic* had a boundary ditch, features which suggest topographical supervision, perhaps by a royal agent such as the king's reeve (*wicgerefa*) in late seventh-century London. Similar officials may have been buried with the glass palm-cups which have been found in or adjacent to all four sites except York. In Ipswich they were with a well-accoutred warrior. A further sign of central control may be the shallow ditches in York's Fishergate that indicate property divisions, which are also recognised, by pit alignments, in *Hamwic*. These imply a concept of property rights and household units, the basis of all later medieval towns even if introduced originally from the surrounding rural society.[10]

More is known about *Hamwic* than the other two large *wic* sites. The distribution of artefacts shows that occupation spread quite rapidly within it. Boundary divisions indicate properties of various sizes, containing timber-built, usually ground-level, houses, also of various sizes. Despite the finds of fragments of glass vessels, with which presumably had come wine, the townspeople seem to have been able to acquire for themselves only a fairly basic series of commodities and a limited, unexciting range of meat, most of which came from quite elderly animals. Except perhaps in the earliest phases, *Hamwic*'s inhabitants were not involved in stock rearing, as they were not eating young casualties from breeding herds. They did not even raise many pigs, hens or geese in their back yards. They derived a little variety from river and estuary fish, but access to wild meat, such as venison, was virtually denied them. Theirs was already an urban diet, but they do not seem to have enjoyed the benefit of an urban market attracting a range of goods from which they could select according to what they could afford. Possibly they had to accept what was supplied to them from the tribute surpluses of kings, who might have conscripted the earliest settlers into the *wics* initially; or it may simply be that a truly urban market takes a long time to establish itself, and that early townspeople did not have strategies for feeding themselves from their back gardens.

Hamwic had several cemeteries, in which a few graves were encircled by ditches, implying low barrows, as have also been found in Ipswich; others had plank-lined chambers, and coffins. There may, therefore, have been wider social

[9] Wade, 'Ipswich', p. 96; W. A.van Es, 'Dorestad centred', in J. C. Besteman, J. M. Bos and H. A. Heidinga, eds., *Medieval Archaeology in the Netherlands* (Assen and Maastricht, 1990), pp. 151–82.

[10] The rural site at Chalton, Hampshire, seems to have been arranged around a formal central area, with fenced-off units; its establishment probably predates *Hamwic*'s: P. V. Addyman and D. Leigh, 'The Anglo-Saxon village at Chalton, Hampshire: second interim report', *Med. Arch.*, 17 (1973), 1–25.

divergence within the *wics* than the bone and most of the artefactual evidence implies, although no 'zoning' has been recognised, except that a large pot-making complex was marginalised at the edge of Ipswich. From the numbers of graves, a sedentary population of some 2,000 or 3,000 has been proposed for *Hamwic*, a figure which might perhaps be revised upwards slightly.[11] Family units can be assumed from child burials, but a preponderance of mature males may mean that there was not a normal population balance. Nevertheless, the differences between the *wic* people and those inland do not seem sufficient to suggest that the former were 'socially marginal';[12] rather, they were one of several new elements, including the Church, in mid-Saxon society. Expansion at *Hamwic* is suggested by the backfilling early in the eighth century of the boundary ditch, though only a few pits were dug on its other side. Some streets were remetalled, and kept clean and free from encroachments, which looks like the continuing control of an authority. There were internal changes: some streets and alleys were secondary, and one overran a cemetery with a wooden church or chapel. Such losses, and intercut burials, indicate a disregard for human remains which is to be seen as part of the developing mentality of urbanism, and the abandonment of kin-identity.[13] Disregard for earlier burials might seem to be evidence of pressure on space, but property sizes remained generous.

Despite the stimulus of the growing *sceatta* silver coinage, the increasing sizes of political groupings, and the probability of agricultural intensification, the excavated *wic* sites do not seem to have grown after the 730s and 740s, and in *c.* 800 York's Fishergate was mostly levelled, and subsequently used on a reduced scale. In the first half of the ninth century, by contrast, Ipswich expanded, with at least two new streets, one overrunning an earlier cemetery. There is no sign of such growth at *Hamwic* at this time; indeed, there were property amalgamations in some parts, though a change in the animal-bone remains suggests the beginnings of more specialised butchery and therefore townsfolk becoming better able to acquire ready-prepared joints. In general, however, fluctuations in eighth- and early ninth-century economic activity there remain elusive; although more *sceattas* than silver pennies, introduced in the later part of the eighth century, have been found, this may simply be because the latter were larger and less easy to lose, not because there were fewer in circulation.

Because of their access to the Rhineland and the Low Countries, urban expansion might most have been expected in East Anglia and Kent, but the evidence is sparse. At Norwich, an enclosure north of the River Wensum is thought to have been dug in the tenth century, but the amount of eighth-century material found there implies a settlement already involved in more than just

[11] In view of Keene's estimate of perhaps some 10,000 for *Lundenwic*, above, p. 188.

[12] The phrase is used by K. Randsborg, *The First Millennium A.D. in Europe and the Mediterranean* (Cambridge, 1991), p. 156.

[13] Morton, ed., *Excavations in Hamwic*, pp. 171–9, where this point is made.

farming and fishing. Thetford has also yielded objects earlier than its excavated features, on both sides of the Little Ouse, and there is good reason to think that there is an eighth-/ninth-century focus to the west of the later town. Some of the East Anglian *sceattas* may have been minted there.[14] Essex perhaps had a *wic* at Harwich, but only the name suggests it; Colchester has produced nothing of the period, though there is a site downriver which could have served; records of coins and other finds at Tilbury on the Thames could be significant; but presumably Essex was locked into London even after loss of direct control.[15] Sandwich in east Kent has a suggestive name, and coin distribution around it may indicate a mint there, but like Fordwich it lacks direct archaeological evidence. There is surprisingly little in eighth-/early ninth-century Canterbury, despite texts such as the record there of a *praefectus regis* that seem to indicate an urban environment.[16] Reeves are mentioned not only in London and Canterbury, but also in Lincoln and Carlisle, where archaeological evidence does not suggest that there were yet significant communities other than ecclesiastical ones. At Lincoln, a grave with a hanging-bowl is seventh century, but despite the name Wigford, significant numbers of eighth-century objects have not been found. Carlisle has produced *sceattas*, a spiral-headed pin and features such as pits, but all may be associated with the nunnery there.[17]

Within emergent Mercia, Chester has produced no artefacts of Anglian date, but a post-Roman dressed-stone building overlain by a late Saxon street near the centre of the old fortress may be the remains of a pre-Viking church. Elsewhere in Chester there has so far been only amorphous 'dark earth', but some sunken-featured buildings outside it may belong to the period. Salt production in Droitwich has fifth-/seventh-century radiocarbon dates, and in the eighth century the river bank was revetted and a trackway was laid down. In Bedford, some Ipswich ware and other sherds might be eighth century, as might a sunken-featured building in Leicester. An excavation within Northampton found a large timber building (for which the best parallels are seventh century) that was replaced by a stone one in the eighth or ninth; the complex may have been secular, ecclesiastical or both, but in any case probably created a focus for later developments. Tamworth had a mill attached to its palace, showing how such places were processing centres, presumably for large quantities of produce brought in as tribute payments, which involved concentrations of labour, as of

[14] For Norwich, B. Ayers, *Norwich* (London, 1994), is a useful summary, with references to excavation reports by himself and others. Work on other places is by A. Rogerson and C. Dallas, and by P. Andrews (Thetford), and in *Archaeologia Cantiana*, 102 (1993), 383–5 (Fordwich); and see below, pp. 642–8, where Brodt also discusses Dunwich.

[15] S. Rippon, 'Essex, *c.* 700–1066', in O. Bedwin, ed., *The Archaeology of Essex: Proceedings of the 1993 Writtle Conference* (Chelmsford, 1996), pp. 117–28.

[16] Reviewed in detail above, pp. 52 and 80.

[17] Work in these places is reported by K. Steane and A. Vince (Lincoln), and by H. Summerson and M. R. McCarthy (Carlisle).

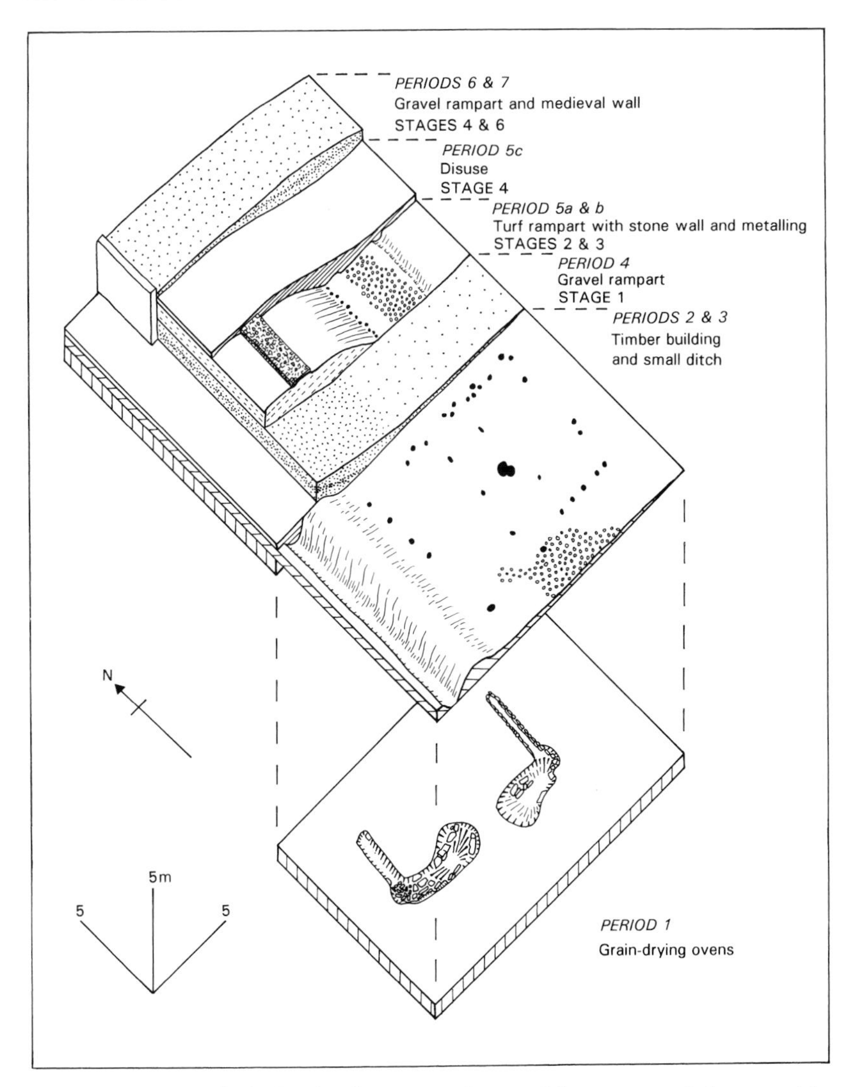

Figure 10.2 Hereford: the development of part of the western defences, with underlying occupation (after Shoesmith). Drawn by K. Knowles.

course did major churches; neither necessitated that a town would develop, but they were obvious catalysts. Hereford is an example, as a grain-drier and traces of occupation – a street or yards – were found below the later rampart (Figure 10.2). Gloucester has evidence of 'dark earth' continuing to build up amongst the Roman ruins; some mid-Saxon sherds have been found, but no features. At Oxford, St Frideswide's church might have built the causeway that acts as the town's spine (Figure 10.3). There are many such places, later to emerge as towns,

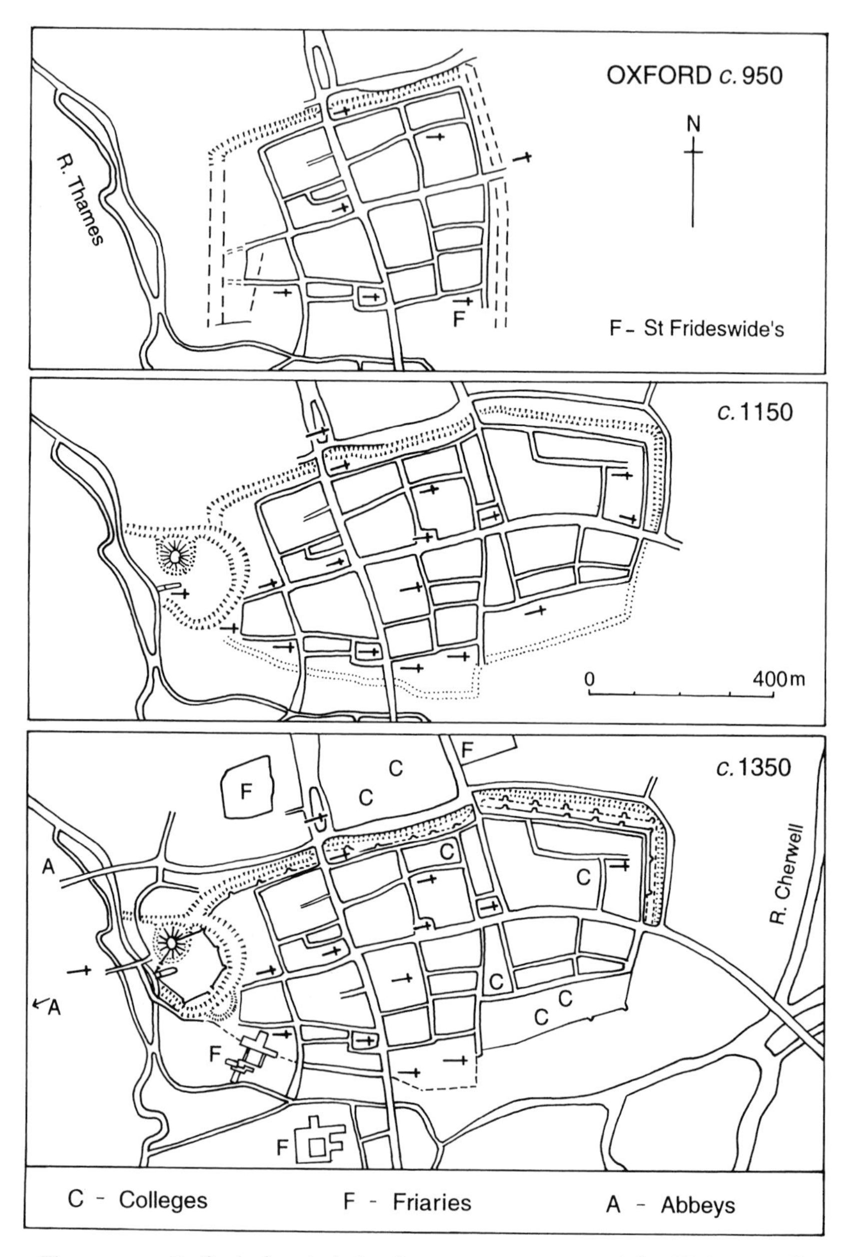

Figure 10.3 Oxford: the city's development *c.* 950–1350 (after Blair, Hassall, *VCH*). Drawn by K. Knowles.

where there were mid-Saxon churches which may have had attached settlements that were incipiently urban. In Wessex, a rich grave in a late seventh-century Winchester cemetery may indicate a small thegnly enclave, but there is almost nothing datable to the eighth century, apart from the bishops' minster.[18]

(ii) FORTRESSES AND URBAN PLANS

By *c.* 800, Viking raids had probably begun to destabilise trade routes, inhibiting expansion. At York's Fishergate, occupation ceased during the middle of the ninth century, and most of *Hamwic* lay deserted soon afterwards. Whether Ipswich suffered a mid-century crisis is not yet known. Against direct attack, the open *wic* sites had no defence, and the absence from within them of cult centres eased the need to defend them to the ultimate. At much the same time, the Burghal Hidage list of fortified places suggests that for Southampton, the old Roman site upstream at Bitterne may have been pressed into service (Figure 10.1 (d)), but the trading centre could not operate without partners, and as a manufacturing centre it was not indispensable. Reuse of Roman walls as in Winchester, or the construction of timber-faced earth banks, ramparts and ditches as in Hereford (Figure 10.2), in that case probably as much against the Welsh as the Vikings, provided enclosures that could shelter streets and houses, as well as markets which a reeve could oversee in the king's interests. The Worcester charter shows the importance of such places by the end of the ninth century. The Burghal Hidage names defended places in Wessex, of which some, like Wareham, already had churches and were 'focal points', and others, like Wallingford, had no known pre-existing churches; both of those went on to become important towns, though this may not have been an initial strategy.[19]

King Alfred had his name put on coins issued at four places not previously recorded as mints, Exeter, Gloucester, Oxford and Winchester, perhaps as an assertion of authority over key places rather than because of any intention to develop them systematically. His use of London as a mint may have been to demonstrate his seizure of it. He does not seem to have used Southampton, probably because anywhere near the coast was vulnerable. A switch of local emphasis to Winchester may have preceded the establishment of the mint there. Its bridge

[18] Work in these places is reported by D. J. P. Mason, K. Matthews, S. Ward and T. J. Strickland (Chester), D. Hurst (Droitwich), D. Baker *et al.* (Bedford), J. H. Williams *et al.* (Northampton), P. A. Rahtz and R. Meeson (Tamworth), C. Heighway and T. Darvill (Gloucester), B. Durham (Oxford), R. Shoesmith (Hereford), and M. Biddle (Winchester). See also discussions above, pp. 35, 128, and below, p. 253.

[19] The Burghal Hidage is discussed in contributions to D. Hill and A. R. Rumble, eds., *The Defence of Wessex: The* Burghal Hidage *and Anglo-Saxon Fortifications* (Manchester, 1996); see also below, Appendix 1a, and above, pp. 35, 53. On Worcester, see above, pp. 81–2, and N. J. Baker *et al.*, 'From Roman to medieval Worcester: development and planning in the Anglo-Saxon city', *Antiquity*, 66 (1992), 65–74.

across the Itchen probably dates to the 850s or early 860s, and a stone building was constructed in the putative thegns' area – touchstones for gold suggest its high-status use. Not far away, a Roman building and street were partly reused, large quantities of window-glass have been found and timbers lining a pit have been dated to *c.* 843–63; the building was soon levelled, but overlying silts may indicate that attempts to recreate a watercourse system were not initially successful. At least two burials took place next, suggesting that the minster had yet to establish disposal rights, before timber buildings occupied the site. By this time, only High Street retained a Roman alignment, and there were new streets, one of which had an Edward the Elder penny and a slightly earlier dirham in its first surfaces. A standard module of length, based on the 16½ foot (5.03 m) pole, may have been used in the new layout. Whether a breach was made in the walls at the same time as the street system was created is uncertain.[20] Despite many important excavations in it, much about Winchester remains unknown, even whether it should be classified as having been a 'large town' – until well into the tenth century, it may have contained few residents who were not directly dependent upon churches or palaces for their livelihoods.

Fewer such doubts apply to York, which, despite Fishergate's abandonment, remained an archiepiscopal centre, and became that of a Viking regime; the area later known as King's Court was *Kuningesgard* in the thirteenth century, a name derived from the Old Norse *Konungsgarðr*, and may show that the south-east gate of the Roman fort was used as its administrative base. It is even possible that the 'Anglian Tower' blocking a breach in the north-west wall dates to this period. Ninth-century turmoil may have caused the concealment of the fine but repaired eighth-century helmet in a pit at Coppergate, outside the walls; bodies had been unceremoniously disposed of in other pits, and a hearth was probably used for glass melting in the second half of the ninth century. Soon afterwards, this whole area between the fort and the River Foss came into denser use (Figure 10.1 (b)), with tenements of widths that were to survive for the next millennium laid out to front on to what was probably a new street. Wickerwork was used for buildings, and also to stabilise stone rubble laid over the river bank to create a landing hard. Burial in York became more orderly, although in at least one

[20] M. Biddle, 'The study of Winchester: archaeology and history in a British town, 1961–1983', *Proc. of the British Academy*, 69 (1983), 93–136; G. D. Scobie, J. M. Zant and R. Whinney, *The Brooks, Winchester: A Preliminary Report on the Excavations, 1987–88* (Museums Service Archaeology Report, 1, Winchester, 1991), pp. 34–9; P. Crummy, 'The system of measurement used in town planning from the ninth to the thirteenth centuries', in S. C. Hawkes, D. Brown and J. Campbell, eds., *Anglo-Saxon Studies in Archaeology and History I* (British Archaeological Reports, British Series, 72, 1979), pp. 149–64. It has been reported that a cemetery at Staple Gardens in the north-west quadrant respected the new streets, but there is still uncertainty about this, a matter that relates not only to the argument for unitary planning, but also to the possibility of a large population prior to the urbanised layout: M. F. Hughes, ed., *Archaeology in Hampshire 1994/5* (Winchester, 1996), p. 46.

churchyard some bodies were laid out in Viking style with objects, one with a coin of 905–15. A burial at the Minster with a piece of caulked clinker planking might be an echo of the Scandinavian boat-burial tradition, suggesting someone of high status who had Viking connections.[21]

York's Scandinavian links are shown by such things as soapstone that reflect cultural preference, and others like mohair and silk that came through the Baltic trade routes from the Arab world. A little pottery was imported from the Rhineland – its paucity a factor of choice, of distance and of the direction of most of the trade contacts, at least until well into the tenth century. Changing modes by then are also seen in the replacement of soapstone by wooden, leather and pottery vessels. Pottery was made in or near York, with some, including glazed wares, coming from Stamford and probably other sources, so there was a little choice. Similarly, meat and fish were a little more varied than they had been at Fishergate, suggesting citizens' increasing ability to choose from a wider selection and to make greater use of back yards, although they were still mostly having to consume quite elderly cattle and sheep. Butchery remained clumsy, however, as though by non-specialists, despite an eleventh-century reference to two stalls *in macello*, which could be translated as 'meat market'.[22]

Most if not all the crafts practised earlier in Fishergate were also practised in tenth-century York, but with some new ones and higher levels of specialisation evident. There was a mint, though perhaps not in the two Coppergate tenements where coin-dies and lead 'trial-pieces' have been found, as they may have been taken there for recycling. Another special product was stone sculpture for the well-to-do, but the Coppergate evidence is also of the growth of a volume market, for instance for base-metal trinkets, producing pewter brooches and the like, with new alloys such as brass also coming into use; an increase is unquantifiable, but seems visible also in pottery, ironwork and glass beads. Much of this may have been for an internally generated market, as the town grew. External distribution of the products is no easier to recognise than before: York-minted coins may have travelled as army payments and as items of wealth, rather than for commercial exchange, in the first half of the tenth century, but one of the 'trial-pieces' suggests a Chester connection. Stone crosses in rural churches indicate local schools of sculptors adapting York designs, rather than that aristocrats were using York masons on their estates. New intramural parish churches,

[21] R. A. Hall, *English Heritage Book of Viking Age York* (London, 1994), with references to the work of J. Bayley (metalworking), J. Lang (sculpture), A. MacGregor (artefacts), A. Mainman (pottery), T. O'Connor (animal bone), P. Ottaway (ironwork), E. J. E. Pirie (coins), D. Tweddle (the helmet and other artefacts) and P. Walton (textiles). For the Minster burials, B. Kjølbye-Biddle in Phillips and Heywood, *Minster*, and see also J. Graham-Campbell, 'Review article: the archaeology of Anglian and Anglo-Scandinavian York', *Early Medieval Europe*, 5/1 (1996), 71–82.

[22] R. A. Hall, 'Sources for pre-Conquest York', in I. Wood and N. Lund, eds., *Peoples and Places in Northern Europe 500–1600; Essays in Honour of Peter Hayes Sawyer* (Woodbridge, 1991), pp. 83–94.

one with its eleventh-century tower surviving, are an aspect of the town's growth. Access between the Foss-side development and the fort was probably improved by removal of the south-east wall, but the date when this occurred is not yet known.

Between 'Anglo-Scandinavian' York and Lincoln there are many similarities, although the latter did not have even an episcopal church, let alone an archbishop's. In its lower town, Silver Street takes a diagonal line between two of the old Roman gates, suggesting that whenever it was laid out there were no restraints on its passage. There is some pottery and other evidence of ninth-century activity, but when the first buildings in Flaxengate were laid out *c.* 900, they were aligned to a road which formed part of the rectilinear plan that mostly exists today, implying the re-establishment of formal control, as do both the careful construction of the cobbled road itself and its subsequent maintenance. Unlike Coppergate, Flaxengate has not produced evidence of separate tenement divisions, a single landlord probably effecting the subsequent series of reconstructions across the whole site. During the tenth century, both banks of the River Witham underwent reclamation, with metalled hards and paths, and timber revetments. Expansion occurred on the south bank of the Witham, along the spinal road through Wigford, marked by a line of churches.[23]

Some of the artefacts, such as soapstone and silk, show Lincoln's Scandinavian connections in the early tenth century, although no Viking-style burials have been found. Coins were being minted at least by the 920s, and large numbers of crucibles and the like show the importance of metalworking and glass melting, the latter presumably to make beads and window glass. Unlike York, evidence of intramural pottery making has been found, dating from the mid-tenth century; the clay was mixed with a lot of shell, and the pottery was made on a wheel – the former was probably a local tradition, the latter not. The numbers of sherds and the scale of operation at the kiln site must indicate volume production, which is confirmed by the quantity of broken pots recovered at Flaxengate. That consumption matched production is shown by the animal-bone record; as in York, slaughtering was mainly on-site and non-specialised. At Flaxengate, meat mostly came from older, though not the most aged, beasts, but elsewhere younger animals are more frequent, culled from local flocks and herds to supply a market that could already afford to reject the toughest meat.

Many of the crucibles used in both York and Lincoln came from Stamford, because of the refractory clays there. Ninth-century Stamford potters used

[23] D. Perring, *Early Medieval Occupation at Flaxengate, Lincoln* (The Archaeology of Lincoln, 9/1, 1981), and contributions in the same series by L. Adams Gilmour (pottery), J. Bayley (metal-working), M. Blackburn, C. Colyer and M. Dolley (coins), P. Chitwood (waterfront), J. Mann (artefacts), T. O'Connor (animal bone) and D. Stocker (churches); also K. M. Dobney, *Of Butchers and Breeds* (Lincoln Archaeological Studies, 5, Lincoln, n.d.).

innovative kilns, and their products briefly included imitations of red-painted continental wares. Wheel-made, glazed pottery was produced in the tenth and eleventh centuries at various sites, apparently on the edges of occupied areas – unlike iron smelting which took place inside them, perhaps because its operatives had greater economic resources rather than because their production was less anti-social. Stamford may have developed from the nucleus of a defended enclosure, an area between that and a bloc of streets being left open for a market; on the other side of the River Welland, another development, perhaps linear like Lincoln's Wigford, may here have originated in the fort recorded as built by Edward the Elder in 918. The chronology and pace of Stamford's growth is less well charted than Lincoln's, but even so it is better than that of the other three 'Five Boroughs', Derby, Leicester and Nottingham.[24]

Further west, an area outside the walls of Chester that had had buildings in the later ninth century was redeveloped in the tenth. A scatter of pins and brooches shows connections with Norse Dublin and York in the first half of the tenth century, but the absence of soapstone suggests that contacts with Scandinavia were indirect. There are, however, few features of the period, and some areas were still being cultivated amongst the ruined buildings, whose still partly upstanding walls impeded redevelopment. Most remarkably, no contemporary coins have been found, although Chester was one of the most active mints. An elite group of churchmen and moneyers may have had a small number of servants and craftspeople to work for them, on a different scale from that seen in York and Lincoln. Northgate Street, which cuts through the *praetorium* area, and the street which overlies the putative church, may be elements of *Æthelflæd's* attempt at regeneration, recorded in the Anglo-Saxon *Chronicle s.a.* 907.[25]

In East Anglia, late ninth- and early tenth-century coins are numerous in Thetford, where there were bank and ditch enclosures on both sides of the Little Ouse. That on the south side was much the larger, but open spaces within it succumbed to expansionist pressure only in the late tenth and early eleventh centuries. Pottery kilns and yards were zoned on the west side, and there were metalled streets, houses and, at least in the eleventh century, churches. Ditch and bank enclosures thought to be late ninth or early tenth century appeared also in Norwich and Ipswich – the only *wic* to re-emerge as a significant port on the same site – though neither seems to have had much internal density until the second half of the tenth century. Colchester, despite its favourable east coast

[24] R. A. Hall, 'The Five Boroughs of the Danelaw: a review of present knowledge', *Anglo-Saxon England*, 18 (1989), 149–206, for summaries and references, in particular to C. Mahany and K. Kilmurry for Stamford.

[25] S. Ward, *Excavations at Chester: Saxon Occupation within the Roman Fortress* (Chester, 1994); K. Matthews, *Excavations at Chester: The Evolution of the Heart of the City* (Chester, 1995); also P. Carrington, *Chester* (London, 1994).

location and mention as a *burh*, is perhaps surprisingly without evidence. Even London made slow progress.[26]

Inland, Oxford may have been the subject of a deliberate plan to augment its existing roads and defences with secondary streets, dated by a coin and Stamford ware to early in the tenth century (Figure 10.3). The width of its main streets, one of which had a wooden drainage channel running down the middle, may imply their use for markets, with frontage properties having space for stalls, but it seems to have remained a very uncrowded town.[27]

In general, therefore, urban growth seems to have been quite slow in the first half of the tenth century, despite whatever boosts were given by mints and enclosures. Lincoln, York and perhaps London and Stamford are the only places that have yet been shown to be appositely termed big towns, with an urbanised life style. Oxford has by now had a representative range of excavations, and the picture there may prove the norm for places that did not have close Scandinavian contacts to ensure long-distance trade. Subsequent falling-away of those contacts was not immediately compensated for by the unification of England and royal use of defended bases. Markets serving internal hinterlands took time to develop, even if they were planned for – conceivably to the extent of fostering crafts such as pot making in future towns such as Northampton, Stafford and Gloucester. Probably an important limiting factor was the decline of European silver stocks, restricting monetary development; English minting levels appear to have been low, even though debasement came only in the 950s.[28]

(iii) EXPANSION

The final third of the tenth century is proving to have been crucial in the development of many towns, with new trading opportunities, refreshed by new silver supplies and coinage reform. An important feature of some later tenth-century towns was a structure unlike any excavated on rural or aristocratic sites. This, the first distinctively urban type, comprised a substantial rectangular cellar, often plank-lined, which probably had ceilings allowing timber superstructures to be used as living space. One in York has been dated by dendrochronology to the 970s.[29] The main function of the cellars seems likely to have been the provision

[26] The most recent work on Thetford is P. Andrews, *Excavations at Redcastle Furze, Thetford, 1988–9* (East Anglian Archaeology, 72, Gressenhall, 1995); see also below, pp. 645–6. For Colchester, P. Crummy, *Aspects of Anglo-Saxon and Norman Colchester* (CBA Res. Rep. 39, Colchester Archaeology Report, 1, 1981), and summary in Rippon, 'Essex'. For London, above, pp. 190–1.

[27] Oxford excavations by T. G. Hassall *et al.* are reported in *Oxoniensia*, 54 (1989), 71–277, and by D. Sturdy, *ibid.*, 50 (1985), 47–94; see also J. Blair, *Anglo-Saxon Oxfordshire* (Stroud, 1994).

[28] D. M. Metcalf, 'Were ealdormen exercising individual control over the coinage in mid tenth-century England?', *British Numismatic J*, 57 (1987), 24–33, and P. Spufford, *Money and its Uses in Medieval Europe* (Cambridge, 1988); see also above, pp. 34–42, for this paragraph and the next.

[29] Those from Coppergate, York, are the best examples; some of the timbers survive to their full

of cool storage space, in which slightly damp conditions would not adversely affect – and would reduce the fire risk to – wool, textiles, hides, furs, wines and foodstuffs. Their size implies a growing capacity to store such things in bulk, perhaps for redistribution in smaller amounts. This is consistent with increasing evidence of markets, outside as well as inside town gates, where suburbs also began to appear. Even though the setting of some cellars well back from tenement frontages, as in Oxford, does not suggest that pressure on space was yet a major factor, a new urban dynamic is implied.

From the 970s, coin output becomes a means of comparison between towns. The number from Exeter may show the importance of tin production in the area, but is also perhaps an indication that the town was developing as a regional centre for the South-West; a pottery established in the early eleventh century may be symptomatic of the latter role.[30] Norwich also seems to have moved forward, challenging Thetford in the eleventh century as the principal East Anglian town. Pot making was introduced there too, although Stamford seems to have retained a monopoly of glazed wares in the area. Distribution from Stamford shows that river and coastal transport was important, but that overland journeys of more than fifty miles were also made. More pottery was taken southwards in the eleventh century, probably because of changes in demand rather than because the Danelaw frontier had been a barrier in the tenth. Lincoln's coins show a similar southwards drift, reflecting the growing economic and demographic pull of East Anglia and the London area, with wool exports to the Low Countries probably increasingly important, even if the cloth industry there somewhat impeded its development in English towns. This Rhineland connection can be seen in imported pottery, though there is much less of it relatively than there had been in the *wic* sites. With more, if not always better-quality, English wares now regularly available, there would have been less point in transporting it except for ship-board use; its paucity even in ports may show that more of the carrying trade was in English hands than before. Rather in the same way, merchants may have brought in foreign coins only in incidental numbers, knowing that there was adequate native currency for their needs, rather than because of formal bans.

The importance of the cloth industry to the burgeoning English towns in the tenth and eleventh centuries cannot be assessed, although the few woven wool, linen and and even silk scraps that survive in particular conditions at least show

height, *c.* 6 feet (1.8 m): Hall, *Viking Age York*, pp. 59–66. If the only light in them came from entrance-way openings, regular use for living or craftworking purposes is precluded. In cases where the earth floor has been identified as a working surface, either there could have been no superstructure except the roof, or the upper floor must have been above ground level, so that the cellar was a semi-basement with at least some light-slits.

[30] J. P. Allan, *Medieval and Post-Medieval Finds from Exeter, 1971–1980* (Exeter Archaeological Reports 3, Exeter, 1994).

that a variety of textiles, some dyed, was available – a corrective to assuming that animal bones and pots are fully representative of the range of townsfolks' choice. The spread of a major technological innovation, the horizontal loom, has implications for greater output and more specialised, male-dominated skills in urban household units. Its early use is difficult to recognise, for the decline in the numbers of loomweights excavated may show only that a tensioned upright loom was being used. Pieces of pierced oak from ninth- and tenth-century contexts in Gloucester have been identified as parts of warping boards from horizontal looms, but wooden survivals like those are rare – wood was more likely to be thrown on to a fire than into a rubbish-pit, and only a few pits have the right anaerobic conditions, usually because they stayed wet at the bottom.[31] Technological advance cannot be assumed to have been uniform; in Lincoln, potters reverted to hand-making methods, as though the wheel was not perceived to have brought advantages for unglazed volume production.

As later in the Middle Ages, there were towns that did not conform to general trends. Although leatherworkers' use of Chester's formerly built-upon extramural area may be indicative both of growing scales of production and of industrial zoning to clear the space within the walls, and a pottery developed in the second half of the tenth century, its minting activity declined from the 970s; some revival occurred in the eleventh century, but by then Chester's Irish trade was being challenged by Bristol, ancestral Norse links to Dublin no longer giving the north-west an advantage over a southern competitor.[32]

A Viking raid could be the reason for the abandonment of Chester's suburb in the late tenth or early eleventh century, but such direct effects can rarely be proved. The aftermath of the Massacre of St Brice's Day in 1002 might, for instance, explain why shell-filled pottery stopped being sent from Oxford to London, but competition from products made closer to the city may have come to exclude the supply from the South Midlands. Nor does Cnut's Anglo-Scandinavian empire seem to have done much to revive York's Danish contacts. The town was maintained – a new building at the rear of one of the Coppergate tenements may have been to provide storage facilities near the Foss bank, but otherwise York appears to have been less vibrant than before. But if Oxford lost its pottery outlet, it was not held back for long, as the original walled area was nearly doubled in size at some time before the Domesday survey of *c.* 1086 (Figure 10.3); the tower by the north gate at St Michael's church still proclaims its prestige. Other Midland towns that now produce more data include Gloucester, with a marked increase in pottery quantities, Hereford, with smith-

[31] Surviving textile scraps may be imports, which limits assessment of the advance of the horizontal loom, but they do show the range; see P. Walton, *Textiles, Cordage and Raw Fibre from 16–22 Coppergate* (The Archaeology of York, 17/5, 1989), on York, and F. A. Pritchard, 'Late Saxon textiles from the City of London', *Med. Arch.*, 28 (1984), 46–76.

[32] Ward, *Chester*; Matthews, *Chester*.

ing slags which correlate with Domesday's evidence of its iron renders, and Worcester, though there the record is still fairly meagre – as it is on the east coast for Colchester, which emerges with a new mint from the 990s, and a new ditch and street plan for which modules based on four-pole units have been suggested, but still with too little pottery to indicate much occupation.[33]

There is no absolute criterion by which to judge when a place became a 'major town', though density of activity despite Viking assaults is being increasingly identified, and parish churches seemingly follow a 'rank-size' correlation. The areas enclosed by walls – which were likely now to be of stone rather than timber – give some scope for measurement, but many had undeveloped space inside them; Cricklade still has an intramural farm, part of a property which Abingdon Abbey acquired in 1008. Although the archaeological evidence from York and Lincoln is that even in the late ninth and early tenth centuries non-agricultural activities predominated, many if not most towns had open spaces for fields within their enclosing walls, as in Winchester where ploughing continued in one quadrant until the expansion of the bishop's palace in the twelfth century. Domesday has references to pasture rights in nearby fields for several towns, presumably for stock rearing. The division between internal and external space was not absolute, and creation of division by enclosure may not have been an immediate consequence of the growth of a new town like Bristol.[34] Despite its omission of London, Winchester and a few other places likely to have had some degree of urban development by 1086, Domesday's records of taxation and numbers of houses (Map 3.1) allow tables to be drawn up that are broadly comparable with those for numbers of known moneyers, though Oxford, Ipswich, Gloucester, Wallingford, Huntingdon (for which there is probably no other information) and Leicester are much higher relatively in the Domesday ranking, while Exeter, Canterbury and Southwark are not in its leading twelve.[35]

Also an indicator of importance are the houses 'attached' to rural estates. These were presumably urban bases where surplus produce could be sold, and purchased goods could be stored. It was probably for this purpose that a bishop of London bought a house in Ipswich in *c.* 950, which was linked to his estate

[33] As well as references above, see B. Durham *et al.*, 'Oxford's northern defences: archaeological studies 1971–1982', *Oxoniensia*, 48 (1983), 13–40; C. Heighway *et al.*, 'Excavations at 1 Westgate Street, Gloucester, 1975', *Med. Arch.*, 23 (1979), 159–213; R. Shoesmith, *Hereford City Excavations*, vol. II (CBA Res. Rep. 46, 1982), and R. Shoesmith, *The Finds* (CBA Res. Rep., 56 and 3, 1985); Crummy, *Colchester*, and subsequent reports in the same series.

[34] On churches, see above, pp. 130–9, and for sizes, R. Morris, *Churches in the Landscape* (London, 1989), pp. 178–92; Cricklade, J. Haslam, 'The towns of Wiltshire', in J. Haslam, ed., *Anglo-Saxon Towns in Southern England* (Chichester, 1984), pp. 87–148 at 106–10 (sadly, the farm has now gone); fields, J. Tait, *The Medieval English Borough* (Manchester, 1936), ch. 3, M. Biddle and D. Keene, 'Winchester in the eleventh and twelfth centuries', in M. Biddle, ed., *Winchester in the Early Middle Ages* (Oxford, 1976), pp. 241–448 at 324, and above, pp. 116–18.

[35] For Domesday Book and mint rankings, see below, Appendix 1b, 2.

at Waldringfield, Suffolk. Nevertheless, the recorded 'contributory' places were almost all (apart from Oxford's and Wallingford's) in the same shire as the towns with which they were associated, so Domesday is either noting a tax-paying system – with anyone who had a house in the nearest market but whose rural estate was in another shire 'contributing' to a different court – or there is some relic in it of a maintenance system. These 'dependent properties' were often owned by aristocrats, who might stay in them when they needed to be present at a court session – and from which they often made their last journey, for burial at a principal church. The Church, as a landlord, was also heavily involved in towns, as is shown by Winchester's 'seven great fiefs', all of which except the king's were held by churches or church leaders. After the Conquest, the new nobility was also fully aware of urban opportunities; Robert of Mortain's annexations in York, royal officeholders in Winchester and twelfth-century charters like that for a property held by the earl of Hereford in Southampton's main street all attest this. At the same time, however, recorded names suggest that the English may have been more successful in retaining their urban than their rural properties.[36]

Another ranking system might be based on the towns into which castles were inserted; London's and York's special importance is shown by their having more than one, and that Oxford and Wallingford both had them by 1071 confirms Domesday's view of their significance, but whether strategic location, administrative role, commercial vitality or numbers of burgesses was the most significant factor in any individual case is never stated. Domesday refers directly to castles in only eleven towns, and then only to explain why houses had been destroyed; they were also often the likeliest cause of loss in others where no explanation was offered, although for Lincoln a careful distinction was made between the 166 destroyed because of the castle and the seventy-four vacant for other reasons – the new cathedral close to the castle, which must have involved some losses, is not cited as one.[37] The transfer of a major church into a larger town had pre-Conquest precedents, as in Exeter; the disruption that this might cause is shown by Norwich, where a developing waterfront zone was transformed into a back area after Bishop Losinga placed his cathedral too near it. Palaces might also be imposed or arbitrarily enlarged, as at Winchester, where the royal kitchens' encroachment on to the south side of the High Street can still be recognised by its narrowing (Figure 10.4).

[36] R. Fleming, 'Rural elites and urban communities in late Saxon England', *P&P*, 141 (1993), 3–37, and above, pp. 81–2.

[37] C. Harfield, 'A hand-list of castles recorded in Domesday Book', *EHR*, 106 (1991), 371–92 at 373–4. See also above, p. 60, on castles, and p. 140, on churches. If a house plot is taken as being as small as the lowest average in Winchester, i.e. 330 square metres, Lincoln's theoretical loss of 54,780 square metres is approximately an area the size of that contained by the streets that now encircle the castle and may indicate the lip of its outer ditch. It is unlikely that the rear of the site would have been so intensively developed, however, so a cleared area for a 'killing-ground' beyond the ditch can be inferred.

Although these impositions affected the larger towns worst, they also stood to gain a little from the need for garrisons, churchmen and building workers to be supplied. Other opportunities were created for a Southampton, well placed for trade with Normandy and the Channel Islands, or a Newcastle where the protection of a garrison led to the development of the waterfront. There were immigrants – 'French' settlers in Shrewsbury, for instance, may have included Flemings – and it is likely that entrepreneurial Jews arrived under a safe-conduct from William I. Unlike earlier aristocratic residential sites, rural castles have little evidence of anything but military activity within their baileys; non-military metalworking, boneworking and other crafts were even more likely to be urban based as a result. By contrast, however, Domesday records three concentrations of rural potters; lower rents, easier access to clay and fuel and restrictions on the use of fire-hazardous kilns may all have contributed to this shift, which was never total, pot making being maintained in Stamford into the thirteenth century perhaps because of its special clays. De-urbanisation may have led to loss of skills and of immediate contact with markets to compete with wood, metal and other materials, leading to loss of quality. Other minor crafts do not seem to have been buoyant within towns, however; the Norman period does not see a continuation of the increase in the metal-trinket market, and making of bone combs seems to have fallen away, although gaming-pieces, a sign of urban leisure pursuits, are more common, and horning increased. Comb making may have been taken over by wood workers, but there were no similar substitutes for base metals.[38]

The return of silver shortages perhaps inhibited urban growth in the second half of the eleventh century and the first two-thirds of the twelfth, allied to heavy taxation and Low Countries competition, which new opportunities in France and beyond in Italy and even Spain may have offset for some towns. At least taxation payments in cash necessitated market involvement, even for rural peasants, and a few towns benefited from reductions in the numbers of places licensed to mint – sixty-five are known for 1083–6, about twenty by the 1130s, nine by 1189. Furthermore, England generally managed to retain a stable weight for its pennies, despite the dearth of silver, which would have created confidence in the currency. Pre-1180 coin-find numbers from published excavations remain small – one from Thetford (compared to thirteen English coins of the pre-Conquest century), seven from York (four), Canterbury three (two), Colchester three (none), Exeter three (none), Oxford none (none).[39]

(iv) URBANISM ESTABLISHED

Despite problems, there were burgesses who were doing well for themselves. One in Oxford probably built the surviving stone-vaulted semi-basement, set close to

[38] A. MacGregor, *Bone, Antler, Ivory and Horn* (London, 1985). For more on Newcastle and its charter, see above, p. 61.

[39] These numbers derive from the various reports cited above. See also above, pp. 118–21.

the main street frontage, that is attributed to the first half of the twelfth century, and heralds the vaults which generally superseded timber-lined cellars. A variation was to have the whole structure above ground level.[40] Remarkable reconstructions of the different trades and services that a medieval town contained have been reconstructed from rentals of twelfth-century Canterbury with its different market places, and from the surveys drawn up for Winchester (Figure 10.4 shows how moneyers concentrated in the main streets, clothworkers being more likely in back streets and near water courses; but 'zoning' was far from absolute).[41]

Substantial buildings must have contrasted markedly with the urban norm, which excavations show to have been of limited size, post-built and thatched: not necessarily flimsy, but still little different from rural farmhouses. In back yards, usually unlined rubbish-pits were not kept clearly separate from wells; animal bones suggest slaughtering wherever was convenient; shallow ditches and gullies may sometimes represent subdivisions within plots, but were invariably open drains. The difference between intramural provisioning and extramural stock rearing is shown by differences in bone assemblages; even those from a site immediately outside the walls, as in Oxford, may be noticeably different from those inside, whereas later the need to dispose of urban rubbish might mean dumping in such areas, so that then the bones outside directly reflect the town's eating habits.[42]

Urban infrastructures were improved, with bridges, stone-built churches, gates and walls. Such building was costly, however, and directly or indirectly had to be paid for, holding back other forms of investment. That castles might be resited, as if on the whim of king or sheriff, as in Gloucester and Canterbury, shows how difficult it must have been for burgesses to resist higher authority. Thetford suffered more than anywhere, but because of river transport problems and competition from Bury, Norwich and Lynn – the last one of three new east coast ports, with Yarmouth and Boston. Lynn is the most investigated archaeologically; the opportunity provided by an informal beach-market, to which merchants probably went to get salt and marsh-reared sheep products, was seized by its ecclesiastical owner, who encouraged development there at the end of the eleventh century. Over the next 200 years, a sequence of land reclamations created new building space which came to enclose the originally open-sided market places. Presumably sales directly from beached boats became increasingly rare.[43]

[40] For buildings, see also below, pp. 182–3, 384–6.

[41] W. Urry, *Canterbury under the Angevin Kings* (London, 1967); Biddle, ed., *Winchester*; and above, pp. 121–2.

[42] M. R. Roberts, 'Excavations at Jowett Walk, Oxford', *Oxoniensia*, 60 (1995), 205–24.

[43] For Gloucester's first castle, T. Darvill, 'Excavations on the early Norman castle at Gloucester, 1983–84', *Med. Arch.*, 32 (1988), 1–49, and for Canterbury's, D. F. Renn, 'Canterbury Castle in the early middle ages', in P. Bennett *et al.*, *Excavations at Canterbury Castle* (Archaeology of Canterbury, 1, Maidstone, 1982), pp. 70–7. The Lynn excavation report is H. Clarke and A. Carter, *Excavations in King's Lynn 1963–1970* (Society for Medieval Archaeology, Monograph 7, 1977). (The attractive idea put forward by D. M. Owen that mounds cast up by salt workings provided a firm surface for settlement has been put in doubt by the Fenlands Project's work.)

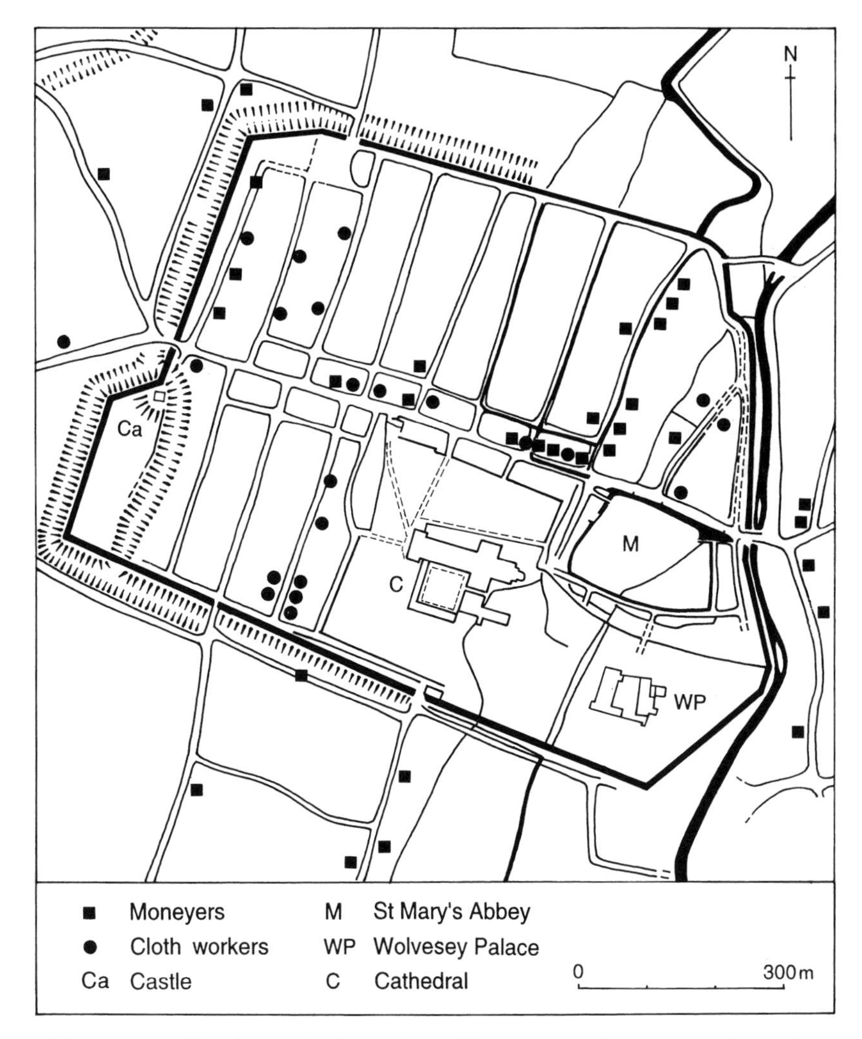

Figure 10.4 Winchester in the mid-twelfth century after the transfer of the New Minster to Hyde Abbey. The locations of the moneyers and clothworkers include some that are uncertain (after Biddle, Keene). Drawn by K. Knowles.

Urban markets were not the only places where goods were sold, since fairs outside Winchester, Boston and London, or far from any major centre, such as St Ives, took many transactions out of towns – the need to provide witnesses and warranties presumably having diminished. On the other hand, the built environment gave greater security for storage and for the handling of bullion, and for the negotiation and record keeping of credit agreements. The native merchants who used the fairs probably had urban bases, as they did later, so although towns lost out on tolls, they did not lose altogether. Towns such as Hereford and Northampton probably enlarged their perimeters, enclosing markets that appear to have formed outside their gates, to protect their toll income. Northampton's pre-eminence in the twelfth-century Midlands is shown by the close-set timber houses lining a central but secondary intramural street near the castle, and the use even of back areas for quite large, semi-cellared buildings.[44] Other towns, like Oxford (Figure 10.3), seem to have been content not to extend their walls further; although both churches and excavations show that suburbs were growing, their use for urban overflow rather than for intensive farming to take advantage of throroughfares leading to the gates is not always distinguishable. A few secondary developments grew to equal their 'parents', like Redcliffe on the opposite side of the River Avon from Bristol (Figure 10.5).

By happy coincidence, the introduction in 1180 of a new and long-lived coin design, the Short Cross, is also the date at which the 'long thirteenth century' is usually taken to have begun. Renewed supplies of silver from central Europe may have helped to create inflation, and increased loss-rates of coins may partly reflect that, but at the same time surely indicate their growing use. Spending power and transaction numbers are shown by the multiplicity of small metal objects; a range of different types of buckle, with plates often ornamented simply with rocked-tracer zigzags, but also sometimes with relief designs, provides just one example. Pottery also breaks out of a monotonous catalogue of sagging-based cooking-pots and lumpy monochrome tripod pitchers into a riot of variegated slips, copper-enriched glazes, applied strips, anthropomorphs, aquamaniles and puzzle-jugs. Many such pots copied expensive metal vessels for the wealthy, and must therefore represent a broader-based market at lower burgess and artisan level. Animal bones show much more evidence of specialised butchery – a better range of meat on offer, less mess in back yards.

As the evidence of craft guilds accumulates, so also did the larger towns move towards self-regulation and monopolistic exclusion, expressed in charters, fee-farming, assays on weights and measures or freedom from merchet. Physically, corporate identity can be seen in hospitals and new gates, and on a smaller scale by town seals, using pictures of walled enclaves, ships or other symbols that a community saw as self-expressive. Royal taxation levies show that by *c.* 1200 London effectively outstripped York by a factor of three; one was a European, the other a provincial, capital. Next as a group came Norwich, Lincoln, Northampton, Dunwich, Exeter and Winchester. Of these, only Dunwich was primarily a port; Exeter and Norwich could be reached by sea-going vessels with varying degrees of difficulty, and Winchester and Northampton not at

[44] On fairs, E. W. Moore, *The Fairs of Medieval England* (Toronto, 1985), and see above, pp. 108–9; Northampton, J. H. Williams, *St Peter's Street, Northampton, Excavations 1973–1976* (Archaeological Monograph, 2, Northampton, 1979), and M. Shaw and S. Steadman, 'Life on a medieval back-street', *Northamptonshire Archaeology*, 25 (1993–4), 127–58.

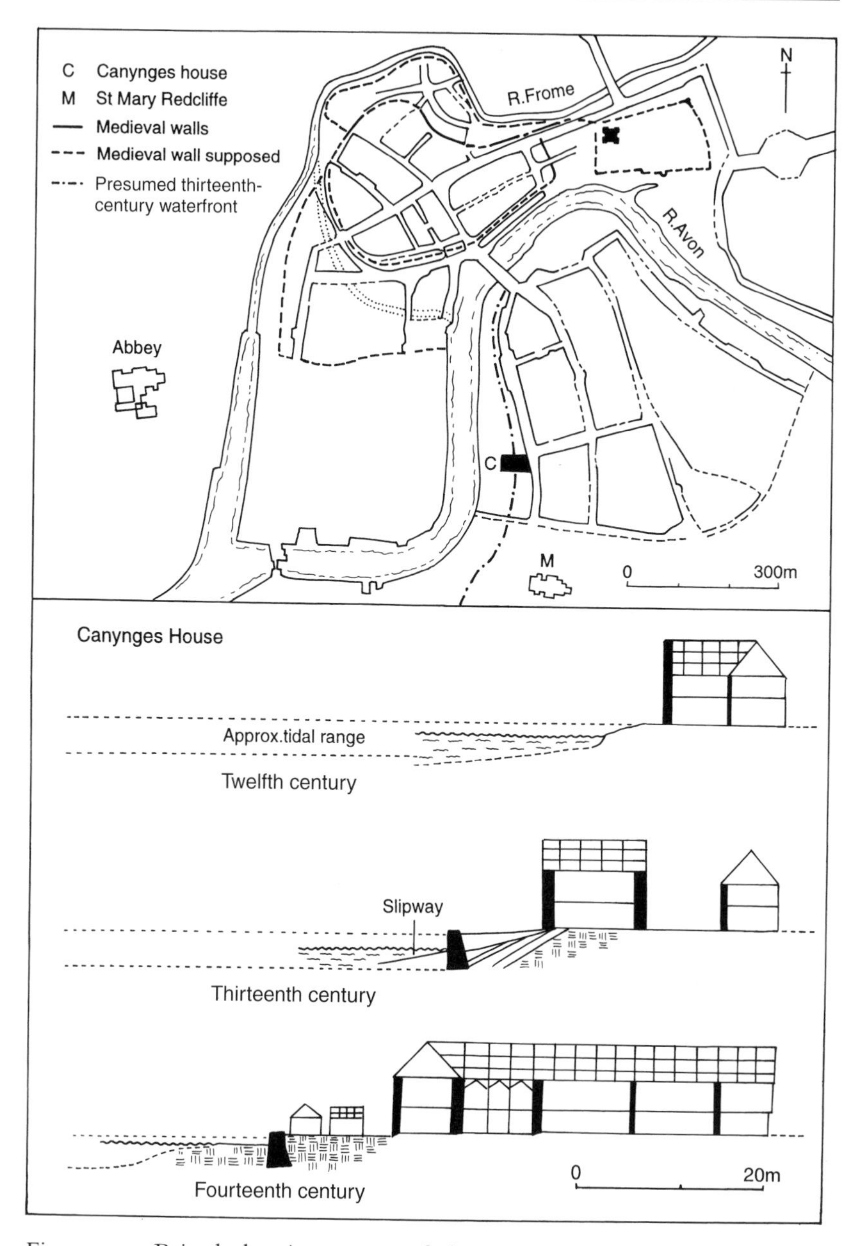

Figure 10.5 Bristol, showing process of plan and foreshore development. The original course of the River Frome may have been to the south of the dotted lines shown here, and the southern extension of the town may have been unwalled on its north side along the river (after Schofield and Vince, and Jones). Drawn by K. Knowles.

all.[45] These towns should perhaps be seen primarily as regional centres, for which redistribution of goods including those from overseas was an important function, but which needed others, notably cloth production, for real prosperity.

During the thirteenth century, these regional centres were joined or surpassed by Bristol, Newcastle, Boston, Lynn, Yarmouth, Coventry and Salisbury – all but the last two of which were ports. In the 1240s, Bristol citizens' initiative built a new bridge across the River Avon and dug a new channel for the River Frome in the 1240s, to improve navigation, though recent excavations suggest that it was the Redcliffe bank of the Avon downstream of the new bridge that saw most waterfront activity, the original shelving river foreshore being built upon with a stone wall, acting as revetment for reclamation (Figure 10.5). A stone-lined slipway at one site is probably typical of many, designed to mitigate the worst effects of the tidal range by allowing boats to be less dependent on beaching, and thus able to reload and float off again with less delay. In the same area, dyeing vats and concentrations of madder roots that have reddened the surrounding soil are an indication of the cloth-finishing trade that helped Bristol to flourish. The late twelfth-century 'Colston's Hall', an aisled building that remained part of one of the most desirable properties in the port, was used during much of its life for large-scale storage, a facility increasingly important as cargo volumes increased in line with boat capacities. Newcastle too has produced madder – and woad for blue colourings – though raw wool was its main export despite the relatively low value of the locally reared fleeces. Coal, despite its bulk, was carried as far south as Dorset, as well as to Calais, and across the North Sea. The growing importance of the Baltic helped Newcastle's trade, as it did that of the other three east coast ports that did so well in the thirteenth century, Boston, Lynn and Yarmouth, all estuary-mouth sites that larger vessels could unload at quickly, but with upriver connections – especially to Lincoln for the first and to Norwich for the third, but to the whole of the South Midlands for the second after the diversion of the River Ouse in the middle of the thirteenth century. These were joined by Hull, able to serve both York and Nottingham, as changing sand-spits altered navigation patterns in the Humber estuary.[46]

[45] Figures based on tables of 'aids' in A. Ballard, *British Borough Charters, 1042–1216* (Cambridge, 1913). For guilds, guards, councils and communities, see above, pp. 64–72.

[46] For Bristol, R. H. Leech, 'The medieval defences of Bristol revisited', in L. Keen, ed., *'Almost the Richest City'* (British Archaeological Association Conference Transactions, 19, 1997), pp. 17–30, and R. H. Jones, 'Industry and environment in medieval Bristol', in G. L. Good *et al.*, eds., *Waterfront Archaeology* (CBA Res. Rep., 74, 1991), pp. 19–26; Newcastle, C. O'Brien *et al.*, *The Origins of the Newcastle Quayside: Excavations at Queen Street and Dog Bank* (Newcastle upon Tyne Society of Antiquaries, Monograph 3, 1988), and R. Fraser *et al.*, 'Excavation on the site of the Mansion House, Newcastle, 1990', *Archaeologia Aeliana*, 23 (1995), 145–213; Hull, P. Armstrong and B. Ayers, *Excavations in High Street and Blackfriargate* (Hull Old Town Report Series, 5, 1987), and P. Armstrong, 'Kingston upon Hull', *Archaeological J*, 141 (1984), 1–4; on

It was not only ports that could be thriving new towns, as New Salisbury shows most clearly (Figure 10.6). Created on a new site in the early thirteenth century, when the bishop decided to move first his cathedral and then his borough to a river valley away from the disturbance of a castle on a cold and arid hilltop, it appears to present a unique opportunity to see how a large town was conceptualised. Even here, however, there were preconditioning factors, notably at least one small settlement, a church and streams, though those were turned to good use for cloth fulling and dyeing, for tanning and for the removal of rubbish by diverting them into water channels down the middle of streets. The cathedral was in a distinct enclosure, later walled and gated. But around the town, an earth bank and ditch was enough, as it was in Lynn: the majesty of a stone wall was not worth the expense. Internally, a large central market, blessed by a chapel, obviated the need for stalls in the streets. Names like Pot Row might suggest zoning – of retailing, not of manufacturing. Despite the apparent uniformity of its grid, Salisbury built up piecemeal, the earliest occupation having been found close to the cathedral. A stone bridge in 1244 completed the infrastructure, and the town was large enough, and rents high enough, to keep two friaries on the outskirts. It is often an indication of a town's prosperity that these new religious orders were not afforded central positions, just as its status may be shown by the numbers of different orders that tried to get a place within it.[47]

Thirteenth-century growth was not universal, and some older towns suffered. After Winchester lost its role as a centre of royal administration during the twelfth century, it had increasing difficulty in meeting its fee-farm dues, although individual town dwellers did not suffer poverty there as they had a fairly lively trade, not least in cloth. One of the wealthiest, John de Tyting, rebuilt for himself between 1299 and 1312 an already substantial property, adding a 'great gate' to his frontage. This led into a courtyard in which a round structure was most probably a dove-cote, as important for its lordly symbolism as for its meat potential. Best of all, perhaps, was that ultimate sign of status, an indoor privy. Yet only two streets away, excavations have shown that an exact contemporary was a row of single-roomed cottages, the first clear example of a terrace, an urban house form as distinctive as a burgess hall, and one with a much longer future.[48]

ships and their cargo capacities, I. Friel, *The Good Ship: Ships, Shipbuilding and Technology in England* (London, 1995), and G. Hutchinson, *Medieval Ships and Shipping* (London, 1994). For further references to waterfronts, see below, pp. 375–6.

[47] For Salisbury, A. Borthwick and J. Chandler, *Our Chequered Past: The Archaeology of Salisbury* (Trowbridge, 1984), and *BAHT*, I; on friaries, L. A. S. Butler, 'The houses of the mendicant orders in Britain', in P. V. Addyman and V. E. Black, eds., *Archaeological Papers from York presented to M. W. Barley* (York, 1984), pp. 123–36, and see above, pp. 144–7.

[48] D. J. Keene, 'The textile industry', in M. Biddle, *et al.*, *Object and Economy in Medieval Winchester* (Oxford, 1991), pp. 200–14 at p. 212; Scobie, Zant and Whinney, *The Brooks*, pp. 40–5; and M. Biddle, 'Excavations at Winchester, 1967', *Antiquaries J*, 48 (1968), pp. 250–84 at 261–6.

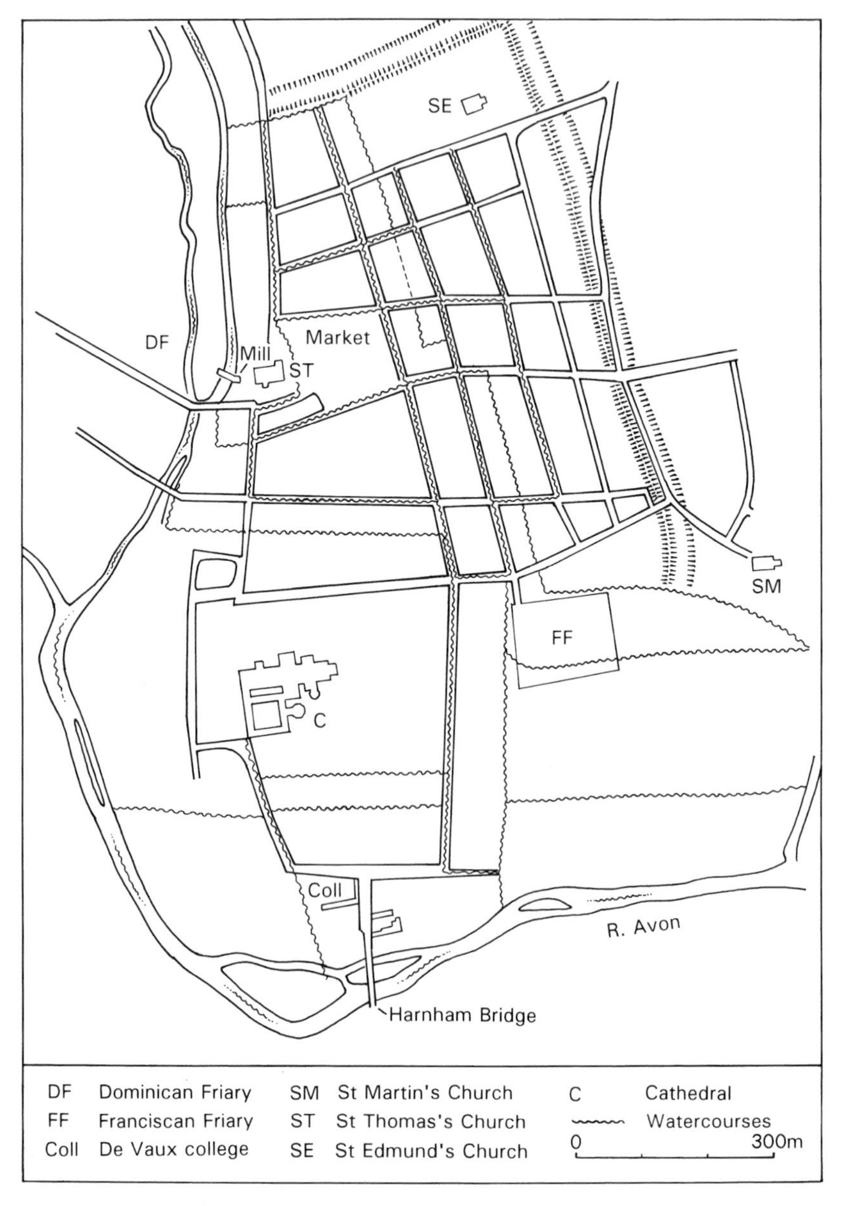

Figure 10.6 Salisbury *c.* 1300. Suburban developments to the west and south not shown (after Lobel, Borthwick and Chandler, and RCHM). Drawn by K. Knowles.

By the end of the thirteenth century, lay subsidies begin to give comparable data on wealth disparity in towns: Shrewsbury, which normally ranked between tenth and twentieth in the national returns, has surviving records that show that nine of its townspeople whose names occur at least three times in the different years' lists paid over £20 in tax on at least two occasions between 1297 and 1332, another fifteen paid £10 or more at least once, twenty-eight over £5, thirty-four over £3, 128 over £1, eighty-five less than £1 and an unknown number nothing at all. Although evasion was an art – at which the widow of Laurence de Ludlow's partner apparently excelled – the figures give some impression of Shrewsbury's wealth hierarchy, though the criteria underrepresent those at the bottom end.[49]

By the end of the thirteenth century, Winchester and Shrewsbury were really no more than shire towns, like Canterbury, Hereford or Gloucester. Lincoln was complaining also, but the worst loss was Dunwich, physically to the sea. Northampton lost Midland superiority to Coventry, which developed the livelier cloth trade. Wallingford also faded, overtaken by Reading down the Thames as well as by Oxford up it, although at the latter declining rents for its tenements allowed a university to infiltrate it almost unnoticed. This had become a formal institution by the early thirteenth century, but only gradually acquired buildings of its own, being attached at first to existing churches. The colleges began to arrive only after the first quarter of the century.[50]

Oxford was surprisingly buoyant in the early fourteenth century, rated the eighth highest for subsidy in 1334. Excluding London, the ten highest-rated towns were valued at just under £12,400 in total; the next ten were worth a further £6,500, the next thirty *c.* £9,500, an average of a quarter of the top ten's.[51] The large towns' wealth is an indication of their national and international importance, but by the end of the thirteenth century they were at the head of a very long list of urbanised places.

[49] D. Cromarty and R. Cromarty, eds., *The Wealth of Shrewsbury in the Early Fourteenth Century* (Shrewsbury, 1993).

[50] R. H. C. Davis, 'The ford, the river and the city', *Oxoniensia*, 38 (1973), 258–67, argued that Oxford was adversely affected by loss of river traffic, caused by increasing numbers of weirs on the River Thames, but this has been discounted by R. B. Peberdy, 'Navigation on the River Thames between London and Oxford in the late middle ages: a reconsideration', *Oxoniensia*, 61 (1996), 311–40.

[51] See below, Appendix 4.

· 11 ·

Small towns 600–1270

JOHN BLAIR

IN PART III of this volume, towns are considered 'small' if they had populations of fewer than 2,000.[1] For the early middle ages such a clear-cut division by size is both impossible and inappropriate – not merely for lack of data. During the ninth to twelfth centuries the urbanising potentials of a variety of places were gradually being realised in a range of different ways, and urban characteristics remained fluid. In 1200 Oxford and Cookham were very different sorts of places; in 800 they may have been quite similar. To apply a cut-off line across the whole period would be nonsensical, though the point comes when certain sorts of town (notably the planned and fortified towns in the tenth century) rise above the line and come within the scope of the previous chapter rather than this one. It seems more useful here to concentrate on processes than on size categories, and to treat the earlier and more modest stages of the urbanisation process as a continuum across these centuries.

Commercial activity is often considered a basic characteristic of urbanism, and it remains true that a place completely lacking a market is hard to define as even a small town. On the other hand, it has come to be realised that much marketing activity in early and high medieval Britain took place in pre-urban or entirely non-urban contexts. *Sceatta* distributions show that by 750, in southern and eastern Britain, exchange was taking place on open-ground sites and places of assembly such as deserted hill-forts; informal trading-places are now known to have remained numerous and important through the middle ages. Again, strong reasons have been adduced for thinking that many of the Angevin period seigneurial towns and chartered markets perpetuated informal but long-standing 'wakes' and other popular trading assemblies. While there can be no serious doubt that local trade expanded during the twelfth and thirteenth centuries, town and market foundations have come to be seen less as the main stimuli of

[1] See below, pp. 505–6.

commercial growth, and more as attempts by lords to control and profit from it.[2]

Likewise, recent scholarship has placed less emphasis on the 'planting' of completely new towns, more on the accretion of elements both planned and unplanned around existing foci.[3] Belatedly adopting a model which has long been familiar in the European context,[4] British historians have become interested in 'primary towns', 'proto-towns' and 'pre-urban nuclei' as formative influences on the urban landscape which becomes clearly visible during the thirteenth century.[5] If the phrase 'proto-town' risks anachronism by embodying a teleological perception of what pre-urban centres were to become, rather than what they were in their own day,[6] the very strong similarities between the kinds of places around which towns grew must mean that they gave some distinct and special impetus to economic growth. These new approaches have run parallel with the development of more informed perceptions of early medieval rural settlement patterns, which emphasise the importance of hierarchical and tribute-collection centres in shifting, dispersed settlement landscapes.

(i) FOCI FOR URBANISATION

The essence of the 'pre-urban nucleus' model is that established places of political, defensive and religious importance offered security, markets for goods and services and foci for regular commercial, social and cult assemblies; hence they

[2] D. M. Metcalf, *Thrymsas and Sceattas in the Ashmolean Museum, Oxford* (London, 1993–4), for *sceatta* distributions; P. H. Sawyer, 'Fairs and markets in early medieval England', in N. Skyum-Nielsen and N. Lund, eds., *Danish Medieval History* (Copenhagen, 1981), pp. 153–68; R. H. Britnell, 'The proliferation of markets in England, 1200–1349', *Ec.HR* 2nd series, 34 (1981), 209–21; C. Dyer, 'The hidden trade of the middle ages: evidence from the West Midlands of England', *J of Historical Geography*, 18 (1992), 141–57. [3] See above, pp. 161–2.

[4] H. Pirenne, *Medieval Cities* (New York, 1956), pp. 39–53; F. L. Ganshof, *Etude sur le développement des villes entre Loire et Rhin au moyen âge* (Paris and Brussels, 1943); E. Ennen, 'Les différents types de formation des villes européennes', *Le moyen age*, 62 (1956), 397–411; C. R. Brühl, 'The town as a political centre: general survey', in M. W. Barley, ed., *European Towns* (London, 1977), pp. 419–30; H. B. Clarke and A. Simms (eds.), *The Comparative History of Urban Origins in Non-Roman Europe* (British Archaeological Reports, International Series 255(i), 1985), especially E. Ennen, 'The early history of the European town' (pp. 3–14), and H. B. Clarke and A. Simms, 'Towards a comparative history of urban origins' (pp. 669–714).

[5] A. Everitt, 'The Banburys of England', *UHY* (1974), 28–38; Sawyer, 'Fairs and markets', pp. 160–4; several essays in J. Haslam, ed., *Anglo-Saxon Towns in Southern England* (Chichester, 1984); C. Dyer, 'Recent developments in early medieval urban history and archaeology in England', in D. Denecke and G. Shaw, eds., *Urban Historical Geography* (Cambridge, 1988), pp. 69–80, at pp. 78–9; G. G. Astill, 'Towns and town hierarchies in Saxon England', *Oxford J of Archaeology*, 10 (1991), 95–117, at 103, 113.

[6] As pointed out by C. Scull, 'Urban centres in pre-Viking England?', in J. Hines, ed., *The Anglo-Saxons from the Migration Period to the Eighth Century* (Woodbridge, 1997), pp. 269–310: a valuable critique of assumptions that such places were urban in the pre-Viking period, which does not, however, undermine the case that they had an *urbanising* role later.

acquired 'suburban' settlements of traders and craftsmen, which in due course might take on a life of their own and flourish independently of the high-status establishments which had spawned them.[7] The nature of the foci, and thus of the dependent settlements, will have varied greatly between cultures, and there are distinctive British versions of this Europe-wide pattern. Four main types of place have been proposed at various times as nuclei for urbanisation: (i) Roman towns and forts; (ii) high-status secular strongholds and royal vills; (iii) hundredal and other local administrative centres; and (iv) cathedrals and monastic centres. In Britain at least, there are grounds for thinking that the fourth category was more influential than the other three.

A fundamental cultural difference between early medieval European regions, in urban origins as in so much else, is the presence or absence of Roman institutions and the physical structures which they produced. Britain certainly had the latter – towns and villas in the lowlands, forts in Wales and southern Scotland – and many of them underlie medieval towns of all sizes. Much effort has been devoted to explaining this fact. Except perhaps at Canterbury (which in some ways makes better sense as a Merovingian city than as an early English one), few would now argue for any continuity in specifically urban forms of life; but in the 1970s a strong case was made for the proposition that some Romano-British walled places survived as seats of secular power, to re-emerge as royal centres and, in due course, as towns.[8] This was the experience of much of post-Roman Europe, and it could certainly have happened in some individual British cases. It must be said, though, that no archaeological evidence has been found for such survival of high-status residences, nor is there written evidence that English or British rulers before the ninth century were in the habit of holding court within Roman walls.[9]

What is abundantly clear is that Roman towns and forts were often used in the seventh century for siting cathedrals and monasteries, and that English rulers, like Frankish and British ones, gave them to monastic founders for this purpose.[10] Again, genuine Christian continuity cannot be disproved in specific cases. But the phenomenon is more convincingly defined as *Romanitas* reimported or, in

[7] Clarke and Simms, 'Towards a comparative history', pp. 672–88, where the very useful 'typology of proto-towns' 'may be compared and contrasted with the one suggested here for Britain. Scull, 'Urban centres in pre-Viking England?', for qualifications.

[8] The classic exposition of this view is M. Biddle, 'Towns', in D. M. Wilson, ed., *The Archaeology of Anglo-Saxon England* (London, 1976), pp. 99–150, at pp. 103–12. For possible continuity at Canterbury, see above, pp. 23, 217.

[9] J. Blair, 'Anglo-Saxon minsters: a topographical review', in J. Blair and R. Sharpe, ed., *Pastoral Care before the Parish* (Leicester, 1992), pp. 226–66, at pp. 239–40 (England); B. Dicks, 'The Scottish medieval town: a search for origins', in G. Gordon and B. Dicks, eds., *Scottish Urban History* (Aberdeen, 1983), pp. 23–51, at pp. 28–34 (Scotland); H. Carter, *The Towns of Wales: A Study in Urban Geography* (Cardiff, 1965), pp. 4–7, and Clarke and Simms, 'Towards a comparative history', pp. 671–2 (Wales).

[10] Blair, 'Topographical review', pp. 235–9.

E. Ennen's phrase, 'continuity in the realm of ideas', a process which could operate beyond as well as within the former Roman frontiers: thus 'the episcopal *civitates* in the Frankish period that had originated in Roman towns became the model for the defended bishops' seats east of the Rhine', which in turn 'became important seed-beds of medieval towns'.[11] The reuse of Romano-British walled places to house minsters was the first stage in their reclamation, a link from Roman to medieval urbanism; but it was a religious and aristocratic link in the first instance, only an urban link at one remove.

Royal and princely strongholds were one of the main kinds of pre-urban nucleus in continental Europe,[12] but it is surprisingly hard to find clear evidence that they assumed this role in Britain. In Scotland it is only a few of the sixth- to eighth-century princely citadels, notably Stirling, Dumbarton, Edinburgh and Dunbar, which emerge as medieval towns,[13] and Scottish urbanisation came so late that even these cases exemplify a high medieval rather than an early medieval phenomenon. There is a striking lack of evidence that English rulers before the ninth century used residential fortresses at all (a circumstance underlined by, for instance, the tiny number of non-monastic sites which were used in this period for issuing royal charters and which have place-names in *-burh*). Perhaps this helps to explain why it is so rare to find reused Iron Age hill-forts underlying English medieval towns, except in those cases (such as Malmesbury and Aylesbury) where the forts also contained minsters.[14]

Large numbers of English *villae regiae* on lowland, mainly undefended, sites are recorded during the seventh to ninth centuries, and their role as long-term settlement foci is often taken for granted; yet evidence from the pre-Viking period scarcely supports this.[15] Each kingdom probably contained two or three places which were genuinely stable royal centres from early times, or which became so in the later eighth to ninth centuries under Carolingian influence; some convincing cases are Faversham and Milton Regis (Kent), Dorchester (Dorset), Wilton (Wilts.) and Tamworth (Staffs.).[16] These royal vills were doubt-

[11] Ennen, 'Early history', pp. 5–7; cf. comments on Ireland by Clarke and Simms, 'Towards a comparative history', p. 672.

[12] Clarke and Simms, 'Towards a comparative history', pp. 681–4.

[13] Dicks, 'Scottish medieval town', pp. 34–40. Note how few of the places listed by E. A. Alcock, 'Enclosed places, AD 500–800', in S. Driscoll and M. Nieke, eds., *Power and Politics in Early Medieval Britain and Ireland* (Edinburgh, 1988), pp. 40–6, show any long-term development into towns or even settlements. [14] Cf. Blair, 'Topographical review', pp. 233–4.

[15] A critical reading of the list in P. H. Sawyer, 'The royal *tūn* in pre-Conquest England', in P. Wormald, D. Bullough and R. Collins, eds., *Ideal and Reality in Frankish and Anglo-Saxon Society* (Oxford, 1983), pp. 273–99, will show how few of the places listed show much continuity before the late ninth century, and then only in Wessex. For the non-correlation between Welsh *maerdrefi* and towns see Carter, *Towns of Wales*, pp. 9–11; W. Davies, *Wales in the Early Middle Ages* (Leicester, 1982), pp. 57–8.

[16] T. Tatton-Brown, 'The towns of Kent', in Haslam, ed., *Anglo-Saxon Towns in Southern England*, pp. 1–36, at pp. 28–32; L. Keen, 'The towns of Dorset', in *ibid.*, pp. 203–7, at pp. 207–8, 230; J.

less as important seed-beds for urban growth as minsters were elsewhere; it can hardly be doubted that Tamworth, for instance, originates as a 'palace-town'. But it has yet to be shown that there were very many of them, and the royal character of nuclei should not be assumed without good cause. For instance, the monumental eighth- and ninth-century halls at the heart of Northampton have been claimed as a Mercian palace; but they stood between two churches, one of them a known minster, and a monastic interpretation seems more reasonable.[17]

From the late ninth century we can recognise a much larger number of royal vills which show stability up to Domesday Book, and which were associated with small towns by 1300. But it is notable how many of these places were also minsters: there are grounds for suspecting that royal settlements were gaining stability by battening on to the inherently more stable monastic settlements. This is demonstrable at Cheddar, and it may explain the 'Kingsbury' names adjoining minsters in several West Saxon towns.[18] The coincidence of this process with the beginnings of urbanisation makes interpretation difficult. For instance, Domesday Book shows Cookham as a rich royal manor with a modestly endowed minster attached, and signals the presence of the later small town, inviting the conclusion that this town grew up at the palace gates; only a chance survival tells us that in the 790s Cookham had been a major minster, fit to be described as an *urbs*, at the centre of its own huge estate.[19]

This chronology does, of course, entail a strong possibility that the palace was the dominant force by the time of the earliest urbanising activity. The decline of minsters, the stabilisation of royal vills and the growth of proto-urban places were going on over much the same time scale, and only archaeology, still rudimentary in this area of study, could come anywhere near to determining cause and effect. It is probably fair to say that ecclesiastical sites had potentially urbanising capacities from the eighth century onwards, but royal sites in England fail to show them until the tenth or eleventh.[20] The same may be true (granted the more exiguous written sources) of Scotland, though there it is in any case only around 1100 that the royal market touns start to emerge as distinctive places of

Haslam, 'The towns of Wiltshire', in *ibid.*, pp. 87–147, at pp. 122–9; Sawyer, 'Royal *tūn*', pp. 293, 298, 296–7; P. Rahtz and R. Meeson, *An Anglo-Saxon Watermill at Tamworth* (CBA Res. Rep., 83, 1992).

[17] J. Blair, 'Palaces or minsters? Northampton and Cheddar reconsidered', *Anglo-Saxon England*, 25 (1996), 97–121, at 98–108.

[18] *Ibid.*, 116–20; Haslam, 'Towns of Wiltshire'.

[19] Great Domesday f. 56v; J. Blair, 'The minsters of the Thames', in J. Blair and B. Golding, eds., *The Cloister and the World* (Oxford, 1996), pp. 5–28, at pp. 14, 23.

[20] A recent critique of the 'monastic town' model in Ireland argues that in the process of urbanisation during the tenth to twelfth centuries, secular centres and enclosures were as important as religious ones: B. J. Graham, 'The town and the monastery: early medieval urbanization in Ireland, AD 800–1150', in T. R. Slater and G. Rosser, eds., *The Church in the Medieval Town* (Aldershot, 1998), pp. 131–54. The evidence marshalled by Graham (who does not take account of the most recent work on England) actually seems to point to a conclusion not dissimilar from the one presented here: a grafting of secular residences and fortresses on to existing religious complexes.

production, processing and exchange rather than mere estate and due-collection centres.[21]

Proto-urban activity at administrative centres is likewise ambiguous. The strong association between markets and hundredal manors in Domesday Book and twelfth-century sources may or may not represent a 'system' of one market per hundred,[22] but in either case it may be that communal trading assemblies, at the sorts of outlying, open-ground sites where hundred courts tended to be held, had been brought quite recently under royal control. Once again, about half of the Domesday markets and boroughs can be recognised as minster sites, as can some two-thirds of the places where coins were struck between Alfred's reign and the Conquest.[23] A similar correlation can be observed with the large cottager communities which often mark out proto-towns in Domesday Book.[24] It is thus unclear how much of the commercial activity which appears to be linked to sites of royal authority may have started during the previous two or three centuries, stimulated by a monastic presence[25] or simply by informal exchange needs.

(ii) SMALL-TOWN ORIGINS 900–1086

The cathedrals and minsters, then, can most clearly be identified as the pre-urban nuclei of British towns. This pattern, which on the whole seems stronger in Britain and Ireland than on the other fringes of the Roman world, reflects various factors, mostly stemming from the distinctive mixture of Roman-derived culture and insular aristocratic life styles which religious communities embodied. Whereas early medieval princely life was itinerant, ecclesiastical life was stationary.[26] The buildings were permanent, organised and of a higher density than any other kind of settlement before the tenth century; in James Campbell's phrase, 'a monastery such as Whitby, with its numerous buildings, its crafts and its maritime contacts must have been considerably more like a town

[21] Cf. R. M. Spearman, 'Early Scottish towns: their origins and economy', in Driscoll and Nieke, eds., *Power and Politics*, pp. 96–110, at pp. 105–8.

[22] For different views: R. H. Britnell, 'English markets and royal administration before 1200', *Ec.H.R.*, 2nd series, 31 (1978), 183–96; J. Campbell, 'Was it infancy in England?', in M. Jones and M. Vale, eds., *England and her Neighbours, 1066–1453: Essays in Honour of Pierre Chaplais* (London and Ronceverte, 1989), pp. 1–17, at p. 14.

[23] These impressionistic calculations are based on the lists in H. C. Darby, *Domesday England* (Cambridge, 1977), pp. 364–70, and D. Hill, *An Atlas of Anglo-Saxon England*, 2nd edn (Oxford, 1984), pp. 131–2.

[24] C. Dyer, 'Towns and cottages in eleventh-century England', in H. Mayr-Harting and R. I. Moore, eds., *Studies in Medieval History Presented to R. H. C. Davis* (London, 1985), pp. 91–106; Blair, 'Minsters of the Thames', pp. 13–14.

[25] As suggested by Sawyer, 'Fairs and markets', pp. 160–1.

[26] Cf. Pirenne, *Medieval Cities*, pp. 44–8. J. W. Bernhardt, *Itinerant Kingship and Royal Monasteries in Early Medieval Germany* (Cambridge, 1993), for links between royal itineration, monasteries and surplus extraction which may have relevance for the earlier English situation.

than were most places'.[27] The inmates of a great minster were numerous, aristocratic and had to be fed the whole year round. Both their provisioning needs and their disposable surpluses must have stimulated trade, which they would have been well-placed to channel;[28] they could have obliged tenants to buy and sell at their markets, for instance to raise cash to pay dues. Such patterns would have been reinforced by the liturgical cycle, which caused a regular influx of laity on Sundays and feasts and made minsters natural places of regular commercial resort; there is widespread later evidence for Sunday markets and for markets in churchyards.[29] Significantly for future urban growth, alms and sanctuary would have attracted the poor and criminal classes, and the specialised supply needs of the communities would have generated lay settlements at the minster gates.[30]

It is in Ireland, where historians have long recognised the 'monastic city', that these processes have been most fully and effectively expounded from written and topographical sources. Kildare in the seventh century is called a *civitas* with *suburbana*, while another early text characterises the circuits of a great monastery from centre to periphery as 'most holy', 'more holy' and 'holy', with the laity allowed in the outer two circles and even the dregs of society allowed in the outermost. Map analysis and aerial photography reveal large, usually curvilinear monastic enclosures, several of which have evolved into small towns where roads and boundaries perpetuate the banks and ditches of the former precincts.[31] For comparative purposes it is of great interest that these Irish proto-towns usually remained in an embryonic state,[32] perpetuating what would have been the typical form of these sites in Britain before the twelfth century.

[27] J. Campbell, *Essays in Anglo-Saxon History* (London, 1986), p. 141; Blair, 'Topographical review', pp. 258–64.

[28] Cf. C. Doherty, 'Exchange and trade in early medieval Ireland', *J of the Royal Society of Antiquaries of Ireland*, 110 (1980), 67–89, at 81–4, for Irish monasteries developing and controlling markets during the ninth to twelfth centuries.

[29] Sawyer, 'Fairs and markets', pp. 160–4; R. H. Britnell, *The Commercialisation of English Society, 1000–1500*, 2nd edn (Manchester, 1996), pp. 84–5, 91–2, for the suppression of churchyard markets after 1200; G. Rosser, 'Religious practice on the margins', in J. Blair and C. Pyrah, eds., *Church Archaeology: Research Directions for the Future* (CBA Res. Rep., 104, 1996), pp. 75–83, at pp. 81–2.

[30] J. Blair, 'Minster churches in the landscape', in D. Hooke, ed., *Anglo-Saxon Settlements* (Oxford, 1988), pp. 35–58, at pp. 47–8.

[31] C. Doherty, 'The "monastic town" in early medieval Ireland', in Clarke and Simms, eds., *Comparative History*, pp. 45–75; L. Swan, 'Monastic proto-towns in early medieval Ireland', in *ibid.*, pp. 77–102; V. Hurley, 'The early Church in the south-west of Ireland: settlement and organization', in S. M. Pearce, ed., *The Early Church in Western Britain and Ireland* (British Archaeological Reports, British Series, 102, 1982), pp. 297–332; E. R. Norman and J. K. St Joseph, *The Early Development of Irish Society: The Evidence of Aerial Photography* (Cambridge, 1969), pp. 90–121, especially the photograph of Armagh on p. 118. There are clearly some problems in interpreting site morphology; but it does not seem to me that Graham, 'Town and monastery', seriously undermines the case that the major enclosed sites were ecclesiastical in origin.

[32] B. J. Graham, 'Irish urban genesis', *J of Historical Geography*, 13 (1987), 3–16; cf. Graham, 'Town and monastery'.

No other early insular culture has texts matching those for Ireland, but comparable physical evidence for enclosed monastic sites, a proportion of which developed into medieval towns, has now been recognised across much of Britain and north-western Europe;[33] the reused Roman and earthwork enclosures are in fact best seen in the same broad context of monastic occupation. In Scotland a much higher proportion of medieval towns seem to have developed out of monastic than royal nuclei. St Andrews, Glasgow and Brechin, eventually significant towns, may be only the most successful and best-recorded among a larger category of old-established kirktouns which grew into proto-urban lay communities. At St Andrews especially, careful topographical analysis has identified the *clachan* or early lay settlement, partly inside and partly outside the early monastic precinct, which was overlain after 1150 by the planned tenements of the burgh.[34] The development of Whithorn (Galloway) from its early monastic nucleus can be traced in remarkable detail thanks to recent excavations, which underline the importance of economic activity and commercial contacts at all stages between the sixth and thirteenth centuries.[35] In pre-Norman Wales 'the picture is not merely one of minimal urbanization but also of minimal trend towards urbanization', but most of the few places which do show faint signs of a proto-urban character were important monasteries.[36] It has been suggested on topographical grounds that several other later medieval Welsh towns show development from enclosed monastic sites, and despite doubts about some individual cases the general point has been strengthened by the discovery in rural contexts of large sub-circular ecclesiastical enclosures resembling the Irish ones.[37]

In England many more of these sites have become towns, sometimes quite substantial ones, so that intensive later development overlies the monastic phases. In these places, furthermore, little archaeology has occurred, except on a very small scale. Study of early medieval 'minster-towns' is as backward as was the study of early medieval planned towns before the campaigns of the 1960s; they pose one of the biggest challenges to urban archaeologists of the next generation. Even so, the modern topography often shows the curvilinear road defining

[33] Blair, 'Topographical review', pp. 231–5.

[34] Dicks, 'Scottish medieval town', pp. 40–4; N. P. Brooks and G. Whittington, 'Planning and growth in the medieval Scottish burgh: the example of St Andrews', *Transactions, Institute of British Geographers*, new series, 2 (1977), 278–95. See also above, pp. 154–5, and below, pp. 718–20.

[35] P. Hill, *Whithorn and St. Ninian: The Excavation of a Monastic Town 1984–91* (Stroud, 1997).

[36] Davies, *Wales in the Early Middle Ages*, pp. 57–8; note that in the early middle ages Chester, Hereford, Newport and Caernarfon, as well as Carmarthen, Llancarfan, Caerwent and Llanllywri, could have been important primarily as ecclesiastical sites. Cf. Carter, *Towns of Wales*, pp. 7–9; and below, pp. 684, 688.

[37] L. A. S. Butler, 'The "monastic city" in Wales: myth or reality?', *Bulletin of the Board of Celtic Studies*, 28(3) (1979), 458–67; L. A. S. Butler, 'Planned Anglo-Norman towns in Wales, 950–1250', in Clarke and Simms, eds., *Comparative History*, pp. 469–504, at pp. 489–99; T. A. James, 'Air photography of ecclesiastical sites in south Wales', in N. Edwards and A. Lane, eds., *The Early Church in Wales and the West* (Oxford, 1992), pp. 62–76.

a precinct, usually as the core of a complex settlement with both organic and planned additions (Figure 11.1).[38] The distinctive material culture of eighth-century minsters is now being widely recognised,[39] but we still know very little about their industrial and service zones, or the associated lay settlements. The ironworking site at Ramsbury, only 500 feet (150 m) from the minster and later cathedral,[40] illustrates a pattern that may well prove to be common. *Sceatta* finds in the environs of minsters are increasing, and may eventually throw light on their role as eighth-century centres of exchange.

Since it has been usual to treat the major, 'planned' towns of tenth-century England as a category apart (and to label them, with anachronistic precision, as '*burhs*'), it is important to stress that they were only one element in a broader spectrum of urbanisation operating over many generations,[41] and were by no means divorced from the much larger number of places that were developing around high-status foci. The tradition of rectilinear planning goes back at least as far as *Hamwic*, and we cannot assume that it was employed only with specifically urbanising intent. The Mercian towns where eighth-century defences have been found or inferred mostly contain minsters, and the primary rectilinear 'defence' at Hereford need be scarcely more than an unusually regular boundary around the cathedral and its adjuncts, later enlarged and fortified: was this any more 'urban' than the eighth-century rectilinear planned settlement beside North Elmham Cathedral?[42] It is striking that some two-thirds of the defended sites listed in the Burghal Hidage either contain or adjoin minsters, including such places as Cricklade, Wareham and Oxford where the bank and ditch have plainly been positioned to encapsulate an existing minster and its precinct.[43] Given that these places evidently did not contain occupation of genuinely urban densities before the late tenth century,[44] their substantial and well-planned fortifications and streets may not, in practice, make them quite so different from less obviously 'planned' towns as has usually been thought.

38 Blair, 'Minster churches in the landscape', pp. 48–50; Blair, 'Topographical review', pp. 231–5.

39 E.g. L. Webster and J. Backhouse, eds., *The Making of England: Anglo-Saxon Art and Culture AD 600–900* (British Museum, London, 1991), pp. 79–107, 133–56.

40 J. Haslam, 'A middle Saxon iron smelting site at Ramsbury, Wiltshire', *Med. Arch.*, 24 (1980), 1–68.

41 Cf. Dyer, 'Recent developments', pp. 74–6, for a healthy antidote to the assumption that the places listed in the Burghal Hidage constitute a coherent group of towns. Also see D. Hill and A. R. Rumble, eds., *The Defence of Wessex* (Manchester, 1996); and above, pp. 225–32.

42 J. Haslam, 'Market and fortress in England in the reign of Offa', *World Archaeology*, 19 (1987), 76–93; Biddle, 'Towns', pp. 120–2; Astill, 'Towns and town hierarchies', 103; P. Wade-Martins, *Excavations in North Elmham Park, 1967–1972* (East Anglian Archaeology, 9, 1980), pp. 37–57, 122–3.

43 Haslam, 'Towns of Wiltshire', pp. 106–10; L. Keen, 'Wareham town walls', *Archaeological J*, 140 (1983), 52–4; J. Blair, *Anglo-Saxon Oxfordshire* (Stroud, 1994), pp. 61–3, 146–8.

44 Astill, 'Towns and town hierarchies', 103–9.

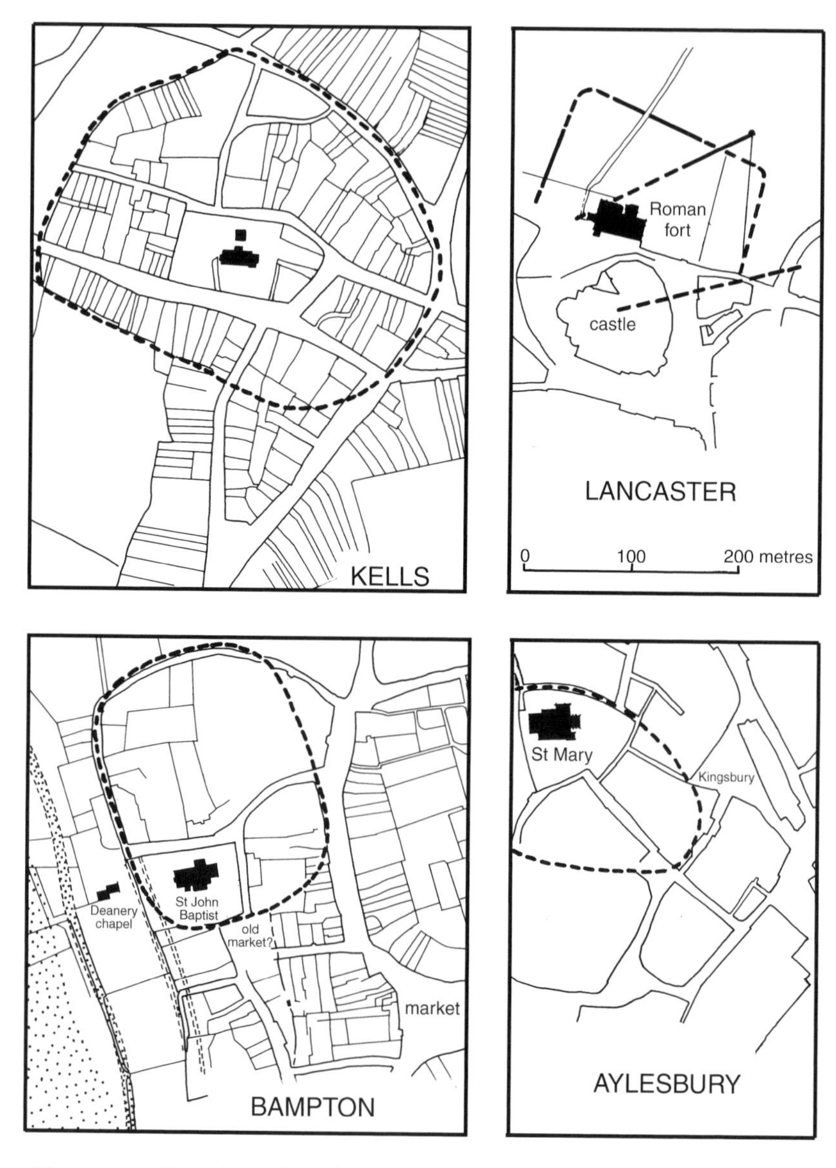

Figure 11.1 Ecclesiastical nuclei and urban growth in early medieval Britain and Ireland: six examples. Postulated monastic precinct boundaries are shown in heavy broken line; defensive Roman walls in heavy continuous line. Depiction of plot boundaries is selective.
Sources: Lancaster after D. Shotter and A. White, *The Roman Fort and Town of Lancaster* (Lancaster, 1980); Bampton after J. Blair, 'Bampton Research Project:

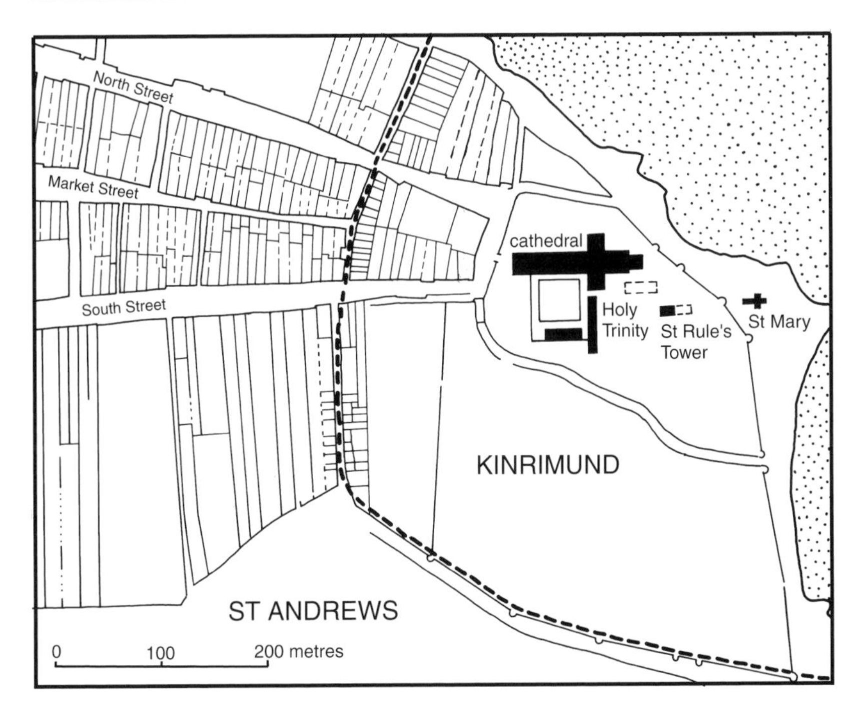

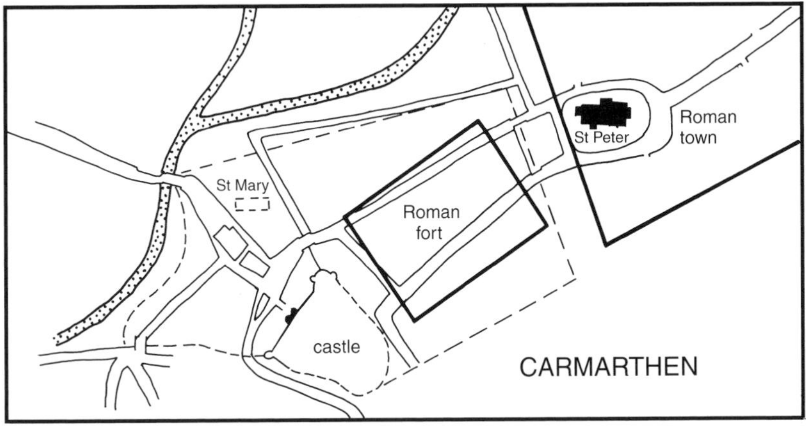

Figure 11.1 (*cont.*)
Bampton town centre: interim report, 1993–97', *South Midlands Archaeology*, 28 (1998); St Andrews after N. P. Brooks and G. Whittington, 'Planning and growth in the medieval Scottish burgh: the example of St Andrews', *Transactions, Institute of British Geographers*, new series, 2 (1977); Carmarthen after I. Soulsby, *The Towns of Medieval Wales* (Chichester, 1983).

All the evidence suggests that from the 970s there was rapid and sustained economic expansion, which stimulated the growth of production and exchange centres. The process had a regional as well as a chronological dimension. Major towns were certainly more developed to the east of Watling Street, and they must have had a more developed rural hinterland and marketing infrastructure: the late medieval contrast between East Anglia and the West Midlands was probably apparent by the year 1000.[45] The archaeological evidence for proto-towns now coming to light seems to confirm this, concentrated as it is in the East Midlands and eastern parts of England.

While we now know a good deal about the origins of large planned towns, and about planned elements in small towns after 1100, the physical and topographical evidence for the development of hierarchical centres into proto-towns during the tenth and eleventh centuries remains little explored. Excavation at such pre-urban nuclei as Northampton, Beverley, Steyning (Figure 11.2), North Elmham, St Neots and Warminster is starting to show the accretion of relatively low-density occupation, sometimes taking the form of enclosed farmstead-type dwellings and sometimes associated with limited industrial activity, on the peripheries of the old religious precincts.[46] Given that the sunken-floored or cellared timber building is a distinctively urban type in the tenth and eleventh centuries, the discovery of simple examples at the incipient minster-towns of Northampton, Steyning and Bampton seems significant.[47] These early stages of settlement nucleation tend to be overlaid by later occupation and thus to leave little trace in the permanent topography, beyond the bare outlines of the triangular market areas which developed at the entrances to minster enclosures.[48]

Emerging proto-towns at the major Benedictine monasteries are among the best documented. A recent study of St Albans suggests that deliberate urban development by the community on the edge of its precinct began as early as

[45] Alan Vince, pers. comm.; Astill, 'Towns and town hierarchies', 108–13; D. A. Hinton, *Archaeology, Economy and Society* (London, 1990), pp. 91–4.

[46] J. Williams, M. Shaw and V. Denham, *The Middle Saxon Palaces at Northampton* (Northampton, 1985), pp. 43–4; P. Armstrong, D. Tomlinson and D. H. Evans, *Excavations at Lurk Lane, Beverley, 1979–82* (Sheffield, 1991), pp. 9–22; M. Gardiner and C. Greatorex, 'Archaeological excavations in Steyning, 1992–95', *Sussex Archaeological Collections*, 135 (1997), 143–71; J. Blair, 'St. Cuthman, Steyning and Bosham', *ibid.* 173–92; Wade-Martins, *Excavations in North Elmham Park*, pp. 125–95; P. V. Addyman, 'Late Saxon settlements in the St. Neots area', *Proc. of the Cambridge Antiquarian Society*, 64 (1973), 45–99; Haslam, 'Towns of Wiltshire', pp. 118–21.

[47] J. H. Williams, *St. Peter's Street, Northampton* (Northampton, 1979), pp. 92–5; Gardiner and Greatorex, 'Excavations in Steyning', 159–61; J. Blair, 'Bampton Research Project: Bampton town centre: interim report, 1993–97', *South Midlands Archaeology*, 28 (1998), 47–54. Cf. above, p. 230.

[48] Cf. T. R. Slater, 'Urban genesis and medieval town plans in Warwickshire and Worcestershire', in T. R. Slater and P. J. Jarvis, eds., *Field and Forest: An Historical Geography of Warwickshire and Worcestershire* (Norwich, 1982), pp. 173–202, at pp. 188–90; Blair, 'Bampton Research Project'.

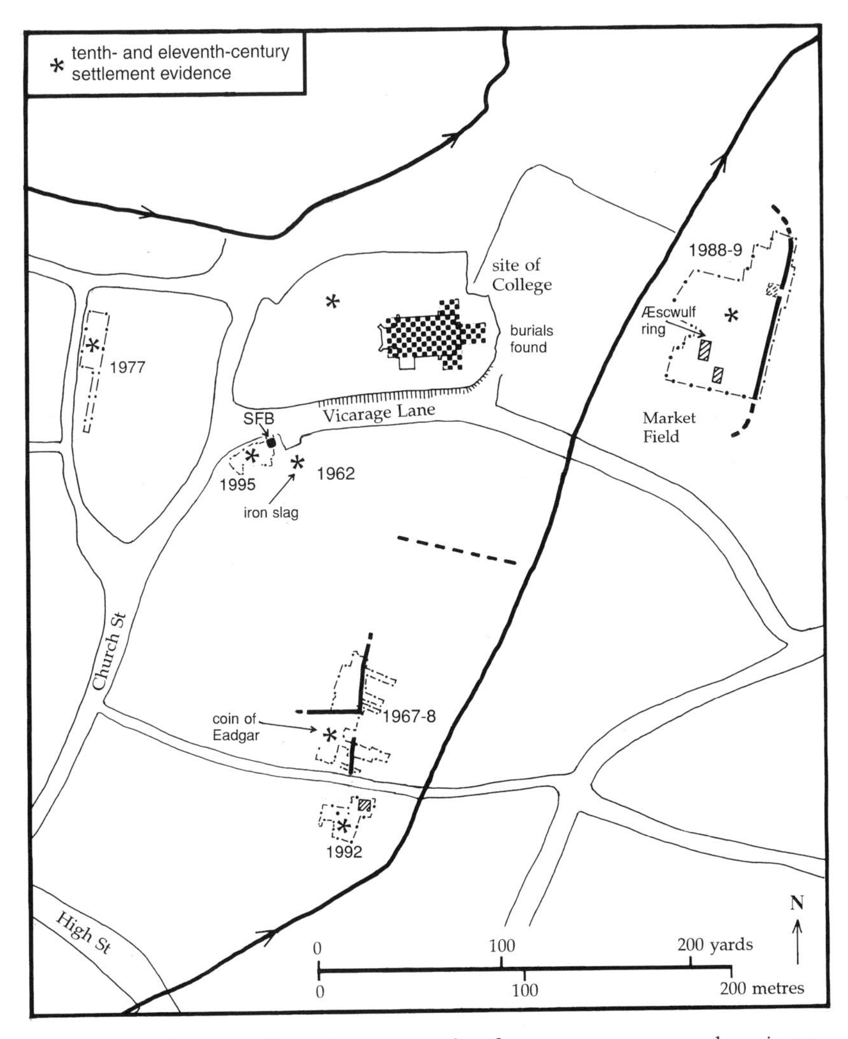

Figure 11.2 Steyning (Sussex): an example of a proto-town around a minster, where archaeology is starting to give some impression of the tenth- and eleventh-century settlement.
Source: after J. Blair, 'St. Cuthman, Steyning and Bosham', *Sussex Archaeological Collections*, 135 (1997).

the tenth century.[49] Other cases are Bury, where a new town 'within a greater perimeter' was laid out at the Abbey gate between 1066 and 1086; Abingdon, with its 'ten merchants dwelling before the gate of the church' in Domesday Book; or Evesham, where the growth of a complex settlement, occupational diversity and a cloth trade can be traced through the late eleventh and twelfth centuries.[50] But the reformed houses had no monopoly: many of the places with mints from the 970s onwards, or with *hagae, burgenses* and markets in Domesday Book, focused on ordinary secular minsters, as did many more places where urban or proto-urban features appeared by 1270. Dependence on an ancient and regionally important church gave these communities, even when they were otherwise little more than market villages, a special status and probably a distinct social character.[51] Parish guilds, which sometimes had a continuous life between at least the eleventh and fourteenth centuries, formed a bridge from the religious life of minster-places to the social life of towns, and it seems possible that more complex patterns of liturgical and guild activity continued to mark the former monastic towns through the twelfth and thirteenth centuries.[52]

(iii) ENTREPRENEURSHIP AND PLANNING 1086–1170

By the time of Domesday Book, both the proto-urban centres and the rural markets were being caught up in major organisational and topographical change. Between the eleventh and mid-thirteenth centuries the small-town landscape was transformed by a new phase of activity, easier to define and better documented: nucleation into regularly laid-out settlements. The phenomenon of the 'planned' or 'planted' town has been more discussed and analysed than any other aspect of British medieval urban topography, especially in the period after 1100 where the capacity to correlate grants of borough and market privileges with

[49] T. R. Slater, 'Benedictine town planning in medieval England: evidence from St. Albans', in Slater and Rosser, eds., *The Church in the Medieval Town*, pp. 155–76. It must be said, though, that the supposed urbanising activities of a mid-tenth-century abbot are known only from a late source, which locates them well before the earliest reliable evidence for a reformed community at St Albans.

[50] Little Domesday f. 372 (and M. Beresford, *New Towns of the Middle Ages* (London, 1967), pp. 156–7, 333–4); Great Domesday f. 58v; R. H. Hilton, 'The small town and urbanisation: Evesham in the middle ages', *Midland History*, 7 (1982), 1–8; T. R. Slater, 'Medieval town-founding on the estates of the Benedictine Order in England', in F.-E. Eliassen and G. A. Ersland, eds., *Power, Profit and Urban Land* (Aldershot, 1996), pp. 70–92; Astill, 'Towns and town hierarchies', 113. For other cases see Beresford, *New Towns*, pp. 326–7.

[51] Cf. Everitt, 'Banburys of England'.

[52] Cf. G. Rosser, 'The Anglo-Saxon gilds', in J. Blair, ed., *Minsters and Parish Churches* (Oxford, 1988), pp. 31–4; G. Rosser, 'The cure of souls in English towns before 1000', in Blair and Sharpe, eds., *Pastoral Care before the Parish*, pp. 267–84; J. Blair, 'Clerical communities and parochial space: the planning of urban mother churches in the twelfth and thirteenth centuries', in Slater and Rosser, eds., *The Church in the Medieval Town*, pp. 272–94.

streets and tenements surviving on the ground has engendered a reassuring sense that written and physical evidence are telling the same story.[53]

To a large extent they are: it is unquestionable that the laying-out of burgages and the obtaining or issuing of a charter were often deliberate and co-ordinated acts of proprietors. As incentives to settle, burgages were offered at money rents and made freely transferable; their tenants were given a variety of privileges, sometimes listed in considerable detail in formulae which were imitated from town to town; and in the larger 'plantations', merchant guilds developed to regulate trade.[54] The twelfth- and thirteenth-century wave of borough charters is the subject of other chapters:[55] suffice it to say here that both the general practice and the individual privileges percolated with remarkable speed from the big towns to the small ones. Soon after 1086 the lord of the small, probably newly planted, town of Burford (Oxon.) gave it a charter conferring burgage tenure and the trading privileges of the Oxford merchant guild.[56] More famously, the privileges of the Norman town of Breteuil were brought after the Conquest to Hereford, whence they became the model at one and two removes for a constellation of small Welsh towns.[57] As formal entities both institutionally and topographically, the proliferation of 'new towns' can be charted through the twelfth and thirteenth centuries with some precision, and classified by date, founder and context.

These were new and specific phenomena in Britain as elsewhere in Europe, especially on its colonising margins. In the German expansion beyond the Elbe, for instance, new settlements and holdings were set out by professional *mensuratores* supervised by 'settlement-men' (*locatores*).[58] It seems a short step back from this to Battle Abbey, William I's foundation a century earlier on the undeveloped commons of Sussex. Its *Chronicle* tells that when the building of the church was well under way,

> a great number of men were recruited, many from neighbouring districts and even some from across the Channel. The brethren who were in charge of the building began to apportion to individuals house-sites of definite dimensions near the boundary of its site. These, with their customary rent and service, can be seen to have remained to this day just as they were then arranged.[59]

[53] The fundamental works are: Beresford, *New Towns*; M. W. Beresford and H. P. R. Finberg, *English Medieval Boroughs* (Newton Abbot, 1973); I. Soulsby, *The Towns of Medieval Wales* (Chichester, 1983); G. S. Pryde, *The Burghs of Scotland* (Oxford, 1965). Cf. above, pp. 161–7.

[54] Beresford, *New Towns*, pp. 198–219; Britnell, *Commercialisation*, pp. 27–8, 147; R. Bartlett, *The Making of Europe* (London, 1993), pp. 167–82, for the European context. Battle (Sussex) had two guild houses: E. Searle, ed., *The Chronicle of Battle Abbey* (Oxford, 1980), pp. 64–6.

[55] See above, pp. 66–71 and 85–9. [56] See above, pp. 61 and 88.

[57] Beresford, *New Towns*, p. 199.

[58] Bartlett, *Making of Europe*, pp. 139–44; cf. Clarke and Simms, 'Towards a comparative history', pp. 692–7. [59] Searle, ed., *Chronicle of Battle Abbey*, pp. 50–3.

Such initiatives may have owed something to the established English tradition of town planning, but in the transformation of settlements from the late eleventh century onwards it must be right to see a new and entrepreneurial professionalism at work.

But this is not the whole story. It has become clear that there is no easy correlation between charters and the growth of real economic activity. Many lords obtained charters to formalise the status of long-standing markets or non-agrarian settlements; many others, like their counterparts across Europe, did so as part of speculative and often never-realised developments of purely rural places; whereas a broad range of settlements with urban characteristics of one sort or another never acquired any formal status.[60] It is also doubtful, given current uncertainties about the chronology of village formation in the parts of Britain where it occurs, how far planned towns should be treated as a category apart from planned villages.[61] The reasonable assumption must be that here, as elsewhere in Europe, the innovations which are so conspicuous on maps and aerial photographs were technical and topographical, and did not fundamentally determine the function of the settlements or status of their inhabitants.

It is helpful to picture nucleation and planning as a new organisational layer overlaid on the pre-nucleated landscape, with its centres of authority on the one hand and its rural markets on the other. Topographically, the critical stage came when the diffuse penumbras of activity which had been growing around hierarchical centres were regularised and concentrated into blocks of formal burgages. At the same time many of the smaller new towns may have assimilated, and thus brought under control, long-standing informal markets which in a dispersed settlement landscape need not have been near habitations at all. That market towns rise above the horizon of written and physical record during this period is as much a result of systematisation as of economic growth.

The earlier stages of this process remain largely obscure. In the bigger towns it was mainly during the century after 950 that occupation intensified, and open courtyard-type properties were subdivided into tenement-plots; arguably it was only then that they decisively outstripped high-status rural sites as centres of production. While it seems likely enough that smaller nuclei developed in a similar kind of way, they show a notable lack of evidence for anything like the formal tenement-plots of, say, York until much later. At Northampton, for

[60] Britnell, *Commercialisation*, pp. 5–28; Bartlett, *Making of Europe*, pp. 167–72.

[61] The recent literature on village nucleation and its chronology is voluminous, and the picture is changing rapidly. For useful perspectives, see for instance: C. Lewis, P. Mitchell-Fox and C. Dyer, *Village, Hamlet and Field: Changing Medieval Settlements in Central England* (Manchester, 1997); S. Oosthuizen, 'Medieval settlement relocation in west Cambridgeshire: three case-studies', *Landscape History*, 19 (1997), 43–55.

instance, settlement spread across the pre-urban focus of the ninth-century halls during the tenth century, but remained unplanned and haphazard until after the Conquest.[62] On present showing, the formation of burgage series in all but the biggest towns may be an eleventh-century innovation.

Thereafter the written evidence grows, and town 'foundations' can be counted decade by decade. In England there is a pattern of predominantly royal, ecclesiastical and castle-associated towns during the seventy years after the Conquest; a dip in the mid-twelfth century; and then a boom during *c.* 1160–1230 which is heavily dominated by lay lords.[63] Granted that many of these places were enlarged not created, and granted too that growth in bureaucratic documentation exaggerates the early thirteenth-century peak, this age of seigneurial entrepreneurs is no fiction. By the 1210s there is often written evidence for burgage formation, and inferences from maps rest on firmer ground. Town planning was part of the accelerating local investment in the built environment between 1160 and 1230 which is also seen, for instance, in the rebuilding and enlargement of manor houses and churches.

In Scotland burgh creation can be traced from the reign of David I (1124–53), and its great age was the twelfth century. Thirty-eight burghs had been founded by 1200, and over the next century the rate of new creations declined sharply. The earliest were royal, but the movement expanded during the twelfth century as ecclesiastical and lay magnates founded their own burghs under royal authority.[64] Royal direction of the process has always seemed especially important, an emphasis modified but not seriously diminished by recent research. It has become evident that in Scotland as elsewhere, burghs were not founded in a vacuum, but developed against a background of royal touns, kirktouns and trading sites. Some of these became burghs, with privileged royal burgesses whose rights and functions were carefully defined; others did not, but continued to function as a lower tier of markets.[65]

Welsh planned towns up to the 1140s were a direct consequence of Norman colonisation, and were therefore concentrated on the southern Marches and south coast. The lack of significant prior urbanisation meant that town formation was dominated, probably more than in any other part of Britain, by the current strategic and political needs. During *c.* 1150–1220 Wales diverges from England in its relative lack of initiatives at grass-roots level, and the few planned towns were insignificant and sometimes short-lived. There was more activity during *c.* 1220–70, not only in the English-controlled Marches and south, but

[62] Williams, Shaw and Denham, *Middle Saxon Palaces*, pp. 43–4; cf. Astill, 'Towns and town hierarchies', 112. [63] Beresford, *New Towns*, pp. 327–38; and see above, pp. 160, 162.

[64] I. H. Adams, *The Making of Urban Scotland* (London, 1978), pp. 14–26; R. Fox, 'Urban development 1100–1700', in G. Whittington and I. D. Whyte, eds., *An Historical Geography of Scotland* (London, 1983), pp. 73–92. [65] Spearman, 'Early Scottish towns', pp. 106–10.

also in the north where the Welsh themselves now started to develop a few small towns such as Nefyn and Pwllheli.[66]

However new in form, 'new towns' were often firmly traditional in their context and circumstances. This is most clearly true of the many small towns which continued in the Anglo-Norman period to be founded at the gates of monasteries. Narrative sources make clear that the functions envisaged by their proprietors were first and foremost to serve the needs of the religious communities, though when the monastery itself had been founded on undeveloped land (as at Battle, above p. 259) the town also had a colonising role. In about 1105 Bishop Gundulf of Rochester

> built a nunnery at [West] Malling [in Kent]. That vill had been a wasteland from of old, with only the occasional inhabitant to till it. With the help of King Henry [I] he made there for the use of the nuns a good-sized town well-suited to merchants, as may be seen today, . . . and crowds flocked from all sides and set up house.[67]

Colonisation aside, there is no fundamental difference between Battle or West Malling (Figure 11.3) and a replanned lay settlement at the gates of an ancient monastery such as Bury. In Scotland, too, several of the twelfth-century burghs were developments, under royal authority but springing from ecclesiastical initiative, around major churches both new and old.[68] These towns therefore continue the old tradition of service-providing *suburbia* and revenue sources attached to centres of authority, with the superficial difference that they are products of an age of planning.

The same might be said of boroughs established beside castles or, less frequently, royal palaces. The great households at royal and baronial *capita* needed service provision as much as did monasteries,[69] and castles had the obvious additional advantage of offering protection. Three-quarters of English towns founded between the Conquest and 1150 adjoined castles, as did virtually all the Welsh towns established in the same period, and the Scottish burghs established up to 1286.[70] In a few twelfth-century cases such as Saffron Walden, Chipping Ongar, Pleshey and Devizes (*de divisis*, i.e. a plantation on the boundary of two manors), the castle earthworks and the enclosing bank of the town

[66] Beresford, *New Towns*, pp. 340–4; Carter, *Towns of Wales*, pp. 10–11, 46–7; Soulsby, *Towns of Medieval Wales*, pp. 4–11. Butler, 'Planned Anglo-Norman towns', notes (pp. 475–6) some slight evidence for an association between commotal centres and Norman castles in Cardiganshire and Caernarfonshire.

[67] R. Thomson, ed., *The Life of Gundulf Bishop of Rochester* (Toronto, 1977), p. 60.

[68] Adams, *Making of Urban Scotland*, pp. 24–5; Spearman, 'Early Scottish towns', pp. 105–8; N. F. Sheard, 'Glasgow: an ecclesiastical burgh', in M. Lynch, M. Spearman and G. Stell, eds., *The Scottish Medieval Town* (Edinburgh, 1988), pp. 116–32.

[69] See above, ch.6, pp. 106–10.

[70] See above, pp. 60 and 173–4.

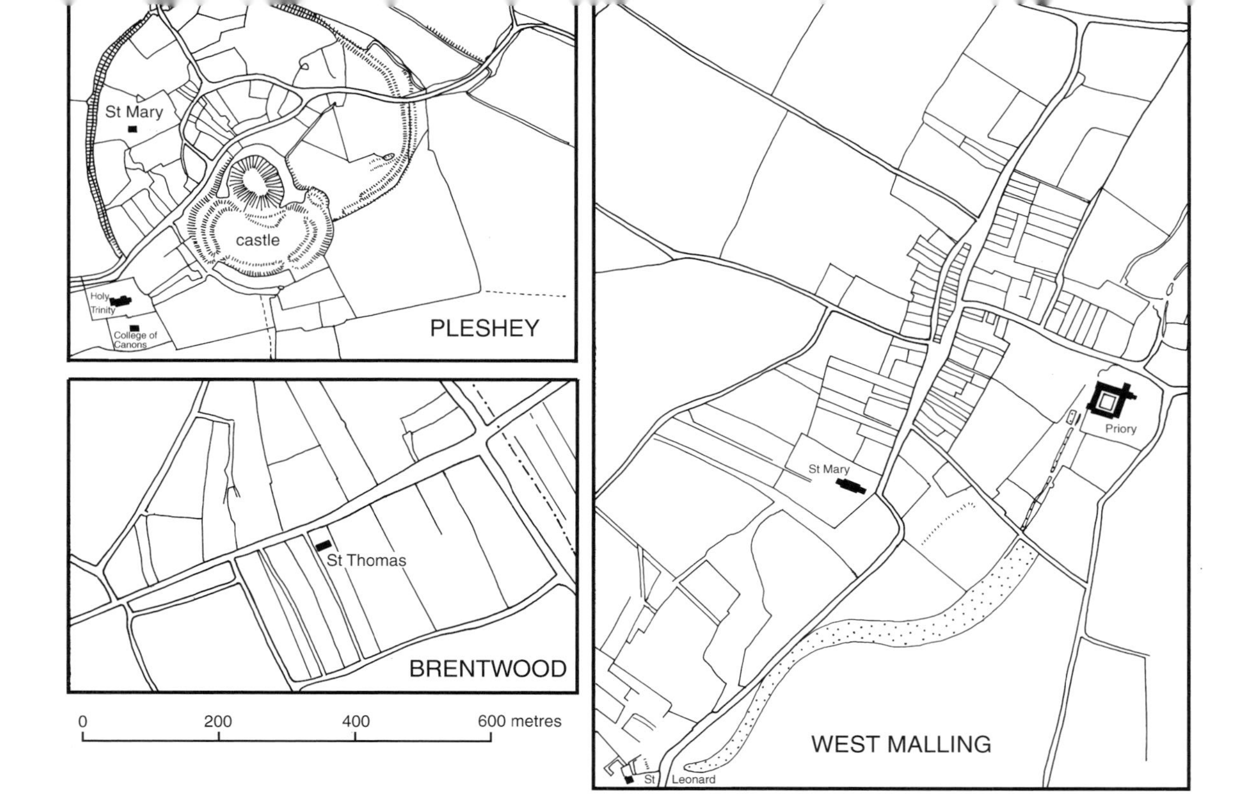

Figure 11.3 Twelfth-century planned towns: three examples.
Sources: Pleshey and Brentwood after M. R. Eddy and M. R. Petchey, *Historic Towns in Essex* (Chelmsford, 1983); West Malling after research by J. Blair.

were evidently planned and laid out in one operation (Figure 11.3).[71] In frontier zones, as at Egremont (Cumb.) around 1200, a founding lord might look to his burgesses for military service and castle guard.[72] More domestically, the men of New Woodstock (Oxon.) claimed that their town came into existence because King Henry II

> often visited his manor-house of Woodstock for love of a certain woman called Rosamond, and at that time there was an empty place outside the park of that manor, and because the king's men were lodged too far from his said manor, the king . . . gave and conceded divers small pieces of land from that empty place to divers men to build lodgings there for the use of the king's men.[73]

Here then is the great residence as magnet for urban growth, a familiar part of the European scene, if less clearly the British, for the past three or four centuries.

(iv) FILLING OUT THE SMALL-TOWN LANDSCAPE 1170–1270

After the 1150s 'new' towns were less frequently additions to high-status foci, and many of them were developments of purely agricultural villages or on vacant sites. In regions of light or dispersed settlement, entrepreneurship on a very small scale was worth trying. Cornwall abounded in tiny planned boroughs which were often barely more than formalised market sites, and in the forest of Arden the minority of settlements which were nucleated at all generally had market charters.[74] In parts of Wales, too, the multiplicity of small boroughs seems excessive for the undeveloped countryside.[75] It is here that British practice comes closest to that on the 'colonial' margins of Europe during the same period, where urban privileges were granted speculatively as incentives for development; it is not surprising that towns in this category include most of the failures.[76]

Generally more successful were foundations strategically sited on main roads and rivers to tap the steadily increasing volume of traffic.[77] A cluster of towns

[71] Beresford, *New Towns*, pp. 125–9; Soulsby, *Towns of Medieval Wales*, pp. 6–11; Butler, 'Planned Anglo-Norman towns', pp. 471–4; J. Schofield and A. Vince, *Medieval Towns* (London, 1994), pp. 42–6; Britnell, *Commercialisation*, pp. 21–2; M. R. Eddy and M. R. Petchey, *Historic Towns in Essex* (Chelmsford, 1983), pp. 82–5, 39–40, 74–7; Bartlett, *Making of Europe*, p. 134, for the European context. [72] See above, pp. 64–5.

[73] *Rotuli Hundredorum* (Record Commission, 1818), vol. II, p. 839.

[74] P. Sheppard, *The Historic Towns of Cornwall: An Archaeological Survey* (Truro, 1980); Chris Dyer, pers. comm. See also above, p. 160, and below, p. 597.

[75] Beresford, *New Towns*, pp. 346–7; and see below, pp. 686, 695.

[76] Bartlett, *Making of Europe*, p. 171; Beresford, *New Towns*, pp. 290–315. However, current work by H. S. A. Fox suggests that the failure of small towns in the south-west may have been exaggerated, and that late medieval Devon was highly urbanised.

[77] Beresford, *New Towns*, pp. 112–24, for water transport. See also above, pp. 156, 162.

on roads leading north-eastwards out of London were developed in the late twelfth century, mainly by ecclesiastical landlords: Chelmsford, Braintree, Brentwood, Epping, Baldock, Chipping Barnet, Royston (Figure 11.3).[78] The chronology of formal market creations in Essex suggests that prime roadside locations became more important after 1200.[79] In west Oxfordshire the route taken by traffic from Gloucester to Oxford allowed the development of Burford and Witney at the expense of the old minster centres at Bampton and Charlbury; in turn, rivalry between the neighbouring lords of Witney and Cogges stimulated planned additions on both sides of the manorial boundary in the 1210s and 1220s.[80]

Yet the newness even of 'new towns' such as this needs qualification. Witney already had an episcopal manor house, Cogges a small baronial castle. A high proportion of successful 'plantations' followed estate development, and were added to a manor house or village nucleus: the planned extensions so often identified as 'Newlands' (Figure 11.4). Even apparently homogeneous and regular town plans can reveal, on close analysis, several stages of enlargement from initial settlements which were in no sense urban. The need for a more sophisticated and sensitive approach to categorising town plans is stressed above by Palliser and Slater;[81] suffice it to say here that most towns were in some sense 'composite', and that attempts to pigeonhole them as 'planted towns', 'developed villages' and 'organic towns' have been more confusing than helpful.[82] During the eleventh to mid-thirteenth centuries the human landscape was transformed not specifically by the planning of towns, but by the planning of settlements at all levels; within that spectrum, it remains a matter for debate whether a clear morphological line is to be drawn between urban and rural.[83]

The material culture of small towns after 1150 also shaded into that of large villages, but with subtle differences which archaeology is starting to define. There is a lack of the industrial residues found in major towns, but the non-agrarian processes (notably clothmaking) which would have been most characteristic of such places are not of a sort to leave many traces. Food assemblages do seem slightly different from those found in villages: there are fewer animals caught in hunting, more selection of meat-joints, more dumps of horn-cores and a higher incidence of hearths and ovens reflecting service industries. On the

[78] Eddy and Petchey, *Historic Towns in Essex*, pp. 32–9, 23–9, 50–3; Schofield and Vince, *Medieval Towns*, pp. 24–8; Beresford, *New Towns*, pp. 435, 452–4.

[79] R. H. Britnell, 'Essex markets before 1350', *Essex Archaeology and History*, 13 (1981), 15–21.

[80] *VCH*, Oxfordshire, XII, p. 58.

[81] See above, pp. 161–2.

[82] Beresford, *New Towns*, for the original definitions. For doubts and qualifications: S. Reynolds, *An Introduction to the History of English Medieval Towns* (Oxford, 1977), pp. 52–6; Slater, 'Urban genesis', pp. 182–3; Schofield and Vince, *Medieval Towns*, pp. 28–9, 34–5.

[83] Contrast D. Palliser, 'Towns and villages in Yorkshire: a sharp divide or a continuum?', *Medieval Settlement Research Group Annual Report*, 8 (1993), 8–9, with T. R. Slater, 'Town plans and village plans: how different?', *ibid.*, 10–12.

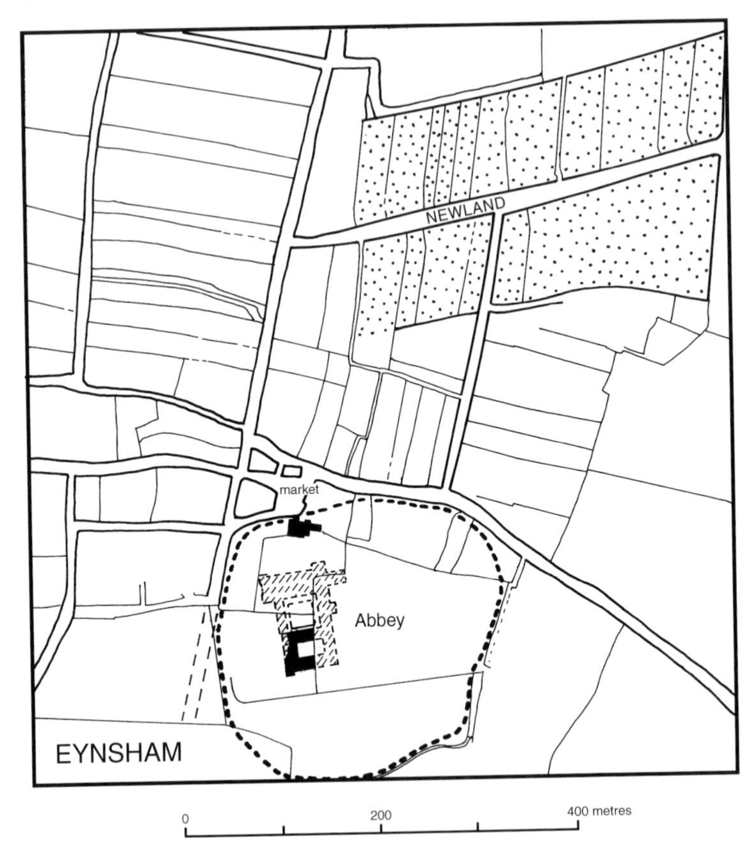

Figure 11.4 Two Oxfordshire 'Newlands'. Eynsham illustrates a planned 'Newland' added in 1215 to an organic market settlement, at the gate of an Anglo-Saxon minster and reformed abbey. At Cogges the 'Newland' was laid out in 1213 by the lord of the adjacent castle and priory, but was economically an adjunct to the earlier planned town of Witney, immediately to the west. *Source:* after *VCH*, Oxfordshire, XII.

other hand the pottery assemblages from villages and small towns are similar in type and range, and lack the diversity of those from big towns.[84]

The distinctiveness of small-town inhabitants is visible from the late eleventh century onwards. Abnormally large groups of Domesday cottars, who seem often to have been market gardeners and suppliers of services, occur not only in the suburbs and environs of substantial towns but also in the emergent proto-urban places.[85] Cottager communities remained a feature of settlements on the

[84] G. G. Astill, 'Archaeology and the smaller medieval town', *UHY* (1985), 46–53.

[85] Above, p. 250 n. 24.

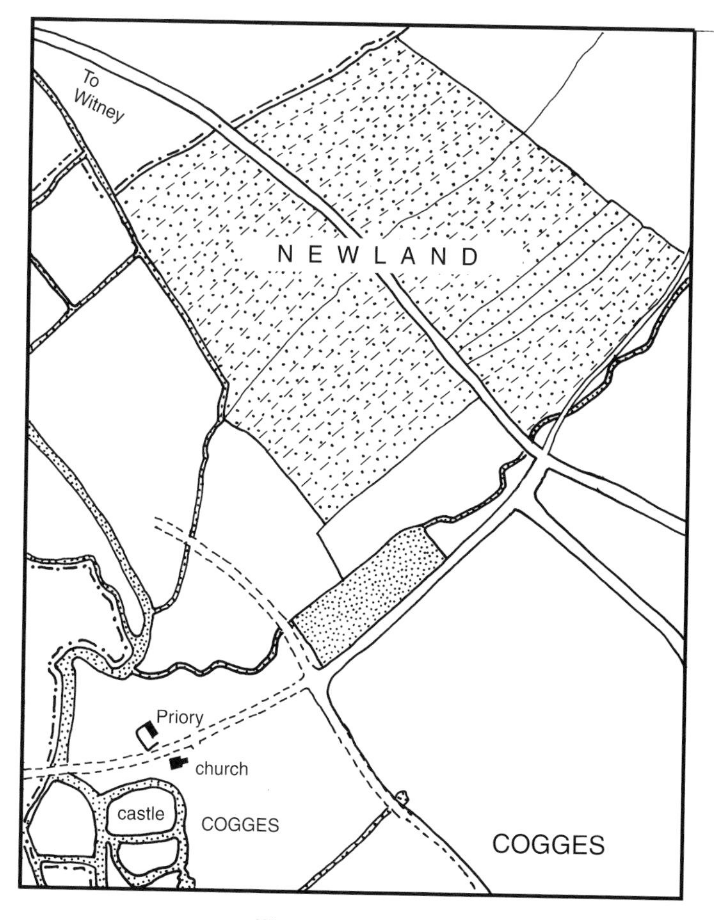

Figure 11.4 (*cont.*)

margins of urbanism for the next three centuries, as did the intermixture of landless messuages – burgages in fact if not in name – with houses attached to normal smallholdings. It is hard to draw a clear line between villages containing scatters of these non-agrarian dwellings, and villages which have acquired distinct 'Newland-type' blocks of messuages with burgage rents. The tenurial make-up of such settlements can often be traced in estate records by the end of the thirteenth century, and deserves more work.[86]

Before 1200, specialisation in small towns can only occasionally be charted.[87] People who took up new houses in Bury St Edmunds between 1066 and 1086

[86] E.g. G. Foard, 'Small towns or large villages? Urban development in Northamptonshire', *Medieval Settlement Research Group Annual Report*, 8 (1993), 9–10. See also Blair, 'Minsters of the Thames', pp. 13–14; R. H. Britnell, 'Burghal characteristics of market towns in medieval England', *Durham University J*, new series, 42 (1981), 147–51. [87] See above pp. 94–9.

included 'seventy-five bakers, ale-brewers, tailors, washers, shoemakers, robe-makers, cooks, porters and agents', who 'daily serve the saint, the abbot and the brethren'.[88] Twelfth- and thirteenth-century surveys show that small towns had a much wider occupational range than purely rural places: artisans such as weavers, fullers, tailors, tanners and saddlers, victuallers such as bakers, cooks and fishmongers, and occasional mercers, merchants and more specialised craftsmen. The tenants of twelfth-century Battle, for instance, included a miller, three bakers, three cooks, a leatherworker, three cobblers, a cordwainer, a weaver, two smiths, a carpenter, a bell-caster, a goldsmith and a 'purger'.[89] Such communities must often have originated to supply crafts and products to their adjacent centres of authority, but by at least the twelfth century they had extended these services to the agrarian settlements of the surrounding regions.

Specialisation and occupational diversity increased greatly during the century after 1170, and many more deeds and rentals survive to indicate local patterns in trade and industry.[90] But it is less clear than it once seemed how far the enlargement of the non-agrarian sector depended on formal town and market creation. By 1270 England had a very commercialised landscape, in which the lower end of the town range shaded into a variety of 'industrial villages' (where occupations might be non-agrarian but also not diverse) and market villages.[91] In a countryside spread thickly with rural markets both chartered and unchartered, supply and specialisation are more important measures of small-town identity than either exchange or legal status.

The landscape of small towns as it had developed by 1270 varied from region to region: in the density of provision, in the prominence or otherwise of visible pre-urban nuclei, in the proportion which show urban attributes before the twelfth-century boom, and in the relative importance of castles, roads and rivers as influences on siting. Plotting the texture of regional patterns, as attempted for one area in Map 11.1, still more explaining them, remain tasks for the future. For instance, it is easy to see why towns with signs of urban potential in 1086 or before tend to have the highest proportion of minster nuclei, less so to see why the regions where such 'primary towns' are numerous should also be rich in ostensibly 'new' towns.[92] The plethora of tiny chartered boroughs and markets in lightly settled western areas is noted above (p. 264); the converse is the extraordinary number of places in highly developed East Anglia which were relatively

[88] Little Domesday f.372.

[89] P. D. A. Harvey, 'Non-agrarian activities in twelfth-century English estate surveys', in D. Williams, ed., *England in the Twelfth Century* (Woodbridge, 1990), pp. 101–11; Hilton, 'Small town and urbanisation', 2; Searle, ed., *Chronicle of Battle Abbey*, pp. 52–9.

[90] Britnell, *Commercialisation*, pp. 79–81; Beresford, *New Towns*, pp. 193–8.

[91] Cf. Dyer, 'Hidden trade'; C. Dyer, 'Towns and villages in the middle ages: how do you tell the difference?', *Medieval Settlement Research Group Annual Report*, 8 (1993), 7–8.

[92] These inevitably impressionistic comments are based on a reading of the various county 'archaeological implications' surveys published during the 1970s and 1980s.

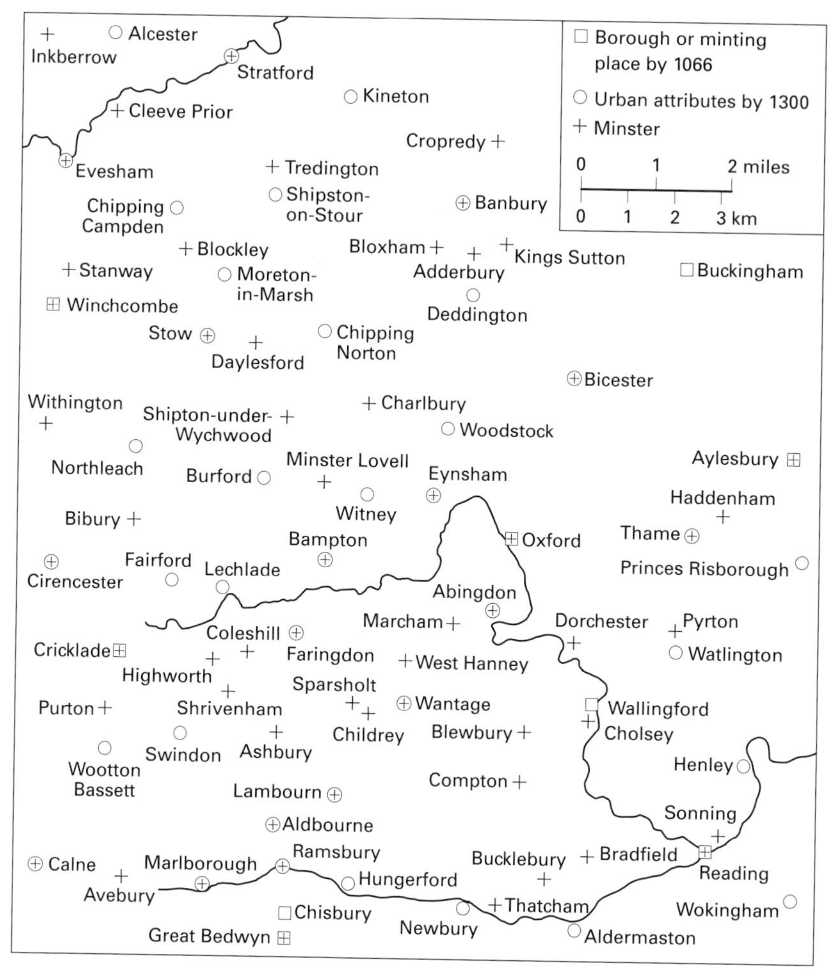

Map 11.1 Origins and hierarchies of towns in the English South Midlands: the correlation between known Anglo-Saxon minsters, tenth- to eleventh-century boroughs and later small towns

populous and important in 1086 and later, but which were juridically indistinguishable from the countryside around.[93]

Forces other than the obvious economic and demographic ones were evidently at work. The fortress policy of tenth-century kings[94] may be a factor, but is clearly not adequate as a general explanation. The survival or non-survival of old territorial patterns, and the associated vested interests, could be more

[93] Cf. Britnell, *Commercialisation*, pp. 8–9; below, pp. 510 and 644. [94] See below, p. 643.

significant. Historians may have paid too little attention to the strength or weakness of inherited structures of authority, initially monastic and royal but by the eleventh century also seigneurial, which determined the incidence of stable centres capable of generating towns. These are factors independent of the total level of commercial activity during the twelfth and thirteenth centuries, which, as East Anglia again illustrates, could still be substantially supported by networks of rural markets.[95] However, the continuing influence of the past on the extent to which such activity was focused into small towns may have been powerful. The small-town landscape of 1270, even its ostensibly recent elements, was the product of layers of social and topographical patterning which had built up over some six centuries.

[95] See below, pp. 643–4.

· PART III ·

The later middle ages 1300–1540

· 12 ·

General survey 1300–1540

BARRIE DOBSON

A CENTURY AGO the most famous of all Cambridge historians of the medieval English town declared that he was 'far from thinking that any one history should be told of all our boroughs'.[1] In some ways F. W. Maitland has proved even wiser and more prophetic than he knew. For many of its readers this present volume may itself suggest that a truly unified history of late medieval British towns is an unattainable ideal. The more intensive the research conducted on individual late medieval towns in recent years, the more apparent seems the singularity of each urban place. Because of the nature of the surviving evidence, nearly all late medieval boroughs tend to be studied as if they were autonomous islands in a non-urban sea – even if in fact their insularity was always more apparent than real. The economic fortunes of all major provincial English towns, from Exeter to Newcastle, were dependent not only on external political, administrative and social pressures but also on all-pervasive networks of national and international trade like those which made them increasingly vulnerable to competition from London merchants in the years before and after 1500.[2] Moreover, when one is able, only too rarely, to examine variations in a town's population and productivity at extremely close quarters during a brief period of time, what tends to be revealed is not stability but a situation of continuous and even alarming short-term volatility.[3] It was only after the middle

[1] F. W. Maitland, *Township and Borough* (Cambridge, 1898), p. 36; cf. F. W. Maitland and M. Bateson, eds., *The Charters of the Borough of Cambridge* (Cambridge, 1901), pp. vii–xxxvii.

[2] A. Dyer, *Decline and Growth in English Towns 1400–1640* (Cambridge, 1995), pp. 7–8. Cf. M. Sellers, ed., *The York Merchants and Merchant Adventurers 1356–1917* (Surtees Society, 129, 1918), pp. 75–9.

[3] See especially C. Platt, *Medieval Southampton* (London, 1973); C. Phythian-Adams, *Desolation of a City* (Cambridge, 1979); R. H. Britnell, *Growth and Decline in Colchester, 1300–1525* (Cambridge, 1986). No less than 40 per cent of the housing stock within the walls of Norwich is now believed to have been destroyed in the two great fires of 1507 and 1508: B. Ayers, *Norwich* (London, 1994), pp. 92–3.

ages were over that new economic and political structures, and eventually the processes of mass industrialisation, gradually began to impose a greater degree of social equilibrium within what had previously been a more or less permanently 'crisis-ridden' urban scene.

(i) THE SHRINKING TOWN?

In such circumstances, any attempt to periodise the history of the late medieval British towns surveyed in this volume, however desirable that objective must obviously be, is foredoomed to at least partial failure. The most significant chronological patterns of urban demography between the early fourteenth and the early sixteenth centuries can lie – even more than those of rural society during the same period – uncomfortably in the eye of the beholder. For a variety of reasons, however, there are good grounds for believing that the decades before and after 1300 did indeed witness the beginnings of a new and considerably less buoyant major phase in British urban history. Thus Hull, created a free royal borough in 1299, was the last English 'new town' of the middle ages to become a prominent seaport; and of the 160 or so other deliberately planned medieval English towns between 1066 and 1344 identified by Maurice Beresford, nearly all had been founded before 1250 and only two were established after 1344.[4] Moreover, only a very small number of these planted towns positively flourished during the course of the fourteenth and fifteenth centuries. Although by 1300 there were no fewer than twenty-five places with borough status in Lancashire, two centuries later only four of these (Liverpool, Preston, Wigan and Lancaster itself) were 'urban' in any meaningful sense of that ambiguous adjective.[5] More alarmingly still perhaps, intensive recent urban archaeological investigation in England, Wales and Scotland suggests that there was considerable later contraction of human settlement within the perimeters of many towns already long and well established before the reign of Edward I.[6] It is hard to resist the general conclusion that by the closing years of the thirteenth century England, Scotland and perhaps even Wales already possessed as many towns, however these might be defined, as the inherently limited demands upon their manufacturing, commercial and administrative services could readily sustain. In southern England at least, the multiplication of small towns and large villages had by then already created a

[4] M. W. Beresford and H. P. R. Finberg, *English Medieval Boroughs* (Newton Abbot, 1973), pp. 37–40, 186; M. Beresford, *New Towns of the Middle Ages* (London, 1967), *passim*.

[5] M. Weinbaum, ed., *British Borough Charters, 1307–1660* (Cambridge, 1943), pp. 65–8; R. A. Donkin, 'Changes in the early middle ages', in H. C. Darby, ed., *A New Historical Geography of England* (Cambridge, 1973), p. 127; N. A. Comfort, *The Lost City of Dunwich* (Lavenham, 1994).

[6] The most notorious case is that of Winchester, where in 1450 it was also alleged that seventeen parish churches in the city had actually 'fallen down': see 'A petition of the city of Winchester to Henry VI, 1450', *Archaeologia*, 1 (1770), 95; *CPR 1436–41*, p. 400; *ibid., 1441–6*, p. 84; D. Keene, *Survey of Medieval Winchester* (Winchester Studies, 2, Oxford, 1985), vol 1, pp. 93–4, 367–8.

situation in which few rural communities were more than a dozen miles from an accessible marketing centre with at least a few urban characteristics.[7]

Moreover, it now seems more likely than not that most traditional assessments of urban population before the first onslaught of the Black Death in 1348–9 underestimate the number of townsmen in late medieval England. In particular, it appears not too implausible that during the early fourteenth century the city of London may have had as many as 80,000 to 100,000 inhabitants, thus ranking with the five or six greatest cities in western Christendom. Similarly, recent research has raised the intriguing possibility that during the century before the Black Death the leading regional urban centres in the kingdom, notably Bristol, Norwich and York, may well have held many more than the 12,000 or so inhabitants with which they have usually been credited.[8] For some recent historians it seems highly probable too that in the first half of the fourteenth century more than 10 per cent of the total English population lived in urban communities of over 2,000 people.[9] How many Englishmen and their families lived in the smaller and more elusive market centres of fewer than 2,000 inhabitants, estimated by Professor Dyer at approximately 700 in Britain as a whole between 1270 and 1540, positively defies calculation.[10] Nevertheless, and however hypothetical all these estimates undoubtedly are, they point to the important conclusion that despite the comparatively large number of its towns, late medieval England – unlike contemporary Flanders or northern Italy – was predominantly a country of widely dispersed rather than densely concentrated urbanisation. Not surprisingly, this generalisation applies even more forcefully to Wales and Scotland, where only three and four towns respectively are likely to have sustained populations in excess of 2,000 at any point in the middle ages.[11] Despite the prominent economic role increasingly played by the city of London and a few other commercial centres, such divergent rather than

[7] R. H. Britnell, *The Commercialisation of English Society, 1000–1500*, 2nd edn (Manchester, 1996), p. 115. For a recent local study of the critical importance of 'local marketing networks', see M. Bailey, 'A tale of two towns: Buntingford and Standon in the later middle ages', *JMed.H*, 19 (1993), 351–71.

[8] D. Keene, 'Medieval London and its region', *LJ*, 14 (1989), 99–111; cf. D. Keene, *Cheapside before the Great Fire* (London, 1985), pp. 19–20. The evidence for supposing that Norwich may have had a population of 25,000 in 1333 is presented in E. Ruttledge, 'Immigration and population growth in early fourteenth-century Norwich: evidence from the Tithing Roll', *UHY* (1988), 15–30.

[9] Britnell, *Commercialisation*, p. 115; cf. R H. Britnell, 'The towns of England and northern Italy in the early fourteenth century', *Ec.HR*, 2nd series, 44 (1991), 22–3.

[10] See below, pp. 506–8; and cf. C. Dyer, 'How urbanized was medieval England ?', in J.-M. Duvosquel and E. Thoen, eds., *Peasants and Townsmen in Medieval Europe* (Ghent, 1995); C. Dyer, 'Medieval Stratford: a successful small town', in R. Bearman, ed., *The History of an English Borough* (Stroud, 1997), pp. 43, 62.

[11] M. Lynch, M. Spearman and G. Stell, eds., *The Scottish Medieval Town* (Edinburgh, 1988); E. Ewan, *Townlife in Fourteenth-Century Scotland* (Edinburgh, 1990), p. 1; R. A. Griffiths, ed., *Boroughs of Mediaeval Wales* (Cardiff, 1978); R. R. Davies, *The Revolt of Owen Glyn Dwr* (Oxford, 1995), pp. 25–30.

convergent characteristics of the British urban scene were to remain remarkably intact throughout the new and at times catastrophic demographic challenges of the late fourteenth century and beyond.

The first outbreak of the Black Death in 1348–9 was unquestionably the most significant turning point in late medieval British urban history, even if a turning point whose consequences for individual towns can often prove extremely difficult to trace and to identify with any precision. Unfortunately, English townspeople have left comparatively little record to posterity of their own personal responses and reactions to this new disaster in their midst. To take only one example, Robert of Avesbury – despite the fact that he was probably attached to the household of the archbishop of Canterbury in Lambeth at the time – wrote extremely little about the effects of bubonic plague in London except to inform his readers that in early 1349 'more than two hundred corpses were buried almost every day in the new burial ground near Smithfield'.[12] But that most English towns were positively decimated by the early outbreaks of the Black Death, probably losing as much as a third of their population between 1347 and the first poll tax returns of thirty years later, there seems little doubt at all. Perhaps the most impressive if indirect evidence of quite exceptionally heavy mortality in any one town derives, ironically enough, from the spectacular increase in the recruitment of new citizens recorded in York's freemen's register, the most comprehensive such register to survive from any town in late medieval Britain.[13] In Wales and Scotland, as well as in England, it seems likely that the mortality caused by the first and many subsequent outbreaks of the Black Death was more severe in town than country.[14] As late as 1487 the first question travelling merchants were likely to ask as they approached a large English town was 'wheder ther was any deth within the Citie or not'. It may not indeed be too melodramatic to envisage London and the major provincial British towns as the most lethal 'death-traps' of late medieval society as a whole.[15]

Perhaps the single most important outcome of the recent spate of detailed research on the demographic and economic fortunes of various late medieval British towns has been to demonstrate that urban reactions to such marked population decline were extremely diverse and not always completely inadequate.

[12] E. M. Thompson, ed., *Robertus de Avesbury de Gestis Mirabilibus Regis Edwardi Tertii* (RS, 1889), pp. 406–7; R. Horrox, *The Black Death* (Manchester, 1994), pp. 64–5.

[13] R. B. Dobson, 'Admissions to the freedom of the city of York in the later middle ages', *Ec.HR*, 2nd series, 26 (1973), 16–22.

[14] J. M. W. Bean, 'Plague, population and decline in England in the later middle ages', *Ec.HR*, 2nd series, 15 (1963), 423–38; J. Hatcher, *Plague, Population and the English Economy, 1348–1530* (London, 1977), pp. 21–30, 44–7; W. Rees, 'The Black Death in Wales', *TRHS*, 4th series, 3 (1920), 115–35; A. Grant, *Independence and Nationhood* (Edinburgh, 1984), p. 75.

[15] A. Raine, ed., *York Civic Records* (Yorkshire Arch. Soc., Record Series, 1939–53), vol. II, p. 4; L. C. Attreed, ed., *York House Books 1461–1490* (Stroud, 1991), p. 541. The remarkable 'paraphernalia which surrounded urban death' is analysed in S. Bassett, ed., *Death in Towns* (Leicester, 1992).

During the generation or so immediately after the first arrival of the Black Death the economic capacities of many of England's largest towns seem to have been positively liberated by the involuntary removal of so many of their non-productive residents.[16] On the other hand, townsmen without the ability or means to respond to their adversities in a flexible manner, even if they lived in cities as ancient and venerable as Lincoln and Winchester, began to articulate a genuinely heartfelt sense of economic distress by at least the early fifteenth century.[17] In due course of time, moreover, few English towns could remain completely immune from the problems created by the continuous erosion of their labour force. No late medieval urban community seems to have been capable of replenishing its population by means of natural regeneration; and for many English towns it became increasingly apparent towards the end of the fifteenth century that 'ther is not half the nombre of good men within your said citie as ther hath been in tymes past'.[18] Thus the population of Colchester may have been reduced by as much as one third between the early fifteenth century and the lay subsidies of the 1520s; and 'if Colchester did not grow throughout most of the period 1300–1525, it is very unlikely that any English town did so'.[19]

(ii) THE GREATER TOWNS: RECORDS AND REGULATION

Few urban historians now accept the view that a decline in a town's population always or necessarily leads to a permanent decline in the wealth and initiative of its leading citizens. Some important cities, notably perhaps London, Edinburgh, Norwich and Exeter, give the impression of entering the sixteenth century with a capacity for enhanced economic, and especially commercial, activity.[20] At a much lesser level the same was quite probably true of many of the small – and usually very poorly documented – market towns of the country.[21] It accordingly

[16] A. R. Bridbury, *Economic Growth* (London, 1962); but cf. C. Phythian-Adams, 'Urban decay in late medieval England', in P. Abrams and E. A. Wrigley, eds., *Towns in Societies* (Cambridge, 1978), pp. 159–85.

[17] The complaints of town governments about their own poverty have of course to be treated with due circumspection; but see, e.g., *CCR 1389–92*, p. 135; *CPR 1436–41*, pp. 317–18; J. W. F. Hill, *Medieval Lincoln* (Cambridge, 1948), pp. 269–72; Keene, *Survey*, *passim*; S. H. Rigby, *Medieval Grimsby* (Hull, 1993), pp. 113–46.

[18] Raine, ed., *York Civic Records*, II, p. 9; Attreed, ed., *York House Books 1461–1490*, p. 549.

[19] Britnell, *Growth and Decline*, pp. 201–2, 267–8.

[20] R. Frost, 'The aldermen of Norwich, 1461–1509: a study of a civic elite' (PhD thesis, University of Cambridge, 1996); E. M. Carus-Wilson, *The Expansion of Exeter at the Close of the Middle Ages* (Exeter, 1963), pp. 29–31; M. Lynch, 'Introduction: Scottish towns 1500–1700', in M. Lynch, ed., *The Early Modern Town in Scotland* (London, 1987); D. M. Palliser, 'Urban decay revisited', in J. A. F. Thomson, ed., *Towns and Townspeople in the Fifteenth Century* (Gloucester, 1988), pp. 15–17.

[21] R. H. Hilton, 'Medieval market towns and simple commodity production', *P&P*, 109 (1985), 3–23; D. Postles, 'An English small town in the middle ages: Loughborough', *UH*, 20 (1993), 7–29; Dyer, 'Medieval Stratford', pp. 43–66; D. L. Farmer, 'Marketing the produce of the countryside, 1200–1500', in E. Miller, ed., *Ag. HEW*, vol. III (Cambridge, 1991), pp. 324–430.

seems important to emphasise that the urban landscape of pre-Black Death England was not utterly transformed by the demographic contraction of the following century. Much has often been made, and rightly so, of the way in which a thriving if highly localised English woollen cloth industry promoted several 'industrial villages' into 'new towns' during this period. Nevertheless, and however high their taxable wealth by the early sixteenth century, places like Castle Combe and Totnes, Hadleigh and Lavenham, still remained very small human communities, not at all capable of challenging the traditional English urban hierarchy.[22] Of the forty English towns most heavily assessed for the Tudor subsidy of 1524–5, all but seven had ranked among the forty wealthiest urban contributors to the lay subsidy of 1334.[23]

There are, however, other reasons why the economic, social and political activity of the forty to fifty most populous and substantial British towns at the beginning of the fourteenth century continues to dominate – despite recent research on their much less well-recorded smaller counterparts – our knowledge of British urban history for the succeeding two centuries. These were the towns which were first induced to articulate, increasingly by the written word, their common procedures, aspirations and grievances. Accordingly, it was this urban elite which constituted a clear majority of the seventy or so towns singled out by the government clerks of Edward I and Edward II for separate representation within the new institution of the English parliamentary Commons.[24] The same group of some forty to fifty towns were also, and predictably enough, subjected to a higher level of national taxation (a tenth as opposed to a fifteenth) during the formative years of the English parliamentary subsidy before 1344.[25] Above all, by the close of the thirteenth century a majority of these major towns had developed – as royal boroughs and in the wake of a long series of grants of various liberties from the crown – not only something of a corporate personality but also a tradition of at least partial self-government, even if at the king's ultimate command. Sooner or later, depending no doubt on the extension of

22 E. M. Carus-Wilson, 'Evidences of industrial growth on some fifteenth-century manors', *Ec.HR*, 2nd series, 12 (1959), 190–205; J. Sheail, 'The distribution of taxable population and wealth in England during the early sixteenth century', *Transactions of the Institute of British Geographers*, 55 (1972), 111–26.

23 R. E. Glasscock, ed., *The Lay Subsidy of 1334* (London, 1975), pp. xxviii–xxxi; and see below, pp. 755–70.

24 By the late fifteenth century the number of English parliamentary boroughs had risen to almost 100: M. McKisack, *The Parliamentary Representation of the English Boroughs during the Middle Ages* (Oxford, 1932), pp. 24–6, 44–5; S. T. Bindoff, ed., *The History of Parliament: The House of Commons, 1509–1558* (London, 1982), vol. I, p. 4.

25 J. F. Willard, 'Taxation boroughs and parliamentary boroughs, 1294–1336', in J. G. Edwards, V. H. Galbraith and E. F. Jacob, eds., *Historical Essays in Honour of James Tait* (Manchester, 1933), pp. 417–35.

urban literacy, the administrative processes of such self-government were certain to produce the habit of writing and of keeping civic records. Not that the compilation and preservation of official documents generated by the internal needs and purposes of a particular borough was an absolutely new phenomenon at the beginning of the fourteenth century.[26] However, the fact remains that only after 1300 (and especially after 1350) does the historian gradually have a proper opportunity to appreciate urban problems as they were actually seen by English townsmen, or at least by their civic councils, themselves. When that happens, the urban historiography of England, as before long of Scotland too, self-evidently enters a new and more informative age.

The creation and, even more, the survival of town records in late medieval Britain is admittedly erratic to a degree; and there is no city in the British Isles, certainly not even London, whose surviving archives are now anything more than the battered remnants of a once much larger civic collection. Nevertheless, the various genres of written document progressively most likely to be conserved by late medieval civic councils undoubtedly reflect the increasing sophistication of town government itself. Thus from a very early date it was royal charters, usually elicited on the initiative of the burgesses themselves, which tended to form the most zealously preserved section of a town's archive.[27] As early as 1300, however, lists of freemen (in a variety of forms), taxation and geld documents, as well as civic custumals and oath books, began to be increasingly necessary for the normal operations of town government. More numerous still were the plea rolls and other judicial documents generated in profusion by the remarkably wide range of mayoral, shrieval and other courts which characterised the exercise of authority in the larger towns of late medieval Britain.[28] Almost as ephemeral, but very revealing where they exist, are the financial records produced by the later medieval British towns. Because of their highly conventionalised format, these borough chamberlains' or treasurers' accounts usually throw clearer light on such detailed items as expenditure on civic entertainment and the reception of magnates than on the economic prosperity of the town as a whole. However, in nearly every case they certainly do reveal how slender were the corporate funds available to the town

[26] G. H. Martin, 'The records of the borough of Ipswich to 1422', *J of the Society of Archivists*, 1 (1956), 87–93; G. H. Martin, 'The origins of borough records', *ibid.*, 2 (1960–4), 147–53; G. H. Martin, 'The English borough in the thirteenth century', *TRHS*, 5th series, 13 (1963), 123–44.

[27] No late medieval British borough seems to have produced a comprehensive cartulary of its holdings of real property: G. R. C. Davis, *Medieval Cartularies of Great Britain: A Short Catalogue* (London, 1958), pp. 140–56.

[28] Britnell, *Growth and Decline*, pp. xii–xvi; J. Laughton, 'Aspects of the social and economic history of Chester in the later middle ages' (PhD thesis, University of Cambridge, 1994); E. P. D. Torrie, ed., *The Gild Court Book of Dunfermline, 1433–1597* (Scottish Record Society, new series, 12, 1986); North Yorkshire County RO, Northallerton: Scarborough Borough Archives, White Vellum Book.

councils of the period.[29] A more direct means of appreciating the problems and preoccupations of the latter is offered by their civic registers and memorandum books. In some fifteenth-century boroughs these registers evolved into comparatively systematic letter books, often recording not only the most important decisions taken by the mayor and council but also some of their most significant incoming and outgoing correspondence.[30]

Perhaps the most important general revelation offered by these and other urban records is that the lives of the inhabitants, and especially the citizens, of late medieval British towns were subjected to intense official regulation. For most townspeople the authority of the mayor and council, implementing royal as well as their own statutes and ordinances, was very great indeed: such authority was much more to be feared than that of the many craft and religious guilds which honeycombed urban society but were usually more powerful in small market towns than in major commercial centres.[31] It was only during periods of exceptional turbulence, most notoriously within the city of London in the 'hurlyng time' between 1376 and 1384, that the 'commons' or *mediocres* of English towns seem to have articulated a more or less coherent programme of opposition to their traditional rulers, the self-styled *bonnes gentz* or *probi homines* of their communities.[32] Throughout Britain urban government may have seemed magisterial in appearance but was almost invariably oligarchic in practice. By the early fifteenth century the mayors of London and most of England's other major boroughs were increasingly elected in rotation from an inner circle of a town's twenty or thirty richest citizens, almost always successful overseas merchants where these existed.[33] Not at all for the last time in the history of Britain's major cities, political and economic power was normally in the hands of a plutocracy,

[29] A town's expenditure on major building enterprises, like its walls and its common or guildhall, usually had to be met from other sources: see R. B. Dobson, ed., *York City Chamberlains' Account Rolls, 1396–1500* (Surtees Society, 192), (1980), pp. xxvi–xxix, 214–15; H. L. Turner, *Town Defences in England and Wales, 900–1500* (London, 1971), pp. 227–43; A. King, 'The merchant class and borough finances of late medieval Norwich' (DPhil thesis, University of Oxford, 1989).

[30] See, e.g., R. R. Sharpe, ed., *Calendar of Letter-Books of the City of London* (London, 1899–1912); M. D. Harris, ed., *Coventry Leet Book or Mayor's Register, 1420–1555*, 4 pts (Early English Text Society, 1907–13); Attreed, ed., *York House Books, 1461–90*, pp. xi–xiii.

[31] H. Swanson, *Medieval Artisans* (Oxford, 1989), pp. 107–26; H. Swanson, 'The illusion of economic structure: craft guilds in late medieval English towns', *P&P*, 121 (1988), 29–48; cf. V. Bainbridge, *Gilds in the Medieval Countryside: Social and Religious Change in Cambridgeshire, c. 1350–1558* (Woodbridge, 1996); E. P. D. Torrie, *Medieval Dundee* (Dundee, 1990).

[32] R. Bird, *The Turbulent London of Richard II* (London, 1949); A. Prescott, 'London in the Peasants' Revolt: a portrait gallery', *LJ*, 7 (1981), 125–43; R. B. Dobson, 'The risings in York, Beverley and Scarborough, 1380–81', in R. H. Hilton and T. H. Aston, eds., *The English Rising of 1381* (Cambridge, 1984), pp. 112–42.

[33] See, e.g., S. Rees Jones, 'York's civic administration, 1354–1464', in S. Rees Jones, ed., *The Government of Medieval York* (Borthwick Studies in History, 3, York, 1997), pp. 134–5; C. M. Barron, 'Richard Whittington: the man behind the myth', in A. E. J. Hollaender and W. Kellaway, eds., *Studies in London History Presented to Philip Edmund Jones* (London, 1969), pp. 211–13.

a plutocracy perhaps most notable for its control of a complex legal and bureaucratic apparatus without the benefit of much in the way of trained bureaucratic personnel. With the important assistance of the common or town clerk and the occasional services of their recorder and other local county lawyers or *legisperiti*, it was one of these aldermen's most critical responsibilities to reconcile the often conflicting interests of their town with those of national government and the higher aristocracy and gentry of their immediate hinterlands.

(iii) TOWNS IN THEIR NATIONAL AND LOCAL CONTEXT

The characteristic tone of what correspondence survives between English, Welsh and Scottish towns and their respective kings and magnates is almost invariably that of a suppliant to his lord and master. How could it be otherwise ? No towns in Britain could fail to be acutely aware that they formed an integral part of the 'communities of the realm' of England or of Scotland. By and large, relations between the late medieval crown and its cities accordingly rested on an unarticulated 'gentlemen's agreement', whereby the royal government conceded considerable powers of self-government to a civic ruling elite: in return it expected assurance of some regular financial and occasional military support as well as due observance of relevant parliamentary statutes and a respectable degree of law and order. On the whole, and although internecine conflicts within urban communities were sometimes difficult to control, it was only occasionally (as in the period associated with the Peasants' Revolt of 1381) that the English government became seriously alarmed at the prospect of a complete collapse of 'peaceful rule' among its towns.[34] For their part, most late medieval town councils were extremely hesitant at the prospect of becoming involved in the factionalism of national political struggle. Indeed, the policies pursued by mayors and aldermen during the Wars of the Roses are more or less impossible to interpret except as a sustained exercise in self-interested and carefully calculated (admittedly sometimes not calculated quite carefully enough) neutrality.[35]

Although the financial contribution of the British boroughs to the purposes of the late medieval English and Scottish monarchies was certainly not insignificant, only rarely can the levies of parliamentary subsidies and traditional fee-farms be said to have been excessively burdensome.[36] More significant were

[34] East Riding of Yorkshire RO, Beverley Corporation Archives, MS BC II/2, f. 17.

[35] J. Gillingham, *The Wars of the Roses: Peace and Conflict in Fifteenth-Century England* (London, 1981), p. 103; cf. A. Goodman, *The Wars of the Roses: Military Activity and English Society, 1452–97* (London, 1981), pp. 202–7.

[36] A. P. M. Wright, 'The relations between the king's government and the English cities and boroughs in the fifteenth century' (DPhil thesis, University of Oxford, 1965), pp. 303–28; L. Attreed, 'The king's interest: York's fee farm and the central government, 1480–92', *NHist.*, 17 (1981), 24–43; L. Attreed, 'Poverty, payments and fiscal policies in English provincial towns', in S. K. Cohn, Jr, and S. A. Epstein, eds., *Portraits of Medieval and Renaissance Living* (Michigan, 1996), pp. 329–33.

the large financial contributions made at various times towards the monarchy's campaigns against the French by exceptionally wealthy English merchants. Thus no Englishman was more active than Sir William de la Pole of Hull in organising financial syndicates on Edward III's behalf during the late 1330s and 1340s; and by the time of his death nearly a century later Richard Whittington had become much the most important of the many London mercers who lent large sums of money to the Lancastrian monarchy.[37] However, the readiness of the merchants of London and other major towns to make and raise loans for the crown could never be taken for granted; and by the last decades of the fifteenth century there seem to have been very few merchants outside London who were lending substantial sums to the royal government at all. For that and other reasons, it seems hard to avoid the somewhat surprising conclusion – still to be properly explained – that outstanding mercantile entrepreneurs were a considerably less common feature of the early Tudor urban scene then than they had been a century or even two centuries earlier.

In any case, and to judge from the increasingly obsequious language of petitions for exemption from the payment of urban fee-farms, it appears that by 1500 the balance of authority between towns and the English central government was moving even further in favour of the latter. On hearing the news of civic disorder within the city of York during the winter of 1494–5, the first Tudor king had no hesitation in invoking the ultimate threat that he might 'put in other rewlers that woll rewle and govern the Citie according to my lawes'.[38] Admittedly, the many minuscule royal boroughs of late medieval Wales had always been recognised – not least by Welsh poets – as tributary agencies of English monarchical power in 'a little corner at the far end of the world'; and north of the border too there was a long tradition of intense regulation of their royal burghs by the Scottish kings.[39] In England such deference was most fulsomely expressed in the highly elaborate speeches and pageants, often meticulously prepared in advance by royal clerks, which accompanied the Tudor monarchs' occasional and usually very brief visits to their major cities. No doubt the bombardment of rose water, artificial hailstones and doggerel verse to which Henry VII was subjected when he rode into York a few months after the battle of Bosworth had a crudely political purpose in attempting to demonstrate the citizens' somewhat suspect 'trueth and hertly affeccion unto the Kinge'.[40] However, such public gestures of respect and obedience were now becoming

[37] E. B. Fryde, *William de la Pole, Merchant and King's Banker* (London, 1988); R. Horrox, *The de la Poles of Hull* (Hull, 1983); Barron, 'Richard Whittington', pp. 197–248.

[38] Raine, ed., *York Civic Records*, II, pp. 115–16.

[39] R. A. Griffiths, *Conquerors and Conquered in Medieval Wales* (Stroud, 1994), *passim*; Davies, *Revolt of Glyn Dwr*, pp. 23–8.

[40] Raine, ed., *York Civic Records*, I, pp. 154–9; cf. L. Attreed, 'The politics of welcome: ceremonies and constitutional development in later medieval English towns', in B. A. Hanawalt and K. L. Reyerson, eds., *City and Spectacle in Medieval Europe* (Minneapolis, 1994), pp. 208–31.

increasingly obligatory. To that extent, and although English burgesses were generally denied the handsome prizes of office under the crown enjoyed by their counterparts in France, the history of the larger medieval English towns seems to close less with displays of great urban self-confidence than with increasing subordination to the royal will and with the symptoms of a genuine, if no doubt inescapable, *trahison des bourgeois*.[41]

A not too dissimilar deferential note usually characterised the attitudes of late medieval townsmen to their neighbouring lords and gentry. Naturally enough, the relationships between town councils and the magnates and gentlemen in their vicinity depended above all on the proximity, the political influence and the acquisitive instincts of the latter. Thus for much of the fifteenth century the city of Exeter had the particular misfortune to be entangled in the bitter conflicts between the Courtenays, earls of Devon, and the Bonville family; and during the late 1440s the aggressive intervention of William de la Pole, duke of Suffolk, disrupted the trade of Norwich and even lost the city its constitutional liberties.[42] Not surprisingly, most English burgesses preferred to regard the lords, gentlemen and senior clergy in their vicinity as prospectively favourable 'good lords', to be presented with gifts of expensive wine, spices and fish on their frequent visits to their town.[43] Not that even benevolent magnates or local gentry and *legisperiti* could 'create trade where none existed'.[44] Only in those exceptional cases where a town's aristocratic or knightly patron was highly influential in central government was he able to make a very positive contribution to its welfare. The services of the prominent Lancastrian retainer, Sir Thomas Erpingham, in helping Norwich to acquire formal incorporation as a county in 1404 provides one example; but perhaps no town in Britain ever rivalled the good fortune of York in possessing – between 1471 and 1483 – a *dominus specialissimus* who went on to become, however briefly, the king of England and accordingly the greatest patron of them all.[45]

(iv) URBAN SOCIETY AND URBAN VALUES

It would accordingly be extremely unwise to make too sharp a distinction between the ranks of urban and rural society. Indeed, in most British towns such

[41] B. Chevalier, *Les bonnes villes de France aux XIVe et XVe siècles* (Paris, 1982), pp. 151–71. For the extreme view that by the 1530s (at Coventry at least) the medieval ideal of urban community was 'already irrelevant', see Phythian-Adams, *Desolation of a City*, p. 277.

[42] R. L. Storey, *The end of the house of Lancaster* (London, 1966), pp. 165–75; P. Maddern, *Violence and Social Order: East Anglia, 1422–1442* (Oxford, 1993), pp. 194–6.

[43] See, e.g., Cambridgeshire County RO, X 70/2–70/10 (Cambridge Borough Treasurers' Accounts, 1423–36); Dobson, ed., *York City Chamberlains' Account Rolls*, pp. 74–5, 110, 169–70.

[44] Attreed, 'Poverty, payments and fiscal policies', p. 343.

[45] S. Walker, *The Lancastrian Affinity, 1361–1399* (Oxford, 1990), pp. 193–4, 200–1; D. M. Palliser, 'Richard III and York', in R. Horrox, ed., *Richard III and the North* (University of Hull, 1986), pp. 51–81.

a distinction would have been almost illusory. The evidence of freemen's registers and (less reliably) of urban toponymic surnames leaves the impression that in the great majority of towns at least a third of their inhabitants were first or second generation immigrants from local villages. In such circumstances it is hardly surprising that closely concerted political activism between townsmen and neighbouring villagers tended to be one of the most widespread, and dangerous, features of the great revolt of 1381.[46] At a much higher level of the social scale, yet another manifestation of the close relationships between the larger British towns and local rural society were the considerable numbers of influential men, and especially widows, who came to form the so-called resident 'urban gentry'.[47] But then the social distinction between leading burgesses and the minor gentry could be very blurred indeed. It has long been known that the merchant class of London was heavily recruited from substantial families in the English countryside, to which they or their descendants usually hoped to return in due course of time. Similar aspirations are also apparent in many other towns. It is accordingly not too difficult to explain why during the course of the fifteenth century many English borough councils were increasingly prepared to accept representation in the parliamentary Commons by county gentlemen. Between 1422 and 1478 the proportion of resident burgesses elected to the Commons fell from 77 to 42 per cent, so striking a decline that it might even be interpreted as yet one more indication of decreasing corporate self-confidence in the case of all but the greatest English boroughs as the middle ages came to a close.[48]

It is indeed easy to forget that late medieval British towns – like all towns at all times – were of the utmost significance for those hordes of anonymous visitors who never resided in them. However, even within the ranks of resident urban society itself, there will never be much prospect of sophisticated prosopographical analysis – except in the case of merchants, civic officeholders and those more substantial traders and craftsmen who (usually from the late fourteenth century onwards rather than earlier) have left their wills and testaments to posterity.[49] Admittedly, these were the individuals, usually enfranchised burgesses – and

[46] H. C. Darby and E. Miller, 'Political history', in *VCH*, Cambridgeshire, II, pp. 398–402; P. Wade-Martins, ed., *An Historical Atlas of Norfolk* (Norfolk Museums Service, Castle Museum, Norwich, 1994), pp. 86–7; R. Hilton, *Bond Men Made Free: Medieval Peasant Movements and the English Rising of 1381* (London, 1973), pp. 186–207.

[47] R. E. Horrox, 'The urban gentry in the fifteenth century', in Thomson, ed., *Towns and Townspeople*, pp. 22–44.

[48] J. S. Roskell, ed., *The History of Parliament: The House of Commons, 1386–1421* (Stroud, 1992), vol. I, pp. 286–91; J. S. Roskell, *The Commons in the Parliament of 1422* (Manchester, 1954), pp. 131–5; McKisack, *Parliamentary Representation*, pp. 100–18.

[49] F. J. Furnivall, ed., *The Fifty Earliest English Wills in the Court of Probate, London, 1387–1439* (Early English Text Society, original series, 78, 1882); and for a particularly scrupulous case study, see P. Heath, 'Urban piety in the later middle ages: the evidence of Hull wills', in R. B. Dobson, ed.,

much less frequently their wives and daughters – who dominated the economic activity of a town as its retailers. Only they had the legal right to 'open windows' and to sell their goods from their houses as well as in the numerous town markets. Much less significant, except perhaps in London, were the Italian, 'Deutsch' and other alien communities revealed by surviving fifteenth-century alien subsidy accounts.[50] Members of the much larger group of resident 'foreigns', i.e. denizen non-citizens who formed the real proletariat of urban society, are even more elusive, tending to appear in the records only when charged with unruly or criminal behaviour. That the major cities, and especially London, harboured colonies of professional thieves, semi-professional prostitutes and other 'marginals' there is naturally no doubt; but of much greater significance to urban society as a whole were the large numbers of countrymen and women who walked into late medieval cities every year in search of short-term employment as domestic servants. In the case of most smaller British towns, many craftsmen may have lived and worked in neighbouring villages but they often sold their labour and their goods – and made their profits and incurred their debts – in what were in effect their local urban markets.[51]

For many members of the British population, however, the attraction of late medieval towns – and especially of the larger towns – had little to do with economic self-interest at all. As so many urban communities in England, Wales and Scotland ultimately owed their foundation and indeed their very existence to a saintly patron, it is hardly surprising that several of the most popular religious cults of the later middle ages were located not in the countryside but in towns. To take the extreme example, in 1420 the mayor and council of Canterbury maintained – most implausibly – that they could accommodate no fewer than 100,000 pilgrims to St Thomas Becket's shrine.[52] Although the thaumaturgical powers of Britain's most popular saints were less widely reported in 1500 than

The Church, Politics and Patronage in the Fifteenth Century (Gloucester, 1984), pp. 209–29. That townswomen are usually much more obscure than their male counterparts can go without saying; but very recent research has shown that they are by no means completely invisible: see, e.g., P. J. P. Goldberg, *Women in England c. 1275–1525* (Manchester, 1995), and – for an especially well-documented case – C. M. Barron and A. F. Sutton, eds., *Medieval London Widows, 1300–1500* (London, 1994).

50 S. Thrupp, 'A survey of the alien population in England in 1440', *Speculum*, 32 (1957), 262–73; S. Thrupp, 'Aliens in and around London in the fifteenth century', in Hollaender and Kellaway, eds., *Studies*, pp. 251–71; J. L. Bolton, ed., *The Alien Communities of London in the Fifteenth Century* (Stamford, 1998).

51 It is accordingly all the more difficult to be confident that many smaller towns were pursuing economic activities 'that were qualitatively rather than quantitatively different from those in their surrounding hinterland': R. B. Dobson, 'Yorkshire towns in the late fourteenth century', *The Thoresby Miscellany*, 18 (Publications of the Thoresby Society, 59 1986), p. 18. Cf. P. J. P. Goldberg, 'Female labour, service and marriage in the late medieval urban North', *NHist*, 22 (1986), 18–38.

52 R. Foreville, *Le jubilé de saint Thomas Becket du XIIIe au XVe siècle (1220–1470)* (Paris, 1959), pp. 177–85.

they had been two centuries earlier, the magnetic attraction of shrines like those of Becket himself, of St Cuthbert of Durham, of St John of Beverley, of St David of Wales and of St Andrew of Scotland certainly survived until their destruction in the 1530s and 1540s.[53] More obviously still, to visit a large provincial town was *ipso facto* to be presented with the opportunity of observing at close quarters the greatest centres of monastic and mendicant spirituality that medieval Britain had to offer. On the eve of the English Reformation, travellers to Oxford were much less likely to be impressed by its university and collegiate buildings than by the remarkable agglomeration – unrivalled even in London – of no fewer than ten different religious houses to the west and north of what was still a comparatively small urban community.[54]

No British town could avoid being heavily influenced by the presence of so large a number of ecclesiastics (sometimes over 5 per cent of the adult male population) in its midst. That influence was always liable to be most intense – and most resented – in the special but not uncommon case of the so-called 'monastic boroughs', where an often substantial urban settlement had long been constitutionally subordinate to a large neighbouring religious corporation. The close and dangerous proximity of two very different types of human community, with very different objectives, provided a recipe for intermittent tension and sometimes almost continuous dispute. Each of these conflicts tended to take its own, highly distinctive, course; but as a general rule they were at their most violent when the towns in question were neither so large that they could largely ignore their monastic neighbours nor so small that they were powerless to resist them. At St Albans and Bury St Edmunds, to take the two best-documented cases of sustained antagonism between English Benedictine abbeys and their urban tenants, the strength of the participants was usually too evenly matched for any degree of comfort.[55] Ironically enough, it was as the dissolution approached that monastic chapters and town councils alike increasingly came to see the advantages of a reasonably amicable *modus vivendi*. Nevertheless, the presence of a large ecclesiastical landlord near an urban community could often delay and even abort the latter's constitutional development until and sometimes beyond the Reformation. Accordingly the cathedral city of Durham had to wait for incorporation under an alderman until the unusually late date of 1565.[56] Admittedly

[53] B. Nilson, 'The development of the major late medieval English cathedral shrines' (PhD thesis, University of Cambridge, 1994); G. Williams, *The Welsh Church from Conquest to Reformation*, 2nd edn (Cardiff, 1976); U. Hall, *St Andrew and Scotland* (St Andrews, 1994), pp. 149–60.

[54] J. Campbell, 'Gloucester College', in *Worcester College Record* (1983), 15–23; J. I. Catto and R. Evans, eds., *The History of the University of Oxford*, vol. II: *Late Medieval Oxford* (Oxford, 1992), pp. 541–63.

[55] H. T. Riley, ed., *Gesta Abbatum Monasterii S. Albani a Thoma Walsingham* (RS, 1867–9); M. D. Lobel, *The Borough of Bury St Edmunds* (Oxford, 1935).

[56] *VCH*, Durham, III, pp. 54–6; M. Bonney, *Lordship and the Urban Community* (Cambridge, 1990), pp. 35–6, 229–35.

pre-Reformation Durham was less a unified urban settlement than a unique and 'crab-like' conjuncture of independent boroughs. Here perhaps is the extreme example in Britain of the general rule that most substantial towns were rarely coherent jurisdictional entities: to a greater or lesser extent they always tended to be honeycombed by a complex and confusing series of ecclesiastical and other franchises.

For most medieval townsmen, such administrative incoherence was no doubt an acceptable price to pay for the opportunity to profit from their role in providing the religious houses inside or near their boundaries with commodities ranging from wine to clothing and from parchment to cutlery.[57] In the special case of the highly differentiated cathedral cities of England, Wales and Scotland, their bishops may have preferred, like the lay aristocracy, to reside in country houses but their cathedrals usually remained the official headquarters of their complex diocesan bureaucracies. By contrast, the role of the many towns which served as royal political, legal and administrative centres in their British localities tended to be more subject to changes in governmental policy and less easy to estimate with any precision. However, even in an age of increasingly decentralised royal justice, the county towns of the English kingdom remained the most important seats of the monarch's innumerable judicial commissions as well as of his sheriffs and his prisons. More striking still, and marking a critical stage in the evolution of both London and Edinburgh towards full-fledged 'capital status', was the dramatic growth of specialised extra-university institutions for the study of non-ecclesiastical law. By the late fourteenth century the Inns of Court had come – at first mysteriously – to dominate the 'west end' of the city of London; and the gradual rise of Edinburgh to legal, and consequently political, hegemony in Scotland probably became irreversible with the formal establishment of the court of session there in 1532.[58]

Where they existed, church and common lawyers were usually the most highly educated and articulate members of urban society. However, they were by no means the only professional groups within the late medieval town. On the evidence of freemen's registers and of civic wills, the fifteenth and early sixteenth centuries witnessed a notable increase in the number of urban residents – even in the smaller towns – who belonged neither to the manufacturing, provisioning nor mercantile crafts but rather to the human service trades or professions. According to its tax assessments in 1436, the three wealthiest individual property owners then

[57] See B. Harvey, *Living and Dying in England, 1100–1540* (Oxford, 1993); cf. R. B. Dobson, 'Cathedral chapters and cathedral cities: York, Durham and Carlisle in the fifteenth century', *NHist*, 19 (1983), 15–44.

[58] J. H. Baker, 'The English legal profession, 1450–1550', in W. Prest, ed., *Lawyers in Early Modern Europe and America* (London and New York, 1981), pp. 16–41; M. Lynch, 'Towns and townspeople in fifteenth-century Scotland', in Thomson, ed., *Towns and Townspeople*, pp. 173–9, 181–4; M. Lynch, *Edinburgh and the Reformation* (Edinburgh, 1981).

resident within the city of London were neither mercers nor grocers but William Venour, curial official and warden of the Fleet Prison; Simon Camp, financial expert and quondam treasurer of the household of Queen Margaret of Navarre; and Thomas Morsted, a surgeon who practised at Westminster as well as from his own home.[59] In offering to those in need of their services an unrivalled concentration of lawyers, men of learning, financial experts, physicians, master masons, illuminators, scriveners, booksellers and eventually printers, London – and Westminster – naturally present a very special case. However, there is little doubt that during the course of the fifteenth century the major provincial towns too became increasingly important centres of what might be characterised as urban professions. At exactly the time when many of the long-established hospitals of Britain were facing increasing poverty and even the prospect of dissolution, the private medical services available within the walls of many towns were greater than they ever had been.[60] Similarly, and although the education of late medieval burgesses is often the most mysterious thing about them, the creation of a wide and complex range of new town schools – with an increasing number of professional schoolmasters – is as much a feature of urban life during the century before as after the Reformation.[61] Indeed, as the progress of that Reformation was itself to reveal, a previous remarkable if unquantifiable increase in urban lay literacy was both the cause and the consequence of a gradual but 'major cultural shift affecting all classes and vocations towards the end of the middle ages'.[62]

How far, and how rapidly, so widespread a change in literacy and cultural attitudes may have gradually transformed the communal ideology of the town before 1540 remains perhaps the most difficult as well as fundamental question in late medieval British urban history. How far, indeed, within the extremely diverse 'rhetoric of urban culture', did these towns enjoy a distinctive communal ideology or mentality at all? The solution to that problem is by no means as easy to discover as it might seem. Fifty years ago Sylvia Thrupp was able not only to demonstrate 'the cultural affinities between merchants and gentlemen' but in particular the way in which the ambitions and aspirations of the richest London

59 S. L. Thrupp, *The Merchant Class of Medieval London* (Chicago, 1948), pp. 378–85.

60 M. Rubin, *Charity and Community in Medieval Cambridge* (Cambridge, 1987), pp. 148–83; C. Rawcliffe, *Medicine and Society in Later Medieval England* (Stroud, 1995); C. Rawcliffe, 'The hospitals of later medieval London', *Medical History*, 28 (1984), 1–21; C. Rawcliffe, 'The profits of practice: the wealth and status of medical men in later medieval England', *Bulletin of the Society for the Social History of Medicine*, 1 (1988), 61–78; N. Orme and M. Webster, *The English Hospital, 1070–1570* (New Haven, 1995), pp. 127–46.

61 N. Orme, *English Schools in the Middle Ages* (London, 1973), pp. 295–321; J. A. H. Moran, *The Growth of English Schooling, 1340–1548: Learning, Literacy and Laicization in Pre-Reformation York Diocese* (Princeton, 1985); and N. Orme, 'Schoolmasters, 1307–1509', in C. H. Clough, ed., *Profession, Vocation and Culture in Later Medieval England* (Liverpool, 1982), pp. 218–41.

62 G. L. Harriss, review of Clough, ed., *Profession, Vocation and Culture*, in *History*, 68 (1983), 502–3, but cf. N. Orme, 'The "laicization" of English school education, 1250–1560', *History of Education*, 16 (1987), 81–9.

citizens were permeated by the ideas of gentility.[63] No doubt for that as well as other reasons, even the most self-assured of British urban governments generally failed to evolve those more conspicuous and enduring visual displays of fully articulated civic pride so common – in their very different ways – within the towns of northern Italy, the Netherlands and even the German *Reich*.

However, it would of course be the most serious of errors to conclude this chapter by judging the corporate and personal values of the late medieval British town according to the standards of other times and other places. What has become more obvious in recent years than ever before is the way in which the then perceived truths of the Christian religion acted as a highly cohesive force among the burgesses of England, Wales and Scotland. The practices and principles of late medieval urban religion were by no means monolithic; and indeed the profound influence of the Christian Church within every possible type of town community was clearly due to the fact that it offered a myriad of different forms, literally something for everybody. That a fervent belief in the benefits of vicarious intercession for the souls of the dead, still very visible on the eve of the Reformation, underpinned the religious practices of the great majority of townsmen and townswomen is especially obvious. Such a belief is most obviously demonstrated by the numerous urban chantry foundations, comparatively insignificant to the wider purposes of the institutionalised Christian Church but so often crucial in the so-called personalisation of late medieval religion. Perhaps more influential still by the late fifteenth century was the role of parish and other religious fraternities in strengthening urban solidarity, above all in the smaller towns.[64] Such manifestations of social cohesion and of 'urban community' were of course never absolute and always vulnerable to affront either by unduly autocratic mayors and councils or by the destitute and the aggrieved. Here, more than anywhere, the evidence available is seriously distorted; and after 1381 the historian rarely has an opportunity to listen to the voices of townsmen who were seriously discontented with their lot. That said, and despite the highly stratified nature of urban society in small towns as in large, it seems apparent that an introspective civic mentality which laid much emphasis upon order, respect for rank and the traditional precepts of Christianity 'generally managed to keep the peace'.[65] On the whole, a high degree

[63] Thrupp, *Merchant Class*, pp. 234–87.

[64] See, e.g., N. P. Tanner, *The Church in Late Medieval Norwich 1370–1532* (PIMSST, 66, Toronto, 1984); C. M. Barron, 'The parish fraternities of medieval London', in C. M. Barron and C. Harper-Bill, eds., *The Church in Pre-Reformation Society* (Woodbridge, 1985), pp. 13–37; C. Burgess, 'For the increase of divine service: chantries in the parish in late medieval Bristol', *JEcc.Hist.*, 36 (1985), 46–65; and B. R. McRee, 'Charity and gild solidarity in late medieval England', *J of British Studies*, 32 (1993), 195–225.

[65] D. G. Shaw, *The Creation of a Community* (Oxford, 1993), p. 289. What it may mean to add that 'later medieval towns, Wells included, worked' (an issue illuminated in G. Rosser, 'Myth, image and social process in the English medieval town', *UH*, 23 (1996), 5–25) is not, however, a question that perhaps even a *Cambridge Urban History* can hope to answer.

of political and social consensus within the late medieval British town seems more evident – and more significant – than its occasional propensity to internal conflict. If so, some of the consequences of such consensus were not to be without their ironies. The acutely divisive and indeed revolutionary changes which in 1540 were about to transform the customary religious and other preconceptions of medieval urban society beyond recognition were usually accepted by townsmen and their families with an acquiescence which must now seem surprising and indeed startling in the extreme.

· 13 ·

Government, power and authority 1300–1540

S. H. RIGBY AND ELIZABETH EWAN

THE NATURE and development of late medieval town government remains an extremely controversial issue amongst urban historians. Was this, as some claim, a time of growing exclusivity and oligarchy[1] or was it an era of increasing popular participation in town government?[2] Was urban political conflict, particularly that of the *communitas* against the mercantile oligarchy, the inevitable result of opposing class interests[3] or were shared ideological norms and a sense of civic community effective in legitimating the authority of town rulers and minimising conflict?[4] Is the concept of 'oligarchy' itself a loaded anachronism when applied to a society which saw the rule of the rich as 'aristocratic' (i.e. rule by the 'better sort' for the 'common profit') rather than as 'oligarchic' (i.e rule by the self-interested few)? Did urban political conflicts revolve around the corruption of individual rulers rather than issues of political principle or a desire for structural change in town government?[5]

S. H. Rigby is responsible for the material on England and Wales; Elizabeth Ewan is responsible for the material on Scotland.

[1] R. H. Britnell, *The Commercialisation of English Society, 1000–1500*, 2nd edn (Manchester, 1996), pp. 225–6; D. M. Palliser, *Tudor York* (Oxford, 1979), pp. 90–1.

[2] A. R. Bridbury, *Economic Growth* (London, 1962), pp. 58–64; C. I. Hammer, 'Anatomy of an oligarchy: the Oxford town council of the fifteenth and sixteenth centuries', *J of British Studies*, 18 (1978), 10.

[3] R. H. Hilton, 'Unjust taxation and popular resistance', *New Left Review*, 180 (1990), 183–4; R. H. Hilton, *English and French Towns in Feudal Society* (Cambridge, 1992), ch. 6; C. Dyer, 'Small-town conflict in the later middle ages: events at Shipston-on-Stour', *UH*, 19 (1992), 183–4; R. B. Dobson, ed., *The Peasants' Revolt of 1381*, 2nd edn (London, 1983), p. 284.

[4] S. L. Thrupp, *The Merchant Class of Medieval London* (Chicago, 1948), pp. 14–27; C. Phythian-Adams, 'Ceremony and the citizen: the communal year at Coventry, 1450–1550', in R. Holt and G. Rosser, eds., *The Medieval Town* (London, 1990), pp. 251–2, 258, 262; G. Rosser, *Medieval Westminster, 1200–1540* (Oxford, 1989), pp. 225, 325–6.

[5] S. Reynolds, *An Introduction to the History of English Medieval Towns* (Oxford, 1977), pp. 135–6, 171; S. Reynolds, 'Medieval urban history and the history of political thought', *UHY* (1982), 14–23; Palliser, *Tudor York*, p. 93; R. H. Britnell, 'Bailiffs and burgesses in Colchester, 1400–1525', *Essex History and Archaeology*, 21 (1991), 105.

(i) THE EXTENT OF SELF-GOVERNMENT

The survival of the records of civic administration generated by the self-governing royal boroughs has tended to give a misleading impression of late medieval town government. In fact, in England, only a minority of towns achieved the degree of autonomy enjoyed by royal towns such as York and Winchester, where the burgesses elected their own mayor and bailiffs to govern the town, to collect royal revenues and account for the fee-farm, and to administer justice in the borough court.[6] By the thirteenth century, many of these self-governing towns had acquired a 'mayor's council' but, in the later middle ages, many added a second or 'common' council. Frequently, as at Lincoln, this was twice the size of the original, which often became known as the council of aldermen.[7] In addition, each town had its own array of civic officials, including chamberlains, coroners, common clerks, recorders, officers to regulate trade, sergeants and many others, including constables, assessors and collectors of taxes, gatekeepers, collectors of mill-tolls and auditors of accounts.[8]

As shire officials were excluded, the scope of government in such self-governing towns was extremely broad, including the levying and expenditure of royal revenues, purveyance, arraying military forces, administering justice and regulating the urban economy.[9] It was these self-governing royal boroughs which were most likely to be required to pay the taxes on moveables at the higher rate in those years when a dual rating system was used and to be called upon to provide representatives at parliaments and merchant assemblies.[10] The main threat to the town officers' jurisdiction was the survival within the boroughs of private sokes and jurisdictions, each with its own courts, officials and markets, as at York where, by 1300, there were at least fourteen such administrative islands within the city. Disputes over jurisdiction were inevitable, as at Exeter where conflict between the city authorities and the cathedral flared up periodically throughout the medieval period. Such friction was not necessarily 'anti-clerical' in origin: the burgesses of Lincoln were as likely to find themselves in conflict with the jurisdiction exercised by the constable of Lincoln Castle as they were with that of the dean and chapter.[11] The Church's spiritual rights could cause

[6] D. Keene, *Survey of Medieval Winchester* (Winchester Studies, 2, Oxford, 1985), vol. II, part I, ch. 3; E. Miller, 'Medieval York', *VCH*, The City of York pp. 70–9.

[7] J. Tait, *The Medieval English Borough* (Manchester, 1936), chs. 10, 11; J. W. F. Hill, *Medieval Lincoln* (Cambridge, 1948), pp. 294–302; Lincolnshire AO, L/1/3/1, White Book, ff. 2v, 3v.

[8] S. H. Rigby, *Medieval Grimsby* (Hull, 1993), pp. 88–102; Palliser, *Tudor York*, ch. 3.

[9] E. T. Meyer, 'Boroughs', in J. F. Willard, W. A. Morris and N. Dunham, eds., *The English Government at Work, 1327–1336*, vol. III (Cambridge, Mass., 1950), pp. 105–41.

[10] J. F. Willard, 'Taxation boroughs and parliamentary boroughs, 1294–1336', in J. G. Edwards, V. H. Galbraith and E. F. Jacob, eds., *Historical Essays in Honour of James Tait* (Manchester, 1933), pp. 417–35.

[11] D. M. Palliser, 'The birth of York's civic liberties, *c.* 1200–1354', in S. Rees Jones, ed., *The*

tension, as in London where disputes over tithe payments lasted for almost a century after 1448, but, in the absence of support from the civic authorities, such conflict remained the exception.[12]

Despite the wide range of functions which towns performed as royal agents, they always remained strictly subordinated to the crown. Given their limited room for manoeuvre, town rulers seem to have been wary of adopting an independent stance in national political conflicts such as the Wars of the Roses. Even London was helpless to resist the king when he decided to seize the city's liberties, as Richard II did in 1392. The city was able to play an important role in national politics only as part of a broader movement, as in the events surrounding the deposition of Edward II in 1326–7.[13] Even in 1460–1, when London's support was crucial for Edward IV's success, the city rulers sought, as they had at the usurpation of Henry IV in 1399, to avoid committing themselves until realism and self-interest no longer made neutrality feasible. Elsewhere, even in a city as important as York, town rulers were even more likely to follow a wait-and-see policy and to follow the prevailing tide.[14] The towns' main political impact came in less dramatic events, in the pressure and petitions that produced parliamentary legislation on trade and finance, as in the anti-alien movement of the fifteenth century, most of whose demands were conceded by Henry VI even though the legislation was not always enthusiastically implemented, even by the townsmen themselves.[15]

However, the majority of medieval English towns were seigneurial foundations, even the largest and wealthiest of which rarely equalled the royal boroughs in their autonomy. Thus, although the seigneurial borough of Boston ranked

Government of Medieval York (Borthwick Studies in History, 3, York, 1997), p. 98; Palliser, *Tudor York*, pp. 87–9; Hill, *Lincoln*, pp. 261–8; L. Attreed, 'Arbitration and the growth of urban liberties in late medieval England', *J of British Studies*, 31 (1992), 212–33; P. C. Maddern, *Violence and the Social Order* (Oxford, 1992), pp. 177–83.

12 J. A. F. Thomson, 'Tithe disputes in later medieval London', *EHR*, 78 (1963), 1–17.

13 C. M. Barron, 'The quarrel of Richard II with London', in F. R. H. Du Boulay and C. M. Barron, eds., *The Reign of Richard II* (London, 1971), pp. 173–201; G. A. Williams, *Medieval London* (London, 1963), pp. 293–8.

14 Barron, 'The quarrel', p. 201; C. M. Barron, 'London and the crown, 1451–1461', in J. R. L. Highfield and R. Jeffs, eds., *The Crown and Local Communities in England and France in the Fifteenth Century* (Gloucester, 1981), pp. 88–109; D. J. Guth, 'Richard III, Henry VII and the city: London politics and the "Dune Cowe"', in R. A. Griffiths and J. Sherborne, eds., *Kings and Nobles in the Later Middle Ages* (Gloucester, 1986), pp. 185–204; A. P. M. Wright, 'The relations between the king's government and the English cities and boroughs in the fifteenth century' (DPhil thesis, University of Oxford, 1965), pp. 363–92; R. B. Dobson, 'The crown, the charter and the city, 1396–1461', in Rees Jones, ed., *The Government of Medieval York*, p. 48. 1485 was an exception in the case of York, see Palliser, *Tudor York*, pp. 42–3.

15 M. McKisack, *The Parliamentary Representation of the English Boroughs during the Middle Ages* (Oxford, 1932), ch. 7; R. A. Griffiths, *The Reign of Henry VI: The Exercise of Royal Authority, 1422–1461* (London, 1981), pp. 169–71, 553–8; A. A. Ruddock, 'Alien hosting in Southampton in the fifteenth century', *Ec.HR*, 16 (1946), 30–7.

fifth amongst English towns in the taxation of 1334 with an assessment of £1,100, it could not compare with even a minor royal borough such as Grimsby (assessed at only £97) in its formal liberties and was, like medieval Southwark, administered as a collection of manors by its overlords. At Grimsby, the townsmen annually elected their own mayor and bailiffs; at Boston, the town bailiffs were the appointees of the honour of Richmond and could serve in office for years before moving to a higher post within the honorial administration. Nor did Boston enjoy the jurisdictional independence of royal boroughs such as Grimsby. In some English seigneurial boroughs, such as Leicester, there was a 'portmanmoot', a court for the townsmen separate from the lord's manorial court, but this was not the case at Boston where the officers of the court, such as the steward and clerk, were honorial appointees.[16]

Nevertheless, despite the absence of formal grants of self-government, the townsmen of many seigneurial boroughs did, in practice, enjoy more autonomy than may appear at first sight. At Wells, the burgesses failed in their struggle to obtain chartered independence in the early 1340s yet eventually still came to exercise a *de facto* self-government through their *communitas burgi*, with its own funds, assembly, court and councillors, and a master who appointed a range of civic officials.[17] Elsewhere, as at Henley, guild merchants could operate as shadow governments in this way,[18] whilst in other towns, such as Lichfield and Stratford, religious guilds possibly took on this function.[19] The tendency for medieval government to be expressed in judicial form and for courts to have broad deliberative and executive functions[20] meant that burgesses of small towns such as Halesowen, Birmingham and Battle, could, like the leading inhabitants

[16] S. H. Rigby, 'Boston and Grimsby in the middle ages: an administrative contrast', *JMed.H*, 10 (1984), 57–62; J. Tait, *Medieval Manchester and the Beginnings of Lancashire* (Manchester, 1904), p. 55; M. Carlin, *Medieval Southwark* (London, 1996), pp. 111–12; A. M. Erskine, 'Political and administrative history, 1066–1509', in *VCH*, Leicestershire, IV (cited below as Erskine, 'Leicester'), p. 12. The court of the Leicester guild merchant was even more free of the earl's control (*ibid.*, p. 25).

[17] Rigby, 'An administrative contrast', 60; D. G. Shaw, *The Creation of a Community: The City of Wells in the Middle Ages* (Oxford, 1993), pp. 114–40, 157–8, 169–72, 264–5, 289; D. R. Carr, 'The problem of urban patriciates: office holders in fifteenth-century Salisbury', *Wiltshire Arch. and NH Magazine*, 83 (1990), 120.

[18] R. B. Peberdy, 'The economy, society, and government of a small town in late medieval England: a study of Henley-on-Thames from *c.* 1300 to *c.* 1540' (PhD thesis, University of Leicester, 1994), pp. 88–102, 139–48, 191–223, 254–64.

[19] R. H. Hilton, *The English Peasantry in the Later Middle Ages* (Oxford, 1975), pp. 83–4, 93–4; Rigby, 'An administrative contrast', 61–2; D. Postles, 'An English small town in the later middle ages: Loughborough', *UH*, 20 (1993), 33; R. B. Dinn, 'Popular religion in late medieval Bury St Edmunds' (PhD thesis, University of Manchester, 1990), vol. I, pp. 122–6.

[20] E. A. Lewis, *The Mediæval Boroughs of Snowdonia* (London, 1912), pp. 122, 127–8; T. Jones Pierce, 'A Caernarfonshire manorial borough: studies in the medieval history of Pwllheli', in J. Beverley Smith, ed., *Medieval Welsh Society: Selected Essays by T. Jones Pierce* (Cardiff, 1972), pp. 167–8; G. A. Williams, *Medieval London* (London, 1963), p. 80.

of rural manors, exercise power in their role as jurors of the local court.[21] However, whatever their relation to the burgesses of their own town, the officials of seigneurial boroughs tended to perform very similar functions on behalf of the crown as did the bailiffs of the royal boroughs.[22] Finally, townsmen within both royal and seigneurial boroughs could serve the crown, as tax and customs collectors, justices and so on, on the basis of personal commissions.[23]

In Wales, the royal boroughs were slower to acquire liberties than English towns and so here the gap between royal and seigneurial boroughs was less marked.[24] In Scotland, by contrast, many towns enjoyed more independence from their overlords than did their English counterparts. A higher proportion of towns were royal burghs, but even seigneurial burghs seem to have enjoyed a fair degree of autonomy and, unlike England, there were few private jurisdictions within the burgh to obstruct local government's control over its citizens. Scottish towns thus differed from each other more in the complexity of their administrative structures than in the degree of their autonomy. The general development of institutions of urban government can be traced from the thirteenth century.[25] Most towns were governed by bailies. Originally the overlord's officials, by the fourteenth century they were usually chosen by the burgesses. In some burghs, a provost or alderman headed the community. Often a town council developed out of the court assizes, although the timing varied considerably from place to place. Berwick enjoyed a council of twenty-four as early as the mid-thirteenth century whereas in Peebles such a body only appeared in the later fifteenth century.[26] Many towns, particularly larger ones such as Edinburgh and Aberdeen, developed more complex systems of government, with a variety of officers similar to those in English towns.[27] In several towns, there was also a guild merchant which generally drew its membership from the 'better sort', although its character could vary; in Edinburgh it was an association of the merchant elite but in Dunfermline its membership comprised about one third of the town's burgesses, both craftsmen and merchants. The guild usually functioned as a branch of local government, being particularly concerned with trading issues. The personnel of guild and town government overlapped and strict jurisdictional boundaries were rarely drawn.[28]

[21] R. H. Hilton, 'Small town society in England before the Black Death', *P&P*, 105 (1984), 68; R. Holt, *The Early History of the Town of Birmingham, 1166 to 1600* (Dugdale Society Occasional Paper, 30, 1985), pp. 11–13; E. Searle, *Lordship and Community* (Toronto, 1974), p. 432.

[22] S. H. Rigby, 'Boston and Grimsby in the middle ages' (PhD thesis, University of London, 1983), p. 119.

[23] S. H. Rigby, 'The customs administration at Boston in the reign of Richard II', *BullIHR*, 58 (1985), 12–24.

[24] Lewis, *Snowdonia*, p. 38.

[25] E. Ewan, *Townlife in Fourteenth-Century Scotland* (Edinburgh, 1990), pp. 40–2.

[26] *Statuta Gilde*, in C. Innes, ed., *Ancient Laws and Customs of the Burghs of Scotland 1124–1424* (Edinburgh, 1868), pp. 80–1, ch. 37; W. Chambers, ed., *Charters and Documents relating to the Burgh of Peebles* (Edinburgh, 1872), p. 166.

[27] Ewan, *Townlife*, pp. 48–50.

[28] E. P. D. Torrie, 'The guild in fifteenth-century Dunfermline', in M. Lynch, M. Spearman and G. Stell, eds, *The Scottish Medieval Town* (Edinburgh, 1988), p. 246.

The distinction between royal and seigneurial burghs was not as strong in Scotland as in England. Prestige and political power in national affairs depended more on the town's economic clout,[29] although distinctions between royal and non-royal burghs became sharper in the sixteenth century. In general, burgesses in royal towns looked after their own affairs, although their bailies continued to account to the Exchequer and to implement royal commands, customs collectors ensured the payment of customs duties and the chamberlain held ayres in the burghs; although less frequently from the fifteenth century. Scottish towns had long consulted together in their dealings with the crown. The Court of the Four Burghs probably developed in the thirteenth century to allow burghs to apportion their share of royal taxation, but it later came to act as a consultative forum for different burghs and helped them formulate common policies to promote in parliament. From 1487 it began to develop into the Convention of Royal Burghs.[30] One result was that the Scottish towns were more uniform in law and custom than English ones, although this contrast should not be overstressed: in 1522 the Convention recognised 'great variance standing in diverse and sundry burghs' in their forms of government.[31] Warfare with England meant that fourteenth-century Scottish monarchs had little time to interfere in burgh life. Indeed, the crown's relative weakness may have stimulated the development of urban self-government. This century also saw the beginning of burgh representation in parliament.[32] The 1424 return of James I from English captivity saw a new royal interest in burgh affairs but, after an initial round of legislation, the towns were generally left to their own devices. The reigns of James III, IV and V (1460–1542) saw a growth in royal intervention in the burghs and a consequent worsening of relations between crown and burgesses. Eventually, in 1546, the Court of Session, the Scottish central court, claimed the right to dismiss any burgh provost. In response, in an attempt to preserve their rights, many burghs drew up copies of their privileges and charters.[33]

Until the mid-fifteenth century, the majority of Scottish burghs were royal. Most non-royal burghs were ecclesiastical: the wave of seigneurial foundations

[29] E. P. D. Torrie, 'The gild of Dunfermline in the fifteenth century' (PhD thesis, Edinburgh University, 1984), pp. 48–9.

[30] D. Ditchburn, 'Trade with northern Europe, 1297–1540', in Lynch, Spearman and Stell, eds., *The Scottish Medieval Town*, pp. 173–4; T. Pagan, *The Convention of the Royal Burghs of Scotland* (Glasgow, 1926), p. 18.

[31] H. MacQueen and W. Windram, 'Laws and courts in the burghs', in Lynch, Spearman and Stell, eds., *The Scottish Medieval Town*, p. 219; M. Lynch, 'Towns and townspeople in fifteenth-century Scotland', in J. A. F. Thomson, ed., *Towns and Townspeople in the Fifteenth Century* (Gloucester, 1988), p. 179; M. Lynch, 'Introduction: Scottish towns 1500–1700', in M. Lynch, ed., *The Early Modern Town in Scotland* (London, 1987), p. 13.

[32] Lynch, 'Introduction', in Lynch, Spearman and Stell, eds., *The Scottish Medieval Town*, p. 9; E. Ewan, 'The community of the burgh in the fourteenth century', in Lynch, Spearman and Stell, eds., *The Scottish Medieval Town*, pp. 229–30, 240.

[33] M. Lynch, 'The crown and the burghs 1500–1625', in Lynch, ed., *Early Modern Town*, p. 69.

happened much later in Scotland (from about 1450) than elsewhere. These new burghs of barony were not represented in parliament nor were they granted foreign trade privileges, although some flouted these restrictions. In those non-royal burghs for which records survive, the burgesses seem to have enjoyed a general autonomy, administering the town through their burgh court although the specific form of local government depended on what was arranged with the burgh superior.[34] In Dunfermline, relations between abbot and town were largely harmonious and local records show little interference by the abbot in town affairs.[35] In Kelso, a struggle between the townspeople and the abbot for control of the town officers and of burgess admissions was resolved by a compromise in 1323.[36]

Given this general political framework, conflicts within towns can be divided into two main groups: those which took place in towns which had yet to win self-government from their lords, and those where the burgesses had won their freedom and where unrest was targeted against the new town rulers.[37] In England, it was amongst boroughs with monastic overlords that the lords' manorial powers seem to have been most resented. Here, the lords often retained control through appointed stewards and bailiffs who ran the courts, collected rents and tolls and regulated the local economy. Even when townsmen obtained the right to nominate candidates for the post of alderman, monastic overlords could retain the power to choose which candidate should serve and abbots always retained the right of confirmation of the candidate elected by the townsmen.[38]

Even though the powers of monastic overlords were not so extreme as to restrict urban growth, they remained a source of irritation to their inhabitants, especially when compared with the independence enjoyed by other towns which were often far less impressive in terms of population and wealth. The result was periodic eruptions of local conflict, whether in the form of litigation by the townsmen against their lords, as at Coventry,[39] or of disorder and riot, as at Bury St Edmunds where the abbot's control of the town officers was a source of friction and periodic open violence from the late twelfth century onwards. The breakdown of central government in 1327 was an opportunity for the townsmen of Bury, like the inhabitants of other monastic boroughs, including St Albans, Abingdon and Dunstable, to press their claims once more. This situation was repeated during the Peasants' Revolt of 1381 when violence erupted against the monastic overlords of Bury, St Albans, Bridgwater, Dunstable and

34 W. M. Mackenzie, *The Scottish Burghs* (Edinburgh, 1949), pp. 80–1.

35 Torrie, 'Guild in fifteenth-century Dunfermline', p. 249.

36 C. Innes, ed., *Liber S. Marie de Calchou* (Bannatyne Club, 1846), vol. II, no. 459.

37 S. H. Rigby, *English Society in the Later Middle Ages* (Basingstoke, 1995), pp. 165–77.

38 N. M. Trenholme, *The English Monastic Boroughs* (University of Missouri Studies, 2, no. 3, 1927), ch. 6; M. D. Lobel *The Borough of Bury St Edmunds* (Oxford, 1935), ch. 2.

39 J. Röhrkasten, 'Conflict in a monastic borough: Coventry in the reign of Edward II', *Midland History*, 18 (1993), 1–18.

Peterborough.[40] At Bury, as elsewhere, the suppression of the Peasants' Revolt effectively meant the end of the townsmen's ambitions. The town's inhabitants had learnt that, unlike the communal movement on the continent, their risings would receive no support from the central government and were thus doomed to failure. As in other monastic towns, it was the Reformation, not the burgesses' struggles, which ended the abbey's control over the town of Bury.[41]

However, persistent conflict was by no means the norm in all English monastic boroughs. At Westminster, friction was the exception and the townsmen were left to order their own affairs so long as the ultimate authority of the abbot was recognised.[42] In those seigneurial boroughs with lay lords, such as Leicester and Boston, co-operation rather than conflict seems to have been even more typical.[43] Co-operation between lord and burgesses was also the norm in the seigneurial towns of the Welsh Marcher lordships where boroughs, as agents of conquest, were faced by the hostility of the native population and so looked to their lords for protection, aid and defence of their privileges.[44]

(ii) CHANGES IN CIVIC LIBERTIES

In contrast with its monastic towns, England's self-governing royal boroughs were able to extend their liberties in the later middle ages without violent conflict. There were three main innovations in the nature of urban franchises in this period. The first was the granting of shire status to a number of towns so that boroughs became shires separate from the county around them, as when Chester became 'the county of the city of Chester', with their own sheriffs, escheators and county courts.[45] The first grant of this kind, that to Bristol in

[40] Trenholme, *Monastic Boroughs*, pp. 5–11, 22–5, 32–45, 55–7; Lobel, *Bury*, pp. 118–57; R. H. Hilton, *Bond Men Made Free* (London, 1977), pp. 202–3; Dobson, *Peasants' Revolt*, pp. 238–51, 271, 279–84, 325–33; S. Blinkhorn and G. Newfield, 'The St Albans charter of 16 June 1381', in P. Barton *et al.*, *The Peasants' Revolt in Hertfordshire* (Stevenage, 1981), ch. 8; R. Faith, 'The "Great Rumour" of 1377 and peasant ideology', in R. H. Hilton and T. H. Aston, eds., *The English Rising of 1381* (Cambridge, 1984), pp. 64–5.

[41] Trenholme, *Monastic Boroughs*, pp. 57, 75–6; Lobel, *Bury*, pp. 157–68. Coventry, where the influence of Queen Isabella was decisive in the townsmen's victory over the prior, was a rare exception to this rule. See A. Gooder and E. Gooder, 'Coventry before 1355: unity or division?', *Midland History*, 6 (1981), 1–38.

[42] Rosser, *Medieval Westminster*, pp. 237–8, 245–7; M. Bonney, *Lordship and the Urban Community* (Cambridge, 1990), pp. 230–3; Shaw, *Wells*, p. 289.

[43] M. Bateson, ed., *Records of the Borough of Leicester* ([London], 1899–1905), vol. I, pp. xxxvii–xl; Erskine, 'Leicester', p. 23; Rigby, 'An administrative contrast', 63–4. For a rare instance of a challenge to the lords of Boston, see Rigby, 'Boston and Grimsby in the middle ages' (PhD thesis), p. 136.

[44] R. R. Davies, *Lordship and Society in the March of Wales, 1282–1400* (Oxford, 1978), pp. 321–3. For an exception, see *ibid.*, p. 94.

[45] Chester City RO, Charters, CH 32; W. de Gray Birch, ed., *The Royal Charters of the City of Lincoln* (Cambridge, 1911), pp. 78–9.

1373, was designed to resolve the specific problems caused by the city's division between the counties of Somerset and Gloucestershire, but once Bristol had acquired this privilege, other cities, such as York (1396), Newcastle (1400), Norwich (1404) and Lincoln (1409) followed suit, and by the mid-fifteenth century even towns such as Hull and Southampton were being made into separate counties.[46] In Scotland, Perth was the first town to receive shire status in 1394.[47]

The second major innovation in town government was the emergence of the doctrine of legal incorporation by which a town became a fictitious personality with the power to sue and be sued, the ability to possess a common seal, the right to make by-laws, the enjoyment of perpetual succession to its liberties and the right to hold lands.[48] In practice, however, incorporation made little difference to town liberties. Its main benefit was the grant of the ability to hold land, an issue which came to the fore following the English crown's extension of the mortmain legislation to the boroughs in 1391.[49] Nevertheless, if corporate status *per se* was of little practical significance, townsmen were still willing to pay to obtain it, as many grants of incorporation were accompanied by a variety of other privileges, including shire status, changes to the borough's constitution and the exclusion from the town of the stewards and marshals of the king's household and of the royal clerk of the market.[50]

Charters of incorporation could also include grants of the third main innovation which occurred in late medieval English (although not Scottish) town government: the elevation of town officers into justices of the peace. The Hull charter of 1440 and the Chester charter of 1506 granted that the mayor, recorder and those who had 'sustained the burden' of being alderman should also be keepers and justices of the peace within the city.[51] Such grants, by excluding the county justices, allowed towns to defend their autonomy in the face of the main innovation in English local government in this period. They may also have been linked with a shift towards the increased authority and prestige of town rulers in

[46] N. P. Harding, ed., *Bristol Charters, 1155–1373* (Bristol Record Society, 1930), pp. 119–23; M. Weinbaum, *The Incorporation of Boroughs* (Manchester, 1937), pp. 54–9, 66–72.

[47] J. M. Thomson *et al.*, *Registrum Magni Sigilli Regum Scottorum* (Edinburgh, 1882–1914), vol. VI, no. 1098.

[48] Weinbaum, *Incorporation*, pp. 65–8; M. Weinbaum, ed., *British Borough Charters, 1307–1660* (Cambridge, 1943), pp. xxiii–vi.

[49] Erskine, 'Leicester', p. 20; *SR*, II, p. 80; S. Reynolds, 'The idea of incorporation in western Christendom before 1300', in J. A. Guy and H. G. Beale, eds., *Law and Social Change in British History* (London, 1984), pp. 27–33.

[50] *CCh.R 1427–1516*, pp. 8, 11; G. H. Martin, 'Doncaster borough charters', in G. H. Martin *et al.*, *Doncaster* (Doncaster, 1995), pp. 18–19.

[51] E. G. Kimball, 'Commissions of the peace for urban jurisdictions in England, 1327–1485', *Proceedings of the American Philosophical Society*, 121 (1977), 465–68; Weinbaum, ed., *Borough Charters*, p. xxiii; *CCh.R 1427–1516*, pp. 10–11; Chester City RO, Charters, CH32; *CPR 1461–7*, p. 330; Erskine, 'Leicester', pp. 26–7.

the later middle ages (see below, p. 309), giving borough by-laws the sanction of royal authority, allowing justices to imprison without bail, extending the town rulers' jurisdiction to criminal cases including riots and disturbances and even granting justices the power to inflict the death penalty.[52] In Scotland, one major development of the late medieval period was the granting of feu-ferme charters to towns, beginning with Aberdeen in 1319.[53] Such charters may not have made much practical difference where towns already paid a yearly ferme but the prestige they gave was evidently regarded as worth paying for, since at least twenty burghs had obtained them by the early fifteenth century. In general, however, urban government in the later middle ages continued within the framework of liberties established by the start of the period. This, and the survival of sources produced from within the towns themselves, has meant that historians have concentrated their attention on internal change in the exercise of urban power.

(iii) POWER AND SOCIAL STATUS

Even within those towns which achieved some degree of self-government, it was always a minority of the population which had any sort of involvement in town government. First, women, even those widows who were successful entrepreneurs and who could be required to contribute to urban taxes, were excluded from any formal role in town government and rarely entered the town freedom in their own right. The fundamental assumption, one so powerful that it rarely needed stating, was, as was said in 1422 when John of Ely was accused of farming the office of assayers of oysters at Queenhithe in London to women, that it was not to the worship of the city 'that women should have such things in governance'.[54] In Scotland, small numbers of women were admitted as burgesses and as guild members in several burghs.[55] They were, however, excluded from guild

[52] S. Rees Jones, 'York's civic administration, 1354–1464', in Rees Jones, ed., *The Government of Medieval York*, pp. 116–20; C. M. Barron, 'Ralph Holland and the London radicals, 1438–1444', in Holt and Rosser, ed., *The Medieval Town*, pp. 173–4.

[53] P. J. Anderson, ed., *Charters and Other Writs Illustrating the History of the Royal Burgh of Aberdeen* (Aberdeen, 1890), no. 8. Berwick received this grant in the late thirteenth century and again in 1329 when it came back under Scottish control, but this lapsed in the 1330s when it returned to English control: R. Nicholson, *Scotland: The Later Middle Ages* (Edinburgh, 1974) p. 108. For other burghs, see the maps in P. G. B. McNeill and H. L. MacQueen, eds., *Atlas of Scottish History to 1707* (Edinburgh, 1996), pp. 306–7, which amplify the list given in W. C. Dickinson, ed., *Early Records of the Burgh of Aberdeen* (Scottish History Society, 1957), p. lxxv.

[54] S. H. Rigby, 'Urban "oligarchy" in late medieval England', in Thomson, ed., *Towns and Townspeople*, p. 70; K. E. Lacey, 'Women and work in fourteenth and fifteenth century London', in L. Charles and L. Duffin, eds., *Women and Work in Pre-Industrial England* (London, 1985), pp. 48, 53; Thrupp, *Merchant Class*, pp. 171–3, 197.

[55] Erskine Beveridge, ed., *The Burgh Records of Dunfermline 1488–1584* (Edinburgh, 1917), pp. 70, 87, 89; R. Renwick, ed., *Extracts from the Records of the Burgh of Peebles* (Scottish Burgh Records Society, 1910) pp. 113, 133, 197; James Marwick, ed., *Extracts from the Records of the Burgh of Edinburgh 1403–1528* (Scottish Burgh Records Society, 1869), p. 2.

and town office, although occasionally the widow of a customs collector could continue her husband's duties for some years after his death.[56]

Secondly, even amongst men, a say in government was the preserve of those who had entered the freedom of the borough, as was stated explicitly at Chester where only those inhabitants admitted to the city franchise had the right to attend the annual election of the mayor and sheriffs or to serve as officers.[57] The proportion of townsmen who were enfranchised varied from town to town. At Exeter, the franchise was particularly exclusive: only 21 per cent of the householders of 1377 (or about 4 per cent of the total population) belonged to the freedom. Although 34 per cent of this group *eventually* entered the freedom, the Exeter franchise was appreciably more restrictive than that of York where over half of the 1377 heads of household may eventually have become freemen.[58] Entry to the borough freedom could be obtained in three ways: by right of inheritance, by purchase and by apprenticeship. At Chester, burgesses' sons paid only 10½d. for the 'fees and wine' associated with their entry to the freedom whereas others paid a fine of 26s. 8d. (although, as elsewhere, this was payable in instalments). Apprentices who had served their term could also enter the freedom at Chester without payment of an entry fine.[59] The fact that the freedom could be bought meant that many towns used entry fines as a means of raising money, as at Exeter where expenditure on the town defences led to a drive to recruit new burgesses.[60] In Scotland, there were, at first, attempts to limit the town freedom to residents but it later became easier to buy the freedom as towns sought new revenues.[61] In such cases, the civic freedom not only offered privilege but was also becoming an obligation for all those who wished to work as independent masters and retailers.

Finally, even within the minority of townsmen who were enfranchised, there were massive social inequalities and corresponding differences in political power. Normally, the correlation between wealth and suitability for office was simply

[56] Marjory Schireham served as custumar in Dundee in the 1320s, while several custumars' wives took over the role after their husbands were killed at Flodden in 1513: *ER*, I, pp. 76, 95, 275, XIV, pp. 48, 50–7, 102–8, 190–1, 199–205, 263–4, 267–8, XV, pp. 55–6, 179–80.

[57] Erskine, 'Leicester', p. 29; Chester City RO, Charters, CH 32, Assembly Book AB1, f. 58v.

[58] M. Kowaleski, *Local Markets and Regional Trade in Exeter* (Cambridge, 1995), p. 96; Palliser, *Tudor York*, p. 148. At Wells, about half of adult males were members of the freedom (Shaw, *Wells*, pp. 142–3).

[59] Chester City RO, Assembly Files A/F/1, f. 10, Mayor's Book MB/5, f. 2v, Assembly Book AB/1, f. 64.

[60] H. Swanson, *Medieval Artisans* (Oxford, 1989), pp. 107–10; Kowaleski, *Exeter*, pp. 98–9; K. J. Allison, 'Medieval Hull', in *VCH*, Yorkshire: East Riding, I (Oxford, 1969), p. 37; Chester City RO, Assembly Book AB1, ff. 58, 69; Assembly File A/F/1, f. 10.

[61] Ewan, *Townlife*, pp. 92–3, 116; M. Lynch, *Edinburgh and the Reformation* (Edinburgh, 1981), p. 10; Torrie, 'Gild of Dunfermline', p. 161; P. S. M. Symms, 'Social control in a sixteenth-century burgh: a study of the burgh court book of Selkirk 1503–1545' (PhD thesis, University of Edinburgh, 1986), pp. 46–7.

taken for granted. Only rarely did it obtain formal expression with the introduction of property qualifications for office, as at Exeter in the 1340s where it was ordained that mayoral candidates were to possess at least 100s. of property.[62] The mercantile political dominance found at Exeter was increasingly the norm in the larger towns of both England and Scotland,[63] a contrast with France where the urban elites of the later middle ages tended to be composed of royal officials, lawyers, clerics, rentiers and financiers.[64] However, in the bulk of small market towns without any substantial overseas trade, the status of town rulers was more modest. At Wells, merchants occupied the office of town master for 42 per cent of the time and gentry for 9 per cent of the time in the period 1377 to 1500 but, despite the relative overrepresentation of these groups, wealthy craftsmen, such as tailors, tanners, weavers, brewers and dyers, occupied the office for almost half the period.[65] In Perth, too, a craft aristocracy played a major role in burgh affairs.[66] British towns lacked the hereditary patriciates to be found on the continent, and town government remained relatively open to those who possessed sufficient wealth.[67] With the occasional exception, such as the butchers who, despite their prosperity, could be seen as a low-status craft and thus excluded from civic office, power and status in the British medieval town were largely determined by wealth.[68]

In the towns of Wales, in both the March and the principality, the distribution of power was complicated by the division between English and Welsh. In theory, according to the Edwardian ordinances, the burgesses of the Welsh towns were to be English and land was not to be demised to the Welsh. Certainly, those of Welsh extraction could be expelled from the boroughs, as at Ruthin in 1359, 1365 and 1376, and their burgages confiscated, as at Hope, Flint and Mostyn in the same period.[69] However, in practice, Welshmen were moving into the

[62] Shaw, *Wells*, pp. 188–9; M. Bailey, *The Bailiffs' Minute Book of Dunwich, 1404–1430* (Suffolk Records Society, 35, 1992), pp. 7–8; Kowaleski, *Exeter*, p. 98, 101–4; Palliser, *Tudor York*, pp. 92–3; R. H. Britnell, *Growth and Decline in Colchester, 1300–1525* (Cambridge, 1986), p. 221.

[63] Thrupp, *Merchant Class*, pp. 80–4; Miller, 'York', p. 79; Britnell, *Growth and Decline*, pp. 32–3, 110–14, 211–12; Lynch, *Edinburgh*, p. 16; H. Booton, 'Economic and social change in later medieval Aberdeen', in J. S. Smith, ed., *New Light on Medieval Aberdeen* (Aberdeen, 1985), p. 47.

[64] Hilton, *English and French Towns*, pp. 101–5.

[65] R. H. Hilton, 'Towns in English feudal society', *Review*, 3 (1979), 6–7; Hammer, 'Anatomy of an oligarchy', 5, 10; Rigby, *Grimsby*, pp. 73–8; Shaw, *Wells*, pp. 164–7.

[66] M. Lynch, 'The social and economic structure of the larger towns, 1450–1600', in Lynch, Spearman and Stell, eds., *The Scottish Medieval Town*.

[67] Hammer, 'Anatomy of an oligarchy', 18–19; Carr, 'The problem of urban patriciates', 133–5; A. D. Dyer, *The City of Worcester in the Sixteenth Century* (Leicester, 1973), pp. 225–6; Palliser, *Tudor York*, pp. 93–4.

[68] Swanson, *Artisans*, pp. 170–1; Shaw, *Wells*, p. 165; E. M. Carus-Wilson, 'Towns and trade', in A. L. Poole, ed., *Medieval England* (Oxford, 1958), vol. I, p. 251; Palliser, *Tudor York*, p. 93; Dyer, *Worcester*, pp. 224–6.

[69] T. Herbert and G. E. Jones, *Edward I and Wales* (Cardiff, 1988), p. 88; Lewis, *Snowdonia*, pp. 41–2, 167, 174, 229–30, 243; R. R. Davies, *Lordship and Society in the March of Wales, 1282–1400*

English foundations even before the end of the thirteenth century whilst the population of some of the Welsh boroughs, such as Pwllheli, Dinefwr and Nefyn, had always been overwhelmingly native in composition.[70] By 1400, most Marcher boroughs had a substantial proportion of Welsh inhabitants, and in some towns they were already a majority, whilst even Cricieth and Harlech had a growing Welsh presence.[71] Welshmen even began to be chosen as town officers, not just in Aberystwyth and Ruthin, always amongst the most integrated of boroughs, but also, by the later fourteenth century, at towns such as Cardigan (where it became common for one of the bailiffs to have a Welsh name and one an English name) and Carmarthen.[72] Glyndŵr's revolt led to a temporary reaction with Henry IV's penal laws reaffirming the ban on Welshmen acquiring land or becoming burgesses in the 'English towns' of Wales, a ban reinforced by local ordinances, as at Brecon in 1408 and 1411.[73] Nevertheless, despite the protests of the burgesses of Conwy, Beaumaris and Caernarfon, the long-term trend was towards the assimilation of the native and settler populations. By the end of the medieval period, as in England and Scotland, wealth, not 'race', was the key social distinction, a process given belated legal recognition by Henry VII, who formally allowed the Welsh to acquire land freely even within the 'English' boroughs, and by the 1536 Act of Union which gave the Welsh the same liberties as the king's other subjects.[74] By this time, however, political power within many Welsh boroughs was falling into the hands of the rural squirearchy, as at Carmarthen where the gentry of the Tywi valley, rather than the town's merchants, came to dominate the borough.[75]

(Oxford, 1978), pp. 316–17, 325–6; P. H. W. Booth and A. D. Carr, *Account of Master John de Burnham the Younger, Chamberlain of Chester, of the Revenues of the Counties of Chester and Flint, Michaelmas 1361 to Michaelmas 1362* (Record Society of Lancashire and Cheshire, 125, 1991), p. lxx.

[70] I. Soulsby, *The Towns of Medieval Wales* (Chichester, 1983), pp. 24, 193; R. A. Griffiths, *Conquerors and Conquered in Medieval Wales* (Stroud, 1994), pp. 266, 344; Jones Pierce, 'Pwllheli', pp. 148, 150.

[71] Davies, *Lordship*, pp. 327, 447; Lewis, *Snowdonia*, p. 260; A. D. Carr, *Medieval Wales* (Basingstoke, 1995), p. 96; D. Walker, *Medieval Wales* (Cambridge, 1990), pp. 63–4, 160–1.

[72] R. A. Griffiths, 'Aberystwyth', in R. A. Griffiths, ed., *Boroughs of Mediaeval Wales* (Cardiff, 1978), pp. 38–9; R. I. Jack, 'Ruthin', in *ibid.*, pp. 250–1; R. A. Griffiths, 'Carmarthen', in *ibid.*, pp. 157, 161; Griffiths, *Conquerors*, p. 293.

[73] Lewis, *Snowdonia*, pp. 181, 253–4, 265; R. R. Davies, *The Age of Conquest: Wales, 1063–1415* (Oxford, 1991), pp. 458–9; Davies, *Lordship*, pp. 307, 325–6, 336–7; R. R. Davies, 'Brecon', in Griffiths, ed., *Boroughs of Mediaeval Wales*, pp. 66–7.

[74] G. Williams, *Recovery, Reorientation and Reformation: Wales, c. 1415–1642* (Oxford, 1987), p. 82; K. Williams-Jones, 'Caernarfon', in Griffiths, ed., *Boroughs of Mediaeval Wales*, pp. 83, 97–101; W. R. B. Robinson, 'Swansea', in *ibid.*, pp. 285–6; R. F. Walker, 'Tenby', in *ibid.*, p. 320; Lewis, *Snowdonia*, pp. 141–2, 221–3, 254–5, 268–71; W. Rees, *The Union of England and Wales* (Cardiff, 1948), p. 56.

[75] Jones Pierce, 'Pwllheli', pp. 171–2; Griffiths, 'Carmarthen', pp. 161, 163; L. B. Smith, 'Oswestry', in Griffiths, *Boroughs*, p. 235;

In Scotland, too, townsmen began to suffer from outside interference in their affairs as the growing regional interests of the great lords after *c.* 1450 led them to pay increasing attention to local burghs. In the period 1450–1530, of eighty new burghs created, fifty-three were dependent on nobles.[76] In 1463, Aberdeen concluded a bond of manrent, a contract guaranteeing protection, with the local magnate, the earl of Huntly, in order to fend off the advances of other north-eastern lords.[77] There was gentry interference too in Perth and Stirling in the sixteenth century, whilst in Edinburgh, the political centre of Scotland, the minority of James III saw the powerful families of Douglas and Hamilton struggling to control the office of provost.[78]

(iv) URBAN POLITICAL THEORY

The social and economic inequalities of the late medieval town were potentially a fertile source of conflict. However, unlike peasant opposition to manorial impositions, which was aimed against some particular landlord, urban economic struggles between merchants and master craftsmen or between masters and their journeymen lacked a single focus. As a result, conflict in late medieval towns often centred on political issues in which the commonalty had a shared sense of identity and a common target for their grievances. In particular, conflict focused on the election of town officials and the belief that town rulers were manipulating the taxation system for their own benefit.[79] Did such conflicts raise issues of political principle and lead to structural change in town government? Or did a consensus about political values mean that popular political movements merely sought to remove corrupt individuals from office?

Medieval urban political theory was based on the commonplace that town government should be carried out for the common good. Town officers swore oaths 'to do right to every person or persons, as well as to poor as to rich, having no reward of any manner of person'; they promised to maintain good custom, avoid evil custom and to defend the widows and orphans of the town. As a result, as a royal writ to the mayor of Northampton said, 'perfect rest, tranquillity, love, plenty, abundance and universal well' would flourish and 'commotions, strifes, debates, poverty, misery and many other inconveniences' would

[76] G. S. Pryde, *The Burghs of Scotland* (London, 1965), pp. 25–6, 51–8.

[77] Booton, 'Aberdeen', p. 52.

[78] M. Verschuur, 'Merchants and craftsmen in sixteenth-century Perth', in Lynch, ed., *Early Modern Town*, p. 39; Lynch, 'Introduction: Scottish towns 1500–1700', p. 22; I. Whyte, *Scotland before the Industrial Revolution* (Harlow, 1995), p. 194.

[79] *Rotuli Parliamentorum* (Record Commission, 1783), vol. VI, p. 432; R. Horrox, 'Medieval Beverley', in *VCH*, Yorkshire: East Riding, VI, pp. 22–4. In Scotland, however, taxation was not such an issue in burgh politics since here government was supported by the 'common good', made up of revenues from such sources as petty customs, leasing of town mills and fishings, burgess entry fees, etc., rather than by regular taxation (Lynch, *Edinburgh*, pp. 21–2).

be avoided.[80] It was assumed that this happy state could best be achieved by, as a royal letter to Lincoln of 1438 put it, the appointment of civic officers from the 'more worthy, more good and true, and more discreet and powerful' men of the city who were 'suitable for occupying and exercising such offices', rather than the appointment of middling persons (*mediocres*) to whom such office would be a burden.[81] The prestige of town officers was further buttressed by their dignity as royal officials[82] and also received religious backing with the emphasis on the need for town officers to attend church services.[83] In Scotland, the role played by religious sanction was even greater. Here each town was united in a single parish and seen as a *corpus Christianum*. Even large burghs regarded themselves as small, close-knit communities, although their reality belied this conception.[84] The authority of town officers throughout Britain was also reinforced by civic ceremonial such as the Corpus Christi processions and pageants which in theory, if not always in practice, were supposed to create 'good unity, charity and concord' amongst the urban community through their reaffirmation of the mutual interdependence of the limbs of the social body 'under the overall direction of the head: the magistracy'.[85]

However, if urban political theory normally expressed a *descending* concept of political power in which town rulers owed their legitimacy to some superior political power, ultimately to God, much day-to-day political practice implicitly embodied an alternative *ascending* concept of power, one in which the basis of political authority lay in some form of popular consent (albeit not conceived of in modern egalitarian terms).[86] The town was a 'public commonwealth' whose citizens had not only the right but also the duty to 'assist, aid and counsel' their mayor even when, as at Lincoln in 1422, this right was restricted to the power to object and argue about, but not to overturn, the decisions of the mayor and aldermen. The mayors themselves were not only royal agents but were also municipal *representatives* who owed their existence not to any chartered grant but simply to the concept of the borough as a self-governing community, free to

[80] Reynolds, 'Medieval urban history', 18–23; Shaw, *Wells*, pp. 178–97; South Humberside Area RO 1/201/1 Mayor's Court Book, f. 124; L. Toulmin Smith, ed., *The Maire of Bristowe is Kalendar* (Camden Society, new series, 5, 1872), pp. 72–3; C. A. Markham, ed., *The Liber Custumarum* (Northampton, 1985), p. 6; W. Hudson and J. C. Tingey, eds., *The Records of the City of Norwich* (Norwich, 1906–10), vol. I, p. 94; M. D. Harris, ed., *The Coventry Leet Book*, part II (Early English Text Society, 135, 1908), pp. 555–6. [81] Birch, *Lincoln*, pp. 95–7.

[82] South Humberside Area RO, 1/102/1 Mayor's Court Book, f. 124r–v; Lincolnshire AO, L/l/1/3/1, White Book, ff. 47v–50v.

[83] C. Phythian-Adams, *Desolation of a City* (Cambridge, 1979), pp. 137–9, Toulmin Smith, *Bristowe*, pp. 74–80. [84] Lynch, 'Towns and townspeople', p. 178.

[85] M. E. James, 'Ritual, drama and the social body in the late medieval English town', *P&P*, 98 (1983), 8–10, 28–9; J. Goldberg, 'Craft guilds, the Corpus Christi play and civic government', in Rees Jones, ed., *The Government of Medieval York*, p. 142; Lynch, 'Towns and townspeople', p. 186.

[86] W. Ullman, *A History of Political Thought: The Middle Ages* (Harmondsworth, 1965), pp. 12–13, 159–61.

order its own affairs.[87] The requirement that town government should be carried out according to custom certainly assumed a tacit consent to such custom by the commonalty. Popular consent could also be given explicit form through the passing of town by-laws and ordinances as at Norwich at the beginning of Henry V's reign when the need for the 'assent of the commonalty' to the ordinances made by the bailiffs and council of twenty-four became a political issue.[88]

The ideology of 'community' was important in Scotland as well. Here, the term 'community of the burgh' was first recorded in the 1290s and quickly became an important concept in urban identity, although the extent to which this 'community' involved any popular voice is debatable.[89] Burgesses were required to attend their town's three annual head courts to give their voice in town business although in larger burghs, such as Edinburgh, this became a practical impossibility in the fifteenth century. In Dundee, by the sixteenth century, the participation of all burgesses was apparently limited to giving consent.[90] Nevertheless, the assent of the community was not merely a formality; in Inverness in 1359 a measure was passed 'with the consent of the *major part* of the community', implying some prior disagreement.[91] The government of smaller towns was particularly likely to involve broader participation. In Selkirk, no formal council existed until the mid-sixteenth century; instead different groups of men were chosen to form inquests to decide on issues in the town court. The court often provided a forum to air personal conflicts which were then resolved by arbitration.[92] In small towns, cliques were usually too small to dominate the population without challenge and a balance between public and private interests could be maintained.[93]

(V) POPULAR MOVEMENTS IN LATE MEDIEVAL TOWNS

It would be wrong, therefore, to see medieval town government as based simply on the assumption that the rule of 'the few best men' would be 'good and

[87] Lincolnshire AO, L/1/3/1, White Book, f. 3v; S. Reynolds, 'The writing of medieval urban history in England', *Theoretische Geschiedenis*, 19 (1992), 50–1; Chester City RO, Assembly Files, A/F/1, ff. 5v, 7; A. Ballard, 'The English boroughs in the reign of John', *EHR*, 14 (1899), 99.

[88] *CPR 1391–6*, pp. 355–6; Hudson and Tingey, eds, *Records of the City of Norwich*, I, pp. 30, 64–70; B. R. McCree, 'Peacemaking and its limitations in late medieval Norwich', *EHR*, 109 (1994), 840, 851.

[89] E. Ewan, 'The community of the burgh in the fourteenth century', in Lynch, Spearman and Stell, eds., *The Scottish Medieval Town*, pp. 228–41; E. P. Dennison, 'Power to the people? The myth of the medieval burgh community', in S. Foster, A. Macinnes and R. Macinnes, eds., *Power Centres* (Glasgow, 1998).

[90] Lynch, 'Social and economic Scottish structure', p. 262; E. P. D. Torrie, *Medieval Dundee* (Dundee, 1990), p. 26.

[91] B. Webster, ed., *Regesta Regum Scottorum VI: The Acts of David II* (Edinburgh, 1982), no. 225.

[92] J. Imrie *et al.*, eds., *The Burgh Court Book of Selkirk 1503–45*, Part I (Scottish Record Society, 1960), *passim*; Symms, 'Selkirk', pp. 18–19, 22–7, 36.

[93] Symms, 'Selkirk', p. 108.

benevolent'.[94] The choice facing townsmen was not that between unquestioning acceptance of the rule of the rich on the one hand and egalitarian democracy on the other. Rather, it was how to reconcile the existence of the principle of rule by the 'better sort' with that of the community's right to consultation and representation. These two principles could coexist, as they did in the Chester charter of 1506 where one sheriff was to be chosen by the mayor, sheriffs and aldermen and one elected by the body of citizens.[95] But the principles of descending and ascending authority could also come into opposition, as at Leicester in 1489 where, in accordance with an act of parliament, the mayor and twenty-four, along with forty-eight of the 'wiser' inhabitants nominated by them, elected Roger Tryng as mayor 'in the name of the whole community', whereas the commonalty of the town, men described in the act as of 'little substance and no discretion', met in accordance with past custom at an assembly of burgesses and elected Thomas Toutheby as mayor. Here, the dispute was not simply about the personal merits of town rulers but explicitly centred on conflicting concepts of the source of legitimate political authority.[96] A similar clash of principles occurred at Selkirk in 1538–9 when the provost attempted to have his own candidate appointed as the chaplain of a parish church altar which was controlled by the community. Even though the provost's nominee was eventually appointed, it was a point of principle on the part of the community of the burgh that the appointment remained within its choice.[97]

That such struggles were not just about individual merit can be seen in those towns where political conflict led to structural reform of government in favour of a greater accountability of the rulers to the commonalty. At Lynn, conflict in the early fifteenth century resulted in concessions to the town's *mediocres* and *inferiores* by its *potentiores* who agreed to consult the lesser inhabitants about financial charges made on them and to allow them involvement in electing officers, and who eventually consented to the creation of a council of twenty-seven to oversee the town's financial affairs.[98] In fifteenth-century Exeter and Wells, pressure from below led not to the creation of a new council, as at Lynn and Norwich, but to enlargement of existing ones, with the addition of 'middling' burgesses to provide a check on the decisions of the 'great' burgesses.[99] At York, popular pressure,

[94] Reynolds, 'Medieval urban history', 18–23; Reynolds, *Introduction*, p. 171; W. H. Stevenson, ed., *Records of the Borough of Nottingham* (London and Nottingham, 1882–5), vol. III, p. 341.

[95] Chester City RO, Charters CH 32.

[96] *Rotuli Parliamentorum*, VI, p. 432; Bateson, ed., *Records of the Borough of Leicester*, II, pp. 319, 324–7.

[97] P. Symms, 'A disputed altar: parish pump politics in a sixteenth-century burgh', *Innes Review*, 42 (1991), 133–5.

[98] McCree, 'Peacemaking and its limitations', *passim*; *HMC*, 11th Report, App. part III, pp. 191–203, 245–6; see also J. Cooper, 'Borough government', in *VCH*, Essex, IX, p. 53.

[99] Tait, *Medieval English Borough*, pp. 310–11, 317–18; Hudson and Tingey, eds., *Norwich*, I, pp. 36, 93–108; B. Wilkinson, *The Mediaeval Council of Exeter* (Manchester, 1931), pp. 6–8, 24–6; Shaw, *Wells*, pp. 170–2.

ranging from petitions to riots, brought about changes in the procedure for electing the mayor in 1464, 1473, 1489, 1504 and 1517, including formal recognition of the role of craft guilds as the representatives of the commonalty, and also involved an attempt by the commonalty to obtain a say in the election of the sheriffs, who were chosen by the council.[100] In Scotland, too, some crafts sought to protect their own interests by securing participation in town government. In the sixteenth century, Edinburgh and Perth bent to pressure from the crafts and made available a few seats on the town council for craft representatives.[101] That urban political strife could raise issues of broader principle is also demonstrated by the struggles in London in the 1440s, where conflict centring on the nomination of Ralph Holland as the popular candidate for the mayoralty raised issues such as the popular basis of authority, the extent of the civic franchise, popular participation in government, the social value of the artisan and equality before the law. The claims made by Holland's supporters in these conflicts reveal a rather different conception of the town rulers and of town government from that provided by the official sources on which we are usually dependent.[102]

Such 'popular' or 'anti-oligarchic' movements were far from being 'democratic' in the modern sense.[103] At Leicester in 1489, London in the 1440s and Lynn in the early fifteenth century, the popular movements accepted that the men chosen as mayors would continue to be drawn from within the ruling elite. Nevertheless, whilst they may not have had the *word* 'oligarchy', in their attempts to prevent town rulers from becoming a self-perpetuating elite who tallaged without consultation, the burgesses of towns such as Lynn certainly seem to have had the *concept*. Their response was not to call upon their rulers to have a change of heart and to repudiate sin, the means which writers of the 'rhetorical' school, such as Brunetto Latini (excerpts of whose *Li Livres dou Tresor* were included in the London *Liber Custumarum*), favoured to obtain good government. Rather, like Marsiglio of Padua and the 'scholastic' theorists, they saw good government not just in terms of personal virtue but also of efficient institutions and of elected officers whose discretionary powers were limited by a series of checks on their actions.[104] The assumption remained that the rich would provide the town

[100] J. I. Kermode, 'Obvious observations on the formation of oligarchies in late medieval English towns', in Thomson, ed., *Towns and Townspeople*, pp. 89–90, 99–102; Rees Jones, 'York's civic administration, 1354–1464', p. 123; Palliser, *Tudor York*, pp. 45–9.

[101] Verschuur, 'Merchants and craftsmen', pp. 40–1; Lynch, 'Social and economic structure', pp. 264–8.

[102] Barron, 'Ralph Holland', pp. 160–83. See also C. R. Friedrichs, 'Urban politics and urban social structure in seventeenth-century Germany', *European History Quarterly*, 22 (1992), 198–202.

[103] Tait, *Medieval English Borough*, p. 338; Reynolds, 'The writing of medieval urban history in England', 50.

[104] Q. Skinner, *The Foundations of Modern Political Thought* (Cambridge, 1978), vol. I, pp. 47–8, 59–60; H. T. Riley, ed., *Munimenta Gildhallae Londoniensi Custumarum* (RS, 1859–62), vol. II, part I, pp. 16–25; Kermode, 'Obvious observations', pp. 89–90, 93, 100–1.

officers; what was at issue was the degree of their accountability to the community as a whole.

Given the assumption that officials would be drawn from the richest inhabitants, conflict between town rulers and the commonalty was often sparked off by individual or factional disputes within the town elite, as at York in 1381 and 1482 or at Norwich in the 1430s.[105] Given the dangers of such 'lites [i.e. strifes] and gruges' within the urban elite, town rulers sought ways of maintaining harmony amongst themselves. Participation in elite guilds was one solution, as at Norwich in the mid-fifteenth century and Leicester in 1477.[106] In Dunfermline, the town's only guild was made up of those who staffed the local government and took on the responsibility of ensuring 'good neighbourhood', friendly relations, between its members.[107]

(vi) THE TRIUMPH OF 'OLIGARCHY'?

However, whilst movements to make town rulers more accountable had some short-term successes, it was the 'descending' rather than the 'ascending' concept of town government which was increasingly dominant in the late medieval period. Thus, the emergence of town councils was not always associated with the extension of popular involvement in town government.[108] Indeed, councils could also be used to restrict popular involvement, as at Grimsby, where a council of twelve of the 'more lawful and discreet men of the town', usually ex-mayors who then served as councillors for years on end, took over some of the duties once carried out by a broader range of burgesses serving on juries in the borough court, a trend also found in many small Scottish towns.[109] Elsewhere, as at Leicester in 1489 (see above, p. 307), councils of burgesses could replace popular electoral assemblies. In England, although not in Scotland, these trends were accompanied by the increasing tendency to appoint aldermen for life and the restriction of candidature for the mayoralty to aldermen, as at Nottingham (1448), Stamford (1462) and Grantham (1463), or at least to those nominated by the aldermen, as at Hull (1443).[110] All of these trends culminated in those towns which adopted 'close corporations', as at Bristol (1499), Exeter (1504) and Lynn

105 R. B. Dobson, 'The risings in York, Beverley and Scarborough, 1380–81', in Hilton and Aston, eds., *The English Rising*, pp. 119–24; Miller, 'York', p. 82; B. R. McRee, 'Religious gilds and civic order: the case of Norwich in the late middle ages', *Speculum*, 67 (1992), 83, 87; Maddern, *Violence*, pp. 183–201.

106 Lincolnshire AO, L1/1/1/1 Council Minutes, f. 36v; Erskine, 'Leicester', pp. 29–30; McCree, 'Religious gilds', 90–3.

107 Torrie, 'Guild of Dunfermline', pp. 249, 256–7.

108 Bridbury, *Economic Growth*, pp. 58–62.

109 Rigby, *Grimsby*, p. 111. For Scotland, see nn. 89 and 90.

110 W. H. Stevenson, *Royal Charters Granted to the Burgesses of Nottingham, AD 1155–1712* (London, 1890), pp. 63–7; *CCh.R 1427–1516*, p. 165; G. H. Martin, ed., *The Royal Charters of Grantham, 1463–1688* (Leicester, 1963), p. 31; *CPR 1441–6*, p. 181.

(1524). At Lynn, the royal charter of 1524 totally swept away the popular element introduced in the early fifteenth century. In future, the town was to be ruled by the mayor, twelve aldermen and eighteen councillors. The eighteen were chosen by the mayor and twelve, and could be removed at will; the twelve were to serve for life. The initial members of the twelve were nominated by the crown; thereafter they were to be selected by the eighteen, who were also to elect a mayor annually from the ranks of the twelve aldermen.[111] In Scotland, parliament gave outgoing town councils the power to choose their own replacements in 1469.[112] Even if we do not choose to describe such changes as representing a trend towards increased 'oligarchy', there seems little doubt that the late medieval period saw a shift from informal plutocracy towards more explicitly exclusive forms of town government which tended to close off even the limited forms of popular participation which had once existed – which is certainly not to say either that towns had once been popular democracies or that all traces of popular influence were eradicated.[113]

Why was this trend dominant in late medieval towns? First, this was a period which witnessed a general growth of oligarchy from the village community to the cathedral cloister.[114] Secondly, less 'democratic' forms of government may, as at Colchester in 1430 and at Leicester, Northampton and York in 1489, have been a response from above to a fear of popular disorder.[115] In Scotland, the 1487 act which attempted to end disorder by restricting the electors to 'the best and worthiest' of the town was introduced mainly in response to disputes in Aberdeen although, ironically, it was ignored there for over a century.[116] Popular protests could easily be dismissed as 'unlawful' by town rulers who had their own sanctions against those who did not accept 'aristocratic' town government. A day in the borough gaol was enough to end the protests of John Astyn of Grimsby who in 1389 refused to pay his assessment for borough taxation and claimed that he would not be ruled by the mayor but only by his 'fellows and equals'.[117]

Thirdly, royal intervention may also have been a force for more 'oligarchic' government. In both Scotland and England, the central government seems to have assumed that town government based on 'descending' power was desirable and that restrictions on the popular voice in elections should be encouraged.

[111] Tait, *Medieval English Borough*, pp. 321, 330–3; *HMC*, 11th Report, App. part III, pp. 206–7.

[112] T. Thomson and C. Innes, eds., *The Acts of the Parliaments of Scotland* (Edinburgh, 1814–75), vol. II p. 95.

[113] Hammer, 'Anatomy of an oligarchy', 5, 10–11.

[114] C. Dyer, 'The English village community and its decline', *J of British Studies*, 33 (1994), 428; T. N. Cooper, 'Oligarchy and conflict: Lichfield Cathedral clergy in the early sixteenth century', *Midland History*, 19 (1994), 54–5.

[115] Miller, 'York', p. 83; *Rotuli Parliamentorum*, VI, p. 432; Britnell, *Growth and Decline*, p. 220.

[116] Lynch, 'Towns and townspeople', p. 174.

[117] Lincolnshire AO, L1/1/1/1 Council Minutes, ff. 2v, 40, 81v; South Humberside Area RO, 1/100 Grimsby Court Rolls, Tuesday after St Lucy, 13 Richard II. See also Dickinson, ed., *Early Records of Aberdeen*, p. 217; Marwick, ed., *Extracts from Edinburgh Records*, p. 86.

Town rulers threatened by popular movements tended to be backed by the crown, whose main concern was the defence of 'order' rather than the resolution of the issues which had given rise to disorder in the first place.[118] Royal charters of the later middle ages displayed a growing interest in the detail of town government, often specifying the officers a community might choose.[119] In England, the royal chancery was a force for the diffusion of methods of government which, as in the case of county status (see above, p. 298) had originally been devised in response to some local problem, although it should be stressed that charters were frequently responses to local petitions and initiatives.[120] Fourthly, town rulers emulated each other in the development of more exclusive forms of government, particularly in the appointment of aldermen for life, an innovation for which London was a particularly influential model.[121]

Finally, whilst economic trends, particularly the shortage of tenants and labourers, tended to favour the success of popular struggles in the countryside,[122] they may have worked against the success of urban popular movements. On the one hand, urban prosperity could result in the growth of oligarchy, as in early fifteenth-century Colchester and late fifteenth-century and early sixteenth-century Exeter where the polarisation of wealth associated with the expansion of the cloth trade saw town government becoming increasingly closed and subject to the control of the wealthy.[123] Yet, paradoxically, economic trends in those towns which suffered from a decline in absolute levels of trade and population and from a shortage of wealthier citizens could also lead to a growth of oligarchy. Decline in trade and population was accompanied by a fall in rents, freemen's entry fines, tolls from trade and mill-fees, and consequent problems in balancing municipal budgets, problems which resulted more from a decline in income than from a proliferation of officers or rising expenditure.[124] Such difficulties led to a search for new forms of income, such as requiring men to pay to be exempt from offices to which they would never expect to be appointed

[118] Wright, 'The relations', pp. 45, 60; Palliser, *Tudor York*, pp. 68–9.

[119] See, for instance, Chester City RO, Charters, CH32, or the Selkirk charter of 1540 which gave the town the right to elect a provost annually (Thomson, *et al.*, *Registrum Magni Sigilli Regum Scottorum*, III, no. 2207).

[120] P. Clark and P. Slack, 'Introduction', in P. Clark and P. Slack, eds., *Crisis and Order in English Towns, 1500–1700* (London, 1972), pp. 22, 46 n. 69; Weinbaum, *Incorporation*, chs. 4, 5; *CCh.R 1427–1516*, pp. 10–11; Martin, ed., *Grantham*, pp. 29–47; Dobson, 'The crown, the charter and the city, 1396–1464', pp. 39–40.

[121] R. R. Sharpe, ed., *Calendar of the Letter-Books of the City of London: Letter Book 'H'* (London, 1907), pp. 409–10.

[122] Rigby, *English Society*, pp. 80–7, 124–34.

[123] Kowaleski, *Exeter*, p. 119; Britnell, *Growth and Decline*, pp. 222–7; Carr, 'The problem of urban patriciates', 120, 134–5.

[124] Lincolnshire AO, L1/1/1/1 Council Minutes, ff. 22v, 33, 33v, 37, 44; Britnell, *Growth and Decline*, pp. 228–9; Rigby, *Grimsby*, pp. 129–36; R. B. Dobson, ed., *York City Chamberlain's Account Rolls, 1396–1500* (Surtees Society, 192, 1980 for 1978–9), p. xxxi; C. Platt, *The English Medieval Town* (London, 1976), pp. 146–7.

in the first place, and encouraged boroughs to cut civic costs, for instance by allowing feudal magnates to appoint and pay the expenses of borough MPs.[125] They may also have led to a growth of more exclusive forms of government as part of a conscious attempt to attract and commit the richer townsmen to participation in town government. After all, although civic office offered power, status and, in some cases, even the possibility of financial profit,[126] it was also time-consuming and potentially costly. The 'poverty of the commonalty' of towns such as Colchester and Grimsby meant that officers often paid the costs of office out of their own pocket with repayment coming perhaps years later, if at all. The late medieval period thus saw not just a growth of the power of town rulers but also an increasing emphasis on the dignity of municipal office and the pomp and ceremonial of town government, as at York where the mayor became 'my lord mayor' and processed preceded by his sergeant carrying the civic sword and mace.[127]

In theory, craft guilds, which proliferated in the late fourteenth and fifteenth centuries, might have been a force to oppose this trend towards more exclusive forms of town government, as at York where representatives of the guilds on the city's common council provided at least some counter to the rule of the mercantile elite.[128] Nevertheless, in general, craft guilds (which anyway were by no means universal in English or Scottish towns) were strictly controlled by the civic authorities. Unlike continental towns, craft representation was very much the exception on British town councils.[129] Thus, neither the urban struggles for independence from monastic overlords nor those which sought to make self-governing towns more 'democratic' were to have much success in the later middle ages. Popular unrest may well have been as inevitable in medieval towns as it was in the countryside, but its achievements were far less significant than the contemporary peasant struggles which helped put an end to serfdom.

[125] J. I. Kermode, 'Urban decline? The flight from office in late medieval York', *Ec.HR*, 2nd series, 35 (1982), 186, 195–6; J. S. Roskell, *The Commons in the Parliament of 1422* (Manchester, 1954), ch. 7; Shaw, *Wells*, p. 53; P. Jalland, 'The "revolution" in northern borough representation in mid-fifteenth century England', *NHist*, 11 (1975), 27–51.

[126] Kowaleski, *Exeter*, pp. 104–5.

[127] South Humberside Area RO, 1/102/1 Mayor's Court Book, f. 39v, 40v; Britnell, *Growth and Decline*, pp. 223–35; Palliser, 'The birth of York's civic liberties, *c.* 1200–1354', p. 89; Erskine, 'Leicester', p. 27; Shaw, *Wells*, pp. 201–2.

[128] Harris, *Coventry Leet Book*, part II, pp. 518–19; Kermode, 'Obvious observations', p. 101.

[129] Swanson, *Artisans*, pp. 110–12, 116; H. Swanson, 'The illusion of economic structure: craft guilds in late medieval English towns', *P&P*, 121 (1988), 30–1, 47; Chester City RO, Assembly Books, AB1, f. 64v; Lincolnshire AO, L1/1/1/1 Council Minutes, ff. 54, 54v; Shaw, *Wells*, pp. 94–5; Kowaleski, *Exeter*, pp. 93, 100–1; T. Smith, *English Gilds* (Early English Text Society, 40, 1870), pp. 299–312; A. S. Green, *Town Life in the Fifteenth Century* (London, 1894), vol. II, pp. 173–82; Lynch, *Edinburgh*, pp. 53–4, 63–4; Whyte, *Scotland*, p. 192; Lynch, 'Towns and townspeople', p. 183; H. Booton, 'The craftsmen of Aberdeen between 1400 and 1550' *Northern Scotland*, 13 (1993), 6–7; F. Rörig, *The Medieval Town* (London, 1967), p. 155.

· 14 ·

The economy of British towns 1300–1540

RICHARD BRITNELL

(i) DEMAND FOR URBAN GOODS AND SERVICES

THERE IS a striking contrast between any analysis of changing demand in the late middle ages and that of earlier centuries. Changes in the period 600–1300, at least at the level of generalisation attempted in Chapter 5, may be summarised with the broad statement that the rising income of landlords, the growth of rural demand and the expansion of long-distance trade were all favourable to the growth of urban incomes over long periods of time. For most of that long period the evidence is not good enough for any much more subtle refinement. No comparable simplicity is viable for the shorter and much better documented period from 1300 to 1540, and it is difficult to generalise about the performance of late medieval urban economies with any firm assurance.

As in the past, the urban households of landlords often contributed a large and distinctive part in the composition of demand affecting townsmen. This was not true only of the small episcopal or monastic towns where it is most obvious. One of the most striking instances is Westminster, where the royal Court with its associated institutions of government, together with Westminster Abbey, and the visitors to both, generated trade both in Westminster itself and in London nearby. Besides numerous manufacturing industries that could prosper in this context, the victualling trades conspicuously benefited. The court and the abbey generated an exceptional demand for meat and so created local employment in grazing and butchering.[1] Heavy dependence upon the presence of large households was the lot of many smaller towns. Oxford and Cambridge are outstanding instances of urban economies heavily reliant on landowning institutions in their midst,[2]

[1] G. Rosser, *Medieval Westminster, 1200–1540* (Oxford, 1989), pp. 138–41, 161.

[2] M. Rubin, *Charity and Community in Medieval Cambridge* (Cambridge, 1987), pp. 35–6; J. Cooper, 'Medieval Oxford', in *VCH*, Oxfordshire, IV, p. 36.

and there are numerous examples of similarly dependent episcopal and monastic towns. From all over their diocese the canons and vicars choral of Wells drew income that they spent in maintaining their individual households, and this body of 200 or so clerical consumers, together with pilgrims to the cathedral, was a major support for the city's lay population, which was about 1,800 in 1377 and about 1,300 in 1524.[3] In Durham many incomes derived from serving and supplying the bishop and the priory in a population whose size was similar to that of Wells, and the occupational structure of the town reflected the particular characteristics of such demand.[4] Local centres of English royal government brought advantages to particular towns, like Ludlow, where the Council of the Marches had its headquarters from 1473 to 1483 and again after 1493, and Carmarthen, which was the centre of royal judicial and financial administration in Carmarthenshire and Cardiganshire.[5]

By implication, in some towns changes in the spending of large households contributed to changes in the level of employment. Between 1300 and 1540 few periods can be unambiguously described as years of rising real income for the greater landlords, though the income of the crown rose considerably from the 1470s. Perhaps the period of economic recovery in the third quarter of the fourteenth century is the most likely to have seen widespread improvements in the expenditure of large households, though much of this increase represented no more than the partial recovery of levels enjoyed earlier in the century. Some periods, by contrast, were so generally unfavourable to landlords that they reinforced economic decline, as in the years *c.* 1400–70.[6] Even Westminster suffered losses of population in the middle of the fifteenth century and a marked economic recession, partly as a result of the reduction of royal expenditure and the movement of the Court to Coventry in the years 1456–60, though it enjoyed exceptional development from the 1460s with the return of government and the subsequent growth of the royal household and administration.[7]

The countryside was incapable of creating a stimulus to urban development in this period comparable to that of the preceding period of equal length. The contraction of rural population during the fourteenth century, and to some extent during the fifteenth, had complex implications for the composition of trade. It had an adverse effect upon demand for cheaper, basic manufactures that had depended upon spending by the relatively poor – such as the cheapest types of clothing. However, writers of the later fourteenth and early fifteenth centuries

[3] D. G. Shaw, *The Creation of a Community* (Oxford, 1993), pp. 46–7, 66–9.

[4] M. Bonney, *Lordship and the Urban Community* (Cambridge, 1990), pp. 35, 156–9, 170–1, 233.

[5] M. Faraday, *Ludlow, 1085–1660: A Social, Economic and Political History* (Chichester, 1991), p. 96; R. A. Griffiths, *Conquerors and Conquered in Medieval Wales* (New York and Stroud, 1994), p. 184.

[6] C. Dyer, *Standards of Living in the Later Middle Ages* (Cambridge, 1989), p. 108.

[7] Rosser, *Medieval Westminster*, pp. 40, 74–92, 171–3; R. A. Griffiths, *The Reign of King Henry VI* (London, 1981), p. 772.

aver that ploughmen were dressing themselves up in clothes of better quality.[8] This observation itself suggests the possibility that rural demand for cloths of higher quality, and other items of finery, had risen; some of this would benefit urban crafts at the expense of rural homespun, and contribute to the rapid development of urban textile industries after 1349. If the new favoured fabrics were the product of crafts in particular towns or regions, this improvement of rural standards of living could have contributed directly to the superior prosperity of some textile towns such as those of Suffolk and Essex. Changes in rural demand cannot be expected to have affected all towns in the same way.

Throughout the fifteenth century there is growing evidence of smaller marketing centres that managed to improve their standing in their local rural economy, often at the expense of older markets nearby. In some cases this success may be attributable to changes in preferred trade routes. Many of the more successful towns of the period, like Knowle (War.),[9] Loughborough (Leics.),[10] Chelmsford (Essex)[11] and Buntingford (Herts.),[12] were on long-established main roads, and owed much of their good fortune to exploiting their position. Other more prosperous towns owed their success to new enterprise in the provision of specialised goods or services. Such, for example, was the case with Thaxted (Essex) and its cutlery. In most cases, unfortunately, the chronology of these towns' development is imperfectly known; reliable information on this point would make an invaluable contribution to the study of fluctuations in internal trade.

Rural standards of living, and the aggregate level of rural demand for goods and services, were not improving all through the period. Much of the gain was associated with the generation or two after the Black Death, and even in this period activity in smaller market towns was often more depressed by the decline in rural population and high raw material prices than stimulated by increases in average spending per head.[13] From about 1420 onwards average improvements in living standards were less marked than earlier, and there were long periods of rural depression when expenditure on manufactures declined. Local studies have frequently demonstrated the vulnerability of minor towns to the problems of the rural economy that surrounded them. Even York and Newcastle-upon-Tyne seem to have suffered from the northern agrarian crisis of 1438–40, so it is not surprising to find evidence that the commerce of local marketing centres like Barnard Castle (Durham) and Richmond (Yorks.) was severely disrupted.[14] In the great

[8] J. Hatcher, 'England in the aftermath of the Black Death', *P&P*, 144 (1994), 16–18, 29–30.
[9] C. Dyer, *Everyday Life in Medieval England* (London, 1994), pp. 294–5.
[10] D. Postles, 'An English small town in the later middle ages: Loughborough', *UH*, 20 (1993), 7–29.
[11] H. Grieve, *The Sleepers and the Shadows* (Chelmsford, 1988), pp. 51–7, 72–5, 78.
[12] M. Bailey, 'A tale of two towns: Buntingford and Standon in the later middle ages', *JMed.H*, 19 (1993), 351–71.
[13] R. H. Britnell, 'The Black Death in English towns', *UH*, 21 (1994), 210.
[14] A. J. Pollard, 'The north-eastern economy and the agrarian crisis of 1438–40', *NHist.*, 25 (1989), 102–3.

depression of the mid-fifteenth century, both large and small towns were universally affected adversely, even those not strongly dependent upon the export of goods abroad.[15] Buntingford (Herts.), having grown up in the later fourteenth century at the expense of older markets at Chipping and Standon, may have experienced a phase of stagnation between 1440 and 1490.[16] Later in the period market towns like Northallerton (Yorks.) in the midst of stagnant rural economies had no basis for expansion or rising prosperity under the early Tudors.[17]

The experiences of boroughs in Wales were perhaps peculiarly diverse because of the strong element of political and military chance that had always shaped their history, and because of their late start of many sound projects. Some – like Caernarfon and Brecon – had exceptional opportunities to go on growing into their local economies into the fourteenth and fifteenth centuries. But even in Wales, urban growth was far from being a general expectation supported by rising economic trends. Many boroughs suffered severely during the course of Owain Glyndŵr's rebellion because they were so closely identified with English interests. This was by no means the only reason for lost rents and depressed trade in the fifteenth century, though, since boroughs in Wales, including the principal ports, often suffered from the same adverse demand characteristics as the English and Scottish. At Newport (Mon.), for example, the difficulties were very long term, since trade showed continuing signs of deterioration throughout the fifteenth century. Table 14.1 shows three indicators of this, the sums levied on fines for breach of the assize of ale, the sums raised on market tolls, and the sums raised on *chenser* fines, which were levied on non-burgesses for the right to trade in the borough. In Cardiff at the end of the fifteenth century, Glyndŵr's rebellion was still being blamed for waste property, but after nearly a hundred years such dereliction testified not so much to the destructiveness of Glyndŵr as to the lack of investment opportunities in the town during the intervening years.[18]

Of all the elements in the demand for urban goods and services, by far the most variable between towns, and the most volatile over time, was demand over long distances, notably the demand for exports. In the course of the fourteenth century the export performance of English urban manufactures cloth improved very considerably, particularly from about the time of the outbreak of the Hundred Years War in 1337.[19] This was chiefly because of a steeply increased

[15] J. Hatcher, 'The great slump of the mid-fifteenth century', in R. H. Britnell and J. Hatcher, eds., *Progress and Problems in Medieval England* (Cambridge, 1996), pp. 266–70.

[16] Bailey, 'Tale of two towns', 365, 368.

[17] C. M. Newman, *Late Medieval Northallerton* (Stamford, 1999), pp. 67–93.

[18] Below, pp. 702–4; Griffiths, *Conquerors and Conquered*, p. 349; R. R. Davies, 'Brecon', and K. Williams-Jones, 'Caernarvon', in R. A. Griffiths, ed., *Boroughs of Mediaeval Wales* (Cardiff, 1978), pp. 64, 68, 84–5.

[19] E. M. Carus-Wilson, *Medieval Merchant Venturers*, 2nd edn (London, 1967), pp. 239–64.

Table 14.1 *Trade-related revenues from the borough of Newport (Mon.) 1402–1522*

	Assize of ale £ s. d.	Tolls £ s. d.	*Chenser* fines £ s. d.
1401–2	9 10 9	2 10 0	11 16 6
1434–5	7 1 4½	1 8 0½	3 7 0
1447–8	4 17 1½	2 0 4	2 18 1
1451–2	4 17 1½	8 0	1 18 9
1456–7	7 11 6	6 8	3 0 0
1497–8	18 6½	5 0	1 15 0
1503–4	1 0 0	13 4	5 16 8
1521–2	18 0	13 4	5 16 8

Source: T. B. Pugh, ed., *The Marcher Lordships of South Wales, 1415–1536: Select Documents* (Board of Celtic Studies, University of Wales, History and Law Series, 20, Cardiff, 1963), p. 171.

duty on English wool exports, aimed at financing the war, that had the effect of protecting English manufactures. A few cloth towns – Salisbury, York, Norwich, Coventry, Colchester – benefited considerably from overseas demand during the later fourteenth century.[20] A number of smaller cloth towns shared in this growth, like Wells.[21] So did some port towns, like Grimsby, where the second half of the fourteenth century has been described as an 'Indian summer'.[22]

However, contrary to the impression sometimes given that the fifteenth and early sixteenth centuries experienced a continuous expansion of cloth exports, the expansive phase of the later fourteenth century ended in the early 1390s, and from then on there was no sustained upward movement of exports for eighty years. Some towns never regained their late fourteenth-century prosperity.[23] Former centres of entrepreneurial triumph, and most spectacularly Coventry, were amongst the most depressed towns of the early sixteenth century.[24] Some towns, most notably Colchester, benefited from a temporary surge in exports to higher levels between 1437 to 1448 which is directly attributable to increasing purchases by Hanseatic merchants in the South-East of England.[25] But that boom fell away at the end of the 1440s, and there was nothing like it again until the 1470s inaugurated a renewed expansion of cloth exports. There were, in fact,

[20] R. H. Britnell, *The Commercialisation of English Society, 1000–1500*, 2nd edn (Manchester, 1996), p. 170. [21] Shaw, *Wells*, pp. 77–8.

[22] S. H. Rigby, *Medieval Grimsby* (Hull, 1993), pp. 114–15. [23] E.g. Wells: Shaw, *Wells*, pp. 78–80.

[24] C. Phythian-Adams, *Desolation of a City* (Cambridge, 1979), pp. 33–67, 281–90.

[25] R. H. Britnell, *Growth and Decline in Colchester, 1300–1525* (Cambridge, 1986), pp. 169–76.

two long periods of deep recession and unemployment in the English textile industries of the fifteenth century, one from 1403 to 1421 and the next from 1449 to the early 1470s. These were also periods of recession in the port towns. Grimsby, for example, suffered acutely from the mid-fifteenth-century slump, and remained depressed well into the sixteenth century; its population in 1540 was perhaps less than half what it had been in 1377.[26] Amongst the Welsh ports, both Cardiff and Aberystwyth seem to have been adversely affected by fifteenth-century economic trends.[27]

The course of Scottish overseas trade was even less encouraging to urban development than that of England. The volume of shipments began to contract after the Wars of Independence, and showed no signs of recovery throughout the period apart from temporary interludes in the 1370s, the 1420s and the late 1530s. The 1450s were particularly depressed. As in England, though to a lesser extent, the prolonged contraction of wool exports was partly compensated by some expansion of cloth exports to Brittany and southern France, especially through Edinburgh, though this development was seriously interrupted in the early fifteenth century, as in England, particularly during the long and acute recession from *c.* 1435 to the 1460s. A significant cloth industry is attested during the fifteenth century at Wigtown in the west, though the principal centres of manufacture were further east, and most of Scotland's cloth exports paid customs in Edinburgh.[28] Wool, which was used for the 'light cloths' of the Netherlands, nevertheless remained Scotland's most important export throughout the period.[29]

Both in England and Scotland the narrowing of horizons for overseas trade in the fifteenth century was associated with its concentration in particular ports. In England the principal beneficiary was undoubtedly London, which was increasing its advantages as a centre of commercial information and credit as well as commanding a powerful trade lobby for protecting London mercantile interests. London led the recovery from the 1470s at the expense of almost all other east coast ports and many of the southern ones.[30] Even Southampton and Exeter, which shared in the late fifteenth-century revival of trade, were showing the

[26] Rigby, *Grimsby*, pp. 126–7. [27] Griffiths, *Conquerors and Conquered*, pp. 317, 349.

[28] M. Lynch and A. Stevenson, 'Overseas trade: the middle ages to the sixteenth century', in P. G. B. McNeill and H. L. MacQueen, eds., *Atlas of Scottish History to 1707* (Edinburgh, 1996), p. 255; M. Lynch, 'The social and economic structures of the larger towns, 1450–1600', in M. Lynch, M. Spearman and G. Stell, eds., *The Scottish Medieval Town* (Edinburgh, 1988), p. 272.

[29] I. S. W. Blanchard, *Northern Wools and Netherlands Markets at the Close of the Middle Ages*, University of Edinburgh, Studies in Economic and Social History, Discussion Paper, 92–3 (Edinburgh, 1992), p. 5; D. Ditchburn, 'Trade with northern Europe, 1297–1540', in Lynch, Spearman and Stell, eds., *The Scottish Medieval Town*, p. 167.

[30] J. L. Bolton, *The Medieval English Economy, 1150–1500* (London, 1980), pp. 255, 315–16, 319; P. Nightingale, 'The growth of London in the medieval English economy', in Britnell and Hatcher, eds., *Progress and Problems*, pp. 103–5.

adverse effects of London's competition by the 1520s. In Scotland a comparable shift occurred away from the earlier regional entrepôts of Aberdeen, Dundee and Berwick towards Edinburgh, which had established itself as an economic capital by 1500, with a wider range of industrial and commercial enterprises than any other Scottish town.[31] After a severe contraction in its trade during the earlier fifteenth century, Edinburgh achieved some recovery in the second half at a time when smaller ports – Dundee, Inverkeithing, Linlithgow, Crail – remained in the doldrums. Away from London and Edinburgh the most independent area of recovery was round the Irish Sea, where Chester and the Clyde ports were expanding their trade in the late fifteenth and early sixteenth centuries, but the total volume of trade in this region was as yet small in relation to that of the east coast and the south.[32]

It is noteworthy that in England the towns that sustained commercial expansion from the 1460s onwards were not those that had participated in the recovery of the later fourteenth. In the intervening period there had been profound changes in the English textile industry, chiefly as a result of the growing commercial hegemony of London. The early Tudor export boom characteristically involved small towns – it begs many questions to call this industry 'rural' – such as Crediton, Tiverton and Totnes in Devon, Stroud and Minchinhampton in Gloucestershire, Westbury, Trowbridge, Bradford-on-Avon and Devizes in Wiltshire, Lavenham in Suffolk, Wakefield, Halifax, Leeds and Bradford in Yorkshire and Kendal in Westmorland.[33] Welsh friezes from the widely scattered Welsh cloth industry were marketed at Ruthin and Oswestry, or carried outside Wales to be sold at Shrewsbury, Ludlow or Bristol.[34]

The grouping of textile towns in particular regions of England implies that there were advantages to be gained from local networks of mercantile organisation and credit. The analysis of such networks has a long way to go, but a few observations can be made with some confidence. In the first place, market networks were relevant primarily to industries whose products entered into international and long-distance trade, notably woollen cloth; they were the creation of mercantile enterprise. Secondly, the existence of interlinked centres of manufacture, as in Devon, Wiltshire, Gloucestershire and Suffolk, did not imply a

[31] Lynch and Stevenson, 'Overseas trade', pp. 242–3, 246, 250.

[32] J. Kermode, 'The trade of late medieval Chester, 1500–1550', in Britnell and Hatcher, eds., *Progress and Problems*, pp. 286–307; A. Stevenson, 'Trade with the south, 1070–1513', in Lynch, Spearman and Stell, eds., *The Scottish Medieval Town*, p. 197.

[33] Bolton, *Medieval English Economy*, pp. 187–92; E. M. Carus-Wilson, 'The woollen industry before 1550', *VCH*, Wiltshire, IV, pp. 133–47; D. Dymond and A. Betterton, *Lavenham: 700 Years of Textile Making* (Woodbridge 1982), pp. 8, 24–7; P. J. P. Goldberg, *Women, Work and Life Cycle in a Medieval Economy* (Oxford, 1992), pp. 75–6; A. J. Winchester, *Landscape and Society in Medieval Cumbria* (Edinburgh, 1987), pp. 118, 128.

[34] G. Williams, *Recovery, Reorientation and Reformation: Wales, c. 1415–1642* (Oxford, 1987), pp. 73, 77.

pattern of provincial autarchy. On the contrary, the trade of these regions often depended heavily on commercial connections through London.[35] Thirdly, the presence of strong regional specialisation was often associated with a localised diffusion of exceptional wealth. It seems likely that the development of Edinburgh in the fifteenth century was associated with a similar reconstruction of trade networks and relocation of enterprise in Scottish industry given that by 1500–5 the city commanded 60 per cent of Scotland's overseas trade (measured by its share of customs receipts).[36]

There is room for discussion here about the relationship between towns and their regions. Some accounts of the late middle ages see urban growth in this period as a response to opportunities for specialisation in supplying distant markets, and would consequently imply that any broader local development was a derived phenomenon, or at least an independent contingency. As in more modern times, high commercial profits in one major branch of commerce could stimulate local investment in other local branches of economic activity.[37] However, there are also grounds for supposing that the character of a town's hinterland was so essential to sustained urban growth that the state of the regional economy should be assigned primary importance.[38] In this interpretation of the period, urban growth, together with the formation of market networks supplying distant markets, was most likely to occur in regions of broadly based economic development. Indeed, the development of industry in the smaller towns of Yorkshire, Suffolk and the West Country may have benefited from the switch of agrarian wealth into industrial investment.[39] The cost advantages of operating outside self-governing boroughs will be discussed later.

If both exports and home demand increased, as in the third quarter of the fourteenth century, many towns expanded in output and population. By contrast, if both domestic demand and foreign demand slumped independently, as in the third quarter of the fifteenth century, there was likely to be a profound and general urban recession. However, because of the relatively slight dependence of the economy upon overseas trade, there was no close relationship between movements of internal and overseas demand, and this is one of the reasons why the urban history of the later middle ages is complex. A town might expand as a result of increasing exports, like Colchester between 1398 and 1412, even in a period of recession in the local rural economy. Periods of strong growth were, in fact, an exceptional good fortune.[40] Many towns had good patches,

[35] M. K. James, *Studies in the Medieval Wine Trade*, ed. E. M. Veale (Oxford, 1971), pp. 204–6; A. E. Welsford, *John Greenway, 1460–1529, Merchant of Tiverton and London: A Devon Worthy* (Tiverton, 1984). [36] Stevenson, 'Trade with the south', p. 197.

[37] Britnell, *Growth and Decline*, pp. 157–8, 212–17, 266–7.

[38] M. Kowaleski, *Local Markets and Regional Trade in Medieval Exeter* (Cambridge, 1995), pp. 327–30.

[39] H. Swanson, *Medieval Artisans* (Oxford, 1989), pp. 143–4, 175.

[40] Britnell, *Growth and Decline*, pp. 69, 90–2, 152–8, 266.

especially in the later fourteenth century, but most were unable to expand their output through most of the period. Many, too, particularly from about 1400, experienced very protracted periods of contracting demand, and it is towns such as these that supply the evidence upon which the case for urban decay in the late middle ages is principally founded.[41]

(ii) THE SUPPLY OF LABOUR AND MATERIALS

As a result of competition between employers for a smaller number of available workers, labour became more expensive throughout the economy, particularly between 1349 and 1410.[42] Rising wages must have placed constraints on the development of export industries after 1349, though there is no reason to suppose that they rose any faster in England than on the continent of Europe. Labour costs characteristically constituted a large share in the selling price of manufactured goods; in Colchester, for example, labour accounted for about half the production costs of a middle-grade woollen textile around 1390.[43] However, in periods of growing cloth exports in the later fourteenth century, commercial profits were sufficiently high in many towns for urban employers to be in the vanguard in bidding labour costs up in order to attract labour from elsewhere. The bailiffs of Colchester were in severe trouble in 1352 for failing to collect the enormous fines, totalling £84 7s. 7d., imposed on townsmen for offences against the Statute of Labourers.[44] There were many reasons for villagers to accept employment opportunities in the towns – to escape from serfdom and conflicts with landlords, to evade the restraints of the Statute of Labourers, or simply because they wanted more interesting lives. During this period, too, the needs of urban employers were to some extent met by widening the labour force to include more women.[45] Given these possibilities of relocating labour to the advantage of urban employers, and the absence of any crises that cannot be explained as crises of demand, there is no reason to believe that scarcities of labour ever blocked urban growth, though at times in the later fourteenth century the need to offer higher wages probably damped it down. For reasons which have already been discussed, the demand for urban labour was much more vigorous in towns experiencing export-led growth than in others, even during the later fourteenth century.

During the fifteenth century, when there were lengthy periods of slackening demand and urban unemployment, migration to towns lost much of its

[41] For a recent survey of the large literature on this topic, see A. Dyer, *Decline and Growth in English Towns 1400–1640* (Basingstoke, 1991).

[42] D. L. Farmer, 'Prices and wages, 1350–1500', in E. Miller, ed., *Ag.HEW*, III (Cambridge, 1991), pp. 520–4.

[43] Britnell, *Growth and Decline*, pp. 61–2.

[44] L. R. Poos, 'The social context of Statute of Labourers enforcement', *Law and History Review*, I (1983), 43–4.

[45] Goldberg, *Women, Work and Life Cycle*, pp. 101, 336–7.

attraction.[46] The growth in textiles manufacture from the 1470s through to the 1540s was a very different phenomenon from the expansion of the later fourteenth century. It did not take place against a general background of labour scarcities or rising labour costs.[47] By taking up the slack in small-town labour markets, and probably attracting labour from decaying textile towns, textile entrepreneurs were able to achieve substantial increases in output without placing any strain upon labour supplies. The early Tudor period is associated in some towns with demands for job protection by workers, and a closing of ranks by male workers to reduce the opportunities available to women.[48]

As a result of the decline in British population between 1300 and 1540 the ratio of people to land altered. Market relationships were sufficiently well established for this change in the availability of resources to be rapidly converted into a change in relative prices, despite reactionary efforts on the part of landlords and governments to protect the status quo. Land and land-related resources generally became relatively cheaper. The decline in rural populations freed resources that could now be used for supplying raw materials to the towns. The urban advantage here was not so apparent in the supply of cereals – wheat, barley and oats in particular were required in large quantities for the feeding of people and horses – because the greater availability of land was offset by higher labour costs. However, there were very significant benefits for the supply of pastoral products – meat, hides and wool – whose production costs were much less affected by rising labour costs, and this is apparent from the movement of relative prices during the 1350s and 1360s.[49] There were periods of the later fourteenth and fifteenth centuries when, for want of any more lucrative way of exploiting their lands, landlords and tenants alike maintained and even expanded their sheep flocks at very low levels of profitability.[50]

One effect of falling urban populations was to reduce the dependence of many towns upon external sources of supply for grain, vegetables and fruit. Even at the height of urban demographic development around 1300 many townsmen cultivated fields. In those towns that contracted during the fourteenth and fifteenth centuries such fields could satisfy a larger part of demand, and waste spaces within towns were converted to gardens and orchards.[51] In this particular there was a move towards self-sufficiency in the mid-fifteenth century, and it probably contributed to the decline of numerous smaller market centres.[52] On

[46] Britnell, *Growth and Decline*, pp. 203–5; Swanson, *Artisans*, pp. 173–4.

[47] Farmer, 'Prices and wages', pp. 523–4.

[48] Goldberg, *Women, Work and Life Cycle*, pp. 155, 337.

[49] D. L. Farmer, 'Prices and wages, 1350–1500', in Miller, ed., *Ag.HEW*, III, pp. 502, 512.

[50] T. H. Lloyd, *The Movement of Wool Prices in Medieval England*, Ec.HR Supplement 6 (Cambridge, 1973), pp. 24–8.

[51] D. Keene, *Survey of Medieval Winchester* (Winchester Studies, 2, Oxford, 1985), vol. I, pp. 153–5.

[52] Britnell, *Commercialisation*, pp. 157–60.

the other hand the growing demand for meat, wool and a wider variety of manufactures created more dependence than before on products drawn from afar.[53] In some cases goods consumed by townsmen were coming longer distances than those characteristic of urban supply before 1300.[54]

(iii) MONEY AND CREDIT

The money stock in circulation in later medieval England continued to be made up exclusively of coined money. Not until after 1540 did paper claims to credit begin to be used as a substitute for coin. This means that the volume of currency was governed by levels of mint output, on the one hand, and the disappearance of currency from circulation on the other. Though mint output for the period 1300–1540 can be calculated with a fair degree of confidence from surviving mint records, there is unfortunately no way of assessing how much coin was exported or melted down, and so estimates of currency in circulation depend on the evidence of recoinages. On such evidence it may be argued that the period began with an exceptionally large currency in circulation, that the money stock contracted sharply in the course of the period but then expanded rapidly towards its end. Britain clearly shared the experience of acute bullion famine which characterised much of the European scene in the fifteenth century.[55] The English evidence is summarised in Table 14.2. The evidence here confirms the deflationary character of economic change during much of the later middle ages. Though there are signs of recovery in the money supply after the low point of the early fifteenth century, the implications of this are not well understood. A great part of the increased monetisation of the later fifteenth century was in gold coinage whose significance for most local trade was slight.[56]

Scottish monetary history presents even more problems than the English in the period 1300–1540 for want of adequate mint records. Mint output remained very much smaller than that of the English mints, partly because of the smaller size of the economy, and partly because Scottish inland transactions continued to depend heavily on imported coins, especially from England. It seems likely that Scottish minting experienced a contraction during the fourteenth century analogous to that of England, and that there was increasing activity in the early sixteenth century, as in England, but such finer detail as the archaeological and

[53] G. G. Astill, 'Economic change in later medieval England: an archaeological review', in T. H. Aston, P. R. Coss, C. Dyer and J. Thirsk, eds., *Social Relations and Ideas* (Cambridge, 1983), pp. 226–30; C. Dyer, *Warwickshire Farming, 1349–c. 1520: Preparations for Agricultural Revolution* (Dugdale Society Occasional Paper, 27, 1981), p. 20.

[54] Britnell, *Growth and Decline*, pp. 246–9.

[55] J. Day, 'The great bullion famine of the fifteenth century', *P&P*, 79 (1978), 3–54; P. Spufford, *Money and its Use in Medieval Europe* (Cambridge, 1988), pp. 339–62.

[56] Spufford, *Money and its Use*, p. 370.

Table 14.2 *Estimates of money stock in circulation in England 1300–1546*

Year	Currency in circulation £m
1300	0.9
1311	1.1
1324	1.1
1350	0.5
1356	0.7
1470	0.9
1526	1.4
1546	1.5

Source: N. J. Mayhew, 'Money and prices in England from Henry II to Edward III', *Agricultural History Review*, 35 (1987), 125; N. J. Mayhew, 'Population, money supply and the velocity of circulation in England, 1300–1700', *Ec.H.R.*, 48 (1995), 244.

documentary evidence permits is inadequate for describing the course of change with quantitative precision.[57]

The use of credit expanded in those towns that developed a stronger commercial economy in the course of the fourteenth century, helped in part by the improved institutional infrastructure created during the century before.[58] However, the development of credit did not, and could not, offset contractions in the money supply. Such evidence as we have suggests that as the currency in circulation contracted so did the amount of credit that those with cash would advance. A study of credit in London between 1350 and 1440 concludes that credit expanded and contracted in direct relationship with changes in the quantity of money in circulation.[59] Dependence on credit, which was particularly striking in the cloth trade, implied a greater capacity for institutional structures and personal connections to influence entrepreneurial opportunities, and this was a strong point in London's competitiveness as a trading city during the fifteenth century. Its credit provisions grew more geared to international markets and more responsive to trade conditions, while those of the provinces remained

57 E. Gemmill and N. Mayhew, *Changing Values in Medieval Scotland* (Cambridge, 1995), pp. 140–2.

58 Britnell, *Growth and Decline*, pp. 98–100; Kowaleski, *Exeter*, p. 202.

59 P. Nightingale, 'Monetary contraction and mercantile credit in later medieval England', *Ec.HR*, 2nd series, 43 (1990), 560–75.

localised and institutionally more rigid.[60] The ability of Yorkshire merchants to compete with Londoners was undermined by the less advantageous credit networks upon which they were able to draw.[61] One of the most lasting consequences of the period of severe recession in the 1450s and 1460s was perhaps to starve out provincial towns from access to funding, and to consolidate the hold of Londoners over credit networks.[62]

(iv) URBAN EMPLOYMENTS AND CHANGES IN RANK SIZE

A general feature of urban economies to be observed is an increase in productivity that permitted urban standards of living to rise, as did those elsewhere. The main sources of increasing productivity related to features of urban change that have already been discussed. The prevailing scarcity of labour for much of the period made it possible for townsmen after 1349 to be more fully employed than their forebears of the thirteenth and early fourteenth centuries. Of course there were fluctuations in the level of trade, and involuntary unemployment remained a recurrent part of the later medieval scene. In years of commercial recession there were real problems which received expression in some of the popular discontent of the mid-fifteenth century.[63] Such discontent serves, however, to demonstrate how normal expectations had changed since the endemic high unemployment of the thirteenth century. The generally better opportunities of employment imply that the average productivity of the labour force was higher.

Table 14.3 illustrates the occupational structure of four towns in the later fifteenth century, as it appears from registers of new freemen and similar sources. Imperfect though this sort of evidence is, it corresponds to the pattern already observed from records of around 1300, suggesting that the provision of food and drink and the manufacture of cloth and clothing together still constituted over half the employment opportunities in these towns. The commercial sector was apparently slightly reduced from the earlier period, probably through the withdrawal of precariously small hucksters and the like from retail trade, and the manufacture of cloth and clothing was proportionately larger. But a broad similarity with the past concealed numerous changes in detail, particularly in the development of trades

[60] J. I. Kermode, 'Medieval indebtedness: the regions *versus* London', in N. Rogers, ed., *England in the Fifteenth Century* (Stamford, 1994), pp. 72–88.

[61] J. I. Kermode, 'Money and credit in the fifteenth century: some lessons from Yorkshire', *Business History Review*, 65 (1991), 475–501.

[62] J. Kermode, 'Merchants, overseas trade, and urban decline', *NHist.*, 23 (1987), 70–1; P. Nightingale, *A Medieval Mercantile Community* (New Haven and London, 1995), pp. 480–9.

[63] J. N. Hare, 'The Wiltshire rising of 1450: political and economic discontent in mid fifteenth century England', *SHist.*, 4 (1982), 16–19; I. M. W. Harvey, *Jack Cade's Rebellion of 1450* (Oxford, 1991), p. 17; M. Mate, 'The economic and social roots of medieval popular rebellion: Sussex in 1450–1451', *Ec.HR*, 45 (1992), 661–75.

Table 14.3 *Occupations of some citizens in York, Canterbury, Norwich and Chester in the later fifteenth century*

	York 1450–1509 % N=3,532	Norwich 1450–99 % N=1,448	Canterbury 1440–99 % N=504	Chester 1450–99 % N=153
Trade				
Food and drink	17	16	28	20
Other	12	10	9	16
Industry				
Textiles and clothing	24	31	28	24
Leather and leather goods	11	12	11	16
Metals	11	7	8	8
Other	6	9	11	12
Services				
Transport	4	5	0	1
Building	5	5	0	2
Other	10	6	5	2

Source: Goldberg, *Women, Work and Life Cycle*, pp. 60–1.

that enhanced labour productivity through developments in specialisation and skill. It was still normal for urban households to have a variety of sources of income, and total dependence upon a single trade was exceptional. The statutory requirement that artisans should confine themselves to a single occupation was weakly enforced, and it is difficult to find any large numbers of prosecutions under the statute.[64] Nevertheless, the growing proportion of townsmen who went through a lengthy apprenticeship and then attached themselves to craft guilds implies a world in which specialisation was more common than in the past. Certainly the Corpus Christi rituals of the fourteenth and fifteenth centuries, constructed as they were about craft institutions, imply that urban authorities perceived townsmen in occupational groupings.[65] This was encouraged in some cases by the growth of local specialisations and dependence on long-distance trade. In others it was encouraged by the wider diffusion of craft goods resulting from higher standards of living. Pin making, which Adam Smith publicised as an instance of advanced occupational specialisation in 1776, was becoming a more specialised craft in the later fourteenth century as a result of a growth of the market.[66] The leather industry developed new specialisations in response to the

[64] 37 Edward III, *c.* 6: *SR*, I, p. 379. [65] M. Rubin, *Corpus Christi* (Cambridge, 1991), pp. 261–3.
[66] C. Caple, 'The detection and definition of an industry: the English medieval and post-medieval pin industry', *Archaeological J*, 148 (1991), 241–55.

greater variety of demand for products made from hides and skins.[67] The development of skills was also fostered by occasional switching into products of higher quality whose production required more careful attention to training. In Colchester between 1415 and 1445 the cloth manufacturers deliberately raised the quality of their standard product in order to cope more satisfactorily with the changing characteristics of the market, and they simultaneously tightened up on apprenticeship rules.[68] Because of their concern for the development and maintenance of skills, later medieval urban administrations often put their weight behind the enforcement of guild regulations. Of course to some extent the regulating of crafts had a protectionist purpose, but it is unlikely to have protected slovenly workmanship since the maintenance of standards was a normal feature of guild ordinances throughout the period. In so far as textiles, pottery or metal wares were 'branded' goods they were known by the name of the town they came from – Colchester russets, Salisbury rays, Coventry blues, Norwich worsteds, Nottingham sculptures in alabaster, Thaxted knives – and only the policing of production standards by urban authorities could protect the reputation of such products against workmen trying to earn extra profits by palming off substandard goods on to dealers.

To some extent, too, but probably a small one, an increase in urban productivity was the result of technological change. In the textile industry the impact of mechanical fulling was probably greater after 1350 than before, partly because a severe decline in grain milling liberated good sites for fulling mills.[69] Of the 202 known fulling mills in medieval Wales, 130 are first recorded between 1350 and 1547.[70] The spread of the spinning wheel in urban industry was another feature of the period from the thirteenth century, though hand-spinning continued to be practised throughout the period. A number of new techniques of leather working can be identified from archaeological remains. It seems likely that technical change was occurring in innumerable minor ways throughout the period, especially in the more specialised urban crafts. However, the archaeological evidence does not allow much stress to be placed on it, and even when new practices are identifiable it is difficult to be confident that they represent productivity growth.[71]

As a result of these changes the average incomes of townsmen increased during the period, so that standards of living were higher in 1540 than in 1300. Because part of this increase in welfare was taken up in the form of improved nutrition, it was of some advantage to farming communities, but urban brewers,

[67] M. Kowaleski, 'Town and country in late medieval England: the hide and leather trade', in P. J. Corfield and D. Keene, eds., *Work in Towns, 850–1850* (Leicester, 1990), pp. 64–5.

[68] Britnell, *Growth and Decline*, pp. 163–8, 185–6.

[69] *Ibid.*, pp. 76, 157; Keene, *Survey*, I, pp. 306–7; Kowaleski, *Exeter*, p. 93.

[70] R. I. Jack, 'The cloth industry of medieval Wales', *Welsh History Review*, 10 (1980–1), 449.

[71] J. Schofield and A. Vince, *Medieval Towns* (London, 1994), pp. 112, 126.

bakers and butchers also benefited even in towns whose population was lower than it had been before the Black Death.[72] Improved living standards also led to increased average expenditure on consumer goods such as clothing, footwear, furnishing and other commodities applied by urban traders.[73] Such improvements in standards of living were not continuous throughout the period; probably the stimulus to urban economies from this source was strongest between 1350 and 1410.

Meanwhile, higher incomes also allowed townsmen to invest more in housing, household goods and other forms of movable wealth than they had done in the past.[74] Even in Winchester, the best documented example of a town whose population contracted in the later middle ages, the size of residential plots increased and houses were often built for the ostentatious display of private wealth and taste. The leading carpenters of the town in the fifteenth century called themselves architects.[75] An increase in average urban wealth is likely to have been very much steeper than the increase in average urban incomes because of the cumulative nature of wealth; even a static income generates steadily increasing levels of personal wealth if it is high enough to permit the continuing purchase of durable goods. This helps to explain why recorded levels of personal wealth were much higher in the English tax assessments of 1524 than in those of 1334, but also demonstrates why this evidence is a very unreliable guide to changes in income between those two years.

English tax records nevertheless show that the accumulation of urban wealth had not proceeded at any uniform rate. The contrasts of urban experience brought about by different commercial opportunities are matched by a considerable change in the rank order of towns in the course of the period under discussion. Table 14.4 shows the leading twenty towns in 1524, as measured by their taxable wealth, and compares this with their ranking in 1334. The contrasts are striking. Of the twenty, half had changed rank position by ten places or more, seven by twenty places or more and four by thirty places or more. All three components of external demand discussed above affected towns differently, but the most important for explaining these changes in urban rank was long-distance trade. The volume and composition of exports varied very considerably from town to town, and the course of overseas trade shaped their fortunes very differently. Because export demand was so important a stimulus to English urban development in this period, those towns with a strong performance in export markets improved their rank order over the period as a whole even in spite of the severe difficulties that most of them faced during prolonged periods of recession. Exeter, Colchester, Bury St Edmunds, Lavenham and Totnes could all attribute

[72] Kowaleski, *Exeter*, pp. 90, 92.

[73] Dyer, *Standards of Living*, pp. 199, 202, 207; Swanson, *Artisans*, p. 174.

[74] Astill, 'Economic change', pp. 236–9.

[75] Keene, *Survey*, I, pp. 143–7, 160, 172.

Table 14.4 *The twenty wealthiest English towns in 1524, with changes in ranking since 1334*

Rank in 1524	Town	Rank in 1334	Rank in 1524	Town	Rank in 1334
1	London	1	11	York	3
2	Norwich	6	12	Reading	40
3	Bristol	2	13	Colchester	53
4	Newcastle	4	14	Bury St Edmunds	26
5	Coventry	10	15	Lavenham	—
6	Exeter	28	16	Worcester	36
7	Salisbury	12	17	Maidstone	—
8	Lynn	11	18	Totnes	—
9	Ipswich	19	19	Gloucester	18
10	Canterbury	15	20	Yarmouth	7

Source: below, Appendixes 4 and 7.

the superior fortunes indicated in Table 14.4 to periods of industrial expansion in clothmaking. Some of the variation of experience amongst Scottish towns can be suggested from the evidence of overseas trade, which shows a very striking contrast over the fifteenth century between the relatively good fortune of Edinburgh and Aberdeen, and the striking deterioration of Cupar, Dundee, Haddington, Inverkeithing, Linlithgow and Perth.[76] But this evidence is not backed up by tax records comparable to those of England for 1334 and 1524, so no very direct comparisons are possible between the two kingdoms.

London's position in this changing scene remains a matter of some uncertainty. The city's taxable wealth increased remarkably relative to other English towns between 1334 and 1524. The capital's history is to that extent one of the major urban success stories of the late middle ages.[77] On the other hand, the volume of export trade passing through is not a reliable indicator of the changing population and wealth of a city of London's size. The changing level of property values in the city shows that it was not immune from the consequences of fifteenth-century recessions.[78] Even on a conservative estimate of London's size at 60,000 inhabitants in 1300 the city's population cannot have been much bigger in 1524, and some estimates of London's population in 1300 are appreciably higher than 60,000.[79] It is possible that London's population had fallen by a

[76] Stevenson, 'Trade with the south', p. 197.

[77] P. Nightingale, 'The growth of London in the medieval English economy', in Britnell and Hatcher, eds., *Progress and Problems*, pp. 99–106.

[78] D. Keene, *Cheapside before the Great Fire* (London, 1985), pp. 19–20.

[79] See below, pp. 396–7; Nightingale, 'Growth of London', p. 105.

quarter or a third, and quite likely that it had known prolonged phases of economic contraction. Colchester's experience suggests that a town could actually increase its population (and ranking) over the period 1300–1540 in spite of very lengthy periods of stagnation and recession.[80]

It is likely that during the later middle ages the bias of urbanisation within Britain swung even more strongly to the South-East of the island than it had been in 1300. The vigorous urban growth in the North and the West during the twelfth and thirteenth centuries had come nowhere near undermining the commercial advantages of the older urbanised zone. Now in the fourteenth and fifteenth centuries there is good reason to suppose, on the evidence of English taxation assessments, that the South and East had become relatively wealthier than the rest of the kingdom.[81] Most of the most successfully developing textile regions were in the region of earliest urbanisation, in Kent, Wessex, Mercia and East Anglia. Even in this part of England there were many sadly decayed towns by 1550 – just as there were growing towns in Wales and Scotland – so the contrast between different parts of Britain is not to be drawn in stark contrasts. It is difficult to believe, however, that the greater concentration of wealth in the South and East, supported by the growing trade of London, did not constitute the most favourable context for urban life. The London region supplies some of the best evidence for renewed urban development in the decades after 1450.[82]

The concept of 'urban decay' in the later middle ages is perhaps otiose, to the extent that the features of decay to be observed most frequently – falling populations, derelict properties, declining rents – were equally characteristic of rural areas. It is misleading if taken to imply declining standards of welfare in the towns since, as in the countryside, the smaller populations of the later middle ages generally enjoyed high levels of employment and better standards of living than their predecessors. It is naive if understood to mean that the history of all towns was the same, since there were great contrasts to be made between different decades and different towns, just as there were during the period of 'urban growth'. Yet though the urban history of Britain over these two centuries and more will never be satisfactorily summarised in two words, it does not thereby reduce to a miscellaneous set of case studies. The changing demand and supply conditions discussed above supply a framework for explaining the widespread contraction of urban economies, while allowing that variety is to be expected as different towns responded to different commercial opportunities and constraints. If defined with care, urban decay describes a widely observable feature of town life between

[80] Britnell, *Growth and Decline*, pp. 265–8.

[81] R. S. Schofield, 'The geographical distribution of wealth in England, 1334–1649', *Ec.HR*, 2nd series, 18 (1965), 483–510.

[82] M. Carlin, *Medieval Southwark* (London, 1996), pp. 143–4; Rosser, *Medieval Westminster*, pp. 174, 177.

1300 and 1550 that contrasts strongly with the more expansive features of the previous centuries of urban growth, and it conveniently draws attention to features of urban history so widespread that they need some general framework of ideas to explain them. It is therefore most unlikely that the idea of urban decay will go away, even if its relevance becomes more precisely circumscribed with the progress of research.

There are three principal aspects of decay for which the evidence needs to be kept as distinct as possible. One concerns urban population, and the extent to which it was declining. The second concerns the extent to which urban trade contracted. This is never directly measurable, but evidence of declining consumption of foodstuffs and raw materials, or evidence of industrial decline, are the most likely sources of information. The third aspect concerns the income received by borough treasurers, or the lords of seigneurial boroughs, and the extent to which this was declining. Such communal or seigneurial income was often only a minute fraction of a town's aggregate income, and its fluctuations have little direct relevance to understanding changes in the urban economy if it was subject to arbitrary legal or political hazards. The problems of the chamberlains of York, for example, were greatly exacerbated when Richard III abolished the tolls on trade in the city, thereby depriving them of a necessary source of income.[83] These three aspects of urban economies may all have changed in similar ways in some cases, but no simple relationship between them can be taken for granted. Urban historians consequently need to exercise as much ingenuity as their sources will allow them in charting these matters separately.

(v) THE REGULATION OF TRADE

During the later middle ages urban economic activity was bound by more complex formal rules than had been the case in earlier centuries. As in the past some of these related to the conduct of markets and fairs, the maintenance of weights and measures and other aspects of everyday trade, and often the enforcement of such laws provoked trouble.[84] A new body of law was imposed on urban authorities by parliamentary statute – these included the whole system of wage regulation under the Statute of Labourers that has already been mentioned, together with numerous rules relating to the discipline of the workforce. It seems likely that after 1349 urban administrations intervened more actively – and more arbitrarily – in policies to regulate the prices of foodstuffs, raw materials and manufactures, since legislation encouraged them to do so.[85] The same concerns are apparent from Scottish burgh records, as in Aberdeen, where price control

[83] L. C. Attreed, ed., *York House Books 1461–1490* (Stroud, 1991), vol. 1, pp. xxi–xxii.

[84] Carlin, *Southwark*, pp. 201–8.

[85] Britnell, *Commercialisation*, pp. 173–5; R. H. Britnell, 'Price-setting in English borough markets, 1349–1500', *Canadian J of History*, 31 (1996), 2–15.

was one of the most frequent matters for formal regulation by the town council during the fifteenth century.[86]

In addition, a greatly increasing number of rules concerned the more public aspects of the urban regulation of manufacture and trade. The role of craft guilds varied considerably between towns for reasons of local politics and other cultural traditions (such as the need to organise mystery plays), but it was not unusual for borough councils to delegate to them the policing of trades; the weavers were made responsible for enforcing rules concerning the quality of cloth, the tanners for the proper treatment of hides, the butchers for ensuring meat was fresh, and so on.[87] The ruling groups in the self-governing towns have been criticised for deterring enterprise within the bounds of their jurisdiction and encouraging the growth of new centres of manufacture, and in particular cases the argument is likely to be sound. The truth of this matter is complex because many of the new regulations of the late Middle Ages benefited commercial enterprise by reducing risks. Merchants had a considerable stake in urban government, and could be expected to modify some of the regulations that seriously hampered their business.[88] But economic regulation at the level of the individual town, however justifiable by local circumstances it seemed, would affect the distribution of investment and entrepreneurship if more rigorous in some places than others. The multiplication of restrictive rules in the interests of urban self-protection was surely one of the things that drove London capital and enterprise away from the established centres of manufacturing into smaller and less heavily governed towns.[89]

In general urban control over manufacturing and trade was even tighter in Scotland than in England because burghs often maintained territorial rights over the surrounding countryside in accordance with royal charters. The boundaries between different regalities were complicated and often disputed, but they constitute a type of urban rights without English analogy in this period. Scottish towns were also more likely than English ones to retain guilds for all urban traders, the descendants of earlier merchant guilds. This meant that powers which in most English boroughs were exercised by the mayor (or bailiffs) and council on behalf of the burgesses were more likely in Scotland to be comprehensively retained by a guild, which functioned rather as a department of burgh government, or as 'a community within a community'. Guilds for separate crafts were correspondingly later to develop in Scotland than in England, though some are in evidence in the fifteenth century. One of the duties of the merchant guilds was to preserve any territorial monopolies their burgh enjoyed. In 1370, for example, the guild

86 Gemmill and Mayhew, *Changing Values*, pp. 25–77.

87 E. Lipson, *The Economic History of England*, vol. I: *The Middle Ages*, 12th edn (London, 1959), pp. 329, 331, 340–2, 356; Kowaleski, *Exeter*, pp. 187–90; Swanson, *Artisans*, pp. 14–17, 55, 116–17.

88 Swanson, *Artisans*, pp. 112–13.

89 Bolton, *Medieval English Economy*, pp. 266–7.

members of Cupar contested the rights of the men of St Andrews to purchase fleeces, skins and hides. In 1448 members of the Dunfermline guild were contesting the right of Kirkcaldy men to trade in goats' milk.[90] Problems of interlocking jurisdictions meant that these trading rights were sometimes too complex to be effectively enforced.[91]

Another of the intractable disadvantages under which older self-governing towns laboured was not, in fact, the effect of economic policing but the costs of their self-government. Burgesses were subject to the payment of scot and lot, tallage, and murage to maintain the status and the fabric of their town, and such burdens were much more easily avoidable in villages and smaller towns.[92] Bridges, gates, roadways, public health and public order had to be maintained by burgesses rather than by the lord of a manor. The administrative apparatus of the borough entailed costs as well. Urban pride was costly when it involved maintaining a presence in parliament or courting local worthies through civic receptions and gifts.[93] This argument is not conclusive, because not all self-governing towns were adversely affected by rural competition in the fifteenth century. However, since none of the arguments to explain industrial relocation in the fifteenth century is very firmly founded in evidence, and since any such argument will need to take account of varieties of local experience, it is rash to rule out the costs of urban self-government without more analysis than the topic has so far received.

[90] E. Ewan, *Townlife in Fourteenth-Century Scotland* (Edinburgh, 1990), pp. 58–63, 66–7; E. P. D. Torrie, 'The guild in fifteenth-century Dunfermline', in Lynch, Spearman and Stell, eds., *The Scottish Medieval Town*, pp. 250–3.

[91] E. P. Dennison, 'Burgh trading liberties', in McNeil and MacQueen, eds., *Atlas of Scottish History*, p. 235.

[92] Britnell, *Growth and Decline*, pp. 220, 227, 232–3; C. Gross, *The Gild Merchant* (Oxford, 1890), vol. I, pp. 53–60; J. W. F. Hill, *Medieval Lincoln* (Cambridge, 1948), pp. 281, 300; Keene, *Survey*, I, pp. 44–5, 80; Kowaleski, *Exeter*, pp. 195.

[93] Britnell, *Growth and Decline*, pp. 234–5.

· 15 ·

Urban culture and the Church 1300–1540

GERVASE ROSSER

WITH SCOTTISH MATERIAL BY E. PATRICIA DENNISON

(i) INTRODUCTION: POINTS OF PERSPECTIVE

IN 1314 the spire of St Paul's Cathedral in London was damaged by a lightning bolt. The repairs accomplished, a man clambered carefully to the scaffold's summit and replaced the great cross, charged with its precious contents of relics which included a fragment of the cross of Christ. From up here, one commanded a panorama of the city. The square mile of the walled area, and the straggling suburbs to east and west and to the south of the River Thames, were all displayed to view. The urban vista was punctuated by the towers of a hundred parish churches and a score of convents, whose smaller scale expressed, from the perspective of the cross of Paul's, their subordinate and ancillary status. Order was additionally revealed in a network of streets still marked by a grid plan imposed four centuries before by an Anglo-Saxon king. From this vantage point the city appeared entire, comprehensible and available for possession. When, in the sixteenth century, the first urban mapmakers were encouraged by municipal councils to publish such another panoptic vision of the city, they made the same climb in order to construct from steeple-tops the impression, before the possibility of human flight, of the bird's-eye, all-encompassing view. Bishop, monarch and magistrate each conceived of the city as a visible entity, conveniently subject to his direction and control.[1]

For assistance with the illustrations I am particularly grateful to Robert Bearman of the Shakespeare Birthplace Trust, Stratford-on-Avon, to John Clark of the Museum of London and to Nigel Ramsay.

[1] St Paul's: G. J. Aungier, ed., *The French Chronicle of London* (Camden Society, 1st series, 28, 1844), p. 38. London topography: *BAHT*, III; above, pp. 190–6, and below, pp. 396–9. London maps in the sixteenth century: S. Prockter and A. Taylor, eds., *The A to Z of Elizabethan London* (Lympne Castle, 1979); H. M. Colvin and S. Foister, eds., *The Panorama of London circa 1544 by Anthonis van den Wyngaerde* (London Topographical Society Publications, 151, 1996); P. Glanville, *London in Maps* (London, 1972), pls. 2–5.

But how many shared the universal vision of Paul's cross? Far below, the teeming alleys and tenements of early fourteenth-century London housed 80,000 individuals, hardly one of whom would ever see the city in this light. Did they remain the blind victims of a design which they were too hemmed in ever to comprehend, still less to alter? Such a conclusion is encouraged by the preponderance of extant sources for the history of late medieval urban culture. The recorded pronouncements of churchmen, kings and city councillors purport to structure every element in the lives of townsmen and women: the space in which they lived, and its boundaries; the time which organised their working days, their festivals and their awareness of the past; their relationship to supernatural powers; their access to knowledge and their forms of artistic expression; their ability to associate in groups. In each of these aspects the late medieval city appears, from the records of authority, to have been the cultural expression of a tiny elite and a tool for its exercise of power over a captive population. Yet a closer scrutiny of the evidence makes clear that the experience of urban culture at that period was a good deal more complex and multivalent than this reductive model. The prevalence of a hegemonic culture, shaped to a large degree by the interests of authority, is apparent, and it would be misleading not to emphasise the constraints thereby imposed upon the majority of townspeople. Nevertheless, the encounter of urban populations with that hegemonic culture was not confined to mute and passive reception. Rather, the sources bear testimony to creative processes of appropriation and reinterpretation, expressive of a wide diversity of attitudes and experiences. From the viewpoint of the magistrates, the town was a vehicle for the imposition of a particular set of hierarchical values. But the practice of urban life never corresponded to the abstract schemata of official lawcodes and moral ordinances. Town rulers could and did do much to delimit the available language of cultural expression. As the following pages will attempt to show, however, they could not predetermine its inflexion and accents in daily use.[2]

(ii) THE DISTINCTIVENESS OF URBAN CULTURE

The implications of this issue have hitherto been underestimated, in so far as historians have remained unaware of the degree to which, by 1300, the society of these islands was affected by urbanisation. The truth has been partially obscured from historical view by the fact that political circumstances, in particular the extensive power of the medieval English monarchy, limited the degree to which towns enjoyed either constitutional autonomy or a legitimised dominance of the

[2] The distinction between official or abstract schemes of social order, and the actual experience of those to whom such abstractions notionally relate, is forcefully drawn by P. Bourdieu, *The Logic of Practice* (1980; trans. Cambridge, 1990), p. 17 and *passim*. A general debt is acknowledged here also to M. de Certeau, *The Practice of Everyday Life* (1974; trans. Berkeley and Los Angeles, 1984), p. 18 and *passim*. Jane Garnett made stimulating contributions to the ideas in this chapter.

countryside, by contrast with the prestigious cities of Flanders and northern Italy. Exceptions were the implanted royal towns of Wales which, because of their role in the process of colonisation, were endowed by the English monarch with powers over the hinterland remotely commensurate with these Flemish and Italian cases; and many of the Scottish burghs, which in a less intensively competitive economic environment than England were endowed with far-reaching economic controls over the countryside.[3] However, the recent realisation that centres of population lacking such rights and numbering just a few hundreds of inhabitants could nevertheless be urban, if a majority of residents were engaged in a variety of non-agrarian activities, has dramatically altered the basis for an understanding of the culture of medieval towns in particular, and indeed of British culture in general.[4] If, as was probably the case, as many as one in five people in late medieval England (and in Wales and Scotland, perhaps one in ten) lived in a town, large or small, and the remainder lived not far away from one,[5] then the old assumption (heavily indebted as it is to more recent romantic and anti-industrial movements) that the contemporary cultural environment was overwhelmingly rural needs to be set aside. The political and economic fact of urbanisation is the theme of other chapters in this volume. The subject of the present one is the variety of social uses which were made of the rhetoric of urban culture. That rhetoric was deployed by many different voices, and it would be an error to identify any single one with the urban experience *tout court*. Rather, urban culture was a powerful, multivalent language which offered itself for appropriation by any of a wide spectrum of town dwellers.

A common assumption, at all social levels, was that the culture of the town distinguished it from the rural other. Of course, as Maitland pointed out, those wishing to understand the development of early towns 'have fields and pastures on their hands'.[6] Pigs ran in the city streets – a phenomenon which the classicist Petrarch would identify as the very antithesis of urbanity – and the continuing economic interdependence of town and agrarian hinterland blurred the cultural distinction between the two.[7] Immigrants from the countryside (whose influx alone enabled town populations, eroded by high levels of mortality, to endure) imported rural patterns of behaviour, muddying modern notions of a link between urbanisation and a supposedly new form of rationality. Folklore

[3] Wales: R. R. Davies, *Conquest, Coexistence and Change* (Oxford, 1987), pp. 373, 473ff. Scotland: E. P. Dennison, 'Power to the people? The myth of the medieval burgh community', in S. Foster, A. Macinnes and R. Macinnes, eds., *Scottish Power Centres* (Glasgow, 1998).

[4] R. Holt and G. Rosser, eds., *The Medieval Town* (London, 1990), Introduction; below, pp. 510–17.

[5] C. Dyer, 'How urbanized was medieval England?', in J.-M. Duvosquel and E. Thoen, eds., *Peasants and Townsmen in Medieval Europe* (Ghent, 1995), pp. 169–83; also D. Keene, 'Small towns and the metropolis: the experience of medieval England', in *ibid.*, pp. 223–38.

[6] F. W. Maitland, *Township and Borough* (Cambridge, 1898), p. 9.

[7] B. G. Kohl and R. G. Witt, eds., *The Earthly Republic: Italian Humanists on Government and Society* (Manchester, 1978), p. 52.

and magic invaded the medieval (as indeed they have continued to do the post-medieval) town, and were not the preserve of any particular social group. The inhabitants of Canterbury continued in the mid-sixteenth century to sprinkle holy water on their rooftops as a protection from lightning; Chaucer's fictional but veristic carpenter, living in the centre of fourteenth-century Oxford, muttered arcane charms against damage to his house; other townspeople sought out wise men to find stolen goods; and educated, cosmopolitan merchants in fourteenth-century Coventry hired a magician to bring about the death of a hated prior.[8] Even into the late seventeenth century, the people of Stornoway continued to pour ale on the sea at Hallowe'en.[9] It would be tempting to conclude that the medieval British town was as infused with rurality as the countryside at the end of the twentieth century is dominated by metropolitan culture. Nevertheless, it was a prevalent perception in the medieval town that its urbanity was distinguished from an alien countryside. The incursions of nature were designated antisocial, when they took the form of bestial dungheaps in the urban street.[10] At other times rurality was found to be comic, vested in the simple rustic of popular fiction who was easily duped by sophisticated citizens. The backwoods gull of Tudor story collections and metropolitan drama had fifteenth-century antecedents in the Chester *Shepherds' Plays* and the *London Lickpenny*.[11] Or again, the rural was appropriated by townspeople as an idealised emblem of beneficent nature: a moralised pastoral image. Such were the twisted trees which Londoners carried into their homes before Easter; the branches used to decorate the streets of Coventry at Midsummer; and the flowers brought to the mayor of Leicester about the spring solstice: 'hawthorn budded forth, bean flowers, and a columbine flower'.[12] One of the defining characteristics of urban culture, in the middle ages as in other periods, was its repeatedly asserted difference from, and control of, the rural world outside.

[8] *Letters and Papers . . . of Henry VIII*, XVIII(2), p. 300 (no. 546.IX); Geoffrey Chaucer, *The Miller's Tale*, lines 3480–1, in F. N. Robinson, ed., *The Works of Geoffrey Chaucer*, 2nd edn (London, 1957), p. 51; H. T. Riley, ed., *Memorials of London and London Life in the XIIIth, XIVth, and Xvth Centuries* (London, 1868), pp. 53, 462, 472, 518; J. Röhrkasten, 'Conflict in a monastic borough: Coventry in the reign of Edward II', *Midland History*, 18 (1993), 1–18, at 3.

[9] E. P. Dennison and R. Coleman, *Historic Stornoway: The Archaeological Implications of Development* (Scottish Burgh Survey, 1997).

[10] E. L. Sabine, 'City cleaning in medieval London', *Speculum*, 12 (1937), 19–43; D. J. Keene, 'Rubbish in medieval towns', in A. R. Hall and H. K. Kenward, eds., *Environmental Archaeology in an Urban Context* (CBA Res. Rep., 43, 1982), pp. 26–30.

[11] R. M. Lumiansky and D. Mills, eds., *The Chester Mystery Cycle* (Early English Text Society, suppl. series, III, IX, 1974, 1986), vol. I, p. 125, vol. II, p. 103; *London Lickpenny*, in E. P. Hammond, ed., *English Verse between Chaucer and Surrey* (New York, 1927; repr., New York, 1965), pp. 237–9.

[12] John Stow, *A Survey of London* (1603), ed. C. L. Kingsford (Oxford, 1908), vol. I, p. 98; R. W. Ingram, ed., *Records of Early English Drama: Coventry* (Toronto, 1981), p. 17; M. Bateson, ed., *Records of the Borough of Leicester*, vol. III: *1509–1603* (Cambridge, 1905), pp. 28–9 (1530).

(iii) THE POLITICS OF URBAN SPACE

That severance was expressed most forcibly by the topographical delimitation of the urban space. Indeed, in Scotland, where stone walls were not usual, the ditch and pallisade which surrounded most towns functioned far more as a psychological than as a physical barrier.[13] The walls which enclosed the larger towns made cultural no less than defensive claims. Towards 1300, the walls of Caernarfon were designed specifically to evoke the appearance of the Byzantine imperial capital of Constantinople (Plate 23). The instigator of this project, King Edward I, thereby presented the newly fortified town to his conquered subjects in Wales as a godsend; precisely as the fulfilment of an ancient Welsh legend which told how the hero Maxim Wledig had seen in a dream a vision of just such a city, in all its distinctive bastions and decorative details, as the new Caernarfon was revealed to be. The fact that the (erroneously supposed) father of the emperor Constantine himself, Magnus Maximus, was traditionally held to be buried locally enabled the English king, by ceremoniously translating the body to the church of Caernarfon, to intensify the positive resonances for the Welsh of his domination of the town.[14] An analogous use of mural symbolism was made by the mayoral council of Colchester when, around 1400, they incorporated into the design of their new civic seal a splendid representation of the city walls: for the origin of these walls, as of the town itself, was attributed by popular tradition to King Cole, the father of St Helen – also alluded to in the iconography – and grandfather of Constantine.[15] Even when the financial burden of maintaining defences, in the relatively peaceful conditions of late medieval England and Wales, led to the neglect of many city walls,[16] the entrance gates which commanded the flow of traffic continued to be used in all British towns to convey images of civic identity, in particular on the occasions of royal progresses (Plate 4). In the smaller kingdom of Scotland, the impact of the royal court upon urban life was particularly felt. By the sixteenth century there was established a formal cycle of royal entries into the principal towns of the realm, including Aberdeen, Dundee and Perth, on which occasions city elders balanced the opportunity to display themselves

[13] E.g. J. Bain, *et al.*, eds., *Calendar of Documents relating to Scotland* (Edinburgh, 1881–1986), vol. IV, p. 459.

[14] A. J. Taylor, 'Caernarfon', in R. A. H. Brown, M. Colvin and A. J. Taylor, eds., *The History of the King's Works* (London, 1963), pp. 369–71.

[15] G. Pedrick, *Borough Seals of the Gothic Period* (London, 1904), pp. 55–8 and pl. XXXVIII; G. Rosser, 'Myth, image and social process in the English medieval town', *UH*, 23 (1996), 5–25, at 8 with references.

[16] H. L. Turner, *Town Defences in England and Wales: An Architectural and Documentary Study AD 900–1500* (London, 1970), pp. 87–94.

against unwelcome disruptions caused by brawling courtiers.[17] It appears, characteristically, to have been initially for the benefit of visiting princes that, in the first half of the sixteenth century, the city fathers of Southampton flanked the north gate of the town with colossal painted representations of the folk-hero Sir Bevis and the giant, Ascupart, whose overthrow by the knight was traditionally held to have saved the city from destruction (Plate 5).[18] In many of these cases urban rulers claimed the right to define the city, and to control access to it, by virtue of legends borrowed from popular tradition. At the same time, however, the very attempt by authority to paint a particular gloss on these stories for the benefit of a wide public is part of the evidence of their independent circulation in a much broader stream of popular culture. Their wide currency and prestige explains their appropriation by ruling elites. But although the magistrates commanded the resources to erect the walls and gates which bounded the city, their published justification for doing so was never more than one possible expression of an inherited cultural language too rich in resonance to be tied to an exclusive meaning. While the wall, and its attendant imagery, proclaimed the ambition of a centralising power to impose within its space a homogeneous culture of civic order, the cultural world inhabited by the townspeople remained obstinately diverse.

The attempt to legislate for the whole physical and moral environment of the town is as old as the civic idea itself. It was a very short time after the declaration of a commune at London had led, at the close of the twelfth century, to the creation of a mayor that the new regime established an 'assize of buildings': a set of standard safety-measures and procedures governing construction which set public welfare above private interest.[19] In Scotland, officers called liners, who monitored plot boundaries and building regulations, are recorded from the earliest days of burghal life.[20] In some English provincial towns this act of urban definition on the part of the political elite came closer to the end of the medieval period. At the small town of Henley-on-Thames the officers of the merchant guild, who were the effective local government, introduced in the course of the

[17] A. A. MacDonald, 'Mary Stewart's entry to Edinburgh: an ambiguous triumph', *Innes Review*, 62 (1991), 101–2; C. Eddington, *Court and Culture in Renaissance Scotland: Sir David Lindsay of the Mount* (East Linton, 1995), pp. 108–10; M. Lynch, 'A royal progress: court ceremony and ritual during the personal reign of James VI', in J. Goodare and M. Lynch, eds., *James VI: Court and Kingship* (forthcoming).

[18] J. Fellows, 'Sir Bevis of Hampton in popular tradition', *Proceedings of the Hampshire Field Club and Arch. Soc.*, 42 (1986), 139–45; A. B. Rance, 'The Bevis and Ascupart panels, Bargate Museum, Southampton', *ibid.*, 147–53.

[19] H. T. Riley, ed., *Munimenta Gildhallae Londoniensis* (RS, 1859–62), vol. 1, pp. 319–32 (for the date see H. M. Chew and W. Kellaway, eds., *London Assize of Nuisance, 1301–1431* (London Record Society, 10, 1973, pp. ix–xi).

[20] E. P. D. Torrie, *Medieval Dundee* (Dundee, 1990), pp. 52–3; Dundee Archive and Record Centre, MS Dundee Burgh and Head Court Book, 30 Mar. 1523; SRO, B20/10/1, MS Burgh Court Book of Dunfermline, pp. 101, 112, 307, 363.

fifteenth century measures for the penning of stray animals, for the purity of the common water supply and for the purchase of land in order to construct 'a public street for the whole community of the town'.[21] The idea of the urban community as a body in need of protection from pollution was objectified in many towns in legislation which banished noxious and antisocial trades – butchers, tanners, bell-founders – to the city limits.[22] In these edicts the principles of public utility and hygiene were invested with a moral emphasis which pervaded alike those civic regulations which related to social groups deemed to be 'marginal': foreigners staying in the town; prostitutes; criminals; the permanently poor. The banishment of all syphilitics in Edinburgh to the island of Inchkeith in 1497, and the exclusion of the poor from St Mary's church in Dundee in the 1520s, were measures increasingly characteristic of city fathers in later medieval Britain at large.[23] As a means to define the core urban culture in terms congenial to the elite, the attempt was repeatedly made to label these categories and either to herd them into designated areas of the town or otherwise to expel them. But the effort to control repeatedly foundered on the complexity and mobility of medieval urban society.

The fortunes of the immigrant to the city present a paradigm of the urban cultural process. In the case of the international merchant coming to London or Southampton for primarily commercial reasons, the host environment imposed conditions expressive of a profound suspicion of cultural pluralism. To the requirement of residence at designated addresses, normally in the household of a native burgess, was added a series of legal and fiscal disabilities. Moreover, in periods of commercial strain the alien groups were at risk from xenophobic attacks. Flemings murdered in the course of the Peasants' Revolt in London in 1381 were identified by the mob because they 'koude nat say Breed and Chese, but Case and Brode (*kaas en brood*)'.[24] Yet these disadvantages did not deny to the foreigner the redeeming sense of a degree of personal choice between engagement with and detachment from the local culture. Some intermarried with the English and Scots, acquired letters of denization and adopted local custom. On the other hand, the wills of Italians resident in fifteenth-century London reveal

[21] P. M. Briers, ed., *Henley Borough Records* (Oxfordshire Record Society, 41, 1960), pp. 33, 34, 57, 72.

[22] E. L. Sabine, 'Butchering in mediaeval London', *Speculum*, 8 (1933), 335–53; E. L. Sabine, 'Latrines and cesspools of mediaeval London', *Speculum*, 9 (1934), 303–21, and 12 (1937), 19–43; Sabine, 'City cleaning'.

[23] *Extracts from the Records of the Burgh of Edinburgh A.D. 1403–1528* (Edinburgh, 1869), pp. 71–2; Dundee Archive and Record Centre, MS Dundee Burgh and Head Court Book, 30 Sept. 1521 and 30 Mar. 1523.

[24] A. A. Ruddock, 'Alien hosting in Southampton in the fifteenth century', *Ec. HR*, 16 (1946), 30–7; A. A. Ruddock, *Italian Merchants and Shipping in Southampton 1270–1600* (Southampton Record Series, 1, 1951); S. L. Thrupp, 'A survey of the alien population of England in 1440', *Speculum*, 32 (1943), 262–73; C. L. Kingsford, ed., *Chronicles of London* (Oxford, 1905), p. 15.

a strategic combination of respectable English executors, together with witnesses drawn from the immigrant community, within which particular features of the city of origin survived translation to make their own contribution to English urban culture. Thus Lucchese residents promoted amidst the Londoners the cult of the miraculous image of Christ in their native city, the 'Volto Santo'; Flemings in Southwark hired a Dutch-speaking priest to celebrate their mass in the local parish church; Welsh and Irish students of law at the Oxford schools congregated in residential halls with their compatriots.[25]

Prostitution was officially linked with crime and identified as a public order issue long before it came to be treated in this light by sixteenth-century magistrates. The dominant concerns of secular authorities were manifested in attempts to confine the profession to particular zones. At Coventry in 1445 and at Leicester in 1467, brothels were banished outside the city walls, as was also becoming the custom in Scotland by this time, allegedly because of the risk of fire.[26] The regulations of the officially recognised 'stews' of Sandwich exemplify the growing attempts at regulation on the part of late medieval city governments. On occasion the houses were forced to close, while city waits blasted trumpets in a biblical gesture of moral outrage.[27] Yet none of these measures was ever effective, because prostitution was only in rare instances a full-time, permanent profession, and was far more commonly a short-term or supplementary occupation taken up by relatively poor women who otherwise practised a variety of trades. The bishop of Winchester might in the name of decency shut the Southwark stews, a renowned resort within his London manor, during sessions of parliament, yet in the taverns of Westminster dozens of alewives continued to offer MPs the same services.[28] In this sense the prostitute was an archetypal medieval townsperson: although her depressed economic status made her vulnerable to punitive legislation, her multiple identities made her an elusive victim of authority.

At the same time, a woman in this social world had only a very limited chance to engage creatively with the dominant culture of the town. Suspected immorality would disqualify her from all officially sanctioned forms of civic life: no

[25] H. Bradley, 'The Italian community in London, *c.* 1350–*c.* 1450' (Ph.D. thesis, University of London, 1992), pp. 291–4; M. Bratchel, 'Regulation and group-consciousness in the later history of London's Italian merchant colonies', *J of European Economic History*, 9 (1980), 585–610; M. Carlin, *Medieval Southwark* (London, 1996), p. 89; J. I. Catto and R. Evans, eds., *The History of the University of Oxford*, vol. II: *Late Medieval Oxford* (Oxford, 1992), pp. 308, and cf. pp. 516–18.

[26] M. D. Harris, ed., *The Coventry Leet Book* (Early English Text Society, orig. series, 134, 135, 138, 146, 1907–13) (continuously paginated), pp. 219–20; M. Bateson, ed., *Records of the Borough of Leicester*, vol. II: *1327–1509* (Cambridge, 1901), p. 291. Cf. Carlin, *Southwark*, pp. 209–10. For the Scottish case see E. Ewan, *Townlife in Fourteenth-Century Scotland* (Edinburgh, 1990), p. 26; Dennison, 'Power to the people?'.

[27] Carlin, *Southwark*, p. 226; R. M. Karras, *Common Women* (Oxford, 1996), pp. 37–43, 50–3.

[28] J. B. Post, 'A fifteenth-century customary of the Southwark stews', *J of the Society of Archivists*, 5 (1977), 418–28; Carlin, *Southwark*, ch. 9; G. Rosser, *Medieval Westminster, 1200–1540* (Oxford, 1989), pp. 143–4; Karras, *Common Women*, *passim*.

evidence has been found of sororities of prostitutes. The same must be said both of criminals and of the poor, two large groups between which there was a significant degree of overlap. Criminality has been little studied in British medieval towns, but Parisian evidence indicates its concentration in a poor, highly mobile class whose members occasionally formed fleeting alliances but tended generally to have the character of isolated aliens within the city.[29] Likewise the absolutely poor – who probably numbered between one third and one half of any urban population in the later middle ages – seem wholly to have lacked any supportive cultural framework, other than as the recipients of burgess charity. Guilds were by definition for the respectable, which precluded the *miserabiles*. Even such an association as 'the guild of poor people of St Austin' of Norwich, while it excluded rich burgesses and offered solidarity to lesser townspeople, did not open its doors to those who had *nothing*; the humblest of urban fraternities demanded material contributions from their members and imposed standards for social behaviour which deliberately distanced these associations from the rootless, migrant poor. The marginality of the latter was often experienced geographically as a life 'on the edge'; typically, Exeter's and Edinburgh's poor were concentrated in the suburban parishes. But they also flowed through the city, in the gaps between the official organisations of respectable townspeople, like the hundred or so homeless migrants observed by tax assessors in late fourteenth-century Shrewsbury, 'fleeing from street to street'.[30] For the vast majority in this situation, the lack of social standing and the inevitable imputations of crime and immorality were an effective barrier to redeeming engagement with the hegemonic culture of the town.

Apart from more or less vain attempts to order society by policies of social zoning, the rulers of medieval towns endeavoured to impose their own structure upon the urban space. From this perspective, a city wall spoke as clearly to residents within as to enemies without its compass. The wall of Norwich, constructed between *c.* 1280 and 1348, claimed for the unitary idea of the city some half-dozen distinct centres of settlement, each with its own history and social character, which together had comprised the polyfocal origins of urban development in the area.[31] At Edinburgh, the construction of the King's Wall across

[29] B. Geremek, *The Margins of Society in Late Medieval Paris* (1971; trans. Cambridge, 1987); C. Hammer, 'Patterns of homicide in a medieval university town: fourteenth-century Oxford', *P&P*, 78 (1978), 3–23.

[30] T. Smith, *English Gilds* (Early English Text Society, 40, 1870), pp. 40–1; W. T. MacCaffrey, *Exeter 1540–1640* (Cambridge, Mass., 1958), pp. 13, 113; H. Summerson, *Medieval Carlisle* (Cumberland and Westmorland Antiq. and Arch. Soc. Extra Series, 25, Kendal, 1993),vol. I, p. 305. On poverty in the Scottish towns see M. Lynch, 'The social and economic structure of the larger towns, 1450–1600', in M. Lynch, M. Spearman and G. Stell, eds., *The Scottish Medieval Town* (Edinburgh, 1988), pp. 261–86, at pp. 263, 275.

[31] J. Campbell, 'Norwich', in *BAHT*, II; A. Carter, 'The Anglo-Saxon origins of Norwich: the problems and approaches', *Anglo-Saxon England*, 7 (1978), 175–204.

the steep slope on the southern side of the city in the 1420s is likely, for a time, to have had the effect of redefining the king's burgh, excluding from it certain poor districts including Cowgate with its associated animals, markets and squalor.[32] It is difficult to determine how far the outlook of inhabitants continued to be affected by such earlier histories, but the fact that the various wards of the City of London were referred to, even in official documents of the later middle ages, as the *patriae* of their occupants is suggestive.[33] On a smaller scale, the history of late medieval Lynn is marked by localist resistance to the centralising policy of the mayor. At one time debate focused on attendance at the senior and official church of St Margaret, next to the guildhall: those living in the quarter just five minutes' walk to the north, around the chapel of St Nicholas, insisted that the distance to St Margaret's was too great, and the way too dangerous to contemplate.[34] It was equally characteristic of a persistent centripetal localism within the later medieval town that residents in different parts of Lynn maintained at the same period two distinct guilds dedicated to the Holy Trinity, one based in the church of St Margaret, the other in the South Lynn church of All Saints.[35] Authority shaped and labelled the spaces and landmarks of the city, but those who moved through and between them persisted in seeing the place from their own perspective.

(iv) TIME, HISTORY, AND MEMORY

Like space, time in the medieval town could not be reduced to unity, but was open to contest and diversity of perception. At the close of the medieval period, mechanical time was explicitly identified as a distinguishing feature of urban life: 'In cities and towns', so the author of the early Tudor *Dives and Pauper* put it, 'men rule them by the clock'.[36] But the regular tolling of the hours was as old as the Benedictine monasteries which, in many towns, had performed this function for centuries and would continue to do so until the dissolution in England and Wales and the Reformation in Scotland. *Pace* a common modern view of the subject, the clock is not necessarily a harbinger of capitalist culture,[37] and the

32 *ex inf.* M. Lynch.

33 E.g. A. H. Thomas, ed., *Calendar of Early Mayor's Court Rolls . . . 1298–1307* (Cambridge, 1924), p. 254.

34 D. M. Owen, ed., *The Making of King's Lynn* (British Academy, Records of Social and Economic History, new series, 9, 1984), pp. 135–9.

35 Norwich, Norfolk County RO, MSS KL/C38/1–31; KL/Gd/77.

36 P. H. Barnum, ed., *Dives and Pauper*, vol. I (1) (Early English Text Society, 275, 1976), p. 120.

37 J. Le Goff, 'Temps de l'église au temps du marchand', *Annales ESC*, 15 (1960), 417–33; J. Le Goff, 'Le temps du travail dans la "crise du XIVe s.": du temps médiéval au temps moderne', *Le moyen âge*, 69 (1963), 597–615; K. Thomas, 'Work and leisure in pre-industrial society', *P&P*, 29 (1964), 50–62; C. Cipolla, *Clocks and Culture, 1300–1700* (London, 1967); R. Tittler, *Architecture and Power: The Town Hall and the English Urban Community c. 1500–1640* (Oxford, 1991), pp. 136–9.

resonance of medieval town bells evoked associations with the liturgy or with a sense of locality at least as strong as that with the timetable of the workshop. Precisely because of its range of connotations, telling the time became a political issue. The erection of town clocks by the townspeople of Dunstable and St Albans in the middle of the fourteenth and at the beginning of the fifteenth century marked the attainment on the part of these secular societies of a degree of autonomy vis-à-vis their monastic lords, who had hitherto claimed a local monopoly on timekeeping as on other affairs.[38] At Stratford-on-Avon the guild of the Holy Cross asserted its status, as the effective if unconstitutional government of the town, by the construction towards 1420 of a public clock with gilded figures and two faces, one internal to the guildhall and the other looking out on to the public street.[39] The making of civic bells could be the focus and expression of a strong sense of local loyalty, most strikingly manifested when, as at Abergavenny in the late fifteenth century, their cost was raised by parishioners who went about 'into the country with games and plays'; or, as at Bridgwater at the same period, they were cast from the old pots, pans and spoons of the townspeople themselves, gathered from door to door through the town.[40] Municipal clocks and bells were thus, before all else, the instruments of *campanilismo*.

The memories of townspeople, similarly, were subject both to manipulation by the elite and, at the same time, to a range of different and contested meanings. Official versions of the past, although often plainly slanted to serve an authoritarian interest, typically drew for their material upon a broad cultural inheritance, and in particular upon the stuff of saint cults, folklore and popular ballads. When the ruling council of Colchester ordered the production of civic annals incorporating the story of the town's foundation by King Cole, that legend was widely current.[41] In the preservation of such legends in written form, a significant role was played by civic officials, such as the mayor of Wycombe, William Redhode, who in 1475 presented to the borough his ledger book, into which he had copied many records of the town; and Robert Ricart, the town clerk of Bristol who at the same period included in his *Kalendar* of memorable information about his city the tale of its first foundation by a descendant of the hero Brutus, a companion of Aeneas of Troy: 'For asmoche as it is righte convenient and accordinge to every Bourgeis of the Towne of Bristowe, in especiall

[38] H. R. Luard, ed., *Annales Monastici*, vol. III (RS, 36, 1866), p. 412; *VCH Hertfordshire* II (London, 1908), pp. 470–1; N. M. Trenholme, *The English Monastic Boroughs* (University of Missouri Studies, 2, no. 3, 1927), pp. 48–9, 74.

[39] J. H. Bloom, ed., *The Register of the Gild of the Holy Cross, the Blessed Mary and St. John the Baptist, Stratford-upon-Avon* (London, 1907), p. 30; subsequently described as 'the town clock called "clockhouse"': Stratford-on-Avon, Shakespeare Birthplace Trust, MS BRT/1/3/84.

[40] G. Williams, *The Welsh Church from Conquest to Reformation* (Cardiff, 1976), p. 459; T. B. Dilks, ed., *Bridgwater Borough Archives 1200–1377* (Somerset Record Society, 48, 1933), pp. 65–6; and cf. Rosser, *Medieval Westminster*, pp. 270–1.

[41] See n. 15 above.

thoo that been men of worship, for to knowe and understande the begynnyng and first foundacion of the saide worshipfull Toune' (Plate 6).[42] The tone and the primary audience in this instance were elitist; but the circulation of these ideas in the popular domain meant that no single group could monopolise their power. The images which they reflected of a town's identity could be appropriated not only by rich burgesses, but also by the unenfranchised. The Coventry tradition of Lady Godiva, for example, was refracted in various ways. The tale of Godiva's naked ride through the city, by which she won freedom from toll for the citizens from her husband, Earl Leofric, was familiar to national chroniclers by 1200. In the second half of the fourteenth century, after the leading citizens had won from the great priory a significant measure of control over their affairs, the mayoral council inserted in the civic church of St Michael a stained-glass window, in which Leofric and Godiva were portrayed with the words: 'I Luriche for the love of thee / Doe make Coventre tol-free'. On the other hand, in the fifteenth century the image of Godiva was invoked by common townspeople complaining of a new tax imposed by the city government. Radical verses were pinned to the door of St Michael's:

> Be it knowen and understond
> This Cite shuld be free & nowe is bonde.
> Dame Good Eve [Godiva] made it free;
> & nowe the custome for woll & the draperie.[43]

This was, moreover, a legend which – like the many stories of female saintly protectors of British towns – offered to the constitutionally marginalised women of the medieval city an opportunity to contribute to the creation of a vision of urban society from which they were not excluded. The currency and the utilisation of such stories about the past thus epitomise the fluid character of medieval urban culture.

Literacy was a familiar medium of that culture, as the textual protest of the Coventry weavers indicates. Elsewhere, written versions of local history were enshrined in public noticeboards.[44] At the same time, however, ballad and story played their own vital part in the oral mediation of popular memory. About 1450 a poem in praise of Abingdon was composed by a local ironmonger, who wished to celebrate the recent completion of a new bridge across the Thames by the collaboration of all the men and women of the town. The focus of these crude but vital verses is upon the communal nature of the enterprise:

[42] L. J. Ashford, *The History of the Borough of High Wycombe from its Origins to 1880* (London, 1960), p. 58; L. T. Smith, ed., *The Maire of Bristowe is Kalendar* (Camden Society, 2nd series, 5, 1872), p. 8.

[43] C. Phythian-Adams, *Desolation of a City* (Cambridge, 1979), p. 173; Rosser, 'Myth, image and social process', 15–17 and references.

[44] G. H. Gerould, '"Tables" in medieval churches', *Speculum*, 1 (1926), 439–40; C. Richmond, 'Hand and mouth: information gathering and use in England in the later middle ages', *J of Historical Sociology*, 1 (1988), 233–52, at 246–7 n. 5.

It was a solace to see in a somer seson,
CCC [300] I wysse workyng at once.
. . .
Wyves went out to wite how they wrought:
V [5] score in a flok it was a fayre syght.
In bord cloths bright white brede they brought,
Chees and chekens clerelych adycht.

A context of commercial rivalry with other towns along the Thames, alluded to in this rousing rhyme, invests some of the imagery with a slightly aggressive tone, expressed also in the final, challenging enunciation of the separate letters of the placename, similar to the chant of a modern football crowd:

> Take the first letter of your forefather with the worker of wax, and I and N, the colour of an ass; set them together, and tell me if you can what it is, then:
>
> A: B: I: N: D: O: N

This rare manuscript survival is testimony to a more general exchange of different and sometimes conflicting versions of the urban past.[45] With a similar refrain, the people of little Musselburgh challenged the nearby capital:

Musselburgh was a burgh
When Edinburgh was nane
And Musselburgh'll be a burgh
When Edinburgh is gane.[46]

Occasional echoes of such oral traditions are heard in reported speech, as when John Leland in Henry VIII's reign was informed by inhabitants of Stamford about the history of their town, where buildings were pointed out which had allegedly once housed the university that had briefly existed in the thirteenth century.[47] This oral urban history was as resistant to control of content as it was fugitive in form.

(v) CHANNELS OF THE SUPERNATURAL

The religious foundations of life in the medieval city were no less contested territory than were conceptions of space and time (Plate 7). Every urban government

[45] F. Little, *A Monument of Christian Munificence* (Oxford, 1871), pp. 121–4; G. Rosser, 'Solidarités et changement social. Les fraternités urbaines à la fin du moyen âge', *Annales ESC*, 48 (1993), 1127–43, at 1140–2.

[46] J. Paterson, *The History of the Regality of Musselburgh* (Musselburgh, 1861), p. 20; E. P. Dennison and R. Coleman, *Historic Musselburgh: The Archaeological Implications of Development* (Scottish Burgh Survey, 1996). 'Burgh' may be a pun on 'brogh', a mussel bed, for which Musselburgh was famous.

[47] John Leland, *Itinerary*, ed. L. T. Smith (London, 1907–10), vol. IV, pp. 89–90; and see F. Peck, *Academia Tertia Anglicana; or, the Antiquarian Annals of Stanford* (London, 1727), pp. 44–5.

clothed itself in a religious guise, claimed indeed to be a sacred object to which reverence was due.[48] Yet for all the potential utility to the elite of this procedure, to see civic religion solely as a tool of social control would be grossly reductive. As was true of ideas about the past, official versions of urban Christianity attempted, with mixed success, to capitalise upon the objects and forms of popular religious practice. A typical instance is the contribution of the secular government of Salisbury to the lengthy, expensive and ultimately successful campaign to secure the papal canonisation of a civic saint, Osmund (Plate 8).[49] The increasingly protective stance adopted by the York city government towards the body and cult of the local hero, St William, was equally characteristic. From the beginning of the fifteenth century the town guild of Corpus Christi was invested by the mayor with an official role as keeper of the precious shrine which was housed in St William's chapel on Ouse Bridge: the annual ceremony of its display during a procession at the feast of Corpus Christi became the vehicle for the secular rulers of the city to declare their alignment with an older-established local cult. The claimed identity of interests between St William, as supernatural protector of York, and the mayoral council, as the town's mundane protector, was further underlined by the rhetorical assertion, contained in an agreement negotiated between the city government and the Corpus Christi fraternity in 1432, that 'the whole city is a member of the guild'.[50] In a similar development the secular rulers of Lincoln around 1500 cultivated an association with a popular local guild of St Anne (originally founded in 1344), helping in the process to make its festival the principal event in the civic calendar. They then declared every inhabitant of the city to be, *ipso facto*, a member of the guild.[51] The adoption of the Virgin Mary as the official patroness of the city of Carlisle, where she appeared on the civic seal in addition to that of the cathedral priory, was likewise inspired by a popular story that in 1385 she had saved the town from destruction by the Scots. Indeed, she was said to appear often to inhabitants of Carlisle, which further encouraged the civic officers to vie with the cathedral canons for the role of the Virgin's chief advocate in the city. A widely held belief that the divine resided in this world in physical objects encouraged the fabrication of civic *palladia*, such as that acquired by the canons of Carlisle in 1451 to satisfy 'the devotion of Christ's faithful people daily flocking there on pilgrimage': 'an image of the Blessed Virgin covered with plates of silver and overlaid with gold, gems and precious stones'.[52] These practices of popular cult and official –

[48] For a comparison see R. C. Trexler, *Public Life in Renaissance Florence* (Ithaca, N.Y., 1980), pp. 132–3, 258–60.

[49] A. R. Malden, *The Canonization of Osmund* (Wiltshire Record Series, 2 1901).

[50] R. H. Skaife, ed., *The Register of the Guild of Corpus Christi in the City of York* (Surtees Society, 57, 1871), p. 252; A. F. Johnston and M. Rogerson, eds., *Records of Early English Drama* (Manchester, 1979), vol. II, s.a. 1432; A. F. Johnston, 'The guild of Corpus Christi and the procession of Corpus Christi in York', *Mediaeval Studies*, 38 (1976), 372–84.

[51] S. J. Kahrl, 'Secular life and popular piety in medieval English drama', in T. J. Heffernan, ed., *The Popular Literature of Medieval England* (Knoxville, 1985), pp. 85–107, at p. 89.

[52] R. B. Dobson, 'Cathedral chapters and cathedral cities: York, Durham and Carlisle in the fifteenth

clerical or lay – patronage amounted to an appropriation of Christianity to express the parochial concerns of particular urban societies. This was the context in which someone could plausibly be reported as saying: 'Of all Our Ladies, I love best Our Lady of Walsingham' – '"and I", saith the other, "Our Lady of Ipswich"'.[53] In countless instances the universal symbolism of the church was translated into a local dialect of civic celebration and civic debate.

This localisation of Catholicism accounts for a number of the known incidences of urban heresy in later medieval England. The particular form taken by a local cult of the Virgin Mary at Coventry led to accusations of Lollardy there.[54] It is similarly probable that a Leicester fraternity of Corpus Christi, which in the early fifteenth century was identified as harbouring Wycliffite supporters, originated as an orthodox society which over time attracted elements committed to controversy concerning transubstantiation.[55] Differences of religious opinion within a particular urban society once again illustrate the potential for divergence or even contradiction between an official statement of orthodoxy and its reception. In 1440 a priest named Richard Wyche was ordered to be burned at London for heresy. But the watching crowd took him for a martyr. They erected a cross at the site, and began to make offerings of money and wax *ex voto* images, until the City authorities dispersed them by casting about animals' dung as a preventative of 'further idolatry'.[56] Difference of religious opinion could also arise within urban families: an anti-papist play, 'The Beheading of John the Baptist', performed on Dundee's playfield at the time of the Reformation, was written by James Wedderburn, the brother of the orthodox vicar of the town.[57] Contrary to the assumptions of an older Protestant historiography, the expression of differences of religious opinion in the towns of the later middle ages was evidence rather of the vitality than of the breakdown of spiritual life. Just as, in the nineteenth century, church attendance was at its highest level in cities where chapel congregations were also large, and indeed where a number of townspeople satisfied different interests by attending both, so late medieval urban religion was characterised by its vigorous diversity. The particular rhetoric of black monks, friars or parish clergy might make exclusive claims to lay allegiance; but in actuality townspeople continued, for a variety of personal and social reasons, to support a range of religious practices: testamentary bequests were made in

century', *NHist.*, 19 (1983), 15–44, at 41–2; G. H. Martin, ed., *Knighton's Chronicle 1337–1396* (Oxford, 1995), p. 336; Summerson, *Carlisle*, I, p. 359.

[53] Thomas More, *The Dialogue concerning Tyndale*, in W. E. Campbell, ed., *The English Works of Sir Thomas More* (London, 1931), vol. II, p. 62 (modern text). See also N. P. Tanner, 'The Reformation and regionalism', in J. A. F. Thomson, ed., *Towns and Townspeople in the Fifteenth Century* (Gloucester, 1988), pp. 129–47.

[54] *VCH*, Warwickshire, VIII, p. 208.

[55] J. Crompton, 'Leicestershire Lollards', *Transactions of the Leicestershire Arch. and Hist. Soc.*, 44 (1968–9), 11–44, at 29–30.

[56] R. Flenley, ed., *Six Town Chronicles of England* (Oxford, 1911), p. 101; J. A. F. Thomson, *The Later Lollards 1414–1520* (Oxford, 1965), pp. 148–50.

[57] A. J. Mill, *Mediaeval Plays in Scotland* (Edinburgh, 1927), p. 88.

varying proportions to convents of every kind, shrines, hermits, sermons, pilgrimages and their own parish churches.[58]

Indeed, one of the distinguishing characteristics of urban life was a degree of choice in lay religious practice. Towns present in intense form the general truth that the medieval church was anything but monolithic. Cities which had been large before the twelfth century were the most prolifically endowed with a variety of churches: Norwich boasted fifty parish churches and half a dozen monastic establishments.[59] Eloquent of the ready exercise of that choice in the greater centres are the quarrels between mendicants and parish clergy over lay preferences in attendance at services or confessions or in patterns of burial.[60] But even in towns of medium size, a marginal or unofficial chapel regularly broadened the scope of religious expression. At Carlisle, the symbolic centre of the city was popularly located in a detached 'chapel' of St Alban. In the mid-fourteenth century the bishop found that this building had never been consecrated, and ordered its closure; but the ban was ineffective, and bequests in the testaments of late medieval townspeople reveal its enduring status as a civic church.[61] No less vivid an image of this religious diversity are the crude images of saints carved in the wall of a subterranean cave in the small Hertfordshire town of Royston (Plate 9).[62]

The legal and fiscal immunities enjoyed by town clergy – who represented perhaps 2 or 3 per cent of the civil population – and the islands of jurisdictional privilege which the greater urban churches represented, were intermittently the focus of active resentment on the part of the burghal elite. These rivalries had no final solution in the medieval period, and their principal effect may have been to offer to humbler townspeople a chance to engage in political debate, as bishop and mayor competed for the status of protector of the community.[63] The extent

[58] N. P. Tanner, *The Church in Late Medieval Norwich 1370–1532* (PIMSST, 66, Toronto, 1984); C. Burgess, '"By quick and by dead": wills and pious provision in late medieval Bristol', *EHR*, 102 (1987), 837–58; P. Heath, 'Urban piety in the later middle ages: the evidence of Hull wills', in R. B. Dobson, ed., *The Church, Politics and Patronage in the Fifteenth Century* (Gloucester, 1984), pp. 209–34; B. A. Kümin, *The Shaping of a Community: The Rise and Reformation of the English Parish c. 1400–1560* (London, 1996), esp. pp. 111–20; R. N. Swanson, *Church and Society in Late Medieval England* (Oxford, 1989), pp. 275–99; J. A. F. Thomson, *The Early Tudor Church and Society 1485–1529* (London, 1993), ch. 9; M. Lynch, 'Religious life in medieval Scotland', in S. Gilley and W. J. Sheils, eds., *A History of Religion in Britain* (Oxford, 1994), pp. 99–124, esp. pp. 120–1.

[59] Tanner, *Norwich*.

[60] A. Williams, 'Relations between the mendicant friars and the secular church in England in the later fourteenth century', *Annuale Medievale*, 1 (1960), 22–95; P. R. Szittiya, *The Antifraternal Tradition in Medieval Literature* (Princeton, N.J., 1986); Swanson, *Church and Society*, pp. 17, 192, 261.

[61] Summerson, *Carlisle*, I, pp. 355–6, II, p. 610.

[62] S. P. Beamon and L. G. Donel, 'An investigation of Royston cave', *Proceedings of the Cambridge Antiquarian Society*, 68 (1978), 47–58. See also G. Rosser, 'Religious life on the margins', in J. Blair and C. Pyrah, eds., *Research Directions in Church Archaeology* (CBA Res. Rep., 104, 1996), pp. 75–83.

[63] G. Rosser, 'Conflict and political community in the medieval town. Disputes between clergy and laity in Hereford', in T. R. Slater and G. Rosser, eds., *The Church in the Medieval Town* (Aldershot,

and violence of these conflicts has been exaggerated by earlier commentators.[64] Moreover, the medieval laity were capable of distinguishing between the legal privileges of religious institutions, which were at times the objects of hatred, and the men and women who inhabited them, who were often no less the objects of affection.[65] Distinctions were also drawn within the clerical body. The poverty and vulnerability of the great mass of urban clergy – five out of six chaplains in fourteenth-century London lacked the security of a parochial benefice[66] – made these very much less the focus of lay hostility than were some of the powerful officeholders of the church. Transcending these differences was the fact that the urban church, in its enormous diversity, represented to the whole spectrum of town dwellers a uniquely potent resource, which to reject would have been almost inconceivable.

In fact, widespread anticlericalism was absent from the towns of later medieval Britain.[67] To set against the occasional scandal born of the close proximity of clerics and laity is the evidence of continuing recruitment from urban families of both secular and monastic clergy, and of ties of respect and affection which linked the groups in multiple ways.[68] Testamentary bequests bear witness to the alliances contracted between lay townspeople and the clergy, both at the parochial level and within the religious houses, all of which, to at least some degree, welcomed the laity into their precincts and services. The mendicant orders, which had been launched with a particular mission to the urban laity, continued at the end of the middle ages to attract a significant proportion of urban benefactions.[69] There appears to be a developing strain of severity in urban lay demands of monastic practice, manifested in bequests to the Carthusians and Observant Franciscans during the century prior to the Reformation.[70] At the same time, however, it would be wrong to dismiss the older houses of Benedictines, the greater of which continued to dispense charity, education and pastoral care to the urban laity.[71] In addition to their benefactions, townspeople

1998), pp. 20–42. For numbers of clergy see Swanson, *Church and Society*, pp. 30–6; Tanner, *Norwich*, pp. 18–21.

[64] The best account remains Trenholme, *Monastic Boroughs*. However, this gives excessive attention to the alleged violence of the disputes. Conflicts were real, but generally contained. For a revisionist case study see P. Rixon, 'The medieval town of Reading' (DPhil thesis, University of Oxford, 1999).

[65] Cf. W. Eberhard, 'Klerus- und Kirchenkritik in der spätmittelalterlichen deutschen Stadtkronistik', *Historisches Jahrbuch*, 114 (1994), 349–80.

[66] A. K. McHardy, 'The churchmen of Chaucer's London: the seculars', *Medieval Prosopography*, 16 (1995), 57–87.

[67] Swanson, *Church and Society*, pp. 259–60; Thomson, *Early Tudor Church*, p. 187; P. Marshall, *The Catholic Priesthood and the English Reformation* (Oxford, 1994), pp. 212–16.

[68] Thomson, *Early Tudor Church*, pp. 291–2; and see refs. in n. 58 above.

[69] Swanson, *Church and Society*, pp. 298–9; J. Röhrkasten, 'Londoners and London mendicants in the late middle ages', *JEcc.Hist.*, 47 (1996), 446–77.

[70] Thomson, *Early Tudor Church*, p. 222.

[71] See B. Harvey, *Living and Dying in England, 1100–1540* (Oxford, 1993), esp. ch. 1, 'Charity'.

expressed their commitment to the local church through guilds and chantries which provided extra priests for under-resourced parishes. It could plausibly be said in 1546 that the large single parish of Stratford-on-Avon, with a total congregation of 1,500, could not be served by the sole offices of the parson, without the assistance he received from the five full-time priests employed by the fraternity of the Holy Cross (Plate 10).[72] At St Helen's Stonegate, York, the presentation of a chantry priest, who would be able to help the parish in addition to praying for the founder, was shared between the Benedictine nuns of Moxby and the York parishioners.[73] Such patronage betrays neither hostility nor indifference on the part of townspeople, but a desire to shape the local church to suit a range of particular concerns.

The role of the Church in urban politics and economic life was no less multifaceted. Notwithstanding his intermittently strained relations with the local Benedictine priory, the mayor of Coventry seized the occasion of a national Benedictine chapter held in the town to offer a civic welcome, in which he sat in splendour between the presidents of the chapter.[74] The economic contribution of ecclesiastical institutions to the urban economy was debated, but could not be ignored. The cloth merchants of Bury St Edmunds believed the late medieval town had outgrown its early economic dependence on the abbey, and the townspeople of Durham after the mid-fourteenth century saw the monks switch their purchasing policy away from the local suppliers in favour of regional merchants, to the city's financial loss.[75] On the other hand, the Church generated a plethora of secondary economic stimuli. At York the chandlers could not be prevented from crowding the approaches to the Minster with stalls selling candles, images and *ex voto* wax limbs to pilgrims.[76] Trends in piety gave rise to – and were in turn fed by – industrial specialisations, such as Nottingham's production of alabaster heads of St John the Baptist (Plate 11).[77] The local economies of most monastic and cathedral towns remained heavily reliant upon the traffic generated by the urban religious communities, and for this reason alone their destruction was unlikely to be seriously contemplated by the townspeople.

The local appropriation of the divine was most powerfully effected by the civic religious drama of the period. Secular drama was in its late medieval origins a distinctively urban cultural form. The noble and princely companies of players

72 Smith, ed., *English Gilds*, p. 222. See also C. Burgess, '"For the increase of divine service": chantries in the parish in late medieval Bristol', *JEcc.Hist.*, 36 (1985), 46–65.

73 Thomson, *Early Tudor Church*, p. 183; E. E. Barker, ed., *Register of Thomas Rotherham, Archbishop of York* (Canterbury and York Society, 1976–), vol. 1, p. 74 (no. 609).

74 L. T. Smith, ed., *The Coventry Leet Book* (London, 1907–13), pp. 588–9.

75 M. D. Lobel, *The Borough of Bury St. Edmunds* (Oxford, 1935), ch. 3; M. Bonney, *Lordship and the Urban Community* (Cambridge, 1990), p. 174.

76 Swanson, *Church and Society*, p. 247 and illustration at p. 233.

77 N. Ramsay, 'Alabaster', in J. Blair and N. Ramsay, eds., *English Medieval Industries* (London, 1991), pp. 29–40, esp. pp. 37–8.

of the Tudor age were the direct descendants and imitators of a rich medieval civic culture of street theatre, which, while indebted to the liturgical drama of the Church, none the less developed a distinctive identity. Again, however, it is necessary to distinguish a range of contemporary perspectives on the medieval civic plays. To the magistracy, they offered a further opportunity for association with a prestigious event, and a chance to show off to wealthy and influential visitors the town's well-governed condition. The mayoral council of York explicitly noted that the presentation of the city's plays at Corpus Christi attracted outsiders and redounded 'to the honour and profit of the city'. For a royal guest, special productions might be scheduled, as they were both at York and Coventry on the occasion of visits by Richard III; not many months later, Coventry's rulers judged it politic to repeat the performance for Henry VII.[78] The chronology of the plays' development suggests a direct link between the attainment of new measures of authority by various urban corporations in the later fourteenth century and the concurrent promotion of more or less elaborate dramatic cycles, largely controlled by the secular government, as a manifestation of presumed legitimacy. That these religious plays were put on in the public street lends some credence to the magistrates' claim to undertake responsibility, alongside the clergy, for the moral welfare of the townspeople at large.[79] Meanwhile, clerics saw in the plays – of which they were probably the authors – a pedagogic opportunity. This was made explicit in the York play of *Pater Noster*, which was dramatised by a particular fraternity in order to explain the meaning of the Lord's Prayer; and in a fictional village preacher's injunction to his ignorant congregation, who could not understand the doctrines of the Creed, to 'go your way to Coventry and there you shall see them all played in Corpus Christi play'.[80] The texts and stage directions of the plays imply a deliberate attempt to create a secular counterpart to the ecclesiastical liturgy. For example, the 'N-Town' cycle introduces such solemn scenes as a debate in Heaven about which of God's Three Persons should save mankind; incorporates passages from the Psalms and other prayers; and orchestrates its players with ceremonious stage-directions,

[78] Johnston and Rogerson, eds., *Records of Early English Drama*, II, p. 11 (and for comparison, L. M. Clopper, ed., *Records of Early English Drama: Chester* (Toronto, 1979), pp. 33, 115); R. Davies, ed., *Extracts from the Municipal Records of the City of York* (London, 1843), pp. 171–3; R. W. Ingram, ed., *Records of Early English Drama: Coventry* (Manchester, 1981), pp. 66, 67–8.

[79] L. M. Clopper, 'Lay and clerical impact on civic religious drama and ceremony', in M. G. Briscoe and J. C. Coldewey, eds., *Contexts for Early English Drama* (Bloomington, Ind., 1989), pp. 102–36, at p. 112. See also R. B. Dobson, 'Craft guilds and city: the historical origins of the York mystery plays reassessed', in A. E. Knight, ed., *The Stage as Mirror* (Cambridge, 1997), pp. 91–105; J. Goldberg, 'Craft guilds, the Corpus Christi play and civic government', in S. Rees Jones, ed., *The Government of Medieval York* (Borthwick Studies in History, 3, York, 1997), pp. 141–63.

[80] Smith, ed., *English Gilds*, pp. 137–8 (the play is mentioned by a Wycliffite preacher: F. D. Matthew, ed., *The English Works of Wyclif* (Early English Text Society, 74, 1880), p. 429); P. M. Zall, ed., *A Hundred Merry Tales* (1526) (Lincoln, Nebr., 1963), pp. 115–16.

including the repeated formal exchange of kisses.[81] Evidence of such extensive dramatic series as this, which treats all history from the Creation to the Last Judgement, survives from only three or four major towns; but the regular performance of single plays on biblical, moral or hagiographical themes was a normal part of urban life. At Reading, the principal urban parish church of St Laurence organised a play of Adam and Eve in one year, of Cain in another, and on a third occasion of The Three Kings of Cologne.[82]

Yet while in mayoral or clerical eyes the civic drama represented a political, economic or educational resource, the perception of both participants and audience could be significantly different in focus. The publishing of the banns of the plays in the surrounding countryside makes it clear that rustic elements were anticipated in the throng;[83] but the most explicit allusions in the surviving texts imply a primarily urban audience, yet one which was broad in its social spectrum. 'Draw therefor nerehande, both of burgh and of towne', Herod invites the crowd in the Wakefield *Magnus Herodes*. In the case of the *Castle of Perseverance*, God's protection is invoked on 'all the good commons of this town that before us stand / In this place'.[84] The organisers, too, were drawn from throughout urban society, as many records of performances make clear. A play called *Vicious*, which formed part of a *Pater Noster* series at Beverley, was presented by 'gentlemen, merchants, and valets' together.[85] Amongst the gathering of both performers and witnesses, the motives for participation ran sometimes obliquely to the ideals of priesthood and magistracy. Part of the attraction was the opportunity for good fellowship. At Kendal and doubtless elsewhere, the various crafts met for festive dinners in order to plan their next performance.[86] And the onlookers included a number like the Wife of Bath who, when her husband was away on business, would make congenial 'visitaciouns': 'To plays of miracles and mariages'.[87] This sociable dimension of urban culture finds its satirical reflection within the plays themselves, as in the Chester *Pageant of Noah's Flood*, in which Noah's wife refuses to come into the Ark without her drinking-companions:

> I will not out of this towne.
> But I have my gossips everychone,
> One foote further I will not gone.[88]

[81] S. Spector, ed., *The N-Town Play* (Early English Text Society, suppl. series, 11, 1991), pp. 111–19, and cf. pp. 74–5, 84–8, 93, 118 and *passim*.

[82] A. F. Johnston, 'What if no texts survived? External evidence for early English drama', in Briscoe and Coldewey, eds., *Contexts for Early English Drama*, pp. 1–19.

[83] Kahrl, 'Secular life and popular piety', pp. 90–1; E. K. Chambers, *The Mediaeval Stage* (Oxford, 1903), vol. II, p. 387.

[84] M. Stevens and A. C. Cawley, eds., *The Towneley Plays* (Early English Text Society, suppl. series, 13, 1994), vol. II, p. 202; Kahrl, 'Secular life and popular piety', p. 90.

[85] Chambers, *Mediaeval Stage*, vol. II, p. 341.

[86] *Ibid.*, p. 373.

[87] Geoffrey Chaucer, *The Wife of Bath's Prologue*, line 558, in Robinson, ed., *Works of Geoffrey Chaucer*, p. 81.

[88] Lumiansky and Mills, eds., *The Chester Mystery Cycle*, vol. I, p. 50.

A play might help to bind actors and audience in other ways; such, at least, was the ambition of Chaucer's parish clerk who played Herod in one of these performances in the hope of winning the fair Alison.[89] These attitudes by no means excluded the probability that for many the plays were also experienced as educational and uplifting. The old Cumberland peasant, who was interviewed by a puritan preacher in 1644 about salvation by Christ, may, as was alleged, have revealed his ignorance:

> 'Oh Sir', said he, 'I think I heard of that man you speak of once in a play at Kendall, called Corpus Christi play, where there was a man on a tree, and blood ran down', &c. And afterwards he professed he could not remember that he ever heard of salvation by Jesus, but in that play.[90]

On the other hand, the misunderstanding between preacher and peasant is no less likely to derive from deliberate irony on the latter's part. More seriously undermining of an authoritarian view was the fact that the plays could become a theatre for the dramatisation of religious debate within the urban community. Thus at York in 1536, the preparations for a performance of a play of St Thomas the Apostle – whose very subject matter treated the theme of doubt – led to riots when it was perceived that the drama was to be used by religious traditionalists as a vehicle for Catholic reaction.[91] The range of perceived meanings varied according to the times and political circumstances. A play such as the Cornish *Life of Meriasek*, performed at Camborne where the church was dedicated to this saint, must traditionally have been seen as the pious and civic celebration of a local hero, in the same spirit as the play of St Thomas Becket staged annually at Canterbury, or that of Helen at Beverley.[92] But it must also be relevant that around 1500, when the unique text of the Meriasek play was copied, there was outspoken hostility in the West Country to the pretensions of the Tudor monarchy. In this context the clash within the play between Meriasek, the virtuous Cornish figurehead, and the invading tyrant with the suggestive name of 'King Teudar', seems certain to have acquired an additional, politically rallying, resonance. Such a reading would account for the particular contemporary interest in the play at Camborne which led to the production of the surviving text, annotated as it is for performance.[93]

[89] Chaucer, *The Miller's Tale*, lines 3383–4, in Robinson, ed., *Works of Geoffrey Chaucer*, p. 50.

[90] A. Douglas and P. Greenfield, eds., *Records of Early English Drama: Cumberland, Westmorland, Gloucestershire* (Toronto, 1986), p. 219.

[91] Chambers, *Mediaeval Stage*, II, pp. 405–6; D. M. Palliser, *The Reformation in York* (Borthwick Paper, 40, York, 1971), p. 7.

[92] Chambers, *Mediaeval Stage*, II, pp. 344ff.; Smith, ed., *English Gilds*, pp. 148–9.

[93] W. Stokes, ed., *The Life of Saint Meriasek: A Cornish Drama* (London, 1872); M. Harris, *The Life of Meriasek: A Medieval Cornish Miracle Play* (Washington, 1977); J. P. D. Cooper, 'Henry Tudor, King Teudar and *Beunans Meriasek*: a dramatic conundrum' (unpublished paper) (I am grateful to John Cooper for showing me this paper – whose emphasis is different from that given here – before its publication).

The local and contemporary setting which the civic plays provided for the great events of Christian history had the effect of lifting the town to a status of cosmic importance: of identifying it as a new Jerusalem. When an angel sounds the last trump in the plays put on at Wakefield, two devils start off up Watling Street – for Wakefield is to be the setting of the Last Judgement.[94] Those, from a wide social spectrum, who assisted in the presentation of these plays were conscious of contributing to an apotheosis of their town, an event which reflected grandeur alike on the community and on its individual members. The transfiguring potential of these occasions was in many cases further intensified by the power of the language of the texts to shock the audience into a sense of active participation. At the opening of the 'N-Town' play of the Passion, a fashionably dressed Demon saunters through the audience, calling out to his friends and implicating all by his engaging manner:

> Gyff me your love, grawnt me myn affeccyon
> And I wyl unclose the tresour of lovys alyawns
> And gyff you youre desyrys afftere youre intencyon.[95]

Such a dramatic moment, within a sequence leading to the revelation of Christ's sacrifice in the very midst of the crowd, created the potential for the individual townsperson to experience a redeeming sense of his or her own contribution to a grand vision of the city.[96]

(vi) THE UPBRINGING OF YOUTH

That perception was fostered in part by a very high degree of lay control over the dramatic proceedings. Without exaggerating the tension between lay and clerical interests, which for the most part were mutually aligned or complementary, it can be observed that the leading role in the provision of education for the young in both English and Scottish towns shifted, between *c.* 1400 and the mid-sixteenth century, from ecclesiastical to lay hands. Great Benedictine monasteries such as Westminster Abbey continued to provide a grammar school education for city boys; but the quantity of new urban foundations by lay patrons, especially in the years after 1500, is striking.[97] On occasion this led to dispute, as at Coventry, where the mayor and council, having set up a public schoolmaster in

[94] Stevens and Cawley, eds., *Towneley Plays*, II, p. 406, and see pp. xix–xxii.

[95] Spector, ed., *The N-Town Play*, p. 248; Kahrl, 'Secular life and popular piety', p. 102.

[96] See also Rosser, 'Myth, image and social process'.

[97] N. Orme, *English Schools in the Middle Ages* (London, 1973), pp. 205–6 and ch. 7, *passim*; J. A. H. Moran, *The Growth of English Schooling, 1340–1548: Learning, Literacy, and Laicization in Pre-Reformation York Diocese* (Princeton, N.J., 1985), ch. 6; C. M. Barron, 'The expansion of education in fifteenth-century London', in J. Blair and B. Golding, eds., *The Cloister and the World* (Oxford, 1996), pp. 219–45; and cf. the cautionary remarks of N. Orme, 'The "laicisation" of English school education, 1250–1560', *History of Education*, 16 (1987), 81–9.

1435, had subsequently to argue against the prior of the cathedral that a citizen should have the right to send his child to school wherever he pleased.[98] Many town schools originated in private benefactions, like that of Agnes Mellors who chose the corporation of Nottingham to oversee the free school which she founded there in 1512.[99] In Scotland the transfer of control of grammar schools from church to town took place a little later than in England, during the course of the sixteenth century.[100] In smaller towns, where a powerful corporation was lacking, the responsibility of supervision was typically entrusted to a guild. The year 1521 saw the endowment of free schools both at Saffron Walden and at Wisbech; in each instance, the lay patron elected a local fraternity to hold the funds and manage the project. At Stratford-on-Avon, free schooling had been provided by the Holy Cross guild, in this case as a corporate guild initiative, for at least a century before this time.[101] Detailed syllabuses are scarcely recorded; but the Saffron Walden case, where the pattern of work was copied from Eton and Winchester, is a reminder that the educational ambitions of these schools should not be underestimated. Not every founder was a Dean Colet, and the free grammar school which he founded in 1509 at St Paul's, replacing the ancient cathedral school, was altogether exceptional.[102] Nevertheless it is striking that, by the end of the middle ages, free grammar school education for boys was being provided, under the aegis of guild or corporation, in most British provincial towns of any size.

The exact impact upon urban culture of this educational provision remains, however, difficult to assess (Plate 12). Naturally it remained optional and, while some schoolmasters themselves discouraged dullards, it may also be guessed that many parents countenanced attendance for their sons for no more than a year or two. To the child seated at his hard bench in the classroom, struggling to answer the master's question while the attendant usher brandished a birch rod, schooling appeared at times to be the agency of tyrannical authority – indeed, of the civil magistracy itself. The notebook of a London schoolboy contains this outburst:

> Wenest thou, huscher, with thi coyntyse
> Iche day beten us on this wyse,
> As thou wer lord of toun?

[98] Harris, ed., *Coventry Leet Book*, pp. 101, 118, 190.

[99] Orme, *English Schools in the Middle Ages*, p. 206.

[100] J. Durkan, forthcoming Scottish Records Society publication on Scottish medieval and early modern schooling.

[101] A. F. Sutton, 'Lady Joan Bradbury (d. 1530)', in C. M. Barron and A. F. Sutton, eds., *Medieval London Widows, 1300–1500* (London, 1994), pp. 209–38, at pp. 228–9; T. Wright, 'Rules of the Free School of Saffron Walden', *Archaeologia*, 34 (1852), 37–41; W. Watson, *An Historical Account of the Ancient Town and Port of Wisbech* (Wisbech, 1827), pp. 657–9; W. J. Hardy, *Stratford-on-Avon Corporation Records: The Guild Accounts* (Stratford-upon-Avon, 1886), p. 12; L. Fox, *The Early History of King Edward VI School Stratford-on-Avon* (Dugdale Society Occasional Papers, 29, 1984), pp. 3–7.

[102] J. B. Gleason, *John Colet* (Berkeley and Los Angeles, 1989), ch. 9.

We had levur scole for-sake
And ilche of us an-other crafte take,
Then long to be in thi bandoun.[103]

But, like all the forms of cultural dominion reviewed in this chapter, the master's sway was neither eternal nor complete. Liberty lay just a season or two away, and in the mean time fantasy supplied a language of revolt. A Londoner's commonplace book of the early sixteenth century contains the following cry of defiance:

I wold my master were an hare,
And all his bokes howndes were,
And I myself a joly hontere;
To blow my horn I wold not spare,
For if he were dede I wold not care![104]

The toys, games and rituals of urban childhood were, no less than lessons in school, handed down to youth from the world of adults: dolls, miniature pots and pans, toy soldiers, paramilitary weapons such as slings and bows and arrows (Plate 13).[105] Yet once again, their employment in playful practice could not be so freely prescribed; the acculturation of each younger generation was a ragged process. On Maundy Thursday and Good Friday, it was customary for children to be given the responsible task of calling people to church, using clappers instead of bells; but the young people of York applied themselves with such unlooked-for enthusiasm to this task that in 1520 a counter-injunction was issued.[106] The satisfaction which youth derives from annoying its seniors continued to be sought by apprentices and sons of citizens who, while enjoying in some respects wider liberty and greater responsibility than their modern counterparts, felt all the more keenly their lack of real independence. In a society in which marriage, with the concomitants of a separate household and attendant political rights, was generally delayed until the late twenties, youth had time on its hands.[107] In the towns young men, in particular, tended to gang together, as reiterated attempts to prevent apprentices from gathering after work make clear. The forms of self-expression of these youth groups were limited, yet they were capable of disturbing their elders' peace, as did the lads who in 1302 rolled a

[103] R. H. Robbins, ed., *Secular Lyrics of the XIVth and XVth Centuries*, 2nd edn (Oxford, 1955), p. 105 (*coyntyse*: cunning; *bandoun*: power); cf. Orme, *English Schools in the Middle Ages*, p. 139.

[104] R. L. Greene, *The Early English Carols* (Oxford, 1977), p. 246.

[105] N. Orme, 'The culture of children in medieval England', *P&P*, 148 (1995), 48–88; also B. Hanawalt, *Growing up in Medieval London* (Oxford, 1993), pp. 78–80, 114–18.

[106] A. Raine, ed., *York Civic Records* (Yorkshire Archaeological Society, Record Series, 106, 1942), p. 70.

[107] P. J. P. Goldberg, 'Marriage, migration, servanthood and life-cycle in Yorkshire towns of the later middle ages: some York cause paper evidence', *Continuity and Change*, 1 (1986), 141–69; M. Kowaleski, 'The history of urban families in medieval England', *JMed.H*, 14 (1988), 47–63, esp. 54–5.

barrel filled with stones down Gracechurch Street in the City of London, to the terror of the neighbourhood.[108] Others took bows and arrows and footballs to St Paul's Cathedral, where they persecuted the pigeons and vandalised the monuments, eliciting in 1385 the frantic condemnation of the bishop.[109] The dean and chapter of Exeter complained similarly around 1448 of 'young persons' who entered the cloister to play at 'the toppe, queke, penny prykke and most atte tenys, by the which the walles of the saide cloistre have be defowled and the glas wyndowes all to brost'.[110] There were occasions when children engaged in sports together with adults; but in such instances as these at London and Exeter, children evidently congregated with their peers, and played in happy defiance of authority. The subversive instincts of youth contributed also to the support given to novel Protestant ideas by the offspring of conventionally pious London citizens in the early sixteenth century.[111]

Naturally, town children grew up playing with one another in the street, more or less unsupervised.[112] But to further the ambition of their seniors that they should become civilised, a variety of fraternities was licensed for their supposedly more decorous pastime. A traditional association of youth with springtime lent children a prominent role in the celebration of May Day which was maintained, with self-conscious pastoralism, in all towns of the later middle ages. The 'May games' presented by local children in Westminster and elsewhere may have involved the dramatisation of stories of Robin Hood and Maid Marion.[113] A probably natural tendency for play to be, in part, divided by gender was acknowledged by the institution, in certain south-western urban parishes, of an annual theatrical performance by the girls alone.[114] A further likely structuring of games around neighbourhood ties seems also to be reflected in the creation of youth organisations with a local focus, such as the two girls' guilds, respectively of Bore Street and Fore Street, in fifteenth-century Bodmin.[115] In a number of towns young men joined guilds of 'bachelors', sometimes teaming up with their peers elsewhere, as did the young merchants of Lynn whose fraternity, founded in 1361 with a significant dedication to the peripatetic John the Baptist, soon recruited members from towns throughout the region.[116] While a few guilds recruited

[108] Thomas, ed., *Calendar of Early Mayor's Court Rolls . . . 1298–1307*, pp. 124–5.

[109] E. Rickert, ed., *Chaucer's World* (Oxford, 1948) pp. 48–9; cf. Riley, ed., *Memorials*, p. 580 (wrestling in St Paul's).

[110] S. A. Moore, ed., *Letters and Papers of John Shillingford, Mayor of Exeter 1447–50* (Camden Society, 2nd series, 2, 1871), p. 101.

[111] S. Brigden, 'Youth and the English Reformation', *P&P*, 95 (1982), 37–67.

[112] E.g. Rickert, ed., *Chaucer's World*, pp. 99–100.

[113] Chambers, *Mediaeval Stage*, I, pp. 174ff. For Robin Hood in Scottish towns, see Mill, *Mediaeval Plays*, pp. 21, 24–5; E. P. D. Torrie, ed., *The Gild Court Book of Dunfermline, 1433–1597* (Scottish Record Society, new series, 12, 1986), f. 49.

[114] J. Mattingly, 'The medieval parish gilds of Cornwall', *J of the Royal Institution of Cornwall*, new series, 10 (1989), 290–329, at 302.

[115] *Ibid.*, 311.

[116] Rosser, 'Solidarités', 1134.

children only, others admitted entire households to membership, providing a context for the integration of family and civil life.[117] All these societies shared a religious dimension, in the common mass and prayers for living and dead members; and a secular dimension, in the collective feast and variable forms of mutual aid. But while the reasons for joining a guild in individual cases were very various, participation offered particular attractions to those unmarried young adults who were always seeking to establish their position in urban society. To the single women who migrated to late medieval towns in large numbers, membership in a fraternity presented the opportunity to form respectable friendships, potentially leading to employment or to marriage. The latter appears to have been an expectation in the Holy Cross guild of Stratford-on-Avon, which charged a single woman only half the normal rate for admission, with the remainder payable when she married.[118] Work opportunities for both men and women were improved by fraternisation with their fellow brothers and sisters of a guild.[119] On the other hand, while such publicly recognised fraternities fostered a culture of respectability which could be invaluable to the otherwise rootless immigrant, other clubs, of more equivocal status, were formed by young journeymen who used the occasions of communal drinking to articulate their particular interests as dependent labourers.[120] To some eyes, this polarisation expressed nothing more than a stage of the life cycle. The journeymen bakers of London, challenged by the masters in 1441 as to their right to hold a fraternity, pointed out that the masters themselves had almost all, in their own youth, belonged to the same society.[121] But workers' guilds were not always so innocent. Although the master cordwainers of York about 1430 forbade confederacies amongst their wage-earning servants, the latter are nevertheless known to have continued thereafter to meet regularly together under the pious cover of a fraternity of St Augustine.[122] The processes of guild formation thus illustrate, once more, the ambivalence of medieval urban cultural forms: legitimised by and ostensibly committed to the establishment, yet in practice susceptible to appropriation for their particular uses by diverse and conflicting interest groups.

117 *Ibid.*; Rosser, 'Communities of parish and guild in the late middle ages', in S. J. Wright, ed., *Parish, Church and People* (London, 1988), pp. 29–55, at p. 34.

118 Rosser, 'Solidarités', 1134; cf. P. J. P. Goldberg, '"For better, for worse": marriage and economic opportunity for women in town and country', in P. J. P. Goldberg, ed., *Woman is a Worthy Wight* (Stroud, 1992), pp. 108–25.

119 G. Rosser, 'Going to the fraternity feast: commensality and social relations in late medieval England', *J of British Studies*, 33 (1994), 430–46; G. Rosser, 'Crafts, guilds and the negotiation of work in the medieval town', *P&P*, 154 (1997), 3–31.

120 G. Rosser, 'Workers' associations in English medieval towns', in J.-P. Sosson, ed., *Les métiers au moyen âge* (Louvain-la-Neuve, 1994), pp. 283–305.

121 R. R. Sharpe, ed., *Calendar of Letter-Books of the City of London* (London, 1899–1912), *Letter-Book K*, pp. 263–6.

122 D. M. Palliser, 'The trade gilds of Tudor York', in P. Clark and P. Slack, eds., *Crisis and Order in English Towns 1500–1700* (London, 1972), pp. 86–116, at pp. 104, 115.

(vii) LEARNING AND BOOKS

Schools, children's fraternities and working men's societies were all amongst the formal means whereby medieval urban culture was both mediated and constantly redefined. That list extended also to the institutions of higher education at Oxford, Cambridge, St Andrews, Aberdeen and Glasgow. These university towns exemplify in exaggerated form the emerging paradigm of persistent diversity within urban cultural unity. The uneasy relationship between 'town' and 'gown' is only the most obvious aspect of this complexity. The urban context of each university was vital to its early development and enduring character, notwithstanding the insularity of the later-developing colleges and the supramundane emphasis of the most prestigious studies undertaken there. In the middle of the period under consideration, around 1400, Oxford was a city of about 5,000 inhabitants, of whom some 1,500 were students, whose minor orders placed them beyond the jurisdiction of the secular magistrates.[123] The consequences of this recipe included some famously bloody clashes, but also a guild of St Thomas which brought together members from both communities.[124] The latent tension of this relationship has never been resolved, although its form has altered from time to time. The internal history of the universities, meanwhile, is conventionally told as the reduction of chaos to order. Between *c.* 1400 and *c.* 1550, both the social organisation and the intellectual training of students were made more directly subject than in the past to the chancellor's control. The requirement that every student reside in a college or academic hall, imposed at Oxford from 1410, was not only – though it was in part – a deliberate assault on the wayward lives of the 'chamber-deacons', those scholars who lived in unlicensed lodgings and allegedly spent their days and nights following the injunctions of the *Carmina Burana*.[125] The new legislation additionally formed part of an attempt by patrons at both universities to check the prevalence of legal and practical studies, and formally to impose an ascendancy of spiritual and theological work: an increased provision of teaching within recognised halls or colleges where students lived was part of an attempt to give a non-materialistic direction to the syllabus. Thus Lincoln College was founded at Oxford in 1427 with a mission to counter Lollard heresy, and in 1473 St Catharine's, Cambridge, was

[123] H. Rashdall, *The Universities of Europe in the Middle Ages*, ed. F. M. Powicke and A. B. Emden (Oxford, 1936), vol. III, ch. 3; Catto and Evans, eds., *History of the University of Oxford*, pp. 488–94; H. E. Salter, *Medieval Oxford* (Oxford Historical Society, 100, 1936), pp. 55–8; A. B. Cobban, *The Medieval English Universities: Oxford and Cambridge to c. 1500* (Aldershot, 1988), pp. 257–74; *VCH*, Oxfordshire, IV, pp. 15–16.

[124] C. I. Hammer, 'The town–gown fraternity of St. Thomas the Martyr in Oxford', *Mediaeval Studies*, 39 (1977), 466–76.

[125] Catto and Evans, eds., *History of the University of Oxford*, p. 502; J. A. W. Bennett, *Chaucer at Oxford and at Cambridge* (Oxford, 1974), p. 34. For the late-medieval legislation see Catto and Evans, eds., *History of the University of Oxford*, p. 624.

established for the exclusive study of philosophy and theology.[126] Yet the schools of Oxford and Cambridge were by the fourteenth century already serving too wide a diversity of professional and cultural interests to be conveniently strait-jacketed before the mid-sixteenth century. They had their roots in the world of practical knowledge – the law, letter-writing, mathematics for accounting and surveying – and more than half of all medieval students abandoned their courses without a degree, having acquired enough of these skills to secure employment in such spheres as estate administration and royal or local government. Some of this practical training could be obtained from the masters of *dictamen*, who covered the lower reaches of the Arts degree course; some was provided by teachers of business methods who operated beyond the fringes of the official university syllabus.[127] The university towns supported theological research at the highest level; they also served the agenda of the majority of students, whose view of education was more pragmatic. Their cultural identity was complex.

The making and ownership of books in wider urban society indicates a similar range of levels of reading. Geoffrey Chaucer, Londoner by adoption and royal servant, appears to have envisaged for his elaborately crafted poetical works a defined literary circle: on the one hand, well-read knights and courtiers such as Sir John Clanvowe; on the other, metropolitan intellectuals like John Gower and Adam Usk.[128] Yet the London merchant who in the fifteenth century owned a copy of William Langland's *Piers Plowman* need not have belonged to such an exclusive group.[129] And when William Caxton chose Westminster to be the site of the first English printing-press in 1476, that experienced business-man must have had in view a potential market comprising not merely the members of the king's Court, but also the MPs, lawyers, legal suitors and pilgrims who constantly flowed through that extraordinarily urbanised place. Indeed, his choice of works for publication – saints' lives, fables, chivalry and selected classical tales, all in English translation – implies the existence of a 'middle-brow' readership of literate townspeople with modest intellectual pretensions. At the same time, the very fact that Caxton also included the *Canterbury Tales* amongst his publications might suggest that the market for Chaucer – and so for other literature – had widened since the late fourteenth century, a development which the advent of cheaper printed editions (although Caxton's Chaucer because of its scale was still a costly volume) must further have encouraged.[130] The stock of books available in the York shop of Neville Mores

[126] Catto and Evans, eds., *History of the University of Oxford*, pp. 602–3. [127] *Ibid*., pp. 497, 523–6.

[128] P. Strohm, *Social Chaucer* (Cambridge, Mass., 1989), pp. 47–83, esp. pp. 63–4.

[129] R. A. Wood, 'A fourteenth-century owner of *Piers Plowman*', *Medium Aevum*, 53 (1984), 83–90; cf. Barron, 'Education in London', p. 242.

[130] H. S. Bennett, *English Books and Readers 1475 to 1557* (Cambridge, 1952); L. Hellinga, *Caxton in Focus: The Beginning of Printing in England* (London, 1982); Rosser, *Medieval Westminster*, pp. 209–15.

in the 1530s is suggestive: the range extended from Latin classics, including poetry and plays, through theology and sermons to legal treatises and other practical manuals.[131] And in Edinburgh by the 1540s there had emerged a literary circle of lawyers and merchants and their wives, with interests in both classical and vernacular literature.[132]

(viii) ARTISTIC PATRONAGE

The potential for personal involvement at most social levels extended also, to a greater degree than has commonly been assumed, into the sphere of musical and artistic production and consumption in the late medieval town. Most visible in the sources are the more exclusive recreations and cultural statements of the mercantile elite. Such a select metropolitan society as the London Puy of around 1300 offered a convivial setting in which wealthy burgesses could show off their sophistication and their skills in musical composition and performance, on a model copied from similar elite cultural associations in the towns of northern France.[133] A later member of the London ruling group, Richard Whittington (d. 1423), proclaimed his status as mayor and friend of the royal family by employing a seal in the form of an antique bust, a gesture towards the Italian Renaissance still extremely rare in England at that date.[134] Yet the Boston guild of St Mary, which in the late medieval period enjoyed a national reputation for the modernity and excellence of its musical life – at least one great early Tudor composer, John Taverner, emerged from this rich training-ground – embraced a socially diverse membership within the town and beyond, enabling both rich and humble participants to identify themselves as musical patrons.[135] At Louth in the same county of Lincolnshire, the parish was also musically ambitious in the early sixteenth century, importing organs of the latest manufacture from Flanders and having numerous 'pricksong' or polyphonic masses copied for the civic choir to perform.[136] At the level of individual

[131] D. M. Palliser and D. G. Selwyn, 'The stock of a York stationer, 1538', *The Library*, 5th series, 27 (1972), 207–19.

[132] T. van Heijnsbergen, 'The interaction between literature and history in Queen Mary's Edinburgh: the Bannatyne manuscript and its prosopographical context', in A. A. MacDonald, M. Lynch and I. B. Cowan, eds., *The Renaissance in Scotland* (Leiden, 1994), pp. 183–225.

[133] A. Sutton, 'Merchants, music and social harmony: the London Puy and its French and London contexts, circa 1300', *LJ*, 17 (1992), 1–17.

[134] C. M. Barron, 'Richard Whittington: the man behind the myth', in A. E. J. Hollaender and W. Kellaway, eds., *Studies in London History Presented to Philip Edmund Jones* (London, 1969), pp. 197–248; J. Alexander and P. Binski, eds., *Age of Chivalry* (London, 1987), p. 283.

[135] The guild's musical fame was noted by John Leland in his *Itinerary*, ed. T. Hearne, vol. VII (1) (London, 1744), p. 37. On Taverner, see S. Sadie, ed., *New Grove Dictionary of Music and Musicians*, (London, 1980), vol. XVIII, pp. 599–602. Further discussion of the guild in G. Rosser, *Medieval English Guilds 900–1600* (Oxford, forthcoming).

[136] R. C. Dudding, ed., *The First Churchwardens' Book of Louth 1500–1524* (Oxford, 1941), pp. 7, 28, 31, 44, 73, 91, 111, 136, 143.

performance, musical instruments were a familiar feature even of relatively modest urban households for long before the generations of Gibbons or Pepys. At Oxford, which archaeology has identified as a medieval centre of musical instrument making, Chaucer's fictional clerk, 'Handy Nicholas', is plausibly depicted with a psaltery at his bedside; and a later, historical clerk of Westminster, Roger Drewe, whose few possessions in his poor lodgings were mostly old and broken, nevertheless possessed several lutes.[137] An early sixteenth-century Londoner, Richard Hill, who worked in an alderman's service, copied into his commonplace book a substantial collection of songs, including at least one, on the murder of the London-born Thomas Becket, which had a local resonance.[138] The civic associations of certain musical compositions are exemplified also in the Coventry Carol, whose inclusion in the Corpus Christi pageant of the Coventry shearmen and tailors underlines its widespread familiarity.[139]

Architectural patronage in the towns of the later middle ages was characterised by a now familiar coexistence of elite determination of the available language with a personal sense of creative involvement spread throughout a wide spectrum of urban society. Municipal buildings were on occasion modelled more or less closely upon princely and aristocratic structures, for reasons relating to the social and political pretensions of the mercantile class, yet with consequences which redounded also upon the prestige and civic pride of the urban society at large. Town halls commonly fell into this category: the most splendid of all, the London Guildhall, was built in the early fifteenth century in direct imitation of the recently completed remodelling of the great royal hall at Westminster, itself now one of the most magnificent in Europe.[140] In smaller towns the scope, indeed the necessity, for a wide range of involvement in such works were commensurately increased. The construction of Abingdon's market cross was undertaken, probably shortly after the grant of a royal charter in 1441, by the town's major fraternity of the Holy Cross, a broad association which involved a very wide sector of the townspeople in its projects. The four-storeyed structure, some sixty feet high, bearing statues of prophets, saints and kings and so richly decorated with coloured paint and gold leaf that in sunlight it dazzled the beholder's eye, gained such wide renown that when, a century later, the citizens of Coventry determined to build the finest cross in the country, they stipulated that

[137] Catto and Evans, eds., *History of the University of Oxford*, p. 367 and n.; Chaucer, *The Miller's Tale*, line 3213, in Robinson, ed., *Works of Geoffrey Chaucer*, p. 48; Bennett, *Chaucer at Oxford and at Cambridge*, p. 31; Rosser, *Medieval Westminster*, p. 211.

[138] R. Dyboski, ed., *Songs, Carols, and other Miscellaneous Poems from the Balliol MS. 354, Richard Hill's Commonplace Book* (Early English Text Society, extra series, 101, 1907).

[139] *VCH*, Warwickshire, VIII, p. 215.

[140] J. Schofield, *The Building of London from the Conquest to the Great Fire* (London, 1984), pp. 107–8; C. M. Barron, *The Medieval Guildhall of London* (London, 1974). On guildhalls in general see Tittler, *Architecture and Power*.

it should be an imitation of that at Abingdon.[141] Participation in such an enterprise by ordinary townspeople might be generalised, as it largely was in this case (although wealthier contributors implanted upon the cross their personal coats of arms). It might alternatively be recognised by specific acknowledgement of the role of particular individuals or groups. The fine stained-glass windows newly installed in the large parish church of St Neot in Cornwall in the 1520s were credited in accompanying inscriptions to a variety of donors, including both wealthy and poorer individuals, and collectivities of young men, maidens and 'the wives of the west part of the parish'.[142] The more modest townsmen and women who contributed to these buildings and their decoration did not determine the hegemonic language in which they were expressed. None the less, precisely because their personal engagement helped to constitute that prestigious hegemony, participation in such collective architectural patronage could be experienced by humble townspeople as a redemptive act.

(ix) CULTURAL RESPONSES TO ECONOMIC CHANGE

It seems possible that the habits of reading and music making as leisure activities spread amongst townspeople during the mid-fifteenth century, at a period when economic recession slowed the pace of urban life. At this time, some elements of the markedly reduced urban population which survived the plague commanded in consequence larger capital resources than their predecessors, enabling many townspeople of middling rank to enjoy enhanced standards of domestic comfort and entertainment, including the acquisition of books.[143] This material context may additionally explain the appearance during the mid- to late fifteenth century of many of the earliest references to the commercialisation of urban sports and games. Fee-charging archery butts, bowling greens and tennis courts all begin to be recorded at this period, typically in suburban locations where they competed for the attention of holidaymaking townspeople.[144] On the other hand, the relatively enlarged contributions of parishioners towards the redecoration and even rebuilding of their churches during the fifteenth century calls for a different interpretation. Within the contracted economy of the period, the very high capital costs of constructing, for example, a new bell-tower called for

[141] M. J. H. Liversidge, 'Abingdon's "right goodly cross of stone"', *Antiquaries J*, 63 (1983), 315–25; *VCH*, Warwickshire, VIII, pp. 143–4.

[142] G. C. Gorham, *The History and Antiquities of Eynesbury and St Neot's in Huntingdonshire and of St Neot's in the County of Cornwall* (London, 1820–4), pp. 233–45; C. S. Gilbert, *A Historical Survey of the County of Cornwall* (London, 1817–20), vol. II, pp. 939–44; Mattingly, 'Gilds of Cornwall', 304.

[143] C. Dyer, *Standards of Living in the Middle Ages* (Cambridge, 1984), ch. 7.

[144] Riley, ed., *Memorials*, p. 571; R. H. Morris, *Chester in the Plantagenet and Tudor Reigns* (Chester, n.d.), p. 330; *VCH*, Warwickshire, VIII, p. 217.

the investment of a large proportion of townspeople's collectively diminished resources. The evidence of churchwardens' accounts, wills and surviving church buildings testifies to a markedly growing lay commitment to local urban churches during the century and a half prior to the Reformation.[145] The church of St Nicholas at Aberdeen was typical of a large class in the support it received, not only from the town authorities, local gentry and nobility, but also from the ordinary townspeople. Gifts were made both in cash and kind, including chalices and other ornaments, and in the labour of local people who helped to maintain the church, for example by repainting the image of St Nicholas. In Scotland, moreover, the lavish support of parish churches and of craft, fraternity and burgh altars was enhanced by the accelerated foundation of collegiate churches after 1400.[146] The participation of the urban laity in fraternities of their own creation tells a similar story. Although the guilds were an ancient phenomenon, they proliferated in the British towns of the fourteenth and, even more, the fifteenth centuries. Amongst their other attractions, they offered to lay men and women the opportunity to determine the particular focus of their devotion, to generate funds for religious images or books, and to hire clergy of their own choice. Spreading secular education evidently fed rising lay expectations of clerical provision; it was normal for such a guild to demand a decent level of learning and sobriety from the priests whom it employed. These enterprises typically complemented, rather than competed with, the parochial establishment. But the extent to which the church, and in particular the urban church, of the late medieval period was becoming controlled by groups of lay parishioners is remarkable.[147]

Yet while the fifteenth and early sixteenth centuries granted to many town dwellers both a diversification of their leisure activities and an increasing role in shaping the patterns of urban religious observance, the social and economic instability of the late medieval town gave rise in addition to new perceptions of welfare needs, and in turn to the creation of a range of more or less novel charitable institutions. The period from the fourteenth to the early sixteenth century was marked far less by the foundation of large, conventual hospitals of a kind more commonly encountered in the twelfth and thirteenth centuries than it was by the launch of a multitude of smaller-scale, neighbourhood initiatives. The modest size of many of the new institutions has led later commentators to an

145 D. Keene, *Survey of Medieval Winchester* (Winchester Studies, 2, Oxford, 1985), vol. I, pp. 116–18, 126–8; Rosser, *Medieval Westminster*, pp. 263–71; and refs. in n. 58 above.

146 *Registrum Episcopatus Aberdonensis* (Spalding and Maitland Clubs, 1845), vol. I, p. 35; Aberdeen AO, MS Sasine Register, vol. I, p. 198, vol. II, p. 199, vol. III, p. 34; *Extracts from the Council Register of the Burgh of Aberdeen* (Spalding Club, 1844–8), vol. I, pp. 83, 68, 85–7; E. P. Dennison and J. Stones, *Historic Aberdeen* (Scottish Burgh Survey, 1997); I. B. Cowan and D. E. Easson, *Medieval Religious Houses: Scotland* (London, 1976), pp. 213–30.

147 Swanson, *Church and Society*, pp. 255–60 (with some qualifying remarks); Rosser, 'Communities of parish and guild'.

erroneously dismissive view of their significance. *Maisonsdieu*, small urban almshouses offering variable support to the very poor, were founded in considerable numbers during the later middle ages, typically by individuals, especially women, who made their own houses available for the purpose. Eighteen are documented in York alone.[148] Fraternities, in addition to providing material assistance to their own members, frequently offered charitable support in a wider sphere. Contrary to the later Protestant claim that Catholic almsgiving was indiscriminate, in practice late medieval urban charity was as a rule carefully targeted to address specific perceived problems. This has been shown to be as true of an old-established source of monastic almsgiving such as Westminster Abbey as it was of the newer lay initiatives which were often pursued through guilds.[149] Many guild hospitals, although open to non-members, excluded the desperately poor; but others, albeit far from adequately, catered for this very group, as did a hostel for sick beggars operated at Charing Cross by the guild of St Mary Rounceval.[150] The Boston fraternity of Our Lady made variable weekly distributions to particular paupers of that town, in addition to its management of a poor house for thirteen long-term residents, who were recruited after interview from towns throughout the region.[151] Other community-run infirmaries specialised in caring for epileptics or the blind.[152] The fragmentary character and humble scale of these and similar charitable ventures in the late medieval town were never commensurate to the actual need; the majority were directed rather to the respectable poor than to the unknown migrant or to the permanently indigent; and the abruptness and extent of the sixteenth-century demographic explosion were alleged by reformers of that period to necessitate a more authoritarian and centralised response to welfare issues.[153] Yet late medieval urban charity offered scope for participation, and consequently for a redeeming sense of personal contribution to the common good, to a very wide range of townsmen and women.

[148] P. H. Cullum and P. J. P. Goldberg, 'Charitable provision in late medieval York: "To the praise of God and the use of the poor"', *NHist.*, 29 (1993), 24–39; P. H. Cullum, '"For poor people harberless": what was the function of the maisonsdieu?', in D. J. Clayton, R. G. Davies and P. McNiven, eds., *Trade, Devotion and Government: Papers in Late Medieval History* (Gloucester, 1994), pp. 36–54; Cowan and Easson, *Medieval Religious Houses: Scotland*, pp. 162–200.

[149] Harvey, *Living and Dying*, ch.1.

[150] Rosser, *Medieval Westminster*, pp. 310–20; another instance at Dunstable: *VCH*, Bedfordshire, III (London, 1912), pp. 366–7.

[151] BL, MS Egerton 2886, ff. 5v, 81v, 274v.

[152] E.g. A. H. Thomas, ed., *Calendar of Plea and Memoranda Rolls of the City of London, A.D. 1381–1412* (Cambridge, 1932), p. 23 (hospital for those who had lost their memory); Rosser, *Medieval Westminster*, p. 320 (fraternity hospital for epileptics). See also M. Carlin, 'Medieval English hospitals', in L. Granshaw and R. Porter, eds., *The Hospital in History* (London, 1989), pp. 21–39.

[153] P. Slack, *Poverty and Policy in Tudor and Stuart England* (London, 1988), pp. 114–22 and passim; P. Slack, *The Impact of Plague in Tudor and Stuart England* (London, 1985).

(x) CONCLUSION: THE MORALITY OF URBAN LIFE

This chapter's review of the medieval rhetoric of urbanism began with a positive image of sophisticated civility opposed to a simpler, and by that token supposedly inferior, culture of the countryside. However, the rhetorical inverse of that image was no less forcefully articulated by contemporary critics of the town. To such observers, complexity was by definition morally equivocal. The widening scale of economic enterprise; the alienating rigmarole of bureaucratic and professional practice; the sheer novelty of so many commodities and relationships in the town, were felt by some moralists to be encouraging townspeople to believe that their world had outgrown the old values of simplicity, honesty and truth. 'Beware guile in borough' was a warning sounded by country people during the Peasants' Revolt; but the sense that the city was a world of 'false seeming', where the only truth was deception, was felt equally by some medieval townspeople.[154] Falsity of appearances was an observed symptom of the unsettling process of social change, as newly rich inferiors aped the fashions of their betters. Thomas Hoccleve ridiculed the monstrosity and pretension of the clothes on which late-fourteenth-century Londoners squandered their livelihoods:

> But this me thinkith an abusion,
> To see one walk in gownes of scarlet,
> Twelve yerdes wyd, with pendant sleves downe
> On the grounde, and the furrour ther-in set
> Amounting unto twenty pounds or bet;
> And if he for it payde have, he no good
> Hath lefte him where-wit for to bye an hood.[155]

Lying was also the full-time occupation, not only of criminal imposters and cheats,[156] but of the ostensibly respectable merchant who traded in adulterated goods,[157] and of the prestigious lawyer whose commitment to profiting from his cases transcended any concern with justice.[158] John Gower's satire may here stand for an extensive genre:

> Fraud also of its trickery
> Oftentimes in mercery
> Cheats people diversely,
> Being full of artifice,

[154] S. Justice, *Writing and Rebellion: England in 1381* (Berkeley and Los Angeles, 1994), pp. 186–7.

[155] Thomas Hoccleve, *The Regement of Princes*, lines 421–7, in *Hoccleve's Works*, vol. III, ed. F. J. Furnivall (Early English Text Society, extra series, 72, 1897), p. 16. See also Chaucer, *The Miller's Tale*, lines 3235ff., 3316ff., in Robinson, ed., *Works of Geoffrey Chaucer*, p. 49.

[156] Riley, ed., *Memorials*, pp. 352, 430–2, 445, 479, 531, 645, 661.

[157] E.g. S. Wenzel, ed., *Fasciculus Morum: A Fourteenth-Century Preacher's Handbook* (University Park, Pa., 1989), p. 345.

[158] E.g. *ibid.*, pp. 319–21.

Of joking and of nonsense,
To make fools of silly people
So as to get their money.[159]

Greed was widely held to be a distinctive characteristic of civic culture, so much so that one preacher's handbook of the fourteenth century explained how the fear of loss of possessions made the majority of townspeople slaves to the elite.[160] The shifting moral universe of the late medieval town seemed to some to justify a relativistic, casuistical morality deployed as a cover for avarice and envy:

> If there is a young merchant, a stranger in some town, perhaps come from poor stock yet smart and flourishing in prosperity . . . will not at once people rise up and become envious of him and say: 'How can he gather so many riches for himself? These things cannot be right!' And thus, in their envious scheming, they will put such a man in some office where, willy-nilly, he will fall into arrears and therby lose his goods and become poor. When they are accused of this, they say that they have done this for the salvation of his soul, to put down the greed and pride that have recently grown in him.[161]

The fact that this image of the urban world as superficial and lacking in moral stability is recurrent, from Juvenal to Walter Benjamin, did not render it any less immediately real to many late medieval town dwellers.

Nor, however, should that rhetorically powerful image of falsity and fragmentation be confused with a balanced description of the urban experience. Once again, an occasionally dominant theme of moral criticism of certain forms of urban behaviour needs to be heard in conjunction with its variations in daily life. Indeed, the attraction, evident at a number of points in this chapter, of an image of urban collective identity lay precisely in the perceived instability both of the townsperson's individual situation and of the moral environment of the city. It was in direct response to the perceived moral uncertainties of urban living that town dwellers sought in various ways, a number of which have been touched upon in the course of this chapter, to build relationships of trust with their neighbours. By selective appropriation of elements of a dominant cultural language, they were able to give voice to a sectional or individual attitude, and by so doing to experience their relationship to the city as positive. The cultural medium of the late medieval town derived its real and perceived force from its users' ability to play with a creative ambiguity; to express in the dignity of a rich and common language the passion of a particular view.

[159] John Gower, *Mirour de l'omme*, lines 25273–9, in G. L. Macaulay, ed., *The Complete Works of John Gower* (Oxford, 1899–1902), vol. I, p. 279, trans. in Rickert, *Chaucer's World*, pp. 27–8.
[160] Wenzel, ed., *Fasciculus Morum*, p. 325. [161] *Ibid.*, p. 155.

· 16 ·

The built environment 1300–1540

JOHN SCHOFIELD AND GEOFFREY STELL

'COMING INTO Canterbury', wrote Charles Dickens in *David Copperfield*, 'I loitered through the old streets with a sober pleasure that calmed my spirits and eased my heart. There were the old signs, the old names over the shops . . . the venerable Cathedral towers . . . the battered gateways.' For Dickens, and for the modern visitor to towns where medieval fabric can still be seen (such as Norwich, which claims to have more surviving medieval churches than any other town in western Europe), the built environment creates a powerful sense of place and a reassuring frame of reference. We can try to reconstruct the former townscape and delve behind it to study the relationship between physical settings and the attitudes which influenced the conduct of medieval life.

The construction of the built environment in medieval British towns reflected both social values and personal initiatives or personal monument making, be it repairing a bridge, erecting a conduit or adding a chapel to the local parish church. But the period was not static. Over the two and a half centuries covered by this chapter, certain developments and underlying trends can be seen.

During the medieval period, several features of construction and amenity first appeared in towns: jetties for the first floor and higher by 1300 (already in London by 1246), dormer windows by 1450 and the flooring over of halls which probably happened in profusion in towns during the fifteenth century before it was necessary or thought fashionable in the countryside. The underlying motors were the conjunction of pressure on space and the availability of cash, generated by trade and other urban pursuits (such as rents), which created the climate for innovation and display, both at the level of grand patronage in a church or the ordinary house.

Secondly, the period before 1300 had been one of large, stark constructions: castles, cathedrals, the great majority of the monastic houses, hospitals and friaries; and most of the examples of town defences in England and Wales. After 1350, with few exceptions, smaller constructions or relatively minor additions to the larger complexes were the norm. At the same time, many towns complained of decay, and some certainly did: to take Lincoln as an example, the number of parish churches fell from forty-six in the fourteenth century to nine in 1549. The suburbs and the back streets were progressively abandoned, and Lincoln, except for the area around the cathedral, became a single-street town which it remained until modern times.

Thirdly, towns at the borders of regions show the contrasts of how the urban mentality differed between those regions, and how a town in this position could change character over time. This is illustrated most potently by Berwick-upon-Tweed, the anglicised built environment of which now betrays few signs of its origins as a major Scottish medieval burgh. Perhaps similar dual natures might be looked for in Welsh border towns.

(i) UNDERLYING INFLUENCES AND LARGER TOPOGRAPHICAL COMPONENTS

An underlying skeleton of the town was often formed by natural features, such as hills and streams, or included a man-made reaction to the elements, such as sea embankments. Many medieval towns were moulded to contours of hills which affected the design and development of the place. Some, like Durham, Edinburgh or Lincoln, still display the crags or steep slopes on which they were built; others, like the City of London, far less so.

Most towns, even the larger ones, had rural overtones. There were barns and probably farms within the walls of many; in the earlier part of the period, all kinds of farmyard animals and fowl roamed the backlands and sometimes the streets. The rural appearance of many of the smaller towns has led to a view that the forms of buildings, especially houses, in the town were only adaptations into a pressurised urban environment of essentially rural prototypes. In the early middle ages, this was no doubt partly true; but also, from the tenth century in medium-sized and larger towns, special urban building forms such as timber cellars had been developed. Other, more institutional buildings were peculiar to towns, so the medieval rural visitor would have seen a mixture of the strange and the familiar.

Once established, towns were constantly adding or losing parts, and adding, replacing or losing individual buildings and monuments. The largest item of expenditure in cash and energy were the town defences (Plate 14).[1] Extensions to circuits sometimes followed growth of population or expansion of building beyond original boundaries, as at Cardiff and Pembroke in the fourteenth century. Rebuilding the defences to define a smaller area than before, which presumably

[1] C. J. Bond, 'Anglo-Saxon and medieval defences', in J. Schofield and R. Leech, eds., *Urban Archaeology in Britain* (CBA Res. Rep., 61, 1987), pp. 92–116.

reflects urban decay or retrenchment, is rare but there are examples at New Winchelsea, where the defences in 1414–15 reduced the area of the town, and at Berwick, where the Elizabethan circuit covered only two-thirds of the area of the fourteenth-century town.

Notable English town walls of the fourteenth century include that in brick at Hull, begun in the 1320s, and the wall of Hartlepool, in stone, dating probably to the years after 1315; later in the century embellishments, including gates, were added at Canterbury and Winchester. Fifteenth-century building or repairs, some perhaps of more symbolic than military significance, took place at Salisbury (two gates and a token bank), Lynn (where the south gate looked as if it had been transposed from a college or monastery) and more practically at London in 1477, when the wall on the north side of the city was given a new parapet and arches along its internal base, probably strengthening against cannon (Henry IV of England had used cannon against the walls of Berwick in 1405). Many towns continued building the defences for generations; for instance Coventry, where nearly two centuries of fund-raising and building from 1355 to 1539 resulted in a circuit of two and a half miles; but even so, only part of the town was enclosed by walls. In general, the town defences of England have been characterised, with few exceptions, as 'too weak, too incomplete and too few'.[2] Comparatively few towns had defences and many that had were poorly constructed, being intended largely for demarcation purposes as in the Salisbury example. Norwich, with twelve gates and nearly forty towers over its two and a half miles, was exceptional in its provision for defence, but typical in that the area of settlement within the walled area was considerably less than the defences circumscribed.

Contrasting markedly with the evidence from England and the European mainland, there is a comparative lack of formal walled defences in Scotland. Clearly, Pedro de Ayala, the Spanish ambassador to the court of James IV, was exaggerating when he wrote in 1498 that 'there is not more than one fortified town in Scotland because the kings do not allow their subjects to fortify them'.[3] So too was John Major in 1521, when he referred to Perth as 'the only walled town in Scotland', by which he included towns 'even with low walls'. He explained that 'the Scots do not hold themselves to need walled cities; and the reason of this may be that they get them face to face with the enemy with no delay, and build their cities, as it were, of men'.[4] Edinburgh was certainly a walled town, but our knowledge of pre-sixteenth-century structures and circuits is

[2] C. Coulson, 'Battlements and the bourgoisie: municipal status and the apparatus of urban defence in later medieval England', in S. Church and R. Harvey, eds., *Medieval Knighthood, V* (Woodbridge, 1995), pp. 137–8.

[3] P. H. Brown, ed., *Early Travellers in Scotland* (Edinburgh, 1891), p. 47. See also *ibid.*, p. 19 and n. 4.

[4] A. Constable, ed., *John Major's History of Greater Britain (1521)* (Scottish History Society, 1st series, 10, 1892), p. 29.

based mainly on documentary record and a few excavated fragments. The certain physical traces are of the so-called Flodden Wall, put up at about the time Major was writing, and the extension known as the Telfer Wall erected over a century later. Stirling, too, retains stretches of its town wall which, possibly replacing earlier earthwork defences, appear to date substantially from the 1540s and later. It is also known that Inverness, Selkirk and Perth possessed defences comprising ditches, ramparts and palisades, with indications that at least one of Perth's gates may have been stone-built. Only Berwick-upon-Tweed preserves substantial visible traces of early defences of stone and lime, and these probably originated in English operations of 1297–8. Further scraps of evidence can be adduced from other towns such as Peebles, but the overall picture is not impressive.[5] The simple fact is that formal urban defences of stone cost a great deal to organise, build and maintain, as the English evidence from York, Hull and Coventry testifies. For the most part, the boundaries of Scottish towns were demarcated by back garden walls, comparable to the rural head dyke, and the points of entry, described formally as ports, were mainly simple gateways designed as much for fiscal and social control as for military security.

In both Scotland and England, some town gates were of masonry but the defences were of earth and timber, giving both strength and prestige to the entry points into the town. This was the case, for instance, at Aberdeen and Pontefract. At Banbury there were four gates, but no walls; Glasgow, Lichfield and Salisbury also had gates across their major streets, but no walls and only token ditches, if at all.[6]

Defences performed many functions besides defence of the town and exclusion of the outsider. Gates, which were often disproportionately splendid in relation to their urban enclosures, were used as accommodation for civic officers, as chapels, lock-ups and meeting rooms. They could also be used to exclude victims of plague. The defensive system included fishponds at Stafford and York, and a lake at Edinburgh; at Hereford water from the town ditch drove mills. Further, defences were only one of several competing considerations for space. Token barriers were enveloped and assimilated; there was frequent encroachment into castle and town ditches by the day-to-day rubbish dumping, and later the wall was used for building on. At London the town ditch by Ludgate was filled up by 1300 to form gardens for a considerable distance along Old Bailey (the extramural street outside the ditch), less than a century after its main documented cutting in 1212.

[5] W. M. Mackenzie, *The Scottish Burghs* (Edinburgh, 1949), pp. 38–44; RCAHMS, *Inventory of Edinburgh* (Edinburgh, 1951), pp. lxii–lxvi, no. 59–60; RCAHMS, *Inventory of Stirlingshire* (Edinburgh, 1963), p. 2, no. 249; RCAHMS, *Inventory of Peebleshire* (Edinburgh, 1967), p. 2, no. 544; R. A. Brown, H. M. Colvin and A. J. Taylor, eds., *The History of the King's Works* (London, 1963), pp. 563–71. See also J. Schofield, 'Excavations south of Edinburgh High Street 1973–4', *Proc. Soc. Antiq. Scot.*, 107 (1975–6), 155–241.

[6] P. D. A. Harvey, 'Banbury', in *BAHT*, I, p. 4; J. H. Kellett, 'Glasgow', in *ibid.*, p. 4.

At Shrewsbury around 1400, a section of town wall was levelled almost down to the plinth, and became the foundation for new houses.[7] Thus one feature of the period reviewed here is that defences became gradually obscured by new or extended houses and yards, although the suburbs further out might be decaying and contracting. The shrinking of settlement outside the town gates would tend to highlight the approach roads, where inns and other suburban functions stayed on. In big places such as London, by contrast, the suburbs were developing again, and this time on a larger scale than before, from the late fifteenth century.

The town often spread in a rather different manner into the adjacent river or sea. A waterfront zone often developed as a narrow strip of reclaimed land along the river bank or shore, modifying it to suit the needs both of landing and exporting of goods, and in time for housing, warehouses and other buildings; even churches. Thus many towns actually increased their area over the medieval period by pushing out into the water. Such reclaimed areas can be identified at ports such as Bristol, Hull, Lynn, Newcastle and Perth.[8]

To take the example of London, all the present land south of Thames Street, which runs for a mile from the Tower of London in the east to Blackfriars in the west, is a reclamation zone; it began in the tenth century, radiating out from a small number of pre-Conquest landing-places and points of congregation on the shore.[9] Excavation on many sites south of Thames Street since 1972 has revealed details of the reclamation process; revetments, buildings and river stairs, waterlogged constructions in timber which can be dated by dendrochronology.[10] Most of this reclamation had however taken place by 1300. Thereafter, river quay walls in stone, found from the twelfth century near public points such as landing-places and bridges in larger ports such as Bristol, Dublin and London, became common on private properties; not requiring constant repair, these walls tended to put an end to the reclamation process itself, in London during the fifteenth century. The waterfront areas of towns were generally not walled (for instance, at London, Hull and Yarmouth), perhaps because access into the town was important; exceptions were in the north at Newcastle and in Wales. By 1540, as shown in a drawing of the London waterfront (Plate 15), this zone in many towns would be an indented, variegated townscape with institutional

7 M. O. H. Carver, ed., *Two town houses in medieval Shrewsbury*, *Trans. of the Shropshire Arch. Soc.*, 61 (1983).

8 G. Milne and B. Hobley, eds., *Waterfront Archaeology in Britain and Northern Europe* (CBA Res. Rep., 41, 1981); G. Milne, 'Waterfront archaeology in British towns', in Schofield and Leech, eds., *Urban Archaeology in Britain*, pp. 192–200; G. L. Good, R. H. Jones and M. W. Ponsford, eds., *Waterfront Archaeology* (CBA Res. Rep., 74, 1991).

9 K. Steedman, T. Dyson and J. Schofield, *Aspects of Saxo-Norman London*, vol. III: *The Bridgehead and Billingsgate to 1200* (LMAS, Special Paper, 14, 1992).

10 E.g. G. Milne and C. Milne, *Medieval Waterfront Development at Trig Lane, London* (LMAS, Special Paper, 5, 1982); G. Milne, *Timber Building Techniques in London, c. 900–c. 1400* (LMAS, Special Paper, 15, 1992).

and private developments packed together, interspersed with cranes of various designs.

Rivers also had to be crossed, or made accessible by bringing roads to them for the loading and unloading of goods and persons. On some major tidal Scottish rivers, a number of towns (for example Dumfries, Glasgow, Perth, Stirling) developed around bridges which were the lowest crossing-point (other than ferries) and which coincided roughly with the tidal limit (and the consequent benefits to navigation).[11] This was, however, not an invariable pattern: Aberdeen and Ayr stood closer to the mouth of the river. To the south in England, Bewdley grew largely after it had migrated to the riverside, following construction of a bridge in 1447, so much so that it could be regarded as a new town, post-dating Queenborough of 1368 which is normally taken to be the last medieval planted town. The effect of building a bridge at one town could be damaging to another: the construction of a bridge over the upper Thames at Abingdon in the fifteenth century was a cause of decay to nearby Wallingford, also on the river, but now placed at a severe disadvantage.

A main road running through a town was probably as important a cause of growth and therefore of congregation of notable buildings as any other.[12] Indeed, the most common and recognisable characteristic of a medieval town, as in succeeding periods, was the traffic jam.[13] The importance of the road to a settlement can be seen in the number of inns which accrued to make the village or town a stopping place along the route. In larger towns the concentration of inns along suburban streets, or round local landmarks such as friaries, shows the strength of traffic along those routes.

A final large topographical element in many towns was the castle; but this will be noted only incidentally here. Nearly all castles in towns were creations of the two centuries before 1300, and had passed their prime by the fourteenth century. After the brilliant Edwardian period of military architecture, castles now displayed a growing tendency to concentrate on amenities rather than defences (with exceptions, such as the gatehouses at Alnwick in 1314, and at Warwick, about 1370). One kind of addition made to several castles in the fourteenth century was a strong tower containing one or more private chambers, as at Richmond or Pickering, or sometimes in tiers, as at Ludlow and Warwick. At the end of the period there is, however, an important flurry of architectural and artistic activity in royal palaces, some of them in towns, such as the Parliament Hall of Stirling Castle, an impressive Renaissance design of 1496, or Henry VIII's Bridewell Palace in London (1518–23), which probably contained the first staircase designed expressly for state occasions. But the main ranges of castles and

[11] E. C. Ruddock, 'Bridges and roads in Scotland: 1400–1750', in A. Fenton and G. Stell, eds., *Loads and Roads in Scotland and Beyond* (Edinburgh, 1984), pp. 67–91 at pp. 81–2.

[12] J. M. Steane, *The Archaeology of Medieval England and Wales* (London, 1985), pp. 104–9.

[13] M. Carlin, *Medieval Southwark* (London, 1996), p. 251.

palaces, by their very nature, were rarely integrated into a town's business or civic life; occasionally (as with Bridewell which was given to the City to become a hospital and workhouse in 1552) the buildings of a palace later took on another function.

(ii) CIVIC BUILDINGS AND STRUCTURES

In Britain, town authorities do not seem to have been much concerned with the wider coordination of planning of streets or areas, or with the deliberate grading of streets by width which can be seen in bastide towns in medieval France, but there was considerable thought given to the provision of amenities.

Towns were above all markets. The market emphasis within late medieval towns found physical expression in civic structures such as market buildings, toll houses, the public weigh-beam, public quays and attention to city gates which were supposed to act as civic turnstiles. By the late thirteenth century covered specialised markets and civic warehouses for food, grain or cloth were to be found, mostly in principal towns; in 1370 at Bristol four places were assigned for the sale of fuel in bulk.[14] London's mid-fifteenth-century Leadenhall market comprised a large market space surrounded by arcades, with two floors of warehouses above, a chapel and a grammar school, the last two endowed by the rich mercer Simon Eyre. The complex was partly a municipal grain store, a feature of several large European cities, and was in this case perhaps prompted by a widespread famine in Europe in 1437–8.[15]

Besides providing a market place, sometimes with covered stalls, the town or its lord was concerned to supply clean water, essential both for consumption and for industries such as textile production; running water drove corn or fulling mills. Many European towns organised a public water supply during the thirteenth century, often following the lead set by religious houses such as the friaries (as in London itself; in the fourteenth century, Gloucester, Lichfield and Southampton relied more directly on the friars to provide the supply). The fourteenth to sixteenth centuries saw extensions to such systems, to reach most parts of the intramural town, and the conduits were often commissioned by individual rich citizens, usually when in civic office. Bristol had several conduits by 1400, and Coventry possessed four in 1483. At other towns, such as Dunfermline, an efficient water system was contrived by combining a stream and a number of built channels which supplied mills, monastery buildings and fishponds.[16] At Exeter, the cathedral made piped water available to the city in

[14] F. B. Bickley, ed., *Little Red Book of Bristol* (Bristol and London, 1900), vol. II, p. 54.

[15] M. W. Samuel, 'The fifteenth-century garner at Leadenhall, London', *Antiquaries J.*, 59 (1989), 119–53.

[16] E. P. D. Torrie, 'The gild of Dunfermline in the fifteenth century' (Ph.D thesis, University of Edinburgh, 1984), pp. 130–2.

1346, but in the early fifteenth century the town itself constructed a separate underground passage from a well outside the walls, down the High Street to a conduit erected in 1441 at the junction of three streets.[17]

Though comprehensive sewerage systems were a thing of the future, town authorities also gave thought to the effective disposal of human and trade waste. At Exeter, in the twelfth century, a stream unequivocally called the Shitbrook conveyed human refuse to the River Exe, but by 1467 the city authorities had provided common latrines over one of the mill-leats on Exe Island in the river.[18] As today, such public facilities were likely to be provided only in the town centres (such as by the main gate of a monastery, as at Westminster). At Southwark, a populous suburb, there seem to have been no public privies until the 1560s; in London generally, by this time, most houses had their own privies, and the authorities tried to insist on their provision in the alleys which were rapidly being filled out with buildings at that time.[19]

The maintenance of bridges, watering places, grates and watercourses was usually the responsibility of the owners of adjacent property, whether private or corporate (such as a parish). Civic officers concerned with both paving the street and (more rarely) cleaning it appear from the late thirteenth century; in Cambridge, Coventry and York a pavage tax was levied on merchandise to pave the town. Traffic regulations, mainly concerned with management of herds of beasts coming into the meat markets, are known in fourteenth-century Bristol, and there were similar regulations in Coventry, London, Nottingham and other towns.[20]

The chief civic building would be the town hall or guildhall. This begins to appear in records in the twelfth and thirteenth centuries, when towns were straining towards self-government. Around the hall, used as a court and for assemblies, would be service buildings (especially kitchens for feasts) and rooms used for storing ammunition and keeping prisoners. At Cardiff, as in many other places, the town hall of 1338 housed both the assizes and the court of common council on the first floor, with the corn market and a variety of traders' stalls below. Timber-framed public halls such as at Canterbury, Coventry, Leicester and Lavenham were adaptations of house designs, but the larger towns in eastern England, during the fifteenth century, could afford guildhalls in stone which are comparable with those in continental towns (London, Lynn, Norwich, York). The porch of the London Guildhall (Plate 16) was embellished with statues of civic virtues (Plate 17), a form of self-assertion by the city which finds parallels in statuary on town halls in many of the larger continental towns.

[17] D. Portman, *Exeter Houses 1400–1700* (Exeter, 1966), p. 16. [18] *Ibid.*, p. 15.

[19] Carlin, *Southwark*, pp. 236–7.

[20] G. T. Salusbury, *Street Life in Medieval England*, 2nd edn (Oxford, 1948), pp. 40–71.

In Scottish burghs, tolbooths (also known as town houses) were the centres of municipal administration, justice and ceremonial. The name, *tolloneum* or *tolbuith*, reflected their function as collection-points for tolls and customs, but from the outset they appear to have been multi-purpose buildings, serving not only as the meeting places for burgh councils and courts but also as prisons. A series of royal grants in the fourteenth century made provision for the building or enlargement of tolbooths in Aberdeen, Dundee, Edinburgh, Irvine and Montrose, but, apart from the outline in the present-day pavement of Edinburgh's 'Heart of Midlothian' (demolished 1817) and the excavated foundations of a tolbooth at Peebles, there are now no surviving traces of Scottish municipal buildings of medieval date, the earliest surviving tolbooths being of the last quarter of the sixteenth century.[21]

The structures and infrastructures of justice, punishment and control were interwoven. Some prisons, such as the royal Fleet Prison in London and the jail at Lydford (Devon), looked like castles; the Fleet had been built in the late eleventh century on an island in the river which shared its name. The heads or quartered remains of famous people denounced as criminals by the state were commonly displayed on poles attached to the top of gates in London and the shire towns, in an expression of the indivisible civic and royal justice which was grimly seen to be done. Town jails were often in or attached to town gates, at least in England, presumably because they were structures of stone which belonged to the commonalty. Some religious and noble lords who claimed local jurisdiction also had jails attached to their houses for those they condemned as malefactors.

(iii) ECCLESIASTICAL BUILDINGS AND STRUCTURES

The fabric of medieval towns was bristling with expressions of religious feeling: carvings of holy persons or scenes inside and outside houses, crosses at road junctions, markets (Plate 18) and at the wayside, parish churches and, slightly removed behind their precinct walls, monastic houses, hospitals and cathedrals.

In England, by 1200, towns both of Roman origin (such as Gloucester, Exeter, Winchester or York and of Saxon origin (such as Ipswich, Norwich or Thetford) possessed many parish churches. A person walking in a fairly straight line across the City of London would pass the doors of sixteen of them.[22] But by 1300, and especially after 1400, the number of churches was in fact declining slowly, particularly in smaller towns. In addition, towns founded after about 1100

[21] G. Stell, 'The earliest tolbooths: a preliminary account', *Proc. Soc. Antiq. Scot.*, 111 (1981), 445–53; RCAHMS, *Tolbooths and Town-Houses: Civic Architecture in Scotland to 1833* (Edinburgh, 1996), pp. 1, 3.

[22] R. Morris, *Churches in the Landscape* (London, 1989); J. Schofield, 'Saxon and medieval parish churches in the City of London: a review', *TLMAS*, 45 (1994), 23–146.

normally had only one church. In Wales, older foundations similarly had more churches, though on a far smaller scale: Chepstow had three churches besides a priory, Haverfordwest had three and Cardiff had two churches and a chapel at the entrance to the castle.

The prevalence of the single-parish burgh is a distinctive institutional and architectural phenomenon of Scottish medieval urban life. In some cases, the burgh might not even possess a separate, purpose-built parish church, the need for a separate building being obviated by the provision of a parish altar within a cathedral or religious house within the town. Those towns that did possess a parish church building came to have only one each, sometimes with dependent chapels within the town and its suburbs. The historical reasons for this development seem to reside partly in the relatively late creation of urban parishes in the twelfth century, alongside the formation of the burghs themselves and a coincidental tightening of the system of appropriation of parish revenues. The result was that, whilst there may have been a choice of churches in the early days of a burgh, as for example at Dundee or Berwick, the tendency was towards one single building that served as the head church of the burgh community.[23]

In the larger English towns, the high number of churches provides evidence of those periods at which more, or less, money was spent on the architectural expression of religious sentiment. In London and York, the fully developed church with three aisles was common by the end of the fourteenth century, though in York in particular this was overtaken by further rebuildings in the next century; in Norwich, however, three-aisled churches appear to be rare before 1450. This would fit with a generally held view that Norwich's period of spectacular growth was in the late middle ages. Occasionally, the main or only town church reflected, in its architecture, the fortunes of the town in growth or decline: the exceptionally fine (perhaps over-grand for a small town) fifteenth-century church at Long Melford (Suffolk) was built on the profits of the cloth trade, whereas at Winchelsea (Sussex) the church is now a chancel without a nave, its arches blocked up in the medieval period as the town died.

From around 1300, but especially in the fifteenth and early sixteenth centuries, town churches were embellished with statues, screens and chantry chapels endowed by individual citizens, both men and women. There was a distinct swing of building energy away from the great religious houses to the parish church and friary, the hospital and almshouse, as devout people (in towns and the countryside) 'voted with their feet for something a little nearer in spirit to themselves'. In London, where there were 108 parish churches by 1300, certain new architectural forms were given their first boost: these semi-private

[23] G. Stell, 'Urban buildings', in M. Lynch, M. Spearman and G. Stell, eds., *The Scottish Medieval Town* (Edinburgh, 1988), pp. 60–80. See also I. B. Cowan, 'The emergence of the urban parish', in *ibid.*, pp. 82–98.

mausolea-chapels on both sides of the chancel, in some cases before aisles were added to the nave of the church during the fifteenth century; and from about 1370, the building of many western towers as belfries. Four of the larger churches (St Mary le Bow, All Hallows Barking, St Bride and St Giles Cripplegate) were designated in 1370 to ring the evening curfew bell, and a century later these four were still regarded as the city timekeepers.[24]

Town churches were also patronised by the crafts. At least ten medieval guilds are recorded in Stamford, for instance, and they were associated with seven of the parish churches. Most have left no physical record of their uses, but a prominent donor provided most of the expense for the surviving fourteenth-century north chapel of St Mary's church, which was probably used by the Corpus Christi guild. In the early sixteenth century Holy Trinity, Coventry, housed not only the archdeacon's court but also eight chapels, three associated with trade groups: mercers, tanners and butchers. The tailors had their own chapel of St George by Gosford Gate, which was probably the focus of civic processions on St George's Day.[25]

The great burgh churches of late medieval Scotland tended to conform to standard patterns of British late medieval ecclesiastical architecture in plan, if not always in style and details. But when the attentions of wealthy individual or corporate patrons, anxious and able to endow altars or chapels, became focused upon just one building, the effects of the chantry movement became particularly exaggerated. The unplanned and mainly lateral growth of the medieval parish church of Edinburgh, St Giles', reflects this process more fully than any other in the way in which it became grossly distended between 1380 and the Reformation in 1560. Although the overall outline of the church was reduced in the course of a programmme of restoration in 1829–33, enough survives to illustrate its late medieval growth, with chapels grouped mainly around the western limb and central body of the church.[26]

There was a comparable growing pressure on internal space. By the Reformation St Giles' contained about forty altars and, like St Mary's, Dundee, had grown to such an extent that it was capable of housing no fewer than three Reformed congregations. Most of the other large burgh churches accommodated two.[27] The church provision in medieval Edinburgh, with only one parish church, is a complete contrast in organisational scale to other larger towns such as London, Bristol, York and Norwich.

[24] C. Platt, *Medieval England: A Social History and Archaeology* (London, 1978), p. 138; Schofield, 'Saxon and medieval parish churches'.

[25] C. Phythian-Adams, *Desolation of a City* (Cambridge, 1979), pp. 160, 173.

[26] G. Hay, 'The late medieval development of the High Kirk of St Giles, Edinburgh', *Proc. Soc. Antiq. Scot.*, 107 (1975–6), 242–60.

[27] M. Lynch, 'Whatever happened to the medieval burgh? Some guidelines for sixteenth- and seventeenth-century historians', *Scottish Economic and Social History*, 4 (1984), 5–20.

The largest number of urban monasteries in towns, by 1300, were Benedictine, though the name of the rule to which each house professed allegiance was not always important. From the early twelfth century houses of the Augustinian canons, and other minor orders of canons, had spread through all kinds of towns. A broad distinction can be made between monastic houses where all the associated domestic buildings of a resident community were necessary, such as Durham or Chester, and secular cathedrals, where the canons were not resident and buildings such as cloisters or dormitories were more formal than necessary, such as at Wells, Salisbury or St Paul's in London.

Apart from local problems of arranging their cloisters and drains because of space restrictions, there is little difference in architecture between urban religious houses of the monks and their rural counterparts. One feature all the urban monasteries and cathedrals shared, however, was an effort to demarcate the precinct within the town itself. In the late thirteenth century, as major towns put effort into their defences, so the major churches within towns fortified their precincts in stone – Norwich in 1276, York, Lincoln and St Paul's in London in 1285 and Canterbury in 1309. In the first half of the fourteenth century, these precincts were embellished or emphasised by prominent gates with a new architecture of octagonal turrets (the earliest probably that at St Augustine's Abbey, Canterbury, in 1308). The urban precinct was becoming, as never before, the heavenly city within a town. Then, during the fourteenth century, the richest churches – the royal chapel of St Stephen Westminster, St Paul's London and the Benedictine abbey at Gloucester (now the Cathedral, which it became in 1541) – produced the first examples of Perpendicular architecture, the polite style which encompassed royal, religious and civic building throughout England until the middle of the sixteenth century. This creation of a new style was probably only possible in towns, where the traditional desire to display in new building was matched by the availability of funds, from institutions which lived off large rents, or from individuals who had made money in trade.

Like the other monastic houses, the majority of hospitals had been founded before 1300; because of their purpose they were sited in suburbs or on the edges of town. They looked like the monastic infirmaries from which they were derived, with a wide, undivided hall;[28] the traditional plan of placing the sick in the body of a large church with the chancel as their chapel continued. Given the level of medical knowledge in the medieval period, hospitals were primarily places to die in: thus the hall-like ward was arranged so that the beds could see the altar in the chapel, and it is not surprising that one of the portals of the Hotel Dieu in Paris carried the inscription 'Here is the House of God and the Door

[28] L. Butler, 'Medieval urban religious houses', in Schofield and Leech, eds., *Urban Archaeology in Britain* pp. 167–76; C. Thomas, B. Sloane and C. Phillpotts, *Excavations at the Priory and Hospital of St Mary Spital, Bishopsgate* (Museum of London Archaeology Service, Monograph 1, London, 1997).

of Heaven'.[29] Some leper hospitals, however, may have given their inmates individual cells in a single range, and by the fifteenth century the courtyard plan is found in hospitals (for instance, St Cross, Winchester, rebuilt by Cardinal Beaufort before the middle of the century) as it was then becoming usual in academic and secular colleges and in almshouses. The latter appeared in the larger towns around 1400, as small establishments for retired old folk, usually around a courtyard and sometimes with a common hall for eating. In some towns the hospital form developed further into extensive, sometimes two-storeyed, plans, such as Browne's Hospital, Stamford (about 1485) and Wigston's Hospital, Leicester (1513).

The urban order *par excellence*, and therefore in themselves evidence of a town's vigour, were the friars, especially the Dominicans (Blackfriars) and Franciscans (Greyfriars). The normal (but by no means universal) extramural siting of friaries is demonstrated by the Welsh towns which were additionally in a troubled frontier zone. At Cardiff, the Blackfriars and Greyfriars both lay outside the town, but near the castle; in other Welsh towns friaries lay at the water's edge (Haverfordwest), across rivers (Brecon), at the limits of settlement or off suburban roads (Carmarthen, Denbigh, Newport (Gwent)). Some friaries, however, were occasionally sited within towns, near market places: at Aberdeen, Maldon, or Lichfield, for instance. The great church of the Greyfriars in London was also next to the Shambles or meat market in the middle of Newgate Street, and in Canterbury the Austin Friars had a gate into the nearby High Street; here, all three friaries were within the walls. Perhaps because the friaries were established later than hospitals, there was often a process of accumulation and consolidation of land to form the friary itself when it lay within the restricted space of the town.[30] The Blackfriars in London had the city wall extended and rerouted around their precinct, to give them a large territory both near the cathedral and yet on the waterfront.

Because they were popular with royal, noble and civic patrons, the main friaries became rich, luxurious complexes. The buildings of the London Blackfriars are vividly described in the fourteenth-century poem *Pierce the Ploughman's Creed*, but this unique architectural description in English medieval literature can stand for one common man's view of all religious houses and cathedrals. The following comes from the free rendering of the text by Clapham and Godfrey:

> Then I gat me forth to look at the Church,
> And found it well and wonderfully built,
> With arches on each side, embellished and carven
> With crockets on their angles and knots of gold
> The wide windows all wrought with numberless writings

[29] M. Girouard, *Cities and People* (New Haven and London, 1985), p. 46.
[30] J. W. F. Hill, *Medieval Lincoln* (Cambridge, 1948), p. 149.

Shining with shapely shields to make a display,
With merchants' marks all figured between
To the number of more than twice two and twenty
(There is no herald that hath half such a roll)
And newly set out as if by a Ragman
Tombs upon tabernacles raised up aloft,
In armour, of alabaster, seemingly clad;
Were knights now clothed in their martial dress –
All, it seemed, saints who were sacred on earth!
And lovely carved ladies lay by their sides
In many gay garments that were beaten gold . . .
And yet these builders will beg a bag full of wheat
Of a poor man that may, for once, pay
Half his rent in a year and half be behind . . . [31]

All these religious buildings formed points of topographic permanence in the town, since they changed character and shape comparatively slowly. It seems that apart from having an effect on their immediate neighbourhoods (in London, the establishment of the Blackfriars may have attracted noble residences to the edges of the new precinct), religious institutions had little more than a marginal influence on the activities of the citizens as an urban community, as illustrated in Winchester.[32] On the other hand, the urban setting influenced the layout and detail of the monastery; in London, the traditional east–west alignment of the large monastic church might be altered by many degrees to fit a constricted site, or the cloister and its buildings placed on the north side of the church so that the reredorter communicated with the nearby city ditch. At Dunfermline, the abbot's lodging was built against the precinct wall in the middle of the fifteenth century, and given a traceried window to overlook the abbot's commercial interests in the town below.[33]

(iv) HOUSES, SHOPS AND OTHER SECULAR BUILDINGS

Around the more permanent and grandiose stone structures lay a restless sea of ordinary houses mostly constructed of less durable materials. Larger properties formed urban residences of some size, usually built around a courtyard on the street side with a garden in the private space behind the main range (Plate 19).

[31] A. W. Clapham and W. H. Godfrey, *Some Famous Buildings and their Story* (London, 1912), pp. 256–7.

[32] L. Butler, 'The houses of the mendicant orders in Britain: recent archaeological work', in P. V. Addyman and V. E. Black, eds., *Archaeological Papers from York Presented to M. W. Barley* (York, 1984), pp. 123–36. For the possible influence of friary preaching on the internal organisation of space in a parish church, see the case of Holy Trinity, Coventry, in Phythian-Adams, *Desolation of a City*, p. 169.

[33] P. Yeoman, *Medieval Scotland* (London, 1995), p. 21.

Many houses in major towns such as Edinburgh, London and York, and in smaller port towns such as Aberdeen and Berwick, were town houses of a lord or prosperous landowner, whether lay or religious, from the countryside or sometimes (as in the case of London) considerably more distant.[34] There were two purposes for such a house: the provision of accommodation for those engaged in the everyday affairs of the house or the see, such as the selling of produce or the buying of goods, especially luxuries; and as the residence of the institution's head when in town. In some small towns such as Bishop's Waltham (Hants.) or the Old Town part of Croydon, the lord's residence was the centre of the place. In the vast majority of cases where their plans can be ascertained, the houses of religious and noble leaders were of courtyard plan. The hall of the property lay normally at the rear of a yard, though occasionally to the side on restricted sites, with a range of buildings (often separately let) fronting the street. Leaders of the merchant community in major towns, such as those who dealt in wine or some other aspect of royal service, also aspired to the style of house with a courtyard and an open hall of lofty proportions.

At corners of major streets, and along commercial frontages, smaller units were the norm from early in the town's history. Below the level of the courtyard house, three very broad types in diminishing size of ground-floor plan can be noted, at least in England. A substantial middling house, filling a whole property, and of three to six rooms in ground-floor plan, would normally have a yard with buildings along one side, or an alley running the length of a long, narrow property. The latter arrangement is illustrated most clearly by properties on waterfront sites, such as in Lynn or south of Thames Street in London. Buildings were usually arranged down the side of the plot behind the street-range which commonly comprised shops, sometimes let separately. Along, usually at the side of, most waterfront properties ran the access alley from the street to the river and the main water supply. This originated for the most part as a private thoroughfare, in some cases becoming public through time and custom.[35]

Smaller, and more uniform in its characteristics, was a house with two rooms on three or more floors. This type is known from documentary and archaeological evidence in London from the early fourteenth century; in several cases such houses form a strip, two rooms deep, fronting but separate from a larger property behind. The ground floor was given wholly over to trade: a shop and a warehouse, sometimes with the two rooms thrown together to form one, or a tavern. The hall lay usually on the first floor at the front, overlooking the street. The

[34] J. Schofield, *Medieval London Houses* (New Haven, 1995), pp. 27–60.

[35] *Ibid.*, 34–6; on Berwick, A. Stevenson, 'Trade with the South', in Lynch, Spearman and Stell, eds., *The Scottish Medieval Town*, pp. 180–206.

kitchen was originally a separate building across a small yard; but later, the kitchen was often placed above ground in the main building, as structures occupied every inch of the small plots. The house with two rooms on several floors is also found in Oxford from 1386, and Exeter and Norwich from around 1500.[36]

The houses of the medieval poor have largely been destroyed without trace in almost every town. These humble dwellings did not survive into the era of engraving, and as in England they commonly lay along street frontages, archaeological excavation has not uncovered them because of later street widening and the digging of cellars, especially in the nineteenth century. Sometimes the existence of buildings, probably forming continuous façades and one room deep, are inferred from the absence of rubbish pits near the line of the street. One-room timber-framed houses of thirteenth- or early fourteenth-century date have been excavated at Lower Brook Street, Winchester, and more substantial examples in stone of the fifteenth century at St Peter's Street, Northampton.[37] In Scotland, as far as is known, humble dwellings tended to be in the backlands; though this impression could be for lack of excavated examples along street frontages. Excavations in Aberdeen and Perth have uncovered parts of nearly forty buildings of the late twelfth to fourteenth centuries, with walls of planks or wattles.[38]

One of the few standing Scottish town houses to have been assigned to the late medieval period was a two-storeyed building with forestair in Church Street, Inverkeithing (Fife). Unfortunately, the building no longer survives, so we are not in a position to check Sir Frank Mears' late fifteenth-century dating and its function as a self-contained merchant-burgess' house set above vaulted stores. Similar forestaired types appear in the panoramic view of St Andrew's (Fife) ascribable to about 1580 but referring to pre-Reformation times (Plate 24).[39]

From surviving and later examples of this building type the existence of a forestair can point to any of several functional variations on the same basic design: examples include inns and ordinary dwellings above warehouses, stores or shops. Two-storeyed flatted or 'stacked cottages' of this general arrangement with families living above and below became a distinctive and characteristic

[36] J. Munby, 'Zacharias's: a 14th-century Oxford New Inn and the origins of the medieval inn', *Oxoniensa*, 57 (1992), 245–309; Portman, *Exeter Houses*, pp. 25–6; A. Carter, 'The building survey', in 'Excavations in Norwich 1976–7', *Norfolk Archaeology*, 36 (1977), 298–304; W. A. Pantin, 'The development of domestic architecture in Oxford', *Antiquaries J*, 27 (1947), 120–50.

[37] M. Biddle, 'Excavations at Winchester: sixth interim report', *Antiquaries J*, 48 (1967), 250–85; J. H. Williams, *St Peter's Street, Northampton, Excavations 1973–76* (Northampton, 1979).

[38] See e.g. J. C. Murray, ed., *Excavations in the Medieval Burgh of Aberdeen 1973–81* (Society of Antiquaries of Scotland Monograph Series, 2, 1982); P. Holdsworth, ed., *Excavations in the Medieval Burgh of Perth 1979–81* (Society of Antiquaries of Scotland Monograph Series, 5, 1987); P. Yeoman, *Medieval Scotland* (London, 1995), pp. 53–85.

[39] F. C. Mears, 'Notes on a medieval burgess's house at Inverkeithing', *Proc. Soc. Antiq. Scot.*, 47 (1912–13), 343–8; National Library of Scotland, MS Acc. 2887, discussed by D. McRoberts, ed., *The Medieval Church of St Andrews* (Glasgow, 1976), pp. 151–2 and frontispiece.

feature of many regions of Scotland, most notably in east central Scotland.[40] It is likely but unproven that they derived from genuine medieval origins.

What was especially startling to visitors to Scotland from the later sixteenth century onwards was the Scottish urban skyscraper, which in the main centres of population rose to four or more storeys in height. Sheer height was not their only special feature. Some were self-contained dwellings in single ownership, others were clearly of multiple occupation and ownership. In notarial instruments recording three-way subdivisions of urban properties in early sixteenth-century Canongate, the divisions agreed upon by the parties appear to have been horizontal as well as vertical, much importance being attached to the forebooths and fore lofts. Inbuilt structural evidence for original flatting, not just later subdivisions for tenants, can be detected in the disposition of original stairs, including forestairs, and in partitions and doorways.[41] By the late sixteenth century the upper floors of the so-called 'John Knox's House' in Edinburgh High Street formed a separate dwelling which was reached by its own newel stair in the front corner of the building. To suggest that such flatting resulted simply or even mainly from the pressures of overcrowding within the security of the town's defences is not a sufficient explanation. It does not explain why similar and indeed more intense conditions in English walled towns did not provoke a similar response.

From the overall plan of a house unit or tenancy we can move to the evolution of some of the rooms and spaces within it.[42] In English towns south of the highland zone, during the thirteenth and early fourteenth centuries, the position of the cellar or undercroft (a cellar with a vaulted ceiling of stone) within the property seems often to reflect a need for easy access from this storage space to the street; and here the expense laid out on vaulting (and presumably colourful decoration) may have been intended to encourage business in or off the street. One type of undercroft with its bays arranged in only a single row or aisle lay along the street frontage, presumably beneath small shops, or occasionally down the side of a property with one end (and its entrance) by the street. On prestigious properties a stone building in this position, on an undercroft of two aisles with columns down the middle (Gisors' Hall, London; Clifton House, Queen

[40] For post-medieval variations on the same basic building design, see G. Stell, 'Scottish burgh houses 1560–1707', in A. T. Simpson and S. Stevenson, eds., *Town Houses and Structures in Medieval Scotland: A Seminar* (Scottish Burgh Survey, 1980), pp. 1–31. See also D. Defoe, *A Tour through the Whole Island of Great Britain* (1724–6; repr., London, 1968), vol. II, p. 693, for reference to the houses of this type and to 'the Scots way of living' in Northumberland.

[41] E.g. G. Donaldson, ed., *Protocol Book of James Young 1485–1515* (Scottish Records Society, 1952), nos. 1120, 1251, 1388 and 1653. For architectural evidence, Stell, 'Urban buildings', pp. 71–4.

[42] For discussions of this topic see P. A. Faulkner, 'Domestic planning from the twelfth to the fourteenth centuries', *Archaeological J*, 115 (1958), 150–84; P. A. Faulkner, 'The surviving buildings', in C. Platt and R. Coleman-Smith, *Excavations in Medieval Southampton, 1953–1969* (Leicester, 1975), pp. 78–124; Schofield, *London Houses*, pp. 61–93.

Street, Lynn) was presumably the hall or focus of the tenement. Though it could be found beneath buildings away from the frontage, the vaulted cellar was usually tied to the street and as a result was often let separately from the buildings above and around it. At Chester, whole streets of undercrofts or cellars, many of them probably separately let, formed the famous Rows during the late thirteenth and fourteenth centuries. Winchelsea (Sussex) was another town in which storage and display of goods was taken seriously on a grand scale, in a number of vaulted and ribbed undercrofts spread through the town.

During the fifteenth century, perhaps as a result of the many economic troubles then being experienced by towns, undercrofts went out of use as places frequented by people coming in off the street. In Southampton, the thirteenth- and fourteenth-century undercrofts there combined the function of shop and warehouse, but undercrofts of the fifteenth century were for basement storage only; and their architecture reflected this change, as they became simpler, less embellished structures. There is a notable concomitant development of the above-ground warehouse (especially for cloths) in larger centres in the fifteenth century. Cloths would suffer if stored in damp cellars, unlike wine which needed cool temperatures. So perhaps the increased trade in draperies demanded, or at least influenced, a partial abandonment of the cellar and the increase in size of shops and warehouses at ground level. The larger shop and warehouse on the ground floor became the basis of the Tudor town house; many towns such as Shrewsbury, Leicester, Gloucester and Bristol were ruled by oligarchies largely of wool and cloth merchants, and by 1540 they had distinctive houses to suit their positions in urban politics and society.

By the end of the medieval period, at least in London, larger houses were specifically divided into suites, comprising rooms or spaces, which were dedicated to trade, family life (especially the parlour and garden) or the preparation of food and domestic storage (kitchen, buttery). In crowded town centres this conscious or subconscious allocation of space to functions had to assume a vertical as well as horizontal dimension. Thus stairs and passages were developed to articulate the house space and provide communication between its parts, in ordinary houses as well as inns. Buildings around a courtyard were linked by galleries, on the first and higher floors. In the early middle ages, especially in small towns, the rich or powerful would have larger, higher houses and the poor would have small cottages. By 1500, this relationship of height was probably being reversed; the larger houses, still the same size, were now not as high as the street-side tenements which screened them from the street.[43]

Several building forms grew out of the general pool of domestic forms: taverns, alehouses, inns and almshouses. Taverns, drinking houses where wine

[43] See house plans of 1607–14 in J. Schofield, *The London Surveys of Ralph Treswell* (London Topographical Society, 135, 1987); further described in Schofield, *London Houses*.

was drunk, are known in undercrofts by the early fourteenth century in London and Oxford. These were no doubt large capital investments. During the fifteenth century the main drinking areas seem to have spread to the ground floor of buildings, and by the sixteenth century the cellar was largely abandoned; the Cheapside area in London was thick with taverns which must have had a frequent trade in company meetings and feasts, possibly in special chambers. On the other hand, smaller late medieval taverns and alehouses, with their drinking rooms at ground-floor level, often resembled private houses and modifications from one function to the other were probably minimal. Inns were naturally extensive establishments, and provided accommodation of some comfort; two surviving examples, the George or Pilgrim Inn at Glastonbury and the New Inn at Gloucester, were mid-fifteenth-century investments by monasteries to house pilgrims.[44] The larger inns displayed innovative architectural features, only some of which were shared with noble residences: two common plan-forms, courtyard or gatehouse. In the first, there were two courtyards (one for receipt of guests, the other a stable yard), and communicating galleries which often went round several buildings. A second and probably far less numerous type comprised a main range which looked like a monastic gatehouse on the street frontage. Inns may have been among the first buildings to have passages and chambers for individuals, two expressions of the developing need for privacy: a guest could ask for a lockable room, and even a self-contained suite of rooms, at London inns by the late fourteenth century.

Houses in medieval towns were made of timber, stone, brick and earth; and the range of materials available had a profound influence on the types of building possible, on decoration and on life-span of buildings.[45] The sources and species of wood were largely local, even in London. The stones used in medieval buildings in towns were almost totally from the immediate region; former Roman towns had a great stock of Roman building material within their walls, which was dug out and reused especially up to the end of the thirteenth century and occasionally later. Houses largely of stone were always the prerogative of the rich, and seem to have been a feature of the thirteenth and fourteenth centuries, as shown by the number of arched foundations of stone found on archaeological sites; after 1400 houses of stone are rare, except in towns near good quarries. Brick was imported from the late thirteenth century and locally produced during the fourteenth century (it was used for many houses in Hull), but was in general use only from the early fifteenth century. When a hospital was

[44] Steane, *Archaeology of Medieval England and Wales*, pp. 115–17; W. A. Pantin, 'Medieval inns', in E. M. Jope, ed., *Studies in Building History* (London, 1961), pp. 166–91.

[45] L. F. Salzman, *Building in England down to 1540* (2nd edn, 1967), is the standard work; see also O. Rackham, *Ancient Woodland* (London, 1980); T. P. Smith, *The Medieval Brickmaking Industry in England, 1400–1450* (British Archaeological Reports, 138, Oxford, 1985); J. Munby, 'Wood', in J. Blair and N. Ramsay, eds., *English Medieval Industries* (London, 1991), pp. 379–406.

built at Ewelme (Oxon.) in 1436, the bricks were made and laid by Flemings.[46] It may be significant that the spread of brick buildings somewhat later in London (for instance the repairs to the city wall in 1477) coincides with the adoption of brick in royal and episcopal palaces, of which there were a great number in the metropolitan area. The first widespread use of brick at Canterbury is in the 1470s; but twenty years later included the whole upper stage of the Bell Harry tower of the cathedral in 1493–7, behind its facing of Caen stone.

Buildings constructed of such durable materials or having stone foundations beneath their timber frames survived to form relative points of permanence within the more rapidly changing surroundings formed by timber buildings. Thus the main buildings of some of the larger houses were a link with former topographic arrangements. By 1540, many town houses must have comprised elements of different dates going back centuries.

The majority of secular constructions were of timber; and certain developments in building construction in timber may be attributed to factors at work in the crowded town. By 1300 jettied buildings were common in the streets of many English towns;[47] engravings show them to have existed in towns of the upland zone and in Scotland. The exploitation of the roofspace, another need arising from density of living, is shown by the development of dormer windows in the first half of the fifteenth century and of the side-purlin roof, presumably at the same time. The technology of the timber frame allowed easy expansion of building units to handle changes in circumstances, such as more functions within the domestic complex or more occupants. Overall, in English towns, the best use was made of town plots by increasing sophistication of carpentry rather than use of stone or brick. Apart from the carpentry, the most important innovation was at the beginning of the period, when from around 1280 timber frames were no longer laid in trenches in the ground, where they decayed quickly, but raised on low walls of stone and later of brick.

Building regulations were developed in the thirteenth and fourteenth centuries, and they may have stemmed not only from practical considerations such as fire prevention, but also from a civic view of the smoother running and beauty of the town. The London regulations (which had been in force from 1200; cases of dispute between neighbours survive from 1301)[48] directed that three foot (1 m) party walls along the sides of properties should be of stone, and these (or their foundations) are commonly found on archaeological excavations. Other

[46] Steane, *Archaeology of Medieval England and Wales*, p. 101.

[47] The 1246 references are to a justices' inquiry into purprestures (encroachments into the street which was deemed to be in the king's possession); it is published as an appendix to the calendar of an eyre (justices' session) of 1244: H. M. Chew and M. Weinbaum, eds., *The London Eyre of 1244* (London Record Society, 6, 1970), nos. 396, 481.

[48] H. M. Chew and W. Kellaway, eds., *London Assize of Nuisance 1301–1431* (London Record Society, 10, 1973), pp. ix–xxx.

rules governed drainage, disposal of sewage, public nuisances and paving, and demanded roofs of fire-proof materials. These regulations appear to have ensured that there was no serious fire in the City of London between 1212 and 1666, a remarkable achievement. There are standing examples of medieval stone party-walls in Dartmouth, Exeter and Plymouth; there were similar but not so full regulations from other towns besides London, and mostly of later in the period, as those concerned with ruinous buildings in Hereford and Nottingham.[49] The 'Neighbourhood Book' of Edinburgh, which recorded the concerns of the town authorities with the positions of mutual gables, lean-tos, stairs and windows, the dangers of ruinous properties and such matters dates from 1529.[50] Such practices were, however, not widespread. Nottingham and Worcester forbade chimneys of wood, but only in the 1490s. In smaller towns roofs of thatch were common until the sixteenth century, and later in the South-West of England. Several towns suffered serious fires, such as two at Cambridge in 1385, which between them destroyed over 100 burgages.

Styles in architecture, and influences from abroad, were naturally to be found mostly on churches, public buildings and the grander residences. Apart from single parallels with buildings in some of the larger towns, affinities with continental Europe are most widespread in Scotland. Here medieval towns, the trading outposts of north-western Europe, exhibited features different from English towns, and similar at least in spirit, if not in exact form, to those of the Low Countries and Tuscany. For example, a number of Scottish town houses are known to have been of semi-fortified tower house form, a particularly impressive late fifteenth-century specimen having served as the solar block of a large town house in Linlithgow, possibly associated with the Knights Hospitallers of nearby Torphichen and copying in part some of the details of the nearby royal palace.[51] Towers in Scotland are also known to have occurred in groups, particularly in the west and south-west of the country. The indications are, though, that most such urban towers were relatively small-scale structures, bearing a closer affinity to the character and grouping of towers in Irish towns than to distant and more lofty ancestors in northern Italy.

Superficially, too, Scottish urban buildings came to assume a recognisable European or certainly a Flemish or Dutch appearance, usually translated into a Scottish building idiom of stone and harl. Certain church architecture, such as the telescopic form of the late fifteenth-century western tower of St Mary's

[49] M. Bateson, ed., *Borough Customs* (Selden Society 18, 21, 1904–6), vol. I, p. 280; W. H. Stevenson, ed., *Records of the Borough of Nottingham* (London and Nottingham, 1882–5), vol. II, p. 386.

[50] Stell, 'Scottish burgh houses', p. 5.

[51] D. MacGibbon and T. Ross, *The Castellated and Domestic Architecture of Scotland* (Edinburgh, 1887), vol. I, pp. 508–14; *Edinburgh Architectural Association Sketch Book* (Edinburgh, 1878–9), vol. II, plates 35–7; G. Stell, 'Architecture: the changing needs of society', in J. M. Brown, ed., *Scottish Society in the Fifteenth Century* (London, 1977), pp. 153–83 at pp. 165–7.

parish church, Dundee, has been convincingly linked to prevailing styles in and around Utrecht in the Netherlands.[52] In the realms of early civic architecture, some Scottish tolbooths such as that at Dunbar also display Dutch overtones in the general form of the five-sided tower, the wood-framed spire and its gableted crowsteps. But the similarities of towers, steeples and belfries are not unexpected, given that so many of the clocks and bells housed within them are of Dutch or Flemish manufacture.[53]

(v) CONCLUSION

As a conclusion to this survey, two questions may be posed. First, how did the medieval townscape react to or reflect the general decline in the fortunes of towns which is often said to be the main characteristic of the period? There was a serious commercial decline in many, if not most, English and Scottish towns from the late fourteenth century until 1500 or later; in Wales, the rebellion of Owain Glyndŵr destroyed or devastated more than forty towns; some were abandoned and the others took generations to recover. The general decline of town life and institutions continued in parts of Wales, for some commentators, until the eighteenth and early nineteenth centuries[54] (but see below, Chapter 22(f)).

This picture of decaying towns, however, requires scrutiny. After the Black Death in 1348–9, because there were considerably fewer people in towns, several processes took place. Shops disappeared from central streets; some houses became larger, while the unwanted margins of settlement crumbled, decayed and were covered with their own version of dark earth, the deposit normally associated with the Saxon centuries. Some of these processes, for instance the amalgamation of properties into larger units, can be seen in other European cities and towns. Within towns, we can expect that the poor and disadvantaged areas suffered disproportionately from the main urban plagues. At the same time, though defences may have been decaying, focal points of civic self-assertion such as gates were rebuilt or refurbished.

52 R. Fawcett, 'Late Gothic architecture in Scotland: considerations on the influence of the Low Countries', *Proc. Soc. Antiq. Scot.*, 112 (1982), 477–96 at 491–2.

53 RCAHMS, *Tolbooths and Town-houses*, pp. 11, 22–3.

54 For general discussions of late medieval decline in towns, see R. B. Dobson, 'Urban decline in late medieval England', *TRHS*, 5th series, 27 (1977), repr. in R. Holt and G. Rosser, eds., *The Medieval Town* (London, 1990), pp. 265–86, and the editors' comments, *ibid.*, 17–18; C. Phythian-Adams, 'Urban decay in late medieval England', in P. Abrams and E. A. Wrigley, eds., *Towns in Societies* (Cambridge, 1978), pp. 159–85; D. M. Palliser, 'Urban decay revisited', in J. A. F. Thomson, ed., *Towns and Townspeople in the Fifteenth Century* (Gloucester, 1988), pp. 1–21. The archaeological evidence from England is reviewed by D. A. Hinton, *Archaeology, Economy and Society* (London, 1990), pp. 191–213. For Scotland, Lynch, Spearman and Stell, eds., *The Scottish Medieval Town*, pp. 6–7; for Wales, I. Soulsby, *The Towns of Medieval Wales* (Chichester, 1983), pp. 24–7 and gazetteer.

Some towns, like Winchester and York, may have suffered particularly in the first half of the fifteenth century when there were widespread difficulties for towns: at York, for instance, very few houses dating from the first half of the fifteenth century have been found, and none in the area of the ancient suburb of Micklegate south-west of the river (in the future this picture may change, when dendrochronology can be applied in quantity to the surviving structures). On the other hand, at Lynn, although there are signs of an early halt to the expansion of the built-up area of the town, there is no evidence of depopulation of streets and buildings. The town remained at a steady level of prosperity from the fifteenth to the seventeenth century. The same can be argued for Saffron Walden, with its notable number of standing buildings.

Secondly, do towns in Britain show regional differences in their medieval built environment – differences which might reflect different forms of town life, or attitude to towns? Medieval British towns have long been viewed as national or regional variations on a European theme. Towns share recognisable patterns of street plans, market places and burgage plots, and they incorporate to a greater or lesser extent standard components such as parish churches and chapels, religious houses, civic and commercial buildings and ranges of house types that are recognisably, if sometimes indefinably, urban. One abiding general impression remains that the differences in the urban built environment from one country or one region to another are principally differences in scale and emphasis, and not essentially differences in kind.

Yet certain towns in border areas may show contrasting attitudes to town planning and to buildings, depending upon who is in possession of the town from time to time. Berwick was the leading burgh in Scotland in the twelfth and thirteenth centuries, and its loss to the English was one of the major long-term effects of the Wars of Independence. Early Berwick had a strong civic and guild organisation; it contained – unusually by western European standards – a considerable amount of monastic property within the town; and at least three early churches in the burgh, St Lawrence, St Mary and Holy Trinity, had reduced themselves, Scottish style, to a single parish church, Holy Trinity, by the end of the thirteenth century.

And thus it has remained. After a thoroughly Scottish start what else there might have been if the English had not wrested the town from the Scots in 1296, and if they had not been able to maintain their grip on it after 1482 is now merely a matter of speculation. Housing in Berwick has developed along English lines; its domestic architecture is quite distinct from Eyemouth a few miles up the coast which has truly Scottish flatted tenements and fisher cottages.

· 17 ·

London 1300–1540

CAROLINE M. BARRON

By the early fourteenth century London was pre-eminent among English urban communities. Whether ranked according to wealth or according to population, its pre-eminence was undisputed.[1] Although London was larger, more populous and wealthier than other English towns, it was distinguished from them not only by size and volume: it developed, in the period covered here, characteristics which were distinctive. London was different not only in scale, but also in kind.

This pre-eminence is reflected in the creation and for the most part survival of a remarkable series of administrative records.[2] Although the chamberlain's records (including the apprentice and freedom registers) were destroyed in a fire in the seventeenth century, the City is rich in custumals, record books and wills and deeds enrolled in the Husting court from the mid-thirteenth century.[3] The pleadings in the mayor's court survive from the end of the thirteenth century and the records of the meetings of the court of aldermen and court of Common Council from 1416.[4] In addition to the City's official records, there survive thousands of testaments enrolled in the ecclesiastical courts,[5] pre-Reformation

[1] See below, pp. 565–72; Appendix 4–7.

[2] For surveys of the surviving records of the medieval city of London, see: H. Deadman and E. Scuder, eds., *An Introductory Guide to the Corporation of London Records Office* (London, 1994), and D. Keene and V. Harding, *A Survey of Documentary Sources for Property Holding in London before the Great Fire* (London Record Society, 22, 1985).

[3] The wills from the Husting court have been calendared: R. R. Sharpe, ed., *Calendar of Wills Proved and Enrolled in the Court of Husting, London 1258–1688* (London, 1889–90); G. H. Martin, *The Husting Rolls of Deeds and Wills 1252–1485: Guide to the Microfilm Edition* (Cambridge, 1990).

[4] A. H. Thomas and P. E. Jones, eds., *Calendar of the Plea and Memoranda Rolls 1324–1482*, 6 vols. (Cambridge, 1924–61); Corporation of London RO, Journals 1–8.

[5] M. Fitch, *Index to Testamentary Records in the Commissary Court of London 1388–1570*, 2 vols. (London, 1969–74); M. Fitch, *Testamentary Records in the Archdeaconry Court of London*, vol. 1 (London, 1979).

records of some thirty of London's parish churches and material of great interest from the archives of the livery companies.[6] Much of this material, particularly that from the city's own administration, has been edited and calendared. Moreover, in the late fourteenth and fifteenth centuries the Londoners developed a taste for 'London chronicles', i.e. histories of England written in the vernacular and divided into mayoral, rather than regnal, years. These chronicles throw some fitful light upon the course of English history, but rather more light on the thought-world of the Londoners who commissioned and bought them.[7]

The importance of London and the richness of its surviving medieval material have ensured that it has not been ignored by historians. In the last twenty years, some 150 books or articles have been published dealing with its history in the period 1300–1540, and there is much work in the pipe-line and still to be done.[8] The interest of historians has shifted from the 'straight' political role of London in national affairs to an interest in the economy of the city and the structure and quality of its communal life. The focus is no longer exclusively on the city's elite but has widened to include the unenfranchised: day labourers, the poor, the clergy, women, aliens, foreigners and children.

(i) THE INHABITANTS AND TOPOGRAPHY OF LONDON

The population of London in 1300 may have been as high as 80,000 to 100,000, probably four times greater than its nearest competitor, Norwich.[9] There may already have been some decline in numbers before the Black Death, but here, as elsewhere, the impact of the plague appears to have been dramatic. The crisis mortality ratio was 16:1 in 1348–9 and 9:1 in 1360–1.[10] In fact the crisis mortality ratio in these outbreaks of plague was higher than in any of the later,

[6] Parish records: see *Churchwardens' Accounts of Parishes within the City of London*, 2nd edn (Guildhall Library, London, 1969); for the records of the city livery companies, see *City Livery Companies and Related Organisations: A Guide to their Archives in Guildhall Library*, 3rd edn (London, 1989).

[7] C. L. Kingsford, *Chronicles of London* (Oxford, 1905); R. Flenley, *Six Town Chronicles of England* (Oxford, 1911); A. Gransden, *Historical Writing in England*, vol. II: *C. 1307 to the Early Sixteenth Century* (London, 1882), ch. 8; M.-R. McLaren, 'The London chronicles of the fifteenth century: the manuscripts, the authors and their aims' (PhD thesis, University of Melbourne, 1991); M.-R. McLaren, 'The aims and interests of the London chroniclers of the fifteenth century', in D. J. Clayton, R. G. Davies and P. McNiven, eds., *Trade, Devotion and Governance: Papers in Later Medieval History* (Stroud, 1994), pp. 158–76.

[8] C. M. Barron, 'London in the later middle ages 1300–1550', *LJ*, 20/2 (1995), 22–33, revised edition in P. L. Garside, ed., *Capital Histories: A Bibliographical Study of London* (Aldershot, 1998), pp. 27–40; H. Creaton, ed., *Bibliography of Printed Works on London History to 1939* (London, 1994).

[9] D. Keene, 'A new study of London before the Great Fire', *UHY* (1984), 11–21, and above, p. 195. For a more conservative view of the size of London's population, see P. Nightingale, 'The growth of London in the medieval economy', in R. H. Britnell and J. Hatcher, eds., *Progress and Problems in Medieval England* (Cambridge, 1996), pp. 89–106, esp. pp. 97–8.

[10] B. Megson, 'Mortality among London citizens in the Black Death', *Medieval Prosopography*, 19 (1998), 125–33.

sixteenth- or seventeenth-century, plague visitations. The population of London was in 1400 probably only half of what it had been in 1300. There are, in the late fourteenth century, frequent references to vacant or ruined tenements; there are more gardens; fewer complaints about encroachments upon common spaces and fewer references to the poor and destitute. The population appears to have remained at this lower figure until the sixteenth century although there is evidence that in some areas, e.g. Westminster, it may have begun to grow again by the late fifteenth century.[11] As the population of England rose during the sixteenth century, so too did that of London, but at first it grew at a faster rate than in the country as a whole. Whatever the intervening fluctuations, it is certain that London in 1540, as in 1300, was easily the most populous city in England. Moreover, because of its size, the attractions of royal government and the court, and its diversified economy, London in the later medieval period was less affected by labour shortages than other English towns.

This fluctuating population lived largely within the Roman city walls (Plate 3). In the last years of the thirteenth century, the circuit of walls in the south-west of the city had been pushed out to meet the Fleet River to the west.[12] In this new enclave Edward I and Archbishop Winchelsey established a house of Dominican friars, hence the later name of Blackfriars. The walls remained important to the Londoners throughout this period, and on several occasions they were guarded to defend the city: in 1381, 1450, 1460, 1471. In 1477 it was even thought advisable to go to the expense of repairing the wall with brick.[13] But Tudor rule, in fact, rendered the defences of London otiose and population expansion made them inconvenient. Moreover, there had always been Londoners who did not live within the walls. Already by 1300 there was ribbon development along the roads leading north from Bishopsgate, Cripplegate and Aldersgate, although there was comparatively little development eastwards from Aldgate. The most substantial suburb, however, lay along Holborn and the Strand, stretching westwards towards the king's court at Westminster, and containing four inns of court and ten inns of chancery as well as a spectacular concentration of inns and taverns; it was recognised as a separate ward, Farringdon Without, in 1394.[14] Beyond these suburbs lay important urban areas, dependent upon the economic might of London, but not upon the mayor's jurisdiction and authority. The vill of Westminster depended upon the patronage of the Benedictine house there and also upon the king's palace nearby, but its ties with London were strong none the less. It was governed in theory by the steward of the abbot and, in practice, by the wardens of the guild of the Virgin's Assumption in St Margaret's parish church.[15] Only in 1587 did Westminster

[11] G. Rosser, *Medieval Westminster, 1200–1540* (Oxford, 1989), pp. 167–82. [12] *BAHT*, III.

[13] *Ibid.*, pp. 45–7.

[14] R. R. Sharpe, ed., *Calendar of Letter-Books of the City of London* (London, 1899–1912)*: Letter-Book H* pp. 407–8. [15] Rosser, *Medieval Westminster*, pp. 39–41, 285–93.

become a self-governing borough. Southwark, across the river, was as populous but, perhaps, more dependent economically upon London. It was divided into five manors and had no centralised organising authority, although there must have been some cohesion since the men of the five manors came together to elect two MPs when required. But the inhabitants of Southwark, unlike those of Westminster, caused numerous problems for the Londoners. The City's appointment of a bailiff for Southwark seems only to have aggravated the problem. Only in 1550 did the city finally secure direct control of one of the five manors; the smallest, if most populous, manor which lay at the bridgehead became the twenty-sixth ward of the city, named Bridge Without.[16]

Most of London's major topographical features and buildings were already in place by 1300: the great Benedictine abbeys, Augustinian houses and the five friaries, all but one within the city walls. The Bridge was a hundred years old, the Tower had just been remodelled by Edward I. But the wealth of the Londoners did not lie idle in their chests and coffers. In the later medieval period great merchants like Sir John Pulteney, Sir William Walworth, Richard Whittington and Sir John Crosby built great houses emulating the earls, bishops and abbots who had already provided themselves with town houses in London or its suburbs.[17] Moreover, the city corporately, but in partnership with private donors, erected two magnificent buildings: the enlarged Guildhall completed in 1411 and the new Leadenhall (market, granary and schools) completed in 1448.[18] The visual impact of these large and stylish buildings must have been considerable. In addition the city renewed the piping and conduits for the water supply and extended it from Cheapside up Cornhill.[19] The prisons at Newgate and Ludgate were rebuilt and a new quay was developed below London Bridge at Billingsgate for the galleys and other larger ships which were trading into the port of London.[20] The king, meanwhile, had commissioned a new custom house, built between Billingsgate and the Tower.[21] These public buildings were complemented by the development of some forty company halls (see Figure 17.5) and by the addition of numerous towers and belfries to the city's parish churches. So, although the basic topography of the city did not change dramatically between the beginning and the end of this period, yet there was much new

[16] M. Carlin, *Medieval Southwark* (London, 1996), pp. 101–27.

[17] *BAHT*, III, pp. 71, 85, 97–8; J. Imray, *The Charity of Richard Whittington* (London, 1968), pp. 16–18.

[18] C. M. Barron, *The Medieval Guildhall of London* (London, 1974); M. Samuel, 'The fifteenth-century garner at Leadenhall', *Antiquaries J.*, 69 (1989), 119–53; M. Samuel, 'The "Ledene Hall" and medieval market' and 'Restructuring the medieval market at Leadenhall', in G. Milne, ed., *From Roman Basilica to Medieval Market* (London, 1992), pp. 39–50, 114–25.

[19] *BAHT*, III, p. 70.

[20] C. M. Barron, 'The government of London and its relations with the crown 1400–1450' (PhD thesis, University of London, 1970), pp. 226–7.

[21] T. Tatton-Brown, 'Excavations at the Custom House site', *TLMAS*, 26 (1975), 103–70.

infilling. Whereas the earlier substantial buildings were all of stone, by the end of the period the use of brick was becoming widespread, for instance in parts of Crosby Hall and at Lincoln's Inn.[22] By 1540 the destructive impact of the dissolution of the monasteries had barely made itself felt, but sixty years later most of the religious houses in London would have been unrecognisable.[23] Lay ownership, population growth and pressure on space had combined to destroy them in London more rapidly, perhaps, than anywhere else.

The urban landscape of London was the creation of people, not nature (Plate 20). Thirteenth-century London had been ruled by dynasties, great families who provided mayors and aldermen over two or three generations,[24] but in this later period no family produced an alderman in two successive generations, let alone a mayor. New men, like Adam Fraunceys from Yorkshire, John Pyel from Northampton, Richard Whittington from Gloucestershire, Simon Eyre from Suffolk, came from the counties of England to people and rule London. If these men produced sons they either seem to have been unsuccessful like young Thomas Eyre, or they chose like Sir Adam Fraunceys to live as gentlemen in the shires.[25] Only a very few aldermen were definitely born in London. What was true of aldermanic families was also true lower down the economic scale. London was a magnet which drew young men and women from all over England. A study of the toponymic surnames of early fourteenth-century London shows that the City attracted men to apprenticeships from the Home Counties (Middlesex, Kent, Essex and Hertfordshire) and, most notably, from the East Midlands dialect area (Cambridgeshire, Huntingdonshire, Norfolk and Suffolk) but also, and increasingly in the course of the fifteenth century, from Yorkshire.[26] The same pattern of long-distance immigration can be observed also in Southwark and Westminster.[27] It seems likely that, as in the sixteenth century, the death rate in London was considerably higher than the birth rate,

[22] J. Schofield, *Medieval London Houses* (New Haven, 1995), pp. 150–2.

[23] E. Jeffries Davies, 'The transformation of London', in R. W. Seton-Watson, ed., *Tudor Studies Presented to A. F. Pollard* (London, 1924), pp. 306–11.

[24] G. A. Williams, *Medieval London* (London, 1963), pp. 50–75.

[25] For Fraunceys and Pyel, see S. J. O'Connor, ed., *A Calendar of the Cartularies of John Pyel and Adam Fraunceys* (Camden, 5th series, II, 1993), and S. J. O'Connor, 'Adam Fraunceys and John Pyel: perceptions of status among merchants in fourteenth-century London', in Clayton, Davies and McNiven, eds., *Trade, Devotion and Governance*, pp. 17–35; for Whittington, see C. M. Barron, 'Richard Whittington: the man behind the myth', in A. E. J. Hollaender and W. Kellaway, eds., *Studies in London History Presented to Philip Edmund Jones* (London, 1969), pp. 197–248; for Simon Eyre, see C. M. Barron in *New DNB* (forthcoming).

[26] E. Ekwall, *Studies in the Population of Medieval London* (Stockholm, 1956); J. Wareing, 'Changes in the geographical distribution of apprentices to the London companies', *J of Historical Geography*, 6 (1980), 241–9; Beryl Nash, 'A study of the freeman and apprenticeship registers of letter book D (1309–1312): The place name evidence' (MA thesis, Royal Holloway, University of London, 1989); see also above, p. 203.

[27] Rosser, *Medieval Westminster*, pp. 182–90; Carlin, *Southwark*, pp. 144–8.

although this is hard to prove. In the absence of parish registers historians have tended to rely, perhaps unduly, on the evidence of wills and have drawn over-gloomy conclusions from the frequent failure to mention children.[28] There may be reasons other than death for these silences. Other studies of the survival rates for the well-documented orphan children of London citizens suggest that two-thirds of these children survived to adulthood.[29] It may be that the persistent failure of London's population to regain its pre-plague levels may have been due less to high mortality than to low fertility. Fewer children may have been born in London either because newly prosperous couples were deliberately limiting their families or because long apprenticeships or servanthoods for girls restricted the years in which they could bear children.[30] Throughout this period, and beyond, immigration remained crucial in maintaining the population of London even at its comparatively low level of about 40,000.

Not all Londoners were citizens (freemen). In the thirteenth century it is not clear how men became freemen, but by 1319 what appears to have been a free-for-all came to an end. Now only those who were presented to the mayor and aldermen and vouched for by six members of the craft they wished to practise could become free of the city.[31] In special cases the freedom might still be sold, e.g. to alien merchants or to royal servants, but this could be done only with the consent of the Common Council. But even the freemen of London comprised only a small group. Of London's 40,000 inhabitants in 1450, half would have been women. Of the 20,000 males, perhaps 7,000 were boys (i.e. under fourteen) and another 1,000 (at least) would have comprised aliens, secular and religious clergy, royal servants and members of aristocratic households. Of the remaining 12,000 males it has been calculated that one in four would have been a citizen.[32] So, about 3,000 men made up the political community of late fourteenth-century London, could become master craftsmen, vote in civic elections and govern their crafts or hold office in the city. The remaining 9,000 or so resident adult males would have been non-citizens, day labourers or journeymen. They might well earn a decent wage but were excluded from the prestige, and expense, of holding a position of authority. It has been suggested that during the sixteenth century the proportion of adult males who were citizens may have risen from *c.* 25 per cent to nearer 70 per cent.[33] This extension of the citizenship coincided with the explosion of the population and may have done some-

[28] S. L. Thrupp, *The Merchant Class of Medieval London* (Chicago, 1948), pp. 191–206.

[29] B. Megson, 'Life expectations of the widows and orphans of freemen in London 1375–1399', *Local Population Studies*, 57 (1996), 18–29.

[30] P. J. P. Goldberg, *Women, Work and Life Cycle in a Medieval Economy* (Oxford, 1992), pp. 345–61.

[31] W. de Gray Birch, ed., *The Historical Charters and Constitutional Documents of the City of London* (London, 1887), pp. 46–7.

[32] A. H. Thomas, ed., *Calendar of Plea and Memoranda Rolls 1364–1381* (Cambridge, 1929), p. lxii.

[33] S. Rappaport, *Worlds within Worlds: Structures of Life in Sixteenth-Century London* (Cambridge, 1989), pp. 47–53.

thing to provide the vast numbers of new immigrants into London with a sense of belonging to, and a responsibility for, the community which they were joining. But when we speak of London taking action corporately in the later middle ages, we are speaking of the citizen body and most probably of that small percentage of citizens who served on the court of Common Council or court of aldermen. At any one time there might have been 200 men involved in civic government, about 75 per cent of the citizen body. On the other hand other citizens would have been serving as churchwardens (*c.* 200), as fraternity wardens (*c.* 200) or as masters or wardens of their trades or crafts (*c.* 150). There would have been some overlap, but it seems reasonable to suggest that at any one time perhaps 25 per cent of the citizen body was involved in some position of responsibility (in relation to their peers). A far higher percentage would have held office of some kind in the course of their lives.

The alien communities were important constituents of the city's population.[34] The Jews had gone by 1300 but were beginning to come back in tiny numbers at the very end of the period. The Italian and Hanse merchants had an influence out of proportion to their numbers and, on occasion, provoked hostility. The Italians in the mid-fourteenth century withdrew from their prominent role in royal finance, but they continued to lend money, more discreetly and more intermittently, to the English crown. They also continued to export English wool and, to a lesser extent, cloth from London and to import wine and a range of luxury goods including spices, expensive silks and velvets, alum, dyes and wine (see Figures 17.1c and 17.2c). The Italian community lived in the north-eastern area of the city and numbered about fifty men (and a few women) who worshipped in the Austin Friars' church where an Italian-speaking friar heard their confessions.[35] Much of the overseas trade of London in this period was facilitated by Italian financial expertise and international contacts. The Hanseatic merchants lived in the Steelyard at Dowgate; there may have been twenty merchants living there at any one time.[36] These merchants enjoyed privileges in London which were not offered to English merchants on a reciprocal basis in the Hanse towns, and this provoked resentment which flared up on occasion as in 1462.[37] But, on the whole, these colonies of alien merchants lived peacefully alongside their English neighbours. They ensured that raw materials from the Baltic lands and from the Mediterranean reached England to nourish domestic

[34] See above, p. 197.

[35] S. Dempsey, 'The Italian community in London during the reign of Edward II', *L J*, 18 (1993), 14–22; H. Bradley, 'The Italian community in London *c.* 1350–*c.* 1450' (PhD thesis, University of London, 1992).

[36] S. Jenks, 'Hansische Vermachtnisse in London: ca.1363–1483', *Hansische Geschichtsblätter*, 104 (1986), 35–111.

[37] M. M. Postan, 'The economic and political relations of England and the Hanse from 1400 to 1475', in E. Power and M. M. Postan, eds., *Studies in English Trade in the Fifteenth Century* (London, 1933), pp. 91–153.

industries, particularly the cloth and building industries. The English mercantile marine rarely ventured further than a cross-Channel trip and it was not until the middle of the sixteenth century that English ships first penetrated the Mediterranean.[38]

Large numbers of immigrant aliens came to settle in London on a permanent basis: in particular men and women from Flanders and Brabant and, in the fifteenth century, from Holland and Zeeland.[39] Some took out letters of denization, but many simply settled in the suburbs, especially in Westminster and Southwark, where they were free to develop their skills as beer brewers, cordwainers, brass founders and brickmakers, and to exploit the London market while being free from the jurisdiction of the mayor and the London craft wardens.[40] These aliens also attracted hostility in times of trouble (e.g. 1381, 1436 and 1518), but they were less likely to do so in a period of labour shortage than in the later sixteenth century when there was too little work to go round. The immigrant 'doche' left their imprint on written English, not least in the language of the river, sea and boats, for it was in Flemish ships that many of the goods came and went in the port of London.[41] The 'doche' were not the only alien immigrants but they were certainly the most numerous. In the early fourteenth century there were French wine importers, and although they disappeared during the wars (1337–1453) the French began to reappear in the early sixteenth century and even formed a fraternity of their own based upon the house of Dominican friars.[42] A few Greeks, refugees perhaps from Constantinople, can be found among the alien taxpayers. The two Effamatos brothers imported and developed the skill of making the gold wire which was used extensively to decorate royal clothing and ecclesiastical vestments.[43] It has been calculated that all the alien communities together may have comprised no more than 2 per cent of the population of London.[44] This is a tiny percentage and yet by their distinctive appearance, languages and skills, these aliens may

[38] G. D. Ramsay, 'The undoing of the Italian mercantile colony in sixteenth-century London', in N. B. Harte and K. G. Ponting, eds., *Textile History and Economic History: Essays in Honour of Miss Julia de Lacy Mann* (Manchester, 1973), pp. 22–49.

[39] C. M. Barron and N. Saul, eds., *England and the Low Countries in the Late Middle Ages* (Stroud, 1995), pp. 12–14. [40] Rosser, *Medieval Westminster*, p. 193; Carlin, *Southwark*, pp. 149–67.

[41] V. Harding, 'Cross-Channel trade and cultural contacts: London and the Low Countries in the later fourteenth century', in Barron and Saul, eds., *England and the Low Countries*, pp. 153–68.

[42] Christ Church College, Oxford, MS 179, Ordinances of the Confraternity of the Immaculate Conception at Blackfriars in London, dated 1517.

[43] J. Harris, 'Two Byzantine craftsmen in fifteenth-century London', *JMed.H*, 21 (1995), 387–403.

[44] S. L. Thrupp, 'Aliens in and around London in the fifteenth century', in Hollaender and Kellaway, eds., *Studies*, pp. 252–72; I. Scouloudi, 'Alien immigration into, and alien communities in, London 1558–1640', *Proc. of the Huguenot Society of London*, 16 (1937–41), 27–49; recent historians have calculated a larger number of aliens in London, bringing the percentage up to a minimum of 6 per cent, see J. L. Bolton, ed., *The Alien Communities of London in the Fifteenth Century* (Stamford, 1998), pp. 8–9.

have contributed more to the diversity and character of London life than their small number might suggest.

(ii) THE GOVERNMENT OF THE CITY

When one considers the large size of London's population, its lack of homogeneity, the high visibility of alien groups, the rapid turnover of families (at least in the male line), the small percentage of the inhabitants who enjoyed political rights (7.5 per cent), it is not surprising if, at times, the government of London seemed insecure. Conflicts within urban communities at this period seem to have arisen from three causes, or a combination of them: conflict between ruling groups (not dynasties at this period), conflicts between those with little political power and those with most, and conflicts between rival crafts and trades.[45] Many of these conflicts were endemic in London but only rarely did they flare up in such a way as seriously to threaten the stability and effectiveness of civic government. The picture in this later period is very different from the almost continuous dynastic rivalries of thirteenth-century London.

This period was an important and formative one in the evolution of civic government in London: charters of privileges and the right of self-government had already been won from the crown by 1300, but now an effective working system had to be created. The mayor, twenty-four aldermen of the wards and the two sheriffs were served by a tripartite civil service: the recorder provided legal expertise, the chamberlain was responsible for the city's finances and the common clerk ran the secretariat.[46] The elaboration of the city's self-government is reflected not only in the keeping of more complete records from the late thirteenth century onwards, but also in the creation of city custumals: the *Liber Horn* and the *Liber Custumarum* compiled by Andrew Horn (d. 1328);[47] *Liber Memorandorum* of the early fourteenth century,[48] and, in the fifteenth century, the *Liber Albus* compiled in 1419 by the common clerk John Carpenter[49] and the *Liber Dunthorne* compiled by William Dunthorne, also the common clerk, in the 1470s.[50] These custumals were attempts to record how the government of London should be conducted both within the city itself and in relation to outsiders, especially the crown.

The most notable development of these centuries was the creation of the Common Council, a body of some 150 to 180 citizens elected from the wards

[45] See above, pp. 210 and 306–9. [46] Williams, *Medieval London*, pp. 76–105.

[47] H. T. Riley, ed., *Munimenta Gildhallae Londoniensis* (RS, 1859–62), vol. II, parts I and II.

[48] Extracts printed as Appendix II to Riley, ed., *Munimenta Gildhallae Londoniensis*, III, pp. 430–56.

[49] Riley, ed., *Munimenta Gildhallae Londoniensis*, I and III.

[50] All these custumals remain in the Corporation of London RO: for those that have 'escaped' see N. R. Ker, 'Liber custumarum and other manuscripts formerly at the Guildhall', *Guildhall Miscellany*, 3 (1954), 37–45.

(although in 1351–2 and again in 1376–84, the constituencies were the crafts). It came to play an increasingly important role in city government; in particular, and in parallel with the evolution of the Commons in parliament, it came to control all the city's financial matters. The citizens of London could not be taxed without its prior approval. To enable the court of Common Council and the court of aldermen to work together effectively, joint committees were frequently set up in the fifteenth century to deal with particular problems such as the conflict with the city rectors over the payment of tithes, or with expensive building projects such as the repair of London Bridge.[51] The early simplicity of the city's civil service gave way to more complicated bureaucracies: the chief officers appointed deputies and came to be served by bevies of clerks and serjeants. The mayor and sheriffs also developed burgeoning households containing permanent officers who might serve successive mayors or sheriffs.[52] By the 1380s the mayor's household was run by his swordbearer or esquire who served successive mayors like a cross between a bodyguard and a butler.[53] Particular officers developed their own areas of responsibility: the common serjeant (deputy to the recorder) was responsible for the city's orphans (*c.* 300 children during the reign of Richard II)[54] and new officers were created: for example in 1385 the city's first 'environmental health' officer was elected and sworn as 'Serjeant to survey the city's streets and lanes'.[55] As the elected mayors and sheriffs came to serve only for a year, so it became more necessary to have a professional and efficient civic bureaucracy. The city's yearly salary bill was growing, but at least those who were paid to do a job carried it out themselves and subcontracting was rare.

In the fifteenth century new pieces were added to the jigsaw of London government. The city companies came increasingly to be used as agents of the mayor and aldermen. The masters and wardens were summoned to Guildhall and allocated tasks such as the raising of money, or of troops to fight in France, or simply to help to keep the peace within the city. The participation of the city companies in the government of London was formally recognised in 1465 when it was decided that the mayor should be elected by the liverymen of the companies led to Guildhall by their masters and wardens.[56] At the beginning of this period all citizens of London could take part in electing the mayor but by the end of the fifteenth century the constituency was limited to the 'better sort' of citizens. It is also apparent that the parishes were themselves developing as administrative units. Churchwardens were elected, accounts were kept (with greater or lesser competence), inventories were compiled and parish officers such as clerks were employed and paid by local subscription. In fact we know more

[51] Barron, 'The government of London', pp. 50–63. [52] *Ibid.*, pp. 51, 103–12.

[53] B. R. Masters, 'The mayor's household before 1600', in Hollaender and Kellaway, eds., *Studies*, pp. 95–114. [54] B. R. Masters, 'The common serjeant', *Guildhall Miscellany*, 2 (1967), 379–89.

[55] Sharpe, ed., *Letter Book H*, p. 275.

[56] R. R Sharpe, ed., *Calendar of Letter Book L* (London, 1912), pp. 132–3.

about parish administration than we do about the wards since almost no ward records survive from the medieval period.[57] The parish, moreover, encompassed all – men, women, children, aliens and clergy – who lived within its boundaries. Its running was not a task reserved exclusively to citizens and the responsibilities were not confined to religious matters: the churchwardens administered doles for the poor, collected rents, compiled inventories and saw to the repair of church buildings. Quite modest men and women formed, or joined, religious fraternities and helped to run their affairs, husband their meagre resources, fulfil their purposes and draw up their rules.[58] Although city government at the top might appear to be moving towards a more oligarchic structure, yet at the grass roots within the wards, parishes and fraternities, men – and women – were able to form their own associations and determine their own governing structures. But although the craft, ward, parish or fraternity may have provided a means of homogenising a fluid immigrant society, many of these immigrants were never assimilated. The few surviving wardmote returns and the records of the church courts bear witness to the existence of many Londoners who lived at the margins of respectability: the poor, the quarrelsome, the vicious, the ill and the criminal.[59] The records of the court of aldermen and of the mayor's court tend to provide a picture of stability and good order but there is much in medieval London which never found its way into the official records of the city. It is worth remembering that the whole world of William Langland, who lived in London for many years, has dropped below the horizon of the historian's vision.[60]

(iii) CONFLICTS AND CEREMONIAL

Certainly there were major conflicts in London which are evident even in the city's formal records. The most serious arose in the years 1376–92 and was caused by acute economic rivalries within the governing elite, in particular a conflict between the drapers led by John of Northampton (a group sometimes categorised as the non-victuallers) and the grocers led by Nicholas Brembre (the victuallers). John of Northampton sought support among the 'small people' of the city and developed a 'reforming' agenda. In 1376 his 'party' secured the election of the Common Council by crafts rather than from the wards, the compilation of the new custumal known as the *Jubilee Book*, which set out the 'good customs'

[57] Deadman and Scudder, eds., *Guide to London Records Office*, p. 18.

[58] C. Burgess, 'Shaping the parish: St Mary at Hill, London, in the fifteenth century', in J. Blair and B. Golding, eds., *The Cloister and the World* (Oxford, 1996), pp. 246–86; C. Burgess, *The Church Records of St Andrew Hubbard Eastcheap c. 1450–c. 1570* (London Record Society, 1999).

[59] For ward records see n. 57 above; for church court records, see R. M. Wunderli, *London Church Courts and Society on the Eve of the Reformation* (Medieval Academy of America, 1981).

[60] C. M. Barron, 'William Langland: a London Poet', in B. A. Hanawalt, ed., *Chaucer's England: Literature in Historical Context* (Minneapolis, 1992), pp. 91–109.

of the city, and the annual election of the aldermen. Brembre, who replaced Northampton as mayor in 1383, set about dismantling the reforms and his successor in the mayoralty, Nicholas Exton a fishmonger, had the *Jubilee Book* burnt in 1387.[61] By 1400 the city government was much as it had been before the upheavals. But, just as the royal government had learnt from the events of 1381, so the city rulers learnt from the discord and street fighting of the 1380s and came to rule in a less partisan spirit. They paid more attention to the reality, as well as the rhetoric, of the 'common good'. The strong royal intervention in the affairs of the city in 1392 may have brought the wealthy ruling aldermen to their senses and to a realisation that the unrestrained pursuit of self-interest was individually, as well as corporately, damaging.[62]

The second outbreak of civic disorder arose in the 1430s. In this case craft rivalries were fought out on constitutional issues. The wealthy, but politically impotent, tailors' craft attempted to secure the election of their alderman, Ralph Holland, as mayor and in this way to gain leverage in their dispute with the drapers. The tailors raised key constitutional questions: were those who had not been involved in the election of the mayor bound to obey the man elected? Were those elected ruling in the common, or in sectarian, interest? The tailors' protest which had originally targeted the mayoral elections of 1439–41 later developed into a general artisan protest about the new royal charter for the city in 1444 which gave to the mayor and aldermen powers as justices of the peace. Not surprisingly, the tailors viewed this as another means whereby the ruling merchant aldermen could dominate, chastise and imprison those who protested. 'This is a commission', Holland claimed, 'not of peace, but of war.' The mayor and aldermen managed to gain control of the situation, Holland was banished from his seat on the aldermanic bench, and it was thirty years before another tailor was elected an alderman.[63]

It is possible that the tailors were in fact protesting about the increasingly oligarchic nature of civic government as they understood it.[64] In fact in the fifteenth century the government of London became both more and less oligarchic. The constituency for electing the mayor was no longer the whole body of the citizens as it had been in the thirteenth century, but was confined to those who were summoned. On the other hand the members of the Common Council now exercised real and effective authority through their control of taxation and

[61] C. Barron, *Revolt in London: 11th to 15th June 1381* (London, 1981), pp. 12–20; P. Nightingale, 'Capitalists, crafts and constitutional change in late fourteenth-century London', *P&P*, 124 (1989), 3–25.

[62] C. M. Barron, 'Richard II's quarrel with London', in F. R. H. DuBoulay and C. M. Barron, eds., *The Reign of Richard II* (London, 1970), pp. 173–201.

[63] C. M. Barron, 'Ralph Holland and the London radicals, 1438–1444', repr. in R. Holt and G. Rosser, eds., *The Medieval Town* (London, 1990), pp. 160–83; M. P. Davies, 'The tailors of London and their guild *c.* 1300–1500' (DPhil thesis, University of Oxford, 1994), pp. 120–7.

[64] See above, pp. 302, 306–12.

participation with the aldermen on joint committees.[65] The base of popular democracy had narrowed but the numbers of the elite had expanded. As we have already seen there were more, albeit less powerful, offices to be filled at company, parish and fraternity level. The events of the 1430s and 1440s seem to have been less of a conflict among the city's ruling elite than a one-man battle waged against the elite by a visionary leader. On the whole the aldermanic body, indeed the governing elite of the city as a whole, seems to have held together remarkably well. Moreover, as has recently been demonstrated, this unity persisted in spite of the strains imposed upon it by the religious differences of the sixteenth century.[66] The aldermen were sensitive to pressure from below and were united in their common anxiety about the need for good order and stability.

What role, if any, did civic ceremonial play in achieving this stability and community spirit in London? Although there were Corpus Christi processions organised by individual fraternities and crafts, such as the skinners, there was no city-wide guild of Corpus Christi and no civic celebration of the body of Christ. Likewise the mayor and aldermen were not members of a single merchant guild but were members of their separate companies. The aldermen did, however, wear a common livery of a scarlet cloak lined with fur, and the mayoral office itself came to be invested with dignity and ceremonial, as the mayor was increasingly addressed as 'lord mayor', and his sword was carried before him by his esquire.[67]

The city of London had two corporate festivities and these both developed in the late medieval period into important civic occasions, encouraged by the self-consciousness of the city companies and by the burgeoning practices of chivalric society. Alongside the coats of arms and the heraldic badges there was always much religious imagery in civic ceremonial. The riding of the newly elected mayor to Westminster to take his oath was, by 1300, a fixed point on the civic calendar and took place on 28 October, the feast of Saints Simon and Jude, although the mayor had been elected on the more significant feast day of Edward the Confessor, 13 October. Originally the mayor rode to Westminster accompanied only by some of the aldermen. By the late fourteenth century it had become customary for members of the city crafts, dressed in their liveries, to accompany the mayor and, by the fifteenth century, the companies fined liverymen who failed to turn up at the ridings.[68] From the 1420s part of the journey

[65] See n. 51 above.

[66] I. Archer, *The Pursuit of Stability: Social Relations in Elizabethan London* (Cambridge, 1991).

[67] I. Archer, C. Barron and V. Harding, eds., *Hugh Alley's Caveat: The Markets of London in 1598* (London Topographical Society, 137, 1988), pp. 82–3.

[68] S. Williams, 'The Lord Mayor's Show in Tudor and Stuart times', *Guildhall Miscellany*, 1, no. 10 (1959), 3–18; M. Berlin, 'Civic ceremony in early modern London', *UHY* (1986), 15–27; Ian Rawlinson, 'Civic processions in later medieval London' (MA thesis, Royal Holloway, University of London, 1995).

took place by barge, a feast at the house of the mayor, or at his company hall, became customary, minstrels came to accompany the procession and in 1481 it was decided to ban the 'disguysyngs' and 'pageouns' which crafts had produced to join the procession from the mayor's house to the water.[69] From being an administrative necessity forced on the city by the demands of the crown, the annual riding had developed into the major civic festival. On this occasion the city celebrated not the festival of Corpus Christi but of Corpus Civitatis Londiniensis. The mayor's riding was expressive not of popular culture but, rather, of the corporate spirit of the city's ruling citizens, of their particular part of the body politic.

There was, however, another London festival which may have been more popular. This was the series of nightly processions known collectively as the Midsummer Watch which took place between 24 and 29 June. On these nights the trained bands of the wards marched through the city to demonstrate their readiness to defend the city from attack. Although John Stow places the origins of this 'marching' back in the mists of time, it may well have been first instituted in the 1380s, but soon developed into a popular festival associated with the charivari of the summer solstice.[70] By 1500 it probably had as little connection with the armed forces of London as the ceremony of the Trooping of the Colour has with the modern British army. The military aspect came to be swamped by torch bearers, pageants, the city waits, giants and morris dancers. In 1539 the king ordered the mayor and aldermen to suspend the Watch on the grounds that it was a threat to public order. Historians, influenced perhaps by John Stow, have tended to see it as a truly popular festivity, a utilitarian exercise which was increasingly taken over by the Londoners to the point that it became a threat to good order and had to be abolished by the crown acting in conjunction with the mayor and aldermen. More recently the Watch has been interpreted as an oppressive and expensive expression of oligarchic rule, imposed on an unenthusiastic populace by London's rulers as a means of asserting their control over civic space. In this interpretation the king, in suppressing the Watch, was acting in a populist manner.[71] Whatever it may once have contributed to community spirit in London, by the early sixteenth century the Marching Watch was considered to have become too great a threat to public order to be allowed to continue. In so far as ceremonial contributed to the cohesiveness and stability of London in these years, it did so less through centralised civic ceremonies than through a myriad of local festivities, of craft and parish and fraternity, which formed a network of interlocking obligations, loyalties and public faces. London was a large city composed of numerous small associations

[69] Sharpe, ed., *Letter Book L*, p. 187.

[70] John Stow, *A Survey of London*, ed. C. L. Kingsford (Oxford, 1908), vol. 1, pp. 101–4.

[71] S. Lindenbaum, 'Ceremony and oligarchy: the London Midsummer Watch', in B. A. Hanawalt and K. L. Reyerson, eds., *City and Spectacle in Medieval Europe* (Minneapolis, 1994), pp. 171–88.

whose memberships overlapped and wove together a network of civic consciousness. It was this that stabilised city government.

(iv) THE CITY AND THE CROWN

It was in its relations with the crown that the city needed, above all, to present a united front. In its position vis-à-vis other English towns London was unchallenged and pre-eminent, but when faced by the power of the crown it was surprisingly vulnerable. It was only in 1297 that Edward I had finally, and reluctantly, restored self-government to London after twelve years of 'direct rule' by a royal warden. In 1392 Richard II again withdrew the city's liberties and their restoration cost the Londoners some £30,000.[72] In the thirteenth century the main issue between the crown and the city was money and, in particular, whether London was liable to pay arbitrary tallage or only voluntary aid to the king. Usually the king was successful in extracting tallage, but by 1300 the issue was on the way to resolution through the introduction of the parliamentary taxation payable on goods and chattels which took the place of the older feudal obligations. Since London now paid taxes as the other shires and towns of England, the point at issue between the city and the crown was not grants, but loans.[73] The crown had cash flow problems and, especially after the collapse of the Italian financiers in the 1340s, turned to the Londoners for help either corporately or from individuals such as John Pyel, Adam Fraunceys, Richard Lyons, Richard Whittington or John Hende.[74] Although the failure of London to supply loans may on occasion, as in 1392, have contributed to friction between the crown and the city, the most significant difficulties focused on lawlessness. By the last quarter of the fourteenth century it looked as if disorder was becoming endemic in the city. It was the failure of the mayor and aldermen to curb street violence which finally provoked Richard II's seizure of the city's liberties. In the fifteenth century the weaknesses, as well as the triumphs, of the Lancastrian dynasty made the kings more dependent upon the city, although the crown by no means always took the action that the city wanted. The sales of London monopolies, the protection of aliens (especially in the sale to the Italians

[72] See n. 62 above.

[73] Edward III, perhaps in deference to the financial strength of London or in partial recognition of the Londoners' claim to be liable only to aid and not to tallage, allowed the City to be taxed at the lower, rural rate of a fifteenth rather than a tenth.

[74] S. J. O'Connor, 'Finance, diplomacy and politics: royal service by two London merchants in the reign of Edward III', *HR*, 67 (1994), 18–39; C. M. Barron, 'London and the crown 1451–61', in J. R. L. Highfield and R. Jeffs, eds., *The Crown and the Local Communities in England and France in the Fifteenth Century* (Gloucester, 1981), pp. 88–109; A. R. Myers, 'The wealth of Richard Lyons', in T. A. Sandquist and M. R. Powicke, eds., *Essays in Medieval History Presented to Bertie Wilkinson* (Toronto, 1969), pp. 301–29; for Whittington, see n. 25 above; for Hende, see entry in *New DNB* (forthcoming).

of licences to avoid the Calais Staple in the 1450s) and the support of sanctuary claims of the clergy, all demonstrated that the crown, in spite of its dynastic weakness, was not obliged to behave in ways which pleased the Londoners.[75] On the other hand the Londoners did supply quite large amounts of cash and, on occasion (e.g. in 1436 and 1449) raised armies for the wars in France.[76] London victuallers supplied the forces at Harfleur and much of the necessary clothing and equipment was made in London workshops.

London was, moreover, the capital of England in part because of its proximity to Westminster. So kings processed through the city before their coronations and, when necessary, the London crowds provided the required 'collaudatio' for usurpers such as Henry IV in 1399 and Edward IV in 1461.[77] The city also provided welcoming ceremonies for royal brides such as Anne of Bohemia in 1381, Margaret of Anjou in 1444 and Catherine of Aragon in 1501, as well as triumphal processions for 'conquering' kings, Richard II in 1392, Henry V in 1415 and Henry VI in 1432.[78] Entertaining pageantry was provided for the visits of foreign heads of state: the Emperor Sigismund in 1415 was met, at the king's command, by the mayor, aldermen and commons at Blackheath where they 'resceyved hym in the best and worthyest maner that they cowde'.[79] In 1522 Charles V was lavishly received in the city and welcomed with addresses from Sir Thomas More and Master Lily, the high master of St Paul's. This welcome at the royal command cost the city nearly £1,000.[80] Although the details of these receptions, the choice of allegories and indeed the costs, were open to negotiation, yet they had come to be considered as an inescapable service rendered by the city to the crown. On the other hand the crowds who gathered to watch the excitements spent their money in London's shops and taverns. There is no doubt that Londoners saw their monarch far more frequently than the inhabitants of other English towns, and they paid for this privilege. In this they were, doubtless, influenced by the 'joyeuses entrées' which the Flemish towns provided for their

75 Barron, 'London and the crown', pp. 90–1; J. Bolton, 'The city and the crown, 1456–61', *LJ*, 12 (1986), 11–24; Barron, 'The government of London', pp. 393–408.

76 Barron, 'The government of London', pp. 457–61.

77 C. M. Barron, 'The deposition of Richard II', in J. Taylor and W. Childs, eds., *Politics and Crisis in Fourteenth-Century England* (Gloucester, 1990), pp. 132–49, esp. p. 143; C. A. J. Armstrong, 'The inauguration ceremonies of the Yorkist kings and their title to the throne', *TRHS*, 4th series, 30 (1948), 51–68.

78 G. Kipling, 'The London pageants for Margaret of Anjou', *Medieval English Theatre*, 4 (1982), 5–27; S. Anglo, 'The London pageants for the reception of Katherine of Aragon, November 1501', *Warburg and Courtauld Institute J*, 26 (1963), 53–89; G. Kipling, 'Richard II's sumptuous pageants and the idea of the civic triumph', in D. M. Bergeron ed., *Pageantry in the Shakespearean Theater* (Atlanta, 1985), pp. 83–103; Barron, 'The Government of London', pp. 468–78; R. H. Osberg, 'The Lambeth Palace manuscript account of Henry VI's 1432 London entry', *Medieval Studies*, 52 (1990), 255–67.

79 A. H. Thomas and I. Thornley, eds., *The Great Chronicle of London* (London, 1938), p. 94.

80 R. R. Sharpe, *London and the Kingdom* (London, 1894–5), vol. I, p. 365.

Burgundian counts, and the frequency of these royal ceremonies may help to explain the absence from London of any notable play cycles.[81] The streets were full of drama: if not a royal procession, then there would be civic and parochial ones. In addition there would be players and musicians performing at the royal court and in the London town houses of the aristocracy. The Londoners did not need to organise play cycles to draw in the crowds, for the crowds were already coming.

But it was not only in ceremonies that the Londoners gained access to their monarchs. The surviving records of the privy council make it clear that the mayor of London, usually accompanied by some of his aldermen, was often summoned to confer with the king and the council, to offer advice or, perhaps, to lodge a complaint. Parliament, moreover, usually met at Westminster and bishops, abbots and lay lords lodged in their town house in, or near, the city. The king, his court and his council were not remote figures, but well known to the ruling elite of London, many of whom supplied their households with furs, silk and velvet, silver and gold plate, woollen cloth for liveries, wine and spices.[82] In the fourteenth century the London merchants seem to have been a class apart: men who dressed in the long robes of clerics rather than the tunics and armour of knights, and who eschewed tournaments and did not fight. They were distinguished by their merchant marks and by their seals which displayed mottos and flora and fauna. Nicholas Exton in 1387 told Richard II that 'the inhabitants of the city were, in the main, craftsmen and merchants, with no great military experience, and it was not permissible for them to devote themselves to warfare save for the defence of the city alone'.[83] In the fifteenth century things began to change: the London aldermen seem to have aspired to gentry status: they adopted coats of arms (see Plate 20) and many of them were knighted by Edward IV. This king invited them to dinner and chose a merchant wife as one of his mistresses.[84] Members of the aristocracy married the widows of London merchants and apprenticed their sons to London merchants.[85] So, by the early sixteenth century, the aldermen of London were less easily distinguished from the aristocracy and from nobles and courtiers than a century earlier. They now shared, in English, a common language, a common chivalric culture and a common concern for overseas trading ventures. What still distinguished the London merchant from the gentleman was the source of his income. Whereas the gentleman lived off an income derived from rents (his livelihood), the

[81] See R. Beadle, *The Cambridge Companion to Medieval English Theatre* (Cambridge, 1994), p. 3.

[82] C. M. Barron, 'Centres of conspicuous consumption: the aristocratic town house in London 1200–1500', *LJ*, 20/1 (1995), 1–16.

[83] B. F. Harvey and L. C. Hector, eds., *The Westminster Chronicle 1381–1394* (Oxford, 1982), p. 217.

[84] A. F. Sutton, 'William Shore, merchant of London and Derby', *Derbyshire Arch. J*, 106 (1986), 127–39.

[85] See K. Bradberry, 'The world of Etheldreda Gardiner', *The Ricardian*, 9 (1991), 146–53.

merchant still lived by barter and sale. Although the successful merchant might use his wealth to buy country estates, like Sir Geoffrey Boleyn, mercer, who purchased the manor of Blickling in Norfolk and established a notable dynasty, yet the wealth was amassed not through landed estates but by trade.[86]

(v) THE ECONOMY OF LONDON

The economic prosperity of London in these centuries was built upon overseas trade, internal distributive trade, manufacturing and the service industry. The economy of London was probably more diversified than that of any other English town and for that reason, if for no other, it was likely to be able to weather the economic storms of population decline and bullion famine in the later medieval period. The role played by Londoners in overseas trade is easiest to chart because of the survival of almost complete runs of royal customs accounts, for the export of wool and cloth, the import of wine and the import and export of a variety of goods subject to petty custom and poundage. Nationally the wool exports declined steadily after the middle years of the fourteenth century, yet London's share of this declining export appears to have risen from 20 per cent in 1280 to 80 per cent in 1540 (see Figures 17.1a and b).[87] Moreover very little of the wool export trade was in the hands of alien merchants: the small share they had enjoyed in the fourteenth century had virtually disappeared by the second half of the fifteenth century (see Figure 17.1c). But it was, of course, cloth which came to dominate the export trade of England, rising from the 10,000 or so cloths exported in the 1360s to the 130,000 cloths of the 1530s (see Figure 17.2a). In this export London gradually built up a virtual monopoly: the London share rose from 10 per cent of the national export in the 1350s to over 80 per cent in the 1530s (see Figure 17.2b).[88] But here the alien exporters, the Italians and the Hanse merchants, clung tenaciously to their share of the cloth export. Even in the sixteenth century the Italians had 10–20 per cent of the cloth export from London and the Hanse merchants about 30 per cent. The denizen merchants rarely controlled more than 50 per cent of the cloth exports through the port of London (see Figure 17.2c). But, clearly, the export of cloth was vitally important to the economy of London in this period, and was largely developed and then monopolised by the Merchant Adventurers' Company of London, who used the hall of the Mercers' Company in Cheapside as their headquarters.[89]

Wine was also an important trading commodity. Although the imports slumped in the course of the fifteenth century from about 10,000 tuns a year to

[86] Thrupp, *Merchant Class*, p. 325; *New DNB*, (forthcoming).

[87] For a detailed discussion of London's role in overseas trade in the fourteenth century, see Nightingale, 'Growth of London', esp. pp. 99–100. [88] *Ibid.*, p. 101.

[89] E. Carus-Wilson, 'The origins and early development of the Merchant Adventurers' organisation in London as shown in their own medieval records', *Ec.HR*, 4 (1932–4), 147–76.

nearer 6,000 in the 1460s, yet by the 1520s imports were higher than a hundred years earlier. London's share of the import trade remained at about 40 per cent throughout the fifteenth century, although the port had cornered a larger share of the trade by the sixteenth century (see Figures 17.3a and b). All the other goods which were traded in and out of England were liable to petty custom at the rate of 3d. in the pound on the value of the goods, and also to poundage, which was levied at the rate of 12d. in the pound. The slump in English trade between 1450 and 1480 is clear (see Figure 17.4a and c), as is the dramatic rise in goods traded which peaked in the 1520s. The value of the goods passing through the port of London had doubled between 1400 and 1540. London's share of these imports and exports had risen from *c.* 45 per cent of the national total to *c.* 70 per cent by the 1540s (see Figure 17.4b and d). Analysis of the petty custom account for London covering the year 1480–1 shows that the main export was cloth.[90] Raw wool was very much in a secondary position and the only manufactured items, apart from cloth, were pewter pots and a few brass items. Tin and lead were the only raw materials exported, and the remaining exports were agricultural items such as butter, cheese, wheat, salt meat, tallow, candles and calf skins. The imported goods were much more varied and, apart from raw materials such as iron, tar, wax, hemp and dyestuffs, consisted largely of manufactured goods, mostly from the Low Countries. About half a million yards of linen came into London in a single year together with numerous linen articles, such as sheets and napkins. Brass and latten cooking pots, candlesticks and basins were imported in large quantities from Dinant, Liège and Cologne, together with armour of many varieties. Through London small manufactured articles flooded into England: clothmaking tools of all kinds, 900 printed books and 30 gross of spectacles in a single year. The sophisticated products of continental workshops were pouring into London in exchange for England's staple export of cloth.

The survival of the customs' accounts enables us to draw a detailed picture of the patterns and commodities of the overseas trade of London. The patterns of England's internal trade are more elusive: no taxes and so no picture. It is easier to glimpse the networks than to analyse them. London drapers appear, at least in the fifteenth century, to have acted as middlemen buying up cloths made all over England and bringing them for sale to Blackwell Hall, which had been established as the city's cloth market in 1396.[91] The same carts and packhorses which brought the cloths to London returned to the villages and towns of England laden with imported goods such as those described in the custom account of 1480–1. Much of this distributive trade seems to have been in the hands of Londoners, since only they could buy and sell goods freely in London

[90] H. Cobb, ed., *The Overseas Trade of London: Exchequer Customs Accounts 1480–1481* (London Record Society, 27, 1990).

[91] Barron, *Guildhall*, pp. 17, 57; Sharpe, ed., *Letter Book H*, p. 449.

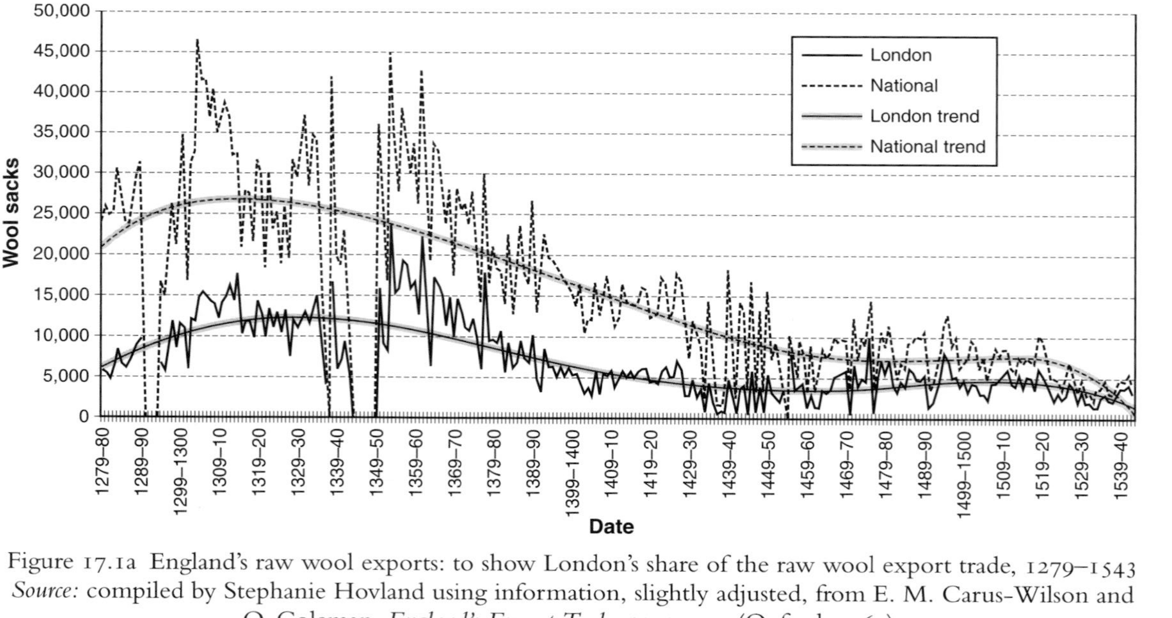

Figure 17.1a England's raw wool exports: to show London's share of the raw wool export trade, 1279–1543
Source: compiled by Stephanie Hovland using information, slightly adjusted, from E. M. Carus-Wilson and O. Coleman, *England's Export Trade, 1275–1547* (Oxford, 1963).

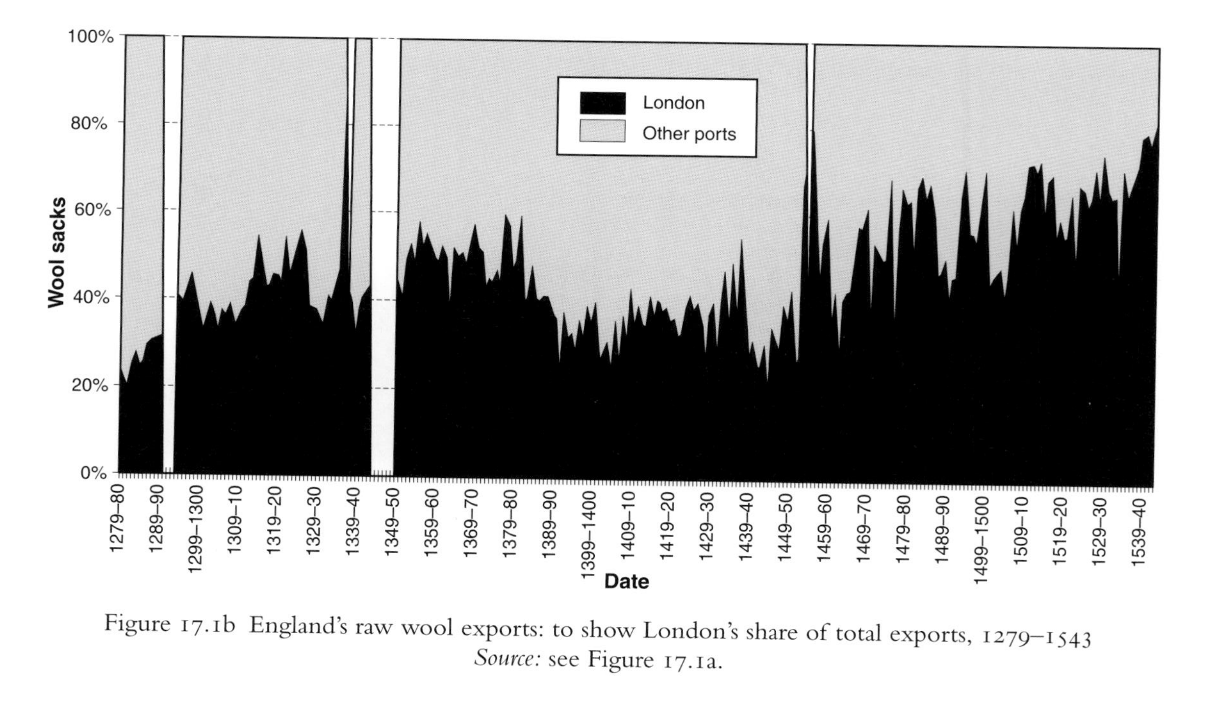

Figure 17.1b England's raw wool exports: to show London's share of total exports, 1279–1543
Source: see Figure 17.1a.

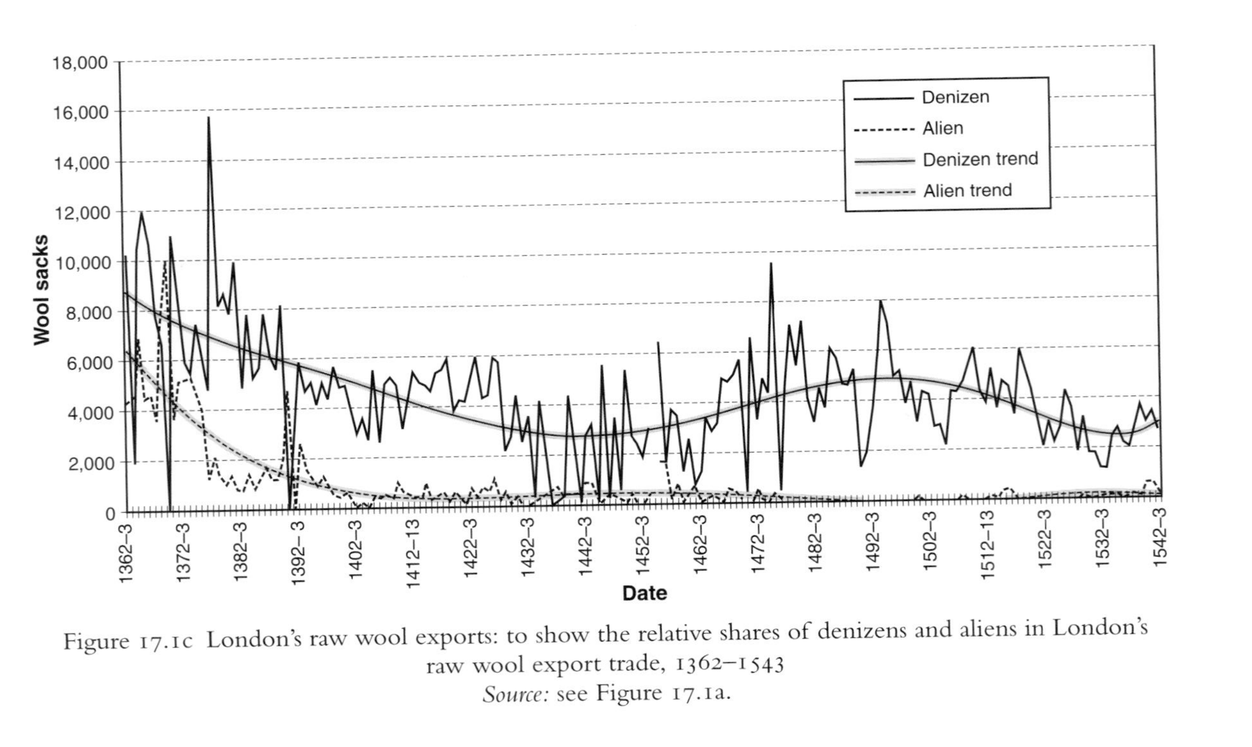

Figure 17.1c London's raw wool exports: to show the relative shares of denizens and aliens in London's raw wool export trade, 1362–1543
Source: see Figure 17.1a.

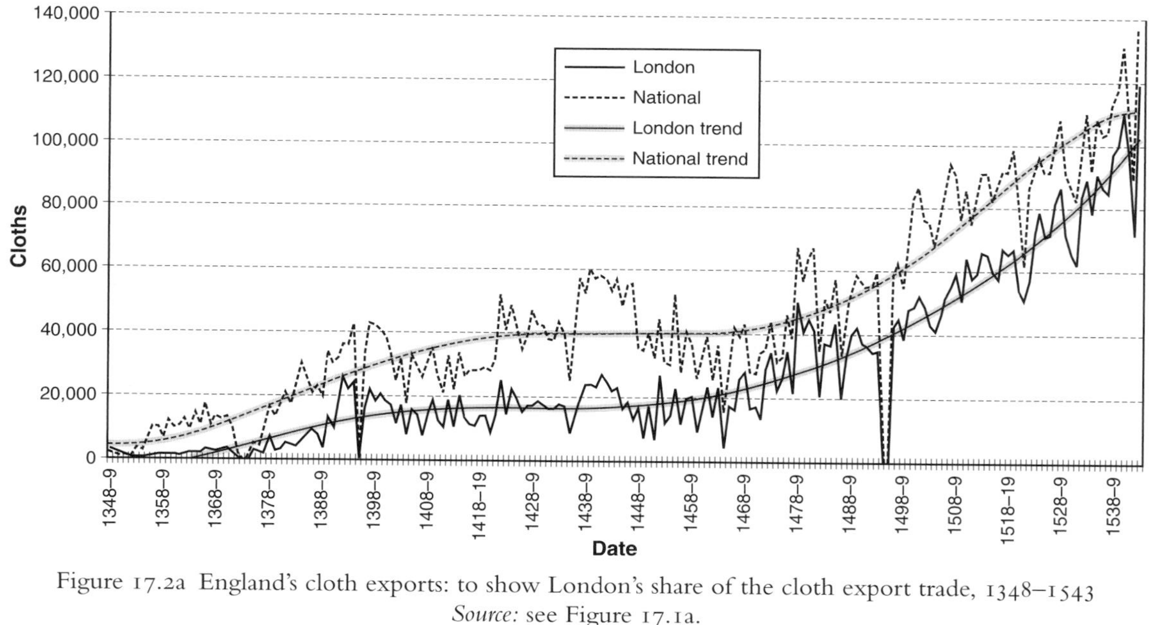

Figure 17.2a England's cloth exports: to show London's share of the cloth export trade, 1348–1543
Source: see Figure 17.1a.

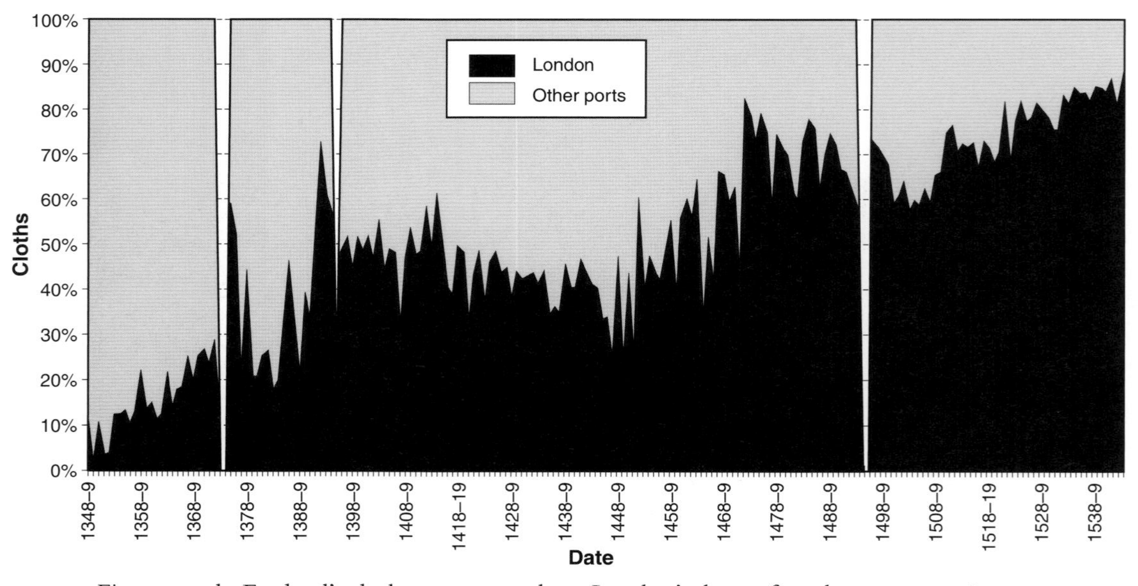

Figure 17.2b England's cloth exports: to show London's share of total exports, 1348–1543

Source: see Figure 17.1a.

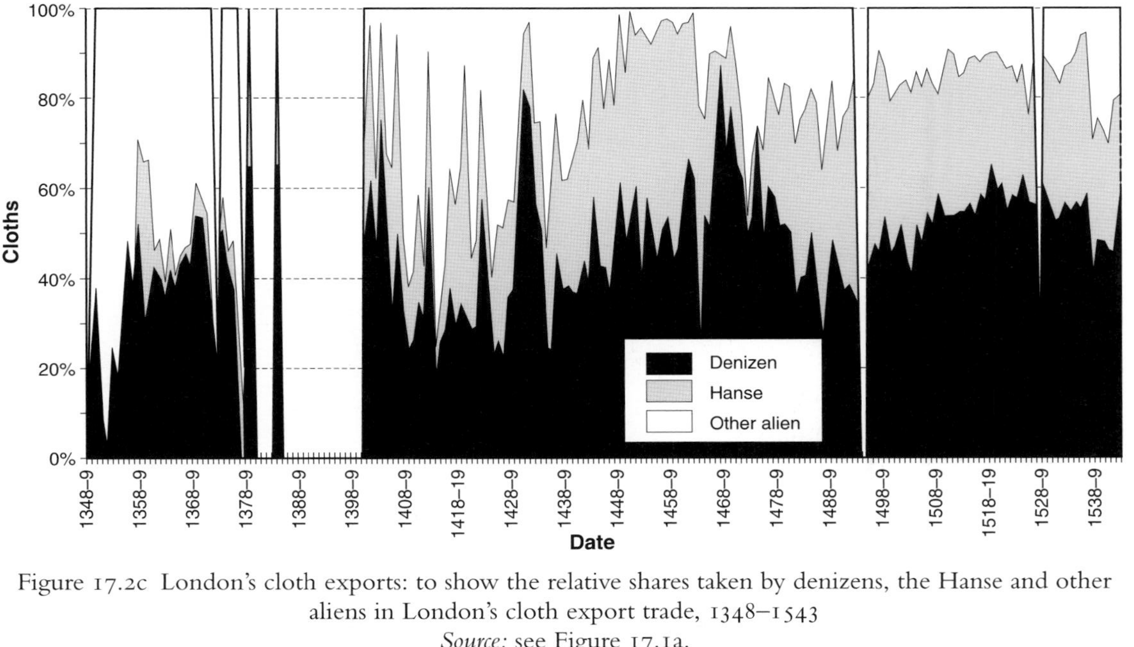

Figure 17.2c London's cloth exports: to show the relative shares taken by denizens, the Hanse and other aliens in London's cloth export trade, 1348–1543
Source: see Figure 17.1a.

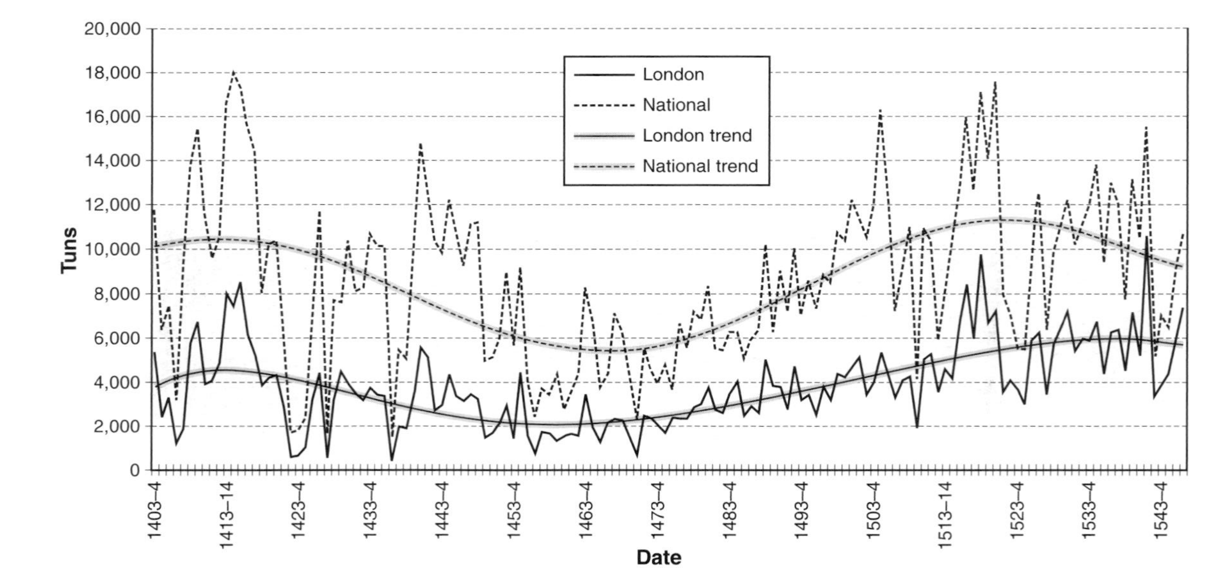

Figure 17.3a England's wine imports: to show the trend of London's share of total imports, 1403–1547
Sources: compiled by Stephanie Hovland using: 1400–1500, information from M. K. James, *Studies in the Medieval Wine Trade* (Oxford, 1971), pp. 108–16; 1500–9, unpublished material kindly supplied by Professor Peter Ramsey; 1509–48, information from Georg Schanz, *Englische Handelspolitik gegen Ende des Mittelalters . . . Heinrich VII und Heinrich VIII* (Leipzig, 1881), pp. 128–45.

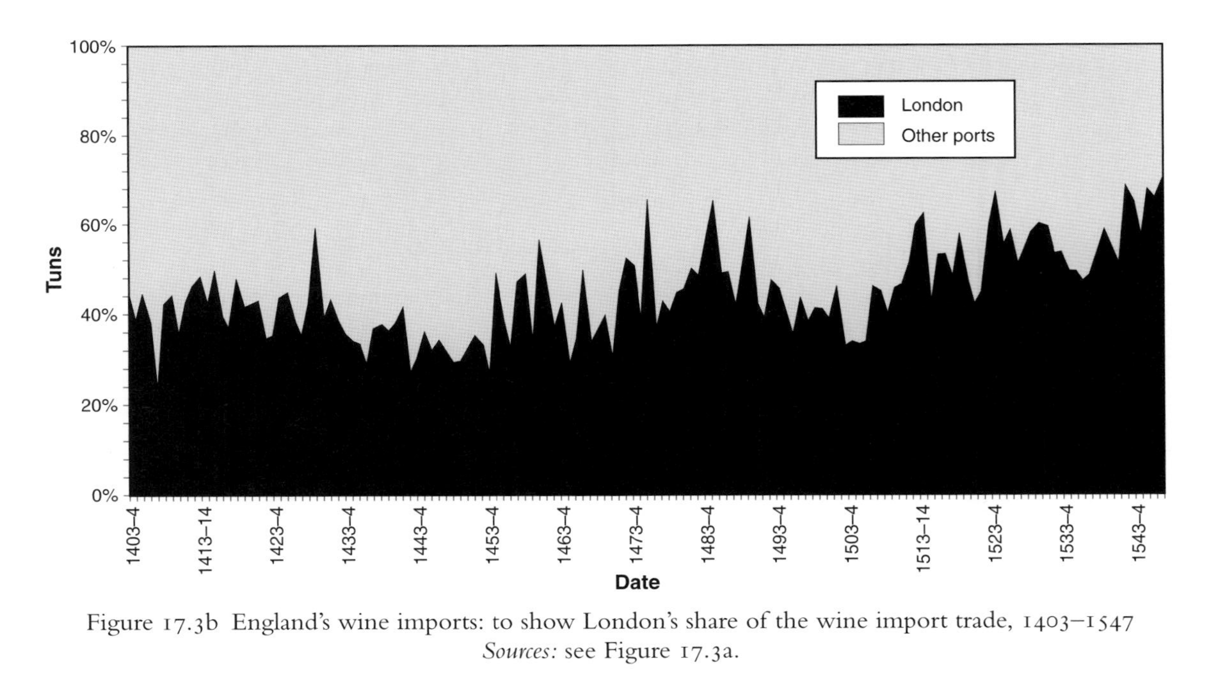

Figure 17.3b England's wine imports: to show London's share of the wine import trade, 1403–1547
Sources: see Figure 17.3a.

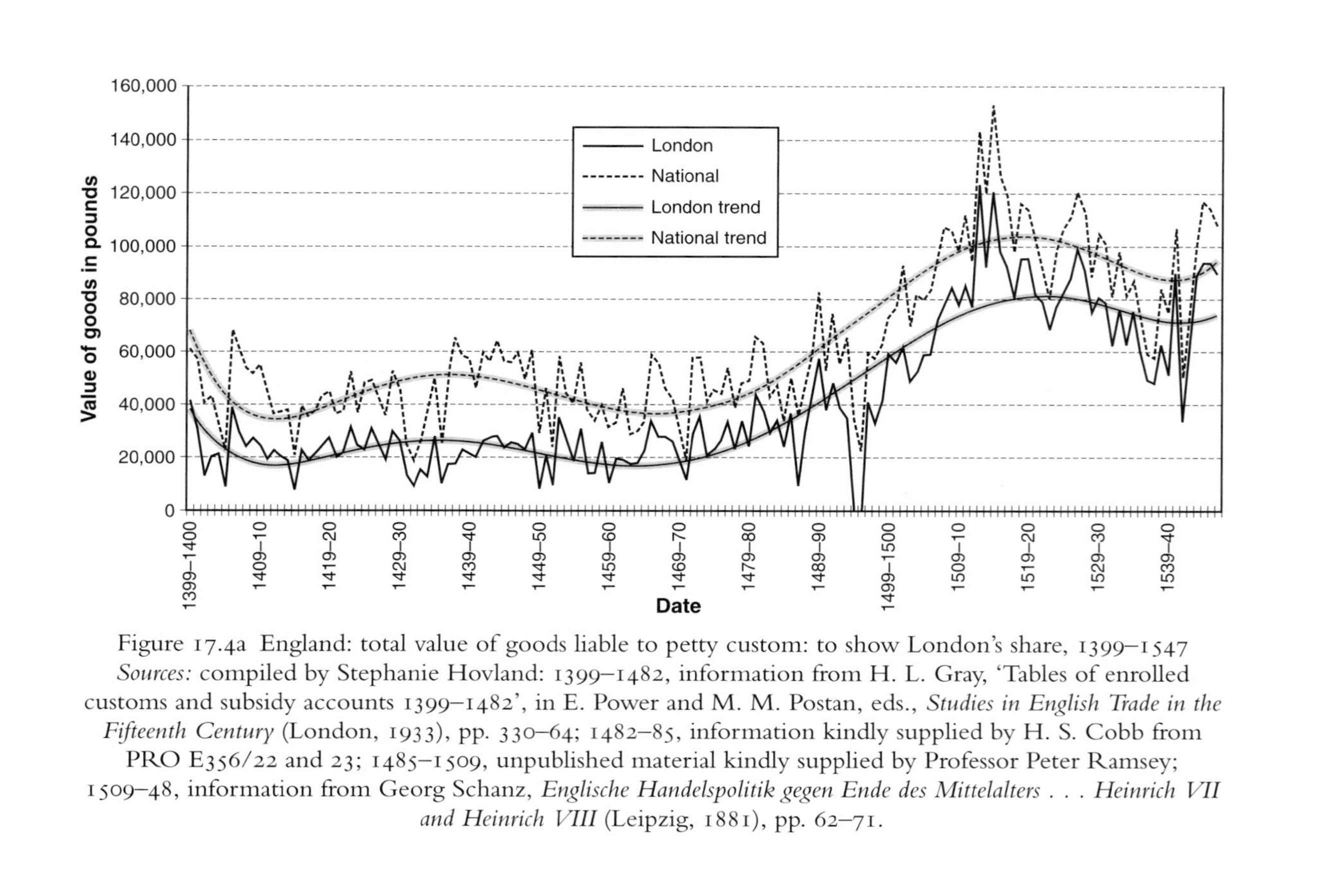

Figure 17.4a England: total value of goods liable to petty custom: to show London's share, 1399–1547
Sources: compiled by Stephanie Hovland: 1399–1482, information from H. L. Gray, 'Tables of enrolled customs and subsidy accounts 1399–1482', in E. Power and M. M. Postan, eds., *Studies in English Trade in the Fifteenth Century* (London, 1933), pp. 330–64; 1482–85, information kindly supplied by H. S. Cobb from PRO E356/22 and 23; 1485–1509, unpublished material kindly supplied by Professor Peter Ramsey; 1509–48, information from Georg Schanz, *Englische Handelspolitik gegen Ende des Mittelalters . . . Heinrich VII and Heinrich VIII* (Leipzig, 1881), pp. 62–71.

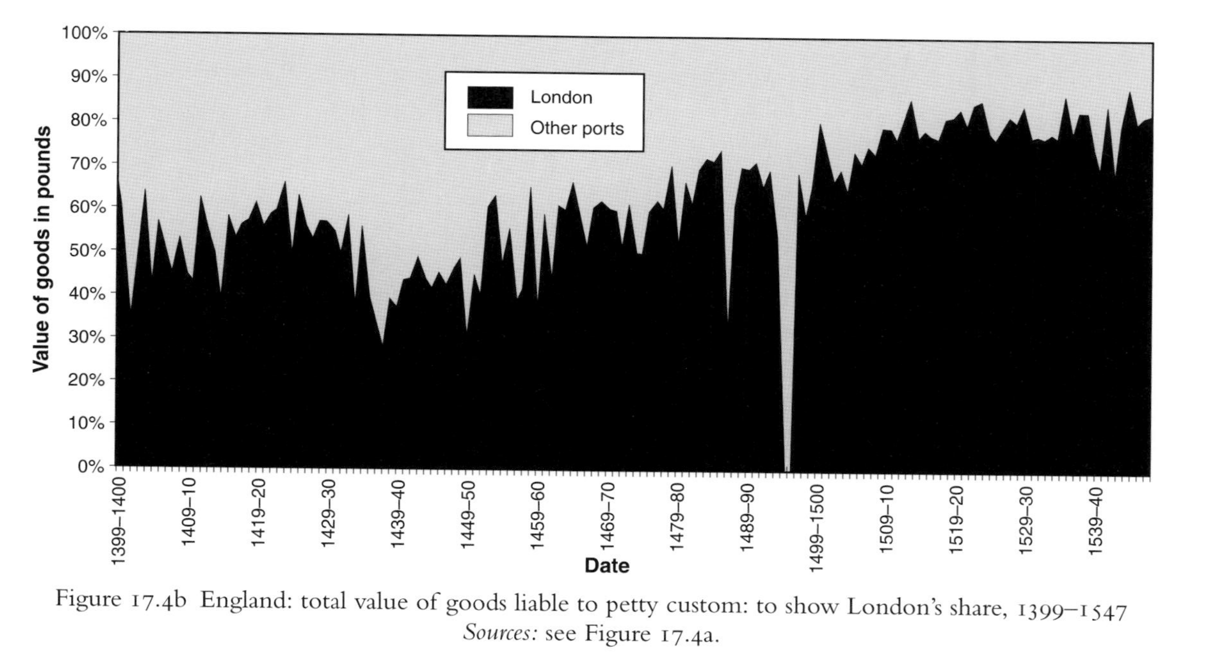

Figure 17.4b England: total value of goods liable to petty custom: to show London's share, 1399–1547

Sources: see Figure 17.4a.

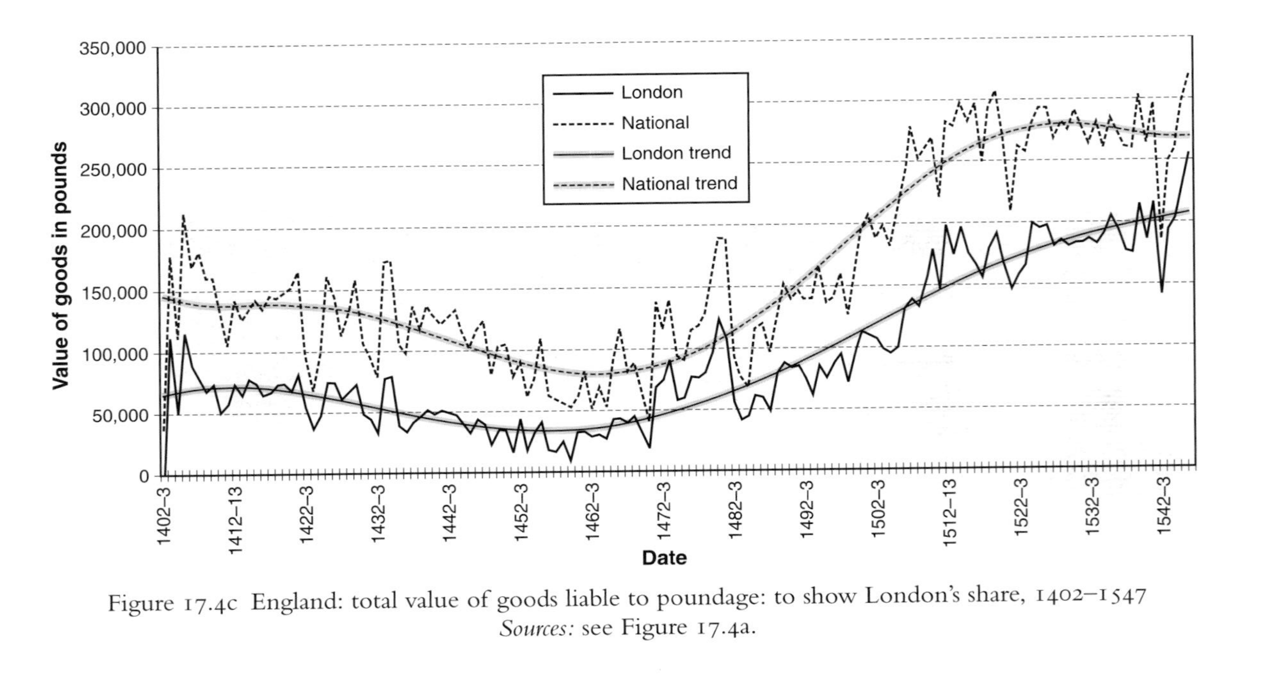

Figure 17.4c England: total value of goods liable to poundage: to show London's share, 1402–1547

Sources: see Figure 17.4a.

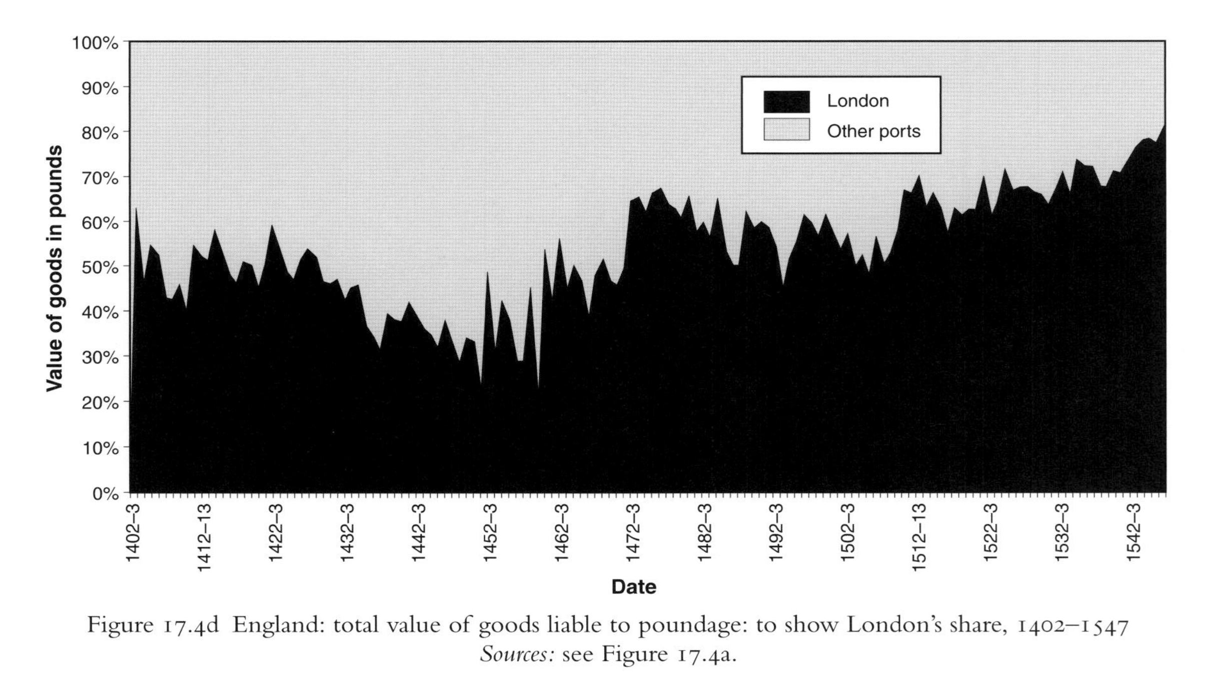

Figure 17.4d England: total value of goods liable to poundage: to show London's share, 1402–1547
Sources: see Figure 17.4a.

and were able to take them elsewhere to sell free of local tolls.[92] The geographical pattern of debts owed to London merchants reveals the far-reaching tentacles of the city's distributive trade.[93]

London merchants were not, however, engaged only in selling goods which had been imported into London. The city was an important centre of manufacture, although this aspect of its economic life is sometimes obscured by the pre-eminence in city government of members of the great 'merchant' companies such as the drapers, mercers and vintners. When the Common Council in 1377 was elected by the crafts of London these included pouchmakers, armourers, girdlers, cutlers, broiderers, bowyers, horners, pewterers, tapicers, weavers, founders, pinners and smiths.[94] Other crafts, moreover, were practised in London which never felt the need for joint action, such as the bookbinders, parchmentmakers, organmakers, mirrorers and seal-engravers.[95] The range of skills practised in London and the variety of goods which were made there and sold from craft workshops either directly to the customer or to middlemen who carried the goods to customers further afield must not be overlooked. It was the Birmingham, as well as the Liverpool, of medieval England. Indeed, some crafts practised in medieval London were probably found nowhere else in England and certainly not on any scale. These were the crafts where demand was infrequent and skill at a premium such as makers of memorial brasses (often known as marbelers), casters of church bells (founders) and painters such as Gilbert Prince.[96] The work of London goldsmiths was valued throughout Europe, and they had few rivals in other English towns. It is clear that not all founders made bells, nor did goldsmiths always fashion the standing cups and pendants which they sold: a craftsman might know the secrets of his trade but choose not to practise it himself but, rather, to run a workshop where he employed servants and trained apprentices whose worksmanship

[92] S. Thrupp, 'The grocers of London: a study of distributive trade', in Power and Postan, eds., *Studies in English Trade*, pp. 247–92; C. Dyer, 'The consumer and the market in late medieval England', *Ec.HR*, 2nd series, 62 (1989), 305–27; I. Archer, *The History of the Haberdashers' Company* (London, 1991), ch. 2 esp. pp. 30–1.

[93] E. Bennet, 'Debt and credit in the urban economy: London 1380–1460' (PhD thesis, University of Yale, 1989), ch. 4; J. I. Kermode, 'Medieval indebtedness: the regions *versus* London', in N. Rogers, ed., *England in the Fifteenth Century* (Stamford, 1994), pp. 72–88. A rising proportion of debts under statute staple were enrolled in London, 33.6 per cent in the 1360s rising to 63 per cent in 1400–10, see Nightingale, 'The growth of London', p. 101.

[94] A. H. Thomas, ed., *Calendar of Plea and Memoranda Rolls 1364–1381* (Cambridge, 1929), p. 243.

[95] E. Veale, 'Craftsmen and the economy of London in the fourteenth century', in Hollaender and Kellaway, eds., *Studies*, pp. 133–51.

[96] J. Blair, 'Purbeck marble', in J. Blair and N. Ramsay, eds., *English Medieval Industries* (London, 1991), pp. 42–56; J. C. L. Stahlschmidt, *Surrey Bells and London Bell-Founders* (London, 1884); C. M. Barron, 'Johanna Hill and Johanna Sturdy, bell-founders', in C. M. Barron and A. F. Sutton, eds., *Medieval London Widows, 1300–1500* (London, 1994), pp. 100–11; J. Alexander and P. Binski, eds., *Age of Chivalry: Art in Plantagenet England 1200–1400* (London, 1987), pp. 131–6, 148–56; D. Gordon, *Making and Meaning: The Wilton Diptych* (London, 1993), pp. 72–3.

he vouched for and sold. The dramatic drop in population in the later fourteenth century appears not seriously to have damaged London's skilled workforce. Richard II was able to find in London the skilled painters, embroiderers, goldsmiths and latoners that he needed to carry out his commissions. It may well be that alien workmen, such as the goldsmith Hans Doubler or the embroiderer André Beauneveu and the painter Hermann Scheere, joined the London workforce and transmitted their skills. Indeed, well into the sixteenth century and beyond 'the metropolis was a centre for production as well as trade . . . three fifths of London's occupations involved some form of production of goods'.[97]

The production of food was clearly important, and guilds of butchers, brewers, poulterers, cornmongers, fruiterers and cheesemongers emerged in the period. But there were other service industries in which there was no element of production, such as apothecaries, gardeners, scriveners, woodmongers, water-bearers, haymongers and hostellers or innkeepers. For these suppliers of food and services it was vital that the population of London should remain buoyant, that the king should live in or near London and that the great men of the realm should inhabit their London houses. When Henry of Derby entertained Richard II in 1397 food was bought in for the great feast: Isabelle Mercer supplied twelve dozen compotes and Agnes 'at Paul's Gate' supplied a further thirty-two.[98] Many Londoners, particularly the poorer ones, lived by servicing the luxurious tastes in food and clothing of the wealthy aristocracy and great London merchants, but the prosperity of the city did not depend, in this period, upon these service industries. Nor was trade alone the source of London's pre-eminence and wealth; indeed, as the tailor John Bale claimed in 1443, the prosperity of the city depended upon the artisans and not the merchants.[99]

Bale might have added that the prosperity of London depended also upon women. Following the plague of 1348–9 women are to be found at work in London and they appear in the records more frequently. They were formally apprenticed to learn a variety of crafts although most seem to have worked in silk in some way. When married they traded as 'femmes soles' and as widows many took up the freedom of the city and ran workshops, took on apprentices and traded goods at home and abroad.[100] London women are found exporting cloths or selling silk embroidery to the royal wardrobe.[101] Many were engaged

[97] A. L. Beier, 'Engine of manufacture: the trades of London', in A. L. Beier and R. Finlay, eds., *London 1500–1700: The Making of the Metropolis* (London, 1986), pp. 141–67, esp. p. 150.

[98] Barron, 'Centres of conspicuous consumption', 10.

[99] Barron, 'Ralph Holland', p. 178.

[100] M. K. Dale, 'The London silkwomen of the fifteenth century', *Ec.HR*, 4 (1933), 324–5; C. M. Barron, 'The "golden age" of women in medieval London', *Reading Medieval Studies*, 15 (1989), 35–58; Barron and Sutton, eds., *Medieval London Widows*; K. Lacey, 'Women and work in fourteenth and fifteenth century London', in I. Charles and L. Duffin, eds., *Women and Work in Pre-Industrial England* (Beckenham, 1985), pp. 24–82.

[101] A. F. Sutton, 'Alice Claver, silkwoman', in Barron and Sutton, eds., *Medieval London Widows*, pp. 129–42.

in making and selling food like the women who made compotes for the Derby feast.[102] Others ran inns and taverns and some chose, or were compelled, to earn their living as prostitutes.[103] Women were needed to fill a gap in the workforce and they were willing and able to do this. What is distinctive about women's work in the period *c.* 1350–*c.* 1500 is that their roles are formally recognised and they are more visible: what is distinctive about their work in London is that girls were apprenticed as boys were; that women took on boys, as well as girls, as apprentices, to learn their own skills, and that they could become freewomen of London and enjoy all the economic advantages of that status.[104] But the absence of any accompanying political rights ensured that when the population began once more to rise, and labour became plentiful, women's work became once more largely informal and invisible.

(vi) CRAFT GUILDS AND COMPANIES

Both the trading and the manufacturing activities of Londoners were organised along guild lines. In 1300 these organisations were in their infancy, although there had been trading/craft guilds in London since at least the twelfth century.[105] The motives which led men of the same craft or trade to associate with each other were diverse: often it was an outside force which propelled them towards collective action: in some cases the force was royal demands and, in others, alien competition.[106] Some craftsmen appear to have associated together because they lived in the same neighbourhood, or because they needed to co-ordinate resistance to a monopolistic purchaser, as with the fusters, who made saddle trees, and the saddlers.[107] The mercers may have formed their first formal association in the early fourteenth century because of concerns about apprenticeship and entry to the city's freedom.[108] There is debate as to whether trade guilds or fraternities were formed from the bottom up or from the top down.[109]

102 See n. 98 above.

103 J. B. Post, 'A fifteenth-century customary of the Southwark stews', *J of the Society of Archivists*, 5 (1977), 418–28; R. Karras, 'The regulation of brothels in later medieval England', *Signs*, 14 (1989), 399–433.

104 For girl apprentices, see C. M. Barron, 'The education and training of girls in fifteenth-century London', in D. E. S. Dunn, ed., *Courts, Counties and the Capital in the Later Middle Ages* (Stroud, 1996), pp. 139–53, esp. pp. 144–7.

105 For earlier craft associations see above, p. 207.

106 E. Veale, 'The "great twelve": mistery and fraternity in thirteenth-century London', *HR*, 64 (1991), 237–63.

107 K. M. Oliver, *Hold Fast, Sit Sure: The History of the Worshipful Company of Saddlers of the City of London 1160–1960* (Chichester, 1995), pp. 18–24.

108 A. F. Sutton, 'The silent years of London guild history before 1300: the case of the mercers', *HR*, 71 (1998), 121–41.

109 H. Swanson, *Medieval Artisans* (Oxford, 1989); M. P. Davies, 'Artisans, guilds and government in medieval London', in R. H. Britnell, ed., *Daily Life in the Late Middle Ages* (Stroud, 1998), pp. 125–50.

The ordinances of the many London crafts which were frequently presented to the mayor and aldermen for approval may represent not so much the wishes of the craft or guild as a whole but, rather, those rules which would best suit the masters in controlling the work of their apprentices and journeymen. The support lent by the mayor and aldermen in the late fourteenth century to the masters of the saddlers, cordwainers and tailors in their attempts to curb the separatist tendencies of their journeymen and apprentices (known as the yeomanry or bachelors of the company) lends some support to this view.[110] But, whatever the divisions of that period, by the fifteenth century the yeomen groups seem to have been harmoniously incorporated into the companies as men not yet of the livery but waiting to enter it, with their own fraternity and feast as in the case of the skinners who had two fraternities, Corpus Christi for the senior members of the craft and a separate fraternity dedicated to St John the Baptist for the younger men.[111]

The fifteenth century probably marks the heyday of the city companies of London. After the flurry of royal interest in voluntary associations in 1388–9, many crafts sought charters of incorporation which licensed them to wear a livery, hold land in mortmain and draw up rules for their internal organisation.[112] Two developments resulted from these charters. In the first place there was a marked acceleration in the building of company halls: whereas there were, perhaps, half a dozen in 1400, there were at least forty-four by 1540 (see Figure 17.5).[113] Even quite modest crafts such as the pinners and tilers contrived to build, or adapt, halls. The second development was that companies began to receive endowments to fund obits for dead members and also to found almshouses (such as that of the tailors in 1405)[114] or schools such as Stockport Grammar School founded by the will of Sir Edmund Shaa, a goldsmith who died in 1488.[115] The companies began to keep more extensive records; they employed clerks and gardeners and rent-collectors; they held feasts and bought liveries which they wore on civic occasions like the mayor's riding to Westminster. The larger companies controlled the working of the apprenticeship system within their craft, although in the lesser and less well-organised crafts this

110 H. T. Riley, ed., *Memorials of London and London Life in the XIIIth, XIVth, and XVth Centuries* (London, 1868), pp. 495–6, 542–4, 609–12, 653.

111 E. Veale, *The English Fur Trade in the Later Middle Ages* (Oxford, 1966).

112 G. Unwin, *The Gilds and Companies of London* (London, 1908), ch. 11; C. M. Barron and L. Wright, 'The London middle English guild certificates of 1388–9', *Nottingham Medieval Studies*, 39 (1995), 108–45, esp. 117–18.

113 Unwin, *Gilds and Companies*, ch. 12; *BAHT*, III; Schofield, *London Houses*, pp. 44–8.

114 M. P. Davies, 'The tailors of London: corporate charity in the late medieval town', in R. Archer, ed., *Crown, Government and People in the Fifteenth Century* (Stroud, 1995), pp. 161–90.

115 T. F. Reddaway and L. E. M. Walker, *The Early History of the Goldsmiths' Company 1327–1509* (London, 1975), pp. 306–7.

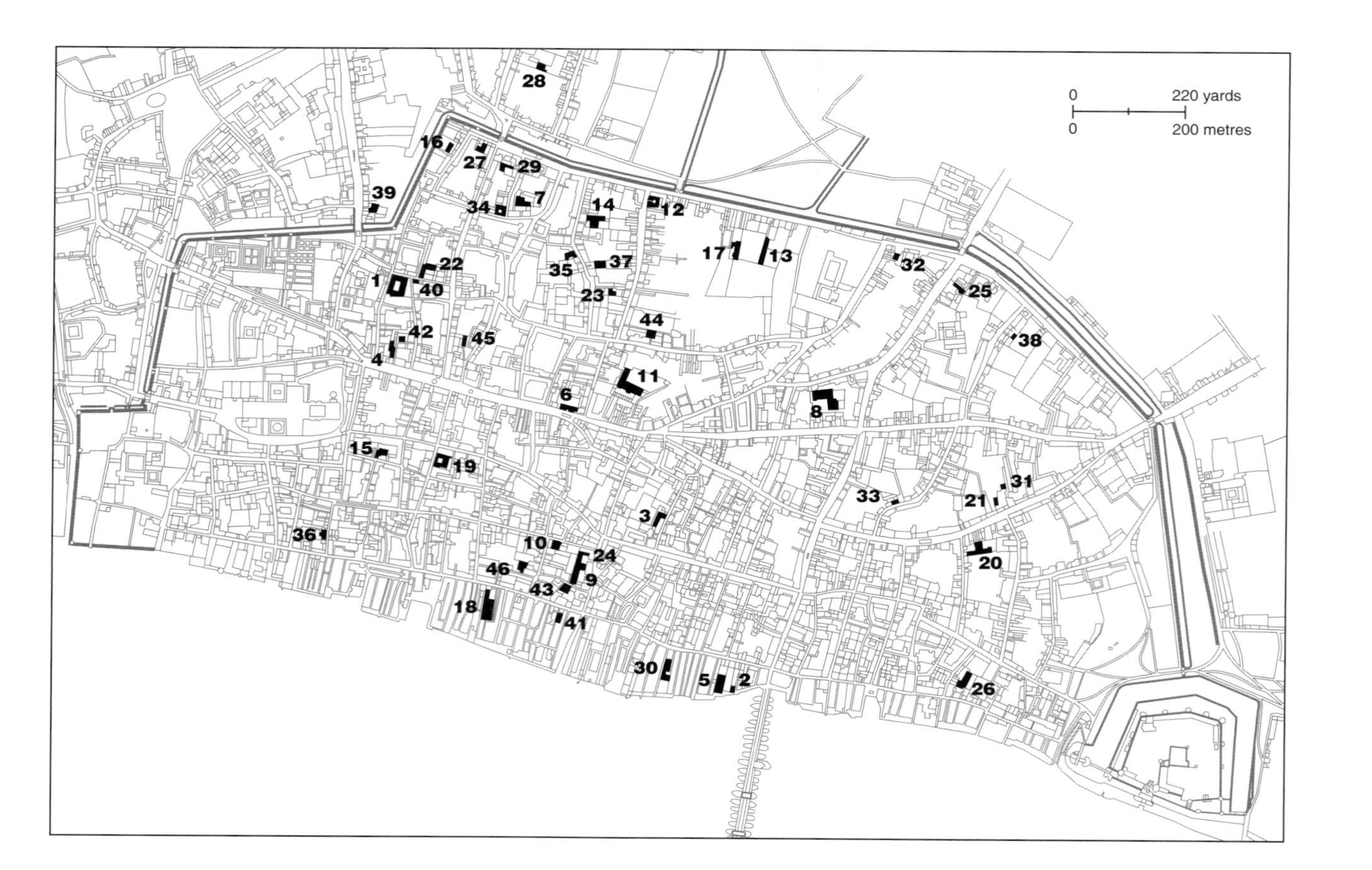
0
220 yards
0
200 metres
28
16
27
29
39
34
7
14
12
17
13
22
35
37
32
1
40
23
25
44
42
45
38
4
11
6
8
15
19
33
31
21
3
36
10
24
20
46
9
43
18
41
30
5
2
26

LONDON COMPANY HALLS
WITH FIRST KNOWN DATES

1	Goldsmiths	1339	24	Tallowchandlers	(1464)
2	Stockfishmongers	1368**	25	Parish Clerks	by 1467
3	Drapers	1385/1408	26	Bakers	(by 1475)
4	Saddlers	1394	27	Bowyers	by 1475
5	Fishmongers	(1398)**	28	Butchers	(by 1475)
6	Mercers	*c.*1400	29	Curriers	(by 1475)
7	Brewers	by 1403	30	Dyers	(by 1475)
8	Merchant Taylors	1404	31	Fullers	by 1475*
9	Skinners	1409	32	Tylers	by 1475
10	Cutlers	1420/2	33	Pewterers	1475
11	Grocers	1427/31	34	Pinners	by 1480
12	Armourers	1428	35	Coopers	*c.*1490
13	Carpenters	1429	36	Blacksmiths	1494/5
14	Girdlers	1431	37	Weavers	1498
15	Cordwainers	by 1440	38	Fletchers	*c.*1500
16	Barbers	1441/5	39	Cooks	1500
17	Leathersellers	1445	40	Waxchandlers	1501/25
18	Vintners	1446	41	Joiners	1518
19	Salters	by 1455	42	Embroiderers	1519/22
20	Shearmen	1455*	43	Innholders	1522
21	Ironmongers	1457	44	Founders	1531
22	Haberdashers	by 1460	45	Stationers	by 1540
23	Masons	by 1463	46	Glaziers	by 1540

Where a date is given in brackets this indicates that the first hall of the company was on a different site from that indicated on the map of company halls in 1540

**The Stockfishmongers and the Fishmongers amalgated on the site of the Fishmongers' Hall in 1536

* The Shearmen and the Fullers amalgamated on the site of the Shearmen's Hall in 1528, and took the name of Clothworkers

Figure 17.5 The Company Halls of London *c.* 1540
Source: BAHT, III.

was still controlled by the mayor and aldermen.[116] The rulers of the craft (the master and/or wardens and court of assistants) oversaw the practice of the craft or trade, and promoted its interests. In the case of the mercers this might involve tackling the royal council over the level of wool and cloth subsidies.[117] In the case of the cutlers it might mean working with other manufacturing crafts to promote a bill in parliament inhibiting the import of manufactured goods from Flanders.[118]

At the heart of almost every craft association or company was a religious fraternity which, in some cases, was more important than the craft. The tailors' fraternity, dedicated to St John the Baptist, attracted more than half its members from outside the craft, and it owned almshouses and offered pensions to its brothers and sisters.[119] Most of the craft religious fraternities were based upon a parish church, often in the area where many of the craftsmen lived, or near to the company hall. The painters in the fourteenth century lived and worked in the extramural part of the suburb of Cripplegate and their fraternity was located in the church of St Giles Cripplegate.[120] The tailors had, originally, founded their fraternity in a chapel in St Paul's Cathedral, but by the middle of the fifteenth century it had been overtaken by their new fraternity in the church of St Martin Outwich next to Tailors' Hall. In fact few crafts chose the cathedral for their religious fraternities. Unlike the crafts of Italian towns such as Bologna, they preferred to 'adopt' a parish church and to locate their fraternity there. The choice of a particular saint provided the craft with a 'logo', a festival day and a particular intercessor replete with appropriate imagery. This image of the saint would embellish the company plate, their record books and their funeral pall. Conversely, the saint's chapel in the parish church would display the arms of the company and of its more wealthy members, in the glass of the windows, on the vestments and on the altar itself.[121] Moreover, the charitable works of the company, whether almshouses, or schools or pensions, were carried out within the religious context of reciprocal prayer and the endless quest for saintly intercession to secure eternal salvation.

[116] J. Ryan, 'Apprenticeship in later medieval London 1200–1500' (MA thesis, Royal Holloway, University of London, 1992).

[117] L. Lyell and F. D. Watney, eds., *Acts of Court of the Mercers' Company 1453–1527* (Cambridge, 1936), see index under 'Custom' and 'Subsidy'.

[118] C. M. Barron, 'London and parliament in the Lancastrian period', *Parliamentary History*, 9 (1990), 343–67, esp. 360–1.

[119] Davies, 'The tailors of London', pp. 161–90.

[120] The Fraternity was dedicated to the Blessed Virgin and St Luke, see the return of 1388, PRO, C47/46/463. Gilbert Prince (d. 1396) left bequests to the fraternity, Sharpe, ed., *Calendar of Wills*, II, pp. 319–20; for the location of London painters, see J. Mitchell, 'The painters of London 1240–1502' (MA thesis, Royal Holloway, University of London, 1989).

[121] Unwin, *Gilds and Companies*, chs. 9 and 13; C. M. Barron, 'The parish fraternities of medieval London', in C. M. Barron and C. Harper-Bill, eds., *The Church in Pre-Reformation Society* (Woodbridge, 1985), pp. 13–37.

(vii) RELIGIOUS LIFE OF LONDON

The religious life of London differed little from that of other English towns in the later medieval period. There was, however, simply more of everything: over a hundred parish churches; over twenty anchorages and perhaps fifty religious houses, almost all of them founded before 1300.[122] There were, however, two important new foundations. London's first Cistercian house was founded by Edward III at East Smithfield, dedicated to St Mary of Graces in thank-offering for his naval victory at Sluys and situated at one of the city's main plague cemeteries in 1348–9. The other cemetery was the site of the second great fourteenth-century foundation, that of the house of Carthusian monks, the Charterhouse, founded by Sir Walter Manny, one of Edward III's war captains, in 1371.[123] Both of these new houses were inspired in part by the cataclysmic deaths in the plague, and were funded out of the profits of the French wars. These houses were exceptional. The characteristic foundations in London in this period were colleges of priests (Guildhall College 1356, Walworth College 1381, Whittington College 1424) and almshouses run either by city companies such as the Tailors, the Skinners, the Mercers and the Parish Clerks, or by parishes such as those administered by the parish fraternity of St Giles Cripplegate.[124] What was distinctive about religion in London was the variety of parish churches, the numerous fraternities and the range of religious houses.

What seems, perhaps surprisingly, to have been absent from London was any institutionalised conflict as occurred at, say, York or Lincoln or Beverley. Perhaps the diversity of religious houses in London fragmented the hostility. No single house in London exercised wide jurisdiction nor owned vast swathes of civic land. The main characteristic of religious life in London, at least at the official level, seems to have been indifference whether to the established religious houses, or to the bishop or to the Cathedral of St Paul. The mayor and aldermen paid official visits to the cathedral at the great festivals and on the Monday, Tuesday and Wednesday following Whitsun when they processed in their livery from St Peter's Cornhill to the cathedral accompanied by the hundred or so city rectors.[125] But the ritual of the civic year was but lightly touched by the practices of the Church. It seems as if there were few occasions when the mayor and aldermen prayed together, but that is not to say that they went rarely to mass: rather each followed his own individual religious light.

[122] For an account of the religious houses of medieval London, see *VCH*, London, I, pp. 407–588; for the anchorages, see J. Collis, 'The Anchorites of London in the late middle ages' (MA thesis, Royal Holloway, University of London, 1992). See also above pp. 211 and 379.

[123] D. Knowles and W. F. Grimes, *Charterhouse* (London, 1954).

[124] Barron, *Guildhall*, pp. 23–4, 33–42; J. Imray, *The Charity of Richard Whittington* (London, 1968); Schofield, *London Houses*, pp. 56–9.

[125] Riley, ed., *Munimenta Gildhallae Londoniensis*, I, pp. 27–30.

There were some particular areas of conflict in which the city, in its corporate capacity, took issue with the Church and turned, unsuccessfully, to the crown for support. From the 1430s off and on until the 1520s, the mayor and aldermen supported various groups of London parishioners in their attempts to resist paying increased (but by no means excessive) tithes. At one point the city funded the sending of an agent to Rome, which was an expensive and unsuccessful move since the agent ended up in prison in Cologne. As time went on the dispute developed into a general resistance to paying other church dues such as those for baptism and burial, and it was this issue which was at the root of the notorious case of Richard Hunne in 1511.[126] The other area of contention between the city and the Church focused on the issue of sanctuary and, in particular, the sanctuary of the collegiate church of St Martin le Grand. The College of St Martin, as Sir Thomas More said, in the 'very bowels' of the city, became notorious for criminals but also as a place where non-citizens could practise their crafts immune from city or company supervision. The sanctuary privileges were a source of revenue for the dean and canons, and there is good evidence that the sanctuaries in London enjoyed a measure of popular support. The mayor and aldermen did not wish to see them abolished, but they did want their inhabitants to be more closely controlled. New regulations were approved in 1457 and the dispute became less acute although it continued to be liable to flare up.[127]

Disputes such as those over tithes and sanctuary were not unique to London, but what seems to have been unusual was the lack of bitterness with which the disputes were conducted. There seems to have been mutual respect and a genuine desire to seek for acceptable solutions. There is, moreover, little evidence to suggest that heresy flourished in London in spite of its size and immigrant population.

When John Wyclif was brought to St Paul's for trial in 1377 the Londoners supported their popular bishop, William Courtenay, in his charges against Wyclif.[128] Obviously some of Wyclif's ideas found adherents in the city. The twelve Lollard conclusions were nailed to the door of St Paul's in 1395, and John Purvey, Wyclif's assistant in the translation of the Bible into English, was able to find obscurity and support in London during the first decade of the fifteenth century.[129] It was, moreover, to St Giles' Fields in London that Sir John Oldcastle

[126] J. A. F. Thomson, 'Tithe disputes in later medieval London', *EHR*, 78 (1963), 1–17; S. Brigden, 'Tithe controversy in Reformation London', *JEcc.Hist*, 32 (1981), 285–301.

[127] I. D. Thornley, 'Sanctuary in Medieval London', *J of the British Archaeological Association*, 2nd series, 38 (133), 293–315; Barron, 'The Government of London', pp. 393–408; G. Rosser, 'Sanctuary and social negotiation in medieval England', in Blair and Golding, eds., *Cloister and the World*, pp. 57–79.

[128] *VCH*, London, I, pp. 211–12.

[129] A. Hudson, 'John Purvey: a reconsideration of the evidence for his life and writing', *Viator*, 12 (1981), 355–80.

rallied the Lollard insurgents at Epiphany 1414. On occasion obdurate Lollards were brought to London for execution: Richard Wyche was burnt on Tower Hill in 1441 and was instantly venerated as a miracle worker by many Londoners. The attitude of the city's rulers was to stamp firmly on any attempt at the popular sanctification of Wyche, not out of concern for the niceties of doctrine, but from anxiety about the preservation of law and order.[130] From the 1470s there are more Lollards prosecuted in London (perhaps because the church courts were becoming more active) and a steady trickle of heretics continued to flow through the London church courts.[131] But there was little to suggest that London might become the stronghold of heretical opposition to the Church which developed in the 1530s and 1540s.[132]

The absence of widespread heresy in London may seem surprising. The vigilance of the mayor and aldermen and the discretion of the ecclesiastical officials may be in part responsible. But the orthodoxy of the city may be a reflection of the high quality of the rectors of the city churches. Non-residence was comparatively rare and the London parishes attracted a high proportion of university graduates. Distinguished and learned clerics were to be found in city churches: men like Gilbert Worthington at St Andrew Holborn, William Byngham at St John Zachary and John Coote and Hugh Damlett at St Peter Cornhill were all notable preachers, concerned with education and with the need to counteract heresy, and they owned substantial personal libraries.[133] Rectors like these were respected in the city, they served on civic committees and were chosen by the mayor and aldermen to preach 'civic' sermons on the days following Easter. Londoners in their turn left money to endow sermons (often specifying that they should be given by a graduate), and for books for their nascent parish libraries. Some of them provided 'Common Profit' books of spiritual instruction which would be passed from man to woman in a chain of commemorative reading and prayer.[134] The surviving parish records suggest a vigorous and varied parish life, with innovations in liturgy and in music, a variety of priests and of services and a degree of parochial self-government and of lay participation (e.g. in the choice of the fraternity priests).[135] These were not the conditions, perhaps, in which heretical ideas were likely to flourish.

[130] J. A. F. Thomson, *The Later Lollards 1414–1520* (Oxford, 1965); for information about Wyche, see C. M. Barron, review of Thomson, *J of the Society of Archivists*, 3 (1967), 257–9.

[131] Wunderli, *Church Courts*, pp. 123–6.

[132] S. Brigden, *London and the Reformation* (Oxford, 1989), chs. 1–4.

[133] C. M. Barron, 'The expansion of education in fifteenth-century London', in Blair and Golding, eds., *Cloister and the World*, pp. 219–45, esp. pp. 228–30; *VCH*, London, I, pp. 228–9.

[134] W. Scase, 'Reginald Pecock, John Carpenter and John Colop's common-profit books: aspects of book ownership and circulation in fifteenth-century London', *Medium Aevum*, 61 (1992), 261–74; J. Catto, 'The king's government and the fall of Pecock, 1457–8', in R. E. Archer and S. Walker, eds., *Rulers and Ruled in Late Medieval England: Essays Presented to Gerald Harriss* (London, 1995), pp. 201–22.

[135] See n. 58 above.

(viii) LONDON AND THE PROFESSIONS

What would certainly have distinguished London from other English towns would have been the range of professional services available. From the end of the thirteenth century men cunning in the common law of England had begun to frequent the royal courts and to compile and study the statutes of the realm. In the course of the fourteenth century these lawyers came to live together in inns in the western suburbs of London, along Fleet Street and Holborn. By the mid-fifteenth century these inns had become formalised as the four great legal inns and the ten lesser inns of Chancery and, together, they constituted London's university and contributed to a series of town and gown conflicts, which usually took the form of battles between the student lawyers and the butchers' apprentices at their common watering hole, the Fleet River.[136] This collection of skilled lawyers provided a body of legal expertise which could be matched nowhere else in England. Men, and women, were drawn to London to pursue cases in the king's courts at Westminster and also to seek legal advice. In the same way it was in London that the most experienced physicians and surgeons were to be found, and the best apothecaries. The physicians did not form themselves into a college until 1518, but there were several of them to be found at any one time in London.[137] Surgeons were more numerous, an elite craft anxious to distinguish themselves from the ubiquitous, but vulgar, barbers who claimed also to be surgeons. In 1493 the surgeons agreed to cooperate with the barbers and formal merger came in 1540.[138]

In a short-lived but remarkable experiment the physicians and surgeons joined together in 1423 to establish a house, or college, where they would hear lectures on medicine, carry out dissections and, most remarkably of all, treat the poor free of charge.[139] Judging from the prices charged by London physicians and surgeons, they were well able to afford this act of charity. The apothecaries were to be found in the Walbrook area in considerable numbers. Many of them in the early part of the period came from the continent, especially from Italy and southern France and they often dispensed medicines directly to patients.[140] Whether

[136] D. S. Bland, *The Early Records of Furnivalls Inn* (Newcastle-upon-Tyne, 1957); J. D. Walker, ed., *Records of the Honorable Society of Lincoln's Inn: The Black Books* (London, 1897–1902), vol. I; R. Roxburgh, *The Origins of Lincoln's Inn* (London, 1973); J. H. Baker, 'The English legal profession 1450–1590', in W. R. Prest, ed., *Lawyers in Early Modern Europe and America* (London, 1981), pp. 16–41; C. M. Barron, *The Parish of St Andrew Holborn* (London, 1979), ch. 3.

[137] C. Rawcliffe, 'Medicine and medical practice in later medieval London', *G St.*, 5 (1981), 13–25; G. N. Clark, *A History of the Royal College of Physicians of London* (London, 1964–72), vol. I.

[138] R. T. Beck, *The Cutting Edge: The Early History of the Barber Surgeons of London* (London, 1974); M. Pelling, 'Barber-surgeons, the body and disease', in Beier and Finlay, eds., *London 1500–1700*, pp. 82–112.

[139] J. F. Smith, *Memorials of the Craft of Surgery in England*, ed. D'Arcy Power (London, 1886), pp. 299–303.

[140] L. G. Matthews, *The Royal Apothecaries* (Wellcome Institute, 1967); G. E. Trease, 'The spicers and

the medical skills of any of these men were to be preferred to the pragmatic wisdom of the wise men and women of the countryside may well be doubted. Margaret Paston warned her son 'be ware . . . what medesynys ye take of any fysissyanys of London. I schal never trust to hem because of yowre fadre and myn onkle';[141] but if the patient wanted sophisticated medical skills then it was in London that these were to be found.

It was also in London that skilled scriveners, bookbinders, limnours (illuminators) and parchmentmakers were to be found. Here could be bought, off the shelf, a book of chronicles, or collection of statutes or a pious work or vernacular romance.[142] In London could be found scribes like William Kingsmill or the poet/clerk Thomas Hoccleve who could draft a single document to order, or like William Ebesham could copy out a whole manuscript.[143] It was in Westminster that William Caxton set up his printing press, and his successor, Wynken de Worde, moved his shop eastwards into Fleet Street.[144] Although by the early sixteenth century there were printers established in other English towns, there was a unique concentration of skill in the western suburbs of London.

Young men apparently flocked to London in the middle years of the fifteenth century in search of education – specifically a Latin education – because of the lack of grammar school masters in towns elsewhere in England. The rising standard of living after the Black Death led to a more general demand for learning of a kind broader than that to be found in the grammar schools, an ability to read, and perhaps write, English, and to cast accounts. In London there were three 'established' grammar schools, at St Paul's, St Martin le Grand and St Mary le Bow, and a new school at St Anthony's Hospital. But there were also many unofficial grammar masters of whom the most distinguished was probably John Sewarde who had a school in Cornhill, and there were also numerous 'dame' schools or scrivener's shops where reading and writing in the vernacular were taught.[145] Girls, in London, also took advantage of these educational opportunities and the daughters of London merchants, and artisan women, seem often to have been able to read, and sometimes to write, English.[146] The places at

apothecaries of the royal household in the reigns of Henry III, Edward I and Edward II', *Nottingham Medieval Studies*, 3 (1959), 19–52; D. Keene, 'The Walbrook study: a summary report' (typescript, Institute of Historical Research, 1987).

[141] N. Davis, ed., *Paston Letters and Papers of the Fifteenth Century*, Part I (Oxford, 1971), p. 291.

[142] C. P. Christianson, *A Directory of London Stationers and Book Artisans 1300–1500* (New York, 1990), pp. 13–44.

[143] Thrupp, *Merchant Class*, p. 159; J. A. Burrow, *Thomas Hoccleve* (Aldershot, 1994); A. I. Doyle, 'The work of a late fifteenth-century English scribe, William Ebesham', *Bulletin of the John Rylands Library*, 39 (1957), 298–325.

[144] A. F. Sutton, 'Caxton was a mercer: his social milieu and friends', in N. Rogers, ed., *England in the Fifteenth Century: Proceedings of the Harlaxton Conference 1992* (Stamford, 1994), pp. 118–48; M. Erler, 'Wynken de Worde's will: legatees and bequests', *The Library*, 10 (1988), 107–21.

[145] Barron, 'Expansion of education'. [146] Barron, 'The education and training of girls'.

St Anthony's were free, as were a certain number of places at St Paul's after Colet's reforms of 1507; but most of this elementary and grammar school education in London would have had to be bought. Doubtless as a result of the availability of teachers, the literacy rate among Londoners was very high: perhaps some 50 per cent of male Londoners at the end of the fifteenth century could read English.[147] If this is correct, then London would appear, in this respect, to have been distinct from other English towns of this period.

The comparatively easy access to books would have contributed to the high rate of literacy. The first public library in England was established at Guildhall in 1423–5, and in the course of the fifteenth century it is clear that parish churches were accumulating small libraries of chained books placed there for the use of parishioners.[148] The inventory of the church of St James Garlickhythe drawn up in 1449 lists two French books, a Bible and a 'boke of Holy Wryte'.[149] The advent of printing brought the possibility of owning books to a wider swathe of the population. As many as 900 books, described as 'diverse histories', were imported into London in 1480.[150] But alongside this developing use of written and printed material, the culture of London would, as elsewhere, have remained largely oral and visual. Sermons and public disputations such as that which raged around the Carmelite house in Fleet Street in the 1460s on the issue of the absolute poverty of Christ, all contributed to the intellectual climate of urban society.[151]

(ix) THE CAPITAL OF ENGLAND

By 1300 London had become the capital of England in the sense of 'head town', the centre of government, the wealthiest and most populous English town. The next 250 years simply confirmed and emphasised this pre-eminence. It is possible that in this period London's region grew larger. In the internal economy of England, the needs of London for grain, coal, tin, wood, stone, cattle and vegetables influenced, or indeed warped, the economies not only of the adjacent counties but also of more distant areas like Cornwall and the North.[152] The local economies of England became dependent upon London. Moreover, as the shortage of manpower became more acute, so London began to draw recruits from further afield, particularly from the North where the 'push' factors of

[147] Thrupp, *Merchant Class*, p. 158.

[148] Barron, *Guildhall*, pp. 33–5; Barron, 'Expansion of education', p. 240 n.92.

[149] Westminster Abbey Muniments, 6644. [150] Cobb, ed., *Overseas Trade*, p. xxxvi.

[151] F. R. H. DuBoulay, 'The quarrel between the Carmelite Friars and the secular clergy of London 1464–1468', *JEcc.Hist.*, 6 (1955), 156–74.

[152] B. M. S. Campbell, J. A. Galloway, D. Keene and M. Murphy, *A Medieval Capital and its Grain Supply* (Historical Geography Research Series, 30, London, 1993); D. Keene, 'Medieval London and its region', *LJ*, 14 (1989), 99–111; F. J. Fisher, *London and the English Economy 1500–1700* eds. P. Corfield and N. B. Harte (London, 1990), ch. 6

endemic warfare and economic recession may have added to the 'pull' factor of London. The growth in wool production and the intensified manufacture of cloth in the different regions of England might well have been damaging to the economy of London, but the London drapers rapidly asserted their control. Cloth was funnelled into London whence it was exported to the hungry markets of Brabant and southern Germany. The merchants of London rose to the challenge posed by the rapid development of the cloth industry and managed to capture the export sales of English cloths for themselves. It was a remarkable achievement.

London's region increasingly came to include areas overseas. As the ports of the east coast declined and the Hanse merchants largely abandoned Hull, Grimsby, Lynn and Boston for their London base, so the trading region of London extended across the North Sea to the Hanseatic ports. The links also between London and Flanders, Holland and Brabant were reinforced and English cloth poured into Antwerp and thence to southern Germany.[153] Italian merchants still brought carricks to Southampton but, increasingly, Venetian and other galleys were finding their way up the Thames to London.[154] Without doubt London was the most cosmopolitan city in England and its economic tentacles were both more numerous and more extended.

The later middle ages also saw the confirmation of London's role as the political capital of England. This was, in part, due to the centralising power of the English monarchy. Edward I developed the practice of summoning the knights of the shires and the burgesses of the towns to meet with him at Westminster. Thus men from all over England were drawn to the city. After 1330 Edward III summoned all his parliaments to Westminster, and this remained the usual place of meeting until the government of Henry VI attempted to break the pattern and summoned parliaments to meet at Reading (1440 and 1449), Bury St Edmunds (1447), Winchester (1449), Leicester (1450) and Coventry (1459). But the practice of summoning parliament to Westminster was re-established under the Yorkists and Tudors, greatly to the economic advantage of the Londoners. The great offices of state, the Chancery and Exchequer, as well as the royal courts, were fixed in or near the Palace of Westminster and the inconvenience of calling a parliament to meet elsewhere was very great. For both political and economic reasons the great lords of church and state found it increasingly necessary to have town houses in or near to London, and so did the knights and country gentlemen who came to London on legal business or to purchase supplies.[155] Not all these visitors had town houses and to cater for these public inns were established. The first of these inns appeared in the mid-fourteenth century

[153] Barron and Saul, eds., *England and the Low Countries*, Introduction.

[154] H. Bradley, 'The Italian community in London *c.* 1350–*c.* 1450' (PhD thesis, University of London, 1992), pp. 76–93.

[155] Barron, 'Centres of conspicuous consumption', 4–9; see above, pp. 215–16.

but a hundred years later they were ubiquitous. The main streets of Southwark and Westminster were lined with hostelries, and it was from the Tabard Inn in Southwark High Street that Chaucer's pilgrims set out for Canterbury.[156] In time the convenience of these London inns rendered the expense of a London town house unnecessary. The Stonors from Oxfordshire had bought a London house in the 1340s but a hundred years later had sold it and chose to stay at public inns in Fleet Street instead. The Pastons never bought a London house and on their frequent visits to London stayed at the George at Paul's Wharf.[157]

The crown fostered the 'capitalisation' of London by becoming increasingly southern in its focus. The war with France tended to focus royal attention in the South where armies were mustered for chevauchées into France. Moreover Edward III increasingly chose to stay at his palaces in the vicinity of London, Sheen, Eltham, Windsor and Woodstock.[158] Although Richard II disliked London and travelled extensively around his kingdom, he nevertheless re-fashioned Westminster Hall as the magnificent setting for an impressive 'imperial' monarchy. In part the failure of Richard III may have been due to the fact that his power base was in the North and not where it was needed in the South, around London. The Tudors shrewdly perceived that although they must control and dominate the North of England yet it was the South that was their heartland. They acknowledged the importance of London and added yet more palaces close to the city: Nonsuch, Hampton Court and Greenwich, as well as Bridewell – constructed well within the mayor's jurisdiction – and Whitehall to take over from Westminster Palace which was not only old-fashioned and inconvenient but also overrun with civil servants.[159]

The size of London, and the diversity of its economy, led to the evolution in the city of certain distinctive characteristics: the links with the monarchy, with royal government and with the aristocracy, both lay and ecclesiastic; the presence of a large and diverse group of aliens, both merchants and artisans within the city and the suburbs; the prominence of women in the skilled workforce and in running workshops and businesses; the presence of professional men such as lawyers, physicians, surgeons and schoolmasters (and schoolmistresses) and the developing vernacular written culture of books, documents and bills fixed to church doors; above all, the interlocking networks of internal and overseas trade centred on London. It would not be until the seventeenth century that the regions of England would begin to challenge the dominant position in the economy and culture of England that London had established in the late medieval period.

[156] Rosser, *Medieval Westminster*, pp. 122–33; Carlin, *Southwark*, pp. 191–208; see above, p. 389.

[157] Barron, 'Centres of conspicuous consumption', 12.

[158] C. Given-Wilson, *The Royal Household and the King's Affinity: Service Politics and Finance in England, 1360–1413* (London, 1987).

[159] S. Thurley, *The Royal Palaces of Tudor England* (New Haven, 1993); G. Rosser and S. Thurley, 'Whitehall Palace and King Street, Westminster', *London Topographical Record*, 26 (1990), 57–77.

· 18 ·

The greater towns 1300–1540

JENNIFER KERMODE

MEASURED IN terms of their populations, twenty or so towns emerge as important provincial centres with some 2,000 taxpayers in 1377. To these must be added Exeter, which doubled in size during the fifteenth century to emerge as the third largest provincial town in 1524–5, and Edinburgh, whose population was growing towards *c.* 12,500 by 1560 (see Table 18.1).[1] York alone achieved a size or status comparable to large European towns such as Antwerp, Bremen or Lyon. Most of the greater towns of Britain were distinguishable from market towns by the scale and intensity of their urbanity: physical size and appearance, complex internal economic and social structures, sophisticated government and regional significance. Even so, few enjoyed the close formal interdependence of a large Italian, French or German town with its *contado* or *umland*.[2] In Britain, administration outside urban liberties commonly remained subject to the crown. Coventry, Gloucester and York were exceptions: Coventry by acquiring some 15,000 acres of the manor of Coventry, Gloucester through its incorporation of thirty or so villages in 1483, and York as the result of its jurisdiction over an adjacent rural wapentake, the Ainsty.[3]

Population size in 1377 reflected the economic vitality of towns which had recovered from the depredations of the Black Death. Though population losses varied, it is likely that many of the greater towns lost a third to a half of their inhabitants between 1348 and 1349.[4] Some, like Boston and Winchester, were already beyond their most successful phase by 1348–9 and retained their rank on

I would like to thank Jane Laughton for help in collecting data.

[1] M. Lynch, *Edinburgh and the Reformation* (Edinburgh, 1981), p. 3.

[2] N. J. G. Pounds, *An Economic History of Medieval Europe*, 2nd edn (London, 1994), pp. 227–8, 255–61.

[3] N. Herbert, ed., *The Gloucester Charter in History* (Gloucester, 1983), p. 53; *VCH*, Warwickshire, VIII, pp. 2–3; *VCH*, City of York, pp. 33–6.

[4] R. H. Britnell, 'The Black Death in English towns', *UH*, 21 (1994), 200–1.

Table 18.1 *Characteristics of the greater towns*

Greater towns	Area within walls/ditch	Walls Roman = earliest circuit	Castle	Headport	Taxpayers 1377	Taxpayers 1524/5	Pre-Conquest centre	Bishopric	Benedictine houses
Beverley		banks	✗	river	2,663	?266	possible	✗	
Boston	*c.* 50 a (20 ha)	banks	✗	✓	2,871	?345	✗	✗	–10
Bristol	*c.* 136 a (55 ha)	11th c.	✓	✓	6,345	1,166	✗	1542	*c.* 11
Bury St Edmunds		12th c.	✗	✗	2,445	645	✗	✗	*c.* 10
Cambridge	156 a (63 ha)	Roman	✓	river	1,902	550	✓	archdeaconry	2 host
Canterbury	*c.* 120 a (48.5 ha)	Roman	✓	river	2,574	784	✓	597	–9
Chester	131.3 a (53 ha)	Roman	✓	✓	—	pop. 5,000[c]	✓	1541[d]	–10
Colchester[e]	108 a (44 ha)	Roman	✓	river	2,955	701	✓	archdeaconry	10
Coventry	*c.* 210 a (85 ha)	1350s	✓	✗	4,817	?725	✗	1102[f]	?10
Edinburgh	140 a (56.6 ha)	1420s	✓	✗	—	pop. ?12,500[g]	N/A	N/A	
Exeter	96.2 a (40 ha)	Roman	✓	✓	1,169	1,050	✓	1046	10
Gloucester	*c.* 128 a (52 ha)	Roman	✓	river	2,239	?466	✓	1541	*c.* 10
Hereford	93 a (37.6 ha)	?8th c.	✓	river	1,903	611	✓	?680	–11
Leicester	*c.* 100 a (40.5 ha)	Roman	✓	✗	2,302	427	✓	679–888	
Lincoln[j]	*c.* 135 a (54.5 ha)	Roman	✓	river	3,569	626	✓	1067	*c.* 1
Lynn	*c.* 300 a (121 ha)	banks	✗	✓	3,127	—	✗	✗	*c.* 1
Newcastle	*c.* 160 a (64.7 ha)	Henry III	✓	✓	2,647	pop. 8–9,000[k]	✗	✗	10
Norwich	*c.* 1.75 sq. miles (388.6 ha)	10th c.	✓	river	3,952	1,423	✓	1094	–1
Oxford	94 a (38 ha)	10th c.	✓	river	2,357	542	✓	1542	3 c
Salisbury	*c.* 205 a (83 ha)	banks	✗	✗	2,373	885	✗	1078	
Shrewsbury		?9th c.	✓	river	1,932	550	✓	✗	1
Winchester	143.8 a (58 ha)	Roman	✓	✗	?2,500	596	✓	662	
Yarmouth	*c.* 133 a (54 ha)	1320s	–1399	✓	1,941	497	✗	✗	–1
York	263 a (106.4 ha)	Roman	✓	river	7,248	?871	✓	625	1

Notes:

– before

+ lesser orders of friars, date of foundation unknown.

* hospitals/? including hospitals extant at the Dissolution but no firm earlier date.

** DB=Domesday borough S=seigneurial R=royal

[a] 10 in 1086. [b] Single reference in 1215. [c] Estimated *c.*3,500 in 1463, *c.*5,000 in 1563. [d] Chester first consecrated 1075, translated to Coventry 1102. [e] Including suburbs. [f] Coventry and Lichfield recognised 1228. [g] Resident ins walled burgh by 1560. [h] Canongate a separate burgh of abbot of Holyrood. [i] Or Candlemas. [j] Excluding suburbs [k] Including Gateshead in 1563. [l] Moved to Jarrow in 1074. [m] By 1400. [n] 9 from 1086–1358.

Table 18.1 *(cont.)*

	Friars *c.* 1300	Earliest known charter	Incorporation	Status**	MPs from 1306	Mayor: earliest reference	Statute Merchant seal	Common/guildhall	Craft guilds after 1400	Craft/company halls	Wards *c.* 1400	Parishes *c.* 1300	Corpus Christi procession/play
	2	1114×16	1573	S	×	×		13th c.	1413:19	✓	14	2	✓
	4+	1204	1545	S	×	×	1285					1	✓
16	4+	1188	1373	DB	✓	1218	1283	✓	1450:26		4–6	18	
7	×	1102	1606	S	×	×		✓	3+		5	2	✓
4	4+	1120	1605	DB	✓	1235		1300			7[a]	17	
	3+	?1155	1448	DB	✓	1448[b]	1336	13th c.			6	22	
	3	*c.* 1136	1506	DB	×	1244	1291	14th c.	*c.* 1500:23		15	9	
	1+	1189	1462	DB	✓	×		1277	1400:*c.*6		4	12	
4	3	1149	1345	R	1326	1345	1336	*c.* 1390	*c.* 1500:33		10	2	✓
	2	12th c.	?1470	R[h]	1326	–1387		*c.* 1369	1523:14		4	1	✓[i]
	2	1154×58	1537	DB	✓	1200	1285	1160	8–9	1470s	4	20	✓
	3	1155	1483	DB	✓	1483	Edward II	13th c.				11	
7	2	1189	1597	DB	✓	1383	1285	✓	20	✓	5	5	✓
5	3+	1229	1589	DB	✓	*c.* 1250	✓	✓	*c.* 17	✓	4–12	9	
	4+	1154	1409	DB	✓	1206	1283	14th c.			4	46	
6	4+	1204	1524	S	✓	?1204		✓	2			1	
10	4+	1100	1400	R	✓	1216	1285	✓	12			4	✓
15	4+	1229	1404	R	✓	1404	1285	13th c.	1449:31		4	?61	
3	4+	1156	1605	DB	✓	1205×9	1285	1229	14		4	14[m]	✓
3	2	1225	1612	S	✓	1249	1351	15th c.	38	✓	4	3	
5	2	1218	1586	DB	✓	×	1283		15		3	?1	
6	5	1155	1588	DB	✓	1200	1283	13th c.	1437:12		6[n]	57	✓
4	3	1208	1608	DB	✓	×						?1	✓
?21	5+	1155×62	1396	DB	✓	*c.* 1212	1283	1256	51	✓	6	45	✓

in sources: A. Ballard and J. Tait, eds., *British Borough Charters 1216–1307* (Cambridge, 1923); D. J. C. King, *stellarium Anglicanum* (New York, 1983); Knowles and Hadcock, *Medieval Religious Houses*; *BAHT*, I and II; J. iofield and R. Leech, eds., *Urban Archaeology in Britain* (CBA Res. Rep. 61, 1987); M. Weinbaum, *The orporation of Boroughs* (Manchester, 1937); J. F. Willard, 'Taxation boroughs and parliamentary boroughs,)4–1336', in J. G. Edwards, V. H. Galbraith and E. F. Jacob, eds., *Historical Essays in Honour of James Tait* anchester, 1933), pp. 417–35; *VCH* (for relevant counties). For taxpayers see below, Appendixes 5 and 6.

the strength of earlier prosperity. Others attracted migrants with sufficient rapidity to make up some of the Black Death losses and to keep ahead of subsequent epidemics in the 1350s and 1360s. In York the rate of burgess admissions increased by 10 per cent in the 1360s, and by 29 per cent in the following decade. Recruitment was strongest in the textile crafts, closely followed by wholesale traders and leather workers.[5] In the longer term, successive epidemics tested the robustness of most towns, leaving only Canterbury, Exeter, Hereford and Norwich with larger populations in the 1520s.

The transformation of England's economy from wool to cloth production with a consequent redirection and expansion of long-distance trade, affected all the greater towns. Those well placed to take advantage of the surge in demand for English cloth in the mid-fourteenth century, like Bristol, Coventry, Norwich and York, recovered population levels fairly rapidly following the Black Death. The multi-functional responsibilities which had promoted older centres continued to underpin many of the greater towns, but others were undermined by the expanding textile industry. Long-term success in textiles largely explains the differences in wealth which opened up between the 1330s and 1520s. Amongst the five wealthiest towns in 1524–5,[6] Coventry, Norwich and Salisbury all manufactured or processed textiles. So did the wealthiest provincial port: Bristol. There is no single factor underlying the success and failure of individual towns. They fulfilled many roles, and explanations must reflect their diversity. Shifts between domestic and international trade, marketing and manufacturing, administrative and institutional functions, complicate the biography of each town and make generalisation problematic.

There was diversity within this conspectus of towns, but they did share a number of characteristics indicative of their regional importance and internal sophistication (see Table 18.1). Some features were visible in smaller centres but were on a larger scale and thus more complex in the greater towns. Their townscapes included more domestic and institutional stone buildings and numerous industrial and commercial premises. Instead of a single, multi-purpose market, most had several permanent market places as well as designated alleys and streets. Edinburgh had fifteen markets in 1477, including one for 'ald greith and gier': some met daily and others twice and thrice weekly. Fairs were often associated with the greater towns, whether run by profit-seeking bishops and abbots, or by town councils.[7]

[5] *BAHT*, II, 'Norwich', p. 16; J. N. Bartlett, 'The expansion and decline of York in the later middle ages', *Ec.HR*, 2nd series, 12 (1959–60), 22–4; *VCH*, City of York, p. 114; see also R. H. Britnell, *Growth and Decline in Colchester, 1300–1525* (Cambridge, 1986), p. 110.

[6] All the data for ranking from Alan Dyer's Appendix 4–7 below.

[7] M. Lynch, M. Spearman and G. Stell, eds., *The Scottish Medieval Town* (Edinburgh, 1988), p. 275; E. Miller and J. Hatcher, *Medieval England: Towns, Commerce and Crafts, 1086–1348* (London, 1995), pp. 166–76; *VCH*, Wiltshire, IV, p. 85.

Growth led to early occupational specialisation and often the fragmentation of chartered guilds merchant into separate craft organisations. Political awareness plus the development of complex government placed the greater towns in the forefront of the push for urban autonomy. Competition demanded reduced transaction costs, and these were achieved in towns where markets were well regulated and the proximity of borough courts ensured that contracts were enforceable.[8] In this important way, trade could be facilitated by the growth of civic jurisdictions, and the crown's grants of Statute Merchant and Statute Staple seals. Greater concentrations of wealth fuelled higher levels of conspicuous consumption, creating a richer urban culture than smaller towns could maintain. Finally, levels of literacy and educational provision were higher. Apart from Yarmouth, all these towns had at least one school, and the presence of literate ecclesiastics perhaps gave the greater towns a distinctive ambience.[9]

(i) LOCATIONS

Antiquity and location were decisive factors, and those towns established as primary centres before or soon after the Conquest were likely to emerge high up the urban hierarchy by the early fourteenth century. Some had begun as strategic posts in Roman or Danish command networks: sixteen were on or close to a Roman road or settlement; fourteen served as Saxon shire towns; and fifteen were Domesday boroughs. Salisbury was refounded on a vacant site, but there were no other 'green-field' plantations. Even *arriviste* Coventry developed on a site of religious antiquity. Several east coast towns were post-Conquest phenomena, growing out of one or more hamlets as outports for older centres. Thus Boston flourished at the mouth of the River Witham as Lincoln's wool port from the early twelfth century and Lynn, promoted by the bishop of Norwich and victor over three competing proximate hamlets, emerged to serve Bury, Cambridge, Ely and more distant Midland towns.[10]

Regional significance and urban vitality attracted ecclesiastical foundations: most often Benedictine abbeys in the eleventh and twelfth centuries, mendicant houses in the thirteenth century. All the greater towns had a major religious foundation and friary, many had several, and some had important religious guilds as well. Their impact on town life was multifarious, and inevitably the impact of

[8] M. Kowaleski, *Local Markets and Regional Trade in Medieval Exeter* (Cambridge, 1995), pp. 202, 337–40.

[9] N. Orme, *English Schools in the Middle Ages* (London, 1973), pp. 296–321; R. B. Dobson, 'Mendicant ideal and practice in late medieval York', in P. V. Addyman and V. E. Black, eds., *Archaeological Papers from York Presented to M. W. Barley* (York, 1984), pp. 109–22.

[10] D. M. Owen, ed., *The Making of King's Lynn* (British Academy, Records of Social and Economic History, new series, 9, 1984), pp. 5–7; S. H. Rigby, '"Sore decay" and "fair dwellings": Boston and urban decline in the later middle ages', *Midland History*, 10 (1985), 52.

the dissolution in England was intense. Most of these towns were also county capitals and thus the venues for county courts and crown adminstration, adding another layer to urban activities. The personnel of lay and secular courts, of estate offices, nuns, monks, friars and royal clerks contributed to the urban melting pot. Large religious institutions could be a mixed blessing, however, sometimes frustrating the constitutional ambitions of seigneurial boroughs such as Beverley and Salisbury but rarely obstructing economic growth in well-located towns such as Bury or Coventry.

The greater towns outpaced rivals because their trade grew faster: a characteristic shared with larger European towns. What differentiated the greater from medium towns was the degree of their investment in commerce.[11] As catalysts in regional expansion, towns channelled regional products, redistributed imported goods and reduced transaction costs through regulated markets. Extensive river networks encouraged long-distance trade, giving their headports unrivalled commercial power. In addition, eight or so river ports, ranging from Cambridge to York, were still accessible to ocean-going ships in the fifteenth century.[12] As export giants like Bristol boomed in the late fourteenth and fifteenth centuries, smaller river ports, like Gloucester, became less directly involved in exports and developed their own upriver trade. Communications could be crucial and the rerouting of north–south traffic over the Thames across the new bridge at Abingdon and away from Oxford in the early fifteenth century spelled disaster.[13]

All but two of the greater towns were situated at crossing points on navigable rivers and working waterways. Edinburgh was one exception and relied on the port of Leith two miles away; a second, land-locked Coventry, was dependent on road transport to outports at Bristol, Boston, Chester, London and Southampton. Strategic location reinforced the importance of major centres so that nobles, or more often the crown, retained control over castle liberties in many of them. Military demands diminished during the late middle ages and their impact remained significant in only a few places such as Newcastle. However, castles routinely serving seigneurial households brought business into urban pockets. For instance, the household expenses of the earl of Leicester amounted to almost £8,000 in 1314–15, with some 100 traders in and around Leicester supplying food.[14]

Towns located between contrasting agricultural regions were advantaged. Thus Lincoln prospered between the Vale of Trent and Lincolnshire Wolds; York

[11] Pounds, *History of Medieval Europe*, pp. 254, 267.

[12] L. C. Attreed, ed., *York House Books 1461–1490*, (Stroud, 1991), vol. I, *passim*; *BAHT*, II, 'Cambridge', pp. 1, 14; Miller and Hatcher, *Medieval England: Towns, Commerce and Crafts*, pp. 144–8.

[13] *VCH*, Oxfordshire, IV, p. 41; J. Masschaele, 'Transport costs in medieval England', *Ec.HR*, 46 (1993), 273.

[14] *BAHT*, II, 'Coventry', p. 1; by 1489 Gloucester's castle had been demolished, *ibid.*, I, 'Gloucester', p. 11; *VCH*, Leicestershire, IV, p. 49.

between the Vale of York, Yorkshire Wolds, the Pennines and the North Sea; Coventry between the upper Avon valley and the Forest of Arden. Collecting regional products, especially wool, cloth and grain *en route* to distant markets, enriched Hereford, Oxford and Salisbury amongst others. Some towns like Beverley, Coventry and Norwich exploited their position to develop domestic manufacturing skills into regionally significant industries such as textile and leather production. Gloucester developed nearby supplies of iron to build up an important metal industry.[15] Ultimately, all towns relied upon their hinterlands, and it is not surprising that there was a higher density of the greater towns, almost one half of them, in prosperous eastern England. Proximity to London markets was a key factor, but the region's excellent natural resources promoted urban growth.

Irrespective of their size, rivers and streams were important for domestic and industrial needs. In Winchester, the Itchen was more important as a power source for fulling mills and for fishing than for communications by the fourteenth century. In Bury local fisheries and water-fowling were important to the town's predominantly textile-driven economy, while Leicester tanners and fishermen exploited the Soar. The craftsmen of land-locked Coventry were easily supplied from the local network of small streams feeding into the River Sherbourne, none of which could transport their products beyond the town boundary.[16]

(ii) DECLINE AND PROSPERITY

Advantaged though the greater towns were by their earlier achievements, their economies were not impregnable. The expansion in cloth manufacturing in the 1350s and 1360s was crucial in changing the balance of individual towns' economies and their place within regional networks. Shifts in trade routes, fluctuations in overseas markets and the growing influence of London affected all the greater towns in England. Most enjoyed a period of prosperity from about 1360 to 1400 or later, to be followed by economic recession. The evidence can be difficult to interpret: external indicators sometimes obscuring internal adjustments. According to the taxation rankings, the economies of Boston and Lynn collapsed during the fifteenth century, yet in the 1540s, their councils could raise large sums to buy up monastic and guild property: £1,646 in Boston. Probably only Bury, Exeter, Hereford and Norwich avoided severe contraction before the mid-sixteenth century.[17]

[15] Herbert, ed., *Gloucester Charter*, p. 21; *BAHT*, I and II, *passim*; *VCH*, Yorkshire: East Riding, VI, pp. 34–41; *VCH*, Wiltshire, VI, pp. 125–6.

[16] D. Keene, *Survey of Medieval Winchester* (Winchester Studies, 2, Oxford, 1985), vol. I, p. 57; R. S. Gottfried, *Bury St Edmunds and the Urban Crisis, 1290–1539* (Princeton, 1982), pp. 113–14; *BAHT*, II, 'Coventry', p. 5; *VCH*, Leicestershire, IV, pp. 41, 45.

[17] A. Dyer, *Decline and Growth in English Towns 1400–1640* (Basingstoke, 1991), pp. 20–36; Claire Cross, 'Communal piety in sixteenth-century Boston', *Lincolnshire History and Archaeology*, 25 (1990), 33–8 at 36.

The experience of some towns during these roller-coaster years was dramatic. Coventry was already the centre of an industrialising district by 1279, but remained a small, relatively obscure place, to emerge into national prominence by the 1370s with a rapidly expanding textile industry.[18] Boston, on the other hand, which had grown quickly from the late twelfth century on a rising tide of wool exports, began to lose ground as a major port in the mid-fourteenth century, sliding into irreversible decline from 1400.[19] Each town's fortunes were largely determined by the mix of its functions and location.

A minority of the greater towns were primary ports: Boston, Bristol, Edinburgh (*via* Leith), Exeter, Lynn, Newcastle, Yarmouth and York (*via* Hull). Generalising about the impact overseas trade had on towns is difficult: Southampton for instance was a busy port but not a prosperous town.[20] Beyond the primary ports, were smaller river ports such as Cambridge, Colchester and Gloucester, and major manufacturing towns: Coventry, Norwich and Salisbury, which were as much a part of the international economy. The link was wool and cloth. Although shrinking as a major export from the 1370s, the wool trade continued to give access to important credit and financial services overseas and to generate sizeable profits for individual merchants. Wool staplers survived alone or in small groups in a few of the greater towns, often exercising an influence disproportionate to their numbers. Theirs were often the largest fortunes amassed by individuals. Five staplers came from two generations of Wigstons in Leicester. All held civic office and the last, William, who died childless in 1536, owned 22 per cent of the taxable property in the town in 1524.[21]

The central role of many of the larger towns was undermined in the fifteenth century as trade diversified into different channels and their merchants faced growing competition from London and Hanseatic merchants. The primary port towns were particularly vulnerable to changes in overseas trade and in the fortunes of their associated inland manufacturing centres. By 1465 Yarmouth no longer served as the outport for Norwich cloth which was now carried overland to London. In the west, Bristol faced a short-term crisis when its wine import–cloth export trade collapsed with the loss of Bordeaux in 1451, but was recovering through diversification by the 1470s. A little further south, Exeter remained relatively untroubled by the major swings in international markets, relying instead on coastal and regional trade and cloth exports. Several east

[18] J. B. Harley, 'Population trends and agricultural developments from the Warwickshire Hundred Rolls of 1279', in A. R. H. Baker, J. D. Hamshere and J. Langton, eds., *Geographical Interpretations of Historical Sources* (Newton Abbot, 1970), pp. 55–68 at 57.

[19] Rigby, '"Sore decay"', 48–51.

[20] J. I. Kermode, 'Merchants, overseas trade and urban decline: York, Beverley and Hull *c.* 1380–1500', *NHist*, 23 (1987), 51–73; O. Coleman, 'Trade and prosperity in the fifteenth century: some aspects of the trade of Southampton', *EcHR*, 2nd series, 16 (1963), 9–22.

[21] *VCH*, Leicestershire, IV, p. 40; see also F. Hill, *Medieval Lincoln*, 2nd edn (Stamford, 1990), p. 279.

coast ports, heavily dependent on trading cloth with the Hanse, faced severe recession: Boston, Lynn and Yarmouth by the mid-fifteenth century, York by the early sixteenth. In the south, Southampton retained its key place as the main entrepôt outside London, serving Coventry, Salisbury and Winchester, until the Italians transferred their business to London in the early sixteenth century.

London and Edinburgh emerged as victors from the restructuring of the domestic economy and concentration of international trade on Antwerp. By 1524–5 London was handling 82 per cent of all English cloth exported and dominated most other trades, and by 1479, Edinburgh was handling 90 per cent of Scotland's exports of wool, fells and hides, and dominated the import and coastal trades.[22]

Long-distance trade was one element in a virtuous circle of trade, investment and industry which the greater towns generated. Ultimately, the prosperity of towns continued to reflect the vitality of their regions so that Hereford and Shrewsbury, Canterbury and York differed because the Welsh Marches were neither as populous nor as commercially developed as the North-East and South-East. However, during the fifteenth century, most of the greater towns had to compete to retain their role as regional centres, when goods could bypass their tolls and evade the restrictive practices of their monopolistic guilds. Their experience was mixed. Whereas Norwich's buoyant economy expanded at the expense of small Norfolk markets which dropped to some thirty by 1500, York city council was driven to advertising its two new and toll-free fairs as far afield as Westmorland in 1502.[23]

(iii) URBAN ECONOMIES

In most towns the 'basic necessities', the provision of food and drink, clothing and building services, generally accounted for 25–33 per cent of freemen, but in particular local circumstances, as in sixteenth-century Cambridge and York, for instance, might absorb 46 to 50 per cent.[24] The rest were engaged in a range of manufacturing processes and trade: merchants, workers in textiles, leather and metalwork being the most numerous. Most of the greater towns had a sophisticated workforce, differentiated by specialist skills. In many, but by no means all, of these towns, occupational demarcation was policed by formal craft organisations.

[22] *BAHT*, II, 'Bristol', p. 16; Lynch, Spearman and Stell, eds., *The Scottish Medieval Town*, p. 269; J. A. F. Thomson, *The Transformation of Medieval England 1370–1529* (London, 1983), pp. 60–1; J. A. F. Thomson, ed., *Towns and Townspeople in the Fifteenth Century* (Gloucester, 1988), p. 177.

[23] *BAHT*, II, 'Norwich', p. 18; A. Raine, ed., *York Civic Records* (Yorkshire Arch. Soc. Record Series 1939–53), vol. II, pp. 166, 172, 175–6.

[24] N. Goose, 'English pre-industrial urban economies', *UHY* (1982), p. 26.

The most powerful crafts emerged from textile and leather production, often as early breakaways from the chartered guild merchant, and, by the fourteenth century, their autonomy was established. The formal recognition of guilds came at different dates according to local conditions, and there is little evidence of craft guilds in most towns before the late fourteenth or even early fifteenth century. Craft guilds became active from time to time, merging and breaking apart to form new composite guilds as circumstances dictated. In Beverley and Winchester, nineteen and twelve or so craft guilds emerged periodically: in Beverley reluctantly to support the Corpus Christi festival.[25] Where permanent guilds did emerge, it may have been as much a consequence of a strongly centralising city council, which found guilds a convenient agency for levying taxes, or as a symptom of industrial prosperity.

Conglomerate craft guilds were another variant. Edinburgh's crafts were of this sort and began to seek formal recognition in 1474. By 1523, fourteen had been 'sealed' by the burgh council.[26] In late fifteenth-century York such combinations were a response to recession and industrial restructuring, but elsewhere the reasons remain obscure. In Shrewsbury in 1525, for instance, the mercers' fellowship included cappers, goldsmiths, ironmongers and pewterers.[27] It is difficult to discern a clear pattern from the available evidence. Newcastle had twelve craft guilds by the mid-fourteenth century, Colchester only two or three textile guilds in the fifteenth century, Exeter eight to nine in *c.* 1400 and York fifty-seven in 1415. In relatively small Hereford there were twenty craft guilds by 1503, thirty-three in very large Coventry by 1522.[28]

The number of specialist occupations was perhaps more indicative of the complexion of employment. Over 125 occupational ascriptions were recorded in late fifteenth-century Norwich and York, eighty to ninety at least in Coventry and Winchester.[29] These estimates cannot be regarded as comprehensive but do suggest the diversity of skills in the greater towns as well as identifying dominant industries. In Norwich, over 39 per cent of workers were taken up in textiles and clothing, 28 per cent in Bristol, 30 per cent in Coventry.[30] Even more revealing, perhaps, is the extent of differentiation within one general group. Gloucester had seventeen different metalworking crafts. In both Winchester and

25 *VCH*, Yorkshire: East Riding, VI, pp. 42–9; Keene, *Survey*, I, p. 333.

26 Lynch, Spearman and Stell, eds., *The Scottish Medieval Town*, pp. 261–2.

27 *VCH*, City of York, p. 91, 96; W. A. Champion, 'The Shrewsbury lay subsidy of 1525', *Trans. of the Shropshire Arch. Soc.*, 64 (1985), 35–46 at 37.

28 R. Johnson, *The Ancient Customs of the City of Hereford* (London, 1882), pp. 118–19; R. Welford, *History of Newcastle and Gateshead* (London and Newcastle, 1883–7), vol. I, p. 114; *VCH*, Essex, IX, pp. 36–7; *VCH*, City of York, p. 91; Kowaleski, *Exeter*, pp. 93, 99–100.

29 Herbert, *Gloucester Charter*, p. 22; Keene, *Survey*, I, table 26; *VCH*, Warwickshire, VIII, p. 155; *VCH*, City of York, pp. 114–16.

30 C. Phythian-Adams, 'Economic and social structure', in *The Fabric of the Traditional Community*, Open University (Milton Keynes, 1980), p. 16.

York there were at least twelve crafts distinguished amongst the leatherworkers, from skinner, tanner and tawyer, to cobbler, cordwainer and shoemaker, and over twenty-two different skills directly associated with textile and clothing production. Supporting technology meant that several metal and wood crafts were as dependent on textiles as they were on other market forces.

At the other end of the scale, individuals practised skills rarely found outside the greater towns. Apothecaries, bell-founders, bookbinders, organmakers and scriveners served a wider catchment than even embroiderers and upholsterers. There can have been little competition for Hereford's harpers, motley weavers or parchmentmakers. The Edinburgh notaries served much of Scotland.[31] Multiple occupation was not uncommon and in an environment with many manufacturing and trading opportunities, flexibility was inevitable, in spite of increasing guild regulation. Thus, Winchester fullers sold more cloth than drapers, and in Chester ironmongers imported wine and merchants kept alehouses.[32]

To these skilled activities must be added two other employment sectors. The first included the untrained and largely unskilled men, women and children who supplied a broad range of services: domestic and industrial servants, labourers, fetchers and carriers. The more sophisticated an economy the larger its supporting base and the unskilled sector in the greater towns was extensive. Unfortunately, it lies beyond our historical reach. The second sector included professional men: lawyers and clerks, employed in religious houses, as salaried officials in diocesan and secular administration, and on hire in ecclesiastical and secular courts. It is difficult to ennumerate these men since they could work outside the jurisdiction of civic authority and yet, in towns accommodating county courts, a diocesan administration, and several religious houses, they were a significant group. In addition, estate administrators and courts generated important traffic of their own, drawing in a mixture of tenants, tradesmen, suppliers of all kinds and individuals with business before the church, city and county courts. Towns acquiring a unique agency enjoyed a boost to flagging fortunes. The Council of the North helped York to overcome some of the effects of the dissolution.[33]

The administrative and judicial roles of the Church extended influence far beyond urban liberties. The courts of bishops, archdeacons, and the metropolitan courts of the two archbishops particularly, affected people throughout vast regions beyond Canterbury and York.[34] Bishoprics and religious houses were

[31] Bell foundry was one of Bristol's regional specialisms. *BAHT*, II, 'Bristol', p. 13; Johnson, *Ancient Customs of Hereford*, p. 116; W. MacLeod and M. Wood, eds., *Protocol Book of John Fowlar 1500–1503* (Scottish Record Society, 64, 1930), *passim*.

[32] Keene, *Survey*, I, p. 309; Chester City RO, Sheriffs' Books 5–8, *passim*; BL Harl. MS 2054 ff. 14v–15v.

[33] D. M. Palliser, *Tudor York* (Oxford, 1979), pp. 264, 192.

[34] C. I. A. Ritchie, *The Ecclesiastical Courts of York* (Arbroath, 1956); B. Woodcock, *Medieval Ecclesiastical Courts in the Diocese of Canterbury* (Oxford, 1952).

extensive landowners in the country and many were based in towns. Benedictine abbeys were established in at least eighteen of the greater towns, three subsequently becoming secular cathedrals following the dissolution. As consumers of goods and services they were important contributors to their local economies, but it is difficult to assess what business returned into towns *via* their links with their tenants and parishes. As the locus of parish and estate authority though, the big hospitals and monasteries generated yet more traffic, swelling the number of customers for town markets.

One of the few towns for which the number of county court visitors has been estimated is Chester. A two or three day session in 1464 required 134 individual jurors, 116 for a session in 1495. The courts met eight or nine times each year, and to the jurors must be added the plaintiffs and defendants. Cheshire operated an unusual system of local control through individual recognisances, and their enrolment required 363 individuals to attend the castle between October 1512 and the following May 1513.[35] The flow of visitors was replicated in other county capitals where outsiders seeking specialist advice and accommodation benefited the whole town: bringing custom to scriveners and innkeepers most immediately. In York, attorneys, scriveners, innkeepers and taverners were amongst the few occupations whose admissions increased slightly after 1450, a trend which persisted into the following century. Inns, taverns and stables clustered along the major thoroughfares of fifteenth-century Gloucester, and in Winchester, decorated signs were displayed by the mid-fourteenth century to attract customers.[36]

There was no competition for these institutionally generated functions, nor yet for the position of regional market, but the relationship between towns and their hinterlands was not invariably symbiotic or constant. The demographic demands of some of the greater towns on their migrant regions exacerbated local pressure. For instance, villages replenishing York became critically depopulated in the fifteenth century. At the same time, in a region such as Essex, agrarian decline in the early fifteenth century released capital and water power. Initially, Colchester fullers exploited both, boosting the town's output, but when rural workers followed their example, competition from the rural textile industry grew and migration into Colchester began to fall away.[37]

Greater towns with a significant industrial sector faced a growing crisis in the early fifteenth century. Some, like York, tried to enforce monopolistic claims over competitors. The council fought a losing battle to have all the lead shipped down the Pennine rivers weighed at the city crane. In 1417 the girdlers tried to

[35] PRO CHES 5/1 4HVIII; D. J. Clayton, *The Administration of the County Palatine of Chester 1442–85* (Chetham Society 3rd series 35, 1990), pp. 134, 230–1. See also Keene, *Survey*, I, p. 398.

[36] *VCH*, City of York, p. 116; Keene, *Survey*, I, p. 167; J. Langton, 'Late medieval Gloucester: some data from a rental of 1455', *Transactions, Institute of British Geographers*, new series, 2 (1977), 265.

[37] Britnell, *Growth and Decline*, pp. 157–8.

claim jurisdiction within a thirty-mile (48.6 km) radius of the city. Winchester, on the other hand, removed all discrimination against non-free traders in 1430, to stimulate a flagging economy.[38]

In some towns, one manufacturing sector developed as another contracted. Coverlet makers, for instance, prospered in Lynn and tapiters in York, while broadcloth manufacture dwindled. New occupations appeared: cappers in Gloucester and hatmakers in York.[39] Several towns adjusted by engaging more closely with rural industry, serving as gathering centres for exports, supplying imported dyestuffs and exploiting local skills to finish rurally manufactured cloth. Salisbury and Norwich, exceptionally, retained their positions as major textile manufacturing towns, a dependency which left them vulnerable to overseas market crises in the mid-sixteenth century. Regional specialisms stimulated extremely localised activities; in Yarmouth 'maisemakers' manufactured boxes for packing herrings, and in Hereford coopers throve constructing barrels for Welsh butter.[40]

Amongst the greater towns, the differences between them derived from the balance between their reliance on manufacturing, on long-distance or local trade and on administrative or other professional activities. Quantifying all the elements in these specific towns is impossible, but some general patterns can be observed. Norwich had accumulated many central functions in its long history. It was a county and diocesan capital, a major regional market and home to several large and wealthy religious houses. It was not a primary port and few Norwich merchants were directly engaged in overseas trade. The city adjusted rapidly from wool gathering to increase its cloth manufacturing in the fourteenth century. By the early sixteenth century, textile production alone accounted for 30 per cent of the skilled workforce and half of all manufacturing. Its economic fortunes remained remarkably buoyant through to the mid-sixteenth century.[41]

Coventry was very different. It had no county functions, but was the seat of a bishop and home to several religious houses. Already wealthy by the 1330s, Coventry lay at the centre of an industrialising region. Exploiting its central Midlands' location, the town grew rapidly in the mid-fourteenth century, through manufacturing cloth and, later on, processing leather. Coventry merchants traded directly with Europe *via* Boston and Southampton, and with Ireland *via* Bristol and Chester, the latter fading towards the end of the fifteenth

[38] Keene, *Survey*, I, pp. 99–100; M. Sellers, ed., *York Memorandum Book* (Surtees Society 120, 125, 1912–15), vol. I, p. 183; *VCH*, City of York, p. 98.

[39] Herbert, *Gloucester Charter*, p. 23; P. Clark and P. Slack, eds., *Crisis and Order in English Towns, 1500–1700* (London, 1972), p. 92; Owen, *Lynn*, p. 56; *VCH*, City of York, pp. 89, 114, 116.

[40] Anon., ed., *A Calendar of the Freemen of Great Yarmouth 1429–1800* (Norwich Arch. Soc., 1910), p. 1; Johnson, *Ancient Customs of Hereford*, pp. 135–8.

[41] Dyer, *Decline and Growth*, pp. 34, 55; *BAHT*, II, 'Norwich', pp. 16–20; *VCH*, Wiltshire, VI, pp. 127–9.

century. Coventry's economy became too reliant on textiles to allow adjustments in the face of disastrous setbacks which dogged the city's fortunes from the 1450s onwards.[42]

Rural competition posed little threat to Coventry but was a major factor in the decline of York. As the northern capital, York had been a key military, ecclesiastical and administrative centre for centuries. It was a major regional market with an economy broadly based in the cloth, leather and metal industries, and supporting a wide range of miscellaneous and rarefied skills. Its overseas merchants waxed prosperous in exporting wool and cloth to the Baltic and Low Countries and importing wine, industrial materials and luxury goods. The 1360s to 1380s marked the apex of York's prosperity and towards the end of the fourteenth century, expansion gave way to contraction. Demand for cloth continued, but York's merchants were increasingly marginalised in overseas markets, and the city's textile workers were undercut by competition from West Riding villages. Although regional production increased, the city played a diminishing role in its export. Plague compounded the city's problems and by the late fifteenth century, very few York merchants, including a handful of Staplers, invested in overseas trade. The city's textile industry had collapsed. What remained were specialised coverlet and linen weavers, and dyers. The dissolution was a further blow, removing accumulated wealth, trading and employment opportunities.[43]

Edinburgh differed from most major English towns in that its economy owed relatively little to manufacturing early on. Retailing and distribution dominated its late fifteenth-century economy and investment in cloth manufacturing was slight. However, by 1558, metalworkers and those processing carcasses and hides accounted for the largest non-mercantile groups. Edinburgh forged ahead of its four possible rivals during the fifteenth century, paying nearly 60 per cent of average customs revenue between 1460 and 1499 and 27 per cent of all burgh taxation by the mid-sixteenth century.[44] When the government finally settled there in the 1530s, adding royal to burgh courts, Edinburgh gained a massive advantage.[45]

(iv) CIVIC AUTHORITY AND REGULATION

The daily life of densely populated towns required a high level of regulation and control. Local government became more complex in the greater towns, first in

[42] *BAHT*, II, 'Coventry', pp. 1–10; C. Phythian-Adams, *Desolation of a City* (Cambridge, 1979); *VCH*, Warwickshire, VIII, p. 157.

[43] Bartlett, 'Expansion and decline', 32; Palliser, *Tudor York*, pp. 208–12, 220–3.

[44] Lynch, Spearman and Stell, eds., *The Scottish Medieval Town*, pp. 269, 273, 276.

[45] A. Grant, *Independence and Nationhood: Scotland 1306–1469* (London, 1984), pp. 148–50: C. A. Malcolm, 'The Parliament House and its antecedents', in *An Introduction to Scottish Legal History* (The Stair Society, 20, 1958), pp. 449–58.

response to expansion, then to decline and decay. The degree of autonomy they enjoyed varied, but however independent or subject to seigneurial intervention, the councils of all the greater towns shared the same concerns. It is likely that they also generated a growing bureaucracy, though perhaps not all shared York's experience of spiralling council costs.[46] The evidence suggests that urban regulation was tightened during the fifteenth century, particularly to protect burgess privilege, and to control every aspect of trade to maximise income from tolls and fines.[47]

Food supply was a critical priority. Although many of the greater towns had retained common grazing for the use of their burgesses, some of whom kept pigs and cattle, none was self-sufficient. Daily supplies were a necessity and were closely supervised and regulated. The bigger a town the more likely it was to have several market places with sites dedicated to specific commodities, as well as purpose-built shops.[48] Burgesses took priority in having the first pick of fresh foods and expected their councils to control prices and quality. Regulation of bread and ale had been devolved to the localities, and the greater towns were often granted the additional rights and responsibilities of the clerk of the market. Butchers seem to have aroused particularly strong suspicions, straddling, as they did, the supply of food and raw materials for leather workers. Butchers and bakers rarely appeared amongst the ruling elite in civic office before 1500, developing a reputation for confrontation in some towns. York's council occasionally encouraged country butchers into the city as a means of lowering prices against the urban monopoly.[49]

Where they existed, craft guilds used their own officers to determine and control the quality of goods, price levels and access to skilled training and trade. Their restrictive tendencies were confirmed and supported by civic rulers, intent on bolstering the privileges of the burgess group. Councils thus approved and enrolled guild regulations into the town records, and pursued transgressors through the local courts. Faced with economic contraction in the fifteenth century, guilds invariably reissued regulations controlling access to their craft by limiting the numbers of apprentices, or the degree of cooperation with non-burgess workers. Craft guilds became as intent as the civic authorities in defining

[46] R. B. Dobson, *York City Chamberlains' Account Rolls, 1396–1500* (Surtees Society 192, 1980), pp. xxxii–iv.

[47] A. S. Green, *Town Life in the Fifteenth Century* (London, 1894), vol. II, chs. 2–6; Raine, ed., *York Civic Records*, II, *passim*; D. H. Sacks, *The Widening Gate: Bristol and the Atlantic Economy, 1450–1700* (Berkeley and Los Angeles, 1991), pp. 55–6, 77.

[48] For example Malcolm, *Introduction to Scottish Legal History*, pp. 449–58; Lynch, Spearman and Stell, eds., *The Scottish Medieval Town*, p. 275; Owen, *Lynn*, p. 25; *VCH*, Oxfordshire, IV, pp. 305–6; *VCH*, Warwickshire, VIII p. 151; *VCH*, City of York, pp. 484–9.

[49] Sellers, ed., *York Memorandum Book*, I, pp. 57–8, 121, 125, 132; *VCH*, City of York, p. 99. See also Norwich where in 1508 an alderman-elect had to renounce his butcher's trade. W. Hudson and J. C. Tingey, eds., *The Records of the City of Norwich* (Norwich, 1906–10), vol. II, p. 107.

and protecting the city liberties to discourage work drifting into the suburbs, as the Edinburgh carders claimed was happening in the 1530s.[50]

Local by-laws and regulations were enforced in local courts, acting autonomously or under the supervision of a lord's steward.[51] The grant of a guild merchant in early charters established the basis for later constitutional developments. The cumulative judicial privileges acquired by boroughs, and provincial capitals in particular, gave them several potential advantages over rivals. Access to a regular court of record and to courts with a wide competence and recognised procedures, created an environment conducive to trade. Such courts were also important agencies for promulgating codes of conduct and encouraging civic-minded standards of behaviour. Close living, alongside industrial workrooms, shops and markets, taverns and bakehouses created dirty and crowded conditions. Councils regulated to control a range of public nuisances, including anti-social behaviour such as night-prowling, and the protection of public spaces and water supplies from industrial waste, scavenging pigs and butchers' debris. They became more concerned about the physical appearance of the townscape, legislating against building encroachments and the use of damaging iron-bound cart-wheels.[52]

Living cheek-by-jowl made people closely aware of space: even a neighbour's gutter could be an offensive intrusion. In Edinburgh, the steeply sloping site and pressure to stay within the security of the defended town put enormous demands on available space as the population grew in the late fifteenth century. The consequent intense infilling led to disputes over loss of light and access. The emergence of a dean of guild court is testimony to the increasing pressure. The dean and provost supervised 'liners', whose duty it was to see boundaries were respected between each tenant and in Edinburgh. The Neighbourhood Book recorded judgements on encroachments and other matters of common concern, such as a woman keeping geese in her upper storey rooms.[53]

Nothing so refined has been found in English towns, although regulation within wards and aldermanries, either through formal ward courts, as in York, leet courts as in Norwich or undertaken personally by aldermen and ward beadles as in Winchester, might have achieved something close. It is likely that their effectiveness was dependent on the number of wards and therefore their individual size. There was no general pattern amongst the greater towns: 156

[50] Sellers, ed., *York Memorandum Book*, I, *passim*; Lynch, Spearman and Stell, eds., *The Scottish Medieval Town*, p. 272.

[51] Salisbury was one of several large towns which had no independent burgess court, *VCH*, Wiltshire, VI, pp. 94–7. See also Beverley and Bury; *VCH*, Yorkshire: East Riding, VI, pp. 20, 28; M. D. Lobel, *The Borough of Bury St Edmunds* (Oxford, 1935), pp. 95–117.

[52] For example Chester City RO, Mayors' Book 15B, ff. 36–7v. Sheriffs' Book 5, ff. 63, 84v, 87; R. C. Morris, *Chester in the Plantagenet and Tudor Reigns* (Chester, 1894), p. 268.

[53] M. Wood, 'The Neighbourhood Book', *The Book of the Old Edinburgh Club*, 23 (1940), 82–100. This was a complaint in York, Attreed, ed., *York House Books*, I, pp. 43–4.

acre (63 ha) Cambridge had seven wards by 1300, 131 acre (53 ha) Chester had fifteen, whereas the one and a half square miles (388.6 ha) of Norwich were regulated through four leet juries up to 1404. Jurisdiction at this level operated house by house, implementing borough ordinances against petty crimes and disorderly conduct, and enforcing personal responsibility for such things as storing kindling safely and street cleaning.[54] Council regulation reflected a mixture of necessary and acceptable control and the emerging ethos of public order and social control which became a characteristic of late medieval city rulers.

In the greater towns merchants invariably dominated civic office, disproportionate to their overall numbers. One effect of the Black Death was to allow the replacement of established rentier patricians by newly enriched overseas merchants, so that, except in towns with a dominant manufacturing base, craftsmen rarely appeared amongst civic rulers. Once removed from council office, the county interest operated through patronage and, less often, as parliamentary representatives. In the greater towns, acquiring the support of royal clerks, nobles and gentlemen was one of many political tactics. Men and women of high status from town and country could associate through membership of such guilds as York's Corpus Christi and St Christopher and St George Guilds, Boston's Corpus Christi Guild and Coventry's Trinity Guild. The last became an integral stage in Coventry's *cursus honorum*.[55]

The strongest and most persistent threat to civic authority was not from the townsfolk but the large religious foundations which graced all the greater towns. Whether colleges, hospitals, abbeys, priories, all were institutions to be reckoned with as obstacles to the expansion and exercise of civic authority. Before clear principles of civic government had developed, rivalry between embryonic councils and (sometimes more urbane) abbots and priors fashioned a definition of jurisdiction to delineate separate areas of control leaving at least one liberty or soke in every large town. The process was riven with animosity. Civic authority could not be exercised within ecclesiastical enclaves, no borough taxes collected nor regulations enforced. In Cambridge, where the situation was peculiarly exacerbated by the presence of the university, the council claimed that its tax base was shrinking as more and more of the residents claimed exemption through service in religious colleges. Disputes continued throughout the late middle ages, extending to common grazing rights and fairs.[56]

54 Keene, *Survey*, I, p. 81; *BAHT*, II, 'Norwich', p. 12; *VCH*, Warwickshire, VIII, p. 271; *VCH*, City of York, pp. 76–7.

55 R. Horrox, 'Urban patronage and patrons in the fifteenth century', in R. A. Griffiths, ed., *Patronage, the Crown, and the Provinces in Later Medieval England* (Gloucester, 1981), p. 156; Phythian-Adams, *Desolation of a City*, pp. 125–6; S. H. Rigby, 'Boston and Grimsby in the middle ages: an administrative contrast', *JMed.H*, 10 (1984), 51–66; E. White, *The St. George and St. Christopher Guild of York* (Borthwick Paper, 72, York, 1987), pp. 14–15.

56 *BAHT*, I, 'Cambridge', pp. 13–14, 'Coventry', pp. 4–9; S. Reynolds, *An Introduction to the History of English Medieval Towns* (Oxford, 1977), p. 116; *VCH*, City of York, pp. 68–9, 82–3.

Walled religious precincts encouraged relative tranquillity within and proclaimed autonomy to the secular world. The crenellated walls of the cathedral close at Salisbury enclosed about 220 acres (86.3 ha), and were pierced by three gates. As at Lincoln, the close contained shops and schools, re-enforcing the impression of a quite separate community.[57] Religious houses were inordinately wealthy, operating as major rentiers throughout their regions as well as inside towns. At the dissolution, the Benedictine abbeys of Canterbury, Gloucester and Winchester were each assessed at over £2,000, Bury and York at over £1,600. St Edmunds at Bury had been the largest rentier in West Suffolk, and St Mary's at York had property throughout the North of England. However, such a wide distribution of properties was exceptional.[58]

Moreover, religious institutions were the major property owners inside towns. In Oxford for example, they owned over 62 per cent of the town's rent income by 1312, and although such a high figure was skewed by the exceptional circumstances of the expanding university, the pattern in other towns was similar. In late fourteenth-century Canterbury, the Church owned 39 per cent of the town, including 27 per cent belonging to the cathedral priory; in Gloucester, the 1455 figure was 59 per cent. It should not be forgotten, however, that there was a lay interest in some 'religious' estates as in the Corpus Christi Guild in Leicester, the largest estate owner there.[59]

(v) SOCIETY

The majority of the residents in all the greater towns were newcomers. High mortality rates resulted in few dynasties. There were notable exceptions like the Bitering/Wyths of Lynn, who survived into five generations before the surviving heiress married a London grocer in the early fifteenth century. Remarriage was common, often resulting in complex family and household structures. A significant population turnover accompanied by a routine influx of outsiders were important factors in shaping social relationships. So were the number of residents, occupational patterns and the physical size and layout of individual towns. There is no doubt that urban society was fluid, rarely socially zoned[60] and enabled many varieties of association. Whether or not it was inherently unstable is a matter for debate.

[57] Hill, *Lincoln*, pp. 121–6; *VCH*, Wiltshire, VI, pp. 70, 74; *VCH*, City of York, pp. 339, 357.

[58] D. Knowles and R. N. Hadcock, *Medieval Religious Houses* (London, 1953), pp. 61, 66, 81–2; Gottfried, *Bury St Edmunds*, pp. 73–9; *VCH*, Yorkshire, III, pp. 107–11.

[59] A. F. Butcher, 'Rent and the urban economy: Oxford and Canterbury in the later middle ages', *SHist*, 1 (1979), 37; Langton, 'Gloucester rental', 269; *VCH*, Oxfordshire, IV, p. 41; *VCH*, Leicestershire, IV, p. 20; see also Owen, *Lynn*, p. 27.

[60] Owen, *Lynn*, pp. 54–5; *BAHT*, II, 'Bristol', p. 13.

Migrants probably followed well-worn routes since migrant regions largely matched economic regions. As towns prospered, their migrant regions expanded and vice versa, giving the greater towns a more diverse migrant base. A similar pattern has been observed in France after 1300.[61] In the early fourteenth century the majority of migrants to Winchester and Leicester came from between 6 to 10 miles (10–16 km) away, whereas the catchment for the majority of Norwich's and York's migrants extended up to 20 miles (32 km), and Boston's up to 25 miles (40.5 km). From the 1350s to 1560s, York continued to draw in most of its new citizens from within 18 miles (30km), 50–75 per cent from Yorkshire, a further 10–15 per cent from the northern counties with a steady flow from Cumbria. There were fewer migrants from further afield by the late fifteenth century: some 3 per cent compared with a possible 15 per cent earlier in the century.[62]

Long-distance trade brought foreigners into the greater towns. Hosting regulations enabled their movements to be monitored while they conducted their business. Some stayed for longer. Brabant merchants, Dutch and German craftsmen became freemen of York; German merchants Henry Wyman and Henry Market were naturalised and held civic office there. A Spaniard, Fernando de Ibarra, married and settled in Chester in the 1530s.[63]

From 1349, most sizeable towns periodically endured high, plague-induced mortality rates. The shortage of labour opened up the market to growing numbers of women in York and probably elsewhere, allowing them access to skilled occupations hitherto denied them. Successive epidemics throughout the fifteenth and early sixteenth century exacerbated the deepening crisis in many towns which had bounced back by 1377. In York, for example, high losses of skilled men in the 1430s and the destruction of merchant businesses sapped the commercial vitality of the town, and insurmountable death rates in Coventry 'fractured' the city in the 1520s.[64] However, towns continued to attract new freemen during the depths of the depression, though there was an increasing tendency for the freemen body to recruit from longer-term residents. Thus, between 1476 and 1566, 28 per cent of new freemen in York entered *via* apprenticeships, a tendency measurable in Bristol in 1532–42.[65]

The distribution of population generally followed the economically vital districts of towns, either clustering around the market places where the need to

[61] Pounds, *History of Medieval Europe*, pp. 268–70.

[62] Keene, *Survey*, I, p. 377; D. M. Palliser, 'A regional capital as magnet: immigrants to York, 1477–1566', *Yorkshire Arch. J*, 57 (1985), 111–13; S. H. Rigby, 'Urban society in early fourteenth-century England: the evidence of the lay subsidies', *Bulletin of the John Rylands Library*, 72 (1990), 181–2.

[63] *VCH*, City of York, pp. 108–9; *CPR 1385–9*, pp. 463, 518; *Letters and Papers*, IX, no. 794.

[64] P. J. P. Goldberg, 'Female labour, service and marriage in northern towns during the later middle ages', *NHist.*, 22 (1986), 18–38; Kermode, 'Merchants, overseas trade and urban decline', 69; Phythian-Adams, *Desolation of a City*, p. 189.

[65] See n. 62.

locate in the commercial centre outweighed the higher rents as in Gloucester and Chester, or close to water because industrial processes like tanning and dyeing demanded a good supply. In Edinburgh, the natural constraints of the site and priority to locate inside the town defences limited options, giving rise to the claim that it was one of the most crowded towns in northern Europe.[66] While overcrowding sometimes pushed people into the suburbs, there were other reasons: a desire to evade close surveillance by civic authorities or because space was needed for livestock fairs. A rival lordship might deliberately encourage suburbs. St Mary's Abbey in York promoted Bootham beyond the city walls, and in Shrewsbury the Abbey Foregate developed in the same way. Most of the greater towns had some suburban extensions by 1300, generally in the form of ribbon development, seen at its most extensive in Lincoln where Wigford stretched about one mile south of the city along the major north–south route. By the early sixteenth century perhaps a quarter of Exeter's residents lived in suburbs and about one half of Winchester's residents, living in the suburbs, were beyond the reach of civic jurisdiction.[67]

There were no clear residential patterns of wealth to echo occupational clustering, though in some towns, Winchester for instance, wealth followed successful groups so that different streets became wealthy in succession, as textile workers and merchants alternately prospered. Zoning by wealth and status was not sharply drawn, though the central streets of late fourteenth-century York were dominated by wealthier, multi-servant households. In the early 1500s, the majority of York's aldermen resided in the central area, perhaps in response to complaints that some had removed their households beyond the city liberties.[68] Multiple occupancy of tenements was common, although one consequence of the shrinking population and falling property values which occurred in the fifteenth century was the amalgamation of subdivided houses into single households. In Gloucester, York and Winchester, for instance, the same process encouraged embellishments to existing properties, more spacious new houses and the creation of larger gardens.[69]

Where the urban area was subdivided into smaller units, wards and parishes, it is likely that more complex social, as well as regulatory, networks flourished. In this context, the number of parishes is probably more significant, though

[66] Chester City RO, Assembly Book 1, ff. 38–41; Keene, *Survey*, I, p. 419; Langton, 'Gloucester rental', 267; *BAHT*, II, 'Norwich', p. 11; Lynch, *Edinburgh and the Reformation*, p. 2.

[67] D. Keene, 'Suburban growth', in M. W. Barley, ed., *The Plans and Topography of Medieval Towns in England and Wales* (CBA Res. Rep. 14, 1976), pp. 79, 81; Champion, 'Shrewsbury lay subsidy', 35.

[68] P. J. P. Goldberg, 'Urban identity and the poll taxes of 1377, 1379, and 1381', *Ec.HR*, 2nd series, 43 (1990), 201–2; Keene, *Survey*, I, pp. 419–20; Palliser, *Tudor York*, p. 105.

[69] Keene, *Survey*, I, pp. 175–6; *BAHT*, I, 'Gloucester', p. 11; *RCHM* (England), *An Inventory of the Historical Monuments in the City of York* (London, 1962–81), vol. III, p. lxiii.

borough and national taxes were collected on the basis of both. The number of parishes functioning in 1300 was usually indicative of the prosperity a town had achieved before the twelfth century. Lincoln, Norwich, York and Winchester were in a league of their own with at least forty-six, sixty-one, forty-five and fifty-four parishes each by 1300. Relative newcomers, Boston, Lynn and Yarmouth, had only one parish, Coventry had two. Edinburgh, like all the Scottish burghs, was a single parish town. When the daily round encompassed more than one market place, as it did in most of the largest towns, it becomes apparent that concepts such as community spirit or even the 'urban village' might not yet be appropriate. Thus a town like York, with its forty-one parish churches, fifty-one or so craft guilds and several market areas in the mid-fifteenth century, might be better described as accommodating several lay communities, rather than comprising a single one.

Where a single parish served a growing population, and was coterminous with the town limits, as in Boston or Lynn, the character of parish life must have been very different from that of multi-parish towns. In so far as individual identity and group loyalty derived from locality, a proliferation of churches could dilute any overarching sense of a single community in a town. The parish provided a convenient structure for social organisation both before and after death, whatever the strength of religious belief amongst the laity. Townsfolk invariably chose burial in their own parish ground, those of higher status inside the church. In Winchester, the cathedral withheld burial rights from the town churches and everyone but the most elevated was buried in the cathedral cemetery.[70] Where urban parishes extended beyond the city walls, as in Leicester,[71] townsfolk and suburbanites gathered together into one congregation. The popularity of religious guilds and confraternities suggested a further subdivision of the congregation, though they might equally serve to bring together a diverse and physically scattered fellowship.[72]

If a system of craft guild organisation had developed, it encouraged another set of loyalties which could extend beyond a single neighbourhood, depending on the physical determinants of individual occupations. Butchers were confined to a shambles in virtually every large town. Resources like a good water supply for fulling and tanning or space for tenters encouraged occupational clustering,

[70] V. Harding, 'Burial choice and burial location in later medieval London', in S. Bassett, ed., *Death in Towns* (Leicester, 1992), p. 125; Keene, *Survey*, I, pp. 107–9; N. P. Tanner, *The Church in Late Medieval Norwich 1370–1532* (PIMSST, 66, Toronto, 1984), pp. 11–12.

[71] *VCH*, Leicestershire, IV, p. 340.

[72] Women seem to have been particularly attracted to religious guilds and fraternities. C. M. Barron, 'The parish fraternities of medieval London', in C. M. Barron, and C. Harper-Bill, eds., *The Church in Pre-Reformation Society: Essays in Honour of F. R. H. Du Boulay* (Woodbridge, 1985), pp. 30–2; P. J. P. Goldberg, 'Women in fifteenth-century town life', in Thomson, ed., *Towns and Townspeople*, pp. 110–11.

but the working requirements of traders were less confining.[73] Proximity to the central market might be desirable, but most wholesalers probably travelled as much outside their towns as they loitered within. Occupational guilds grew to meet generally similar needs: the regulation of their craft or trade and the collective funding of social and welfare provisions.

However small or impoverished, occupational guilds and companies reinforced their common purpose with their own rituals to bind apprentices, journeymen and masters into a corporate whole. In this, they matched civic ritual, intended to achieve the same bonding through a blending of religious celebration and displays of secular power. The process in Coventry has been closely observed.[74] Success was no doubt achieved some of the time, but journeymen were as likely to form their own 'confederations' as concur with guild aldermen. The York cordwainers' and tailors' guilds invoked council regulations to suppress alternative fraternities amongst their journeymen. Squabbles marred many Corpus Christi celebrations,[75] which most of the greater towns marked with processions in addition to festivities on Rogation Sunday, Candlemas and other days specific to individual towns. Oxford, for instance, celebrated the feast of St Giles and Salisbury, St George's day.[76]

Processions and festivals were an important part of medieval life and, like so much else, blended religious, social and secular needs into a single rhetoric. Indeed, the Trinity Guild in Coventry and St George's Guild in Norwich became integral to civic government.[77] Perhaps as a function of the size of greater towns, or because there was a frustrating mix of opportunity combined with inequalities of wealth and power, civic rulers worked hard to impose their corporate philosophy with increasing intensity from the late fourteenth century. The councils of Bristol and York mounted elaborate ceremonies to impress visiting dignitaries and their own citizens.[78] Foundation myths were deployed to establish the antiquity of borough authority, and hence to legitimise the rule of oligarchy. Colchester had King Coel, Coventry – Lady Godiva, Oxford – King Mempric and York – King Ebrauk.[79]

[73] Textile workers congregated in Bristol and Coventry. M. H. M. Hulton, *'Company and Fellowship': The Medieval Weavers of Coventry* (Dugdale Society Occasional Papers, 31, 1987), p. 5; Keene, *Survey*, I, p. 64; *BAHT*, II, 'Bristol', p. 12; *VCH*, Wiltshire, VI, p. 133.

[74] C. Phythian-Adams,'Ceremony and the citizen: the communal year at Coventry, 1450–1550', in Clark and Slack, eds., *Crisis and Order*, pp. 59–80.

[75] Sellers, ed., *York Memorandum Book*, I, pp. 191, 193, II, pp. 79, 156–8; Hudson and Tingey, eds., *Records of Norwich*, II, p. 230; A. F. Leach, ed., *Beverley Town Documents* (Selden Society 14, 1900), pp. 33–6.

[76] *VCH*, Oxfordshire, IV, p. 71; *VCH*, Wiltshire, VI, p. 96; *VCH*, Yorkshire: East Riding, VI, p. 45.

[77] B. R. McRee, 'Religious gilds and civic order: the case of Norwich in the late middle ages', *Speculum*, 67 (1992), 69–97; Phythian-Adams, *Desolation of a City*, pp. 118–22.

[78] L. Attreed, 'The politics of welcome: ceremonies and constitutional development in later medieval English towns', in B. A. Hanawalt and K. L. Reyerson, eds., *City and Spectacle in Medieval Europe* (Minneapolis, 1994), pp. 208–31; Sacks, *The Widening Gate*, pp. 178–9.

[79] *VCH*, Essex, IV, p. 19; *VCH*, Oxfordshire, VI, p. 3; Attreed, ed., *York House Books*, II, p. 482.

Even so, disaffection erupted periodically for remarkably similar causes amongst these towns: intra-elite rivalry, ambition for a wider electoral role, suspicion of corruption and fear of the loss of common lands. These remained concerns throughout the late medieval period and into the sixteenth century. The rhetoric of corporateness and community invoked by town rulers confirmed the suspicions of those excluded from power.[80] A minority of townsfolk, the burgesses (22–50 per cent of resident adult males) had access to political power.[81] They comprised the economically significant group buying into a long-term attachment to the town. This was by no means an automatic choice made by those eligible to become freemen. The financial and personal costs, which were acceptable in a buoyant economy, may have become a deterrent during a depression. A daily or annual licensing system for non-free foreigners was essential in the greater towns to allow country suppliers access to urban markets. From time to time, qualifying journeymen might prefer to remain foreigners and many towns allowed individuals the flexibility of opting in or out. In fifteenth-century Canterbury, for instance, there was a separate category of 'intrants', paying an annual fine to work and trade in the city. Their association with the town was, on average, for less than six years.[82]

There is little evidence to suggest that differences of wealth *per se* provoked direct antagonism, even though individuals amassed considerable cash fortunes, becoming millionaires in contemporary terms. The most famous, like the two William Canynges of Bristol, were often merchants, and of as much interest as the money the Canynges expended on St Mary's Redcliffe was the *palazzo* the family occupied. It had a lofty, timber-roofed hall, two courtyards and a stone tower amongst other features. William II owned at least fourteen ships and employed 800 mariners at his peak.[83] Different economic environments brought non-merchants to the fore. John Norris, a barker, grew sufficiently wealthy from Leicester's leather industry to serve as mayor and be counted as one of the eight leading citizens in 1505. There was little industry in Cambridge but fortunes could be made in specialist retailing and innkeeping. The Vescy family became gentry from profits accumulated as apothecaries and grocers.[84]

[80] J. I. Kermode, 'Obvious observations on the formation of medieval urban oligarchies', in Thomson, ed., *Towns and Townspeople*, pp. 87–106.

[81] J. I. Leggett, 'The 1377 lay poll tax return for the city of York', *Yorkshire Arch. J*, 43 (1971), 128–46; Phythian-Adams, *Desolation of a City*, p. 132; D. G. Shaw, *The Creation of a Community* (Oxford, 193), pp. 140, 142–3.

[82] A. F. Butcher, 'Freemen admissions and urban occupations', unpublished paper, Urban History Conference (1983).

[83] *BAHT*, II, 'Bristol', p. 12; J. W. Sherburne, *William Canynges (1402–1474) Mayor of Bristol* (Bristol Historical Association Local History Pamphlets, 1985), pp. 13–15. See also *VCH*, Yorkshire: East Riding, I, pp. 77, 79, for the de la Pole's Courthall in Hull.

[84] *BAHT*, II, 'Cambridge', p. 14; W. M. Palmer, ed., *Cambridge Borough Documents*, vol. I (Cambridge, 1931), pp. 87, 114, 157; *VCH*, Leicestershire, IV, p. 42.

It was less common, though, for townsfolk to build up large landed estates.[85] Where they did so, it was often before manufacturing or commerce had fully developed. Thus, in late fourteenth-century Bury, investment in property was a characteristic of the burgess elite. One mercer, Nicholas Fornham, owned some of the best arable land in greater Bury. His contemporary, a butcher Thomas Hammond, left sufficient property in and around the town to propel his three sons directly from burgess to gentry status. Once textiles came to dominate the town, there seemed to be fewer large burgess estates. Generally, nobles and gentlemen were the wealthiest non-institutional landowners, with a handful of exceptional burgesses.[86]

The range of wealth within and between towns was wide, as the 1524–5 lay subsidies demonstrate. In Coventry, the top 5 per cent of the population owned nearly 75 per cent of the taxable wealth while the bottom 75 per cent of the population owned about 4 per cent. Half of the Coventry residents were too impoverished to be assessed. In comparison, 66 per cent of Yarmouth's population was too poor to be assessed and twenty-three men owned half of the town's wealth. But Yarmouth was a poorer town, and whereas in Coventry sixty-four men had been assessed at over £40, two at over £1,000, only twenty-three Yarmouth men were assessed at over £40; the highest assessment was £200. The larger the town, it has been claimed, the greater the inequalities of wealth distribution and, yet, in some of the middling towns like Yarmouth and Leicester, wealth could be concentrated within a tight circle of families: the Byschops in Yarmouth and the Wyggestons in Leicester.[87]

Although most wealthy households were likely to be found in the central parishes of the greater towns, small, artisan households jostled against larger mercantile households. In late fourteenth-century York, in the central streets dominated by merchants, about half of household heads were married and about a third of the unmarried population was in service. The average York household was probably between 3.91 and 4.58, those of poorer artisans being smaller. Inevitably, merchant households were generally materially more comfortable and socially more complex, often including cousins and distant kin accommodated as domestic servants. One characteristic of large-town society was the high number of domestic servants: one third of all the households recorded in York in 1377 had servants, the mercantile trades employing over half of all servants,

[85] W. G. Hoskins, 'English provincial towns in the sixteenth century', in W. G. Hoskins, *Provincial England* (London, 1963), pp. 77–8, 86–114; J. I. Kermode, *Medieval Merchants* (Cambridge, 1998), ch. 9; Langton, 'Gloucester rental', 271.

[86] Gottfried, *Bury St Edmunds*, pp. 143–53; For York see *Feudal Aids* (HMSO, 1906), vol. VI, pp. 544–6; *VCH*, City of York, pp. 108–9.

[87] W. G. Hoskins, *The Age of Plunder* (London, 1976), pp. 40–2; Phythian-Adams, 'Economic and social structure', pp. 34–5.

employing an average of two per household.[88] Servants were not confined to the very wealthy households, and in Coventry maybe 45 per cent of those assessed at the lowest rate of £2 in 1524–5 could afford live-in servants.[89]

(vi) CONCLUSION

The greater towns fostered a civic mentality to meet their political and social needs, establishing an urban culture which shaped England's fortunes in the centuries to come. The economic robustness of the majority derived from the broad mix of their activities which allowed them to accommodate losses in one area by falling back on to a more limited range of functions. Even so, between 1300 and 1550, several towns did not have the resilience to adapt to profound demographic and economic changes and allowed newcomers like Reading and Maidstone to move into the urban hierarchy. Beverley was overtaken by Hull, and Gloucester lost ground to Worcester, but both, like other 'failures', retained many characteristics of advanced urbanity and continued to play a significant role in their own region.

[88] Goldberg, 'Female labour', 18–38; Goldberg, 'Urban identity and the poll taxes', 199, 201; Goldberg, *Women, Work and Life-Cycle*, pp. 187–9; Leggett, '1377 lay poll tax return', 128–46.

[89] Phythian-Adams, 'Economic and social structure', p. 34.

· 19(a) ·

Port towns: England and Wales 1300–1540

MARYANNE KOWALESKI

As the chief gateways of an island kingdom perched on the periphery of Europe, English and Welsh port towns served a crucial function not only in linking Britain with the continent and neighbouring islands, but also in facilitating inter-island trade and communications. Presiding over this traffic and trade was a wide social and cultural mix of peoples: merchants and mariners, pilgrims and pirates, rich and poor, native English and foreigners who traded by coast and overseas, embarked for distant lands, fished nearby waters, built and owned the country's ships and manned the royal navy. While this concentration of distinctive occupational groups and visitors clearly differentiated seaports from inland settlements, so too did their special relationship with the crown, which relied on the inhabitants of port towns to transport troops and supplies, to collect the hefty revenues associated with royal customs and to police the staple system. Port towns also occupied a significant place in the urban hierarchy; eight of the twenty wealthiest English towns in 1334, seven of the most populous towns in 1377 and half of the twenty wealthiest towns in 1524–5 were port towns. In Wales, six of the ten largest towns around 1300 were seaports.

(i) WATERFRONTS AND PORT ADMINISTRATION

This chapter will focus primarily on coastal towns with immediate access to the sea, treating riverine ports only when they were customs headports, such as Exeter and London, or when they could be easily reached by ocean-going ships. Exeter, in fact, was a port town only in an administrative sense since it enjoyed no direct access to the sea, relying instead on its outport four miles south at

The author wishes to thank Judith Bennett, David Sylvester and Robin Ward for their comments on an earlier version of this chapter, and Wendy Childs and T. H. Lloyd for their comments on the calculations in Tables 19.1 and 19.4.

Topsham, which itself is located at the head of a narrow-channelled estuary, six miles from the open sea. Exeter's distance from the sea accounts for the absence of mariners, shipbuilders and fishers among the town's inhabitants; only in its concentration of overseas merchants and alien residents did Exeter resemble a true port town. Other large ports also suffered from difficulties of access because of their riverine locations; at Chester, silting of the narrow channel of the Dee forced larger vessels to unload at outports, some as far as sixteen miles away, on to smaller craft or carts for transport to Chester. Ships sailing into Bristol had to contend with an extreme tidal range as well as a seven mile journey up the narrow winding Avon; these hazards in the long run helped to refine the skills of Bristol mariners and promoted the construction of ships renowned for their sturdiness.[1]

Despite these disadvantages, riverine ports enjoyed better access to inland markets, more protection from the ravages of the sea and greater security from enemy raids than did estuarine ports or those bordering the sea. The exposed eastern ports in particular suffered from severe flooding, coastal erosion and the silting up of their havens. Violent storms in the early fourteenth century almost completely submerged the town of Ravenser Odd on the Yorkshire coast and washed away as many as 600 buildings in the Suffolk port of Dunwich. Sea storms and coastal erosion were especially deleterious on the Sussex coast, where the old settlements of Hythe, Romney, Winchelsea and Hastings had to be resited further inland. The inning of the tidal marshes from Romney to Pevensey also prompted extensive silting that eventually choked most of the harbour entrances and limited the ability of vessels to dock at the many small ports along this coast; by the early sixteenth century, New Romney, where only a century earlier the sea had lapped at its streets, was actually two miles from the sea. Further west, a savage tempest in 1377 destroyed the Cobb, the huge breakwater of Lyme Regis, as well as nearly eighty houses and fifty ships.[2] Destructive acts of nature like these imposed considerable financial burdens on port towns; the investment required to build and repair sea walls and causeways, dredge harbours and river channels and open new shipping lanes was enormous, while coping with the economic impact of the material destruction and the loss of shipping and trade further sapped the ability of many port towns to pay for necessary repairs and preventative measures.

[1] M. Kowaleski, *Local Markets and Regional Trade in Medieval Exeter* (Cambridge, 1995); K. P. Wilson, 'The port of Chester in the fifteenth century', *Transactions of the Historical Society of Lancashire and Cheshire*, 17 (1965), 1–15; P. W. Elkin, 'Aspects of the recent development of the port of Bristol', in G. L. Good, R. H. Jones and M. W. Ponsford, eds., *Waterfront Archaeology* (CBA, Res. Rep., 74, 1991), pp. 27–35.

[2] J. A. Williamson, 'The geographical history of the Cinque Ports', *History*, new series, 11 (1926), 97–115; M. Bailey, '*Per impetum maris*: natural disaster and economic decline in eastern England, 1275–1350', in B. M. S. Campbell, ed., *Before the Black Death* (Manchester, 1991), pp. 184–208; John Hutchins, *The History and Antiquities of the County of Dorset*, 3rd edn, ed. W. Shipp and J. W. Hudson (Westminster, 1861–73), vol. II, p. 44.

Port towns in exposed coastal locations also incurred heavy costs when attacked by enemy forces, a danger visited in particular on towns facing the French coast during the Hundred Years War. The Sunday morning raid by the French on Southampton in October 1338 was so devastating that it took decades for the town to rebuild, recover lost rents and restore confidence in the local administration. French raids in 1338–40 also targeted Folkestone, Dover, Hythe, Romney, Rye, Winchelsea, Hastings, Portsmouth and Teignmouth, which all saw parts of their town burned and shipping destroyed. Hit-and-run raids by the French in 1377–85 created further havoc all along the southern coast of England and as far north as Gravesend at the mouth of the Thames; in 1384 they almost completely destroyed Winchelsea. Ports in north-eastern England were subject both to Scottish and French raids; in 1378, Scarborough was plundered by a combined force of Scots, French and Spanish. Another spate of attacks centring more on the western ports occurred in 1403–5 when Haverfordwest in Wales, as well as several Cornish, Devon and Dorset ports were raided by fleets of French and Spanish ships. Norman and Breton forces inflicted an especially heavy toll in 1457 when they assaulted Sandwich, killing the mayor and other officials, abducting many wealthy inhabitants for ransom and burning and pillaging as they went; they were eventually repulsed with the help of reinforcements from Rye and Hythe, but not before they had carried off most of the ships anchored in the haven. On their way home they sacked Fowey in Cornwall, setting fire to half of the town. In Wales, the revolt led by Owain Glyndŵr in the opening years of the fifteenth century targeted many of the Welsh seaports because of their strategic value, causing significant damage to Carmarthen, Caernarfon and Beaumaris, among others. To address these threats, port towns invested heavily in seaward defences, including fortified towers, chains strung across harbour entrances, artillery fortifications and reinforced stone walls.[3]

Port towns met the expenses associated with these destructive acts of nature and human hand through royal, corporate and individual funding. To finance the construction of a new harbour entrance in 1392 (no fewer than four entrances had to be built between 1300 and 1410 because of continual silting), Yarmouth levied a 1s. tax on every last of herring; it later received an allowance of £500 out of the port's royal customs to help meet the estimated £1,000 cost of the entrance built in 1409. English kings bestowed on Tenby in South Wales an unprecedented ten grants of quayage from 1328 to 1461 for the construction

[3] N. H. Nicolas, *A History of the Royal Navy* (London, 1847), vol. II, pp. 35–6, 40–1, 260–3, 285–6, 354–5, 357–9, 362–4, 369, 374, 377–80; C. Platt, *Medieval Southampton* (London, 1973), pp. 107–16; M. Hughes, 'The fourteenth-century French raids on Hampshire and the Isle of Wight', in A. Curry and M. Hughes, eds., *Arms, Armies and Fortifications in the Hundred Years War* (Woodbridge, 1994), pp. 121–43; J. W. Rowntree, 'The borough, 1163–1500', in A. Rowntree, ed., *The History of Scarborough* (London, 1931), p. 123; Hutchins, *Dorset*, I, pp. 5–6, and II, pp. 45, 449–50; D. Gardiner, *Historic Haven: The Story of Sandwich* (Derby, 1954), pp. 138–9.

and repair of its quay and walls. To aid Southampton's recovery from the devastating effects of the French raid, Edward III awarded tax relief to several local ecclesiastical landlords, provided funds to fortify the town defences and requisitioned armed men and supplies from lords in neighbouring counties. The cost of rebuilding houses and the maintenance of the defences, however, fell on to the shoulders of local townsfolk. Similar arrangements occurred in other port towns; the king helped by making murage grants to fortify seaward defences or by granting relief from taxation or reductions on the fee-farm, but in the long run the bulk of these expenses had to be met through local taxation and individual investment.[4]

Local funding was especially important in the development and maintenance of a town's waterfront, including the construction of breakwaters, quays, jetties, beacons, tidal mills, cranes, weigh-beams and other port facilities. While the bigger projects were financed through local taxation or royal grants, most waterfront development was funded through individual efforts, especially by merchants. Some 90 per cent of the tenements on the medieval London waterfront, for example, were in private hands and it was their owners who paid for the land reclamation, revetments, river walls, timber jetties, stairs and stone docks on the river edge of their properties. Piecemeal private investment was also crucial in the development of the medieval waterfronts at Lynn, Hull and many other ports. But during the later middle ages such individual projects fell into disfavour, and civic authorities began to exercise more control over construction and repairs on the waterfront. Regulations to steer all commercial traffic to the public wharves reflected this more direct management, as did increased amounts of civic-sponsored investment. Late medieval port towns funded waterfront projects through special taxes, such as the tallage collected at Hull in 1443–4 for the repair of the haven and jetties, or the early fifteenth-century 'scotts' imposed on the value of residents' goods in New Romney to pay for repairs to the town's sluices and other projects.[5] In late fifteenth-century Sandwich, the construction of a dike and new waterway was subsidised by compelling each city ward to furnish a certain number of labourers, with the city providing food and drink to the workers.[6]

[4] A. Saul, 'English towns in the late middle ages: the case of Great Yarmouth', *JMed.H*, 8 (1982), 83; Platt, *Southampton*, pp. 112–16; D. M. Palliser, 'Town defences in medieval England and Wales', in A. Ayton and J. L. Price, eds., *The Medieval Military Revolution* (London, 1995), pp. 105–20.

[5] T. Dyson, *The Medieval London Waterfront* (London, 1989), pp. 19–23; V. A. Harding, 'The Port of London in the fourteenth century: its topography, administration and trade' (PhD thesis, University of St Andrews, 1983), pp. 10–73; G. Milne, 'Waterfront archaeology in British towns', in J. Schofield and R. Leech, eds., *Urban Archaeology in Britain* (CBA Res. Rep., 61, 1987), pp. 192–200; D. M. Owen, ed., *The Making of King's Lynn* (British Academy, Records of Social and Economic History, new series, 9, 1984), pp. 193–205; K. J. Allison, 'Medieval Hull', *VCH*, Yorkshire: East Riding, I, pp. 24, 40, 75–6; Kent RO, NR/FAC.2, ff. 57v–66v.

[6] Gardiner, *Historic Haven*, pp. 196–8.

Seigneurial investment tended to be a factor only in the smaller ports; at Minehead, where the Luttrells developed the harbour; at Hartlepool, where the town's 'herring house' at the edge of the harbour was built by the Brus family; and at Topsham, where the Courtenay earls of Devon financed warehouses, shops, and a crane at the quay.[7]

The return on waterfront investment in warehouses, cellars, cranes and weigh-beams was usually recouped in the form of rents or fees. The town of Hull, for example, farmed its weigh house for as much as £49 in 1422/3, while Sandwich collected £10 in 1454/5 for the farm of tronage.[8] Most lucrative were a whole host of port and shore duties for the use of town facilities, including anchorage, ballastage, bushellage, cranage, keelage and towage, to name only a few; to these were also added the basic local customs (usually assessed by amount and type of commodity and occasionally by value), as well as temporary grants of quayage, murage, pavage and pontage. Small port towns might only collect one or two of these customs, but the larger towns assessed an impressive array of these charges on incoming and departing ships, goods and merchants. Exemptions from some or all of these local customs were available based on personal status, place of residence and whether the goods were for personal consumption or sale. In the frequent disputes which arose over these exemptions, port towns assiduously protected their right to collect port duties not only in long legal campaigns, but also by the purchase of expensive charters. Much was at stake here since local customs often provided a significant share of a port town's annual revenues.[9]

The collection of port duties and supervision of the port was usually the responsibility of one or more of a town's chief officers, such as the mayor or receiver. By the late middle ages, some of the larger ports appointed special 'water bailiffs' who in turn worked with a group of deputies and clerks. From the mid-fifteenth into the early sixteenth century, other officials were also occasionally appointed in the larger ports, such as the pesager and six men who supervised packing at Southampton, or the Keeper of the Quay at Bristol. On occasion some of these port offices fell into private hands or were farmed out for long periods by the town. Salaried port workers were common in all ports with an active overseas trade; they included lodemen (pilots, who were especially

[7] F. Hancock, *Minehead in the County of Somerset: A History of the Parish, the Manor, and the Port* (Taunton, 1903); R. Daniels, 'Medieval Hartlepool: evidence of and from the waterfront', in Good, Jones and Ponsford, eds., *Waterfront Archaeology*, p. 48; Devon RO, W1258/G6/50.

[8] J. I. Kermode, 'Merchants and local government in some northern towns (York, Hull and Beverley), during the 14th and 15th centuries' (PhD thesis, University of Sheffield, 1990), Appendix 2; Kent RO, Sa/FAt 2.

[9] N. S. B. Gras, *The Early English Customs System* (Cambridge, MA, 1918), pp. 21–35, 153–99; Harding, 'Port of London', pp. 89–111; H. S. Cobb, ed., *The Local Port Book of Southampton for 1439–40* (Southampton Record Series, 5, 1961); M. Kowaleski, ed., *Local Customs Accounts of the Port of Exeter 1266–1321* (Devon and Cornwall Record Society, new series, vol. 36, 1993).

prevalent in riverine or estuarine ports), cranemen, porters (for whom scales of charges were set especially early in Hull and Bristol), as well as the temporary workers hired to dredge the harbour, dig new sluices or strengthen the seaward defences.[10]

(ii) PORT TOWNS AND THE CROWN

Alongside the local port administrators were those appointed by the king (or occasionally elected by the town) to guard the crown's interests; these royal agents proliferated from 1275 when the national customs system was regularised. To facilitate the collection of royal customs due on imports and exports, the crown divided up the coastline into thirteen customs jurisdictions, each managed from a specially designated customs headport. In the early fifteenth century, the number of headports rose to fifteen with the addition of Bridgwater, carved out of the Bristol jurisdiction, and Plymouth/Fowey, separated out from the massive jurisdiction of Exeter (Map 19.1). Superimposed on this royal customs system was the staple system which, in order to promote revenue collection for the crown, sought both to channel foreign merchants to designated home staples in England and to direct English exports to a compulsory staple port abroad. The ordinance of 1353 eventually fixed the home staples of wool, woolfells, hides and lead at Newcastle, York, Lincoln, Norwich, Westminster, Canterbury, Chichester, Winchester, Exeter, Bristol and Carmarthen. Exports from the inland towns in this group left through the closest customs headport: York to Hull, Norwich to Yarmouth, Westminster to London, Canterbury to Sandwich and Winchester to Southampton.[11]

Each of the fifteen customs headports usually had two customs collectors, as well as a controller, searcher and tronager, all drawn largely from among the town's chief merchants. To these could be added collectors for petty custom and subsidies, a surveyor, wine gauger, numerous deputies and clerks, as well as salaried workers such as packers, porters and boatmen. The crown's interest in customs collection thus stimulated further royal investment in port towns: through fees and other perquisites given to the customs officials; through wages paid to various port workmen; through the construction or rental of customs houses, warehouses, weigh-beams; and through the purchase of the many ancillary items needed to pack, store and transport goods. In the main ports of entry

[10] Cobb, *Southampton*, pp. xli–l; J. W. Sherborne, *The Port of Bristol in the Middle Ages* (Bristol Branch of the Historical Association Local History Pamphlets, 1965), pp. 15–21.

[11] For the changing boundaries of the customs jurisdictions of the headports, see E. M. Carus-Wilson and O. Coleman, *England's Export Trade, 1275–1540* (Oxford, 1963), pp. 175–93. For the staple system, see T. H. Lloyd, *The English Wool Trade, in the Middle Ages* (Cambridge, 1977); W. M. Ormrod, *The Reign of Edward III* (New Haven, 1990), pp. 190–4.

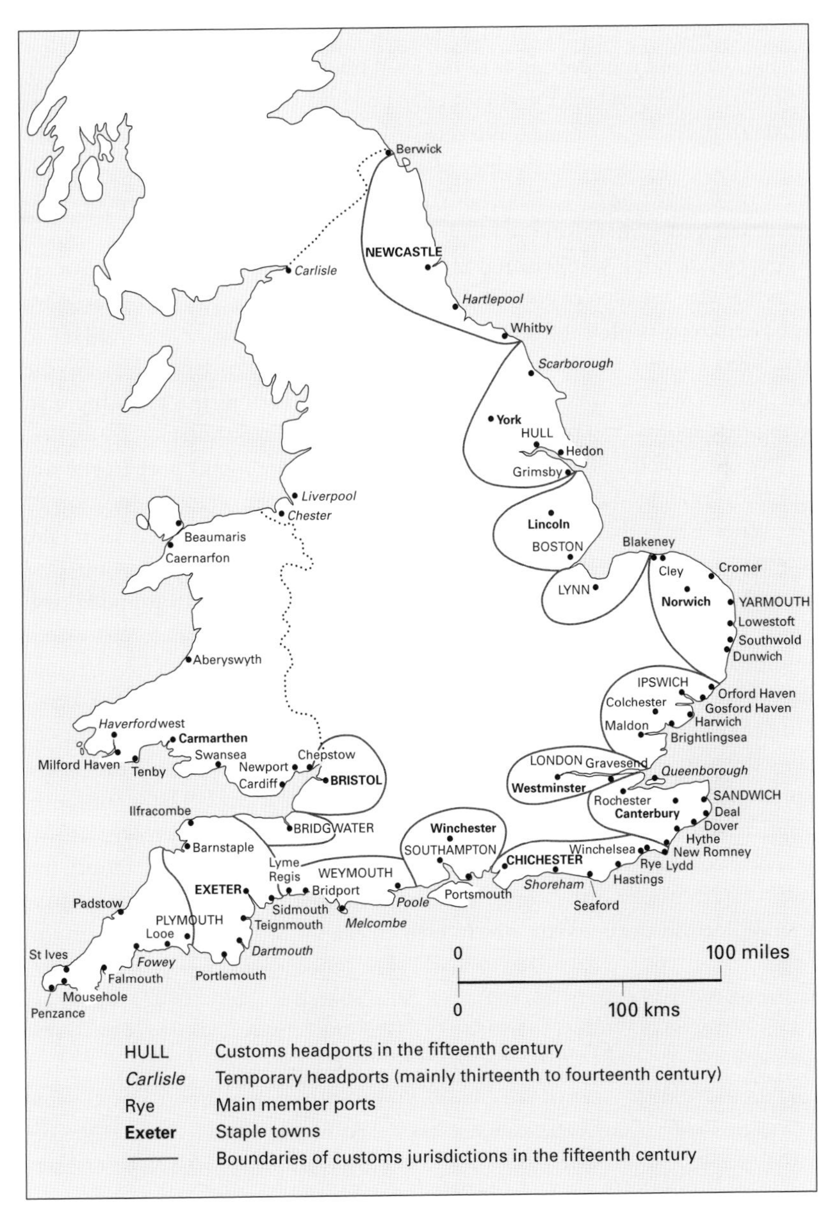

Map 19.1 Customs headports and jurisdictions in the fifteenth century

for wine, the king's butler and his staff were also active taking wine prisage, storing wine and transporting it to the royal household.[12]

In Wales, the royal butler normally exercised jurisdiction only over the crown's northern ports since baronial lords retained rights to wine prisage in the southern ports; the ports of the duchies of Lancaster and Cornwall, and the palatinates of Chester and Durham, also collected prisage in the name of their privileged lords rather than the king.[13] In Wales after about 1350, royal customs on exports of wool, woolfells and hides and imports and exports of other merchandise were usually not collected in the southern baronial ports of Haverford and Pembroke, while the lordships of Glamorgan and Gwent seem always to have been entirely outside the royal customs system. Carmarthen became the sole staple town for Wales in 1353, although Welsh loyal to the English crown were often allowed to take their wool directly to the English staples.[14]

The close relationship between the royal government and port towns was especially evident during periods of warfare when the strategic location of deepwater ports, their shipping and their manpower became crucial to the country's naval efforts. Indeed, the English kings often deliberately acquired or planted port towns for their strategic value. In Wales, Edward I founded new towns around castles and usually situated them on the coast where they could be provisioned by sea. In England he pursued a similar policy; when he purchased Wyke upon Hull from Meaux Abbey, he built a new quay (known as King's Staith), laid out over fifty new plots, fortified the town and soon began using the port as a supply base for his Scottish campaigns, a role that the newly named Kingston-upon-Hull was to play for centuries.[15] The continuing conflicts with France, moreover, almost certainly stimulated the crown's efforts to secure control over the ports of Plymouth (in the 1290s) and Dartmouth (by 1327); by transferring the rights to these two south Devon ports, as well as several Cornish ports to the newly created duchy of Cornwall in 1337, the

[12] Gras, *English Customs*, pp. 94–100; M. H. Mills, 'The collectors of customs', in W. A. Morris and J. R. Strayer, eds., *The English Government at Work, 1327–1336*, vol. II (Cambridge, Mass., 1947), pp. 168–200; R. L. Baker, *The English Customs Service, 1307–1343: A Study of Medieval Administration* (Transactions of the American Philosophical Association, new series, vol. 51, part 6, 1961).

[13] In Chester, and in most Cornish ports, this lord was the king. In the duchy of Cornwall some royal customs were collected either by the havener of the duchy or by collectors attached to the headport jurisdictions of Exeter or Plymouth/Fowey. Customs at Chester were recorded in the accounts of the palatinate of Chester, but ports in the palatinate of Durham, such as Hartlepool, were included in the royal customs accounts. Ports in the duchy of Lancaster, such as Liverpool, only occasionally appeared in the royal customs accounts; wine prisage was included in the duchy's own accounts.

[14] E. A. Lewis, 'A contribution to the commercial history of medieval Wales', *Y Cymmrodor*, 24 (1913), 86–188.

[15] M. Beresford, *New Towns of the Middle Ages*, 2nd edn (Gloucester, 1988); Allison, 'Hull', pp. 11–27.

crown solidified control of a string of strategic harbours on the eve of the Hundred Years War.

The crown's closest and oldest relationship with port towns was with the Cinque Ports, a confederation of south-eastern port towns which enjoyed tax exemptions, a special judicial system and other liberties, ostensibly in exchange for providing the king with fifty-seven ships (with crews of twenty-one mariners) for fifteen days each year. The original headports of the confederation were Sandwich, Dover, Hythe, Romney and Hastings, along with the 'ancient towns' of Winchelsea and Rye; several of these ports had royal privileges predating the Conquest. Attached to each of these ports were 'member' ports which together brought the total number of communities in the liberty of the Cinque Ports to thirty-nine port towns and villages, ranging from Grange in northern Kent to Seaford in Sussex, with Brightlingsea in Essex the only outlier. For the crown, the strategic and political value of the Cinque Ports, located in a position to control the English Channel, was more important than their ship service, which was paltry compared to the months-long service the navy usually required.[16]

Since the English kings had no permanent navy, they depended almost wholly on port towns to furnish mercantile vessels (and their crews) in order to transport troops and supplies, patrol the coast and engage the enemy at sea. Naval impressment and purveyance dearly cost port towns and their residents. Ships could sail into a harbour on a trading venture and be suddenly impressed to carry troops overseas, thereby forgoing the profits of freightage and commercial revenues. Impressed ships could be captured or destroyed and their crews held to ransom or even killed. Towns also paid the price corporately when they responded to crown requests for a specified number of ships; the civic authorities either hired vessels and their crews (at no small cost) or were required to build new ships to fulfil this service. Demands like these on port towns have led many scholars to stress the relatively greater burden shouldered during the war by coastal areas compared to inland regions.[17] The impact of naval impressment on even small fishing ports is evident in a 1347 petition from Budleigh in east Devon; it reported that continual service to the king had cost its residents three ships, twelve boats and 141 men.[18]

But the king's wars also promoted economic development in some port towns.[19] Ports of embarkation for naval fleets, especially Plymouth, Southampton, Portsmouth and Sandwich, profited from the supply and outfitting of large military and diplomatic expeditions, particularly when ships and their crews

[16] N. A. M. Rodger, 'The naval service of the Cinque Ports', *EHR*, 110 (1996), 636–51; K. M. E. Murray, *The Constitutional History of the Cinque Ports* (Manchester, 1935).

[17] J. W. Sherborne, 'The Hundred Years War: the English navy: shipping and manpower 1369–1389', *P&P*, 37 (1967), 163–75.

[18] *Rotuli Parliamentorum* (Record Commission, 1783), vol. II, p. 203.

[19] M. Kowaleski, 'The port towns of fourteenth-century Devon', in M. Duffy, S. Fisher, B. Greenhill, D. J. Starkey and J. Youings, eds., *The New Maritime History of Devon*, vol. I (London, 1992), pp. 70–1.

were forced to wait for weeks until favourable winds or sufficient stores and carriers arrived. War profiteering also benefited merchants in the northern ports like Newcastle, Hull and Scarborough which served as supply points during the Scottish wars.[20] And naval impressment was not entirely without rewards; shipowners usually collected compensation based on carrying capacity (tontight), at the rate of 3s. 4d. per ton for each three-month period of service, while shipmasters earned 6d. and mariners 3d. per day of service, plus bonuses.[21] Municipal coffers also profited when town-owned ships were employed in commercial ventures; New Romney, for example, earned over £85 one year from freightage and a share in sales of wine, wheat and herring transported to Bordeaux and to Sandwich.[22] Besides providing employment to mariners, war also stimulated shipbuilding and prompted royal investment in port facilities and defences. The wartime contributions of port towns like Hull, Plymouth and Dartmouth were, moreover, rewarded with new urban liberties, while other port towns regularly enjoyed murage and quayage grants or moneys from the royal customs to improve their fortifications and harbours.

(iii) TRADE AND SHIPPING

Some idea of the relative standing of English customs headports in overseas trade can be gleaned from the first extant list of customs revenues, a fifteenth charged on the value of imports and exports in 1203–4 (Table 19.1).[23] The prominence of the eastern ports (from Newcastle to Chichester), which controlled an impressive 88 per cent of the value of the country's trade, reflects the early dominance of wool in English exports. Production of high-quality wool was concentrated in eastern England during this period, which explains in large part the high profile of Boston's customs jurisdiction; it alone handled 29 per cent of overseas trade, followed by London, Hull and Lynn. The busiest western port was Southampton, through which passed some 14 per cent of the value of overseas trade. When English wool exports peaked (about 1304–9), the eastern ports still dominated the export of wool, but London's share of this trade had begun to grow at the expense of other ports.[24]

[20] B. Waites, 'The medieval ports and trade of north-east Yorkshire', *Mariner's Mirror*, 63 (1977), 138; E. Gillet and K. A. MacMahon, *A History of Hull*, 2nd edn (Hull, 1989), pp. 62–70; C. M. Fraser, 'The life and death of John of Denton', *Archaeologia Aeliana*, 4th series, 37 (1959), 303–25.

[21] The tontight rate varied from a high of 7s. to a low of 2s. per ton; T. J. Runyan, 'Ships and mariners in later medieval England', *J of British Studies*, 16 (1977), 7–8.

[22] Kent RO, NR/FAC.2, f. 63v.

[23] Note that the exact dates, items covered and persons taxed in 1203–4 are not completely clear. Bristol, the Welsh ports and Chester were not included in the tax, thereby heightening the share of the eastern ports somewhat, although the former ports never exported much wool in this period (a fact which reinforces the view that this tax mainly reflects wool exports).

[24] Carus-Wilson and Coleman, *England's Export Trade*, pp. 41, 122.

Table 19.1 *The relative importance of English headports in overseas trade 1203–1204 and 1478–1482*

Customs Headports	Total value of overseas trade 1203–4 £	%	1478–82 £	%
Newcastle	3,030	4.1	2,063	.1
Hull	11,460	15.4	62,567	4.4
Boston	21,555	29.0	39,909	2.8
Lynn	9,780	13.1	10,626	.7
Yarmouth	1,005	1.4	14,925	1.0
Ipswich	540	.7	29,299	2.1
London	12,555	16.9	871,158	60.9
Sandwich	720	1.0	79,117	5.5
Chichester	1,950	2.6	11,685	.8
Southampton	10,680	14.4	109,606	7.7
Melcombe/Weymouth	—	—	31,089	2.2
Exeter and Dartmouth	255	.3	42,489	3.0
Plymouth and Fowey	840	1.1	13,422	.9
Bridgwater	—	—	9,850	.7
Bristol	—	—	103,353	7.2
Total	74,370	100.0	1,431,158	100.0

Sources: the 1203–4 figures come from a tax of one fifteenth on imports and exports; see Gras, *English Customs*, pp. 217–22, and Lloyd, *English Wool Trade*, pp. 9–13. The tax included thirty-five ports, but they have here been divided up into the customs jurisdictions under which they fell in the fifteenth century. Melcombe/Weymouth probably accounted with Southampton in 1203–4. The 1478–82 figures come from the national customs accounts; these years were chosen because they are the only time the accounts distinguish Hanseatic from Other Alien (i.e. non-Hanseatic) shares of petty custom. The overall total value of a headport's trade was calculated by adding the value of wine imports (at £4 per tun) to the total value of aliens' merchandise plus the total value of denizens' merchandise (which was derived by subtracting, from poundage, the petty custom valuation minus the Hanseatic petty custom valuation, and then subtracting the value of Other Alien cloth exports, and adding the value of denizen cloth and wool exports). The overall petty custom and poundage valuations are taken from E. Power and M. M. Postan, eds., *Studies in English Trade in the Fifteenth Century* (London and New York, 1966), pp. 330–60, as are the tunnage amounts for sweet and non-sweet wine, although the tunnage imported was corrected to that given in M. K. James (*Studies in the Medieval Wine Trade* (Oxford, 1971), pp. 114–15) when her figures for non-sweet wine imports were higher. Cloth and wool export figures are from Carus-Wilson and Coleman, *England's Export Trade*, pp. 67–8, 106–7. Denizen wool exports are here valued at £6 per sack, alien wool exports at £8 per sack, denizen and Hanseatic cloth exports at £1 15s. each, and Other Alien cloth exports at £2 each. Note also that these figures should be treated with great caution since they are only estimates based on wholesale valuations that are subject to some debate by scholars. Their accuracy is further limited by small gaps in the accounts for some ports and, perhaps more seriously, the inclusion of additional months to the accounts for other ports, notably London and Southampton.

By the first decade of the fourteenth century, London's share of the country's overseas trade had mounted to about 36 per cent,[25] and by the third quarter of the fifteenth century, it had shot up to an extraordinary 61 per cent (Table 19.1).[26] Southampton ranked a distant second, while Bristol ranked third, followed by Sandwich and Hull. Although the figures on the value of overseas trade in 1203–4 and 1478–82 are not strictly comparable, they do provide a very rough indication of the shifts that had occurred over almost three centuries. It is clear that London's growth came largely at the expense of the eastern ports, with Hull, Boston and Lynn suffering the greatest decline. In contrast, the western ports flourished, since they, with the exception of Southampton, hosted considerably more overseas trade in the late fifteenth century than they had in the early thirteenth century.

The late medieval decline of the eastern ports stemmed in part from the fall in wool exports and the rise of cloth exports. Although the volume of cloth exports exceeded wool exports only after the mid-fifteenth century, they had surpassed wool exports in value a good deal earlier. Cloth made in the eastern half of the country drew on the higher quality wool available in these regions, but the less expensive cloth exports through the western ports proved more successful in foreign markets by the mid-fourteenth century, when the customs accounts first allow us to view the distribution of cloth exports by port. By 1352–62, the western ports from Southampton to Bristol were responsible for exporting an impressive two-thirds of all cloth exports (Table 19.2). Thereafter their relative share of the cloth export trade declined in the face of the amazing growth of London, whose cloth exports rose from 13 per cent of the realm's cloth exports in 1352–62, to 40 per cent by 1430–40, and 61 per cent by 1500–10. Yet the boom in cloth exports from London more adversely affected the eastern than western ports; by the early sixteenth century cloth exports from the eastern ports had fallen in both absolute and relative terms, whereas the volume of cloth exports through the western ports increased, with the customs jurisdiction of Exeter and Dartmouth registering the largest relative gains.

Although wool and cloth accounted for the bulk of the country's export trade during the middle ages, some ports also exported local products. Devon and Cornish ports, for instance, dominated the export of tin, much of which until the very late fifteenth century was first transhipped by coast to London or

[25] E. Miller and J. Hatcher, *Medieval England: Towns, Commerce and Crafts, 1086–1348* (London, 1995), pp. 213–14; they calculated the annual average value of overseas trade in each port by using the customs figures for alien trade in 1303–11, wool exports in 1304–9 and wine imports in 1300–1, which together they claim accounted for about four-fifths of the total value of overseas trade.

[26] From 1473 to 1495, the London accounts included cloth exports (mostly by aliens) packed in London but shipped from outports, especially Southampton; this practice tends slightly to inflate cloth exports (and therefore the valuations in Table 19.1) for London and understate them for Southampton (especially the alien trade); see H. S. Cobb, 'Cloth exports from London and Southampton in the later fifteenth and early sixteenth century: a revision', *Ec.HR*, 2nd series, 31 (1978), 601–9.

Table 19.2 *The relative importance of English headports in the cloth export trade in three periods 1352–1510*

Customs Headports	*1352–62* Annual average in cloths of assize (No.)	%	*1430–40* Annual average in cloths of assize (No.)	%	*1500–10* Annual average in cloths of assize (No.)	%	Change in total cloth exports from 1352 to 1430 %	from 1430 to 1510 %
Newcastle	(10)	.1	(72)	.2	(30)	.1	+86	−140
Hull	(306)	4.2	(2,911)	6.7	(2,461)	3.0	+89	−18
Boston	(587)	8.0	(1,028)	2.3	(54)	.1	+76	−1803
Lynn			(1,420)	3.3	(755)	.9		−88
Yarmouth	(465)	6.3	(682)	1.6	(194)	.2	+89	−251
Ipswich			(3,603)	8.3	(1,722)	2.1		−109
London	(956)	13.0	(17,597)	40.4	(49,501)	60.7	+95	+64
Sandwich	(97)	1.3	(854)	2.0	(175)	.2	+89	−388
Chichester	(48)	.7	(66)	.1	(159)	.2	+27	+58
Southampton	(1,466)	20.0	(8,414)	19.3	(10,547)	12.9	+84	+20
Melcombe/Weymouth			(802)	1.8	(2,587)	3.2		+69
Exeter and Dartmouth	(755)	10.3	(1,122)	2.6	(8,268)	10.2	+61	+86
Plymouth and Fowey			(797)	1.8	(759)	.9		−5
Bridgwater	(2,651)	36.1	(75)	.2	(412)	.5	+36	+82
Bristol			(4,087)	9.4	(3,916)	4.8		−4
Total	(7,341)	100.0	(43,530)	100.0	(81,540)	100.0		

Source: Carus-Wilson and Coleman, *England's Export Trade*, pp. 75–7, 93–5, 112–13. Each period consists of ten years, but adjustments were made to compensate for ports with missing data in some years. In 1352–62, Lynn accounted with Boston, Ipswich with Yarmouth, Melcome/Weymouth with Southampton, Plymouth and Fowey with Exeter, and Bridgwater with Bristol.

Southampton for export overseas.[27] Newcastle was known for its coal exports, and Yarmouth specialised in herring, Bridport in rope, Portlemouth in south Devon in slate, Anglesey in millstones. The Kent and Sussex ports concentrated on the export of wood, while those in East Anglia and Kent were known for exports of grain.[28]

Wine was the premier commodity imported to medieval England, promoted in no small part by the crown's acquisition of Gascony in 1152. At Exeter, for example, wine imports alone accounted for 70–80 per cent of the value of the port's import trade in the late fourteenth century.[29] Even in the late 1440s, on the eve of England's loss of Bordeaux, wine imports represented about one third of the value of the country's entire import trade.[30] Since demand for wine was heaviest in the more densely populated and prosperous eastern half of England, almost two-thirds of imported wine came through the eastern ports in the fourteenth century (Table 19.3). As the Hundred Years War intensified, however, the supply available declined while the transport costs to England rose; these conditions favoured the western ports which, with their easier access to Gascony and growing shipping power, increased their share of the wine trade while that of the eastern ports declined.[31]

Coastal trade, which went unrecorded in the national customs accounts, played a crucial role in redistributing foreign imports of wine and other goods from the original port of entry to other British ports for distribution and sale. In all, some 75 per cent of goods arriving at the port of Exeter travelled via coastal routes and was thus never entered in the national port customs accounts. Although hard data are scarce, a similar situation probably prevailed in most of England's smaller ports; at Colchester's outport of Hythe, for instance, it appears that about 80 per cent of the vessels mooring there in the 1390s sailed via the coast.[32] These figures warn against accepting the neat figures in the royal customs accounts as wholly indica-

[27] J. Hatcher, *English Tin Production and Trade before 1550* (Oxford, 1973), pp. 98–106, 112–16, 119–31, 164–93.

[28] PRO E122 *passim*; J. B. Blake, 'The medieval coal trade of North East England: some fourteenth-century evidence', *NHist.*, 2 (1967), 1–26; C. M. Fraser, ed., *The Accounts of the Chamberlains of Newcastle upon Tyne 1508–1511* (Society of Antiquaries of Newcastle-upon-Tyne, 3, 1987); A. Saul, 'The herring industry at Great Yarmouth *c.* 1280–*c.* 1400', *Norfolk Archaeology*, 38 (1981), 33–43; J. Pahl, 'The rope and net industry of Bridport', *Proc. of the Dorset Natural History and Archaeological Society*, 82 (1961), 143–6; R. A. Pelham, 'Timber exports from the Weald during the fourteenth century', *Sussex Archaeological Collections*, 69 (1928), 170–82; B. M. S. Campbell, J. A. Galloway, D. Keene and M. Murphy, *A Medieval Capital and its Grain Supply* (Historical Geography Research Series, 30, London, 1993), pp. 47–55, 69–71, 92.

[29] Kowaleski, *Exeter*, pp. 251, 254 n. 110.

[30] E. M. Carus-Wilson, *Medieval Merchant Venturers*, 2nd edn (London, 1967), p. 271 n. 1.

[31] M. K. James, *Studies in the Medieval Wine Trade* (Oxford, 1971). See Table 19.3 for the wine imports and Table 19.5 for the wine-carrying trade. Some wine was also imported from Germany (going mostly to London) and Iberia (primarily to London and the West Country ports).

[32] R. H. Britnell, *Growth and Decline in Colchester, 1300–1525* (Cambridge, 1986), p. 70. The ability to gauge the extent of coastal trade elsewhere is limited by the paucity of surviving local port customs accounts and their failure (with the exception of those for Exeter) to record exempt merchants, ships and cargoes.

Table 19.3 *The relative importance of English headports in the overseas import trade of non-sweet wine in two periods 1350–1500*

Customs Headports	1350–1, 1371–2 and 1405–15 Annual average (Tuns)	%	1461–71 and 1490–1500 Annual average (Tuns)	%	Change in port's annual average between the two periods
Newcastle	(45)	.5	(134)	1.9	+50%
Hull	(972)	10.1	(426)	6.1	−39%
Boston	(208)	2.2	(32)	.4	−73%
Lynn	(318)	3.3	(75)	1.1	−62%
Yarmouth	(194)	2.0	(43)	.6	−64%
Ipswich	(196)	2.0	(79)	1.1	−42%
London	(3,504)	36.3	(2,731)	39.0	−12%
Sandwich	(724)	7.5	(191)	2.7	−58%
Chichester	(108)	1.1	(96)	1.4	−5%
Total eastern ports	(6,269)	65.0	(3,807)	54.3	−24%
Southampton	(897)	9.3	(419)	6.0	−36%
Melcombe/Weymouth	(235)	2.4	(170)	2.4	−16%
Exeter & Dartmouth	(589)	6.1	(495)	7.1	−9%
Plymouth & Fowey	(341)	3.5	(426)	6.1	+11%
Bridgwater	(82)	.9	(144)	2.0	+28%
Bristol	(1,230)	12.8	(1,548)	22.1	+11%
Total western ports	(3,374)	35.0	(3,202)	45.7	−3%
Grand total	(9,643)	100.0	(7,009)	100.0	−16%

Source: James, *Wine Trade*, pp. 98, 108–9, 113, 116. Note that appropriate adjustments were made to compensate for periods of missing data.

tive of a headport's trade. The proportion of coastal trade at any one port could also alter over time, as it did in late fifteenth-century Exeter when the port was able to draw on increased cloth production in its hinterland to attract more overseas shippers directly to its port, thereby reducing its dependence on coastal trade.[33]

The control of English overseas trade by aliens varied widely from port to port. In the early fourteenth century, aliens controlled about 57 per cent of the country's overseas trade, but they were especially prominent in London and Boston which together handled 71 per cent of the realm's alien trade (Table 19.4).[34] By 1478–82,

[33] W. R. Childs, 'Devon's overseas trade in the late middle ages', in Duffy, Fisher, Greenhill, Starkey and Youngs, eds., *A New Maritime History of Devon*, I, pp. 84–6.

[34] Miller and Hatcher, *Medieval England: Towns, Commerce and Crafts*, p. 213, offer a rough calculation of the relative strength of the alien and denizen trade in the early fourteenth century. See also T. H. Lloyd, *Alien Merchants in England in the High Middle Ages* (Brighton and New York, 1982).

Table 19.4 *The relative importance of English headports in the alien overseas trade 1324–1329 and 1478–1482*

Customs Headports	% of total alien trade 1324–9	% of total alien trade 1478–82	% of port's trade in alien hands 1478–82	% of alien trade held by Hansa 1478–82	% of alien trade held by Other aliens 1478–82
		excluding wine	excluding wine	excluding wine	excluding wine
Newcastle	1.2	—	4.5	0	—
Hull	6.3	3.5	30.9	6.8	.8
Boston	30.7	.8	9.7	1.6	.2
Lynn	5.2	1.1	52.5	1.6	.6
Yarmouth	1.9	.8	25.1	.1	1.4
Ipswich	4.6	1.1	17.2	1.6	.6
London	40.2	65.4	37.1	86.4	47.9
Sandwich	2.1	6.6	41.4	1.9	10.5
Chichester	.6	.7	31.1	0	1.2
Southampton	6.3	14.6	67.3	0	26.7
Melcombe/Weymouth	.1	2.3	38.3	0	4.3
Exeter and Dartmouth	.4	1.9	26.5	—	3.5
Plymouth and Fowey	.3	.5	25.3	0	.9
Bridgwater		—	2.3	0	.1
Bristol	.1	.7	4.1	0	1.3
Total	100.0	100.0		100.0	100.0
Average			35.5		
Total £ value per annum	26,466	116,088		52,720	63,368

Sources: the figures for 1324–9 are based on the enrolled customs accounts, as printed in Lloyd, *Alien Merchants*, pp. 211–26; the figures were adjusted slightly for some ports to compensate for missing data and are the only figures in this table that include wine imports. Values were calculated as follows: £4 per cloth, £3 for a cwt of wax, £6 5s. for a sack of wool, and £20 for a last of hides, as employed by Miller and Hatcher, *Medieval England: Towns, Commerce and Crafts*, p. 213. Because these values were closer to retail than wholesale prices (which were only used in the customs accounts to cite the value of general merchandise), they are not strictly comparable to the customs valuations for 1478–82, which were wholly based on wholesale prices.

The years 1478–82 were chosen because their enrolled customs accounts, unlike those for other years, distinguish the Hanseatic and Other Alien (i.e. non-Hanseatic alien) shares of overall petty custom paid. For the sources used and method followed in calculating these figures, see Table 19.1, above. Note that the figures for percentage of alien and Hanseatic trade do not include wine imports since the customs accounts do not distinguish between alien and denizen wine imports. The value of the Hanseatic trade was calculated by adding the value of the Hanseatic portion of the petty custom and wax imports (as in Lloyd, *England and the German Hanse*, pp. 382–4), with wax valued at £2 per cwt, to the value of the Hanseatic cloth exports. The value of the Other Alien trade was calculated by subtracting the value of the Hanseatic petty custom from the overall value of alien trade; this latter was derived by adding the petty custom valuation to the value of alien wool exports, Other Alien cloth exports, Hanseatic cloth exports and Hanseatic wax imports.

when we have a particularly accurate picture of the aliens' share of each customs headport's overseas trade, their control of overseas trade had fallen to about 35 per cent. They (notably the Italians) were especially powerful in the headport of Southampton, where their influence considerably reduced the returns from trade to local merchants.[35] Alien merchants also invested heavily in the overseas trade of Lynn (where the Hansards were especially strong), Sandwich (where the Italians and Flemish were prominent) and the Dorset ports of Melcombe and Weymouth (where Breton and Channel Island traders were active). Although London hosted the most alien trade (65 per cent), the aliens' share of London's total trade was only 37 per cent. The ports with the lowest percentage of alien trade were generally on the fringes: Newcastle, where the Scottish trade was higher than elsewhere in England, and Bristol and Bridgwater, where the Irish and Welsh were busiest.

The most influential foreign-trading partners of the English ports were the merchants of the German Hanseatic League, who controlled the bulk of the Baltic trade in raw materials to England. Although the differential customs rates on alien wool exports largely priced the Hansards out of the wool trade, their other trading privileges in England, including a lower customs rate on cloth exports, enabled them to capture a significant portion of trade at the eastern ports, particularly in London, Hull and Lynn (Table 19.4).[36] Italian merchants also commanded a substantial portion of English overseas trade. The Genoese preferred Southampton, but the Venetians focused on London until the mid-1450s when anti-alien riots compelled them to switch to Southampton. Sandwich also attracted trade from the Venetians, who used it as a convenient outport for London; indeed, the Italians tended to treat even Southampton as an outport of London, finding it cost-efficient to send their imports by cart overland to the capital.[37]

The maritime trade of the ports of Wales and north-western England, regions largely outside the customs jurisdictions of the English crown, is harder to quantify. Beaumaris hosted the most overseas trade of the North Welsh ports, while the busiest ports in South Wales were the staple port of Carmarthen, Tenby (whose ships carried more wine from Bordeaux than any other Welsh port) and the ports of Milford Haven.[38] Ships from Ireland, Brittany and Iberia

[35] O. Coleman, 'Trade and prosperity in the fifteenth century: some aspects of the trade of Southampton', *Ec.HR*, 2nd series, 16 (1963), 9–22.

[36] T. H. Lloyd, *England and the German Hanse, 1157–1611* (Cambridge, 1991), esp. pp. 74–82; W. R. Childs, *The Trade and Shipping of Hull 1300–1500* (East Yorkshire Local History Series, 43, 1990), pp. 28–9, 37–8.

[37] A. A. Ruddock, *Italian Merchants and Shipping in Southampton 1270–1600* (Southampton Records Series, 1, 1951); M. E. Mallet, 'Anglo-Florentine commercial relations, 1465–1491', *EcHR*, 2nd series, 15 (1962), 250–65; E. B. Fryde, 'Italian maritime trade with medieval England (*c.* 1270–*c.* 1530)', *Recueils de la société Jean Bodin*, 32 (1974), 343–63.

[38] Lewis, 'A contribution to the commercial history of mediaeval Wales'; A. D. Carr, *Medieval*

also occasionally docked at such Welsh ports as Cardiff and Caernarfon. Most Welsh trade was coastal, however, concentrating on exchange with other Welsh ports, Bristol and the north Devon and Somerset ports. At Chester, the Irish trade dominated, although in the second half of the fifteenth century alien merchants from Brittany, Gascony and Spain began to bring in cargoes of wine and iron. Chester also served as a depot for Coventry's trade with Ireland in the fifteenth century, and began to serve a similar role for Manchester in the late fifteenth and sixteenth centuries. Liverpool saw only occasional coastal traffic until the sixteenth century when its lack of customs dues began to attract Irish and Midland traders away from Chester.[39] Ports further north, such as Carlisle, also carried on an Irish trade, and traded with Scottish ports when political conditions allowed. Several early fifteenth-century customs accounts show a lively import trade in cattle and horses, and an export trade in cloth and leather goods at Carlisle.[40]

From the thirteenth to the early sixteenth century, three trends in the maritime trade of British ports stand out. One is the rising dominance of London, which went from controlling roughly 17 per cent of the country's overseas trade at the beginning of the thirteenth century to approximately 61 per cent near the end of the fifteenth century (Table 19.1). The second trend is the general decline of the other eastern ports; they enjoyed a substantial hold on the country's overseas trade in the early thirteenth century, but saw their fortunes fall with the decline of the wool trade in the later middle ages and the rising dominance of London.[41] Continual troubles with the Hanseatic League, culminating in the Anglo-Hanseatic War of 1468–72, also damaged the fortunes of the eastern ports because so many of them depended on their Hansard trading partners. Other problems that beset many of the eastern ports in the late middle ages included continual silting and coastal erosion, which reduced the quality of their harbours, and the decline of the herring industry, the backbone of the prosperity of Yarmouth and a whole string of smaller ports from Norfolk to

Anglesey (Anglesey Antiquarian Society, 1982), pp. 113–15. In 1372–86, eleven of the Welsh ships at Bordeaux were from Tenby (Table 19.6). Tenby also contributed eight of the Welsh ships in naval service (Table 19.5). See also R. F. Walker, 'Tenby', in R. A. Griffiths, ed., *Boroughs of Mediaeval Wales* (Cardiff, 1978), pp. 289–320.

[39] K. P. Wilson, 'The port of Chester in the later middle ages' (PhD thesis, University of Liverpool, 1965), pp. 79–138, and K. P. Wilson, ed., *Chester Customs Accounts 1301–1566* (Record Society of Lancashire and Cheshire, 110, 1969).

[40] PRO E122/39/8, 39/9.

[41] For detailed studies of eastern ports that illustrate the causes of decline enumerated here, see J. Kermode, 'Merchants, overseas trade, and urban decline: York, Beverley and Hull *c.* 1380–1500', *NHist.*, 23 (1987), 51–73; Childs, *Trade and Shipping of Hull*; S. H. Rigby, *Medieval Grimsby* (Hull, 1993), pp. 113–46; S. H. Rigby, '"Sore decay" and "fair dwellings"': Boston and urban decline in the later middle ages', *Midland History*, 10 (1985), 47–61; Saul, 'English towns in the late middle ages'; K. J. Wallace, 'The overseas trade of Sandwich, 1400–1520' (MPhil thesis, University of London, 1974).

Sussex.[42] Increasing competition from the Dutch in shipping and fishing also adversely affected many of the eastern ports.[43]

The rise of the western ports in the late middle ages represents the third trend. By exploiting their easy access to expanding markets in Brittany, Gascony, Iberia and Ireland in the late middle ages, and capitalising on the growing production of cloth and tin in their hinterlands, the western ports increased their overall share of England's overseas trade (Tables 19.2 and 19.3).[44] In contrast to the eastern ports, Southampton was the only western port to suffer from London's growing dominance.[45] With the exception of Southampton, alien interests also tended to be weaker in the western ports (Table 19.4), leaving more scope for profit-taking by denizen merchants and insulating the western ports from the severe trade disruptions with the Normandy and Picardy during the Hundred Years War, and the Hanseatic League and Norway during the mid to late fifteenth century. The western ports also profited from an expansion of their fishing industry in the late middle ages, led by the especially impressive development of the south-western and Welsh fisheries.[46] By the late fifteenth century, 'Westernmen' had even begun to fish the waters of eastern England.[47] And despite the hardships caused by naval impressment and enemy raids, the western ports appear not to have suffered as badly as the eastern ports from the events of the Hundred Years War; indeed, the use of Portsmouth and Southampton as naval bases for ship assembly and shipbuilding, along with the heavy reliance on ships from Dartmouth, Plymouth, Fowey and Bristol in the royal navy probably stimulated shipbuilding and investment in these western ports.[48]

One of the most visible signs of the growth of the western ports was their increasing prominence in the country's ship-carrying trade, which can be measured in several ways. The overall naval contribution of the western ports, for

[42] For silting and erosion, see above, n. 2. For the decline of the herring trade, see Saul, 'The herring industry at Great Yarmouth'; P. Heath, 'North Sea fishing in the fifteenth century: the Scarborough fleet', *NHist.*, 3 (1968), 53–69; M. Bailey, 'Coastal fishing off South East Suffolk in the century after the Black Death', *Proceedings of the Suffolk Institute of Archaeology and History*, 37 (1990), 102–14. The Rye fisheries also declined but recovered in the 1440s; A. J. F. Dulley, 'The early history of the Rye fishing industry', *Sussex Archaeological Collections*, 108 (1969), 55–8.

[43] D. Burwash, *English Merchant Shipping 1460–1540* (Toronto, 1947), pp. 152–9; A. Beaujon, *The History of the Dutch Sea Fisheries* (London, 1884).

[44] For details on this expanding trade, see E. M. Carus-Wilson, *The Expansion of Exeter at the Close of the Middle Ages* (Exeter, 1963); D. T. Williams, 'Medieval foreign trade: the western ports', in H. C. Darby, ed., *An Historical Geography of England before A.D. 1800* (Cambridge, 1951), pp. 266–97; W. R. Childs, 'The commercial shipping of south-western England in the late fifteenth century', *Mariner's Mirror*, 83 (1997), 272–92; and items in n. 1 and 10, above.

[45] A. A. Ruddock, 'London capitalists and the decline of Southampton in the early Tudor period', *Ec.HR*, 2nd series, 20 (1949), 137–51.

[46] M. Kowaleski, 'The expansion of fishing in southwestern England in the later middle ages', *Ec.HR*, 2nd series, 53 (2000), 429–54.

[47] A. Finn, ed., *Records of Lydd* (Ashford, 1911), pp. 210, 243–4, 279, 323.

[48] Kowaleski, 'Port towns of fourteenth-century Devon'; *VCH*, Hampshire, v, pp. 360–8.

example, rose compared to the shipping furnished by the eastern ports during the Hundred Years War (Table 19.5). Especially noticeable is the decline in shipping from several of the larger eastern ports like Boston and Yarmouth, and the rise of shipping from Devon and Cornwall, which by the 1440s was providing over one third of all vessels in royal service. A similar decline in eastern shipping is evident in the wine-carrying trade from Bordeaux (Table 19.6). The eastern ports dominated this trade in the early fourteenth century, but began to lose ground to the western ports in the second half of the fourteenth century. By the mid-fifteenth century ships from the western ports, especially from Devon, Cornwall and Bristol, represented 73 per cent of the wine fleet from England and Wales, a domination which became even more marked after Bordeaux passed into French hands. Ships from the western ports also carried almost 80 per cent of the pilgrims who travelled by sea from England to Santiago in northern Spain.[49]

While the geographic proximity of the western ports to Gascony and Spain probably promoted the use of western shipping on the wine and pilgrim routes, the relative decline of eastern shipping in all three indexes of the carrying trade is striking. A study of commercial shipping in late fifteenth- and early sixteenth-century ports supports this point. Although English shipping generally prospered and grew during this period, the ships of the western ports captured a larger share of overseas trade and competed more successfully against foreign carriers than did the vessels of the eastern ports.[50]

(iv) THE MARITIME COMMUNITY

Long-distance trade by sea fostered an especially strong merchant class in port towns. By serving both as middlemen between a port's hinterland and foreign markets, and as royal administrators of the national customs, staple and navy, port town merchants had many and varied opportunities for profit. The king also sought their support in his efforts to raise port customs to finance the war effort and their advice on matters concerning foreign trade and shipping. Among the port town merchants who advanced to positions of national prominence were the de la Poles of Hull, who through lending money to the crown rose to be peers of the realm; William Soper, who migrated to Southampton as a merchant's

[49] For the pilgrim trade, and more details on shipping in south-western ports, see Childs, 'Commercial shipping', 277–84.

[50] Burwash, *English Shipping*, pp. 145–64. There is some evidence, however, that the shipping and trade of the smaller ports of Norfolk and Suffolk fared better than the larger head ports of eastern England; see Tables 19.5 and 19.6, below, and N. J. Williams, *The Maritime Trade of the East Anglian Ports 1550–1590* (Oxford, 1988). There is also some support for this view in G. V. Scammell, 'English merchant shipping at the end of the middle ages: some east coast evidence', *Ec.HR*, 2nd series, 13 (1961), 327–41.

Table 19.5 *The naval service of English and Welsh ships in three periods 1336–1450*

	1336–46		1377–95		1439–50	
Home ports	(N)	%	(N)	%	(N)	%
Northumberland and Durham	(8)	.7	(2)	.3	—	—
Newcastle	(18)	1.5	(11)	1.9	(2)	.6
Yorkshire	(14)	1.2	(9)	1.6	(3)	.9
Hull	(34)	2.9	(30)	5.2	(9)	2.6
Lincolnshire	(39)	3.3	(18)	3.1	—	—
Boston	(23)	2.0	(9)	1.6	(5)	1.5
Norfolk	(12)	1.0	(5)	.9	(40)	11.8
Lynn	(31)	2.7	(37)	6.4	(3)	.9
Yarmouth	(112)	9.6	(18)	3.1	(2)	.6
Suffolk	(55)	4.7	(1)	.2	(11)	3.3
Ipswich and Orwell Haven	(23)	2.0	(12)	2.1	(2)	.6
Essex	(35)	3.0	(9)	1.6	(3)	.9
Colchester	(16)	1.4	(16)	2.8	(2)	.6
London and Thames	(52)	4.5	(42)	7.3	(13)	3.8
Kent	(67)	5.7	(13)	2.3	(21)	6.2
Sandwich	(31)	2.6	(18)	3.1	(14)	4.1
Sussex	(33)	2.8	(10)	1.7	(4)	1.2
Rye and Winchelsea	(47)	4.0	(8)	1.4	(18)	5.3
Total eastern ports	(650)	55.6	(268)	46.6	(152)	44.8
Hampshire	(57)	4.9	(34)	5.9	(11)	3.2
Southampton	(36)	3.1	(13)	2.3	(13)	3.8
Dorset	(32)	2.7	(12)	2.1	(14)	4.1
Weymouth and Melcombe	(33)	2.8	(5)	.9	(9)	2.7
Devon	(65)	5.6	(25)	4.4	(25)	7.4
Dartmouth	(52)	4.4	(57)	9.9	(34)	10.0
Plymouth	(48)	4.1	(41)	7.1	(14)	4.1
Cornwall	(33)	2.8	(6)	1.0	(27)	8.0
Fowey	(60)	5.1	(18)	3.1	(22)	6.5
Somerset and Gloucestershire	(3)	.3	(11)	1.9	(4)	1.2
Bristol	(36)	3.1	(53)	9.2	(4)	1.2
Wales	(4)	.3	(17)	3.0	(4)	1.2
Chester and Liverpool	(2)	.2	(4)	.7	(2)	.6
Total western ports	(461)	39.4	(296)	51.5	(183)	54.0
King's ships	(42)	3.6	(2)	.3	—	—
Unidentified	(17)	1.4	(9)	1.6	(4)	1.2
Grand total	(1170)	100.0	(575)	100.0	(339)	100.0

Sources: to minimise record bias, the table focuses on the larger naval expeditions since they required country-wide impressments. A ship was counted once for each

Table 19.5 (*cont.*)

expedition in which it served. **1336–46:** M. Lyon, B. Lyon and H. S. Lucas, eds. *The Wardrobe Book of William de Norwell 12 July 1338 to 27 May 1340* (Brussels, 1983), pp. 363–86; H. J. Hewitt, *The Organization of War under Edward III, 1338–62* (Manchester, 1966), pp. 182–6. The 1346 figures are drawn from the so-called Calais Roll, which some scholars view with suspicion because it survives only in sixteenth-century copies; the proportions of ships from individual ports, however, appear reasonable in light of other impressments. The 1346 figures in this table are based on the collated version printed in Nicolas, *A History of the Royal Navy*, II, pp. 507–10, and emended in places by further comparison with versions in J. Charnock, *A History of Marine Architecture* (London, 1800–2), vol. I, pp. xxxviii–xliii; BL Cotton MS Titus E. III. f. 262; Harleian MS 78, ff. 16–17; Harleian MS 246, ff. 15v–16v; Harleian MS 3968, ff. 131v–3. **1377–95:** PRO E101/37/25, 40/9, 40/19, 40/36, 40/40, 41/26, 41/27, 41/28, 41/29, 41/30, 41/31, 41/32. **1439–50:** PRO E101/53/25, 53/39, 54/4, 54/10, 54/14; and M. Oppenheim, *A History of the Administration of the Royal Navy and of Merchant Shipping* (London, 1898), p. 26.

apprentice and became a wealthy merchant-shipowner and keeper of Henry VI's ships; and the very wealthy William Canynges of Bristol, who owned at least ten ships (with a capacity of over 3,000 tons), and employed some 800 men in his shipping enterprises.[51] Port town merchants, especially those from Bristol, also paved the way for England's voyages of discovery; their entrepreneurial spirit was evident in Robert Sturmy's early voyages to the Mediterranean in the 1440s, as well as in the Bristol-funded voyages across the Atlantic in the 1480s and 1490s, when John Cabot's quest for the Northwest Passage to the riches of Asia laid a foundation for European expansion westwards.[52]

Shipowners like William Canynges acquired vessels not only through purchase but also by building others. Most of the larger port towns supported some shipbuilding, as shown by the royal orders to furnish purpose-built galleys for the navy; Newcastle, York and London even had shipwrights' guilds. Many shipyards were located along sheltered riversides; in the fifteenth century, for example, the shipyards of Smallhythe, a small port a few miles upriver from Rye, built vessels for the king and for the town of New Romney. Although there were no permanent royal dockyards in the middle ages, the crown regularly depended on shipyards near London, Smallhythe, the River Hamble and especially Portsmouth (where Henry VII invested £194 to build a great dry-dock in 1495)

[51] R. Horrox, *The De La Poles of Hull* (East Yorkshire Local History Society, 1983); S. Rose, ed., *The Navy of the Lancastrian Kings: Accounts and Inventories of William Soper, Keeper of the King's Ships, 1422–1427* (Navy Records Society, vol. 123, 1982), pp. 6–27; J. Sherborne, *William Canynges 1402–1474* (Bristol Branch of the Historical Association, 1985).

[52] D. H. Sacks, *The Widening Gate: Bristol and the Atlantic Economy, 1450–1700* (Berkeley, 1991), pp. 32–6.

Table 19.6 *The relative importance of English and Welsh ports in the Bordeaux wine-carrying trade in three periods 1372–1483*

	1372–86		1442–9		1482–3
Home ports	Ships %	Tuns %	Ships %	Tuns %	Ships %
Newcastle	1.7	1.7	1.1	1.1	
Yorkshire	.8	.9	.7	2.1	
Hull	4.9	7.3	7.4	10.1	
Lincolnshire and Grimsby	1.4	1.1	.4	.2	
Norfolk and Suffolk	.5	1.0	—	—	
Lynn	3.6	4.3	1.9	3.4	
Yarmouth	3.7	3.9	.7	.3	
Ipswich	3.2	3.1	1.5	1.5	
Essex and Colchester	1.9	2.4	.7	.7	
London and Thames	7.3	9.9	8.5	12.7	16.0
Kent and Sandwich	2.0	2.8	1.5	1.0	
Sussex and Winchelsea	1.7	2.2	2.7	1.8	2.0
Total eastern ports	32.7	40.6	27.1	34.9	18.0
Hampshire	4.7	5.2	1.5	.9	4.0
Southampton	3.6	4.5	2.2	2.4	
Dorset and Weymouth	2.0	1.6	4.5	4.3	4.0
Devon	4.2	3.2	8.6	4.9	10.0
Dartmouth	12.7	11.6	12.3	13.5	22.0
Plymouth	14.9	12.6	5.2	2.8	12.0
Cornwall	1.9	.8	13.0	8.2	12.0
Fowey	7.6	5.1	8.2	7.6	8.0
Somerset and Gloucestershire	1.5	.8	1.1	.5	
Bristol	11.0	11.6	10.4	14.4	6.0
Wales and Tenby	3.0	2.3	5.9	5.6	4.0
Liverpool	.2	.1	—	—	
Total western ports	67.3	59.4	72.9	65.1	82.0
Total	100.0	100.0	100.0	100.0	100.0
Total sums (N)	591	49,601	195	28,860	50

Sources: PRO E101/179/10 (1372–3), 180/2 (1374–5), 182/5 (1377–8), 182/6 (1378–9), 182/11 (1379–81), 183/11 (1385–6), 194/3 (1442–3), 195/19 (1448–9); BL Add. MS 15,524 (1444–5); M. G. Ducaunnes-Duval, ed., 'Registre de la Comptablie de Bordeaux, 1482–1483', *Archives historiques du département de la Gironde*, 50 (1915), 78–141.

to build and maintain its ships. Only in the reign of Henry VIII were more permanent royal dockyards established on the Thames at Deptford, Woolwich and Erith.[53]

Mariners, fishers, pilots, ropers and anchorsmiths were other distinctive occupations in port towns. Not particularly well paid, mariners had to endure cramped quarters aboard ship, as well as the constant fear of violent storms or capture by hostile forces. To counteract the danger of capture, several English and French port towns forged agreements for the ransom and exchange of captured mariners. The mariners of Lydd and New Romney, for example, had a long-standing arrangement with their Norman counterparts; a captured shipmaster was to be ransomed for six nobles plus expenses for each week he was held, and a mariner paid three nobles plus expenses, along with one half noble for his safe-conduct. Captured fishing boats could be freed on payment of 40s. Such arrangements did not apply, however, to merchants who could be held for whatever ransom they could bring. Several south Devon ports had a similar agreement with the Breton port of St Malo that stipulated higher rates of ransom for captured merchants and shipmasters than for mariners and soldiers, and also charged sums for board and a 'passport'. The risk of capture was sufficiently great that individual mariners also planned ahead by mortgaging their property to ensure funds would be available in the event they were held for ransom.[54]

On occasion, mariners also formed guilds, as they did at Newcastle, York, Hull, Grimsby, Boston, Lynn and Bristol, although many of their guilds were oriented more towards religious functions than training and supervision.[55] Within towns, mariners tended to settle near the waterfront, as they did in Bristol, but many who crewed the ships of the larger port towns actually resided in nearby rural settlements along the coast.[56] Mariners' terms of employment were largely regulated by the Laws of Oleron, a body of customs recognised throughout western Europe. Hired for the duration of a voyage, their pay, while small, included food and drink and could be supplemented by the free freightage they

[53] I. Friel, *The Good Ship: Ships, Shipbuilding and Technology in England 1200–1529* (London, 1995), pp. 27–67, contains the best recent overview of shipbuilding.

[54] H. R. Watkin, *Dartmouth* (Devonshire Association Parochial Histories, 5, 1935), pp. 105–6, 400–1; Kent RO, NR/FAC.2, m. 72v. The New Romney agreement seems also to have included other Kentish ports; see G. J. Mayhew, 'Rye and the defence of the Narrow Seas: a 16th century town at war', *Sussex Archaeological Collections*, 120 (1982), 149–60.

[55] C. M. Fraser, 'The early hostmen of Newcastle upon Tyne', *Archaeologia Aeliana*, 5th series, 12 (1984), 178; A. Storey, *Trinity House of Kingston upon Hull* (Kingston upon Hull, 1967); M. Sellers, ed., *York Memorandum Book*, vol. II (Surtees Society, 125, 1914), pp. 215–16; L. R. Simon, 'Grimsby's mariners guild in the second half of the sixteenth century', *Lincolnshire Historian*, 2 (1955), 27–30; N. Camfield, 'The guilds of St Botolph's', in W. M. Ormrod, ed., *The Guilds in Boston* (Boston, 1993), p. 27; F. B. Bickley, ed., *Little Red Book of Bristol* (Bristol and London, 1900), vol. II, pp. 186–92.

[56] Sherborne, *Port of Bristol*, p. 19; Kowaleski, 'Introduction', *Local Customs Accounts of the Port of Exeter*, pp. 18–20.

were often granted to transport goods, and by additional fees they earned for loading and unloading goods. Minimum wages set down in 1375, for example, gave mariners sailing between London and Bordeaux during vintage time 8s. plus carriage of a tun of wine on the return voyage.[57] The most skilled mariners became shipmasters and not only captained the ship during voyages, but also often took responsibility for buying and selling goods on behalf of merchants.

Many port town residents also depended on fishing for part or all of their livelihood. Yarmouth's annual herring fair from August to November attracted hundreds of ships and traders from all over England and the continent, making it England's pre-eminent centre of the fish trade. Yarmouth's residents, like those in other fishing ports, invested heavily in fishing boats and nets, as well as in smoke-houses, salt-houses and barrels for curing fish. The industry itself usually ran on the 'share' system whereby all involved were assigned part of the catch. Owners of capital equipment, such as the boat and nets, usually took more shares, while those contributing their labour, which included the fishers as well as those who packed the fish, also received a share of the profits. The importance of the fish trade to the port town economy is evident in the monopolies that towns such as Yarmouth, Blakeney and Dunwich enforced on landing and selling fish in their districts, and in the tolls that towns like Aberystwyth and Beaumaris charged fishing boats and their catch.[58]

Both English fishers and seamen were schooled in the ways and profits of piracy by the crown's increasing reliance on privateers to harass enemy shipping during the Hundred Years War. The profits that mariners, shipmasters and ship-owners could expect to reap from a heavily loaded Hanseatic cog or Spanish carrack must also have often proved tempting. Almost every port town had some in its midst who dabbled in piracy, but the Devon and Cornish ports were especially infamous in the late middle ages. Men like John Hawley of Dartmouth, a merchant who owned twelve ships and served as his town's mayor fourteen times, easily veered from privateering to piracy, although he managed to secure pardons for his worst offences and ended up an extremely wealthy landowner and holder of several royal appointments. Cornish privateer/pirates included Mark Mixtow of Fowey, who after attacking a Genoese carrack off the Portuguese coast, cavalierly put its crew ashore destitute in a strange land. And when a West Country squadron led by Robert Winnington of Dartmouth captured over 100 ships of the Hanseatic salt fleet in 1449, it sparked an international incident that further worsened Anglo-Hanseatic relations.[59]

[57] T. Twiss, ed., *The Black Book of the Admiralty* (RS, 55, 1871), vol. I, p. 139. Burwash, *English Shipping*, pp. 35–81, provides the best discussion of seamen's work conditions.

[58] See items in n. 42, above, and L. F. Salzman, *English Industries in the Middle Ages* (London, 1964), pp. 258–76; R. A. Griffiths, 'Aberystwyth', in Griffiths, ed., *Boroughs of Mediaeval Wales*, p. 36; E. A. Lewis, *The Mediaeval Boroughs of Snowdonia* (London, 1912), pp. 197–9, 207.

[59] G. V. Scammell, 'War at sea under the early Tudors: some Newcastle upon Tyne evidence',

As the kingdom's gateways to coastal and continental traffic, port towns also hosted a multitude of native and foreign visitors. Many of these foreigners married English spouses and became denizens, some even rising to positions of considerable authority in their towns, such as Edmund Arnold, a Gascon who settled in Dartmouth and eventually became mayor.[60] More numerous than these prominent foreigners, however, were the servants, labourers and artisans who migrated to England from abroad. Their ranks included many whose maritime occupations may have made their assimilation into port town society easier, such as John Shipewrogt of Normandy, who settled in Wareham in Dorset, the Scottish fishermen and their wives who resided in Whitby, and the numerous foreign shipmen who made Boston or Lynn their home.[61]

Many port towns regulated their alien residents, taxing them at a higher rate, for example, or requiring them to register their trade with the local authorities, or forbidding them to enter certain occupations. The tendency for aliens to settle in the same neighbourhood, as the *Doche* did in Southwark, or to carry out much of their business within discrete communities, like the Hanseatic *Kontore* in Boston, Lynn and London, also reflects the segregation of foreigners within medieval port towns. In the fifteenth century, the English became more hostile to the aliens in their midst, motivated in part by jealousy of unreciprocated privileges extended to foreign merchants like the Hansards, and by a growing nationalism in the face of the country's war with France. In 1439, parliament passed the first of many subsidies assessed on alien residents, although wealthier and well-connected foreigners generally escaped the tax. Alien hosting regulations, which had been on the books in many towns for years, also began to be more rigorously enforced. National legislation in 1439 required all foreign traders to lodge with an English host and provide him or her with daily reports of their business, which the host then reported to the Exchequer. Anti-alien sentiment was particularly strong in London, which had a long history of discrimination and attacks on foreigners, especially the Flemish. In 1456, the attacks on the Italians were so severe that many moved their activities elsewhere, especially to Southampton where they felt more welcome.[62]

Archaeologia Aeliana, 4th series, 38 (1960), 73–97; C. L. Kingsford, *Prejudice and Promise in Fifteenth-Century England* (Oxford, 1925), pp. 78–106; J. C. Appleby, 'Devon privateering from early times to 1688', in Duffy, Fisher, Greenhill, Starkey and Youings, eds., *A New Maritime History of Devon*, I, pp. 90–2.

[60] Watkin, *Dartmouth*, pp. 70, 184, 272.

[61] PRO E179/103/83, 270/31/42, 136/206/3, 149/126/3. See also M. Carlin, *Medieval Southwark* (London, 1996), pp. 149–67, for a discussion of the wide variety of occupations pursued by alien immigrants.

[62] M. S. Giuseppi, 'Alien merchants in England in the fifteenth century', *TRHS*, 9 (1895), 75–98; Carlin, *Southwark*, pp. 149–67; Lloyd, *England and the German Hanse*, references under 'Steelyard'; A. A. Ruddock, 'Alien hosting in Southampton in the fifteenth century', *Ec.HR*, 16 (1946), 30–7; S. Thrupp, 'A survey of the alien population of England in 1440', *Speculum*, 32 (1957), 262–73; R. Flenley, 'London and foreign merchants in the reign of Henry VI', *EHR*, 25 (1910), 644–55.

Given the resentment that the merchant class harboured against the privileges of foreign merchants, as well as the personal experience that many port town residents had of the damaging effects of enemy raids, it is not surprising that hostility to aliens could be especially strong in port towns. But it is important to remember that flare-ups occurred mainly in the fifteenth century and were far worse in London than elsewhere. The hosting regulations seem mainly to have been honoured in Hull, London and Southampton, and even there enforcement could be lax and excluded the Hansards and Genoese altogether. Later collections of the alien subsidies, moreover, considerably widened the number of foreigners exempt from tax. Port towns had long practice in accommodating visitors and residents of different customs and ethnicities for they were, after all, regular and essential parts of the maritime economy. English merchants, mariners and fishermen, moreover, had much in common with their counterparts in neighbouring or distant port towns; their lives oscillated to the same distinctive rhythms – dependent on unpredictable tides and winds, as well as the seasonal demands of water carriage, fishing and trade.

· 19(b) ·

Port towns: Scotland 1300–1540

DAVID DITCHBURN

IN SCOTLAND, as in England, ports were the kingdom's gateway to Christendom. Few of medieval Scotland's towns were, however, natural ports. Of fifty-five established burghs by 1300, twenty-three were located on inland sites.[1] Although eleven others were on navigable rivers, most of these arguably owed their origins less to maritime access than to land routes which converged on estuarine fording points. Of the twenty-one coastal burghs many, such as Cromarty and Cullen, were of such minimal economic significance that they can be scarcely classified as either ports or towns. Even among those which did develop a regular maritime trade, the topography of some suggests that maritime access was of secondary significance to their early development. Although, for instance, noted in the early twelfth century as one of only three trading centres north of Forth, it remains uncertain whether Inverkeithing developed around the natural harbour at the mouth of the Keithing burn or around the main thoroughfare which was located on considerably higher ground to the north. A similar observation has been made of Crail and could be made of Montrose, where the distinctive place name of the harbour, Strumnay, suggests a separate origin from that of the adjacent town.[2]

There were few exceptions to the predominantly landward vista of the early Scottish burghs. Aberdeen was probably one, particularly if the plausible identification of its early nucleus as adjacent to the Denburn harbour is accepted.[3] Dundee and Ayr were probably others. These coastal towns were well positioned to exploit the commercial expansion of the twelfth and thirteenth

1 G. S. Pryde, *The Burghs of Scotland* (London, 1965), nos. 1–38, 82–105.

2 *RRS*, I, no. 243; J. Wordsworth *et al.*, 'Excavations at Inverkeithing, 1981', *Proc. Soc. Antiq. Scot.*, 113 (1982), 520; A. T. Simpson and S. Stevenson, *Historic Crail: The Archaeological Implications of Development* (Scottish Burgh Survey, 1981), p. 22.

3 E. P. D. Torrie, 'The early urban site of new Aberdeen: a reappraisal of the evidence', *Northern Scotland*, 12 (1992), 1–18.

centuries, an expansion spawned chiefly by a new Anglo-Norman elite demanding the importation of wine and wheat and the more or less simultaneous emergence of large quantities of wool available for export to the Netherlandish draperies. It was this trade which necessitated ports and, perhaps fortuitously, fluvial towns discovered that the rivers on which they were located often afforded access to burgeoning commercial activity. For landward towns, muscling in on maritime trade was more problematic. Cupar and Elgin directed their overseas trade through several nearby ports, while Dunbar and Haddington used respectively Belhaven and Aberlady.[4] Other towns acquired legal rights over satellite ports: Edinburgh, for instance, gained (South) Leith in 1329 and Linlithgow acquired Blackness in 1389.[5] Even then, access to satellite ports, and jurisdiction over them, was sometimes contentious. In the late fifteenth century Cupar merchants found the highway to the port of Motray obstructed by a local laird, while it was only in 1398 that Edinburgh acquired lands beside the harbour at Leith. Jurisdictional disputes between Edinburgh and the lords of Restalrig, concerning their respective rights in Leith, continued to fester into the sixteenth century.[6]

(i) WATERFRONTS AND PORT ADMINISTRATION

Port facilities across Scotland were normally simple, often amounting to no more than a beach-head bereft of man-made constructions.[7] The agreement made in 1394 between the burgesses and abbot of Arbroath for the construction of a timber-encased stone harbour was far from typical and the attention which it has received from historians is actually reflective of the paucity of harbour constructions elsewhere in the fourteenth century.[8] While there are signs of development at some smaller ports from the later fifteenth century, even at the busier harbours constructions were late and limited.[9] Though used as a port by the early four-

[4] For Cupar, 'port of Eden', 'port of Motray' and Tayport, see, for example, *ER*, v, pp. 189, 226, 260, 299, 337, 375, 427, 494, 554, 624; for Elgin and ports at Findhorn, Aberdeen and Spynie, *ibid.*, iv, p. 625, viii, p. 632; C. Innes, ed., *Registrum Episcopatus Moraviensis* (Bannatyne Club, 1837), no. 163; for Dunbar and the port of Belhaven, and for Haddington and the port of Aberlady, *ER*, iii, *passim*.

[5] *RRS*, V, no. 381; *RMS*, i, no. 776.

[6] G. Neilson and H. Paton, eds., *Acts of the Lords of Council in Civil Causes*, vol. ii (Edinburgh, 1918), pp. 38–9, 177, 187; J. Colston, *The Town and Port of Leith* (Edinburgh, 1892), pp. 3–7; A. B. Calderwood, ed., *Acts of the Lords of Council*, vol. iii (Edinburgh, 1993), p. 312.

[7] A. Graham, 'Archaeological notes on some harbours in eastern Scotland', *Proc. Soc. Antiq. Scot.*, 101 (1968–9), 202–3.

[8] *Liber S. Thome de Aberbrothoc* (Bannatyne Club, 1848–56), vol. ii, no. 42. For improvements to the navigational channel rather than the harbour at Lossie, see Innes, ed., *Reg. Moraviensis*, no. 163.

[9] D. Adams, 'The harbour: its early history,' in G. Jackson and S. G. E. Lythe, eds., *The Port of Montrose* (Tayport, 1993), p. 27; G. S. Pryde, ed., *Ayr Burgh Accounts 1534–1624* (Scottish History Society, 1937), pp. 80, 88–9; E. P. D. Torrie and R. Coleman, *Historic Kirkcaldy: The Archaeological Implications of Development* (Scottish Burgh Survey, 1995), pp. 13–15.

teenth century, it was not until 1465 that permission was granted for the construction of harbour works at Blackness.[10] Evidence of constructions at Perth is also meagre, until a new harbour was constructed in the early sixteenth century.[11] Dundee, apparently, did possess stone-built harbour facilities, but although from 1447 vessels entering the port were subject to a levy earmarked for the maintenance of the harbour, by 1560 the town's harbour was in a state of decay.[12] At Aberdeen a (probably timber) jetty and a quay were recorded by 1398. In the later fourteenth or early fifteenth century a granite-built harbour wall was also constructed although this was superseded by a new harbour, apparently built in the later fifteenth or early sixteenth century. Only then, too, did fortifications appear to defend the harbour against attack.[13] At Leith, Edinburgh's acquisition of the shoreside lands in 1398 was partly with a view towards 'enlarging, lengthening and constructing' the port and improving access through the construction of new roads. Later imposts levied at the port were earmarked for the 'augmentation of the fabric' of the harbour.[14] This perhaps included the erection of beacons, a feature evident at Aberdeen by the later fifteenth century, but there is no Scottish evidence of harbour-side cranes in the medieval period.[15] Similar, however, to the imposts introduced at Dundee, those authorised at Leith in 1428, 1445 and 1471 were also intended to fund harbour repairs.[16] Repairs, as opposed to new constructions, seem to have been common and were necessitated at Dundee and Aberdeen by silting, which impeded harbour entry, and, at Aberdeen and Leith, by shipwrecks. At Leith, by 1457, these were said to be frequent and the cause of 'heavy and inestimable damages', while at Aberdeen it was perhaps the obstruction caused by wrecks which made the harbour unusable between 1430 and 1434 and again between 1447 and 1451. A Gdansk vessel was certainly wrecked at the harbour in the intervening years.[17]

If evidence of harbour construction in Scotland is limited, that for waterfront buildings is even more so. At Leith construction work began in 1434 of a shoreside building which was to serve as a royal residence, storehouse and armoury. Such a large building was unusual, and not completed until 1500, but warehouses, cellars and shops were perhaps the norm in Scotland as elsewhere in

[10] J. Bain *et al.*, eds., *Calendar of Documents relating to Scotland* (Edinburgh, 1881–1986), vol. IV, no. 461, V, nos. 440, 464, 472, 475, 492; *RMS*, II, no. 257.

[11] D. Bowler and R. Cachart, 'Tay Street, Perth: the excavation of an early harbour site', *Proc. Soc. Antiq. Scot.*, 124 (1994), 485–7.

[12] E. P. D. Torrie, *Medieval Dundee* (Dundee, 1990), p. 37.

[13] J. Murray, ed., *Excavations in the Medieval Burgh of Aberdeen, 1973–81* (Edinburgh, 1982), pp. 37–45; E. P. Dennison and J. Stones, *Historic Aberdeen* (Scottish Burgh Survey, 1997), pp. 83–4.

[14] Colston, *Port of Leith*, pp. 3–15.

[15] Aberdeen, City Archive, Council Register, vol. VI, p. 598. Documentary evidence of beacons at Leith dates from the sixteenth century (J. D. Marwick, ed., *Extracts from the Records of the Burgh of Edinburgh* (Scottish Burgh Record Society, 1869–92) vol. II, pp. 275–6).

[16] Marwick, ed., *Edinburgh Records*, I, pp. 3, 7, 25.

[17] *ER*, IV, pp. 535, 566, V, pp. 306, 341, 389, 431; Aberdeen, City Archive, Council Register, vol. V(2), p. 684. The wreck of a Spanish barge in the harbour is noted in 1484 (*ibid.*, vol. VI, p. 598).

Europe.[18] Ports brought profits to local communities, and not just through trading. By the later middle ages the ancient royal shipping tolls, now known as the petty customs, were retained by the burghs themselves. Since most ports were an integral part of a larger burgh, responsibility for collecting these dues, and for port administration and jurisdiction generally, fell to those twin pillars of the burgh community, the council and the guild merchant. In the satellite port of Leith alone did an official with specific port responsibilities, the water baillie, appear. The water bailie presided over his own court, but apparently only from *c.* 1490, in Leith itself. He was, moreover, elected by Edinburgh's burgesses and presumably performed similar functions in Leith to those which bailies elsewhere performed with the added duty of ensuring that Leith's inhabitants did not infringe the rights of Edinburgh's burgesses.[19]

(ii) PORT TOWNS AND THE CROWN

In addition to the petty customs a system of national customs dues, the 'great customs', was introduced in the later thirteenth century in imitation of that already operative in England. Unlike the English system, the range of taxable commodities remained restricted. Imports, with the exception of those from England and Ireland, were not normally taxed until 1597. In the fourteenth century financial emergencies usually resulted in an increase in the rate of existing customs dues, rather than in an extension of duty to other commodities. Although by the fifteenth century the traditionally taxed exports of wool, woolfells and hides had been supplemented by imposts on woollen cloth, salt, coal, fish and a variety of skins, several exemptions from payment, especially on salt, skins and fish, were granted.[20] In practice, therefore, many exports too remained untaxed.

From the fourteenth century, all Scottish exports, in theory, were directed to an overseas staple, which was normally located at either Bruges or Middelburg. With the exception of Edward I's unpopular experiment of funnelling all exports through Berwick, there was no domestic staple.[21] Customs dues were normally levied at the first port of departure. The crown appointed custumars

[18] A. T. Simpson, S. Stevenson and N. Holmes, *Historic Edinburgh, Canongate and Leith* (Scottish Burgh Survey, 1981), pp. 82–3; E. Ewan, *Townlife in Fourteenth-Century Scotland* (Edinburgh, 1990), p. 7.

[19] For the role of the bailie see above, p. 295; for the water bailie of Leith, see Marwick ed., *Edinburgh Records*, I, pp. 59, 90, 133, 150, 193, 208, 220.

[20] E.g. *RMS*, II, nos. 507, 1529, 1566; P. J. Anderson, ed., *Charters and Other Writs Illustrating the History of the Royal Burgh of Aberdeen* (Aberdeen, 1890), nos. 17–18; R. Renwick, ed., *Charters and Other Documents relating to the Burgh of Stirling, 1124–1705* (Scottish Burgh Record Society, 1884), no. 21.

[21] F. W. Maitland, ed., *Memoranda de Parliamento* (RS, 1893), p. 184; D. Macpherson *et al.*, eds., *Rotuli Scotiae in Turri Londinensi* (London, 1814–19), vol. I, p. 40.

(normally two in each burgh, normally men and normally burgesses) to levy customs, to purchase goods and to make payments on its behalf; the custumars then presented their accounts (normally annually) to the peripatetic meetings of the royal Exchequer. The custumars were assisted by a tronar, who weighed goods on a public weigh-beam ('tron'), and a clerk of the cocket, who sealed a certification of customs payment for merchants and maintained duplicate records of customs payments for the crown.[22] Abroad, a conservator with jurisdictional powers was appointed by the crown to oversee and protect the interests of Scottish traders in the Low Countries.[23] Custumars and conservator apart, there was little other routine crown interference in maritime affairs, though serious judicial issues and contentious diplomatic business of interest to the port towns were the preserve of various crown courts and officers, including the Admiral or his deputes, who were usually of burgess origin.[24]

(iii) TRADE AND SHIPPING

The commodities of Scottish trade were remarkably similar to those passing through English ports, with a few notable exceptions, such as the absence of tin and lead shipments from Scotland. More significant differences between the two countries emerge in the comparative importance of exported and imported commodities. Scottish cloth exports, for instance, were comparatively small, whereas wool retained its pre-eminence among exports far longer in Scotland than it did in England.[25] Scotland also had fewer direct dealings with southern Europe. In the fourteenth century the bulk of Scottish exports were directed to Flanders and it was from here that the majority of imports probably also arrived. From the later fifteenth century, while Flanders still attracted a substantial proportion of Scottish trade, contacts with Normandy, Scandinavia, the eastern

22 Ewan, *Townlife*, pp. 74–5, 127–9; A. Murray, 'The customs accounts of Kircudbright, Wigtown and Dumfries, 1434–1560', *Transactions of the Dumfries and Galloway Natural History and Antiquarian Society*, 3rd series, 40 (1961–2), 136–42.

23 A. Stevenson, 'Trade between Scotland and the Low Countries' (PhD thesis, University of Aberdeen, 1982), pp. 185–201.

24 W. C. Dickinson, ed., *Early Records of the Burgh of Aberdeen, 1317, 1398–1407* (Scottish History Society, 1957), pp. cxii-cxiv; D. Ditchburn, 'Trade with northern Europe, 1297–1542', in M. Lynch, M. Spearman and G. Stell, eds., *The Scottish Medieval Town* (Edinburgh, 1988), pp. 174–5.

25 On the commodities of trade see Ditchburn, 'Trade with northern Europe', pp. 166–9; A. Stevenson, 'Trade with the south', in Lynch, Spearman and Stell, eds., *The Scottish Medieval Town*, pp. 180–202, *passim*; I. Blanchard, 'Northern wools and Netherlands markets at the close of the middle ages,' in G. Simpson, ed., *Scotland and the Low Countries 1124–1994* (East Linton, 1996), pp. 76–88; D. Ditchburn, 'A note on Scandinavian trade with Scotland in the later middle ages', in G. Simpson, ed., *Scotland and Scandinavia 800–1800* (Edinburgh, 1990), pp. 73–89; D. Ditchburn, 'Cargoes and commodities: Aberdeen's trade with Scandinavia and the Baltic, *c.* 1302–*c.* 1542', *Northern Studies*, 27 (1990), 12–22; A. Stevenson, 'Medieval commerce', in Jackson and Lythe, eds., *Montrose*, pp. 16–26.

Baltic and England become substantially more important, with England emerging as a major market for fish and a supplier of diverse manufactured products which had hitherto mainly been purchased in Flanders.[26]

The volume of Scottish trade in the later middle ages should not, however, be exaggerated.[27] The west and north exported little directly abroad, and although international traffic from these regions was supplemented by coastal traffic (in the north ferrying goods to and from ports such as Aberdeen, Dundee and Leith),[28] ship movements were probably small. In the 1360s and 1370s on average fewer than five ships departed annually with custumed goods from Inverness, the most important northern port; by the 1450s fewer than two did.[29] This decline in vessel movements partly reflected a decline in Scottish custumable exports which occurred from the 1380s and which reached a nadir in the early fifteenth century. Responses to this decline varied. Aberdeen, commercially unchallenged by other towns in the north-east, resorted temporarily to piracy to shore up its legitimate trade;[30] in central Scotland the two dominant towns, Perth and Dundee, attempted to expunge each other's trade by asserting conflicting privileges over the Tay's commerce;[31] and in the south-east, where older trading patterns had already been broken up by the loss of Berwick and the redirection of its trade through the Forth, Linlithgow and Edinburgh sought legal security over their satellite ports in 1389 and 1398.

In the event competition for the shrinking export trade merely confirmed earlier trends. Trade through east coast ports had long since been more substantial than that from other regions; but it now came to be increasingly concentrated on a handful of ports. Aberdeen, Dundee, Perth, Linlithgow and Edinburgh between them accounted for over three-quarters of Scotland's entire custumable exports between 1400 and 1410. These larger towns enhanced their position by exercising an economic domination well beyond those legally recognised trading precincts, or 'liberties', in which burgesses held exclusive trading rights.[32]

[26] Ditchburn, 'Trade with northern Europe', pp. 165–6; Stevenson, 'Trade with the south', pp. 200–1; evidence of England's importance derives mainly from a study of the English customs accounts (PRO E122/various classifications).

[27] M. Lynch and D. Ditchburn, eds., 'Economic development', in P. G. B. McNeill and H. L. MacQueen, eds., *Atlas of Scottish History to 1707* (Edinburgh, 1996), pp. 238–265; see also the works cited in n. 25 above.

[28] E.g. H. Booton, 'Inland trade: a study of Aberdeen in the later middle ages,' in Lynch, Spearman and Stell, eds., *The Scottish Medieval Town*, pp. 153–5; SRO, E71/12/5 (for Dundee); E71/29/2; E71/29/4 (for Leith).

[29] *ER*, II, pp. 97, 196–7, 242–3, 269, 320, 380, 408, 482, 531, 568, 615, V, p. 421, VI, pp. 303, 392.

[30] D. Ditchburn, 'The pirate, the policeman and the pantomime star: Aberdeen's alternative economy in the early fifteenth century', *Northern Scotland*, 12 (1992), 19–34; see also D. Ditchburn, 'Piracy and war at sea in late medieval Scotland', in T. C. Smout, ed., *Scotland and the Sea* (Edinburgh, 1992), pp. 35–58.

[31] W. Hay, ed., *Charters, Writs and Public Documents of the Royal Burgh of Dundee* (Dundee, 1880), no. 22. [32] See below, p. 722, for further details regarding trading liberties.

Aberdeen's zone of economic domination extended from Elgin and Forres in the north-west to Montrose in the south; by the mid-sixteenth century Dundee acted as a channel for regional exports stretching from Montrose to Anstruther (via, and including, its old rival Perth), with goods from Aberdeen and the Spey in the north and from Dunfermline and Kirkcaldy in the south also occasionally passing through the port.[33] Within the dominant group, however, Edinburgh and its port of Leith were already pre-eminent, and Leith's share of overseas trade continued to grow: by the 1470s more than half of Scotland's overseas trade was custumed there; and by the 1530s more than two-thirds.[34] Leith's overall dominance masks the different pace at which it acquired supremacy in particular exports. Its domination of the wool trade, for example, came much sooner than its command of the hide trade.[35] If anything, however, the customs figures underestimate Leith's overall significance, for it handled not only the exports of Edinburgh and its environs, but also goods cocketed elsewhere in the Forth and as far north as Dingwall and Tain, including some from the three other 'great towns of Scotland', Perth, Dundee and Aberdeen.[36]

Leith's domination of Scottish trade, and especially its role as a funnel through which the trade of other ports was channelled, suggests that in an economic sense all of eastern Scotland acted as its hinterland. Explanations for Leith's commercial supremacy are more difficult to determine. It certainly gained from Berwick's demise, but a combination of geographical and practical factors probably also contributed to its rise. Leith was closer to the larger foreign markets than most other Scottish ports and was a convenient location at which to assemble convoys of merchant vessels. More important, perhaps, was the growing concentration of governmental institutions and royal residences near the port. This provided a larger and more predictable demand for imports than elsewhere, thereby attracting incoming vessels to the port. With substantially more frequent vessel movements than elsewhere, it made sense for merchants from elsewhere to channel their exports via Leith. The alternative was a sometimes lengthy wait for a vessel which could adversely affect profits: whereas the custumars of Banff reported in 1389 that no ship had visited their port for some time, in the 1380s an average of almost eighteen ships departed from Leith annually, a figure which was to rise to over thirty in 1510–11 and 1512–13.[37] Yet whatever its reason, Leith's domination of later medieval Scottish trade was remarkable. Indeed, its

[33] Booton, 'Inland trade', pp. 153–5; SRO, E71/12/5; Torrie, *Medieval Dundee*, p. 82.

[34] *ER*, III, pp. 514–27, 539–53, 564–77, 590–603, 613–34, IV, pp. 1–21, 40–57, 72–91, 104–20, M. Lynch and A. Stevenson, 'Overseas trade: the Middle Ages to the sixteenth century', in McNeill and MacQueen, *Atlas of Scottish History*, p. 250.

[35] M. Lynch, Spearman and G. Stell, 'Towns and townspeople in fifteenth-century Scotland', in J. A. F. Thomson, ed., *Towns and Townspeople in the Fifteenth Century* (Gloucester, 1988), pp. 175–7.

[36] SRO, E71/29/2; E71/29/4.

[37] *ER*, III, pp. 52, 65, 86, 116, 132, 150, 168, 186, 203, 213; SRO, E71/29/2; E71/29/3. (These two sixteenth-century accounts are for eight-month periods only.)

domination of trade, coupled with the unusual centrality of the harbour to its economic vitality, makes Leith arguably the only true port town in medieval Scotland. It remains difficult, however, to determine the balance of Scotland's trade. Some have assumed that it was in substantial deficit throughout the later medieval period. Such assumptions lack credibility.[38] They are based too exclusively on the data for a narrow range of custumable exports, take little cognisance of other signs of prosperity in later Scotland and confuse a probable decline in the volume of trade, resulting from demographic trends, with a balance of payments problem. By the fifteenth century, at least, the signs are that Scotland was well able to pay for its extensive range of imports.

(iv) THE MARITIME COMMUNITY

The occupational structure of Scottish port towns is difficult to determine. While merchants directed the political life and commercial activity of the ports (some, as in England, entering government service) definition of the term 'merchant' is itself problematic, for not all merchants participated in overseas trade, while, by the sixteenth century at least, not all overseas traders were, in the conventional sense of the word, merchants.[39] The mercantile elite aside, particular employment opportunities arose in Scottish as in English ports for shipbuilders, mariners, pilots, ferrymen, fishermen, coopers, carters and porters or pynours. Little specific is known about most of these occupations, though the Aberdeen pynours, who included several women as well as men, had become a recognised but not incorporated trade by the later fifteenth century, a status similar to that enjoyed by mariners in at least some ports by the sixteenth century.[40] The proportion of port populations engaged in maritime-related employment remains uncertain, but it may be assumed that it was higher in Leith, where the port was the *raison d'être* of the settlement, than it was Aberdeen and Dundee, where the port was merely an adjunct to other economic activity. This, certainly, is the impression given by a study of property holdings in Canongate's small port of North Leith, where all of the identifiable property holders in *c.* 1500 were engaged in activities directly related to the workings of a port.[41] Such occupa-

[38] The negative case is postulated in Stevenson, 'Trade with the south', p. 198; Ditchburn, 'Trade with northern Europe', p. 176 [but I retract !]. The more optimistic case is put by E. Gemmill and N. Mayhew, *Changing Values in Medieval Scotland* (Cambridge, 1995), ch. 6. See also n. 19, above.

[39] M. Lynch, 'The social and economic structure of the larger towns, 1450–1600', in Lynch, Spearman and Stell, eds., *The Scottish Medieval Town*, pp. 262, 273.

[40] J. Bulloch, *The Pynours: Historical Notes on an Ancient Aberdeen Craft* (Aberdeen, 1887). By 1576 Leith mariners had for some time been in receipt of 'prime gilt', an impost used to support sailors in need; a similar fund was established at Kirkcaldy in 1591 (Marwick, ed., *Edinburgh Records*, IV, p. 54; Torrie and Coleman, *Historic Kirkcaldy*, pp. 13–14).

[41] S. Mowatt, *The Port of Leith* (Edinburgh, 1993), pp. 64–8.

tional specialisation in satellite, as opposed to integrated, ports, if such it was, was probably intensified by the restrictions on commercial activity in the satellite ports imposed by, or at the behest of, their burghal superiors. In the 1480s, for example, Edinburgh persuaded the crown to confirm a number of prohibitions on commercial activity by (South) Leith's inhabitants. They were forbidden from holding markets in Leith and forging partnerships with Edinburgh burgesses in 'merchandice-making'.[42] Still, even in Leith, other industries emerged: a brewery and maltmen, for example, are recorded there in the early sixteenth century.[43]

Foreign vessels routinely visited at least the larger Scottish ports. Their arrival brought an occasional influx of soldiers and, at ports such as Whithorn, pilgrims, but more especially merchants and mariners. Not all behaved themselves: a brawl between French and Spanish sailors is recorded 'on the schoyr of Leith', for instance, in 1496.[44] Central to the business and leisure interests of these foreigners were taverns and inns, whose keepers not only provided accommodation but who, by statute of 1426, were also expected to witness currency transactions involving foreigners.[45] The innkeeper's role was as much that of watchful eye over the foreigner as host. His policing duties were but one component in the regulation of alien commercial activity, much of it, in theory, designed to uphold the interests of the urban community as a whole by, in practice, discriminating against outsiders. Foreign merchants did not generally acquire commercial privileges or preferential customs rates, and one common ground for resentment of aliens elsewhere was thus not present in Scotland. But there were other reasons, too, for the apparent lack of friction between natives and aliens. For one, visits by foreigners were normally seasonal, concentrated in the months between spring and autumn, and of short duration;[46] for another their number was comparatively small. Between 1331 and 1333, when aliens were subject to additional customs dues at all ports except Berwick, substantial foreign activity is evident only at Aberdeen, Dundee and Inverkeithing.[47] By the early sixteenth century visits by foreign merchants had declined further: fewer than twenty out of almost three hundred consignments for export were handled by clearly identifiable foreigners at Dundee, for instance, in 1527.[48]

If transient aliens were limited, resident aliens were even scarcer. Thirteenth-century Berwick, with its Flemish mercantile entrepôt at the Red Hall, had been

[42] Marwick, ed., *Edinburgh Records*, I, pp. 46, 50.

[43] T. Dickson and J. B. Paul, eds., *Accounts of the Lord High Treasurer of Scotland* (Edinburgh, 1877–1916), vol. III, pp. 12, 222, V, pp. 206, 229.

[44] Neilson and Paton, eds., *Acts of Council*, II, pp. 38–9.

[45] T. Thomson and C. Innes, eds., *Acts of the Parliaments of Scotland* (Edinburgh, 1814–75), vol. II, p. 9. Legislation of 1424–7 repeatedly called for the establishment of inns in all burghs (not specifically ports), suggesting that there was a dearth of such accommodation (*ibid.*, pp. 6, 10, 14).

[46] Stevenson, 'Trade between Scotland and the Low Countries', p. 317.

[47] A. Stevenson, 'Foreign traffic and bullion exports, 1331–1333', in McNeill and MacQueen, *Atlas of Scottish History*, pp. 248–9.

[48] SRO, E71/12/1.

an exception snuffed out by the Anglo-Scottish wars.[49] Subsequently, even Leith failed to attract a large community of resident foreigners. Experiments in the early fifteenth century by some Hansards to station resident factors proved short-lived and it is tempting to assume that loneliness contributed to the suicide of their factor in Edinburgh in 1425.[50] With few resident foreigners, it follows that the topography of Scottish towns was largely undisturbed by the needs of such a community: whereas Scots abroad often possessed their own shrines and inhabited the same areas of a town, frequently giving their name to a particular street, there were no similar developments in later medieval Scotland's ports.

[49] Stevenson, 'Trade with the south', p. 188. For other foreigners in Berwick, see Ditchburn, 'Trade with northern Europe', p. 162.

[50] C. Sattler, ed., *Handelsrechnungen des Deutschen Ordens* (Leipzig, 1887), pp. 11, 20, 23, 28; K. Hohlbaum *et al.*, eds., *Hansisches Urkundenbuch* (Halle, Leipzig and Weimar, 1879–1939), vol. VI, no. 618; *ER*, IV, p. 412.

· 20 ·

Small towns 1270–1540

CHRISTOPHER DYER

(i) NUMBERS AND LOCATION OF SMALL TOWNS

A FIRST STAGE in understanding late medieval small towns must be to ask how many there were, and where they were located. But how do we recognise the small towns among the thousands of rural settlements? Those places can be identified which enjoyed the status of boroughs (in England and Wales) and burghs in Scotland. But that can only initiate the inquiry, because we know that many small boroughs and burghs existed only in law and never developed into urban settlements. Other places, especially in eastern England, became towns without gaining the privileges of a borough. The clerks used the word 'vill' to describe both rural and urban places, and in doing so echoed common speech, in which a wide range of settlements were called 'towns'. Without clear guidance from contemporary terminology, we must apply our definition of a town, searching for evidence of a compact and permanent settlement, in which a high proportion of the inhabitants pursued a variety of non-agricultural occupations. In addition, we might hope to find that the town served as the commercial, administrative or religious centre of its locality, and that it had the topographical characteristics of closely set houses, narrow plots and a market place.

Small towns are defined here arbitrarily as containing fewer than 2,000 inhabitants. Places have accordingly been excluded if they are found to exceed that figure at any time in the period, but some of them did not remain consistently

I am very grateful to the following who have helped me in the preparation of this chapter, and especially Table 20.1: M. Bailey, M. Beresford, J. Blair, P. Clark, S. Coleman, R. Croft, H. Dalwood, R. Edwards, G. Foard, H. Fox, J. Galloway, M. Gardiner, J. Hare, D. Hinton, J. Laughton, M. Mate, P. Northeast, J. Sheail, P. Stamper, J. Williams and A. Winchester. D. Crocker, H. Lovell, R. Peberdy and J. Sheail allowed me to use material from their unpublished theses. B. Harvey and R. Smith showed me articles in advance of publication. R. Griffiths saved me from error. S. Rigby made some useful criticisms. P. Dennison tutored me in Scottish urban history.

large. No lower limit has been imposed, though we would expect that most towns would be larger than the surrounding villages, and in practice the great majority of small towns had populations in excess of 300. Perhaps a uniform rule should not be applied over very diverse regions. In the West and North of Britain very few towns rose above 2,000 inhabitants, and places like Carlisle, Carmarthen or Glasgow, which had populations below that total for all or part of our period, none the less played an important role in their regions as centres of trade, government and religion. Similarly, at the bottom of the urban hierarchy, the very small knots of traders and artisans that gathered in Abergele, Ottery St Mary or Prestwick seem significant centres in relation to their neighbouring hamlets.

The definitions cannot be applied easily because of the incomplete nature of the evidence. The size of populations, and the degree of occupational diversity, have to be judged from surveys, rentals, tax lists, wills and court rolls. Lords tended not to intervene in the internal affairs of towns as closely as they did in their manors, so their records contain limited amounts of detail. A few towns escaped close documentation because they were sited across manorial, parish and even county boundaries. Written evidence is in especially short supply for the lesser Scottish towns. Archaeological research throws some light on size of towns, and the activities that went on within them, but excavation has been concentrated on large towns.

Small towns can therefore be identified and counted only with considerable difficulty. The numbers are subject to large margins of error, and will no doubt be improved and refined in the future (Table 20.1). In England about 660 places are known to have acquired burgage tenure or were called boroughs by 1509.[1] However, 124 of these have to be deducted because some early medieval boroughs had lapsed by 1270, the beginning of our period; some cannot be regarded as separate places, like the three settlements with burgage tenure which formed suburbs of Totnes; and others lack any convincing evidence that they ever developed urban characteristics. We must also leave aside the fifty-two towns which cannot be regarded as 'small'. Then a compensatory addition must be made of the towns defined in social, economic and topographical terms, but which did not have burgesses, burgage tenure or charters conferring borough privileges. This produces a total of 667 small towns which existed at some time between 1270 and 1540. Most had been founded before 1270, but a few late developers flourished around 1300, and then went into terminal decline, while others appear to have gained urban characteristics late in the period. The number of small towns at any one time must be estimated at around 600.

[1] M. W. Beresford and H. P. R. Finberg, *English Medieval Boroughs* (Newton Abbot, 1973); M. Beresford, 'English medieval boroughs: a hand-list: revisions, 1973–81', *UHY* (1981), 59–65; A. Crosby, 'The towns of medieval Lancashire: an overview', *Regional Bulletin for the Centre for North-West Regional Studies*, new series, 8 (1994), 7–18. Professor Beresford has kindly informed me of eight others discovered since 1981.

Table 20.1 *The small towns of England*

County	No. of small towns in the period 1270–1540	Area of county (in 000s of acres)	Area of land in county per town (in 000s of acres)
Bedfordshire	6	300	50
Berkshire	10	450	45
Buckinghamshire	11	480	44
Cambridgeshire	5	560	112
Cheshire	11	620	56
Cornwall	22	870	40
Cumberland	9	970	108
Derbyshire	10	640	64
Devon	48	1,650	34
Dorset	17	620	36
Durham	10	620	62
Essex	21	960	46
Gloucestershire	25	770	31
Hampshire (and Isle of Wight)	22	1,020	46
Herefordshire	10	540	54
Hertfordshire	16	400	25
Huntingdonshire	8	230	29
Kent	45	970	22
Lancashire	14	1,030	74
Leicestershire	9	520	58
Lincolnshire	22	1,690	77
Middlesex	2	220	110
Norfolk	21	1,300	62
Northamptonshire	9	630	70
Northumberland	16	1,280	80
Nottinghamshire	7	520	74
Oxfordshire	11	470	43
Rutland	2	97	49
Shropshire	17	860	51
Somerset	31	1,030	33
Staffordshire	18	690	38
Suffolk	32	940	29
Surrey	10	450	45
Sussex	24	900	38
Warwickshire	17	560	33
Westmorland	5	500	100
Wiltshire	27	860	32

Table 20.1 (*cont.*)

County	No. of small towns in the period 1270–1540	Area of county (in 000s of acres)	Area of land in county per town (in 000s of acres)
Worcestershire	12	440	37
Yorkshire			
East Riding	10	740	74
North Riding	14	1,350	96
West Riding	31	1,610	52
Total	667		46 (median area)

In Scotland and Wales we are much more dependent on counting the burghs and boroughs because of the scarcity of detailed evidence.[2] In Scotland 149 burghs are recorded before 1540, but a number have to be eliminated because of doubts on both legal and economic grounds. This leaves us with four 'large' towns and 118 which are candidates for the 'small-town' category. Fifty-three of these were 'burghs of barony' or 'burghs of regality' which were established between 1450 and 1540, in addition to the sixty-five burghs which had been founded by 1450. It is difficult to establish which of either legal category had urban characteristics. In Wales, 105 places have been listed as towns, mostly because they had some claim to be boroughs. There are doubts about the urban nature of twenty-six of these, and if three 'large' places are also removed, we are left with seventy-six potential small towns. At the beginning of our period there were about fifty Welsh towns; many were founded after 1270, and after some cases of chronic decline about fifty were left by the early sixteenth century.

This statistical exercise, which can be seen to depend on unavoidable speculations, can be concluded with a figure of 861 small towns which are likely to have existed in Britain in the later middle ages, and in any one year between 1270 and 1540 about 700 were functioning as urban communities. They were unevenly distributed (Map 20.1). In Scotland they lay thickest in the eastern part of the country from the Moray Firth to the borders, with a good scatter across the central belt and in Galloway. In Wales they were initially most numerous in the south, but the north gained many foundations in the period of Edwardian conquest between 1277 and 1307. Boroughs and burghs in these two countries are relatively numerous in relation to the overall population, and this is paralleled

[2] G. S. Pryde, *The Burghs of Scotland* (London, 1965); I. H. Adams, *The Making of Urban Scotland* (London, 1978), pp. 20–7; I. Soulsby, *The Towns of Medieval Wales* (Chichester, 1983).

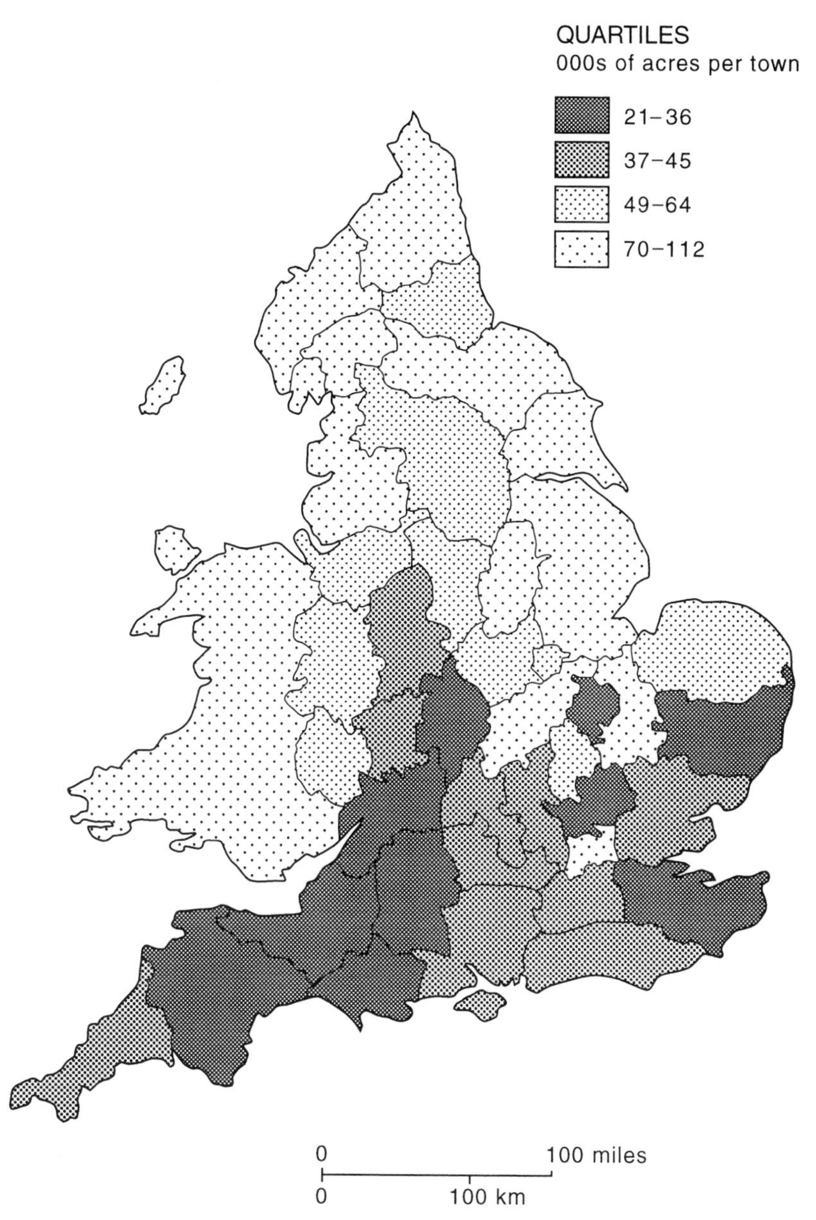

Map 20.1 Density of small towns in England and Wales 1270–1540

by the high density of boroughs found in thinly populated western England. Devon, for example, leads the English counties with a total of seventy-five boroughs, while the large, rich and populous county of Norfolk could muster only six. To some extent the balance is redressed if the towns which were not boroughs are brought into the picture, and the boroughs which do not seem to have become urban are removed. This gives Norfolk a more credible total of twenty-one small towns, but Devon is still left with forty-eight, and high densities are recorded in other western counties (Table 20.1). In parts of the East, such as Cambridgeshire and Nottinghamshire, towns seem rather scarce. There can be no simple economic or demographic explanation of these discrepancies. One factor must be the ambitions of lords of the West, who, without rich arable resources, founded boroughs in the hope of profit. In upland areas more market centres were needed because of the difficulties of transport across hills and steep valleys.[3] A close correlation can be observed between industrial development and the proliferation of market towns, which gave Devon, Suffolk and Kent many small towns, but left mainly agricultural counties like Bedfordshire or the East Riding of Yorkshire with fewer, more widely spaced centres. Regional economies and cultures were expressed in distinct patterns of urbanisation, just as rural settlements and farming systems differed from district to district.

(ii) URBAN FUNCTIONS OF SMALL TOWNS

The quantity of small towns must contribute to our assessment of the importance of the urban sector in medieval society. In Wales around 1300, the town dwellers (almost entirely in small towns) are thought to have amounted to almost a fifth of the whole population. In England at the same time, if the mean population of small towns lay around 750, then 600 small towns could have contained 450,000 people, almost a half of the urban total, or a tenth of that of the whole country. Throughout Britain in *c.* 1300 there was a small town for every 8,000 country people.[4] For most peasants, a small town would have provided their nearest contact with the urban world, and they could have chosen between two or three. Even a remote village in north Derbyshire, such as Eyam, had access to Bakewell, Tideswell and Castleton which all lay within six miles, and Sheffield and Chesterfield at a distance of twelve miles.

But can these places really be regarded as towns? We might feel uneasy at including minuscule settlements like Castleton in the same category as York. There are good reasons for thinking of such modest places as properly urban,

[3] M. Kowaleski, *Local Markets and Regional Trade in Medieval Exeter* (Cambridge, 1995), p. 49.

[4] Soulsby, *Towns of Medieval Wales*, pp. 22–3; on English and Scottish population R. M. Smith, 'Demographic developments in rural England, 1300–48: a survey', in B. M. S. Campbell, ed., *Before the Black Death* (Manchester, 1991), pp. 48–51; R. Nicholson, *Scotland: The Later Middle Ages* (Edinburgh, 1974), p. 2.

even if they differ in many respects from the cities in the upper ranks of the hierarchy.

Let us begin with the agrarian dimension of small-town life, because this often causes problems for those who feel that cows and corn are incompatible with urbanism. Small towns must be carefully distinguished from town-like settlements in which agriculture predominated, or which did not develop in size or occupational variety. Traders and craftsmen might take up permanent residence in villages with chartered markets, as at Pinchbeck in Lincolnshire, but if the great majority of the inhabitants made their living from the land, these places cannot be called towns.[5] Villages which contained so many smallholders and part-time craftsmen that they might be equated with the 'open village' of the nineteenth century still count as villages. Markets, both official and informal, might grow on road sides at the edge of parish or manor, and some became towns, like Stony Stratford, but many remained small and restricted in their range of occupations. Some villages adjacent to large towns developed into quasi-suburbs, as at Sowe near Coventry, but their mainly peasant population remained. On major road junctions or ferry points groups of inns formed, as had happened by 1379 at Cawood on the Yorkshire Ouse; ostlers and their servants, however, cannot constitute a town on their own. Likewise, industrial villages, with a concentration of peasant-weavers or peasant-miners and few other occupations, must remain in our classification as rural settlements. Drawing a dividing line through the rather fuzzy categories of very small towns, market villages and industrial villages leaves the historian with few easy choices.[6]

Applying such definitions cannot resolve many ambiguous cases. Fortunately, there were types of small town with clearly separate urban economies. When a new town was founded on a piece of land carved out of the fields of an existing village, in legal and administrative terminology the 'borough' was kept distinct from the 'foreign', and the settlements stood apart, with a 'bond end' where the peasants still lived. The restricted size of the borough's territory – 150 acres (61 ha) at Baldock for example or 95 acres (38 ha) at Boroughbridge – could not possibly have provided a living for the town's inhabitants.[7] They could acquire land beyond their own fields, but in the Cotswold towns, or at Leeds, most households depended on their urban occupations, leading to quite a sharp division between town and country.[8] More problematic were the many towns with extensive fields,

[5] G. Platts, *Land and People in Medieval Lincolnshire* (Lincoln, 1985), pp. 197, 301.

[6] C. Dyer, 'The hidden trade of the middle ages', *J of Historical Geography*, 18 (1992), 141–57; R. B. Dobson, 'Yorkshire towns in the late fourteenth century', *Publications of the Thoresby Society*, 59 (1986), 18; J. Patten, 'Village and town: an occupational study', *Agricultural History Review*, 20 (1972), 1–16; L. R. Poos, *A Rural Society after the Black Death: Essex, 1350–1525* (Cambridge, 1991), pp. 35–41.

[7] M. Beresford, *New Towns of the Middle Ages* (London, 1967), pp. 452–3, 523–4; the general point is discussed on pp. 220–5.

[8] R. H. Hilton, *The English Peasantry in the Later Middle Ages* (Oxford, 1975), pp. 76–81; J. W. Kirby, ed., *The Manor and Borough of Leeds* (Thoresby Society, 57, 1983), pp. xlvii–lix.

or closely integrated into a rural settlement. Caernarfon had been provided with nearly 1,500 acres (600 ha) of land, and its burgesses usually held agricultural land. At Lutterworth in Leicestershire the houses of the town were mingled with those of an extensive peasant settlement, and the fields contained 69 yardlands (1,725 acres (690 ha)). Such places should surely still be regarded as having an urban economy, providing that there was a sufficient variety of occupations among the inhabitants, and agrarian activities did not exercise a dominating influence. At Ayr, for example, 24 rigs (about 6 acres (2.4 ha) of land) were attached to each burgage, which was not enough to feed a family.[9] One fourteenth-century Ayr tenant acquired as much as 64 acres (26 ha), but there can be no doubt that the majority of the population of more than 1,000 pursued mainly non-agricultural activities. The farming interests of better-off townspeople and nearby villagers has been explored through the wills of the inhabitants of four Kentish small towns in the fifteenth and early sixteenth centuries.[10] Among the town dwellers (from Ashford, Hythe, Milton and Sittingbourne) 35 per cent bequeathed agricultural land, compared with 71 per cent of country people. Some of the testators from the towns must have been renting out their country property, as only a fifth of them mentioned cattle or corn. No impermeable barrier divided town from country, but there were important differences of degree.

The agrarian side of small towns should be regarded as a positive advantage for the inhabitants. The town population was secured against grain shortages by access to arable, and could obtain cheap supplies of pasture, firewood or turf from common land. Horses which had an essential role in trade were kept in large numbers – 120 of them were pastured near Carmarthen in the late thirteenth century.[11] Land gave a secure investment for commercial profits, and rents, or money from the sale of property, could be ploughed back into business ventures. The inhabitants of large towns likewise cultivated fields, and acquired agricultural land, sometimes in great quantity, but no one doubts the urban status of Cambridge or Aberdeen, where these activities are well known. The towns' direct involvement in rural life through collective and individual landed assets provided one element in the constant interaction between town and country.

Studies of large towns rightly emphasise their central place function, by which they acted as administrative and ecclesiastical centres as well as venues for trade. By defining an upper limit of 2,000 we are counting as 'small' some quite impor-

[9] R. A. Griffiths, ed., *Boroughs of Mediæval Wales* (Cardiff, 1978), pp. 74–101; J. Goodacre, *The Transformation of a Peasant Economy: Townspeople and Villagers in the Lutterworth Area, 1500–1700* (Aldershot, 1994), pp. 8–29; E. Ewan, *Townlife in Fourteenth-Century Scotland* (Edinburgh, 1990), pp. 109–10; W. Dodd, 'Ayr: a study of urban growth', *Ayrshire Archaeological and Natural History Collections*, 10 (1970–2), 306–24.

[10] A. J. F. Dulley, 'Four Kent towns at the end of the middle ages', in M. Roake and J. Whyman, eds., *Essays in Kentish History* (London, 1973), pp. 61–3.

[11] Griffiths, ed., *Boroughs of Mediæval Wales*, p. 150.

tant places: English county towns such as Stafford and Lancaster, many Scottish heads of sheriffdoms, like Banff and Peebles, as well as cathedral cities like St Andrews in Scotland and St David's in Wales. A much larger number of small towns inherited from the period before 1270 a position at the head of such administrative units as hundreds, commotes, jurisdictional liberties, baronies and large manors. A high proportion were linked with a monastery or important church. In Cornwall and Devon the newly smelted tin was stamped at nine 'coinage' towns giving an official boost to Bodmin, Lostwithiel and Truro, which served the busiest mining districts.[12] Minor centres of government and worship were being renewed and changed after 1270, for example, by the building of new castles in North Wales, or by the rise in status of some aristocratic residences like Thornbury under the dukes of Buckingham, or the foundation of new collegiate churches at Higham Ferrers or Ruthin. A large number of small towns were, however, associated with no greater focus of power than a manor house or a chapel, and depended on their market to establish influence over the surrounding countryside.

The small towns' fully urban character can be tested by examining their occupational diversity. The large towns could have more than a hundred separate occupations, but small towns could usually muster between twenty and forty. They can be calculated by gathering all of the occupational surnames in the period before 1348 when the names are most likely to reflect the trade or craft of the bearers, or their fathers or husbands. Thirty-eight separate non-agricultural occupations have been recorded for Godmanchester for example. Occupational descriptions in a series of borough court records or in the poll tax allows the identification of between twenty-eight and thirty-five different trades and crafts at Halesowen, Hedon or the Cotswold towns of Stow-on-the-Wold and Winchcombe. In some towns the annual court leet systematically amerced a wide range of different traders and artisans for breaking regulations on price and quality. At Basingstoke, which lies near to the upper limit of our small-town category, seventeen are listed in 1399, but the figure rises to twenty-eight in 1464, going beyond the usual butchers, bakers, carpenters, tailors, smiths and shoemakers to include such specialists as a brasier, haberdasher and hosier. Excavated finds of raw materials, waste products and tools can indicate a wide range of trades. For example, at Elgin most of the processes of clothmaking, including dyeing, seem to have been practised, together with iron, bronze and glassworking, and the carving of bone and antler.[13]

[12] G. R. Lewis, *The Stannaries: A Study of Medieval Tin Miners of Cornwall and Devon*, repr. (Truro, 1965), pp. 44–5; J. Hatcher, *English Tin Production and Trade before 1550* (Oxford, 1973), pp. 76–9.

[13] J. A. Raftis, *A Small Town in Late Medieval England* (PIMSST, 53, Toronto, 1982), p. 135; R. H. Hilton, 'Small town society in England before the Black Death', in R. Holt and G. Rosser, eds., *The Medieval Town* (London, 1990), pp. 76–80; R. H. Hilton, 'Lords, burgesses and hucksters', *P&P*, 97 (1982), 9–12 (Halesowen); Humberside RO, DDHE/20,21 (Hedon borough records);

The smallest towns tended to provide a living for a few representatives of each occupation, with perhaps only one or two weavers, tailors, smiths, coopers, shoemakers and so on, thus catering for the varied needs of their hinterlands. Variety was institutionalised in market places where space was allocated for the stalls of different traders. Loughborough had a mercery, drapery, ironmongery and butchers' shambles. More remarkable for a very small town, Newmarket in the fifteenth century divided its market between butchers, drapers, ropers, mercers, barkers (tanners), ironmongers, cheesemongers and cordwainers.[14] If small towns had a concentration of those pursuing similar trades, it was among sellers of food and drink. A high proportion of any list of traders will be taken up with brewers, bakers, butchers, fishmongers and cooks, and low grade retailers who distributed foodstuffs prepared by others, notably the gannockers, tapsters, or tranters who dealt in ale. Even the smallest town would regularly record each year (through the enforcement of the price regulating assize of bread and ale) twenty or thirty brewers and sellers of ale, and a half-dozen bakers. In some places the food and drink trades account for a high proportion of the town's occupations – 41 per cent of those at Howden in 1379, for example.[15] Trade in food and drink gave much part-time or occasional employment, especially to women. Concentrations of those engaged in other trades are encountered less often, but groups of textile workers can be found quite frequently, and in a few places ironworkers bulked large in the population. Very rarely were our small towns sufficiently sophisticated in their economies or government for their artisans to be organised into fraternities, though six 'craft guilds' are recorded at Loughborough, and two at Ruthin.[16]

The small town's social range is rightly said to have been more limited than that of the great cities. It lacked both an elite of great aristocrats and merchants, and swarms of beggars and criminals at the other end of the social scale. This generalisation needs to be qualified: first, the landed gentry figured prominently in small-town society. In some seigneurial boroughs the founders' successors continued to live in the town, like the lords of Birmingham, who

Footnote 13 (*cont.*)
J. R. Boyle, *The Early History of the Town and Port of Hedon in the East Riding of the County of York* (Hull and York, 1895); Hilton, *English Peasantry*, pp. 78–9 (Stow and Winchcombe); F. J. Baijent and J. E. Millard, *A History of the Ancient Town and Manor of Basingstoke* (London, 1889), pp. 240–88; R. M. Spearman, 'Workshops, materials and débris – evidence of early industries', in M. Lynch, M. Spearman and G. Stell, eds., *The Scottish Medieval Town* (Edinburgh, 1988), pp. 137–45 (Elgin).

[14] D. Postles, 'An English small town in the later middle ages: Loughborough', *UH*, 20 (1993), 15; P. May, *Newmarket, Medieval and Tudor* (Newmarket, 1982), p. 45.

[15] R. Smith, 'A periodic market and its impact upon a manorial community: Botesdale, Suffolk and the manor of Redgrave, 1280–1300', in Z. Razi and R. Smith, eds., *Medieval Society and the Manor Court* (Oxford, 1996), pp. 450–81; P. J. P. Goldberg, 'Urban identity and the poll taxes of 1377, 1379, and 1381', *Ec.HR*, 2nd series, 43 (1990), 211.

[16] Postles, 'Loughborough', 14; Griffiths, ed., *Boroughs of Mediæval Wales*, pp. 255–7.

occupied a moated house near the market place. Similarly, the impressive tower of the lords of Alloa overlooked their new burgh of barony at the end of the fifteenth century. In North Wales the constable of the castle sometimes served as the mayor of the adjacent borough. Everywhere, gentry who had no feudal link with the town are found acquiring urban property, especially in the fifteenth century – at places as varied as Chelmsford, Henley-on-Thames and Caernarfon. These purchases might have simply been investments, for the sake of good returns in rent, but the houses were also used as residences, and aristocratic families in Cumberland like the Huttons and Lowthers stayed on occasion in Penrith, and town-dwelling gentry appear in places as small as Pershore and Coggeshall.[17]

The second reservation about the restricted structure of our towns relates to the merchants, who would not be expected to congregate in places which traded on a small scale in low value goods over short distances. However, wool merchants, often in ones and twos, are found at Birmingham, Melton Mowbray, Darlington and Hartlepool. They did not operate on a restricted scale – a Basingstoke merchant in 1274 was handling fifty-two sacks of wool worth more than £300. Nor were they local in their horizons, as Nicholas Adele de la Pole from Andover, where there was a concentration of wool merchants in the 1270s, was buying wool as far afield as Faringdon in Berkshire and Tewkesbury in Gloucestershire, and then shipping it overseas through Southampton.[18] The presence of the wealthy Gloucestershire woolmongers of Northleach and Chipping Campden has left its mark in their tombs and the impressive late fourteenth-century house of William Grevil, the 'flower of the wool merchants of the whole of England'. With the rise of clothmaking, a number of small fifteenth-century towns, such as Bradford-on-Avon, Trowbridge and Lavenham came under the economic domination of wealthy clothiers. As some small towns were also ports, they were also more likely to contain at least a few merchants.[19]

[17] L. Watts, 'Birmingham moat: its history, topography and destruction', *Transactions of the Birmingham and Warwickshire Arch. Soc.*, 89 (1978–9), 1–77; A. T. Simpson and S. Stevenson, *Alloa* (Scottish Burgh Survey, 1983); G. Stell, 'Urban buildings', in Lynch, Spearman and Stell, eds., *The Scottish Medieval Town*, p. 61; H. Grieve, *The Sleepers and the Shadows* (Chelmsford, 1988), pp. 78–9 (Chelmsford), 38 (Coggeshall); R. B. Peberdy, 'The economy, society and government of a small town in late medieval England: a study of Henley-on-Thames from *c.* 1300 to *c.* 1540' (PhD thesis, University of Leicester, 1994), pp. 169–72; Griffiths, ed., *Boroughs of Mediæval Wales*, pp. 86, 90–3 (Caernarfon); A. J. L. Winchester, *Landscape and Society in Medieval Cumbria* (Edinburgh, 1987), pp. 121–9 (Penrith); J. S. Roskell, *The Commons in the Parliament of 1422* (Manchester, 1954), pp. 230–1.

[18] T. H. Lloyd, *The English Wool Trade in the Middle Ages* (Cambridge, 1977), pp. 50–3, 132; R. A. Pelham, 'The trade relations of Birmingham during the middle ages', *Transactions of the Birmingham Arch. Soc.*, 62 (1939), 32–40; C. M. Fraser, 'The pattern of trade in the North-East of England, 1265–1350', *N Hist.*, 4 (1969), 50–2; Baijent and Millard, *Basingstoke*, p. 185.

[19] E. M. Carus-Wilson, 'The woollen industry before 1550', *VCH*, Wiltshire, IV, pp. 134–6, 141–4; A. Betterton and D. Dymond, *Lavenham: Industrial Town* (Lavenham, 1989), pp. 6–15, 25–49.

In the absence of a large group of merchants the elite in most small towns consisted of traders who may have had wider horizons and larger profit margins than most artisans, but were still confined to dealing in relatively mundane commodities in their localities. Typical occupations of the leading townsmen at such places as Axbridge, Chelmsford, Okehampton and Thornbury were tanners, dyers, waxchandlers, butchers, cornmongers, innkeepers and even a cook.[20] The core of the small-town community was provided by artisans and small-scale retailers, using the labour of their own families and no more than one or two employees, and confining their activities to a single workshop or stall.

As in any town or village, wage-earning labourers made up a substantial minority of the householders. Servants, full-time employees living with their masters, have been seen as especially characteristic of urban society, often accounting for more than a fifth of the population recorded in the poll taxes, but their numbers varied in the small towns. In Yorkshire in 1379 the percentage of servants rose as high as 22 and 16 at Howden and Ripon, but could be as low as 6 at Sheffield. Throughout England the lay subsidy of 1524–5 suggests that small towns contained concentrations of wage earners. Labourers and servants together frequently accounted for more than 40 per cent of the inhabitants.[21] In any series of borough court records servants appear as an unruly group, but they also carried more responsibility than we would expect from their subordinate social and legal position. They seem often to have negotiated sales on behalf of their employers, leading to a butcher and his servant being jointly accused of dealing in bad meat. But they also traded on their own account, and could sue or be sued for their debts or trespasses. For example, at Andover in 1387 John, servant of John Swon, brought a plea of debt to recover 1s. 3d. from Thomas Frome.[22] Some employers held their servants in high regard judging from the bequests to them of goods and even property in fifteenth- and early sixteenth-century wills, such as John Bird of Woodbridge, who in 1462 left to Robert his servant the loom 'on which Ella my daughter, used to weave'.[23]

[20] H. Lovell, 'Axbridge, Somerset: history of a Domesday borough, with special reference to the growth of local government' (MPhil thesis, University of London, 1970), p. 51; Grieve, *The Sleepers and the Shadows*, pp. 80–1; Kowaleski, *Exeter*, p. 303; R. H. Hilton, 'Towns in English feudal society', in R. H. Hilton, *Class Conflict and the Crisis of Feudalism* (London, 1985), p. 177; R. H. Hilton, 'Low-level urbanisation: the seigneurial borough of Thornbury in the middle ages', in Razi and Smith, eds., *Manor Court*, pp. 482–517.

[21] Goldberg, 'Urban identity and the poll taxes', 199; J. Yang, *The Wage Earners of England 1500–1550* (Hangzhou, 1991), pp. 94–114, 212–17.

[22] Hampshire RO, 37M88 2/HC/14 (Andover borough court rolls, 1387–8, have especially plentiful references to activities of servants). A butcher and servant were accused jointly of selling meat of a drowned pig at Pershore in 1392: PRO SC2/210/72.

[23] Suffolk RO, Ipswich branch, J421/2 (from a transcript kindly made available to me by Mr Peter Northeast).

Small towns attracted fewer social marginals than large cities, partly because they lacked the concentration of very wealthy households and institutions from which beggars could make a living. The sudden growth of a new town, as at Halesowen after 1270, created considerable social problems as single women without regular jobs, petty traders, lodgers and transients gathered to form a Rabelaisian underworld. In more settled towns there were still those who did not fit easily into a conventional official framework; up to thirty-four men in early fifteenth-century Alcester were reported in the borough court to be 'out of assize', that is, failing to take the oath that would bring them into the self-policing organisation of the frankpledge. Fears of disorder were raised by travellers and temporary lodgers, identified as Welsh in the Gloucestershire towns of Thornbury and Moreton-in-Marsh, and as Scots at Northallerton in Yorkshire. At Tiverton in Devon in 1451 John Irissheman, described as a pauper, caused alarm by living 'suspiciously'. Even among the established population the stresses and temptations of urban life could lead to social ruin: the two daughters of Hugh the Baker of Burton-on-Trent had evidently turned to prostitution and had by 1319 entered local legend as Agnes 'Dear' and Emma 'Better cheap'. Numbers cannot be calculated, but small towns judging from regular complaints and clean-up campaigns must have harboured their fair share of brothels and prostitutes.[24]

(iii) HINTERLANDS AND TRADE

The commercial functions of small towns are reflected in their hinterlands. The marketing zone can be reconstructed by mapping the places of residence of parties to pleas of debt recorded in court rolls, and also the place of origin of outsiders paying to acquire trading privileges. Research on a dozen small towns shows that between 41 and 67 per cent of debtors and traders came from within 6.2 miles (10 km), and the great majority within 15.5 miles (25 km). Some Welsh towns were granted a market monopoly within a specified radius – 15 miles at Aberystwyth, 8 miles for Caernarfon. The Scottish burghs were also given market privileges in defined territories. These could be quite large. Peebles, for example, was supposed to have a trading monopoly within an area measuring 22 miles (35 km) from east to west, and 28 miles (45 km) from north

[24] Hilton, 'Small town society in England', pp. 82–96; Warwickshire County RO, CR1886/141–8 (Alcester court rolls, 1424–48); Hilton, 'Hucksters', 13 (Thornbury); Westminster Abbey Muniments, 8358, 8359 (unruly Welsh at Moreton, 1377, 1414); C. Newman, 'Local court administration within the liberty of Allertonshire, 1470–1540', *Archives*, 22 (1995), 22; D. G. Stuart, ed., 'A rental of the borough of Burton, 1319', *Collections for a History of Staffordshire*, 4th series, 16 (1994), 23; Suffolk RO (Ipswich branch), HD64/1/28, refers to a couple who kept 'a bordelhouse' at Orford, Suffolk, in 1479, where they 'entertained the wives of their neighbours against the will of their husbands'. The same town (HD64/1/29) contained 'a lane called *Gropecuntlane*'.

to south, and Rutherglen was granted trading rights over a substantial part of Lanarkshire.[25]

The country can be divided into a series of marketing territories, in which each town had its sphere of influence, but hinterlands overlapped, and neighbouring towns competed. In Wales and Scotland the privileged burgesses had to defend their monopolies: traders in the country or even out at sea were brought before courts in fourteenth-century Wales for not using the borough markets. Caernarfon sought to prohibit trade at Bangor, just as Ayr conducted disputes with nearby Irvine. These conflicts show that the monopolies were taken seriously, but also that in practice they were broken.[26] In England the effects of competition can be seen in the shape of the hinterlands. Hedon in East Yorkshire dominated the trade of Holderness to the east of the town, but had few contacts with villages to the west which looked to Beverley and Hull (Map 20.2). Andover's trade was restricted by the influence of towns to the south, giving its hinterland a lopsided appearance (Map 20.3). Successful towns often lay on the frontiers of contrasting rural landscapes, and their markets acted as points of contact between buyers and sellers with complementary needs – those with arable and pastoral specialisms, for example. Small towns could stretch their trading horizons if they could host a successful fair. St Ives' (Hunts.) international event was hard to match, but those at Chipping Campden and Winchcombe were not so unusual in attracting dealers throughout their region and beyond.[27]

Who bought and sold in these commercial territories? The aristocracy had an important role in the trade of larger towns, and indeed we can show that their involvement extended to small market centres. The produce of lords' demesnes in Oxfordshire was sometimes sold in markets such as Witney and Aylesbury. But wool was usually sold by private treaty to a big city merchant, and grain was often carried to a large town or a port where a better price could be obtained. The greater lords bought joints of meat or baskets of fish from market towns, and the monks of Durham around 1300 patronised merchants in Darlington and Hartlepool, but their more bulky and expensive supplies tended to come from fairs or major towns and ports. Small towns caught the trade of the aristocracy when they were on the move, or if a major residence stood nearby, like the castles which dominated many Welsh boroughs. In the early fifteenth century the Talbot family spent much time at their house at Blakemere in Shropshire and

[25] C. Dyer, 'Market towns and the countryside in late medieval England', *Canadian J of History*, 31 (1996), 17–35; Griffiths, ed., *Boroughs of Mediæval Wales*, pp. 33, 79; R. Fox, 'Urban development, 1100–1700', in G. Whittington and I. D. Whyte, *An Historical Geography of Scotland* (London, 1983), p. 83; J. M. Houston, 'The Scottish burgh', *Town Planning Review*, 25 (1954–5), 116.

[26] Griffiths, ed., *Boroughs of Mediæval Wales*, p. 98; I. J. Sanders, 'Trade and industry in some Cardiganshire towns in the middle ages', *Ceredigion*, 3 (1959), 319–36; E. Torrie, 'The guild in fifteenth-century Dunfermline', in Lynch, Spearman and Stell, eds., *The Scottish Medieval Town*, p. 259; Ewan, *Townlife*, pp. 144–5.

[27] Dyer, 'Market towns'.

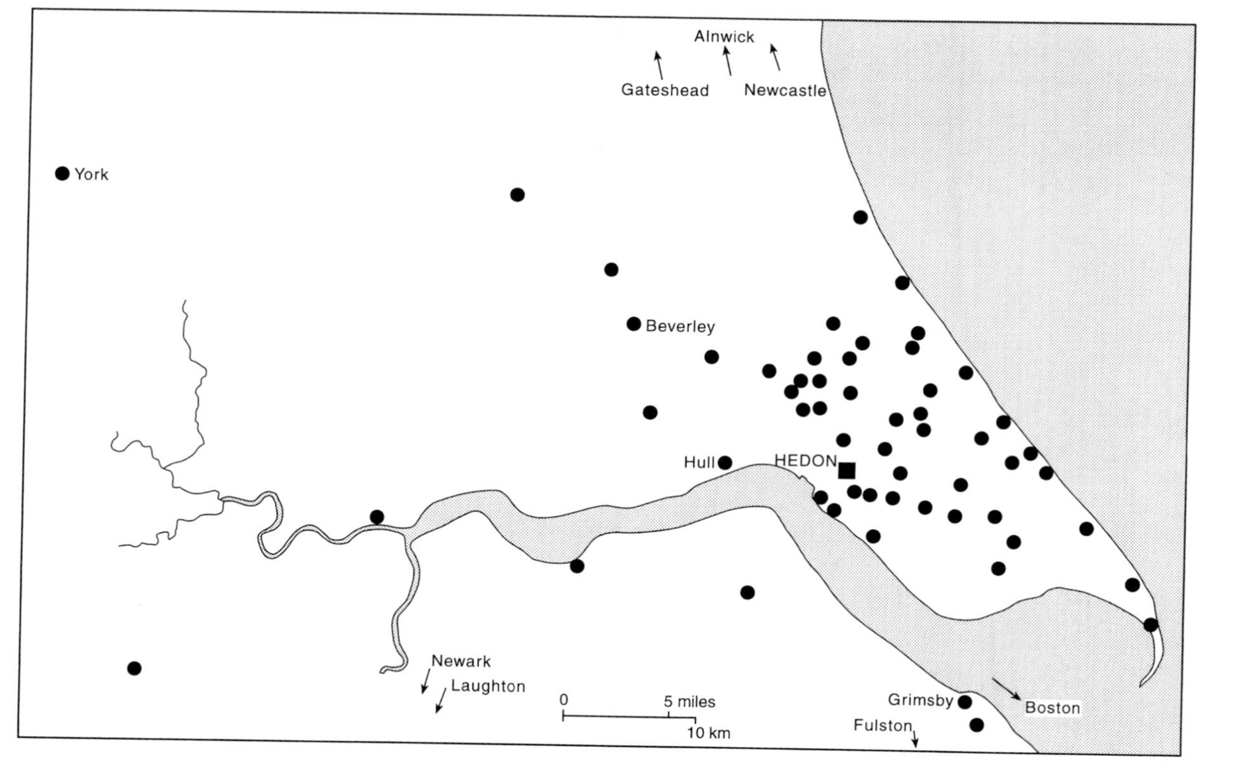

Map 20.2 The hinterland of Hedon (Yorks.)
Each dot represents evidence of a trade contact, usually a debt recorded in the borough court.

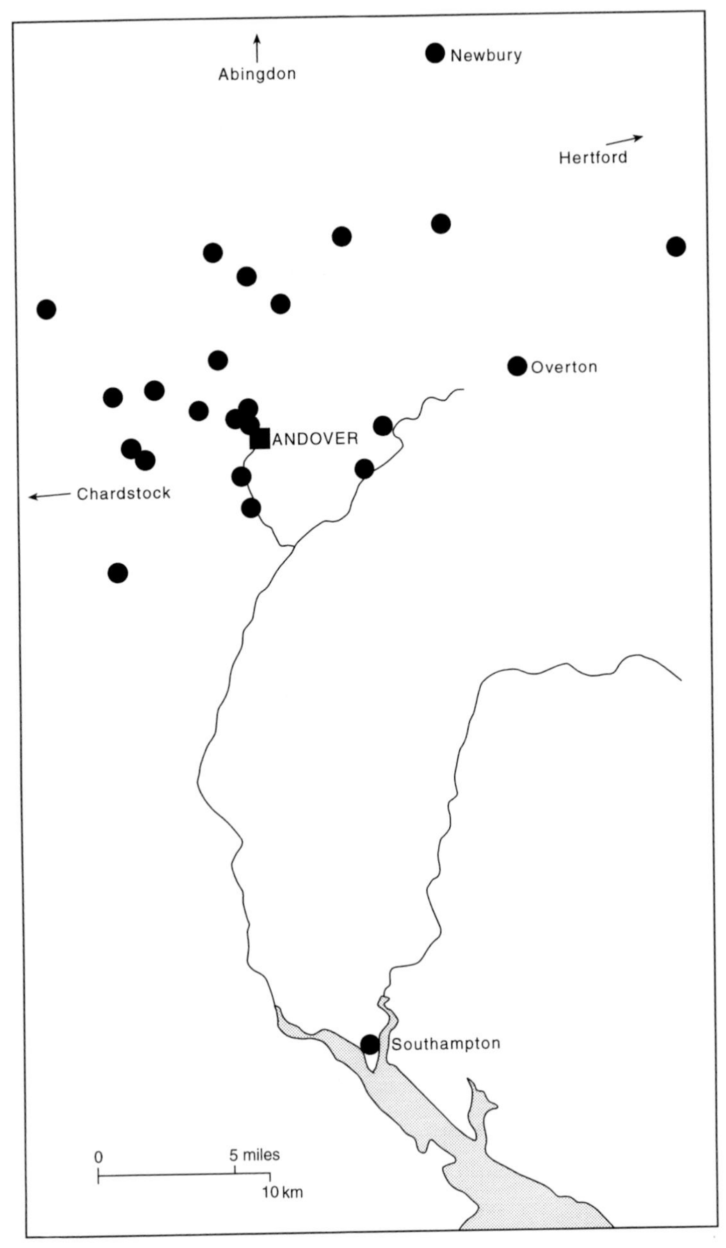

Map 20.3 The hinterland of Andover (Hants.)
Each dot represents evidence of a trade contact, usually a debt recorded in the borough court.

bought hundreds of gallons of ale from the market town of Whitchurch. Rich consumers might be attracted by local specialisms, like the eels of Forfar and the rabbits of Crail bought by the Scottish royal household in the fourteenth century.[28] The everyday routine of the small-town economy depended on the regular sales and purchases of those living in its hinterland, who included gentry and clergy, but above all thousands of peasants, rural artisans and wage earners with modest means, who cumulatively disposed of large quantities of goods and cash. The range of products sold – inexpensive clothing, shoes, ironware and above all basic food and drink – reflected the needs of this clientele.[29]

Hinterlands can be defined in more human terms as the areas from which migrants reached the towns. They were generally more extended than the marketing zones. The new Welsh towns provide a rather special case because they were set up to colonise conquered territory, and the burgesses were often recruited from England. Holt, for example, in the first thirty-five years after its foundation in 1282, drew settlers from as far afield as Derby and Doncaster as well as nearby Flintshire and Cheshire. Older towns attracted people both from local villages and from well beyond the normal reach of their market. Burton-on-Trent's tenants in 1319 included people named from forty-nine places, and twenty-six of these had travelled more than 10 miles (16 km).[30] When surnames cease to provide a guide to migration patterns, the movements of serfs can be traced from manorial records. Favourite destinations for peasants from the Huntingdonshire manors of Ramsey Abbey were Ramsey itself, St Ives and St Neots, all within a dozen miles (20 km), but again individuals migrated much further, like Simon Duntyng of Hemingford Abbots, who moved more than 40 miles (64 km) to Daventry in 1377.[31]

Trade depended on communications by road rather than river for most inland small towns. Some of the most successful small towns were sited on major routes, notably Chelmsford on the main road from the capital to Colchester. Andover and Alton with their many inns developed a specialised function as stopping points for long-distance traffic. The carts which carried imported goods from

[28] D. Postles, 'Markets for rural produce in Oxfordshire, 1086–1350', *Midland History*, 12 (1987), 19; D. L. Farmer, 'Marketing the produce of the countryside, 1200–1500', in E. Miller, ed., *Ag.HEW*, vol. III (Cambridge, 1991), pp. 324–430; C. Dyer, 'The consumer and the market in the later middle ages', *Ec.HR*, 2nd series, 42 (1989), 305–26; Fraser, 'Pattern of trade', 50–2; B. F. Harvey, 'The aristocratic consumer in the long thirteenth century', *Thirteenth-Century England*, 6 (1997), 17–37; Ewan, *Townlife*, p. 67.

[29] C. Dyer, 'Were peasants self sufficient? English villagers and the market, 900–1350', in E. Mornet, ed., *Campagnes médiévales: l'homme et son espace. Etudes offertes à Robert Fossier* (Paris, 1995), pp. 653–66.

[30] D. Pratt, 'The medieval borough of Holt', *Transactions of the Denbigh Historical Society*, 14 (1965), 9–74; Stuart, ed., 'Burton', 12–13.

[31] J. A. Raftis, *Tenure and Mobility: Studies in the Social History of the Medieval English Village* (Toronto, 1964), pp. 167–82.

Southampton in the fifteenth century often headed for large towns, but a significant number had as their destinations Abingdon, Burford, Devizes and similar places, and even took the long haul to Chesterfield.[32]

Small towns were integrated into wider commercial networks. They gathered in the produce of the countryside by a number of different mechanisms. Peasants brought to market both carts loaded with grain and baskets of eggs, butter and fruit. Cornmongers and woolmongers went out to buy in the villages. In districts which developed rural industries, small towns provided meeting and collection points for the scattered artisans and traders. Circuits of markets developed so that traders could acquire goods on successive days, selling them at a venue at the end of the week. So the minor Lancashire market held at Rochdale on Wednesdays could feed into the locally important Saturday market at Manchester.[33] Commodities were consumed in the small town itself, but much would be passed on to larger towns. We find Aberdeen receiving in the fifteenth century malt from Elgin and timber from Banff. In Devon, Okehampton and Tiverton tanners supplied leather to Exeter.[34]

Goods also flowed down the commercial chain from the ports and large towns to small-town retailers. Merchants in Bristol sent wine to the taverns of Leominster, and 8 lb. of pepper sold by John Pope of Ramsey in 1411 (at an exorbitant price, the court was told) presumably came ultimately from a London grocer. Even cheap goods might have a source in the larger towns: in 1466 a Norwich merchant was selling herring (said to be rotten) in the Norfolk market town of Hingham, and Nottingham bakers took their bread for sale in Castle Donington in the early sixteenth century.[35] Small town industries obtained raw materials from the larger cities. Devon tanners bought their skins from Exeter butchers, and clothmakers everywhere were supplied with their oil and dyestuffs by importing merchants. In each region we can identify a commercial hierarchy of towns dependent on one another. Usk and Newport in South Wales were dominated by Bristol traders who bought wool and hides, and also provided manufactured and imported goods for the local retailers: Chester had a similar role in North Wales. London, of course, dominated the small towns of South-East England, drawing its grain from a ring of specialist centres, notably

[32] E.g. K. F. Stevens, ed., *The Brokage Books of Southampton for 1477–8 and 1527–8* (Southampton Record Society, 28, 1985).

[33] G. H. Tupling, 'The origins of markets and fairs in medieval Lancashire', *Transactions, Lancashire and Cheshire Antiquarian Society*, 49 (1933), 75–94; T. Unwin, 'Rural marketing in medieval Nottinghamshire', *J. of Historical Geography*, 7 (1981), 231–51.

[34] H. W. Booton, 'Inland trade: a study of Aberdeen in the later middle ages', in Lynch, Spearman and Stell, eds., *The Scottish Medieval Town*, pp. 154–5; Kowaleski, *Exeter*, pp. 302–6.

[35] M. K. James, *Studies in the Medieval Wine Trade* (Oxford, 1971), p. 187; E. B. DeWindt, ed., *The Court Rolls of Ramsey, Hepmangrove and Bury, 1268–1600* (Toronto, 1990), p. 677; P. Nightingale, *A Medieval Mercantile Community* (New Haven and London, 1995), pp. 365–71, 383–5, 439–40; Norfolk RO, MCR/B/26 (Hingham court rolls); Postles, 'Loughborough', 28–9.

Faversham, Ware and Henley-on-Thames. A knife-making industry grew at Thaxted, for which the London merchants probably supplied capital and credit and distributed the products throughout the country.[36] Even among the small towns commercial inequalities can be identified, by which in the West Midlands, for example, the lesser centres of Alcester and Shipston-on-Stour depended on the ironmongers and drapers of Evesham, Stratford-on-Avon and Chipping Campden for more specialised goods.[37]

The trading network encouraged migration between towns. This could lead to movement from one modest centre to another, like the Ramsey tanner who went to work in St Ives (Hunts.) in 1400. And sometimes people moved from large to small towns. People called 'de London' are found in small towns in Essex in 1327, and a Chester merchant became mayor of Flint in the early fourteenth century. But in many cases traders sought the opportunities offered by a larger place, after a successful small-town career. The Elmes family of fifteenth-century Henley-on-Thames had developed a niche in the wool trade, and later William Elmes moved to Stamford in Lincolnshire.[38] More conventionally ambitious small-town business men went to make their fortune in the capital. One of the functions of the small towns was perhaps to initiate newcomers into urban life before they moved on to greater things.

Small-town trade was conducted on a limited scale. Many disputes in the courts arose from the sale of small items such as a shirt or a pair of shoes, worth no more than a few pence. But we should not presume too petty a level of commerce. The mean size of debts which were the subject of pleas varies from town to town, but transactions were generally larger than those found in the countryside (see Table 20.2). At Basingstoke, with the lowest level of individual debt, the mean recorded debt is equivalent to two or three weeks' earnings for a skilled worker, and in most towns the average debt corresponds to the purchase price of a horse or ox. Individual workshops had a limited production capacity, but their cumulative output could be impressively large. In the drink trade, dozens of ale-wives in a single small town might be selling in total tens of thousands of gallons each year. A fulling mill at Cockermouth was rented out in 1270 for £11 6s. 8d., which must mean that it was processing well over a thousand yards of cloth.[39]

[36] P. Courtney, *Medieval and Later Usk* (Cardiff, 1994), pp. 116–17, 128–31; R. R. Davies, *Conquest, Coexistence and Change* (Oxford, 1987), pp. 168–70; G. Williams, *Recovery, Reorientation and Reformation: Wales 1415–1642* (Oxford, 1989), pp. 70, 77–8; D. Keene, 'Small towns and the metropolis: the experience of medieval England', in J.-M. Duvosquel and E. Thoen, eds., *Peasants and Townsmen in Medieval Europe* (Ghent, 1995), pp. 223–38. [37] Dyer, 'Market towns', 30.

[38] DeWindt, ed., *Court Rolls of Ramsey*, p. 627; J. C. Ward, ed., *The Medieval Essex Community: The Lay Subsidy of 1327* (Essex RO Publication, 88, 1983), pp. 35, 105; Davies, *Conquest, Coexistence and Change*, p. 168; Peberdy, 'Henley-on-Thames', pp. 176–82, 244.

[39] C. Dyer, 'Small-town conflict in the later middle ages: events at Shipston-on-Stour', *UH*, 19 (1992), 190; A. J. L. Winchester, 'Medieval Cockermouth', *Transactions of the Cumberland and Westmorland Antiq. and Arch. Soc.*, 86 (1986), 109–28.

Table 20.2 *Debts recorded in small town courts*[a]

Place	County	Dates of recorded debts	No. of debts	Mean size of debt[b]
Alcester	War.	1424–68	51	9s. 9d.
Andover	Hants.	1387–8	87	9s. 3d.
Basingstoke	Hants.	1386–1450	79	4s. 1d.
Droitwich	Worcs.	1329–1412	180	8s. 0d.
Eynsham	Oxon.	1453–67	10	5s. 8d.
Hedon	Yorks. East Riding	1368–1473	23	11s. 4d.
Pershore	Worcs.	1329–93	35	4s. 4d.
Stratford-on-Avon	War.	1499–1509	56	5s. 6d.
Thornbury	Glos.	1324–66	329	4s. 7d.
Wimborne	Dorset	1372–1400	43	6s. 10d.

Notes:

[a] Differences between the mean size of debts in these towns may reflect the character of each town's trade, but will also be influenced by the limits on the size of the debt recoverable in a borough court (in at least three cases debts over 40s. could not be pursued in the court) and by the degree to which debts (usually very small ones) would be recovered by informal processes outside the court. Debts arose from a wide range of transactions, including the sale of goods, loans, payment of wages and rents etc.

[b] Debts have been calculated to the nearest penny (d.).

Sources: Alcester: Warwickshire. County RO, CR 1886/141–70; Andover: Hampshire RO, 37 M 85 2/HC/14; Basingstoke: Baijent and Millard, *Basingstoke*, Hampshire RO, 148 M 72 2/1/8; 2/1/58; Droitwich: Birmingham Reference Library, photographic copies of Droitwich borough records; Eynsham: BL Harleian rolls F21, F35; Hedon: Humberside RO, DD HE/20, 21A; Pershore: Westminster Abbey Muniments 21937–42, 21944–6, 21949–60; PRO SC2/210/71, 72; Stratford: Shakespeare Birthplace RO, DR 75, nos. 4, 7; Thornbury: Hilton, 'Seigneurial borough of Thornbury', p. 503; Wimborne: Dorset County RO, D/BKL 1 CJ 1/1/2, 6, 8; D/FRY 1042.

Market revenues which in many small towns yielded £5 or £10 per annum in the decades around 1300 represent thousands of transactions, when a penny or halfpenny was levied on the sale of an animal or cartload of grain. The actual total of purchases would have been larger, because numerous traders were exempt from toll, and many bargains were struck away from the market place – in the fields, on the roads and in inns. Trade was not confined to market days, which helped to swell the volume of commerce in small towns rather than market villages. Court cases at Hedon reveal that on one day in August 1423, 700 quarters of wheat changed hands, and over nine months in 1427–8 550 hides were sold.[40] The profits that could be gained in the small town are signalled by the sums that traders were prepared to pay to join a guild merchant, or to acquire the freedom of the borough from a lord. In the fifteenth century at Alcester the charge varied from 6d. to 2s. 3d., but the 'liberty' of Hedon cost 20s.; at Bridport and Stirling 40s. was demanded, while at Dunfermline it cost 40s. to join the guild, but 6s. 8d. to become a burgess.[41]

Any degree of specialisation would seem to be the antithesis of the small town's role of providing a wide range of services to its locality. Agnes, wife of Thomas Woodward of Ramsey who provides an example of a general trader, was said in 1400 to have been selling candles, cheese, butter, eggs, herring and other types of fish, oatmeal and wax.[42] Within a household a woman often pursued a trade (commonly ale brewing or selling) different from that of her husband or father. On the other hand, if a town were to grow, it needed to develop a distinctive product with an appeal beyond its immediate hinterland. The specialism might derive predictably from a local raw material, like salt at Droitwich and Nantwich, the iron of Trellech, Thetford's rabbit skins or Corfe's marble. Others, however, owed at least as much to the ingenuity and initiative of the traders – no natural resource alone determined Thaxted's knife industry, Bridport's ropes or Burton's beer. A function as a port must have helped specialism to develop, as in the case of Bridport. Iron working was an appropriate trade in south Staffordshire, but why did Rugeley make knives, while Walsall produced horse bits? Birmingham attracted bladesmiths though there was no iron and coal in the immediate vicinity. Flax was widely grown in East Anglia, but it was the Norfolk town of Aylsham that became famous for its linen. Sometimes the presence of a centre of demand encouraged the specialism: the simnel bread of High Wycombe and Walden's saffron found their main market in the capital. Of course, the many minor cloth towns of the fifteenth century catered for a much wider European export market, where names such as Stroud became well known.

A final confirmation of the wealth generated by the small-town economy comes from the property market. The rapid turnover in the tenancy of burgages, messuages, cottages and market stalls, and in parcels of garden and arable on the edge of the town, can be glimpsed from series of deeds or court rolls. But the same is often true of the rural land market, and land values give a better standard of comparison. The normal annual rent under burgage tenure, 6d.–18d., was fixed. But some lords kept more control of rents, and charged entry fines on new lettings which reflected changes in demand. At Pershore in the fourteenth

[40] Humberside RO, DDHE/20.

[41] Warwickshire County RO, CR1886/141–170; Humberside RO, DDHE/20; Dorset County RO, DC/BTB C54; Torrie, 'Dunfermline', p. 247; C. Gross, *The Gild Merchant* (Oxford, 1890), pp. 289–351.

[42] DeWindt, ed., *Court Rolls of Ramsey*, p. 629.

century, cottages were being rented annually for as much as 2s. and 3s. 4d., and messuages (full burgage plots, as they would be called in more privileged towns) paid 5s., 6s. and 8s. In 1337 a new tenant was expected to find an entry fine of 100s. for a messuage.[43] These are much higher sums than those collected from local rural tenants, and if the rent for a messuage is converted into shillings per acre, it was twenty times higher than would be paid for agricultural land. In other towns (Axbridge, Christchurch and Dorchester, for example) the value of property is reflected in the rents for sublettings, and in the money paid to purchase a burgage: cottage rents were as high as 4s. per annum, burgages paid 10s.–18s., and a tenement in a prominent site sold for more than £20, all comparable with property values in large towns.[44] That these sums were related to trading profits can be proved by noting the purchase price and rents, often as high as those for a house, paid for a stall or seld occupying a few square yards in the market place. Shops and selds at Stratford-on-Avon in 1296–1346 were bought for 30s. and 60s. each, and rents varied between 3s. and 10s. per annum.[45] Such was the intensity in the use of space that land changing hands could have its dimensions specified in deeds in feet and even inches. At Dunfermline the 'liners' (officials charged with settling boundary disputes) in a case in 1522 ruled that a gap of 5 inches (127 mm) should be allowed between neighbours for an eavesdrip.[46]

The powerful market of great cities exercised a strong influence on land use in the surrounding countryside, and a much weaker, but still comparable, effect is found in the vicinity of small towns. Horticulture developed on the edge of the town, in for example a group of gardens north of the built-up area at Stratford-on-Avon. The butchers and drovers of Warwick and Birmingham ensured that plentiful areas of cattle pasture lay near to the town where animals could be kept in transit.[47]

(iv) GOVERNMENT AND POLITICS

In general, the greater the size of the town, the more independent would be its system of government, and the majority of small towns were ruled by lords, whether as seigneurial boroughs in England and Wales, burghs of barony in Scotland or simply as adjuncts of manors. Important exceptions to this rule (as well as the occasionally large seigneurial boroughs) are the small towns which

43 PRO SC2/210/71, 72; Westminster Abbey Muniments, 21937–42, 21944–6, 21949–51.

44 Lovell, 'Axbridge', pp. 89–110; Dorset County RO, DC/CC 1/2, 1/3; C. H. Mayo, ed., *The Municipal Records of the Borough of Dorchester, Dorset* (Exeter, 1908).

45 Shakespeare Birthplace Trust RO, F. C. Wellstood, calendar of medieval records of Stratford borough.

46 E. Beveridge, ed., *The Burgh Records of Dunfermline* (Edinburgh, 1917), document no. 7.

47 C. Dyer, *Everyday Life in Medieval England* (London, 1994), p. 123; R. Holt, *The Early History of the Town of Birmingham* (Dugdale Society, Occasional Papers, 30, 1985), pp. 10–11; C. Dyer, *Warwickshire Farming, 1349–c. 1520* (Dugdale Society Occasional Papers, 27, 1981), pp. 17–18.

grew up on royal estates, like Andover, Woodstock and Windsor, or places founded as *burhs* before the Conquest such as Cricklade. Many of these small royal towns gained from the beneficent rule of the crown, and were granted such privileges as the right to form a guild merchant, and to pay their dues as a fee-farm. In Scotland the many small royal burghs founded in the twelfth and thirteenth centuries were granted feu-ferme rights in the fourteenth century, and many of them acquired guild merchants, including places as small as Cupar. In Wales the rash of new royal towns set up after 1277 similarly enjoyed extensive rights, despite their limited size. When after 1345 the English crown granted the privileges known to modern historians as incorporation, a score of small towns benefited, including the small seigneurial borough of Much Wenlock in 1468.[48]

Some lords conceded rights of self-government to their towns, and so we find places like Burford, High Wycombe and Brecon possessing some of the trappings normally found further up the urban hierarchy, such as fee-farms, guild merchants, common seals and mayors. But most lords kept closer control. Monks have a reputation as particularly repressive landlords, and the best-known struggles between townsmen and lords occurred in monastic towns, at Abingdon, Cirencester, Dunstable and St Albans. Both monastic and other types of lord could be reluctant to recognise the normal tenurial and personal freedoms. Tenants might be regarded as serfs, or their lords would expect them to do labour services. Much more often the tenants were granted some form of free tenure, but with such obligations as entry fines and heriots (death duties). Townspeople were commonly required to use the lord's mill and oven. The lord held the town court, presided over by his representative, at which bailiffs or reeves were appointed, who were responsible to the lord for such matters as collecting rents. Occasional rebellions and the more frequent minor frictions show that townspeople aspired to win complete freedom in the tenure of their holdings, and some measure of autonomy in jurisdiction, the raising of money and the choice of officials. On the St Albans estate the people of the small market centre of Chipping Barnet agitated for decades, culminating in a revolt in 1417, to hold their land by charter and to be able to transfer it outside the lord's court. At Cirencester the townspeople campaigned for a borough to be separate from the manor, and for a guild merchant.[49]

Did the restrictions of seigneurial government hold back the economy of the town? There were obvious advantages for traders to have free disposal of property,

[48] On incorporation, M. Weinbaum, *The Incorporation of Boroughs* (Manchester, 1937), pp. 132–3; W. F. Mumford, *Wenlock in the Middle Ages* (Shrewsbury, 1977), pp. 116–22.

[49] On the general issue, D. Knowles, *The Religious Orders in England* (Cambridge, 1948–59), vol. II, pp. 263–9; R. H. Hilton, *English and French Towns in Feudal Society* (Cambridge, 1992); on the two specific cases, D. W. Ko, 'Society and conflict in Barnet, Hertfordshire, 1337–1450' (PhD thesis, University of Birmingham, 1994), pp. 317–46; E. A. Fuller, 'Cirencester: the manor and the town', *Transactions of the Bristol and Gloucestershire Archaeological Society*, 9 (1884–5), 298–344; C. D. Ross, ed., *The Cartulary of Cirencester Abbey* (Oxford, 1964–77), vol. I, pp. xxxvi–xl.

whereby they were better able to raise capital from sales and mortgages, and see less of their profits creamed off through rents and dues. The leading townsmen no doubt hoped to compete more successfully with outsiders if they were able to manipulate the market. But some seigneurial towns flourished, and the less successful places seem to have been limited more by the character of their hinterland than by the rule of their lord. Agitations were partly motivated by resentment at the glaring inequalities of privileges between towns. Townspeople were often able to make progress by moderating seigneurial rule or indeed bypassing the lord's government. Many lords, bishops and lay aristocrats, in particular, were willing to arrive at some compromise by which the town was governed in their name, while in reality the elite of the community, the people who would have held office if the town had achieved autonomy, occupied such positions as bailiffs and jurors. Scottish lords in the mid-fourteenth century allowed the burgesses some say in the choice of bailies. The lord might retain the function of accepting new recruits into the ranks of burgesses – they were after all his tenants – but the existing community could gain the right to approve new burgesses. This was enshrined in the Walsall charter of 1309, and was conceded to Westerkelso in 1323.[50]

In almost every English small town with detailed records we find some form of fraternity, or group of feoffees attached to a chapel or chantry, which while serving religious and social functions had a prominent role in public life. Chapels and fraternities might be the only focus for communities which had mushroomed in remote spots, like Buntingford and Maidenhead.[51] In boroughs which had been traditionally governed by their lords, fraternities which began to resemble shadow governments might sometimes look subversive, like that at Chipping Campden which in 1387 was accused of behaving violently towards people from rival towns. But they were generally sober and conservative bodies, which could develop comprehensive roles. The fraternity of Henley-on-Thames held an annual assembly in the fifteenth century at which the warden (in effect the mayor), bailiffs, constables, bridgewardens and churchwardens were elected. Here the fraternity took on the whole government of the town, supervising law and order, repairing the bridge and church and regulating the market. It also accumulated property, and exercised considerable power as an urban landlord. Rents from Henley were still paid to its lord, but his influence was very weak compared with the concentration of authority in the hands of the fraternity.[52] The importance of small-town fraternities is

[50] K. F. Brown, 'Two Walsall charters', *Transactions of the South Staffordshire Arch. and Hist. Soc.*, 17 (1975–6), 70, 72–3; Ewan, *Townlife*, p. 54.

[51] M. Bailey, 'A tale of two towns: Buntingford and Standon in the later middle ages', *JMed.H*, 19 (1993), 351–71; G. G. Astill, *Historic Towns in Berkshire* (Reading, 1978), p. 43.

[52] Hilton, *English Peasantry*, pp. 91–4; R. H. Hilton, 'Medieval market towns and simple commodity production', *P&P*, 109 (1985), 17–19; P. M. Briers, ed., *Henley Borough Records: Assembly Books I–IV, 1395–1543* (Oxfordshire Record Society, 41, 1960); Peberdy, 'Henley-on-Thames', pp. 88–103, 191–224.

confirmed by their frequent conversion shortly after the end of our period, with the dissolution of chantries, into secular town governments as corporations or the 'town estate'.

Small-town governments, judging from by-laws and court cases, had concerns common to all urban authorities. They attempted to defend the market from profiteers by forbidding forestalling and regrating. Just as in any large city, a bell rang over the market place at Northallerton or Chesterfield to signal that the dealers could buy only after the domestic consumers had satisfied their needs.[53] The governments regulated weights and measures, supervised bread and ale prices and imposed quality controls on butchers who sold diseased meat, or tanners with substandard leather. They sought to maintain peace and order, by setting the watch, enforcing the law against violence and theft and by providing mechanisms for settling disputes. If the court procedures for recovering debts or seeking damages for trespass failed, the warring parties might have to accept arbitration, with fierce penalties for those who persisted in their quarrel. They made efforts, with varying effectiveness, to maintain a clean and safe environment by ordering householders to remove the manure heaps and stacks of timber and firewood from the street outside their houses. Small towns had no assize of nuisance, but the borough court dealt with latrines and drains which caused offence to neighbours and visitors, and attempted to prevent the pollution of water supplies. They advocated fire precautions, an ever present danger in all towns. By-laws at Ruthin in 1364, issued typically *after* an outbreak, required the removal of piles of fuel to the outskirts, and the provision of thatch hooks and vats of water in the streets.[54]

These apparently well-meaning attempts to make towns decent and secure, together with the brotherhood and amity proclaimed by the fraternities, and the claims of rulers of towns to be acting in the interests of the community, may give the impression that small towns achieved relative harmony. This is not supported by the numerous petty offences reported to the courts leet, including each year in many towns a dozen or more violent assaults with the use of fists, knives and cudgels, in which everyone, servants, householders and women, seem to have participated. Medieval crime is notoriously difficult to quantify, but the combination of violence and trespasses, the need for arbitration and the occasional record of gossip, insults and defamation could suggest that the intensity of small-town life created a heated and quarrelsome atmosphere. The leading figures, just as in the large towns, were prone to faction. The Andover guild merchant saw some bitter quarrels among its members in the early fourteenth century. One 'brother' accused another of being a '*bribour*, robber and ribald' in 1311, and in

[53] Newman, 'Allertonshire', 21; J. M. Bestall, *History of Chesterfield* (Chesterfield, 1974), p. 65.

[54] R. I. Jack, 'The fire ordinances of Ruthin, 1364', *Transactions of the Denbighshire Historical Society*, 28 (1979), 5–17.

a serious incident in 1327, a tumultuous year in many English towns, Robert le Kyllere was said to be planning with fifty-five accomplices to destroy some prominent colleagues. He was expelled, but he had a capacity for survival, and was elected warden nine years later.[55]

The gentry became involved in urban politics and society by joining fraternities and helping in their deliberations. At Windsor the new constitution of 1474 allowed gentlemen and lawyers to be recruited to the council, so that they could give the benefit of their 'power' and 'authority'. In Scotland, burghs, and individual townsmen, from the late fifteenth century sought the protection of local aristocrats by entering into indentures of manrent. Nairn, for example, was bound in 1472 to Hugh lord Fraser of Lovat. Scottish legislation sought ineffectively to prevent such alliances, and to stop the gentry holding burghal office. English and Welsh townspeople were recruited into retinues, and joined in aristocratic disputes. The people of High Wycombe were ordered in 1490 not to wear badges or liveries. Gentry interest in town politics led to outbreaks of violence in three West Midland market towns in the early fifteenth century, fomented by the unruly Burdet family. A practical example of the advantage of an alliance with the gentry comes from Axbridge, which was the scene of a long-running property dispute between 1480 and 1506. Thomas Waleys evicted his tenant, John Haynes, after he had paid no rent for five years. Haynes enlisted the aid of a gentry supporter, Thomas St Barbe, and Waleys' son William made an alliance with Thomas Stafford esquire.[56]

Small towns tended to oligarchical government, based on very narrow elite groups. Chesterfield was ruled by twelve 'honest' men, whose deliberations were kept secret, and twelve men also selected the mayor and other officers at Lyme Regis. At Much Wenlock in the late fifteenth century a council of six elected the officers. Guild merchants formed select groups also – that at Dunfermline had fifty members, a third of the burgesses, in the fifteenth century. The fraternities might seem to have offered a wider degree of participation, but some of these look like very exclusive clubs. The Trinity Guild at Wisbech, with its sixty-six members, had an inner circle of twelve to eighteen jurors who chose the officers. The Windsor fraternity contained thirty of the 'substantiallest and wisest men of the town', who were picked by the mayor and aldermen from the 'wisest and honestest' persons.[57] We hear of cooptions, of officeholding for life and

55 Hampshire RO, 37M80 3/GI/11; Gross, *Gild Merchant*, pp. 317–20, 331.

56 C. Carpenter, 'Town and "County" the Stratford Guild and political networks of fifteenth-century Warwickshire', in R. Bearman, ed., *The History of an English Borough* (Stroud, 1997), pp. 62–79; R. R. Tighe, *Annals of Windsor* (London, 1858), vol. I, pp. 399–403; J. Wormald, *Lords and Men in Scotland: Bonds of Manrent, 1442–1603* (Edinburgh, 1985), pp. 137–42; L. J. Ashford, *The History of the Borough of High Wycombe* (London, 1960), p. 81; Dyer, 'Shipston-on-Stour', 204–7; Lovell, 'Axbridge', pp. 158–65.

57 Bestall, *Chesterfield*, pp. 94–5; Dorset County RO, DC/LR B1/2; Mumford, *Wenlock*, pp. 123–31; Torrie, 'Dunfermline', p. 246; *VCH*, Cambridgeshire, IV, pp. 255–6; Tighe, *Windsor*,

other devices to keep government in the hands of a small elite. This type of rule may have worked, but not without friction. Sometimes the town constitution was committed to writing precisely because of an outbreak of criticism, for example, by 'evil disposed persons' in Chesterfield in 1480. The Windsor rules allowed for anyone mocking a member of the fraternity to be imprisoned for two days. The elite's sanction against dissidents of expulsion from guilds and fraternities had real teeth because it threatened their livelihood.

Some of the policies of these governments were openly designed to favour the rich, like the High Wycombe by-law of 1511 which ordered any dyer, fuller or weaver who deceived or 'hindered' a clothier to pay compensation.[58] But as few market towns had enough merchants to make the control of artisans a major issue, a more frequent theme in small-town government was the need to maintain order among potentially unruly and idle sections of society. A campaign against gambling, especially with dice, appears to have been launched in a number of towns in the period 1410–25, from Basingstoke to Bradford. Apprentices (who played bowls, frequented alehouses and carried knives) became a special concern at the former town in the early sixteenth century.[59] The concern to get people to bed at an early hour, to suppress games, to combat prostitutes and vagabonds and in general to impose social controls (recurring in by-laws all over England) has been seen as a form of early puritanism. In line with this tendency hospitals and almshouses were founded or encouraged, and they became the characteristic institution of the small town, almost as clear an emblem of the settlement's status as the friary for the larger towns.

Minor towns have been said to have lacked civic buildings.[60] Certainly English and Scottish small towns, unlike those in Wales, were not usually provided with walls, but their larger neighbours were also often unwalled, and do not seem to have suffered any great disadvantage. Often a great deal depended on individual townspeople, so the streets were supposed to be maintained piecemeal by householders, who at Eynsham in 1476 had to be reminded of their duties by the borough court. Likewise, roads and bridges were often funded by bequests in wills, which, unless a town was supported by an unusually wealthy benefactor, would result only in small-scale improvements. Modest sums could accumulate into an impressive expenditure, like the total of £550 bequeathed before 1540 in thirty-five wills from Lavenham for road works.[61] Houses were built and

pp. 399–403; S. Bond, 'The medieval constitution of New Windsor', *Berkshire Arch. J.*, 65 (1970), 21–39.

[58] R. W. Greaves, ed., *The First Ledger Book of High Wycombe* (Buckinghamshire Record Society, 2, 1947), pp. 62–3.

[59] Baijent and Millard, *Basingstoke*, pp. 258, 311, 320, 322; D. H. Crocker, 'The medieval manor of Bradford in the West Riding of Yorkshire, 1066–1399' (MPhil thesis, University of Leeds, 1974), pp. 534–5.

[60] P. Clark, 'Introduction', in P. Clark, ed., *Small Towns in Early Modern Europe* (Cambridge, 1995), p. 7.

[61] BL, Harleian roll F 35; and Betterton and Dymond, *Lavenham*, pp. 16, 113–15.

maintained in many cases by their tenants, and in seigneurial boroughs building agreements were written into the terms of new tenancies, or the court made orders for repair work, but these were not always observed. Town governments made efforts within their limited resources to provide appropriate public buildings, and were capable of remarkable initiatives. An important focal point for most small towns was the guildhall or (in Scotland) town house or tolbooth where council meetings and courts could be held, and which were often combined with a market hall. Other facilities which were sponsored by town governments included the hospitals and almshouses. That at Sherborne in Dorset cost more than £80 in the late 1430s, raised by collections encouraged by the elite, in order to provide the town with an impressive institution, as well as to serve pious and social purposes. Expenditure on improvements could be covered by toll collections licensed by the crown, such as pavage grants which were by no means confined to large towns – Atherstone was allowed in 1343 to collect money to pave the streets, because 'in wet weather [it] is dirty'.[62] A few small towns even boasted a public water supply – Chelmsford had a conduit, and more surprisingly so did the minor Shropshire town of Newport, begun in 1309. The leading figures in small towns recognised the advantage to their trade of improved communications, which led to some ambitious investments. The burgesses at Arbroath in conjunction with the abbot in 1394 set to work on building a new harbour. The Holy Cross fraternity at Abingdon embarked on a new bridge in 1416 designed to divert trade from Wallingford.[63] Finally, town governments and fraternities contributed substantially to domestic buildings by constructing and maintaining the houses from which they drew rent income. The quality of the physical fabric of some small towns which could win the praise of visitors like John Leland must be judged as one of the achievements of urban governments in this period.

(v) URBAN CULTURE

Did the inhabitants of small towns acquire an urban outlook or was their mentality nearer to that of the countryside? It would be easy to argue that they were so heavily involved in the rhythms of agriculture, under such strong influence from the gentry, and in such constant contact with the peasantry, that their way of life was essentially rural. Against this view must be set the range of institutions found in our towns (especially those with populations of about 800 or more), the evidence for a civic consciousness and their role as cultural centres for their hinterlands.

[62] C. H. Mayo, *Historic Guide to the Almshouses of St. John, Sherborne* (Oxford, 1933), pp. 20–4; Grieve, *The Sleepers and the Shadows*, pp. 86–7; E. Jones, 'Historical notes of Newport, co Salop', *Transactions of the Shropshire Arch. Soc.*, 8 (1885), 248–52; Hilton, 'Market towns', 12.

[63] Ewan, *Townlife*, p. 6; K. Rodwell, ed., *Historic Towns in Oxfordshire* (Oxford, 1975), p. 33.

Market towns contained more institutions than did villages. Truro was provided with a hospital and three or four chapels; Manchester by the end of our period had no fewer than eight endowed chantries in addition to its collegiate church.[64] Some eastern English towns had a number of fraternities, as did the villages, but the wealthy and influential urban fraternities were more dominant institutions than in the country. For the better-off, the fraternity feasts and drinkings punctuated the urban year, and the solidarity of the brothers and sisters was presented in public processions, like the St George's day event at Poole.[65] The clergy employed by chapels, chantries and fraternities gave townspeople a closer contact with literacy, and indeed a high proportion of all town dwellers must have had at least an ability to read by the end of our period. The standard list of schools in the middle ages shows that about half of them were located in small towns. Endowed schools are inevitably better documented, and if we take into account more informal arrangements for teaching, and include the elementary schools, at least 200 of our small towns must have had educational facilities for part of our period.[66] The growing use of documents in town government led not just to a proliferation of accounts, court records and deeds, but also to the keeping of an authoritative record of important decisions or property transfers – two examples of these prestigious registers are the *Domesday* of Dorchester which was instituted in 1414, and the *Ledger Book* of High Wycombe begun in 1475.[67]

Distinctive institutions, solemn processions and books of evidences, all contributed to a sense of civic pride and common purpose. Just as in larger towns, the rhetorical flourishes extolling the 'profit and utility' of the whole community were taken seriously. At Axbridge the guildhall window carried the inscription: 'God that is lord of all, Save the council of this hall' expressing the sense of importance of the elite. At the same place a fourteenth-century town chronicle, deploying impressive historical scholarship, recounted a legendary origin for the town, emphasising its close relationship with Anglo-Saxon kings, thereby diminishing the importance of its more recent lords, the bishops of Bath and Wells. A more popular myth was celebrated at Droitwich, where festivities marked the anniversary of a famous son, St Richard of Wych, who had miraculously restored the flow of the brine on which the town's economy depended.[68]

Small towns acted as cultural centres both for the townspeople and those living in the hinterland. Drama included a Corpus Christi play at Ashburton, a

[64] P. Sheppard, *The Historic Towns of Cornwall* (Cornwall Committee for Rescue Archaeology, n. d.), pp. 23–6; M. Morris, *Medieval Manchester: A Regional Study* (Greater Manchester Archaeological Unit, 1983), pp. 41–2.

[65] H. P. Smith, *The History of the Borough and County of the Town of Poole* (Poole, 1948), vol. I, p. 197.

[66] N. Orme, *English Schools in the Middle Ages* (London, 1973), pp. 322–5; J. A. H. Moran, *The Growth of English Schooling, 1390–1548* (Princeton, N.J., 1988), pp. 237–79.

[67] Mayo, ed., *Dorchester*; Greaves, ed., *High Wycombe*.

[68] Lovell, 'Axbridge', pp. 9, 314–17; D. N. Klausner, ed., *Herefordshire, Worcestershire* (Records of Early English Drama, Toronto, 1990), p. 370.

spectacular event judging from the amount of cash spent by the churchwardens on costumes. Performances by the town players and waits tend to be recorded when they put on a show at another town, as when the Liskeard players paid a visit to Barnstaple in 1538.[69] Country people were also drawn to the town by the coarser pleasures of plentiful ale, bullbaiting, dancing bears and street entertainers. We think of music as an amateur activity, or as being performed by itinerants, but most series of small-town records contain a reference to a resident musician (a harper or piper is most common) who appears to have made a living from his skill.

(vi) CONCLUSION – CHANGE

We expect to find, from studies of the larger towns, a pattern of urban growth in the late thirteenth and early fourteenth centuries, with varied experiences, including some decline, in the subsequent 200 years. But did small towns have a different history? Certainly small towns expanded in number between 1270 and 1350, as more than a hundred English boroughs, another thirty in Wales and fifteen Scottish burghs were either founded in those decades, or are mentioned in documents for the first time. Individual towns grew in size judging from the numbers of burgages reported in surveys or rentals. Cowbridge in Glamorgan, which contained only 58 burgages in 1262, had become one of the largest towns in Wales by 1306 when 278 burgages had been created.[70] On the other hand, the small towns sometimes departed from the general trend with a number of failures even during the period of general urban expansion. Some new foundations, whether because of misjudgements in their siting, or as victims of competition, went into decline. Newport in south-west Wales, which had been founded in the late twelfth century, lost part of its built-up area by the end of the thirteenth. Such was the upheaval in the urban network in the thirteenth century that some apparently well-established places declined, such as Ilchester. The Welsh and Scottish wars adversely affected a number of previously prosperous places.[71]

Small towns have been brought into the controversy over late medieval urban decline. The proponents of decline have argued that large numbers of very small market centres disappeared, but this fate was suffered by village markets rather than market towns.[72] The optimists point to the undoubted success stories

[69] J. M. Wasson, ed., *Devon* (Records of Early English Drama, Toronto, 1986), pp. 17–23, 30–8.

[70] Soulsby, *Towns of Medieval Wales*, p. 115.

[71] K. Murphy, 'Excavations in three burgage plots in the medieval town of Newport, Dyfed, 1991', *Med. Arch.*, 38 (1994), 55–82; M. Aston and R. Leech, *Historic Towns in Somerset* (Bristol, 1977), pp. 67–79; G. W. S. Barrow, 'The aftermath of war. Scotland and England in the late thirteenth and early fourteenth centuries', *TRHS*, 5th series, 28 (1978), 108–11.

[72] M. Mate, 'The rise and fall of markets in southeast England', *Canadian J of History*, 31 (1996), 59–86; D. M. Palliser and A. C. Pinnock, 'The markets of medieval Staffordshire', *North Staffordshire J of Field Studies*, 11 (1971), 49–59.

among places which were able to benefit from the growing prosperity of the peasants and rural artisans in their hinterlands. Many small towns undoubtedly lost population. Both rentals and archaeology tell us of abandoned houses, leading to the desertion of a whole section of the town at Wimborne.[73] Everywhere the rents and fee-farms were falling, sometimes by more than 50 per cent. The greatest concentration of decline is found in Wales, where about thirty of the seventy-six small towns had suffered serious contraction, and in a number of cases, virtual disappearance, by the early sixteenth century. There are relatively few examples of growth in Wales to offset this picture.[74] In Scotland there are grounds for expecting a deterioration in the economies of the lesser towns because of the concentration of external trade in a few large centres in the fifteenth century, but we cannot ignore the remarkable foundation of dozens of burghs of barony after 1450, some of which gave the well-established towns cause for concern.[75]

In England rentals and surveys giving the numbers of burgages, messuages, tenements or tenants in the late thirteenth and early fourteenth centuries, though difficult to interpret, can be compared with the numbers of taxpayers recorded in the poll taxes of 1377–81 and the subsidies of 1524–5. From a sample of thirty-three, the majority, twenty-six, seem to have been reduced in size during the fourteenth and fifteenth centuries. Five remained a similar size, and another five show signs of growth. Most towns therefore seem to have followed the generally downward tendency in the national population, which halved in this period, but a few were able to move against the tide. The changes in a much larger sample can be traced between 1377–81 and 1524–5 (Table 20.3), which covers the period after the famines and plagues of the period 1315–69, but still allows the fortunes of the towns to be compared with the general movement in population. At first sight this seems to support an optimistic view, as more small towns expanded than declined, against both the national trend which was probably stagnant or falling slightly, and the experience of the large towns, the majority of which declined. However, even this sample of 127 towns cannot be treated as representative, because Devon has through an accident of documentary survival provided so many cases, and the almost universal success of its small towns distorts the total. Comparison between regions suggests that as well as Devon, other clothing districts produced a number of expanding towns, in Essex, Somerset and Wiltshire, while in the Midlands, from Staffordshire to Oxfordshire, most small towns either declined or stood still. As when considering the decline of the larger towns, varying reasons can be given

[73] G. G. Astill, 'Archaeology and the smaller medieval town', *UHY* (1985), 49; Dorset County RO, D/FRY DI/5331.

[74] Soulsby, *Towns of Medieval Wales*; R. Griffiths, 'The medieval boroughs of Glamorgan and medieval Swansea', *Glamorgan County History* (Cardiff, 1936–88), vol. III, pp. 333–77.

[75] M. Lynch, 'Towns and townspeople in fifteenth-century Scotland', in J. A. F. Thomson, ed., *Towns and Townspeople in the Fifteenth Century* (Gloucester, 1988), pp. 173–89.

Table 20.3 *Changes in small-town populations 1377–1381 to 1524–1525*

	No. in sample	No. in decline	No. with little change	No. growing
Berkshire	2	1	0	1
Cambridgeshire	2	1	0	1
Cornwall	4	0	2	2
Devon	28	1	3	24
Essex	13	2	6	5
Gloucestershire	7	3	3	1
Hampshire	2	0	1	1
Leicestershire	5	4	1	0
Lincolnshire	1	1	0	0
Norfolk	4	0	2	2
Northamptonshire	8	3	4	1
Oxfordshire	9	5	2	2
Rutland	1	1	0	0
Somerset	6	3	0	3
Staffordshire	13	10	2	1
Sussex	1	0	0	1
Warwickshire	1	0	0	1
Wiltshire	20	11	2	7
Total	127 (100%)	46 (36%)	28 (22%)	53 (42%)

Notes:
The figure for each town was calculated by doubling the numbers of taxpayers in 1377 (the conventional multiplier of 1.9 may be a little low in the light of new evidence that the tax exempted the householding poor, not just mendicants, and that there were considerable omissions in some towns). For 1379 and 1381 multipliers of two and three were used to give a minimum and maximum figure. In view of the controversies about the size of the multipliers for 1524–5, again a minimum and maximum were used of five and seven. If the minima and maxima from the two periods overlapped, the town was judged to belong to the middling category, showing no definite movement.
Sources: For the poll taxes the main source were the texts being prepared by Dr C. Fenwick and Dr R. Smith for publication by the British Academy, and for 1524–5, the tables in J. Sheail, 'The regional distribution of wealth in England as indicated by the lay subsidy returns of 1524/5' (PhD thesis, University of London, 1968), in both cases supplemented by the various published lists for individual counties.

for the problems of different places – some could not maintain their specialisation, like Trellech, but more commonly the problem must have been changes in the hinterlands, such as those dependent on the grain-based agrarian economies of parts of the Midlands. Competition might damage a town, especially if it had been badly sited in the period of foundation. It must still be emphasised that our small towns performed relatively well in difficult times. For the majority of towns either to grow or maintain their numbers, which is still true if Devon is set on one side, was a remarkable achievement in a period when thousands of rural settlements were shrinking or being deserted. Devon deserves special mention as an unusually dynamic county, where Ashburton, for example, could rise from about 550 people in 1377 to near 1,000 in 1524–5.

Finally, a little noticed feature of the end of our period is the small but significant new wave of town foundations – Scottish burghs were established and a number of English towns were encouraged with new grants of privilege, such as Bewdley and Sutton Coldfield, though we do not always know if they were successful in economic terms. Informal trading centres were also emerging without the benefit of charters and privileges, often in regions experiencing growth in pastoral farming and rural industry. Places such as St Ives (Cornwall), Stourbridge (Worcs.) and Stroud show that small-town economies were capable of new growth as well as survival and renewal.

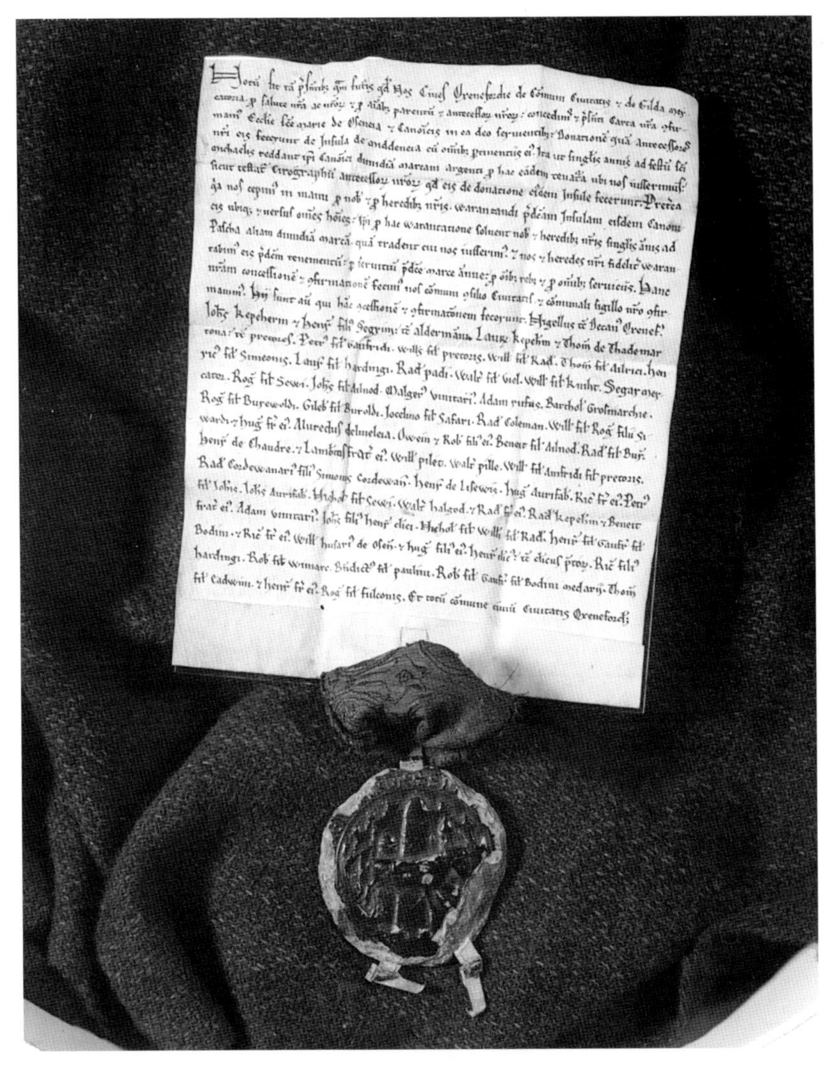

1 The seal of the town of Oxford 1191.
This is the earliest surviving municipal seal in Britain, appended to a charter of 1191. It depicts a walled city, identified by the superimposition of an ox, and the inscription (damaged) reads 'The seal of the commune of all the citizens of the city of Oxford.'

2 The mace of the town of Ilchester, early thirteenth century.
The head of this mace of Ilchester in Somerset dates from the mid-thirteenth century or earlier, and was the staff of office of the bailiffs who governed the town from the thirteenth to the nineteenth centuries. It is the oldest surviving municipal mace or equivalent for any British town. The figures are an angel and three kings, possibly representing the Magi; the inscription has been variously interpreted. The rest of the staff is probably early nineteenth century in date.

3 London, Westminster and Southwark in the mid-sixteenth century.
From G. Braun and F. Hogenberg's atlas *Civitates Orbis Terrarum*, first published in 1572. This reproduction (from the Guildhall Library, London) is of the second state of the map, which appears in editions of the atlas published in 1574 and later, and which shows the Royal Exchange, built 1566–70. The map, however, shows the spire of St Paul's Cathedral which was destroyed in 1561, and appears to be derived from an earlier, more detailed survey of between 1547 and 1559. The extent of the built-up area is very much as it would have been *c.* 1300, despite the city's renewed expansion after 1500. The line of the city walls on the north bank of the River Thames is clearly visible and largely retained the form it had in Roman times.

4 Matrix seal of the burgh of Dunfermline, *c.* 1589.

5 The Bargate, Southampton, showing the early sixteenth-century paintings of Sir Bevis and the giant Ascupart.

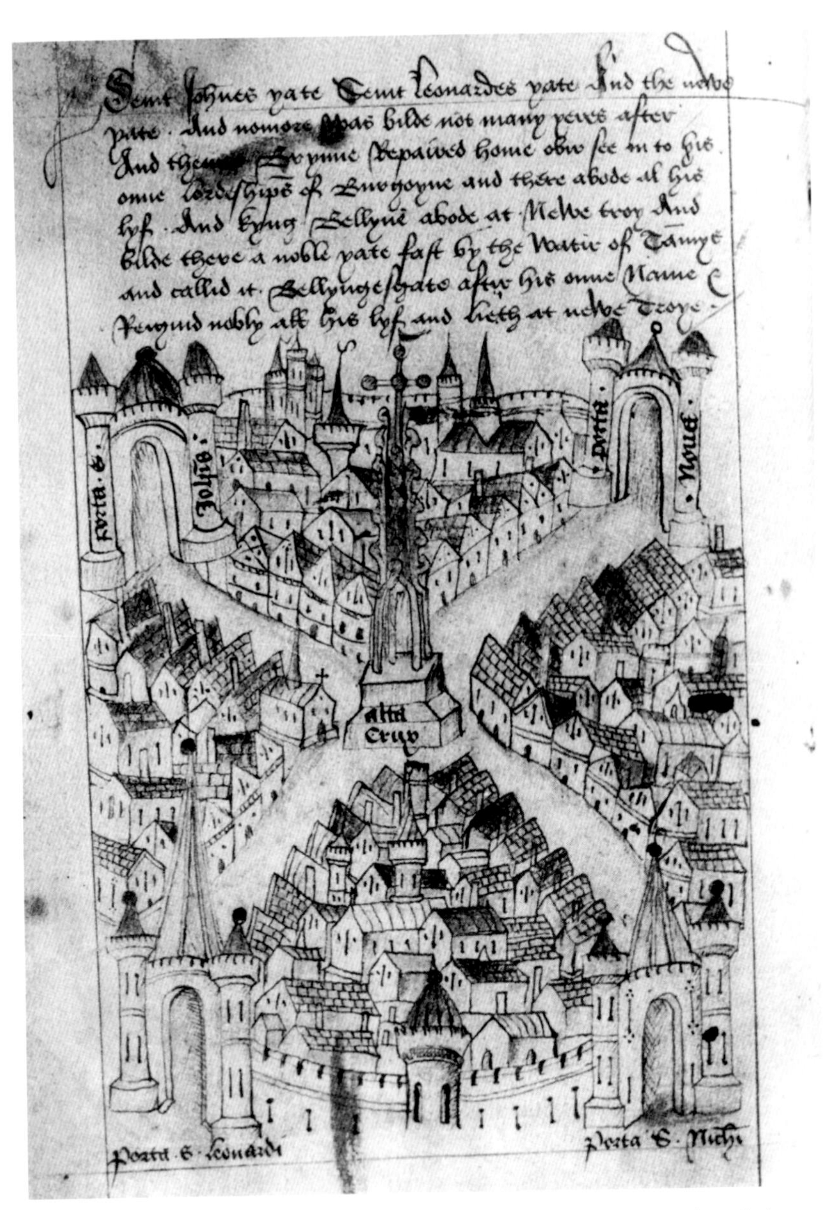

6 Fifteenth-century map of Bristol at the time of its legendary foundation, from the *Kalendar* of the town clerk, Robert Ricart.

7 Holy Trinity church, Hull. This late medieval parish church is the largest in Britain.

8 Late medieval pilgrim badge commemorating St Osmund of Salisbury.

9 Late medieval carvings of saints and religious subjects on the wall of Royston Cave, Herts.

10 Fifteenth-century guildhall, almshouses and guild chapel of the fraternity of the Holy Cross, Stratford-on-Avon.

11 Alabaster head of St John the Baptist, English (? Nottingham), fifteenth century.

12 The Gild Court Book of Dunfermline. Merchants' marks, 1559.

13 Toy soldier on horseback from London. Lead, *c.* 1300.

14 Micklegate Bar, York, by Moses Griffith in 1777. The gate retained its fourteenth-century barbican until 1826.

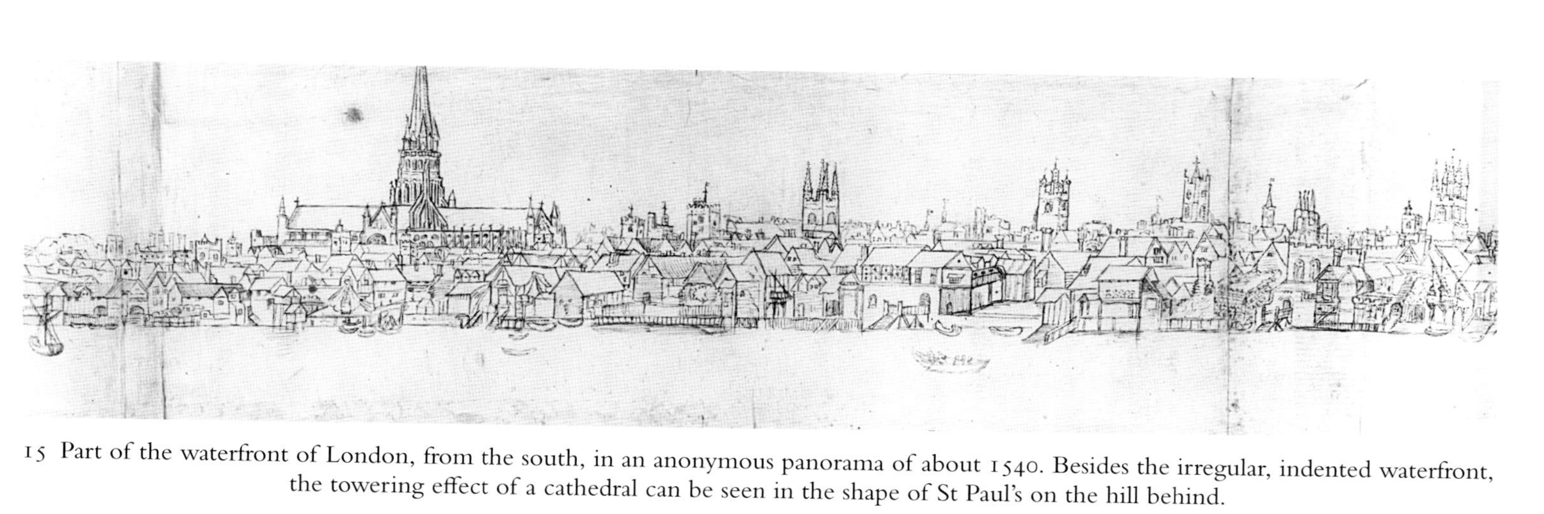

15 Part of the waterfront of London, from the south, in an anonymous panorama of about 1540. Besides the irregular, indented waterfront, the towering effect of a cathedral can be seen in the shape of St Paul's on the hill behind.

16 Guildhall, London; a reconstruction of the fifteenth-century hall and adjacent Guildhall Chapel by Terry Ball and Caroline Barron.

17 Statues from the Guildhall porch, London, drawn in 1783 by John Carter. He thought them to represent Discipline, Justice, Fortitude and Temperance.

18 Mercat cross, Banff; late fifteenth-century head depicting the Crucifixion.

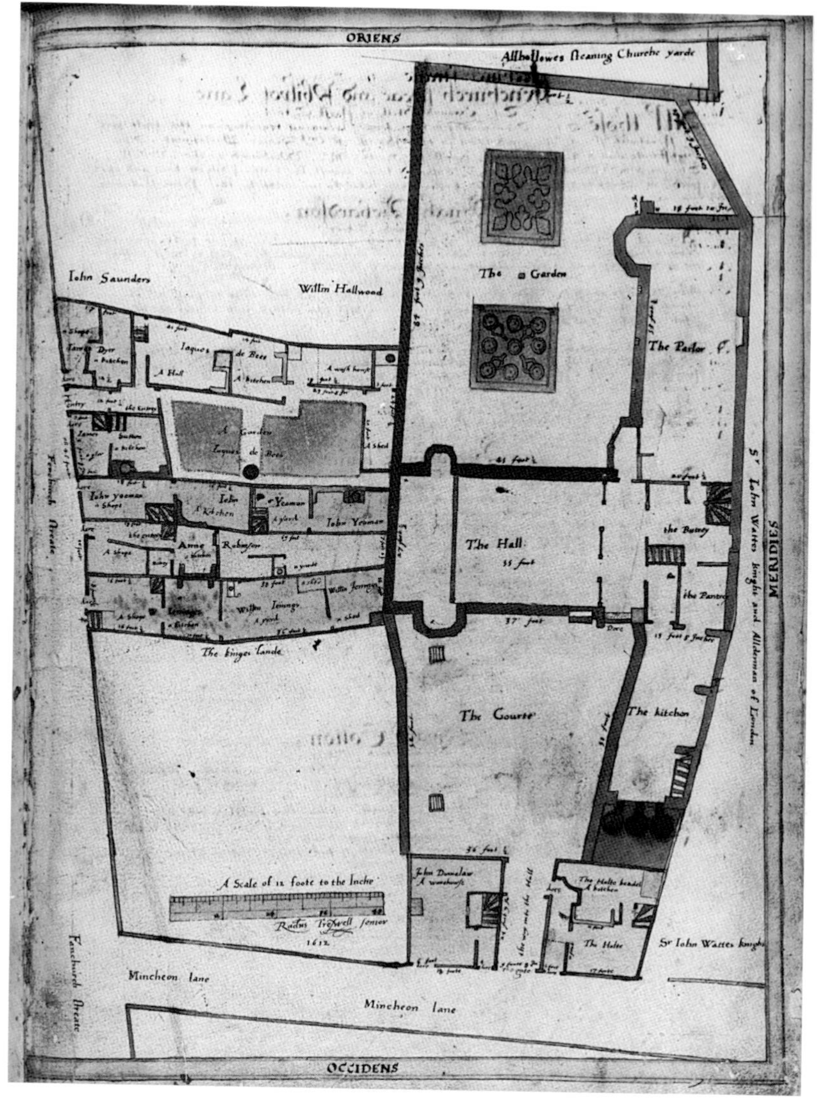

19 Survey of property in Mincing Lace and Fenchurch Street, City of London, by Ralph Treswell in 1612. This shows Clothworkers' Hall, a courtyard house and an adjacent block of ordinary houses in Fenchurch Street. All the buildings shown here, with the exception of the parlour of Clothworkers' Hall of 1594, were probably of pre-1550 construction.

20 One of twenty-six coloured drawings of the London aldermen *c.* 1446–9, probably by Roger Leigh, Clarenceux King of Arms, depicting John Olney, mercer, who was mayor in 1446–7. The name of his ward, Coleman Street, where he was alderman from 1435 to 1457, is recorded at the base of the placard of blank shields.

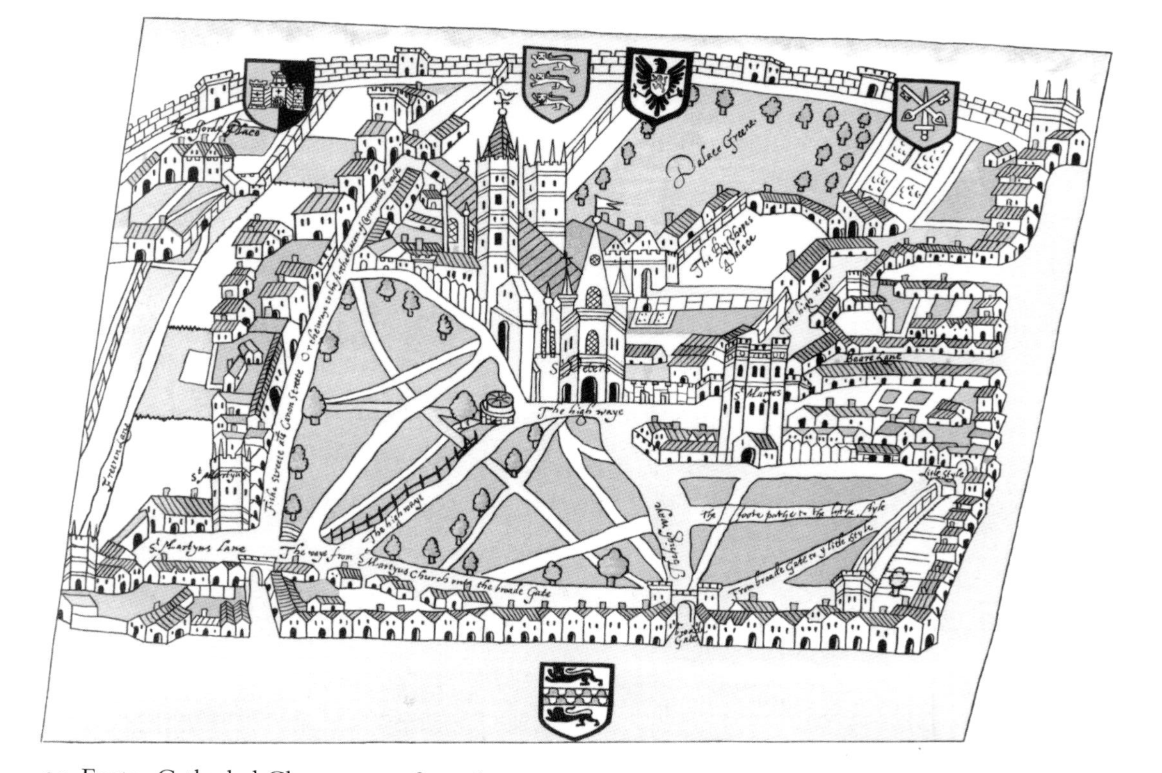

21 Exeter Cathedral Close *c.* 1590 from the manuscript of John Hooker. The Close was the liberty of the Dean and Chapter and was walled and gated.

22 Pembroke, from the south-east. The port town developed in stages from the early castle (*c.* 1100) along the protected (and walled) peninsula, eventually including two parishes based on St Mary's (shown) and the later thirteenth-century St Michael's (to the east, beyond the photograph). It had fortified bridges near the north and west gates, and a strong east gate; two [illegible] at either end of the main street

23 Caernarfon, from the north-east. The port town and administrative capital was surrounded by water and walls. Roman, Norman and Welsh occupation was followed by Edward I's castle (from 1283) and defended borough. It had no church until St Mary's was built in the north-west corner (1307); town mills stood beyond the east gate, and the market place (left) was beneath the castle's east wall.

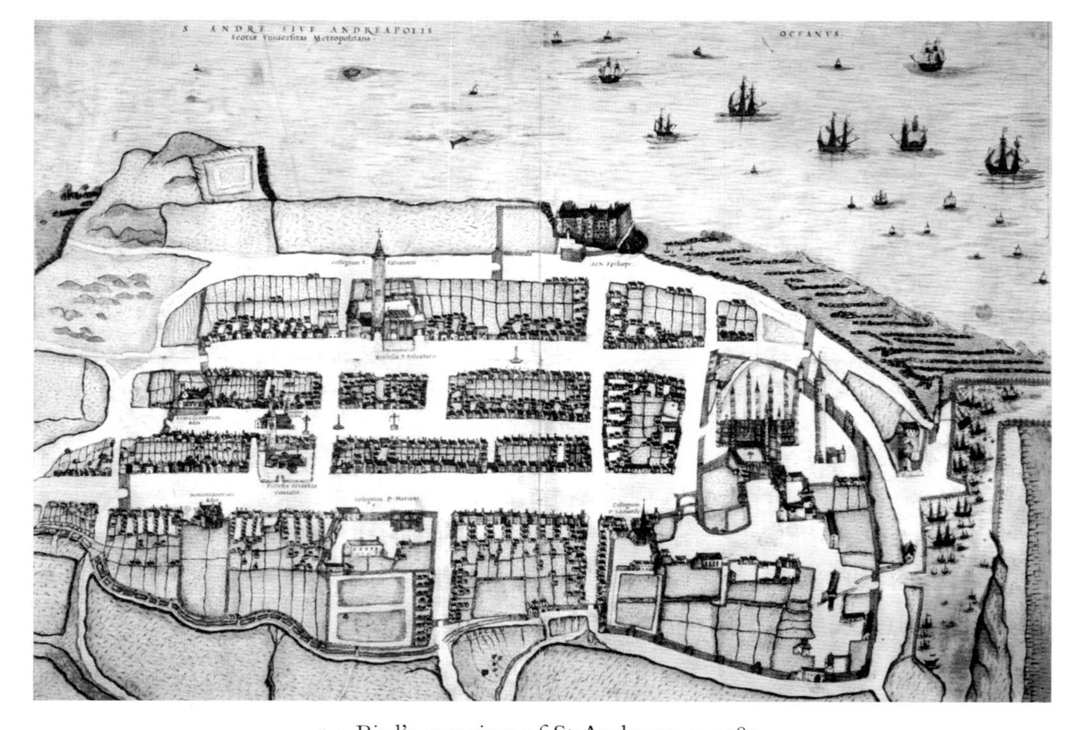

24 Bird's-eye view of St Andrews, *c.* 1580.

25 A fifteenth-century view of Stirling from John Fordun's *Scotichronicon*, showing one of the earliest illustrations of houses in Scottish towns.

· PART IV ·

Regional surveys

· 21 ·

Regional introduction (England and Wales)

DEREK KEENE AND D. M. PALLISER

FEW REGIONS of Europe, certainly in lowland territories, owe their identities solely to inherent characteristics of soil, relief or people. The ecology has been unstable, not least on account of human influence. Long-term cycles in the extent and density of settlement, and some catastrophes, have shaped the ways in which natural resources have been used to best advantage. More intensive use has, through exchange, promoted regional specialism in production and culture, and has generated material and mental infrastructures which can persist through disruptive episodes. Political frameworks, power and tradition are products of those processes and at the same time strongly influence them. Language, for example, is a signifier of local identity which owes as much to politics as to inheritance or migration. Often, the regional boundary markers according to different sets of criteria will not coincide, even in a territory where the physical landscape seems well defined. Moreover, in order to identify the character of a region it is necessary to look beyond it: to other regions within the territory, nation or state, to influences outside that larger space and to the possibility that the region itself may straddle the boundary of that space.

Markets and towns play a central role in the formation of territorial and regional identities, and the following surveys explore that interplay over nine centuries. Overall the period is characterised by growth in the resource base, both human and natural, from a level which was initially very low. That development was interrupted by invasions and natural disasters, occasioning severe demographic setbacks, but there was a continuity to the process which is apparently absent from the transition from late Roman to early medieval times in southern Britain. Nevertheless, the significance of Roman rule for town life in later Britain should not be underestimated, for it left an ideology and an infrastructure which have had continuing influence. Furthermore, it may not have been until the eighteenth century that material conditions resembling those under Roman rule were restored. The principles of organisation, however, were very different from those which underlay the Roman episode of urbanisation, and the framework of urban life in southern Britain today is essentially the creation of the middle ages, as are the nation and state within which that region lies.

Is it legitimate to identify whole regions of medieval England in terms of towns? Yves Barel has argued that there was a medieval 'urban system', but it is doubtful if such a phrase can be used of any except the most highly urbanised parts of medieval Europe. However, Jacques le Goff, while taking issue with Barel in terms of French towns, has argued that 'there was an urban "network" (*réseau*)'.[1] 'Network' has perhaps not quite the right connotations for medieval or even early modern British towns, but we can certainly think in terms of urban *regions*. A widely used model for early modern England has a dominant capital city as a first-order town, followed by a handful of provincial capitals, each of which had its own cluster of smaller towns within its 'province'. W. G. Hoskins memorably declared that 'in each province of England, above all in the peripheral regions, certain towns played the part of capital cities to their regions – Norwich and York, Exeter and Salisbury, Newcastle and Bristol, for example'. His simplified model has been refined for the early modern period by Peter Clark and Paul Slack, and in later literature by Peter Clark and others, especially in the successor volume to this. Inevitably, the evidence for the medieval centuries is less detailed, but to deny any existence of urban regions – or to dismiss the whole of Britain as 'the region of London' as J. C. Russell has done – is erroneous.[2] Certainly by the twelfth century some writers thought of England as divided into regions focusing on cities, among which London was the 'queen metropolis' or 'head of the realm',[3] and it can legitimately be argued that provincial capitals were even more the focal points of their regions between the eleventh and thirteenth centuries than they were later. The more integrated urban system of the later middle ages was based much more on the dominance of London than on a structured hierarchy of first-, second- and third-order towns on the Christaller model, although there certainly were ways in which lesser towns interacted with larger ones, both directly and through intermediate centres.

Work on the English capital at the Centre for Metropolitan History makes a good basis for seeing a London region of Home Counties proportions by the

[1] Y. Barel, *La ville médiévale* (Grenoble, 1975), *passim*; J. le Goff, ed., *Histoire de la France urbaine*, vol. II: *La ville médiévale* (Paris, 1980), pp. 18 ff.

[2] W. G. Hoskins, *Provincial England* (London, 1963), p. 86; P. Clark and P. Slack, *English Towns in Transition 1500–1700* (Oxford, 1976); P. Clark, ed., *The Cambridge Urban History of Britain*, vol. II: 1540–1840 (Cambridge, 2000); J. C. Russell, *Medieval Regions and their Cities* (Newton Abbot, 1972), pp. 121–31.

[3] L. J. Downer, ed., *Leges Henrici Primi* (Oxford, 1972), pp. 44–5; H. E. Butler, ed., *The Chronicle of Jocelin of Brakelond* (London, 1949), p. 77; K. R. Potter, ed., *Gesta Stephani* (London, 1955), pp. 3, 7.

thirteenth century at latest, and other regions can be identified which also had their dominant towns. East Anglia, for instance, was heavily dominated by Norwich in the later middle ages, and South-West England, less strongly, by Salisbury and Exeter. It would be misleading to argue that all of England and Wales could be mapped in terms of regions dependent on the largest towns, but the regional divisions followed in the next chapter do, we believe, represent provinces or regions within which dominant towns, rival towns or groups of towns played an important role.[4] Clearly the regions we have chosen could easily be divided into sub-regions, as some contributors have indicated in their regional surveys; equally, others could be seen as overlapping into even larger regions, with London, for instance, spreading its influence into much of the Midlands, East Anglia and even the North.[5] Another anomaly is the position of Bristol, usually among the largest three provincial towns, which uneasily straddles two of our chosen regions, and is therefore discussed under both. Nevertheless, the scheme adopted is, we believe, as reasonable as can be devised to discuss the relationships of towns and the countryside in areas smaller than the realm. The fluid and multi-layered character of *all* English regional divisions, however, has to be borne in mind. Some large continental cities in the middle ages were able to monopolise the trade of their hinterlands, and even to take them under their full political and economic control, as with the *contadi* of the great Italian cities, which 'could inhibit the evolution of more extensive inland marketing networks. England, however, was a uniform and extensive polity, with a relatively unrestricted market system. That was one factor which promoted the growth of London and the early dynamism of English agriculture.'[6]

Even though the creation of a united English state in the tenth century weakened some aspects of local identity, notably the political loyalties to older kingdoms, a regional approach can still be helpful in understanding urban changes over time. Some regions experienced more prosperity, or more depression, than others. A good argument has been made, for example, that towns in the Danelaw – what became the North and East of a united England – were commercially more advanced in the ninth and tenth centuries than those in Wessex and western Mercia, partly at least because of a thriving North Sea economy rather

[4] The English regions are defined as follows: *South-East*: Bedfordshire, Berkshire, Buckinghamshire, Essex, Hampshire, Hertfordshire, Kent, Middlesex, Oxfordshire, Surrey, Sussex; *South-West*: Cornwall, Devon, Dorset, Somerset, Wiltshire; *Midlands*: Derbyshire, Gloucestershire, Leicestershire, Lincolnshire, Northamptonshire, Nottinghamshire, Rutland, Staffordshire, Warwickshire, Worcestershire; *East Anglia*: Cambridgeshire, Huntingdonshire, Norfolk, Suffolk; *North*: Cheshire, Cumberland, Durham, Lancashire, Northumberland, Westmorland, Yorkshire. *Wales and the Marches* is taken to include the whole of Wales together with Herefordshire, Monmouthshire and Shropshire, though the last is also partly covered as a Midland county.

[5] London's impact on the Newcastle coal trade was already apparent before *c.* 1200.

[6] B. M. S. Campbell, J. A. Galloway, D. Keene and M. Murphy, *A Medieval Capital and its Grain Supply* (Historical Geography Research Series, 30, London, 1993), p. 2.

than Scandinavian influences.[7] The dominance of the West Saxon dynasty from the tenth century effected some changes, including the development of Exeter and the South-West, while the rise of London and the Norman connections after 1066 further affected regional fortunes. Nevertheless, apart from London, six of the ten highest-taxed towns in 1334 may be described as east coast ports, coastal or inland (York, Newcastle, Boston, Norwich, Yarmouth and Lincoln). In the mid-fifteenth-century depression, however, that very east coast belt was, at least in part, the region most affected by urban 'decline', as trading advantages shifted to ports with good access to the markets of the Low Countries. York, Lincoln, Beverley, Boston, Lynn and others all fared worse as Norwich, Exeter, Reading and others prospered.[8]

It seems clear from the following surveys that there were significant regional variations throughout the middle ages, including the concentration of important towns in southern and eastern England, the early development of an urban network centred on London and the curious contrast between regions with important towns but few privileged boroughs (notably East Anglia) and the less-urbanised South-West with its multitude of small boroughs. Towns like Norwich, Bristol and York, and above all London, played a dominant role in creating an extensive network of urban specialisation, with distinctive products in large and small towns, regional links between them and considerable links between London and the regions. Clearly, the links were selective and patchy, and the lives of even some townspeople and countryfolk close to London or the provincial capitals might be little affected by them, but the basis was already there for more extensive and intensive development in the early modern period.

[7] A. Vince, 'The urban economy in Mercia in the 9th and 10th centuries', in S. Myrvoll, ed., *Archaeology and the Urban Economy* (Bergen, 1989), pp. 136–59.

[8] A. D. Dyer, *Decline and Growth in English Towns 1400–1640* (Basingstoke, 1991), pp. 40–2; A. J. Pollard, *North-Eastern England during the Wars of the Roses* (Oxford, 1990), pp. 43–80.

· 22(a) ·

The South-East of England

DEREK KEENE

(i) GENERAL CHARACTERISTICS AND TRANSITIONS

THE MANY sources throwing light on the existence, function and significance of the towns of south-eastern England during the middle ages are, as for other regions, fragmentary and incomplete. Measures of urbanisation are crude and below the top rank of towns indicators of urban function are lacking. The contemporary terminology for towns can mislead, although in the South-East, unlike East Anglia, those settlements whose urban status achieved formal recognition broadly corresponded to those which can be demonstrated to have been towns by virtue of social or economic function (Map 22.1). Thus, much of the discussion is concerned with the 150 or so places within the eleven counties surrounding London which at some time during the period were legally identified as towns (Map 22.2).[1]

This definition of south-eastern England, more extensive than that adopted in many regional studies, emphasises the capacity of the region for internal communication and for interaction with commercial networks overseas. The definition also acknowledges the role of London in shaping the region. Since Roman times London has been the dominant city of the British Isles and one of the most substantial in Western Europe. Yet over at least the first half of the period London occupied a site which was marginal in relation to kingdoms whose heartlands lay far from the city. Nevertheless, it was a powerful attraction and perhaps at times a seat of power shared between competing authorities. A continuing theme throughout the period, therefore, concerns London's integrating function,

[1] Most of the towns are listed in M. Beresford, *New Towns of the Middle Ages* (London, 1967); M. W. Beresford and H. P. R. Finberg, *English Medieval Boroughs* (Newton Abbot, 1973); and M. Beresford, 'English medieval boroughs: a hand-list: revisions, 1973–81', *UHY* (1981), 59–65. D. Hill, *An Atlas of Anglo-Saxon England*, 2nd edn (Oxford, 1984), pp. 126–44, covers the pre-Conquest period.

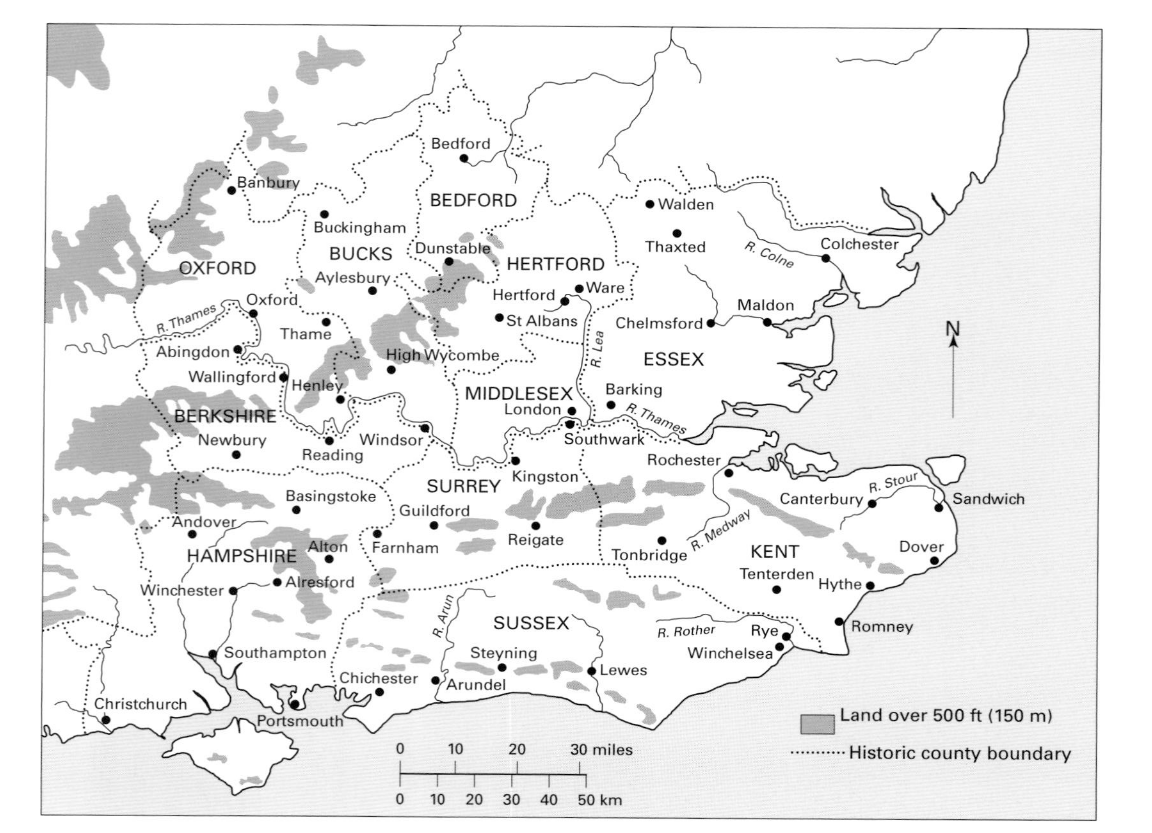

Map 22.1 The South-East of England and its principal towns during the later Middle Ages

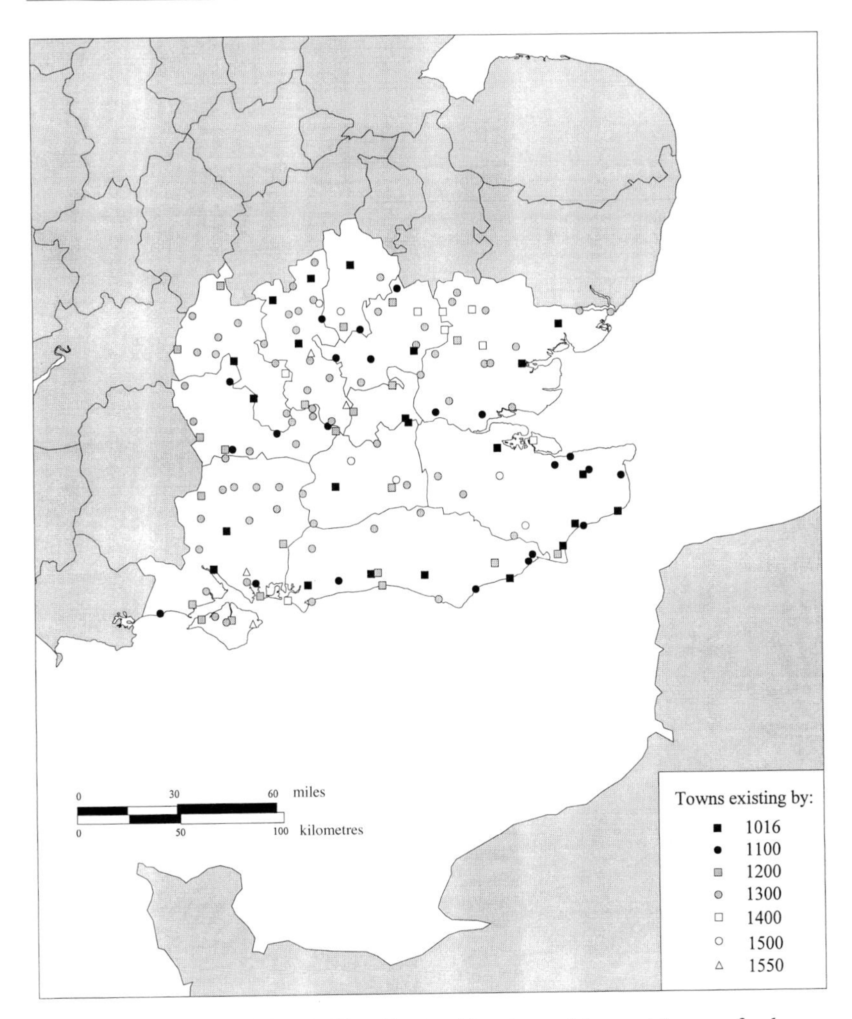

Map 22.2 Towns of South-East England by date of first evidence of urban status *c.* 900–1550

In most cases the evidence for the classification is noted in M. W. Beresford and H. P. R. Finberg, *English Medieval Boroughs* (Newton Abbot, 1973), and M. W. Beresford, 'English medieval boroughs; a hand-list: revisions, 1973–81', *UHY* (1981). Several of the lesser towns existing before 1100 have been identified by their status as mints (see C. E. Challis, *A New History of the Royal Mint* (Cambridge, 1992), table 2). The county boundaries shown here and in Maps 22.4–22.7 are approximate only, and derive from a modified version of a map first produced by Professor Marjorie K. McIntosh of the University of Colorado. I am grateful to Professor McIntosh for permission to use the map, and Dr J. A. Galloway of the Centre of Metropolitan History for undertaking the modifications as part of the 'Market networks in the London region *c.* 1400' project, funded by the Leverhulme Trust, at the Centre for Metropolitan History.

manifested in its special impact on the countryside and towns around it and in the way it gave shape to the English state whose capital it became shortly before 1300. London was the one stable element in an urban system in which a host of lesser towns, including sub-regional centres, continuously shifted rank.

Despite the force of London, older notions of regional identity, cutting across what we might, from a modern perspective, identify as the 'London region', retained some power. A twelfth-century author thought of Winchester as the 'head of the kingdom and the laws', but of London and Kent as areas with their own legal customs.[2] Contemporaries perceived England as a territory divided into regions focusing on cities, among which London was the 'queen metropolis', and London came commonly to be recognised as the 'head of the realm'.[3] Later in the middle ages London played a strong, but not well-understood, role in the evolution of standard English, yet even then London does not seem to have shaped contemporary perceptions of dialect difference. Those focused on the contrast between the North or the Danelaw, on the one hand, and the South or South-West on the other, while Norfolk and Kent were perceived as having distinctive forms of speech of their own,[4] thus revealing a culture, familiar in the twentieth century, in which London lacked a clear identity. Consideration of towns within the region should be sensitive to the evolution of cross-cutting, multi-layered notions of local identity and to the fact that contemporaries may not have perceived realities seemingly indicated by sources available to us.

London lies almost exactly at the centre of this region, which extends up to about 75 miles (120 km) in all directions, while other major medieval cities within it were about 60 miles (100 km) distant as the crow flies. The influence of those cities extended beyond the formal boundaries of the region, as did that of London itself. The distinctive standing and culture of the other cities was weakened as the power of London grew. Thus before the twelfth century the second city of the kingdom, and in some sense its capital, lay within the region, while afterwards English cities of second and even third rank lay well outside it.

The region owes much of its unity to physical factors. Water routes were a key influence. The Thames, at times and to varying degrees navigable downstream from Oxford, made accessible an extensive hinterland to the west of London. Other rivers were less significant, although the River Lea and the Essex estuaries provided access to several towns, while the Medway, the Stour and the Rother opened up large parts of north and east Kent and the Weald. Sussex rivers, navigable over shorter stretches, likewise served fertile inland districts and conditioned the siting and prosperity of towns. The Itchen and Test, however, were probably never navigable far above Southampton. The mouths of the major

[2] L. J. Downer, ed., *Leges Henrici Primi* (Oxford, 1972), pp. 44–5. [3] See above, p. 542.

[4] J. S. Brewer, J. F. Dimock and R. G. F. Warner, eds., *Giraldi Cambrensis Opera* (RS, 1861–91), vol. VI, p. 177; T. Turville-Petre, *England and the Nation: Language, Literature, and National Identity, 1290–1340* (Oxford, 1996), pp. 20–1, 143.

waterways opened across the sea to continental ports and river systems which had been important for British trade since before the Romans. In the middle ages the South-East, and especially parts of Kent, was thus closely associated with that area of intensive production and exchange which focused on the Strait of Dover and straddled the North Sea basin.[5] Roman writers noted the proximity of Britain to Germany and Gaul, and for Julius Caesar the inhabitants of Kent were the most civilised of the Britons.[6] Coastal trade unified much of eastern and southern England, from the Humber to the Solent, with the Thames estuary and Thanet as the fulcrum. About 970 York merchants landed at Thanet; later the men of Hastings promoted the Yarmouth herring fair; there were close trading connections between Colchester, Sandwich, Rye and Winchelsea, and between Lynn and Canterbury.[7] Havens and ports near Thanet became the focus of English naval interests.[8] Throughout the middle ages the intensive activity in the eastern and in some coastal parts of the region stood in sharp contrast to the more leisurely ways inland and to the west: London was on the threshold between these contrasting areas.

Harwich, at the eastern coastal limit of the region, was about the same distance from the mouth of the Rhine as Southampton, at the western coastal limit, was from the mouth of the Seine. London was equally well placed for both. Patterns of trade and culture reflected these proximities. The scale of London's market and its capacity for communication, both inland and along the coast, made it central for much of England. In handling bulky goods, London had more potential for developing close links with the coastal districts of the region and with the opposite shores of the sea than with its more immediate hinterland. Thus, in terms of transport costs a territory extending down the Thames valley from just below Oxford and then along ever narrowing coastal strips to north Norfolk and central Sussex was more accessible from London than were northern Hampshire, parts of northern Essex and the Weald, all closer as the crow flies.[9] By this measure, London was nearer to Bruges or St-Omer than to Oxford. Moreover, the difficulties of rounding North Foreland meant that Southampton and other south coast ports had less ready access to London by sea than ports on the Wash or the Humber which were about the same sailing distance from the capital.

The region was also shaped by its road system, the main framework of which, radiating from London, was a Roman inheritance. The Roman road through

[5] P. Barnwell, 'Kent and England in the early middle ages', *SHist.*, 16 (1994), 1–20.

[6] P. Salway, *Roman Britain* (Oxford, 1984), pp. 42, 39.

[7] A. S. Green, *Town Life in the Fifteenth Century* (London, 1894), vol. II, p. 49 n; *VCH*, Sussex, II, pp. 126–8, IX, pp. 8–9; D. Whitelock, ed., *English Historical Documents c. 500–1042* (London, 1979 (orig. publ. 1955)), pp. 227, 284; R. H. Britnell, *Growth and Decline in Colchester, 1300–1525* (Cambridge, 1986), pp. 13, 19; *VCH*, Essex, IX, p. 27.

[8] N. A. M. Rodger, 'The naval service of the Cinque Ports', *EHR*, 111 (1996), 636–51.

[9] B. M. S. Campbell, J. A. Galloway, D. Keene and M. Murphy, *A Medieval Capital and its Grain Supply* (Historical Geography Research Series, 30, London, 1993), fig. 7.

Silchester to the south-west was replaced by a more southerly route aiming for Winchester and Southampton. Political geography, as well as trade, favoured the emergence of other routes, including that north from Southampton to the upper Thames valley and the Midlands, and the road from London to Oxford, both reflecting the establishment of Oxford as a strategic centre. Land and water transport systems were complementary. Roads transmitted commodities and information whose value was high by comparison with the cost of carrying them, and so were important for gaining commercial, political or military advantage. Roads between London and the ports east of Southampton provided the most rapid access to the Channel.[10] Roads which ran parallel to water routes transmitted news more swiftly than the goods being carried by boat and so facilitated the efficient operation of trade. The most important of that type linked London and Canterbury, via the bridge at Rochester. Central to the identity of the kingdom, it provided rapid access to the continent, and linked the metropolis of the English Church with the seat of secular power. Canterbury, in association with its outports and with the bastion of the realm at Dover, was a key site from which to watch the continent, and at which to wait for a passage, receive important visitors, handle money and bullion and stockpile goods for trade. The cult of the London-born St Thomas the Martyr, and the Canterbury pilgrimage, were resounding expressions of these vital connections.

Traffic influenced the lesser towns of the region as way stations, as markets feeding local products into wider distributive systems, as break-points for consignments of goods brought into the locality and as interchanges between land and water routes. Conversely, the promotion of a town might, as with Thame or Henley, significantly change the regional pattern of routes.[11] Investment in land transport is apparent from the eighth century onwards, and the stock of bridges was essentially complete by 1300.[12] The same seems also to have been true of investment in water transport, such as the construction of the substantial quays needed to handle the growing volume of trade.[13] The human contribution to the physical infrastructure of the region in the pre-canal age was essentially complete before the Black Death.

Within the region, the chalk ridges of the North and South Downs, the Chiltern Hills and the Berkshire and north Hampshire Downs, rising in places to more than 800 feet (250 m) above sea level, were significant barriers to movement. Elsewhere, the soils of the region included extensive tracts of clay, especially in Essex and Middlesex. Important zones of deep, well-drained loams and alluvial soils in northern and eastern Kent, along the Thames valley and near the Sussex coast were highly productive. Over much of the region different soils

[10] *VCH*, Sussex, VI, pp. 140, 156–7.
[11] Campbell, Galloway, Keene and Murphy, *Medieval Capital*, pp. 47–9, 174.
[12] D. F. Harrison, 'Bridges and economic development, 1300–1800', *Ec.HR*, 45 (1992), 240–61.
[13] See pp. 375 and 470.

were intermixed, and agrarian practice effectively combined a variety of resources. Throughout the period the Chiltern Hills and the Weald, both relatively difficult of access, contained extensive tracts of woodland. Clearance of wood for cultivation was great by 1350, but the region nevertheless remained more wooded than England as a whole, in part because of London's large demand for fuel. Little is known of population densities before 1086 and of farming practice before the late thirteenth century, but evidence from those dates indicates a pattern in which continuities are striking. In 1086 eastern Kent and parts of coastal Sussex contained some of the highest rural population densities in England. Much of the rest of the region was underpopulated by comparison with southern England as a whole, although the limited areas of dense population along the Thames immediately above London and in the middle and upper Thames area are notable. The picture is similar for the fourteenth century. By that date northern Kent and the vicinity of Southampton had also emerged as prosperous areas, and Bedfordshire had been drawn into a Midland region of dense population in the hinterland of the Wash. North and east Kent, and to a lesser extent Sussex, were notable for intensive farming systems, which resembled those of Norfolk and the densely settled parts of Flanders and northern France a short distance across the sea. This was as much an outcome of commerce and urbanisation, and of opportunities for diversification, including sea fishing, as of the inherent qualities of the soil. Within the region as a whole, however, these busy districts were offset by the relative sparsity of population elsewhere, so that while the region contained 21 per cent of the land area of England in the fourteenth century it held no more than 26 per cent of the population and 30 per cent of taxed wealth, the latter undoubtedly indicating the commercial character of the region and its largest city (Table 22.1).[14]

Under Roman rule the South-East, containing a third of the *civitas* capitals of Britain, was notable for its degree of urban order.[15] Five of the capitals were again important centres in the seventh century or later, and of the principal medieval towns of the region only Oxford lacked a substantial Roman predecessor. Roman ways of thinking contributed an element to the urban culture of the region, which contained more than a third of medieval English episcopal sees. Yet while the Roman urban system primarily served the needs of a land-based empire to control a wide territory and to ensure the orderly distribution of money and goods, later urban networks, up to 1300 and beyond, came into being

[14] See R. E. Glasscock, ed., *The Lay Subsidy of 1334* (London, 1975), maps I and II; E. Miller, ed., *Ag.HEW*, vol. III (Cambridge, 1991), pp. 28–85; R. Smith, 'Human resources', in G. Astill and A. Grant, eds., *The Countryside of Medieval England* (Oxford, 1988), pp. 188–212; Campbell, Galloway, Keene and Murphy, *Medieval Capital*, *passim*; J. A. Galloway, D. Keene and M. Murphy, 'Fuelling the city: production and distribution of firewood and fuel in London's region, 1290–1400', *Ec.HR*, 49 (1996), 447–72.

[15] J. S. Wacher, *The Towns of Roman Britain* (London, 1975), fig. 3.

under locally based warrior aristocracies which required access to, and drew profit from, trade. Some Roman towns continued as foci of power after the formal end of imperial rule. Suggestions of continuity of settlement and authority from Roman to English rule at Canterbury, Dorchester, London and Winchester are far from conclusive. *Verulamium* and Silchester may have survived as seats of British authority into the sixth century, and were the only two *civitas* capitals in the region whose sites did not subsequently come to be reused as urban centres. That may indicate the influence of immediately post-imperial political structures in shaping urban survival, failure or regrowth, but it is equally significant that neither of those towns had access to the sea.[16]

Four factors shaped the pattern of town development over the period as a whole. The first was population and the potential it provided for specialisation and exchange. Those forms of urban life which emerged in the immediately post-Roman centuries were sustained by a much less densely settled countryside than had been the case under Roman rule. After considerable, but not quantifiable, growth the region in 1100 may have contained fewer than half the number of inhabitants it had had in AD 200, a total which may not have been equalled until about 1300 when the medieval population was at its peak.[17] The second factor was overseas trade, reviving in the late seventh and eighth centuries, then suffering a setback but growing again from the late tenth century onwards. The dynamics of this growth were continental rather than insular in origin and the towns of the South-East were important in linking Britain to those wider networks of exchange. Indeed, the activities of the sailors and merchants of the English south coast ports must have been largely responsible for Mediterranean perceptions, by the mid-twelfth century, of the waters to the north of Spain as 'the sea of the English'.[18] The third factor embodied the political structures and the pattern of warfare in the region. The Viking invasions of the ninth century provide the most dramatic instance, for while they undermined one urban system the reaction to them promoted the emergence of a newly ordered network of towns. Nevertheless, the later Danish invasions, the Norman Conquest and the loss of Normandy each influenced the pattern of urban prosperity. Finally, there was the accumulation of networks of knowledge and trust, in train before the ninth century and more clearly apparent from the tenth century onwards, which sustained urban growth and specialisation. This was one of the major and lasting legacies of the period: its survival through the demographic catastrophe of the fourteenth century presents a striking contrast to the discontinuity after the end of Roman rule. This was part of a wider European process which had a profound influence on the towns of the region, and underlay the growth of London.

[16] The most recent assessment of the 'continuity issue' is D. G. Russo, *Town Origins and Development in Early England, c. 400–950 A.D.* (Westport, Conn., 1998).

[17] Salway, *Roman Britain*, p. 544.

[18] R. Dozy, ed., *Description de l'Afrique et de l'Espagne par Edrîsî* (Leiden, 1866), p. 206; C. W. David, *De Expugnatione Lyxbonensi* (New York, 1936), pp. 54–7.

(ii) COMMERCIAL CENTRES, DEFENCE AND MARKETS FROM THE SEVENTH TO THE ELEVENTH CENTURY

Between the seventh and the ninth century the recognisably urban settlements in the South-East were the trading sites, or 'wics', at London and Southampton. With areas of well over 150 and 100 acres (60 and 40 ha), respectively, they were densely built-up and carefully ordered settlements. Ipswich, just outside the region, was similar in character. The primary function of these towns was trade with counterparts in the Low Countries and northern France. [19] Equally important as a commercial phenomenon, although less well understood as a physical settlement, was the cluster of sites in the easternmost part of Kent, including ports at Reculver, Richborough and Sandwich, toll stations at Sarre and Fordwich and the suburb of Canterbury itself. Collectively, in terms of population and business, this cluster of settlements may have exceeded London, and the use of coinage seems to have spread thence into other parts of the region.[20]

These towns were associated with seats of royal and episcopal authority at Canterbury, London and Winchester, all former Roman capitals and now serving as the chief cities of three distinct peoples. Much of their trade doubtless served the needs of elite groups, but the size of the settlements and the evidence for manufactures and local trade indicates that their economies were complex and had much in common with the larger towns of the region at a later date. Fundamental aspects of their organisation, however, remain obscure. Religious communities and secular rulers probably organised craft production and the distribution of the surplus from their estates. That perhaps both contributed to the life of the *wics* and stimulated the emergence of smaller settlements with some urban characteristics. Abingdon, Barking, Bedford, Hertford, Kingston, Oxford and Steyning serve as examples of monastic sites, meeting places, royal vills or sites for royal burial which may have been centres of some significance in this period, and which later were to be towns.[21] On the other hand, at least one site where money and crafts are evidenced seems to have been

[19] See above, pp. 218–21.

[20] D. M. Metcalf, 'Monetary circulation in southern England in the first half of the eighth century', in D. Hill and D. M. Metcalf, eds., *Sceattas in England and on the Continent* (British Archaeological Reports, British Series, 128, 1984), pp. 27–69; N. P. Brooks, *The Early History of the Church of Canterbury* (Leicester, 1984), pp. 22–30; *Med. Arch.*, 35 (1991), 170; D. A. Hinton, 'Coins and commercial centres in Anglo-Saxon England', in M. A. S. Blackburn, ed., *Anglo-Saxon Monetary History* (Leicester, 1986), pp. 11–26; S. Kelly, 'Trading privileges from eighth-century England', *Early Medieval Europe*, 1 (1992), 3–28

[21] *VCH*, Sussex, VI, p. 220; J. Haslam, ed., *Anglo-Saxon Towns in Southern England* (Chichester, 1984), pp. 56–7; *Med. Arch.*, 30 (1986), 136–7; *ibid.*, 31 (1987), 126; *ibid.*, 34 (1990), 182–3; B. A. E. Yorke, *Kings and Kingdoms in Early Anglo-Saxon England* (London, 1990), pp. 45, 55, 116; S. Keynes, *An Atlas of Attestations of Anglo-Saxon Charters* (Cambridge, 1995), *passim*.

no more than the rural residence of an elite household.[22] We know too little about such places satisfactorily to define any 'urban network'. Nevertheless, it is clear that the major urban sites had access to the sea and that in addition there were noteworthy distributions of settlements with some urban features along the south coast and along the Thames from its estuary up to Oxford. These were areas which had been notable for wealth during the sixth century. The upper Thames valley and what is now south Bedfordshire contained distinctive clusters of such sites, which may indicate traffic between those areas and the Wash. There are signs of commerce at Colchester, and, as in later periods, trade between London and East Anglia.[23] As Mercian power grew, London and the Thames valley became vital elements in a political and commercial nexus extending from the Midlands to eastern Kent. Southampton served the West Saxons in a similar fashion. Control of London and Kent was a central issue in relations between the kingdoms.

The *wics* were undefended, and in those Roman cities in use during this period the space within the wall may have been a relatively empty elite preserve. That seems possible in the cases of London, Canterbury and even Winchester, but the recent discovery within the walls at Winchester of an apparently eighth- to ninth-century cemetery containing several hundred interments suggests the presence there of a sizeable non-aristocratic population.[24] Outside the immediate confines of royal and minster precincts it was perhaps the practical considerations of land use and commerce, rather than a purely social allocation of space, which determined the use of these walled cities.

The Viking invasions undermined these arrangements, destroyed Mercian authority and bore especially hard upon Canterbury and eastern Kent.[25] The West Saxon reaction to the invasions, including the establishment of defended sites and the means of manning and supplying them, reordered the framework of urban life, with an emphasis on the strategic control of the Wessex heartland and the areas progressively recovered from the invaders. That, along with the tenth-century policies concerning markets and mints, promoted regularity in the concentration of business and a degree of urbanisation, especially in inland districts. Some of the new urban sites were defended bridgeheads or short-lived refuges, but at others substantial walled circuits enclosed regular layouts of streets or plots presumably intended to house substantial populations. The space within the Roman walls of Winchester was disposed in this way, while activity at Southampton declined sharply. At London the commercial focus of the settlement moved from outside

[22] J. R. Fairbrother, *Faccombe Netherton: Excavations of a Saxon and Medieval Manorial Complex* (London, 1990).

[23] Metcalf, 'Monetary circulation'; Hinton, 'Coins'; A. Vince, *Saxon London* (London, 1990), pp. 107, 112–14.

[24] *Med. Arch.*, 30 (1986), 149; *ibid.*, 34 (1990), 188. The most recent, but unpublished, view on this cemetery, however, is that it dates from the tenth century and later.

[25] Barnwell, 'Kent'.

to within the walls. On the upper Thames a large walled town was established at Wallingford and a somewhat smaller one at Oxford, testifying to the resources concentrated in that district and to the strategic necessity of controlling the Thames valley and the road into recently recovered Mercian territory. Defended centres were also established at Hertford, Bedford and Buckingham and further north. On the south coast the Roman city of Chichester, not hitherto a significant site for settlement and trade (that may have been at the episcopal seat of Selsey), was brought back into use, and an almost equally large defended site was established at Lewes. Details are lacking for Kent.[26]

These formal arrangements were not immediately accompanied by a revival of earlier prosperity. Much of the tenth century appears to have been characterised by the development of an internal network of markets and towns, rather than by commercial growth associated with long-distance trade.[27] London's contacts were with the Oxford region rather than overseas. About 970 Wallingford was described as a 'modest city replete with commerce', testimony to the importance of internal trade along the Thames, and in the mid-eleventh century its inhabitants owed carrying services to neighbouring settlements and downriver to Reading, indicating the way in which the town served its hinterland and distributed produce further afield.[28] Oxford, better situated for traffic to the north, came to overtake Wallingford, although the latter remained an important strategic centre.[29] It was not until the later tenth century, however, that London's overseas trading contacts were definitively re-established, reflecting the increasing intensity of production and exchange in northern France and the Low Countries. The new flow of German silver lubricated this growth and made Cologne a trading centre of special importance for the region. Ceramics suggest that in Wessex and the south specialised industrial production for an extended market also developed at that time, but that in this respect the region lagged behind the Midlands and other parts of the Danelaw.[30] Thus early tenth-century towns in the upper Thames valley may have been more vigorous than those to the south and south-east.

A sense of the tenth-century urban hierarchy can be gained from the size of defended areas *c.* 900, numbers of moneyers *c.* 930 and mint outputs *c.* 1000.[31]

[26] Hill, *Anglo-Saxon Atlas*, pp. 85–6; J. Campbell, E. John and P. Wormald, *The Anglo-Saxons* (Oxford, 1982), pp. 152–3; Haslam, ed., *Anglo-Saxon Towns in Southern England*, pp. 315–30.

[27] S. H. Jones, 'Transaction costs, institutional change, and the emergence of a market economy in later Anglo-Saxon England', *Ec.HR*, 46 (1993), 658–78.

[28] M. Lapidge and M. Winterbottom, *Wulfstan of Winchester: The Life of St Æthelwold* (Oxford, 1990), pp. 64–6; *VCH*, Berkshire, I, p. 325.

[29] *VCH*, Berkshire, III, pp. 523–4.

[30] See above, pp. 191, 543–4; *Med. Arch.*, 38 (1994), 308 (review of D. Piton, ed., *Travaux du Groupe de Recherches et d'Etudes sur la Céramique dans le Nord-Pas-de Calais* (Berck-sur-Mer, 1993)).

[31] Hill, *Anglo-Saxon Atlas*, pp. 126–30; D. M. Metcalf, 'The ranking of boroughs: numismatic evidence from the reign of Æthelred II', in. D. Hill, ed., *Ethelred the Unready* (British Archaeological Reports, British Series, 59, 1978), pp. 59–201. See Table 22.1.

Early in the century London was undoubtedly the principal centre of business and population. Winchester was a large and apparently growing city and the main seat of royal authority, but Canterbury had more moneyers, and in that respect almost equalled London. Rochester, Chichester, Lewes and Southampton were also significant towns, each with as many moneyers as Exeter. The prominence of the two Kent towns, however, may reflect their traditional status as mints rather than their present prosperity. At the beginning of the century land in Winchester near the main market street was already very valuable, while during its last three decades major building programmes at the city's great minsters and evidence for specialised craft districts suggest further growth.[32] In the late tenth century lesser market towns with mints such as Aylesbury and Guildford, both on important roads, emerged to complement, if not rival, established centres such as Buckingham, Bedford and Hertford. St Albans, promoted by the abbey and its estate economy, may belong to the same group of emerging inland market towns.[33] Ports were equally vigorous, and among the seventeen towns in the region which emerged as mints between *c.* 930 and *c.* 1020, eight were inland and seven, including Hastings, Romney and Steyning, were on the south coast, indicating the growth of Channel trade. Colchester came rapidly to the fore as sixth town of the region, demonstrating the importance of links across the North Sea.

In the early eleventh century London dominated the towns of the South-East. Winchester, in the second rank of English towns by size and wealth and in the first by virtue of its political and cultural standing, had a mint output less than half of London's (Table 22.1). By that measure, the next most important towns of the region were Southwark and Canterbury, followed or sometimes equalled by Oxford, Lewes, Colchester and Wallingford. Oxford became a major town, significant for its hinterland, its links with London, as a royal centre and as a national meeting place, especially when conflicts between northern and southern interests were to be resolved.[34] The network of towns, providing a framework of public order as well as commerce and crafts, was dominated by former Roman cities and by major new urban centres on the upper Thames. The smaller towns lay predominantly on the coast and north of a line between Oxford and Maldon, demonstrating the significance of the northern inland part of the region for small-scale local marketing. The renewed significance of 'nodal areas' of commercial and urban (or proto-urban) activity apparent before the ninth century is striking: London, east Kent, central coastal Sussex, the Solent, the upper Thames and Bedfordshire (Map 22.2).

London and Southwark together seem at this period to have accounted for about half the urban activity of the region, as measured by mint output, while

[32] M. Biddle, ed., *Winchester in the Early Middle Ages* (Oxford, 1976), pp. 454–5.

[33] P. Taylor, 'The early St. Albans endowment and its chronicles', *HR*, 68 (1995), 119–42.

[34] *VCH*, Oxfordshire, IV, pp. 3–10, 22, 35.

the region as a whole accounted for about half the urban activity of England (Table 22.1). This indication of the concentration of urban life in the South-East bears comparison with later measures of the 'urban potential' of the region (see below), and demonstrates the significance of its close connections to the continent. *A priori* it would seem that the towns of the region already operated within an urban system which was to some degree integrated, and within which they developed complementary roles. Direct evidence of this is hard to come by, but the relations between London and Winchester are indicative. Londoners were the most prominent visitors to Winchester in the 960s, and later in the century their city gained precedence over the West Saxon capital as a site associated with the national standard of measurement.[35] Traffic between the two cities presumably contributed to the growth of Guildford, while the Thames was almost certainly used in trade between the Oxford region and London. The twelfth-century (or earlier) rules concerning rights of pre-emption from the Lorraine merchants in London indicate that the city's trade was of great interest to the other towns of the region: first the king's representative had made his purchases from the Lorrainers, then, the merchants of London, Oxford and Winchester in succession made theirs, before the market was opened to traders from other towns.[36] The regular sequence of small and large towns along the south coast in this period suggests an integrated response to coastal and inland traffic.

(iii) GROWTH AND INTENSIFICATION: ELEVENTH TO FOURTEENTH CENTURY

The eleventh century witnessed substantial urban growth, indicated by the physical expansion and increasing density of settlements and by the foundation of parish (or proto-parochial) churches at centres such as London and Oxford. By the measure of parish churches Winchester was perhaps half the size of London and significantly larger than Oxford and Canterbury.[37] The overall distribution of towns remained more or less unchanged, but the emergence of new towns in already urbanised areas along the coast and the Thames valley and in the counties to the north of London, as well as the appearance of local hierarchies, indicates intensifying use of market centres (Map 22.2). Borough farms and the totals of burgesses or town properties recorded in Domesday Book reveal the increasing predominance of London, now perhaps three times wealthier than Winchester.[38] Other major centres were Wallingford and Oxford, while distinctly below them came Canterbury, Colchester and Lewes, after which the

[35] Biddle, ed., *Winchester*, pp. 461, 556–7.

[36] M. Bateson, 'A London municipal collection of the reign of John', *EHR* 17 (1902), 480–511, 707–29, esp. 500.

[37] See above, pp. 134–5.

[38] J. Tait, *The Medieval English Borough* (Manchester, 1936), p. 184; Biddle, ed., *Winchester*, p. 500; H. C. Darby, *Domesday England* (Cambridge, 1977), pp. 364–8.

Table 22.1 *Principal towns in the South-East estimated as a proportion of regional values*

	Percentages of regional total, in rank order													
	Mint output								Valuation for tax[a]					
	c. 1000[b]		c. 1020[c]		c. 1050[d]		c. 1086[e]		1334[f]		1377[g]		1524[h]	
Principal towns	L & S[h]	47	L & S	56	L & S	39	L & S	30	L & S	6.6	L & S	6.9	L & S	28.8
	London	38	London	50	London	37	Winchester	19	London	6.5	London	6.5	London	27.5
	Winchester	19	Winchester	15	Winchester	15	Canterbury	18	Oxford	0.5	Colchester	0.9	Southwark	1.3
	Southwark	9	Southwark	6	Canterbury	7	London	17	Winchester	0.4	Canterbury	0.8	Canterbury	0.9
	Canterbury	7	Oxford	6	Hastings	7	Southwark	13	Canterbury	0.3	Oxford	0.7	Reading	0.7
	Lewes	4	Canterbury	3	Lewes	5	Dover	7	S'hampton[j]	0.3	Winchester	0.7	Colchester	0.7
	Colchester	3	Colchester	3	Oxford	5	Oxford	5	Newbury	0.2	?		Newbury	0.4
	Oxford	3	Lewes	3	Chichester	5	Wallingford	4	Barking	0.2	S'hampton	0.3	St Albans	0.3
	Wallingford	3	Hertford	2	Wallingford	4	Lewes	3	Reading	0.2	Southwark[k]	0.3	S'hampton	0.3
	Rochester	3	Wallingford	2	Steyning	3	Chichester	3	Abingdon	0.2	Chichester	0.3	Oxford	0.3
	Hertford	2	Bedford	2	Colchester	3	Colchester	1.5	Banbury	0.2	Maidstone	0.2	Windsor	0.3
	Lympne	2	Dover	2	Bedford	2	Hastings	1.5	St Albans	0.2	Newbury	0.2	Winchester	0.3
	Dover	2	Maldon	1.5	Dover	2	Romney	1.5	Colchester	0.15	Thaxted	0.2	Maldon	0.2
	Maldon	2	Chichester	1.5	Hertford	2	S'hampton	1.5	Chichester	0.15	Writtle	0.2	Basingstoke	0.2
	Bedford	1	S'hampton	1.4	Southwark	2	Steyning	1.5	Dunstable	0.12	Tenterden	0.2	Barking	0.2
	Chichester	1	Rochester	0.7	Sandwich	1	Sandwich	1	Kingston	0.12	Maldon	0.2	Chichester	0.2
	S'hampton	0.5	Hastings	0.6	Romney	0.8	Hythe	1	Andover	0.12	Banbury	0.2	Kingston	0.2
	Hastings	0.4	Romney	0.4	Rochester	0.8	Bedford[l]	0.6	Bedford	0.12			Rochester	0.2
Other towns with values (N)	(6)	1.2	(5)	0.75	(7)	2.3	(5)	1.8	(102)	6.0		?	(101)	6.0

All towns with values	100	100	100	100	16.1	?	41
Regional total	100	100	100	100	100	100	100
London as % England	19	21	14	9	1.9	1.7	12
L & S as % England	23	23	16	16	2	1.7	12
Region as % England	49	41	41	53	30	26.0	42

Notes and sources:

[a] Valuations are lacking for many towns which should appear in this group, especially for towns in Kent and Sussex.

[b] Metcalf, 'The ranking of boroughs'.

[c] Based on the recorded coins of Cnut's Quatrefoil type in K. Jonsson, 'The coinage of Cnut', in A. R. Rumble, ed., *The Reign of Cnut: King of England, Denmark and Norway* (London, 1994), pp. 193–230, Table 11.9.

[d] Based on total recorded coins by mints under Edward the Confessor, A. Freeman, *The Moneyer and the Mint in the Reign of Edward the Confessor, 1042–1066* (British Archaeological Reports, British Series, 145(i), Oxford, 1985).

[e] Based on mid ranges of the estimated mint output of the Paxs type of William I: D. M. Metcalf, 'Continuity and change in English monetary history, *c.* 973–1086', *British Numismatic Journal*, 50 (1980), Appendix VII.

[f] Glasscock, ed., *Lay Subsidy*. The following places, whose recorded values lie within the range covered by the table, have been excluded on the grounds that the values probably reflect the scale of their rural territories rather than the urban nucleus: Chipping Norton, Haslemere, Leighton Buzzard, Luton, Uxbridge, Waltham (Essex), Wargrave, Writtle.

[g] C. Fenwick, 'The English poll taxes of 1377, 1379 and 1381: a critical examination of the returns' (PhD thesis, London School of Economics, 1983), and figures kindly provided by Richard Smith. Many town totals are missing. The values are those recorded which represent more than 0.15 per cent of the regional total.

[h] J. Sheail, *The Regional Distribution of Wealth in England as Indicated by 1524/5 Subsidy Returns*, ed. R. W. Hoyle (Kew: List and Index Society, 1998).

[i] London and Southwark.

[j] Southampton.

[k] Based on total in M. Carlin, *Medieval Southwark* (London, 1996), p. 137.

[l] Maldon and Rochester have the same value.

other towns were very much less significant. The larger towns contained substantial populations, with totals (perhaps minima) of 6,000 people at Canterbury and 9,000 at Winchester, and well over 20,000 at London, although all such estimates should be treated with caution.[39] In the larger towns craft specialisation was well advanced.[40]

Military events had a distinctive impact. Within Cnut's Danish empire, London gained a new strategic significance as a centre of authority and the collection of tribute enhanced the standing of its mint. The emergence of Sandwich, an outport of Canterbury but perhaps already associated with London, points to the importance of east Kent both for trade and the assembly of ships. Defence and the need to control the Channel explain the ship-service owed by south coast ports and the origins of the special privileges of the Cinque Ports.[41]

The impact of the Norman Conquest was more dramatic. Control of cities and communications was essential to holding the kingdom. Key urban sites, and some lesser ones, were quickly secured by the erection of castles, involving the displacement of inhabitants and lasting changes in the form and aspect of towns.[42] The Conquest also influenced the output of coin, foreshadowing the way in which the structure of the Anglo-Norman realm was to influence its towns.[43] Minting was concentrated in southern areas most firmly under the control of the new regime, and so the towns of the South-East increased their share of national output. Royal uncertainty concerning the city of London may be indicated by the sharp fall in its share, although a corresponding increase in Southwark's contribution seems to demonstrate the continuing importance of London, in its broadest sense, as a commercial and fiscal centre. The special, but short-lived, significance of the Canterbury and Dover mints expresses the firm control of Kent.[44] Increases in the size and value of Sussex port towns between 1066 and 1086[45] suggest their closer links with Normandy. Winchester's enhancement as a minting centre reflects its new situation within a cross-Channel axis of power, as well as the investment which flowed from the new regime stamping its mark on the heart of the English kingdom.

[39] Brooks, *Early History of the Church of Canterbury*, p. 32; Biddle, ed., *Winchester*, p. 440; D. Keene, *Survey of Medieval Winchester* (Winchester Studies, 2, Oxford, 1985), vol. I, pp. 366–8. London is estimated in relation to the other two. See above, pp. 194–6.

[40] Biddle, ed., *Winchester*, pp. 427–39.

[41] Haslam,ed., *Anglo-Saxon Towns in Southern England*, pp. 16–21; R. Eales, 'An introduction to the Kent Domesday', in *The Kent Domesday* (London, 1992), pp. 1–77, esp. pp. 32, 39; Rodger, 'Naval service'.

[42] D. J. C. King, *Castellarium Anglicanum: An Index and Bibliography of the Castles in England, Wales and the islands* (Millwood, N.Y., 1983).

[43] Table 22.1 and D. M. Metcalf, 'Continuity and change in English monetary history, *c.* 973–1086', *British Numismatic J*, 50 (1980), 20–49, and 51 (1981), 52–90.

[44] Eales, 'Kent Domesday', pp. 43–9.

[45] *VCH*, Sussex, I, pp. 387–9, 391–2, 395, 407, 435.

Since well before the Conquest the larger towns had been places of special interest for the king and other lords as places of assembly, occasional residence, rent income and trade.[46] Under the peripatetic style of government, changes in the geography of power influenced the prosperity of towns. London certainly increased its prominence by the early thirteenth century, when it was three to four times wealthier than the second and third cities nationally and seven times more so than the second city in the South-East.[47] Yet throughout the Anglo-Norman period London was at the far eastern limit of the English territory habitually visited by the king, which was shaped primarily by an axis extending north from the Solent to Oxford and Northampton.[48] Passage to and from Normandy acquired a new significance in government, estate management and trade: it was the main factor behind the spectacular twelfth-century growth of Southampton. Oxford's rise to second town of the region by the mid-thirteenth century reflects the new governmental pattern, as well as its role as a meeting place now favoured by clergy from north and south. Oxford was as much a town of the Midlands as of the South-East.[49] Colchester's relative decline[50] may also be an outcome of political geography, as well as of the growth of Yarmouth and Ipswich. The importance of the new axis is indicated by the cluster of new towns in the vicinity of the Solent and those further to the north (Map 22.2). Newbury grew up on a site of military significance in Stephen's reign where the road north crossed a major east–west route. The new town quickly overshadowed the older one of Thatcham nearby, and by the thirteenth century there was a small Jewish community there.[51]

Other new towns of the period appear within the already urbanised parts of the region, especially to the north of London, along some of the principal roads radiating from London, and along the middle stretches of the Thames (Map 22.2). Winchester lost some of its standing as a national centre in the early twelfth century, and more later with the settling of governmental functions in London, but it remained an important royal seat and the site of the only major international fair south of the Thames until the reign of Edward I when, in recognition of the power of London, royal interests suddenly focused more sharply on the capital.[52] During the second half of the thirteenth century and in the early fourteenth Winchester seems, along with Canterbury and at times Southampton, to have been in the third rank after Oxford, although by then all towns in

[46] R. Fleming, 'Rural elites and urban communities in late-saxon England', *P&P*, 141 (1993), 3–37.
[47] Biddle, ed., *Winchester*, p. 501.
[48] T. K. Keefe, 'Place-date distribution of royal charters and the historical geography of patronage strategies at the court of King Henry II Plantagenet', *Haskins Society J*, 2 (1990), 179–88.
[49] *VCH*, Oxfordshire, IV, p. 13; J. I. Catto, ed., *The History of the University of Oxford*, vol. I: *The Early Oxford Schools* (Oxford, 1984), pp. 12–17; J. F. Hadwin, 'The medieval lay subsidies and economic history', *Ec.HR*, 2nd series, 36 (1983), 200–17.
[50] *VCH*, Essex, IX, pp. 26–7.
[51] *VCH*, Berkshire, IV, p. 136.
[52] See above, pp. 214–15.

the South-East, other than London, were outranked by provincial centres which lay well outside the region, including York, Bristol, Lincoln and Norwich, which came to the fore in the twelfth century, and perhaps Newcastle and Yarmouth, which became prominent during the thirteenth. Oxford ranked no higher than eighth or ninth among English towns. According to the 1334 valuations, London was five times greater than the second city nationally and seven times that of the third, but it was more than twelve times greater than Oxford. In terms of population, as indicated by the poll tax assessments of 1377, London's dominance was not quite so marked. This pattern of urbanisation indicates the strengthening of regional networks outside the South-East and the emergence of a more clearly structured national system of towns, while London became ever more dominant.[53]

Many of the thirteenth-century new towns contributed to the intensification of local networks. In two areas, however, they appear where there had been no small towns before (Map 22.2). In the extreme north-west of the region, Oxford perhaps stimulated small-town development in its hinterland. A swathe of new towns also appeared in the relatively sparsely inhabited territory extending from northern Hampshire through Surrey into the inland parts of Sussex. Some were on roads from London to the coast. The continuing emergence of towns in response to traffic is indicated by the evenly spaced group along the road between Guildford and Winchester. The monasteries, which had long been important nuclei for town growth, were in the twelfth and thirteenth centuries joined by the peripatetic owners of great estates, such as the bishop of Winchester, who promoted towns as a way to take advantage of the increasing density of resources and exchange. Some towns, like Banbury,[54] grew up at the estate centres where lords consolidated their power. Reigate, the castle town of the Warenne family, was a focus for their Surrey estates, but also a staging post between their residence in Southwark and their town of Lewes, where William de Warenne had erected a strong castle after the Conquest. This axis shows how castles, large towns and small towns could complement one another in establishing territorial control. Close to Reigate, and perhaps deliberately set up to rival it, was the smaller castle town of Bletchingley, belonging to the Clare family, whose local headquarters lay further east at the castle town of Tonbridge, established soon after the Conquest.[55] In a similar fashion the great royal castle at Windsor, controlling the Thames valley above London, stimulated town growth.

Many of the small towns of the region lacked strong urban identities. At least fifty-nine of the 125 towns assessed in 1334[56] were valued at less than £87, the value for Farnham and representing 0.05 per cent of the total valuation of the

[53] See Table 22.1 and below, Appendix 4, 5. [54] *BAHT*, I, 'Banbury', pp. 1–2.

[55] *VCH*, Surrey, III, pp. 229–34, IV, pp. 253–5; *VCH*, Sussex, VII, pp. 1, 19–23; Eales, 'Kent Domesday', p. 44. [56] Glasscock, *Lay Subsidy*.

region and 0.8 per cent that of London. The least town in this group, the bishop of Winchester's Newtown, near Newbury, was in 1334 valued at 0.01 per cent of London and in 1301–2, when it apparently had neither market stalls nor tolls, contained seventy-five houses or plots and was worth almost £8 a year to the bishop. Overton, another of the bishop's new towns, had thirty-two stalls, sixteen selds (shops) and about eighty houses, generated £12 13s. 6d. income in 1301–2, and was valued at 0.49 per cent of London in 1334. New Alresford had fulling mills, tolls, stalls and about 150 houses, brought in £20 2s. 6d. in 1301–2, and was valued at 0.65 per cent of London in 1334. On this evidence, New Alresford probably had at least 650 inhabitants. All three towns appear to have been bigger in the thirteenth century.[57] Slightly more substantial towns could offer a wider range of services and crafts. Baldock, founded by the Templars near where the Icknield Way crossed the London road, had at least eleven specialised occupations, including that of goldsmith, in 1185.[58] In 1334 it ranked forty-sixth or lower among the towns of the region (1.21 per cent of London) and was of about the same standing as Reigate, the small but developing industrial town of Thaxted, and the small ports of Maldon and Portsmouth. Such places were perhaps twice as populous as New Alresford. Occupational diversity in these towns reflected their standing, but may not have changed much between the twelfth and the fourteenth century. Around 1300 Winchester and London had about 70 and 175 occupations, respectively.[59] In 1327 seventeen occupations were recorded at Barking, a settlement beside the abbey and lacking formal urban status, by comparison with fourteen at the more populous town of Colchester. In the same return, Thaxted and Maldon had nine and fifteen occupations, respectively.[60]

Small towns developed niches of their own and contributed to the increasingly structured market system.[61] The men of the established town of Andover quickly obtained trading privileges at Newbury, which occupied a more advantageous position for traffic.[62] Throughout the later middle ages the fortunes of many small towns, such as Buntingford or Abingdon, shifted in response to local changes in routes, themselves often influenced by the flow of London business.[63] Rural landlords responded to such developments. In the thirteenth century the bishops of Winchester shifted from a policy of shipping the produce of their upper Thames manors downriver for sale in London to one of selling it locally,

[57] Beresford, *New Towns*, pp. 442–3, 445–7; M. Page, ed., *The Pipe Roll of the Bishopric of Winchester, 1301–2* (Hampshire Record Series, 14, 1996), pp. 99, 111, 328–9.

[58] Beresford, *New Towns*, pp. 452–3.

[59] P. J. Corfield and D. Keene, eds., *Work in Towns, 850–1850* (Leicester, 1990), p. 7.

[60] D. Keene, 'Small towns and the metropolis: the experience of medieval England', in J.-M. Duvosquel and E. Thoen, eds., *Peasants and Townsmen in Medieval Europe* (Ghent, 1995), pp. 223–38, esp. pp. 236–7; J. C. Ward, ed., *A Medieval Essex Community: The Lay Subsidy of 1327* (Chelmsford, 1983).

[61] Keene, 'Small towns'.

[62] *VCH*, Berkshire, IV, p. 136.

[63] *VCH*, Oxfordshire, IV, p. 41; M. Bailey, 'A tale of two towns: Buntingford and Standon in the late middle ages', *JMed.H*, 19 (1993), 351–72.

whence at least some of it was distributed via intermediate markets to the capital.[64] Many small towns distant from London were stimulated by the demands of the capital, for which they served as entrepôts or gathering points for rural produce. Henley may have been established in this way as a market for corn, and certainly became one in response to the economic forces which favoured the production of wheat and firewood for the London market in its hinterland and its emergence as the head of regular navigation on the Thames. Richard earl of Cornwall may have promoted Henley, which took trade from Wallingford, although in 1334, when valued at £96, Henley still ranked well below Baldock. Wycombe (£90 in 1334) enjoyed the double advantage for a cornmarket town of being on the busy main road between Oxford and London and of having ready access to the Thames at Marlow, while the cornmarket of Faversham (not valued in 1334) could serve London and the even greater demands of Flemish towns with almost equal ease. Other small towns developed industrial specialisms by virtue of local resources and their links with London: Thaxted's cutlery business, and at Kingston the trades in timber, fish and horses and the pottery industry, were all to some degree driven by the London market.

London also interacted distinctively with some of the larger towns. In the mid-thirteenth century, Winchelsea, one of the Channel ports most accessible by road from London, was noted as being of special interest to the Londoners, probably on account of its role as an entrepôt for the wine trade. Sandwich enjoyed a similar role. In the twelfth century the king's chamberlain of London, who purchased wine and other imported luxuries for the crown, had responsibilities in Sandwich as well as London, and in 1303, when the 'new custom' was established, it was at first envisaged that London's custom zone would include Sandwich.[65] The Canterbury connections of leading London mercantile families during the twelfth and thirteenth centuries demonstrate their strong interest in that commercially strategic part of Kent. The easterly direction of much of London's trade is also indicated by city fishmongers' interests in Yarmouth.[66] At the same time, the intensity of London's connections with the more westerly parts of the region diminished, especially as Winchester lost its former position as a centre of power and business and came to be more closely connected with districts to the west than those to the east. The sharp fall-off in London's migration field towards the south-west may reflect the same phenomenon, as well as the contribution which the more densely populated districts to the north and east of the city made to its population.[67]

[64] Campbell, Galloway, Keene and Murphy, *Medieval Capital*, pp. 55, 89.

[65] Keene, 'Small towns'; *Calendar of Fine Rolls*, I, pp. 466–8.

[66] See above, p. 203; A. Saul, 'Great Yarmouth in the fourteenth century: a study of trade, politics and society' (DPhil thesis, University of Oxford, 1975), pp. 350–1.

[67] Biddle, ed., *Winchester*, p. 503; Keene, *Survey*, I, pp. 377–9, II, p. 1121; P. H. Reaney, *The Origin of English Surnames* (London, 1967), pp. 345–51 and fig. IV.

(iv) URBAN CULTURE AND DENSITY

During the twelfth and early thirteenth centuries the urban culture of the region was shaped by its four major cities, London, Winchester, Canterbury and Oxford. Their citizens had distinctive roles at coronation feasts, an indication of the influence of towns in shaping the realm.[68] Likewise, the administrative customs of London and Winchester, which paralleled each other, served as exemplars for other towns in their hinterlands. The influence of London, however, was from the beginning more extensive than that of Winchester and ultimately, along with that of Oxford, eroded that of the former West Saxon capital (Map 22.3). Nevertheless, the institutions and social life of these towns continued to set standards of urban culture for the region, and in the early fourteenth century, despite the striking degree to which London had moved ahead, they remained the main concentrations of human and material resources after the capital, with Southampton, and perhaps Sandwich and Winchelsea, ranking after them. Then came a long tail of well over a hundred smaller towns valued in 1334 at less than 4 per cent of London and less than half of Winchester. Many of these small towns presumably had very limited horizons, but even in the lowest group by value, which included market centres of apparently no more than local significance such as Overton (£54 in 1334), there were to be found towns like Lewes (£40), Henley (£50) and Arundel (£53) which had deep-rooted, specialised identities as centres of power or trade. Many of these smaller places had acquired a distinctively urban culture, expressed in administrative institutions, guilds and communal buildings.[69]

Indicators of urbanity, other than wealth or size, cannot readily be compared in more than a few cases. Town walls were important expressions of urban identity, but only about fifteen towns in the South-East had effective defensive circuits in the early fourteenth century. Several circuits were later strengthened in response to the threat of invasion, but there were no medieval additions to this total. Most towns were too insignificant for investment in walls, the existence of which reflected Roman origins, a strategic role in the earlier middle ages (Oxford, Wallingford and perhaps Bedford), or a situation on the south coast exposed to attack from France. In a few cases (Lewes, Pleshey, Sandwich, Tonbridge), the defences owed their origin to the role of the town as a centre of magnate power, especially during civil war. The towns of the South-East made a notable contribution to the defence of the realm (Map 22.4). Among other indicators of standing, the most readily comparable is the town's endowment with religious institutions – cathedrals, religious houses, friaries and hospitals – measured by means of a weighted score (Map

[68] W. Urry, *Canterbury under the Angevin Kings* (London, 1967), p. 106; Biddle, ed., *Winchester*, p. 503; *VCH*, Oxfordshire, IV, pp. 9, 50. [69] See above, pp. 94–9 and 532–4.

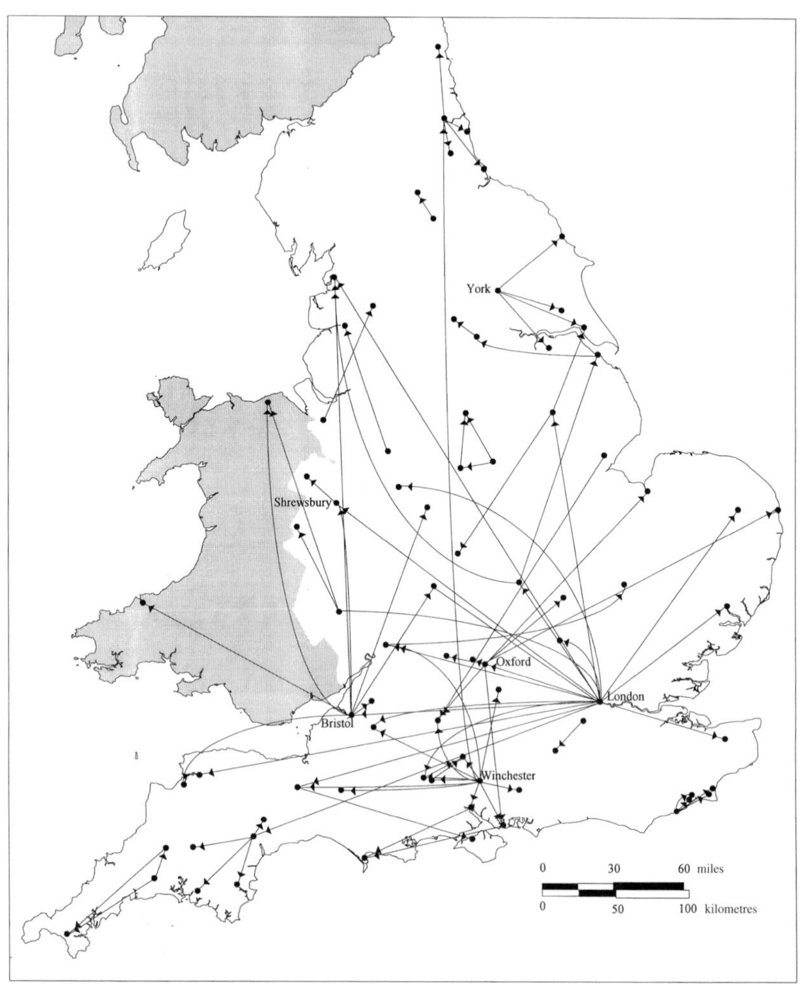

Map 22.3 Affiliation of borough customs up to 1256
In each relationship indicated by a line, the arrow points towards the town whose customs were modelled on those of the other town. The significance as models of London, Winchester and Oxford in this period is striking. Later, London was much more predominant. The exercise is limited to England and Wales and is based on C. Gross, *The Gild Merchant* (Oxford, 1890), vol. I, pp. 244–53.

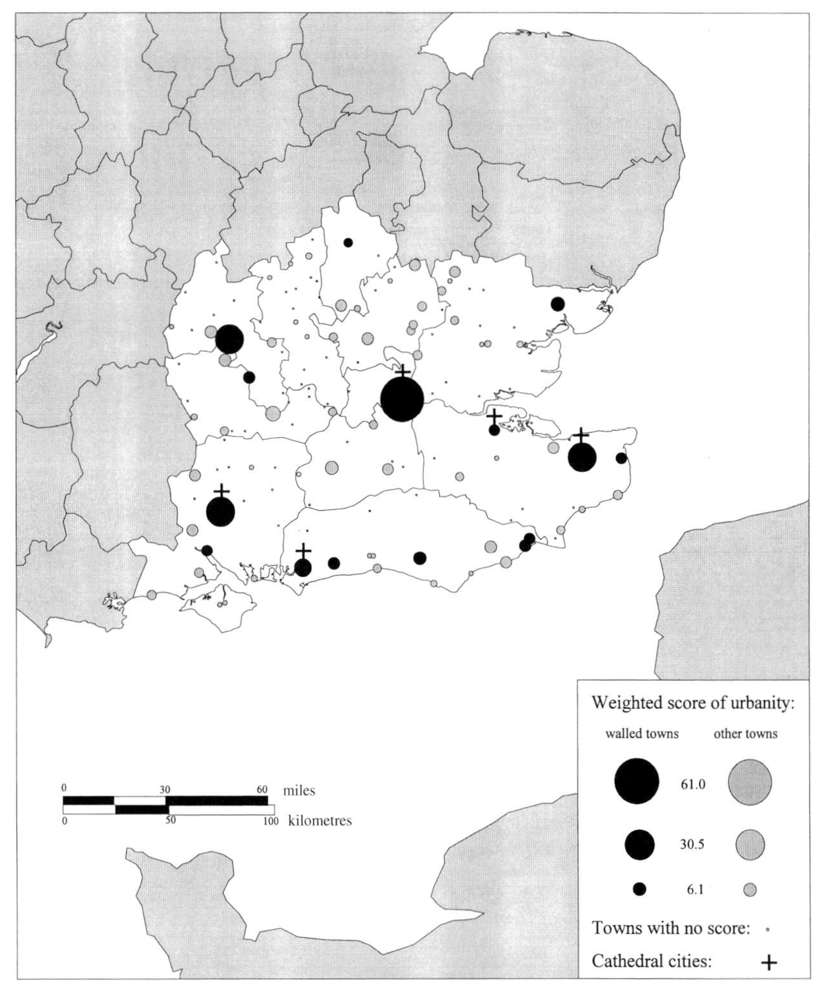

Map 22.4 Towns of South-East England *c.* 1300 according to their significance as urban centres

For the 'weighted score of urbanity', see p. 265 and n. 70. Towns such as Tonbridge and Pleshey, whose defences appear to have originated as the outer defensive circuits of the castles whose dependencies they were, are not shown here as walled towns.

Sources: D. J. C. King, *Castellarium Anglicanum* (Millwood, N.Y.), and H. L. Turner, *Town Defences in England and Wales* (London, 1970).

22.3).[70] By this measure, London emerges as housing by far the most elaborate urban culture (with a score of 68), followed after a considerable interval by Canterbury, Oxford and Winchester (28) and then by Chichester, Southwark and Reading (9), Colchester (8) and Guildford and Lewes (7). Nine other towns, of which six were ports, were marked as distinctively urban by possession of a friary. Wallingford's relatively high score (6), but lack of a friary, reflects its early prosperity and decay since the twelfth century. Other centres of early wealth or special patronage, such as Chichester, Guildford, Lewes and Arundel (6), also score relatively highly. It is noteworthy that seven of the top seventeen towns of the region measured by the assessment of 1334 (Table 22.1), lacked friaries and did not score as highly as Guildford. In several of these the presence of a powerful abbey inhibited the foundation of a friary; in some, subsidy valuations were enhanced by the inclusion of rural areas; and in others, like Newbury (score 3), the town was of relatively recent growth. Scores calculated for the early sixteenth century reveal a very similar picture. The degree to which the urban culture of the region emerged from a long process of accumulation before 1300 is especially striking.

Some towns, notably Bedford, Winchester, Canterbury, London and Oxford, had a distinct character as seats of royal government in their shires, as indicated by the presence of royal castles, county courts and gaols.[71] But in other counties the picture was confused by the changing fortunes of towns, the lack of a dominant urban centre or considerations of territorial lordship. Thus despite always being the 'natural capital' of Essex, Colchester was not usually allowed to function as a seat of authority,[72] and in Buckinghamshire, where there was no dominant town before Wycombe established itself on the back of London trade, Aylesbury was chosen because its castle was in royal hands. Hertfordshire and Berkshire each experienced a similar mismatch between the seat of county administration and the shifting focus of urban prosperity.

Major towns were also recognised as centres of pilgrimage. St Thomas the Martyr, St Frideswide and St Swithun brought much business to Canterbury, Oxford and Winchester up to the end of the period, and shaped ideas of the region and its identity. Londoners made the most of their connection with St Thomas, even in the commercial world of the fifteenth and sixteenth centuries.[73] At Oxford

[70] Scores were attributed for religious institutions (D. Knowles and R. N. Hadcock, *Medieval Religious Houses*, 2nd edn (London, 1971)) as follows: cathedrals and Benedictine abbeys, 5; Cistercian and Carthusian houses, 4; alien and other dependent priories, houses of Augustinian canons, Templars and Hospitallers, 3; friaries, 2; hospitals and secular colleges, 1. Parish churches were excluded from the exercise since their numbers are significant only up to the twelfth century. An unweighted score provides a similar, but less differentiated, picture.

[71] See above, pp. 65–6. The gaol is a key indicator of the seat of shire government: R. B. Pugh, *Imprisonment in Medieval England* (Cambridge, 1968), esp. pp. 57–86.

[72] Cf. above, p. 54.

[73] The Merchant Adventurers of London adopted St Thomas as their patron: J. Imray, *The Mercers' Hall* (London Topographical Society, 143, 1991), p. 13.

and Winchester a sense of the identity conferred by English patron saints persisted beyond the Reformation. How far that expressed an awareness of contrast between the present decay and former glory of the two towns is not known, but it is certain that by 1500 Winchester's chief claims to fame were its great churches and the icons of its legendary history rather than its repute as a centre of government and trade.[74]

Urban culture played an important part in the interaction between town and country. Rustics and landed magnates looked to the towns, but the wealthier townsmen were also influential figures in the countryside, especially around London. The first mayor had a ring of strategically situated estates and seats around the city which indicate both his standing as a landowner and the part he played in the commercial exploitation of the resources of the region. He had many comparable successors. The country houses and memorials of such men expressed the permeating influence of the great city, and there were similar signs within the less extensive territories of other towns.[75]

Towns contributed to the relative density of population in the South-East. By comparison to England as a whole, the region contained a total of towns in proportion to its area but, according to the poll tax assessment of 1377, a greater share of population (Table 22.2). If the population of England in 1300 was 4.75 million and was distributed broadly as it was in 1377, then the density of population in the region was 111 persons per square mile (43 per square km). That was a figure very much lower than those estimated for contemporary Flanders, Picardy or the Laonnais, although in parts of Essex, and on the coastal fringes of Kent and Sussex, densities at least equalled those in Picardy. The concentration of substantial towns in the region fell far short of that in Flanders and Artois, and, in contrast to the cities of the Low Countries, London was physically distant from its English rivals (Map 22.5).[76] Moreover, the taxed wealth located in towns of all sizes in South-East England in 1334 cannot have been much more than 16 per cent of the regional or 5 per cent of the national total (Table 22.1). Despite the notable concentration of English urban resources in the South-East, the region was distinctly less urbanised than adjacent areas of the continent.

The main urban functions were concentrated in large, widely separated towns. The relative absence of towns within 12 to 20 miles (20–30 km) of London (Maps 22.2, 22.3) is to be explained by the attraction of its market rather than by its legal privileges. The long-established role of the larger towns as centres of authority within an extensive and politically unified territory was also important in forming the system.[77] Moreover, the soils and topography of the region, and its relative isolation from wider networks of trade – except through London

[74] Keene, *Survey*, I, p. 105, II, pp. 1405–6, 1440.

[75] See above, pp. 206 and 411–12; S. L. Thrupp, *The Merchant Class of Medieval London* (Chicago, 1948), pp. 226–31, 279–87; Keene, *Survey*, I, pp. 227–9; D. Keene, 'Henry FitzAylwin', *New DNB* (forthcoming).

[76] See above, p. 196; A. Saint-Denis, *Apogée d'une cité: Laon et le Laonnais aux XIIe-et XIIIe-siècles* (Nancy, 1994), pp. 511, 514–17.

[77] See above, pp. 53–6.

Table 22.2 *Counties of the South-East as a proportion of regional values*

	Percentage of regional total											10 square km per unit, 1300	
County	Area	Coins *c.* 1000	Coins *c.* 1020	Coins *c.* 1050	Popn 1086	Coins *c.* 1086	Friaries *c.* 1300	Towns *c.* 1300	Value 1334	Popn 1377	Tax 1524	Market	Town
Beds.	4	1	2	2	5	<1	6	4	6	6	3	6	24
Berks.	7	3	2	4	8	4	3	11	9	6	5	6	13
Bucks.	7	<1	<1	<1	6	0	0	11	6	7	4	5	13
Essex	15	5	5	4	18	2	11	13	11	14	12	5	24
Hants.	15	19	17	15	12	21	14	17	11	11	8	9	18
Herts.	6	2	2	2	6	<1	0	8	5	5	4	5	16
Kent	15	13	6	12	15	28	14	10	16	16	15	4	31
Middx.	3	38	53	34	3	17	17	2	10	9	31	9	37
Oxon.	7	3	1	5	8	5	5	8	12	7	4	8	20
Surrey	7	9	6	2	5	13	3	5	5	5	6	8	28
Sussex	14	6	5	9	12	9	14	12	10	10	8	7	24
Total	100	100	100	100	100	100	100	101	100	100	100	6	21
Region as % England	21	49	41	41	?	53	22	22	30	26	42	—	—

Sources: see Table 22.1. For 'Friaries *c.* 1300', see p. 568 and n. 70. For 'Towns *c.* 1300', see p. 545 and n. 1. For numbers of markets, see R. H. Britnell, 'The proliferation of markets in England, 1200–1349', *Ec.HR*, 2nd series, 34 (1981), 209–21; M. Mate, 'The rise and fall of markets in Southeast England', *Canadian J of History*, 31 (1996), 59–86; B. A. McLain, 'Factors in market establishment in medieval England: the evidence from Kent, 1086–1350', *Archaeologia Cantiana*, 177 (1997), 88–103.

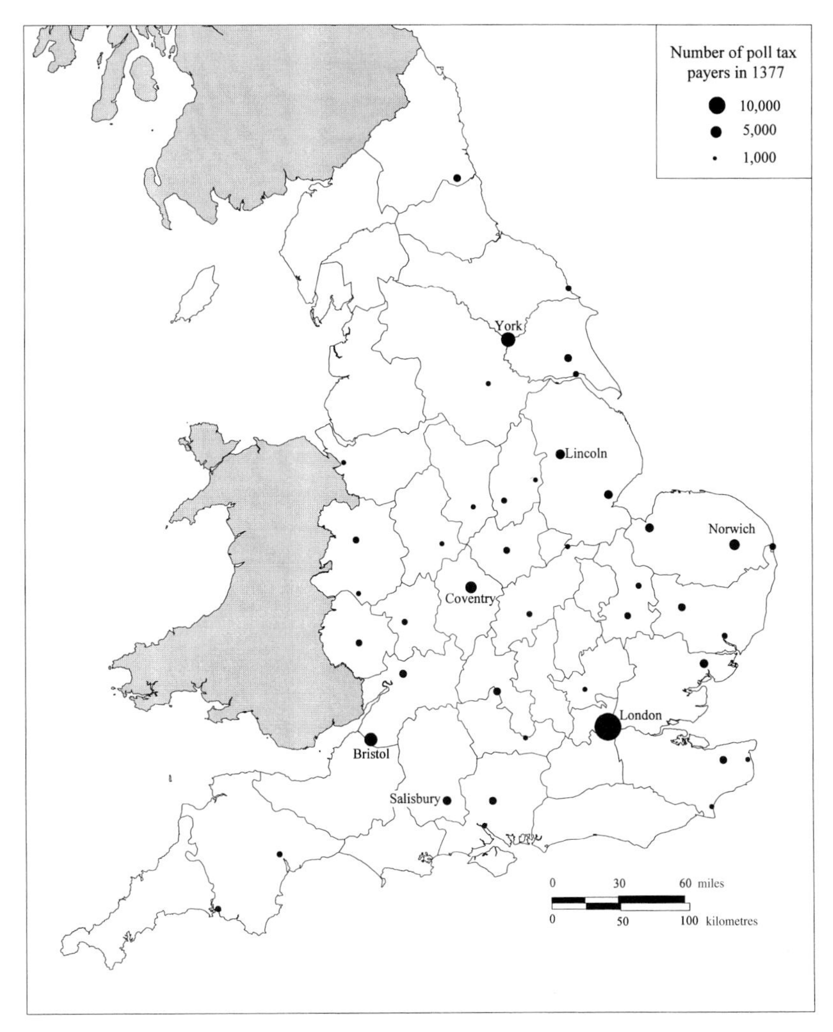

Map 22.5 Principal English towns 1377

Towns with 1,000 or more taxpayers are shown. In the absence of 1377 returns, the 1381 figures have been used for Scarborough and Southwark, while Chester, St Albans, Reading, Romney and Sandwich have been assumed to have had 1,000 taxpayers each. The exercise was undertaken by Dr J. A. Galloway (see caption to Map 22.2).

Source: C. C. Fenwick, 'The English poll taxes of 1377, 1379 and 1381: a critical examination of the returns' (PhD thesis, University of London, 1983), the first part of which is now in print as C. C. Fenwick, ed., *The Poll Taxes of 1377, 1379 and 1381* (British Academy Records of Social and Economic History, new series, 27, 1998).

and the ports on the periphery – did not favour the emergence of intensive rural settlement across wide areas. In Flanders and the Laonnais, by contrast, the towns were individually less prominent within densely populated countrysides, and had grown up rapidly from relatively insignificant beginnings. Winchester, Oxford and London, each remote from the most densely populated parts of the region, were very different, although in its setting Canterbury more nearly resembled the towns across the sea.

The establishment of towns was uneven, both spatially and chronologically, and reflects local differences both in exposure to commercial and political influence and in the dates at which maximum sustainable numbers of towns were attained (Map 22.2; Tables 22.3–5). In 1100 Kent had the greatest density of towns, but the slowest rate of increase thereafter, so that by 1300 it had the lowest density. This reflects its early commercialisation and the sparse settlement over much of its inland area, features also relevant to the spread of Sussex towns. The commercialisation of Kent continued, however, so that by 1300 it had the greatest density of markets of the counties in the region. Over the twelfth century, Hampshire and Hertfordshire experienced the greatest rates of increase in the number of towns, while Berkshire came to contain the greatest density. In part these were responses to the increase in inland traffic and to the structure of Anglo-Norman rule. Essex and Buckinghamshire gained relatively few towns in the twelfth century, but with Oxfordshire experienced a striking increase during the thirteenth. Buckinghamshire ended up with high densities of towns and markets, while Oxfordshire ranked lower on both counts. Essex ended up with one of the lowest densities of towns, but one of the highest of markets, possibly reflecting the localised character of exchange over much of the county and industrial activity in its villages, which was already apparent in the thirteenth century. Population density alone did not generate towns: thus Bedfordshire in 1300 had a low density of towns, but a high density of markets. Population growth, local networks of traffic and exchange, exposure to overseas commerce and the geography of lordship interacted in complex ways to shape the pattern of lesser towns.

(v) CHANGE, 1300–1540

The striking changes in the towns of the South-East during this period arose from the continuing dynamic of an established urban system; from the sharp fall in the general level of the population following the fourteenth-century famine and pestilences; from a consequent rise in the general standard of living, which promoted new patterns of consumption and crafts and, probably, an increase in the intensity of exchange; and from developments in European networks of trade. The intensification of markets and production in Flanders and Brabant was particularly influential. Above all the period was marked by a further, and especially

Table 22.3 *Most prominent towns in each county of the South-East as a proportion of that county and the region*

	Most prominent towns as a percentage of county and region														
	c. 1020 (coins)			*c.* 1050 (coins)			1334 (subsidy)			1377 (poll tax)			1524 (subsidy)		
County	Town	% cty	% reg.	Town	% cty	% reg.	Town	% cty	% reg.	Town	% cty	% reg.	Town	% cty	% reg.
Beds.	Bedford	100	1.9	Bedford	100	2.4	Bedford	2	0.1	?			Bedford	4	0.1
Berks.	Wallingford	100	1.9	Wallingford	98	3.9	Newbury	3	0.2	?			Reading	13	0.7
Bucks.	Buckingham	50	0.2	Buckingham	50	0.3	Newport P.	2	0.1	Wycombe	2	0.05	Wycombe	4	0.1
Essex	Colchester	66	2.9	Colchester	79	2.9	Colchester	1	0.1	Colchester	6	0.1	Colchester	6	0.7
Hants.	Winchester	92	15.3	Winchester	100	14.5	Winchester	3	0.4	Winchester	7	0.4	Southampton	4	0.3
Herts.	Hertford	100	2.3	Hertford	100	1.8	St Albans	3	0.2	?			St Albans	9	0.3
Kent	Canterbury	40	3.2	Canterbury	58	7.0	Canterbury	2	0.3	Canterbury	5	0.35	Canterbury	6	0.9
Middx.	London	100	50.4	London	100	37.4	London	68	6.5	London	67	6.5	London	88	27.0
Oxon.	Oxford	100	5.6	Oxford	100	4.8	Oxford	5	0.5	Oxford	9	0.5	Oxford	7	0.3
Surrey	Southwark	98	5.6	Southwark	71	1.6	Haslemere	3	0.1	Southwark	6	0.1	Southwark	21	1.3
Sussex	Lewes	54	3	Hastings	35	6.8	Chichester	2	0.1	Chichester	2	0.1	Chichester	3	0.2

Sources: see Table 22.1.

Table 22.4 *Densities of population and towns in the South-East, 1100–1500*

County	Recorded population per square km		10 square km per town				Change 1100–1300
	1086	1377	1100	1200	1300	1500	(1100 = 100)
Beds.	3.0	17	40	30	24	20	60
Berks.	3.3	12	37	23	12	12	32
Bucks.	2.6	13	64	48	13	12	20
Essex	3.5	13	100	80	24	20	24
Hants.	2.3	10	105	42	18	18	17
Herts.	2.8	12	41	27	16	14	39
Kent	2.9	15	40	40	31	29	77
London and Middx.	?	47	73	37	37	37	51
Middx. only	3.0	15	—	—	—	—	
Oxon.	3.4	14	196	65	20	18	9
Surrey	2.1	9	98	65	28	22	29
Sussex	2.5	10	47	34	24	27	51
Region	2.9	13	62	41	21	19	34

Sources: see p. 545 and n. 1. For recorded populations in 1086 and 1377, see Table 22.1 n. [g] and Darby, *Domesday England*, pp. 364–8.

sharp, increase in the significance of London as a centre of business and in its impact on the towns of the region.

By the late fourteenth century most towns, including London, were significantly smaller than they had been in 1300. Most were smaller still in 1500. By that date there were signs of growth in the outlying parts of London, but it may not have been until the mid-sixteenth century that the capital regained its former size.[78] The overall contraction was far less visible in London than elsewhere, and bore most heavily on Winchester which had lost its former role as a centre of power and international trade. Winchester's expanding clothing industry, succeeding its trade in wool as a source of prosperity, enabled it to retain some standing into the early fifteenth century, although by then it had lost parish churches, many houses had been replaced by garden plots and the interests of its more prosperous citizens were turning towards London. Its subsequent decay was even more striking. Even so, Winchester displayed many features which reflect a general shift in the balance of resources towards traders, craftsmen and urban communities during the late middle ages, including an

[78] See above, pp. 397–9.

Table 22.5 *Numbers of towns and the rates of their foundation in the South-East 1100–1500*

	Number and percentage of towns								Rate of change (earlier date = 100)			
	1100		1200		1300		1500					
County	N	%	N	%	N	%	N	%	1100–1200	1200–1300	1100–1300	1300–1500
Beds.	3	7	4	6	5	4	6	3	133	125	167	120
Berks.	5	11	8	12	15	11	15	10	160	187	300	100
Bucks.	3	7	4	6	15	11	16	11	133	375	500	107
Essex	4	9	5	8	17	13	20	14	125	340	425	118
Hants.	4	9	10	15	23	17	23	16	250	230	575	100
Herts.	4	9	6	9	10	8	12	9	150	167	250	120
Kent	10	23	10	15	13	10	14	10	100	130	130	108
Middx.	1	2	2	3	2	2	2	1	200	100	200	100
Oxon.	1	2	3	5	10	8	11	8	300	333	1,000	110
Surrey	2	5	3	5	8	5	9	6	150	267	400	112
Sussex	8	18	11	17	16	12	14	10	138	145	200	88
Region	45	102	66	101	134	101	142	98	150	202	302	107

Sources: see p. 545 and n. 1.

increase in personal consumption, improvements in housing, investment in civic building and ceremonial and the embellishment of those parish churches still needed by the reduced population. At Winchester, however, that phase came to an end sooner than at other provincial centres. Oxford also suffered severely, losing its diversified commerce and crafts, and coming primarily to serve the scholars (themselves less numerous than before) whose halls and colleges extended their occupation of deserted areas within the walls.[79]

In the fourteenth century London and its suburbs contained about 7 per cent of the assessed wealth and population of the South-East: by the 1520s they accounted for 29 per cent, a proportion which was rising. The urban resources of the region became ever more concentrated in London. In 1334 the total assessed wealth of the towns other than London was three times that of the capital, but by the 1520s no more than half. At the latter date, Southwark in its own right ranked as the second town of the region (Table 22.1). This perhaps reflected the increasing orientation of London interests towards Kent and the Channel, for suburban settlements on the north bank of the Thames did not increase their wealth to a comparable degree.[80] These overall developments both promoted and were reinforced by the increasing royal and governmental focus on the capital. Between the reigns of Edward III and Henry VIII royal residences were ever more concentrated around and within London, the protection of which was increasingly significant in the national strategy.[81] Yet even if we discount London, the towns of the South-East came to contain a greater share of the region's wealth than they had had in the early fourteenth century (Table 22.1).

The reasons for the increasing concentration on London are clear. From the late thirteenth century onwards certain English textiles gained a strong position in international markets, to which they were distributed by the dynamic trading centres of the Low Countries, especially Bruges and then Antwerp. Those centres added value to the English product, and supplied high-quality manufactured goods in return. This pattern of trade favoured textile-producing districts in the South-East and adjoining regions, and promoted London as an export and distributive centre.[82] The Low Countries market also assisted London to become the principal site for the manufacture of another English niche product, pewter.[83] London thus steadily accumulated a critical mass of functions as a

[79] Keene, *Survey*, *passim*; *VCH*, Oxfordshire, vol. IV, pp. 28–9, 40–4.

[80] See above, p. 192.

[81] R. A. Brown, H. M. Colvin and A. J. Taylor, eds., *The History of the King's Works* (London, 1963), vol. I, pp. 112, 241–8; D. J. Turner, 'Bodiam, Sussex: true castle or old soldier's dream house', in W. M. Ormrod, ed., *England in the Fourteenth Century: Proceedings of the 1985 Harlaxton Symposium* (Woodbridge, 1986), pp. 267–77; S. Thurley, *The Royal Palaces of Tudor England: Architecture and Court Life, 1460–1547* (New Haven and London, 1993), pp. 2, 56–7, 67–9.

[82] See above, pp. 412–28.

[83] D. Keene, 'Metalworking in medieval London: an historical survey', *J of the Historical Metallurgy Society*, 30/2 (1996), 95–102.

market, as a seat of craft and entrepreneurial skills and as a source of information, credit and patronage. At the same time it became increasingly subordinate to markets overseas.

This pattern was already present in the fourteenth century, as indicated by measures of 'urban potential' based on English urban populations in 1377 (Maps 22.5, 22.6). This indicates the relative potential for intensive interaction (the essence of urban life) in different regions according to the 'weight' and spatial distribution of their principal urban centres. It demonstrates the very high potential of London and its vicinity, and the sharp fall-off to the south and south-west by comparison with districts to the north of the capital, where, as we have seen, even small towns lay thicker on the ground. Unfortunately, the exercise cannot take account of the influence of towns overseas, which would undoubtedly have extended the area of highest potential well to the east of London. This deficiency can be remedied by examining the residential pattern of those in debt to Londoners in a large sample of cases from the central court of common pleas around 1400 (Map 22.7). The numbers of debts indicate a relationship between the major towns which corresponds closely to that demonstrated by the poll tax values (Map 22.5), and so they provide a measure of the level of commercial activity at each place as well as of the closeness of its connection to London. The lack of business to the south and south-west of London is striking, as is its density along the Thames valley upstream of the city, to the north in Hertfordshire and southern Cambridgeshire, in Essex and adjacent parts of Suffolk and in northern and eastern Kent.

The towns that came to the fore after London express this potential (Table 22.1). Colchester owed its new standing to its textile industry and its role as a market for the cloths of its hinterland. The increase in the town's relative prosperity over the fourteenth century was so great that it may have actually grown in size, despite the severe depopulation of parts of Essex. This trend did not continue through the fifteenth century, when Colchester's trade came increasingly to depend on London.[84] Textiles, as well as the general concentration of trade on the Thames estuary, promoted the fortunes of Canterbury, Maidstone (which first clearly emerges as a town *c.* 1400), Rye and other Kent towns, while both Reading and Newbury owed at least some of their new standing to their role as clothing towns. In 1524 the most prominent towns (Table 22.1) and those of the top thirty which had increased their share of the region's taxed wealth by three or more times since 1334, indicate where the bases of small-town prosperity lay. They included ports such as Manningtree, Harwich, Maldon and Lewes, of which the last was establishing a role as a county town.[85] Sandwich and Rye probably belonged to this group. Other towns, such as St Albans, Kingston,

[84] Britnell, *Growth and Decline*, where the case for the physical expansion of the town is less well founded than that for its relative increase in prosperity. [85] Pugh, *Imprisonment*, p. 77.

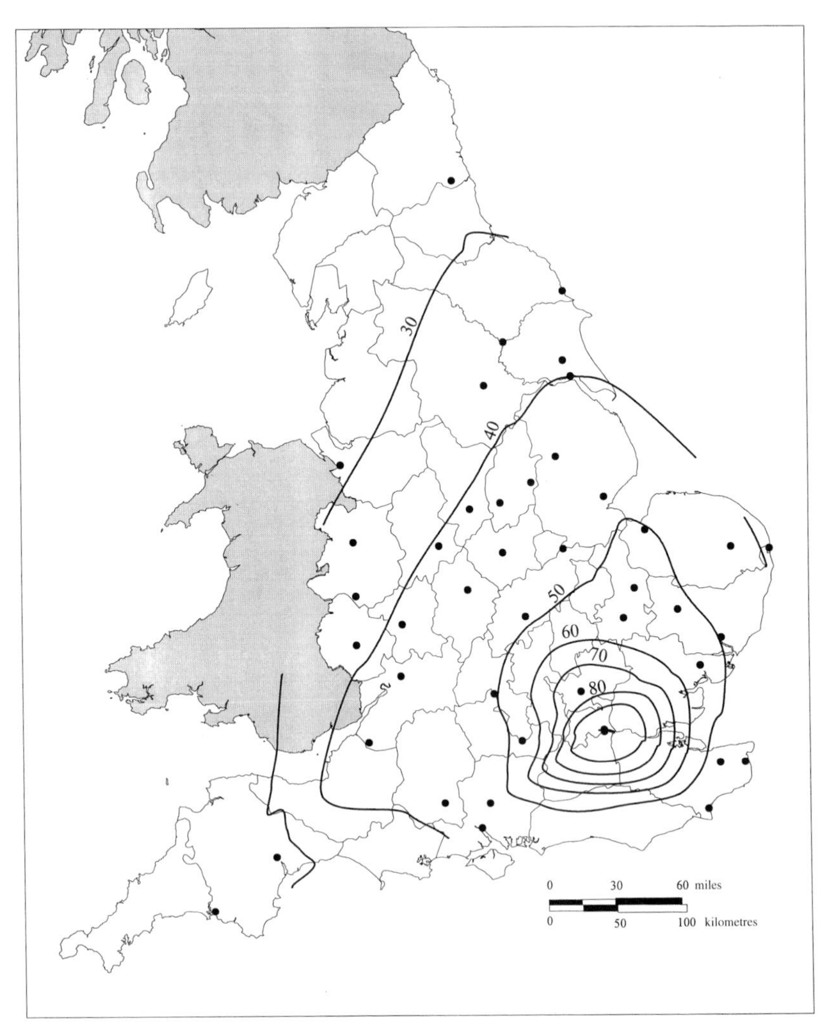

Map 22.6 Urban potential in England 1377
This map indicates the potential for interaction at the principal English towns by means of a value for each town (expressed as a percentage of the maximum value encountered) which takes account of the population of each place (see Map 22.5) and its distance as the crow flies from all other towns covered by the exercise. In this case the population values of seaports (including London) were doubled, so as to take account of the transport advantages they enjoyed. The spread of values is expressed by means of isopleth lines. The method closely resembles that described in J. de Vries, *European Urbanization, 1500–1800* (London, 1984), pp. 154–8, where the formulae used are given. An exercise which does not weight the values of the seaports produces a very similar picture, although one in which the isopleth lines for values of 60 and below lie further from London to the north and north-west, so as to include Coventry, Leicester and Northampton as part of a region of 'relatively high potential' associated with the capital. The exercises were undertaken by Dr J. A. Galloway (see caption to Map 22.2).

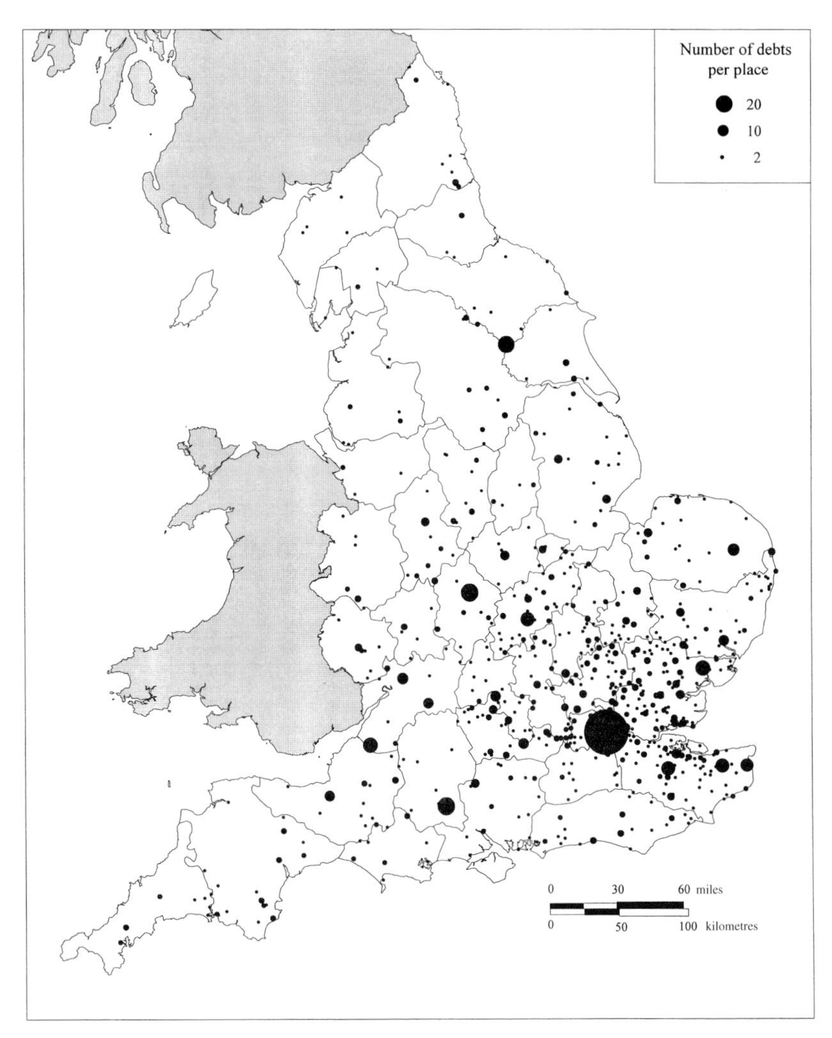

Map 22.7 Residence of debtors to Londoners *c.* 1400
The exercise is based on a sample of 7,806 cases from the Common Plea Rolls (PRO, CP40) for the Michaelmas terms in 1384, 1404 and 1424. In particular, it concerns those 1,409 debts owed to Londoners by individuals whose place of residence is identified. The sample was drawn from cases laid in Beds., Berks., Bucks., Essex, Herts., Kent, London, Middx., Northants. and Surrey, but since London plaintiffs laid their pleas in London the exercise presents a reliable picture for England as a whole. Moreover, there was evidently an association between the significance of provincial centres and their credit relationship with the capital (cf. Map 22.4). The exercise was undertaken by Dr J. A. Galloway and Dr M. Murphy as part of the 'Market networks' project (see Map 22.2).

Henley, Saffron Walden and Maidstone (which may have ranked with St Albans or Southampton),[86] and a number of much smaller towns to the north and east of London, including Romford and Royston, served as markets supplying the capital with basic commodities such as corn, malt, livestock, leather and stone.[87] A third group, including Farnham, Alton and Basingstoke, seem primarily to have served the traffic on main roads to London, and by the early fifteenth century a distinct category of innkeeping towns can be recognised, comprising places as different as Alresford and St Albans. The rise to local prominence of many of these small towns contrasts with the decay of some older and larger centres.[88]

Some south coast ports, and certainly Sandwich, benefited from the increasing easterly focus of commerce (Map 22.7), but direct overland connections with London were also important. Rye became a major fishing port, and the rapid conveyance of fresh fish to the discriminating tables of the capital, an important part of its trade in the sixteenth century, was already established by the 1420s when the rippiers who traded the fish occur at villages on the road from Rye to London.[89] For London merchants Rye perhaps assumed the role formerly played by Winchelsea, and by the 1490s London street-names had been adopted for districts of the town, demonstrating the colonising power of metropolitan commercial culture also apparent at Stourbridge fair.[90] Road traffic between London and Southampton demonstrates the way in which London interests came to permeate the South. With the growth of the Bordeaux trade and that of the Mediterranean galleys, for both of which Flanders was an important destination, Southampton became well suited as an outport for London, and in the fifteenth century Londoners regularly had Gascon and Mediterranean goods carted thence to the capital. London pewterers supplied themselves with Cornish and Devon tin by the same route. Londoners also used Southampton as a base for their distributive trade, supplying wine to Oxford and elsewhere, and raw materials for cloth finishing to textile centres such as Winchester, Salisbury and Coventry.[91]

Londoners also supplied cloth finishers and other craftsmen at smaller towns: dyers at St Albans, Maidstone, Tenterden and Cranbrook; cutlers at Thaxted; and tanners at Maidstone, who returned the tanned hides to leatherworkers in the

[86] P. Clark and L. Murfin, *The History of Maidstone: The Making of a Modern County Town* (Stroud, 1995), pp. 27, 42.

[87] M. K. McIntosh, *Autonomy and Community: The Royal Manor of Havering, 1200–1500* (Cambridge, 1986), pp. 144, 229–34.

[88] *VCH*, Hertfordshire, II, pp. 480–1; Keene, *Survey*, I, pp. 92–3.

[89] A. J. F. Dulley, 'Four Kent towns at the end of the middle ages', *Archaeologia Cantiana*, 81 (1966), 95–108; G. Mayhew, *Tudor Rye* (Falmer, 1987), pp. 38–9; PRO CP40/655.

[90] *HMC*, 5th Report, App., p. 497; C. H. Cooper, *Annals of Cambridge* (Cambridge, 1842–53), vol. I, pp. 222, 246.

[91] O. Coleman, ed., *The Brokage Book of Southampton, 1443–1444* (Southampton Records Series, 4 and 6, 1960–1).

capital. Textile finishing in Essex, however, was less directly under London's influence and received its imported supplies via Colchester, reflecting the particular geography of North Sea and Channel shipping.[92] London's role in articulating the markets and in supplying goods and credit for urban industry, both within the region and at vigorous industrial centres outside it, was firmly established.

Such metropolitan strength, however, had a negative aspect, for within a productive system which in aggregate remained smaller in scale than two centuries before, London's appropriation of markets and the power to add value reduced the scope for enterprise at lesser centres. Moreover, the metropolis itself lost functions to Antwerp, with the result that while it increased its concentration of wealth and its attraction to mobile labour and the poor, the opportunities it presented for skilled employment diminished in relative terms. Thus, even the capital experienced problems in the latter part of the period, while second-rank towns, burdened with fiscal obligations which were inappropriate to their present resources, perceived themselves as suffering parlous decay. That was even the case with Canterbury, which enjoyed a standing within the region and the nation higher than ever before.

On the eve of the Reformation the towns of the South-East embodied physical characteristics, functions and memories (some true and some false), of which elements had originated up to 1,600 years earlier. Some of those identities expressed cultures which were more localised than, or cross-cut, that of the region itself. There were towns, though minor ones, which still expressed a strong sense of the magnate interests to which they owed their origin. Others, especially London, Canterbury, Winchester and Oxford, represented aspects of national identity more strongly than most other cities in the realm. This was dramatically demonstrated in the carefully managed visit of the emperor Charles V in 1522. Landing at Dover, he was met by the king and was then formally received into the kingdom in the city of Canterbury. The two monarchs processed to London, where their entry into the city lavishly proclaimed the diplomatic message of the visit. Following entertainments and negotiation at Hampton Court and Windsor, they journeyed to see King Arthur's Round Table at Winchester, where it was all too apparent that the resources of that city and its hinterland were no longer sufficient to sustain a royal visitation on this scale: members of the two courts were lodged at Salisbury until the emperor set sail from Southampton.[93] The strongest force linking the towns of the region and

[92] PRO CP40/495, 571, 655 (debt relations between London grocers, who supplied dyestuffs, and Colchester men were rare); Clark and Murfin, *Maidstone*, pp. 29–30.

[93] S. Anglo, *Spectacle, Pageantry and Early Tudor Policy* (Oxford, 1997 (orig. publ. 1969)), pp. 181, 184–206; J. S. Brewer, ed., *Letters and Papers, Foreign and Domestic, Henry VIII*, vol. III, part 2 (London, 1867), nos. 2361, 2388; *Calendar of State Papers Spanish* II, no. 441; R. Brown, ed., *Calendar of State Papers and Manuscripts relating to English Affairs, Existing in the Archives and Collections of Venice* (London, 1869), no. 486.

sustaining their prosperity was now that of a commercial interest focusing on London and shaping the overseas relationships of the state. That interest had always been present in the systems (to varying degrees coherent or comprehending the region as a whole) which had determined the affairs of its towns. The evolution of those systems, of the connections between the towns and of the opportunities they offered, explains the variations in the fortunes of towns. The progressive elaboration of infrastructure, the development of market hierarchies and the general demographic background, provide only partial accounts of the urban character of the region. Contingency and catastrophe, not necessarily originating within the region, could be powerful forces in shaping its towns, as their fortunes during the sixteenth and seventeenth centuries were again to show.

· 22(b) ·

The South-West of England

T. R. SLATER

The south-west comprises the modern counties of Cornwall, Devon, Dorset, Somerset and Wiltshire. This region bestrides the divide between highland and lowland England.[1] The majority of the region comprises the older, harder rocks of upland Britain, together with the more acidic soils derived from those rocks, the consequent pastoral farming systems, an ancient *bocage* landscape and a dispersed pattern of rural settlements. There are few large towns (Map 22.8). The upland moors of Mendip and Exmoor and the granite bosses of Dartmoor and Bodmin Moor add transhumance and mineral exploitation of silver, tin and lead to the economic equation, whilst the long, indented coastline to both the north and south of the peninsula brought opportunities for fishing, coastal trading and links with South Wales, Ireland, north-west France and Iberia. However, the south coast is altogether more sheltered than the north with its steep cliffs and lack of inlets.

In contrast, Wiltshire, Dorset and east Devon are part of the lowland zone with fertile clay vales, chalk and limestone escarpments and plateaux. Soils are more fertile, the climate is drier, mixed farming systems predominate and nucleated village settlements are the norm.[2] However, there were also large areas of lowland heath on the poor sandy soils of south-east Dorset, and extensive downland pastures on the chalk of Salisbury Plain which could be exploited to feed huge flocks of sheep. Whereas water was in short supply on the downs, the opposite was true in the marshlands of the Somerset Levels which provide a third distinctive local landscape of much richer pastureland.

This division between upland and lowland, between pastoral and mixed farming, was reflected, too, in the political divide of the early medieval period, with the lowland regions of Dorset, Somerset and east Devon being absorbed

[1] A. H. Shorter, W. L. D. Ravenhill and K. J. Gregory, *Southwest England* (London, 1969), pp. 10–53.
[2] B. Cunliffe, *Wessex to AD 1000* (London, 1993), pp. 1–10.

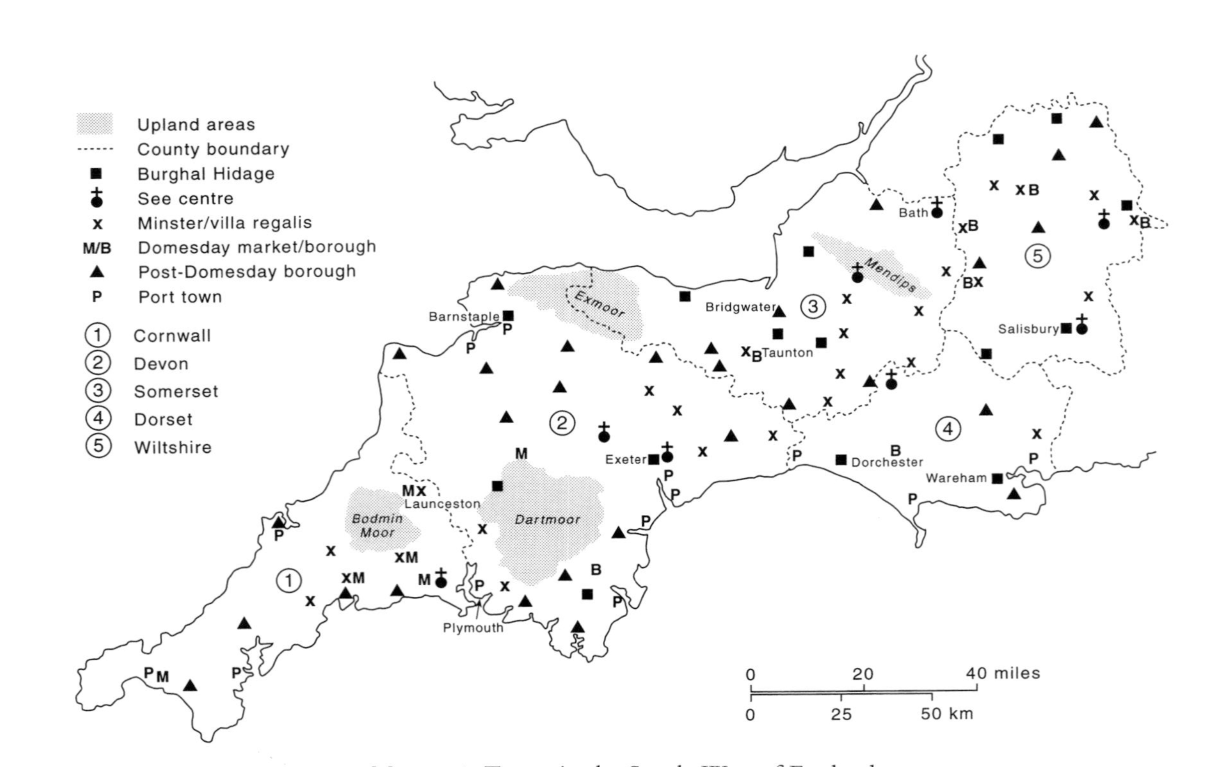

Map 22.8 Towns in the South-West of England

into the kingdom of Wessex by the early seventh century, whereas much of Devon was not incorporated until the early eighth century and Cornwall later still.[3] The cultural divide provided by the Tamar is still reflected in current society and this was certainly more so in medieval times. This physical, economic and cultural pattern is inevitably reflected, too, in the development of towns in the region. The South-West is a region of small, late-founded, manorial boroughs. Movement westwards through the region sees a pattern of progressively smaller, later-founded towns with small trading regions. There are only two large towns, Exeter and Salisbury, though Bristol began to spew over the Avon into Somerset soon after the Conquest.

(i) LATE ROMAN AND DARK AGE CENTRES

The Roman urban inheritance was concentrated in the eastern parts of the region. There were two large *civitas* capitals at Exeter (*Isca*), serving the Dumnonii, and Dorchester (*Durnovaria*), serving the Durotriges, whilst just beyond the regional boundary of the upper Thames was Cirencester (*Corinium*), capital of the Dobunni.[4] There was a rather smaller, later town at Ilchester (*Lendiniae*) on the Fosse Way which may have served as capital of the northern part of the Durotriges' territory in the fourth century, together with the religious cult centre at Bath (*Aquae Sulis*) around the hot springs. There was a port at Sea Mills (*Portus Abonae*) at the mouth of the Avon and an industrial lead-mining settlement at Charterhouse on the Mendips. Small towns or large villages are attested archaeologically at Mildenhall (*Cunetio*) near Marlborough, *Verlucio* near Calne, Whitewalls near Malmesbury, Wanborough, and at *Sorviodunum*, to the south of Old Sarum, on the road to Dorchester. Further south-west there were other such settlements at Camerton on the Fosse Way in Somerset and at North Tawton (*Nemetostatio*) in Devon. Most of these places have finds from the first to fourth centuries.[5]

Relatively little evidence of the occupation of the late Roman period has been excavated for these towns. However, the defensive use of the amphitheatre at Cirencester, the late Roman settlement around the cemetery at Poundbury, west of Dorchester, and the evidence for the slow abandonment of Exeter are known. In Bath, archaeology shows that the sacred spring within the walls continued to be used in the fifth and sixth centuries.[6] Also documented is the continued

[3] F. M. Stenton, *Anglo-Saxon England*, 2nd edn (Oxford, 1947), p. 233; J. R. Maddicott, 'Trade, industry and the wealth of King Alfred', *P&P*, 123 (1989), 3–51.

[4] J. S. Wacher, *The Towns of Roman Britain*, 2nd edn (London, 1995) pp. 302–77.

[5] B. C. Burnham and John Wacher, *The 'Small Towns' of Roman Britain* (London, 1990), pp. 34, 62–70, 148–52, 165–76, 208–11.

[6] Wacher, *Towns of Roman Britain*, p. 332; C. J. S. Green, 'The cemetery of a Romano-British community at Poundbury, Dorchester, Dorset', in S. M. Pearce, ed., *The Early Church in Western Britain and Ireland* (British Archaeology Reports, 102, 1982), pp. 61–76; S. Esmonde Cleary, *The Ending of Roman Britain* (London, 1989), pp. 125–6; B. Cunliffe, *Roman Bath Discovered*, 2nd edn (London, 1984); B. Cunliffe and P. Davenport, *The Temple of Sulis Minerva at Bath*, 2 vols. (Oxford, 1988).

importance of international trading links between the South-West and the western Mediterranean and Iberia where the many late fourth-/fifth-century *amphorae* found in Exeter are significant evidence. Another place with many such wine *amphorae* from the sub-Roman period is the *emporium* at Tintagel where tin may have been traded in return in the late fifth to early sixth centuries.[7]

There is considerable evidence for the presence of a substantial Christian community in the late Roman South-West. The mausolea and gypsum burials at Poundbury, and other Christian artefacts from the town, show that Dorchester had such a community, though the Poundbury cemetery shows no evidence of continuity into the medieval period.[8] At Exeter, there are sub-Roman Christian burials in the forum dating from the end of the fifth century suggesting a church there. This cemetery was in use again from middle Saxon times into the post-Conquest period around the minster church of St Peter (on the later site of St Mary Major).[9] St Sidwells, outside the north-east gate, is another place which could have been a late Roman cemetery site with a mausoleum developing into a cult centre and shrine attracting pilgrims. Charles Thomas suggests that Somerset and Dorset was one of the areas where the evidence for sub-Roman Christianity is strongest.[10] However, it was also an area in which the evidence for a sub-Roman pagan revival was strong, especially in Somerset.[11] There are many rural Celtic church sites along the coasts of Devon, and in Cornwall, notably Padstow, where a town was ultimately to develop around 'the holy place of St. Padarn'.

In the Dark Age period, hill-forts were reoccupied at South Cadbury and Cadbury Congresbury and possibly at Chisbury and Malmesbury.[12] The rebuilding of the defences and gates at South Cadbury, the lordly hall within those defences and the Mediterranean *amphorae* of the late fifth/early sixth centuries all suggest a high-status centre with a call on more than the immediate population. Another fortress re-established by the British population was at Old Sarum since it was at *Searoburh* that Cynric put the Britons to flight in 552. The Anglo-Saxon Chronicle reference to the battle of Dyrham in 577, and the capture of Bath, Cirencester and Gloucester, suggests later memories of possible political

[7] J. P. Allan, *Medieval and Post-Medieval Finds from Exeter, 1971–80* (Exeter Archaeological Reports, 3, 1983); C. G. Henderson, 'Exeter', in G. Milne and B. Hobley, eds., *Waterfront Archaeology in Britain and Northern Europe* (CBA Res. Rep., 41, 1981), pp. 119–22; C. Thomas, *A Provisional List of Imported Pottery in Post-Roman Western Britain and Ireland* (Redruth, 1981), *passim*; Esmonde Cleary, *Ending of Roman Britain*, p. 185; Wacher, *Towns of Roman Britain*, pp. 342–3.

[8] Esmonde Cleary, *Ending of Roman Britain*, pp. 125–7.

[9] J. Allan, C. Henderson and R. Higham, 'Saxon Exeter', in J. Haslam, ed., *Anglo-Saxon Towns in Southern England* (Chichester, 1984), pp. 385–414.

[10] C. Thomas, *Christianity in Roman Britain to AD 500* (London, 1981), pp. 240–74.

[11] Haslam, ed., *Anglo-Saxon Towns in Southern England*, pp. 87–140.

[12] Esmonde Cleary, *Ending of Roman Britain*, p. 179; P. Rahtz and P. Fowler, 'Somerset AD 400–700', in P. Fowler, ed., *Archaeology and the Landscape* (London, 1972), pp. 187–221; Haslam, ed., *Anglo-Saxon Towns in Southern England*, pp. 87–140.

central-place functions for these three places in the Dark Ages.[13] It is these two themes, the political and the ecclesiastical, that provide most of the evidence for the development of central-place functions in the South-West of England in the early medieval period.

(ii) MINSTER CHURCHES AND *VILLAE REGIAE*

Over much of the South-West, whatever the uncertainties of the evidence for direct settlement continuities, it is clear that the majority of Roman settlements of any size were succeeded by Anglo-Saxon royal estate centres, the so-called *villae regiae,* or by minster churches, and frequently by both. The royal centres served a semi-peripatetic household and John Blair suggests that it was the minster which was the more stable element. The type-site is the 'royal palace' at Cheddar, excavated by Philip Rahtz. Its massive timber long hall of pre *c.* 930 was surrounded by outbuildings but the full extent of the complex is not known. Blair has recently suggested that it was a hunting lodge which had encroached on a minster enclosure.[14]

In common with many such places in this period, administrative, ecclesiastical and defensive functions were separated on the south side of the Mendips. The earliest evidence of urbanism was the ninth-century fortress at Langport which was still recognisably urban at Domesday but, by then, Ilchester had surpassed both it and Somerton with its market, port, good road connections and multiplicity of churches. Ilchester was probably developed as a town by King Edgar, perhaps as a consequence of the revival of the lead and silver mines of Mendip. It had a mint from 973 to1280, there were at least eight documented medieval churches and there may have been ten or more. St Mary Major was the principal town church, but St Andrew's, Northover, in the transpontine suburb, was the early minster and may have derived from a Roman cemetery church.[15] At Domesday there were 109 burgesses and the market was worth £11 but, thereafter, it declined as Bridgwater developed further downstream.

Wilton was another *villa regia* of this type with dispersed central-place functions. There is a 'Kingsbury' name at its settlement core and it was the administrative centre of the fifty-hide royal manor which included the hill-fort of Old Sarum and the settlement outside at *Searisbyrig*. St Mary's nunnery at Wilton is first recorded in 830 and was successively enriched and refounded first by Alfred,

[13] Stenton, *Anglo-Saxon England*, pp. 21–9.

[14] P. A. Rahtz, 'The Saxon and medieval palaces at Cheddar, Somerset', *Med. Arch.*, 6–7 (1962–3), 53–66; D. M. Wilson, ed., *The Archaeology of Anglo-Saxon England* (London, 1976), pp. 65–8; but see J. Blair, 'Palaces or minsters? Northampton and Cheddar reconsidered', *Anglo-Saxon England*, 25 (1996), 97–121.

[15] Maddicott, 'Trade, industry', 44–5; M. Aston and R. Leech, *Historic Towns in Somerset* (Bristol, 1977), pp. 67–75; R. W. Dunning, 'Ilchester', in *VCH*, Somerset, III, pp. 179–203.

and then by Archbishop Dunstan and King Edgar in *c.* 974. Edgar also established the mint at Wilton whilst Alfred had made it one of the *burhs* of Wiltshire. In 1003 Wilton was ravaged by Swein and his army and most of the population and the moneyers moved to the safety of the hill-fort at Old Sarum.[16]

Dorchester, with its Roman urban antecedents, was probably another *villa regia*. The first arrival of the Vikings in England is recorded there about 789 when they slew the royal reeve as he was escorting them to the king's hall, having mistaken them for merchants rather than marauders.[17] A long series of ninth-century charters suggests that the Wessex kings regularly spent Christmas at Dorchester and perhaps Easter too. Athelstan made it a town in the 930s. The mint was established with a single moneyer, and the place is recorded as a *civitas*. Two moneyers are known to have been active in the town in the reign of Ethelred II and two are recorded in Domesday Book.[18] The Roman defences were refurbished and three churches with roughly equal parish areas were founded within the walls. They were not subordinate to the minster outside the walls at Fordington, and Laurence Keen has suggested that this implies their establishment under royal authority, again, presumably, by Athelstan. The street and plot pattern consists of a simple cross of streets linking the four gates with back service lanes to all streets and a regular tenement pattern which is similar to the 'High Street' layout in Winchester.[19] These contrasts between the temporal development of the shire centres of Somerton/Ilchester, Wilton and Dorchester are instructive of the differences to be found in the growth of central-place functions in royal administrative centres.

Minster churches were founded in some numbers in the eastern part of the region by the early eighth century. This followed the establishment of the new see of Sherborne for the kingdom of Wessex west of Selwood by King Ine in 705. The first bishop, Aldhelm, as abbot of Malmesbury, had already founded new communities in Cricklade in *c.* 700 and Frome which, like Malmesbury itself, were endowed from large royal estates. From Sherborne his foundations included Bradford-on-Avon by 709, Bruton, Warminster in *c.* 705 and Wells, beside the powerful springs which gave name to the place.[20] The majority of these places fit a simple model of settlement development where the combination of *villa regia* and minster church, often standing side-by-side in adjacent enclosures led, in the ninth and tenth centuries, to developing central-place

[16] Haslam, ed., *Anglo-Saxon Towns in Southern England*, pp. 122–8.

[17] Anglo-Saxon Chronicle; L. Keen, 'The towns of Dorset', in Haslam, ed., *Anglo-Saxon Towns in Southern England*, pp. 203–48; B. Yorke, *Wessex in the Early Middle Ages* (Leicester, 1995), p. 300.

[18] Keen, 'Towns of Dorset', pp. 239–41; D. Hill, *An Atlas of Anglo-Saxon England* (Oxford, 1981), p. 83.

[19] Keen, 'Towns of Dorset', pp. 233–4; see the fine eighteenth-century town plan reproduced in C. C. Taylor, *Dorset, the Making of the Landscape* (London, 1970), plate 39.

[20] Haslam, ed., *Anglo-Saxon Towns in Southern England*, pp. 87–146.

functions and the increasing control of marketing for taxation purposes. The limitation of coin minting to these centres was for the same reason and added another central-place function. The surviving topography of cruciform church, a 'Kingsbury' place-name, a market place nearby and a 'Silver Street', suggestive of the location of moneyers, is characteristic of many later towns in all parts of the South-West except for Cornwall.[21]

(iii) *WICS*, *BURHS* AND MINTS

There were other patterns of central-place development, however. One such was the development of long-distance trading centres linking Wessex with other kingdoms, both in Britain and overseas, from the eighth century onwards. In eastern and south-eastern England these trading *emporia*, or *wics*, are widely recognised because of the significance and volume of trade in the North Sea–Baltic Sea coastal zone. A number have been extensively excavated, most notably that at *Hamwic*. There has been little attempt to recognise such trade centres elsewhere in the South-West, however. That is not to say that they did not exist, only that they were smaller and undocumented. The early trading centre at Tintagel on the north Cornish coast has already been referred to; on the south coast the great sandy beach beside St Michael's monastery is a prime candidate for such a sea-based trading centre since it is clear from the earliest records that trading on the beach preceded the formal founding of the town at Marazion, whose place-name derives from the Cornish for 'market'. The seasonally occupied trading beach at Bantham is another likely minor trading *emporium* exchanging products with Brittany, Iberia and Ireland, as well as along the south coast. The huge oyster shell dumps at Poole represent the detritus of an important trading activity of a rather later period.[22] A site requiring further archaeological investigation on the south coast is Weymouth. This was originally a royal estate, though by the thirteenth century it was in the hands of the bishops of Winchester. Its earliest name was Wyke Regis and, by 1244, there were two separate boroughs facing one another across the estuary. The *wic* place-name in such a location and with such a history of port trading is suggestive of an hitherto unrecognised *emporium*.[23] Another possible site with a *wic*

[21] Blair, 'Palaces or minsters?', 97–121; and see above, pp. 246–58.

[22] Yorke, *Wessex in the Early Middle Ages*, pp. 294–6; C. Thomas, '"Gallici nautae de Galliarum provinciis" – a sixth/seventh century trade with Gaul reconsidered', *Med. Arch.*, 34 (1990), 1–26; F. M. Griffith, 'Salvage observations at the Dark Age site at Bantham Ham, Thurlestone in 1982', *Proc. of the Devon Arch. Soc.*, 44 (1986), 39–57; P. A. S. Pool, *The History of the Town and Borough of Penzance* (Penzance, 1974), pp. 19–21; I. P. Horsey, *Excavations in Poole 1973–1983* (Dorset Natural History and Archaeological Society Monograph Series, 10, 1992); I. P. Horsey and J. M. Winder, 'Late Saxon and Conquest-period oyster middens at Poole, Dorset', in G. L. Good, R. H. Jones and M. W. Ponsford, eds., *Waterfront Archaeology* (CBA Res. Rep., 74, 1991), pp. 102–5.

[23] RCHM (England), *Dorset*, vol. II *The South East*, part II (London, 1970), pp. 330–9; M. Beresford, *New Towns of the Middle Ages* (London, 1967), pp. 429–50.

place-name is Bath. Bathwick was on the east bank of the Avon, opposite the Roman town. It may have been no more than a dairy farm but more attention needs to be paid to *wic* place-names on river bank sites in urban locations. Bath was an important place strategically, on the border between the kingdoms of Mercia and Wessex, and a trading *emporium* under royal protection might not be unexpected before the two kingdoms merged in the early tenth century and the superior site of Bristol began its rapid rise to become the regional economic capital.

In the ninth and tenth centuries new defended sites began to supersede some of these early trading places. The Burghal Hidage of 914x19[24] lists sixteen fortresses in the region originating at least from Alfred's reorganisation of the defence of Wessex against the Vikings. Clearly, many of these had not even the pretensions to urban status. Chisbury, Lyng and Halwell were adapted hill-forts only.[25] The urban status of Axbridge, Langport, Pilton, Watchet and Wilton *burhs* in the tenth century is contentious. All had demonstrable functions additional to defence but these did not necessarily make them towns. Malmesbury, Lydford, Bridport and Shaftesbury were promontory *burhs* and were seemingly intended to have full urban functions.[26] Bath and Exeter reused Roman urban sites for their defence. Cricklade and Wareham have distinctive grid street plans within new earthwork defences and were seemingly intended to be at the top of the urban hierarchy, but excavations have shown that much of intramural Cricklade, at least, remained vacant and the same may have been true at Exeter. Almost all these fortresses were established on existing royal estates and some of them certainly had earlier defences and central-place functions. For example, the Viking army were using Wareham as a *faesten* in 875–6 and Exeter in 876–7, suggesting that these places were defensible, and both had important early minster churches.[27] The Vikings frequently raided Watchet, too, one of the few sheltered anchorages on the north Somerset coast.

The Somerset group of forts at Axbridge, Lyng and Langport were seemingly designed to protect the royal palaces at Somerton and Cheddar and the Mendip silver and lead mines.[28] Some of the fortresses were superseded by a further group of fortified towns which David Hill postulates are the work of Athelstan, but which Jeremy Haslam suggests are the work of Edward the

[24] D. Hill and A. R. Rumble, *The Defence of Wessex* (Manchester, 1996), p. 11.

[25] N. Brooks, 'The unidentified forts of the Burghal Hidage', *Med. Arch.*, 8 (1964), 74–90; D. Hill, 'The Burghal Hidage – Lyng', *Proc. of the Somerset Arch. and NHSoc.* 109 (1967), 64–6; T. R. Slater, 'Controlling the South Hams: the Anglo-Saxon *burh* at Halwell', *Transactions of the Devonshire Association for the Advancement of Science*, 123 (1991), 57–78.

[26] Haslam, ed., *Anglo-Saxon Towns in Southern England*, pp. 111–17, 221–3, 256–9.

[27] Stenton, *Anglo-Saxon England*, pp. 250–1; Haslam, ed., *Anglo-Saxon Towns in Southern England*, pp. 106–10; D. A. Hinton and C. J. Webster, 'Excavations at the church of St Martin, Wareham, 1985–86, and "minsters" in south-east Dorset', *Proc. of the Dorset NH and Arch. Soc.* 109 (1987), 47–54.

[28] Maddicott, 'Trade and industry', 44–7.

Elder.[29] This contentiousness also applies to the location and function of some of these places since in some it is likely that defence and trade continued on two separate sites. Thus Barnstaple may well be the original *burh* of Pilton (it was in its parish), but it is also possible that it superseded an earlier fortress at Pilton Camp hill-fort. Bridport *burh* may have been the hill-fort of Bredy, the town being laid out only in the early tenth century.[30] Totnes, too, was a fully defended town in the tenth century and it may have replaced, or been a supplement to, the defensive capabilities of Halwell, but J. R. Maddicott has suggested that its early trade and wealth derived from the Dartmoor tin industry and that the same is true for the successful urban *burh* at Lydford.[31] The relationships between Old Sarum and Wilton, between Chisbury and Bedwyn, and Langport and Ilchester may have been similar with inaccessible hill-fort sites being abandoned for places where landholders could more easily make a profit from urban tolls, rents and fines.

The evidence of mints indicates trading status and the development of another central-place function.[32] Only Exeter had one in Alfred's time, probably from the 890s; Bath was added early in his reign by Edward the Elder, and Bridport, Langport, Shaftesbury and Wareham mints were operating by the end of his reign. Clearly the south coast trading ports of Wessex had mints but the north did not and whilst some large *burhs* certainly had mints others (such as Malmesbury and Cricklade) did not. Dorchester acquired a mint under Athelstan and Barnstaple and Totnes were added by 957 under Eadwig. Ilchester, Malmesbury and Wilton followed under Edgar in 973 and Lydford under Edward the Martyr in 975. Axbridge, Bristol, Bruton (briefly), Crewkerne, Cricklade, Milborne Port (briefly), Salisbury, South Cadbury (temporarily replacing Ilchester for a decade), Taunton, Warminster and Watchet and the first Cornish mint at Launceston followed under Ethelred II, mostly in 997. Bedwyn, Frome and Petherton (briefly) had mints before 1066. Metcalf has provided a ranking of these places based on the number of surviving coins.[33] Exeter stands out as the provincial centre for the South-West and is the eighth-ranked town in the kingdom. Of the other towns in the South-West only Bath, Ilchester, Wilton, Shaftesbury, Salisbury, Totnes, Lydford, Bristol, Wareham and Watchet stand out as second-rank centres.

[29] D. Hill, 'Trends in the development of towns during the reign of Ethelred II', in D. Hill, ed., *Ethelred the Unready* (British Archaeological Reports, 59, 1978), pp. 213–26; J. Haslam, 'The towns of Devon', in Haslam, ed., *Anglo-Saxon Towns in Southern England*, pp. 249–84.

[30] The B manuscript of the Burghal Hidage provides an insertion to explain that Pilton was Barnstaple, see Hill and Rumble, eds., *Defence of Wessex*, pp. 36–67; for Bridport see N. Brooks, 'The administrative background to the Burghal Hidage', in Hill and Rumble, eds., *Defence of Wessex*, p. 134 and references.

[31] Maddicott, 'Trade and industry', 36–7.

[32] Hill, *Anglo-Saxon Atlas*, pp. 126–33, maps and summarises this information; see also Maddicott, 'Trade and industry', *passim*; D. M. Metcalf, 'The ranking of boroughs: numismatic evidence from the reign of Ethelred II', in Hill, ed., *Ethelred the Unready*, pp. 182–210.

[33] See below, Appendix 1b.

William of Malmesbury notes that Athelstan was responsible for the rebuilding of Exeter's walls with 'squared stone' using the Roman remains as its core.[34] The city was attacked at least three times in the early eleventh century by the Danes which is suggestive of both its administrative importance and its wealth. Its topography suggests that it was replanned in a similar manner to Winchester in the late ninth or tenth century. The northern part of High Street is the only medieval street that follows a Roman alignment exactly. There are the characteristic back lanes behind part of High Street and an intramural street around the western and southern defences. There are churches on or beside the four gates and a majority of the city's sixteen parish churches and six chapels seem to have been in existence by 1086. Late Saxon pottery suggests that the principal overseas trading contacts were with the coastal ports of Normandy and Brittany, and some contact with the Loire valley, but there was little contact with the Rhineland. There was also a pottery in the city itself.[35]

(iv) CATHEDRALS, MONASTERIES, CASTLES AND TOWN WALLS

The majority of the monasteries revived by Dunstan and King Edgar in the later tenth century were in rural locations but might be endowed with the rents from urban houses and markets for their support, or they developed towns on their estates to improve their finances. An example is Glastonbury where the town wraps itself around the precinct of the great abbey but it was seemingly not urban before the twelfth century. Similarly with Tavistock Abbey, which established a small town beside its precinct in the twelfth century by extending an existing settlement, and Milton and Buckfast Abbeys which did the same in the thirteenth century. The minster town of Bodmin was clearly the most important centre in Cornwall in 1086 with its market and sixty-eight houses (burgesses in the Exon. Domesday).[36] It was the nunneries, however, which had the largest urban holdings in the South-West. The abbess of Wilton had rents from the borough worth £10 17s. 6d. and twenty-five burgesses; the abbess of Shaftesbury had 151 burgesses in that town who, thanks to the destruction of properties following the Conquest, were living in only 111 houses. Shaftesbury Abbey also held Bradford-on-Avon where there were thirty-three burgesses paying 35s. 9d. and a market worth 45s. in 1086.[37]

[34] D. Whitelock, ed., *English Historical Documents*, vol. I, (Oxford, 1955), pp. 277–83.

[35] Allan, Henderson and Higham, 'Saxon Exeter'.

[36] Aston and Leech, *Historic Towns in Somerset*, pp. 57–65; H. P. R. Finberg, *West Country Historical Studies* (Newton Abbot, 1969), pp. 104–28; Shorter, Ravenhill and Gregory, *Southwest England*, pp. 112–31.

[37] H. C. Darby and R. Welldon Finn, *The Domesday Geography of South-West England* (Cambridge, 1967), pp. 50–61.

The dioceses of the South-West were not based in towns until after the Conquest. Sherborne was certainly more rural than urban.[38] Similarly, from 909, when the diocese was divided into four, Crediton, Ramsbury and Wells, and from 1027, St Germans were all essentially rural. Consequently, Archbishop Lanfranc's ordinance of 1075, that cathedrals should properly be in towns, particularly affected the South-West, though reforming bishops had already got diocesan reorganisation under way. In 1058, Sherborne was united with Ramsbury and a new see established at Old Sarum which was neither properly urban nor a convenient site as experience was subsequently to prove. The first cathedral was begun in 1075 and completed by 1092 in the north-west quadrant of the hill-fort.[39] In Devon, by contrast, everything was concentrated at Exeter which developed rapidly from the tenth century after its deliberate refoundation by Alfred perhaps to exploit his control of Dartmoor tin.[40] Exeter became a cathedral city when Bishop Leofric transferred his see from Crediton to St Peter's minster in 1050. The bishop was a substantial landholder in Exeter with a church (St Stephen's) and forty-nine houses, two of which had been destroyed by fire in 1086.[41] The Norman cathedral was begun in 1112–14 and the choir was completed and consecrated in 1133. The whole was completed by about 1200 (Plate 21).

The Wells see was moved to Bath in 1088 by its first Norman bishop in the year that Bath was ravaged by rebels from Bristol. This may be why the king was happy to sell his Bath estate to Bishop John of Tours in 1091. In 1086 the abbey had twenty-four burgesses, a mill and twelve acres of meadow in the town; the addition of the substantial royal holding made Bath a monastic town and the rebuilding of the precinct began almost immediately in 1091. It incorporated nearly a quarter of the walled city since there was a bishop's palace, as well as the abbey church and its cloister and buildings. Bishop John (1088–1122) was interested in medical matters, which may be why he had moved the see to Bath. He incorporated the King's Bath into the precinct. The *Gesta Stephani* (*c.* 1148) is the first medieval reference to the baths, the writer noting that 'sick persons from all England resort thither to bathe in these healing waters'. It was probably John who rebuilt the Roman enclosure and surrounded it with arched semi-circular recesses and an upper balustrade which survived almost unaltered into the late seventeenth century.[42] As well as urban holdings in the see town, bishops also held land elsewhere. The bishop of Winchester had a flourishing borough at Taunton with sixty-four burgesses rendering 32s. for example, and the bishop of Coutances, in Normandy, had substantial holdings in Barnstaple and Exeter.

[38] K. Barker, 'The early Christian topography of Sherborne', *Antiquity*, 54 (1980), 229–31; Keen, 'Towns of Dorset', pp. 208–13.

[39] RCHM (England), *Ancient and Historical Monuments in the City of Salisbury*, vol. I (London, 1980), pp. 1–23. [40] Maddicott, 'Trade and industry', 3–51.

[41] Allen, Henderson and Higham, 'Saxon Exeter', pp. 398–404.

[42] B. Cunliffe, 'Saxon Bath', in Haslam, ed., *Anglo-Saxon Towns in Southern England*, pp. 345–59.

The Domesday record of towns in the South-West is far from systematic and it is difficult to make comparisons between places. Thirty settlements were boroughs and another five have evidence of urbanism.[43] From the disparate evidence it is clear that Exeter was the largest town by far and had a population of at least 2,000. Shaftesbury was next in the hierarchy, followed by Bath, both with a minimum of 1,000 population; Wareham came next, and then Totnes, Ilchester, Malmesbury and Bridport. Most of these larger towns had suffered considerable destruction in the twenty years from the Conquest partly as a result of the construction of castles. The Devon boroughs had seen forty-eight houses wasted in Exeter, forty in Lydford and thirty-eight in Barnstaple. In Dorset the boroughs seem to have suffered grievously at the hands of Hugh, the sheriff; there were 122 waste properties in Shaftesbury, 150 in Wareham, twenty in Bridport and twenty-eight in Dorchester whilst the number of houses had been reduced by eighty-four in this latter town over the twenty years from 1066.[44] However, Norman lords were clearly also in the process of founding new towns. At Okehampton, Baldwin de Brionne had four burgesses and a market and at Yeovil there were twenty-two men and twenty-two *masurae*. There were also boroughs of longer standing held by secular lords. The most significant of these urban holdings was probably that of Judhel of Totnes where there were 110 burgesses in his fief. The town was flourishing because of its role in the Dartmoor tin trade, though silt from the industry was beginning to clog the river wharfage. Contributory burgesses attached to rural estates are listed for only some of the Domesday boroughs, most notably for Bath, Cricklade, Malmesbury, Wareham and Wilton, enabling the market and administrative areas of towns over much of Wiltshire to be suggested.[45]

The late eleventh and twelfth centuries were notable in towns as a period of new building by the Norman elite which provided work for masons, carpenters, quarrymen, glaziers and others. Quarrying on Purbeck, Portland and Portlemouth expanded and Corfe, for example, developed as a small town dominated by the yards of Purbeck quarrymen and masons.[46] Early earthwork and timber castles were quite quickly reconstructed in stone; churches and cathedrals were rebuilt in newly fashionable Romanesque styles, and borough defences and gates were refurbished or constructed for the first time in stone. Such change was probably most noticed in Cornwall where the count of Mortain was intent on ensuring that the shire was more integrated into the kingdom. New castles were constructed at Launceston, Trematon and Liskeard and earlier Sunday markets under the control of the Church were moved to the castle sites to ensure that boroughs flourished as trading centres at the heart of these estates. Launceston

[43] Darby and Welldon Finn, *Domesday Geography*, *passim*.
[44] *Ibid.*, pp. 50–9, 117–21, 279–84.
[45] *Ibid.*, pp. 52–9, 198.
[46] RCHM (England) *Dorset* vol. II: *The South East*, part I, pp. xxxvii, 52–3.

was the most successful of these new planned towns and was walled and gated in the thirteenth century, but its new church of St Mary did not become parochial until 1380.[47]

In Devon, Plympton Erle provides a classic example of a small borough, founded probably in *c.* 1110–20, with market and burgages laid out along a single street beside the earthwork defences of the massive motte and bailey castle constructed by Richard de Redvers, earl of Devon, in 1107. Though Plympton remained head of the honour, the castle was not reconstructed in stone following its slighting in the civil war between Stephen and Matilda.[48] In contrast, Judhel's castle, on the highest point of the ridge on which Totnes had been developed, has a fine surviving stone shell keep. Judhel also founded a Benedictine priory, giving it the town's parish church, before he forfeited his estates in 1088. He returned to favour under Henry I and was granted the borough and honour of Barnstaple where he proceeded to build a similar castle and to found a Cluniac priory.[49]

The castle which dominates the northern corner of Exeter was King William's, built in 1068 after the revolt of the Exeter citizenry the previous year. Their success in repelling an eighteen-day siege following King William's conquest is testament to the strength of the stone walls and gates of the city. At Old Sarum the castle was built by 1070 at latest and became the seat of the sheriff. It was a massive ring motte and ditch in the centre of the Iron Age hill-fort with the bailey comprising the eastern half of the fort. Bishop Roger acquired the castle in 1130 and built part of the stone wall around the hill-fort defences, effectively making castle and cathedral a single fortified complex.[50] Bishop Roger was also responsible for the construction of the motte and bailey, deer park and borough at Devizes and the castle at Sherborne. These works were to be of great consequence in the civil war between Stephen and Matilda, as was the castle constructed at Taunton by Henry de Blois, bishop of Winchester, in 1138.[51] Ditches around the castle and town were added in 1216 and the subsequent strength of Taunton Castle made it important to kings as well as bishops.

The towns which developed from Anglo-Saxon *burhs* were initially fortified at least with earthwork and timber defences and ditches; a few had stone walls and gates before the Conquest, most notably Totnes, together with those places within the confines of Roman circuits: Bath, Dorchester and Exeter, where the Roman walls could be repaired or, at the least, form a source of supply for building stone. Barnstaple and Malmesbury also maintained their earlier defensive circuits. As at

[47] Beresford, *New Towns*, p. 405.

[48] R. Bearman, *Charters of the Redvers Family and the Earldom of Devon 1090–1217* (Devon and Cornwall Record Society, 37, 1994), pp. 1–43.

[49] S. Rigold, *Totnes Castle, Devon* (London, 1971); H. R. Watkin, *A History of Totnes Priory and Medieval Town* (Torquay, 1914).

[50] RCHM, *City of Salisbury*, pp. 208–13.

[51] P. Leach, *The Archaeology of Taunton* (Gloucester, 1984), pp. 5–28.

Taunton, ditches were still considered adequate for the defence of Salisbury in the fourteenth century. In 1367, the bishop granted the townspeople the right to have four gates and an eight-perch wide ditch around the city but, even by 1440, it was unfinished.[52]

Murage grants provide dating evidence for wall building or reconstruction and repair at Totnes in 1264, at Bridgwater in 1269, at Melcombe in 1338, at Wells in 1341, at Bath in 1369, at Plymouth in 1378, 1463 and 1485, at Ilfracombe in 1418 and at Poole in 1433. These last were in response to the constant French threat to coastal towns along the south coast. There were also castles and gun ports guarding the entrances to the estuaries, notably at Dartmouth where a chain could also be stretched from shore to shore if enemy ships approached.[53] The murage grants for Bristol begin in 1232 and continue to the end of the fifteenth century. The 1232 grant relates specifically to the Redcliffe suburb, where the so-called Port Wall was constructed jointly by the men of Redcliffe and the tenants of the Knights Templar. It was complete by 1240, together with the two gates which led into axial streets of the suburb.[54] At Exeter, in 1215, the burgesses received 100 marks from the 1214 tallage towards enclosing the town and in 1216 they were ordered to clear houses from the wall and ditch. In 1218, a further 100 marks was diverted for the same purpose.[55]

(V) MARKETS, FAIRS AND BOROUGHS

Somerset, Devon and Cornwall had the highest number of boroughs in medieval England. It is tempting to see this as a reflection of a highly developed economy, but all the evidence goes to show that the opposite was the case and that the south-western economy was growing only slowly. H. P. R. Finberg and Maurice Beresford have suggested that the lack of earlier towns in Devon and Cornwall encouraged feudal lords to develop their estates with new small towns to enhance rents and encourage economic development. Others have pointed to the difficulties of transport in the region and the considerable regional diversity of products.[56]

Founding a town was in fact the final stage of what was usually a three-phase process which began with the acquisition of a market charter or one for a fair. This could be for an existing farming community, for a place where some trading

[52] RCHM, *City of Salisbury*, p. xxxvii.

[53] H. L. Turner, *Town Defences in England and Wales* (London, 1970); B. H. St J. O'Neill, 'Dartmouth Castle and other defences of Dartmouth Haven', *Archaeologia*, 85 (1935), 129–53.

[54] M. D. Lobel and E. M. Carus-Wilson, 'Bristol', in *BAHT*, II, p. 7.

[55] I. Burrow, 'The town defences of Exeter', *Transactions of the Devonshire Association for the Advancement of Science*, 109 (1977), 13–40.

[56] M. W. Beresford and H. P. R. Finberg, *English Medieval Boroughs* (Newton Abbot, 1973); M. Beresford, 'English medieval boroughs: a hand-list: revisions, 1973–81', *UHY* (1981), 59–65; M. Kowaleski, *Local Markets and Regional Trade in Medieval Exeter* (Cambridge, 1995), pp. 41–80.

was already taking place unofficially or, most speculatively, for a new site without permanent settlement. There have been no detailed studies of the markets and fairs of any of the South-West shires other than Maryanne Kowalewski's for Devon. Here, as elsewhere in England, the number of market and fair sites was considerably in excess of the places which later acquired borough charters. Fairs were especially concentrated around the fringes of Dartmoor, including Bampton, Ashburton and Crediton, where they were held in the autumn for sale of livestock for fattening and slaughter. At least one third of markets were at places with easy access to the sea, perhaps reflecting the difficulty of land transport, but only Exeter had markets on three days of the week. The biggest fairs were in Exeter, too, at the beginning of Lent, in early August and early December.[57]

In Cornwall there were thirty-eight small boroughs, all newly developed or enhanced from the late eleventh century onwards. The earlier church, the manorial centre and the town were often in different locations with different names. The new towns were mainly strung out along the two main roads that traverse the county, or were estuarine ports, usually established nearer the sea than the older church or manorial centres. By 1300, the earl of Cornwall had ten boroughs in the shire (as well as Bradninch, in Devon) and several were successful local market centres with a wide variety of local craftsmen, traders and retailers amongst the population. Lostwithiel, for example, first founded in the 1190s close to Restormel Castle, the duchy administrative centre, gained a borough charter in 1268 and had 377 burgages in 1337, representing a population of perhaps 1,800 people.[58] It is worth noting that many of the earl's boroughs had burgage rents of only 6d., half that of boroughs in most parts of the country and perhaps reflecting the difficulty of persuading traders to settle in Cornwall. The earl of Cornwall was exceptional; only the earls of Devon of other secular magnates in the South-West founded more than two or three boroughs.

Devon had seventy-one boroughs, more than any other county, the majority being creations of the thirteenth century. In the twelfth and thirteenth centuries Devon was the largest European source of tin. Four towns gained much of their wealth from the stannaries which stamped tin and collected the taxes due prior to export, but other places close to Dartmoor benefited from the demand for foodstuffs from the miners. Roadside foundations on the road from the Tamar to the Dorset border were a notable feature of the south Devon towns. In 1308, for example, Chudleigh was recorded as a *novus burgus* of the bishop of Exeter. The bishops also founded a successful borough at Ashburton, which was both astride the main road and a stannary town; at Crediton, where the ancient minster settlement was expanded with a street borough in 1231x42, and at West

[57] Kowaleski, *Exeter*, pp. 41–80. [58] Beresford, *New Towns*, pp. 406–8.

Teignmouth, which grew into a successful small port.[59] Okehampton dominated the road to the north of Dartmoor in much the same way as Ashburton did to the south and, by 1274, the four burgesses of Domesday had increased to 140. Livestock marketing was especially important here.

A number of lords founded new boroughs in close competition with one another or to take advantage of existing trade. Bridgetown Pomeroy is a classic 'bridgehead suburb' across the River Dart from Totnes, but it was a separate borough administratively, and a successful one, with fifty-five burgesses in 1273.[60] On a rather grander scale, the Redcliffe suburb of Bristol occupied a similar position, which was emphasised still further because it was across the county boundary in Somerset until the city was made a county in 1373. It was a carefully planned development divided between two lords: the Fitzharding family held the western half, whilst the eastern half had been granted to the Knights Templar. The Redcliffe borough was in existence by the mid-twelfth century but there was a second phase of development in the 1240s when new quays, a new bridge and the Port Wall were constructed.[61] Two urban developments laid out side by side by separate lords are also a feature of Newton Abbot and Newton Bushel at the head of the Teign estuary, Kingsbridge and Dodbrooke, occupying a similar situation at the head of the Kingsbridge estuary, and Sutton Priors and Sutton Vautort (which were to become Plymouth) at the head of Plymouth Sound. All were single street towns without spacious market places and it must always have been difficult to distinguish one borough from the other.

That did not prevent lords going frequently to the law courts to guard their privileges. At Wimborne, where the lords of Kingston Lacy had extended the settlement and acquired their own market, they and the minster community were frequently in dispute over the two adjacent markets, whilst port customs dues were at the heart of disputes between Weymouth and Melcombe Regis until they were amalgamated in 1571.[62] Such disputes were comparatively minor when compared with the complex of jurisdictions in Exeter. Like most cathedral cities, Exeter had separate fees controlled by the bishop, by the dean and chapter, by the crown and by at least four other individuals or corporate bodies. The 1280s saw one such period of dispute between secular and ecclesiastical authorities. The bishop was in dispute with the dean and chapter and in 1283 the precentor, William Lechlade, was set upon and murdered by men of the town favouring the dean. Two years later Edward I himself travelled to Exeter at Christmas to resolve the case. After trial in the great hall of the castle, the mayor

[59] W. G. Hoskins, *Devon*, 2nd edn (Newton Abbot, 1972), pp. 320–1, 366–7, 378–9, 491–2.

[60] Beresford, *New Towns*, p. 420.

[61] Lobel and Carus-Wilson, 'Bristol', pp. 7–8.

[62] Beresford, *New Towns*, pp. 429–30; J. Blair, 'Minster churches in the landscape', in D. Hooke, ed., *Anglo-Saxon Settlements* (Oxford, 1988), pp. 48–9; J. Blair, 'Wimborne minster', *Archaeological J*, 140 (1983), 37–8.

of the city, Alured de Porta, and the porter of the South Gate, were summarily hanged for opening the gate and allowing the murderers to escape. Soon after, the bishop gained royal permission to enclose the cathedral close with stone walls so that it could be secured at night.[63]

In the 1280s, too, there were serious disputes between the town and Isabella, countess of Devon, who blocked the River Exe with a weir. This destroyed both the salmon fishery upstream and the port functions of the city. Relationships between the city and the earl continued to flare up into violence or legal dispute through the next century. In the 1330s it was the tolls from the Lammas fair which were in dispute whilst, at the same time, Hugh Courtenay, the third earl of Devon, reinforced the Exe weir and built a new quay and crane at his port of Topsham downstream.[64] There were further disputes with the cathedral community in the 1440s when formal processions to the cathedral by the mayor and commonalty were attacked by the canons' servants who pushed 'their back parts even into the mayor's lap'. Two local magnates had to be called in to resolve the disputes.[65] There were also disputes between the various ecclesiastical institutions, especially over the burial of the dead, which was the sole right of the cathedral. In 1301, the dean and chapter, asserting their right to burial fees, were in dispute with the black friars over the burial of Sir Henry Rawley. His corpse lay unburied 'till it stank' at the gates of the friary while the dispute remained unresolved.[66]

The region contains the most spectacularly successful of all planned new towns in the shape of Salisbury which, by the early fourteenth century, had become the most important town of the region. Richard I gave sanction to remove the cathedral from its inconvenient location within the ramparts of Old Sarum to a new site beside the Avon meadows. A market charter for the new town was acquired in 1219 and a fair in 1221. The borough charter, from Bishop Richard, followed in 1225 and was confirmed by the king in 1227. A second church, St Thomas', was provided and, in 1269, as the town expanded rapidly, a third, St Edmund's was built for the northern extension of the city. The parish boundary divided the large rectangular market place. Plots were laid out within the grid street blocks to dimensions of seven x three perches at the standard burgage rent of 12d. The whole settlement took up 260 acres (105 ha) of which the cathedral close was *c.* 83 acres (33.6 ha), the town 120 acres (48.5 ha) and the rest common moor. Water channels were laid down the streets and were an

[63] W. G. Hoskins, *Two Thousand Years in Exeter* (Chichester, 1960), pp. 32–4; S. Izacke, *Remarkable Antiquities of the City of Exeter* (London, 1724), pp. 21–3.

[64] Hoskins, *Two Thousand Years in Exeter*, pp. 49–50; A. M. Jackson, 'Medieval Exeter, the Exe and the earldom of Devon', *Transactions of the Devonshire Association for the Advancement of Science*, 104 (1972), 57–79; Kowaleski, *Exeter*, p. 59.

[65] G. Rosser, 'Conflict and political community in the medieval town: disputes between clergy and laity in Hereford', in T. R. Slater and G. Rosser, eds., *The Church in the Medieval Town* (Aldershot, 1998), pp. 20–42.

[66] Izacke, *Antiquities of Exeter*, p. 31.

important part of the plan, feeding from the mill leat. The necessity for appropriate gradients dictated the eccentricities of the plan from orthogonal rectilinearity.[67] The royal charter had allowed for the alteration of roads and bridges for the improvement of the city and so, in 1244, Bishop Bingham built the great bridge over the Avon to the south of the city with its hospital and bridge chapel. Wilton was effectively bypassed by this development and its trade captured. In 1377, there were 3,226 taxpayers, making Salisbury the sixth largest town in England, not including the suburb of Fisherton which had been developed by Richard Aucher, or Old Sarum where there were ten taxpayers remaining. A rental of 1455 refers to over 400 tenements, 120 cottages and 100 shops and there were two large friaries, a college and two hospitals.[68]

Salisbury is exceptional in the scale and regularity of its planning. The other major new town in Wiltshire is also exceptional. Devizes was founded in 1135x39, most probably by Bishop Roger of Salisbury who had built a castle there in *c.* 1120, but by 1141 the castle was in Matilda's hands and, though the manor was returned to the bishop in 1149, the castle, park and borough were to remain with the crown. Its spacious semi-circular plan is determined by its layout around the castle and it was probably developed in two phases, each served by a church and market place.[69] Most other new towns in the South-West are planned on the basis of a single street, with burgages on each side, and it was the passing traders on the road who were the basis of their prosperity. A good example of this type of borough is Honiton, founded by William de Redvers, earl of Devon before 1211. It sits astride the main road to Exeter and its burgages were laid out over a distance of more than half a mile, probably in several phases. De Redvers held two other boroughs in Devon, Plympton and Tiverton, besides others in Hampshire. Such one-street boroughs could also be laid out to urbanise previous rural settlements with central-place functions. Chard is an episcopal example developed in 1206x34 by the bishop of Bath and Wells beside an earlier settlement with fifty-two new one-acre burgages on both sides of a new High Street on the main road from Salisbury to Exeter.[70]

(vi) THE URBAN HIERARCHY IN 1334

Despite the deficiencies of the 1334 lay subsidy as a means of devising an urban hierarchy, it provides a convenient snapshot of the region at the end of the period

[67] RCHM, *City of Salisbury*, pp. xxix–xl; Beresford, *New Towns*, pp. 506–8.

[68] K. H. Rogers, 'Salisbury', in *BAHT*, I; E. Nevill, 'Salisbury in 1455', *Wiltshire Arch. and NH Magazine*, 115 (1911), pp. 66–91.

[69] Beresford, *New Towns*, p. 504; see M. Aston and J. Bond, *The Landscape of Towns* (London, 1976), p. 89, for plan.

[70] Bearman, *Charters of the Redvers Family*, pp. 17–37; Aston and Leech, *Historic Towns in Somerset*, pp. 31–4.

Table 22.6 *Rank order of towns in the South-West in 1334*

Rank	Borough	Valuation
1	Salisbury	£75 0s. 2d.
2	Exeter	£40 12s. 4d. (includes Exe Island)
3	Plymouth (Sutton Priors + Vautort)	£34 12s. 8d.
4	Bridgwater	£26 0s. 0d.
5=	Bodmin	£20 0s. 0d.
5=	Shaftesbury	£20 0s. 0d.
5=	Ottery St Mary (ancient demesne)	£20 0s. 0d. (includes rural parish)
8	Wells	£19 0s. 0d.
9	Barnstaple	£18 14s. 0d.
10	Dartmouth	£17 6s. 8d. (includes Southtown + Kingswear at 1/15)
11	Corsham	£15 0s. 0d. (not borough, taxed 1/15)
12	Chippenham	£14 0s. 0d. (excludes Rowden, ancient demesne)
13	Bath	£13 6s. 8d.
14	Wyke Regis and Weymouth (ancient demesne)	£12 14s. 10d. (includes Elwell)
15	Glastonbury (and 12 hides)	£12 6s. 8d. (not borough, taxed 1/15)
16	Truro	£12 1s. 10d.
17	Malmesbury	£11 10s. 10d.
18	Melksham (ancient demesne)	£10 10s. 0d. (includes rural parish)
19	Taunton	£10 3s. 4d.
20	Bridport	£9 19s. 5d.

of urban growth in the thirteenth century (Table 22.6).[71] In the South-West only five towns were amongst the fifty most wealthy nationally so, despite the urbanisation of the thirteenth century, the region remained largely rural with a plethora of small boroughs but few larger towns. Salisbury was the wealthiest town in the region, twelfth in the national ranking. Its function as the principal market centre for the wool from the flocks on the Wiltshire Downs, as well as an intermediate centre between the Midlands and Southampton for overseas export and

[71] R. E. Glasscock, ed., *The Lay Subsidy of 1334* (London, 1975), pp. 29–35, 49–78, 258–75, 332–48.

import commodities, had led to its rapid growth. The wealth of Exeter's inhabitants was assessed at just over half that of Salisbury and it was twenty-second in the national hierarchy. The city was an important port for the coasting trade and was the distributive centre for much of Devon.[72]

The next two towns are rather different. Plymouth's wealth is disguised by the fact that it was a place divided between three lordships, only one of which was a borough. It was only with incorporation, in 1439, that it gained its present name. Its growth was a consequence of its superb harbour which, though open to prevailing south-westerly winds, was much used from the thirteenth century onwards for the assembling of naval fleets. Its merchants were dominated by traders in wine from Gascony.[73] Bridgwater was next in the hierarchy, and it, too, was a developing port town. Though 11 miles (18 km) from the sea, it had developed rapidly from *c.* 1200 when William Brewer had built his castle, rebuilt the bridge over the Parrett and its causeways and established a market, borough and eight-day fair. The port customs were subsumed under Bristol until the early fifteenth century but the wealth of its merchant community, trading with Wales, Ireland and Gascony, was reflected in the high valuation of the town.[74] Bridgwater served Somerset in much the same way as Exeter served Devon but it lacked the institutional development of Exeter and was always in competition with Taunton for the local market trade of the region.

The next group of towns in the wealth-derived hierarchy of 1334 were a very different group of places. Bodmin, taxed at £20, was the market and administrative centre for Cornwall and, though it was the fifth most wealthy town in the South-West, ranked only seventy-sixth in the national hierarchy. Shaftesbury, Ottery St Mary and Wells were all dominated by ecclesiatical institutions but, whereas Shaftesbury and Wells were thriving market towns, Ottery's wealth was inflated by its very large minster parish where rural wealth cannot be differentiated from urban. The same is true of Chippenham and Corsham. In all these places the rural textile industry, which was to bring new wealth to them, was just beginning to develop. Barnstaple and Dartmouth, the ninth and tenth most wealthy towns in the region, were lesser ports serving north and south Devon respectively. The merchant community in both places traded overseas and inflated their valuations over and above similar sized towns elsewhere. Dartmouth, like Plymouth, was much used for assembling naval expeditions since its deep-water harbour was even more sheltered and defensible. It developed across five separate manors. Besides what became the borough of Clifton–Dartmouth–Hardness, there was also Southtown and, across the harbour in Brixham parish, was Kingswear. It is notable that merchant wealth was concentrated in the port towns. None of the Stannary towns around Dartmoor, for

[72] *VCH*, Wiltshire, VI, pp. 124–8, 132–5; Kowaleski, *Exeter*, pp. 179–234.

[73] Kowaleski, *Exeter*, pp. 231–6.

[74] *VCH*, Somerset, VI, pp. 196–220.

example, was other than a very small town, though Ashburton had a Jewish merchant, Joel, who farmed the taxes on tin between 1169 and 1188.[75]

(vii) PORTS AND HARBOURS

There was considerable change in the port geography of the South-West in the post-Conquest period. This was a consequence of the changing pattern of long-distance trade; of changes in ship technology and the change from small shallow-draught vessels to bigger vessels requiring deep-water anchorages and quay walls; of geomorphological changes to coasts and rivers; and of changing commodities being traded. Excavations on the Redcliffe river frontage in Bristol have shown very clearly the way in which slipways were succeeded by quay walls in the thirteenth century.[76] In Poole and Plymouth, successive quaysides were rebuilt out from the original strand line as urban refuse was tipped to make up ground. Poole was a new port town of the thirteenth century developed on a gravel spit on the north shore of Poole Harbour. It took the place of Wareham as that town's quays became less accessible as the outer parts of Poole harbour silted up and ships got larger.[77] This same process of port succession can be observed on the Dart, which was affected by silt from Dartmoor tin mining so that the port function of Totnes gave way to Dartmouth; at Exeter, where almost all ships docked at its outport of Topsham and only small lighters could reach the city quay, whilst a little later access was blocked entirely by a weir across the Exe;[78] at Ilchester which was too far up the River Parrett to enable larger boats to have access and so was succeeded by Bridgwater further downstream; and by the rapid rise of Plymouth in succession to Plympton in the fourteenth century, and Falmouth in sucession to Penryn and Truro in the fifteenth century.

Kowaleski has shown how a small oligarchy of Exeter merchants had controlling interests in the waterborne trade of that city from the fourteenth century. Imports and coasting were far more important than exports and international trade, and conflict with the earl of Devon ensured that the customs accounts were compiled especially fully. Wine and woad were the most valuable commodities imported in the thirteenth century; together with garlic and onions, they betoken cross-Channel links with Gascony and Brittany. The coasting trade dealt in products such as herring and grain coming from the ports of the East

[75] P. Russell, *Dartmouth: A History of the Port and Town* (London, 1950), pp. 21–6; G. R. Lewis, *The Stannaries: A Study of the English Tin Miner* (Cambridge, Mass., 1924), pp. 233–8.

[76] R. H. Jones, 'Industry and environment in medieval Bristol', in Good, Jones and Ponsford, eds., *Waterfront Archaeology*, pp. 19–26.

[77] J. Barber and C. Gaskell-Brown, 'Plymouth', in Milne and Hobley, eds., *Waterfront Archaeology*; I. P. Horsey, 'Poole', in Milne and Hobley, eds., *Waterfront Archaeology*, pp. 145–6; I. P. Horsey, 'Poole: the medieval waterfront and its usage', in Good, Jones and Ponsford, eds., *Waterfront Archaeology*, pp. 51–3.

[78] Jackson, 'Medieval Exeter', 57–79; Kowaleski, *Exeter*, pp. 222–4.

and South-East of England, whilst the merchants also controlled the fishery of the whole Exe estuary. Earl Hugh Courtenay did much to develop the port facilities of Topsham after 1293, including the provision of a new market, wharf and crane.[79] The most important exports were woollen cloth. By the mid-fourteenth century exports from Devon ports represented 15 per cent of English cloth exports. This is probably a substantial underrepresentation since much cloth was taken by smaller craft to Bristol and Southampton before its final export and this sector would not be registered as from Devon. In the late fourteenth century the greatest production of cloth was channelled through Barnstaple but, by the fifteenth century, east Devon had developed more rapidly and more cloth was going out through Exeter.[80]

Of the smaller ports, Teignmouth developed in the thirteenth century and, like Poole, Melcombe Regis, Exmouth and East Looe, amongst others, was built on a sandy spit at the estuary mouth. Teignmouth was destroyed by the French in 1340 and took a long time to recover. Melcombe, too, was burnt in 1377 and in 1380 and, by 1401, Lyme Regis was 'so wasted and burned by attacks of the sea and assaults of the King's enemies and frequent pestilences that scarcely a twentieth part of it is now inhabited.'[81] Dartmouth had the largest deep-water fleet in the South-West in the thirteenth century and dominated the Bordeaux wine trade and trade with Iberia through to the fifteenth century. The port was especially significant in the war effort with the French through the fourteenth century, providing more ships than any other port. It was also a port of embarkation for pilgrims going to Compostella as were Plymouth, Fowey and Bristol.[82] Plymouth began to develop from the fourteenth century, because of royal patronage through the duchy of Cornwall. Its exports were more varied than Dartmouth and it had a broader hinterland. However, all these places, including Exeter, were of minor significance when compared with the provincial centres of Southampton and Bristol just beyond the regional bounds.

(viii) LATE MEDIEVAL DEVELOPMENTS

Bubonic plague probably entered England through a ship arriving in Melcombe Regis in the early summer of 1348.[83] Following the economic and social devastation of the Black Death, the 1377 poll tax returns provide a different ranking based on adult population, excluding only the very poor and church people. Salisbury is still at the top of the rankings with 3,373 recorded taxpayers, the

[79] M. Kowaleski, *Local Customs Accounts of the Port of Exeter 1266–1321* (Devon and Cornwall Record Society, 36, 1993); Kowaleski, *Exeter*, pp. 222–79.

[80] Kowaleski, *Exeter*, pp. 19, 232–8; E. M. Carus-Wilson and O. Coleman, *England's Export Trade, 1275–1547* (Oxford, 1963).

[81] J. H. Bettey, *Wessex from AD 1000* (London, 1986), p. 113.

[82] C. M. Storrs, *Jacobean Pilgrims from England to St James of Compostella* (London, 1994), pp. 173–82.

[83] R. Horrox, *The Black Death* (Manchester, 1994), pp. 63–4.

seventh most populous town in the country. Exeter and Plymouth are next biggest with 1,700 and 1,600 taxpayers respectively, standing together in the national hierarchy at twenty-third and twenty-fourth. Only half their size were Wells, Bridgwater and St Germans, with between 750 and 1,000 taxpayers. The last was neither a borough nor sufficiently wealthy to appear in the 1334 hierarchy. Barnstaple was a little smaller with 680 taxpayers, whilst Bath, Taunton, Melksham and Dartmouth had between 500 and 600 taxpayers. No other towns in the South-West were sufficiently large to feature in the national hierarchy (see Appendix 5).

The fifteenth and early sixteenth centuries was a period of considerable change in the urban hierarchy of the South-West when the region became both more urbanised and more industrialised. The woollen cloth industry transformed both the countryside and the urban centres of the region since, although production moved to the countryside around the water-power sites of fulling mills, marketing took place in the older-established towns. In Wiltshire and eastern Somerset the broadcloth industry dominated and became increasingly focused on the small market centres of the county border, such as Frome, Warminster, Trowbridge and Bradford-on-Avon, where there were few social or cultural restrictions to limit the expansion of the increasingly capitalised industry. They became, in effect, some of England's first specialist industrial towns.[84] At first, this cloth was exported to the Low Countries for dyeing and finishing but, by the later fifteenth century, dyestuffs were imported through Bristol and Southampton. Bristol did not share in the wealth generated by the export of cloth until the late fifteenth century, when the wine trade with Bordeaux and Spain and Portugal also revived. Bristol merchants rebuilt the bridge over the Avon together with many of the parish churches of the city in this period, whilst William Canynges, whose family dominated the trade with Iceland, used much of his fortune to rebuild the great parish church of St Mary Redcliffe.[85]

In Devon and Somerset it was the lighter, coarse rough woollens known as 'dozens' or 'straits' that dominated the industry. The core of textile production was in east Devon, where Crediton, Tiverton, Cullompton, Ottery St Mary and Colyton became sufficiently wealthy to enter the national urban hierarchy of 100 wealthiest places in 1524–5 (see Appendix 7). The last three, with between 230 and 250 taxpayers, were more rural than urban, despite their wealth and population, since the industry was largely domestic in character and was integrated into the farming year. However, there is no doubting the wealth generated by clothmaking or its scale of expansion. Whereas in 1380 Devon generated 1 per cent of England's cloth exports, by 1500 it generated 10 per cent. Exeter was the principal market centre and entrepôt for this trade to the extent that it had overtaken

[84] R. Leech, *Early Industrial Housing: The Trinity Area of Frome* (RCHM (England), Supplementary Series, 3, 1981), pp. 1–18. [85] Lobel and Carus-Wilson, 'Bristol'.

Salisbury in the hierarchy by 1524–5 and was perhaps the sixth largest city in the country. Taunton, Marlborough, Totnes and Glastonbury were other places which grew rich and populous as a result of the late medieval cloth industry.

Exeter's merchants and manufacturers were organised in powerful guilds of tailors, weavers, fullers and shearmen by the mid-fifteenth century and the great Guildhall in the centre of the city was rebuilt in 1460.[86] The wealth of the merchant community is still reflected in many of these towns in surviving timber-framed houses, such as those in Totnes and Dartmouth, and inns in which merchants and traders could stay. The New Inn in Exeter, for example, was built in 1445 by the dean and chapter, with shops in front of it, and was leased by the corporation for many years thereafter. The magnificent George in Glastonbury is another inn of this period, whilst Salisbury has three surviving late medieval inns, including the Blue Boar built in 1444.[87] Another characteristic late medieval urban building deriving from merchant wealth was the endowed almshouse. Exeter had seven such establishments founded between 1407 and 1540 but few other towns had more than one.[88]

Salisbury, too, came to be dominated by the textile industry with dyers concentrated in those tenements backing on to the river and weavers, tailors and tuckers scattered through the town, their racks occupying marginal chequers. It was also a market for cloth produced in rural south Wiltshire and London merchants and drapers attended the Lady Day cloth fair to purchase the fine striped cloth known as 'rays' which was the Salisbury speciality. Tanners, parchment makers and glovers were the other principal late medieval occupations in the city.[89] Leather goods were also the principal product of Yeovil and Ilchester in the later medieval period.

Tin production on Dartmoor reached its peak in 1521 but it was a poorly capitalised industry despite the value of the ore. Thereafter, production declined until a new capitalised phase of the industry developed in the seventeenth century. However, new sources of tin had begun to be worked in Cornwall and led to the late medieval development of many of the port towns of that shire, such as Padstow and Fowey, whilst Bodmin's status, in the midst of the metalliferous region, was enhanced further. By 1524–5, it was the fifty-first ranked town in England in terms of number of taxpayers.[90] By contrast, Plymouth, whose earlier growth was at least partly stimulated by the tin industry, fell on hard times in the fifteenth century and, despite being only the second town in England to be incorporated, in 1439, it fell rapidly down the urban hierarchy to forty-fourth place in 1524–5 since it had little share in the cloth industry though its merchant

[86] Kowaleski, *Exeter*, p. 19; S. R. Blaylock, 'Exeter Guildhall', *Proc. of the Devon Arch. Soc.*, 48 (1990), pp. 123–78. [87] RCHM, *City of Salisbury*, p. xlvi.

[88] N. Orme and M. Webster, *The English Hospital 1070–1570* (New Haven, 1995), pp. 181–5.

[89] *Ibid.*, pp. xli–xlii; *VCH*, Wiltshire, IV, pp. 115–47.

[90] J. Hatcher, *English Tin Production and Trade before 1550* (Oxford, 1973), pp. 8–26, 89–118.

fleet continued to export it (see Appendix 7). In the fifteenth century, deep-sea fishing began to grow in significance for all the South-West ports, but especially those of south Devon and Cornwall where Brixham grew rapidly as a fishing port, and places such as Fowey, Looe and Dartmouth had fishing fleets of some size. Herring was the main catch to begin with but later hake and cod came to the fore. The fleets ranged further and further into Atlantic waters and eventually, in the sixteenth century, began to fish the Grand Banks off Newfoundland. Much of this fish was subsequently sold through Exeter merchants and markets, the Lenten fair being dominated by the sale of fish. Poole, too, shared in this industry together with importing timber and produce from northern France and the Bay of Biscay.[91] New stone quays characterised many of the more prosperous ports in the late medieval period, including Exeter, Dartmouth and Poole. From the 1470s, the South-West saw the fastest rate of growth in overseas trade of any region of Britain.

[91] Horsey, 'Poole: the medieval waterfront'.

· 22(c) ·

The Midlands

CHRISTOPHER DYER AND T. R. SLATER

THE MIDLAND region contains unspectacular countryside, except at its western and northern margins, and varied geology. The dominating features of its geography are three of the major drainage basins of England: the Severn, the Trent and the Ouse/Nene/Welland (Map 22.9). These river systems gave shape to sub-regions, provided easy transport routes to other parts of the country and ensured the prosperity of towns located on their banks and crossing places. The West Midlands is focused on the Severn, Warwickshire Avon, Wye and Teme valleys, whilst the Wiltshire Avon and the upper Thames form its southern bounds. The shire towns (except Stafford) were all located beside these rivers (Map 4.1). So, too, was the entrepôt trading centre of Bristol which became the largest city of the region since it was able to serve a large part of the South-West too. The Severn was navigable to Welshpool on the Welsh border. In contrast, the Trent was navigable only a few miles upstream from Nottingham, which is the only shire town located beside it, though Stafford, Leicester and Derby are on tributaries. The entrepôt of the Trent valley is Hull, which served the whole Yorkshire Ouse basin of the North of England too. The rivers draining the South-East Midlands reached the North Sea via the fenlands and their successful navigation depended on constant maintenance. Boston and Lynn were the major port towns, but the shire towns are also located on the principal rivers.[1]

Despite its gentle topography, the underlying geology produces a patchwork of distinctive *pays*. In the East Midlands the rocks and the drainage trend north-east/south-west. The chalk escarpment of the Chilterns provides a distinctive physical divide with the South-East of England. A broad clay vale separates the

[1] H. C. Darby and I. B. Terrett, *The Domesday Geography of Midland England* (Cambridge, 1954), pp. 417–55; J. F. Edwards and B. P. Hindle, 'The transportation system of medieval England and Wales', *J of Historical Geography*, 17 (1991), 123–34; J. Langdon, 'Inland water transport in medieval England', *J of Historical Geography*, 19 (1993), 2–6.

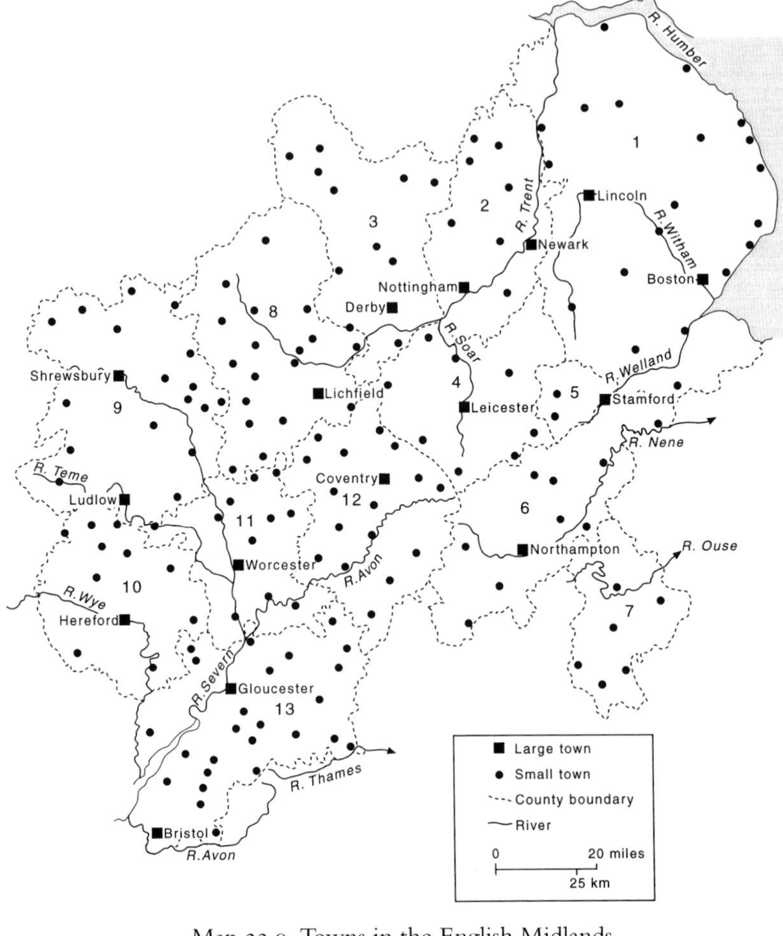

Map 22.9 Towns in the English Midlands

1 Lincolnshire
2 Nottinghamshire
3 Derbyshire
4 Leicestershire
5 Rutland
6 Northamptonshire
7 Bedfordshire
8 Staffordshire
9 Shropshire
10 Herefordshire
11 Worcestershire
12 Warwickshire
13 Gloucestershire

chalk from the limestone escarpment of the Cotswolds and the Northampton uplands and both chalk and limestone form narrow ranges of hills in Lincolnshire. The fenland marshes dominated a large tract of country in the east and the shallow waters of the coastal fringe were suitable for salt production. The Jurassic limestone provided some of the finest building stone in England from which the region's churches, cathedrals and castles benefited immeasurably. It also provided the pastures for huge flocks of sheep in the later medieval period.

The southern parts of the West and East Midlands were the granary of high medieval England; open-field farming and nucleated villages predominated on the Jurassic scarplands and on the clay vales to the north-west from Bristol to Lincoln. Beyond the line of the Warwickshire Avon, however, a more wooded countryside took over, with mixed farming systems on the more acidic soils and sandstones and gravels of the northern and western Midlands. Here, too, were coal seams outcropping to the surface around Coventry, in the Black Country, central Staffordshire, north of Nottingham, north-west Leicestershire and in east Shropshire, in all of which regions coal was mined in the medieval period. The northern and western margins of the region are part of highland England. The southern tip of the Pennine ridge forms gritstone and limestone uplands in Staffordshire, Derbyshire and Nottinghamshire which were pastoral countrysides, where they were not bleak moorlands or extensively forested, as in Sherwood. Lead was extracted from the Carboniferous limestones. Similar landscapes are found on the hills of Shropshire and Herefordshire in the west.

(i) FROM LATE ROMAN TO EARLY MEDIEVAL MIDLAND TOWNS: 400–1100

The Midlands was well developed and urbanised under Roman rule. *Civitas* capitals of considerable size and sophistication were established at Cirencester (*Corinium*), Wroxeter (*Viroconium*) and Leicester (*Ratae*). There were major *coloniae* at Gloucester (*Glevum*) and Lincoln (*Lindum*); important industrial settlements at Droitwich, Worcester and Water Newton; small towns at Alcester, Ancaster, Great Casterton, Irchester, Kenchester and Towcester; a number of small posting stations on the major roads which seem to have acquired some central-place functions in the late Roman period, such as Wall and Penkridge; and small market centres like Duston and Bourton-on-the-Water. The Roman communication system had a continuing significance throughout the medieval period, including the main roads leading from London, such as Watling Street and Ermine Street, the Fosse Way which brought the north-east of the region into contact with the south-west, countless minor roads, and the waterway, the Foss Dyke, which connected Lincoln to the Trent.

In the towns themselves in the two centuries after 400, there is much evidence for abandonment and dereliction. At Gloucester the post-Roman period is marked on a number of excavated sites by a layer of dark earth, implying that much of the city was either totally deserted, or used for agriculture. Throughout the region the Roman towns shrank drastically in size, ceased to be involved in large-scale industry or trade using coins and can no longer be regarded as urban. They retained political and religious roles. The sequence of occupation on the site of the baths basilica at Wroxeter continued through the fifth and sixth centuries. The Roman stone buildings were dismantled and replaced by timber structures, some of them flimsy, but including a large and substantial hall, which could have been the residence of a political leader or a bishop.[2] At Cirencester, too, there is evidence for a late Roman Christian community, and for the conversion of the amphitheatre into a stronghold of a British ruler in the early fifth century. Elsewhere there is evidence for some late defensive reorganisation, such as the blocking of gate passages to leave only a single carriageway at Kenchester. The tradition that Bath, Cirencester and Gloucester were captured after the defeat of three rulers at the battle of Dyrham in 577 suggests that some central-place functions survived at these former Roman cities.[3]

Christianity played an important role as a bridge between the Roman towns and their early medieval successors. Some Roman churches survived in use into the middle ages, as is plausibly argued in the case of St Helen's, Worcester. In some cases Roman masonry was incorporated into medieval churches and still survives, as at the Jewry Wall at Leicester. At St Mary-de-Lode, in Gloucester, the discovery of a Roman oratory under the later church suggests that Christian worship had an uninterrupted history on the same site. In the centre of the forum at Lincoln a sequence of churches was built from the late Roman period into the early middle ages, with their long axes laid out in relation to Roman structures.[4] The Anglo-Saxon migrants into the western Midlands did not need to be converted to Christianity by St Augustine and his successors after 597 because they had already come into contact with British Christians, and the bishops' sees at Lichfield, Worcester and Hereford were established in the seventh century at places where British churches already existed.

So although urban life was extinguished in the fifth and sixth centuries, the Roman sites continued in use either as centres of secular power, or religious cults, and when towns revived again they developed on, or near to, the ruins of Roman precursors. This did not lead to an exact recreation of the Roman pattern. Often the site moved, leading to the medieval town's development at a distance of some miles: Shrewsbury succeeded Wroxeter, Northampton grew near Duston, and Newark replaced *Ad Pontem* (East Stoke). There were structural differences too, because the Roman urban hierarchy was not perpetuated – Cirencester, once an important Roman provincial capital, was never more than a modest market town in the middle ages, and the large medieval town of

[2] C. M. Heighway, 'Anglo-Saxon Gloucester to A. D. 1000', in M. L. Faull, ed., *Studies in Late Anglo-Saxon Settlement* (Oxford,1984), pp. 38–9; R. White and P. Barker, *Wroxeter: The Life and Death of a Roman City* (Stroud, 1998), pp. 118–36.

[3] J. S. Wacher, *The Towns of Roman Britain*, 2nd edn (London,1995), pp. 322–3; B. C. Burnham and J. Wacher *The 'Small Towns' of Roman Britain* (London,1990), pp. 70–6.

[4] S. Bassett, 'Churches in Worcester before and after the conversion of the Anglo-Saxons', *Antiquaries J*, 69 (1991), 225–56; W. Rodwell, 'Churches in the landscape: aspects of topography and planning', in Faull, ed., *Late Anglo-Saxon Settlement*, pp. 1–23; K. Steane and A. Vince, 'Post-Roman Lincoln: archaeological evidence for activity in Lincoln from the 5th to the 9th centuries', in A. Vince, ed., *Pre-Viking Lindsey* (Lincoln,1993), pp. 72–4.

Northampton was apparently the successor to a very minor Roman market centre. Only Gloucester, Lincoln and Leicester occupied high positions in the ranking order both in the Roman and medieval periods. And of course many medieval towns were entirely new.

The first phase of medieval urbanisation, in the period 650–850, might appear to have missed the Midlands, as the most famous *-wic* settlements are found on the south and east coasts. Lincoln may have been an early trading site, though we lack firm indications of this from the archaeology. Instead, the north Lincolnshire site of Flixborough has produced evidence for a wide range of craft activities and trade contacts. These were located in a relatively small settlement adjacent to either a secular lord's residence, or a minster church.[5] Perhaps a number of sites of this type fulfilled some of the functions of the *wic* settlements in other parts of England. Of course, the Midlands could have obtained imported goods from the Mercian *wic* of London, and perhaps also from *Hamwic*. Seventh- and eighth-century coins of the *sceatta* series circulated in the Midlands, which were presumably used in trade.[6] Likely centres of exchange include Droitwich, a *wic* (though the place-name element is normally translated as 'salt-making place') which was trading in salt by the eighth century.[7] Gloucester had some occupation throughout the post-Roman period, and a deposit of wood and bone in the centre of the city, dated to the ninth century, suggests some intensive economic activity, albeit of a rather unsophisticated type.[8] Mercian kings, probably in the late eighth or early ninth centuries, fortified Hereford, Tamworth and Winchcombe, no doubt to protect the royal residences and important churches sited in those places, but also enclosing enough space for streets and houses. A metalled road and four houses of the eighth or ninth centuries have been excavated at Hereford, whilst at Tamworth a mill, built on the edge of the fortified area in the ninth century, may have served a permanent population, as well as the itinerant royal household. Other places, such as Derby, Gloucester and Warwick, had some administrative importance for the Mercian monarchy, and at Northampton excavation has shown how large and impressive high-status buildings of this period could be, notably an eighth-century hall with stone foundations 123 feet (43 m) long. Usually thought to have belonged to a royal palace, it could have been a residential building attached to a monastery, as it stood next to St Peter's church. Large timber

[5] S. Bassett, 'Lincoln and the Anglo-Saxon see of Lindsey', *Anglo-Saxon England*, 18 (1990), 1–32; Steane and Vince, 'Post-Roman Lincoln', pp. 71–9; C. P. Loveluck, 'A high status Anglo-Saxon settlement at Flixborough, Lincolnshire', *Antiquity*, 72, no. 275 (1998), 146–61.

[6] D. M. Metcalf, *Thrysmas and Sceattas* (London, 1993); M. Blackburn, 'Coin finds and coin circulation in Lindsey', in Vince, ed., *Pre-Viking Lindsey*, pp. 80–90.

[7] D. Hooke, 'The Droitwich salt industry', *Anglo-Saxon Studies in Archaeology and History*, 2 (British Archaeological Reports, 92, 1981), 123–69.

[8] Heighway, 'Anglo-Saxon Gloucester', pp. 39–40.

buildings stood near to St Mary's church in Nottingham and went through successive rebuildings from the eighth to the eleventh centuries, suggesting a residence of high status before 900, and its continued use in the period of Danish domination.[9] There were also important churches, both cathedrals and monasteries, at such places as Leicester, Worcester and Gloucester which may have served as nuclei around which grew trading and craft activities. However, we should not forget that dozens of royal residences and minster churches – places like Gumley in Leicestershire or Tredington in Warwickshire – remained rural in subsequent centuries.[10]

We cannot identify an urban hierarchy, or even be confident of the existence of urban settlements, until the period 850–1100. The top ranks of the urban hierarchy were filled by places which were fortified (given *burh* status according to one terminology) when the Midlands were disputed between the Danes and the English in the late ninth and early tenth centuries. The Danes fortified the 'five boroughs' of Derby, Leicester, Lincoln, Nottingham and Stamford, while Alfred's daughter Æthelflæd and her husband Ethelred are recorded as providing Worcester with walls in the 890s and, in 912–16, Æthelflæd was credited with the fortification of Bridgnorth, Stafford, Tamworth and Warwick. Shrewsbury, too, is likely to have been defended at this time. Also, Gloucester's Roman walls were refurbished, the defences of Hereford and Winchcombe upgraded and fortifications at Northampton built. Bedford became a double fort, protecting both ends of the bridge across the Ouse.[11]

[9] P. A. Rahtz, 'The archaeology of West Mercian towns', in A. Dornier, ed., *Mercian Studies* (Leicester, 1977), pp. 107–29; R. Shoesmith, *Hereford City Excavations*, vol. I: *Excavations at Castle Green* (CBA Res. Rep., 36, 1980); R. Shoesmith, *Hereford City Excavations*, vol. II: *Excavations on and Close to the Defences* (CBA Res. Rep., 46, 1982); P. Ellis, 'Excavations in Winchcombe, Gloucestershire, 1962–1972: a report on excavation and fieldwork', *Transactions of the Bristol and Gloucestershire Arch. Soc.*, 104 (1986), 95–138; P. Rahtz and R. Meeson, *An Anglo-Saxon Watermill at Tamworth* (CBA Res. Rep., 83, 1992); J. H. Williams, M. Shaw and V. Denham, *Middle Saxon Palaces at Northampton* (Northampton,1985); J. V. Beckett, ed., *A Centenary History of Nottingham* (Manchester,1997), pp. 32–3.

[10] These are conveniently mapped in D. Hill, *An Atlas of Anglo-Saxon England* (Oxford,1981), pp. 83, 160–1.

[11] These statements, and subsequent information about these towns in the period 850–1100, are based on Rahtz, 'Archaeology of West Mercian towns'; Shoesmith, *Hereford City Excavations*; R. A. Hall, 'The Five Boroughs of the Danelaw: a review of present knowledge', *Anglo-Saxon England*, 18 (1989), 149–206; M. Carver, 'Early Shrewsbury: an archaeological definition in 1975', *Transactions of the Shropshire Arch. Soc.*, 59 (1973–4), 225–63; S. R. Bassett, 'Anglo-Saxon Shrewsbury and its churches', *Midland History*, 16 (1991), 1–23; M. Carver, *Underneath Stafford Town* (Birmingham, n.d.); T. R. Slater, 'The origins of Warwick', *Midland History*, 8 (1983), 1–13; M. Gelling, *The West Midlands in the Early Middle Ages* (Leicester,1992), pp. 146–67; J. H. Williams, 'From "palace" to "town": Northampton and urban origins', *Anglo-Saxon England*, 13 (1984), 113–36; *VCH*, Gloucestershire, IV, pp. 5–12; C. Mahany, A. Burchard and G. Simpson, *Excavations in Stamford, Lincolnshire, 1963–1969* (Society for Medieval Archaeology Monograph, 9, 1982); J. Haslam, 'The origin and plan of Bedford', *Bedfordshire Arch. J*, 16 (1983), 29–36.

Towns did not necessarily grow within the defensive circuits. Chirbury was fortified, but along with a number of similar places on the Welsh border did not become urbanised. Some of the forts, such as Gloucester and Lincoln, were probably already developing urban functions before their Roman walls were put into order. The Worcester charter can be interpreted to mean that the market, streets and court dealing with trading offences were all new in the 890s, but it is more likely that they had all existed before 890, and that the charter was merely recording a settlement of financial and other matters between the secular rulers and the bishop.[12] The earthworks of the new fortifications were not generally built on 'green-field' sites, but around existing royal or church centres, so they were reinforcing the significance of 'central places' already serving as focal points for their districts.

The new status and administrative functions of the more important fortified places encouraged urbanisation. A dozen became shire towns at which courts were held, taxes collected and coins minted. The region stands out because all of its shires (except Rutland, a special case) were named from the towns at their centres, unlike the older system of local government in the south. Gloucester, Hereford and Worcester acquired rectilinear arrangements of main streets and back lanes, while in the East Midlands the streets grew piecemeal, giving them a less orderly appearance: at Lincoln and Northampton for example.[13] The development of properties and plots at Worcester began with the division of the land along the High Street into parcels of about ¾ acre (0.3 ha), with a street frontage of 160 feet (50 m), which were then subdivided into smaller building plots. Houses in the city were attached to rural estates, presumably providing, among other benefits, outlets in the town for the sale of rural produce.[14] Houses have been excavated in Flaxengate in Lincoln. They were timber structures 16 feet (5 m) wide and about 30–45 feet (10 m–15 m) long, built close together from the late ninth century onwards, and subject to successive rebuildings in the succeeding centuries.[15] The size of the settlements grew, with the fortified area becoming fully occupied – 43 acres (17 ha) at Worcester, 60 acres (24 ha) at Northampton, and even larger areas at Lincoln and Stamford. Suburbs were appearing outside the gates at Worcester, Stamford and other towns. These places were clearly urbanising in the sense that they were growing in size and becoming dense and permanent settlements.

[12] For different views, H. B. Clarke and C. C. Dyer, 'Anglo-Saxon and early Norman Worcester: the documentary evidence', *Transactions of the Worcestershire Arch. Soc.*, 3rd series, 2 (1968–9), 27–33; N. P. Brooks, 'The administrative background to the burghal hidage', in D. Hill and A. Rumble, eds., *The Defence of Wessex* (Manchester,1996), pp. 143–4.

[13] J. H. Williams, 'A review of some aspects of late Saxon urban origins and development', in Faull, ed., *Late Anglo-Saxon Settlement*, pp. 25–34.

[14] N. J. Baker and R. Holt, 'The city of Worcester in the tenth century', in N. P. Brooks and C. Cubitt, eds., *St Oswald of Worcester* (London, 1996), pp. 129–46.

[15] D. Perring, *Early Medieval Occupation at Flaxengate, Lincoln* (Lincoln Archaeological Trust, Archaeology of Lincoln, IX–1, 1981), pp. 36–45.

The other essential urban characteristic, a variety of occupations, emerges from the excavated evidence for industry: at both Northampton and Lincoln, for example, metalworking, textile production, glass and pottery making, bone working and the building trades were practised. Pottery making was introduced into a number of towns, which is especially striking at Stafford because in that north-western part of the region there appears to have been no tradition for making and using pottery since the end of the Roman period. The new urban pottery manufacture is found in relatively minor towns, such as Torksey, as well as the shire towns of Leicester and Northampton. But the most remarkable story of innovation in manufacture is found at Stamford where, towards the end of the ninth century, a continental potter, almost certainly from the town of Huy, now in Belgium, settled at Stamford and brought with him advanced techniques which allowed him to introduce an entirely new ware, made of a white or pale fabric, with a lead glaze coloured pale green or yellow. Stamford's rural marketing zone, judging from the distribution of pottery, extended over a radius of 15 miles (24 km), and early Stamford ware also occurs at Northampton, suggesting a trading network that linked towns.[16]

The result of early medieval urbanisation can be assessed through Domesday Book and other sources of about 1100. In the west, the towns of the Severn/Avon river system included five large places with populations probably exceeding 1,000 – in ascending order of size Hereford, Warwick, Worcester, Gloucester and Bristol. Domesday has no detailed description of Bristol, but its population could have been greater than Gloucester's 2,500–3,000, because it rendered £84 annually, compared with £60 at Gloucester. Shrewsbury's population had probably exceeded 1,000 immediately before the Conquest. The smaller towns of this subdivision of the region had a chequered history – Winchcombe, once an important Mercian centre and briefly the head of its own shire, was now demoted. The fortification at Quatford/Bridgnorth (its precise location is controversial) appears at this time not to have grown into a town. Droitwich had reached a modest size appropriate for a specialised industrial centre. There are signs of real urban growth in the Avon valley. The monastery of Pershore had apparently promoted a town at its gates, though Domesday records the burgesses as belonging to Westminster Abbey, which had recently been granted sections of the original Pershore estates. Evesham Abbey had acquired the right to hold a market just before the Norman Conquest, and its embryonic urban community appears in Domesday as twenty-seven bordars (smallholders) 'serving the court', and 'men living there' who paid a rent of 20s. Tewkesbury seems to have just begun its development also with a settlement of

[16] W. Giertz, 'Middle Meuse Valley ceramics of Huy-type: a preliminary analysis', *Medieval Ceramics*, 20 (1996), 33–64; K. Kilmurry, *The Pottery Industry of Stamford, Lincolnshire, c. A.D. 850–1250* (British Archaeological Reports, 84, 1980), pp. 155–75.

bordars, and thirteen burgesses, and Wigmore grew beside the new castle. In Gloucestershire, markets are mentioned at Berkeley, Cirencester and Thornbury, suggesting at least the first stage of the emergence of those small towns. Coventry, which lies near the north-eastern edge of the Severn/Avon river system, is described in 1086 as a rural manor but, by 1102, was regarded as sufficiently urban to become the see of the bishopric previously based at Lichfield and later Chester. It was probably growing, unnoticed by Domesday, outside the gates of the wealthy Benedictine monastery founded before the Conquest.[17]

In the Trent/Soar river system, the towns increased in size as one moved down the rivers to the east, with the small shire towns of Stafford and Derby to the west, and the once important Mercian centre of Tamworth, but both Leicester and Nottingham went well over the 1,000 population limit. Lincoln, which was joined to the Trent by its canal, the Foss Dyke, was by far the largest town in the Midlands, with a population of about 6,000 before the Conquest, and nearer to 5,000 in 1086. Grantham, like Lincoln in the valley of the Witham, had a population of about 1,000. The smaller towns of the Trent valley, with populations of hundreds, were Torksey and Newark, and Louth was of comparable size. Hints of new towns are less plentiful than in the west of the region, though a trading settlement was growing around the new castle at Tutbury, and markets which might suggest the beginnings of smaller towns were held at such places as Melton Mowbray and Barton-on-Humber.

To the south of the region, in the Ouse/Nene/Welland river system, the upstream town of Bedford seems to have been relatively small, but Huntingdon, lower down the same river, and Northampton, on the Nene, had well over 1,000 people. Stamford was much larger, with more than 2,000, and Lincoln can be linked with this subdivision of the region as well as with the Trent valley. Again, markets were recorded, sometimes producing much toll money, at places which

[17] All of these generalisations are based on Domesday, presuming that the total of burgesses, houses, etc., for each town should be multiplied by five to allow for families and households. The Domesday figures for Gloucester and Winchcombe have been corrected in the light of near contemporary surveys: H. B. Clarke, 'Domesday slavery (adjusted for slaves)', *Midland History*, 1 (1972), 38–9. Discussion of individual places in this period include H. A. Cronne, ed., *Bristol Charters 1378–1499* (Bristol Record Society, 11, 1946), pp. 20–2; C. Dyer, *Everyday Life in Medieval England* (London, 1994), p. 252; C. J. Bond, 'The topography of Pershore', *Vale of Evesham Historical Society Research Papers*, 6 (1977), 18–26; R. H. Hilton, 'The small town and urbanisation – Evesham in the middle ages', in R. H. Hilton, *Class Conflict and the Crisis of Feudalism* (London, 1985), pp. 187–93; A. Hannan, 'Tewkesbury and the earls of Gloucester: excavations at Holm Hill, 1974–5', *Transactions of the Bristol and Gloucestershire Arch. Soc.*, 115 (1997), 79–231; R. H. C. Davis, *The Early History of Coventry* (Dugdale Society Occasional Paper, 24, 1976), p. 17; R. Goddard, 'Lordship and the growth of Coventry, 1043–1355' (PhD thesis, University of Birmingham,1998), pp. 23–52; K. Lilley, 'Trading places: monastic institutions and the development of high-medieval Coventry', in T. R. Slater and G. Rosser, eds., *The Church in the Medieval Town* (Aldershot, 1998), pp. 177–208.

later became towns: Higham Ferrers, Leighton Buzzard, Luton, Oundle and Spalding. As before, we must suspect that some urban centres were omitted by Domesday, notably Peterborough where a community of about 1,000 people were living outside the gates of the monastery in the early years of the twelfth century, and there are hints of commercial activity at Grimsby.[18]

Domesday is not very informative about urban functions and the occupations of the inhabitants. The iron bars rendered to the king from Gloucester hint at the output of artisans receiving their supplies of metal from the Forest of Dean. Commerce is suggested by the forty-two men settled at Tutbury who 'live only from their trade', and merchants are mentioned at Nottingham. The tolls collected from some markets – 40s. at Spalding for example – must imply a high volume of transactions. And the tendency for the places at the top of the hierarchy to be those near the mouths of the river systems – Bristol and Lincoln – implies that they benefited from the volume of trade at the end of the communications network. Large sums of money flowing through the towns explain the high payments to the crown recorded, though they might include dues collected in the attached hundreds and shires. The varied size of the payments is generally in agreement with other indicators of the town's position in the hierarchy. Lincoln heads the list with £100, and £75 from its moneyers. Leicester, Gloucester, Shrewsbury and Worcester paid various sums between £23 and £60, and poorer places proportionately less – £9 at Stafford, and £4 10s. 0d. at Tutbury.

High-ranking towns tended to have important administrative roles, and their size reflected the wealth of their surrounding countryside – Lincoln lay at the centre of a large and populous shire, while Stafford's shire was thinly populated and poor. Lincoln was made into a bishopric in 1072, in recognition of its secular importance, and this new function helped the development of the town. But a cathedral or large monastery on its own did not guarantee success, and the Norman churchmen were shocked to find a bishop's see located in such an insignificant place as Lichfield. A better guide to the institutional complexity of different towns is provided by their numbers of churches – Lincoln is thought to have had thirty-five by 1100, Gloucester ten and Leicester six or seven. The lesser places managed with one or two, though they might have been of considerable size and wealth, like Stafford's church of St Mary which was served by thirteen canons, with a parish extending far beyond the town.[19] Domesday tells us that, in the larger and more important towns, houses belonged to lords based in the surrounding countryside – there were a dozen landowners at Leicester, for example. The smaller towns were ruled by a single lord.

[18] E. King, 'The town of Peterborough in the early middle ages', *Northamptonshire Past and Present*, 6 (1980–1), 187–95; S. H. Rigby, *Medieval Grimsby* (Hull, 1993), p. 7.

[19] J.W. F. Hill, *Medieval Lincoln* (Cambridge, 1948), p. 147; *VCH*, Gloucestershire IV, p. 14; *VCH*, Leicestershire, IV, p. 49; *VCH*, Staffordshire, VI, pp. 238–9.

The well-defined hierarchy of 1086 gives the urban system of the Midlands the semblance of maturity. The most prominent places remained the leading towns in the region in the later middle ages, except for Coventry and Boston, which grew rapidly in the twelfth and thirteenth centuries. Towns had made a considerable impact on their local societies by 1086, judging from their size in relation to the population as a whole – the towns of Gloucestershire (making a reasonable estimate for Bristol) contained more than a tenth of the county's population. The proportion was much lower in Warwickshire – only about one in twenty of its people lived in towns. Most Midland counties lay somewhere between these extremes – 8 per cent of town dwellers in Lincolnshire, and 7 per cent in Nottinghamshire are reasonable estimates. The urban hierarchy seems weak because it lacked a network of market towns. There must have been opportunities for exchange in Derbyshire, for example, outside the market at Derby, though this is the only trade centre mentioned in Domesday. The market at Chesterfield, first recorded in 1165, may have had an earlier history, and in the south of the shire people could have used Burton-on-Trent, where traders and artisans were living beside the monastery by the early years of the twelfth century.[20] But we must suspect that local trade was mainly conducted through gatherings in churchyards or at the gates of lords' houses. The gaps in the urban network are especially glaring in the north of the region, where upland Derbyshire and Staffordshire, north Shropshire and Nottinghamshire apparently lacked any town. These blank spaces must point to the incomplete and underdeveloped state of the urban systems of the Midlands before 1100.

(ii) NEW TOWNS, BOROUGHS AND MARKETS

The West Midland region after about 1100, in contrast with the East Midlands, is characterised by the creation of large numbers of new towns. The most successful were those founded early, in economically strategic locations, by powerful lords. The three West Midlands' bishops were all town-founders but not all their towns were successful. The bishop of Worcester established only two boroughs, one of which, Stratford, was an extremely successful small town. It was a minster church site at the heart of a large episcopal estate; several long-distance routes used the ford over the Avon; it had good local road links; and it was at the boundary of two farming regions, one pastoral and one arable. The bishops of Hereford founded five small boroughs on their estates, again centred on minster church sites; all except Prestbury became successful small towns. The bishops of Coventry and Lichfield, despite founding two markets and three boroughs, were

[20] J. M. Bestall, *History of Chesterfield* (Chesterfield, 1974), p. 30; J. Walmsley, 'The boroughs of Burton-upon-Trent and Abbots Bromley in the thirteenth century', *Mediaeval Studies*, 35 (1973), 339–53.

economically successful only with the see town of Lichfield itself. Stratford, Lichfield, Bishop's Castle and Ledbury were all carefully planned settlements with regular burgage series, designed market spaces and ordered streets. The bishops were also concerned to participate in the physical expansion of their see cities by planning new market spaces, suburbs and roads, thereby opening land for development.[21]

Benedictine monasteries were similarly involved in developing the economies of their estates in this region by founding new towns, often in close association with new stone bridges at strategic river crossings. Examples include the rapid expansion of Burton by five successive abbots on the north bank of the Trent; the development of Pershore, jointly by Pershore and Westminster Abbeys; of Evesham a few miles further up the Avon valley, mostly before 1150; and the little Cotswold borough of Northleach, founded by Gloucester Abbey in the 1220s where the road from Oxford to Gloucester crossed the Fosse Way.[22] The most successful towns tended to be those in which abbeys themselves were the major institution, though disputes often arose between townspeople and monastery. Abbots were also involved in the deliberate expansion of existing settlements, such as Reading Abbey's new house plots regularly laid out along all the approach roads to Leominster after the minster estate had been gifted to them by Henry I. The cathedral priory at Coventry laid out a new street through an orchard to provide land for development and also was responsible for the infilling of the market place with house plots, whilst Shrewsbury Abbey held the east suburb of that town, beyond the English Bridge, as a separate borough.[23]

The crown was responsible for relatively few new towns in this period, but two successful developments beside important castles were, first, Bridgnorth, where the castle was begun by Robert de Belesme and the town established in its outer bailey; subsequently it was expanded in three major phases by Henry I and Henry II following Robert's rebellion; and, secondly, Newcastle-under-Lyme, where the castle had been built by the earl of Chester, but the town was established by Henry II, probably in 1172–3 on the road to Chester. The other successful royal new town was Newport (Salop.), also founded by Henry I. The remaining new towns were the responsibility of secular feudal lords great and small. Amongst the most successful were Ludlow, founded by the de Lacy family

[21] T. R. Slater, 'Ideal and reality in English episcopal medieval town planning', *Transactions, Institute of British Geographers*, new series, 12 (1987), 191–203; R. Bearman, ed., *The History of an English Borough* (Stroud, 1997), pp. 30–62; J. Hillaby, 'The boroughs of the Bishop of Hereford in the late 13th century, with particular reference to Ledbury', *Transactions of the Woolhope Naturalist's Field Club*, 40 (1970), 10–35; M. Beresford, *New Towns of the Middle Ages* (London, 1967), pp. 450–2, 500–1.

[22] T. R. Slater, 'Medieval town-founding on the estates of the Benedictine Order in England', in F.-E. Eliassen and G. A. Ersland, *Power, Profit and Urban Land* (Aldershot, 1996), pp. 70–92.

[23] K. D. Lilley, 'Coventry's topographical development: the impact of the Priory', in G. Demidowicz, ed., *Coventry's First Cathedral* (Stamford, 1994), pp. 72–96.

in the late twelfth century beside their great castle overlooking the River Teme and astride an important road from Hereford to Shrewsbury, and Tewkesbury at the heart of the honour of the earls of Gloucester, founded in the mid-twelfth century. Status was less the key to successful urbanism than early foundation and good location, however. Thus the little boroughs of the de Ferrers earls of Derby (Newborough and Uttoxeter) were founded in the mid-thirteenth century as part of an attempt to assart the Forest of Needwood, whilst even Tutbury, founded soon after the Conquest beside the de Ferrers' castle, failed to thrive in this pastoral and forest region. By contrast, Birmingham's lord, Peter, purchased a market charter from the crown in 1166, his successor granted burgage tenure to anyone wanting to settle in the new town for a rent of only 8d. a year (compared with the more usual 12d.) and by the 1230s the town was thriving.[24] With these few notable exceptions the West Midland new towns were tiny places. However, in the hierarchically ordered urban marketing system, they played a vital role as the places in which country people sold surplus produce for cash to pay rents and acquire manufactured goods. These little towns rarely had a market catchment area which extended beyond five or six miles; they were mostly developed in the middle years of the thirteenth century; their markets did not compete because they were held on different days; this enabled traders to move round a succession of these markets before selling on in the larger market towns. Despite their small size, however, the majority of the places with borough charters were clearly urban in their social and occupational structure. In this they differed from those settlements which failed to progress beyond the acquisition of a market charter.[25]

The East Midlands differed profoundly: there were few new towns in the twelfth and thirteenth centuries, less evidence of large-scale planning of urban settlements, and fewer small marketing centres. Maurice Beresford suggests only nine places in the six East Midland shires as new plantations. However, these did include Boston, the second most successful new town and outport of Lincoln, which dominated the Midland trade with the North Sea and Baltic countries. It was founded by the Breton earl of Richmond in the late eleventh century and, besides its port and marketing functions, developed one of the great international fairs of Europe, extending over eight days at the feast of St Botolph (17 June). It was already in existence by 1125, when it was held in the churchyard. In 1190, the profits of the town were £3 16s. 0d. but the fair already yielded

[24] Beresford, *New Towns*, pp. 486–8; R. Holt, *The Early History of the Town of Birmingham 1166 to 1600* (Dugdale Society Occasional Papers, 30, 1985), pp. 3–8.

[25] C. C. Dyer, 'The hidden trade of the Middle Ages: evidence from the West Midlands of England', *J of Historical Geography*, 18 (1992), 141–57; T. R. Slater, 'The urban hierarchy in medieval Staffordshire', *J of Historical Geography*, 11 (1985), 115–37; R. H. Hilton, 'Lords, burgesses and hucksters', *P&P*, 97 (1982), 3–15; R. H. Hilton, 'Small town society before the Black Death, *P&P*, 105 (1984), 53–78.

£50. 7s. 7d. The geographical extent of the port's market function can be judged from the fact that most of the monastic institutions of eastern and northern England maintained a house for trading purposes in the town, whilst its exports were probably second only to London by the early thirteenth century.[26]

Though there were fewer new towns with borough status, more places became urban with the help of only a market charter and older established places were extended, often in carefully devised, planned developments. William Peverel's French borough of Nottingham doubled the area of the town soon after the Conquest and, though the two parts of the city had separate legal systems for many years, they were united through the huge triangular market place that linked the two communities. A similar extension of the borough happened at Northampton after the Conquest, whilst at Peterborough, the abbot laid out an extensive market place and new burgages for traders and craftspeople in the early twelfth century.[27] Only seven places in Leicestershire had burgage tenure and Nottinghamshire had only three chartered boroughs. Some quite significant market towns such as Market Harborough, Mansfield and Southwell prospered with only market and fair charters. T. Unwin's analysis of the markets of Nottinghamshire suggests that only Southwell and East Retford competed with the Friday and Saturday markets in Nottingham in the weekly cycle, whilst in Derbyshire and Nottinghamshire, two-thirds of the market charters date from the period 1200–75.[28]

Some of the East Midland fairs were of national importance; Lenton Priory's great twelve-day Martinmas fair at Nottingham brought in traders from all over England in the thirteenth century, whilst fairs at Northampton, Stamford and especially Boston attracted merchants from overseas. Most towns had three-day fairs on the feast day of their patron saint, and some of these gained a reputation for particular commodities: the bishop of Lincoln's fair at Horncastle, for example, was mainly a horse fair.[29]

(iii) THE URBAN HIERARCHY IN *C.* 1330

The lay subsidies of the early fourteenth century show how these new-founded and extended towns fitted into the urban hierarchy of the region. The first point to make is that when towns are ranked by their taxable wealth almost a quarter of the 100 most wealthy places in England are in the Midland region. Bristol was easily the second wealthiest city of the kingdom in the 1330s, and Boston, Lincoln and Coventry were among the leading ten. Of the shire towns, Lincoln

[26] Beresford, *New Towns*, pp. 463–5; Hill, *Lincoln*, pp. 314–22.

[27] M. W. Barley and I. F. Straw, 'Nottingham', in *BAHT*, I.

[28] M. W. Beresford and H. P. R. Finberg, *English Medieval Boroughs* (Newton Abbot, 1973), pp. 135, 146–7; T. Unwin, 'Rural marketing in medieval Nottinghamshire', *J of Historical Geography*, 7 (1981) 231–51.

[29] W. Addison, *English Fairs and Markets* (London, 1953), p. 165.

is followed by Shrewsbury, Hereford and Gloucester, all of which were ranked in the top twenty towns (see Appendix 4). Despite the wealth of Lincolnshire and the pre-eminence of the North Sea trade networks, Boston was open to fiercer competition from other east coast ports, such as Hull, Lynn and Yarmouth, so that its prosperity was subject to greater fluctuation when compared with Bristol. Bristol dominated the West Midlands' local trading networks via the Severn and its tributaries and it had an important regional coasting trade in the South-West and South Wales. In the mid-twelfth century it had been the embarkation point for the Anglo-Norman invasion of Ireland and its links with Dublin, Drogheda and Waterford, already strong, were enhanced further. Its principal commodity was wine from Gascony. Up to 3,000 tuns per year was imported in the thirteenth century (some ¾ million gallons). Other products included salt (from Gascony) and woad from Picardy for the West Midland and West Country cloth industry. The diversion of the River Frome, in 1240, to create new quays is a reflection of developing maritime trade and merchant wealth, whilst the community was also building the Port Wall to enclose the Redcliffe suburb at the same time.[30]

Lincoln's wealth and position in the hierarchy was a reflection of its trade, manufacturing, marketing and secular and ecclesiastical administrative position in the wealthiest part of England. The royal castle and the new cathedral, episcopal palace and houses of the canons, dominated the upper town, known as the Bail. Its trading links were enhanced when the Foss Dyke was reopened in 1121 to link the River Witham to the Trent, but most of Lincoln's exports, especially wool and cloth, went through Boston. The significance of the city is well reflected by its Jewish community, probably the largest after London's, until their expulsion from England in 1290. They included Aaron the Rich, one of the wealthiest merchants and financiers in the kingdom, who, from 1166 until he died in 1185 lived in the Bail to safeguard his wealth; another, Joseus of York, may have built one of the surviving Romanesque stone houses with undercroft and shops on Steep Hill. The enormous wealth of the fen-edge parishes of the Holland division of Lincolnshire meant that, by the fourteenth century, Lincoln's craft manufacturing was extremely diversified and this is reflected in the fourteen different craft guilds in the city.[31] Though the Jews of Lincoln were one of the larger urban communities, Jews were found in all the shire towns, including the smaller places such as Warwick, as well as other middle-ranked towns such as Bridgnorth.[32]

Coventry was at the crossroads of England; midway between Bristol and Lincoln and London and Chester. Its early development was centred on a market

[30] E. Carus-Wilson, 'Bristol', in *BAHT*, II.

[31] Hill, *Lincoln*, pp. 217–38; J. V. Beckett, *A Regional History of England: The East Midlands from AD 1000* (London, 1988), pp. 53–66.

[32] J. Jacobs, ed., *The Jews of Angevin England* (London, 1898).

place established by the Benedictine monastery founded by Earl Leofric and Godgifu in 1043; the addition of the see, transferred from Chester, and the earl of Chester's castle and estate to the south of the abbey, was accompanied by the development of a wool trade and then a textile industry. However, though the wool merchants and mercers were the most important groups in the city, in the thirteenth century Coventry was also a centre of luxury metal trades such as jewellery, of locksmiths and of leathermaking and soap manufacture. It was also a town of divided lordship with the major merchants living in Earl Street, in the earl of Chester's half of the town, whilst the market place was within the prior's part of the city. It was only in 1355 that it became united under a mayor and council.[33] Coventry was the largest town of the central Midlands and its size meant that the trading capabilities of the nearby shire centres, especially Warwick, but also Leicester (ranked thirty-eighth in 1334) and Northampton (ranked twenty-ninth), were partially eclipsed. The first two were dominated by the castles and estates of their respective earldoms, and locally marketed textiles, tanning and shoemaking were important in all three. Derby's prosperity (it ranked thirty-third in 1334) was at least partly based on the wealth generated by the trade in lead from the Peak District, exports going down the Trent to Hull. Staffordshire's larger towns were in competition with one another for the trade of a generally poor county. Thus the shire town, which ranked ninety-eighth in 1334, was only marginally more wealthy than Lichfield, with its cathedral community, and Newcastle-under-Lyme, with its castle beside the road to the north-west.[34]

In contrast, the Welsh border shire towns, Shrewsbury, Hereford and Gloucester, dominated their counties and were in thirteenth, sixteenth and eighteenth places in the 1334 hierarchy. Shrewsbury and Gloucester had major Benedictine abbeys (three in the latter case), a river port function and, together with Hereford, had extended their commercial links to encompass the sale of Welsh wool production and the marketing of cattle on the hoof destined for the meat markets and tanneries of the Midlands and South-East. Worcester, which ranked thirty-sixth, had river port functions, too; it was dominated by ecclesiastical institutions which included three friaries, two nunneries and three hospitals as well as the Benedictine cathedral priory. Ironmaking, using the resources of the Forest of Dean, was especially significant in the economy of Gloucester where there was an important armaments industry near the castle making shields, spurs, arrows and horseshoes; there were also needle makers, bell-founders and goldsmiths, and the Severn fisheries, especially for lampreys.[35] Below these shire towns in the urban hierarchy were Cirencester, the market centre for the Cotswold wool trade,

[33] J. C. Lancaster, 'Coventry', in *BAHT*, II; P. R. Coss, ed., *The Early Records of Medieval Coventry* (British Academy, Records of Social and Economic History, new series, 11, 1986), pp. xv–xlii.

[34] Beckett, *East Midlands*, pp. 53–66; Slater, 'Urban hierarchy'.

[35] L. E. W. O. Fulbrook-Leggatt, *Anglo-Saxon and Medieval Gloucester* (Gloucester, 1952), pp. 42–52; *VCH*, Gloucestershire, IV, pp. 22–8.

Bridgnorth and Ludlow, which were secondary wool market centres for the Welsh borders, and Tewkesbury with its great Benedictine abbey at the confluence of the Severn and Avon.

The surviving early fourteenth-century detailed subsidy assessments for Shrewsbury enable us to say a little more about the economy of that town. Dominating the community, and taking the position as bailiffs in local government, were the wealthy merchants; men such as John de Lodelowe, Richard Stury and John Gamel whose father had been the master mason responsible for building the town's walls. They traded in the enormous quantities of wool that was brought into the town from Wales and the borders; in 1313, twenty-five merchants between them exported 1,090 sacks (some 400,000 fleeces); wine, cloth, silks, furs and other luxuries were being imported. Profits were invested in land in Shrewsbury itself, in the surrounding rural area and in other towns, while these merchants were also the bankers of the local community. Gamel was trying to recover debts of more than £140 from fourteen individuals in 1314, for example. Below them in the hierarchy were lesser merchants, widows of merchants, mercers, butchers, brewers, tanners, corvisors and a few professionals drawn from the ranks of the clergy.[36]

In the East Midlands, Newark (ranked twenty-fourth in 1334) and Nottingham (twenty-fifth) competed for the trade of the mid-Trent valley. The latter was the more significant town in the twelfth century as its bridge over the Trent carried the road from London to York. However, the construction of the bridge at Newark deflected much of the traffic eastwards leading to the growth of both Newark itself, and Grantham (which ranked immediately below Leicester in 1334) and East Retford. Stamford (ranked twenty-seventh) and Peterborough (forty-second) had the advantage of links to the Wash down the Welland and Nene respectively and Stamford was on the Great North Road. It was an important wool market in the twelfth century and had a developing cloth industry in the thirteenth. Grimsby was one of many smaller port boroughs on the east coast; it had strong links with Norway from where pine boards, hawks and falcons, and squirrel furs (some 12,000 for the king in 1234) were amongst the imports.[37] The sheep pastures of Lincolnshire generated enormous wealth, reflected not only in the rapid growth of market and port towns such as Louth, Sleaford and Wainfleet, but also the fen-edge villages which were assessed only a little below Boston and Lincoln in 1334.

(iv) MIDLAND TOWNS AT THE END OF THE FOURTEENTH CENTURY

The poll taxes of 1377–81 provide us with our best opportunity in the late middle ages to assess the size of the Midland towns, and to examine their range

[36] D. Cromarty and R. Cromarty, eds., *The Wealth of Shrewsbury in the Early Fourteenth Century* (Shrewsbury, 1993), pp. 53–61. [37] Rigby, *Grimsby*, pp. 1–8.

of occupations.[38] These incomplete documents can be supplemented with records of those paying aulnage on the sales of cloth, and litigation over debts in borough court rolls. The poll taxes come after the Black Death and subsequent epidemics, but in most cases the size of towns relative to each other had not changed greatly. However, in the period after the epidemics the uneven health of the economies of towns was reflected in their varied rate of recovery. Gloucester and Brackley, for example, probably never returned in the later middle ages to their population level of *c.* 1300, but Coventry actually grew in size in the fourteenth century despite the plagues. The robustness of the 'new towns' was tested and, by the time of the poll taxes, places like Newborough (Staffs.) and New Eagle (Lincs.) had clearly failed to survive as urban communities.[39] We are therefore observing, in 1377–81, towns which had stood up with varying degrees of success to the crises of the fourteenth century.

Continuing with the subdivisions of the region based on river valleys, we begin with the Severn/Avon basin. The population figures are based on the assumption that about a half of the population contributed to the first poll tax of 1377, with a smaller proportion in the later poll taxes, down to about a third in 1381. We know that there was much evasion in the 1379 and 1381 assessments, but we remain uncertain about the numbers of people who were exempted or who evaded in 1377, so round figures will be used. Bristol dominated the Severn valley with a population in excess of 12,000, but near to the upper reaches of the Avon stood Coventry which was climbing towards 10,000 people. Gloucester was the third largest town with about 4,500, closely followed by Shrewsbury, Hereford and Worcester, in descending order, each of which contained between 4,000 and 3,000 inhabitants. Ludlow rose just above the 2,000 level, and Bridgnorth and Cirencester both probably fell just below it. Warwick, overshadowed by Coventry, belongs with about eighty small towns in the Severn/Avon basin providing a living for populations mostly below 1,500. Some of these market towns could be very small, with even well-established places in Herefordshire, like Bromyard and Ross-on-Wye, barely able to muster 500 people, and Whitchurch (Salop.) apparently contained fewer than 200. The small towns were especially numerous in the West Midlands, with an average of sixteen per county.

In the Trent/Soar basin Lincoln remained the largest centre of population with approximately 7,000, and Boston's *c.* 5,700 put it into a position not far

[38] Subsequent references to the poll tax are based on C. C. Fenwick, 'The English poll taxes of 1377, 1379 and 1381' (PhD thesis, University of London, 1983); C. C. Fenwick, ed., *The Poll Taxes of 1377, 1379 and 1381: Part 1* (British Academy Records of Social and Economic History, new series, 27, 1998); L. M. Midgley, 'Some Staffordshire poll tax returns', *Staffordshire Record Society*, 4th series, 6 (1970), 1–25; W. Boyd, ed., 'The poll tax of AD 1379–81', *Staffordshire Historical Collections*, 17 (1896), 155–205; C. M. Barron, 'The fourteenth-century poll tax returns for Worcester', *Midland History*, 14 (1989), 1–29.

[39] D. M. Palliser, *The Staffordshire Landscape* (London, 1976), pp. 149, 151; Beresford, *New Towns*, pp. 465–6, 487–8.

behind. Among the inland towns Leicester contained about 4,400 people, and (in descending order) Nottingham, Newark, Derby and Lichfield had populations varying between 3,000 and 2,000. The rise of Lichfield eclipsed the county town of Stafford (with rather less than a thousand inhabitants), which was also inferior in population to Newcastle-under-Lyme (with just over a thousand). Three Lincolnshire centres, the ports of Grimsby and Wainfleet, and the inland wolds town of Louth, all had populations in the region of 1,400. The number of smaller towns is less than in the Severn/Avon basin. Staffordshire has as many as eighteen, and in Lincolnshire there were twenty-two, scattered over its very large area. The counties of Derby, Nottingham and Leicester could only each muster seven to ten small towns.

Finally, the Ouse/Nene/Welland valleys had a low concentration of small towns, comparable with the counties immediately to the north, with only twenty-five in the three counties of Bedford, Huntingdon and Northampton. Admittedly, some of these were quite large – Huntingdon had almost 2,000 people, with Peterborough not far behind with *c.* 1,700, while Bedford and Dunstable probably contained more than 1,000, and Towcester and Daventry just below 1,000. Stamford was in decline, but the tax collectors could still find 1,218 taxpayers, implying, if we take into account a section of the town that was omitted, a population in excess of 2,600. This means that it had fallen behind Northampton with almost 3,000 people.

The patterns of urban development in the region were clearly the product of complex changes. To some extent the three subdivisions of the region coincided with the hinterlands of the towns and the flow of trade. A good deal of the surplus agricultural produce of the Severn/Avon region went down by river and road to Bristol. Towards the end of the fourteeenth century we know of the activities of dealers in the districts around Tewkesbury and Cheltenham collecting the grain of that rich arable district, which was carried by boat to Bristol.[40] Wool came from Herefordshire, Shropshire and the Cotswolds, though by the end of the fourteenth century an increasing quantity of cloth went to Bristol from the industrialising districts in the Cotswolds. Timber, wood, iron and coal were supplied from the Forest of Dean. In return boats from Bristol carried fish and imported goods, especially wine, up the Severn to Gloucester, Tewkesbury, Worcester, Bridgnorth and Shrewsbury for distribution overland.[41] In a similar fashion, Boston had in the early fourteenth century exported a great deal of East Midland wool, Lincolnshire salt and also Derbyshire lead, and it imported wine

[40] R. H. Hilton, *The English Peasantry in the Later Middle Ages* (Oxford, 1975), p. 89.

[41] E. M. Carus-Wilson, *Medieval Merchant Venturers* (London, 1954), pp. 4–13; S. A. C. Penn, 'Social and economic aspects of fourteenth century Bristol' (PhD thesis, University of Birmingham, 1989), pp. 8–60; C. Dyer, 'Trade, towns and the Church: ecclesiastical consumers and the urban economy of the West Midlands, 1290–1540', in Slater and Rosser, eds., *The Church in the Medieval Town*, pp. 61, 63, 67–8.

for distribution over the region. With the decline in the wool trade Boston could supply the English clothmakers with dyestuffs, and export finished cloth, as well as continuing to import fish, and Hanseatic goods like timber and pitch.[42] But these activities depended on extending trade well beyond the watersheds that divided the river valleys, because Boston provided an outlet for Coventry's cloth. Its fair had, in the early fourteenth century, been attracting customers well inside Bristol's hinterland: the monks of Worcester priory were buying cloth, spices and fish there.[43]

The rise of Coventry helped to unify the commerce of the region, as its location at the meeting point of the watersheds meant that it could trade to the south into the Avon and Severn valleys, and indeed had important dealings with Bristol; it also looked west beyond Birmingham toward southern Shropshire and even to Chester; to the north and east into Leicestershire; and to the south-east into Northamptonshire and the Nene valley. As well as the evidence of the commercial links with the region reflected in debts, the membership of the Trinity Guild shows that Coventry had a cultural and social influence extending into Lincolnshire as well as over the West Midland counties.[44] In short, it had become the regional capital, uniting the various urban networks. But we must not forget that the apex of the urban hierarchy of the region was occupied, not by Coventry, Lincoln or Bristol, but to an ever greater degree by London, as the merchants of the capital sold goods, and took over more of the export trade. While we cannot divide the region in the late fourteenth century into self-contained parcels, we are aware of important differences between the West and East Midlands. The western counties had many more towns, so they record a high density of boroughs and small towns, and they also show a higher proportion of urban dwellers, with figures of 20 per cent and more, compared with 15 per cent or even lower percentages in the East Midlands.

How were the experiences and opportunities of the people who lived in towns of varied rank affected by their position in the hierarchy? An important distinction between the larger and smaller towns was created by the presence of merchants. Wealthy traders can be detected in numbers in all of the towns with 2,000 or more inhabitants, such as the draper, dyer and butcher who paid the highest contributions to the 1381 poll tax for Worcester. Of the 134 Bristol traders who paid the aulnage tax on cloth sales in 1395–6, 39 appear in other documents as merchants, and they formed the majority who are recorded as dealing in more than thirty cloths in the year. A prominent position in the commercial life of a town gave the merchants political power as well – 100 of the 209 common councillors recorded in 1340–1410 can be identified as merchants.[45]

[42] S. H. Rigby, ' "Sore decay" and "fair dwellings": Boston and urban decline in the later middle ages', *Midland History*, 10 (1985), 48–51. [43] Dyer, 'Trade, towns and the Church', p. 61.

[44] C. Phythian-Adams, *Desolation of a City* (Cambridge, 1979), pp. 19–30.

[45] Penn, 'Fourteenth century Bristol', pp. 102–4, 187–91.

Merchants were not entirely absent from the smaller towns, but they tend to stand out from the artisans and small-scale traders who made up the bulk of the population. At Stow-on-the-Wold most of the 167 taxpayers in 1381 paid 6d. or 12d., but Thomas Kys and John Hickus, both described as merchants, contributed 6s. each. The wealth of the towns at the top of the hierarchy attracted a large number of poor. The tax assessors at Shrewsbury complained that a hundred men and women were avoiding them by 'wandering and fleeing from street to street and place to place'.[46]

The larger towns were characterised by a deep social structure, from the very rich to the miserably poor, and also a greater breadth of occupations. The poll tax for Worcester mentions forty-six different crafts and trades, while at the larger town of Leicester sixty occupations are mentioned among those being admitted to the guild merchant in the fourteenth century.[47] Smaller towns usually provided a living for a narrower range of specialisms: twenty-five non-agricultural occupations appear in the 1381 tax list for Melton Mowbray. These activities were related to the size of the town's hinterlands, and the types of customer they attracted. Within their main marketing radius of 7 miles (11 km), small towns provided venues for the sale of agricultural produce, and supplied the mundane needs of a clientele without pretension – peasants buying boots, horseshoes and foodstuffs. Large towns also catered for their local customers: lists of traders at Gloucester in 1380–1423 show that 80 to 90 per cent of them came from within 16 miles (24 km).[48] But larger towns also served a wider hinterland with more specialised and expensive goods. Among Leicester's recorded occupations were two jewellers and an 'ymager', and a number of bell-founders, whose products can still be found in church towers throughout the region and beyond.[49] The relationship between towns and their customers can be explored by examining the purchases of consumers, like the gentry Bozoun family of Woodford in Northamptonshire, who in 1348 bought their meat regularly from the small market town of Higham Ferrers, while the monks of Pershore bought relatively little in the small town at their gates, but obtained their wine, fish and other goods at Worcester, Gloucester, Coventry and Oxford.[50] The landed aristocracy made contact with the larger towns by living in their town houses, as did the Catesbys at Coventry in the 1390s, by joining fraternities, and by associating themselves with religious houses, like the Greyfriars at Stamford where the earl

[46] H. Summerson, *Medieval Carlisle* (Kendal, 1993), p. 305.

[47] M. Bateson, ed., *Records of the Borough of Leicester* ([London], 1899–1905). The calculation has been made by Dr Jane Laughton, for whose help we are very grateful.

[48] C. Dyer, 'Market towns and the countryside in late medieval England', *Canadian J of History*, 31 (1996), 17–35; *VCH*, Gloucestershire, IV, pp. 46–7, 50.

[49] Bateson, ed., *Borough of Leicester*. Based on information kindly provided by Dr Jane Laughton and Alex Bayliss.

[50] C. Dyer, 'The consumer and the market in the later middle ages', *Ec.HR*, 2nd series, 42 (1989), 316; Dyer, 'Trade, towns and the Church', pp. 60–3.

of Kent was buried in 1361.[51] Small towns were close to the peasantry, not just through trade, but also because, in the East Midlands, it was not uncommon at towns like Daventry and Oundle for peasants and those pursuing non-agricultural occupations to live in close proximity on the same streets. In the western Midlands the new boroughs were more often physically and socially separated from the older peasant communities near which they had been founded.

The presence of rural industry gave some market towns opportunities to specialise, and so we find metal industries developing in south Staffordshire, like knife-making at Rugeley, which used the raw materials and extractive industries in the neighbourhood.[52] In general, though, the flow of trade within the region followed the conventional pattern in which the larger towns supplied more specialised goods to the small-town retailers – debt pleas show Simon Spycer of Northampton being owed money by a man from Daventry, very likely for spices, and a draper from Northampton was apparently supplying a draper in Oundle.[53] More basic commodities, and especially foodstuffs, flowed up from small town markets to the larger towns, such as cattle, which were sold in small towns such as Birmingham, and were eventually bought by Coventry and London butchers. Another important pattern in the trade of the region connected *pays* with complementary needs and resources. In 1401, for example, grain from the arable fields of south Warwickshire was traded northwards from Stratford to towns in the wooded and pastoral districts – Birmingham, Coleshill, Dudley and Walsall. Wood, timber, cattle, dairy products and iron and leather goods flowed in the opposite direction.[54]

The Midland towns depended on road transport for their trading network. The Severn, the Trent, the lower reaches of the Ouse and Nene and the rivers of south Lincolnshire all carried valuable traffic, but the central part of the region could be served only by carts and pack horses. The larger towns enjoyed the advantages of a navigable waterway, but Leicester and Northampton had developed on rivers that were not continuously navigable, and Lichfield, and above all Coventry, prospered in this period entirely on the basis of the road system. A few smaller towns were river ports, and a remarkable commercial centre grew at Yaxley in Huntingdonshire, on the Nene, where fish from the east coast were distributed via the road network.[55] The infrastructure of road transport had

[51] N. W. Alcock, 'The Catesbys in Coventry: a medieval estate and its archives', *Midland History*, 15 (1990), 1–36; J. S. Hartley and A. Rogers, *The Religious Foundations of Medieval Stamford* (Nottingham, 1974), pp. 42, 62, 64. [52] Dyer, 'Hidden trade', p. 151.

[53] We are grateful to Dr J. Galloway of the Centre for Metropolitan History, University of London, for this information from his database of debts in common pleas records, 1403 and 1424.

[54] Holt, *Birmingham*, p. 10; C. Dyer, 'Medieval Stratford: a successful small town', in Bearman, ed., *Stratford-upon-Avon*, pp. 54, 57, 184.

[55] J. Masschaele, *Peasants, Merchants, and Markets* (Basingstoke, 1997), pp. 214–17. On a later period, J. Greatrex, ed., *Account Rolls of the Obedientiaries of Peterborough* (Northamptonshire Record Society, 23, 1984), pp. 120, 142.

reached a high level of development by the fourteenth century, with bridges and causeways carrying the main roads (and many minor ones) over rivers. Inns gave shelter and fodder for travellers in every town, and along important roads, or where roads made contact with navigable rivers, as at Wansford on the Nene. Inns often played an important role in the economy of small towns.[56]

The degree of self-government of the Midland towns was to some extent correlated with their size, in that the old shire towns tended to be royal boroughs. However, Boston was a seigneurial borough, as was Coventry until 1345. The leading men of towns under the rule of lords often found means for consultation and decision making through a religious fraternity, which was able to provide unofficial means of government. The Holy Cross fraternity at Chesterfield did not hide its role as in 1389 its brethren were sworn to support 'all their liberties' within and outside the town.[57] The number and size of institutions, such as friaries and hospitals, and the richness of the cultural life, notably the drama performed at Corpus Christi, help to distinguish the larger places from the small towns.

(v) DECLINE AND GROWTH 1400–1540

In the fifteenth and early sixteenth centuries, Midland towns, in common with those of other regions, show signs of falling population, physical contraction and economic difficulties. However, some towns maintained their size and wealth, and a few expanded. Here these tendencies will be analysed using the subdivisions of the region based on the river systems, and taking into account the varied fortunes of towns at different levels of the urban hierarchy. The subsidy assessments of 1524 and 1525, though inferior in value to the poll taxes as evidence for population, indicate the relative size of towns towards the end of this period.

The most consistent evidence for decline in this period comes from the larger towns of the Trent/Soar and Ouse/Nene/Welland river systems. Boston lost about half its population between 1377 and 1524/5, from about 5,700 to 2,000–2,500, and in the national ranking order it fell from tenth to fifty-first. As a port its prosperity was directly related to the flow of goods, and these declined sharply: in the 1390s about 3,000 sacks of wool and 3,000 cloths passed annually through the town, but by the 1540s the comparable figures were 200 sacks and 100 cloths. Imports fared no better, as the wine trade slumped, and the Hanseatic merchants transferred their activities to London. The harbour was silting up, and St Botolph's fair, already declining in 1400, was reduced to a very modest occasion. Leasehold rents totalling £98 were gathered in the town by

[56] E.g. in 1406–7 four ostlers are recorded in Market Harborough and three at Melton Mowbray: PRO E101/258/2, mm. 6d, 7 (we owe this reference to Dr Jane Laughton).

[57] P. Riden and J. Blair, eds., *History of Chesterfield*, vol. v (Chesterfield, 1980), p. 127.

its lord in 1434–5, but these had dwindled to £46 by 1493–4.[58] Lincoln slipped from sixth to twelfth in national size rankings between 1377 and 1524/5, and probably lost about a third of its population during those years. In 1428 seventeen of its parishes were reported as having fewer than ten households and, by 1515, the constables were being told by city authorities worried by the number of ruined buildings not to allow further demolition of houses.[59] Stamford's pre-1350 decline continued in the fifteenth century. It may have reached 5,000 people in *c.* 1300, but this had become about 3,000 in 1377 and nearer to 2,000 in the early sixteenth century. Two of its churches disappeared in the fifteenth century.[60] At the end of the thirteenth century it had been considerably larger than Leicester and Northampton, but sank below them by the end of our period. Leicester probably lost about half its population between the early fourteenth and early sixteenth century, and was ranked thirty-third in 1524/5, having been eighteenth in 1377. Nottingham declined from twenty-eighth to fiftieth, and the population of Grimsby fell from *c.* 1,500 to *c.* 900 in the century and a half after 1377. Grimsby, like Lincoln, was successful in obtaining reductions to the annual fee-farm that was paid to the crown. Northampton appears to be an exception to this story of gloom. Although it was pardoned part of its fee-farm payments in 1462, 1478 and 1484, and was said at the last date to be 'desolate', it kept its ranking order (twenty-eighth and twenty-seventh) and maintained its population (about 3,000) between 1377 and 1524/5, though it had been larger in the thirteenth century. Its fair, once a very important event for the whole region, dwindled until it had only local significance.[61] Derby and Lichfield retained their positions in the ranking order, and the latter increased modestly in size.

The small towns in the hinterlands of these declining larger centres had mixed fortunes, most being reduced in size but in varying degrees. There were some shifts in the hierarchy, as when, for example, in the early sixteenth century, Loughborough outstripped Melton Mowbray to become the second largest town in Leicestershire. Melton, with its very busy market and favoured position on the transport network, had prospered earlier, but between the first and last decades of the fifteenth century its market tolls fell from an annual £8 to £3, and in the middle of the century its subsidy assessment was reduced (abated) by

[58] The 1524/5 figures derive from Appendix 6 to this volume, and J. Sheail, *The Regional Distribution of Wealth in England as Indicated in the 1524/5 Lay Subsidy Rolls* (List and Index Society, Special Series, 28 and 29, 1998). For Boston see Rigby, 'Boston and urban decline', 47–61.

[59] Hill, *Medieval Lincoln*, pp. 287–8.

[60] D. Roffe, ed., *Stamford in the Thirteenth Century* (Stamford, 1994), pp. 4, 40; the 1377 figure includes an estimate for Stamford Baron; Hartley and Rogers, *Religious Foundations*, pp. 29, 31. We owe this information, and most of that cited in the following eight footnotes, to Dr Jane Laughton, for whose help we are very grateful.

[61] Rigby, *Grimsby*, pp. 115–29; C. A. Markham, ed., *The Records of the Borough of Northampton* (Northampton, 1898), vol. 1, pp. 91–101.

the unusually high proportion of 38 per cent.[62] Brackley had also done well in the thirteenth century, but in the fifteenth it qualified for a large subsidy abatement of 41 per cent. Leland, visiting in 1539, commented that it was a 'poor town', and its population probably fell from about 1,000 in 1301 to 600 in 1524/5. Like Melton, Brackley lost its high position in its county's hierarchy in 1334, and in terms of population was outstripped in 1524/5 by Oundle and Towcester.[63] Louth had ranked fifty-eighth among English towns in 1377, but it does not appear in the first hundred in 1524/5.

No clear patterns emerge from an overview of the fortunes of the smaller towns of the East Midland river basins. There is ample anecdotal evidence of symptoms of decay which makes them seem to resemble Boston, Lincoln and Stamford. Their populations fell, apparently by more than a half at Hallaton, from about 500 to 200 in 1377–1524/5; houses were ruinous and plots fell vacant, for example at Daventry; shops lacked tenants and rents fell, at Towcester; subsidy assessments were abated in the mid-fifteenth century in most towns, normally by about 10 per cent. After a devastating fire in 1409, Higham Ferrers' market revived in a few years, but the fee-farm was at first remitted, and then reduced permanently, suggesting that the town suffered some economic weakness that prevented full recovery.[64] As we have seen, three of the larger market towns lost ground, and it might be tempting to contrast them with two much smaller places, Lutterworth, which judging from a rental of 1509 had much the same population then as in 1377 (about 500), and Oundle, where the numbers of shops were increasing (though there were fewer stalls) towards the end of the fifteenth century, and the rents of the mills rose between 1471 and 1512.[65]

We can suggest some general factors which might explain the tendency of the towns of the Trent and Nene river systems to decline at this time. The decline in wool exports damaged Boston, and may have had repercussions in the inland wool towns like Melton and Brackley. There was little compensatory growth in a cloth industry, and towns once famous for their clothmaking, such as Lincoln and Stamford, had, by 1400, ceased to have a major role in the industry. In this region there is little evidence for a migration of industry into the countryside.

[62] D. Postles, 'An English small town in the later middle ages: Loughborough', *UH*, 20 (1993), 7–29; PRO E179/133/70 m.1; Leicestershire RO, 71'22 (PD 3/12); Melbourne Hall MSS, x94 Lothian, Box 34/2–8.

[63] PRO E179/155/105; E179/155/159 m. 6; L. Toulmin Smith, ed., *The Itinerary of John Leland in or about the Years 1535–1543* (London, 1907–10), vol. II, pp. 35–7.

[64] A. E. Brown, *Early Daventry: An Essay in Early Landscape Planning* (Leicester, 1991), pp. 22–3, 27–8; I. Jack, ed., *The Grey of Ruthin Valor* (Bedfordshire Record Society, 46, 1965), pp. 66–8; R. M. Serjeantson, *The Court Rolls of Higham Ferrers* (n.p., but *c.* 1918), part 2, pp. 13–14, 17–18, 49–50, part 3, p. 33.

[65] J. Goodacre, *The Transformation of a Peasant Economy: Townspeople and Villagers in the Lutterworth Area 1500–1700* (Aldershot, 1994), pp. 46, 59–60; Northamptonshire RO, Westmorland MSS, Box 5, v, 4/4 and 4/5.

But any study of the larger towns reveals a good deal of craft production continuing and sometimes growing. Northampton, perhaps the most successful of the larger towns in the early sixteenth century, provided work for more than seventy different occupations, in which the leather trades figured prominently, but also dyers and eleven furbours working in the arms industry. In view of the failure of rural industries to grow in opposition to those in the towns, the argument cannot be invoked that the 'craft guilds' discouraged enterprise by their restrictive attitudes. At Northampton, as in other towns, the crafts were regulated by the town authorities, with the aim of controlling sectional interests and maintaining order, like the weavers who in 1432 were said to be involved in 'unfitting contests and debates' with their journeymen.[66] The small towns (which usually lacked 'craft guilds') housed small-scale industries, and we find minor specialisms like flax trading and linen weaving at Higham Ferrers and Market Harborough, and a wealthy glover lived at Kettering in the late fifteenth century.[67]

The decline of the great fairs and the rise of London took trade in luxuries away from the merchants of the large towns, and diverted commerce from ports like Boston. Londoners even extended their influence into small towns like Market Harborough.[68] Some towns in the East Midland wolds, such as Louth and Melton Mowbray, often contained in their hinterlands a number of villages which were deserted in the fifteenth century, and these local concentrations of depopulation must have had an adverse effect on urban economies.[69]

Finally, the overall tendency of towns to decline should not imply that de-urbanisation was in progress in the East Midlands. It is true that some places by the early sixteenth century – Market Bosworth and Mountsorrel in Leicestershire, for example – seem to have lost any claim to urban status, but earlier evidence of their modest size and lack of varied occupations makes us doubt whether they could at any stage of their history be regarded as towns. Most village markets, founded before 1348, had ceased to exist by the sixteenth century, but the market towns continued to perform their functions as local centres of trade and social contact.[70] The small towns served the needs of their local rural hinter-

[66] A. Dyer,'Northampton in 1524', *Northamptonshire Past and Present*, 6 (1979), 73–80; Markham, ed., *Borough of Northampton*, I, pp. 268–74.

[67] Northamptonshire RO, Higham Ferrers court rolls, Box x687, x688; Leicestershire RO, 1st Register Book, ff. 329v–330; Northamptonshire RO, Early Wills Book, f. 97r.

[68] J. E. Stocks and W. B. Bragg, *Market Harborough Parish Records to AD 1530* (London, 1890), pp. 169–70, 185; *Early Chancery Proceedings* (PRO, 1901–36), III, bundle 181, no. 43, V, bundle 478, no. 47.

[69] C. Lewis, P. Mitchell-Fox and C. Dyer, *Village, Hamlet and Field: Changing Medieval Settlements in Central England* (Manchester, 1997), pp. 152–3.

[70] The judgements about the urban status of these settlements is based on work for the ESRC funded project on 'Urban hierarchy and functions in the East Midlands' (no. R0002359022; award holders P. Clark, C. Dyer and A. Grant). On the survival of markets, A. Everitt, 'The marketing of agricultural produce', in J. Thirsk, ed., *Ag.HEW*, vol. IV (Cambridge, 1967), pp. 473–5.

land, like the villages within a 6-mile (13 km) radius whose inhabitants visited the market at Melton most frequently. They also acted as 'thoroughfare' towns, providing services for travellers. The larger towns also continued to cater for wealthier customers and more specialised demands, like the goldsmiths, bookseller and clockmaker who made their livings at Lichfield.[71] The cultural life of the communities, and their sense of civic pride, does not seem to have been lost in this period. Fraternities flourished, even as many as six in minor market towns, such as Wellingborough. Colleges, almshouses, hospitals, guildhalls and schools added high-quality buildings to the townscapes and contributed both to civic dignity and the quality of life. There was evidently some cash to spare for prestigious projects even in a 'desolated' town, and the survival of a few houses until the present, and comments like Leland's that Boston could boast 'fair' buildings shows that individuals could still make a good living. The subsidy assessments of 1524/5 reveal super-rich magnates like William Wiggeston at Leicester, who paid more than a quarter of the town's taxes.[72] The towns continued to attract migrants from the country, but in contrast with earlier periods, the loss by mortality and emigration exceeded the flow of newcomers. Many agricultural communities were shrinking in size, so that in most districts the towns accounted for a similar proportion of the population as in the thirteenth and fourteenth centuries. All of this should lead us to regard towns in 1400–1540 as experiencing in most cases a setback rather than a catastrophe.

Coventry deserves separate treatment as it stood between the river systems of the Midlands, so does not belong exclusively to any of our sub-regions. It attained its peak as a regional capital in the 1430s, when there were about 10,000 inhabitants. Vacant building plots were noted in 1442, and they seem to have grown in number in the 1470s and 1480s, but the main decline in population came in the early sixteenth century, down to about 6,000. Coventry shows many of the symptoms of 'urban decline', with the shrinkage of its broadcloth industry, which was not fully replaced by the rise of cap making in the late fifteenth century. The crafts complained about the costs of their participation in the Corpus Christi plays, and members of the elite were refusing to take up civic offices, even the mayoralty. Among a number of signs of social tension Lawrence Saunders led a protest in 1480 against the restricted access by ordinary citizens to the common pastures. After an episode of high food prices in 1520, 565 houses were found to be empty, and the city was experiencing a demographic crisis, not just in falling numbers overall, but in a shortage of children which foretold a bleak future. Despite all of these problems, Coventry remained, even after its crisis in the 1520s, the largest inland urban centre in the Midlands, and it still supplied imported and

[71] *VCH*, Staffordshire, XIV, p. 119.

[72] On fraternities, the best sources are Northamptonshire RO, Early Wills Book and Will Books for the early sixteenth century; on Wiggeston, W. G. Hoskins, *Provincial England* (London, 1965), p. 73.

manufactured goods, especially to wealthier consumers, over a wide hinterland. Its cattle fair remained important. It numbered among its citizens Richard Marler, one of the richest merchants in England.[73]

The changing fortunes of the towns of the Severn/Avon river system present a much more varied pattern than those to the east of Coventry. The largest centres generally kept their position in the national ranking order between 1377 and 1524/5, with Bristol in third place, and Gloucester seventeenth. Shrewsbury and Worcester rose a little, and Hereford, ranked at twenty-first in 1377, appears in thirteenth position in 1524/5. In the early sixteenth century five towns in the Severn/Avon basin (excluding Coventry) appear in the leading twenty-five towns of England, but only one from the eastern side of the Midland region. Of course, these rankings measure only relative size, and the largest towns of the west lost population, in the case of Bristol by a third, from about 12,000 in 1377 to about 8,000 in 1524/5, and Gloucester dipped from 4,500 to 3,000–3,500. However, in contrast with the almost universal fall in the population of the East Midland towns, Hereford and Shrewsbury remained much the same size, and Worcester probably increased somewhat, from about 3,000 to 3,500. There were signs of physical decay, such as the 300 houses said to be in disrepair in Gloucester in 1487–8.[74]

Similarly, in the smaller towns reductions in population are not hard to find – at Cirencester there were probably about 1,500 inhabitants in 1377, and well below 1,000 in the early sixteenth century. In the early fourteenth century, Thornbury had about 500–600 people and, two centuries later, was said by Leland to have lost its clothing industry and that 'idleness . . . reigneth', which helps to explain its relatively low population of 300–400.[75] Other small towns, while no doubt shrinking in size, still maintained a certain vigour. Pershore appears from its court records to have been an active place, with many brewers and some prostitutes, as well as artisans employed in making gloves and cloth. The people of nearby Evesham also seem to have enjoyed some prosperity as they paid three times as much to the 1524/5 subsidy as in 1334, in contrast with Warwick and Winchcombe, whose assessments remained at much the same level.[76] Stratford lost some population in the period, and suffered from dilapidated houses and decayed rents. Its cloth industry met with hard times, yet new activities developed after the mid-fourteenth century, such as oil milling and selling the locally produced plaster and, in the fifteenth century, there was an impressive campaign of civic and private building.[77] Birmingham, which served as a general market centre for its district, and specialised in tanning and ironworking, attracted favourable comments from Leland on its 'pretty' street and busy artisans. The population of around a thousand in the early fourteenth century had risen to about

[73] Phythian-Adams, *Desolation of a City*, *passim*.   [74] *VCH*, Gloucestershire, IV, p. 36.

[75] R. H. Hilton, 'Low-level urbanisation: the seigneurial borough of Thornbury in the middle ages', in Z. Razi and R. Smith, eds., *Medieval Society and the Manor Court* (Oxford, 1996), pp. 489–95.

[76] Hilton, *English Peasantry*, pp. 81–2, 90–1; Hilton, 'Evesham in the middle ages', p. 190.

[77] Dyer, 'Medieval Stratford'.

double that figure in the 1540s.[78] For the smaller north Warwickshire towns of Atherstone and Nuneaton, with populations above 500 in the early sixteenth century, no evidence of serious shrinkage is visible in their abundant fifteenth-century records – on the contrary they show every sign of lively commercial and industrial activity at the centre of their small but prosperous hinterlands.[79] The very small town of Shipston-on-Stour presents a direct contrast with Higham Ferrers in its recovery from a damaging fire. Shipston around 1400 was embroiled in conflicts, both internally, and with its lord, and this was followed by a period of economic mediocrity in the mid-fifteenth century. After a fire in 1478, the tenants were able to rebuild more than fifty destroyed houses within four years, and went on to enjoy increased prosperity indicated by high market stall rents in the 1480s, and rising land values in the 1490s.[80]

The West Midland towns impress much more than their eastern counterparts with the quantity of late medieval buildings, both public and private, which still stand. It is not just the small and relatively remote centres, such as Weobley, which retain groups and terraces of timber-framed buildings. They are to be seen in small towns in the more modernised areas east of the Severn, such as Henley-in-Arden, Tewkesbury and Winchcombe, and an impressive number of medieval buildings are still standing or were recently demolished in Ludlow, Shrewsbury and Worcester. These survivals to some extent reflect the subsequent history of the towns, as old houses were not replaced, but we cannot avoid observing that a great deal of high-quality building was going on in the towns of the sub-region in the period 1380–1550.[81]

The Severn/Avon region maintained its higher level of urbanisation through the testing times of the later middle ages. Basing our calculations on the 1524/5 taxpayers, it appears that more than a quarter of the population of Gloucestershire and Warwickshire lived in towns, compared with 16 and 17 per cent in Leicestershire and Lincolnshire. These high western figures reflect the size of the larger towns, but also the cumulative total of the people living in the market towns. What lay behind the greater persistence of urban prosperity in the western counties of the Midlands? A structural factor which helped towns to grow and then encouraged their survival can be identified in the contrasting *pays*. The Feldon and Arden of Warwickshire, the wolds, vale and forest in Gloucestershire, the woodlands and champion Vale of Evesham in Worcestershire, all encouraged

[78] Holt, *Birmingham*; but the population figures are too low, as he missed T. Smith and F. Brentano, eds., *English Gilds* (Early English Text Society, 40, 1870), pp. 247, 260; Smith, ed., *Leland's Itinerary*, II, pp. 96–7.

[79] A. Watkins, *Small Towns in the Forest of Arden in the Fifteenth Century* (Dugdale Society Occasional Papers, 38, 1998), pp. 19–21.

[80] C. Dyer, 'The great fire of Shipston-on-Stour', *Warwickshire History*, 8 (1992–3), 179–94.

[81] These buildings await systematic study, but a beginning is D. Lloyd and M. Moran, *The Corner Shop* (Ludlow Research Papers, 2, Birmingham, 1978). Also J. T. Smith, 'Shrewsbury: topography and domestic architecture to the middle of the seventeenth century' (MA thesis, University of Birmingham, 1953).

markets because each *pays* had distinctive products which it needed to exchange through urban markets – timber and fuel from the woodlands, for example, in return for grain from the champion districts. In the Welsh border counties the contrasts between the valleys and the pastoral uplands were even more marked. The rural economies of these *pays* were more specialised and had more distinct frontiers than the *pays* further east. Towns like Atherstone, Nuneaton and Alcester in Warwickshire stood at points where Arden met Feldon, and Chipping Campden and Wotton-under-Edge in Gloucestershire served as channels of trade over the Cotswold escarpment. Indeed, larger towns such as Worcester and Gloucester functioned as funnels for exchanging the produce of contrasting regions on either side of the Severn. After 1400, the *pays* became more specialised, as the regions already tending to pastoralism turned even more land over to grazing, and the woodlands weathered the crises of the period more successfully than the champion Feldon and wold *pays* which were devoted before the Black Death to cereal cultivation.[82]

The western counties also saw industrialisation in the countryside, notably the coal mining and iron working east of the Severn, in south Shropshire, south Staffordshire and northern Worcestershire, and the clothmaking of south Gloucestershire and north Worcestershire. Such developments were not always to the detriment of small towns, which could act as marketing centres for the artisans, and it is no accident that the best examples of the growth of new towns in this period are located in these industrialising regions: at Stourbridge, near Worcestershire's border with Staffordshire, and Stroud in the clothing district of Gloucestershire.[83] Not all industry was located in the countryside, and Worcester's increasing size at this time must be mainly attributed to its growing cloth production, which in 1468–9, according to dubious aulnage returns, amounted almost to 500 cloths and, in 1511, one merchant, William Mucklowe, was carrying near to that number of cloths in one year to fairs at Bergen-op-Zoom and Antwerp.[84]

(vi) CONCLUSION

The Midlands region was urbanised rather slowly before 1100, but in the next two centuries established a network and hierarchy of towns, which were to endure into modern times. In the 200 years after the Black Death the shifts in the hierarchy, and the overall changes in the size of communities, reveal the Severn valley and its tributaries as having a more dynamic urban life than the eastern parts of the region.

[82] C. Dyer, *Warwickshire Farming: 1349–c. 1520* (Dugdale Society Occasional Papers, 27, 1981), pp. 9–13.

[83] Dyer, 'Hidden trade', 148; *VCH*, Gloucestershire, XI, pp. 99–145.

[84] A. D. Dyer, *The City of Worcester in the Sixteenth Century* (Leicester, 1973), pp. 91–108.

· 22(d) ·

East Anglia

BÄRBEL BRODT

(i) GEOGRAPHICAL BACKGROUND

BY THE strictest definition, East Anglia corresponds to the medieval diocese of Norwich: Norfolk, Suffolk and south-eastern Cambridgeshire. For the purposes of this chapter the whole of Cambridgeshire and Huntingdonshire are included (Map 22.10). East Anglia had wide areas of high fertility and a good climate. The long curve of its coastline ensures easy access to the sea even for inland places; sailing distances to important parts of the continent are short.[1] Although there are many harbours for small craft, good major harbours are few and liable to be affected by recurrent problems both of erosion and of silting.[2] In the early part of our period the configuration of the central part of the East Anglian coastline was very different from what it is now. A great estuary extended to within a few miles of Norwich[3] which was probably the major port for the area. The estuary silted up and was drained in or by the eleventh century. It was this which allowed the development of Yarmouth on a sandbank[4] at the estuary's mouth. Inland communication by water was of fundamental importance. The rise of Yarmouth and of Lynn[5] is largely to be explained by each lying near the focus of a major river system. A lesser one converged near Ipswich. There is evidence that minor rivers were much more important for transport in the middle ages than was later the case.[6] The road system of

[1] An average of some 230 miles (368 km).

[2] B. Brodt, '"Do not go too near the edge. The sea has not finished yet". East Anglian coasts and harbours', in K. Friedland, ed., *Hansisches Colloquium King's Lynn 1998* (forthcoming).

[3] J. Campbell, 'Norwich', in *BAHT*, II.

[4] A. W. Ecclestone and J. L. Ecclestone, *The Rise of Great Yarmouth: The Story of a Sandbank* (Yarmouth, 1959).

[5] D. M. Owen, ed., *The Making of King's Lynn* (British Academy, Records of Social and Economic History, new series, 9, 1984); V. S. Parker, *The Making of King's Lynn* (London, 1971).

[6] J. C. Baringer, 'The rivers of Norfolk and north Suffolk', in L. M. Munby, ed., *East Anglian Studies* (Cambridge, 1968), pp. 1–17.

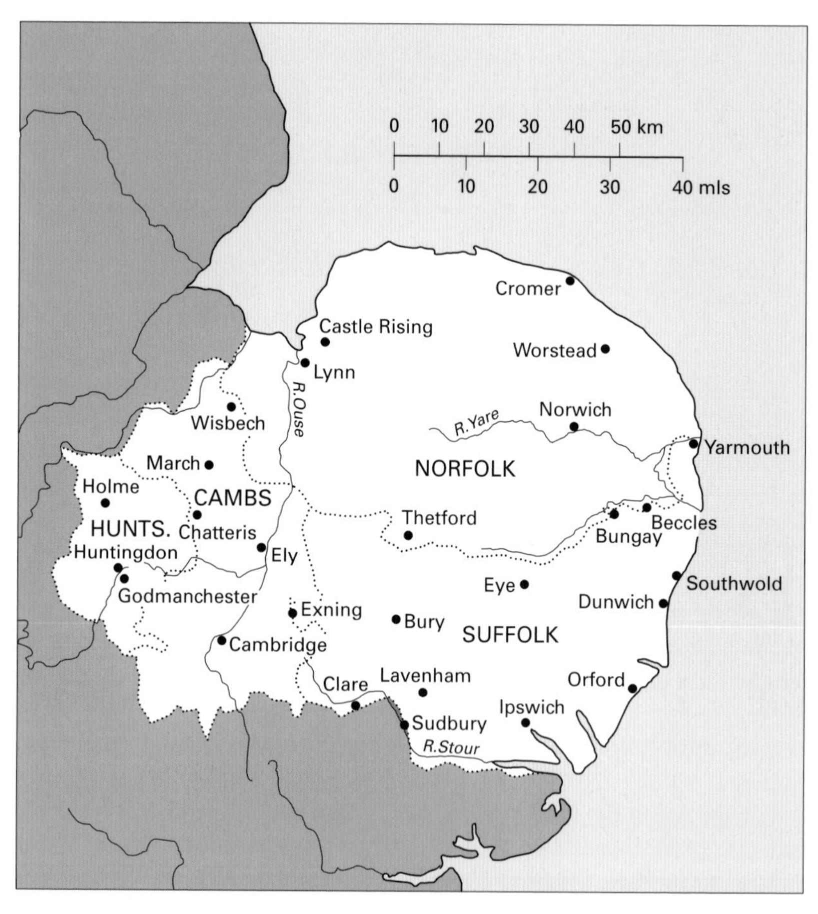

Map 22.10 Towns in East Anglia

medieval East Anglia has been imperfectly studied. It is, however, likely that the significance of Norwich as a great hub for far-reaching roads is old. The non-agricultural natural resources of East Anglia were extensive. Most important was the major herring fishery centred on Yarmouth, a national food resource whose importance possibly antedated its first documentation in the eleventh century. In south-east Norfolk there was an immense source of fuel. The Broads are tremendous peat diggings whose exploitation had started by the twelfth century if not earlier, and which were flooded out of use in the fourteenth century. Some resources may have been more important than at first appears. For example there has been no adequate study of the extensive system of chalk mines which lie under Norwich. Chalk may have been especially important for the manufacture of lime.

(ii) ROMAN EAST ANGLIA

In Roman times all or most of East Anglia in the narrow sense was included in the *civitas* of the Iceni. The capital was *Venta Icenorum*, three miles south of Norwich. *Venta* was a substantial place of some 35 acres (14 ha) within the walled area.[7] It is unusual among *civitas* capitals in being today a deserted site. As with the other two such instances (Silchester and Wroxeter) a major medieval town developed not far off. It is not clear when *Venta* was deserted; the evidence of two major Anglo-Saxon cemeteries not far from its walls is ambiguous. A likely reason for the move of the major focus of activity to Norwich is that there the water communications are much better. There was an important Roman port at Caistor-by-Yarmouth, a few miles north of Yarmouth. A characteristic problem is produced by there having been a small Roman town near North Elmham which became a major ecclesiastical centre. Not far off lies a very large cremation cemetery[8] at Spong Hill. This combination suggests a kind of continuity of focus which may have continued elsewhere without being so suggestively indicated. The major Roman centre in later Cambridgeshire was a walled settlement just outside Cambridge itself (rather confusingly called by the Anglo-Saxons *Grantacaestir*). It is rare among such places in that we have a categorical statement (from Bede) that it was deserted.[9] In Huntingdonshire there was a specialised manufacturing town, the pottery centre at Great Chesterton.

(iii) THE ANGLO-SAXON PERIOD

The extent to which life continued on urban sites between *c.* 400 and *c.* 700 is unknown, but the picture becomes a little clearer in the seventh and eighth centuries. The key site here is Ipswich, where archaeology[10] has shown that here was a major *emporium* which extended over an area of more than 124 acres (50 ha). There is evidence for considerable contacts with Frisia, the Rhineland and Gaul. Kilns have been found showing that pottery, 'Ipswich ware', was produced here on a substantial scale from the mid-seventh century or earlier. (This was the first wheel-made pottery produced in post-Roman Britain.) It is sobering to note that Ipswich is not mentioned in any written source until 993. Although its history between the eighth century and the tenth is incompletely explored, it may well

[7] J. S. Wacher, *The Towns of Roman Britain*, 2nd edn (London, 1995), p. 251; D. G. Russo, *Town Origins and Development in Early England, c. 400–950 A.D.* (Westport, Conn., 1998), pp. 70–2.

[8] See J. N. L. Myres and B. Green, *The Anglo-Saxon Cemeteries of Caistor-by-Norwich and Markshall* (Society of Antiquaries Research Reports, 30, 1972).

[9] C. Plummer, ed., *Venerabilis Baedae, Opera Historica: Historiam Ecclesiasticam* (Oxford, 1896), vol. I, p. 245 (= Book iv, chapter 19).

[10] S. Dunmore, 'The origin and development of Ipswich: an interim report', *East Anglia Archaeology Report*, 1 (1975), 57–67.

have had a continuous urban life for three completely undocumented centuries. The *wich* element in Ipswich's name is one which seems to be significantly associated with *emporia* sites, and which makes one wonder about the early significance of Dunwich and Norwich. Archaeological inquiry[11] at Dunwich is hindered by the fact that the medieval town has disappeared under the sea, but it is worth noticing that there is a plausible case for supposing Dunwich to have been the *Domnoc* which was the site of the first East Anglian see.[12]

The nature of Norwich's pre-tenth-century past[13] is obscure. We can only say that there was some Roman and Dark Age activity on parts of its site. When one remembers the vast extent of the medieval city (over a square mile) and the long period in which the now recognised *emporium* sites at London and York were undiscovered, the possibility that there was such a site in or near Norwich must remain open.

In East Anglia as in the whole of England it is crucial for the historian of the proto-urban past to identify the 'significant places' of the earlier Anglo-Saxon period. Irrespective of the term used to describe them, there is no doubt that places which form the nuclei of 'primary towns' are of major political significance. The search for royal vills and for 'old minsters' – often but by no means always the same – is crucial here. Take Hadleigh in Suffolk. The Annals of St Neots, a twelfth-century Latin version of the Anglo-Saxon Chronicle, inform us that Hadleigh was a *villa regalis* and that the first Danish king of East Anglia, Guthrum, was buried there. The special significance of unchartered Hadleigh, a more than merely petty urban significance, continued in the nineteenth century when it was one of the richest livings in England.[14]

(iv) DOMESDAY AND BEYOND

Our best introduction to the East Anglian towns[15] of the later Anglo-Saxon period is Domesday Book. One should not engage in argument on the subject

[11] S. E. West, 'Excavation of Dunwich town, 1970', *Proc. of the Suffolk Institute for Archaeology and History*, 32 (1970–2), 25–33.

[12] J. Campbell, 'The East Anglian sees before the Conquest', in I. Atherton, E. Fernie, C. Harper-Bill and H. Smith, eds., *Norwich Cathedral* (London, 1996), p. 3.

[13] A. Carter, 'The Anglo-Saxon origins of Norwich: the problems and approaches', *Anglo-Saxon England*, 7 (1978), 175–204.

[14] J. Campbell, 'The Church in Anglo-Saxon towns', in J. Campbell, *Essays in Anglo-Saxon History* (London, 1986), pp. 139–55, esp. 153–4.

[15] The somewhat questionable list in Beresford and Finberg consists of: Cambridge, Linton, Swavesey (Cambs.); Alconbury Weston,* Brampton,* Godmanchester, Hartford,* Holme, Huntingdon, King's Ripton,* Offord Cluny* (Hunts., those marked * may well have been simply ancient demesne and were included in the list for tax purposes); Castle Rising, Yarmouth; Lynn, New Buckenham, Norwich, Thetford (Norfolk); Beccles, Bungay, Bury St Edmunds, Clare, Dunwich, Exning, Eye, Ipswich, Orford, Southwold, Sudbury (Suffolk). M. W. Beresford and H. P. R. Finberg, *English Medieval Boroughs* (Newton Abbot, 1973).

of urban definition. It is better simply to lay out some of the basic information revealed in Domesday in relation to 1066 and 1086. Four places appear as of special economic importance associated with, as we learn from the *Liber Eliensis*, a special juridical significance: Cambridge, Ipswich, Norwich and Thetford. Their population in 1086 varied between 1,500 in Cambridge, around 1,600 in Ipswich, around 2,000 in Thetford and hardly less than 5,000 in Norwich.[16] Their value to the crown at the same date appear as £14 (Cambridge) £25 (Ipswich), £70 (Norwich) and £76 (Thetford).[17] Their status in the English urban hierarchy according to these criteria was high: Norwich was second only to York, Thetford and Ipswich held fifth and sixth places, while Cambridge ranked thirteenth.[18] There had been one major urban development in association with a great Benedictine abbey: the entrepreneurial Abbot Baldwin, formerly of St Denis, had extended and reshaped Bury St Edmunds on a major scale. On a masterful grid pattern no fewer than 342 new houses had been built[19] between 1066 and 1086. There was nothing comparable in association with the other great abbeys of the region, Ely, Ramsey and St Benet at Holme. Probably the most striking feature about the 'new' Bury was its market place: the Great Market was created at the junction of Guildhall Street and Abbeygate Street. The old market to the south of the abbey, St Mary's Square, retained its function only partly – as a horse market.

A number of other places are described by Domesday in such a way as to indicate a status which for one reason or another might be called urban or proto-urban. These were Beccles, Bungay, Castle Rising, Clare, soon to be headquarters of a large honour, Dunwich, Ely with its vast cathedral, Exning, Eye, closely associated with the Malets, Yarmouth, Huntingdon, Linton in south Cambridgeshire, Sudbury, Wisbech and Wymondham. It is worth observing that here the number of places which appear to have had some kind of legally defined urban status in 1086 was considerably fewer in relation to the size of the population than in a number of other shires. One likely explanation for this is that the granting of urban status in much of Wessex and the Midlands was related to the construction of fortresses, especially by King Alfred and King Edward the Elder. East Anglia had been conquered by quick campaigns and the same considerations would not have applied. Also, in East Anglia the places with urban status were a rather mixed bag. Beccles,[20] for example, looks like a clear example

[16] See H. C. Darby's *Domesday Geography of Eastern England*, 3rd edn (Cambridge, 1971), for the actual recordings of messuages, burgesses, borders, etc., and bear in mind that he refers to concluding population figures as minimal ones. The Norwich population may well have been as high as 10,000. [17] J. Tait, *The Medieval English Borough* (Manchester, 1936), p. 184.

[18] C. Stephenson, *Borough and Town* (Cambridge, Mass., 1933), appendix iii.

[19] J. T. Smith, 'A note on the origin of the town plan of Bury St. Edmunds', *Archaeological J*, 108 (1951), 162–4. Still the best general account of Bury is M. D. Lobel, *The Borough of Bury St Edmunds* (Oxford, 1935). [20] B. Brodt, *Städte ohne Mauern* (Paderborn, 1997), pp. 189–94.

of something which probably did not have a significant Anglo-Saxon past. Domesday contains no indication of Beccles having been a major estate centre or its church having been a head minster. But Beccles was situated at an important point on the waterway system, the abbey of Bury was an important landowner there and Domesday's description indicates that it was an economically attractive and growing place. It is interesting to notice that the abbey of Bury also owned the church of St Lawrence in Norwich. Like Beccles, this church owed a substantial herring render to the abbey and perhaps not entirely by coincidence stands on a high bluff besides the Wensum, very much as Bury's church of St Michael at Beccles stands on a high bluff overlooking the Waveney.

Domesday shows that there were many places which appear to have had sufficient population and consequence to have ranked as minor towns in other circumstances or other counties, but which so far as we can tell had no juridical distinction from the surrounding countryside. This was a long continuing and also a very revealing phenomenon. Thus in our shires, these places are amongst those which appear with recorded populations of more than sixty, or with a valuation of more than £10: Bassingbourn, Woodditton, Eltisley, Cherry Hinton (Cambs.), Paxton, Buckden, Bluntisham, Somersham, Spaldwick (Hunts.), Wymondham (Norfolk), Eye, Beccles, Clare and Sudbury (Suffolk). We are tracing here a set of circumstances familiar enough to geographers though sometimes neglected by historians in which the definition of distinctions whether contemporary or modern between 'town' and 'village' is not necessarily of determinative significance. For many purposes we have to think in terms of a hierarchy, at the bottom of which is the simplest hamlet with two or three poor peasant families and at the top a metropolis providing a very wide variety of goods and services. What the Domesday data in part draw our attention to is that there were quite a number of steps on this ladder and that some may have been quite high up judged by economic criteria, but not by governmental or juridical ones.

These Domesday data have been used somewhat roughly. An obvious and crucial question arises about the relationship between economically significant places of the kind with which we have just been dealing and the nature and distribution of rural markets. Domesday mentions a limited number of markets outside places which by any criteria were towns. In Norfolk, for example, these were Holt, Dunham and Litcham.[21] In days gone, it was supposed that one could trace the 'proliferation of rural markets' by considering the royal grants of market rights which appear in considerable numbers in particular in the thirteenth century. It is now generally recognised that the proliferation of charters is likely to have been in large part a product of an increasing royal demand for charter evi-

[21] D. Dymond refers to the close proximity of Dunham and Litcham, both in Launditch Hundred and only 2 miles (3.2 km) apart, and hints at commercial competition. D. Dymond, *The Norfolk Landscape* (London, 1985), p. 88.

dence for rights and the general climate of social and legal thought in which written evidence gained a weight and significance which it had lacked in previous centuries, rather than necessarily a growth in the number of markets. So there may have been, and probably were, a number of rural markets in the eleventh and twelfth centuries which are not documented until the thirteenth century or later. In association with this there has to be considered the possibility that there was an orderly system of markets in late Anglo-Saxon England which would have persisted after the Conquest, such that every hundred had its market.

The consideration of Domesday indicates that ordered efforts at economic expansion of the kind of which the most striking example is Abbot Baldwin's extension to Bury were not confined to major towns. Thus we not only find that Bury appears to have been running a new and flourishing urban settlement at Beccles, but that the value of Wymondham[22] which belonged to the abbey of St Albans tripled between 1066 and 1086 to £60. It is worth noticing here that the value to the crown of only eleven or twelve English towns exceeded £60 in 1086.[23] The relationship between major ecclesiastical houses and urban development is brought out in a particular way by the history of the see of East Anglia. The Anglo-Saxon *sedes* of this see was at North Elmham. Not very long after the Conquest it was moved to Thetford in accordance with a general policy. In 1094 it was subsequently moved to Norwich. Bishop Herbert de Losinga's campaign for the building and endowment of the new cathedral and the cathedral monastery had large urban elements. Losinga also took an active interest in the East Anglian seaports. He established a foothold at Lynn which was to lead to its becoming until the dissolution a largely episcopal town, and he made an attempt on Yarmouth which although not altogether successful did leave the cathedral church with the patronage of the great parish church of St Nicholas.

In the context of significant places the dense population of East Anglia has to be noted.[24] The sheer density of the population in certain areas was bound to ensure that there were some settlements such as to present problems of definition, for those who are interested in them, as to what was a large village and what was a very small town. A particularly East Anglian expression of these circumstances is the existence of many settlements which had more than one church.

What was the condition of the major towns of East Anglia at the time of the Conquest and what was the impact of the Conquest upon them? Let us look at some of them. From the ninth to the late eleventh century Thetford[25] was one of the largest and most important towns in England and then it declined rapidly.

[22] Brodt, *Städte ohne Mauern*, pp. 189–94.

[23] Tait, *Medieval English Borough*, p. 184; M. Biddle, ed., *Winchester in the Early Middle Ages* (Oxford, 1976), p. 500.

[24] Brodt, *Städte ohne Mauern*, pp. 85–100.

[25] F. Blomefield, *The History of the Ancient City and Burgh of Thetford* (Fersfield, 1739); J. Wilkinson, *The Architectural Remains of the Ancient Town and Borough of Thetford* (London, 1822); A. Crosby, *A History of Thetford* (Chichester and London, 1986).

Originated around a ford at the confluence of the Little Ouse and the Thet, and a major centre for pottery and metalworking,[26] Thetford in 869 served as the winter base for the Danish army. It was a mint from 959 to 1189 and covered an area of approximately 185 acres (75 ha). Domesday Book[27] records 943 burgesses in 1066 which indicates that Thetford has to be compared with York, Lincoln and Norwich. Surprisingly, its value was a moderate £36. Twelve churches were recorded, most of them on the Suffolk side of the Little Ouse, and a Benedictine priory had been established shortly after 1020. In 1072 the bishop of East Anglia left North Elmham – temporarily – in favour of Thetford. The reasons for Thetford's decline invite speculation, but the facts are obvious as early as 1086 when Domesday Book notes a marked fall in the number of burgesses to 720 and records no fewer than 224 empty messuages.[28] The remarkable increase in value to £76, however, may be linked to its relatively new status of bishop's see. Possible explanations for the decline include the competition from Abbot Baldwin's new creation at Bury St Edmunds, silting of the Little Ouse which could have made the river less navigable, and from not later than 1200 a likely degree of competition from Lynn.

The salient features of Norwich were above all the large number of recorded inhabitants and burgesses suggesting a population which cannot have been less than 5,000 and could have risen as high as 10,000. By 1086 at least fifty of the maximum number of sixty-odd medieval churches of Norwich were already there;[29] the identification of the churches both enables one to establish the extent of the urban area and to show that in some parts the settlement must have been very dense. The picture which emerges is that of an inhabited area whose size was little short of that of the city in all later centuries up to the nineteenth.[30] In many areas there must have been serious open space between the built-up parts, but the distribution of the churches combined with the archaeological evidence shows the likelihood that the built-up area would have been adequate to accommodate a population at the maximum indicated by the Domesday figures. Obviously, the question arises as to how this city had grown up. As is common with towns in this period our information other than that which derives from archaeology is exceedingly thin. Norwich grew[31] up where two probable

[26] S. Dunmore and R. Carr, 'The late Saxon town of Thetford', *East Anglian Archaeology*, 4 (1976).

[27] P. Brown, ed., *Domesday Book, Norfolk* (Chichester, 1984), vol. II, ff. 118b–19.

[28] These messuages did not fall victim to the clearing of a site for the Norman castle, as this was erected outside the defences in the east of the town.

[29] Norwich's Domesday entry is one of the longest; it covers nearly three folios. Little Domesday, ff. 116–18. Seventeen churches were situated north of the river; the most remarkable density is in St Benedict's Street where seven churches were founded in just over a quarter of a mile.

[30] Around 617 acres (250 ha).

[31] A. Carter, 'The Anglo-Saxon origins of Norwich: the problems and approaches', *Anglo-Saxon England*, 7 (1978), 175–204, who has argued that Norwich developed out of a number of villages, viz. Needham, Conesford, Westwic and Coslany.

Roman roads crossed, and at the lowest bridging point of the Wensum. After the name first appears on coins of Æthelstan, there is nothing in writing until an account of the destruction of the city by Cnut. Next there are a tiny handful of pre-Conquest charter references and that is the total of what we have from before 1066. The only non-archaeological evidence for the importance of Norwich before 1086 is that relating to the number of its moneyers and its mint output. Finally, there is the topographical impact the Norman Conquest had on the town. Around 1075 a royal castle was erected on the end of a spur overlooking the valley. Domesday Book states that the raising of its motte and ramparts necessitated the destruction of ninety-eight properties. Immediately to the west of the castle the Normans established a major, largely planned, extension, known as the New or French Borough. Its main focus was a large sloping market place. The extension was to survive as a distinct legal entity until about 1200; by 1086 at least 125 French burgesses with considerable economic and cultural influence had moved in. The second major topographical change was the erection of a cathedral in 1096 under Herbert de Losinga. The cathedral, 400 yards (365 m) away from the castle, was to serve the whole of East Anglia and to be served by a community of sixty Benedictine monks. The establishment of the cathedral precinct led to the destruction of at least two parish churches; numerous houses were taken down, the courses of streets were altered.

Yarmouth, next to Norwich and Thetford the third major pre-Conquest town of Norfolk, grew[32] on a sandbank off the Yare. By the time of the Conquest it was a small but obviously well-established trading and fishing community. Domesday Book[33] calls it a *burgus* and notes seventy burgesses, indicating a population of maybe 500. Domesday Book also specifically mentions twenty-four fishermen at Yarmouth in 1066 who belonged to the manor of Gorleston on the Suffolk side of the Yare, and it refers to a church at Yarmouth dedicated to St Benet, but its exact position in the town cannot be identified. The church was served by a priest sent from Norwich. Used only during the herring season it ceased to exist shortly after the Conquest. In 1101 bishop Herbert de Losinga was given permission to build a new church, St Nicholas, which was consecrated in 1119. The church is situated at the north-eastern edge of Yarmouth, overlooking the vast market place and is claimed to be the largest parish church in England.[34] When Yarmouth received its first murage grant in 1260,[35] the main topographical features were already completed. The built-up area was long and thin with three major streets in north–south direction; the east–west connections between these were formed by around 150 narrower lanes and alleys, the Yarmouth 'rows'.

[32] A. Carter, 'Great Yarmouth – an introduction', *Archaeological J*, 137 (1980), 300–03.

[33] Little Domesday, ff. 118, 118b, 283a.

[34] Until St George's was built in 1714, St Nicholas was Yarmouth's only church.

[35] The walled area eventually consisted of around 321 acres (130 ha).

In Suffolk, next to Bury St Edmunds, Ipswich[36] was clearly the most important town at the time of the Conquest. It developed first on the west bank of the Gipping, in the proximity of the Roman *Combretonium* and fairly close to the 'Peddars Way'.[37] In the course of the seventh century Ipswich came into being at the present site at the corner of the Orwell estuary; its topography suggests a natural growth, with the market on Cornhill and the church dedicated to St Mildred one of its centres. Thanks to its natural advantages, particularly the harbour, Ipswich grew to roughly 247 acres (100 ha) in the middle ages. It was probably guarded by a surrounding ditch in Anglo-Saxon times; but rather surprisingly considering its scale and importance it never came to be properly walled.[38] Although the Normans erected a castle just outside the town, for unknown reasons Ipswich was devastated at some stage after the Conquest.[39] There been 538 burgesses in 1066 but their number had in 1086 dropped to 220, half of whom were described as *pauperes*,[40] and 328 messuages lay waste. Despite this, the town's value had risen by £5 and Ipswich was soon to recover its former strength.

The Suffolk harbour town of Dunwich[41] rivalled Ipswich at the time of Domesday. Dunwich was most unusual in being largely the property of a lay landowner other than the king: in 1066 it belonged to Eadric of Laxfield, and the abbey of Ely also held eighty burgesses there.[42] Twenty-four Frenchmen are mentioned and the number of burgesses had increased from 120 in 1066 to 236 in 1086. However, there were also 180 *pauperes*. The number of churches had risen from one to three. There had been a dramatic increase in the value of Dunwich from £10 in 1066 to £50, plus an extra 60,000 herrings. But there are hints in Domesday Book that Dunwich was already suffering from sea erosion which was ultimately to destroy it.

Cambridgeshire was one of the shires with no settlement to which Domesday attributed urban status other than that from which it took its name. Cambridge developed at a river crossing. Situated at the southern edge of the fens, it dates back to Roman times when there was *Duroliponte* on the left bank of the navigable river Cam. As stated above, Bede explicitly mentions the settlement as deserted in the seventh century, but there was a revival to come. The bridge that

36 G. H. Martin, 'The borough and merchant community of Ipswich' (PhD thesis, University of Oxford, 1956); L. J. Redstone, *Ipswich through the Ages* (Ipswich, 1948).

37 Originally called Gippeswice. Cf. N. Scarfe, *The Suffolk Landscape* (London, 1972), pp. 98–100.

38 On the rather intriguing phenomenon of towns without walls in East Anglia see Brodt, *Städte ohne Mauern*.

39 Redstone, *Ipswich*, p. 26.

40 A. Rumble, ed.,*Domesday Book, Suffolk* (Chichester, 1986), vol. II, ff. 290, 294b, 421b.

41 Called a city in 803: W. de Gray Birch, ed., *Cartularium Saxonicum*, (London, 1885–93), no. 312. See also T. Gardner, *An historical account of Dunwich, antiently a city, now a borough* (London, 1754); R. Parker, *Men of Dunwich* (London, 1978).

42 Little Domesday, I, ff. 311b, 312, 331b, 333b, II, ff. 385b. Eadric of Laxfield was dispossessed and Dunwich became part of Robert Malet's holdings.

gave the town its name was first mentioned in 875. The settlement had shifted towards the right side of the river and it was protected by ditches and wooden gates at the time of the Danish invasions; it was, however, never fortified by a stone wall. At some time in the tenth century Cambridge was established as the administrative centre of *Grantabricscire*; it had the equivalent of a hundred court, a market and a mint. Domesday Book calls it a *burgus* and shows that the town was divided into ten wards[43] with an estimated population of around 1,500. South of the bridge were probably six pre-Conquest churches,[44] while the plots on the northern side were more given to governmental buildings. The Conquest resulted in the erection of a motte and bailey castle[45] above the river in 1068 which together with the Huntingdon castle ensured William's control over the region. The county's administration remained centred in the town, with its headquarters in the new castle.

What else is there especially noteworthy in East Anglia at the time of Domesday? One striking aspect is the number of markets mentioned not only in connection with but also outside 'towns'. The most peculiar of the four counties under consideration here was Suffolk. Markets were mentioned in Bury, Ipswich and Dunwich – the Suffolk *burgi*. But there were also markets at Beccles, Blythburgh, Clare, Eye, Haverhill, Hoxne and Kelsale; in Sudbury and Thorney which is now better known as Stowmarket. This list is remarkably long; longer still when compared to other counties in Domesday Book, but perhaps less surprisingly if we reflect that Suffolk was then the most densely populated English shire.

(V) THE LEGAL FRAMEWORK

When one looks at the period *c.* 1100 to *c.* 1400, a dominant feature is the very large number of town charters issued in the late twelfth and the thirteenth centuries. Royal charters went out to Bury St Edmunds in 1102–3, to Cambridge in 1120–31, to Dunwich in 1200, to Yarmouth in 1208, to Ipswich in 1200 and to Norwich in 1194.[46] The first two are different from the numerous and fairly similar group of urban charters issued by Richard and by John. On 3 April 1102–3 Henry I let it be known that 'the monastery and burgesses, and all residents of St Edmunds [Bury]' and all the manors of St Edmund are to have the same liberty which they enjoyed under Cnut and Edward.[47] No secular person or royal official is to meddle with the borough, except the abbot and convent and their officials.

[43] *Custodie*; frequently to be found in the Danelaw.
[44] St Clement, St George, St Botulph, St Edward, St Benet and St Peter.
[45] Twenty-seven houses had been destroyed during its erection.
[46] A. Ballard, ed., *British Borough Charters 1042–1216* (Cambridge, 1913), pp. xxvi–xxxii.
[47] C. Johnson, *et al.*, eds., *Regesta Regum Anglo-Normannorum 1066–1154*, vol. II: *Regesta Henrici Primi 1100–1135* (Oxford, 1956), no. 644.

Abbot, convent and burgesses are free from toll and other customs in all the fairs and markets of the realm. The Cambridge charter[48] decrees that any ship is forbidden to put in at any strand (*litus*) in Cambridgeshire, except at the strand of the king's borough of Cambridge. No carts are to be loaded anywhere except in the borough of Cambridge nor is anyone to take toll except there. A noteworthy feature of the Bury charter is the assumption that there were privileges which the burgesses shared with the abbey and which had already been defined. The interesting thing about the Cambridge charter is its exclusive concern with an economic monopoly. Usually, the emphasis of the charters of Richard's and of John's reign was different. In them we find the question of the fee-farm, references to the highest ranking official, usually called *praepositus* who is in charge of the safe deliverance of the farm, and also the first signs of internal self-government.

Charters, supplemented by urban ordinances and custumals can provide important insight into internal urban government. Two major examples are Ipswich and Norwich. Ipswich is a most interesting case, as here burgesses and inhabitants took the institutions of urban government well beyond the limits of what was indicated by the royal charter, first granted on 25 May 1200. Ipswich was made a *liber burgus*, the *praepositus* had to deliver the annual fee-farm of £65 at the Exchequer, the burgesses were to elect two bailiffs to replace the royal reeves and there were to be four elected coroners to assist the bailiffs. No mention was made about modes of election or indeed of provision for a council. Here the burgesses thought a step beyond the words of the charter. On 29 June, the inhabitants assembled outside St Mary Tower and elected the two bailiffs and four coroners for one year only.[49] Furthermore, it was decided to elect annually two councils, one to consist of *duodecim capitales portmenni* and the second to consist of sixty *probes et legales homines*. The election mode was substantially altered in 1309, when the council of sixty was reduced to twenty-seven representatives of the urban parishes, and membership in the upper house became for life.[50] In 1317 the number of coroners was reduced to two.[51]

Norwich received important privileges by royal charter on 5 May 1194.[52] The annual fee-farm was fixed at £108 and the inhabitants were to elect the *praepositus* or reeve who had to deliver it to the Exchequer. The reeve was also to preside over the municipal assembly. Norwich was organised into four leets, Conesford, Mancroft, Wymer and Over-the-Water.[53] Neither the office of coroner, nor a

[48] *Ibid.*, no. 1729.

[49] The 1320 ordinance changed the election date to 8 September. The annual election was first confirmed by royal charter in 1378. *CCh.R 1341–1417* p. 249; see R. Canning, *The Principal Charters which have been Granted to the Corporation of Ipswich in Suffolk* (London, 1754), pp. 10–11 on Richard II's confirmation.

[50] Martin, 'Ipswich', p. 43.

[51] *CCh.R 1300–26*, pp. 344–5.

[52] W. Hudson and J. C. Tingey, eds., *The Records of the City of Norwich* (Norwich, 1906–10), vol. I, pp. 12–13. Norwich received the rights and privileges of London.

[53] For leet boundaries and subdivisions see map in Campbell, 'Norwich'; A. King, 'The merchant class and borough finances in later medieval Norwich' (PhD thesis, University of Oxford, 1989), map 2.3.

council – both well established – are mentioned. One of the major changes in the city administration took place without any apparent preliminary royal grant: around 1223 the office of reeve was abandoned and that of four bailiffs was installed instead,[54] probably to ensure a higher degree of internal control. In the years that followed the bailiffs were assisted by a council of twenty-four, but we have to wait until 1379[55] before its existence was formally acknowledged. In 1404 Norwich became a county in its own right,[56] while at the same (and in this sense late) time the office of mayor was introduced. The office of bailiff is abandoned and replaced by provision for two sheriffs. Mayor and sheriffs are to be elected annually. Although the body is not mentioned in the 1404 charter, membership in the council of twenty-four (by now known as aldermen, to be elected in equal numbers per ward) had in fact become a life-long one. But shortly after this charter internal unrest broke out in Norwich, kindled by a disputed shrieval election. It is most noteworthy that the introduction of the royal charter makes explicit mention to the cause of the unrest: the lack of 'written' election procedures and that the inhabitants of Norwich were willing enough to pay 100 marks for the charter which was issued in 1417.[57] Life-long membership in the aldermanic body was legitimised. Concessions, however, were made to the 'inhabitants' by establishing a further council of sixty members, to be annually elected on the basis of the population figures within the four leets.[58] The charter is in abundant detail as regards the actual election procedure. This was to remain the last change in the internal administration of the city until the Municipal Reform Act of 1835. It must be noted as a most striking feature of the East Anglian towns under consideration here how few and far between were the constitutional changes which affected their civic authorities.

(vi) PLANTATIONS, PROGRESS AND PROBLEMS

Another such feature of East Anglia is the foundation of new chartered towns. Any selection has to include Newmarket, Clare, Orford and Lynn which represent a market foundation, two creations in immediate connection with establishing a royal and seigneurial stronghold and finally a monastic venture with the most obvious economic intentions in mind. Between 1217 and 1223 Richard de Argentein moved the market from Exning at the extreme west of Suffolk, forming a legal enclave in Cambridgeshire, some three miles to the south-east

54 Hudson and Tingey, eds., *Records*, I, p. xxv; F. Blomefield, *An Essay towards a Topographical History of Norfolk* (Norwich and Lynn, 1739–75), vol. III, p. 45.

55 15 February, charter by Richard II, see Hudson and Tingey, eds., *Records*, I, pp. 29–30.

56 On towns with county status see Bärbel Brodt, 'Verfassungsnorm und kommunale Wirklichkeit. Englische Provinzmetropolen zwischen Spätmittelalter und früher Neuzeit' (Habilitations-thesis, University of Münster, forthcoming).

57 Hudson and Tingey, eds., *Records*, I, pp. 36–7.

58 Twelve for Conesford, sixteen for Mancroft, twenty for Wymer and twelve for Over-the-Water.

and founded Newmarket.[59] The market was confirmed by royal charter in 1227, and at the same time de Argentein was granted an annual fair.[60] Newmarket remained small, covering an area of less than 25 acres (10 ha). It was a most untypical new settlement – its lord was extremely reluctant to grant any rights and privileges to the inhabitants who cannot have numbered more than 300; its plan was not carefully laid out, it grew rather naturally without more than a hint of a focus on its two churches, All Saints on the Cambridgeshire side of the settlement, and St Mary in the Suffolk part. In the 1334 lay subsidy it was assessed at the rural fifteenth with £7. It was never fortified, it was never taxed as a borough, there is no reference to a functioning internal government, it was never represented at the eyre, it also failed to attract religious orders and no internal provision was made for the aged and infirm. In short, the urban status attributed to it by some historians should be reconsidered.[61] Clare was different. It was mentioned as a market in Domesday and some forty-three burgesses are recorded there.[62] Its value was an impressive £40 both in 1066 and 1086. William I granted Clare together with some 170 other manors to Richard de Bienfaite; his heirs were to be better known under the name de Clare.[63] Much of the medieval importance of this place derived from its being the *caput* of a great honour,[64] and in the 1090s the family erected a massive castle there. From 1262 the sources distinguish clearly between the manor and the borough of Clare. There are references to borough rents and income derived from the borough markets and mills. There was also a borough court with view of frankpledge. Developing in a bend of the River Stour to an area of around 25 acres (10 ha), the streets of medieval Clare are mentioned by name in the court rolls, and one, Mill Lane, led down to the Austin Friary which had been founded in 1248, the first house of the order in England. Accounts of Clare's population vary; the lay subsidy of 1327 lists only twenty-five taxpaying inhabitants, while the 1377 poll tax notes no fewer than 425, which suggests a population of up to 800.[65] From 1310 onwards our sources mention urban officers, originally installed by the lord, but from 1331 elected

59 See M. Beresford, *New Towns of the Middle Ages* (London, 1967), p. 490.

60 PRO C 60/18 membr. 3; *CChR 1226–57*, p. 11.

61 I am here referring to Beresford and Finberg's list, in *English Medieval Boroughs*.

62 In 1066, 75 inhabitants had to pay tax, in 1086 there were 127 of them, 43 explicitly referred to as burgesses. Little Domesday, f. 389b.

63 G. A. Thornton, *A History of Clare Suffolk* (Cambridge, 1930); also G. A. Thornton, 'A study in the history of Clare, Suffolk, with special reference to its development as a borough', *TRHS*, 4th series, 11 (1928), 85; J. C. Ward, 'The honour of Clare in the early middle ages', *Proc. of the Suffolk Institute for Archaeology and History*, 30 (1965), pp. 94–111. The best study on the Clares is M. Altschul, *A Baronial Family in Medieval England: The Clares 1217–1314* (Baltimore, Md., 1965); see also W. Rye, 'De Clares of Clare in Suffolk', *Genealogist*, new series, 37 (1921), 169–73.

64 Other examples in East Anglia include Bungay, Southwold, Castle Acre and Castle Rising.

65 *Suffolk in 1327, being a Subsidy Return* (Woodbridge, 1906) (=Suffolk Green Books 9), no. 11; C. C. Fenwick, 'The English poll taxes of 1377, 1379 & 1381: a critical examination of the returns' (PhD thesis, University of London, 1983), p. 635.

annually by the inhabitants. Most prominent of these were the bailiffs and the ale tasters. In 1313 the burgesses and inhabitants were granted special mercantile rights, and a market court was established in 1343. Although Clare never received an urban charter, its urban character cannot be doubted.

It has been stated[66] that the Bigod ambition led to the creation by Henry II of the castle and new town of Orford in the Suffolk hundred of Plomesgate in 1165. Henry laid out the town of roughly 22 acres (9 ha) on a simple grid pattern between the castle and the newly founded church of St Bartholomew.[67] A market was established by 1102.[68] Overlooking the Orford Ness, Orford monopolised the trade of the tidal Alde River until well into the sixteenth century, when Aldeburgh started to rise at Orford's expense. In 1256 Orford was called a *liber burgus*: this was confirmed in 1326 with freedom from toll for its inhabitants in the entire realm.[69] In 1298 and 1306 Orford was represented in parliament, and it was taxed as a borough six times between 1313 and 1336, while in 1334 it was assessed on the tenth with £10.[70] It was beyond doubt a successful urban foundation although it seems to have been declining a little towards the end of our period.

None of the East Anglian foundations, however, proved to be as successful as that remarkable monastic venture, Lynn.[71] This foundation lay beside the River Ouse, in a corner of the East Anglian bishop's manor of Gaywood and just north of a village already mentioned in Domesday Book, South Lynn, where salt making was of major economic importance.[72] There were already resident merchants when Bishop Herbert de Losinga in 1095 dedicated a new church,[73] St Margaret, with an accompanying Benedictine monastery in the area between Purfleet and Millfleet. The borough was granted considerable mercantile privileges and put under the jurisdiction of the monastery. By 1146 another church, dedicated to St James, was founded there. By 1174 north of the borough, a plantation called Newlands had been set up,[74] with a system of parallel streets, fortification,[75] market and an individual church, St Nicholas. In

[66] Scarfe, *Suffolk Landscape*, p. 162.

[67] V. B. Redstone, 'Orford and its castle', *Proc. of the Suffolk Institute for Archaeology and History*, 10 (1898), 205–30; R. A. Roberts, 'Orford Castle', *J of the British Archaeological Association*, new series, 34, (1928), 82–6. [68] Beresford, *New Towns*, p. 489.

[69] Patent Roll, 26 Edw. III, part 1, membr. 29; Ipswich RO, HD 64/1/30; *CCh.R 1300–26*, p. 482.

[70] J. F. Willard, 'Taxation boroughs and parliamentary boroughs, 1294–1336', in J. G. Edwards, V. H. Galbraith and E. F. Jacob, eds., *Historical Essays in Honour of James Tait* (Manchester, 1933), pp. 417–35, esp. p. 433–4; R. E. Glasscock, ed., *The Lay Subsidy of 1334* (London, 1975), p. 294.

[71] Brief account by B. Brodt, 'King's Lynn', in *Lexikon des Mittelalters* (Munich and Zurich, 1980–98), col. 1159; H. Harrod, *Report on the Deeds and Records of the Borough of King's Lynn* (King's Lynn, 1874); H. J. Hillen, *History of the Borough of King's Lynn*, 2 vols. (Norwich, 1907).

[72] The relevant entry in Domesday Book records some 180 active salterns close to Lynn.

[73] Brodt, *Städte ohne Mauern*, pp. 234–44.

[74] Beresford, *New Towns*, p. 467; see Plan in Owen, *Lynn*, p. 23.

[75] Fortified between 1146 and 1176; H. L. Turner, *Town Defences in England and Wales* (London, 1970), see p. 126 on mural grants.

1204 both settlements[76] received the privileges of Oxford[77] and became a *liber burgus* under the overlordship of the bishop of Norwich;[78] at the same time a guild merchant is mentioned. Until 1216 the *praepositus* is the highest ranking official in Lynn; from that date the office of mayor is established and Lynn sent members to parliament from 1283 onwards. Only three years later the Hanseatic League established a *Kontor* in the thriving harbour which became one of the leading East Anglian ports through which corn, wool and cloth were traded along the English coasts and to the continent. New quays were built at the end of the thirteenth century and Lynn was one of the staple ports in Edward III's reign. In 1334 it was assessed to the tenth with £ 50,[79] and the poll tax of 1377 recorded 3,127 taxpaying inhabitants, which points to a population of up to 8,000 or 10,000.[80]

Lynn belongs to the same category as Bury: ecclesiastical owned towns. But there they vary. There was far less tension between Lynn and the bishop of Norwich than there was between Bury and its abbot. Contrary to current ideas, it should be pointed out that civic unrest in monastic boroughs was not automatically directed at the institution, but rather against individual officeholders. Looking at what happened in Bury in 1304, in 1327 or, indeed, during the so-called Peasants' Revolt of 1381, one can be in two minds as to whom the movements were directed against.[81] In 1304 the inhabitants failed in their demands, but in 1327, the local unrest was centred around the urban aldermen, and this time it was backed by the crown.[82]

The question of civic unrest can be further highlighted by looking at Norwich and the disputes between the priory and the townspeople which reached a climax in 1272. The frequent disputes usually centred around the prior's claim of view of frankpledge in the areas under his jurisdiction[83] and exemption from taxation there. In 1272 violence broke out; citizens broke into the Close, burnt part of the cathedral and killed some of the prior's servants. Norwich was taken into the king's hand and put under papal interdict. A settlement was finally

[76] They covered an area of around 200 acres (80 ha) in the fourteenth centry.

[77] Four years later Yarmouth became the second East Anglian borough to receive the Oxford liberties. In the case of Lynn, oddly enough, the first of three in that year was issued by King John in Lambeth on 17 January 1204. This was followed by one of the bishop on 24 March 1204, again to be confirmed by the king on 4 September. It is most striking, however, that none of the three charters mention the fee-farm. See Brodt, *Städte ohne Mauern*, pp. 148–51.

[78] The counts of Arundel, lords of neighbouring Castle Rising, however, continued to hold a complicated share in Lynn.

[79] Only once was Lynn assessed as a *villa* (otherwise quite common for monastic boroughs): in 1316. See Willard, 'Taxation boroughs', pp. 433–4. On 1335 see Glasscock, *Lay Subsidy*, p. 197.

[80] Fenwick, 'Poll Taxes', pp. 230, 501.

[81] For an overview see *CPR 1301–7*, pp. 283–4.

[82] M. D. Lobel, 'A detailed account of the 1327 rising at Bury St. Edmunds and the subsequent trial', *Proceedings of the Suffolk Institute for Archaeology and History*, 21 (1933), 215–31; R. S. Gottfried, *Bury St Edmunds and the Urban Crisis 1290–1539* (Princeton, N.J., 1982), pp. 222–30.

[83] The Cathedral Precinct, Holmestreet, Ratten Row, Tombland, Spitteland, and Great Newgate. Campbell, 'Norwich', p. 12.

reached in 1276 when the citizens had agreed to pay 1,000 marks for the rebuilding of the cathedral. In 1306 the city agreed to the prior's claim to view of frankpledge,[84] but the city coroners had the right to enter it.

(vii) ECONOMY AND POPULATION TOWARDS THE CLOSE OF THE MIDDLE AGES

East Anglia's agricultural economy included the substantial production of wool. Its most important industry was the manufacture of cloth, much of it for export.[85] The picture emerges that Yarmouth was the most important port for wool export, while Lynn seems to have dominated the broadcloth export. There was an emergence of small and minor towns which was closely connected to the worsted production[86] whose influence can already be felt by the time of the 1334 lay subsidy.[87] For example, in Tunstead hundred (Norfolk), North Walsham is assessed at £15; Worstead was assessed at very nearly as much.[88] The average assessment for the twenty-five places in the hundred was just under £5. Neither Worstead nor North Walsham had the juridical status of towns, but their high assessments mark them out as places of unusual economic standing. Just consider the much poorer shire of Staffordshire, where neither of the two most important boroughs, Stafford and Lichfield, had quite so high an assessment as these Norfolk industrial villages.[89] Of course, had such villages been assessed on the same basis as Stafford and Lichfield, that is to say, at the rate of a tenth rather than a fifteenth, their assessments would have probably been significantly higher yet. It must have been a serious consideration that places which had a juridical urban status as interpreted by the Exchequer paid a higher rate than those which did not. The most extraordinary East Anglian example of a place which one would have thought to have paid the rate of a tenth, but in fact paid that of the fifteenth, was Bury St Edmunds.[90] The fiscal

[84] With the exception of Great Newgate which was granted to the city in 1305.

[85] See E. M. Carus-Wilson and O. Coleman, *England's Export Trade, 1275–1547* (Oxford, 1963), pp. 40–55 for wool exports from East Anglian ports, and pp. 75–87 for cloth exports.

[86] Unfortunately neglected by Carus-Wilson and Coleman. See A. Beardwood, *Alien Merchants in England, 1350–1377: Their Legal and Economic Position* (Cambridge, Mass., 1931), appendix C.

[87] Glasscock, *Lay Subsidy*; see also M. W. Beresford, *Lay Subsidy and Poll Taxes, the Lay Subsidies, pt. i, 1290–1334; pt. ii, After 1334. The Poll Taxes of 1377, 1379 and 1381* (Canterbury, 1963), esp. pp. 1–18.

[88] Glasscock, *Lay Subsidy*, p. 202.

[89] The crown derived its highest income from Norfolk in 1334: £3,487 (*ibid.*, pp. 192–208). It obtained £1,439 from Suffolk (a nationwide fifth-ranking; *ibid.*, pp. 284–96), and relatively modest sums from Cambridgeshire and Huntingdonshire: £1,011 and £444 respectively. On 'industrial villages', see *ibid.*, p. 277.

[90] £24. Bearing in mind Beresford's and Finberg's list of East Anglian boroughs, others, i.e. Beccles, Bungay, Castle Rising, Clare, Exning, New Buckenham, Newmarket, Southwold and Sudbury were likewise taxed on the rural fifteenth; Beccles, Exning and Sudbury, paying well above £14 – more than for example Huntingdon (£12), Dunwich (£12) or Orford (£10). The leading East Anglian boroughs were assessed with £100 (Yarmouth), £94 (Norwich), £64 (Ipswich), £50 (Lynn) and £46 (Cambridge). See Brodt, *Städte ohne Mauern*, pp. 127–36.

disadvantages of urban status are most strikingly illustrated by the fact that during the remainder of the fourteenth century and for the whole of the following, no place in East Anglia received the new status of a town by charter.

Our next fairly comprehensive source is the poll tax returns, surviving in varying degrees from the taxes between 1377 and 1381. Some sectors of the East Anglian economy seem to have a history of fairly continuous prosperity in the fourteenth century, in particular in relation to the production of worsted. The customs accounts, although imperfect, indicate high exports of worsteds from Yarmouth. There had, however, been major changes in urban fortunes in the fourteenth century, above all attributable to the Black Death and successive outbreaks of the plague. The changes were particularly apparent in Norwich and in Yarmouth. In Norwich it looks as if the impact of the plague had led to the abandonment of several churches; in the case of St Catherine's (St Winwaloy's) the parish became almost completely uninhabited. A rent roll of city property in 1357 described many tenements and most shops and stalls in the market as ruinous and without tenants. In 1369 the size of the market was decreased to enlarge St Peter Mancroft's churchyard.[91] But Norwich recovered and by the end of the middle ages its population was probably higher than it had been before. The 1377 poll tax recorded 3,952 taxpayers, indicating a population of around 5,000. By 1524 it was probably around 10,000. In the case of Yarmouth it was a combination of war and plague which led to a decline of the town.[92] Plague probably reduced the town's population by a third; war brought piracy and disrupted trade, outweighing Yarmouth's advantages obtained from government contracts and supplying Berwick and Calais. Fifth among provincial towns in 1334, Yarmouth was seventeenth in 1377,[93] and ranked eighteenth in 1524.

[91] Campbell, 'Norwich', p. 16nn. 24–6.

[92] A. Saul, 'Great Yarmouth in the fourteenth century. A study in trade, politics and society' (PhD thesis, University of Oxford, 1975), pp. 259–69.

[93] With 1,941 recorded taxpayers.

· 22(e) ·

Northern towns

JENNIFER KERMODE

(i) THE NATURE OF THE REGION

THE PACE and pattern of urbanisation in northern England was more varied than the traditional image of an undeveloped backwater might suggest (Map 22.11). Certainly this is an area with a high proportion of upland over 500 feet (180m) and large tracts of uncultivated marginal land where economic activity was invariably measured lower than in other English regions. Yet, within a region divided north–south by the spine of the Pennines and east–west by the Lakeland massif and North Yorkshire Moors, the dominant characteristic of northern settlement history was its variety.

Both coasts are penetrated by navigable rivers draining large basins. The resultant landforms created different soil types which changed over comparatively short distances, to include thin sands and gravels, acid moorlands, estuarine fens, alluvial flood plains, the inland mosses of Lancashire and Cheshire and the well-drained eastern lowlands. The difficult terrain dictated land communications. These had been established by the Romans and survived for the most part as the only routes feasible: north–south on either side of the Pennines following lowland plains and valley routes (Eden–Lune), trans-Pennine across the south Pennines from Tadcaster to Chester *via* Manchester, north-west from upper Teesdale across Stainmore to the Solway, and west along Hadrian's wall.[1]

It is within this context that the history of northern towns must be seen. This was a sparsely populated region and towns were generally small: only four had 2,000 or more taxpayers in 1377 and only three were ranked in the top twenty in England by wealth in 1524–5. Urban settlements emerged earlier and more rapidly in the south of the region and east of the Pennines. Several

I would like to thank Sandra Mather for drawing Map 22.11.

[1] T. W. Freeman, H. B. Rogers and R. H. Kinvig, *Lancashire, Cheshire and the Isle of Man* (London, 1966), pp. 7–21, 31–3; N. J. Higham, *The Kingdom of Northumbria AD 350–1100* (Stroud, 1993), pp. 2–9.

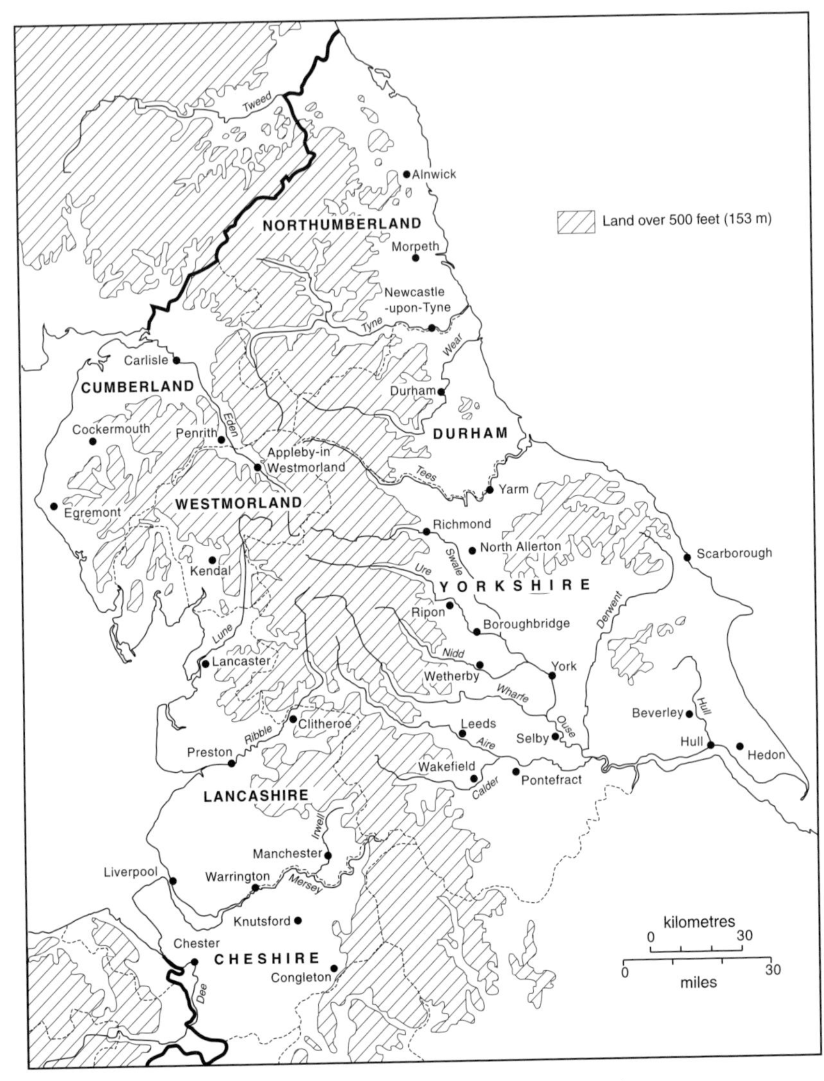

Map 22.11 Towns in northern England

administrative and economic networks emerged within the region, the most significant centring on Carlisle, Chester, Newcastle and York.

Northern towns were of many types and reflect the characteristics of frontier territory, with towns maintaining active defences against Vikings, Welsh and Scots, and serving as supply depots. Although there were important local differences, pastoral farming predominated throughout the region, with the largest towns commonly associated with livestock fairs and wool markets.

Mineral deposits, notably coal, iron ore and lead, as well as the salt in central Cheshire, became important elements in the region's growing economy. Rural mineral extraction generally affected towns indirectly, though Boroughbridge and Newcastle were exceptions.

The evidence for the early middle ages is uncertain since there is no Domesday survey for almost half the region. Distinguishing between recognisable towns and potential centres which failed to fledge is problematic. Places such as Hexham and Conisbrough, which combined religious and royal associations in the seventh century probably encouraged trade and might be regarded as displaying some urban qualities. There were other small, proto-urban centres such as Middlewich, but whose status and history nevertheless remain obscure. Together with York and Chester, there may have been twelve or so urbanising places in *c.* 900. Losses and gains had left the stock at about fifteen by *c.* 1086, but only York and Chester could claim to be fully fledged towns. By 1300, there were approximately 110 towns in the north, the majority emerging in the thirteenth century. By 1550, numbers had risen to about 140.

East of the Pennines, development was most intense in the twelfth to early thirteenth centuries, visible through the formal confirmation of markets and promotion of boroughs. Some fifty-seven places were advanced, compared with thirty west of the Pennines. Development in the west came later, during the fourteenth century, but many of those promotions failed. Perhaps because of the three Palatinates (Chester, Durham and Lancaster), and numerous, extensive baronies, the incidence of seigneurial sponsorship throughout the North was high, with only about a quarter of boroughs in receipt of royal charters. In many of the smaller towns, therefore, burgess participation in government was limited and capital resources were as likely to be financed by their lords as through the collective investment of merchants or burgesses. Another ingredient in northern government, the wardenships of the Marches, became an extension of distant royal government after Richard II's reign, until the Council of the North consolidated its authority under the Tudors.[2]

Scottish raiding was the real challenge to northern vitality. It disturbed and occasionally destroyed monastic wool production and cattle farms, as well as overrunning and capturing individual towns. The impact was mixed, and there is no doubt that, individually, Carlisle and Newcastle benefited from military investment. On the Welsh border, Chester was less often subject to raids, but was similarly advantaged.[3] Further pressure was put on marginal centres by natural disasters. Bad weather and sheep murrain of the early fourteenth century hit the

[2] J. A. Tuck, 'War and society in the medieval North', *NHist.*, 21 (1985), 48–9.

[3] H. E. Hallam, ed. *Ag.HEW*, vol. II (Cambridge, 1988), pp. 258–9; A. J. Pollard, *North-Eastern England during the Wars of the Roses* (Oxford, 1990), pp. 30–80; H. Summerson, *Medieval Carlisle* (Cumberland and Westmorland Antiq. and Arch. Soc. Extra Series, 25, Kendal, 1993), vol. I, pp. 395–8; Tuck, 'War and society', 43.

North badly and in the 1430s, plague, a series of severe winters and food shortages plunged much of the North-East into an economic recession.[4]

Distance from national arteries was most critical in the North-West, where settlements easily became isolated by natural physical barriers. It took nine days by road to Carlisle from London in 1514, two to three from Doncaster to Carlisle in 1536. The costs incurred in long-distance trade were discouraging, but sometimes poor quality wool could be worth exporting if other costs were avoided. In the 1390s, Richard de Redness, a Carlisle merchant, exported locally supplied wool through Hull at under half the regular customs rate. By the 1430s, the evidence of debts suggests occasional trade links between Carlisle and Coventry, York, Hull and London.[5] Political isolation occurred too: only four North-West towns were represented in parliaments in the 1280s and 1290s, compared to thirteen in the North-East. Thereafter Hull, Scarborough and York regularly returned MPs, Carlisle until *c.* 1450.[6]

From the mendicants' perspective, few northern places appeared inviting in the thirteenth century. Twenty-one northern towns were selected for friaries: two-thirds were established east of the Pennines. Chester, Newcastle and York were favoured with four or more, but thirteen other towns accommodated only a single friary.[7] Monastic orders had different priorities and even the smallest towns attracted them. Their investment in property created a network of connections across the region. Hexham, Holm Cultram, Lanercost, Melrose, St Bees and St Leonard's York all owned property in Carlisle; Holm Cultram, houses in Newcastle, Hartlepool and Boston; Birkenhead Priory, a warehouse in Liverpool; Vale Royal, houses in Chester.[8] Religious foundations generated a variety of cultural and commercial environments, which many northern towns, like Thirsk and Wigan, experienced at a remove because they had neither friary nor monastery. Hospitals were more common, endowed in most instances by the town's lord.

Soil type and location largely determined settlement in this region. Commerce flourished in the east with coastal and overseas trade into Europe as key factors, whereas trade in the west was limited to Irish Sea partners. The chronology and pattern of urbanisation was distinctively different in four sub-

[4] D. Hey, *Yorkshire from AD 1000* (London, 1986), p. 86; A. J. Pollard, 'The north-eastern economy and the agrarian crisis of 1438–40', *NHist.*, 25 (1989), 88–105; A. J. Winchester, 'Medieval Cockermouth', *Transactions of the Cumberland and Westmorland Antiquarian and Arch. Soc.*, 86 (1986), 112.

[5] E. Miller and J. Hatcher, *Medieval England: Towns, Commerce and Crafts, 1086–1348* (London, 1995), p. 244; Summerson, *Carlisle*, pp. 341, 419, 558.

[6] M. McKisack, *The Parliamentary Representation of the English Boroughs during the Middle Ages* (Oxford, 1932), pp. 7–11, 19; Summerson, *Carlisle*, p. 445.

[7] D. Knowles and R. N. Hadcock, *Medieval Religious Houses* (London, 1953), pp. 182–208.

[8] Summerson, *Carlisle*, pp. 75, 138–9, 558; *VCH*, Lancashire, IV, p. 9; *VCH*, Cheshire, V, (forthcoming).

regions, Cumbria, Cheshire and Lancashire south of the Lune, Northumbria and Yorkshire, and these will frame our discussion of urban history across the five northern counties.

(ii) CUMBRIA (CUMBERLAND, WESTMORLAND, NORTH LANCASHIRE)

Containing, as it does, the Lakeland massif and north Pennines, this region was both economically advantaged by its mineral deposits and disadvantaged by the sparsity of arable land. Coal and iron were exploited for local use, lead for sale beyond the region, often *via* Newcastle, and the silver supplied mints in Durham and York. Wool produced by religious houses attracted Italian buyers by the 1280s, and was supplying the expanding textile industry in Cockermouth, Egremont, Kendal and Penrith by the 1320s.[9]

Cumbria had the slowest rate of urbanisation of the northern regions. Even by 1550 there was only a handful of sizeable towns, Carlisle, Cockermouth, Kendal, Lancaster and Penrith. None came close to the major towns of the other northern regions in terms of size or wealth. Carlisle had 678 taxpayers in 1377 and a possible population in 1540 of a mere 1,500, yet in the context of a sparsely populated and difficult terrain, it was a success. It was the only place with pre-Conquest urban pretensions. William Rufus built a castle there in 1092, but there is no evidence of any urbanising settlements in the region before the late twelfth century. At that time several towns were promoted from baronial *capita* such as Appleby and Egremont; others, like Kendal and Penrith, from parochial centres. The siting of friaries suggests that by the 1230s, in addition to Carlisle, only Appleby, Lancaster and Penrith appeared ripe for development.[10]

Location was critical. Thriving towns like Appleby, Brough, Kendal and Penrith were located in valleys and therefore on major roads; Cockermouth, between the upland massif and the coastal plain. Keswick was at the confluence of three valleys and close by the lead deposits in the Derwent fells. Carlisle and Lancaster developed as river ports. Apart from Egremont, there was no successful town close to the sea. Several attempted borough promotions, Dalton, Flookburgh, Warton and Ulverston, were located on the coast, suggesting that Morecambe Bay and the Solway were important as trade routes, for fishing grounds and as sources of evaporated salt. Holm Cultram Abbey's three attempts to plant towns on the southern Solway shore in the early thirteenth century were washed away.[11]

[9] A. J. Winchester, *Landscape and Society in Medieval Cumbria* (Edinburgh, 1987), p. 117–20.
[10] Summerson, *Carlisle*, pp. 10–13, 512; Winchester, *Cumbria*, p. 126.
[11] M. Beresford, *New Towns of the Middle Ages* (London, 1967), pp. 415–16; Summerson, *Carlisle*, pp. 21–2; Winchester, *Cumbria*, p. 122.

Carlisle was the natural choice for a border outpost. It stood at the junction of two surviving Roman roads, and of three rivers, with access to the Solway Firth. Fortifications dominated royal attention, and military authority was complemented by the creation of the bishopric in 1133. Within fifty years, Carlisle had acquired a guild merchant, annual fair and two weekly markets with a trading monopoly over the neighbouring countryside. Early settlers, possibly from Lincolnshire, were soon joined by others from Ireland, Flanders and France. By 1231, the town had its own mayor and was held at farm.[12] During the next three centuries Carlisle developed its own modest textile, leather and metal industries, collected wool and became the redistribution centre for linen from Ireland, fish and salt from the Solway, leather and cloth from Cockermouth and Penrith. Despite embargoes against trade with the Scots, Carlisle continued to import cattle and horses from south-west Scotland, sending cloth, flour, leather and malt back. [13]

Between the 1190s and 1230s, economic stirrings were reflected in a flurry of seigneurial borough promotions and market charters throughout the region, some granted to settlements at early church sites like Kendal, Penrith and Ulverston. By 1300, maybe twelve boroughs had been created but most failed due to competition from better placed rivals. Egremont was successful and a typical seigneurial plantation. Head of the barony of Copeland, it was laid out at the foot of the Norman castle. Fullers, dyers and weavers were mentioned in its *c.* 1202 charter and tolls were levied on livestock, linen and woollen cloth, herrings, leather and iron. Cockermouth, another baronial *caput*, had corn and fulling mills, three smithies, a dyeworks and a population of possibly around 1,000 in *c.* 1270, exploiting its location between two dramatically different terrains.[14]

Lancaster is a rare example of a castle town in Cumbria, becoming the *caput* of Roger de Poitou's new honour when he built a castle there in 1102.[15] It was one of several mottes strung along the Lune valley, marking the defence in depth behind William Rufus' new frontier at Carlisle.[16] Charters of 1193 and 1199, and John's foundation of the hospital of St Leonard's, were intended to promote the town but industry and commerce were slow to develop.[17] The town remained

[12] Summerson, *Carlisle*, pp. 27, 32, 59, 62, 65, 89.

[13] Summerson, *Carlisle*, pp. 340, 345–50, 423; Winchester, *Cumbria*, p. 127.

[14] A. J. Ballard, ed., *British Borough Charters 1042–1216* (Cambridge, 1913), p. 160; Winchester, *Cumbria*, pp. 124–7; Winchester, 'Cockermouth', 109–28; J. Munby, 'Medieval Kendal: the first borough charter and its connexions', *Transactions of the Cumberland and Westmorland Antiquarian and Arch. Soc.*, 85 (1985), 95–114.

[15] D. Kenyon, *The Origins of Lancashire* (Manchester, 1991), p. 154; A. White, ed., *A History of Lancaster, 1193–1993* (Keele, 1993), pp. 18–20.

[16] M. Morris, ed., *The Archaeology of Greater Manchester*, vol. 1: *Medieval Manchester* (Manchester, 1983), p. 17.

[17] W. Farrer, ed., *Lancashire Inquests, Extents, and Feudal Aids* (Record Society of Lancashire and

small, despite acquiring a guild merchant and mayor. The creation of the county Palatine in 1351, for which Lancaster became the administrative headquarters, brought in business but the town was held back by a succession of disasters which made recovery difficult, including Scottish destruction in 1322 and 1389, and epidemics in 1349, 1423 and 1466.[18]

Devastation by the Scots was a phenomenon shared by the most northerly towns and was almost continuous after 1300. Carlisle's strategic location became a mixed blessing. It was occupied several times by the Scots, but the crown's periodic investment in the castle and walls generated employment: £126 was spent on repairs in 1391–4, £5,000 in 1541–2. As the headquarters for the wardens of the western March from Richard II's reign, Carlisle was drawn into gentry politics, its merchants thereby profiting as victuallers but also facing closely pressed tax demands. Some relief was gained when the fee-farm was reduced from £80 to £40 in 1461. The town's fortunes fluctuated until border politics achieved a relative stability in the late fifteenth century. By the early sixteenth century, Carlisle's markets were supplying most of north Cumberland and south-west Scotland, and French wine was traded into the town by merchants from Kirkcudbright and Wigtown. Lord Dacre was buying green ginger, peppers and comfits there in the 1520s. The population remained, however, fairly static.[19]

Many smaller towns shared Carlisle's roller-coaster experience, but destruction was not inevitably followed by recovery. Appleby, for example, barely survived as a town following the Scots' raid of 1322, and for several newer foundations, such attacks were too much. By 1500, only five or six Cumbrian places could claim urban status, with only Carlisle and Lancaster supporting a semblance of urban culture.[20]

(iii) SOUTH LANCASHIRE AND CHESHIRE

South of Lancaster and Lonsdale, high moorlands give way to flat landscape, bordered in the east by the Pennines and in the south and west by the Ellesmere moraine and Clwyd hills.[21] This was a mainly pastoral economy, though coal and salt had been part of the Romans' regional interests. Edward I's castle building generated an exceptional market for fuel during the 1280s and 1290s, but local demand remained low and there is no evidence of an active trade out of the region. Brine salt, on the other hand, was an important natural resource, extracted in central Cheshire from Roman times and shipped out through Chester.

Cheshire, 48, 1903), pp. 184, 187; 54 (1907), p. 23; 70 (1915), pp. 152–3; White, ed., *Lancaster*, pp. 33–7, 40. [18] White, ed., *Lancaster*, pp. 41–4.

[19] Summerson, *Carlisle*, pp. 394, 406–14, 448, 488, 549, 567.

[20] R. E. Glasscock, ed., *The Lay Subsidy of 1334* (London, 1975), p. 36; Winchester, *Cumbria*, pp. 127–9.

[21] Freeman, Rogers and Kinvig, *Lancashire, Cheshire and the Isle of Man*, pp. 10–12, 15–19, 27–9, 42.

A network of saltways developed, some following surviving Roman routes. Middlewich, Northwich and Wigan grew around Roman staging posts; Preston, Stockport and Warrington near Roman river crossings; Chester and Manchester had been Roman settlements.[22] Anglian settlers came late to this region and although there were centres of Christianity, there is little evidence of town life outside Chester. Of the three salt 'wics', Middlewich and Northwich were sites of continuing industrial significance and possibly urban characteristics; Middlewich becoming a major parochial and hundredal centre. Viking bases around the Irish Sea generated traffic between York, Chester and Dublin. Following the defeat of the Danes in 910, *burh* building across north Cheshire and south Lancashire created a network of fortresses, but only Manchester and Runcorn (Halton) emerged as potential towns and then not until the fourteenth century.

In 1086, burgesses were recorded only in Chester and Penwortham. Chester was already capital of a region which included adjacent North Wales, west Cheshire and the mid-Mersey valley. It is likely that Chester was partially occupied from at least the sixth century and St John's collegiate church was possibly founded in 689. By the end of the ninth century new building was underway and metal and earthenware were being manufactured for long-distance trade. Three of Chester's eventual nine parishes had formed before 910 and the city walls were extended south later in the century.[23]

Trade with Ireland was building up and Cheshire became a shire at about this time with Chester as its administrative centre, a role of greater importance following the creation of the Palatinate. The city had its own reeve and doomsmen. Moneyers were active there from the early tenth to mid-twelfth century. In 1092 St Werburgh's was founded anew as a Benedictine monastery and St John's was briefly elevated to cathedral status when Bishop Peter moved his seat from Lichfield to Chester in 1075. By 1066, there were some 564 *domus* in the city and suburbs, twenty-one occupied by clergy. By 1086, over 200 *domus* had been destroyed, perhaps due to the construction in 1070 of a castle on the site of the late Saxon fort.[24]

Chester had already achieved a level of urbanisation by 1086 that few other medieval English towns ever reached, yet it remained comparatively small and poor by national standards. It was the solitary example, west of the Pennines, of developments characteristic of larger medieval towns. In addition to St

[22] *Ibid.*, p. 33; J. Hatcher, *The History of the British Coal Industry*, vol. I: *Before 1700* (Oxford, 1993), p. 131; G. D. B. Jones, *Roman Manchester* (Altrincham, 1974), pp. 1–9; Morris, *Medieval Manchester*, pp. 2–5; *VCH*, Cheshire, I, p. 329.

[23] N. J. Alldridge, 'Aspects of the topography of early medieval Chester', *J of the Chester Arch. Soc.*, 64 (1981), 5–31; P. Carrington, *English Heritage Book of Chester* (London, 1994), pp. 50–64; *VCH*, Cheshire, I, pp. 104, 239, 241, 244, 249–58, 268–9.

[24] Carrington, *Chester*, pp. 64–5; *VCH*, Cheshire, V, (forthcoming); *ibid.*, III, pp. 261, 268–9.

Werburgh's, several religious houses, including three mendicant orders, settled there. The city achieved self-government and eventually independence as a county in 1506. Chester was the principal entrepôt for the North-West. Facing west and away from England's lucrative trades in wool and cloth, its trading partners were Ireland and the small ports on the Irish Sea coasts. Imports included yarn, cloth, fish, hides, cattle on the hoof and some wine *via* Bristol. Exports included salt, some cloth, but scarcely any wool. Trade began to pick up in the 1470s and Mediterranean goods arrived from Spain and Portugal. Imported wine and Spanish iron and return cargoes of hides and Lancashire cloth became the staples of its trade. More Cestrians began to invest in trade, replacing the earlier dominance of Dubliners. Even so, the city oligarchy remained a hybrid of country and mercantile interests.[25]

From time to time, defence needs boosted the city's economy, funding an unusual number of stone domestic buildings, possibly including the unique Rows. These continuous, first-floor shopping galleries, were built over street-level undercrofts on the four central streets. A fire in 1278, and the economic boom generated by Edward I's conquest of North Wales, may have given impetus to their development.[26] Conversely, as a border town Chester was vulnerable to depredation, the most severe following an attack by Owain Glyndŵr's rebels.[27] Craft guilds were slow to form. There were some thirty by 1499/1500 and over 170 different occupations recorded between *c.* 1350–*c.* 1480, including such threshold occupations as apothecaries and bookbinders. Chester workers finished cloth of Irish and Welsh manufacture, as well as producing their own from imported yarns. Local butchers, tanners and glovers processed Irish hides and skins before selling them on to London or overseas.[28]

In the north of the region six burgages recorded at Penwortham in 1066 suggest Anglian antecedents but even this early advantage could not prevent the rise of the town of Preston on the opposite bank of the Ribble. Penwortham was sited at an important nodal point, focused on the tidal limit of the Ribble and its confluence with the Darwen, and became the *caput* of a Norman barony. Political readjustments soon downgraded the older site to the advantage of its rival. Preston had served as the meeting place between north and south of Lancashire from at least the eleventh century. A royal borough from 1079 and with river access to the sea, Preston flourished as entrepôt between three distinctive

[25] J. Kermode, 'The trade of late medieval Chester, 1500–50', in R. H. Britnell and J. Hatcher, eds., *Progress and Problems in Medieval England* (Cambridge, 1996), pp. 286–306; *VCH*, Cheshire, v, forthcoming. [26] Carrington, *Chester*, pp. 77–8.

[27] Jane Laughton, 'Aspects of the social and economic history of late medieval Chester 1350–*c.*1500' (PhD thesis, University of Cambridge, 1993); K. P. Wilson, 'The port of Chester in the fifteenth century', *Transactions of the Hist. Soc. of Lancashire and Cheshire*, 117 (1965), 1–16.

[28] BL Harl. MS 2104, f. 4.; Kermode, 'Chester trade', pp. 301–4; Laughton, 'Aspects of Chester', ch. 4.

regions.[29] It had the only functioning guild merchant in the region, apart from Chester's, though of a unique type in that 55 per cent of its members in 1415 were leather workers. Its status and economy were boosted when the Palatinate chancery was based there from the fifteenth century, a recognition of its dominance of central and west Lancashire.[30]

There was only one successful castle town south of the Lune: Clitheroe. This is assumed to be Roger of Poitou's castle, built to protect the newly created barony and guarding the western approaches to the Aire Gap. Urban development must be assumed because there was a fair in 1205, and by 1258, sixty-six burgages lined the single market street.[31]

Market and borough promotions came relatively late to this region. Only Liverpool, Preston and Frodsham can claim chartered privileges dating from between 1179 to 1209. Low densities of population fostered petty boroughs and market towns: maybe forty in Lancashire south of the river Lune, and about twenty-four in Cheshire, not including Flint. The majority were promoted between 1260 and 1300, with a steady trickle continuing through the fourteenth century. The majority of these 'boroughs' failed to develop: for example, Ormskirk, sponsored by Burscough Priory in 1286, was administered as a manor in 1524.[32]

Lordship weighed heavily. In Cheshire there were no alternative noble patrons to the earls of Chester. With the creation of the earldom sometime in the eleventh century, it became the practice of successive earls to exploit the county for their own profit, farming estates to royal servants on short-term leases. When the earl was the king, the issues from the county were more easily diverted to pay military costs, especially in Wales from 1272.[33] North of the Mersey, the impact of the duchy and Palatinate of Lancaster were perhaps less exploitative, but with the exception of Liverpool and Wigan, which became royal boroughs in 1207 and 1246 respectively, all the other putative boroughs in this region were seigneurial.[34]

[29] Kenyon, *Lancashire*, pp. 160, 163; Morris, *Medieval Manchester*, p. 31; H. B. Rodgers, 'Preston: the interrelations of town and region' (MA thesis, University of Manchester, 1950), pp. 10, 42–52, 107–8.

[30] A. Crosby, *The History of Preston Guild: 800 Years of England's Greatest Carnival* (Preston, 1991), p. 25; R. Somerville, *History of the Duchy of Lancaster*, vol. I: *1265–1603* (London, 1953).

[31] Beresford, *New Towns*, p. 460; *31st Report Dep. Keeper PRO*, Appendix, p. 6; J. Caley and W. Illingworth, *Placita de Quo Warranto* (London, 1818), p. 382.

[32] *PP 1888 HC LIII First Report of the Royal Commission on Market Rights*; M. W. Beresford and H. P. R. Finberg, *English Medieval Boroughs* (Newton Abbot, 1973), pp. 73–6, 131–5; G. H. Tupling, 'An alphabetical list of markets and fairs of Lancashire recorded before the year 1701', *Transactions of the Antiq.Soc. Lancashire and Cheshire*, 51 (1936), 86–110.

[33] A. E. Currie, 'The demesne of the county Palatine of Chester in the early fifteenth century' (MA thesis, University of Manchester, 1977), pp. 284 *et seq.*; H. J. Hewitt, *Medieval Cheshire* (Chetham Society, new series, 88, 1929), p. 4.

[34] Beresford and Finberg, *English Medieval Boroughs*, pp. 131–5.

It may be that this high incidence of seigneurial control was one of the factors limiting urban growth west of the Pennines, combined with a sluggish regional economy. Two centres with Roman antecedents, Manchester and Warrington, continued to develop urban features, but their progress to self-government was blocked by their lords. In Warrington, for instance, the Botiller family rescinded the chartered freedoms they had granted in 1292, by taking back the town's government into their manorial court in 1300. Even so, Warrington grew into an important market town. The commodities paying tolls at its bridge in 1310 came from distant as well as local suppliers and included goats, pigs, fleeces, fish, nails, horseshoes, brass and copper, Spanish iron and wine *en route* from Chester to Macclesfield and south Yorkshire perhaps, Breton woad to the textile centres in and around Manchester.[35]

However, seigneurial parsimony was only one factor affecting urban fortunes and in the case of Liverpool, even such a powerful sponsor as the king had difficulty overcoming the disadvantages of poor location. When King John created a new borough in 1207, he was seeking an independent port of embarkation to Ireland, an alternative to the earl of Chester's port at Chester. Liverpool was one of the few planned towns in the North-West, and was laid out on a block of land alongside a tidal creek: *le pool*. Perhaps as many as 168 burgages were created in the new grid of seven streets, each with holdings in the town fields. John invested heavily in Liverpool, giving it extensive privileges: a market, annual fair, possibly a mill and a chapel.[36]

His investment paid off, though slowly. The presence of several brewers in 1324 and two goldsmiths in 1346 suggests Liverpool was already outpacing regional competitors in specialist services. In 1346, there were 196 burgess householders, a sizeable population, no doubt reduced by plague in 1360. By 1379 there were eighty-six taxpayers, of whom one third were peasant farmers and the remainder were tradesmen.[37] Port services probably accounted for the town's resilience as communications into the hinterland improved. There were three ferries across the Mersey by the early 1300s, with inns at Birkenhead for waiting passengers. By the late fifteenth century, Liverpool was well positioned to compete with Chester just when south-east Lancashire's textile industry took off. By the 1560s Liverpool had taken over Irish yarn imports and cloth.[38]

Urban development south of the Mersey reflected the geological differences between east and west Cheshire. Fertile west Cheshire was dominated by the city of Chester but supported no other towns of significance. East Cheshire was traditionally less agriculturally productive but, serving the Pennines uplands as well,

[35] W. Beamont, *The Annals of the Lords of Warrington* (Manchester, 1872), pp. 136–9; *VCH*, Lancashire, III, pp. 262–3.

[36] Beresford, *New Towns*, p. 461; Kenyon, *Lancashire*, pp. 174–5.

[37] PRO, E179/130/24, 28; *VCH*, Lancashire, IV, pp. 8–9.

[38] Kermode, 'Chester trade', pp. 306–7; *VCH*, Lancashire, IV, pp. 8–9.

had sufficient vitality for small towns to prosper. The Cheshire boroughs of Congleton, Knutsford, Macclesfield and Stockport ringed the eastern border of the Cheshire plain. Their urban life began to take shape in the late thirteenth century, albeit with intrusive seigneurial support which allowed only limited participation in borough government. However, they grew into small market towns, each with distinguishing concentrations of industry by the fifteenth century: Congleton and Stockport had shoemakers and glovers, Knutsford, cutlers and glovers.[39]

In central Cheshire's salt-producing area, brine boiling concentrated around Middlewich, Nantwich and Northwich. Probably only Nantwich could claim urban status before the fifteenth century. Urbanisation associated with an industrial complex was rare as was the extent of external control.[40] Combermere Abbey owned one quarter of Nantwich, and the remainder became part of the earldom of Chester. Many of the salthouses were owned or leased by outsiders: Wenlock Priory, Vale Royal, Basingwerk, Chester citizens and local gentry. By the early fifteenth century, the presence of a goldsmith, leather and clothing craftsmen suggests a degree of industrial and commercial specialisation developing quite apart from salt.[41]

By the early sixteenth century, this remained a region of small towns. Estimates suggest that even the larger towns had populations of only *c.* 600–1,000. Chester stood alone with a population of between 3,500 and 4,000.

East of the Pennine ridge the basins of the rivers Tyne, Tees and Ouse delineate three sub-regions. None was autonomous, but whereas there was a recognisable focus in the north, on Durham then Newcastle, and in the south on York, there was no obvious central place in the Tees valley.[42] Teesdale provided access over the Pennines to Cumbria, outlets for produce from North Yorkshire and south Durham, customers for imports through Hull and Newcastle. At least nine centres emerged along both banks, developing associations to the north and south through trade, political expediency and administrative obligations, but only Barnard Castle, Darlington, Richmond and Yarm developed into recognisable towns. For the convenience of the present discussion, the Teesside towns will be shared between north and south.

[39] PRO, CHES 25/11, 12; 29/123, 125, 129, 130; Miller and Hatcher, *Medieval England: Towns, Commerce and Crafts*, pp. 307, 318.

[40] D. A. Hinton, *Archaeology, Economy and Society* (London, 1990), p. 142.

[41] M. Bennett, *Community, Class and Careerism: Cheshire and Lancashire Society in the Age of Sir Gawain and the Green Knight* (Cambridge, 1983), p. 116; Hewitt, *Medieval Cheshire*, pp. 109–11, 117; J. Oxley, 'Nantwich: an eleventh-century salt town and its origins', *Transactions of the Hist. Soc. of Lancashire and Cheshire*, 131 (1981), 1–19.

[42] A. J. Pollard, 'All maks and manders: the local history of the Tees valley in the later middle ages', *Cleveland History*, 65 (1994), 17–19, 25–6.

(iv) NORTHUMBRIA (NORTHUMBERLAND AND DURHAM)

At first sight, the River Tees appears to mark the end of arable lowland with the uplands of the Pennines and Cheviots to the west and north. However, north of the Tees, the long coastal plain, Glendale and the dales of the rivers Coquet, Rede, Tees, Tyne and Tweed create a patchwork of *pays*. Where the land is exposed to bitter north-east weather, the growing season is short and in the middle ages, favoured barley and oats, though some wheat was grown. This was a predominantly pastoral region, producing cattle for distant as well as local consumption, and a short staple wool of such poor quality that, although it found markets overseas, was periodically exempted from full export duties.[43]

Rich deposits of coal, lead and iron generated a scatter of industrial districts away from towns.[44] Coal became the region's main source of income: the deposits were exceptionally thick and easy to mine, and the growing demand from London and towns as far away as Exeter could be supplied by water.[45] Lead was worked from the late twelfth to early thirteenth century when many mines were abandoned. Some were re-established in the 1370s and others the following century. Iron was found in Weardale and a bloomery was smelting there in the fifteenth century. Limestone, marble, millstone and slate were quarried in east County Durham, again in a rural setting.[46]

Given such a variety of resources and richness of industrial material, it is perhaps surprising that even by 1550 there were few sizeable towns north of the Tees. In 1066, apart from the possibility of Durham, there were no towns north of the Tees but within two centuries the region had been transformed by the development of village markets, small towns and the rise of Newcastle. A castle was begun in 1080 on an empty site on the north bank of the Tyne, where the Roman *Pons Aelius* had stood. Its medieval successor used the same crossing point, infringing the bishop of Durham's liberty on the south bank and fuelling a continuous complaint finally resolved in the bishops' favour in 1416.[47]

Newcastle was a conspicuously successful foundation. Within a generation, a town and port grew up at a speed matched and facilitated by its acquisition in Henry I's reign of burghal privileges, the 'Laws of Newcastle'. By then, Newcastle's burgesses were claiming a monopoly within the town and its hinterland, over

[43] *Rotuli Parliamentorum* (Record Commission, 1783), vol. IV, pp. 250–1, V, p. 503; R. Newton, *The Northumberland Landscape* (London, 1972), pp. 22–7; J. F. Wade, 'The overseas trade of Newcastle-upon-Tyne in the late middle ages', *NHist.*, 30 (1994), 43.

[44] R. Welford, *A History of Newcastle and Gateshead in the Fourteenth and Fifteenth Centuries* (London and Newcastle, 1884), pp. 78, 86.

[45] E. Miller, ed., *Ag.HEW*, vol. III (Cambridge, 1991), p. 356; Hatcher, *Coal Industry*, pp. 70–3; M. Kowaleski, *Local Markets and Regional Trade in Medieval Exeter* (Cambridge, 1995), p. 239.

[46] *Ag.HEW*, III (1991), p. 356; Hatcher, *Coal Industry*, pp. 70–3; M. Kowaleski, *Local Markets and Regional Trade in Medieval Exeter* (Cambridge, 1995), p. 239.

[47] Beresford, *New Towns*, pp. 432–3; Welford, *Newcastle and Gateshead*, pp. 200, 359.

buying wool and hides, and making, dyeing and retailing cloth. Coal was important by 1214, when John finally granted the town independence at a farm of £100, because, he was advised, the town's income was so 'increased with coal'. By 1200 Newcastle had four churches, a bridge chapel, a Benedictine nunnery and a hospital.[48] Thereafter it prospered as a port, despite being 9 miles (15 km) upriver from the sea. Potential rivals, North and South Shields, planted at the river mouth in the early thirteenth century by the priors of Tynemouth and Durham respectively, were eclipsed.

The town invested in new quays, and by the 1280s may have been exporting over 15,000 hides annually, a direct product from the hinterland vaccaries of religious and lay estates.[49] Wool, albeit of mixed quality, was Newcastle's major international commodity and, in 1275, Newcastle became a licensed wool port, a home staple in 1326 and, in 1353, head customs port for the coast between Berwick and Scarborough. Trade brought Italians into the town in the 1280s, Hugh Gerardino of Lucca marrying a local widow and settling there to trade in wool and hides. By 1304–9, Newcastle accounted for 3 per cent – 5 per cent of England's overseas wool and wine trade. Later trade diversified into wine, woad, lead and millstones.[50]

Coal remained basic to Newcastle's wealth. Mining was probably minimally affected by Scottish raids, allowing the town to prosper during periods of hostilities. London was already a major customer by 1300, soon joined by most major east coast ports.[51] Newcastle won a crucial victory in 1350, when Edward III granted the burgesses extraction rights in common lands disputed with Tynemouth Priory.[52] A wealthy elite emerged, comprising merchants, local gentry, royal officials, even fullers. In 1311, they could afford to lend Edward II over £633, and in the 1330s, Newcastle merchants were making loans to Scottish earls: Angus and Athol.[53] By 1334, Newcastle was rated fourth in the kingdom, just below York, and with maybe 80 per cent or more of York's taxable wealth. By 1377, there were 2,647 taxpayers listed in Newcastle and by 1524, Newcastle may still have ranked fourth, and with at least twice York's assessed wealth.

Newcastle, like Carlisle, was strategically important. A mint was set up in 1249 and walls begun in 1265, their maintenance generating continuous employment.

[48] V. J. Brand, *The History and Antiquity of Newcastle upon Tyne* (London, 1789), vol. I, pp. 67–85, 425–9; E. Miller, 'Rulers of thirteenth century towns: the cases of York and Newcastle upon Tyne', in P. R. Coss and S. D. Lloyd, eds., *Thirteenth-Century England*, vol. I (Woodbridge, 1986), p. 129; Newton, *Northumberland*, p. 166.

[49] C. O'Brien *et al.*, 'Excavation at Newcastle quays: the crown court site', *Archaeologia Aeliana*, 5th series 17 (1989), 141; Welford, *Newcastle and Gateshead*, pp. 316–18.

[50] C. M. Fraser, 'The pattern of trade in the North-East of England, 1266–1350', *NHist.*, 4 (1969), 56–8; T. H. Lloyd, *The English Wool Trade in the Middle Ages* (Cambridge, 1977), pp. 54, 68–9.

[51] J. B. Blake,'The medieval coal trade of North-East England', *NHist.*, 2 (1967), 1–26; Miller and Hatcher, *Medieval England*, p. 147.

[52] Wade, 'Overseas trade', p. 40.

[53] Tuck, 'War and Society', 39; Welford, *Newcastle and Gateshead*, p. 21.

From the 1280s, the Scottish wars made Newcastle a forward military base, frequently visited by the king or his household. The king's wagons and carts were kept in Newcastle in the 1320s. Berwick and the Scottish castles were supplied from Newcastle with everything from coal to corn mills. Commandeered ships were commissioned in the port, and local merchants supplied victuals as well as trans-shipping food from as far afield as Canterbury.[54]

No other North-East town rivalled Newcastle, but its growth should not obscure other developments. Between 1100 and 1250, maybe thirty-six potential towns were acknowledged in Northumberland and County Durham. Smaller towns developed close to sites of earlier Anglian centres, or were planted at the mouths of major rivers or upstream at major crossings. The Rivers Tyne and South Tyne attracted at least six urban promotions. There may have been some proto-urban development at the former royal vills of Bamburgh, Corbridge, Newburn-on-Tyne, Rothbury and Warkworth, and the Anglian monastic settlement at Hexham, all of which re-emerged as town sites soon after the Conquest. But, in the event, urban life soon faded at Newburn, and was very limited at Bamburgh and Rothbury.[55]

Baronial castles probably initiated urbanisation at Alnwick, Bamburgh, Mitford, Morpeth, Norham and Warkworth.[56] Additional new towns were created as outports: at Warenmouth for Bamburgh and at Alnmouth for Alnwick. The former failed but Alnmouth had some success until it was destroyed by the Scots in 1336. Alnwick became the regional market for the north of Northumberland. It did rather better than most small market towns in that it achieved several important borough attributes: burgage tenure, a borough court and seal and probably a guild merchant. By *c.* 1300 cloth was manufactured there and, soon after, the town acquired new lords when the Percy family made the castle its principal seat. At Morpeth the castle was built to guard a ford across the Wansbeck, possibly in 1090. The town developed quickly, by 1138, but was on the opposite bank. One of England's earliest bridges replaced the ford in the early thirteenth century to be used by the re-routed main road north. As a consequence, nearby Mitford failed but Morpeth flourished to become the main market town for central Northumberland. Its outport, Newbiggin, had some modest success as a small port, acquiring a fair in 1204, a licence to sell sea coal, and boasting exotic spices, almonds and figs for sale in its market.[57]

[54] Welford, *Newcastle and Gateshead*, pp. 3, 18–19, 48, 56, 62, 86, 91, 102–3, 109.

[55] R. H. Britnell, 'Boroughs, markets and trade in northern England, 1000–1216', in Britnell and Hatcher, eds., *Progress and Problems*, pp. 46–67; Newton, *Northumberland*, pp. 85–92, 144–67.

[56] C. Hunter Blair, 'The early castles of Northumberland', *Archaeologia Aeliana*, 4th series, 22 (1944), 116–68.

[57] E. Bateson *et al.*, eds., *A History of Northumberland* (Newcastle, 1893–1940), vol. III, p. 31, vol. V, pp. 252, 350, 456; Beresford, *New Towns*, pp. 470–5; Fraser, 'Pattern of trade', 47; Newton, *Northumberland*, pp. 147–8; G. Tate, *The History of the Borough, Castle, and Barony of Alnwick* (Alnwick, 1866–9), vol. I, *passim*.

One of the curiosities of this region was the enthusiasm with which clerics created boroughs; another was the struggle for Durham itself to coalesce into a single urban centre. Hugh du Puiset, bishop of Durham, created five or six boroughs in the mid-twelfth century, the prior of Durham two and the prior of Tynemouth one. Only Norham, in Tweedsdale, quickly established itself as a market town. Durham comprised six separate areas, five of which might be regarded as boroughs subject to at least two different seigneurs: the prior and the bishop. Formal identity was defined in terms of lords and not the 'town' of Durham, and by the fifteenth century, life was dominated by the officials, clerks and notaries of the prior and bishop. The single market place served all the residents, encouraging a semblance of urbanity. Street names reflect the clustering of different occupations, mainly basic services, but a weaving industry had developed by the fifteenth century and a variety of skilled crafts surfaced from time to time between 1250 and 1500, reflecting the highly specialised demands of rich clerics and county families. Not every medieval town could boast an apothecary or scabbard maker.[58]

None the less, Durham retained a hybrid quality not uncommon in medieval towns. Townsfolk were still engaged in seasonal agriculture after 1500. There were six corn mills reflecting the multiplicity of lordship, and two fulling mills, unused for most of the fifteenth century. Durham was one of the northern towns where craft guilds formed, but perhaps as much in response to the needs of the Corpus Christi procession as through economic dynamism. The Corpus Christi guild, responsible for the play cycle and procession, was refounded in 1437.[59]

(v) YORKSHIRE

The vast plain of the Vale of York dominated the centre of the county with its subsidiary, the Vale of Pickering, running between the bleak moors and wolds. There was coal and ironstone in South Yorkshire, lead in the Pennine dales and large deposits of iron in Eskdale in the North York Moors, exploited by the canons of Guisborough from the thirteenth century. The contiguity of distinctively different landforms and resources determined much of the eventual urban pattern. Towns sprang up along the edge of the uplands: the River Ouse and its many tributaries provided alternative sites, the lower reaches of the Ouse, in particular, attracting urban promotions.[60]

Yorkshire was already populous by 1066, when there were over 1,830 settlements. East Yorkshire was close to being fully exploited and was one of the wealthiest areas in the country. However, there is little evidence of urban life except in York, and perhaps Dadsley (Tickhill). A Norman motte built at

[58] M. Bonney, *Lordship and the Urban Community* (Cambridge, 1990), pp. 41–9, 55–6, 154.
[59] *Ibid.*, pp. 183–4, 191. [60] Hey, *Yorkshire*, pp. 7–9; Pollard, *North-Eastern England*, p. 38.

Doncaster, where the strategic river crossing had been protected by an Anglo-Saxon *burh*, presaged urbanisation, but the town emerged much later.[61]

York had endured a succession of occupation from its Roman inception. Its location commanding the fertile Vale of York, the 'great north road', and extensive Ouse river system, were crucial to its continuing importance, confirmed by its adoption by Northumbrian and then Scandinavian kings. The minster occupied a site within the Roman forum, but the Vikings shifted the commercial focus outside, to their industrial workshops in Coppergate, Fossgate and Ousegate on the banks of the River Foss. Micklegate, the major road entering the city from the south, moved east and away from its earlier Roman alignment, fixing the crossing at the present site of the Ouse Bridge.[62]

By *c.* 980, York was a densely populated city, enriched through Scandinavian trade and enjoying advantages as the centre of a diocese, established in 625, which stretched across the Pennines and up to the Scottish border. Metropolitan dignity had come to York in 735 and thereafter, as the seat of the archbishop, the city became unquestionably the capital of the North. By 1065, York contained at least fourteen churches and 1,600–1,800 houses and, like many other settlements in the North, was on the verge of major change.[63]

Following the upheaval of rebellion and its repression by William's forces, large new honours like Pontefract, Richmond and Skipton were created with castles built to consolidate the conquest. York had two. Strategic considerations sited many of these baronial and royal castles along the edge of the uplands and at river crossings, giving them potential advantages in communications and as centres for exchange between pastoral and arable *pays*. These castles stimulated the development of towns: at least ten in the North Riding, and seven in the West Riding. East Riding towns remained exceptional in having no major castles. The 'castle towns' which prospered were invariably promoted to borough status irrespective of the survival of the castle: in the North Riding, Helmsley, Kirkbymoorside, Malton, Pickering, Richmond, Scarborough and Thirsk by 1200, Northallerton by 1298; in the West Riding, Knaresborough, Pontefract and Tickhill by 1200, Harewood, Sheffield and Skipton by 1300.[64]

Pontefract is a good example of a successful castle town, laid out in the shadow of the Norman castle built by Ilbert de Lacy to guard the Aire Gap. The castle was one of the largest in the West Riding, dominating the Vale of York and dwarfing Pontefract. The town was made the head of a deanery, a profitable extension of its functions. It flourished to such an extent that, as the scale of

[61] M. Harvey, 'Planned field systems in eastern Yorkshire: some thoughts on their origin', *Agricultural History Review*, 31 (1983), 91–103; H. C. Darby and I. S. Maxwell, *The Domesday Geography of Northern England* (Cambridge, 1962), pp. 7, 92, 170.

[62] R. A. Hall, *English Heritage Book of York* (London, 1996), pp. 27–37.

[63] D. M. Palliser, *Domesday York* (Borthwick Paper, 78, York, 1990); *VCH*, City of York, pp. 2–25, 365.

[64] Beresford and Finberg, *English Medieval Boroughs*, pp. 157–92.

commerce increased, the original market place shrank under the encroachment of streets designated to the sale of different commodities. By the 1270s, it was a primary wool market. In 1334, it was not assessed as a borough, but at £18 was the highest rated centre in the riding, with more skilled craftsmen and merchants than any other West Riding town.[65] By 1377, Pontefract had 1,085 taxpayers.

Administration was an effective force in urban growth, often generating a livelihood for a town in an otherwise weak economy. Skipton Castle, up against the Lancashire border, was headquarters for the administration of a large forest area and venue for the honour courts of the barony. A lot of business was generated for the town, which, although developing as an important market and textile finishing centre, retained a strongly unskilled element. In 1379, Skipton taxpayers included seventy-nine labourers, forty-eight traders and craftsmen. Of these thirteen worked in textiles, including a Flemish weaver and his son.[66]

Towns grew through other associations. The Benedictine abbey at Selby was founded in 1069 and soon transformed the existing village by investing in staithes and a market place. Whitby expanded under the patronage of its Benedictine abbey, Bridlington benefited from its Augustinian priory, while Beverley and Ripon grew around minster churches, under the lordship of the archbishop of York. Beverley had the advantage of pilgrims attracted to St John's shrine, and, by the 1120s, had become a borough with its own hansehus, had an annual fair, and, by the end of the century, was manufacturing its distinctive cloth for export.[67]

The absence of fortifications in many East Yorkshire towns suggests that their primary function was trade. Scarborough had had a castle and walls since *c.* 1158, but its later history as a minor international port suggests that trade and fishing soon became dominant. Hedon was planned as a port by the earl of Aumale, lord of Holderness. His new town was begun soon after 1138, and by *c.* 1140 was used by St Leonard's Hospital, York, for collecting corn. In 1202, Hedon purchased the right to trade in dyed cloths and by 1203–4 was thriving as the main port for the produce of Holderness, rating ahead of Yarmouth in a tax on merchant property. It had two weekly markets and two annual fairs. By the early thirteenth century, this prosperous small town had three churches and generated sufficient profits to invest in a new haven for ships.

Late in the thirteenth century, Hedon was one of a half dozen primary centres for wool collection and export in East Yorkshire. Its prosperity was short-lived. Hull began to grow and Hedon's access to the sea was *via* a small creek of the Humber, susceptible to silting. Oversea trade diminished and the town was thrown back on to a mixture of manufacturing, and its tile and lime kilns. In 1377

[65] Glasscock, ed., *Lay Subsidy*, p. 390; Lloyd, *Wool Trade*, p. 64.

[66] [No editor], 'The rolls of the collectors in the West Riding of the lay subsidy', *Yorkshire Arch. J*, 7 (1882), p. 151.

[67] *VCH*, Yorkshire: East Riding, v, pp. 19, 34, 39.

there were 482 taxpayers in Hedon, perhaps a concentration of fullers, and certainly brewers', butchers' and shoemakers guilds in the early fifteenth century.[68]

Other small port towns collapsed under the shadow of precocious neighbours. Competition and risk were integral to the process of urban promotions and development and speculative investment reached a peak in Yorkshire in the late twelfth and early thirteenth centuries. For instance, Maurice Paynell grafted his new town of Leeds on to the Anglo-Scandinavian settlement at Kirkgate in 1207 and around the same time, St John's Priory at Pontefract was laying out its new town, Barnsley, to take advantage of traffic on several cross-country routes including the saltway from Cheshire. To these commercial promotions can be added such towns as Wakefield, a droving centre for animals in from the Calder valley vaccaries, which flourished and became an influential industrial centre by the 1330s. Bawtry was another foundation of *c.* 1200, a port on the River Don for Derbyshire lead and mill-stones, and wool in the 1290s. The planners diverted the Roman road from its original course, into the large rectangular market at the centre of their new town's grid street pattern.[69]

Success was not guaranteed. Compared with the majority of the older 'castle towns', where large market places consolidated the shift from purely administrative functions, many speculative promotions failed. Several new towns, promoted along the banks of the Rivers Ouse and Humber, by abbots of St Mary's and archbishops of York, failed due to the spectacular success of Edward I's sponsorship of Hull. Edward purchased Wyke upon Hull in 1293, enlarged the quay, and improved the roads from York, Beverley and Hessle. He extended the duration of the markets and fairs, built a ditch around the town and in 1297 designated Hull as one of the nine English ports through which wool and leather could be traded. Hull was granted borough status in 1299. Wyke was already the sixth port in the kingdom by 1203–5 and after Edward's investment in his renamed Kingston-upon-Hull, expansion accelerated making it one of the most successful 'new towns' in England. Former competitors, Scarborough, Hedon and Patrington, had to fall back on fishing and coastal shipping. Ravenser Odd was washed away: a dramatic victim of the tidal changes attacking much of Holderness and the north Lincolnshire coast.[70]

By 1300 there were probably about forty towns in Yorkshire. Thereafter there were no new promotions, although several smaller centres grew and acquired new privileges. By 1334, it was clear that the areas which emerged relatively unscathed from the crises of the 1310s were around York, Beverley, Hull and Scarborough in East Yorkshire, and Doncaster and Pontefract in the South. Of

[68] Lloyd, *Wool Trade*, p. 64; *VCH*, Yorkshire: East Riding, v, pp. 173–9.

[69] Beresford, *New Towns*, p. 524; D. Hey, *The Making of South Yorkshire* (Ashbourne, 1979), p. 58; Hey, *Yorkshire*, p. 43; Lloyd, *English Wool Trade*, p. 64.

[70] Beresford, *New Towns*, pp. 509–16, 521–2; Hey, *Yorkshire*, pp. 46–7; *VCH*, Yorkshire: East Riding, I, pp. 11–21.

the eighty Yorkshire communities assessed at £4 and more, sixty were in the West Riding, twelve in the East and only eight in the North.[71] Even allowing for the differences in geographical size, this imbalance between the three Ridings marked a trend which climaxed in the emergence of the south Pennine textile industry as a major force behind England's Industrial Revolution.

Nationally, only the four East Yorkshire towns were rated in the top forty, but their positions were not impregnable, and a combination of natural disasters, pestilence, domestic economic shifts, and changes in international markets, challenged their regional dominance. The Black Death killed maybe 40–5 per cent of the rural population of Yorkshire, more in the crowded towns. Pestilence returned during the 1360s and 1370s but the evidence of the poll taxes suggests that the recovery of many towns was at the expense of rural communities, probably, in the same process, increasing women's access to urban employment. By 1377, around thirty places in Yorkshire had over 300 taxpayers. The four East Yorkshire towns and Pontefract were credited with over 1,000, Doncaster with 800, Hull's non-urban neighbour, Cottingham with 767, Selby, Tickhill, Whitby and probably Ripon ranged from 580 to 680, and the remaining twenty smaller towns with 300–600 taxpayers.[72] All the smaller towns were in the North Riding. The relative prosperity of York, Beverley and Scarborough created opportunities, fuelling the struggle between factions ambitious for political power in the risings of 1381.[73]

Northallerton was a small town with a population of some 372 taxpayers by 1377 and was one of a dozen or so market centres which maintained a modest level of exchange within the North Yorkshire, Teesside, region. A town by 1197, Northallerton's position on the main north road traversed by Edward I on his way to Scotland might explain why it was granted representation in parliament in 1298. The privilege was not repeated. From time to time, textile finishing became prominent: in 1301, a fuller and two dyers (one a woman) paid taxes, and in the 1390s, Northallerton men were paying ulnage on cloth of unspecified origin. Finishing remained a small but persistent element in Northallerton's economy: shearmen and dyers were still selling their skills to local rural producers in the 1490s, but the town itself was in the doldrums until the 1540s. A regionally important livestock fair developed there before 1555.[74]

Perhaps more critical for Yorkshire towns, though, was the restructuring of the national economy from wool to cloth production. York weavers had already

[71] Glasscock, ed., *Lay Subsidy*, pp. 356–95.

[72] R. B. Dobson, 'Yorkshire towns in the late fourteenth century', in *The Thoresby Miscellany*, 18 (Publications of the Thoresby Society, 59, 1986), pp. 1–21; P. J. P. Goldberg, 'Female labour, service and marriage in the late medieval urban North', *NHist.*, 22 (1986), 18–38; Hey, *Yorkshire*, pp. 89–91.

[73] R. B. Dobson, 'The risings in York, Beverley and Scarborough, 1380–1381', in R. H. Hilton and T. H. Aston, eds., *The English Rising of 1381* (Cambridge, 1984), pp. 112–42.

[74] Miller and Hatcher, *Medieval England*, p. 109; H. Heaton, *The Yorkshire Woollen and Worsted Industries from the Earliest Times up to the Industrial Revolution*, 2nd edn (Oxford, 1965), pp. 1–8.

established a guild by 1163, and a monopoly in making dyed and striped cloths. Beverley and York were leading centres, but Knaresborough, Malton, Thirsk, Ripon and Scarborough were also engaged in cloth production. York weavers were complaining of undercutting by rural competitors in 1237. The number of textile centres was growing inexorably and, by 1300, included Hedon, Leeds, Northallerton, Pickering, Pontefract, Selby, Whitby and Yarm.[75] Thereafter, and at an accelerating pace, the manufacturing and finishing, especially of the cheaper kerseys, was undertaken away from, and at the expense of, the older urban centres. By 1379, this transformation was well established in the West Riding, accelerating the growth of several small towns such as Barnsley, Bradford, Leeds and Wakefield. Other specialist concentrations were visible in 1379: notably of locksmiths and cutlers in and around Sheffield.

Remarkable by their absence in small towns were mercers, merchants and general traders. This was a crucial difference between the large and small towns. Pontefract had more traders than most small towns, a dozen or so in 1379, while Doncaster, Ripon and Tadcaster boasted three or four, and Leeds one. The enormous gap between them and York could not be more graphically illustrated: between 1375 and 1378, York admitted nine or more chapmen, mercers and merchants to the freedom each year.[76] However, in the fifteenth century, textile production became as important to urban success as trade. The rise of the West Riding textile industry not only undermined the older centres, but also Teesside towns. By 1478, West Riding production outstripped all other northern producers and from the 1470s fulling mills were closing or contracting throughout North Yorkshire and Teesside: in Darlington, Barnard Castle, and Ripon.[77]

In many respects, the relative decline of the larger towns is easier to chart than the rise of their competitors and is well known. York, Beverley, Hull and Scarborough were of national significance, with York second only to London in 1377. By 1524–5, all four had slipped, York to maybe fifth with a population loss of perhaps one half to *c.* 8,000 by 1548, Beverley to perhaps twenty-fourth with a population loss of about one quarter to 3,900 in 1548. In regional terms, though, York, Beverley and Hull were still major centres in the early sixteenth century.

Scarborough is one of the enigmas of Yorkshire. The town's history was chequered and we know too little of it. The common activities developed: clothmaking in the twelfth century, wool collection and export in the thirteenth and early fourteenth. More unusual perhaps was the local pottery, producing ware

[75] Miller and Hatcher, *Medieval England*, pp. 100, 109–10; Hey, *Yorkshire*, p. 85; Heaton, *Woollen and Worsted Industries*, pp. 1–8; *VCH*, City of York, p. 44.

[76] F. Collins, ed., *Register of the Freemen of the City of York* (Surtees Society, 1, 1897), pp. 73–9; Miller and Hatcher, *Medieval England*, p. 113; [no editor], 'The rolls of the collectors in the West Riding of the lay subsidy', *Yorkshire Arch. J*, 5 (1879), 6 (1881), 7 (1882).

[77] Heaton, *Woollen and Worsted Industries*, pp. 75–9; Pollard, *North-Eastern England*, pp. 72–3.

widely sold throughout the North and in Scotland before 1300. Salt from northern France was amongst Scarborough's imports in the early fourteenth century, an adjunct of its fishing. This was probably the bedrock of Scarborough's economy. Although briefly investing in deep-sea fishing around Iceland, from *c.* 1412–*c.* 1417, Scarborough reverted to inshore fishing. As elsewhere, Scarborough's retreat may have been driven by London investment.[78]

York's fortunes rested on a more complex mix of activities than any other northern town. As home to wealthy religious foundations in addition to the minster, diocese and archbishopric, the city serviced the needs of one of the largest and, perhaps, most self-indulgent consumer populations in the North. The emerging city government also sharpened its constitutional claws in disputes with wealthy religious foundations, determined to establish their own liberties within the city. The tenants of massive religious estates such as St Mary's Abbey, which extended into all the northern counties, brought further business to local merchants and craftsmen, as did the clients of ecclesiastical courts. In addition, York's strategic location kept it under the royal gaze and drew the city into national and county politics. The result was a rich mix of skills, commerce and cultures, unrivalled outside London.

The needs of sophisticated consumers were met by an unusual agglomeration of highly skilled craftsmen: bell-founders, bookbinders, embroiderers, glaziers, jewellers and upholsterers for instance. At their peak before the 1430s, York's international merchants accounted for over half the wool and cloth traded through Hull, and one third of wine and miscellaneous imports. They supplied the city and region with textile requirements such as dyestuffs and teasels, with wine, Mediterranean fruit and spices, silks and brocades, all financed from their sales of wool and cloth. Continental luxuries, like overseas travel, coloured the lives of provincial townsfolk. York was a cosmopolitan city importing ideas alongside almonds and liquorice, and, on one occasion, the text of a play from northern Europe.[79]

The city's social and occupational structure reflected this commercial potpourri, with over 125 different occupational ascriptions recorded and at least fifty craft guilds for most of the fifteenth century. Some fifteen religious guilds and fraternities nurtured more intimate associations than could perhaps be achieved by the city's forty-one or so parishes. Such abundant provision created an impressive array of spires and towers which sharply contrasted with the single church most towns possessed.

In 1400 York was still England's leading provincial city. It was beholden to no one except the king, from whom the city was held at farm, set at £100 since the

[78] Miller and Hatcher, *Medieval England*, pp. 77, 84, 100, 164, 410; P. Heath, 'North-Sea fishing in the fifteenth century: the Scarborough fleet', *NHist.*, 3 (1968), 62–3.

[79] H. Swanson, *Medieval Artisans* (Oxford, 1989); *VCH*, City of York, pp. 99–103.

Conquest. Over the centuries, successive kings had demanded loyalty, cash, troops, hospitality and sanctuary and in return York had steadily acquired constitutional privileges until royal charters of 1393 and 1396 gave it the status of an independent incorporate county. Constitutional precocity was matched by sophisticated internal politics and an ambitious mercantile oligarchy. Its physical size, wealth, occupational specialisation, complex government, public regulation, number of churches and religious houses, scale of trade, multiple markets, sophistication and education of its society were massively different from even its closest rivals, Beverley and Newcastle. In spite of the recession which was affecting the city by the 1430s, York remained an important centre of secular and ecclesiastical administration and regional market.[80]

(vi) CONCLUSION

That the wealthiest and most sophisticated towns lay to the east of the Pennines is not surprising. By every measure, agricultural, commercial, industrial and institutional, the east had major advantages and so urbanised earlier and faster than the west. The contrasts were stark, with a handful of sizeable towns in Cumbria by 1550, a dozen or so in south Lancashire and Cheshire, and some 120 east of the Pennines. Easier access to minerals and to distant markets partly explains the difference between the two northernmost regions. Carlisle remained a small town in its remote backwater, whereas Newcastle became a wealthy and rising industrial port town. In the west, although Chester had no rivals, neither was it supported by a network of satellite towns and remained constrained by its underdeveloped hinterland. The most successful medieval centres, Beverley, Hull, Scarborough and York, lay in the south-east where a combination of excellent communications, early regional development, access to distant ports and a productive hinterland encouraged a high level of urbanisation.

[80] J. N. Bartlett, 'The expansion and decline of York in the later middle ages', *Ec.HR*, 2nd series, 12 (1959–60), 17–33; D. M. Palliser, 'A crisis in English towns? The case of York, 1460–1640', *NHist.*, 14 (1978), 108–25; *VCH*, City of York, pp. 25–116.

· 22(f) ·

Wales and the Marches

RALPH A. GRIFFITHS

(i) A FRAMEWORK

IN 1300 Wales was almost as urbanised a country as England (Map 22.12). The current view, based largely, if tentatively, on the surviving records of a lay subsidy imposed on Wales by Edward I in 1292–3, is that Wales' population at that time was about 300,000 souls.[1] It had about 100 towns and chartered boroughs, albeit they were on average smaller in size than those of England; only a minority is likely to have had more than 1,000 inhabitants each. The proportion of Wales' population that lived in these towns seems not to have been significantly smaller than town-dwelling proportions in England (estimated at 15 per cent) or Spain; fewer than one fifth of these town dwellers were of Welsh descent. Furthermore, in 1300 townsmen and country dwellers from Wales were regular visitors to the substantial, prosperous border towns of Chester, Oswestry, Shrewsbury, Ludlow, Leominster, Hereford, Tewkesbury, Gloucester and, by sea and ferry, to Bristol, whose own merchants customarily plied their trades in many a Welsh town.[2]

Wales in 1300, then, was an urbanised society to a significant degree. This may seem surprising in view of the fact that Gerald of Wales (*c.* 1146–1223), who knew southern Wales especially well and had travelled widely through much of the country, implied that the Welsh population:

[1] Much of this paragraph is based on K. Williams-Jones, ed., *The Merioneth Lay Subsidy Roll, 1292–3* (Cardiff, 1976), pp. xli–lxv, civ–cxi. Cf. R. H. Britnell, *The Commercialisation of English Society, 1000–1500*, 2nd edn (Manchester, 1996), p. 115. J. C. Russell's classic *British Medieval Population* (Albuquerque, 1948), p. 351, estimated that 2.66 per cent of Wales' population lived in towns before the great plague.

[2] E.g. R. A. Griffiths, 'Medieval Severnside: the Welsh connection', in R. R. Davies, R. A. Griffiths, I. G. Jones and K. O. Morgan, eds., *Welsh Society and Nationhood* (Cardiff, 1984), pp. 70–89, reprinted in R. A. Griffiths, *Conquerors and Conquered in Medieval Wales* (Stroud, 1994), pp. 1–18.

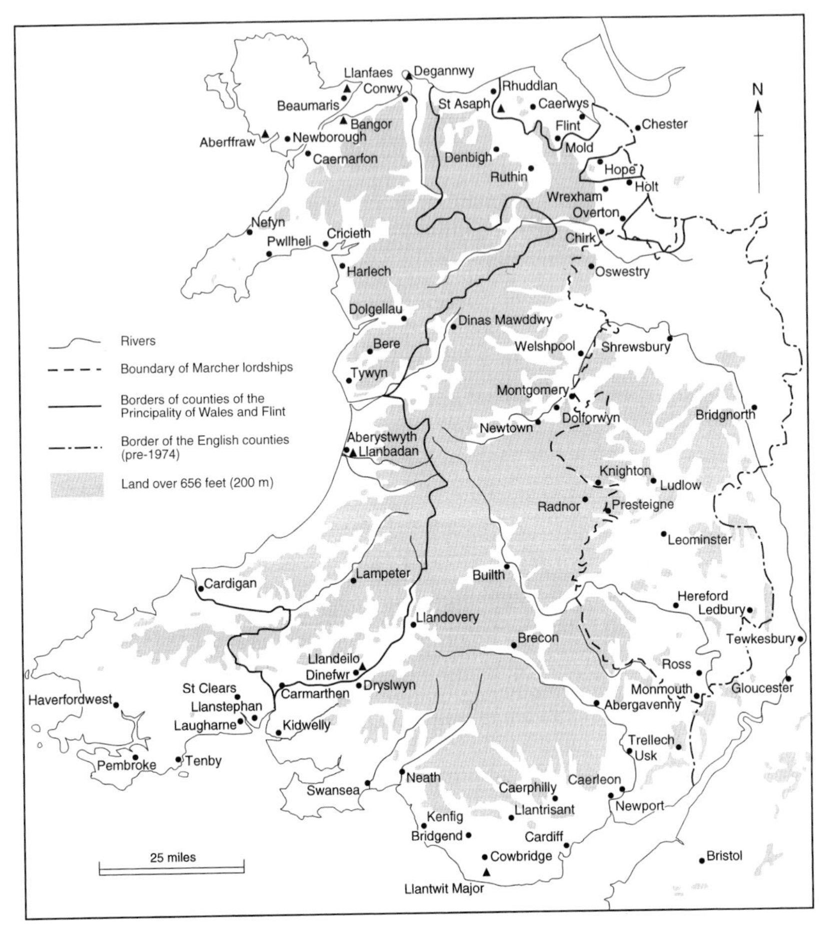

Map 22.12 Towns in Wales and the Marches

> do not live in towns, villages or castles, but lead a solitary existence, deep in the woods. It is not their habit to build great palaces, or vast and towering structures of stone and cement. Instead they content themselves with wattled huts on the edges of the forest, put up with little labour or expense, but strong enough to last a year or so.
>
> They do not have orchards or gardens, but if you give them fruit or garden produce they are only too pleased to eat it. Most of their land is used for pasture. They cultivate very little of it, growing a few flowers and sowing a plot here and there.

And again, 'they pay no attention to commerce, shipping or industry, and their only preoccupation is military training'. That may well have been generally so in the past though Gerald's oft-quoted description is myopic and stylised.[3] By Gerald's day scores of Anglo-Norman towns had been founded, some of them already had Welsh inhabitants, and the impact and influence of urban life and activities were not limited to those who lived protected by the towns' defences. A century and a quarter earlier still, say in 1070, it is difficult to detect any towns at all in Wales, though not impossible. In short, Wales between 1070 and 1300 experienced a major change of mood in its landscape, its political and social organisation and in its economic and cultural life, and this change was the result of purposeful immigration and reorganisation of unprecedented force.[4]

It seems likely that at the time of the lay subsidy of 1543, the population of Wales was about 10 per cent smaller than it had been in 1300, before natural disasters, famine and plague, and war and rebellion had taken their substantial toll in the fourteenth and early fifteenth centuries.[5] The proportion of the population living in towns in 1543 had fallen in some places and risen in others since Edward I's day, but taken in aggregate Welsh towns appear to have been as populous under Henry VIII as they had been under King Edward. Proportionately and numerically, more people of Welsh descent were town dwellers by the mid-sixteenth century, and immigrant families were less of a distinctive breed and fewer of them preserved their *arriviste* character. This suggests that by the time of the Acts of Union, Wales was a more integrated society in terms of native and immigrant, town and countryside, than at any time in the past. Scarcely any new towns had appeared after 1300 – not even primarily market and commercial centres – despite the ending of the era of conquest and the coming of comparative peace to Wales as a whole.

Three important factors underpin this pattern of development. The first is the nature of the topography and landscape of Wales, both land and marine. The highland core and lowland peripheries – the latter especially extensive in the south, the east and, to a lesser extent, the north – influenced the distribution of the country's medieval population and its exposure to the external world: the valleys and vales fanned out to luscious plains that extended into the English Midlands and across relatively sheltered waterways in the north and the south, and across the more boisterous seas to Ireland. These geographical imperatives

[3] Gerald of Wales, *Journey through Wales and the Description of Wales*, transl. L. Thorpe (London, 1978), pp. 233, 251–2, from J. F. Dimock, ed., *Giraldi Cambrensis Opera*, vol. VI: *Itinerarium Kambriae et Descriptio Kambriae* (RS, 1868), pp. 180, 200–1. The *Descriptio* was written *c.* 1194; for a critique, see R. Bartlett, *Gerald of Wales, 1146–1223* (Oxford, 1982), chs. 6, 7, and H. Pryce, 'In search of a medieval society: Deheubarth in the writings of Gerald of Wales', *Welsh History Review*, 13 (1987), 265–81.

[4] For this chronology, see I. Soulsby, *The Towns of Medieval Wales* (Chichester, 1983), table 1 (p. 6); M. Beresford, *New Towns of the Middle Ages*, 2nd edn (Gloucester, 1988), tables XII.1, 2 (pp. 341–2).

[5] Williams-Jones, *Merioneth Subsidy*, pp. xlviii-lxv; L. Owen, 'The population of Wales in the sixteenth and seventeenth centuries', *Transactions of the Cymmrodorion Society* (1959), pp. 99–113.

allowed the urban centres of Bristol, Gloucester, Hereford, Shrewsbury, Chester and Dublin a major impact on town development in Wales. These imperatives had, too, changing significances over time, the so-called 'Irish Sea province' waning in importance from the thirteenth century, and the Severnside connection and Cheshire and its hinterland becoming more intensively significant from 1070 onwards.[6] In sparsely populated upland districts, a small market town and administrative or religious centre might have as much influence on its rural hinterland, relatively speaking, as a larger town might have in more densely populated, lowland countryside.

A second factor is the peculiar history of authority and lordship in Wales, both secular and ecclesiastical. In the post-Roman era, Wales had a multiplicity of kingdoms and kings, and a number of notable religious communities. By the eleventh century, prior to the Anglo-Norman invasions, both sources of power and authority had been subject to centripetal forces so that a relatively small number of royal and religious centres had come to tower over the rest in terms of status and size. In the secular world, there was Aberffraw in Anglesey, facing Ireland and the seat of the rulers of Gwynedd, or, even earlier, Degannwy, the twin hill-fortress of Welsh rulers on the northern coast which may have been occupied as early as the sixth century and continued to be fought over by Saxon, Welsh and Anglo-Norman from the ninth century to the thirteenth.[7] In the religious sphere, there was Llandeilo Fawr (the Great) in the broad Tywi valley, and Llantwit Major, close to the coast in Glamorgan, both sizeable communities sustained by the traditions of Dark Age saints and spiritual and educational activities.[8] Llanbadarn Fawr, second only to St David's as a venerable Christian site in western Wales, and a centre of scholarly and artistic distinction on the eve of the Norman invasions, was then described as 'a high city (*metropolis*) where the holy bishop Padarn led an outstanding life', 'the metropolis of St Padarn'.[9] At the very least, such centres as Llandeilo Fawr, Llantwit Major and St David's, and also Bangor in the north, had lively market places close to their churches by the thirteenth century.

[6] Cf. Gerald of Wales' comment (*c.* 1194) on trade with England and across 'The Irish Sea, [and] the Severn Sea', in *Description*, transl. Thorpe, p. 267 (Dimock, *Opera*, VI, pp. 218–19).

[7] W. Davies, *Wales in the Early Middle Ages* (Leicester, 1982), pp. 20, 24, 89, 97.

[8] L. A. S. Butler, '"The monastic city" in Wales: myth or reality', *Bulletin of the Board of Celtic Studies*, 28 (1979), 458–67; H. Pryce, 'Ecclesiastical wealth in early medieval Wales', in N. Edwards and A. Lane, eds., *The early Church in Wales and the West* (Oxford, 1992), p. 30; on Llandeilo Fawr, see J. W. Evans, 'Aspects of the Early Church in Carmarthenshire', in H. James, ed., *Sir Gâr: Studies in Carmarthenshire History* (Carmarthen, 1991), pp. 245–9, and R. A. Griffiths, 'A tale of two towns: Llandeilo Fawr and Dinefwr in the middle ages', in *ibid.*, pp. 205–8, 217–18 (reprinted in Griffiths, *Conquerors and Conquered*, pp. 254–6, 267–8).

[9] M. Lapidge, 'The Welsh-Latin poetry of Sulien's family', *Studia Celtica*, 8/9 (1973–4), 84–5 (quoted from Ieuan ap Sulien's 'Carmen . . . de vita et familia Sulgeni', late eleventh century), and 'Vita Sancti Paterni' in A. W. Wade-Evans, ed., *Vitae Sanctorum Britanniae et Genealogiae* (Cardiff, 1944), pp. 260–1 (*c.* 1120). See also J. L. Davies and D. P. Kirby, eds., *Cardiganshire County History* (Cardiff, 1994–), vol. I, pp. 270–1.

From the 1070s to the 1280s this pattern of lordship was transformed by military conquerors from the east, Anglo-Norman and English kings and nobles, whose conquests produced renewed political morcellation, territorial fragmentation and foreign immigration, spearheaded by castle building and new religious foundations, and sustained economically, financially and in other ways by the deliberate creation of towns and chartered boroughs (Plate 22). The intensity of the morcellation and colonisation in scores of lordships led, by the time the phases of subjugation and conquest had ended by 1300, to a generous provision of towns whose original *raisons d'être* had already begun to disappear. In the meantime, the consequence was that few homesteads or settlements in Wales, except in the remoter parts of the highlands, were beyond half a day's journey from a town and its influences. It meant, too, that in this dynamic frontier society, native and immigrant, Welsh and non-Welsh, could hardly fail to interact and, in many cases, integrated one with another, in towns as well as in the countryside, more speedily here than there, more peacefully and completely in some places than in others.[10]

A third factor is the social structure associated with these developments, and its economic base. In the early middle ages, Wales was a land of free and bond communities settled in homesteads, with local, district lordship sustained by predominantly food renders and services in kind. If there were supply or market centres, they existed less to satisfy a wide demand than to ensure the immediate self-sufficiency of the royal courts and religious communities. Rather than commercial centres in a sparsely populated land, these courts and communities (such as Aberffraw and Degannwy, and including Llandeilo Fawr and Llantwit Major) were centres of clustered populations sustaining themselves by agriculture and services, and usually situated close to the coast.[11] Major changes in lordship from the late eleventh century onwards exploited the topography, landscape and resources of Wales in rather different (or at least more intensive) ways, in time creating different social and economic structures, as well as military, political and religious ones, though not immediately destroying the older order and its structures. Coasts, estuaries and havens, in a country with an exceptionally long coastline, received greater emphasis, and even the native rulers of Gwynedd were developing their estates at Pwllheli and Nefyn in the Lleyn peninsula, and at Llanfaes in Anglesey, as small towns and fishing ports in the second half of the twelfth century.[12] For the immigrants after 1070, protection,

[10] See R. R. Davies, 'Frontier arrangements in fragmented societies: Ireland and Wales', in R. Bartlett and A. Mackay, eds., *Medieval Frontier Societies* (Oxford, 1989), esp. pp. 87–92.

[11] Davies, *Wales in the Early Middle Ages*, ch. 2.

[12] R. R. Davies, *Conquest, Coexistence and Change* (Oxford, 1987), pp. 164–5. The twelfth-century *Historia* of Gruffydd ap Cynan, king of Gwynedd, refers to harbours at Nefyn and the unidentified 'Abermenai', which seems to be more than a haven or landing stage. A. Jones, ed., *The History of Gruffydd ap Cynan* (Manchester, 1910), pp. 112–15, 137, 156–7.

privilege and profit in an alien environment were the chief priorities, and easy, direct access to England by land and sea was imperative. Political and religious lordship increasingly coincided in the new lordships – and all this at a time of rising population. The surge of town foundations in these circumstances brings to mind Colin Platt's comment of 1976: 'while it is true that prominent natural features . . . were never unimportant in the shaping of a town plan, it should be remembered that towns are the most artificial of all human creations and that they reflect, more than anything, the social habits of the men who made them'.[13]

(ii) SOURCES AND OPPORTUNITIES

The difficulties confronting the historian of medieval Welsh towns are well known. There is, to date, a lack of convincing evidence of continuous settlement and urban life, as opposed to the continuous occupation of sites, in any Welsh town from the Roman period to the Anglo-Norman invasions. There is, too, a disconcerting patchiness in the surviving written evidence even for the post-Norman period. And apart from the pioneering study of E. A. Lewis, *The Mediæval Boroughs of Snowdonia*, there have been few authoritative studies of individual medieval Welsh towns written in the twentieth century to place the subject on a footing firm enough to realise its potential.[14]

On the other hand, several promising avenues have been identified more recently and are now being explored. First, Wales has a long and vigorous poetic tradition from at least the ninth century in which praise-poetry is a prominent genre. Whether focused on, and patronised by, notable Welsh men and occasionally women, including some of immigrant ancestry, or less frequently and incidentally directed at some of the Welsh and border towns, this tradition was not generally urban in tone in the middle ages. However, poets of the fourteenth and fifteenth centuries, in particular, let slip their feelings towards the towns and their 'English' inhabitants: in some cases, perhaps, these were the stereotypical idiom of the poetic tradition itself, and were expected of poets by their patrons and audiences; or else they may reflect deeply ingrained rural prejudices. In the middle of the fourteenth century, Dafydd ap Gwilym (*fl.* 1320–70), Wales' greatest poet and a down-to-earth commentator on the social scene, could record a playful encounter in a town's inn situated opposite stout stone walls; and in the course of a poem in honour of Holy Cross Chapel in Carmarthen, Dafydd offered a glimpse of life in the busy town.[15] After the revolt of Owain Glyndŵr,

[13] C. Platt, *The English Medieval Town* (London 1976), pp. 43–5.

[14] E. A. Lewis, The *Mediæval Boroughs of Snowdonia* (London, 1912). R. A. Griffiths, ed., *Boroughs of Mediaeval Wales* (Cardiff, 1978), by its selection of eleven individual studies, and Soulsby, *Towns of Medieval Wales*, with its gazetteer, point ways forward.

[15] D. Johnston, 'The serenade and the image of the house in the poems of Dafydd ap Gwilym',

by which time Welsh-born burgesses were to be found in all Welsh towns and chartered boroughs, poets expressed admiration for the larger towns, where they were doubtless welcomed. Sion Cent (*c.* 1400–30/45) commended the inhabitants of Brecon and the bustle of its burgesses' busy lives in what was one of the largest of all Welsh towns.[16] Later in the century, Guto'r Glyn (*c.* 1435–*c.* 1493) saw Oswestry, the gateway to England, as the London of Wales, with 'wine filled homes, [and] lands of orchards', whose inhabitants were the 'best band, delightful'. To his contemporary, Tudur Aled (*c.* 1465–*c.* 1525), Oswestry's commercial Willow Street 'is the best store under Christ'; he admired the town's officials, and its shopkeepers with their

> Well-made coffers at rare price,
> Cummin, box, excellent wine,
> Sugar, fine fabrics, velvet, fulled cloth,
> Cheapside itself in silk shops,
> Each ware from the whole strange world.

In one of his verses, Guto went further: Oswestry (he said) was 'the best of cities, far as Rome'.[17] These exaggerations were the metaphors of admiration; the most sublime was Huw Cae Llwyd's judgement on late fifteenth-century Brecon, 'the Constantinople of Wales'.[18] These poetic descriptions are fascinating revelations of the place of an urban culture in Wales in the turbulent later middle ages, and reflect on the evolution of an integrated society of Welsh and immigrant, town and country folk.

Study of the place-names of Wales has lagged behind the work of the English Place-Name Society, but a major project now under way will eventually provide Wales with an authoritative series of volumes comparable to England's.[19] For a country which, especially in the two centuries from about 1070, received waves of immigrants, many of whom were absorbed into towns and chartered boroughs, these studies will provide a surer understanding of the social, economic and topographical implications of urban nomenclature. The advances so far made in Flintshire, Glamorgan and Pembrokeshire have poured cool water on

Cambridge Medieval Celtic Studies, 5 (1983), 1–20; A. P. Owen, 'Englynion Dafydd Llwyd ap Gwilym Gam i'r Grog o Gaer', *Ysgrifau Beirniadol*, 21 (1996), 13–36.

[16] H. Lewis, T. Roberts and I. Williams, eds., *Cywyddau Iolo Goch ac Eraill*, new edn (Cardiff, 1937), p. 269 line 11, quoted in R. R. Davies, 'Brecon', in Griffiths, ed., *Boroughs of Mediaeval Wales*, pp. 63–4.

[17] I. Williams and J. Ll. Williams, eds., *Gwaith Guto'r Glyn* (Cardiff, 1939), pp. 183–4, transl. in J. P. Clanchy, *Medieval Welsh Lyrics* (London, 1965), pp. 219–21, and quoted in L. B. Smith, 'Oswestry', in Griffiths, ed., *Boroughs of Mediaeval Wales*, pp. 219, 228, 232; T. G. Jones, ed., *Gwaith Tudur Aled* (Cardiff, 1926), vol. I, p. 262, quoted in Smith, 'Oswestry', p. 224 (transl. D. J. Bowen), and in A. Breeze, *Medieval Welsh Literature* (Dublin, 1997), pp. 153–4 (transl.). Cf. D. Johnston, ed., *Gwaith Lewys Glyn Cothi* (Cardiff, 1995), no. 208, on Oswestry.

[18] L. Harries, ed., *Gwaith Huw Cae Llwyd ac Eraill* (Cardiff, 1953), no. 118 lines 8–9, transl. in Davies, 'Brecon', p. 61.

[19] Sponsored by the Board of Celtic Studies of the University of Wales.

one of the more intriguing puzzles of urban origins in Wales, namely, the possible influence of Viking, especially Hiberno-Norse, contacts with the southern and northern coasts in the later tenth and eleventh centuries.[20] Many of those contacts were violent and destructive, the religious centres of coastal Wales suffering repeated raids from 961 until the end of the tenth century. In 988, for instance, the religious communities at Llanbadarn Fawr, St Dogmaels and St David's were severely ravaged by Viking marauders. Other Scandinavian forays towards the Dee and Severn estuaries have been associated – by historical intuition rather than with certainty – with possible staging-posts, even Norse trading communities, in such places as the Wirral and at Cardiff, Swansea (Sveinn's hill or island) and Milford Haven. But H. R. Loyn's suggestion that historians may have been inclined to underestimate Scandinavian and Scandinavian Irish influence on such growing towns as Chester, Bristol and even Swansea and Cardiff has not received any significant support from place-name scholars since his review of the evidence in 1976.[21] One problem is that whatever Scandinavian influence there was would have been quickly overlaid by the Anglo-Norman influx, so that to distinguish between Germanic name forms that are Old Norse or Old English requires great care. Moreover, if Norsemen settled in coastal Wales, they would hardly have done so very much before the end of the tenth century, and soon afterwards the Norman conquerors arrived. Norse naming of prominent landmarks, headlands, promontories, rocks and islands, suggesting the kinds of contact which seafarers would make, is reasonably well attested in North-East and especially South Wales, and in many cases these names have persisted to our own day; but the earliest surviving references to them are later than the Norse period itself. One or two have been authenticated in and near Cardiff, but no trace of Scandinavian occupation or settlement has yet been unearthed there by archaeologists.[22] Indeed, would archaeologists be able to recognise a Welsh Viking settlement, let alone have the opportunity to excavate any that might lurk beneath a later town? Viking Hedeby, at the base of the Jutland peninsula, has been identified as an early town because it was replaced by a new settlement across the river at Schleswig early in the eleventh century: would it have been so easily discoverable if the site had been continuously occupied (as Cardiff has been) without a break for a further 900 years?[23]

[20] G. O. Pierce, *The Place-Names of Dinas Powys Hundred* (Cardiff, 1968); G. O. Pierce, 'The evidence of place-names', in H. N. Savory, ed., *Glamorgan County History*, vol. II: *Early Glamorgan* (Cardiff, 1984), pp. 456–92; H. W. Owen, *The Place-Names of East Flintshire* (Cardiff, 1994); B. G. Charles, *The Place-Names of Pembrokeshire*, 2 vols. (Aberystwyth, 1992).

[21] H. R. Loyn, *The Vikings in Wales* (London, 1976); W. Davies, *Patterns of Power in Early Wales* (Oxford, 1990), pp. 52–90.

[22] B. G. Charles, *Old Norse Relations with Wales* (Cardiff, 1934); B. G. Charles, *Non-Celtic Place-Names in Wales* (London, 1938).

[23] K. Schietzel, 'Haithabu [Hedeby]: a study on the development of early urban settlements in northern Europe', in H. B. Clarke and A. Simms, eds., *The Comparative History of Urban Origins*

Archaeology is, however, tentatively substantiating a Scandinavian presence elsewhere along the northern and, to a lesser extent, the southern coasts of Wales. A number of coin and silver finds from the late tenth and the first half of the eleventh centuries, along with evidence from stone crosses and the Irish annals, suggest that both seaways were well-used runs, with coastal contacts, perhaps even settlements, at various points between the Norse centres of York, Man, Chester and Dublin.[24] If Scandinavians settled there, by the eleventh century they are likely to have been trading rather than persisting in raiding. It may not be a coincidence that two of the largest Viking coin hoards have been discovered near Degannwy, on a hill on the opposite side of the Conwy estuary from the medieval borough of Conwy. Degannwy was a Welsh royal centre possibly as early as the sixth century, and some evidence there dates from the late Roman period. It may have been occupied by the Norsemen, and although evidence for a civil settlement alongside the early fortress is uncertain thereafter, tenements of a Welsh settlement are noted from the mid-thirteenth century, and markets and fairs and a ferry were being encouraged by Henry III in 1251. Degannwy eventually fell victim to the continuing warfare between Welsh and English: Henry III abandoned his plans to found a new borough there, and in 1283 Edward I preferred a more secure harbour site across the river-mouth at Conwy.[25]

Site-specific and enthusiastic the findings of archaeologists may be, but their art has been revolutionised in Wales over the past twenty years, since the establishment of the four Archaeological Trusts; moreover, in recent years, their remit has extended from 'rescue archaeology' and 'watching briefs' to more directed investigation. The Dyfed and Powys Trusts have begun to survey medieval 'small boroughs' and village marts, and the ambitious '*llys* and *maerdref*' (court and township) survey of the Gwynedd Trust may reveal more about the estates and settlements of Welsh rulers (as at Aberffraw, Rhosyr and Llanfaes in Anglesey) than the surviving documentary evidence and law-books are able to do.[26] The

in Non-Roman Europe (British Archaeological Reports, International Series, 225(i), Oxford, 1985), part 1, ch. 6. Cf. the Viking towns founded in Ireland, at Dublin, Waterford, Wexford, Cork and Limerick, from the ninth century: B. J. Graham and L. J. Proudfoot, *An Historical Geography of Ireland* (London, 1993), pp. 38–40.

[24] G. C. Boon, *Welsh Hoards, 1979–1981* (Cardiff, 1986), part 1. For recently discovered Viking remains in Anglesey, suggesting settlements and trade, see N. Edwards, 'A possible Viking grave from Benllech, Anglesey', *Transactions of the Anglesey Antiq. Soc. and Field Club* (1985), pp. 19–24; M. Redknap, 'Excavation at Glyn, Llanbedrgoch, Anglesey', *Archaeology in Wales*, 34 (1994), 58–60; 35 (1995), 58–9 (tenth-century date).

[25] Soulsby, *Towns of Medieval Wales*, pp. 120–1; D. Stephenson, *The Governance of Gwynedd* (Cardiff, 1984), p. 79.

[26] E.g., D. Longley, 'The royal courts of the Welsh princes of Gwynedd, AD 400–1283', in N. Edwards, ed. *Landscape and Settlement in Medieval Wales* (Oxford, 1997), ch. 4; J. Kissock, '"God made nature and men made towns": post-Conquest and pre-Conquest villages in Pembrokeshire', in *ibid.*, ch. 10.

Royal Commission on Ancient and Historical Monuments of Wales is developing a National Monuments Record whose database absorbs the Sites and Monuments Records of the Trusts. This will make more readily available comparative data for the whole of Wales. Already well advanced is its comparative study of medieval and early modern domestic buildings, both rural and urban. A clear contrast has emerged, for example, between town buildings in the South-West of Wales – solid, stone buildings with constructional affinities with Somerset and Devon and of which the fifteenth-century 'Merchant's House' at Tenby is a splendid survivor – and those in the rest of Wales, from the South-East to the North-West, where town buildings in Brecon, Builth, Ruthin, Conwy, Beaumaris and elsewhere preferred dwarf stone walls surmounted by timber superstructures which stand comparison with the sophisticated houses of Cheshire and the West Midlands.[27] The entire county of Radnor has had all of its early surviving domestic buildings surveyed in detail, including the later medieval, half-timbered houses in the towns of Presteigne and Knighton. Such investment in building, seemingly in the century following the Glyndŵr rebellion, suggests a measure of prosperity and economic recovery in at least some of the towns of later medieval Wales. Topographical artists of the stature of the Buck brothers in the 1740s, and Thomas Rowlandson, John Varley and the Sandby brothers, recorded scenes and buildings in Welsh towns like Welshpool, Rhuddlan, Cardiff and Cowbridge in the eighteenth century, when medieval markets, houses and halls survived amid elegant rebuilding, and before industrialisation obliterated large numbers of them.[28] Their drawings and paintings supplement and explain the findings of architectural historians.

A more recent initiative of the Royal Commission is in the field of aerial photography. Site, layout and the interrelationship of military, religious, commercial and domestic buildings and burgage plots in such well-known medieval towns as Pembroke, Carmarthen, Conwy and Caernarfon often become clearer when viewed from the air, and other photographs reveal what examination at ground level or by map does not reveal of the configuration of the small Carmarthenshire town of St Clears, and those remains of burgages and buildings of the diminutive town that once stood within the bailey of Dryslwyn Castle in Edward I's reign and which seem gradually to have decayed during the later middle ages after the entire Tywi valley had passed into English hands.[29]

[27] P. Smith, *Houses of the Welsh Countryside*, 2nd edn (London, 1988), pp. 103–33, 372–3 (Map 7), 380–1 (Map 10), 392–3 (Map 11), 435 (Map 26c).

[28] *Ibid.*, Plate 15; D. Robinson, *Cowbridge* (Swansea, 1980), pp. 33–45 (with illustrations of surviving buildings); for Monmouth's buildings of *c.* 1800–30, see *Thomas Tudor (1785–1855), an Artist from Monmouth* (Aberystwyth, 1996).

[29] C. Musson, *Wales from the Air: Patterns of Past and Present* (Aberystwyth, 1994), pp. 48, 62, 58; P. Crew and C. Musson, *Snowdonia from the Air* (Aberystwyth, 1966), pp. 38–9; T. James and D. Simpson, *Ancient West Wales from the Air* (Carmarthen, 1980), nos. 18, 27.

The value of the surviving archives of the crown and Marcher lords to the study of the medieval Welsh town requires little stress, except to note their patchy and often uninformative nature: town and borough charters (in some cases surviving only in much later copies, as for Brecon); the financial accounts of receivers and lesser officials, who often, in the later middle ages, held their towns at farm and hence recorded few details of urban activities; extents, surveys and rentals; and a small number of royal tax or subsidy returns like those of 1292–3 and 1543–5. The surviving collections of sixteenth- or seventeenth-century town ordinances, regulations and customs are not always easy to interpret. Those of Cowbridge were compiled in 1610/11 'worde by worde agreable to the oulde decaied Roule withe other more Ordinaunces added thereunto', and the strikingly similar ordinances of Kenfig were copied, sometime after 1572, from an older roll which is recorded as dating from 1330, before the town decayed dramatically. When the Neath ordinances were written in 1542, no mention was made of an earlier collection, but the family resemblance between the ordinances of Cowbridge, Kenfig and Neath suggests that Glamorgan's medieval boroughs may have modelled their individual rolls of ordinances on those of one or more of their neighbours, with only partial regard to the appropriateness of every clause.[30]

Exceptional in its potential for the historian is one group of records which, because of their number and the richness of their detail, have not hitherto been fully exploited, namely, the court rolls of the lordship of Dyffryn Clwyd in North-East Wales, including Ruthin, which was founded as a post-Conquest borough in Edward I's reign.[31] A project at Aberystwyth has committed part of this remarkable archive to a database. The rolls for the period 1294–1307 were calendared many years ago; the new project is concentrating on those for the period up to 1422, with special attention to 1340–52 and 1389–99, decades that have been specially chosen to coincide with the Black Death, and to cover the period prior to the devastating attack of Owain Glyndŵr on Ruthin and other towns in the region in September 1400. The analysis of the data reveals, amongst other things, the character of the English settler community and its relationship with the indigenous population, the extent of criminality and violence, the place of the clergy and of women, personal naming practices, the principal landholding families and their role in the town of Ruthin, the longevity or otherwise of

[30] R. A. Griffiths, 'The study of the medieval Welsh borough', in Griffiths, ed., *Boroughs of Mediaeval Wales*, pp. 5–8; P. Moore, ed., *The Borough Ordinances of Cowbridge in Glamorgan* (Cardiff, 1986); W. de Gray Birch, *A History of Neath Abbey* (Neath, 1902), pp. 260–5; *Archaeologia Cambrensis*, 4th series, 2 (1871), 246–56.

[31] A. D. M. Barrell, R. R. Davies, O. J. Padel and L. B. Smith, 'The Dyffryn Clwyd court roll project, 1340–52 and 1389–99: a methodology and some preliminary findings', in Z. Razi and R. Smith, eds., *Medieval Society and the Manor Court* (Oxford, 1996), pp. 260–97. The rolls for Edward I's reign only were published by R. A. Roberts, ed., *The Ruthin Court Rolls* (London, 1893).

men and women, their mobility and the tempo and character of the land market.

These sources and approaches make possible a commentary on several issues of medieval urban history to which the Welsh experience is peculiarly relevant: continuity of site and urban development, circumstances of town growth and decline, relations between native and immigrant, and between townsfolk and countryfolk.

(iii) CONTINUITY

The issue of continuity of occupation of sites and of urban characteristics has its own peculiar interest in Wales, not least because of the country's history of invasion, conquest and immigration. Wales had only two Roman *civitates* or civil capitals, Carmarthen and Caerwent, and of these only Carmarthen developed a medieval town; significantly, it became one of the largest in Wales. Caerwent was ignored by the Anglo-Normans, who preferred to exert their lordship from the former legionary fortress of Caerleon nearby, with its superior defences and river access to the Severn. It is striking, however, how many Roman forts in Wales, especially those with a *vicus* settlement adjacent, were the sites of later towns.[32] Either the military considerations in the minds of Roman planners were still potent factors in the siting of medieval castles and their supportive towns, as at Caernarfon, Usk and Cardiff as well as at Caerleon, and possibly at Monmouth and Chepstow too; or else in the late eleventh and twelfth centuries sufficient remained of defences, building materials and traditions to attract would-be townsfolk and even to determine the configuration of later streets. Where the main Roman road westward from Caerleon to Neath crossed the several rivers that tipped into the Severn, *vici* were established to serve the villas of the fertile Vale; at most of these sites later towns were founded to complement the Norman castles and religious houses – at Newport, Cardiff, Cowbridge, Kenfig and Neath, even not far south of the road at *Sveinn's eia* (Swansea) and further westward at Loughor and, of course, Carmarthen.[33] Inland the broader valleys of the Wye, Usk and Tywi carried Roman roads to

[32] J. S. Wacher, *The Towns of Roman Britain*, 2nd edn (London, 1995), pp. 378–94; W. Davies, 'Roman settlements and post-Roman estates in south-east Wales', in P. J. Casey, ed., *The End of Roman Britain* (Oxford, 1979), pp. 153–73.

[33] I. D. Margary, *Roman Roads in Britain*, 3rd edn (London, 1973), ch. 8; B. Jones and D. Mattingly, *An Atlas of Roman Britain* (Oxford, 1990), pp. 153–74; R. Shoesmith, *Excavations at Chepstow, 1973–74* (Bangor, 1991). Cf. the continuity of settlement from Roman Chester, in T. J. Strickland, 'The Roman heritage of Chester: the survival of the buildings of *Deva* after the Roman period', in R. Hodges and B. Hobley, eds., *The Rebirth of Towns in the West AD 750–1050* (CBA Res. Rep., 68, 1988), pp. 109–18; A. T. Thacker, 'Early medieval Chester: the historical background', in *ibid.*, pp. 119–24. For Roman ruins at Caerleon and Carmarthen which Gerald of Wales saw and described in the 'Journey through Wales' (*c.* 1191), see *Journey*, trans. Thorpe, pp. 114–15, 138 (Dimock, *Opera*, VI, pp. 55, 80).

Roman sites that also attracted the Anglo-Norman colonists to establish their towns at Monmouth, Abergavenny, Usk, Llandovery and, with a slight shift to a better defended site at a river junction, at Brecon.[34] Recent excavations beneath Cowbridge in the Vale of Glamorgan, astride the old Roman portway, revealed a small Roman town, possibly outside an early military fort.[35] Other *vici*, however, withered and died, especially beyond the more densely populated areas of southern Wales.

The sites of Roman forts also attracted the Christian faithful to found their early churches, shrines and monasteries well before the Anglo-Norman invasions. Carmarthen is a likely example, although others gave rise to no more than hamlets or villages – until, in the case of Merthyr Tydfil (an anchorites' *martyrium*), quite modern times.[36] On the other hand, one of the Saxon *burhs* has been identified on the Welsh side of Offa's Dyke: it was part of a defensive network that already included Gloucester, Hereford, Worcester and Chester. *Cledemutha*, beside the River Clwyd and dating from 921, when Edward the Elder was anxious to protect his Mercian kingdom from Norse attack, was planned as a sizeable fortified site; it lay cheek by jowl with the later Norman castle and town of Rhuddlan. *Cledemutha* was close to, but not beneath, the Norman buildings, perhaps because the Saxon fortifications were still standing in William the Conqueror's reign.[37] Such Roman, Christian and Saxon sites were, in several instances, made over to the newer religious orders of the Normans, as at Carmarthen, Chepstow and Rhuddlan, and that suggests that parts of the earlier fabric survived, helping to determine later planning decisions – as well as attracting later settlers to the general site.

This was a phenomenon similar to that being revealed by archaeologists at Chester and Gloucester, and evidence of continuity of occupation from Saxon to Anglo-Norman times is becoming more secure at Bristol, Hereford and Shrewsbury as a result of excavation. The example and influence of these western Saxon towns should not be ignored as far as the pattern of clustered populations further to the west is concerned. Chester and Gloucester had been major Roman military and civil settlements and seem to have become significant Christian centres thereafter; urban life revived more strongly in both with their refortification early in the tenth century, giving them a royal and religious

[34] E.g. D. R. Evans, 'Excavations at 19 Cross Street, Abergavenny, 1986', *Monmouthshire Antiquary*, 11 (1995), 5–53; C. N. Maylon, 'Excavations at St Mary's Priory, Usk', *ibid.*, 9 (1993), 29–42.

[35] J. Parkhouse and E. Evans, *Excavations in Cowbridge, 1977–88* (Oxford, 1996), with a preliminary summary in B. C. Burnham and J. Wacher, *The 'Small Towns' of Roman Britain* (London, 1990), pp. 296–300.

[36] S. Victory, *The Celtic Church in Wales* (London, 1977), pp. 22, 30–1; Davies, *Wales in the Early Middle Ages*, pp. 25, 57–8 (with a map of 'Some possible pre-urban nuclei').

[37] J. Manley *et al.*, 'Cledemutha: a late Saxon burh in North Wales', *Med. Arch.*, 31 (1987), 13–46; H. Quinnell and M. Blockley, *Excavations at Rhuddlan, Clwyd, 1969–73, Mesolithic to Medieval* (York, 1994).

importance and a planned settlement pattern.[38] Shrewsbury was not an important Roman site, but by the tenth century it too was flourishing as a royal and ecclesiastical centre. Hereford may have had the greatest significance for Wales among these Saxon towns: it was the only one to have been the headquarters of a bishop (and from an early date), it had easiest access by Roman road to central and southern Wales and it was one of the earliest of the Mercian refortified sites, with a regular settlement pattern by *c.* 700 and walls a century or so afterwards. Although Bristol emerged later, the Severn Sea had long been a significant means of communication with southern Wales, and the town's origins in the tenth and eleventh centuries, as a result of local economic and political factors in an age of maritime links with Scandinavian Ireland, may reflect what was happening, on a smaller scale, in Norse posts along the southern Welsh littoral.[39] Moreover, the influence of these towns may have extended through substantial parts of Wales before the Norman conquest, when they became the early springboards for invasion and – especially Hereford – exemplars for Anglo-Norman urban organisation.

Within Wales, native rulers and communities doubtless had their horizons broadened by the Anglo-Norman foundations after 1070, even if the emergence of newer towns did not lessen ethnic hostilities for some considerable time. In independent Wales, prior to Edward I's conquests, the rulers of Gwynedd appear to have encouraged towns at places like Pwllheli, Nefyn and Tywyn on the north-west coast, at Llanfaes in Anglesey, and at Caernarfon. Their choice of sites, some with Roman or early religious associations, was appreciated by Edwardian town planners at the end of the thirteenth century: the port and court which are known to have existed earlier at Caernarfon were absorbed by the chartered borough which Edward I established in 1283 (Plate 23).[40] Nefyn seems to have been a centre of urban activity and occupations from the 1140s onwards, when Welsh lords granted Haughmond Abbey, near Shrewsbury, several interests there.[41] Llanfaes, which had become a flourishing Welsh town and port by the end of the twelfth century, proved less convenient for the new rulers, and when the seaside fortress and borough at Beaumaris were founded in 1295, Llanfaes was allowed to decay, its buildings were stripped by the new builders,

[38] 'A. T. Thacker, 'Chester and Gloucester: early ecclesiastical organisation in two Mercian burhs', *NHist.*, 18 (1982), 199–211; Thacker, 'Early medieval Chester'.

[39] See P. Ottaway, *Archaeology in British Towns* (London, 1992), pp. 141–2, in general; Griffiths, in Davies, Griffiths, Jones and Morgan, eds., *Welsh Society and Nationhood*, pp. 70–89 (Griffiths, *Conquerors and Conquered*, pp. 1–18).

[40] K. Williams-Jones, 'Caernarfon', in Griffiths, ed., *Boroughs of Mediaeval Wales*, pp. 73–7.

[41] T. Jones Pierce, 'The old borough of Nefyn, 1355–1882', *Transactions of the Caernarfonshire Hist. Soc.*, 18 (1957), 36–53. For grants of lands in Nefyn to Haughmond Abbey in the mid- and late twelfth century, see U. Rees, ed., *The Cartulary of Haughmond Abbey* (Cardiff, 1985), nos. 784–803; with commentary in Stephenson, *Governance of Gwynedd*, pp. xviii no. 10, 197 n. 11 (mentioning burgesses there), 202.

and many of the Welsh townsfolk were given a new borough ('Newborough') on an entirely different site, though one that was close to the Welsh court (*llys*) complex at Rhosyr.[42] Further east, an urban settlement of some significance had emerged in the Clwyd valley under the rule of Welsh princes. After the conquest in 1282, it continued to develop as the borough of Ruthin, an administrative centre with a collegiate church and a new castle, and a thriving market that served the new Marcher lordship of Dyffryn Clwyd (or Ruthin). It was the only borough in the late medieval lordship, but none of the Greys' tenants was more than a day's journey from its commercial and other facilities.[43]

It is not unreasonable to imagine the more numerous kings in earlier Wales encouraging royal courts that demonstrated the functions and services of later towns, whether at Aberffraw or Degannwy or Dinefwr. It is known that they offered lodgings for officers, troops, smiths, physicians, priests and carpenters by 1200 at least.[44] The same may have been true of the larger and more famous religious communities that were the hub of religion in pre-Norman Wales: places like Llantwit Major with its little Severnside port, or Llandeilo Fawr at a crossing of the River Tywi, or, of course, St David's and Bangor, the most distinguished centres of all, whose communities have had a continuous existence down to our own day. These may not have been sizeable towns in the middle ages, still less chartered boroughs, but they may have had urban traits and functions that simply failed to develop strongly in tune with the demands of Anglo-Norman conquerors from the eleventh century onwards. This colonising process so conditioned contemporaries' perception of a town, and the language they used to refer to towns, that Gerald of Wales believed that the Welsh were not town dwellers – or at least preferred not to live in towns of the newer Anglo-Norman style.[45]

Centres of authority and lordship, both secular and religious, seem to have attracted people in such numbers, and activities of such sort, as to provide conditions for town life that were not irretrievably disrupted by political changes during the two and a quarter centuries after 1070. The English urban institutional framework and its terminology give the impression that something

[42] Lewis, *Snowdonia*, pp. 52–3; Stephenson, *Governance of Gwynedd*, pp. 58–9, 79. For N. Johnstone's report on the recent excavation of Rhosyr, revealing coins minted in Canterbury and Berwick, and thirteenth-century pottery from eastern England and Bordeaux, see *British Archaeology* (1997), and 'An investigation into the location of the royal courts of thirteenth-century Gwynedd', in Edwards, ed., *Landscape and Settlement*, ch. 5 (with Rhosyr, pp. 65–7).

[43] Barrell, Davies, Padel and Smith, 'The Dyffryn Clwyd project'; R. I. Jack, 'Ruthin', in Griffiths, ed., *Boroughs of Mediaeval Wales*, ch. 10.

[44] Stephenson, *Governance of Gwynedd*, pp. 4–5, 60–1 (Aberffraw); Griffiths, in James, ed., *Studies in Carmarthenshire History*, pp. 205–26 (Griffiths, *Conquerors and Conquered*, pp. 262–3).

[45] Above pp. 681–2. Cf. the urban characteristics of such Irish religious and royal centres as Kildare and Kells before the Norman period: A. Simms *et al.*, eds., *Irish Historic Towns Atlas*, vol. 1 (Dublin, 1996), nos. 1, 4.

entirely new was being introduced. Yet charters rarely marked the creation of towns: they were granted in order to confirm, define, refine or publicise townsmen's privileges and to promote urban activities and life styles under royal or seigneurial surveillance. In particular, charters of privilege were prospectuses to develop markets, and recruit and encourage settlers with trades and craft skills; yet individual privileges were not always implemented, nor indeed were they always entirely appropriate to the towns that received them.[46] Such charters were usually based on those of existing towns, and frequently on Hereford's, directly or indirectly, perhaps because William fitz Osbern, earl of Hereford (d. *c.* 1071), a pioneer among the Norman invaders of Wales, had brought the portfolio of liberties of the Norman town of Breteuil to the *caput* of his new English earldom; and perhaps also because of Hereford's unique position as a long-established episcopal, commercial and political centre at a convergence of routes leading into Wales and where immigrants could be recruited and assembled most conveniently. Nor did an initial charter necessarily signal the foundation of a town at a location previously unoccupied by a community of one sort or another; more often than not, charters were granted to towns whose sites had Roman, Christian or other associations worth exploiting by later planners. Even in Edward I's reign, when rapid measures were required after the collapse of the principality of Gwynedd in 1282–3, it was relatively rare for a charter to inaugurate a town.

Cardiff's earliest known charter seems to have been granted by Robert, earl of Gloucester and lord of Glamorgan (d. 1147), a generation after the Anglo-Norman town emerged on a site with a Roman and possibly Scandinavian past, rather than at the early religious centre of Llandaff which did not have immediate access to the Severn channel. The earliest reference to this charter appears in the grant of privileges made by Robert's son William, earl of Gloucester (d. 1183), to Cardiff's burgesses, and including arrangements for the organisation of their commercial life. These privileges and customs were understandably modelled on those of the earl's town of Tewkesbury, with the addition of certain of Hereford's customs.[47] They may have been specifically designed to encourage a town that was the *caput* of Glamorgan, the successor lordship of the kingdom of Morgannwg. They were less appropriate to the more exposed towns of Kenfig and Neath towards the western edge of the conquered kingdom, where a

[46] Lewis, *Snowdonia*, pp. 279–94, for a selection.

[47] G. T. Clark, ed., *Cartae et alia munimenta quae ad dominium de Glamorgancia pertinent*, 2nd edn (Cardiff, 1910), vol. I, pp. 94–7, 104, vol. II, p. 248; J. H. Matthews, ed., *Cardiff Records* (Cardiff, 1898–1911), vol. I, pp. 10–11. For commentary, see D. G. Walker, 'Cardiff', in Griffiths, ed., *Boroughs of Mediaeval Wales*, pp. 111–13; R. A. Griffiths, 'The boroughs of the lordship of Glamorgan', in T. B. Pugh, ed., *Glamorgan County History*, vol. III: *The Middle Ages* (Cardiff, 1971), pp. 335–6; W. Rees, *Cardiff: A History of the City*, revised edn (Cardiff, 1969), p. 54.

Roman fort (Neath) and other evidence of pre-Norman occupation (Kenfig) have been unearthed; yet Earl William included both among the list of his towns in England and Wales to which he confirmed the detailed terms of Cardiff's grant.[48]

Exceptionally, no prior settlement is known on the site of Haverfordwest, whose first charter was granted by William Marshal, earl of Pembroke (d. 1219), a century after Henry I began the town with Flemish and other immigrants. In those early days, the link between Haverford (or Herford) west and Hereford (east) was explicit in encouraging the new development.[49] Elsewhere, a new charter may have been accompanied by a change of site to accommodate a more thriving town in the changed political and demographic circumstances of the thirteenth century. At Montgomery, the Anglo-Norman castle mentioned in Domesday Book, and any associated settlement it may have had, were abandoned in favour of Henry III's new and larger fortress, begun in 1223 one and a half miles away, with a substantial town which received its walls in the following decade and, in 1227, a charter whose terms were based on that of Hereford.[50]

The castle and town planned at Aberystwyth in 1277 occupied a site from which a few Welsh tenants had to be dislodged to make way for the building works. However, this new urban site was barely 2 miles (2.5 km) from the distinguished early monastic site of Llanbadarn Fawr. The new integrated castle and town had open access to the sea to ensure good communications, protection and support in the recently won English lordship of northern Cardiganshire – needs which Llanbadarn Fawr could not meet. But the earlier community's importance to Aberystwyth is reflected in the fact that Llanbadarn Fawr and Aberystwyth – a major religious centre and a Welsh fortress – were a market centre and fishmongery, where tolls were imposed on traders, at least half a century before the Edwardian castle and town were constructed nearby. Furthermore, Llanbadarn Fawr's large church remained the parish church of Aberystwyth, and indeed Edward I's new town at first was called Llanbadarn. Its charter was granted immediately, on 28 December 1277, in order to place the

[48] Soulsby, *Towns of Medieval Wales*, pp. 149–50, 189–90; G. G. Francis, ed., *Original Charters and Materials for the History of Neath and its Abbey* (Swansea, 1845), no pagination; P. V. Webster, 'The Roman period', in Savory, ed., *Glamorgan County History*, II, p. 287; J. K. Knight, 'Glamorgan, A.D. 400–1100: archaeology and history', in *ibid.*, pp. 333–4.

[49] Charles, *Non-Celtic Place-names*, p. 79; Soulsby, *Towns of Mediaeval Wales*, pp. 139–40. Flemish was still spoken at Haverfordwest towards the end of the twelfth century: Gerald of Wales, *Speculum Duorum*, ed. M. Richter *et al.* (Cardiff, 1974), pp. 37, 39.

[50] *CPR 1216–25*, p. 414; Soulsby, *Towns of Medieval Wales*, p. 185. Gwenwynwyn of Cyfeiliog, lord of old Montgomery, had a town there in 1215 when he granted to the monks of Strata Marcella use of his lands nearby: G. C. G. Thomas, ed., *The Charters of the Abbey of Ystrad Marchell* (Aberystwyth, 1997), no. 62.

new urban community on a sound economic footing and to attract reliable additional settlers.[51]

Following Edward I's conquests in North Wales a few years later, it became common to associate town foundation with initial charters, as in the case of Edward's *bastides* at Flint and Harlech; though once again, some of Edward's foundations – Beaumaris, Caernarfon and Cricieth spring to mind – utilised sites which may previously have been occupied by clustered communities. At Beaumaris, Edward wanted a more appropriate site on Anglesey's southern shore, dominating the Menai Strait and easily sustained by sea. It was the last of Edward's foundations in Gwynedd. It was situated just half a mile (1 km) from Llanfaes, the town patronised by the princes of Gwynedd in the thirteenth century. This older town was demolished and some of its inhabitants were transported to Beaumaris, to join other Welshmen who seem to have been already settled on the site. Work on the castle began in April 1295, and in September 1296 a charter was issued for the adjacent borough, based on Hereford's privileges.[52] It acquired a new collegiate church, despite the presence of a church at Llanfaes and a Franciscan friary founded there (*c.* 1237–45) by Prince Llywelyn ab Iorwerth; perhaps these religious foundations were too closely associated with the defeated regime. The remaining Welsh townsmen of Llanfaes, probably the majority – were moved some 15 miles (24 km) away to the former royal settlement at Rhosyr which Edward I appropriately designated 'Newborough'. No castle was built alongside, but careful provision was made to enable the Welsh burgesses to continue to pursue an urban life style, and in 1303 Newborough received a charter which adopted Rhuddlan's privileges, and they in turn were derived from Hereford.[53]

Military conquests and the subsequent political settlements gave a great spur to urban development in Wales between 1070 and 1300, and although English example (most notably *via* Hereford) and immigration were prominent features in choosing a site for development, continuity and traditions of communal life were also of cardinal importance.

[51] R. A. Griffiths, 'Aberystwyth', in Griffiths, ed., *Boroughs of Mediaeval Wales*, p. 32 (Griffiths, *Conquerors and Conquered*, p. 311); R. A. Roberts, 'Cymru Fu: some contemporary statements', *Transactions of the Cymmrodorion Society* (1895–6), p. 122; *CCh.R 1257–1300*, p. 206 (in full in *Archaeologia Cambrensis*, original documents supplement vol. 1 (1877), pp. xxxiv–xxxv); R. A. Griffiths, 'The three castles at Aberystwyth', *Archaeologia Cambrensis*, 126 (1977), 74–87 (Griffiths, *Conquerors and Conquered*, pp. 322–36); Thomas, ed., *Charters of Ystrad Marchell*, no. 77, which records a grant made to the abbey, *c.* 1229–35, by Owain ap Gruffydd, grandson of the Welsh ruler, the Lord Rhys, of exemption from trading tolls at Llanbadarn Fawr and Aberystwyth.

[52] G. Usher, 'The foundation of an Edwardian borough: the Beaumaris charter, 1290', *Transactions of the Anglesey Antiq. Soc. and Field Club* (1967), 1–10, correcting Lewis, *Snowdonia*, p. 282; Soulsby, *Towns of Medieval Wales*, pp. 78–80, 166–7, 194–6.

[53] Above p. 689; Lewis, *Snowdonia*, pp. 40–1, 283.

(iv) CRISES AND CHANGE

The question of whether towns were prosperous or in decline after 1300 may be asked of Wales as of elsewhere in Western Europe. Yet this may not be the most appropriate question, for with the ending of the English conquest in the 1290s, the mingling of English and Welsh communities that was well under way by then, and the greater degree of peace and stability that resulted, it was rather a case of a shaking-out, 'a winnowing', of the hundred or so towns which earlier political and military imperatives had created. There was a reordering, rather than a general decay, of urban life, in the course of which some towns expanded and prospered while others contracted, withered or died. That does not necessarily imply a rejection of town life by the Welsh, the immigrants or the mixed communities, or a stunting of urban activities, or an attenuation of civility in Wales. In places, there was a surge in town foundation and growth in the thirteenth century and at the beginning of the fourteenth, supported by an increase in the population to levels not reached again until the late sixteenth century. Welshpool, for example, a native Welsh seigneurial foundation of the mid-thirteenth century in an area of settlement that goes back to Roman and early Christian periods, had 106 taxpayers in 1292–3 and by 1309 had 173 burgesses.[54] The town of Carmarthen was booming earlier in the century. It acquired town walls after a murage grant of 1233, shops and a new church, St Mary's, were in existence by 1252, and a survey in 1268 reveals a mature, busy town: more than a dozen substantial families owned half the listed properties, some had Bristol connections, and textile and food trades were flourishing; a few of the burgesses were Jews, some families had come from the West Midlands or other Welsh towns, and already some Welsh people were settled in the thriving town.[55] Monmouth experienced several decades of prosperity after it was acquired by the house of Lancaster in 1267: its fortifications were partly rebuilt in stone, new burgages were laid out and more sophisticated buildings were erected; its still surviving fortified gateway and bridge across the River Monnow towards the defended suburb of Over Monnow replaced an earlier wooden bridge whose piles have recently been uncovered.[56] At Cowbridge, the linear development of the town along the Roman road extended outside the west gate in the late thirteenth century, and stone and timber cottages from this period, albeit smaller

[54] Soulsby, *Towns of Mediaeval Wales*, pp. 265–8; R. Morgan, 'The foundation of the borough of Welshpool', *Montgomeryshire Collections*, 65 (1997), 7–24.

[55] R. A. Griffiths, 'Carmarthen', in Griffiths, ed., *Boroughs of Mediaeval Wales*, pp. 143–52 (Griffiths, *Conquerors and Conquered*, pp. 177–81); T. James, 'Medieval Carmarthen and its burgesses', *Carmarthenshire Antiquary*, 25 (1989), 9–26.

[56] R. Shoesmith, 'Excavations in Monmouth, 1973', *Monmouthshire Antiquary*, 6 (1990), 5–15; P. Courtney, *Medieval and Later Usk* (Cardiff, 1994), pp. 118ff; M. L. J. Rowland, *Monmouth Bridge and Gate* (Stroud, 1994).

than those located within the gate, have recently been excavated.[57] The original settlement within the walls at Kidwelly was reported in 1401 to be 'ruinous, waste, and desolate', but that situation is largely explained by the earlier growth of the borough across the River Gwendraeth into a larger, undefended and flourishing suburb near the Benedictine priory.[58] This was also the age when the friars constructed their large houses in some of the larger towns of Wales. By 1242 a Dominican friary had been built outside Cardiff's west gate; somewhat later, the largest Dominican friary in Wales was established at Brecon, in the suburb outside the town walls and across the River Usk; at Denbigh, the Carmelite friary was founded in 1289. The popularity of these orders would have attracted many visitors; their friaries secured the patronage of wealthy townsfolk and others; they contributed to towns' wealth and became prestigious burial places. At Carmarthen, the Franciscan friary, founded *c.* 1280, was a place where Welsh and English, townsfolk, gentry and poets could spend their last days and be buried.[59]

At the same time, changes of a different sort were beginning to modify the urban map of Wales. Political change sounded the death knell of some towns. At Dryslwyn, the tiny borough lodged by Edward I within the bailey of Rhys ap Maredudd's hill-top castle, after the defeat of Rhys' rebellion in 1287–8, barely lasted half a century; after the castle lost its military value in the new royal shire of Carmarthen, the borough was all but abandoned in the mid-fourteenth century.[60] Further north, the market centre which Prince Llywelyn began to develop in 1273 to support his provocative fortress at Dolforwyn, west of Montgomery, was abandoned almost as soon as his castle was seized and granted to Roger Mortimer; it was then neglected as Mortimer proceeded to establish a market and fair at what soon became Newtown, further up the Severn, at a spot where it was unlikely to compete with Welshpool and Montgomery downriver. Whether or not Dolforwyn had been designed as a permanent market or something akin to the modern street market, by 1321 it could be described as a grange, which probably meant merely a collection of farm buildings.[61] Trellech, not far south of Monmouth, was one of the largest towns in thirteenth-century Wales,

[57] Robinson, *Cowbridge*, pp. 37ff; Soulsby, *Towns of Medieval Wales*, pp. 115–17; Griffiths, 'The medieval boroughs of Glamorgan', pp. 339–40.

[58] R. R. Davies, *The Revolt of Owain Glyn Dŵr* (Oxford, 1995), p. 15.

[59] Rees, *Cardiff*, pp. 33–4; Davies, 'Brecon', pp. 61, 69; J. Manley, 'The cemetery of Denbigh priory', *Transactions of the Denbighshire Hist. Soc.*, 37 (1988), 55–6; Griffiths, 'Carmarthen', pp. 159–63 (Griffiths, *Conquerors and Conquered*, pp. 185–8); James, 'Medieval Carmarthen'. The Dominicans had five houses in Wales, the Franciscans three and the Carmelites two.

[60] R. A. Griffiths, 'The revolt of Rhys ap Maredudd, 1287–8', *Welsh History Review*, 3, 2 (1966), 141–2 (Griffiths, *Conquerors and Conquered*, pp. 78–9); P. Webster, 'Dryslwyn Castle', in J. R. Kenyon and R. Avent, eds., *Castles in Wales and the Marches* (Cardiff, 1987), pp. 89–104, for recent excavations.

[61] Soulsby, *Towns of Medieval Wales*, pp. 130–1, 209–11; Stephenson, *Governance of Gwynedd*, p. xxxiv.

situated on the extensive Marcher estates of the Clare earls of Gloucester; today it is the sleepiest of villages, at last attracting the archaeologist. It possibly had 378 burgages in 1288, but after the widespread rebellion of 1294–5, 102 of them were declared vacant and may never have been reoccupied. The last of the Clares fell at Bannockburn in 1314 and Trellech, which seems to have been an important centre of the Clares' iron industry, was all but abandoned. By then, there was less need for Trellech as a commercial or industrial centre in a more peaceful age and situated so close to Monmouth, Abergavenny and Usk. The plague in 1369 delivered the *coup de grace*: forty years later, forty-eight burgages were still being recorded as vacant 'because of the Second Pestilence'.[62] Visitations of plague dealt several towns a lethal blow: in 1349 seventy-seven people died in Ruthin in a fortnight, and Monmouth was badly hit, and at Carmarthen the king's two customs collectors died probably of the disease.[63] Yet all three towns recovered.

More serious threats to urban existence were posed in some cases by the environment. Archaeologists have recently shown that Monmouth was disastrously affected by flooding during the rainy years of the early fourteenth century. The Wye and the Monnow, which all but surrounded the town, rose to unprecedented levels in the period 1315–45, according to archaeometric analysis; this led to the collapse of houses, leaving a thick leaven of silt. Yet Monmouth survived this and the plague, and in the long term its prosperity was largely unaffected.[64] More destructive were longer-term changes that affected the South Wales coast and its port towns in the later middle ages. It is not known for how long townsmen had been resisting encroaching sand and silting estuaries along the coasts of Gwent, Glamorgan and Carmarthenshire; in the upper Severn estuary in the vicinity of Newport, both Roman and medieval maritime remains have been uncovered in the levels where once there was a haven and there is now land – most startlingly, in recent years, a complete medieval boat wrecked while carrying iron ore.[65] By the fourteenth century, when political and demographic circumstances made the challenge of resisting nature all the more difficult, the town of Kenfig was in danger of being overwhelmed by dunes; the situation

[62] R. Howell, 'Excavations at Trellech, Gwent, 1991–93: an investigation of a decayed medieval urban settlement', *Monmouthshire Antiquary*, 11 (1995), 71–86; Beresford, *New Towns*, pp. 73, 256; W. Rees, *South Wales and the March, 1284–1415* (Oxford, 1924), p. 247 (quoting PRO, SC6/928/19–23). For Trellech's declining financial situation, see G. A. Holmes, *The Estates of the Higher Nobility in the XIVth Century* (Cambridge, 1957), pp. 107, 163.

[63] W. Rees, 'The Black Death in Wales', *TRHS*, 4th series, 3 (1920), 120 (reprinted in R. W. Southern, ed., *Essays in Medieval History* (London, 1968), p. 184); Courtney, *Medieval and Later Usk*, p. 129; PRO, SC6/1306/1 m. 1 (1349–50, Carmarthen); Griffiths, 'Carmarthen', p. 154 (Griffiths, *Conquerors and Conquered*, p. 183).

[64] *Archaeology in Wales*, 30 (1992), on excavations.

[65] N. Nayling, 'The excavation, recovery and provisional analysis of a medieval wreck from Magor Pill, Gwent Levels', *Archaeology in the Severn Estuary*, 6 (1995), 85–95.

worsened in the fifteenth century and later so that today only the peaks of its castle-tower and a hill-top church remain, creating a time capsule awaiting the archaeologist.[66] At Kidwelly, a flourishing port for much of the middle ages, the seas began to retreat so that larger ships could no longer enter the River Gwendraeth and approach the landing-stage of this walled town. Even Carmarthen, one of the largest towns in later medieval Wales, had to cope with the formation of a sand-bar in the Tywi estuary which, by the early fifteenth century, was being circumvented by transferring wine and other cargoes from sea-going vessels to smaller ballingers at a quay downriver.[67] Similar comment may be offered about the River Dee's estuary, for the town of Overton decayed before the middle ages were ended, and Flint and Holt also declined. Steady deterioration of the river artery made recovery from the ravages by Welsh rebels in 1294–5 and 1400–3 virtually impossible.[68]

Periodic rebellion took its toll of a number of towns. Trellech and Newport in the South-East, Denbigh and Flint in the North-East, and Bere and Harlech in North-West Wales were besieged in the rebellion of 1294–5, when much of Caernarfon was razed to the ground. This experience edged Trellech and Bere towards a decay that environmental factors, plague and declining population virtually completed.[69] In the decade after 1400, many more towns were mauled by rebels and often more severely. Owain Glyndŵr's first attacks on those towns of North-East Wales in the vicinity of his own estates reflect his personal resentments at the outset of the revolt. On 18 September 1400 he set fire to Ruthin before moving on to savage Denbigh, Rhuddlan, Flint, Hawarden and Holt.[70] The news of the attack on Ruthin reached Shrewsbury the next day, when the town council swiftly demanded that all Welsh residents of the town provide surety for their loyalty. It may have been a precaution, or else Shrewsbury was appraised of Owain's plans, for on 22–3 September he set fire to Oswestry and Welshpool, less than 20 miles (32 km) from Shrewsbury's gates.[71] In 1401, an assault on Conwy by Owain's Anglesey kinsmen partially destroyed the town and its walls. Later threats to Caernarfon by land and sea prompted a group of nineteen burgesses to estimate their losses in goods and trade at £1,275.[72] At Harlech,

[66] Griffiths, 'The medieval boroughs of Glamorgan', p. 354.

[67] Griffiths, 'Carmarthen', p. 155 (Griffiths, *Conquerors and Conquered*, p. 183); T. James, 'Shipping and the River Towy: problems of navigation', *Carmarthenshire Antiquary*, 22 (1986), 27–37.

[68] Soulsby, *Towns of Medieval Wales*, pp. 135–7, 144–7, 211–12.

[69] Griffiths, ed., *Boroughs of Mediaeval Wales*, pp. 30–1, 81–2, 170, 197; Lewis, *Snowdonia*, pp. 54, 183, 225–31; above pp. 700–1.

[70] J. E. Lloyd, *Owen Glendower* (Oxford, 1931), pp. 31–2; Davies, *Glyn Dŵr*, p. 102; Soulsby, *Towns of Medieval Wales*, p. 136. At Ruthin at least the damage was limited: Jack, 'Ruthin', p. 259.

[71] *CPR 1399–1401*, p. 359; D. R. Walker, 'An urban community in the Welsh borderland: Shrewsbury in the fifteenth century' (PhD thesis, University of Wales (Swansea), 1981), p. 328; Lloyd, *Glendower*, p. 32.

[72] Lewis, *Snowdonia*, pp. 184–5 (Caernarfon), 248–9 (Conwy); Williams-Jones, 'Caernarfon', pp. 88–9.

whose castle fell to the rebels in 1403 after a long siege, John Collier, who came from a long-established immigrant burgess family, claimed that he had lost 165 head of cattle, 40 horses, 100 sheep, 100 goats and £40 worth of other goods: Collier was merely the most spectacular victim among a group of Harlech's burgesses.[73] When the rebels took their depredations to southern Wales, the havoc was no less. During the descent on Kidwelly in 1403, several burgesses were killed and many townsmen fled with their wives and children after much of the old town within the walls was destroyed; they were discouraged from returning when, in the following year, the borough was ransacked and partly burnt.[74] The situation was little better in the larger, regional capital of Carmarthen: in 1403 more than fifty inhabitants were killed in a rebel attack, during which houses were razed to the ground; whilst in 1404, many townsmen retired from a town whose walls were partly demolished and whose future security was put in question. Thomas Dier, a prominent Carmarthen burgess and wool merchant, claimed that he had lost goods worth £1,000 in the attack of 1403 alone.[75] Not even Pembrokeshire was safe. Glyndŵr's French allies attacked and burned Haverfordwest in 1405, as well as threatening a number of other castles and boroughs in North and South Wales from the sea.[76] And in the South-East, burgages, mills and fisheries were destroyed at Usk and Caerleon, presumably when Glyndŵr attacked them in August 1402: 'Like another Assyrian, the rod of God's anger, he vented his fury with fire and sword in unprecedented tyrannies', lamented a shocked Adam of Usk when the news reached him in Rome.[77] Loyalists (or the faint-hearted) in Wrexham were perhaps more fortunate in being able to protect their life and moveables: early in the revolt, some of them retired behind the walls of Chester, only 11 miles (17 km) away.[78]

In such circumstances, the burden of urban defence was materially and financially crippling. The destruction of town walls and the sacking and razing of houses required considerable remedial investment which not all towns were able to secure in the years that followed Glyndŵr's revolt. For one thing, trade was severely disrupted during the emergency, and this disruption extended to

[73] Lewis, *Snowdonia*, p. 202 (from PRO, E163/6/38); *CPR 1401–5*, p. 293.

[74] Davies, *Glyn Dŵr*, pp. 269–77; F. C. Hingeston-Randolph, ed., *Royal and Historical Letters during the Reign of Henry the Fourth* (RS, 1860), vol. 1, pp. 160–2 (3 October 1403).

[75] Davies, *Glyn Dŵr*, p. 194; H. Ellis, ed., *Original Letters Illustrative of English History*, 2nd series (London, 1827), vol. 1, pp. 14–15; R. A. Griffiths, *The Principality of Wales in the Later Middle Ages*, vol. 1: *South Wales, 1277–1536* (Cardiff, 1972), p. 335 (and sources cited); Griffiths, 'Carmarthen', p. 155 (Griffiths, *Conquerors and Conquered*, p. 183).

[76] Davies, *Glyn Dŵr*, pp. 194–5, which is cautious about a widespread French impact.

[77] Holmes, *Higher Nobility*, pp. 104–5, 107, 162; C. Given-Wilson, ed., *The Chronicle of Adam Usk, 1377–1421* (Oxford, 1997), pp. 160–1. Usk Castle was attacked again in March 1405 and presumably the town suffered once more (*ibid.*, pp. 212–13). In that year, Adam's petition to the pope on behalf of Usk Priory noted 'the burning and pillaging and other misfortunes resulting from the war which is raging in those parts' (pp. 192–3).

[78] Davies, *Glyn Dŵr*, p. 220.

the high seas and to the border counties, where Chester and Shrewsbury bemoaned their loss of commerce, the substantial commitment to the king's military expeditions that was required of them (for all the business which royal armies may have brought to Chester, Shrewsbury, Hereford and Bristol) and the prohibition on the sale of foodstuffs and arms to the rebels.[79] At Carmarthen, for instance, several merchant-burgesses suffered for their loyalty to the crown. John Sely, a merchant of both Carmarthen and Llanstephan, shipped food and other supplies from England and Ireland to victual the coastal fortresses between Aberystwyth and Swansea in 1403 and 1404; his ship was seized in the port of Carmarthen by rebels. Thomas Rede, a prominent merchant of Carmarthen and Bristol, was probably much worse off towards the end of the revolt (he died in 1412) than at its beginning, for he made substantial loans to Prince Henry, partly for the defence of Carmarthen.[80] All told, this rebellion was the most widespread, concerted and intensive assault on a major sector of the civilian population of the king's dominions in the fourteenth and fifteenth centuries.

(v) WELSH AND ENGLISH

It should not be assumed that towns were the objectives of Glyndŵr's rebels (nor even of the rebels of 1294–5) simply because they were 'oases of Englishness' (to use R. R. Davies' phrase) created by foreign immigration. Englishness was 'a matter of perceptions and attitudes as well as of descent and language' in medieval Wales.[81] Whilst exploitation and rebellion fuelled resentment and distrust between English immigrants and their descendants, on the one hand, and the native population, on the other, at one time or another all Welsh towns accepted Welsh-born residents who adopted an urban life style and the association with Englishness that went with it. In the aftermath of Glyndŵr's rebellion, in 1411, Henry IV confirmed Brecon's liberties in a charter to 'the burgesses . . . whom we regard as English, as much on their father's side as on their mother's side'.[82]

Early foundations like Cardigan and Carmarthen, and later Edwardian towns like Aberystwyth, Dinefwr and Ruthin, had Welsh inhabitants from the local-

[79] *Ibid.*, pp. 246–7, 255–6, 281; *Rotuli Parliamentorum* (Record Commission, 1783), vol. III, pp. 618–19 (Shrewsbury's laments); *HMC*, 8th Report, App I, p. 359a (Chester's role); *Deputy Keeper's Reports*, vol. 36 (1875), pp. 60, 63, 78, 102, 198, 226, 475 (Cheshire recognisance rolls, 1402–4); J. G. Jones, 'Government and the Welsh community: the north-east borderland in the fifteenth century', in H. Hearder and H. R. Loyn, eds., *British Government and Administration* (Cardiff, 1974), pp. 60–2; R. Griffiths, 'Prince Henry's war: armies, garrisons and supply during the Glyndŵr rising', *Bulletin of the Board of Celtic Studies*, 34 (1987), 171–2.

[80] *CPR 1401–5*, p. 293; PRO, E101/43/38/1/28; DL42/16 f. 63r;/18 f. 11. For Sely as bailiff of Carmarthen, and Rede as mayor of the town, see Griffiths, *Principality of Wales*, I, pp. 336–7, 113–14, 347.

[81] Davies, *Glyn Dŵr*, p. 28.

[82] J. R. Alban and W. S. K. Thomas, 'Charters of the borough of Brecon, 1276–1517', *Brycheiniog*, 25 (1992–3), 31–55; Davies, 'Brecon', pp. 66–7.

ity or elsewhere in Wales, for the migrations of the middle ages with town development in view did not depend solely on recruitment in the English border shires, still less from further afield, important though these reservoirs of potential migrants were in an age of expanding population.[83] Cardigan, indeed, has the rare distinction of being an Anglo-Norman town which was captured by Rhys ap Gruffydd, overlord of Deheubarth, in 1165, barely half a century after its beginnings; for a generation it lay in Welsh hands and prospered. It is true that the Lord Rhys allowed some of the inhabitants to depart with half their possessions, but evidently others stayed, as did several clergy attached to the Benedictine priory which was a daughter house of Chertsey Abbey in Surrey. Rhys preserved the link with Chertsey and confirmed the priory's charter in the 1170s; he held court at Cardigan and organised in 1176 a festival of the arts there (allegedly the first eisteddfod); and he refortified the castle in stone and installed a Welsh constable. The town itself must surely have attracted some Welsh inhabitants during the Lord Rhys' time, and it was certainly a thriving urban centre in the mid-thirteenth century when it reverted to royal control.[84]

Some of Edward I's new burgesses at Dinefwr came from South Wales alongside others from England, to judge by their names.[85] The surviving records of Edwardian foundations in North Wales indicate that a number of their new burgesses were involved in the construction of local castles and town buildings. Personal property and borough privileges were offered to keep builders, masons and other craftsmen and their servants at their task at, for example, Flint, Rhuddlan, Caernarfon, Caerwys, Hope and Overton.[86] Yet even here, a minority of the early burgesses were Welsh: in 1292 three of seventy known burgesses of Flint had Welsh names, and so did four of the forty-three at Caerwys, and twenty-two of the fifty-seven at Overton.[87] Admittedly, Edward I proclaimed that all burgesses in his new boroughs should be of English birth and that the borough lands should not be devised to Welsh people; but these were unattainable goals, and in any case his archbishop of Canterbury, John Peckham, regarded urban development as a means of civilising the Welsh.[88] Accordingly, Aberystwyth had a mixed society from the start

[83] E.g. Jack, 'Ruthin', p. 250; Griffiths, 'Aberystwyth', pp. 38–9 (Griffiths, *Conquerors and Conquered*, p. 314).

[84] J. Williams ab Ithel, ed., *Annales Cambriae* (RS, 1860), p. 50; E. M. Pritchard, *Cardigan Priory in the Olden Days* (London, 1904), pp. 145, 148; R. A. Griffiths, 'The making of medieval Cardigan', *Ceredigion*, 11 (1990), 105–10 (Griffiths, *Conquerors and Conquered*, pp. 282–8). The Lord Rhys also captured Llandovery, but nothing is known of its town under his rule: Soulsby, *Towns of Medieval Wales*, p. 162.

[85] Griffiths, 'A tale of two towns', p. 215 (Griffiths, *Conquerors and Conquered*, pp. 264–5).

[86] A. J. Taylor, 'The earliest burgesses of Flint and Rhuddlan', *Flintshire Hist. Soc. J*, 27 (1975–6), 152–60. [87] *Ibid.*

[88] C. T. Martin, ed., *Registrum Epistolarum Johannis Peckham* (RS, 1882–4), vol. III, pp. 776–7.

in 1277, and by the end of the fourteenth century the same seems to have been true of Harlech and Cricieth. Edward I's ordinances were observed increasingly in the breach.[89]

At times of stress or difficulty, most notably in the aftermath of the plagues, the Edwardian ideal was preached anew at Ruthin, Hope, Flint and Montgomery. Welsh residents in certain towns experienced waves of resentment at their presence and their enjoyment of urban privileges. In 1345, a year of particular tension in North Wales, the burgesses of Rhuddlan complained that Welshmen had been proceeding against them in the court of King's Bench for the past ten years in order to breach their privileges, and had attacked them physically when they met at St Asaph's fair in 1344.[90] Such hostility was not simply a matter of race or birth: it was more complex, arising from conflicting rights and customs in an urban environment, each town market and fair jealous of its charters and privileges.

The resentment was not eased by the way in which incomers, including Welsh folk, seized the opportunities presented by the plague to exploit the land market and attempt to purchase available messuages and tenements left vacant by death or flight. In 1353 the burgesses of Flint (among them Ithel de Birchover, soon to be bailiff of Flint in 1355–6) opened negotiations with the Black Prince's officials for a confirmation of their charter and the town's boundaries, and in the months that followed several actions were initiated against Welshmen who were holding burgages in the town. The new charter was acquired on 20 September 1360; but Ithel was undeterred for, in June 1361, he was fined 66s. 8d. for having acquired a burgage and 2.5 acres (1 ha) in Flint which used to belong to John Adynet, and a further 20 acres (8.1 ha) there.[91] At Hope, a new royal charter of 1351 specifically excluded the Welsh from the town, and burgages formerly held

[89] Griffiths, 'Aberystwyth', pp. 38–9 (Griffiths, *Conquerors and Conquered*, pp. 314–15); Davies, *Conquest, Coexistence and Change*, pp. 421–2.

[90] J. G. Edwards, ed., *Calendar of Ancient Correspondence concerning Wales* (Cardiff, 1935), p. 232; D. L. Evans, 'Some notes on the history of the principality of Wales in the time of the Black Prince', *Transactions of the Cymmrodorion Society* (1925–6), pp. 42–4; *Register of Edward, the Black Prince*, 4 parts (London, 1930–3), III, p. 4; R. R. Davies, *Lordship and Society in the March of Wales, 1282–1400* (Oxford, 1978), p. 17.

[91] *Register of Edward, the Black Prince*, III, p. 121; *Deputy Keeper's Reports*, vol. 36 (1875), p. 184; P. H. W. Booth and A. D. Carr, eds., *Account of Master John de Burnham the Younger, Chamberlain of Chester, of the Revenues of the Counties of Chester and Flint, Michaelmas 1361 to Michaelmas 1362* (Manchester, 1991), pp. 55, 58–61, 63, 192. For Adinet or Adynet, a diminutive of Adam, see P. H. Reaney, *The Origins of English Surnames* (London, 1967; repr., 1987), p. 152. On the other hand, Thomas of Worcester, one of Flint's bailiffs in 1360–1, negotiated a £10 fine for half a burgage which formerly belonged to Madog 'Le Reve' and half a messuage which belonged to Madog 'le Cook', evidently two respectable Welsh townsmen of Flint; yet in the following year, one of the two bailiffs of Flint was named Cynwrig de Fakenhale, doubtless a man with Welsh forebears, like Ithel de Birchover. Booth and Carr, eds., *Account of John de Burnham*, pp. 65, 55.

by Welsh tenants appear to have been confiscated, although a Welsh burgess of Hope could still be identified in 1360.[92]

About the same time, at Caerwys in Flintshire, both of the bailiffs were Welsh men. As such, Cynwrig ap Roppert ab Iorwerth and Ednyfed ab Ieuan were even granted the farm of the town for six years in August 1358, and Cynwrig was a substantial figure: he was made sheriff of Flintshire for three years from September 1360 and constable of Flint Castle – provided he appointed an Englishman as his deputy![93] Peoples might be of different birth and have a different history, but in the affairs of urban life they were learning to share the same environment – until other, more extreme, tensions arose. Further south, at Ruthin, within fifty years of 1282, a Welshman called Ieuan Ceri was living in Welsh Street; in the 1340s he was a modestly prosperous burgess-tradesman, brewing ale, selling cattle, horses and oxen, lending money 'to lubricate the market in commodities and land' in the town and surrounding district (and he could be charged with usury on at least two occasions), and he evidently capitalised on the disruption of 1349 to invest some of his commercial capital in a new upper-storey *solarium* for his house in the town. He was part of a Welsh community in Ruthin: as early as 1324, two of the tailors of Ruthin were Welshmen and so were as many as eleven of the butchers.[94]

New charters granted to the southern towns of Carmarthen (in 1386), Laugharne (1389) and St Clears (1393) stated that no burgess should henceforward be 'convicted or adjudged by any Welshman . . . but only by English burgesses and true Englishmen'.[95] Such formalities of discrimination were widespread and they turned to practical victimisation during Glyndŵr's rebellion. In Oswestry, among the border towns, Welshmen were no longer trusted (1401) to help guard the gates, and in Chester tight restrictions were imposed (1403) on the movements of Welsh people.[96] Yet within Wales matters were not everywhere as clear-cut. Lord Charlton's charter granted to Welshpool in 1407, when the rebellion was far from over, implied that loyal Welshmen might still be burgesses, but other Welsh folk were to be treated harshly.[97] These towns were situated not too far from the Cheshire plain. Elsewhere, the opportunities open to Welsh burgesses, and the

[92] D. L. Evans, ed., *Flintshire Ministers Accounts, 1328–53* (Flint, 1929), p. xliv; *Register of Edward, the Black Prince*, III, p. 46; Booth and Carr, eds., *Account of John de Burnham*, p. lxx.

[93] *Deputy Keeper's Report*, vol. 36 (1875), p. 409; Booth and Carr, eds., *Account of John de Burnham*, pp. 57, 55, 193.

[94] Barrell, Davies, Padel and Smith, 'Dyffryn Clwyd project', p. 294; M. Rogers, 'The Welsh Marcher lordship of Bromfield and Yale, 1282–1485' (PhD thesis, University of Wales (Aberystwyth), 1992), pp. 282–94.

[95] Davies, *Glyn Dŵr*, p. 28; Griffiths, 'Carmarthen', pp. 157–8 (Griffiths, *Conquerors and Conquered*, pp. 184–5).

[96] Davies, *Glyn Dŵr*, pp. 290–2; *Deputy Keeper's Report*, vol. 36 (1875), p. 102 (4 September 1403).

[97] Davies, *Glyn Dŵr*, p. 291; see *Montgomeryshire Collections*, 7 (1874), 343–6, for the charter.

tensions that could result, may have been greater. In the south, where rebels had been highly destructive, townsfolk seem to have been more nervous: in Brecon in 1408 the bailiffs were forbidden to receive any Welshman as a burgess; although it was decreed at Kidwelly in 1407 that no Welshman should be a town official, no similar ban seems to have been imposed on admission to the body of burgesses.[98]

For all the suspicion, fear and social resentments which the Glyndŵr rebellion accentuated, some townsmen of Welsh descent stood loyal to the king, their town and their own interests. Thomas ap Dafydd, bailiff of Brecon during the rebellion, helped to defend the town against Glyndŵr's forces.[99] Contrariwise, several townsmen of English descent were prepared to join the rebels, among them a scion of a loyalist immigrant family at Tenby, David Perrot; less surprisingly, Welsh-born burgesses like John Llwyd of Carmarthen turned rebel. The towns of Wales, bastions of royal and seigneurial rule, defended themselves against the rebel armies and suffered accordingly; though many an urban community had its dissidents.[100]

The towns in Glyndŵr's day – perhaps even in the 1290s – were obvious centres of privilege and English loyalty that gave credibility and focus to the rebellion. Welsh townsmen – and there were many – sometimes spurned the disaffected and contemplated the opportunities of more settled times ahead. Once the passions of rebellion were spent, the process of urban integration of communities could resume. It took several decades before trust between Welsh and English in the towns could be restored or established, and distinctions and suspicions overcome; attempts were periodically made (as in the 1440s) to confirm or revive discriminating laws and customs against Welshmen aspiring to be burgesses in 'English towns' in Wales.[101] Nevertheless, faced with the social realities, more than one town felt able to share its administration between the communities: at Wrexham by 1466, the English tenants were presenting one of the bailiffs, and the Welsh townsmen the other; at Holt by the 1470s, it was common to have one English and one Welsh bailiff each year, in defiance of the letter of Thomas fitz Alan's charter of 1411; and the same pattern seems to have been followed at Cardigan after the rebellion was over.[102] By the end of the fifteenth century, even in the administrative capital of the king's northern prin-

[98] Davies, *Glyn Dŵr*, p. 291; Davies 'Brecon', pp. 66–7.

[99] Davies, 'Brecon', pp. 58, 66.

[100] R. Turvey, 'The Marcher shire of Pembrokeshire and the Glyndŵr rebellion', *Welsh History Review*, 15 (1990–1), 159, 161; Griffiths, *Principality of Wales*, I, pp. 292, 337.

[101] *Rotuli Parliamentorum*, V, pp. 104, 138–9; R. A. Griffiths, 'Wales and the Marches', in S. B. Chrimes, C. D. Ross and R. A. Griffiths, eds., *Fifteenth-Century England, 1399–1509* (Manchester, 1972; repr., Stroud, 1995), p. 154.

[102] B. Evans, 'Grant of privileges to Wrexham (1380)', *Bulletin of the Board of Celtic Studies*, 19 (1960), 42–7; Rogers, 'Welsh Marcher lordship of Bromfield and Yale', pp. 282–94 (Holt); Griffiths, *Principality of Wales*, I, pp. 419–36; Griffiths, 'The making of medieval Cardigan', 120 (Griffiths, *Conquerors and Conquered*, p. 293). Ordinances of Henry VIII's reign that prevented Welshmen from the hills from becoming burgesses of Neath reflected tension between town and country

cipality, Caernarfon, wealth and reputation, rather than ethnic origin, were the key to position and prominence in the borough. This was recognised more widely by Henry VII when he formally allowed Welsh men to acquire land freely in the so-called 'English' boroughs of northern Wales where the distinctions may have remained the sharpest.[103]

(vi) THE LATER MEDIEVAL TOWNS

In the fifteenth century, population levels were beginning to rise, environmental disasters had partly abated and political changes were in train that relieved the royal and seigneurial pressures from many towns whilst at the same time removing certain crucial supports from others. It was this combination of factors which produced the 'winnowing' of Wales' numerous towns, so that some prospered and others did not. This can hardly be said to amount to urban decline. Prosperous towns were fewer in number but many were as large, if not larger, than in the past. And alongside the thriving there appeared a breed of country markets, often on sites different from those of decayed towns, but supplementing the economic and social services provided by earlier towns and chartered boroughs in a countryside that was experiencing more peaceful conditions. This urban reorientation was often accompanied by a lively land and tenement market in the later middle ages, along with the development of suburbs and a growing integration of countryside and town, not least by means of the urbanisation of rural landowners.

It is in the nature of towns that they have a close relationship with their hinterlands, and not even Wales' castellated boroughs with masonry defences carefully integrated with towering fortresses – as at Conwy and Caernarfon still – were isolated islands. In the case of small towns, which predominated in much of Wales, the relationship between town and country, and between townspeople and countryfolk was an intimate one. It seems likely that in all towns the townsmen had always occupied properties outside the towns' defences – indeed, the opportunity to do so was doubtless included in the package of privileges offered to potential immigrants from the twelfth century onwards. Such arrangements are clear in Edward I's reign: burgage holders in towns like Denbigh were also owners of curtilages outside the walls and of portions of land in the surrounding countryside.[104] By 1305 there were 52 burgages inside the walls and 183 outside them, so dramatic was the town's growth.

rather than between Welsh and English – and may in part have originated earlier: R. A. Griffiths, 'The boroughs of the lordship of Glamorgan', p. 354; above p. 691.

103 Williams-Jones, 'Caernarfon', pp. 93–101; J. B. Smith, 'Crown and community in the principality of North Wales in the reign of Henry Tudor', *Welsh History Review*, 3 (1966–7), 157–8.

104 D. H. Owen, 'Denbigh', in Griffiths, ed., *Boroughs of Mediaeval Wales*, pp. 169–70, 174–5; D. H. Owen, 'The two foundation charters of the borough of Denbigh', *Bulletin of the Board of Celtic Studies*, 28 (1979), 253–66.

When other towns experienced plague-induced crises in the 1350s and 1360s, both Conwy and Beaumaris were expanding, partly by absorbing the lands of former bond settlements nearby which had previously sustained the economic and social structures of princely Gwynedd. Burgesses acquired the holdings of Welsh clans, and the process whereby Bartholomew Bolde of Conwy, whose forebears had migrated from Lancashire, achieved this between 1420 and 1453 has been reconstructed from his surviving archive.[105] In the south at Llanstephan, the sole surviving lay cartulary from Wales, that of the Fort family, shows a similar process at work much earlier during the late thirteenth and fourteenth centuries, but then Llanstephan was situated in a part of Wales that was a land of peace much earlier; the Bolde experience suggests that for all the turbulence at the turn of the fourteenth and fifteenth centuries, the process was not halted.[106] The Boldes and the Forts were of immigrant descent, but close study of the family of Sir Rhys ap Thomas, Henry VII's and Henry VIII's lieutenant in Wales, indicates that in the fifteenth century the native-born were able to do just as well – in this case by turning the decayed town of Dinefwr into a country estate and by buying properties in Carmarthen which made one of the very largest towns in Wales into a family fiefdom.[107]

A number of towns showed signs of lively industrial development during the later fourteenth and fifteenth centuries, including in their suburbs or on their outskirts and especially in the cloth industry. Fulling mills were built at Swansea, Kidwelly, Carmarthen and Llanelli along the southern coast, and at Ruthin and Chirk in the north-east; at Ruthin guilds of weavers and fullers had been formed to manage their trade and personal interests by the 1440s, and there was a corvisers' guild there in 1496.[108] These towns had ready access to markets for manufactured Welsh cloth as far as London and sometimes overseas. Elsewhere, coal mining and iron smelting were part of the economy, and before the end of the fourteenth century Llansamlet, to the north of Swansea, was the site of coal mines producing presumably for export.[109]

[105] D. H. Owen, 'The middle ages', in D. H. Owen, ed., *Settlement and Society in Wales* (Cardiff, 1989), p. 211; T. Jones Pierce, 'The *Gafael* in Bangor manuscript 1939', *Transactions of the Cymmrodorion Society* (1942), pp. 158–88 (reprinted in T. Jones Pierce, *Medieval Welsh Society* (Cardiff, 1972), ch. 7).

[106] R. A. Griffiths, 'The cartulary and muniments of the Fort family of Llanstephan', *Bulletin of the Board of Celtic Studies*, 24 (1971), 311–84 (Griffiths, *Conquerors and Conquered*, ch. 14). The Forts were presumably of immigrant descent in the twelfth or thirteenth century, though their original home is unknown.

[107] R. A. Griffiths, *Sir Rhys ap Thomas and his Family: A Study in the Wars of the Roses and Early Tudor Politics* (Cardiff, 1993), esp. pp. 73–4.

[108] R. I. Jack, 'The cloth industry in medieval Wales', *Welsh History Review*, 10 (1981), 443–60; R. I. Jack, 'Fulling mills in Wales and the March before 1547', *Archaeologia Cambrensis*, 130 (1981), 70–130.

[109] W. R. B. Robinson, 'Swansea', in Griffiths, ed., *Boroughs of Mediaeval Wales*, p. 268. Cf. Monmouth and Trellech (until its decay in the fourteenth century): above pp. 700–1.

Some towns were acquiring sturdier, larger buildings in the later middle ages, including stone hall houses in the fourteenth century and imposing churches which doubtless reflected the prosperity of town inhabitants as well as their lively faith; here one thinks of Cowbridge, Brecon, Cardiff and Tenby, and the northern towns of Gresford and Mold whose church building was patronised by the Stanley family towards the end of the fifteenth century. By the middle of the fifteenth century more elaborate hall-houses were being built, as in Ruthin – with upper storey solars where previously the halls were open to the rafters.[110] Prosperity and considerations of safety made slates and tiles popular in some towns, as Jean Creton noticed of Conwy on his visit with Richard II in 1399.[111] At Brecon, the new tower of St Mary's church in the middle of the borough was paid for by Edward Stafford, duke of Buckingham (d. 1521).[112] Public buildings appeared, a court house with shops below at Wrexham by 1391, a town hall and a court house at Holt before 1500.[113]

Carmarthen, Pembroke, Cardiff, Brecon, Monmouth, Newport, Denbigh and Caernarfon retained an importance when other centres of government like Cardigan, Aberystwyth, Kidwelly, Usk and Holt, whose administrative role derived from seigneurial lordship and political morcellation, were losing theirs. The former, larger towns were regional centres whose position was confirmed by the reorganisation of government and justice in the Acts of Union.[114] It might be thought that the growth of Bristol and, to a lesser extent, Chester as entrepôts for their regional economies, and the proximity of Hereford, Gloucester and Shrewsbury, three of the wealthier towns in England in 1334, might have prejudiced the development and commercial vitality of Welsh towns and ports in the Severn and Dee valleys; but this seems not to have been the case.[115] Rather did Carmarthen merchants divide their time and their wealth between their home town and the metropolitan city, and South Wales ports grew in association with

[110] Above pp. 690, 707; E. Hubbard, *The Buildings of Wales: Clwyd* (London, 1986), pp. 168, 390; *An Inventory of the Ancient Monuments in Glamorgan*, vol. III: *Medieval Secular Monuments*, Part II: *Non-Defensive* (Cardiff, 1982), pp. 134–6, 144–5, 197–8; Smith, *Houses of the Welsh Countryside*, plates 15, 66, 67, 71. And for the half-timbered town houses in all but the three south-western counties, *ibid.*, maps 10 (pp. 380–1), 11 (pp. 392–3).

[111] C. Given-Wilson, ed., *Chronicles of the Revolution, 1397–1400* (Manchester, 1993), p. 140.

[112] E. G. Parry, 'Brecon: topography and townscape, part 1: origins and early development, 1093–1521', *Brycheiniog*, 21 (1984–5), 12–20.

[113] Rogers, 'Welsh Marcher lordship of Bromfield and Yale', pp. 282–94, 352–7.

[114] W. Rees, *The Union of England and Wales* (Cardiff, 1948), pp. 55ff.

[115] M. O. H. Carver, ed., *Medieval Worcester: An Archaeological Framework* (*Transactions of the Worcestershire Archaeological Society*, 3rd series, 7 (1980)), p. 9; M. O. H. Carver, ed., *Two Town Houses in Medieval Shrewsbury* (*Transactions of the Shropshire Archaeological Society*, 61 (1983 for 1977–8)), p. 68; R. H. Hilton, 'Low-level urbanization: the seignorial borough of Thornbury in the middle ages', in Razi and Smith, eds., *Medieval Society and the Manor Court*, p. 484. For Chester's declining fortunes from the mid-fourteenth century, see Booth and Carr, eds., *Account of John de Burnham*, pp. xli–ii, lxv.

Bristol rather than failed in competition with it. By 1500, Bristol's population had had a significant well-to-do element of Welsh descent for several centuries, to judge by personal nomenclature and the recorded occupiers of tenements in the city. Contacts with Welsh towns were frequent in the thirteenth century, and as early as 1218 wool was being exported from Carmarthen to Bristol; its role as an assembly point for armies and supplies during phases of the conquest of Wales strengthened the link. By 1300, Thomas de Kenfig occupied a tenement in Broad Street; and John de Monmouth had a messuage in Wine Street which, when Richard de Monmouth inherited it by 1325, had two halls fronted by four shops; and a tailor, John de Cardiff, and his wife were leasing a tenement in Wine Street by 1390. These need not have been Welsh-born Bristolians, but in the fifteenth century merchants with unmistakable Welsh names had migrated to Bristol. Among the prominent Vaughan clan, David Vaughan was a tenant in Wine Street by 1405, at the height of the rebellion, and Richard Vaughan was a substantial merchant, with several properties in the city's commercial districts at the turn of the fifteenth and sixteenth centuries.[116] Bristol's westward interests from the sixteenth century onwards may also have aided some of the Welsh ports.

In this process of shaking out or 'winnowing', market centres emerged during the fifteenth century for no other than local commercial reasons, and they gradually acquired the characteristics of town life. One thinks of Dolgellau, which had only three taxpayers in 1292–3, when the nearby Welsh and, more recently, Edwardian borough of Bere still met the crown's military needs. But by 1543, Bere was no more and Dolgellau had twenty-three taxpayers; a few years earlier, John Leland had described it encouragingly as the 'best village' in the area, and it was still growing.[117] Dinas Mawddwy, in the same region, often thought the poorest town in Wales, was a new borough, created by charter in 1395, when it had as many as thirty-five burgesses. In the south, Bridgend was developing as a market when nearby Kenfig was overblown by sand and Aberafan was shrinking into villagedom.[118]

Townsfolk – even those in the more modest towns – shared a common, collective urban identity, no matter how appropriate or inappropriate or derivative were their charters, privileges or ordinances. This identity was strongest in the more robust towns of later medieval Wales and it could be expressed in grants and charters of personal and communal privileges, or the construction or extension (as at Tenby) of stone walls and gateways, usually at a town's expense through

[116] R. H. Leech, ed., *The Topography of Medieval and Early Modern Bristol: Part 1* (Bristol, 1997), pp. 25–6, 38, 62, 94, 136, 149, 166, 169, 179, 185, 190, 197; C. Burgess, ed., *The Pre-Reformation Records of All Saints, Bristol, Part 1* (Bristol, 1995), for Vaughans and others with distinctive Welsh names. See Griffiths, 'Medieval Severnside', pp. 86–9 (Griffiths, *Conquerors and Conquered*, pp. 12–14). [117] Soulsby, *Towns of Mediaeval Wales*, pp. 131–3.

[118] *Ibid.*, pp. 126–7; Pugh, ed., *Glamorgan County History*, III, pp. 359–60. For market centres of the late thirteenth century, see D. Pratt, 'Llanrhaeadr-ym-Mochnant's market charter, 1284', *Transactions of the Denbighshire Hist. Soc.*, 34 (1985), 57–90; *CCh.R 1257–1300*, pp. 213, 276.

taxation (or murage) of its trade. It could be fortified by frequent tension between town dwellers and country folk, during which the townsfolk saw themselves as loyal English, even though a variable proportion of townsmen in every town after 1300 was of Welsh descent. The burgesses of the chartered boroughs in particular expressed their identity through communal acts: by petitioning and lobbying for further privileges and for confirmation of existing ones, as Cardigan and Carmarthen did in 1386–95 against each other's interests;[119] by organising town life through ordinances or by-laws, as at Cowbridge, Carmarthen and Wrexham;[120] by victimising vagrants and 'foreigners'; by investing in conspicuous town building and improvements; by establishing merchant and craft guilds, as at Brecon, Cardiff and Ruthin;[121] by insisting on attending their own town (or hundred) court; by authenticating a town's decisions with a common seal 'of the commune' or 'of the commonalty';[122] by taking manifest pride in origin myths that had Roman, Arthurian, Christian or other roots (as at Carmarthen, Caernarfon, Oswestry and Caerleon); by standing on their dignity and privileges against powerful religious institutions in the vicinity, as at Carmarthen against the Augustinian priory and its urban community of 'Old' Carmarthen; and by cherishing religious relics which, as at St Mary's priory in Cardigan, could make a town famous.[123]

At this same time, the relationship between countryside and town, between country dweller and townsman, between Welsh-born families and the descendants of immigrants, was becoming closer and the differences between them less apparent. At Carmarthen in the fifteenth century, the country gentry took to serving as mayors, and presumably had town houses.[124] At Cowbridge the Carne family of the Vale had its town house, and several Gower landowners had one foot in the town of Swansea. Back in the 1290s, there were few signs of rural Welsh people taking such a stake in the towns; by the end of the fifteenth century it had become common.[125] John Leland commented on fifty-eight Welsh towns

[119] Griffiths, 'Making of medieval Cardigan', pp. 117–18 (Griffiths, *Conquerors and Conquered*, p. 292 and references cited).

[120] Above p. 691; D. Pratt, 'Bromfield and Yale: presentments from the court roll of 1467', *Transactions of the Denbighshire Hist. Soc.*, 37 (1988), 43–53; J. Davies, 'Apud Carmarthen: "A booke of ordinaunces"', *Carmarthenshire Antiquary*, 29 (1993), 27–38.

[121] Davies, 'Brecon', p. 68; D. G. Walker, 'Cardiff', in Griffiths, ed., *Boroughs of Mediaeval Wales*, p. 126; Jack, 'Ruthin', p. 256.

[122] For example, Griffiths, 'Making of medieval Cardigan', p. 116 (Griffiths, *Conquerors and Conquered*, p. 291). In general, see D. H. Williams, *Catalogue of Seals in the National Museum of Wales* (Cardiff, 1993–), vol. I, pp. 47–53.

[123] Williams-Jones, 'Caernarfon', pp. 73–6; Griffiths, 'Carmarthen', pp. 132–8; Smith, 'Oswestry', p. 219; Griffiths, 'Making of medieval Cardigan', pp. 123–4 (Griffiths, *Conquerors and Conquered*, pp. 295–6).

[124] Griffiths, *Principality of Wales*, I, pp. 347–53.

[125] Robinson, *Cowbridge*, pp. 67ff; Robinson, 'Swansea', pp. 283–4; R. K. Turvey, 'The Perrots and their circle in South-West Wales during the later middle ages' (PhD thesis, University of Wales (Swansea), 1988), pp. 310–65.

which he visited during his travels in Wales, rather more than half of the towns known in the middle ages. His adjectives and judgements imply that he thought that about thirty of the fifty-eight were either stagnant or in decline. Some he understood to have been seriously blighted by Glyndŵr's rebellion and still bore the marks: Montgomery was 'deflorichid' by Glyndŵr, and Radnor was 'partely destroied' by the rebels.[126] Even if this is an accurate view, what it represents is not the general decay of urbanity in Wales but rather the consequences of discrimination in development.

In short and in aggregate, Welsh towns were almost as populous in the early sixteenth century as they had been in the 1290s. Where the population of individual towns had fallen it had occurred predominantly in the mountainous districts, or where towns in close proximity were in competition economically or administratively with one another. There was still a thriving urban economy which was not necessarily – certainly not simply – dependent on prosperous, immediate hinterlands. Rather could it capitalise on Wales' exceptionally long coastline, its contacts with Bristol, Chester and the greater centres of the West Midlands, and of course on its sea-borne trade which, as Star Chamber cases from the early sixteenth century make plain, brought French, Breton, Spanish and Portuguese vessels to Milford Sound and the Severn estuary.[127] Commerce, devolved administration, relative peace and the integration of town and countryside sustained this vitality.

[126] L. T. Smith, ed., *The Itinerary in Wales of John Leland* (London, 1906) (p. 41).

[127] For example, Griffiths, *Sir Rhys ap Thomas*, pp. 93–4; H. James and T. James, 'Ceramic and documentary evidence for Iberian trade with West Wales', in B. Vyner and S. Wrathwell, eds., *Studies in Medieval and Later Pottery in Wales Presented to J. M. Lewis* (Cardiff, 1987), pp. 225–34.

· 23 ·

Scotland

E. PATRICIA DENNISON AND GRANT G. SIMPSON

(i) GEOGRAPHICAL AND GEOLOGICAL SETTING

THE HISTORY of urbanisation in Scotland is predetermined by the geography and geology of northern Britain. Often assumed to be a country of sharp divide between Highland and Lowland, its physical nature, however, is more complex. It was not merely the mountainous areas of the Highlands that were seemingly unapproachable from the more gentle Lowland terrain; but the south-west regions of Galloway and Ayrshire were equally divorced from the east coast; and the southern border region of the country, in its very lack of natural, physical definition, often had a somewhat different agenda from the other parts of Scotland.

Even a cursory glance at the west coast of northern Britain, from Lancashire to the northern Highlands of Scotland, reveals the linkages that were to dominate this seaboard. Travel by water was to form the easiest method of contact for the western Highlands, Islands, Galloway and Ayrshire; and the predominant communication points and influences for these areas were to be not the Lowland basin centred around the River Forth, but Ireland and the North of England.

The east coast, by contrast, used the sea to look to mainland Europe, and in particular northern France, the Low Countries, Scandinavia and the Baltic. They were more approachable, in terms of both ease and time of travelling, than the less accessible parts of Scotland. Rivers, such as the Tweed, the Forth, the Tay and the Dee, all providing natural harbours, would become the foci for this contact. Perth and Stirling, at the highest navigable points of the Rivers Tay and Forth respectively, were to play crucial roles in Scotland's history; and Berwick, Dundee and Aberdeen, with their good harbourage, were to dominate the economic scene; but increasingly under the hegemony of Edinburgh through its pre-eminent port of Leith.

It was inevitable that the southern regions of Scotland would have close links with England; but these were not always to be harmonious. The boundary between the two countries was disputed for centuries. The Scots, for example, under David I (1124–53) invaded the North of England in 1135, ostensibly in support of the claim to the English throne of his niece, Empress Matilda. The net result was the annexation of Cumberland by 1138; and between 1140/2 and 1151 of Northumberland and Westmorland, or 'Kentdale', and a strong Scottish influence well into Yorkshire. This 'English empire', south of Lothian, was held until 1157.[1] Nominal authority over the three most important southerly Scottish towns, Edinburgh, Roxburgh and Berwick, was then lost to England in 1174, only to be later regained. Throughout the Wars of Independence (from 1296) and well into the fourteenth century, the Scottish border region experienced occupation and domination at times by both Scottish and English rule. Such a lack of firm frontiers and the loss, albeit temporary, of crucial centres had an inevitable impact on urban settlements further north;[2] and would continue to do so until formal definition was achieved in the latter part of the fourteenth century, compounded by alternating national control of Berwick and its ultimate loss in 1482.

A land of geographic and geological contrasts, Scotland was provided with a climate harsher than that of its southern neighbour; this would have implications not only for communications and trade (the Tay, for example, was known to freeze between Dundee and Perth); but also for the health of the population, which probably suffered more than has been recognised in the past from the effects of, for example, pulmonary infections and pneumonic plague. It was, however, a landscape that was well wooded, which facilitated construction of dwellings (see pp. 182–3). The maps of the cartographer Timothy Pont, drawn in the last decade of the sixteenth century, are testament to the lasting afforestation of Scotland throughout the middle ages. Hard woods, such as oak timbers, were used in large impressive buildings, often being re-utilised in less prestigious sites. There was also a more than adequate supply of soft woods, which required minimum preparation prior to use. Alder, ash, elm, beech and willow proved the mainstay of lesser dwellings. Peat and coal were plentiful, as was salt, of the coarse variety; the land could support not only reared animals, but also a variety of wild game; and the rivers and seas provided an excellent source of fish. Even though the country was not, as a whole, blessed with a clement climate or major stretches of fertile soil, the Scottish diet of fish and meat, supplemented with vegetables such as kale, with a staple of cereals, in particular oats, was a relatively healthy one.

[1] I. Blanchard, 'Lothian and beyond: the economy of the "English empire" of David I', in R. H. Britnell and J. Hatcher, eds., *Progress and Problems in Medieval England* (Cambridge, 1996), pp. 23–43.

[2] E. P. Dennison and R. Coleman, *Historic Melrose* (Scottish Burgh Survey, 1998).

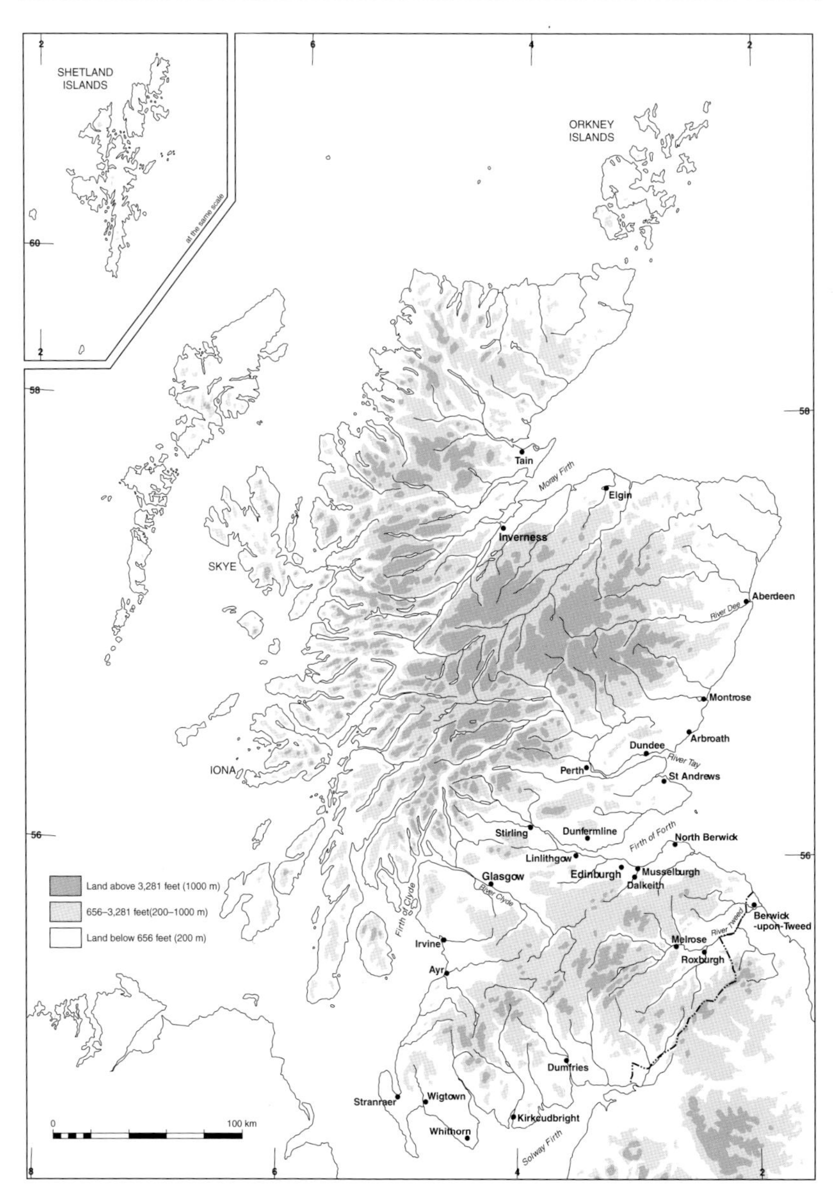

Map 23.1 Towns in Scotland

(ii) EARLY URBAN SETTLEMENT

It was in this geophysical setting that the first Scottish towns emerged; and the geographical advantages of particular sites were some of the strongest influences on the choices of specific settlement sites (see p. 717). Less clear is when this happened. The earliest documentary evidence for burghs, settlements deliberately created with specific legal rights, is as late as the first half of the twelfth century. But there is no reason to conclude that this was when towns first appeared. Annalistic evidence suggesting the existence of urban settlements of some kind is extant from before the twelfth century; and it is unwise to assume that the appearance of formal written evidence and the emergence of towns were coincidental. There was no intrinsic need for early burghs to have written records of foundation and privilege, and even burghs founded by David I and his successors may have received their rights by word of mouth, rather than by written charter.

Indeed, for much of the period under review the path of the urban historian is troubled by the paucity of source material. The earliest continuous urban archive, that for Aberdeen, begins as late as the very end of the fourteenth century; and even this record has a loss of registers for 1413–33. A number of guild merchant and burgh court records survive from the fifteenth century; but it is only towards the end of this time that they survive in any meaningful volume. Scottish urban historians are, in many cases, forced to rely for pre-fifteenth century evidence largely on charters, where they survive; the *Leges Burgorum*, reputedly of the reign of David I, drawn up perhaps for Berwick, and to become the basic foundation for the rulings of specific Scottish burghs; the *Statuta Gildae*, the statutes of the guild of Berwick, the earlier part of which is attributed to 1249 and the later specifically dated 1281 and 1294; and ecclesiastical records in the form of cartularies of religious houses.[3]

Although in England the later Saxon and Viking periods saw the establishment of a number of urban centres on erstwhile Roman sites, this was not the case in Scotland. Civilian settlements attached to *vici*, as, for example, at Inveresk beside Musselburgh, at Newstead by Melrose and possibly Elginhaugh beside Dalkeith, are known; but all the evidence suggests that these were never truly independent urban settlements. Groupings of people with both an agricultural and a trading base, as at Traprain Law, may begin to suggest some form of proto-urban society; but although there may be seen here some facets of urbanisation, it would be difficult to claim that towns were in existence by the late Roman period. The typical pattern of settlement in much of Scotland was

[3] For a fuller discussion of the available source material, see I. Flett and J. Cripps, 'Documentary sources', in M. Lynch, M. Spearman and G. Stell, eds., *The Scottish Medieval Town* (Edinburgh, 1988), pp. 18–41.

one of pastoral *toun*, dependent on a basically agricultural substructure. By the late eleventh century, however, in spite of the lack of archaeological evidence and an inadequate documentary record, the historian becomes alerted to the existence of communities that might be categorised as urban.

There are numerous instances. Dunfermline, for example, was a burgh by 1124x27 at latest.[4] A charter of David I of *c.* 1128, however, confirming the grants of preceding kings to the church of Dunfermline, records the donations of King Malcolm Canmore (1058–93) and Queen Margaret to the township, indicating the existence of settlement before burghal status.[5] A royal hunting lodge, with an associated church, had focused as the setting for the marriage of King Malcolm Canmore to the Princess Margaret in 1067x70. And, even as early as this date, a 'royal activity centre' could readily have come into existence, offering both service and supplies. Referred to as an 'oppidum' in Fordun's chronicle, it is reasonable to assume that the small township had, at least, a trading, proto-urban existence.[6]

Aberdeen, also, is known to have been a burgh by the reign of David I;[7] and, during this time, it was of sufficient stature to house the peripatetic king and his court and at least one charter was issued from the town.[8] Further evidence, however, reveals that Aberdeen was a flourishing trading township by the early decades of the twelfth century, at latest. A grant of *c.* 1180 by William I (1165–1214) to his burgesses at Aberdeen, Moray and north of the Mounth stated that they should enjoy their free hanse as they had in the time of David I – a specific reference to the existence of settlements of both native and foreign traders and of established trade.[9] This is further confirmed by the grant in 1136 to the bishop of Aberdeen of the tithes of all ships coming into Aberdeen, indicating that the haven of Aberdeen was well known to, and well frequented by, both ships and merchants.[10] As early as the reign of Alexander I (1107–24), it was already one of the three major trading centres north of the Forth.[11] It is most unlikely that it suddenly burst on the mercantile scene in the early years of the twelfth century; and its origins probably lie, as with Dunfermline, in the eleventh century.

Twelfth-century St Andrews (Plate 24) is a further example that reveals the existence of some form of pre-burghal nucleus. Kinrimund, the religious focal point and supposed shrine of St Andrew, can be traced back to at least the eighth

[4] *Registrum de Dunfermelyn* (Bannatyne Club, 1842), no. 26. Although this charter is undated, it was a grant of King David I, who succeeded in 1124; and one of the witnesses was Robert, bishop elect of St Andrews, consecrated in 1127. [5] *Ibid.*, no. 1.

[6] W. F. Skene, ed., *Johannis de Fordun: Chronica Gentis Scotorum* (1871–2), liber v, xv (p. 213); A. O. Anderson, ed., *Early Sources of Scottish History, 500 to 1286* (Edinburgh, 1922), vol. II, p. 25.

[7] *Registrum Episcopatus Aberdonensis* (Spalding Club, 1845), vol. I, p. 6.

[8] G. Barrow *et al.* eds., (*RRS*), I, no. 80. [9] *Ibid.*, II, no. 153.

[10] *Reg. Episc. Aberdonensis*, I, p. 4. [11] *RRS*, I, no. 243.

century and perhaps a century more.[12] It is unlikely to have been able to exist for four centuries without the support of some ancillary secular settlement. Indeed, the town's charter of 1144x53 erecting it to burghal status specifically refers to the existing *toun*;[13] and, in 1189x98, the burgesses were given the right to move the market cross to the new market place from 'the place where the clochin used to be'. This was, without doubt, the Gaelic 'clachan' meaning a hamlet – the *toun* or pre-burghal nucleus of St Andrews.[14]

These three burghs were not unique in having origins stretching back beyond their formal receipt of legal rights. Similar evidence arises for many other towns. Dumbarton, Dundee, Nairn and Perth[15] are merely four further examples of towns with known pre-burghal nuclei. Indeed, there were probably very few burghs erected in the twelfth century on totally green-field sites.

What is clear is that this policy of establishing burghs, whether by elevation of an existing township or by deliberate plantation, was a Scottish facet of the growth in urbanisation throughout Western Europe in this period. David I and his successors had much to gain from the creation of burghs. Not only did their presence offer a means of extending royal control but, equally, the resultant stimulus to manufacturing and trade brought increased revenue to the crown. And it was not merely the crown that benefited. Lay and religious magnates were also permitted, with royal approval, to establish dependent burghs, as in Glasgow, Arbroath and Dundee, which respectively had a bishop, abbot and secular lord as overlords.

A map of Scotland showing twelfth-century burghs is an accurate indicator of royal influence. But we should not dismiss the possibility that other settlements displaying urban characteristics may have existed, but have escaped recognition as they were never raised to burghal status. This might partly be explained by their being outwith the arena of active royal control. It is striking that, in the second half of the twelfth century, in Galloway and Moray, both on the fringes of central power, royal burghs were founded after the failure of revolts against crown authority in these areas. Such burghs might become strongholds or outposts for governmental control. The Highlands, where royal grip was less firm, were not planted with burghs. Rather, burghs skirted the edges. Inverness and Dumbarton are notable examples of early Scottish burghs in such strategic

[12] R. G. Cant, 'The development of the burgh of St Andrews in the middle ages', in *Three Decades of Historical Notes* (St Andrews, 1991), p. 44.

[13] A. C. Lawrie, *Early Scottish Charters* (Glasgow, 1905), no. clxix.

[14] For a full discussion of the pre-burghal nucleus of St Andrews, see N. P. Brooks and G. Whittington, 'Planning and growth in the medieval Scottish burgh: the example of St Andrews', *Transactions, Institute of British Geographers*, new series, 2 (1977), 291–2.

[15] E. P. Dennison and R. Coleman, *Historic Dumbarton* (Scottish Burgh Survey, 1999); E. P. D. Torrie, *Medieval Dundee* (Dundee, 1990), pp. 15–20; E. P. Dennison and R. Coleman, with R. G. Macpherson, *Historic Nairn* (Scottish Burgh Survey, 1999); A. A. M. Duncan, *Scotland* (Edinburgh, 1975), pp. 467–9.

positions. There were strong political reasons, as well as geographic factors, in favour of the concentration of burghs along the eastern and south-west margins of Scotland.

To facilitate this policy of founding burghs, foreigners, in particular Flemish and English immigrants, were encouraged to settle in the new Scottish burghs: Mainard the Fleming, Elfgar and Arnald (Ernald) in St Andrews; Baldwin and Swain in Perth; and Geoffrey Blount in Inverness, for example.[16] They brought with them ideas already prevalent in their own homelands; and, in consequence, much of early burghal life in Scotland was based on the pattern already established in other countries. It is not coincidental that the *Leges Burgorum* reflect in several chapters the 'customs' of Newcastle-upon-Tyne and, to a lesser degree, those of Winchester, Northampton and Nottingham; all of which, in turn, owed much to the customs of Breteuil.

A further incentive to populate burghs in Scotland was the notion of 'kirseth' (a Norse term in origin). This was a period of time, usually one year, during which a burgess was permitted to establish his home on the allotted burgage plot, free of taxation. In burghs that were less desirable a longer period might be granted. An immunity period of five years was, for example, granted to those who would settle in Dumbarton. The quite exceptional ten years granted at Dingwall is a comment on the remoteness and lack of attractiveness of the new burgh. Initially, the possession of a 'biggit' or built burgage plot was one of the essential qualifications for burgess-ship. The right to burgage tenure was inalienable if inherited, except *in extremis*, and protected by the king's peace and later by burgh law.[17]

The granting of burgh status assured other fundamental rights for its privileged inhabitants – the burgesses.[18] Most striking in a strongly hierarchical society was the relative freedom of the urban individual: while the authority of the burgh and its superior were fully recognised, some bonds which functioned beyond the burghs were non-existent within them. A burgess, for example, had

[16] *Liber Cartarum Prioratus Sancti Andree in Scotia* (Bannatyne Club, 1841), 124; W. M. Mackenzie, *The Scottish Burghs* (Edinburgh, 1949), p. 36.

[17] *Leges Burgorum*, *c.* 99, for example, in C. Innes, ed., *Ancient Burgh Laws* (Scottish Burgh Records Society, 1868).

[18] There are no extant charters to burghs prior to 1160, and many of those known to have existed soon after this, such as the ones bestowing liberties on Edinburgh, Perth and Berwick, were lost or otherwise destroyed. Extrapolation is therefore necessary from surviving evidence, such as the charter to Inverness by William I (1165–1214) (*RRS*, II, no. 213) or from the charter granted to Perth about 1205 (*ibid.*, no. 467); and also from the early laws relating to the burghs (*ibid.*, no. 475); H. L. MacQueen and W. J. Windram, 'Laws and courts in the burghs', in Lynch, Spearman and Stell, eds., *The Scottish Medieval Town*, pp. 208 and 209. *Leges Burgorum* and the less frequently quoted *Constitutiones Regis Willelmi* offer an early insight into burghal rights and customs (SRO, PA5/1). MacQueen and Windram in 'Laws and courts in burghs', pp. 209–10, discuss the provenance and dating of these laws; BL, Add. MS 18111; *Fragmenta Quaedam Veterum Legum et Consuetudinum Scotiae Undique Collecta* in *APS*, I.

the right to bequeath his property by means of his will. The harshest punishment under burgh law was banishment from the community, for this meant loss of all personal rights and privileges.

The Scottish burgh was far more than a structure possessing constitutional liberties. It was a community organised for trade.[19] To judge from the percentage of clauses dealing with mercantile matters in early burghal legislation,[20] it was recognised as such as early as the twelfth century. In practice this brought several advantages, but perhaps of most significance to burgesses was, first, the freedom from payment of toll to the owner of a market, thus enabling a burgess to travel at will around the country buying and selling; and, secondly, the burghal community gained the right to have its own market, at which it could exact toll from others. In some burghs the establishment of a guild merchant further enabled the town to take full advantage of its newly gained economic privileges.[21]

Some burgh charters make specific reference to a more radical and far-reaching privilege: while burghs were, in theory, to have a marketing monopoly, many of them were also granted the sole right to trade over an extended rural hinterland. Concessions of this nature were unknown in such territorial breadth in the rest of Europe. In effect, for many a Scottish burgh, a theoretical economic *contado* was established: all inhabitants in a specified landward area were obliged to market their goods in the burgh of their locality.

In these elements of the economic structure the contrast is striking between Scotland and England. In that kingdom privileges with regard to trade monopolies were remarkably limited. No one was compelled to go to a particular town for trading purposes; and trade overseas was not restricted to royal boroughs. While it would be an exaggeration to say that Scottish towns functioned like Italian city-states, the linkage of a Scottish town to its hinterlands was crucial and in this respect, as in many others, medieval Scotland functioned very much in the style of continental Europe.

(iii) THE GROWTH OF TOWNS

The relationship between a town and its surrounding countryside, along with the extent and prosperity of this rural neighbourhood, naturally had a profound influence on the emerging economic success of the town. When a representa-

[19] W. C. Dickinson, 'Burgh life from burgh records', *Aberdeen University Review*, 21 (1945–6), 224; F. W. Maitland, *Domesday Book and Beyond* (Cambridge, 1897), p. 193. This was the case for the most privileged towns in Western Europe.

[20] A. Ballard, 'The theory of the Scottish burgh', *SHR*, 13 (1916), 16.

[21] *Leges Burgorum*, c. 94; *Assise Regis Willelmi*, c. 39. Guilds merchant received official sanction in *Assise Regis Willelmi*, when it was decreed that merchants of the realm were to have their guild with the liberties to buy and sell in all places within the bounds of liberties of burghs, to the exclusion of all others.

tive selection of burghs is considered, a clear indication of the fundamental importance of their geographical setting emerges. Throughout most of the middle ages, Edinburgh, Aberdeen and Dundee, followed closely by Perth, dominated the national economic scene. Berwick, also, although frequently denied to Scotland from 1333, maintained an importance in the Scottish economy.[22] Its fluctuating status, until it finally became English in 1482, meant a decline in its role in Scottish trade; but as a counterbalance Edinburgh's fortunes were much enhanced. It was not coincidental that geographically these burghs were placed within large, relatively fertile, rural catchment areas; and on the east coast with ready access to Scotland's trading partners, around the North Sea and on the Baltic. In particular, Edinburgh had a vast hinterland, reaching from the Forth to well into the borders after the loss of Berwick. Aberdeen was granted the entire sheriffdom of Aberdeen as its trading liberty by Alexander II (1214–49).[23] Robert I's (1306–29) charter of 1327 to Dundee likewise bestowed an extensive trading monopoly over a fertile hinterland which included rich monasteries: only burgesses of Dundee were to be permitted to buy wool and skins within the sheriffdom of Forfar; all goods brought to the shire by foreign merchants were to be offered first for sale at Dundee; and foreign merchants were to trade within the sheriffdom solely with Dundee merchants.[24]

Such provisions were also made for smaller burghs. Rutherglen, for example, was granted the lower ward of Lanarkshire by David I in 1179x1189.[25] Ayr had a rural hinterland that marched with Rutherglen, covering an area approximately the size of modern Ayrshire.[26] In 1363, David II (1329–71) decreed that the four regality burghs of the abbey of Dunfermline – Dunfermline, Kirkcaldy, Musselburgh and Queensferry – should have the sole right to trade throughout the full confines of the regality of Dunfermline.[27] In practice, this meant an apportioning of the monopoly area by the four burghs, Kirkcaldy and Dunfermline having distinct commercial hinterlands north of the Forth. Neighbouring Inverkeithing had its hinterland defined by the reign of William I, as between the water of Leven and the water of Devon and with its north-eastern boundary marching with the jurisdiction of Cupar.[28]

The importance of such instances of this patchwork of monopolistic trading privilege throughout the country was not whether it was ultimately enforceable in fine detail; but rather the economic influence it bestowed on particular burghs, an influence that these urban communities valued highly and fought to

[22] Many Scottish goods continued to be exported through Berwick.

[23] P. J. Anderson, ed., *Charters and Other Writs Illustrating the History of the Royal Burgh of Aberdeen* (Aberdeen, 1890), no. 3.

[24] Dundee District Archive and Record Centre, CC1, no. 16.

[25] Duncan, *Scotland*, pp. 475–6; *RRS*, III, no. 244.

[26] *RRS*, II, no. 462.

[27] *Reg. de Dunfermelyn*, no. 390.

[28] SRO, PS/1/69. G. Home, ed., *Charters and Other Muniments Belonging to the Royal Burgh of Cupar* (Cupar, 1882), no. 3.

maintain against the encroachment of ambitious burghal neighbours (and also a few rural markets such as Kelso and Brechin).[29] Without this underpinning from the locality, a burgh had little likelihood of flourishing economically.

The domination of a town over a neighbouring region, sometimes an extensive one, was enhanced wherever urban parishes stretched beyond the burgh limits and covered a wide rural area. Many parishes were merely coextensive with the burgh, for example, Anstruther Wester, Pittenweem and Anstruther Easter. Even as late as the mid-eighteenth century, their parishioners numbered only 1,100, 385 and 939 respectively.[30] Haddington, however, with a parish stretching over 36 square miles (90 sq. km), Hamilton with 25 square miles (62.5 sq. km) and Dunfermline with 20 square miles (50 sq. km), according to the same census, accommodated 3,975, 3,815 and 8,552 parishioners respectively.[31] Not only would such a considerable landward parish play a major role in the urban balance of power over its hinterland, but it inevitably drew the links of town and country even closer.[32]

The economic importance of the greater burghs was further enhanced by their merchants' monopoly of overseas trade in staple goods.[33] A grant normally bestowed on royal burghs (although some ecclesiastical and baronial burghs such as St Andrews, Dunfermline and Dunbar were also so favoured), it benefited financially not only the burghs themselves but equally the crown: from the early fourteenth century, from which time the records are extant, the great customs on hides, wool and woolfells exports were an important source of royal revenue. In 1319, Aberdeen was granted feu-ferme status,[34] soon to be followed by other Scottish burghs. The significance may have been more symbolic than innovatory, possibly merely officially recognising an existing practice; but the formal granting of all burgh revenues, other than the great customs, to burghs in return

[29] Duncan, *Scotland*, 479.

[30] 'Webster's analysis of population 1755', in J. G. Kyd, ed., *Scottish Population Statistics* (Scottish History Society, 1952), pp. 41 and 38.

[31] *Ibid.*, pp. 13, 30 and 39. These areas are approximate only, calculated by multiplying the length and breadth of the parishes, as stated by Webster. The maps produced by the Institute of Heraldic and Genealogical Studies (Canterbury, 1982) indicating parish boundaries in Scotland, while not totally agreeing in detail, and perhaps more accurate, do, however, confirm the general hypothesis.

[32] Neighbourliness did not extend to parishioners from outwith the burgh precincts during the time of plague, although limited access was granted to stranger parishioners in Kirkcaldy in 1585 to attend the parish church (L. MacBean, ed., *The Kirkcaldy Burgh Records* (Kirkcaldy, 1908), p. 11).

[33] See D. Ditchburn, 'Trade with northern Europe, 1297–1540', in Lynch, Spearman and Stell, eds., *Scottish Medieval Town*, pp. 161–79; and A. Stevenson, 'Trade with the South, 1070–1513', in *ibid.*, pp. 180–206.

[34] Anderson, ed., *Charters and Other Writs*, no. 8. A royal grant in feu-ferme gave to a burgh in perpetuity the right to pay to the crown one annual fixed sum in respect of all burgh rents and other proceeds, excepting the 'great customs' on exports. It is possible that Berwick already held this privilege in the later part of Alexander III's reign (*Calendar of Inquisitions Miscellaneous*, vol. II (London, 1916), no. 1601).

for a fixed annual sum was a measure of the crown's acknowledgement of the ability of burghs independently to control their own financial affairs. For the first time a burgh was permitted to act as an administrative entity in relationship to its superior. Towns were also the places where money circulated, and it was from towns that coinage was issued: early mints were sited in the main burghs, as was the practice in the rest of Europe, and in 1250–1 Alexander III (1249–86) authorised mints in sixteen, a pattern to be followed in various important towns throughout the middle ages.[35] The ransoms agreed before the return to Scotland of David II in 1357 and James I (1406–37) in 1424 were raised only with significant input from the burghs and their merchants.

Financial acumen was to result in political power. The seals of six *communitates villarum* – Berwick, Roxburgh, Stirling, Edinburgh, Aberdeen and Perth – had been appended to Scotland's treaty with France in 1295,[36] foreshadowing a more significant role for burghs in national politics in the following century. Burghal representatives were first officially called to attend parliament in 1326 at Cambuskenneth, although they may have been present earlier in the reign of Robert I.[37] From 1341, burghal financial contributions were made to central funds and burgess participation in parliament from this time became increasingly commonplace.[38] The appointment of burgesses to prominent government positions is a sure indication of the changing role of the burgh in national politics. Adam Tore in control of the new mint in Edinburgh in the 1350s, William de Leith steward in the queen's household in 1359 and John Mercer of Perth rendering the chamberlain's accounts in 1376 were merely forerunners of a new breed of burgesses as government officials.[39] There can be no doubting the primary reason for the political emergence of the third estate: money gave burghs power, and power attracted money.

There could not, however, be consistency in the expression of power within burghs over a period of time, and neither was there consistency in the balance of power between burghs at any one time. Gradually a pyramid was to develop, with a shifting foundation, a jockeying for middling status and an increasingly constricting stranglehold at the summit. When, towards the end of the middle ages, a proliferation of new burghs entered the fray in an attempt to grasp for themselves some of the authority bestowed on established burghs by their charters and the old burgh laws, the traditional power that was vested in the burgh community was challenged.

The establishment of new burghs and consequent redefining of trading precincts, the power base of the medieval burgh, undermined the status quo. Irvine,

[35] G. W. S. Barrow, *Kingship and Unity* (London, 1981), p. 97. [36] *APS*, I, p. 453.

[37] A. A. M. Duncan, 'The early parliaments of Scotland', *SHR*, 45 (1966), 51. It is not insignificant that this parliament agreed on a yearly contribution of a tenth to support the royal household.

[38] E. Ewan, *Townlife in Fourteenth-Century Scotland* (Edinburgh, 1990), pp. 147–9, traces the emergence of the third estate in parliament. [39] *Ibid.*, p. 126.

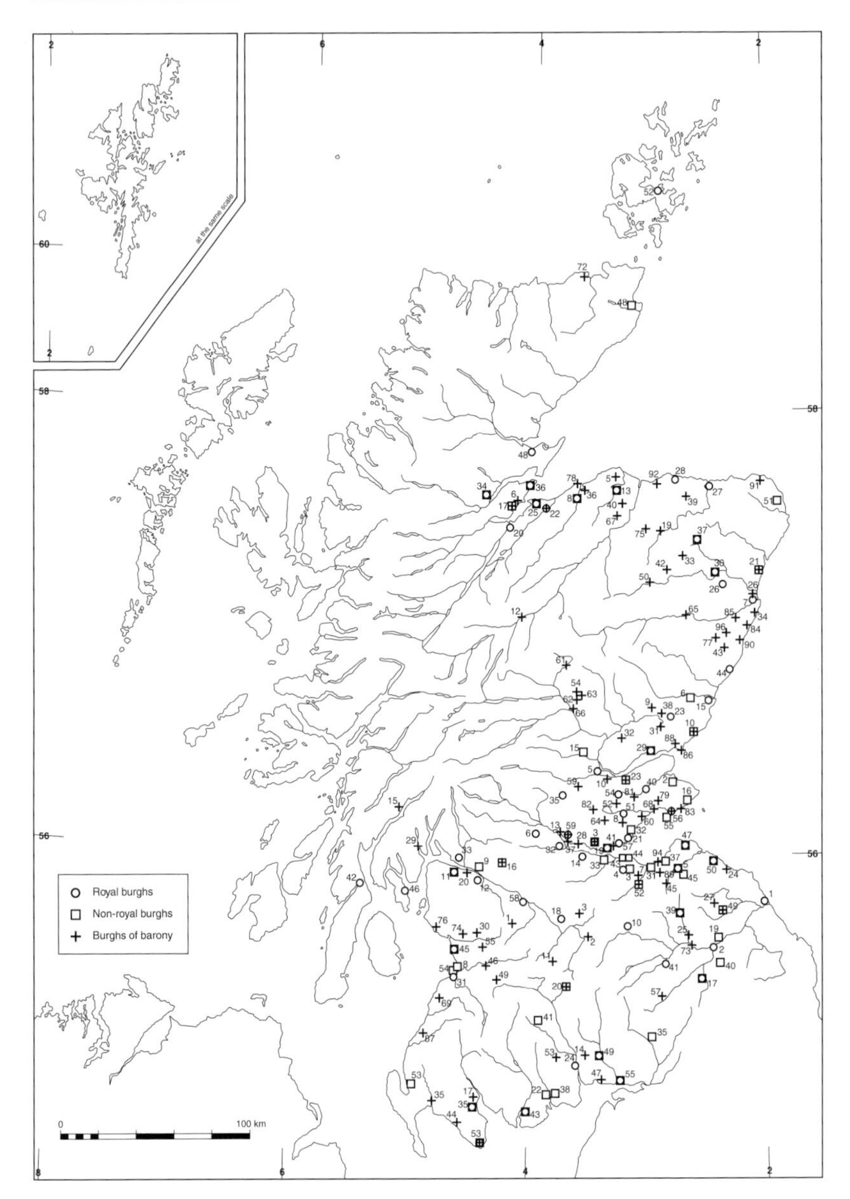

Map 23.2 Scottish burghs before the Reformation

Note: the information on the above map, and the lists which follow, is based on G. S. Pryde, *The Burghs of Scotland: A Critical List* (London, 1965). Some burghs changed their status in the course of time. Such instances are indicated by super-imposing symbols on the map and by adding symbol cross-reference numbers in the list. 'Non-royal burghs' are those possessed under crown authority by certain magnates, such as earls, barons, bishops and abbots, in the period before the technical term 'burgh of barony' was introduced in 1450.

Key to Map 23.2

ROYAL BURGHS – ○

No.	Burgh	Date	
1	Berwick-upon-Tweed	1119×24	
2	Roxburgh	1119×24	
3	Dunfermline	1124×27	□25 +21
4	Edinburgh	1124×27	
5	Perth	1124×27	
6	Stirling	1124×27	
7	Aberdeen	1124×53	
8	Forres	1130×53	□26
9	Haddington	1124×53	□4
10	Peebles	1152×53	
11	Renfrew	1124×47	□5
12	Rutherglen	1124×53	
13	Elgin	*c.* 1136	□27
14	Linlithgow	*c.* 1138	
15	Montrose	1124×53	
16	Crail	1150×52	□7
17	Jedburgh	1124×53	□34
18	Lanark	1124×53	
19	Inverkeithing	1153×62	□11
20	Inverness	1153×65	
21	Kinghorn	1165×72	
22	Auldearn	1179×82	+58
23	Forfar	1184	
24	Dumfries	1186	
25	Nairn	*c.* 1190	□28
26	Kintore	1187×1200	
27	Banff	1189×98	
28	Cullen	1189×98	
29	Dundee	1191×95	□13
30	Inverurie	1195	□12
31	Ayr	1203×1206	
32	Airth	1195×1203	
33	Dumbarton	1222	
34	Dingwall	1227	□36
35	Auchterarder	1246	
36	Cromarty	1264	□30
37	Fyvie	1264	□50
38	Wigtown	1292	□42
39	Lauder	1298×1328	□29
40	Cupar	1327	
41	Selkirk	1328	
42	Tarbert	1329	
43	Kirkcudbright	1330	□46
44	Inverbervie	1341	
45	Irvine	1372	□18
46	Rothesay	1401	
47	North Berwick	1425	□47
48	Tain	1439	
49	Lochmaben	1440	□34
50	Dunbar	1445	
51	Falkland	1458	
52	Kirkwall	1486	
53	Whithorn	1511	□39 +4
54	Auchtermuchty	1517	
55	Annan	1532	□1
56	Pittenweem	1541	+70
57	Burntisland	1541	
58	Hamilton	1549	+16
59	Clackmannan	1153×64(?)	

NON-ROYAL BURGHS – □

No.	Burgh	Date	
1	Annan	12 cent.	○55
2	St Andrews	1124×44	
3	Canongate	1128×53	
4	Haddington	1152×57	○9
5	Renfrew	1147×53	○11
6	Brechin	1165×71	
7	Crail	1165×71	○16
8	Prestwick	1165×74	
9	Glasgow	1175×78	
10	Arbroath	1178×82	+23
11	Inverkeithing	1190×95	○19
12	Inverurie	1191×95	○30
13	Dundee	1191×95	○29
14	Dunbar	13 cent.	○50
15	Dunblane	13–14 cent.	
16	Kirkintilloch	1211×14	+71
17	Rosemarkie	1214×86	+95
18	Irvine	1214×49	○45
19	Kelso	1237	
20	Crawford	1242×49	+56
21	Newburgh	1261	+48
22	Urr	1262	
23	Newburgh	1266	+22
24	Lochmaben	1296	○49
25	Dunfermline	1303	○3 +21
26	Forres	1312	○8
27	Elgin	1312	○13
28	Nairn	1312	○25
29	Lauder	1313×28	○39
30	Cromarty	1315	○36
31	Musselburgh	1315×28	
32	Kirkcaldy	1315×28	
33	South Queenferry	1315×28	
34	Jedburgh	1320	○17
35	Staplegorton	1320	
36	Dingwall	1321	○34
37	Seton	1321	
38	Buittle	1325	
39	Whithorn	1325	○53 +4
40	Prenderleith	1328×29	
41	Sanquhar	1335	+18
42	Wigtown	1341	○38
43	North Leith	1367	
44	South Leith	1367	
45	Nungate of Haddington	1367	

Key to Map 23.2 *(cont.)*

46 Kirkcudbright	*c.* 1369	○43	
47 North Berwick	1381×88	○47	
48 Wick	1393–4		
49 Langton	1394	+51	
50 Fyvie	1397	○37	
51 Rattray	1395×97		
52 Dalkeith	1401	+80	
53 Inermessan	1426		
54 Newton-upon-Ayr	1446		
55 Earlsferry	unknown		

BURGHS OF BARONY – +

1 Strathaven	1450		
2 Biggar	1451		
3 Carnwath	1451		
4 Whithorn	1459	○53	□39
5 Spynie	1451		
6 Fortrose	1455		
7 Roslin	1456		
8 Leslie Green	1458		
9 Kirriemuir	1459		
10 Abernethy	1459		
11 Douglas	1459		
12 Kingussie	1464		
13 Port of Menteith	1467		
14 Torthorwald	1473		
15 Inverary	1474		
16 Hamilton	1475	○58	
17 Myreton	1477		
18 Sanquhar	1484	□41	
19 Huntly	1488		
20 Paisley	1488		
21 Dunfermline	*c.* 1488	○3	□25
22 Newburgh	*c.* 1488	□23	
23 Arbroath	*c.* 1488	□10	
24 Dunglass	1489		
25 Earlston	1489		
26 Old Aberdeen	1489		
27 Duns	1490		
28 Culross	1490		
29 Kilmun	1490		
30 Newmilns	1491		
31 Glamis	1491		
32 Keithick	1492		
33 Rayne	1493		
34 Torry	1495		
35 Ballinclach	1497		
36 Kinloss	1497		
37 Alloa	1497		
38 Auchterhouse	1497		
39 Fordyce	1499		
40 Belliehill	1500		
41 Aberdour	1501		
42 Clatt	1501		
43 Fettercairn	1504		
44 Merton	1504		
45 Pencaitland	1505		
46 Auchinleck	1507		
47 Ruthwell	1508		
48 Newburgh	1509	□21	
49 Cumnock	1509		
50 Kildrummy	1509		
51 Langton	1510	□49	
52 Strathmiglo	1510		
53 Terregles	1510		
54 Dalnagairn	1510		
55 Mauchline	1510		
56 Crawford	1511	□20	
57 Hawick	1511		
58 Auldearn	1511	○22	
59 Dunning	1511		
60 Wemyss	1511		
61 Kirkmichael	1511		
62 Balnakilly	1511		
63 Balnald	1511		
64 Corshill-over-Inchgall	1511		
65 Kincardine O'Neill	1511		
66 Dunkeld	1512		
67 Turrif	1512		
68 Largo	1513		
69 Maybole	1516		
70 Pittenweem	1526	○56	
71 Kirkintilloch	1526	□16	
72 Scrabster	1527		
73 Dryburgh	1527		
74 Kilmaurs	1527		
75 Doune	1528		
76 Saltcoats	1529		
77 Kincardine	1532		
78 Findhorn	1532		
79 Drumochy	1540		
80 Dalkeith	1540	□52	
81 Pitlessie	1541		
82 Kinross	1541		
83 Anstruther Wester	1541		
84 Cowie	1541		
85 Durris	1541		
86 Panmure (Easthaven of)	1541		
87 Ballintrae	1541		
88 Newbigging	1541		
89 Tranent	1542		
90 Arbuthnot	1543		
91 Fraserburgh	1546		
92 Portsoy	1550		
93 Clackmannan	1551	○59	
94 Prestonpans	1552		
95 Rosemarkie	1554	□17	
96 Fordoun	1554		

for example, was confirmed in 1372 as possessing a hinterland stretching over Cunningham and Largs, so reducing the effective control of Ayr, though this potential threat, as evidenced in the sixteenth-century tax returns, was held in check by the gradual silting up of Irvine's harbour.[40] For Inverkeithing in the fifteenth and sixteenth centuries, rights over Culross, the extent of the parish of Kinghorn, the petty customs of Dysart and the customs of St Luke's fair at Kinross all became matters of contention;[41] and the erection of Burntisland and Culross into royal burghs in 1586 and 1592 respectively[42] further threatened Inverkeithing's hold over its hinterland. Smaller burghs also, at times, found themselves dominated by the larger: Kintore and Fyvie would probably have considered themselves outwith the jurisdiction of Aberdeen, but by the late fourteenth century the latter was claiming that Fyvie, now a baronial burgh, along with others such as Inverurie, fell within its rural hinterland.[43]

From the fourteenth century, moreover, a power struggle developed over a share of declining customable overseas trade, which was not to see a sustained resurgence until the end of the sixteenth century. While the expanding, even booming, wool trade had played a vital part in the burghal and national economy in the twelfth and thirteenth centuries, the Wars of Independence combined with the effects of the Black Death were effectively to see its demise. By the mid-fourteenth century, almost as a forewarning of things to come, Bruges recognised Edinburgh, Aberdeen, Perth and Dundee as 'the four great towns of Scotland'.[44] Such an assessment was based solely on overseas customable trade, and may be reinforced by the customs returns: in the 1370s 58 per cent was paid by the 'big four'.[45] They were, however, followed fairly closely by Linlithgow and Haddington, which were able to take advantage of their geographical situation after the loss of Berwick to the English. But consolidation by the big four regional centres was ultimately to be the overriding factor. The fortunes of lesser towns varied according to the staple commodity most in demand. But there developed an increasing control of the most important commodities by Edinburgh: inexorably of the wool trade which by the 1530s reached 83% of the national total,[46] and then of the hide exports – 67.7 per cent by 1535–9 and 84.3 per cent by 1595–9.[47] Its control of cloth exports for the same periods was equally dramatic, being respectively, 71.8 per cent and 85.4 per cent.[48] Although

[40] *Muniments of the Royal Burgh of Irvine* (Edinburgh, 1890), vol. I, no. 4.

[41] W. Stephen, *A History of Inverkeithing and Rosyth* (Aberdeen, 1921), pp. 8–10.

[42] *RMS*, V, no. 934; *APS*, III, pp. 584–6.

[43] P. G. B. McNeill and H. L. MacQueen, eds., *Atlas of Scottish History to 1707* (Edinburgh, 1996), pp. 231–2.

[44] K. Hohlbaum, ed., *Hansisches Urkundenbuch* (Halle, 1882–6), III, no. 131.

[45] Perth was responsible for 9 per cent, Dundee 10 per cent, Aberdeen 15 per cent and Edinburgh 24 per cent. M. Lynch, 'Towns and townspeople in fifteenth-century Scotland', in J. A. F. Thomson, ed., *Towns and Townspeople in the Fifteenth Century* (Gloucester, 1988), p. 175.

[46] *Ibid.*, p. 176.

[47] McNeill and MacQueen, eds., *Atlas of Scottish History*, p. 253.

[48] *Ibid.*, p. 255.

cheap cloth was not to be subject to duty until 1597, lesser towns could not but be affected, even though some would move out of certain commodities in response to the increasing stranglehold, only to find themselves soon squeezed out of their new market.[49] Some east coast ports, however, such as Montrose, which in the sixteenth century took advantage of the overseas fisheries market, particularly salmon, were to have a short-lived prosperity.[50] In the same period, on the other hand, Pittenweem and the other east Fife burghs would see their revenues from fish exports, in particular their control of 57.7 per cent of herring, radically undermined, although the cheaper end of the market, 63.4 per cent of cod exports, was less affected.[51] Customs accounts, of course, reflect only a partial picture – local trade, which is not documented in financial figures, may have played a more significant role in the average burgh economy; and the increasing use of Edinburgh's harbour of Leith by ships from other burghs and of stranger merchants' part-loads in Edinburgh ships gives a certain bias in Edinburgh's favour.[52] Even with such reservations, however, it is clear that, on the basis of the available figures, for many middling and smaller towns,[53] the fifteenth and sixteenth centuries increasingly were years of lurching from one crisis to another.

The expression of power, and indeed the very nature of that power, whether political, economic or constitutional, varied from town to town and from time to time. Although the growing domination of Edinburgh bore similarities in character, if not in scale, to that of London, no Scottish burgh would ever reach, or even aspire to, the pinnacles of greatness in size and authority of many successful European cities, such as the Italian city-states. Considered in their context, however, it is difficult not to conclude that Scottish burghs held a power in the nation quite disproportionate to their size.[54]

(iv) THE PEOPLE IN THE TOWNS

In attempting to analyse who the town dwellers were we must confront several basic issues. How many were they, for example? Guess-work figures have sug-

[49] Lynch, 'Towns and townspeople', p. 177.

[50] Montrose enjoyed 14.1 per cent compared with Perth's 13.8 per cent, Dundee's 15.1 per cent, Aberdeen's 41.9 per cent and Edinburgh's mere 5.7 per cent of the salmon export trade in 1535–9, McNeill and MacQueen, *Atlas of Scottish History*, p. 256.

[51] *Ibid.*, p. 258. Within sixty years, although still commanding 69.4 per cent of the less lucrative cod exports, Pittenweem and the other Fife coast burghs could muster only 22.5 per cent of the herring trade, compared with Dumbarton's 44.5 per cent, and were totally unable even to consider competing with Edinburgh's domination of the salmon exports since it now controlled 41.4 per cent, compared with Aberdeen's 34.3 per cent.

[52] Staatsarchiv Bremen, 1/Bc/1445, Juli 15.

[53] The exceptions were probably small, specialised fishing ports, which may account for their phenomenal rise in the tax rolls at this period. We are indebted to Professor M. Lynch for his views on customs and tax rolls.

[54] A. Grant, *Independence and Nationhood* (Edinburgh, 1984), p. 69.

gested that in the later middle ages only about 10 per cent of a national population of around 700,000 were townspeople.[55] Firm population figures for individual towns are non-existent, but it is entirely clear that all Scottish urban units were small by European city standards, most of them very small. In the thirteenth century Berwick was the wealthiest town in Scotland and some documentation from 1302 has been used to produce a population estimate as low as 1,500, while exaggerated figures in chronicle accounts of the sack of the town in 1296 might be adjusted downwards to suggest at least 3,000.[56] Dunfermline, a significant ecclesiastical burgh, has been reckoned to have about 1,000–1,100 inhabitants by 1500; and Edinburgh in 1560 (by then the capital) may have held about 12,500.[57] A few detailed town censuses emerge in the seventeenth century: Old Aberdeen, for example, again under ecclesiastical authority, had in 1636 precisely 832 inhabitants, excluding the staff, students and servants of King's College.[58] In the later middle ages only a few major towns, such as Edinburgh, Perth, Dundee and Aberdeen would have had more than 2,000 people; and, since small burghs were numerous, the average town must have held less than 1,000: by modern standards, a mere village. What follows is that these towns were tiny, close-knit structures where intimate neighbourhood contacts and interrelationships were all at the core of daily existence.

Equally fundamental is the question of who the townspeople were in terms of their origins: social, familial and locational. The answers vary not only from place to place, but also over periods of time. Early medieval burgesses, as already indicated, were often incomers, either in themselves or in their family backgrounds: persons named 'of (King's) Lynn', 'of Leicester', and 'of Winchester' betray English roots, while Scottish town or countryside names also occur: 'of Berwick', 'of Haddington', 'of Fingask', 'of the Mearns'. Although it is difficult to trace in detail, there was a continuing process of immigration into towns, from both urban and rural sources of population. The origins of many inhabitants remain obscure, since their names are either simple patronymics or are, apparently, descriptive of the possessor's trade or craft. It has been said of those named in the earliest Aberdeen records, around 1400, that '"surnames" . . . appear merely to designate the individual's trade'.[59] And at a lower level there were those who remain largely or totally invisible to us. Historians often say 'little enough

[55] R. Nicholson, *Scotland: The Later Middle Ages* (Edinburgh, 1974), p. 2; S. G. E. Lythe and J. Butt, *An Economic History of Scotland, 1100–1939* (Glasgow, 1975), p. 4.

[56] W. C. Dickinson, *Scotland from the Earliest Times to 1603*, 3rd edn (Oxford, 1977), p. 114; H. Maxwell, trans., *Chronicle of Lanercost* (Glasgow, 1913), p. 115.

[57] Torrie, *Medieval Dundee*, p. 59; M. Lynch, 'The social and economic structure of the larger towns, 1450–1600', in Lynch, Spearman and Stell, eds., *The Scottish Medieval Town*, p. 279.

[58] G. G. Simpson, *Old Aberdeen in the Early Seventeenth Century: A Community Study* (Aberdeen, 1975), p. 5.

[59] W. C. Dickinson, ed., *Early Records of the Burgh of Aberdeen, 1317, 1398–1407* (Scottish History Society, 1957), p. 247.

about the luckless weaver and fuller, and nothing at all about the really poor and destitute, for those men never put their names to parchment'.[60] Yet at the upper levels of town society elite groupings were developing, at least in larger towns, before the twelfth century ended. It has been noted that, 'although the prominent burgesses of Perth were of cosmopolitan origin, by the early thirteenth century they were forming a number of small dynasties or clans within the town'.[61] Society in later medieval Aberdeen, for example, was dominated, both socially and politically, by eleven outstanding families, whose internal relationships can be displayed in family trees, often with a good deal of detail.[62]

Origins and the nature of social unity can be further illuminated if we touch on the use of languages in the towns. Immigrants brought their own tongues and 'Scandinavianized Northern English, or Anglo-Danish, was certainly the principal, though probably not the only, language of the early Scottish burghs.'[63] From Old Norse *gata* derived *gate*, meaning a street; from Flemings who visited or settled came their word *caland* which became *callan*, a customer, merchant or youth: a significant term in a trading context. Down to roughly about 1200 Gaelic was still the commonest tongue in Scotland and must have been heard then in the streets of towns within reach of the Highland line, such as Inverness, Elgin, Aberdeen, Perth and Dumbarton. Even in some border towns Gaelic may not have been unknown in that era. We cannot know how many town clergy actually spoke in Latin to one another, but the daily services in the parish church were in that language. But the linguistic pattern in the towns does not retain this varied structure as we move into the later middle ages. Before the end of the fourteenth century the northern English mentioned above 'had become the dominant spoken tongue of all ranks of Scots east and south of the Highland line, except in Galloway where a form of Gaelic appears to have survived'.[64] This 'Inglis', or 'Scottis' as it was also named from the late fifteenth century, became the pre-eminent speech in towns. That position is reflected also in the various burgh records which survive, at first patchily, from about 1400. Some of the earliest of them are in Latin, but 'from the 1450s, Scots is increasingly the language of record', in the practice of town clerks.[65] The forward march of Scots usage was 'perhaps in part influenced by an impulse towards national solidarity when the nation was beleaguered in the War of Independence'.[66] By the end of the middle ages a commonality of language in towns was the norm, and that language – Scots – was one of the two national

[60] A. A. M. Duncan, 'Perth: the first century of the burgh', *Transactions of the Perthshire Society of Natural Science*, Special Issue (1974), 48. [61] Duncan, *Scotland*, p. 493.

[62] H. W. Booton, 'Burgesses and Landed Men in North-East Scotland in the Later Middle Ages: A Study in Social Interaction' (PhD thesis, University of Aberdeen, 1987), chapters I and II and appendix A. [63] M. Robinson, ed., *Concise Scots Dictionary* (Aberdeen, 1985), p. ix.

[64] *Ibid.*

[65] Lynch, Spearman and Stell, eds., *The Scottish Medieval Town*, p. 25, esp. nos. 35, 57 above.

[66] Robinson, ed., *Dictionary*, pp. ix–x.

tongues, Gaelic being the other. A travelling merchant, a royal administrator or a bishop on visitation would find the same tongue predominantly in use in every town he reached; and that tongue gave cohesion to the Lowland regions of the kingdom, within which the towns had a significant place.

The life of the Scots-speaking town dwellers can be characterised best by looking at four abstract elements and attaching the practicalities of existence to each of them. The daily round involved for them all: proximity, community, hierarchy and variety. The fact of your proximity to other people was probably the single most obvious physical feature of urban living. This closeness has emerged already in comments on population size, on visible town boundaries, whether defences or end-of-rig walling, and on the horizontally occupied flats in the urban skyscrapers of some larger Scottish towns. But the consistent form of house-and-street relationship tells the same story. The crowding of houses on the street frontages, with long, narrow rigs behind, indicates an urgent desire to make contact with the customers who thronged that street. The open market area of every burgh also betokens not only the centrality of trading, but also the frequent public intermingling of folk. As a medieval town inhabitant, your neighbour mattered greatly to you: his house and garden lay immediately alongside yours, his noise and activity intruded on your life, his midden smells invaded your space, his plague infected you and your family (Plate 25).

This physical contiguity links too with social cohesion, which can be illustrated in several ways. Intermarriage of burghal families is frequently documented and the economic and social significance of heiresses in burgh life is very evident. In Aberdeen from the start to the end of the fifteenth century it had become twice as common for a non-burgess to marry the daughter of a burgess of guild.[67] The negative side of close social relationships emerges too from recorded details of the quite frequent personal disputes, including both verbal and physical attacks. Catherine Lyne, an inhabitant of Old Aberdeen, for example, miscalled one of the town bailies by addressing him as 'swetie hatt, clipit brecis and blottit hippis' (sweaty hat, short trousers and bloated hips). She gives a vivid picture of a fat official but she suffered for her invective, since as punishment she was banished from the town.[68] On a more positive and pleasurable note, days of festivity and merriment must have brought most of the community together in commingling relaxation. The list of recorded public entertainments is long and varied: Corpus Christi plays, processions and pageants; plays involving Robin Hood and the Abbot of Unreason; morris dancing; summer bonfires – all were elements of the occasional social whirl.[69]

A sense of community is conveyed to us at every turn. In the records the phrase 'community of the burgh' occurs as early as the thirteenth century and

[67] Booton, *Burgesses and Landed Men*, pp. 158*ff*. [68] Simpson, *Old Aberdeen*, p. 7.

[69] A. J. Mill, *Medieval Plays in Scotland* (Edinburgh, 1927); see also above, p. 338.

in later times becomes very common. From that century onwards burghs frequently possessed seals and the legend on each refers to 'the common seal of . . .' or 'the seal of the community of . . .'. 'The common profit of the town' was also a favourite piece of wording. It can be readily argued that such phraseology must quite often have represented in practice the wishes of some elite group or clique: the dominantly wealthy or politically powerful.[70] But stated duties were at least formally attached to the position of any burgess, as a full member of the community: for example, attendance at the three head or principal courts of the burgh each year was officially expected, and defaulters were fined for absence. That rule may well have been breached at times and may have been less prominent in the later middle ages, but at least the ideal of common responsibility was visible. And in a more practical way the feeling of community emerges particularly strongly in later medieval times, when care for the urban parish church is prominently on record. This was achieved in many towns, for example, by appointment of one or more kirk-masters, who were secular officials, not churchmen, charged with supervision of the building work on and around the church, and maintenance of its fabric. These masters of works display the concern of the community for its own religious observances. And strong support for services in a local church can be noted too in the active processes of founding altarages (*anglice* chantries): by the Reformation in 1560 the parish church of St Giles in Edinburgh had at least forty of these and Holy Trinity parish church in St Andrews had about thirty.[71] The frequency of services within any such major urban church displays that building and that institution as a focus for community activity to a degree utterly unlike the habits of urban populations in present-day Britain.

It was well recognised that within the community a functioning hierarchy existed: John Ireland, a fifteenth-century Scottish intellectual, remarked that 'thar is gret ordoure and dignitie ascendand fra the lauborare ore sempil persoune to the hier stag mare and mare'.[72] Above the level of burgh society itself was the legal superior of the burgh: the king as formal overlord of every royal burgh, and the baron, bishop or abbot, by royal permission, as possessor of his own baronial burgh. The degree of authority exercised by superiors varied, but each burgh usually had its own principal officer, the *prepositus* (later provost), sometimes called alderman, aided by some form of council, plus a group of bailies or magistrates. The community and the jurisdictional power structure here merged together, for, by law, every new burgess had to swear fealty to the

[70] J. H. Stevenson and M. Wood, *Scottish Heraldic Seals* (Glasgow, 1940), I, pp. 52–82; see also above, p. 306.

[71] M. Lynch, *Edinburgh and the Reformation* (Edinburgh, 1981), p. 28; R. G. Cant, *The Parish Church of the Holy Trinity, St Andrews* (St Andrews, 1992), p. 7.

[72] Johannes de Irlandia, *The Meroure of Wyssdome*, III, ed. C. McDonald (Scottish Text Society, 4th series, XIX, 1990), p. 92.

bailies and to the community of the burgh. The significance of hierarchy can be observed when its operation occasionally breaks down, as in the frequent disputes, for example, among the craft guilds of Aberdeen about their positions in the Corpus Christi processions, the organising of which was the responsibility of the bailies.[73] Yet although political and social hierarchy leaps at us from the records, the inner workings of the structure are not yet sufficiently explored. It is not enough to say, in the words of one recent historian, that 'much of the history of the medieval town can properly be explained in terms of its institutions'.[74] There is truth in the comment, but where a sufficient quantity of late medieval and early modern records exists, as it does for Aberdeen, for example, the activities and interrelationships of families will be found to be of striking interest. The formalities of power and public office are readily visible, but within the interstices of that apparatus families are visible rising and falling, and households can be observed in operation as the social units which must often have meant more in the lives of the town inhabitants than the formal decisions of the officials who caused the hierarchy itself to tick over. The tensions between public authority and personal attitude are visible in the comment of an Aberdeen inhabitant in 1545 directed against Thomas Menzies of Pitfoddels, landed gentleman and frequently provost of the town, to the effect that the protestor 'did not care for all his power or his stane house'.[75]

The French historian Jacques le Goff has rightly remarked that 'for the men from the fields, the forest, and the moors, the town was at once an object of attraction and repulsion'.[76] Within its boundaries lay both variety and excitement. In a simple physical sense it was remarkable, as we have noted, on account of its density of buildings and of people. Yet it included within its operations agricultural activities too: in the long rigs behind the burgess frontages there were garden crops and orchards, as well as smaller domestic animals such as pigs and fowls. Many a burgess was in part a farmer also, hence the dung-heaps on the public streets which town councils frequently attempted to prohibit or remove. And the social mix of the town was also varied and complex. In addition to the hierarchical range from the significantly wealthy to the poverty-stricken, others intermingled. Kings and their households visited, living in the nearby royal castle, or at a religious house, or even in the house of a burgess or at an inn. From the twelfth century onwards aristocrats owned town properties: in a charter of about 1161, King Malcolm IV granted the royal steward 'one full toft [house site] for his lodging in every burgh of the king'.[77] Religious houses, too, purchased town tenements and used them as

[73] Mill, *Medieval Plays*, p. 64. [74] Lynch, 'Social and economic structure', p. 267.

[75] J. Robertson, *The Book of Bon-Accord: A Guide to the City of Aberdeen* (Aberdeen, 1839), p. 105.

[76] J. Le Goff, *Medieval Civilization* (Oxford, 1988), p. 293.

[77] G. W. S. Barrow, ed., *Acts of Malcolm IV, King of Scots, 1153–65* (*RRS.*, I, no. 184).

bases for business and as stopping-points for their abbots when travelling.[78] The major towns at least, therefore, welcomed occasional important visitors whose main concerns in life were centred elsewhere. Town inhabitants were accustomed to rubbing shoulders with, or at least gazing at, a changing kaleidoscope of great persons and their numerous hangers-on.

In addition to mixing with non-burgess figures passing through, a few burgesses, even as early as the thirteenth century, can be seen turning their eyes to ownership of rural properties and so becoming an element in the laird or gentry class. This trend in the later middle ages has been briefly investigated in print and deserves careful attention.[79] Only a small minority followed this route of non-urban land acquisition. But a change of focus is involved and, for a tiny group at least, capital acquired through trade and burgh rents was evidently available to permit purchase of rural estates. The motivation may have been partly economic, but the increased status gained by a burgess-laird must also have counted for much. By the later fourteenth century we meet, for example, the figure of John Mercer, burgess of Perth, rich enough to impress an English chronicler by his 'inestimable wealth'; trusted sufficiently to be engaged on diplomatic missions in David II's reign; and powerful enough to acquire land by marrying into the family of Murray of Tullibardine, in Perthshire, and so to create a niche in landed society for his descendants, as the Mercers of Aldie and Meikleour.[80] In the words of Nicholson, 'investment in land was a stepping-stone to gentility'.[81]

To those outside the town walls the inhabitants within them looked different: in personal aims, social attitudes and institutional functioning. But the walls did not create rigidly defined enclaves. Scottish medieval town dwellers interacted with those in their hinterlands and far beyond. Integration within the kingdom was a primary keynote of all that was done by the people in the towns.

(v) FUTURE STUDIES

Where does the topic of Scottish medieval towns need to go from here? In many aspects it remains essentially rather underresearched, even though a variety of methodologies are viable and should increasingly be brought into operation. Topographical and cartographical studies are now being undertaken by the Burgh Survey team at Edinburgh University, but are required for many more towns, both large and small.[82] Perth has been the subject of a small, but detailed

[78] W. Stevenson, 'The monastic presence in Scottish burghs in the twelfth and thirteenth centuries', *SHR*, 60 (1981), 97–118.

[79] R. Nicholson, 'Feudal developments in late medieval Scotland', *Juridical Review* (1973), 9–16; Ewan, *Townlife*, pp. 100–16.

[80] Nicholson, *The Later Middle Ages*, pp. 153, 194–5; Ewan, *Townlife*, p. 127.

[81] Nicholson, *The Later Middle Ages*, p. 457.

[82] In the new series of Burgh Surveys, commissioned by Historic Scotland, and researched and

study of its medieval townscape, on the model of Professor Conzen's Alnwick.[83] Aberdeen is fortunate in that a two-volume general history of the town, funded by the local authority, is in preparation and will be published in, or soon after, 2000.[84] Such researches will effectively relate each town to its site and illuminate its layout and built environment.

Correspondingly, the breakdown investigation of property data, possibly by computerised methods, can certainly clarify the social and economic character of the various sectors of a town and permit study of development over time. A major record source awaits full-scale analysis in the Aberdeen Burgh Register of Sasines, for example, which survives from 1484 onwards. Archaeological conclusions too require to be expanded and more broadly drawn on many topics. Why have we no national study as yet, for example, of what the finds of pottery imports from abroad in Scottish towns can tell us about the country's ceramic trading interests in the middle ages? Recent archaeological research, for example in Whithorn and St Andrews,[85] has given us vital insights into early urban life and can, without doubt, further clarify our knowledge. Also, much more social analysis of urban communities is required. How strong were the 'urban patriciates'? And how did landed interests and burgh families intermesh? We have already noted that from the thirteenth century onwards burgesses bought themselves into the landed class: did that change work smoothly and did it grow at a steady pace?

It is a truism that a town is a complex organism and requires study from many viewpoints. The keynote of future urban studies in Scotland must be integration of methodologies. This has increasingly been visible in scholarly effort within the last twenty years. There remains much to be achieved, however; and a multidisciplinary approach must be further encouraged if we are to gain a fuller, rounded understanding of the medieval Scottish town.

written in the Centre of Scottish Urban History, Dept of Scottish History, University of Edinburgh, the towns of Kirkcaldy, Stranraer, Stornoway, Musselburgh, Hamilton, Coupar Angus, Forfar, North Queensferry, Melrose, Dalkeith, Cumnock, Linlithgow, Dumbarton, Nairn and Dunblane have been studied.

[83] R. M. Spearman, 'The medieval townscape of Perth', in Lynch, Spearman and Stell, eds., *Scottish Medieval Town*, pp. 42–59.

[84] E. P. Dennison, D. Ditchburn and M. Lynch, eds., *A New History of Aberdeen* (East Linton, forthcoming) vol. I; H. Fraser and C. Lee, eds., *ibid.*, vol. II (East Linton, forthcoming).

[85] J. Lewis, 'Excavations at St. Andrews, Castlecliffe, 1988–90', *Proc. Soc. Antiq. Scot.*, 126 (1996), 605–88; P. Hill, *Whithorn and St Ninian: The Excavation of a Monastic Town, 1984–91* (Stroud, 1997).

· PART V ·

Conclusion

· 24 ·

Conclusion

D. M. PALLISER

WE HAVE in this volume surveyed the towns of three countries over a span of nine centuries. The reader who has followed our contributions so far, or is about to engage with the urbanisation charted by Peter Clark and his colleagues in Volume II, may well expect some broad insights underlying our detailed analyses. What are the most significant of them?

First, towns before the sixteenth century were collectively more important, populous and wealthy than is still often acknowledged by historians of later periods. After the earliest period of intermittent urbanisation (or reurbanisation) in England between *c.* 600 and 850, there followed what Christopher Dyer has characterised as 'a period of sustained urban growth' between *c.* 880 and 1080.[1] This is a claim fully confirmed by the studies in Part II of this volume, and should not unduly surprise us, for the growth of towns was only one of a series of important economic developments in late Anglo-Saxon England, changes which were perhaps 'more significant than any which took place in the sixteenth century or even later'.[2] Dyer's 'second period of urbanization', this time involving Britain as a whole, lies between the late eleventh and early fourteenth centuries, and is much better known. Richard Britnell suggests that for England, where the statistics are best, towns may have accounted for almost 10 per cent of the national population by 1086 and up to 15 per cent by about 1300; Dyer would go further and see a doubling of the proportion living in towns. Without question, the absolute numbers of urban inhabitants must have declined over the century or so after 1348–50, but it is likely that towns still maintained or even

[1] Christopher Dyer, 'How urbanized was medieval England?', in J.-M. Duvosquel and E. Thoen, eds., *Peasants and Townsmen in Medieval Europe* (Ghent, 1995), p. 178.

[2] James Campbell, 'The late Anglo-Saxon state: a maximum view', *Proceedings of the British Academy*, 84 (1994), 53.

increased their *relative* share of the national total.[3] Furthermore, Britnell has suggested that the process of commercialisation continued in the fourteenth and fifteenth centuries, and that towns prospered through their part in it: 'tax assessment suggests that the urban share of England's wealth was higher in the early sixteenth century than in 1334'.[4] His survey of the period for this volume suggests that the broad picture is applicable to British towns as a whole, and not only to England, though it is fair to add that the subject is a controversial one.[5]

Secondly, our knowledge of medieval British towns is still very uneven. The great bulk of research has concentrated on some forty or fifty of the largest and wealthiest towns; and yet despite, or perhaps, because of, its huge survival of documentary and archaeological evidence, London has been comparatively neglected. It is therefore very welcome that that neglect is now being remedied, in work much of which is surveyed and taken further in this volume. What Derek Keene and Caroline Barron are able to show is the enormous importance of London in relation to other towns, a relative importance which if anything increased after 1348.[6] Less surprisingly, given the more restricted evidence available, the 800 or more small towns of medieval Britain have also been understudied; Dyer's substantial survey, the first of its kind, fills a real gap, and demonstrates abundantly that most of them, however small, were true urban communities, with distinctive social and economic characteristics marking them off from their rural neighbours.[7] There has also been a geographical imbalance of coverage, with until recently much more work on English than on Welsh and Scottish towns; that is now, fortunately, being remedied, and we have tried to do justice to the towns of all three countries so far as the evidence allows.

Clearly, demographic and economic indicators are crucial in assessing the importance and the changing fortunes of medieval towns, given that our definition of them stresses a concentration of population and a diversity of occupations.[8] Nevertheless, over the last half-century, scholars have perhaps overstressed the economic dimensions, and it is welcome that recent research has followed a broader agenda. On the one hand, historians have explored more fully urban society and culture, including both material culture (where archaeological evidence is especially illuminating) and mental culture, attitudes, customs and beliefs. There has also been more research on urban topography, morphology and architecture – the physical stage, as it were, on which life was played. On

[3] R. H. Britnell, *The Commercialisation of English Society, 1000–1500*, 2nd edn (Manchester, 1996), pp. 49, 115, 170; Dyer, 'How urbanized was medieval England?', pp. 174–80.

[4] Britnell, *Commercialisation*, p. 170; but cf. p. 233 n. 24

[5] Above, Chapter 14. For cogent scepticism about the data, see S. H. Rigby, 'Late medieval urban prosperity: the evidence of the lay subsidies', *Ec.HR* 2nd series 39 (1986), 411–16.

[6] Above, Chapters 9, 17. [7] Above, Chapter 20.

[8] However, some of the crucial indicators have not been, and perhaps cannot be, satisfactorily quantified: see S. H. Rigby, 'Urban decline in the later middle ages: some problems in interpreting the statistical data', *UHY* (1979), 46–59; Rigby, 'Late medieval urban prosperity'.

the other hand, there has also been a welcome return to those political and constitutional aspects of town life which were the staple fare of British medieval urban history until the 1950s, but which have since fallen out of fashion.

Undeniably, political and jurisdictional relationships – within towns, between towns and their overlords, and between towns and the state – are of great importance, and for that reason our surveys of power and authority have been given pride of place after the general period overviews. Lords of towns – whether kings, secular magnates or churchmen – were crucial to their development and were often their founders, perceiving them as valuable resources of skills and capital. The venerable debates about feudalism and the rise of towns are not directly addressed in this volume, but however we define feudalism, if indeed it is any more than a historian's construct, there is little support any longer for the view of towns as 'non-feudal islands in feudal seas'.[9] As Rodney Hilton puts it, 'far from being an antagonistic element within feudal society, towns would be one of its essential constitutive components'.[10] There is still, however, less consensus about potential political antagonisms *within* towns, especially between the urban ruling groups and the lesser townsfolk. For the late middle ages, evidence of conflicts and discontent is relatively abundant, but scholars – including contributors to this volume – are divided about how to read that evidence: some would take a broadly consensual view of urban society and see the evidence of conflict and sedition as abnormal, while others would stress 'class' conflict and see the recorded evidence as only the tip of an iceberg. Similar differences lie behind the debate over late medieval 'oligarchy', which is more than a matter of semantics and which reflects real differences in historians' perceptions of town life. These are debates which we cannot have hoped to resolve here, partly because, after 1381, we are rarely able 'to listen to the voices of townsmen who were seriously discontented'.[11] One of our contributors, in a recent survey of towns in fifteenth-century Europe, certainly takes the view that despite great differences in wealth and some instability, urban 'commons' in England, as in France and the Empire, 'were usually content with the government they received at the hands of their ruling elites'.[12]

Barrie Dobson makes this judgement in a section he calls 'A crisis of confidence?', a reminder that the fourteenth and fifteenth centuries are often viewed in rather negative terms as an age of recession. There can be no doubt,

[9] Michael Postan, 'The trade of medieval Europe: the North', in M. Postan and E. E. Rich, eds., *The Cambridge Economic History of Europe*, vol. II, 1st edn (Cambridge, 1952), p. 172; repr. unaltered in M. Postan and E. Miller's 2nd edn (Cambridge, 1987), p. 221.

[10] R. H. Hilton, *English and French Towns in Feudal Society* (Cambridge, 1992), p. 18. Cf. C. Dyer, 'Were there any capitalists in fifteenth-century England?', in J. Kermode, ed., *Enterprise and Individuals in Fifteenth-Century England* (Stroud, 1991), p. 7.

[11] Above, p. 289.

[12] R. B. Dobson, 'Urban Europe', in C. Allmand, ed., *The New Cambridge Medieval History*, vol. VII (Cambridge, 1998), p. 140.

of course, of the major change around the early fourteenth century when a long period of demographic growth came to an end and was followed by nearly two centuries of decline and stagnation. It was a combination of this turning point, together with the greatly increased survival of town records after about 1300, which persuaded us to make that the main chronological division of our volume. Whether, however, we should link demographic shrinkage to urban fortunes and characterise the late middle ages as a period of urban 'decay', 'crisis' or even 'de-urbanisation', as was commonly argued in the 1970s and 1980s, is more questionable, and recent surveys of the debate stress the complexity both of the evidence and of its interpretation.[13] The experience of different towns and different urban regions could be very different, while there was also variation over time. The debates about urban fortunes over two centuries mask, for instance, the change from prosperity for many towns in the late fourteenth and early fifteenth centuries, through a deep depression in the mid-fifteenth century, to a 'less uniformly dismal' scene by about 1500.[14] Furthermore, standards of living may have been rising in towns even if their populations shrank.

Other aspects of medieval British towns are, however, not so much debatable as simply underresearched. It will have become clear from many of our contributions that much more work remains to be done, and that some topics cannot yet be built into syntheses. This is especially the case with the analysis of urban populations, where there has been no general description of the data and findings for half a century, but where current research, especially on English taxation returns of the fourteenth century, promises much.[15] Studies are now proliferating of urban women and children, two important groups of 'legal marginals', including the exploitation of previously neglected sources, but again not yet sufficiently so for a convincing general account.[16] The archaeological exploration of cemeteries is increasingly providing much new anthropological evidence, but again without as yet sufficient syntheses. Similarly, there is now a huge volume of archaeological data on the material culture of medieval house-

[13] D. M. Palliser, 'Urban decay revisited', in J. A. F. Thomson, ed., *Towns and Townspeople in the Fifteenth Century* (Gloucester, 1988), pp. 1–21; A. D. Dyer, *Decline and Growth in English Towns 1400–1640* (Basingstoke, 1991). See also the articles by Rigby cited in n.8.

[14] John Hatcher, 'The great slump of the mid-fifteenth century', in R. H. Britnell and J. Hatcher, eds., *Progress and Problems in Medieval England* (Cambridge, 1996), pp. 266–70.

[15] J. C. Russell, *British Medieval Population* (Albuquerque, 1948), was a valuable pioneering study but badly needs replacing. See, however, C. Fenwick, ed., *The Poll Taxes of 1377, 1379 and 1381: Part 1* (British Academy Records of Social and Economic History, new series, 27, 1998).

[16] The phrase 'legal marginals' is that of David Nicholas, *The Later Medieval City 1300–1500* (Harlow, 1997), p. 258. Good case studies include P. J. P. Goldberg, *Women, Work and Life Cycle in a Medieval Economy* (Oxford, 1992), and J. M. Bennett, *Ale, Beer and Brewsters in England: Women's Work in a Changing World 1300–1600* (Oxford, 1996). Excellent urban sections are in H. Leyser, *Medieval Women* (London, 1995), pp. 154–65, 175–80. B. A. Hanawalt, *Growing Up in Medieval London: The Experience of Childhood in History* (Oxford, 1993), can, however, be recommended only with reservations.

holds, but much of it is published in 'finds reports', though a handful of town studies are now drawing on it for a broader picture of real value to historians.[17] There are also still too few syntheses of the evidence of standing buildings, apart from the urban inventories of the Royal Commission on Historical Monuments.

There remain also real lacunae in the study of urban law, customs, culture and *mentalités*, although Gervase Rosser and Pat Dennison valuably survey much of the field.[18] An important key to the understanding of medieval urban life is the collections of customs and by-laws in the form of custumals, but although much of their evidence was published and analysed almost a century ago,[19] study of them has scarcely advanced since. Within what we may call urban culture, the vernacular drama of the so-called cycle plays or Corpus Christi plays has been thoroughly studied,[20] but other aspects, such as the spread and standardisation of the English language itself and the part of the towns in that dissemination, need more work. R. R. Davies has pointed out, in suggestive asides, that towns played a key role in the spread of the English language both in Scotland and Wales.[21] The transmission of literacy and learning, in particular the extent of school attendance, also needs more work on the fragmentary sources, though there have been some valuable regional surveys of school provision, much of it located in the towns.[22] Other topics could easily be added, but this list may suffice to show that the study of medieval British towns is very far from exhausted.

As noted earlier, [23] British towns had come a long way by the early sixteenth century. Their numbers had increased to perhaps the maximum sustainable in a pre-industrial economy: certainly very few new towns were established in the following two centuries except in Scotland. The populations of those towns were in many cases, apparently, still below their pre-1348 peak, but there is strong support for the belief that many townspeople around 1500 enjoyed a collective life richer and more complex than in any earlier period. There were economic and social pressures which created instability, sometimes acutely, but as in the early modern period those pressures were usually contained without violence or breakdown. Nevertheless, it has to be remembered that there are limits to generalising about British towns at this period, and especially about glossing over the real differences – political and legal as well as economic and social – between

[17] Notably M. Biddle *et al.*, *Object and Economy in Medieval Winchester* (Oxford, 1991); Sue Margeson, *Norwich Households: The Medieval and Post-Medieval Finds from Norwich Survey Excavations, 1971–1978* (East Anglian Archaeology Report, 58, Norwich, 1993); G. Egan, *The Medieval Household* (Medieval Finds from Excavations in London, 6, 1998).

[18] Above, Chapter 15. [19] M. Bateson, ed., *Borough Customs* (Selden Society, 18, 21, 1904–6).

[20] Notably by the Records of Early English Drama (REED) project. See the valuable bibliography in R. Beadle, ed., *The Cambridge Companion to Medieval English Theatre* (Cambridge, 1994), pp. 344–64.

[21] R. R. Davies, 'The peoples of Britain and Ireland, 1100–1400: IV Language and historical mythology', *TRHS*, 6th series 7 (1997), 7, 8.

[22] See esp. Chapter 15 above, refs. cited in n. 97. [23] Above, p. 15.

England and Scotland, and Scottish towns still differed strikingly from English and Welsh towns in important ways.[24]

Finally, it may be appropriate to consider the changes of the 1530s and 1540s, when we conclude our survey and where Volume II begins. The current historical climate stresses continuities rather than revolutions, but divisions there must be in a multi-period survey, and a better claim can be made for the 1530s and 1540s in urban terms than for most. That period witnessed, in England and Wales, a whole complex of events which we loosely call 'the English Reformation', and which transformed not only the political and ecclesiastical landscape but also the culture and rhythms of urban and rural life. Independently of ourselves, Robert Tittler had been coming to a similar conclusion, in arguing that 'the Reformation marks a distinct watershed . . . in English urban history'.[25] Certainly the catalogue of changes affecting English and Welsh towns in the 1530s and 1540s is impressive in its scope: not only changes to doctrine and Church organisation, but also the abolition of institutions central to urban life (the friaries, hospitals, chantries and religious guilds, and often schools as well, usually rather more significant than the monastic houses), the destruction or emasculation even of parish churches, the wholesale transfer of property, and the abolition or curtailment of a host of rituals, processions, ceremonies, pageants and plays which gave shape to the seasonal and yearly round of townspeople, as well as meaning and colour to their lives. Even more importantly, the very existence of urban collective memory was threatened, and urban rulers had to work hard to create alternatives.[26] Such a radical transformation did not all happen at once, being not fully completed even in England until after 1558. Scotland was, of course, still a separate country with its own urban framework and ecclesiastical traditions: there, the Reformation took place only in the 1560s – though it was then more rapid and thorough than England's. Nor could one possibly argue that the whole of urban life suffered a breach in continuity. Nevertheless, if we wish to find a division with real relevance to British towns, the decades of the Reformation make more sense than most alternatives.

[24] Above, p. 14.

[25] Robert Tittler, *The Reformation and the Towns in England: Politics and Political Culture, c. 1540–1640* (Oxford, 1998), pp. 335–6. Cf. also P. Collinson and J. Craig, eds., *The Reformation in English Towns 1500–1640* (London, 1998), and Peter Clark, ed., *The Cambridge Urban History of Britain*, vol. II: *1540–1840* (Cambridge, 2000), esp. ch. 8.

[26] Robert Tittler, 'Reformation, civic culture and collective memory in English provincial towns', *UH*, 24 (1997), 283–300.

APPENDIX

Ranking lists of English medieval towns

ALAN DYER

INTRODUCTION

These listings attempt to supply basic information which might be used to estimate the relative size and wealth of English medieval towns over this long time span. They should always be used with care and more than a touch of cynicism. None of the documentary sources was created to serve the ends which historians have imposed upon it. Early administrations were inefficient and surviving records subject to damage and omissions of which we are unaware. Political influence allowed towns to escape their full tax burden and other factors of which we are usually ignorant led to inexplicable increases or reductions in their recorded financial obligations. Urban statistical assessments are bedevilled by the problem of defining the area which the town may legitimately be said to have covered: in the lists below some attempt has been made to include immunities and suburbs, and to exclude rural populations beyond the town limits, but this is frequently impossible to achieve, and some of the smaller towns may well have inflated values for this reason.

IA PRE-CONQUEST TOWNS: AREA WITHIN FORTIFICATIONS OF ANGLO-SAXON *BURHS*

Over 60 acres

1. London
2. Canterbury
   Chester
   Chichester
   Colchester
   Dorchester
   Exeter
   Wallingford
   Wareham
   Winchester

Under 60 acres

11. Warwick
12. Tamworth
13. York
14. Gloucester
15. Hereford
16. Wilton
17. Stafford
18. Nottingham
19. Ilchester
20. Christchurch
21. Dover?
22. Cambridge
23. Stamford
24. Old Sarum
25. Durham
26. Barnstaple
27. Malmesbury
28. Bath
29. Rochester
30. Guildford
31. Maldon
32. Buckingham
33. Shaftesbury
34. Bristol
35. Lewes

36. Shrewsbury
37. Lydford
38. Totnes

Source: D. Hill, *An Atlas of Anglo-Saxon England* (Oxford, 1981), p. 143.

1B PRE-CONQUEST TOWNS: NUMBER OF SURVIVING COINS FROM EACH MINT 973–1066

1. London and Southwark 10,758
2. York 4,805
3. Lincoln 4,342
4. Winchester 2,932
5. Stamford 1,712
6. Chester 1,550
7. Thetford 1,485
8. Exeter 1,360
9. Canterbury 1,265
10. Norwich 1,083
11. Oxford 754
12. Cambridge 679
13. Lewes 605
14. Ipswich 510
15. Dover 485
16. Wallingford 480
17. Bath 476
18. Gloucester 474
19. Ilchester 379
20. Colchester 378
21. Huntingdon 365
22. Northampton 359
    Shrewsbury 359
24. Wilton 356
25. Hastings 352
26. Hereford 344
27. Chichester 313
28. Rochester 312
29. Shaftesbury 307
30. Leicester 294
31. Sarum (Salisbury) 293
32. Hertford 272
33. Totnes 260
34. Lydford 250
35. Bristol 246
36. Worcester 245
37. Bedford 243
38. Warwick 202
39. Maldon 172

40. Barnstaple 161
41. Derby 150
    Nottingham 150
43. Wareham 142
44. Cricklade 121
45. Steyning 114
46. Watchet 103

Confined to mints with totals over 100.
Source: D. M. Metcalf, *An Atlas of Anglo-Saxon and Norman Coin Finds, c. 973–1086* (London, 1998), pp. 293–301. Professor Metcalf's figures are derived from H. B. A. Petersson's tabulation of 44,350 coins.

2 RANKING OF DOMESDAY TOWNS 1086

The information given by Domesday Book on the 112 towns to which it refers is fragmentary, inconsistent and extremely difficult to interpret. Some places which may well have possessed urban characteristics were omitted from it, while the truly urban character of some of the places listed below might be questioned. We may be less uncertain about some of the upper ranks of the urban hierarchy, but below this level any system of specific ranking such as is attempted below for later dates must be pointless. What appears here is an attempt to suggest tentative orders of magnitude. Entries are frequently incomplete, so that in many cases the figures given should be regarded as partial. Numbers are derived from the total number of 'properties' listed (*mansurae, mansiones, hagae* and *domus*); where there are ambiguities which might raise this total, or totals of *homines* are also given, a second and higher number is given after a / mark. Groups III onwards are given in alphabetical order.

I
London – no record.

II
York 1,036/1,576
Lincoln 939
Winchester ?? (very incomplete)
Norwich 881
Thetford 750/783
Bristol ?? – no record

III
Bury St Edmunds 342/652/859
Canterbury 599
Colchester 439
Dunwich 316/598
Exeter 399
Gloucester 98+ (but 528 *c.* 1100)
Lewes 458
Oxford 477
Sandwich 415/445
Stamford 415+
Wallingford 545

IV
Bath 185/205
Cambridge 324

Chester 282/320
Chichester 242
Derby 156
Dover 29+/449+
Grantham 111+85
Hereford ?200+
Huntingdon 256/380
Hythe 231
Ipswich 212/273
Leicester 383
Maldon 183+
Northampton 296
Nottingham 233/353
Shaftesbury 217/328
Shrewsbury 151/203+
Southampton 151/230
Warwick 244+?100
Worcester 160+

V
Arundel 17, Ashwell 14, Axbridge 32, Barnstaple 69, Beccles 26, Bedwyn 25, Berkhamsted 52, Bodmin 68, Bradford-on-Avon 33, (?Bridlington 4), Bridport 121, Bruton 17, Buckingham 25/52, Calne 74, Clare 43, Clifford 16, Cricklade 35+, Dadsley 31, Dorchester 90, Droitwich 151, (?Ewias Harold 2), Eye 25, Fordwich 86, Guildford 81, Hastings 24, Hertford 54, Ilchester 108, Langport 39, Louth 80, Lydford 69, Malmesbury 101, Milborne Port 69, Milverton 1, Newark 56, Okehampton 4, Penwortham 6, Pershore 28, Pevensey 111, (?Pocklington 15), Reading 59, Rhuddlan 18, Rochester 115+, Romney 156, Rye 64, St Albans 46, Seasalter 48, Stafford 146/159, Stanstead Abbots 7, Steyning 123, Sudbury 138, Tamworth 22, Tanshelf 60, Taunton 64, Tewkesbury 13, Tilshead 66, Torksey 102, Totnes 111, Tutbury 42, Twynham 39, Wareham 146, Warminster 30, Wilton 30, Wimborne Minster 22, Winchcombe 29 (but 141 *c.* 1100), Windsor 95, Yarmouth 70.

VI No information.
Bedford, Frome, Marlborough, Newport Pagnell,
Old Sarum, Quatford, Wigmore

VII Burghal status disputed.
Watchet, Yeovil.

Source: H. C. Darby, *Domesday England* (Cambridge, 1977) pp. 364–8, and other authorities.

3 RANKING OF TOWNS IN FARMS, TALLAGES AND AIDS 1154–1312

These taxes varied so greatly in their incidence, and records are preserved so irregularly, that they defy close analysis within a limited space. The more important towns which paid them are here classified in six groups of descending magnitude: where the amounts levied in the later part of this period varied strikingly from earlier ones, two groups are given. This analysis is advanced with even greater caution than usual. London's payments were always well above those of any provincial town. Towns are listed alphabetically within each class.

I
Bristol, Lincoln, Northampton (II later), Norwich, York

II
Canterbury, Dunwich (VI later), Exeter (III later), Winchester

III
Cambridge, Gloucester, Ipswich, Oxford, Stamford

IV
Bedford, Berkhamsted, Colchester, Doncaster, Hereford, Huntingdon, Marlborough, Newcastle-upon-Tyne (III or II later), Nottingham, Rochester, Southampton (III later), Worcester (III later)

V
Carlisle?, Chichester, Cirencester, Derby, Grimsby, Hertford, Hull, Newcastle-under-Lyme, Orford, Scarborough, Shrewsbury (III or II later), Stafford, Yarmouth (II later)

VI
Buckingham, Guildford, Ilchester, Maldon, Malmesbury, Tamworth, Wilton

Sources: S. K. Mitchell, *Taxation in Medieval England* (New Haven,1951); S. K. Mitchell, *Studies in Taxation under John and Henry III* (New Haven, 1914); J. F. Hadwin, 'The last royal tallages', *EHR*, 96 (1981).

4 RANKING OF TOWNS BY TAXABLE WEALTH: THE SUBSIDY OF 1334

Sums preceded by a ? have been revised on the basis of the taxation record of the period 1252–1332 presented by J. F. Hadwin ('The medieval lay subsidies and economic history', *EcHR*, 36, (1983)) in order to produce figures which are more consistent with previous assessments when the 1334 figure seems misleading; this is a hazardous process, and the resulting estimates should not be regarded with excessive respect. Where adjusted, the actual assessment follows in square brackets. The figures given are the total sums assessed – the amounts paid are generally one tenth or one fifteenth of these values. These figures were apparently based on earlier assessments of the value of land and moveable goods, but from 1334 onwards became a standardised total sum. The problem of whether suburbs and outlying members are or are not included in these figures is very hard to resolve, and this factor should be borne in mind, especially with lower rankings.

1. London £11,000
2. Bristol ?£1,900 [£2,200]
3. York ?£1,620 [too low?]
4. Newcastle-upon-Tyne £1,333
5. Boston £1,100
6. Norwich ?£1,100 [£946]
7. Yarmouth £1,000
8. Oxford £914
9. Lincoln ?£900 [£1,000]
10. Coventry ?£750 [nominal, too low?]
11. Lynn £770
12. Salisbury £750
13. Shrewsbury ?£700 [£940]
14. Winchester £625
15. Canterbury £599
16. Hereford ?£550 [£600]
17. Southampton £511
18. Gloucester ?£510 [£540]
19. Ipswich ?£500 [£650]
20. Beverley £500
21. Cambridge ?£500 [£466]
22. Newbury £412
23. Plymouth £400
24. Newark £390
25. Nottingham £371

26. Bury St Edmunds £360
27. Stamford £360
28. Exeter ?£350 [£406]
29. Northampton £350
30. Luton £349
31. Barking £341
32. Ely £315
33. Derby £300
34. Hull ?£300 [£333]
35. Scarborough ?£300 [£333]
36. Worcester ?£300 [£200]
37. Swaffham £300
38. Leicester £294
39. Grantham £293
40. Reading £293
41. Sudbury £281
42. Peterborough ?£275 [originally £385]
43. Huntingdon ?£270 [originally £263 – includes Godmanchester]
44. Marshfield £270
45. Pontefract £270
46. Abingdon £269
47. Banbury £267
48. St Albans £266
49. Waltham Abbey £263
50. Bridgwater £260
51. Doncaster £255
52. Cirencester £250
53. Colchester ?£250 [£260]
54. Leighton Buzzard £249
55. Godalming £248
56. Barton-on-Humber £246
57. Bicester £245
58. Bridgnorth £244
59. Tewkesbury £243
60. Ludlow £240
61. Sleaford £240
62. Wainfleet £233
63. Louth £230
64. Yaxley £227
65. North Walsham £225
66. Chipping Norton £221
67. Ringwood £221

68. Chichester £220
69. Worstead £218
70. East Dereham £218
71. Beccles £213
72. Dunstable £212
73. Kingston-on-Thames £211
74. Melton Mowbray £210
75. Andover £200
76. Bodmin £200
77. Chipping Campden ?£200 [originally £255 with 2 villages]
78. Hatfield £200
79. Ottery St Mary £200
80. Shaftesbury £200
81. Bedford £196
82. Market Deeping £195
83. Whitby £195
84. Wymondham £195
85. Ware £194
86. Wells £190
87. Barnstaple £187
88. Painswick £186
89. Truro £182
90. Hemel Hempstead £180
91. Witney £179
92. Fairford £174
93. Mildenhall £173
94. Petworth £170
95. Thetford £160
96. Faringdon £156
97. Guildford £151
98. Stafford £144
99. Chippenham £140+? [originally £173 with Rowden]
100. Bath £133

Excludes Cinque ports and counties of Chester and Durham, western Shropshire and the stannary men of Devon and Cornwall.
Kent data deficient.

Source: R. E. Glasscock, ed., *The Lay Subsidy of 1334* (London, 1975).

5 RANKING OF TOWNS BY TAXPAYING POPULATION: THE 1377 POLL TAX

These figures show the total number of recorded taxpayers. Every layperson over the age of fourteen (with the exception of the very poor) should have been included.

1 London 23,314 [plus outparishes?]
2. York 7,248
3. Bristol 6,345
4. Coventry 4,817
5. Norwich 3,952
6. Lincoln 3,569
7. Salisbury 3,373 [includes Fisherton Anger]
8. Lynn 3,127
9. Colchester 2,951
10. Boston 2,871
11. Beverley 2,663
12. Newcastle-upon-Tyne 2,647 [excludes Gateshead]
13. Canterbury 2,574
14. Winchester ?2,500
15. Bury St Edmunds 2,445
16. Oxford 2,357
17. Leicester 2,302
18. Gloucester 2,239
19. Yarmouth 1,941
20. Shrewsbury 1,932
21. Hereford 1,903
22. Cambridge 1,902
23. Exeter 1,666
24. Hull 1,557
Worcester 1,557
26. Plymouth 1,549
27. Ipswich 1,507
28. Northampton 1,477
29. Nottingham 1,447
30. Ely 1,394
31. Scarborough 1,393
32. Stamford 1,340
33. Chester about here?
34. Newark 1,178
35. Ludlow 1,172

36. Southampton 1,152
37. Pontefract 1,085
38. Derby 1,046
39. Lichfield 1,024
40. Newbury ?1,000
41. Durham about here?
42. Huntingdon 984 [excludes Godmanchester]
43. Hadleigh ?917 [estimate based on 1381 return]
44. Wells 901
45. Bridgnorth ?900 [Hoskins' estimate]
46. Bridgwater 888
47. Barking ?880 [Hoskins' estimate]
48. Chichester 869
49. Peterborough 850
50. Maidstone 844 [may include rural area]
51. Doncaster 800
52. Reading ?800 [estimate based on incomplete 1381 return]
53. Barnstaple 788
54. Cottingham? 767
55. St Germans 766
56. Cirencester ?746 [estimate based on 1381 return]
57. Grimsby ?700 [estimate based on 1381 return]
58. Louth 684
59. Dartmouth 683
60. Tickhill 680
61. Carlisle 678
62. Wainfleet 678
63. Thaxted 668
64. Whitby 640
65. Wilton 639
66. Writtle 600
67. Selby 586
68. Cranbrook 576
69. Bath 570
70. Rochester 570
71. Newcastle-under-Lyme 550
72. Tenterden 546
73. Taunton 539
74. Banbury 531
75. Wolverhampton? [large parish, 783 *cum membris*]
76. Mildenhall ?517 [estimate based on 1381]
77. Eccleshall 511

78. Kirkbymoorside 511
79. Melksham 511
80. Mere 489
81. Hedon 482
82. High Wycombe 482
83. Wakefield 482
84. Waltham 480
85. Ripon ?480 [estimate based on 1379 return]
86. Sheffield? [555, a large parish]

Counties of Durham and Chester excluded.
A consensus of authorities would indicate that total populations for these towns might generally be achieved by employing a multiplier of about 1.75–1.9.

Source: J. C. Russell, *British Medieval Population* (Albuquerque, 1948), pp. 118–46, as amended and extended by C. C. Fenwick, 'The English poll taxes of 1377, 1379 and 1381. A critical examination of the returns' (PhD thesis, University of London, 1983); cf. the rankings listed in W. G. Hoskins, *Local History in England*, 3rd edn (London, 1984), pp. 277–8.

6 RANKING OF TOWNS BY TAXPAYING POPULATION: SUBSIDY OF 1524–1525

Maximum number of recorded taxpayers in either year. The subsidy was assessed on landed income (rare in towns), moveable goods and what amounts to a poll tax on the better-off wage earners. The treatment of wage earners seems to have varied between towns, with some tendency to tax them in either 1524 or 1525, rather than in both years: consequently the total number of individuals appearing in one tax list or the other (where both survive) is usually greater than the figures given below would suggest. The proportion of households totally omitted is highly debatable, and varied between towns.

1. London [no figures survive]
2. Norwich 1,423
3. Bristol 1,166
4. Newcastle-upon-Tyne? [not taxed]
5. York ?(871) [underassessed?]
6. Exeter 1,050
7. Coventry ?(725) [underassessed]
8. Salisbury 885
9. Canterbury 784
10. Colchester 701
11. Bury St Edmunds 645
12. Lincoln 626
13. Hereford 611
14. Chester? [not taxed]
15. Winchester 596
16. St Albans 580
17. Gloucester ?(466) [underassessed?]
18. Cambridge 550
19. Shrewsbury 550
20. Oxford 542
21. Reading 531
22. Worcester 499
23. Yarmouth 497
24. Beverley ?(266) [original defective, and underassessed]
25. Ipswich 484
26. Maidstone 480 [may include rural area]
27. Northampton 477
28. Durham? [not taxed]
29. Southampton 450
30. Rochester 437

31. Crediton 433 [includes rural area]
32. Huntingdon 433 [includes Godmanchester]
33. Leicester 427
34. Newbury 414
35. Lichfield 391
36. Saffron Walden 380
37. Dover around here? [not taxed]
38. Derby around here? [underassessed]
39. Doncaster around here? [underassessed]
40. Hull 338
41. Rye? [not taxed]
42. Lynn about here? [return defective]
43. Hadleigh 311
44. Plymouth 310
45. Stamford ?308
46. Beccles 307
47. Chichester 301
48. Ely 300
49. Taunton 300
50. Nottingham 295 [underassessed?]
51. Boston ?295 [return defective]
52. Tiverton 289 [includes rural area?]
53. Wymondham 287
54. Bodmin 285
55. Basingstoke 284
56. Carlisle? [not taxed]
57. Windsor 267
58. Alton 260
59. Barking 256
60. Wisbech 252
61. Spalding 250 [includes large rural element?]
62. Ottery St Mary 250
63. Kingston-on-Thames 249
64. Cullompton 245
65. St Columb 240
66. Marlborough 237
67. Colyton 236
68. Cirencester ?(119) [underassessed]
69. Dunwich 235
70. Walsingham 232
71. Sudbury 231
72. Aylsham 231

73. Barnstaple 230
74. Wells 221
75. Totnes 220
76. Enfield 219
77. Shaftesbury 213
78. Bath 212
79. Bishops Hatfield 210
80. Glastonbury 209
81. Ramsey 209
82. Lewes 207
83. Lavenham 199
84. Maldon 193
85. St Neots 193
86. Woodbridge 192
87. Wellingborough 188
88. Croydon 185
89. Pontefract 181
90. Modbury 179
91. Petworth 178
92. Holbeach 174
93. Torrington 173
94. Dorchester 171
95. Selby 170
96. Wolverhampton 168
97. Ilminster 165
98. Oundle 164
99. Penryn 164
100. Manchester 163

The original tax excluded the counties of Durham, Chester, Northumberland, Cumberland and Westmorland and the towns of Ludlow and the Cinque ports. An attempt has been made to suggest the position of some of the more prominent towns affected by these omissions (though not Kendal), but there must be some which have not been included. Returns from Kent are very defective, and several lesser towns must be affected there. Underassessment was undoubtedly a factor in the assessment of the subsidy, as is often shown by comparison with evidence from the as yet unanalysed returns of the subsidies of the 1540s. Gloucestershire and Somerset clearly escaped the searching assessment of other counties, though one cannot assume that all the towns within their boundaries were uniformly affected. From the North Midlands to the North in general, underassessment was very common – Lancashire for instance was grossly undertaxed by comparison with the South. For this reason a number of medium-sized and smaller northern towns do not appear, but an attempt has been made in the lists above to inflate the status of several larger northern towns, such as Beverley; Derby and Doncaster appear at estimated levels. Where estimates have been used, they are based on the population reflected in the chantry certificates of the 1540s and the ecclesiastical census of 1563, with a cautious allowance for growth after the 1520s. They should of course be regarded with great caution, yet to have omitted these towns altogether, or even to have allowed them to appear at an improbably low level, would have been to allow an avoidable and greater distortion to have affected many of the other rankings. No agreement exists about the inflation factor to be applied to these numbers to raise them to estimates of full population totals, but a multiplier of 6.0–7.0 would probably be about right in many cases.

Source: J. Sheail, 'The regional distribution of wealth . . . in the lay subsidy returns (1524–5)' (PhD thesis, University of London, 1968), with additions from other sources.

7 RANKING OF TOWNS BY TAXABLE WEALTH: THE SUBSIDY OF 1524–1525

Maximum sum paid in any one year. These amounts are predominantly contributed by the tax paid on moveable goods: they chiefly reflect therefore the size and wealth of the business community, and are only indirectly related to population size.

1. London [no figures survive]
2. Norwich £749
3. Bristol £479
4. Newcastle-upon-Tyne [based on population estimate]
5. Coventry £448
6. Exeter £441
7. Salisbury £411
8. Lynn £302
9. Ipswich £282
10. Canterbury £269
11. York ?£230 [probably higher if underassessed]
12. Reading £223
13. Colchester £204
14. Bury St Edmunds £180
15. Lavenham £180
16. Worcester £171
17. Maidstone £169 [may include rural area]
18. Totnes £144
19. Gloucester £134
20. Yarmouth £125
21. Rye? [estimate]
22. Hereford £124
23. Chester around here?
24. Lincoln £124
25. Newbury £121
26. Boston £111
27. Hadleigh £109
28. Hull £108 [probably higher]
29. Leicester £107
30. Oxford £105
31. Shrewsbury £101
32. Southampton £101
33. Stamford £100
34. Beverley ?£63 [underassessed]

35. Cambridge £97
36. St Albans £95
37. Windsor £94
38. Dover around here?
39. Northampton £91
40. Taunton £86
41. Winchester £86
42. Durham around here?
43. Marlborough £85
44. Plymouth £85
45. Huntingdon £82 [includes Godmanchester]
46. Ottery St Mary £79
47. Dorchester £77
48. Beccles £74
49. Crediton £74 [includes rural area]
50. Maldon £72
51. Basingstoke £67
52. Barking £66
53. Long Melford £65
54. Chichester £63
55. Colyton £63
56. Kingston-on-Thames £62
57. Gravesend £61
58. Saffron Walden £61
59. Sudbury £61
60. Wells £61
61. Cullompton £60
62. Shaftesbury £60
63. Farnham £59
64. Nayland £59
65. Walsingham £58
66. Cirencester £58
67. Alton £55
68. Bruton £55
69. Luton £55
70. Witney £55
71. Abingdon £54
72. Tiverton £53 [includes rural area?]
73. Guildford £52
74. Devizes £50
75. Modbury £50
76. Thaxted £49

77. Godalming £48
78. Bath £45
79. Woodbridge £45
80. Wymondham £45
81. High Wycombe £44 [includes some rural settlements]
82. Peterborough £44
83. Wisbech £44
84. Lewes £43
85. Glastonbury £42
86. Henley-on-Thames £41
87. Dunwich £40
88. Spalding £39
89. Barnstaple £38
90. East Dereham £38
91. Aylesbury £37
92. Croydon £37
93. Bodmin £37
94. Lichfield £36
95. Newark £36
96. Aylsham £34
97. Oundle £34
98. St Neots £34
99. Thetford £34
100. Burford £33

Exclusions and sources: as for the previous list for 1524/5.
Fewer attempts have been made to amend these rankings than were made there, since reliable alternative figures for the taxable value of individual towns are very difficult to establish; as a result, towns which were excluded from the tax such as Carlisle, Kendal, Ludlow and Rye do not appear; also omitted are a number of towns which were either underassessed or lack credible data, such as Derby, Doncaster, Ely and Rochester. This will have the effect of raising the ranking of the towns which would have appeared below them by comparison with the preceding list.

RANKING SUMMARY OF THE MORE IMPORTANT TOWNS MENTIONED IN APPENDICES

	1a	1b	2	3	4	5	6	7
							Payers	Wealth
	Area	Mint	1086	Tallage	1334	1377	1524/5	1524/5
Abingdon					46			71
Banbury					47	74		
Barking					31	47	59	52
Barnstaple	26	40	V		87	53	73	89
Bath	28	17	IV		100	69	78	78
Beccles			V		71		46	48
Beverley					20	11	24	34
Bodmin			V		76		54	93
Boston					5	10	51	26
Bridgnorth					58	45		
Bridgwater					50	46		
Bristol	34	35	II	I	2	3	3	3
Bury St Edmunds			III		26	15	11	14
Cambridge	22	12	IV	III	21	22	18	35
Canterbury	2	9	III	II	15	13	9	10
Carlisle				V		61	56	
Chester	2	6				33	14	23
Chichester	2	27	IV	V	68	48	47	54
Cirencester				V	52	56	68	66
Colchester	2	20	III	IV	53	9	10	13
Coventry					10	4	7	5
Derby		41	IV	V	33	38	38	
Doncaster				IV	51	51	39	
Dorchester	2		V				94	47
Dover	21	15	IV				37	38
Dunwich			III	II/VI			69	87
Durham	25					41	28	42
Ely					32	30	48	
Exeter	2	8	III	II/III	28	23	6	6
Gloucester	14	18	III	III	18	18	17	19
Grantham			IV		39			
Guildford	30		V	VI	97			73
Hadleigh						44	43	27
Hereford	15	26	IV	IV	16	21	13	22
Hull				V	34	24	40	28
Huntingdon		21	IV	IV	43	42	32	45
Ipswich		14	IV	III	19	27	25	9
Lavenham							83	15

RANKING SUMMARY OF THE MORE IMPORTANT TOWNS MENTIONED IN APPENDICES (*cont.*)

	1a	1b	2	3	4	5	6	7
							Payers	Wealth
	Area	Mint	1086	Tallage	1334	1377	1524/5	1524/5
Leicester		30	IV		38	17	33	29
Lewes	35	13	III				82	84
Lichfield						39	35	94
Lincoln		3	II	I	9	6	12	24
Ludlow					60	35		
Luton					30			69
Lynn					11	8	42	8
Maidstone						50	26	17
Maldon	31	39	IV	VI			84	50
Marlborough			VI	IV			66	43
Newark			V		24	34		95
Newbury					22	40	34	25
Newcastle-upon-Tyne				III/II	4	12	4	4
Northampton		22	IV	I/II	29	28	27	39
Norwich		10	II	I	6	5	2	2
Nottingham	18	41	IV	IV	25	29	50	
Ottery St Mary					79		62	46
Oxford		11	III	III	8	16	20	30
Peterborough					42	49		82
Plymouth					23	26	44	44
Pontefract					45	37	89	
Reading			V		40	52	21	12
Rochester	29	28	V	IV		70	30	
Rye			V				41	21
Saffron Walden							36	58
St Albans			V		48		16	36
Salisbury	(24)	(31)	(VI)		12	7	8	7
Scarborough				V	35	31		
Shaftesbury	33	29	IV		80		77	62
Shrewsbury	36	22	IV	V/III	13	20	19	31
Southampton			IV	IV/III	17	36	29	32
Stamford	23	5	III	III	27	32	45	33
Sudbury			V		41		71	59
Taunton			V			73	49	40
Thetford		7	II		95			99
Totnes	38	33	V				75	18
Waltham					49	84		
Wells					86	44	74	60

RANKING SUMMARY OF THE MORE IMPORTANT TOWNS MENTIONED IN APPENDICES (*cont.*)

	1a Area	1b Mint	2 1086	3 Tallage	4 1334	5 1377	6 Payers 1524/5	7 Wealth 1524/5
Winchester	2	4	II	II	14	14	15	41
Windsor			V				57	37
Worcester		36	IV	IV/III	36	24	22	16
Yarmouth			V	V/II	7	19	23	20
York	13	2	II	I	3	2	5	11

Select bibliography

The following list concentrates on recent work, and makes no attempt to be comprehensive. For further references see the bibliographies by Gross, Martin and McIntyre listed below, and the annual bibliography in the journal *Urban History*. Primary sources, whether printed or unpublished, are not generally included. Works are cited by alphabetical order of authors, except for volumes of the *RCHM*. Composite volumes are generally listed under editors' names, but not the separate chapters by author.

Adams, I. H., *The Making of Urban Scotland* (London, 1978)

Addyman, P. V., and Black, V. E., eds., *Archaeological Papers from York Presented to M. W. Barley* (York, 1984)

Aldsworth, F., and Freke, D., *Historic Towns in Sussex: An Archaeological Survey* (London, 1976)

Andrews, P., ed., *Excavations at Hamwic*, vol. II (CBA Res. Rep., 109, 1997)

Astill, G. G., 'Archaeological theory and the origins of English towns – a review', *Archaeologia Polona*, 32 (1994)

Astill, G. G., 'Archaeology and the smaller medieval town', *UHY* (1985)

Astill, G. G., *Historic Towns in Berkshire: An Archaeological Appraisal* (Reading, 1978)

Astill, G. G., 'Towns and town hierarchies in Saxon England', *Oxford J of Archaeology*, 10 (1991)

Aston, M., and Bond, J., *The Landscape of Towns* (London, 1976)

Aston, M., and Leech, R., *Historic Towns in Somerset: Archaeology and Planning* (Bristol, 1977)

Aston, T. H., Coss, P. R., Dyer, C., and Thirsk, J., eds., *Social Relations and Ideas: Essays in Honour of R. H. Hilton* (Cambridge, 1983)

Atherton, I., Fernie, E., Harper-Bill, C., and Smith, H., eds., *Norwich Cathedral: Church, City and Diocese, 1096–1996* (London, 1996)

Atkin, M., 'The Anglo-Saxon urban landscape in East Anglia', *Landscape History*, 7 (1985)

Attreed. L., 'Arbitration and the growth of urban liberties in late medieval England', *J of British Studies*, 31 (1992)

Attreed, L., 'The politics of welcome: ceremonies and constitutional development in later medieval English towns', in Hanawalt and Reyerson, eds., *City and Spectacle*

Attreed, L., 'Poverty, payments and fiscal policies in English provincial towns', in S. K. Cohn, Jr, and S. A. Epstein, eds., *Portraits of Medieval and Renaissance Living: Essays in Memory of David Herlihy* (Michigan, 1996)

Ayers, B., *Norwich* (London, 1994)

BAHT, I: M. D. Lobel, ed., *Historic Towns: Maps and Commentaries of Towns and Cities in the British Isles, with Historical Commentaries, from Earliest Times to 1800: Volume I* (London and Oxford, 1969)

BAHT, II: M. D. Lobel, ed., *The Atlas of Historic Towns: Volume II: Bristol, Cambridge, Coventry, Norwich* (London, 1975)

BAHT, III: M. D. Lobel, ed., *The British Atlas of Historic Towns: Volume III: The City of London from Prehistoric Times to c. 1520* (Oxford, 1989)

Bailey, M., 'A tale of two towns: Buntingford and Standon in the later middle ages', *JMed.H*, 19 (1993)

Baker, N. J., Dalwood, H., Holt, R., Mundy, C., and Taylor, C., 'From Roman to medieval Worcester: development and planning in the Anglo-Saxon city', *Antiquity*, 66 (1992)

Ballard, A., ed., *British Borough Charters 1042–1216* (Cambridge, 1913)

Ballard, A., and Tait, J., eds., *British Borough Charters 1216–1307* (Cambridge, 1923)

Barley, M. W., ed., *The Plans and Topography of Medieval Towns in England and Wales* (CBA Res. Rep., 14, 1976)

Barley, M. W., ed., *European Towns: Their Archaeology and Early History* (London, 1977)

Barron, C. M., 'Centres of conspicuous consumption: the aristocratic town house in London 1200–1500', *LJ*, 20/1 (1995)

Barron, C. M., 'The fourteenth-century poll tax returns for Worcester', *Midland History*, 14 (1989)

Barron, C. M., '"The golden age" of women in medieval London', *Reading Medieval Studies*, 15 (1989)

Barron, C. M., 'London in the later middle ages 1300–1550', *LJ* 20/2 (1995)

Barron, C. M., *The Medieval Guildhall of London* (London, 1974)

Barron, C. M., 'The parish fraternities of medieval London', in C. M. Barron and C. Harper-Bill, eds., *The Church in Pre-Reformation Society: Essays in Honour of F. R.H. Du Boulay* (Woodbridge, 1985)

Barron, C. M., 'Ralph Holland and the London radicals, 1438–1444', in *A History of the North London Branch of the Historical Association . . .* (London, 1970); repr. in Holt and Rosser, eds., *The Medieval Town*

Barron, C. M., 'The social and administrative development of London 1300–1550', *Franco-British Studies*, 17 (1994)

Barron, C. M., and Saul, N., eds., *England and the Low Countries in the Late Middle Ages* (Stroud, 1995)

Barron, C. M., and Sutton, A. F., eds., *Medieval London Widows, 1300–1500* (London, 1994)

Barrow, G. W. S., *Kingship and Unity: Scotland 1000–1306* (London, 1981)

Bassett, S. R., 'Anglo-Saxon Shrewsbury and its churches', *Midland History*, 16 (1991)

Bassett. S. 'Churches in Worcester before and after the conversion of the Anglo-Saxons', *Antiquaries J*, 69 (1991)

Bassett, S. ed., *Death in Towns: Urban Responses to the Dying and the Dead, 100–1600* (Leicester, 1992)

Bateson, M., ed., *Borough Customs* (Selden Society, 18, 21, 1904–6)
Beadle, R., *The Cambridge Companion to Medieval English Theatre* (Cambridge, 1994)
Bearman, R., ed., *The History of an English Borough: Stratford-upon-Avon, 1196–1996* (Stroud, 1997)
Benton, J. F., *Town Origins: The Evidence from Medieval England* (Boston, Mass., 1968)
Beresford, M., 'English medieval boroughs: a hand-list: revisions, 1973–81', *UHY* (1981)
Beresford, M., *New Towns of the Middle Ages: Town Plantation in England, Wales and Gascony* (London, 1967; 2nd edn, Gloucester, 1988)
Beresford, M., and Finberg, H. P. R., *English Medieval Boroughs: A Hand-list* (Newton Abbot, 1973)
Beresford, M. W., and St Joseph, J. K. S., *Medieval England: An Aerial Survey*, 2nd edn (Cambridge, 1979)
Biddle, M., 'The study of Winchester: archaeology and history in a British town, 1961–1983', *Proc. of the British Academy*, 69 (1983)
Biddle, M., 'Towns', in Wilson, ed., *Archaeology of Anglo-Saxon England*
Biddle, M., ed., *Winchester in the Early Middle Ages: An Edition and Discussion of the Winton Domesday* (Winchester Studies, 1, Oxford, 1976)
Biddle, M., and Hill, D., 'Late Saxon planned towns', *Antiquaries J.* 51 (1971)
Biddle, M., *et. al.*, *Object and Economy in Medieval Winchester* (Winchester Studies, 7, ii, Oxford, 1991)
Blackburn, M. A. S., ed., *Anglo-Saxon Monetary History: Essays in Memory of Michael Dolley* (Leicester, 1986)
Blair, J., *Anglo-Saxon Oxfordshire* (Stroud, 1991)
Blair, J., 'Palaces or minsters? Northampton and Cheddar reconsidered', *Anglo-Saxon England*, 25 (1996)
Blair, J., ed., *Minsters and Parish Churches: The local Church in Transition 950–1200* (Oxford, 1988)
Blair, J., ed., *St Frideswide's Monastery at Oxford: Archaeological and Architectural Studies* (Stroud, 1990; repr. from *Oxoniensia*, 53 (1988))
Blair, J., and Golding, B., eds., *The Cloister and the World: Essays in Medieval History in Honour of Barbara Harvey* (Oxford, 1996)
Blair, J., and Ramsay, N., eds., *English Medieval Industries: Craftsmen, Techniques, Products* (London, 1991)
Blair, J., and Sharpe, R., eds., *Pastoral Care before the Parish* (Leicester, 1992)
Boffey, J., and King, P., eds., *London and Europe in the Later Middle Ages* (London, 1995)
Bolton, J. L., *The Alien Communities of London in the Fifteenth Century: The Subsidy Rolls of 1440 and 1483–4* (Stamford, 1998)
Bonney, M., *Lordship and the Urban Community: Durham and its Overlords, 1250–1540* (Cambridge, 1990)
Bridbury, A. R., *Economic Growth: England in the Later Middle Ages* (London, 1962)
Bridbury, A. R., 'English provincial towns in the later middle ages', *Ec.HR*, 2nd series, 34 (1981); repr. in his *The English Economy from Bede to the Reformation* (Woodbridge, 1992)
Britnell, R. H., 'The Black Death in English towns', *UH*, 21 (1994)
Britnell, R. H., *The Commercialisation of English Society, 1000–1500* (Cambridge, 1993; 2nd edn, Manchester, 1996)

Britnell, R. H., 'English markets and royal administration before 1200', *Ec.HR*, 2nd series, 31 (1978)
Britnell, R. H., *Growth and Decline in Colchester, 1300–1525* (Cambridge, 1986)
Britnell, R. H., 'Price-setting in English borough markets, 1349–1500', *Canadian J of History* 31 (1996)
Britnell, R. H., 'The proliferation of markets in England, 1200–1349', *Ec.HR*, 2nd series, 34 (1981)
Britnell, R. H., 'The towns of England and northern Italy in the early fourteenth century', *Ec.HR*, 44 (1991)
Britnell, R. H., ed., *Daily Life in the Late Middle Ages* (Stroud, 1998)
Britnell, R. H., and Campbell, B. M. S., eds., *A Commercialising Economy: England 1086 to c. 1300* (Manchester, 1995)
Britnell, R. H., and Hatcher, J., eds., *Progress and Problems in Medieval England: Essays in Honour of Edward Miller* (Cambridge, 1996)
Brodt, B., *Städte ohne Mauern: Stadtentwicklung in East Anglia im 14. Jahrhundert* (Paderborn, 1997)
Brooke, C. N. L., and Keir, G., *London, 800–1216: The Shaping of a City* (London, 1975)
Brooks, D. A., 'The case for continuity in fifth-century Canterbury re-examined', *Oxford J of Archaeology*, 7 (1988)
Brooks, D. A., 'A review of the evidence for continuity in British towns in the 5th and 6th centuries', *Oxford J of Archaeology*, 5 (1986)
Brooks, N. P., *The Early History of the Church of Canterbury* (Leicester, 1984)
Brooks, N. P., and Cubitt, C., eds., *St Oswald of Worcester: Life and Influence* (London, 1996)
Brooks, N. P., and Whittington, G., 'Planning and growth in the medieval Scottish burgh: the example of St Andrews', *Transactions Institute of British Geographers*, new series, 2 (1977)
Brown, R. A., Colvin, H. M., and Taylor, A. J., *The History of the King's Works: The Middle Ages* (London, 1963)
Burnham, B. C., and Wacher, J., *The 'Small Towns' of Roman Britain* (London, 1990)
Butcher, A. F., 'Rent and the urban economy: Oxford and Canterbury in the later middle ages', *S Hist*, 1 (1979)
Butler, L. A. S., and Morris, R. K. eds., *The Anglo-Saxon Church: Papers on History, Architecture, and Archaeology in Honour of Dr H. M. Taylor* (CBA Res. Rep., 60, 1986)
Cam, H. *Liberties and Communities in Medieval England: Collected Studies in Local Administration and Topography* (London, 1963)
Campbell, B. M. S., ed., *Before the Black Death: Studies in the 'Crisis' of the Early Fourteenth Century* (Manchester, 1991)
Campbell, B. M. S., Galloway, J. A., Keene, D., and Murphy, M., *A Medieval Capital and its Grain Supply: Agrarian Production and Distribution in the London Region c. 1300* (Historical Geography Research Series, 30, London, 1993)
Campbell, J., 'Bede's words for places', in P. H. Sawyer, ed., *Places, Names and Graves* (Leeds, 1979); repr. in Campbell, *Essays*
Campbell, J., 'The Church in Anglo-Saxon towns', in D. Baker, ed., *The Church in Town and Countryside* (Oxford, 1979); repr. in Campbell, *Essays*

Campbell, J., *Essays in Anglo-Saxon History* (London, 1986)
Campbell, J., ed., *The Anglo-Saxons* (Oxford, 1982)
Carlin, M., *Medieval Southwark* (London, 1996)
Carus-Wilson, E. M., *The Expansion of Exeter at the Close of the Middle Ages* (Exeter, 1963)
Carus-Wilson, E. M., 'The first half-century of the borough of Stratford-upon-Avon', *Ec.HR*, 2nd series, 18 (1965); repr. in Holt and Rosser, eds., *The Medieval Town*
Carus-Wilson, E. M., *Medieval Merchant Venturers* (London, 1954; 2nd edn., London, 1967)
Carus-Wilson, E. M., 'Towns and trade', in A. L. Poole, ed., *Medieval England*, vol. I (Oxford, 1958)
Carus-Wilson, E. M., and Coleman, O., *England's Export Trade, 1275–1547* (Oxford, 1963)
Carver, M. O. H., *Arguments in Stone: Archaeological Research and the European Town in the First Millennium* (Oxford, 1993)
Carver, M. O. H., *Underneath English Towns: Interpreting Urban Archaeology* (London, 1987)
Carver, M. O. H., ed., *Medieval Worcester: An Archaeological Framework* (Transactions of the Worcestershire Arch. Soc., 3rd series, 7, 1980)
Childs, W. R., 'Commerce and trade', in C. Allmand, ed., *The New Cambridge Medieval History*, vol. VII (Cambridge, 1998)
Childs, W. R., *The Trade and Shipping of Hull 1300–1500* (East Yorkshire Local History Series, 43, 1990)
Christie, N., and Loseby, S. T., *Towns in Transition: Urban Evolution in Later Antiquity and the Early Middle Ages* (Aldershot, 1996)
Clarke, H., and Ambrosiani, B., *Towns in the Viking Age* (Leicester, 1991; revised edn, London, 1995)
Clarke, H., and Carter, A., *Excavations in King's Lynn 1963–1970* (Society for Medieval Archaeology, Monograph 7, 1977)
Clarke, H. B., and Simms, A., eds., *The Comparative History of Urban Origins in Non-Roman Europe* (British Archaeological Reports, International Series, 255, 1985)
Clemoes, P., and Hughes, K., eds., *England before the Conquest: Studies in Primary Sources Presented to Dorothy Whitelock* (Cambridge, 1971)
Clough, C. H., ed., *Profession, Vocation and Culture in Later Medieval England: Essays Dedicated to the Memory of A. R. Myers* (Liverpool, 1982)
Conzen, M. R. G., *Alnwick, Northumberland: An Essay in Town-Plan Analysis* (Publications of the Institute of British Geographers, 27, 1960)
Conzen, M. R. G., 'The use of town plans in the study of urban history', in H. J. Dyos, ed., *The Study of Urban History* (London, 1968)
Corfield, P. J., and Keene, D., eds., *Work in Towns, 850–1850* (Leicester, 1990)
Coss, P. R., ed., *The Early Records of Medieval Coventry* (British Academy, Records of Social and Economic History, new series, 11, 1986)
Coulson, C., 'Battlements and the bourgeoisie: municipal status and the apparatus of urban defence in later medieval England', in S. Church and R. Harvey, eds., *Medieval Knighthood, V* (Woodbridge, 1995)
Cowie, R., and Whytehead, R., 'Lundenwic: the archaeological evidence for Middle Saxon London', *Antiquity*, 63 (1989)
Creaton, H., ed., *Bibliography of Printed Works on London History to 1939* (London, 1994)

Darby, H. C., *Domesday England* (Cambridge, 1977)
Darby, H. C., ed., *A New Historical Geography of England* (Cambridge, 1973)
Davies, R. R., *Conquest, Coexistence and Change: Wales 1063–1415* (Oxford, 1987); republished as *The Age of Conquest: Wales, 1063–1415* (Oxford, 1991)
Davis, R. H. C., *From Alfred the Great to Stephen* (London, 1991)
Dawes, J. D., and Magilton, J. R., *The Cemetery of St Helen-on-the-Walls, Aldwark* (The Archaeology of York, 12/1, York, 1980)
Denecke, D., and Shaw, G., eds., *Urban Historical Geography: Recent Progress in Britain and Germany* (Cambridge, 1988)
Dennison, E. P., 'Power to the people? The myth of the medieval burgh community', in S. Foster, A. Macinnes and R. Macinnes, eds., *Scottish Power Centres* (Glasgow, 1998)
Dennison, E. P., and Stones, J., *Historic Dunblane: The Archaeological Implications of Development* (Scottish Burgh Survey, 1998)
Dennison, E. P., and Coleman, R., *Historic Hamilton: The Archaeological Implications of Development* (Scottish Burgh Survey, 1996)
Dennison, E. P., and Coleman, R., *Historic Melrose: The Archaeological Implications of Development* (Scottish Burgh Survey, 1998)
Dennison, E. P., and Stones, J., *Historic Aberdeen: The Archaeological Implications of Development* (Scottish Burgh Survey, 1997)
Dobson, R. B., 'Admissions to the freedom of the city of York in the later middle ages', *Ec.HR*, 2nd series, 26 (1973)
Dobson, R. B., *Church and Society in the Medieval North of England* (London, 1996)
Dobson, R. B., 'Urban decline in late medieval England', *TRHS*, 5th series, 27 (1977); repr. in Holt and Rosser, eds., *The Medieval Town*
Dobson, R. B., 'Urban Europe', in C. Allmand, ed., *The New Cambridge Medieval History*, vol. VII (Cambridge, 1998)
Dobson, R. B., 'Yorkshire towns in the late fourteenth century', in *The Thoresby Miscellany*, 18 (Publications of the Thoresby Society, 59, 1986)
Dobson, R. B., ed., *The Peasants' Revolt of 1381*, 2nd edn (London, 1983)
Duncan, A. A. M., *Scotland: The Making of the Kingdom* (Edinburgh, 1975)
Duvosquel, J.-M., and Thoen, E., eds., *Peasants and Townsmen in Medieval Europe: Studia in Honorem Adriaan Verhulst* (Ghent, 1995)
Dyer, A., *Decline and Growth in English Towns 1400–1640* (Basingstoke, 1991; repr., Cambridge, 1995)
Dyer, C., *Everday Life in Medieval England* (London, 1994)
Dyer, C., 'Market towns and the countryside in late medieval England', *Canadian J of History*, 31 (1996)
Dyer, C., 'Small-town conflict in the later middle ages: events at Shipston-on-Stour', *UH*, 19 (1992)
Dyer, C., *Standards of Living in the Later Middle Ages: Social Change in England, c. 1200–1520* (Cambridge, 1989)
Dyson, T., 'King Alfred and the restoration of London', *LJ*, 15 (1990)
Eddy, M. R., and Petchey, M. R., *Historic Towns in Essex: An Archaeological Survey* (Chelmsford, 1983)
Egan, G., *The Medieval Household* (Medieval Finds from Excavations in London, 6, London, 1998)

Eliassen, F.-E., and Ersland, G. A., *Power, Profit and Urban Land: Landownership in Medieval and Early-Modern North European Towns* (Aldershot, 1996)
Everitt, A., 'The Banburys of England', *UHY* (1974); revised version, 'The primary towns of England', in his *Landscape and Community in England* (London, 1985)
Ewan, E., *Townlife in Fourteenth-Century Scotland* (Edinburgh, 1990)
Fawcett, C. B., *Provinces of England*, revised edn., W. G. East and S. W. Wooldridge (London, 1960)
Fenwick, C. C., ed., *The Poll Taxes of 1377, 1379 and 1381: Part 1* (British Academy Records of Social and Economic History, new series, 27, 1998)
Fleming, R., 'Rural elites and urban communities in late Saxon England', *P&P*, 141 (1993)
Fryde, E. B., *Studies in Medieval Trade and Finance* (London, 1983)
Galloway, J. A., Keene, D., and Murphy, M., 'Fuelling the city: production and distribution of firewood and fuel in London's region, 1290–1400', *Ec.HR*, 49 (1996)
Gelling, M., *The West Midlands in the Early Middle Ages* (Leicester, 1992)
Gemmill, E., and Mayhew, N., *Changing Values in Medieval Scotland: A Study of Prices, Money, and Weights and Measures* (Cambridge, 1995)
Gilchrist, R., and Mytum, H., eds., *Advances in Monastic Archaeology* (British Archaeological Reports, British Series, 227, 1993)
Glasscock, R. E., ed., *The Lay Subsidy of 1334* (British Academy, Records of Social and Economic History, new series, 2, London, 1975)
Goldberg, P. J. P., 'Mortality and economic change in the diocese of York, 1390–1514', *N Hist.*, 24 (1988)
Goldberg, P. J. P., 'Urban identity and the poll taxes of 1377, 1379, and 1381', *Ec.HR*, 2nd series, 43 (1990)
Goldberg, P. J. P., *Women, Work and Life Cycle in a Medieval Economy: Women in York and Yorkshire, c. 1300–1520* (Oxford, 1992)
Goldberg, P. J. P., ed., *Woman is a Worthy Wight: Women in English Society c. 1200–1500* (Stroud, 1992)
Goldberg, P. J. P., ed., *Women in England c. 1275–1525: Documentary Sources* (Manchester, 1995)
Good, G. L., Jones, R. H., and Ponsford, M. W., eds., *Waterfront Archaeology: Proceedings of the Third International Conference on Waterfront Archaeology* (CBA Res. Rep., 74, 1991)
Grant, A., *Independence and Nationhood: Scotland 1306–1469* (Edinburgh, 1984)
Grant, L., ed., *Medieval Art, Architecture and Archaeology in London* (British Archaeological Association Conference Transactions for 1984, 1990)
Gras, N. S. B., *The Early English Customs System* (Cambridge, Mass., 1918)
Green, A. S., *Town Life in the Fifteenth Century* (London, 1894)
Greep, S., ed., *Roman Towns: The Wheeler Inheritance* (CBA Res. Rep., 93, 1993)
Grenville, J., *Medieval Housing* (London, 1997)
Grierson, P., and Blackburn, M., *Medieval European Coinage*, vol 1: *The Early Middle Ages (5th–10th Centuries)* (Cambridge, 1986)
Grieve, H., *The Sleepers and the Shadows. Chelmsford: A Town, its People and its Past*, vol. 1: *The Medieval and Tudor Story* (Chelmsford, 1988)
Griffiths, R. A., ed., *Boroughs of Mediaeval Wales* (Cardiff, 1978)

Gross, C., *A Bibliography of British Municipal History* (New York, 1897; 2nd edn, with preface by G. H. Martin, Leicester, 1966)

Gross, C., *The Gild Merchant: A Contribution to British Municipal History* (Oxford, 1890)

Hadwin, J. F., 'From dissonance to harmony in the late medieval town', *Ec.HR*, 2nd series, 39 (1986)

Hadwin, J. F., 'The medieval lay subsidies and economic history', *Ec.HR*, 2nd series, 36 (1983)

Hall, A. R., and Kenward, H. K., eds., *Environmental Archaeology in an Urban Context* (CBA Res. Rep., 43, 1982)

Hall, R. A., *English Heritage Book of Viking Age York* (London, 1994)

Hall, R. A., *English Heritage Book of York* (London, 1996)

Hall, R. A., *The Excavations at York: The Viking Dig* (London, 1984)

Hall, R. A., 'The Five Boroughs of the Danelaw: a review of present knowledge', *Anglo-Saxon England*, 18 (1989)

Hall, R. A., ed., *Viking Age York and the North* (CBA Res. Rep. 27, 1978)

Hallam, H. E., ed., *Ag.HEW*, vol. II (Cambridge, 1988)

Hanawalt, B. A., and Reyerson, K. L., eds., *City and Spectacle in Medieval Europe* (Minneapolis, 1994)

Harrison, D. F., 'Bridges and economic development, 1300–1800', *Ec.HR*, 45 (1992)

Hartmann, W., ed., *Europas Städte zwischen Zwang und Freiheit: Die europäische Stadt um die Mitte des 13 Jahrhunderts* (Regensburg, 1995)

Harvey, B., *Living and Dying in England, 1100–1540: The Monastic Experience* (Oxford, 1993)

Haslam, J., *Early Medieval Towns in Britain c. 700 to 1140* (Princes Risborough, 1985)

Haslam, J., 'Market and fortress in England in the reign of Offa', *World Archaeology*, 19 (1987)

Haslam, J., ed., *Anglo-Saxon Towns in Southern England* (Chichester, 1984)

Haslam, J., and Edwards, A., *Wiltshire Towns: The Archaeological Potential* (Devizes, 1976)

Hatcher, J., *The History of the British Coal Industry*, vol. I: *Before 1700* (Oxford, 1993)

Heighway, C. M., 'Anglo-Saxon Gloucester to A.D. 1000', in M. L. Faull, ed., *Studies in Late Anglo-Saxon Settlement* (Oxford, 1984)

Hemmeon, M. de W., *Burgage Tenure in Mediaeval England* (Cambridge, Mass., 1914)

Herbert, N., ed., *The Gloucester Charter in History* (Gloucester, 1983)

Highfield, J. R. L., and Jeffs, R., eds., *The Crown and Local Communities in England and France in the Fifteenth Century* (Gloucester, 1981)

Hill, D., *An Atlas of Anglo-Saxon England* (Oxford, 1981; 2nd edn, Oxford, 1984)

Hill, D., and Rumble, A., eds., *The Defence of Wessex: The Burghal Hidage and Anglo-Saxon Fortifications* (Manchester, 1996)

Hill, J. W. F., *Medieval Lincoln* (Cambridge, 1948; 2nd edn., Stamford, 1990)

Hilton, R. H., *Class Conflict and the Crisis of Feudalism: Essays in Medieval Social History* (London, 1985; 2nd edn, London, 1990)

Hilton, R. H., *English and French Towns in Feudal Society: A Comparative Study* (Cambridge, 1992)

Hilton, R. H., *The English Peasantry in the Later Middle Ages* (Oxford, 1975)

Hilton, R. H., 'Lords, burgesses and hucksters', *P&P*, 97 (1982); repr. in his *Class Conflict*

Hilton, R. H., 'Medieval market towns and simple commodity production', *P&P*, 109 (1985)

Hilton, R. H., *A Medieval Society: The West Midlands at the End of the Thirteenth Century* (London, 1966)

Hilton, R. H., 'Small town society in England before the Black Death', *P&P*, 105 (1984); repr. in his *Class Conflict*, 2nd edn only, and in Holt and Rosser, eds., *The Medieval Town*

Hilton, R. H., 'Towns in English medieval society', *UHY* (1982); repr. in Holt and Rosser, eds., *The Medieval Town*

Hilton, R. H., and Aston, T. H., eds., *The English Rising of 1381* (Cambridge, 1984)

Hindle, B. P., *Medieval Town Plans* (Princes Risborough, 1990)

Hinton, D. A., *Archaeology, Economy and Society: England from the Fifth to the Fifteenth Century* (London, 1990)

Hodges, R., *The Anglo-Saxon Achievement: Archaeology and the Beginnings of English Society* (London, 1989)

Hodges, R., *Dark Age Economics: The Origins of Towns and Trade A.D. 600–1000* (London, 1982)

Hodges, R., and Hobley, B., eds., *The Rebirth of Towns in the West AD 750–1050* (CBA Res. Rep., 68, 1988)

Hollaender, A. E. J., and Kellaway, W., eds., *Studies in London History Presented to Philip Edmund Jones* (London, 1969)

Hollister, C. W., 'London's first charter of liberties: is it genuine?', *JMed.H*, 6 (1980); repr. in his *Monarchy, Magnates and Institutions in the Anglo-Norman World* (London, 1986)

Holt, R., and Rosser, G., eds., *The Medieval Town: A Reader in English Urban History, 1200–1540* (London, 1990)

Hooke, D., ed., *Anglo-Saxon Settlements* (Oxford, 1988)

Huffman, J. P., *Family, Commerce, and Religion in London and Cologne: Anglo-German Emigrants, c. 1000–c. 1300* (Cambridge, 1998)

James, M. E., 'Ritual, drama and the social body in the late medieval English town', *P&P*, 98 (1983)

Johnston, A. F., and Rogerson, M., eds., *Records of Early English Drama: York* (Manchester, 1979)

Karras, R. M., *Common Women: Prostitution and Sexuality in Medieval England* (Oxford, 1996)

Keen, L., ed., *'Almost the Richest City': Bristol in the Middle Ages* (British Archaeological Association Conference Transactions, 1997)

Keene, D., *Cheapside before the Great Fire* (Economic and Social Research Council, London, 1985)

Keene, D., 'London in the early middle ages 600–1300', *LJ*, 20/2 (1995)

Keene, D., 'Medieval London and its region', *LJ*, 14 (1989)

Keene, D., 'New discoveries at the Hanseatic Steelyard in London', *Hansische Geschichtsblätter*, 107 (1989)

Keene, D., 'Suburban growth', in Barley, ed., *Plans and Topography of Medieval Towns*; repr. in Holt and Rosser, eds., *The Medieval Town*

Keene, D., *Survey of Medieval Winchester* (Winchester Studies, 2, Oxford, 1985)

Keene, D., and Harding, V., *Historical Gazetteer of London before the Great Fire*, vol. I: *Cheapside* (Cambridge, 1987)

Keene, D., and Harding, V., *A Survey of Documentary Sources for Property Holding in London before the Great Fire* (London Record Society, 22, 1985)

Kelly, S., 'Trading privileges from eighth-century England', *Early Medieval Europe*, 1 (1992)

Kermode, J. I., 'Medieval indebtedness: the regions *versus* London', in N. Rogers, ed., *England in the Fifteenth Century: Proceedings of the 1992 Harlaxton Symposium* (Stamford, 1994)

Kermode, J. I., *Medieval Merchants: York, Beverley and Hull in the Later Middle Ages* (Cambridge, 1998)

Kermode, J. I., 'Urban decline? The flight from office in late medieval York', *Ec.HR*, 2nd series, 35 (1982)

Kermode, J. I., ed., *Enterprise and Individuals in Fifteenth-Century England* (Stroud, 1991)

Knowles, D., and Hadcock, R. N., *Medieval Religious Houses: England and Wales* (London, 1953; 2nd edn, London, 1971)

Kowaleski, M., 'The commercial dominance of a medieval provincial oligarchy: Exeter in the late fourteenth century', *Mediaeval Studies*, 46 (1984); repr. in Holt and Rosser, eds., *The Medieval Town*

Kowaleski, M., 'The history of urban families in medieval England', *JMed.H*, 14 (1988)

Kowaleski, M., *Local Markets and Regional Trade in Medieval Exeter* (Cambridge, 1995)

Kowaleski, M., 'The port towns of fourteenth-century Devon', in M. Duffy, S. Fisher, B. Greenhill, D. J. Starkey and J. Youings, eds., *The New Maritime History of Devon*, vol. 1 (London, 1992)

Langton, J., 'Late medieval Gloucester: some data from a rental of 1455', *Transactions, Institute of British Geographers*, new series, 2 (1977)

Leech, R., *Historic Towns in Gloucestershire* (Bristol, 1981)

Leech, R., *Small Medieval Towns in Avon: Archaeology and Planning* (Bristol, 1975)

Lewis, E. A., *The Mediæval Boroughs of Snowdonia: A Study of the Rise and Development of the Municipal Element in the Ancient Principality of North Wales down to the Union of 1536* (London, 1912)

Leyser, H., *Medieval Women: A Social History of Women in England 450–1500* (London, 1995)

Lilley, J. M., *et al.*, *The Jewish Burial Ground at Jewbury* (The Archaeology of York, 12/3, 1994)

Lipman, V. D., *The Jews of Medieval Norwich* (London, 1967)

Lloyd, T. H., *Alien Merchants in England in the High Middle Ages* (Brighton and New York, 1982)

Lloyd, T. H., *England and the German Hanse, 1157–1611: A Study of their Trade and Diplomacy* (Cambridge, 1991)

Lloyd, T. H., *The English Wool Trade in the Middle Ages* (Cambridge, 1977)

Lloyd, T. H., *The Movement of Wool Prices in Medieval England*, *Ec.HR* Supplement 6 (Cambridge, 1973)

Lobel, M. D., *The Borough of Bury St Edmunds: A Study in the Government and Development of a Monastic Town* (Oxford, 1935)

Lobel, M. D., ed., *The British Atlas of Historic Towns*: see under *BAHT*

Loyn, H. R., 'Boroughs and mints A.D. 900–1066', in R. H. M. Dolley, ed., *Anglo-Saxon*

Coins: Studies Presented to F. M. Stenton (London, 1961); repr. in Loyn, *Society and Peoples*

Loyn, H. R., *Society and Peoples: Studies in the History of England and Wales, c. 600–1200* (London, 1992)

Loyn, H. R., 'Towns in late Anglo-Saxon England: the evidence and some possible lines of enquiry', in Clemoes and Hughes, eds., *England before the Conquest*; repr. in Loyn, *Society and Peoples*

Lynch, M., Spearman, M., and Stell, G., eds., *The Scottish Medieval Town* (Edinburgh, 1988)

McCarthy, M. R., and Brooks, C. M., *Medieval Pottery in Britain AD 900–1600* (Leicester, 1988)

Mackenzie, W. M., *The Scottish Burghs* (Edinburgh, 1949)

McKisack, M., 'London and the succession to the crown during the middle ages', in R. W. Hunt, W. A. Pantin and R. W. Southern, eds., *Studies in Medieval History Presented to F. M. Powicke* (Oxford, 1948)

McKisack, M., *The Parliamentary Representation of the English Boroughs during the Middle Ages* (Oxford, 1932)

McClure, P., 'Patterns of migration in the late middle ages: the evidence of English place-name surnames', *Ec.HR*, 2nd series, 32 (1979)

McNeill, P. G. B., and MacQueen, H. L., eds., *Atlas of Scottish History to 1707* (Edinburgh, 1996)

McRee, B. R., 'Peacemaking and its limitations in late medieval Norwich', *EHR*, 109 (1994)

McRee, B. R., 'Religious gilds and civic order: the case of Norwich in the late middle ages', *Speculum*, 67 (1992)

Maddern, P. C., *Violence and the Social Order: East Anglia 1422–42* (Oxford, 1992)

Maddicott, J. R., 'Trade, industry and the wealth of King Alfred', *P&P*, 123 (1989)

Madox, T., *Firma Burgi* (London, 1726)

Mahany, C., Burchard, A., and Simpson, G., *Excavations in Stamford, Lincolnshire, 1963–1969* (Society of Medieval Archaeology, Monograph 9, 1982)

Maitland, F. W., *Domesday Book and Beyond* (Cambridge, 1897)

Maitland, F. W., *Township and Borough* (Cambridge, 1898)

Martin, G. H., 'Domesday Book and the boroughs', in Sawyer, ed., *Domesday Book*

Martin, G. H., 'The Domesday boroughs', in A. Williams and R. W. H. Erskine, eds., *Domesday Book Studies* (London, 1987)

Martin, G. H., 'The English borough in the thirteenth century', *TRHS*, 5th series, 13, (1963); repr. in Holt and Rosser, eds., *The Medieval Town*

Martin, G. H., and McIntyre, S., *A Bibliography of British and Irish Municipal History*, vol. 1: *General Works* (Leicester, 1972)

Martin, G. H., *et al.*, *Doncaster: A Borough and its Charters* (Doncaster, 1995)

Masschaele, J., 'Market rights in thirteenth-century England', *EHR*, 107 (1992)

Masschaele, J., 'The multiplicity of medieval markets reconsidered', *J of Historical Geography*, 20 (1994)

Masschaele, J., *Peasants, Merchants, and Markets: Inland Trade in Medieval England, 1150–1350* (Basingstoke, 1997)

Masschaele, J., 'Transport costs in medieval England', *Ec.HR*, 46 (1993)

Masschaele, J., 'Urban trade in medieval England: the evidence of foreign gild membership lists', in P. R. Coss and S. D. Lloyd, eds., *Thirteenth Century England, V* (Woodbridge, 1995)

Metcalf, D. M., *An Atlas of Anglo-Saxon and Norman Coin Finds c. 973–1086* (London, 1998)

Metcalf, D. M., 'The monetary history of England in the tenth century viewed in the perspective of the eleventh century', in Blackburn, ed., *Anglo-Saxon Monetary History*

Metcalf, D. M., 'The ranking of boroughs: numismatic evidence from the reign of Æthelred II', in D. Hill, ed., *Ethelred the Unready* (Oxford, 1978)

Miller, E., 'The English economy in the thirteenth century', *P&P*, 28 (1964)

Miller, E., 'The fortunes of the English textile industry in the thirteenth century', *Ec.HR*, 2nd series, 18 (1965)

Miller, E., 'Rulers of thirteenth century towns: the cases of York and Newcastle upon Tyne', in P. R. Coss and S. D. Lloyd, eds., *Thirteenth Century England, I* (Woodbridge, 1986)

Miller, E., ed., *Ag.HEW*, vol. III (Cambridge, 1991)

Miller, E., and Hatcher, J., *Medieval England: Rural Society and Economic Change, 1086–1348* (London, 1978)

Miller, E., and Hatcher, J., *Medieval England: Towns, Commerce and Crafts, 1086–1348* (London, 1995)

Mills, D., *Recycling the Cycle: The City of Chester and its Whitsun Plays* (Toronto, 1998)

Milne, G., *Timber Building Techniques in London, c. 900–c. 1400: An Archaeological Study of Waterfront Installations and Related Material* (LAMAS Special Paper, 15, 1992)

Milne, G., and Hobley, B., eds., *Waterfront Archaeology in Britain and Northern Europe* (CBA Res. Rep., 41, 1981)

Mitchell, S. K., *Taxation in Medieval England* (New Haven, 1951)

Moore, E. W., *The Fairs of Medieval England: An Introductory Study* (PIMSST, 72, Toronto, 1985)

Morris, R., *Churches in the Landscape* (London, 1989)

Morton, A. D., ed., *Excavations at Hamwic*, vol. I (CBA Res. Rep., 84, 1992)

Munro, J. H., *Textiles, Towns and Trade: Essays in the Economic History of Late-Medieval England and the Low Countries* (Aldershot, 1994)

Murray, K. M. E., *The Constitutional History of the Cinque Ports* (Manchester, 1935)

Newton, K. C., *Thaxted in the Fourteenth Century* (Chelmsford, 1960)

Nicolaisen, W. F. H., Gelling, M., and Richards, M., *The Names of Towns and Cities in Britain* (London, 1970)

Nightingale, P., *A Medieval Mercantile Community: The Grocers' Company and the Politics and Trade of London, 1000–1485* (New Haven and London, 1995)

Nightingale, P., 'Monetary contraction and mercantile credit in later medieval England', *Ec.HR*, 2nd series, 43 (1990)

O'Connell, M. G., *Historic Towns in Surrey* (Surrey Arch. Soc. Research, 5, 1977)

Orme, N., *English Schools in the Middle Ages* (London, 1973)

Ottaway, P., *Archaeology in British Towns: From the Emperor Claudius to the Black Death* (London, 1992)

Owen, D. M., ed., *The Making of King's Lynn: A Documentary Survey* (British Academy, Records of Social and Economic History, new series, 9, 1984)

Palliser, D. M., 'A crisis in English towns? The case of York, 1460–1640', *NHist.*, 14 (1978)

Palliser, D. M., *Domesday York* (Borthwick Paper, 78, York, 1990)

Palliser, D. M., 'English medieval cities and towns: new directions', *JUH*, 23/4 (1997)

Palliser, D. M., 'A regional capital as magnet: immigrants to York, 1477–1566', *Yorkshire Arch. J*, 57 (1985)

Palliser, D. M., 'Town defences in medieval England and Wales', in A. Ayton and J. L. Price, eds., *The Medieval Military Revolution* (London, 1995)

Palliser, D. M., *Tudor York* (Oxford, 1979)

Palliser, D. M., 'Urban society', in R. Horrox, ed., *Fifteenth-Century Attitudes: Perceptions of Society in Late Medieval England* (Cambridge, 1994)

Pantin, W. A., 'Medieval English town-house plans', *Med. Arch.*, 6–7 (1962–3)

Parker, V., *The Making of King's Lynn: Secular Buildings from the 11th to the 17th Century* (London and Chichester, 1971)

Penn, K. J., *Historic Towns in Dorset* (Dorset Natural Hist. and Arch. Soc., Monograph 1, 1980)

Pevsner, N., *et. al.*, *The Buildings of England* (Hamondsworth, 1951–)

Phythian-Adams, C., 'Ceremony and the citizen: the communal year at Coventry, 1450–1550', in P. Clark and P. Slack, eds., *Crisis and Order in English Towns, 1500–1700* (London, 1972); repr. in Holt and Rosser, eds., *The Medieval Town*

Phythian-Adams, C., *Desolation of a City: Coventry and the Urban Crisis of the Late Middle Ages* (Cambridge, 1979)

Phythian-Adams, C., 'Urban decay in late medieval England', in P. Abrams and E. A. Wrigley, eds., *Towns in Societies: Essays in Economic History and Historical Sociology* (Cambridge, 1978)

Platt, C., *The English Medieval Town* (London, 1976)

Platt, C., *Medieval Southampton: The Port and Trading Community, A.D. 1000–1600* (London, 1973)

Platts, G., *Land and People in Medieval Lincolnshire* (Lincoln, 1985)

Pollard, A. J., *North-Eastern England during the Wars of the Roses: Lay Society, War, and Politics 1450–1500* (Oxford, 1990)

Portman, D., *Exeter Houses 1400–1700* (Exeter, 1966)

Postles, D., 'An English small town in the later middle ages: Loughborough', *UH*, 20 (1993)

Pryde, G. S., *The Burghs of Scotland: A Critical List* (London, 1965)

Raftis, J. A., *Early Tudor Godmanchester: Survivals and New Arrivals* (PIMSST, 97, Toronto, 1990)

Raftis, J. A., *A Small Town in Late Medieval England: Godmanchester 1278–1400* (PIMSST, 53, Toronto, 1982)

Rahtz, P., and Meeson, R., *An Anglo-Saxon Watermill at Tamworth* (CBA Res. Rep., 83, 1992)

RCHM (England), *Ancient and Historical Monuments in the City of Salisbury*, vol. 1 (London, 1980)

RCHM (England), *An Inventory of the Historical Monuments in the City of York* (London, 1962–81)

RCHM (England), *An Inventory of the Historical Monuments in the Town of Stamford* (London, 1977)

RCHM (England), *Salisbury: The Houses of the Close* (London, 1993)

Records of Early English Drama (Toronto, 1979–)

Reed, M., ed., *English Towns in Decline: 1350 to 1800* (Centre for Urban History, University of Leicester, Working Paper, 1, 1986)

Rees Jones, S., ed., *The Government of Medieval York: Essays in Commemoration of the 1396 Royal Charter* (Borthwick Studies in History, 3, York, 1997)

Reynolds, S., *Ideas and Solidarities of the Medieval Laity: England and Western Europe* (Aldershot, 1995)

Reynolds, S., *An Introduction to the History of English Medieval Towns* (Oxford, 1977)

Reynolds, S., *Kingdoms and Communities in Western Europe 900–1300* (Oxford, 1984; 2nd edn., Oxford, 1997)

Reynolds, S., 'Medieval urban history and the history of political thought', *UHY* (1982); repr. in Reynolds, *Ideas and Solidarities*

Reynolds, S., 'The rulers of London in the twelfth century', *History*, 57 (1972); repr. in Reynolds, *Ideas and Solidarities*

Reynolds, S., 'Towns in Domesday Book', in J. C. Holt, ed., *Domesday Studies* (Woodbridge, 1987)

Reynolds, S., 'The writing of medieval urban history in England', *Theoretische Geschiedenis*, 19 (1992); repr. in Reynolds, *Ideas and Solidarities*

Richardson, H. G., *The English Jewry under Angevin Kings* (London, 1960)

Rigby, S. H., 'Boston and Grimsby in the middle ages: an administrative contrast', *JMed.H*, 10 (1984)

Rigby, S. H., 'The customs administration at Boston in the reign of Richard II', *Bull.IHR*, 58 (1985)

Rigby, S. H., *English Society in the Later Middle Ages: Class, Status and Gender* (Basingstoke, 1995)

Rigby, S. H., 'Late medieval urban prosperity: the evidence of the lay subsidies', *Ec.HR*, 2nd series, 39 (1986)

Rigby, S. H., *Medieval Grimsby: Growth and Decline* (Hull, 1993)

Rigby, S. H., '"Sore decay" and "fair dwellings": Boston and urban decline in the later middle ages', *Midland History*, 10 (1985)

Rigby, S. H., 'Urban decline in the later middle ages: the reliability of the non-statistical evidence', *UHY* (1984)

Rigby, S. H., 'Urban society in fourteenth-century England: the evidence of the lay subsidies', *Bulletin of the John Rylands Library*, 72 (1990)

Rodwell, K., ed., *Historic Towns in Oxfordshire: A Survey of the New County* (Oxford, 1975)

Roffe, D., ed., *Stamford in the Thirteenth Century: Two Inquisitions from the Reign of Edward I* (Stamford, 1994)

Röhrkasten, J., 'Conflict in a monastic borough: Coventry in the reign of Edward II', *Midland History*, 18 (1993)

Rollason, D., Harvey, M., and Prestwich, M., eds., *Anglo-Norman Durham 1093–1193* (Woodbridge, 1994)

Rollason, D. W., ed., *Sources for York History to AD 1100* (The Archaeology of York, AY/1, York, 1998)

Rosser, G., 'Crafts, guilds and the negotiation of work in the medieval town', *P&P*, 154 (1997)
Rosser, G., 'Going to the fraternity feast: commensality and social relations in late medieval England', *J of British Studies*, 33 (1994)
Rosser, G., *Medieval Westminster, 1200–1540* (Oxford, 1989)
Rosser, G., 'Myth, image and social process in the English medieval town', *UH*, 23 (1996)
Rosser, G., 'Workers' associations in English medieval towns', in J.-P. Sosson, ed., *Les métiers au moyen âge* (Louvain-la-Neuve, 1994)
Rubin, M., *Charity and Community in Medieval Cambridge* (Cambridge, 1987)
Rubin, M., *Corpus Christi: The Eucharist in Late Medieval Culture* (Cambridge, 1991)
Russell, J. C., *British Medieval Population* (Albuquerque, 1948)
Russo, D. G., *Town Origins and Development in Early England, c. 400–950 A.D.* (Westport, Conn., 1998)
Salzman, L. F., *Building in England down to 1540* (Oxford, 1952; 2nd edn, 1967)
Saul, A., 'English towns in the late middle ages: the case of Great Yarmouth', *JMed.H*, 8 (1982)
Sawyer, P. H., *Anglo-Saxon Charters: An Annotated List and Bibliography*, revised edn, S. E. Kelly (n.p., 1994)
Sawyer, P. H., 'Early fairs and markets in England and Scandinavia', in B. L. Anderson and A. J. H. Latham, eds., *The Market in History* (London, 1986)
Sawyer, P. H., 'Fairs and markets in early medieval England', in N. Skyum-Nielsen and N. Lund, eds., *Danish Medieval History: New Currents* (Copenhagen, 1981)
Sawyer, P. H., 'The royal *tūn* in pre-Conquest England', in P. Wormald, ed., *Ideal and Reality in Frankish and Anglo-Saxon Society* (Oxford, 1983)
Sawyer, P. H., ed., *Domesday Book: A Reassessment* (London, 1985)
Schofield, J., *The Building of London from the Conquest to the Great Fire* (London, 1984)
Schofield, J., 'The capital rediscovered: archaeology in the City of London', *UH*, 20 (1993)
Schofield, J., *Medieval London Houses* (New Haven, 1995)
Schofield, J., and Leech, R., eds., *Urban Archaeology in Britain* (CBA Res. Rep., 61, 1987)
Schofield, J., and Vince, A., *Medieval Towns* (London, 1994)
Schofield, J., Palliser, D., and Harding, C., *Recent Archaeological Research in English Towns* (CBA, 1981)
Scull, C., 'Urban centres in pre-Viking England?', in J. Hines, ed., *The Anglo-Saxons from the Migration Period to the Eighth Century: An Ethnographic Perspective* (Woodbridge, 1997)
Searle, E., *Lordship and Community: Battle Abbey and its Banlieu, 1066–1538* (Toronto, 1974)
Serjeantson, D., and Waldron, T., eds., *Diet and Crafts in Towns: The Evidence of Animal Remains from the Roman to the Post-Medieval Periods* (British Archaeological Report, 199, 1989)
Shaw, D. G., *The Creation of a Community: The City of Wells in the Middle Ages* (Oxford, 1993)
Sheeran, G., *Medieval Yorkshire Towns: People, Buildings and Spaces* (Edinburgh, 1998)
Shoesmith, R., *Hereford City Excavations*, vol. I: *Excavations at Castle Green* (CBA Res. Rep., 36, 1980)
Shoesmith, R., *Hereford City Excavations*, vol. II: *Excavations on and Close to the Defences* (CBA Res. Rep., 46, 1982)

Slater, T. R., *The Analysis of Burgages in Medieval Towns* (University of Birmingham, Dept of Geography, Working Paper, 4, 1980); revised version as 'The analysis of burgage patterns in medieval towns', *Area*, 13 (1981)

Slater, T. R., 'Ideal and reality in English episcopal medieval town planning', *Transactions, Institute of British Geographers*, new series, 12 (1987)

Slater, T. R., 'The origins of Warwick', *Midland History*, 7 (1983)

Slater, T. R., 'The urban hierarchy in medieval Staffordshire', *J of Historical Geography*, 11 (1985)

Slater, T. R., ed., *The Built Form of Western Cities: Essays for M. R. G. Conzen on the Occasion of his Eightieth Birthday* (Leicester and London, 1990)

Slater, T. R., and Rosser, G., eds., *The Church in the Medieval Town* (Aldershot, 1998)

Smith, T., *English Gilds* (Early English Text Society, 40, 1870)

Soulsby, I., *The Towns of Medieval Wales* (Chichester, 1983)

Spearman, R. M., 'Early Scottish towns: their origins and economy', in S. Driscoll and M. Nieke, eds., *Power and Politics in Early Medieval Britain and Ireland* (Edinburgh, 1988)

Stafford, P., *The East Midlands in the Early Middle Ages* (Leicester, 1985)

Steedman, K., Dyson, T., and Schofield, J., *Aspects of Saxo-Norman London*, vol. III: *The Bridgehead and Billingsgate to 1200* (LAMAS Special Paper, 14, 1992)

Stenton, F. M., *Anglo-Saxon England* (1st edn, Oxford, 1943; 2nd edn, 1947; 3rd edn, 1971)

Stephenson, C., *Borough and Town: A Study of Urban Origins in England* (Cambridge, Mass., 1933)

Stocker, D., *St Mary's Guildhall, Lincoln* (Archaeology of Lincoln, 12/1, CBA, 1991)

Summerson, H., *Medieval Carlisle* (Cumberland and Westmorland Antiq. and Arch. Soc. Extra Series, 25, Kendal, 1993)

Swanson, H., 'The illusion of economic structure: craft guilds in late medieval English towns', *P&P*, 121 (1988)

Swanson, H., *Medieval Artisans: An Urban Class in Late Medieval England* (Oxford, 1989)

Swanson, R. N., *Church and Society in Late Medieval England* (Oxford, 1989)

Tait, J., *The Medieval English Borough: Studies on its Origins and Constitutional History* (Manchester, 1936)

Tanner, N. P., *The Church in Late Medieval Norwich 1370–1532* (PIMSST, 66, Toronto, 1984)

Tatton-Brown, T., 'The topography of Anglo-Saxon London', *Antiquity*, 60 (1986)

Thacker, A., 'Chester and Gloucester: early ecclesiastical organisation in two Mercian burhs', *NHist.*, 18 (1982)

Thomson, J. A. F., 'Tithe disputes in later medieval London', *EHR*, 78 (1963)

Thomson, J. A. F., ed., *Towns and Townspeople in the Fifteenth Century* (Gloucester, 1988)

Thrupp, S. L., *The Merchant Class of Medieval London* (Chicago, 1948; repr. Ann Arbor, 1962)

Torrie, E. P. D., *Medieval Dundee: A Town and its People* (Dundee, 1990)

Tout, T. F., 'The beginnings of a modern capital. London and Westminster in the fourteenth century', in T. F. Tout, *Collected Papers* (Manchester, 1934), vol. III.

Trenholme, N. M., *The English Monastic Boroughs* (University of Missouri Studies, 2, no. 3, 1927)

Turner, H. L., *Town Defences in England and Wales: An Architectural and Documentary Study AD 900–1500* (London, 1970)

Urry, W., *Canterbury under the Angevin Kings* (London, 1967)
Verhulst, A., *Rural and Urban Aspects of Early Medieval Northwest Europe* (Aldershot, 1992)
Vince, A., *Saxon London: An Archaeological Investigation* (London, 1990)
Vince, A., ed., *Aspects of Saxo-Norman London*, vol. II: *Finds and Environmental Evidence* (LAMAS Special Paper, 12, 1991)
Vince, A., ed., *Pre-Viking Lindsey* (Lincoln, 1993)
Wacher, J. S., *The Towns of Roman Britain* (London, 1975; 2nd edn, London, 1995)
Weinbaum, M., *The Incorporation of Boroughs* (Manchester, 1937)
Weinbaum, M., ed., *British Borough Charters, 1307–1660* (Cambridge, 1943)
Wilkinson, B., *The Mediaeval Council of Exeter* (Manchester, 1931)
Willard, J. F., 'Taxation boroughs and parliamentary boroughs, 1294–1336', in J. G. Edwards, V. H. Galbraith, and E. F. Jacob, eds., *Historical Essays in Honour of James Tait* (Manchester, 1933)
Williams, G. A., *Medieval London: From Commune to Capital* (London, 1963; 2nd edn, London, 1970)
Wilson, D. M., ed., *The Archaeology of Anglo-Saxon England* (London, 1976)
Wright, A. P. M., 'The relations between the king's government and the English cities and boroughs in the fifteenth century' (DPhil thesis, University of Oxford, 1965)
Wright, S. J., ed., *Parish, Church and People: Local Studies in Lay Religion 1350–1750* (London, 1988)
Yates, N., and Gibson, J. M., eds., *Traffic Management and Politics: The Construction and Management of Rochester Bridge, AD 43–1993* (Woodbridge, 1994)
Yorke, B. A. E., 'The bishops of Winchester, the kings of Wessex and the development of Winchester in the ninth and early tenth centuries', *Proc. of the Hampshire Field Club and Arch. Soc.*, 40 (1984)
Yorke, B. A. E., 'The foundation of the Old Minster and the status of Winchester in the seventh and eighth centuries', *Proc. of the Hampshire Field Club and Arch. Soc.*, 38 (1982)
Yorke, B. A. E., *Kings and Kingdoms in Early Anglo-Saxon England* (London, 1990)
Young, C. R., *The English Borough and Royal Administration, 1130–1307* (Durham, N.C., 1961)

Index

Note: page numbers in italic refer to Tables and Figures